LOWNDES AND RUDOLF

The Law of General Average and The York-Antwerp Rules

AUSTRALIA
LBC Information Services
Sydney

CANADA and USA
Carswell
Toronto : Ontario

NEW ZEALAND
Brooker's
Auckland

SINGAPORE AND MALAYSIA
Thomson Information (S.E. Asia)
Singapore

BRITISH SHIPPING LAWS

LOWNDES AND RUDOLF

The Law of General Average and The York-Antwerp Rules

TWELFTH EDITION
BY

D. J. WILSON, A.C.I.I.
Member and past Chairman of the Association of Average Adjusters

J. H. S. COOKE, M.A.,
of Lincoln's Inn, Barrister

LONDON
SWEET & MAXWELL
1997

Published in 1997 by
Sweet & Maxwell Limited
of 100 Avenue Road
Swiss Cottage, London NW3 3PF.
Typeset by Selwood Systems, Midsomer Norton
Printed and bound in Great Britain by Hartnolls Ltd,
Bodmin, Cornwall

A CIP catalogue record for this book
is available from The British Library

ISBN 0421 56450 4

THE LAW OF GENERAL AVERAGE

First Edition	(1873)	By Richard Lowndes
Second Edition	(1874)	
Third Edition	(1878)	
Fourth Edition	(1888)	
Fifth Edition	(1912)	By Edward L. de Hart and George Rupert Rudolf
Sixth Edition	(1922)	

THE YORK-ANTWERP RULES

First Edition	(1926)	By George Rupert Rudolf

LOWNDES & RUDOLF: THE LAW OF GENERAL AVERAGE AND THE YORK-ANTWERP RULES

Seventh Edition	(1948)	By A. J. Hodgson and George Rupert Rudolf
Eighth Edition	(1955)	By J. F. Donaldson and C. T. Ellis
Ninth Edition	(1964)	By J. F. Donaldson, C. T. Ellis and C. S. Staughton
Tenth Edition	(1975)	By Sir John Donaldson, C. S. Staughton and D. J. Wilson
Eleventh Edition	(1990)	By D. J. Wilson and J. H. S. Cooke
Twelfth Edition	(1997)	By D. J. Wilson and J. H. S. Cooke

PREFACE TO THE TWELFTH EDITION

The passage of a century and a quarter has proved that it was clearly quite unnecessary, but in his Introduction to the First (1873) edition of *The Law of General Average*, Richard Lowndes apologised *"for offering to the public a volume on a topic that might be supposed a hackneyed one"*. The present editors feel similarly obliged to offer their readers an apology for producing yet another edition of this hackneyed topic so soon on the heels of the previous Eleventh edition, but trust that this also will be deemed unnecessary and the book found useful, as "user friendly", and even the "good read" that was reported of its predecessor!

The production of the Eleventh edition was a fairly mammoth task, involving as it did the fusion and complete overhaul of the two essentially separate works by *Lowndes* and by *Rudolf*, and the incorporation of a further 40 per cent of new material. When it was published in late 1990, the editors felt entitled—and certainly hoped—to be able to sit back and relax until at least the millennium, at which time in normal circumstances one might have expected the next due revision of the York-Antwerp Rules to take place. Yet the printers' ink was scarcely dry on that Eleventh edition when, in December 1990, following the solitary change to Rule VI earlier in the year consequent on the 1989 International Convention on Salvage, the Comite Maritime International decided to undertake a full review of *all* the Rules of the York-Antwerp Rules!

This required that the editors abandon their relaxation, return to their lasts, and follow closely the various projected draft Rules and early discussions, culminating with the full CMI Conference at Sydney in October 1994 at which the York-Antwerp Rules 1994 were promulgated. These included an entirely new Rule Paramount and important new provisions relating to pollution and damage to the environment, while a prospective new Rule on Rates of Exchange required us to take on the role of the *Financial Times* and add an essay on SDRs to Section 6.

In the area of case law the developments have been less extensive. The decision in *The Alpha* to the effect that no requirement of reasonableness was to be implied into the numbered Rules was obviously of great importance at the time, but where the latest 1994 Rules apply its effect has been nullified by the Rule Paramount. The decision of the

House of Lords in *The Bijela* has necessitated some revision of the commentary on Rule XIV.

The bulk of the manuscript for this latest edition, much of it the only copy, was handed to the publishers in January 1996 at their office at South Quay in London's Dockland, and almost immediately was involved in very real peril and almost a *general average* of its own. It was lying on a desk there when the building was seriously damaged by a bomb explosion. For a whole month no-one from the publishers was allowed in the building, and the draft might have been destroyed in the bombing or salvage operations, but certainly exposed to the elements and liable to be blown away. Fortunately, it was retrieved, but to the consequences of the bombing we request that all errors and misprints found in this edition should be attributed!

If there is a dent in the "user friendly" image of the new edition (and that, hopefully, of a temporary nature only), it is likely to be our chosen prefix for the paragraphs dealing with the new Rule Paramount and the existing Rule of Interpretation, neither of which can properly be said to constitute a regular *lettered* or *numbered Rule*. We decided upon **PRE**.(01 etc), short for *Pre*liminary or *Pre*fatory, and readers will find that the commentary on these early Rules commences at page 63.

We gratefully acknowledge the kind permission granted by the Association of Average Adjusters to copy their Rules of Practice relating to General Average; the United States Association of Average Adjusters to copy their Notes on the Rule of Practice dealing with Air Freight; and the Committee of Lloyd's in respect of their standard security documents and Salvage Agreement.

D.J.W.
Radlett,
HERTS WD7 8JA

J.H.S.C.
20 Essex Street,
LONDON WC2R 3AL

TABLE OF CONTENTS

SECTION 1
HISTORICAL INTRODUCTION

SECTION 2
SOME PRINCIPLES OF THE LAW OF CARRIAGE BY SEA

SECTION 3
THE HISTORY AND DEVELOPMENT OF THE YORK-ANTWERP RULES

SECTION 5
DETERMINING the PLACE and LAW of the ADJUSTMENT and ENFORCING RIGHTS of CONTRIBUTION

SECTION 6
THE CURRENCY OF THE ADJUSTMENT, RATES OF EXCHANGE, AND THE PROBLEM OF SET-OFF 40.01–40.57

SECTION 7
GENERAL AVERAGE AND INSURANCE

APPENDICES

TABLE OF CASES

(Paragraph numbers in **bold** type provide a fuller account of the case details.)

TABLE OF STATUTES

YORK-ANTWERP RULES

SECTION 1

HISTORICAL INTRODUCTION

1. ORIGINS OF THE LAW OF GENERAL AVERAGE

The Rhodians

The first known statement of the law of general average is a small fragment of ancient Greek legislation, which forms the text for a chapter in the Digest of Justinian: "*Lege Rhodia cavetur ut si levandae navis gratia jactus mercium factus est, omnium contributione sarciatur quod pro omnibus datum est.*"[1] "The Rhodian law decrees that if in order to lighten a ship merchandise has been thrown overboard, that which has been given for all should be replaced by the contribution of all." This short sentence contains both the principle and a perfect example of the peculiar communism to which seafaring men are brought in extremities. What is given, or sacrificed, in time of danger, for the sake of all, is to be replaced by a general contribution on the part of all who have been thereby brought to safety. This is a rule which from the oldest recorded times has been universal amongst seafaring men, no matter to what country they belonged, being obviously founded upon the necessities of their position. **00.01**

"While the Phoenicians and the Carthaginians were making a commerce truly universal, a career less vast, but yet not without importance, was opening itself to the navigation of the Greeks, and especially"—for Greece itself was late in entering upon the field—"the Greek colonies in Asia Minor and the adjacent islands. These, surrounded by fertile lands, intersected with bays and rivers, not far off from one another, and yet very diversified in their agricultural products, early profited by the facilities their position gave them, to exchange their commodities, and to carry them into Phoenicia, which was a sort of *entrepôt*."[2] Thus sprung up a commerce, which appears to have been of some importance, though, perhaps, not extending very far beyond the limits of the Aegean Sea. Rhodes is one of the cities decorated by the title of "mistress of the sea". In the Punic wars, according to Polybius, Rhodes took the Roman side, and did good service in attacking the war-vessels of the Carthaginians— **00.02**

[1] Digest XIV.2.1.
[2] Collection des Lois Maritimes, J. M. Pardessus (1837) Intr. xxvi, xxvii.

as cruisers perhaps.[3] Cicero says of the Rhodians that they were a people whose naval power and discipline remained even to times within his own memory.[4] Pardessus considers it probable that the Rhodians borrowed their maritime laws from the Phoenicians, though he hardly offers any particular reasons for the conjecture.[5]

00.03 However, to say that Greeks from Rhodes were the first to express the principle of general average in words, and so give it currency, throws very little light on its true origin. It must have been already very ancient and very widespread as a practice before it became so neatly formulated. It must be remembered that in olden times, for perhaps thousands of years, the merchants or owners of cargo used, almost of course, to sail with their wares from port to port like pedlars. In these little vessels, mostly navigating the Mediterranean or Aegean Sea, where storms quickly spring up and subside, occasions would be frequent where shipwreck could only be averted by lightening the ship of portions of her cargo, a measure which, however beneficial to the rest, might to one man on board mean ruin. His consent to such a sacrifice could only be bought by a promise—first express, then customary and taken for granted—that when, or if, the ship came safe to shore, all who had profited by his loss would pay their share to make it good.

The Romans

00.04 The Romans, the great improvers of other people's inventions, have given us a good specimen in the chapter of the Digest of Justinian headed *De Lege Rhodia de Jactu*. The sentence above quoted takes the place of honour, as a sort of text, and is followed by a fragmentary collection of short judgments or opinions. It is not easy to trace the principle of arrangement,[6] unless it be, first, to show by examples (such as the cutting away of a mast) that the case of throwing cargo overboard is only to be treated as an illustration of some more general principle; secondly, to establish that this rule of contribution is to be restricted to such sea-losses as flow from a voluntary sacrifice for the sake of all, leaving every loss, whether of ship or cargo, which is the result of pure accident, to lie where it falls; and thirdly, when these two points are made clear, to determine some of the more complicated questions which arise in carrying the principle consistently into operation.

For an example under the third head, in the opinion of Julianus a claim for contribution to the cost of temporary repairs at a port of refuge (Hippo) failed, since the expenditure was incurred rather to fit out the ship than to save the cargo (*sumptus instruendae magis navis, quam*

[3] Park, Ins. Intr. xlvii.
[4] Pro. leg. Manil. c. 13.
[5] 1 Pard. Intr. xxix.
[6] But see Buckland's *Manual of Roman Private Law*, p. 23.

conservandarum mercium gratia factus est).[7] Some of the texts are not concerned with general average at all, the last in the chapter being an explanation of the difference between lump-sum freight and freight calculated on the quantity of cargo carried or discharged.[8] Another records a case of shipwrecked seamen who "were plundered by the tax-farmers who live in the Cyclades Islands". The rescript of the Emperor Antoninus ran:

> Let it be judged by the Rhodian law which deals with nautical matters, so far as that is not directly contrary to our own law. For I am lord of the whole world, but the law is lord of the sea.[9]

This may have been an early recognition of the difficulties encountered even by the most powerful nations in seeking to regulate the international transactions of merchants exclusively by their own laws.[10]

The Middle Ages

After the fall of the Roman Empire, its laws fell into oblivion. In the recollection of seafaring men, however, or as tradition, or as a rule commending itself on account of its utility, the outlines of this chapter *de jactu* retained a hold, in some degree over the seafaring population of Europe, and were reproduced, in a simpler and ruder form, in the several collections of sea laws which belong to a later period. **00.05**

The Rolls of Oleron

Of the codes or collections of customs here spoken of, perhaps the most important, as that which had the most extended authority, is one called the Rolls or Judgments of Oleron. Their origin is lost in obscurity, but from internal evidence we may conclude that they were a collection of judgments, probably delivered in some court of Bordeaux, and having reference to the commerce in wine which had its centre in that city. According to Selden these rolls were revised by Richard I on his return from the Holy Land during his stay at the Isle of Oleron, and were declared to be the law of the sea, under the title of *la ley Olyroun*.[11] Be that as it may, for some reason or other these judgments obtained, and held for some centuries, over the greater part of Europe a very con- **00.06**

[7] Digest XIV, 2.6. See now Rule XIV of the York-Antwerp Rules.
[8] Digest XIV.2.10.
[9] *Ibid.* XIV.2.9.
[10] In 1935 a translation of *The York-Antwerp Rules 1924* by G. R. Rudolf (a constituent part of this present work) was published in the Soviet Union. The foreword commended the book for its utility, but added: "It can be definitely stated that with the evolution of a socialist society there will be no need of any general average rules."
[11] Selden: *Mare Clausum*, lib. 2, cap. 24; 1 Pard. 289.

siderable authority. They were copied into the Black Book of Admiralty.[12] In 1402 Parliament petitioned Henry IV to require the Admirals to govern their decisions exclusively by the laws of Oleron, the ancient laws of the sea, and the common law of England.[13] The old laws of Flanders,[14] of Catalonia,[15] of Genoa,[16] and of Holland,[17] in like manner contain clauses literally copied from the judgments of Oleron.

00.07 So far as concerns general average all that is said in the Rolls of Oleron is the following:

> ART. 8. A ship leaves Bordeaux or elsewhere, and it happens that a storm takes it at sea and the ship cannot escape without throwing out goods from within. The master is bound to say to the merchants: "Signors, we cannot escape without throwing out the wines and the goods." The merchants, if there are any, shall signify their good will who shall agree to this jettison, and that the master's reasons are most clear; and if they do not agree, the master ought, nevertheless, not to fear to throw out as much as shall seem to him good, swearing himself and the third of his crew on the Holy Gospels, when he shall have come safe ashore, that he did it of no malice, but to save their lives, the ship, the goods, and the wines. Those which have been thrown out ought to be appraised at the rate of those which shall come safe, and shall be divided pound by pound amongst the merchants; and the master ought to share on account of the ship or his freight, at his choice, to restore the damage. The mariners ought to have each a ton (*tonnel*) free, and the rest shall contribute to the jettison according to what he has, if he defends himself on the sea like a man; and if he does not defend himself, he shall have nothing free; and the master shall be believed upon his oath. And this is the judgment in this case.[18]
>
> ART. 9. It occurs that the master of a ship must cut away his mast by force of tempest; he ought to call the merchants and show them that it is fitting to cut the mast to save the ship and the wares; and sometimes it occurs that one cuts cables and the anchors to save the ship and the wares. These ought to be counted pound by pound like jettison; and the merchants ought to share and pay without delay before their goods are put out of the ship; and if the ship was held fast (*en dur siege*) and the master was delayed by their debate, and there was collusion, the master ought not to suffer, but he ought to have his freight on those wines as he will take for the others. And this is the judgment in this case.[19]
>
> ART. 35. It is ordered and established for custom of the sea that, when it occurs that one makes jettison from a ship, it is well written at Rome that all the merchandise and effects contained in the ship should share in the jettison, pound for pound; and if there are cups of silver more than one in

[12] 1 Pard. 309; Twiss, *Black Book*, p. 97.

[13] Rotuli Parliamentorum, Vol. 3, p. 498; 4 Pard. 197, where it is erroneously treated as an Act of Parliament.

[14] 1 Pard. 375.

[15] 5 Pard. 362.

[16] 4 Pard. 521.

[17] 1 Pard. 406.

[18] *Rolls of Oleron*, Art. 8; 1 Pard. 328. In explanation of this franchise allowed to the sailors, it may be mentioned that by Art. 31, those seamen who have agreed to be paid as wages a certain proportion of the freight shall each be allowed one ton free of freight. This ton was likewise, it appears, free of contribution to average if its owner behaved well.

[19] *Rolls of Oleron*, Art 9; 1 Pard. 329.

the ship, they ought to contribute to the jettison [*ou faire gré*], and one cup also, if it is not borne at table for the service of the mariners; robes and linen if they are not yet cut, or have not yet been worn, all shall contribute to the jettison. And this is the judgment in this case.[20]

Other Old Sea-laws of Europe

Most of the other old sea-laws of Europe, such as the law of Wisbuy,[21] **00.08** the laws of Amsterdam, of the Hanseatic League, of Flanders, of Genoa, and Catalonia, either set forth literal translations of these three articles, or reproduce their substance, albeit with less drama and vivacity. Everywhere jettison and the cutting away of a mast and slipping a cable are the first examples of a general contribution; to which are gradually added, in later codes, some instances of extra-ordinary expenditure for the common safety, such as the expense incurred in lightening a stranded ship.

2. Basis of General Average

Bargain Made on the Spot

It will be observed that in the judgments of Oleron, as in all the sea- **00.09** laws of Europe which adopted and developed those judgments, the idea which lies at the foundation of this contribution is that of a bargain or agreement made between the captain and the owners of the cargo at the moment of danger: on the part of the latter a consent to part with their goods; on the part of the former, and likewise of the latter as amongst themselves, an undertaking to make rateable compensation in case safety shall be attained. Of this idea there is no trace in the Roman law, the terms of which would rather lead one to suppose that the rule was laid down as obligatory on grounds of natural equity.

Delegation to Master

In later times a great revolution in maritime commerce took place **00.10** when merchants gave up their migratory habits, and began to carry on their business from counting-houses on shore, and by means of factors or agents or branch-houses at the principal ports with which they traded.

[20] 1 Pard. 329. This article is No. 32 in the manuscript of the English Admiralty. It is not found in any other copy, printed or MS. (1 Pard. 329, n. 1).

[21] Tradition ascribes the origin of the law of Wisbuy to a Convention of Mariners and Merchants from all parts of Europe, meeting on the occasion of some great fair or mart at Wisbuy in the Baltic.

This change was certainly originated by Italians. The great merchant cities, and especially Genoa, Pisa, Florence and Venice, held, in the fourteenth and fifteenth centuries, a position at the head of maritime commerce which it is difficult for us now to realise. Each city was an independent republic, and the leading merchants, as the wealthiest, soon began to busy themselves in politics, and become persons of importance on shore. Their long voyages grew, no doubt, extremely inconvenient. It became absolutely necessary to invent some system of delegation. The faculty of invention was not wanting in the quick-witted Italians, at that time by far the most highly cultivated people in Europe. Accordingly, within no very great space of time, the many remarkable inventions necessary to complete the complicated machinery of modern commerce followed one another: bills of exchange, book-keeping by double entry, an elaborate system and law of *commando* or agency, and marine insurance, being among the number. Then, by degrees, owners of cargo began to live ashore, a habit which naturally spread until it became practically universal. This absence of the merchants inevitably led to a great increase in the power and responsibility of the master, particularly on occasions such as a jettison or sacrificing of a part.

Continuing Need for General Average

00.11 Lowndes raised the question whether, at this early stage, the abolition of the system of contribution towards sacrifices for the common safety may not have been considered. There is no evidence that it was, but during the last hundred years or more there have been intermittent calls for abolition on various grounds. Earlier editions of this work dealt at some length with arguments for and against abolition,[22] and in Appendix 5 the subject is again considered in some detail. However, for present purposes it may be sufficient to state the principal points only.

First, there is no doubt that adjustment is in many cases (but not all) an expensive and complicated process, and that it may lead to delay in the settlement of accounts.[23] Secondly, the benefit and burden of general average contribution are in most cases (but not all) ultimately enjoyed or borne by the insurers of the contributing interests, and it may be supposed that they could make an appropriate alteration to premium rates (up or down) if general average contribution were abolished. Against abolition, there is first the difficulty that all parties to a particular adventure, and perhaps their insurers, must expressly so agree before every possible right to receive contribution is extinguished. More important, perhaps, is the point that the master's position in circumstances of danger would become more difficult. At present he may have to choose

[22] 9th ed., para. 11 and App. 4.

[23] In *Chandris v. Argo Insurance Co. Ltd* [1963] 2 Lloyd's Rep. 65, Megaw J. found that there were cases where it had not been reasonably possible to complete an adjustment within six years of the sacrifice or expenditure.

between a number of possible measures to save ship and cargo, and this is a responsible task. "On its being performed with coolness, courage and discretion, the whole property and the lives of all depend."[24] But the master does not need to consider on whom the loss or expense will fall, for whatever course he adopts it will be borne by the same interests in the same proportions. If there were no general average contribution he would be faced with that additional problem, and might subsequently be accused either by his owners of neglecting the interests of his employers, or by the owners of the cargo of allowing purely nautical considerations to be overriden by concern about the burden that would fall on his owners. So in *Australian Coastal Shipping Commission v. Green*[25] Mocatta J. said:

> "If the authorities and the words of the rules permit it, it is desirable that when the master or other agents of the owners of a vessel has or have to consider, often in circumstances of great difficulty and urgency, what course to take for the common safety for the purpose of preserving from peril the property involved in a common maritime adventure, it is important that technicalities of the law should not, unless this is unavoidable, give rise to a conflict of interests, and thus fetter or influence the choice to be made in the best interests of all concerned."

3. Origin of the word "Average"

Early References

The word "average" is of much later origin than the thing. However, there are to be found in the *Constitutum Usus* of the City of Pisa, a code dating from about A.D. 1160, some faint traces of the growth of a technical term out of the common Italian word *avere*, the having of property. The code is written in a sort of Italianised or mongrel Latin; the captain, for example, is called *capitaneus*, the sailors *marinarii*, and so forth. The word *avere* is used throughout the code to denote the basis of contribution or contributory value; thus, the jettison and damage through jettison, it says, shall be equalised over "*totum avere*", all the property remaining in the ship. In another place it speaks of those whose *avere* (property) has been cast out, and those whose *avere* is safe.[26] In a later Pisan code, A.D. 1298, a regulation concerning jettison is headed, "*de divisione haveris projecti*".[27] In a Genoese code, A.D. 1341, the word *averia*, or *avaria*, for it is spelt both ways, has come to mean expenses or losses for the common good, and as such forming charges upon the *avere* or entire property.[28] In a statute of Ancona of 1397, the word *varea* 00.12

[24] *Barnard v. Adams* (1850) 10 Howard's S.C. 270 at 286.
[25] [1971] 1 Q.B. 456 at 465; affirmed by the Court of Appeal, *ibid.*
[26] 4 Pard. 580–581.
[27] *Ibid.* 593.
[28] *ibid.* 521.

is used to denote the contribution itself.[29] And in a Venetian code of the fourteenth century we find the phrase *dividatur per avariam* used to express a general contribution.[30] All sorts of theories have been propounded as to the origin of the word "average", which in this sense is universal in all the languages of Europe under various thin disguises, as *avarie, haverei*, and the like.[31] These theories, however, are purely conjectural, whereas here we have something like the vestiges of the actual growth of this peculiar technical expression.

Guidon de la Mer, 1556–1584

00.13 Coming now to a much later period, between the years 1556 and 1584, we find, in the remarkable treatise called the *Guidon de la Mer*,[32] the first express definition of general average. The work is a digest, or authoritative code, of the law of insurance, apparently intended for the use of the then newly constituted consular court of Rouen. Incidentally, however, it touches on other branches of maritime law, such as affreightment, bottomry and general average.

> "The insurer", it says, "is bound to indemnify his merchant for the expenses, losses (*mises*), average, and damage which occur to the merchandise from the time of loading, the whole of which is comprised in this word *average*, which receives several divisions. The first is called common or gross average, that which arises by jettison, for ransom or composition, for cables, sails, or mast cut for the saving of the ship and merchandise, the compensation for which is levied upon (*se prend sur*) the ship and merchandise; for which reason it is called common."[33]

Ordonnance of Louis XIV, 1681

00.14 The Ordonnance of Louis XIV, in 1681, gave the force of law to a definition of general average, evidently modelled upon this of the *Guidon*.

> "Every extraordinary expense", it says, "which is made for the ship and merchandise conjointly or separately, and every damage that shall occur to them from their loading and departure until their return and discharge, shall be reputed *average*. Extraordinary expenses for the ship alone, or for the merchandise alone, and damage which occurs to them in particular, are

[29] 5 Pard. 139.
[30] *Ibid.* 97.
[31] See Manley Hopkins, *Handbook of Average* (4th ed.), pp. 3 *et seq.*, where the different meanings and the derivation of the word are discussed at length. See also "Average", in Professor Skeat, *Etymological Dictionary*. The learned professor, one of the greatest authorities on the etymology of the English language, says that the word is a Mediterranean maritime term of unknown origin. In the *New English Dictionary*, edited by Sir James Murray, its derivation is also stated to be uncertain.
[32] For a fuller account of the *Guidon*, see Lowndes, *Marine Insurance*, Intr. xxiv.
[33] 2 Pard. 387. Examples of general average are afterwards given (*ibid.* 392–396), some of them evidently taken from the Digest of Justinian.

simple and particular average; and extraordinary expenses incurred and damage suffered, for the common good and safety of the merchandise and the vessel, are gross and common average. Simple averages are borne and paid by the thing which shall have suffered the damage or caused the expense, and the gross and common shall fall as well upon the vessel as upon the merchandise, and shall be equalised over the whole at the shilling in the pound" (*au sol la livre*).[34]

The Ordonnance set an example which was followed throughout Europe. In 1721 was published the Ordinance of Rotterdam which in like manner begins with a definition in similar terms: **00.15**

"All damage arising from anything that is voluntarily done for the preservation of ship or goods, or for preventing greater and more apparent mischief, shall be deemed general average, and be borne by ship and cargo."[35]

The Ordinance of Bilbao says:

"A gross average is that which arises from the means interposed to free the ship and its lading from shipwreck or loss."[36]

English Origins

England was almost the only maritime country which did not possess a code of sea-law. Its early commercial law appears to have been regulated by the merchants themselves. The name of Lombard Street, until recently, on English policies of insurances,[37] attests the tradition which attributes to settlers from the Lombard cities, probably in the times of the Medici, the introduction to England of the practice of marine insurance. Pardessus gives the text of a statute of the time of William I concerning jettison, which, however, is not to be found in the Statute Book, and cannot be safely treated as authentic.[38] A statute of Elizabeth I recorded that questions of insurance and trade had theretofore been dealt with by certain older merchants, "grave and discreet persons", appointed by the Lord Mayor of London, "as men by reason of their experience fittest to understand such matters".[39] This statute constituted a special mercantile tribunal to take their place; but the tribunal never found much favour **00.16**

[34] Ordonnance. tit. 7, Arts. 2, 3; 4 Pard. 380.

[35] 2 Magens 95. The Ordinances of Stockholm (A.D. 1750), of Konigsberg (1730) and of Hamburg (1731), contain similar definitions. (2 Mag. 204, 236, 279.)

[36] 2 Mag. 396.

[37] The policy which is set out in the First Schedule to the Marine Insurance Act 1906, includes the words "And it is agreed by us, the insurers, that this writing or policy of insurance shall be of as much force and effect as the surest writing or policy of assurance heretofore made in Lombard Street. . . ."

[38] 4 Pard. 203.

[39] 1 Marshall, *Insurance*, p. 25.

amongst the merchants, and speedily fell into decay.[40] In the meanwhile, according to such books as Beawes, Magens and others, published by mercantile men for use among themselves, the rules followed in these matters consisted of a body of customs, in which were embedded provisions borrowed without visible discrimination from the various codes and sea-laws of all the countries of Europe. When, in London, Lloyd's coffee-house came to be the headquarters of the business of marine insurance, it became also, naturally, the headquarters of information as to these customs, which hence acquired the title of "the Customs of Lloyd's".

00.17 The researches of a member of the Association of Average Adjusters[41] have brought to light what is almost certainly the earliest recorded instance of a dispute concerning contribution towards a jettison being considered by the English courts. The case was heard in the Court of King's Bench in the Trinity Term of the year 1285, that is to say about twenty years after the promulgation of the Rolls of Oleron, and was a successful attempt to prevent the modification of existing customs to accord with the law as there stated. The report is as follows[42]:

> "The barons of the Cinque Ports of The Lord King and likewise all the sailors of Yarmouth and others in the realm of England complained to the Lord King that, when it happened that one of them hired his boat out to bring wines or other goods from overseas to England, Gascony, Ireland or Wales, and it was imperative because of an oncoming storm at sea for those on board ship to jettison in order to save that ship, sometimes ten or twenty or thirty barrels, sometimes forty or a greater or lesser number, and from time immemorial it has been established and conceded to the same barons that the ship in which those wines or wares were ought with all its tackle to be free from making or contributing to any aid for the aforesaid jettisoning, provided that the sailor loses his freightage for the barrels or wares thrown out into the sea, Gregory de Rokesle, Henryle Waleys and other of the Lord King's merchants, within the Lord King's territory, not only of England and Gascony but also of Ireland, compel the aforesaid barons of the Cinque Ports and other sailors of the King's realm to appraise their ships with all the apparatus and sailing tackle belonging to those ships and along with the wines and other goods on board ship in order to make acquittance for the wines or goods thrown in this way into the sea at their will, and to restore to him who owned them what had been thrown into the sea, to the most grievous loss of those barons and sailors [and] in defiance of the liberties granted to those same barons, etc.
>
> And the aforesaid Gregory and Henry came along with many merchants of England and Gascony. And, after hearing the arguments of those merchants as well as those of the aforesaid barons and sailors, it is decreed, granted, and definitively adjudged by the Lord King and his council that, in the first place, henceforth the ship in which the wares or wines were with all its apparatus, the ring carried on the finger of the ship's captain, the

[40] *Ibid.* p. 26.
[41] The late Mr F. E. Vaughan.
[42] Sayles, *Select Cases in the Court of King's Bench*, Vol. 1. (*Selden Society Publications*, Vol. 55, pp. 156–157, 1936) reproduced by kind permission of the Society.

sailors' victuals, the implements used in making their meals, the jewelry, belt and silver cup from which the ship's captain drinks, if he possesses any, shall be freed from contributing to any aid for the aforesaid jettisoning into the sea. And also the sailors shall keep the freightage of the wines and other goods on board ship which have been saved. And the ship's captain shall lose his freightage for the barrels or goods thus thrown into the sea. And all other goods on board ship, of the sailors as well as of the merchants, such as wines, merchandise, money in gross, beds and other goods and wares, with the exception of the aforesaid apparatus and tackle for the ship, the sailors' victuals, the implements for making their meals, the jewelry, belt and silver cup, the ring and the freightage for goods which have been saved, as aforesaid ought henceforth to be appraised for the purposes of making an aid in acquaintance for the wines or goods thrown out of the ship into the sea through a storm at sea."

It is not till the year 1799 that any trace can be found of the actual term "general average" in the English courts of law. "General average", said Lord Stowell, in the Court of Admiralty, "is for a loss incurred, towards which the whole concern is bound to contribute *pro rata*, because it was undergone for the general benefit and preservation of the whole".[43] This definition was practically superseded by one laid down two years later in the Court of King's Bench by Lawrence J., in the case of *Birkley v. Presgrave*,[44] on which, as will be shown in paragraphs 00.19 to 00.30, below, and generally in Rule A, the English law of general average has been constructed.[45] **00.18**

It is interesting to note that the first statutory mention of the profession of "average adjuster" is to be found in the Compensation (Defence) Act 1939, which by section 8 enacted that the third member of the Shipping Tribunal[46] shall be "a person appearing to the Lord Chancellor to have special qualifications as an average adjuster or accountant". Thus 140 years after Lord Stowell's recognition of general averages a legal conception, the average adjuster as an individual appears in the Statute Book.

[43] *The Copenhagen* (1799) 1 C.Rob. 289. The first reference to "general average" in an American court occurred one year earlier: *Campbell v. The Alknomac* (1798) Bee 124; Fed. Cas. 2350. The word "average" to denote a general average contribution is, however, found in the report of *Hicks v. Palington* (1590) Moore 297, and of *Marsham v. Dutrey* (1719) Select Cases of Evidence 58. See also *Sheppard v. Wright* (1698) Show. P.C. 18. MacKinnon L.J. in his presidential address to the Association of Average Adjusters on May 10, 1935, referred to the *Select Pleas in the Court of Admiralty* published by the Selden Society, and edited by the late R. G. Marsden. He instanced several earlier cases in which general average is mentioned; in a charterparty of the *Jesus*, dated 1562, in a claim settled by arbitration in 1540 arising out of the voyage of the *Trinity James* from Normandy to the Thames and in an arbitration award in 1575 for "contribution or average every man according to the rate of his goods", where part of the cargo of the *Elizabeth* had been seized to satisfy the demands of the tolner of the King of Denmark in lieu of the arrest of the ship.

[44] (1801) 1 East 220 at 228.

[45] For the meaning of the word "average" in the context of the phrase "free from average" in a contract for the sale of a ship, see *Kelman v. Livanos* [1955] 1 W.L.R. 590.

[46] *I.e*, the Shipping Claims Tribunal.

4. Basis of the Right to General Average in the Modern Law

00.19 Is the right to general average founded on authority merely, no matter whether that of the Rhodian, or Roman, or any later positive law, or of immemorial custom, or on some more primary grounds? And, if the latter, are they grounds of natural equity or utility, or do they rest on some contract between the parties, originally perhaps express, but which in course of time has come to be constantly implied, or on some theory as to agency?

The older English law writers on average, probably following Emerigon and other French lawyers, based this right simply on natural justice:

> "This obligation ... is founded on the great principle of distributive justice; for it would be hard that one man should suffer by an act which the common safety rendered necessary, and that those who received a benefit from that act should make no satisfaction to him who had sustained the loss."[47]

00.20 In proportion as the subject of general average came to be more familiar, it seems to have been felt to be more consonant with the spirit of the English common law that, in seeking to place this right of contribution on a secure basis, some implied contract or implied agency should, if possible, be found for it to rest on. Several such easily presented themselves. It might be supposed, for instance, that, at the time of shipping or entering into the contract for shipping the goods, all shippers impliedly contract with the shipowner and with each other, that the master shall have authority in case of danger to make all needful sacrifices, to the expense of which they, the shippers, will contribute their share; or it may be supposed that a similar engagement is made between the parties, at the moment of danger, treating them as if on the spot, as they originally were; or, again, if an implied agency is preferred, the master may be supposed to have, in virtue of his office, an authority to do for each cargo-owner, as well as for the shipowner, whatever any one of those parties would have had the duty or the power to do had he been on the spot; so that the master's act should on each occasion be taken to be, and treated as if it were, the act of his appropriate principal.

00.21 At first sight there is little to be gained in seeking to lay down the precise basis of the right. The same could be said of the doctrine of frustration, whereby a contract is held to be dissolved by supervening events. Arguments as to whether this results from an implied term in the contract, or from the construction of the contract, or from an independent rule imposed by law[48] are of little practical interest, unless they have a

[47] Park, *Insurance* (8th ed.), p. 277. See also Abbott, *Shipping* (5th ed.), p. 344 and *The Star of Hope* (1869) 9 Wall. 203 at 230.
[48] See, *e.g. Davis Contractors Ltd v. Fareham U.D.C.* [1956] A.C. 696.

bearing on the test to be applied in order to establish frustration, or on the consequences which flow from it. Otherwise they merely provide an interesting reflection of changing judicial views as to the force of the doctrine of freedom of contract. However, this is unfortunately not always the case with the right to general average contribution. It may be important to determine the nature of the right, for example, in order to select the appropriate rule on which to found jurisdiction,[49] or to consider whether a claim to contribution is barred by some statutory or contractual period of limitation.[50]

Some Judicial Opinions

In *The Gratitudine*[51] Lord Stowell said: **00.22**

> "Though in the ordinary state of things [the master of a ship] is a stranger to the cargo, beyond the purposes of safe custody and conveyance, yet in cases of instant and unforeseen and unprovided necessity the character of agent and supercargo is forced upon him, not by the immediate act and appointment of the owner, but by the general policy of the law; unless the law can be supposed to mean that valuable property in his hand is to be left without protection and care."

In *Simonds v. White*,[52] Abbott C.J. said:

> "The principle of general average ... if of very ancient date, and of universal reception among commercial nations. The obligation to contribute, therefore, depends not so much upon the terms of any particular instrument as upon a general rule of maritime law. The obligation may be limited, qualified, or even excluded by the special terms of the contract as between the parties to the contract."

In *The Hamburg*[53] Lord Kingsdown said:

> "The character of agent for the owners of the cargo is imposed upon the master by the necessity of the case, and by that alone. In the circumstances supposed, something must be done, and there is nobody present who has authority to decide what shall be done. The master is invested by presumption of law with authority to give directions on this ground, that the owners have no means of expressing their wishes."

In *Aitchison v. Lohre*,[54] Lord Blackburn said:

> "It may be as well here to point out that the liability of the articles saved to contribute proportionally with the rest to general average and salvage, in

[49] See paras. 30.29 *et seq.*, post.
[50] See paras. 30.37–30.41, post.
[51] (1801) 3 C.Rob. 240 at 257. Approved by Lord Roche in *Morrison S.S. Co. v. Greystoke Castle; The Cheldale* [1947] A.C. 265.
[52] (1824) 2 B. & C. 805 at 811.
[53] (1864) 2 Moo. P.C.C. (N.S.) 289 at 321; 33 L.J.Adm. 116 at 118.
[54] (1879) 4 A.C. 755 at 760.

noways depends on the policy of insurance. It is a consequence of the perils of the sea, first imposed, as regards general average, by the Rhodian law many centuries before insurance was known at all, and as regards salvage by the maritime law, not so early but at least long before any policies of insurance in the present form were thought of."

In *Pirie v. Middle Dock Co.*,[55] Watkin Williams J. said:

"It is a law founded upon justice, public policy, and convenience, and rests ... upon reasons which are so obvious that it is not surprising to find that it is older than any other law or rule in force ... This principle of law must, in my judgment, be regarded as incorporated in and forming part of the unwritten common law of England."

Bramwell L.J., delivering the judgment of the Court of Appeal in *Wright v. Marwood*,[56] said:

"When such sacrifice is made, as was here, for the common good, as a rule it comes within general average, and must be borne proportionally by those interested. It is not necessary to say what is the origin or principle of the rule, but, to judge from the way it is claimed in England, it would seem to arise from an implied contract *inter se* to contribute by those interested."[57]

The way that general average was then claimed may be ascertained by reference to the record in *Anderson v. Ocean Steamship Co.*[58] The statement of claim there alleged that:

"the Defendants promised that they would contribute and pay their just share and proportion in respect of the said goods of any general average loss that might arise or happen to the said ship during the said voyage."

Lord Blackburn said:

"I think that the promise stated in the first paragraph of the Statement of Claim is one that would be implied by law in every contract for the carriage of goods."[59]

This was the zenith of the contract theory.

00.23 A year earlier the rule of law theory had begun to gain support with the judgment of Brett M.R. in *Burton v. English*[60]:

"How does such a claim [for jettison of cargo] arise? In theory it arises from an act done by the master of a ship, not as the servant of the ship-owner, but as the servant of the cargo-owner, a relation which is imposed on him by the necessity of the case. It arises by reason of a voluntary sacrifice by the cargo-owner for the benefit of the ship and cargo, and not from any act

[55] (1881) 4 Asp.Mar.Law Cas. 388 at 390; 44 L.T. 426.
[56] (1881) 7 Q.B.D. 62 at 67.
[57] See to the same effect, Maclachlan, *Merchant Shipping* (5th ed.), p. 734n.
[58] (1884) 10 A.C. 107.
[59] *Ibid.* at 115.
[60] (1883) 12 Q.B.D. 218.

done for the ship-owner at all. By what law does the right arise to general average contribution? Lord Bramwell in his judgment in *Wright v. Marwood*,[61] considers it to arise from an implied contract; but although I always have great doubt when I differ from Lord Bramwell, I do not think that it forms any part of the contract to carry, and that it does not arise from any contract at all, but from the old Rhodian laws, and has become incorporated into the law of England as the law of the ocean. It is not as a matter of contract, but in consequence of a common danger, where natural justice requires that all should contribute to indemnify for the loss of property which is sacrificed by one in order that the whole adventure may be saved. . . .[62]

"The acts of the captain with reference to properly or improperly jettisoning part of the cargo are not both done by him in the same capacity; one is done by him as the agent of the cargo-owner, and the other as the servant of the shipowner."

Bowen L.J., delivering his judgment in the same case, summed up the matter discussed in this section so as quietly to indicate that we were not, after all, to suppose it to be of any great practical importance. He said:

"In the investigation of legal principles, the question whether they arise by way of implied contract or not often ends by being a mere question of words. General average contribution is a principle which comes down to us from an anterior period of our history, and from the law of commerce and the sea. When, however, it is once established as part of the law, and as a portion of the risks which those who embark their property upon ships are willing to take, you may, if you like, imagine that those who place their property on board a ship on one side, and the shipowner who puts his ship by the quay to receive the cargo on the other side, bind themselves by an implied contract which embodies this principle; just as it may be said that those who contract with reference to a custom impliedly make it a part of the contract. But that way, although legally it may be a sound way, nevertheless is a technical way of looking at it. This claim for average contribution, at all events, is part of the law of the sea, and it certainly arises in consequence of an act done by the captain as agent, not for the shipowner alone, but also of the cargo-owner, by which act he jettisons part of the cargo on the implied basis that contribution will be made by the ship and by the other owners of cargo."[63]

In *Strang, Steel & Co. v. A. Scott & Co.*[64] Lord Watson, after referring **00.24**
to the Rhodian law[65] and the judgments in *Wright v. Marwood* and *Burton v. English*,[66] said:

[61] (1881) 7 Q.B.D. 62.

[62] (1883) 12 Q.B.D. 218 at 220–221, cited by Bailhache J. in *Austin Friars S.S. Co. v. Spillers and Bakers* [1915] 1 K.B. 833 at 837, and by Greer L.J. in *Tate & Lyle Ltd v. Hain Shipping Co.* (1934) 39 Com.Cas. 259 at 280.

[63] *Burton v. English* [1883] 12 Q.B.D. 218 at 223.

[64] (1899) 14 A.C. 601 at 607–608. The advice was that of Lords Watson, Fitzgerald, Hobhouse and MacNaghten.

[65] See para. 00.01, *ante*.

[66] See paras. 00.22–00.23, *ante*.

"Whether the rule ought to be regarded as a matter of implied contract, or as a canon of positive law resting upon the dictates of natural justice, is a question which their Lordships do not consider it necessary to determine. The principle upon which contribution becomes due does not appear to them to differ from that upon which claims of recompense for salvage services are founded. But, in any aspect of it, the rule of contribution has its foundation in the plainest equity. In jettison, the rights of those entitled to contribution, and the corresponding obligations of the contributors, have their origin in the fact of a common danger which threatens to destroy the property of them all; and these rights and obligations are mutually perfected whenever the goods of some of the shippers have been advisedly sacrificed, and the property of the others has been thereby preserved."

00.25 In *Milburn v. Jamaica Fruit Importing Co.*,[67] where the York-Antwerp Rules 1890 applied, A.L. Smith L.J. expressed views on this point which agree with that of Lord Esher, saying:

"The foundation of a general average claim is ordinarily not that of contract, but is founded upon a loss which arises in consequence of extraordinary sacrifices made or expenses incurred for the preservation of the ship and cargo in the time of peril, and which must be borne proportionately by all who are interested."

Similarly, Vaughan Williams L.J. says:

"The liability to contribute in no sense results from the contract of carriage, but exists wholly independently of the contrast of carriage, by virtue of the equitable doctrine of the Rhodian law, which as part of the law maritime has been incorporated in the municipal law of England."[68]

Two brief references to the point may be found in the speeches of the House of Lords in *Hain S.S. Co. v. Tate & Lyle*.[69] Lord Atkin, speaking of a claim for contribution, said: "No doubt the claim does not arise as a term of the contract."[70] Lord Maugham described the lien for contribution as "a right resting not on the charterparty but on the general maritime law".[71]

00.26 In *Morrison S.S. Co. v. Greystoke Castle; The Cheldale*,[72] when the carriage was under the York-Antwerp Rules 1924, Scott L.J. said:

"The common law of the sea in regard to general average imposes the duty to disburse on the master of the ship, and equally imposes the duty to

[67] [1900] 2 Q.B. 540 at 546, 550.

[68] The same view has been expressed in several decisions of the American courts: see *The Roanoke* (1893) 59 Fed.Rep. 161; *Marwick v. Rogers* (1895) 163 Mas. 50; *The Eliza Lines* (1896) 61 Fed.Rep. 308 at 325. "The principle on which this contribution is founded is not the result of a contract, but has its origin in the plain dictates of natural law": Story, *Equity Jurisprudence*, p. 490. In *Marwick v. Rogers* it was held that the cesser clause in a charterparty could not relieve the owner of cargo, who was also the charterer, from liability to contribute.

[69] (1936) 41 Com.Cas 350.

[70] *Ibid.* at 357.

[71] *Ibid.* at 372.

[72] [1945] P. 10 at 14.

> contribute on the other parties to the adventure, whenever an event causes danger of loss to the whole adventure."

In this case in the House of Lords, Lord Porter said[73]:

> "It is more consistent with the realities of the case to hold that the shipowner is directly liable to pay those whom he employs, but nevertheless in incurring the debt and making the payment is acting not only for the ship but also on behalf of all the interests concerned.... So in the present case the owners ... pledged their own credit as principals to answer for the general average expenditure, but yet acted as agents for the contributories including the [cargo-owners] in incurring the expense."

Lord Roche expressed a similar view,[74] and Lord Uthwatt said[75]:

> "[General average] acts are in law done on behalf of all in the sense that they are done by the actor as agent for all. The acceptance of this view relates the consequences of the general average act to a definite and intelligible principle."

The problem has arisen in two cases decided in 1971/72 where it had been agreed that any dispute arising "out of" or "under" the contract of carriage should be referred to arbitration, and that any claim should be deemed to be waived unless made within 12 months of discharge. In both cases the York-Antwerp Rules 1950 applied, and made some slight difference to the shipowners' claim for general average contribution, if only in respect of commission and interest. Likewise in both cases it was alleged that the shipowners were at fault in the events which led to the general average act, from which fault they could only claim exemption (and thus recover contribution) by relying on exceptions in the contract of carriage. **00.27**

In *Alma Shipping Corporation v. Union of India*[76] Roskill J. said that, since the York-Antwerp Rules were incorporated by contract, and since the shipowners would need to rely on the exception of negligent navigation in the contract "... the present claim is clearly a dispute arising under this charterparty...." Mocatta J. reached a different conclusion in *E. B. Aaby's Rederi A/S v. Union of India*,[77] on the ground that an undertaking similar to an average bond had been given by the cargo interests before discharge, and that neither the time limit nor the arbitration provision in the contract of carriage provided an answer to a claim brought upon that undertaking. But the judge would otherwise have reached the same conclusion as Roskill J.

Mocatta J. said:

[73] [1947] A.C. 265 at 294.
[74] *Ibid.* at 281–283.
[75] *Ibid.* at 311–312.
[76] [1971] 2 Lloyd's Rep. 494 at 501.
[77] [1972] 2 Lloyd's Rep. 129.

> "... it is clear that whatever be the origins of the common law as to general average, the present claim to contribution depends in many respects on the provisions of the contract of carriage, which regulated the place where and the practice according to which the adjustment was drawn up, affected the *quantum* of contribution and is, in all probability, on the limited facts as to the casualty at present known, vital on the issue whether this was due to the fault of the plaintiffs, which if established, would defeat the claim."[78]

00.28 Only the second of these two cases went to the Court of Appeal.[79] The decision of Mocatta J. was upheld, but part of his reasoning and that of Roskill J. in the earlier case were overruled. The Court of Appeal held that (1) a claim for general average contribution was not such a claim as had to be made within the 12-month time limit; (2) (affirming Mocatta J.) a claim under the letter of undertaking was not affected by the time limit.

In the House of Lords[80] it was held that in general a claim for contribution would have been a claim arising out of the charterparty. For although general average is not necessarily the creature of contract, the application of the York-Antwerp Rules made some difference as to the quantum of contribution, the charterparty provided for general average to be settled in London rather than in accordance with the law of the port of discharge, and the terms of the charterparty might well be relevant to rebut a defence of fault. However, the decision of Mocatta J. and the Court of Appeal was upheld, on the ground that neither the arbitration clause nor its time limit applied to a claim under the letter of undertaking. Equally they would not (*per* Viscount Dilhorne) or might not (*per* Lord Salmon) have applied to a claim under a Lloyd's general average bond.[81]

00.29 The view that rights and obligations in general average may arise independently of contract, express or implied, was reaffirmed by Lord Diplock in *Castle Insurance v. Hong Kong Shipping Co.*,[82] but he also pointed out that a claim for general average will in practice be contractual:

> "Under that branch of English common law into which the *lex mercatoria* has long ago become absorbed, the personal liability to pay the general average contribution due in respect of any particular consignment of cargo that had been preserved in consequence of a general average sacrifice or expenditure lies, in legal theory, upon the person who was owner of the consignment at the time when the sacrifice was made or the liability for the expenditure incurred. In practice, however, the personal liability at common law of whoever was the owner of the contributing consignment of cargo at

[78] *Ibid.* at 134.

[79] [1973] 1 Lloyd's Rep. 509.

[80] [1974] 3 W.L.R. 269.

[81] *Ibid.* at 281, 283. For the terms of the Lloyd's general average bond see para. 80.02, *post*. In *The Percy Jordan* (1968) A.M.C. 2195 it was held (1) that a claim upon a general average undertaking was subject to the same statutory period of limitation as a direct claim for general average contribution; and (2) that the place where the claim arose was the port of discharge.

[82] [1984] A.C. 226 at 233, P.C.

the time of the general average act is hardly ever relied upon. There are two reasons for this. The first is that the contract of carriage between the shipowner and the owner of the consignment, whether the contract be contained in a charterparty or a bill of lading, invariably nowadays (so far as the decided cases show) contains an express clause dealing with general average and so brings the claim to contribution into the field of contract law."

Principles Established by the Cases

It is submitted that, on the preponderance of authority, a claim for general average contribution is not based upon contract if the same claim could be made without the aid of the York-Antwerp Rules and in accordance with the law and practice of the port of discharge. But if that is not so, the claim is contractual.[83] Even if the claim itself is not founded on contract, it may give rise to a dispute which arises out of the contract owing to the nature of the defence to the claim.[84] Where two shippers have each agreed with the shipowner that the Rules shall apply, and one shipper claims general average contribution from the other shipper, it is submitted that the Rules apply as a matter of implied contract between them.[85] **00.30**

[83] In *Castle Insurance v. Hong Kong Shipping Co.* [1984] A.C. 226 at 233, P.C. Lord Diplock's remarks may go rather further and support the view that a claim is contractual whenever there is a contract between the claimant and the respondent which deals with general average, whether or not the provisions of the contract affect the claim in the instant case.

[84] *Cf. Re Polemis and Furness, Withy & Co.* [1921] 3 K.B. 560.

[85] In *British Shipping Laws*, Vol. 3: Carver, paras. 1349–1350, the view is preferred that the obligation to contribute is one imposed by law. As to the case of a claim by one shipper on another, it is there suggested (citing *Thomson v. Micks Lambert* (1933) 39 Com.Cas. 40, *Grange v. Taylor* (1904) 9 Com.Ca 223 and *United States Shipping Board v. Durrell* [1923] 2 K.B. 739) that either the Rules apply by reason of implied contract or agency, or they are not applicable at all to such a claim. See para. 30.28, *post*.

SECTION 2

SOME PRINCIPLES OF THE LAW OF CARRIAGE BY SEA

Although the law of carriage by sea lies outside the scope of this work and reference should in case of need be made to the specialised works on the subject,[1] a brief reference to the general principles may not be out of place. The main importance of these principles in the context of general average is that the question may arise whether the accident which gave rise to the sacrifice or expenditure was caused by the actionable fault of one of the parties to the adventure, with the consequences described later in this work.[2] Another question which frequently arises in the adjustment of general average is whether the common maritime adventure has been or might be frustrated by damage to the ship or cargo, or by delay.[3] **00.31**

1. THE CONTRACT OF CARRIAGE

The shipowner usually engages by his contract to deliver the goods entrusted to his care, subject to certain excepted causes of loss or damage. But the shipowner's obligations may not be limited and exhausted by what appears on the face of the contract, for obligations may be implied by law: **00.32**

> "Underlying the contract, implied and involved in it, there is a warranty by the shipowner that his vessel is seaworthy, and there is also an engagement on his part to use due care and skill in navigating the vessel and carrying the goods. Having regard to the duties thus cast upon the shipowner, it seems to follow as a necessary consequence, that even in cases within the very terms of the exception in the bill of lading" (or charterparty) "the shipowner is not protected if any default or negligence on his part has caused or contributed to the loss."[4]

This statement of the common law is admirable in its simplicity and clearness. It may, however, be misleading if it is not borne in mind that

[1] See, *e.g. British Shipping Laws*, Vols. 2 and 3; Carver, *Carriage by Sea* (13th ed., 1982); *Scrutton on Charterparties* (20th ed., 1996).

[2] See paras. D.01 *et seq.*, *post.*

[3] See paras. 00.37–00.41, *post.*

[4] *Per* Lord Macnaghten in *Wilson v. Owners of Cargo per Xantho* (1887) 12 App.Cas. 503 at 513. See also the judgment of Lord Blackburn in *Steel v. State Line S.S. Co.* (1877) 3 App.Cas. 72 at 87.

the contract may contain an express exception of loss caused by negligence or, as the case may be, initial unseaworthiness.

00.33 Substantially to the same effect is a passage in the judgment of Willes J. in *Grill v. Iron Screw Collier Co.*,[5] which has frequently been quoted in subsequent cases.[6] The passage is as follows:

> "I may say that a policy of insurance is an absolute contract to indemnify for loss by perils of the sea, and it is only necessary to see whether the loss comes within the terms of the contract, and is caused by perils of the sea: the fact that the loss is partly caused by things not distinctly perils of the sea, does not prevent its coming within the contract. In the case of a bill of lading it is different, because the contract is to carry with reasonable care, unless prevented by the expected perils. If the goods are not carried with reasonable care, and are consequently lost by perils of the sea, it becomes necessary to reconcile the two parts of the instrument, and this is done by holding that if the loss through perils of the sea is caused by the previous default of the shipowner he is liable for this breach of his covenant."

Effect of negligence or breach of warranty of seaworthiness

00.34 Thus it will be seen that the effect of negligence in the carriage of the cargo is that the shipowner is liable for any loss or damage that happens to the cargo in consequence of the negligence, even though the immediate cause of the loss be a peril excepted by the contract of carriage, provided always that negligence be not itself an expected peril. Similar results follow upon a breach of the implied warranty of seaworthiness[7], subject to a like proviso.

Deviation

00.35 The shipowner further impliedly engages in every contract of affreightment that the ship shall proceed on the voyage without departure from her proper course and without unreasonable or unjustifiable delay. Any breach of this undertaking is called a deviation.

In considering whether there has been a deviation in any particular case, it must not be forgotten that the contract of affreightment may, and usually does, contain a wide clause giving liberty to deviate.[8]

[5] (1866) L.R. 1 C.P. 600 at 611.

[6] *e.g.* the speech of Lord Herschell in *Wilson v. Owners of Cargo per Xantho* (n. 4, *supra*) at 510.

[7] *Kopitoff v. Wilson* (1876) 1 Q.B.D. 377; *Cohn v. Davidson* (1877) 2 Q.B.D. 455; *Steel v. State Line* (n. 4, *supra*); *The Glenfruin* (1885) 10 P.D. 103. The shipowner also impliedly warrants that the ship is reasonably fit to receive and carry the cargo: see *Tattersall v. National S.S. Co.* (1884) 12 Q.B.D. 297; *McFadden v. Blue Star Line* [1905] 1 K.B. 697. This fitness is sometimes regarded as being included in the warranty of seaworthiness. See *Owners of Cargo ex Maori King v. Hughes* [1895] 2 Q.B. 550 at 557; *Sleigh v. Tyser* [1900] 2 Q.B. 333.

[8] See *British Shipping Laws*, Vol. 3; Carver, *Carriage by Sea* (13th ed.), paras. 1176–1186; Scrutton (20th ed.), pp. 261–264.

Effect of unjustifiable deviation

The legal effects of a deviation are more far reaching than those of any other breach of the contract of affreightment.[9] Deviation is a fundamental breach of the contract of carriage which gives the cargo owner the right to elect whether (1) to waive the breach and affirm the contract or (2) to treat the contract as abrogated. If he affirms, all the terms of the contract continue to apply to the adventure, but the cargo owner can claim damages (or exercise his rights and remedies in relation to actionable fault[10]) in respect of any loss or liability to contribute *caused* by the deviation.[11] If he treats the contract as abrogated, it ceases to apply, and the shipowner thereafter holds the goods as a common carrier—that is to say he is strictly liable for any loss or damage unless caused by act of God, the Queen's enemies or inherent vice,[12] and he can prove that the loss would have occurred even if there had been no deviation. **00.36**

So far as general average contribution is concerned, unjustified deviation, unless the contract be affirmed, has the following effect:

(a) The shipowner's *contractual* right to contribution is destroyed[13]; he will thus lose any right to claim under the provisions of the contract of affreightment, for example to claim contribution in accordance with the York-Antwerp Rules or to hold liable a consignee (not being the owner of the goods at the time of the general average) who would otherwise have been liable under the terms of the bill of lading.[14]

(b) It is an unresolved question whether the shipowner's right to contribution *at common law* is likewise destroyed. In *Hain S.S. Co. v. Tate & Lyle*[15] Scrutton L.J. expressed the view that all rights of contribution of all parties (including innocent cargo owners) were destroyed, because:

[9] See *British Shipping Laws*, Vol. 3; Carver, *Carriage by Sea* (13th ed.), paras. 1187–1204; *Scrutton on Charterparties* (20th ed.) pp. 258–261; *Hain S.S. Co. v. Tate & Lyle* (1934) 49 Ll.L. Rep.123, C.A.; (1936) 41 Com.Cas. 350, H.L.

[10] See paras. D.01 *et seq., post.*

[11] See *Hain S.S. Co. v. Tate & Lyle* (n. 9, *supra*) at 371, H.L., *per* Lord Maugham.

[12] Possibly also subject to statutory exceptions, such as that of fire under the Merchant Shipping Act 1995; see Carver (*op. cit.*), para. 1196.

[13] See *Hain S.S. Co. v. Tate & Lyle* (*supra*). In *Drew Brown v. The Orient Trader* [1973] 2 Lloyd's Rep. 174 the Canadian Supreme Court, applying U.S. law, held that the effect of the *New Jason* clause in the bill of lading was that the carrier could recover general average loss caused by a fire which broke out after a deviation, it not being shown that the fire was *caused* by the deviation. It is clear, however, that English law is to the opposite effect.

[14] See paras. 30.54 *et seq., post*, as to the persons against whom proceedings for contribution will lie. Although the contractual liability of a consignee (not being the owner of the goods at the relevant time) is destroyed by the deviation, the shipowner may exercise a lien on the cargo in order to obtain security; see paras. 30.56 *et seq., post.*

[15] At 131. See also in H.L. *per* Lord Atkin at 357, and the dissenting judgment of Spence J. in *Drew Brown v. The Orient Trader* (*supra*).

"they were not parties by agreement to the adventure after the deviation. The basis of general average contribution, the 'common adventure' had been destroyed by the deviation..."

However, while there is undoubtedly much to be said for this point of view, there remains room for debate on the question, since general average at common law does not depend on agreement, and a deviation does not render unlawful the shipowner's possession of the goods during the remainder of the voyage,[16] which may therefore be said still to retain the essential features of a common adventure.[17] In practice, because of the strict liability of a shipowner for loss or damage after deviation, there would be few cases in which a cargo owner would be unable to defend the shipowner's claim for contribution on the ground of actionable fault.[18]

(c) The cargo owner who claims contribution from the shipowner may elect to waive the deviation and claim in accordance with the provisions of the contract of carriage. However, it will usually be more advantageous to him to rescind the contract and to hold the shipowner strictly liable, as a common carrier, for the whole loss.

(d) The rights of cargo owners *inter se* is a difficult question. The owner of sacrificed cargo cannot waive the deviation and proceed against the other cargo owners in accordance with the contract, since the latter, also being innocent parties, have their own separate right to elect whether to affirm or rescind. The question whether any rights of contribution survive at common law has already been discussed in head (b) above. There seems little justification for depriving a cargo owner of his common law right of contribution as a result of a deviation by the shipowner.

It is an unresolved question whether deviation abrogates the contract of carriage from the beginning, or whether the contract continues to apply up to the moment of deviation.[19] It is submitted that the better view is the latter.

The effect of a deviation on the liability of a consignee who has entered into an average bond is dealt with in Section 5, Part 2, "Enforcing Rights of Contribution", paragraphs 30.56 *et seq.*, below.

[16] *Hain S.S. Co. v. Tate & Lyle* (n. 9, *supra*), at 371, H.L., *per* Lord Maugham.

[17] See also *British Shipping Laws*, Vol 3; Carver, *Carriage by Sea* (13th ed.), para. 1198.

[18] See paras. D.01 *et seq.*, *post.*

[19] *Cf. British Shipping Laws*, Vol 3; Carver, *Carriage by Sea* (13th ed.), para. 1200; *Scrutton on Charterparties* (20th ed.), p. 259. See also *Suisse Atlantique Soc. d'Armement v. Rotterdamsche Kolen Centrale* [1967] 1 A.C. 361; *Photo Production v. Securior* [1980] A.C. 827, *Kenya Railways v. Antares* [1987] 2 Lloyd's Rep. 424.

Effect of Frustration

Frustration is the main exception to the basic rule that contracts are absolute—that is; they must be fulfilled however difficult, inconvenient or expensive performance may become. It occurs when, as a result of some extraneous event outside the control of either party, further performance of the contract becomes physically impossible, or illegal[20] or "something radically different from that which was undertaken by the contract."[21] **00.37**

In the absence of frustration, or some express provision in the contract, the adventure can only be lawfully[22] terminated by carriage to the contractual destination or by express agreement between the carrier and cargo interests.

Frustration of the adventure does not bring to an end accrued rights to contribution in general average.[23] Its importance in matters of general average is that when it occurs it will usually cause the common adventure to end before arrival at the contractual destination and this premature termination of the adventure may affect the valuation of the contributing interests, the law governing the adjustment and the period over which port of refuge expenses are allowable.

Frustration of the adventure at a port or place of refuge

Frustration may result from many types of event, such as war, ice, or total loss of ship or cargo, but in the context of general average the issue most likely to arise is whether damage to the ship or the cargo suffered as a result of an accident on the voyage, or the delay consequent thereon, is sufficiently serious to frustrate the contract and thus to terminate the adventure at a port or place of refuge. In essence, the test to be applied in such a case is the same as in any other. In *Hill v. Wilson*[24] where both ship and cargo were damaged on a voyage to Hull and the ship put into Copenhagen as a port of refuge, Lindley J. stated that in order to uphold an adjustment made at Copenhagen, in accordance with Danish law, **00.38**

[20] In general, supervening illegality by the proper law of the contract or by the law of the place of performance will bring about frustration.

[21] See *Davis Contractors v. Fareham U.D.C.* [1956] A.C. 696 at 729, *per* Lord Radcliffe.

[22] It may also be terminated by a breach of contract which the innocent party is entitled to, and does, treat as a repudiation of the contract.

[23] One reason is that, although the obligation to contribute will normally arise out of the contract (see paras. 00.29–00.30, *ante*) the Law Reform (Frustrated Contracts) Act 1943, does not apply to contracts for the carriage of goods by sea other than time charterparties or charterparties by demise. In any event, it is submitted that a provision regarding general average is severable from the remainder of the contract of carriage and is intended to apply to all general averages, including those which occur in circumstances which bring about the frustration of the adventure (*cf. Heyman v. Darwins* [1942] A.C. 356). Where the Act does apply, see s. 2(3).

[24] (1879) 4 C.P.D. 329 at 333. The passage quoted here was relied upon in *Assicurazioni Generali v. The Bessie Morris S.S. Co.* [1892] 1 Q.B. 571; [1892] 2 Q.B. 652, C.A.

against the cargo owners the shipowner would have to prove that the voyage terminated there:

> "either by agreement or by necessity, *i.e.* the occurrence of circumstances beyond the control of the [shipowner], and such as rendered the completion of the voyage on the terms originally agreed upon physically impossible, or so clearly unreasonable as to be impossible in a business point of view."

It is worthwhile investigating in a little more detail the circumstances in which this test is fulfilled, and we shall do so under three headings:

00.39 (1) *Damage to the ship.* The shipowner is obliged to repair and continue the voyage if the cost of repairs will be less than the repaired value of the ship plus the value of freight still at risk,[25] provided that the repair can be effected and the voyage completed without such delay as would frustrate the adventure. In all such cases, it is the cost and the duration of such repairs as are necessary to complete the voyage, and not of permanent repairs, which are the relevant consideration.[26]

(2) *Damage to the cargo.* Damage to the cargo will frustrate a contract when the cargo is rendered unfit for onward carriage from the port of refuge, and cannot be reconditioned without frustrating delay or without such expenditure as would render it commercially "impossible" in the sense described above.

(3) *Delay.* Unavoidable delay in prosecuting the voyage from the port of refuge will give rise to frustration if it is so great as to destroy the commercial purpose of the voyage. It is impossible to lay down any general rule as to the length of delay which will have this result, but the following factors are relevant:

   (a) The length of time which the voyage would normally be expected to last. A delay of one month on a voyage which would normally last one week would be more likely to give rise to frustration than if the normal length of the voyage were six weeks.

   (b) The nature of the cargo—(for instance, a cargo of bananas could not survive a long delay whereas a cargo of iron ore could remain indefinitely in a vessel).

   (c) Whether the cargo is intended for a particular market or a particular use which makes it of fundamental importance that it should arrive promptly.

00.40 Frustration will occur as soon as it is possible to make a reasonably reliable and well-informed estimate that the damage to ship or cargo is so great, or the delay is likely to be so long, as to be sufficient to frustrate

[25] *Moss v. Smith* (1850) 9 C.B. 94; *Jackson v. Union Marine Insurance* (1874) L.R. 10 C.P. 125; *Assicurazioni Generali v. The S.S. Bessie Morris Co.* (n. 24, *supra*); *Carras v. London & Scottish Assurance* [1936] 1 K.B. 291.

[26] *Kulukundis v. Norwich Union Fire Insce. Co.* [1937] 1 K.B. 1.

the adventure under the principles described above. It is not necessary to wait until the facts are known with absolute certainty. In *Bank Line v. Capel*[27] where the issue was whether delay caused by a requisition of the ship had frustrated a time charter, Lord Sumner explained the correct approach as follows:

> "The probabilities as to the length of the deprivation and not the certainty arrived at after the event are also material. The question must be considered at the trial as it had to be considered by the parties, when they came to know of the cause and the probabilities of the delay and had to decide what to do. Rights ought not to be left in suspense or to hang on the chances of subsequent events. The contract binds or it does not bind, and the law ought to be that the parties can gather their fate then and there."

The Shipowner's Right to Tranship

The general rule is that frustration occurs automatically once the frustrating event has happened and its effect on further performance of the contract is known or can be predicted with sufficient certainty; the cargo interests are thereupon bound and entitled to take possession of their cargo at the port of refuge, unless some new agreement is entered into between the parties. **00.41**

To this rule there is one important exception, namely that the shipowner has an implied right to tranship the cargo and complete the voyage in another ship, provided that the cargo is fit to stand the voyage and that the voyage can be completed without unreasonable delay. The shipowner is under no obligation to exercise this right,[28] but if he wishes to do so he must act promptly.

2. Hague Rules and Similar Legislation

Exceptions Clauses and the Hague Rules

Shipowners for years successfully endeavoured to protect themselves by clauses in their contracts of affreightment which exempted them from responsibility for the negligence of their servants, or for losses brought **00.42**

[27] [1919] A.C. 435 at 454.

[28] The shipowner may be *obliged* to tranship where the ocean voyage is effectively at an end so that, *e.g.* the voyage could be completed by transhipment into lighters: see *Kulukundis v. Norwich Union Fire Insce. Co.* (*supra*) at 16–17, *per* Greer L.J. *Cf. Western Sealanes Corp. v. Unimarine* [1982] 2 Lloyd's Rep. 160 at 166–167.

about by the unseaworthiness of the vessel.[29] However, it is necessary in this connection to distinguish between contracts of affreightment which are made by charterparty and those which are contained in or evidenced by bill of lading. To contracts of the first sort the common law still applies; the parties are free to make any bargain they please, although if the shipowner wishes to protect himself against liability for breach of any implied term or warranty he must do so in clear and unambiguous language. But a contract covered by a bill of lading (including any bill of lading issued under charterparty if and when the holder of the bill of lading is a person other than the charterer) may now be subject, both in this country and in most maritime countries, to the provisions of the Hague Rules as applied by various statutes. These Rules may also be incorporated in a bill of lading, or indeed a charterparty, by agreement.

00.43 In the United Kingdom the Hague Rules were first given statutory effect by the Carriage of Goods by Sea Act 1924. Amendments to the Rules were formulated in the Brussels Protocol of 1968, and the amended Rules form the Schedule to the Carriage of Goods by Sea Act 1971,[30] which applies to bills of lading issued on or after June 23, 1977.[31] Further amendment to the financial limits of the carrier's liability for loss or damage, was made by the Protocol of 1979, which has been given statutory force by the Merchant Shipping Act 1981.

Whether or not the Rules apply to a contract of carriage, where not incorporated by express agreement, will depend on the proper law of the contract and the extent to which the courts in which the action is brought will give effect to that law.[32] Where English law applies, the effect of the Carriage of Goods by Sea Act 1971, and of the amended Rules, is that the Rules apply:

(1) where the port of shipment is in the United Kingdom;
(2) where the bill of lading provides that the Rules are to govern the contract; or
(3) where the bill of lading relates to carriage between different states; and
 (a) the bill of lading is issued in a contracting state,[33] or
 (b) the carriage is from a port in a contracting state,[34] or

[29] The warranty of seaworthiness will, however, only be excluded by stipulation so clear as to admit of no other construction: see *Gilroy v. Price* [1893] A.C. 56; *McIver v. Tate Steamers* [1903] 1 K.B. 362, C.A.; *Rathbone v. McIver* [1903] 2 K.B. 378, C.A.; *Elderslie S.S. Co. v. Borthwick* [1905] A.C. 93; *Nelson Line v. James Nelson & Sons Ltd.* [1908] A.C. 16; *South American Export Syndicate v. Federal Steam Nav. Co.* (1909) 14 Com.Cas. 228; *Fiumana Societa di Navigazione v. Bunge & Co.* [1930] 2 K.B. 47, and *British Shipping Laws*, Vol. 2; Carver, *Carriage by Sea* (13th ed.), paras. 159–167.

[30] 1971, c.19.

[31] The Carriage of Goods by Sea Act 1971 (Commencement) Order 1977, S.I. 1977 No. 981.

[32] See *Vita Food Products v. Unus Shipping Co.* [1939] A.C. 277.

[33–34] A contracting state is a state which is a party to the Protocol of 1968, whether or not a party to the Protocol of 1979: see the Merchant Shipping Act 1981, s. 2(6). For a list of contracting states, see the Carriage of Goods by Sea (Parties to Convention) Order 1985, S.I. 1985 No. 443.

(c) the contract provides that the amended Rules or legislation giving effect to them is to govern the contract.[35]

There are many countries, including the United States, which have not adopted the amended Rules. As a result, it is frequently the unamended Rules which will apply.[36] References to the Hague Rules in the remainder of this section apply equally to either version unless the contrary is expressly stated.

Under the Hague Rules the carrier is entitled to the benefit of extensive rights and immunities, unless the contract expressly provides to the contrary, and these rights and immunities operate in effect as exceptions clauses. Thus if the necessity for the general average act arose through the "act, neglect or default of the master, mariner, pilot, or the servants of the carrier in the navigation or in the management of the ship" (Article IV, rule 2) there would be no actionable fault on the part of the carrier, and he could claim contribution. The detailed application of these rights and immunities lies outside the scope of this work, but brief mention must be made of one or two of the more important effects of the Rules. **00.44**

Effect of Hague Rules on Obligation to make Ship Seaworthy

At common law, the shipowner, in every contract of affreightment, impliedly engaged with the shipper of goods by reason of the warranty of seaworthiness that his ship, on the commencement of her voyage, was seaworthy for that voyage and supplied with a competent crew.[37] Section 2 of the 1924 Act (section 3 of the 1971 Act) abolishes the implied absolute warranty of seaworthiness, where it applies, but substitutes an implied warranty that the carrier will use due diligence to secure that his ship is so seaworthy and supplied. **00.45**

Effect of Hague Rules on Duty to Care for the Goods

Article III, rule 2 of the Hague Rules provides that the carrier shall "properly and carefully load, stow, carry, keep, care for and discharge the goods". This reflects the duty at common law to carry goods carefully. In order to reconcile this provision with the exception of negligent navigation or management of the ship, it is necessary to draw what is **00.46**

[35] See the Carriage of Goods by Sea Act 1971, s.1(3), (6), and Art. X of the amended Rules.

[36] For the application of the unamended Rules see *British Shipping Laws*, Vol. 2; Carver, *Carriage by Sea* (13th ed.), paras. 571–578.

[37] See paras. 00.32–00.34, *ante*.

often a narrow distinction between negligence in the care of the cargo, and negligence in the management of the ship as a whole. Thus a failure to close the hatches when in port has been held to be negligence towards the cargo rather then the ship,[38] as has a failure correctly to operate the refrigeration machinery used for cooling the cargo.[39] On the other hand a failure properly to secure the tarpaulins on the hatch covers, with the result that seawater entered the holds on the voyage, was held to be negligence in the management of the ship.[40]

Effect of the Hague Rules on Deviation

00.47 So far as deviation is concerned the Rules have made little difference. The provisions of Article IV, rule 4, provide:

> Any deviation in saving or attempting to save life or property at sea or any reasonable deviation shall not be deemed to be an infringement or breach of these Rules or of the contract of carriage, and the carrier shall not be liable for any loss or damage resulting therefrom.

The only result appears to be that so far as contracts to which the Rules apply are concerned, the deviation to be justifiable must be reasonable (which in particular includes a deviation to save life or property). As to what is a reasonable deviation see *Stag Line v. Foscolo Mango & Co.*[41] and *Danae Shipping v. T.P.A.O.*[42]

Effect of Hague Rules on Provisions regarding General Average

00.48 It is uncertain to what extent the Hague Rules affect the parties' freedom to contract on such terms as they wish with regard to general average. The Rules contain the following provisions relevant to this question:

Article III, Rule 8

> Any clause, covenant or agreement in a contract of carriage relieving the carrier or the ship from liability for loss or damage to or in connection with goods arising from negligence, fault or failure in the duties and obligations provided in this Article or lessening such liability otherwise than as provided in these Rules, shall be null and void and of no effect.
>
> A benefit of insurance in favour of the carrier or similar clause shall be deemed to be a clause relieving the carrier from liability.

[38] *Gosse Millerd v. Canadian Govt. Merchant Marine* [1929] A.C. 223.
[39] *Foreman & Ellams v. Federal S.N. Co.* [1928] 2 K.B. 424.
[40] *International Packers v. Ocean S.S. Co.* [1955] 2 Lloyd's Rep. 218.
[41] [1932] A.C. 328. For a detailed discussion of the effect of Art IV, r. 4, see *British Shipping Laws*, Vol. 2; Carver, *Carriage by Sea* (13th ed.), paras. 546–550 and *Scrutton* (20th ed.), pp. 447–449.
[42] [1983] 1 Lloyd's Rep. 498.

Article IV Rule 3

The shipper shall not be responsible for loss or damage sustained by the carrier or the ship arising or resulting from any cause without the act, fault or neglect of the shipper, his agents or his servants.

Article V

Nothing in these Rules shall be held to prevent the insertion in a bill of lading of any lawful provision regarding general average.

It is clear that Article V overrides Article IV, rule 3, with the result that the shipper's liability to contribute in general average is not affected by absence of fault on his part. However, it seems unlikely that Article V was intended to override Article III, rule 8, so as to allow wider exemption clauses to operate in respect of claims in general average. **00.49**

Whether this intention has been achieved is doubtful. Although the purport of the word "lawful" in Article V is unclear, if the words of the Article are given their ordinary meaning it is difficult to resist the conclusion that no provision of the Rules, including Article III, rule 8, may be invoked in order to invalidate a "provision regarding general average" which would otherwise be lawful. Moreover in *Goulandris Bros Ltd v. B. Goldman & Sons Ltd*[43] it was held by Pearson J. that the words "loss or damage" in the 1924 version of Article III, rule 6 (which provides that the carrier shall be discharged from liability unless suit is brought within one year) do not include liability to contribute in general average. If that is so, the words "loss or damage to, or in connection with, goods" in Article III, rule 8 can scarcely include liability to contribute.[44]

Hence the effect of Article III, rule 8 and Article 5 appears to be that a contract of affreightment which was subject to the Rules could lawfully provide that the shipowner should be entitled to general average contribution, notwithstanding any breach of the obligations imposed by Article III, rules 1 and 2. Such provisions though not unknown[45] are rare, and the result is one which the courts might be reluctant to reach; but it is submitted that it must follow, unless the decision of Pearson J. in *Goulandris Bros Ltd v. B. Goldman & Sons Ltd*[46] as to the meaning of **00.50**

[43] [1958] 1 Q.B. 74.

[44] Although they are not limited to physical loss or damage: *G. H. Renton & Co. Ltd v. Palmyra Trading Corporation* [1957] A.C. 149. *Cf. Adamastos Shipping Co. Ltd v. Anglo-Saxon Petroleum Co. Ltd* [1959] A.C. 133.

[45] Both the 1978 and the 1994 editions of the widely-used Congenbill contain, in addition to a clause paramount and a New Jason clause, the following provision:

> "Cargo's contribution to General Average shall be paid to the Carrier even when such average is the result of a fault neglect or error of the Master, Pilot or Crew."

On the face of it, this provision entitles the carrier to general average contribution even where the fault or neglect is in the care of the cargo rather than in the navigation or management of the ship and would therefore involve a breach of the Hague Rules: see para 00.46, *ante*.

[46] See n. 43, *supra*.

"loss or damage" is reconsidered,[47] and unless the court is prepared to give a very restrictive interpretation to Article V.

The Harter Act

00.51 Contracts for the carriage of goods on Atlantic voyages sometimes contain a clause incorporating the provisions of the "Harter" Act, a statute of the United States, passed in 1893, to regulate the trade between the United States and foreign ports. Sections 1 and 2 of the Act prohibit and avoid clauses which relieve the shipowner from the duty to take care of the cargo and provide a seaworthy ship; but section 3 enacts that if the shipowner has exercised due care to make the vessel seaworthy, neither he, the vessel, her agent, nor her charterers shall be liable for damage or loss arising from (*inter alia*) faults or errors in navigation, or in the management of the vessel.[48] The Supreme Court of the United States has held that this exemption in the Act has not the effect of entitling the shipowner to claim a contribution for a general average loss due to the negligence of his servants.[49] It may be argued that the incorporation of the Harter Act in an English contract should have the same effect as is attributed to it by American law, so that, notwithstanding the decisions in *The Carron Park*[50] and *Milburn v. Jamaica Fruit Importing Co.*,[51] the shipowner is not entitled to contribution for a loss due to the negligence of his servants in the navigation or management of the vessel. It has, however, been held that the legal result, if the contract is expressed to be subject to the provisions of the Act, is only the same as if the

[47] The decision on the effect of Art. III, r. 6, was not essential to the result, and was reached without the benefit of the decision of the House of Lords in *Adamastos Shipping Company Ltd v. Anglo Saxon Petroleum Company Ltd* (n. 44, *supra*). However, it has been said that the incurring of a liability to contribute is not "loss" within the meaning of the Merchant Shipping Act 1894, s. 503: see *Greenshields, Cowie and Co. v. Stephen and Sons Ltd* [1908] A.C. 431, H.L.; *Louis Dreyfus v. Tempus Shipping* [1931] A.C. 726 at 739, *per* Lord Dunedin.

[48] For a consideration of this Act, and the effect of its incorporation into an English bill of lading, see *Dobell v. S.S. Rossmore Co.* [1895] 2 Q.B. 408.

[49] *The Irrawaddy* (1898) 171 U.S. 187. Before the Act any clause in a bill of lading which exempted the shipowner from liability for the negligence of himself or his servants was considered by the U.S.courts to be contrary to public policy and void. Section 3 only provides a defence where none existed previously; it does not entitle a shipowner to claim general average contribution consequent upon negligence, since it does not mention general average. Equally (or perhaps *a fortiori*) the section does not exonerate the shipowner from liability to contribute in general average to the loss of cargo; for otherwise he might be in a better position if his servants had been negligent than if they had not: *The Jason* 225 U.S. 32 (1910); *The Ernestina* 259 Fed.Rep. 772 (1919). And the shipowner's sacrifices and expenditure must be taken into account in any claim by cargo for contribution, notwithstanding his negligence or that of his servants; in this manner such a claim may be reduced or wholly extinguished: *The Strathdon* 94 Fed.Rep. 206 (1899); 10 Fed.Rep. 600 (1900).

[50] (1890) 15 P.D. 203.

[51] [1900] 2 Q.B. 540.

material clauses of the Act were written into the contract.[52] It is therefore submitted, that under an English contract incorporating the Act, the shipowner would not be precluded by the decision of the Supreme Court from claiming contribution; the incorporation of the Act is only equivalent to the insertion of a negligence clause in the terms of the Act.

The Jason Clause and the New Jason Clause

In consequence of the decision in *The Irrawaddy*[53] a negligence general average clause is almost invariably included in bills of lading under which general average is likely to be adjusted in the United States. If this be the *Jason Clause*,[54] the shipowner's right to general average contribution is expressed to be subject to the condition that he shall have exercised due diligence to make the ship seaworthy and properly manned, equipped and supplied; if he has not, it matters not that there was no causal connection between his failure and the casualty.[55] In the *New Jason Clause*, on the other hand, the right is subject only to the condition that the casualty shall not have resulted from a cause for which the shipowner is responsible by statute, contract or otherwise.[56] **00.52**

Despite the provenance of the *Jason Clause* and the *New Jason Clause* one or other of them (and sometimes both) is from time to time included in a contract of carriage where general average is to be adjusted elsewhere than in the United States. The question has been raised, whether this has the result of reducing the shipowner's rights.[57] **00.53**

Thus in *Goulandris Bros Ltd v. B. Goldman and Sons Ltd*,[58] it was argued that, whatever the effect of Rule D, of the York-Antwerp Rules, the result of incorporating a *New Jason Clause* in the bill of lading was that the cargo owner had a pure defence to a claim for general average whenever the danger arose from the actionable fault of the shipowner. However, since Pearson J. decided the issue in favour of the cargo owner on the construction of Rule D itself, he did not deal with this question.

In *E. B. Aaby's Rederi v. Union of India (No. 2)*,[59] it was argued that

[52] *Dobell v. S.S. Rossmore Co.* [1895] 2 Q.B. 408, C.A., "They then introduce into their bill of lading the words of the Harter Act, which I decline to construe as an Act, but which we must construe simply as words occurring in this bill of lading": *per* Lord Esher. See also *Rowson v. Atlantic Transport Co.* [1903] 2 K.B. 666, C.A.

[53] See para. 00.51, n. 49, *ante*.

[54] *The Jason* 225 U.S. 32 (1910).

[55] *The Isis* (1934) 48 Ll.L.R. 35. In one case the general average clause has been held itself to determine the shipowners' duties under the contract, as far as concerned general average: *Schade v. National Surety Corporation* (1961) A.M.C. 1225.

[56] For a discussion of the history of these clauses, see *Drew Brown Ltd v. The Orient Trader* [1972] 1 Lloyd's Rep. 35 at 47–48; [1973] 2 Lloyd's Rep. 174.

[57] See *post*. See also *The Makedonia* [1962] 1 Lloyd's Rep 316 at 341.

[58] [1958] 1 Q.B. 74 at 106. For the decision in this case on Rule D, see para. D.23, below.

[59] [1976] 2 Lloyd's Rep. 714. The argument was not pursued in the Court of Appeal [1978] 1 Lloyd's Rep. 351.

the effect of the incorporation of a *Jason Clause* in the bill of lading was to deprive the shipowner, who had failed to exercise due diligence to make the ship seaworthy, of a right to contribution, even if the unseaworthiness in question was not the cause of the casualty. The bill of lading incorporated the Hague Rules, and references to the Harter Act had been deleted. Donaldson J. rejected this argument, holding that the effect of the clause did not detract from the ordinary right of the shipowner under English law or under the York-Antwerp Rules to recover contribution unless his actionable fault was the cause of the peril.

The Hague Rules in the United States

00.54 The Carriage of Goods by Sea Act 1936 gave effect with slight modifications to the Hague Rules[60] and enacted (section 13) that it should apply to all foreign trade to and from the ports of the United States. By section 12, however, the Harter Act remained applicable before loading and after discharging cargo. It would therefore appear that so far as general average is concerned, the decisions under the Harter Act are of academic interest only, except on the point mentioned in paragraph 00.51, above.

The Hamburg Rules 1978

00.55 For the sake of completeness it remains to mention the Hamburg Rules 1978, which were intended to replace the Hague Rules as an internationally adopted code, applying compulsorily to contracts for carriage of goods by sea other than charterparties. These Rules are contained in the U.N. Convention on the Carriage of Goods by Sea concluded at Hamburg in 1978, but it is only very recently that the Convention has been ratified by a sufficient number of states to bring it into force. The United Kingdom has ratified the Convention, but it has so far taken no steps to introduce legislation to give legal effect to the Rules, and it remains uncertain whether it will ever do so. A small number of states, mainly non-maritime, have given legal effect to the Hamburg Rules, but at present it seems improbable that they will gain international acceptance and become an effective replacement for the Hague Rules.

Where the Hamburg Rules do apply, they render the carrier prima facie liable for loss, damage or delay while the goods are in his charge during the voyage or at the port of loading or discharge. In order to avoid liability the carrier must prove "that he, his servants or agents took all measures that could reasonably be required to avoid the occur-

[60] In the U.S. the Brussels Protocol of 1968 (see para. 00.43, *ante*) has not yet been enacted or brought into force.

rence and its consequences". At the risk of over-simplication it may be said that probably the most important difference in practical terms between the Hamburg Rules and the Hague Rules is that under the Hamburg Rules the carrier will always incur liability for loss, damage or delay caused by negligence, and that there is no exception of "act, neglect or default ... in the navigation or in the management of the ship". It is hardly necessary to mention that the absence of this exception would greatly increase the number of cases in which a claim for contribution can be successfully defended on the ground of actionable fault.

The Carrier's Obligation to Incur General Average Expenditure

The shipowner is not released from his duty to care for the cargo **00.56**
merely because an accident occurs which necessitates extraordinary measures, involving either sacrifice or expenditure. If the carrier ought reasonably to have taken such measures, he will be liable to the owner of the cargo which is damaged by his failure to do so.

In *Notara v. Henderson*[61] a cargo of beans, wetted by seawater when the ship was involved in a collision, was discharged at a port of refuge. The shipowner failed to take any steps to dry the beans, as a result of which they suffered much greater damage than would otherwise have been incurred. It was held that the shipowner was liable for this damage. Although not responsible for the collision, the shipowner was under a duty to care for the cargo after the collision and he ought reasonably to have arranged for the beans to be dried. If he had done so, the costs of drying the beans could have been recovered from the shipper as a particular charge.[62]

The principle in *Notara v. Henderson*[63] is equally applicable to the case **00.57**
of general, as well as particular average, and it exposes the fallacy of an assertion which is sometimes advanced, namely that the making of a sacrifice or the incurring of expenditure cannot be a general average act if the shipowner is under a duty under the contract of carriage to make or to incur it. The proper inquiry is whether the shipowner is obliged to make the sacrifice or incur the expenditure *and to bear the whole burden thereof himself as part of the cost of performing his contractual obligations.* In a case concerned with temporary repairs,[64] after pointing out that it was the shipowner's obligation under the contract of carriage to effect the repairs and complete the voyage, Hobhouse J. continued:

[61] (1870) L.R. 5 Q.B. 346; (1872) L.R. 7 Q.B. 225.

[62] See *ibid.* at 354, *per* Lord Cockburn C.J., and at 233, 235, per Wills J.

[63] See n. 61, above.

[64] *Marida v. Oswal Steel; The Bijela* [1992] 1 Lloyd's Rep. 636 at 643 (reversed on another point [1994] 2 Lloyd's Rep 1, H.L.). The claim was for the cost of temporary repairs of accidental damage under Rule XIV of the York-Antwerp Rules, and the case is discussed in the context of that Rule.

"The existence of the obligation is not decisive of the question before me. Many types of general average expenditure are incurred by the master in the fulfilment of his duties to the interests involved in the common adventure, including to the cargo-owners, and the function of general average is to provide a superimposed scheme for the sharing of the burden of that expenditure in an equitable fashion."

Thus if, under the principles examined in this work, the shipowner is entitled to contribution in general average toward his sacrifice or expenditure from the other parties to the adventure, he is not to be deprived of that entitlement on the ground that he would have been in breach of his obligations toward those other parties if the master had failed to act as he did. However, slightly different considerations may apply when the claim is for substituted expenses, and these are discussed in commentary on Rule F of the York–Antwerp Rules.

Obligations of the Shipper

00.58 The contract of carriage usually imposes on the charterer or shipper certain obligations with regard to the nature of the goods shipped. If goods shipped in breach of those obligations are sacrificed because they had become a danger to the ship or to other cargo on board, the shipper will be precluded from claiming contribution in general average on the grounds that the peril arose by his actionable fault.

Dangerous goods

00.59 In addition to any express terms of the contract which may prohibit the shipment of certain types of goods, there is at common law an implied warranty on the part of the shipper that he will not ship dangerous goods without giving notice to the shipowner of their dangerous character.[65] If the dangerous character is obvious from the description given to the shipowner, the shipowner is deemed to have notice, and no further warning is necessary[66] unless the goods possess some special characteristic which gives rise to special risks, or requires the use of special precautions during the voyage.[67]

00.60 It is a matter of controversy whether the implied obligation of the shipper is absolute, or whether it is to give notice of those dangerous

[65] *Brass v. Maitland* (1856) 26 L.J.Q.B. 49; 6 E. & B. 470; *Bamfield v. Goole & Sheffield Transport Co.* [1910] 2 K.B. 94; *Ministry of Food v. Lamport & Holt* [1952] 2 Lloyd's Rep. 371; *Atlantic Oil Carriers v. British Petroleum* [1957] 2 Lloyd's Rep. 55 at 95.

[66] *Acatos v. Burns* (1878) 3 Ex.D. 282; *Greenshields Cowie & Co. v. Stephens & Sons* [1908] A.C. 431.

[67] *Atlantic Oil Carriers v. British Petroleum* (*supra*).

characteristics of which he was, or ought to have been, aware.[68] An absolute obligation is frequently imposed by the express terms of the contract; and where the Hague Rules apply, Article IV, rule 6 provides:

> Goods of an inflammable, explosive or dangerous nature to the shipment whereof the carrier, master or agent of the carrier, has not consented, with knowledge of their nature and character, may at any time before discharge be landed at any place or destroyed or rendered innocuous by the carrier without compensation, and the shipper of such goods shall be liable for all damages and expenses directly or indirectly arising out of or resulting from such shipment.
>
> If any such goods shipped with such knowledge and consent shall become a danger to the ship or cargo, they may in like manner be landed at any place or destroyed or rendered innocuous by the carrier without liability on the part of the carrier except to general average, if any.

The effect of the first paragraph appears to be that the liability of the shipper is absolute. All that the carrier need prove is that (1) the goods were of an inflammable, explosive or dangerous nature, and (2) he did not consent to their shipment with knowledge of their nature and character. In these circumstances, the shipper is liable to compensate the carrier for all losses resulting from the shipment. Also he is denied any right of contribution in general average, since the words "without compensation" are, it is submitted, wide enough to apply to contribution.

Position of consignee when dangerous goods are shipped

Under both the common law and the Hague Rules, it is the shipper upon whom the obligations relevant to the shipment of dangerous goods are imposed, and it is an unresolved question whether those obligations are transferred to a consignee or indorsee by virtue of the Bills of Lading Act 1855, or to the holder of the bill of lading by virtue of the Carriage of Goods by Sea Act 1992.[69] This question could be of importance in the context of a claim for general average if dangerous goods, shipped in breach of contract, were sacrificed after property had passed from the shipper to the consignee. If the contractual obligations are also transferred, the shipowner would be able to establish actionable fault on the part of the consignee, and would avoid liability to contribute on that ground,[70] whereas otherwise he would have to pursue a separate action **00.61**

[68] *Cf.* Carver, *op. cit.*, paras. 1108–1110, Scrutton, *op. cit.*, Art. 53. In *Effort Shipping v. Linden Management* [1994] 2 Lloyd's Rep. 171; [1996] 1 Lloyd's Rep. 577, C.A., it was held that the obligation was absolute. An appeal to the House of Lords is understood to be pending.

[69] See *Ministry of Food v. Lamport & Holt* [1952] 2 Lloyd's Rep. 371 at 382; *British Shipping Laws*, Vol 2; Carver, *Carriage by Sea* (13th ed.), para. 95; *Scrutton on Charterparties* (20th ed.), p. 40. In *Effort Shipping v. Linden Management* (see n. 68, *supra*) it was held that, under the Bills of Lading Act 1855, the shipper was not divested of his liability in respect of dangerous cargo upon the indorsement of the bill of lading. The question whether the indorsee was also liable did not arise.

[70] See paras. D.01 *et seq.*, *post*.

against the shipper. However, the effect of the first paragraph of Article IV, rule 6[71] of the Hague Rules is that no claim in general average arises out of the sacrifice of dangerous goods shipped without the carrier's consent. Thus, where the Hague Rules apply, it will be irrelevant whether the claim for contribution is brought by the shipper or by the consignee.

General Average Sacrifice as a Defence

00.62 The character of a defence that exists in general average sacrifices has long been recognised[72] and has been considered by the Supreme Court of Canada in a case of some importance, *Federal Commerce and Navigation Co. Ltd v. Eisenerz G.m.b.H.*[73]

The vessel *Oak Hill*, owned by the appellants, loaded two part cargoes of pig iron at Sorel, P.Q., for carriage to Genoa. Owing to the negligence of the pilot, for which the appellants were by contract not responsible, the vessel stranded in the St. Lawrence River and put into the port of Levis, P.Q., as a port of refuge for repairs. It was necessary to discharge and subsequently reload the pig iron in order that repairs could be carried out and, during the course of these operations, the cargoes became intermingled and to a limited extent lost and destroyed. The respondent, as owner of the cargo, claimed for the full amount of the loss and damage. The appellants relied on Rule XII of the York-Antwerp Rules 1950 as a defence.

If the facts had stopped there, the appellants would (as the Supreme Court evidently considered) have had a defence to the claim. It is submitted that this defence would not have rested on Rule XII, which affords the owner of cargo lost or damaged at a port of refuge a right to general average contribution; it would have rested on the inherent characteristic of all general average sacrifices, that the shipowner is not liable for loss of or damage to cargo resulting from a general average act, except to the extent of his contribution.

00.63 It was found that the loss and damage was caused by the negligence of the master and of general average surveyors appointed by the shipowners. The appellants contended that the port of Levis was so ill-equipped for the reception of pig iron that the mixing and breaking might have taken place without anybody's negligence, but this contention was rejected. The Supreme Court held the appellants liable. Ritchie J. said:

> "In entering upon the general average act and in making all reasonable and necessary expenditures consequent thereon, the master is to be taken as

[71] See para. 00.60, *ante*.
[72] See, *e.g.* the judgment of Lord Stowell in *The Gratitudine* (1801) 3 C.Rob. 240 at 257; quoted para. 1.02, *post*.
[73] [1970] 2 Lloyd's Rep. 332; [1975] 1 Lloyd's Rep. 105.

> acting with the implied authority of the cargo owners as well as the ship, but this authority does not extend so as to identify the cargo owners with the negligence of the master or those employed by him in carrying out the general average procedure or to derogate from his overriding responsibility to care for the cargo in his capacity as the servant of the shipowner."[74]

If taken out of context this reasoning goes too far. A master who is entitled in an emergency to throw cargo overboard is, it is submitted, to that extent released from his overriding responsibility to care for the cargo. But the decision itself is that when a master fails to exercise reasonable skill and care in the course of a general average act, the shipowners are liable notwithstanding that the master is for the time being acting to some extent as the agent of all parties to the adventure.

[74] [1975] 1 Lloyd's Rep. 105 at 114.

SECTION 3

THE HISTORY AND DEVELOPMENT OF THE YORK-ANTWERP RULES

Introduction

In England and indeed in every country in the world possessing a maritime trade the principle exemplified by the Rhodian law[1] has been adopted; and the adjustment of losses caused by a sacrifice in time of peril at sea, so that the burden shall not fall to be borne by one but all, forms a well recognised and common incident of almost daily occurrence among all those engaged in maritime commerce. **00.64**

But almost of necessity the exact losses which must be regarded as general average, their method of calculation and the manner in which they shall be borne, vary considerably with the law of the country concerned. Thus on this important subject, which constantly affects those engaged in overseas commerce, it is unsafe to hazard an opinion even as to what constitutes a general average sacrifice or loss, let alone the correct method of dealing with it, without reference to the pages of voluminous textbooks or the intricate sections of a foreign code.

It is not surprising, therefore, that attempts have been made from time to time to bring about some common international agreement on the subject of general average, to the extent even of abolishing it altogether.[2]

Glasgow Resolutions 1860

Preliminaries

The movement for attaining international uniformity may be dated from the year 1860. Early in that year an appeal was made to the National Association for the Promotion of Social Science, London, by Lloyd's, the Underwriter's Association of Liverpool, and several other important commercial bodies, to take up this work. In response to this appeal the National Association issued a circular letter, dated May 3, 1860, which was addressed to all the maritime countries of Europe, and to the United States. **00.65**

[1] See para. 00.01 *ante*.
[2] See para. 00.11, *ante*, and App. 5, *post*.

This letter read as follows:

"The system of general average is one which, to prevent confusion and injustice, pre-eminently requires that the same principles should be acknowledged amongst the chief maritime nations. So far is this from being the case, however, that some of the most important rules vary not only in the same country, but in the same port. Uncertainty in law is always an evil; and, in regard to general average, the evil is peculiarly felt. The ship may be owned in one country, insured in another, her cargo owned and insured in several, and the port of destination, where the general average is made up, may be in a country which has different rules to any of the others. What is considered to be particular average on ship in one port is held to be general average in another, so that the owner of an outward-bound ship may find himself unable to recover his loss either from his underwriters at home, or as general average abroad; or on the other hand, he may be in a position to indemnify himself fraudulently twice over. A similar remark would apply to special charges on freight and on cargo. A very large portion of the most important questions rest in England nominally upon the decision of that extremely vague authority, 'the custom of Lloyd's', but really depends upon the idiosyncrasy of the particular adjuster who may be entrusted with the papers. Hence arise many cases where apparently injustice must be done to assurer or assured. Either the assured finds himself saddled with a loss against which he believed himself insured, or the underwriter pays one which was not considered in the premium.

Much loss is occasioned to the mercantile community and to the country at large, and much valuable time is worse than wasted through business being impeded by misunderstandings and irritated feelings.

A still more crying evil, resulting from the present uncertainty of law and custom, is the opening which it leaves for every sort of abuse. Attempts are daily being made to introduce charges of the most outrageous description, which do not even go into the pocket of the shipowner, but which he feels himself helpless to resist from want of a law to appeal to; and he naturally considers himself hardly used should charges which he himself has paid be refused by his underwriters, though these last are obliged to refuse in justice to themselves and to prevent the innovation becoming a precedent.

The evils of such a state of things are notorious and unquestioned, though it may be doubted whether many which are distinctly traceable to it, and are therefore removable, are clearly realised as proceeding from this source. Probably the chief reason which has hitherto prevented any general movement in favour of this reform is an exaggerated estimate of the difficulties in the way of carrying it out. The difficulties are, no doubt, considerable, but they are far from being insuperable, and the importance of the end amply justifies an attempt to grapple with them.

Both the assured and the underwriter are interested in placing their mutual relations upon a footing which would effect a saving of time and temper, and would secure them against the annoying pecuniary loss to which they are at present exposed. It is not of so much importance how the disputed points of general average are settled, as that they should be settled. Most of the questions are in the end merely matters of account between one set of underwriters and another, and it would make little difference to any underwriter upon which interest it might be determined the charge should fall. It is true that there are points, such as the allowance of wages and provisions in a port of refuge, which would raise questions between shipowner and underwriter, but for the sake of both it is to the last degree desirable that these should not be left as a bone of contention between assurer and assured, as they are at present, *e.g.* when goods to America are insured in England.

The evils of the present system have already caused much dissatisfaction in America as well as in this country, and will become more and more intolerable as the commerce of the world increases, which it seems likely to do with a rapidly hitherto unexampled. The time then would seem to have come, when an attempt should be made to remove this most unnecessary element of irritation between assured and underwriter.

In the hope of coming to an understanding upon this question, the Council of the National Association for the Promotion of Social Science have determined that it shall be brought forward for discussion at their next meeting at Glasgow on Monday, September 24 next, and the following days; and we earnestly trust that you will find it in your power to send representatives of your body to that meeting, as it is very desirable that delegates from the commercial bodies in different parts of the world which are chiefly interested should be present."

A few days before the Conference assembled at Glasgow, the following memorandum was issued: **00.66**

"The adjustment of a general average is governed by the laws and customs of the State in which it is adjusted. The laws and customs of different States vary materially, and that which is general average in one country is not general average in another. It is admitted that this is a great practical grievance, and the object of this meeting is to put an end to it.

The following are the principal points on which differences exist:

1. Damage done to ship and cargo by voluntary stranding.
2. Damage done to ship and cargo in extinguishing a fire.
3. Chafage and breakage of cargo after jettison.
4. Damage done to cargo by discharging it at a port of refuge.
5. Cutting away the wreck of masts accidentally carried away.
6. Expenses of warehouse rent on cargo, re-shipping it, and outward port charges, at a port of refuge, when the original ship carried on the cargo from that port.
7. Carrying a press of sail.
8. Wages and provisions for the crew during the delay caused by putting into port.
9. Contributing values of ship, freight, and cargo.

The opinion of the meeting will be taken on each of these points:

1st. As to the principle which should govern it—*i.e.* whether the loss is, or is not, in principle, allowable in general average.

2nd. As to the expediency of adopting a practical rule to modify or prevent abuse of that principle."

The Glasgow Conference

The Conference was opened on September 25, 1860, under the presidency of Lord Brougham. The proceedings lasted for three days, during which papers were read and discussions ensued, and finally the following resolutions were adopted: **00.67**

"1. That the meeting hereby requests the Council of the Association to assist by their counsels such person or persons as may be approved of by them, in drawing up a Bill, with a view to its being enacted into a law by the legislative authorities of the several nations of the world, which Bill shall define, as clearly as may be, the term 'general average,' and describe more or less fully the cases intended to be included within the definition, and which shall also specify the nature of the loss, damage, or expense allowable in general average, and the principle on which the amount of the loss, damage, or expense shall be ascertained; also, furnish a rule or rules for ascertaining the contributory values of the interests concerned, and which shall contain such matters as the person or persons drawing up the Bill may think it advisable to insert. That upon such Bill being drawn up and printed, copies thereof shall be transmitted to the several Chambers of Commerce, Boards of Underwriters, Shipowners' Associations, and other commercial societies in different parts of the world, accompanied by a copy of this resolution, and a request to them to examine and return the said copies, with such alterations or amendments as they may think proper to make therein, within six months from the time of the receipt thereof. That, upon the return of the said copies, or upon the expiration of the said six months, the said Bill shall be revised by the person or persons drawing up the same, enlightened by the information acquired as aforesaid. That, upon the Bill being perfected in the manner aforesaid, it be recommended to the legislative authorities of all commercial nations to enact the same into a law.

2. That, in the meantime, the meeting resolves to circulate as widely as possible, for general information, the rules embodied in the resolutions which have been passed by the meeting, as those which, under a uniform system, it might be desirable to consider."

The Rules

00.68 Eleven working Rules, largely on the subjects detailed in paragraph 00.66, above, were passed and embodied in the Glasgow Resolutions, and the full text of each is quoted in Appendix 2A between paragraphs 60.19 and 60.27, below.

York Rules 1864

Aftermath of Glasgow Conference

00.69 It will be seen from the first of the two general resolutions quoted above that the Glasgow Conference decided to proceed on the lines of legislation rather than by the path of voluntary agreement. The terms of the resolution indicate that the ultimate aim was uniform legislation in the various countries concerned, but by committing itself to the drafting of a Bill, which by its terms clearly indicated that it was a draft of a Bill to be introduced into Parliament, the Conference ran a grave risk of being misunderstood as to its real aim and intention.

00.70 Unexpected delays took place in drafting and instead of the six months which the Glasgow Conference, it appears, had allotted to the task of translating their eleven resolutions into a parliamentary draft, some two years elapsed before the draft Bill made its appearance. It was entitled "Draft of a Bill intituled An Act to Consolidate and Amend the Laws relating to General Average Sacrifices and General Average Contributions", and consisted of 126 sections. Those who may wish to study its provisions are referred to Wendt's *Maritime Legislation*, in which it is printed in full.[3] The Bill was subjected to severe criticism by experts and after careful scrutiny, a committee appointed by the National Association for the Promotion of Social Science reported that of the 126 sections:

29 sections could not be agreed upon and were left open for public discussion;
22 sections were recommended for amendment;
30 sections were recommended to be struck out altogether;
5 sections should be altered by the draftsmen of the Bill as instructed;

and only 40 sections were passed as originally drafted.

This report was presented to a conference held at the Guildhall, London, in June 1862. No public discussion took place on the Bill. The delegates proceeded to consider its terms in private and various amendments were suggested, but in the end it was decided to proceed no further with the onerous work of remodelling the Bill, but to leave to a committee the task of deciding upon and drafting "a Bill, or series of resolutions, having for object the establishing of one uniform system of general average throughout the mercantile world". This committee, which consisted of 16 members, had for its Chairman, Dr E. E. Wendt, and for its Secretary, Mr Richard Lowndes, and was composed of representatives from the United States, Holland, Belgium, Denmark, as well as from Great Britain. As a start, this committee drew up a statement of the various arguments on each side of what were regarded as the principal questions of general average in dispute, which was issued in 1863 to all the members of the committee, together with a "Projet de Code" submitted by Messrs Engels and van Peborgh, of Antwerp, a compilation of the Danish law on general average and a translation of the German Code of 1862. Opinions and criticisms were invited, and these, together with the documents referred to, were published in January 1864, under the title of "Transactions of the International General Average Committee". **00.71**

York Congress

Shortly afterwards, it was decided that the Third International General Average Congress should meet at York on September 26, 1864, and a draft Bill[4] was circulated in advance as a basis for discussion at the Congress. **00.72**

[3] Wendt (3rd ed.), pp. 71–94.
[4] See Wendt (3rd ed.), pp. 126–128.

The following resolution was passed unanimously before the Congress proceeded to consider the terms of the draft Bill in detail:

> "That the object of this Congress is simply to carry out the Glasgow resolution passed on September 27, 1860; and, that it is by no means intended that the Bill should be passed only by the English Legislature, but that, in the terms of that resolution, it should, when perfected, be recommended to the legislative authorities of all commercial nations, to enact the same into a law."

00.73 The Congress continued its labours for three days and at its conclusion 11 rules (The York Rules[5]) were agreed to.

On the motion of Lowndes the following resolutions, among others, were carried as to the future procedure to be adopted:

> "That the draft Bill as now amended in Congress, ought, in the opinion of this Congress, to be the basis of International General Average Law.
>
> That in order to carry out this object, associations should be formed, or other measures taken, in each of the countries represented in Congress, and in other countries where practicable, for the purpose of causing this Bill to become the law and practice of such country.
>
> That this end should be pursued through the Legislatures of each country where applicable, and also, pending legislation, by means of clauses to be introduced into bills of lading and charter parties.
>
> That the clauses recommended for this purpose be the following: 'All claims for general average to be settled in conformity with the International General Average Rules, framed at York in 1864'.
>
> That the representative or representatives of each country or place, as named above, shall charge himself or themselves with the task of organising an association or committee for such place, or taking such other measures as in his judgment shall be best conducive to the carrying out of the purposes laid down in the foregoing resolutions."

York and Antwerp Rules 1877

00.74 In accordance with the last-quoted resolution, many of the delegates to the York Conference published reports on the subject, which led to public discussions on the new rules. Repeated attempts were also made through the Associated Chambers of Commerce to obtain Imperial legislation on the basis of the York Rules, but these led to no practical results, and no doubt the indifference, if not the opposition, of Lloyd's to legislation on these lines had considerable influence on the attitude of the government authorities. The movement for international uniformity, launched with such vigour and hope in 1860, languished for more than 10 years, although it is recorded by Lowndes[6] that in 1871 the Italian Government proposed a Congress at Naples for the discussion, among

[5] See App. 2A, paras. 60.18–60.29, *post*.
[6] 4th ed., p. 669.

other things, of the practicability of establishing a uniform code of general average in all countries.

In 1875, however, the subject was brought to notice again at the third annual Congress of the Association for the Reform and Codification of the Law of Nations, held at The Hague in that year, when one of the members drew attention to the desirability of reviewing the laws of general average. In 1876, at the next Congress of the Association, a paper was read by Mr Hach, of Bremen, reviewing the history of the movement and proposing that it should be continued on the lines of considering the practicability of a code, which, it is to be noted, should contain a definition of general average. After discussion, a committee was appointed "to consider the subject of general average".

Antwerp Conference 1877

As a result, a meeting was called for August 30, 1877, at Antwerp, for the purpose of making a further and serious attempt to obtain international agreement on the subject. The meeting was presided over by Sir Travers Twiss and was attended by 68 delegates. **00.75**

The delegates from Lloyd's protested against the York Rules being adopted as a basis for discussion, and proposed that uniformity could best be achieved by the abolition of general average; but the expressed feeling of the meeting was clearly against such an expedient and the consideration of the York Rules was then proceeded with.

After three days' discussion these rules were finally approved with certain modifications, of which the most important were: **00.76**

> "1. In the first, the exception in favour of timber or deals jettisoned from deck was deleted, so that no jettison of deck cargo should be allowed in general average.
>
> 2. To the third rule, the provision was added that no compensation was to be allowed to packages which had been on fire.
>
> 3. In the seventh and eighth rules, the clauses relating to the exemption from contribution to port of refuge expenses of cargo left at such port, were deleted.
>
> 4. In the tenth rule, the basis for the contributing value of freight was altered from three-fifths of the gross amount to the gross freight less port charges and crew's wages, incurred after the general average act."

A twelfth rule was also added, reading as follows:

> "The value to be allowed for goods sacrificed shall be that value which the owner would have received if such goods has not been sacrificed."

A proposal to preface the rules with a definition of general average met with no favour.[7]

[7] For full details of the York and Antwerp Rules, see App. 2A, paras. 60.18–60.29, *post*.

Adoption of York and Antwerp Rules

00.77 The delegates from Lloyd's joined in the discussions at the Conference, but expressly dissociated themselves from the general approval of the new rules that was given by the meeting. At the conclusion of the proceedings, it was resolved that local committees should immediately take steps to ensure consideration of the revised rules "and the favourable attention and action of their respective governments". Vigorous steps to this end were undoubtedly taken; and in Britain, in 1878, the General Shipowners' Association convened a meeting in London of shipowners, underwriters and others, which passed the following resolutions:

> "1. That in the opinion of this meeting it is desirable that the York and Antwerp Rules of general average be carried into operation.
> 2. That in the opinion of this meeting the most effectual mode of procedure will be by a general agreement on the part of shipowners, merchants and underwriters to insert in bills of lading and charterparties the words, 'general average, if any, payable according to York and Antwerp Rules,' and in policies of insurance to add to the foreign general average clause the words, 'or York and Antwerp Rules,' so that the clause will run thus:—'general average payable as per foreign adjustment (or custom) or York and Antwerp Rules, if so made up.'
> 3. That a definite date should be fixed for the proposed change, and the date recommended by this committee is January 1, 1879."

It is interesting to note that all reference to legislative action is omitted in these resolutions, apparently for the first time.

00.78 At the next Conference of the Association for the Reform and Codification of the Law of Nations, held at Guildhall, London, in 1879, it was reported that the owners of more than two-fifths of the entire registered tonnage of Great Britain had agreed to include the rules in their bills of lading and charterparties, that a large number of the mutual insurance associations had adopted them and that underwriters generally, despite the continued opposition of Lloyd's, were agreeing to the inclusion of the new foreign general average clause without additional premium. This general approval of the rules was, no doubt, facilitated by certain decisions in the English courts, which gave effect to the principles underlying several of the rules, even though the practice of average adjusters in this country had up to then been to a contrary effect. It was stated by Lowndes at the general meeting of the Association of Average Adjusters in 1880 that all except two of the York Rules had been adopted into the law and practice of this country. Encouraging figures were also given at the 1879 Conference of the progress which had been made in other countries, and it appeared that almost without exception shipowning and underwriting bodies, and indeed all the great mercantile communities, in the United States, the British Colonies and on the European Continent, had approved the new rules and given effect to them in contracts of affreightment and policies of insurance.

York-Antwerp Rules 1890

Liverpool Conference

After the rules had undergone the practical test of some ten years' operation, it was recognised that they did not entirely conform with the changing needs of commerce and that some revision was desirable. The Association of Average Adjusters took the initiative in the matter and drafted a report suggesting various amendments in and additions to the rules for submission to the Conference of the Association for the Reform and Codification of the Law of Nations, held at Liverpool in 1890. The proceedings lasted for four days, during which the report presented by the Association of Average Adjusters was very fully discussed and criticised, as a result of which certain amendments in the existing rules were agreed and a few entirely new rules were adopted. The resulting group of 18 rules was entitled the York-Antwerp Rules 1890,[8] and adopted almost universally throughout the world. **00.79**

It may be added here that at the Antwerp Conference of 1903, a further rule was recommended for adoption entitled "Antwerp Rule 1903", which read as follows: **00.80**

> "Rights to contribution in general average shall not be affected though the danger which gave rise to the sacrifice, or expenditure, may have been due to default of one of the parties to the adventure; but this shall not prejudice any remedies which may be open against that party for such default."

This rule embodied the law of most countries on the particular point, but was never very generally adopted in contracts of affreightment.

Shortcomings of 1890 Rules

The 1890 Rules did not by any means cover the whole area of disputed territory. They consisted merely of a group of rules dealing with certain specific points—points upon which the law or practice was known to differ at the time when the first conferences on the subject were held, added to or amended at succeeding conferences in the light of further experience of their working or the development of commercial requirements. The rules were based on no coherent and logical principle. The adherents to the rival doctrines of "benefit of the adventure" and "common safety", for instance, could each claim that the principle they supported was exemplified in the rules, and each could equally claim that the others' views were clearly refuted thereby. This lack of a guiding principle underlying the rules was not a matter of mere academic objection. It had practical consequences of a far-reaching nature. Commerce was constantly developing in directions and by means which it **00.81**

[8] See App. 2B, paras. 60.39–60.63, *post*.

was impossible to prophesy from year to year. With these conditions of change ever present, any code of rules confined to certain limited points of practical importance at any given date must continue to grow out of date and to lose its value for use in commercial contracts. It is hardly a matter of surprise, therefore, that the movement for international uniformity did not cease after 1890.

Proposals for further reform

00.82 In 1895 an article appeared in the January issue of the *Law Quarterly Review* by Mr (later His Honour Judge) Dowdall Q.C., in which he revived the idea of a code for international adoption, and proceeded to state the terms of such a code, consisting of 32 sections, which dealt with the definition of general average, the calculation of general average losses, the method of contribution thereto, and the means of enforcing payment.

00.83 The Conference of the International Law Association, held in London in 1910, was the occasion of an important development in the movement towards uniformity. Mr Dowdall returned to the subject which he had made peculiarly his own, and read a paper on the "Codification of the Law of General Average". In this he submitted:

> "that a great service would be rendered to the commercial community and a great advance made if it were possible to effect a systematic and comprehensive survey of all the various contemporary laws and practice of average adjustment *as regarded in the light of intelligible principles*, pointing out those considerations of expediency which in special circumstances make it necessary to depart from those principles or to raise presumptions of fact by which those principles should on occasion be superseded."

As a result, a resolution was unanimously passed;

> "that the President be requested to nominate a committee to collate in detail the law of general average among the various maritime nations in relation to the principles by which the law is governed."

The report of the committee was presented to the Paris Conference in 1912.

00.84 On the motion of Kennedy L.J., it was decided to refer the matter back to the committee, with the instruction to prepare upon the basis of the report an *avant projet* or model form of the law of general average. At the Madrid Conference held in 1913, the *avant projet* prepared by the committee was presented. A resolution was passed at the Conference provisionally accepting the *avant projet*, and the convenor of the committee (Mr Dowdall) was subsequently authorised to obtain the opinions of those interested, in order that the matter might be widely discussed before the next Conference of the International Law Association, which was to be held at The Hague in September, 1914, The *avant projet*, with some minor alterations, was thereupon printed and circulated under the title of a "Draft International Code relating to General Average" in the spring of 1914.

The reception of the draft Code by the mercantile community was not a favourable one on the whole, although there were not wanting many expressions of admiration for the thorough manner in which it had been prepared. Certain bodies, notably the Liverpool Steamship Owners' Association, which expressed its approval of the Code subject to certain minor amendments, and the Liverpool Underwriters' Association, which passed a resolution in favour of the principle of codification, gave encouragement to the project, but it was clear from the reports which were received that the business community as a whole did not welcome the idea of codification and preferred to retain the York-Antwerp Rules, possibly in an amended form, as the common basis for the regulation of general average. **00.85**

A committee of the Newcastle Chamber of Commerce reported in favour of a revision of the York-Antwerp Rules and a combination of them with sections embodying general principles, the germ of an idea which found development in the York-Antwerp Rules of 1924, as will be seen later. **00.86**

Further consideration of the draft Code, however, and indeed of all other attempts towards international agreement, was suddenly suspended by the outbreak of the First World War, and needless to say, nothing further was heard of the project until after peace was declared and the citizens of the world had had an opportunity of re-establishing some degree of order in their affairs, both political and social, which hostilities had so rudely interrupted.

York-Antwerp Rules 1924

Invitations were issued by the International Law Association to a meeting to be held at Gray's Inn on January 16, 1924, for the purpose of considering the best means of procedure to be adopted to attain some practical result which would commend itself to the mercantile community. The meeting was held under the chairmanship of Sir Henry Duke (later Lord Merrivale) and was attended by representatives of shipowning and underwriting bodies, average adjusters and others interested in the subject, as well as by certain representives from the Continent. As a result of a long discussion the following resolution was carried unanimously: **00.87**

> "That a settlement of the difference which exist with regard to general average will be aided by co-operation among the business interests concerned with a view to:

(a) Formulation of Rules of Practice so far as the same are not now expressed or are insufficiently expressed in the York-Antwerp Rules, and in due course:—

(b) The ascertainment and authoritative statement of the law of general average so far as international agreement thereon exists or can be obtained, and

That this meeting agrees that it will be of public advantage that the International Law Association shall continue its action with a view to promoting these objects."

00.88 In May 1924 Sir Norman Hill, at the International Conference of Shipowners held in London, moved the following resolution, which was carried unanimously:

"That this Conference takes note of the movement of the International Law Association to secure greater international uniformity and certainty in general average law and practice throughout the world and is of the opinion that the object in view can best be obtained by:

(1) A revision of the York-Antwerp Rules to bring them into line with modern requirements.

(2) The embodiment in the revised rules of a general declaration of the principles underlying the rules of practice therein contained, so that such principles may be accepted and applied in those cases which are not provided for in such rules."

00.89 This was shortly followed by the summoning of a meeting of the General Average Committee of the International Law Association at Gray's Inn, which was held under the chairmanship of the Right Hon. Lord Phillimore on June 16, 1924. The position which had now been reached was put before the meeting by Sir Norman Hill, and after a lengthy discussion on the whole question of how uniformity could best be attained, the following resolution was adopted:

"That it is desirable that a draft be prepared for consideration of the Conference at Stockholm, embodying:

(1) A revision of the York-Antwerp Rules, and therein

(2) A declaration of the general principles applicable to general average.

And that, in preparing No. 1, the drafting committee take for its guidance the revision made by the Average Adjusters' Association of the United Kingdom with the modifications suggested by the French, Dutch, German, Swedish, Norwegian and Belgian committees and any further reports which national committees may send in.

And that, in preparing No. 2, the drafting committee do take into consideration the draft code prepared by His Honour Judge Dowdall, K.C., and the *Avant Projet* of Monsieur Dor."

00.90 The drafting committee appointed by the meeting in accordance with the above resolution consisted of Sir Norman Hill, Bart., His Honour Judge Dowdall, K.C., Maître Léopold Dor and Mr G. R. Rudolf, with Mr A. F. Greenwood as secretary. Its report was issued on July 24, 1924. The Committee's draft revision contained a definition of principles (lettered rules), followed by the rules (numbered) dealing with points of practice, which were simply the 1890 Rules amended (Rule XVIII being omitted) with the addition of six new rules.

Stockholm Conference

The thirty-third Conference of the International Law Association was opened at Stockholm in the presence of His Majesty the King of Sweden on September 8, 1924. The consideration of the drafting committee's report was undertaken by the General Average section of the Conference, and the international character of the meetings may be gauged from the fact that delegates attended from the United States, Great Britain (including the vice-chairman of Lloyd's), France, Germany, Holland, Belgium, Norway, Sweden, Denmark, and Japan. The proceedings were presided over by Sir Norman Hill, and lasted for four days, at the end of which the new rules were finally agreed, under the title of the York-Antwerp Rules 1924, and were adopted on the following day by the general Conference.[9] The report accompanying the draft of the 1924 Rules, as presented to the Conference, contained the following clauses: **00.91**

> "3. The draft prepared by the drafting committee has been considered by this Conference in detail and amended as has been found necessary.
> 4. In the opinion of this Conference the draft as so amended will attain the objects to which the International Shipping Conference directed its attention, *viz.*:
> First, Bring the York-Antwerp Rules 1890 into line with modern requirements.
> Second. Establish principles which may be accepted and applied in those cases which are not provided for in such rules.
> 5. This Conference therefore resolves that the rules as so amended be placed before the commercial and shipping interests for consideration, and, if approved by them, for ratification and use by voluntary agreement in the same manner as the York-Antwerp Rules 1890.
> 6. This Conference further resolves that, if the draft be not ratified by the commercial and shipping interests generally, the International Law Association be requested to arrange for further consideration of the draft by the interests directly concerned at a Conference to be specially convened for that purpose."

The new rules were immediately published in the press and were also circulated shortly after to the leading mercantile bodies throughout the world, and it was soon evident that they met with a very general measure of approval. No serious criticism of their provisions was raised, except in the United States, and the business community as a whole accepted the rules as a satisfactory solution of their demand for a revision which would provide a greater degree of uniformity in all cases of general average, whether under modern or future conditions of commerce. **00.92**

[9] For the text of the Rules, see App. 2B, paras. 60.30–60.69, *post*.

In the United States, however, the new rules were not received with the same approval, and special clauses providing for the partial application of the 1924 Rules became common.[10]

York-Antwerp Rules 1950[11]

The Makis Case

00.93 It was clearly the intention of the framers of the 1924 Rules, and of the Stockholm Conference which adopted them, that all cases provided for by the numbered rules should be considered as general average, and that the lettered rules laid down general principles to be applied in those cases not specifically covered by the numbered rules.

In 1928 however, the decision in *Vlassopoulos v. British & Foreign Marine Insurance Co. Ltd*,[12] upset all preconceived ideas on this point.

It was held in that case that the lettered rules constituted a code of general average, and that the numbered rules were to be regarded as specific examples. This meant that all the matters covered by the numbered rules were subject to the over-riding principles laid down in the lettered rules.

The Makis Agreement

00.94 The situation following this decision caused embarrassment in commercial circles in this country and to overcome the difficulty an agreement was made in January 1929 between leading shipowners and underwriters in the United Kingdom. This agreement, known as the "Makis Agreement", was as follows:

> "The main object of the York-Antwerp Rules is to secure uniformity of practice in cases of General Average.
>
> In consequence of the decision in the case of *Vlassopoulos v. British & Foreign Marine Insurance Co. Ltd.* (that of the "Makis"), reported at 31 Lloyd's List Law Reports, p. 315, questions have arisen as to the intention of the parties in framing the York-Antwerp Rules 1924, and it is desirable to set doubt at rest by agreeing that the rules shall be construed as if they contained the following provision:

[10] The clause most generally used (prior to the adoption of the 1950 Rules) was that appearing in the Standard bill of lading required to be used by the Maritime Commission and which was mandatory during the Second World War. This clause, which was used by most lines (with some minor changes dependent on the trade in which the vessel was engaged) read as follows:

> "General average shall be adjusted, stated and settled, according to Rules 1–15 inclusive, 17–22 inclusive and Rule F of York-Antwerp Rules 1924, at such port or place in the U.S. as may be selected by the carrier and as to matters not provided for by these Rules, according to the laws and usages at the port of New York."

[11] For the text of the Rules, see App. 2B, paras 60.30–60.69, *post*.

[12] [1929] 1 K.B. 187.

> 'Except as provided in the numbered Rules 1 to 23 inclusive, the adjustment shall be drawn up in accordance with the lettered Rules A to G inclusive.'
>
> And it is hereby agreed that both outstanding and future cases shall be dealt with on this basis.
>
> This agreement shall be communicated to the Association of Average Adjusters of the United Kingdom with the request that all their Members and Associates shall act upon it."

The agreement was, of course, only binding upon the signatories, but it was generally respected by all concerned and ensured that the practice remained in line with that existing in other countries.

The general position regarding the 1924 Rules remained unsatisfactory, and after the Second World War had ended it soon became evident that these Rules should be revised. The development during that war of the American merchant marine rendered it more than ever important that a set of rules should be framed which would be acceptable without reservation by United States interests.

Movement for revision of 1924 Rules

The question of revising the 1924 Rules was first raised at a Conference of the Comité Maritime International (a body devoted wholly to matters of maritime concern) at Antwerp in September 1947, with particular reference to Rule XXII; and the International Law Association was invited to consider the desirability of amending this Rule so as to substitute for the legal rate of interest prevailing at the final port of destination a fixed rate of interest for all countries. **00.95**

The Conference of the International Law Association in Brussels in 1948, acceded to this request and adopted a resolution in the following terms:

> "1. Rule XXII be amended as follows: Notwithstanding anything contained in Rule XXII the rate at which interest shall be allowed under that Rule shall in all cases be 5 per cent, per annum and that Rule and the York-Antwerp Rules 1924 shall be read together and known as the York-Antwerp Rules 1924/1948.
>
> 2. That the desirability of amending other of the York-Antwerp Rules and the best method of doing so in co-operation with the Comité Maritime International be referred to the Executive Council."

It will be noted that this resolution went further than the original request made by the Comité Maritime International and paved the way for a general revision of the Rules.

The International Law Association agreed to an arrangement whereby the Comité Maritime International was to undertake the task of examining the 1924 Rules with the object of facilitating their general adoption, and the Permanent Bureau of the Comité Maritime International invited its British branch, the British Maritime Law Association, to take the lead in investigating the position and in co-ordinating the work of the other national branches.

00.96 The British Maritime Law Association met in London in July 1948 under the Chairmanship of Sir Leslie Scott, and a sub-committee was appointed to examine and report on any amendments desirable with a view to facilitating the general adoption of the York-Antwerp Rules.

Committees were also set up by the national branches of the Comité Maritime International in Belgium, Denmark, France, Holland, Norway, Sweden and in the United States, and all the reports, memoranda and minutes of the British sub-committee were circulated to these national committees.

International Commission

00.97 The views of these committees were ascertained and co-ordinated by the British Maritime Law Association Sub-Committee, for consideration by an International Commission appointed by the Permanent Bureau of the Comité Maritime International.

The Commission met in London on July 4 and 5, 1949. Each Rule was considered in detail and decisions were reached on all points of difference. A drafting committee was appointed and instructed to prepare a draft of the amended Rules in accordance with decisions reached, to be submitted to the Permanent Bureau for circulation to the various national associations.

Amsterdam Conference 1949

00.98 New draft Rules and various reports were placed before the Conference of the Comité Maritime International held at Amsterdam in September 1949, and after being considered and discussed fully were, with a few amendments, adopted and designated "The York-Antwerp Rules".

Delegates of all the nations represented, including the United States, agreed to recommend the adoption of the new Rules by their respective countries, and in a very short time the York-Antwerp Rules 1950 were adopted generally without reservation.

York-Antwerp Rules 1974[13]

00.99 Although the 1950 Rules were almost universally accepted, in the ensuing 20 years criticisms came to be made. These were in part the result of change in commercial procedures and shipping techniques, but in larger measure directed towards simplifying the task of average adjustment.

After valuable work by the Association Internationale de Dispacheurs Européens and the International Union of Marine Insurers, in November 1969 the Bureau Permanent of the Comité Maritime International

[13] For the text of the Rules, see App. 2B, paras 60.30–60.69, *post*.

resolved to set up an international sub-committee to study the subject. Mr William Birch Reynardson was appointed chairman and Mr Henri Voet rapporteur.

A preliminary report and questionnaire were then circulated to national associations comprising the Comité Maritime International. Apart from questions directed to a number of specific Rules, these called for comment on matters not dealt with in the 1950 Rules, including the formalities of securing general average contribution, a franchise to eliminate small contributions, and a standard form of non-separation agreement. The replies were considered by a working group whose report was considered by the international sub-committee, which then appointed a drafting committee with Mr Lloyd Watkins as secretary. In February 1973 a draft text for the revised Rules was circulated to national associations. It was accompanied by the report of the President, which contained the following passage commenting on the revisions proposed at that time: **00.100**

> "The object of this detailed work was to clarify and simplify the Rules. After over twenty years it is not surprising the 1950 Rules were criticised in certain material respects.
>
> The concept of General Average should not be allowed to be shrouded in academic mystique.... The principles upon which it is based must be clear and simple. If not, then unnecessary costs and delays will ensue. To be acceptable in the future the system must be seen to be both equitable and commercially viable.... It is hoped that the simplifications and clarifications which have been made will aid the practitioner and facilitate the drawing up of adjustments with the minimum of expense and delay."[14]

Hamburg Conference

The XXXth Conference of the Comité Maritime International was held at Hamburg from April 1 to 5, 1974. Over four hundred delegates representing 29 countries attended. The 1973 draft for revised York-Antwerp Rules was largely approved by the Conference, subject to important exceptions relating to Rules E, XIII and XVII[15] and to other changes of lesser importance. At the plenary session on April 4, 1974, each of the revised Rules was approved by a vote showing a substantial majority, except in the case of Rule XIII where the vote on the 1973 draft was a tie and the Swedish amendment re-introducing deductions "new for old" in a *modified form* was carried. The following resolution, proposed by Mr William Birch Reynardson, was then carried unanimously: **00.101**

> "The delegates representing the National Associations of Maritime Law of those States as set out hereunder[16]:

[14] C.M.I. Documentation, 1974, I.58.

[15] These are noted in the commentary on the Rules in question, paras. E.02, 13.04–13.05, 17.08, *post*.

[16] The resolution was carried by 29 States.

1. Having noted with approval the amendments which have been made to the York-Antwerp Rules 1950 and which have been incorporated into a revised text of Rules to be known as the York-Antwerp Rules 1974.
2. Recommend that the York-Antwerp Rules 1974 should be applied in the adjustment of General Average claims as soon as is practical after July 1, 1974."

York-Antwerp Rules 1974, as amended 1990

00.102 The average lifespan of any set of York-Antwerp Rules is in the region of 25 years, and it might normally have been expected that the 1974 edition would survive for the remainder of the century. In April 1989, however, an International Convention on Salvage attended by representatives from 66 nations was held in London, the principal purpose of which was to amend the terms of the 1910 Brussels Convention for the Unification of Certain Rules of Law relating to Assistance and Salvage at Sea in view of the great present day concern for the protection of the environment, particularly with regard to substantial physical damage to human health or to marine life or resources in coastal or inland waters by pollution and contamination, etc.

By Article 8 of the 1989 Convention, salvors owe a duty to carry out salvage operations with due care and, in performance of that duty, to exercise due care to prevent or minimise damage to the environment. However, to ensure that adequate incentives are available to salvors, and particularly where the prospect of successfully salving maritime property with a worthwhile value might be small, Article 14 introduces a new special compensation which is payable when the ship or cargo to be salved threatens damage to the environment and the values of the property salved were insufficient by themselves to provide an adequate reward. The special compensation is payable by the owner when the salvage operations had prevented or minimised damage to the environment, and is at least equivalent to the expenses incurred by the salvors, and in very special circumstances, even up to 200 per cent of the expenses.

00.103 Having completed their deliberations and adopted various recommendations and resolutions, the Conference added an Attachment 2 to their report:

> "CONSIDERING that payments made pursuant to article 14 are not intended to be allowed in general average
>
> REQUESTS the Secretary-General of the International Maritime Organisation to take the appropriate steps in order to ensure speedy amendment of the York-Antwerp Rules, 1974, to ensure that special compensation paid under article 14 is not subject to general average."

This request was implemented at a Conference of the Comite Maritime International held in Paris in June 1990 when an amendment was made to Rule VI (alone) of the York-Antwerp Rules 1974, the full text of which is quoted in paragraph 6.17, below. The Rules, *in toto*, were to be referred to as the "York-Antwerp Rules 1974, as amended 1990", and it was recommended that they should be applied in the adjustment of claims in general average as soon as practicable after October 1, 1990.

York-Antwerp-Rules 1994

At the conclusion of the official meeting of the Comite Maritime International held in Paris in June 1990 at which Rule VI was amended (see paragraph 00.103, above), an informal meeting gave consideration to the important question of whether a full review of the York-Antwerp Rules was timely. Rules, other than Rule VI, also had an impact on pollution damage to the environment and the cost of avoiding or minimising same, and further reasons for a full review included the following: **00.104**

1. Changes in modern shipping techniques and the tendency for liner and container services to be more and more widely used made it relevant to examine the principles of general average to ensure that it was appropriate in the present commercial and legal world, and to reaffirm that in all respects the York-Antwerp Rules reflected modern commercial, technical, environmental and legal developments.
2. If (as in fact transpired), UNCTAD intended to begin its own critical examination of the topic, it was highly desirable that, by reason of its own work, the CMI should be able to offer to UNCTAD the very best possible advice in their deliberations.
3. The European Association of Average Adjusters (AIDE) had already taken the first steps in a re-examination of the principles of general average and the York-Antwerp Rules and offered its full co-operation with the CMI.

Market soundings both in the United Kingdom and abroad indicated a general acceptance to review the York-Antwerp Rules, and at their meeting in December 1990 the Council of the CMI decided on this course and appointed Mr David Taylor to head an International Sub-Committee.

Their first task was to prepare a Preliminary Report and a Questionnaire in two main parts. Part A sought general background information to provide a full awareness of legal, commercial and technical operating development which had occurred since the previous review in 1974, while Part B sought opinions on the form and substance of the Rules together with proposals for specific amendments and additional subjects on which the then current Rules were silent. **00.105**

This was circulated by the CMI Secretariat to national associations in July 1991 and some 20 replies had been received when the working group came to consider them in January 1992. Among those additional topics proposed for inclusion in the new Rules were:

Cost of measures to protect the environment imposed on the vessel in a port of refuge
Currency of Adjustment and Rates of Exchange
Tug (or pushboat) and Barges
Contributing interests such as Passenger Vehicles, Containers, etc., also Contributory Values on Multimodal Transport
Differential Salvage Awards
Non-Separation Agreements
Time Limits for the production of documents to the adjuster

The Working Group completed their analysis of the responses to the Questionnaire in March 1992; in December a first meeting of the International Sub-committee was held in Brussels; and in July 1993 a situation Report was circulated to national associations preparatory to a final meeting of the International Sub-Committee in Paris in December 1993. By this time, those most intimately concerned with the day-to-day practice of general average had largely thrashed out between themselves the likely substance of the new York-Antwerp Rules to be discussed and promulgated at the full CMI Conference to be held at Sydney in October 1994.

00.106 These periodic reviews of the York-Antwerp Rules presuppose that the institution of general average enjoys a widespread support within the maritime community, but as extensively recorded in Appendix 5, and particularly paragraph 90.02, below, strong calls for reform of the system have been made throughout the years, commencing even prior to the York Rules in 1864, and the proposed revision in 1994 prompted a resurgence of similar criticisms.

UNCTAD produced in November 1991 *General Average—A Preliminary Review*, to be followed in March 1994 with *The Place of General Average in Marine Insurance Today*, both extremely well-researched and developed papers. In turn, the International Union of Marine Insurers (IUMI), after their Conference at Berne in 1992, established a small working group to review marine insurers' experience of general average. This included the compiling and in-depth analysis of data of over a thousand general average incidents during recent years and the issuing of an impressive Report—*General Average and its Impact on Marine Insurance*—in June 1994. The Report indicated that the general average system appeared to operate heavily in favour of shipowners and detrimentally to shippers, and that the shipowners who most benefited from general average were the owners of old and sub-standard shipping; far from encouraging maritime safety, general average was subsidising poor standard shipping.

Perhaps of more immediate impact, the President of IUMI wrote to the President of CMI on September 27, 1994 expressing concern at several proposals for changes in the Rules which implied a continued expansion of general average and stating that *under no circumstances could IUMI accept expansion from the existing Rules.*

Professor William Tetley Q.C. of Canada also issued a thoughtful pre-conference paper entitled *Restraining the Expansion of General Average and the Abolition of Artificial General Average.*

Sydney Conference

Thirty nine national maritime law associations attended the CMI Conference at Sydney between October 2 to 8, 1994, together with numerous observers, and there is little doubt that the three-pronged attack referred to above resulted in a containment of any proposals of an expansionary nature in the new Rules. The attack, however (and particularly from IUMI and Professor Tetley), came a little late, and it is also to be noted that a number of sound proposals for *reducing* allowances in general average were successfully held at bay. **00.107**

At a plenary session on October 7, 1994 the text of the new York-Antwerp Rules was unanimously adopted by the 36 Member Association voting, together with the following resolution:

> "The Marine Association of Australia and New Zealand as the host Association proposes with pleasure that the delegates representing the National Associations of Maritime Law of the States listed hereunder[17]:
> 1. Having noted with approval the amendments which have been made to the York-Antwerp Rules, 1974, as amended 1990.
> 2. Propose that the new text be referred to as the York-Antwerp Rules, 1994.
> 3. Recommend that the York-Antwerp Rules, 1994 should be applied to the adjustment of claims in General Average as soon as practicable after 31st December 1994."

In his concluding Report, Mr David Taylor, Chairman of the International Sub-Committee, stated that:

> "The theme, which has been the theme of all recent periodical reviews of the York-Antwerp Rules, has been ... to seek to simplify general average procedures, to clarify doubtful issues with a common goal of trying to ensure that the general average regime continues realistically to respond to the shipping, insurance, financial, trading and environmental techniques of the 1990's."

[17] The resolution was carried by 39 States.

SECTION 4

THE YORK-ANTWERP RULES 1994

Introduction

The York-Antwerp Rules 1994, like all their predecessors,[1] apply only when the parties to the contract, whether it be of affreightment, of marine insurance[2] or of some other nature,[3] so agree; and they fall to be construed in the same manner as any other contractual terms which have been reduced into writing. Thus it is submitted that, in an English court, the actual intentions of the draftsmen of the Rules are not admissible aids to their construction, although they are interesting and important as a guide to the international commercial interpretation of the Rules.[4] On the other hand reference may be made to decisions on the construction of the earlier Rules in so far as the wording remains unaltered and their construction is not affected by the "Rule of Interpretation" which precedes the lettered rules. In the following pages each of the Rules is considered under three main headings, namely: **PRE.01**

(1) English law and practice on the subject-matter of the Rule, and independently of the contractual provisions of the Rule itself.
(2) Historical development and practice under the Rule since its introduction in 1860 or subsequently.
(3) Construction of the individual words and phrases in the 1994 Rule.

Under the third heading an attempt has been made to forecast the construction which could be put upon each Rule by an English court in the light of such decisions as there have been and the English legal rules of construction.

[1] See App. 2, paras. 60.18 *et seq.*, *post.*
[2] For the relevant provisions of the Institute Clauses, see paras. 50.84 and 50.86, *post.*
[3] See *Thomson v. Micks Lambert & Co.* (1933) 47 Ll.L.R. 5 (average bond).
[4] In *Vlassopoulos v. British and Foreign Marine Insurance Co.* [1929] 1 K.B. 187, Roche J. refers at 196 and 198 to the intentions of the draftsmen, but it is suggested that he was not considering their actual intentions but the intentions which must be imputed to them and to the parties who by contract had adopted the Rules.

If general average is adjusted otherwise than in accordance with English law, the Rules may be interpreted differently,[5] although the wording was the work of international committees.[6] It is outside the scope of this work to consider such differences.

[5] For the system of law which should govern the adjustment, see paras. 30.01 *et seq.*, *post*, also Rule G.

[6] See Section 3, paras. 00.64 *et seq.*, *ante*.

Rule of Interpretation

Historical Development and Practice

The 1890 Rules were numbered only and dealt with specific situations, and whether or not they should be treated as general average; they laid down no general principles. However, in *Anglo-Grecian Steam Trading Co. Ltd v. T. Beynon & Co.*,[1] Roche J. held that under those Rules it was not sufficient for a person claiming contribution in general average to prove the state of facts required by any individual numbered Rule unless he could also prove that there had been a general average act in accordance with the general law, which he held to be expressed in section 66(2) of the Marine Insurance Act 1906.[2] **PRE.02**

In 1924 lettered Rules dealing with general principles were introduced in an effort to obtain international uniformity. The inter-relationship of the general law, the lettered and the numbered Rules was considered by Roche J. in *Vlassopoulos v. British and Foreign Marine Insurance Co.*[3] In that case the ship's foremast collapsed at the loading port, causing a derrick to fall into the hold, and allowances were claimed in respect of the expenses incurred while the repairs were being carried out. The repairs were necessary for the safe prosecution of the voyage, and most of the expenses claimed therefore fell within the relevant provisions of Rules X and XI. However, neither ship nor cargo were at any time in peril, and on that ground allowance was refused. The judge described the relationship between the lettered and the numbered Rules as follows:

> "In my judgment the true construction is this: that certain general Rules are laid down in order that if the parties choose to adopt the Rules by way of contract, as these parties have done, they may not be troubled thereafter by questions which arise under the old Rule XVIII as to what, if any, general law is to apply. They may have if they choose a self-contained code. ... But when this has been done and a general set of Rules provided laying down the general principles which are to operate, then the Rules go on to deal with certain specific cases, and I am satisfied on the true construction of the Rules that those cases are dealt with not by way of mere illustration, but in order to make definite and certain what the Rules decide about certain cases which are on the border line and which might be held to be on one side or the other of the line which is to be drawn under the general Rules. ... It is, I think, as if the Rules had provided that Rules A, B, C,

[1] (1926) 24 Ll.L.Rep. 122. The report incorrectly refers to the 1924 Rules.
[2] See para. A.05, *post*.
[3] [1929] 1 K.B. 187.

and so forth constitute the general rules for general average and then followed the words: 'And in particular 1, 2, 3, 4' and so on 'are cases of general average.'"[4]

PRE.03 Whatever may have been the intention of the parties in the case referred to above (which concerned the *S.S. Makis*), the construction propounded by Roche J. did not accord with international practice or meet with the approval of the leading British shipowners and underwriters, who subsequently concluded an Agreement, commonly known as the "Makis Agreement",[5] which provided: "Except as provided in the numbered Rules 1 to 23 inclusive, the adjustment shall be drawn up in accordance with the lettered Rules A to G inclusive." It is in this Agreement that the Rule of Interpretation has its origin.

York-Antwerp Rules 1950 and 1974

RULE OF INTERPRETATION

PRE.04 In the adjustment of general average the following lettered and numbered Rules shall apply to the exclusion of any Law and Practice inconsistent therewith.

Except as provided by the numbered Rules, general average shall be adjusted according to the lettered Rules.

York-Antwerp Rules 1994

Two changes were made in the Rule, both merely consequences of the adoption of the Rule Paramount in the 1994 Rules,[6] and having no wider significance. First, the reference to the *lettered and numbered* Rules was omitted, in order to ensure that the Rule Paramount (which is neither lettered nor numbered) fell within the provisions of the first paragraph of the Rule. Secondly, an express reference to the Rule Paramount was inserted in the last paragraph of the Rule.

RULE OF INTERPRETATION

In the adjustment of general average the following Rules shall apply to the exclusion of any Law and Practice inconsistent therewith.

Except as provided by the Rule Paramount and the numbered Rules, general average shall be adjusted according to the lettered Rules.

[4] This construction was accepted by Tucker J. in *Athel Line v. Liverpool and London War Risks Insurance Association Ltd* [1944] 1 K.B. 87.

[5] Text of this Agreement is set out, para. 00.94, *ante*.

[6] See paras. PRE.21 *et seq., post*.

Second Paragraph

CONSTRUCTION

First Paragraph

The first paragraph of the Rule ensures that the Rules shall not be construed as a mere codification of any national law or any practice, national or international. They thus take effect as a contract between the parties and fall to be construed in the same manner as any other contract. They do not, however, constitute a complete or self-contained code and need to be supplemented by bringing into the gaps provisions of the general law which are applicable to the adjustment.[7] The practice of adjusters at the place of adjustment may also supplement the Rules, but law or practice on a matter which is fully dealt with by the Rules, for example a practice as to the interpretation of the Rules, is excluded by the Rule of Interpretation. In *Marida Ltd v. Oswal Steel; The Bijela*[8] evidence as to the practice of adjusters in interpreting Rule XIV was held on this ground to be inadmissible. Having stated the general Rule that evidence of usage is admissible to explain or supplement the terms of a contract, but not to contradict or nullify them, the judge continued[9]: **PRE.05**

> "But the matter does not rest there. There is an express provision in the Rule of Interpretation in the York-Antwerp Rules. That provides that in the adjustment of general average the lettered and numbered rules shall apply to "the exclusion of any Law and Practice inconsistent therewith". Therefore any attempt by the defendants to prove a practice that is inconsistent with the true construction of the rules is legally irrelevant and must be refused."

Second Paragraph

The second paragraph in effect reverses the decision in the *Makis* case.[10] Thus if the facts support a claim in general average under the numbered Rules, it matters not that there has been no general average act within the meaning of Rule A. Equally if the numbered Rules negative any claim in general average arising out of the loss in question (see, for example Rule I) no claim can be made under the lettered Rules although the facts fall within the scope of such Rules. There may be cases where any claim in general average is negatived, not expressly, but by implication from the wording of the numbered Rules, with the same result. However, it must be a clear implication from the wording of the Rule that *any* claim in general average is negatived. It is not sufficient that the claim **PRE.06**

[7] *Goulandris Bros Ltd v. B. Goldman & Sons Ltd* [1958] 1 Q.B. 74 at 91, *per* Pearson J.
[8] [1992] 1 Lloyd's Rep. 636, reversed on another point [1994] 2 Lloyd's Rep. 1.
[9] *Ibid.* at 642.
[10] See para. 3.02, *ante*.

should merely be excluded from the scope of the numbered Rule in question.

PRE.07 If a claim in general average can be established under one of the numbered Rules, it does not follow that all the lettered Rules must be disregarded in relation to that claim. In the first place, if a claim is advanced under one of the numbered Rules "it is the wording of the numbered Rule which has to be construed but it should be construed taking into account the general principles of the York-Antwerp Rules as stated in the lettered Rules".[11] Secondly, the Rule of Interpretation requires that the numbered Rules shall override the lettered Rules only to the extent that there is inconsistency between them in any particular case.

PRE.08 Determining whether inconsistency exists is in some instances most difficult, but in cases of doubt the sensible approach would seem to be to keep in mind that many of the numbered Rules were introduced with the specific intention of resolving vexed questions, and differences in local law or practice, which regularly arose in applying the principles of general average in certain particular situations, and to seek to identify those particular issues which the numbered Rule in question was intended to resolve.

For example, it is reasonably clear from its origins, content and wording that Rule VII is intended to resolve the question whether the running of the ship's machinery, when afloat or when ashore, is an *extraordinary* measure, and whether the resulting damage is *intentionally* incurred and therefore a *sacrifice*. Thus if a claim is made under Rule VII for damage to machinery or boilers it is irrelevant to inquire whether the requirements of Rule A relating to these three matters have been fulfilled; Rule VII is intended to provide a complete answer of its own on these questions. It is equally clear that Rule VII is not intended to impinge on the matters covered by Rules B, D, E and G,[12] which will therefore remain applicable to any claim under that Rule. Rule F is also unlikely to give rise to problems in this context, since by its nature it has no relevance to the case where the claim falls within the scope of a numbered Rule, its purpose being to allow recovery of expenses, not falling within the lettered Rules, which are substituted for another expense which would have been recoverable under the numbered Rules. Where matters become much more problematic is in considering whether Rule

[11] *Per* Hobhouse J. in *Marida v. Oswal Steel; The Bijela* [1992] 1 Lloyd's Rep. 636 at 644.

[12] Rule G will, of course, give way to such numbered Rules as may be inconsistent with it, in particular Rules XVI and XVII. In its 1993 "Review of the law of General Average and Revision of the York-Antwerp Rules" A.I.D.E. raised the question whether the Rule of Interpretation should be re-worded to reflect "the distinction in practice, that whereas Rules A, C and G are subordinated to the numbered rules, the matters treated in Rules D, E and F are in effect paramount".

C, or the remaining requirements of Rule A, apply to a claim under Rule VII.

In *Corfu Navigation Co. v. Mobil Shipping; The Alpha*[13] it was held that the provisions of Rule C and Rule E remained applicable to a claim under Rule VII, but that the requirement of reasonableness under Rule A did not.[14] So far as concerns Rule E this is clearly correct, but as regards Rule C it seems an oversimplification. Rule VII contains provisions of its own on causation, and seems to be designed to provide a complete code on causation so far as concerns the chain of events between the endeavours to refloat and the damage to the machinery or boilers. However, the Rule does not purport to provide its own code beyond that point, and the question whether losses and expenses consequential on the damage to the machinery or boilers (such as loss of charter hire, costs of repairs or expenses of an adjustment) are recoverable in general average is therefore governed by Rule C. Many of the numbered Rules require a similar distinction to be drawn. So far as concerns the requirement of reasonableness under Rule A, it is this aspect of the decision in *The Alpha* which gave rise to the most concern and was the reason for the introduction of the Rule Paramount in 1994.[15] It seems unlikely that Rule VII was consciously intended to dispense altogether with the requirement of reasonableness, or to substitute some different requirement.[16] On the other hand several of the numbered Rules expressly incorporate a requirement of reasonableness (or of *necessity*, which is if anything a more stringent test), and this militates against the view that such a requirement is automatically imported into every numbered Rule. As a matter of construction of the 1974 Rules it must therefore be accepted that the decision in *The Alpha* is probably correct. **PRE.09**

Other numbered Rules which have given rise to similar problems are Rules X(b) and XI(b). On the face of it, these Rules confer allowances in general average for *inter alia* expenses incurred at a port of loading or of call during delay caused by repairs to accidental damage, where the repairs are necessary for the safe prosecution of the voyage. As we have already seen, it was held in *Vlassopoulos v. British & Foreign Marine Insurance Co; The Makis*[17] that a requirement of peril was to be incorporated into the numbered Rules, and this decision led to the Rule of Interpretation. But even after the Rule of Interpretation had been introduced a similar approach to that in *The Makis* was adopted in the **PRE.10**

[13] [1991] 2 Lloyd's Rep. 515 at 519 (York-Antwerp Rules 1974)

[14] In the 10th and 11th editions of this work the view was expressed that neither Rule C nor Rule A would apply to a claim under Rule VII.

[15] See paras. PRE.21 *et seq., post.*

[16] In *Anglo-Grecian Steam Trading Co. Ltd v Benyon & Co.* (1926) 24 Ll.L.Rep. 122, which concerned voluntary stranding under the 1890 Rules, Roche J. said: "it is necessary for the plaintiffs to satisfy me and for me to be satisfied that the vessel was *reasonably* and intentionally run on shore."

[17] [1929] 1 K.B. 187.

U.S.A., in *Orient Mid-East Lines v. A Shipment of Rice; The Orient Transporter*,[18] where it was said that "the numbered Rules do not do away with the requirement that a ship must be in peril before the law of general average applies". However, this decision was not followed in *Eagle Terminal Tankers v. Insce. Co. of USSR; The Eagle Courier*[19] or in *Ellerman Lines v. Gibbs Nathaniel; The City of Colombo*,[20] where it was concluded that Rules X(b) and XI(b) are not subject to any overriding requirement of peril. This conclusion seems inescapable on the wording of those Rules.

PRE.11 Under the 1994 Rules, the Rule A requirement of reasonableness has by virtue of the Rule Paramount been made an essential of any claim, whether under the lettered or the numbered Rules. However, the very fact that this one requirement has been singled out for special treatment in this manner is an indication that under the 1994 Rules the remaining requirements of Rule A are not paramount, and are not to be imported into the numbered Rules.

[The next paragraph is PRE.21.]

[18] (1974) A.M.C. 2593 (YAR 1950), U.S. Ct. of Appeals 5th.
[19] (1981) A.M.C. 137, U.S. Ct. of Appeals 2nd.
[20] (1986) 26 D.L.R. (4th) 161; (1986) A.M.C. 2217.

Rule Paramount

Historical background

In the preceding paragraphs we have observed that the Rule of Interpretation has the effect that the numbered Rules override the lettered Rules in the case of inconsistency, but that it provides little or no guidance on the question whether inconsistency arises in any given case. The problem, which is also touched upon in the commentary under Rule A,[1] usually arises in determining which, if any, of the provisions of the lettered Rules are applicable to a claim under the numbered Rules. The extent of the problem was brought into sharp focus in 1991 by the decision of the English court in *Corfu Navigation v. Mobil Shipping; The Alpha.*[2] It was held in that case that a claim under Rule VII for damage to machinery sustained during attempts to refloat a grounded ship was not subject to the requirement of reasonableness in Rule A, and was therefore entitled to succeed even though the attempts to refloat by using the ship's engines had been unreasonable. It was the view of many that the decision, although unfortunate, was correct as a matter of construction of the Rules. **PRE.21**

York-Antwerp Rules 1994

As a result of the decision in *The Alpha* there was a widespread view among delegates at the Sydney Conference in 1994 that the Rules should be changed so as to make it clear that the requirement of reasonableness embodied in Rule A should apply to all claims whether under the lettered or numbered Rules. The U.S. delegation had proposed a Rule Paramount which would contain, as overriding provisions, both the requirement of reasonableness and the exclusion of pollution liabilities and clean-up costs. The latter provision was eventually transferred to Rule C, but the Conference accepted the U.S. proposal to the extent of adopting a Rule Paramount which made reasonableness an overriding requirement. **PRE.22**

This course did not meet with universal approval. Some delegates, including the British M.L.A., took the view that the numbered Rules already contained their own requirement of reasonableness (or necessity)

[1] See para. A.94, *post*.
[2] [1991] 2 Lloyd's Rep. 515; see also para. PRE.09, *ante*.

wherever this was appropriate,[3] and that to require the adjuster to determine the reasonableness of the measures adopted would require him to resolve questions of navigation and ship management which could frequently only be done with the assistance of consultants, thereby increasing the costs of the adjustment; it would also encourage protracted analysis, with the aid of hindsight, of decisions often taken in the heat of the moment. However, the majority of the delegates regarded these considerations as being of lesser importance than the need to exclude from allowances losses resulting from measures which it was unreasonable to adopt, and an attempt by the French delegation in plenary session to delete the Rule was defeated, as was a suggestion by the British delegation that the objections to the Rule could be reduced if it were so expressed as to exclude from allowance sacrifices or expenditure "if *unreasonably* made or incurred".

Rule Paramount

In no case shall there be any allowance for sacrifice or expenditure unless reasonably made or incurred.

Construction

PRE.23 The Rule must be read in the context of the Rule of Interpretation, which expressly provides that the Rule Paramount overrides the lettered Rules in the event of inconsistency. The title of the Rule probably owes its origin to the phrase "Clause Paramount" which is frequently found in charterparties and bills of lading in order to describe a clause which incorporates the Hague Rules into the contract of carriage "and which overrides any express exemption or condition which is inconsistent with it".[4] It follows that, although the York-Antwerp Rules contain no explicit provision that the Rule Paramount overrides all of the numbered Rules, it is inherent in its title that it should have this effect. The result is that it is a requirement of any claim whether under the lettered or numbered Rules, just as it is under English law, that the sacrifice or expenditure should be reasonably made or incurred.

[3] This view is not easy to accept. There are no grounds for suggesting that any of the numbered Rules were adopted for the purpose of excluding or modifying the requirement of reasonableness. It is true that some of the provisions of the numbered Rules are expressly made subject to a requirement of reasonableness, whereas others are not, but it is difficult to discern any rationale behind these differences in treatment, which seem to owe as much to chance as to design. See para. A.94, *post*.

[4] *Nea Agrex v. Baltic Shipping* [1976] Q.B. 933 at 943, *per* Lord Denning M.R.

"reasonably made or incurred." The wording is identical to that of the corresponding provisions of Rule A (and of English law[5]), the effect of which is discussed at paragraphs A.84 to A.86, below. Thus any claim, whether under the lettered or numbered Rules, will be subject to the identical test of reasonableness. In spite of the rejection of the wording proposed by the British delegation, referred to above,[6] it seems likely that the approach to the interpretation of the Rule Paramount will follow that adopted in practice under Rule A[7]; the sacrifice or expenditure will be deemed to have been reasonably made or incurred unless the contrary is established, and the master will be given the benefit of the doubt. **PRE.24**

In determining whether a sacrifice was reasonably made, what must be considered is the reasonableness of the decision to adopt the measure which involves or causes the sacrifice. If the measure in question is then carried out in a negligent manner, that does not deprive it of its character as a general average act; however, any additional loss or damage resulting from that negligence may be excluded from general average by Rule C (if the claim is under the lettered Rules), and those parties whose property has been lost or damaged thereby may pursue any remedies available to them in respect of the negligence.[8]

The Rule Paramount provides a defence to a claim in general average if the sacrifice or expenditure was unreasonable, even though the claimant was not himself responsible for the unreasonable conduct. Thus a cargo owner whose cargo is unreasonably jettisoned by the master, or damaged by unreasonable attempt by the master to extinguish a fire on board, will have no claim for contribution, at any rate against those interests who were not guilty of unreasonable conduct. It may be that in such a case the shipowner would be estopped from invoking the unreasonable conduct of his own servants or agents in order to resist a claim for contribution, and in any event, unless he is protected from liability by an exceptions clause, he will be liable in damages for the loss caused thereby. **PRE.25**

[5] I.e. the Marine Insurance Act 1906, s.66(2): see para. A.05, *post*.

[6] See para. PRE.22, *ante*.

[7] See para. A.84, *post*.

[8] *Cf. Federal Commerce and Navigation Co. v. Eisenerz* [1970] 2 Lloyd's Rep. 332; [1975] 1 Lloyd's Rep. 105. See also para. 00.62, *ante*, para. 12.11, *post*.

Rule A

Definition of General Average

A.01 **There is a general average act when, and only when, any extraordinary sacrifice or expenditure is intentionally and reasonably made or incurred for the common safety for the purpose of preserving from peril the property involved in a common maritime adventure.**

...[1]

Such are the bare words defining what constitutes a general average act, and it will here be our purpose to analyse and explain each phrase of this succinct definition. First, however, it may be of value to quote some of the earlier legal definitions from which the wording of the Rule has been distilled, and even before recounting the antecedents, to repeat Rule A word for word, highlighting the essential features so that they may be recognised in the reading of the earlier legal pronouncements:

There is a general average act when, and only when, any ...

EXTRAORDINARY ...

SACRIFICE OR EXPENDITURE IS ...

INTENTIONALLY and ...

REASONABLY made or incurred for the ...

{ COMMON SAFETY for the purpose of preserving from ...
{ PERIL the property involved in a ...

COMMON MARITIME ADVENTURE.

Earlier Legal Definitions

A.02 The first modern case in which the sanction of an English court of common law was given to the principle of general average was that of *Birkley v. Presgrave*,[2] in 1801. The principle, indeed, does not appear to have been contested at the trial of this case, but was treated in argument

[1] A second paragraph was added to Rule A in 1994, but as this is not concerned with the *definition* of general average, it will be discussed, in paras. A.88 and A.98, *post*.

[2] 1 East 220.

as a thing long established and well known, and the dispute was only as to some particular point of its application. One of the judges, however, Lawrence J., began his judgment with the following sentence:

> "All loss which arises in consequence of extraordinary sacrifices made or expenses incurred for the preservation of the ship and cargo comes within general average, and must be borne proportionably by all who are interested."[3]

This was no new departure, but a direct continuation of the historical antecedents discussed in Section 1 of this book in paragraphs 00.01 *et seq.*, above. Nevertheless the words of Lawrence J. have always been treated as of the highest authority. They were adopted and used as a test in *Covington v. Roberts*[4] and *Job v. Langton*,[5] and in *Svendsen v. Wallace*,[6] Brett M.R. said:

> "It has been considered to be one of the many happy expositions of mercantile law made by that learned person, in terms so broad and yet so accurate, as to shew that he was one of the greatest mercantile lawyers who has ever adorned our profession in this country."

Variations, substantially however amounting to much the same thing, have been offered by other judges. **A.03**

> "In order to give rise to a charge as general average, it is essential that there should be a voluntary sacrifice to preserve more subjects than one exposed to a common jeopardy. An extraordinary expenditures incurred for that purpose is as much a sacrifice as if, instead of money being expended for the purpose, money's worth were thrown away. It is immaterial whether a shipowner sacrifices a cable or an anchor to get the ship off a shoal, or pays the worth of it to hire those extra services which get her off": *Kemp v. Halliday*,[7] *per* Blackburn J.

> "The claim for general average arises where part of a cargo or ship is destroyed in order to rescue the remainder from some impending peril. If, during a voyage, by stress of weather or otherwise, a vessel is in immediate danger of being lost, and part of the cargo is thrown overboard, or a mast is cut away, as a means of preventing the total loss of vessel and cargo, that loss, being incurred for the common benefit of all concerned, shall not be sustained by the owner of the ship alone, but by a general contribution from all": *Hallett v. Wigram*,[8] *per* Wilde C.J.

[3] *Ibid.* at 228. The words "all loss" in this definition, said Gorell Barnes J. in *The Leitrim* [1902] P. 256–266, must read with some limitation; they ought not to cover losses which "are the result of 'accidental circumstances' affecting the loser, and are not losses which the other persons interested ought in ordinary course to be treated as concerned with". For the test as to remoteness, see paras. C.01–C.14, *post*.
[4] (1806) 2 B. & P.N.R. 378.
[5] (1856) 6 E. & B. 779 at 790.
[6] (1884) 13 Q.B.D. 69 at 73.
[7] (1865) 6 B. & S. 723 at 746; 34 L.J.Q.B. 233 at 242.
[8] (1850) 9 C.B. 580 at 601; 19 L.J.C.P. 281 at 288.

"It is a loss incurred for the general benefit of the ship and cargo, to which those who have received the benefit are by law liable to contribute rateably": *Cargo ex Galam*,[9] *per* Lord Kingsdown.

"Wherever under extraordinary circumstances of danger to both ship and cargo a voluntary sacrifice of money [*read*, property or money] is made in order to save both ship and cargo, by the expenditure of which both ship and cargo are saved, the person who has made the voluntary sacrifice is entitled to call upon the others, whose property has been saved by the voluntary sacrifice made on their behalf, as well as on his own, for general average contribution": *Ocean Steamship Co. v. Anderson*,[10] *per* Brett M.R. (Lord Esher).

"If loss or expense is occasioned by reason of some extraordinary course taken, or risk incurred, for the benefit of all concerned, then those who, by reason of their being exposed to a common danger, are interested in that course being taken or that risk incurred, must contribute their share": *Walthew v. Mavrojani*,[11] *per* Bovill C.J.

"General average contribution is defined to be a contribution by all the parties in a sea adventure to make good the loss sustained by one of their number on account of sacrifices voluntarily made of part of the ship or cargo to save the residue and lives of those on board from an impending peril, or for extraordinary expenses necessarily incurred by one or more of the parties for the general benefit of all the interests embarked in the enterprise": *The Star of Hope*,[12] *per* Clifford J.

A.04 In cases of doubt or difficulty, however, the English courts still recognise the importance of the original maxim of the Rhodian law.[13]

"General average is founded on the Rhodian law; which, however, in terms did not extend further than to cases of jettison, but its principle applies and it has been applied to all other cases of voluntary sacrifice for the benefit of all, that is, if properly made."[14]

"The classical writers stress that general average arises when the master of a vessel gives something for the sake of all (*quod pro omnibus datum est*)": *Australian Coastal Shipping Commission v. Green*,[15] *per* Lord Denning M.R.

[9] (1863) 33 L.J.Ad. 97 at 102. See further *Johnson v. Chapman* (1865) 19 C.B. (N.S.) 563 at 583; *Fletcher v. Alexander* (1868) L.R. 3 C.P. 375 at 381; *Walthew v. Mavrojani* (1870) L.R. 5 Exch. 116 at 124; *Stewart v. West India and Pacific S.S. Co.* (1873) L.R. 8 Q.B. 88 at 93; *Whitecross Wire Co. v. Savill* (1882) 8 Q.B.D. 653 at 661, 662.

[10] (1883) 13 Q.B.D. 651 at 662.

[11] (1870) L.R. 5 Exch. 116 at 119.

[12] (1869) 9 Wall. 203 (U.S. Sup.Ct.). This and many other American decisions tend to show that, in the U.S., measures to ensure the completion of the adventure may give rise to general average, although the property was not in physical danger.

[13] See the judgment of Watkin Williams J. in *Pirie v. Middle Dock Co.* (1881) 4 Asp. M.C. 388 at 390. Parsons, referring to this maxim, says: "This law was in force in the commerce of the Mediterranean and Adriatic seas more than a thousand years before the Christian era; nor can there be a better definition of the law of general average as it is in force today." (Boston, *Law of Shipping* (1869), p. 339.)

[14] *Anderson v. Ocean S.S. Co.* (1884) 10 A.C. 107 at 114.

[15] [1971] 1 Q.B. 456 at 484.

Statutory Definition

General average is not a doctrine forming part of the law of insurance; it belongs to the law of carriage by sea. Nevertheless it has important consequences in the field of marine insurance, and section 66 of the Marine Insurance Act 1906 contains a definition of a general average loss and of a general average act. There is judicial authority[16] for the proposition that this will now prevail for all purposes. Although the application of the Act is clearly confined to marine insurance, it was intended to codify the law and thus may be regarded as of a wider application.[17] The relevant provisions are as follows: **A.05**

> **66.**—(1) A general average loss is a loss caused by or directly consequential on a general average act. It includes a general average expenditure as well as a general average sacrifice.
>
> (2) There is a general average act where any extraordinary sacrifice or expenditure is voluntarily and reasonably made or incurred in time of peril for the purpose of preserving the property imperilled in the common adventure.

It is clear that Rule A of the York-Antwerp Rules, introduced at the Stockholm Conference in 1924, is modelled very closely on the English statutory definition, and it may be useful to print the two definitions together for ease of comparison: **A.06**

(MIA) *There is a general average act where any ...*
(YAR) There is a general average act when, and only when, any ...

(MIA) *EXTRAORDINARY ...*
(YAR) **EXTRAORDINARY** ...

(MIA) *SACRIFICE or EXPENDITURE is ...*
(YAR) **SACRIFICE or EXPENDITURE** is ...

(MIA) *VOLUNTARILY and ...*
(YAR) **INTENTIONALLY** and ...

(MIA) *REASONABLY made or incurred in ...*
(YAR) **REASONABLY** made or incurred for the ...

(MIA) *TIME OF PERIL for the purpose of preserving the property ...*
(YAR) **COMMON SAFETY** for the purpose of preserving from ...

(MIA) *IMPERILLED in the ...*
(YAR) **PERIL** the property involved in a ...

(MIA) *COMMON ADVENTURE.*
(YAR) **COMMON MARITIME ADVENTURE**.

[16] *Austin Friars S.S. Co. v. Spillers and Bakers Ltd* [1915] 1 K.B. 833 at 835, *per* Bailhache J.
[17] *Australian Coastal Shipping Commission v. Green* [1971] 1 Q.B. 456 at 478.

A.07 We now look more closely at the five essential features, all of which must be present to constitute a general average act:

(1) INTENTIONAL
(2) PERIL (COMMON SAFETY)
(3) COMMON MARITIME ADVENTURE
(4) EXTRAORDINARY
(5) REASONABLE

1. NECESSITY FOR INTENTIONAL ACT

A.08 In order that a sacrifice or expenditure may constitute a general average act, under the terms of Rule A it must be INTENTIONAL, while English legal decisions and the statutory definition use the word *voluntary*. When Rule A was being discussed in 1924 at the Stockholm Conference it was urged by some of the delegates that the word "voluntarily" was capable of several interpretations, none of which implied quite the same decisiveness as "intentionally". Many acts might be done voluntarily without implying any precise intention. After careful consideration of this some what refined point the Conference elected to adopt the word "intentionally" as emphasising more clearly the idea of deliberate choice. This was also designed to avoid the argument that an act was not voluntary when it resulted from overwhelming pressure of circumstances.

From a practical point of view, the use of the word *intentional* (or *voluntary*) is to distinguish the resultant loss from one that is entirely *accidental* in origin. Thus, if a vessel strands and rips open her bottom, the damage to the ship and to the cargo in any affected hold is the direct and immediate result of an accident, and the respective owners of the ship and the damaged cargo will each bear their own losses without contribution. But if, in order to refloat the stranded vessel and her cargo,

cargo is jettisoned, and/or
lighters are hired to offload the cargo, and/or
salvage tugs are employed, and/or
the ship's engines are damaged by working them when aground,

each or any of these losses, although having its origin in the initial accidental stranding, is really the result of an *intentional* act and will generally be admissible as general average.

A.09 Losses incurred by accident or through superior force are not made good in general average. The act must be the result of the exercise of reasoning power and discretion, directed to the particular problem of saving the vessel and cargo concerned. In *Athel Line Ltd v. Liverpool and London War Risks Association Ltd*,[18] two vessels of the plaintiff line, sailing in convoy from Bermuda to the United Kingdom, put back to Bermuda under order of the convoy commodore. These orders were pursuant to Admiralty instructions, owing to the convoy ahead having been attacked by an enemy raider with considerable loss thereto. The plaintiffs' vessels lost six days on their voyage and extra fuel and stores were consumed. Accordingly the plaintiffs claimed from their War Risk underwriters the ships' contribution towards these expenses in general average under Rules A and X(a) of the York-Antwerp Rules 1924. Tucker J. held that the language of Rule A was inappropriate to cover mere obedience to lawful orders of a superior authority, and that the plaintiffs could not rely upon the acts of the masters of the vessels as general average acts. He also decided that the plaintiffs could not rely upon the acts of (1) the commodore, or (2) the Admiralty, as in his view of the facts the orders were given as part of the general naval and strategic dispositions in the North Atlantic, and not for the sole purpose of preserving from peril the property involved in the adventures in the plaintiffs' two vessels.

Must General Average Act be that of the Master?

A further important question is whether an intentional sacrifice or expenditure, in order to constitute a general average act, must be ordered or at any rate authorised by the master, or whether it may be the act of the crew or of a stranger to the adventure. The master is no doubt in most cases the proper person to decide whether a sacrifice or expenditure must be made or incurred, the conduct of the adventure and the care of the ship and cargo having been entrusted to him. If, however, an emergency arises at a time when the master is absent or for any other reason incapable of acting, a sacrifice or expenditure made or incurred under the direction of the mate or other officer discharging the master's duties would without doubt be treated as a general average act if it could have been so treated if performed by the master. Yet there may be exceptional cases in which a sacrifice has reasonably been made without any order from him (or his substitute), or even against his wish; and the question may arise in such cases whether the owner of the property sacrificed is entitled to contribution. There is little English authority on the point. **A.10**

In *Price v. Noble*,[19] a claim for contribution was made in respect of the jettison of the ship's guns and part of her stores and tackle, after she had been captured by a French privateer and while she was in the possession of a prize master and crew. The mate of the ship and two of **A.11**

[18] [1944] K.B. 87.
[19] (1811) 4 Taunt. 123.

the crew had, however, been left on board; and in the emergency of the storm the prize crew called the mate to their aid in navigating the ship, and it was with his assistance and on his advice that the jettison was made. Afterwards the ship was recaptured, and her owner brought an action for a contribution in general average, and obtained a verdict which the defendants moved to set aside on the ground that the jettison was not ordered by the master, but by strangers to whom the respective owners of the ship and cargo had not entrusted their safety. The court, however, held that, as the goods had been jettisoned for the benefit of the residue of the property, the shipowners were entitled to contribution. It is true that Mansfield C.J. said in his judgment that the prize crew had consulted the mate and entrusted him with the navigation, and that the stores seem to have been thrown overboard by his direction; but it seems clear that the mate's evidence to this effect was only used by his Lordship for the purpose of showing that the jettison was necessary. As the ship and cargo were in the possession of the prize crew, the mate's position was that of an adviser to the prize master, and the power to decide whether the sacrifice should be made or not was in the hands of the latter.[20]

A.12 In *Papayanni v. Grampian S.S. Co.*[21] the facts were that the defendant's ship, *The Birkhall*, being on fire, was taken by her master into the port of Philippeville, where the crew were unable by their own exertions to extinguish the fire. The captain of the port, to whom intimation of the state of affairs had been given, came on board, and ordered the ship to be scuttled. The master afterwards stated that in his opinion "it was the best thing for the ship and cargo to scuttle the ship, though he was only obeying the orders of the captain of the port, and had nothing to do with it". The action was for a general average contribution, and, as reported, the judgment of Mathew J. is contained in the following words:

> "This evidence shows that what was done was in the interest of ship and cargo. There is no evidence that there was any other motive for scuttling the ship. The captain, who had not parted with the possession of his ship, did not object. There seems to be clear evidence that he sanctioned what was done. The loss must be adjusted as a general average sacrifice."

The statement that the master "sanctioned" what was done suggests that Mathew J. based his judgment on a finding that the master was a party to the sacrifice. From the report, however, it seems clear that the master did not propose the scuttling of the ship, that he was not consulted about it, and was powerless to prevent it. Under these circumstances his approval of the sacrifice seems only material as being evidence that the

[20] There seems to have been no suggestion in any of the judgments that as the ship and cargo had not yet been condemned by a Prize Court, the prize master might be regarded as the person who had succeeded to the master's duty to the owners of the property to take the necessary steps for its preservation, and not as a stranger to the adventure.

[21] (1896) 1 Com.Cas. 448.

scuttling was a proper measure; and it is improbable that the learned judge intended to found his decision on the master's assent, except in so far as it was evidence of the necessity of the sacrifice.

In both these cases, therefore, the only view consistent with the facts seems to be that the sacrifice was made *by a stranger to the adventure*; and they support the conclusion that it is not essential that the sacrifice should have been made under the authority of the master, but that the real question is whether it was necessary for the general safety. Such a rule is consistent with the principle of natural justice on which the law of general average is said to be founded; and if this be the correct view, it follows that a sacrifice made by the crew without the master's assent, and even against his wish, may be general average, though the fact that the master was opposed to the sacrifice would be strong evidence that it was not imperative, and the clearest proof of its necessity would therefore be required. **A.13**

A different rule has, however, been laid down by a majority in the Supreme Court of the United States. In *Ralli v. Troop*,[22] a case of a ship on fire, which was scuttled by the harbour authorities, it was held that: **A.14**

> "The power and duty of determining what part of the common adventure shall be sacrificed for the safety of the rest, and how and when the sacrifice shall be made, appertain to the master of the vessel, *magister navis*, as the person intrusted with the command and the safety of the common adventure, and of all the interests comprised therein, for the benefit of all concerned, or to some one who, by the maritime law, acts under him or succeeds to his authority."

Applying this rule, the court held that a sacrifice of vessel or cargo by the act of a stranger to the adventure gives no right of contribution, and that the port authorities were strangers to the maritime adventure and to all interests included therein.[23]

In 1944 this question was again argued at length before Tucker J. in *Athel Line Ltd v. Liverpool and London War Risks Association Ltd.*[24] Upon the view taken of the facts by the learned judge, it was not necessary to decide the point, and he observed that it was undesirable that he should express any opinion with regard to it. He did, however, say that "there was no clear authority". All the cases above referred to

[22] 157 U.S. 386 (1894).

[23] See also *Minneapolis, etc., S.S. Co. v. Manistee Transit Co.* 156 Fed.Rep. 424 (1907); *Wamsutta Mills v. Old Colony Steamboat Co.* 137 Mass. 471 (1883); *Andree-Moran No. 16* (1930) A.M.C. 631. This line of authority has been much criticised. *Cf. The Roanoke* (1893) 46 Fed.Rep. 297; 53 Fed.Rep. 270; 59 Fed.Rep. 161; and *The Beatrice* (1924) A.M.C. 914, where the work of extinguishing the fire was done by the fire department, but by request of the owners with the approval of the officers and crew and for the safety of the particular ship and cargo, and it was held that the fire department was acting as the agent of the shipowner and that the damage done in putting out the fire was recoverable as general average (*Ralli v. Troop* distinguished).

[24] [1944] K.B. 87.

were cited and it was suggested that there might be a difference between English and American law in this respect.

A.15 A different aspect of aspect of the same problem is now far more common, where the master does not exercise his own judgment but acts on the orders of his owners, or the owners themselves carry out the general average act. For example, in *Australian Coastal Shipping Commission v. Green*[25] tugs were summoned not by the masters of the two vessels concerned but by the plaintiffs' shore officers. It was not argued that on this ground the hiring of the tugs could not be general average acts. No doubt the masters there assented to the steps that their employers had taken. However, it is submitted that the decision was right on a wider ground: the shipowner, as employer of the master, is entitled if he wishes and the opportunity occurs, to call in the discretion which he has entrusted to the master, and to make the decision himself or by others of his servants or agents.

If the master and crew abandoned a vessel completely and with no expectation of returning to her, measures taken by a stranger in order to bring her to safety would not be of a general average nature, under English law, but see Rule VI. Nor would be measures taken to destroy a vessel, for example because of a risk of pollution.

A.16 At the Stockholm Conference in 1924 an amendment was in fact moved to add the words "by the master or his representative" after the word "incurred", but was withdrawn. It may be assumed, therefore, that the intention of the Conference was that, provided the act otherwise possesses the necessary qualification required by Rule A, the fact that it was not specifically ordered by the master will not bar a claim to allowance in general average. Nor is it required by Rule A that the sacrifice must be preceded by a consultation between the master and the crew, as provided by many foreign codes. These must be regarded as wise omissions, for provisions to this effect would certainly narrow the scope of general average unduly. Provided that the act possesses the true elements of general average, the fact that the master was absent or, in the emergency of the moment, acted on his sole initiative, should not on grounds of policy deprive the interest selected to suffer of compensation in general average.

2. Necessity for Peril

A.17 Of the five essential features necessary to constitute a general average act, perhaps the most important is that there must be present a situation

[25] [1971] 1 Q.B. 456.

of real and substantial PERIL whereby the COMMON SAFETY of the adventure is threatened.

Unfortunately, this subject of peril is also one of the most difficult to deal with comprehensively. The infinite variety of circumstances surrounding almost every maritime casualty make it impossible to formulate any general proposition with sufficient precision to enable those concerned to ascertain at a glance whether any particular situation has the necessary degree of peril to be treated as general average. However, by examining some of the decisions of the courts and other situations encountered in everyday practice, some working guidelines may be deduced.

There are, of course, certain situations of such extreme danger and gravity that there would and could be no dispute that ship and cargo were in peril, for example:

(1) a loaded vessel heavily aground on rocks for half her length and with one or more holds flooded;
(2) a loaded tanker ablaze in the Arabian Gulf after a missile attack;
(3) a vessel with her deck cargo of steel pipes shifted, and listed 45° in heavy seas; or
(4) a loaded vessel after a serious collision, with the engine room and the adjacent cargo hold flooded.

At the other end of the spectrum, it would hardly be suggested that the ship and cargo were in peril if, for instance:

(5) A vessel struck a quay wall on leaving port and merely indented the shell plating above the waterline, in no way reducing her strength or impairing her ability to continue the voyage in the normal manner.

It is between these two extremes, however, that the situation is less clear.

Is a Danger to Life Sufficient?

In practice the case is not likely to arise in which the ship and cargo **A.18**
are not imperilled by a danger which threatens the lives of the persons on board the vessel; and if the effect of sacrificing part of the property in fear of death has been to save that which remains, it may well be that a court would not inquire whether the saving of the property was actually in the mind of the master when he directed the sacrifice, but would impute such a motive to him. Yet if there could be a case in which a portion of the ship or cargo has been sacrificed in fear of death, without any expectation or possibility of advantage to the owners of the property which remains, there are no authorities except the dictum set out below

which supports the view that there would be a liability to contribute to general average.[26]

A.19 In *Montgomery v. Indemnity Mutual Marine Insurance Co.*,[27] Vaughan Williams L.J., delivering the judgment of the Court of Appeal, said:

> "It is not, we think, true to say that it is only the danger to the ship, freight or cargo which necessitates and justifies sacrifice by the master of either a portion of the cargo or a portion of the ship. This may be done in fear of death, and if it is done upon a proper occasion all must contribute to the loss."

The contrary view was expressed in the American case of *Shoe v. Low Moor Iron Co.*,[28] as one of two grounds on which the right to contribution was denied.

It is to be noted that a jettison of cargo to enable the ship to receive the passengers and crew of *another* vessel in distress would not constitute a general average sacrifice. In *Dabney v. New England Co.*[29] the Supreme Court of Massachusetts held that the sacrifice had not been made to avoid a danger to the original adventure.

Must a Total Loss of Ship and Cargo be Envisaged if Nothing be Done?

A.20 As a general principle, it is probably true to state that for an act to be considered a general average act, it must have been undertaken to preserve the ship and cargo from a situation which *might* or could develop into an actual or commercial total loss of the ship and cargo—other than by mere decay—before arrival at her final destination. Thus, it is to be assumed, for instance, that:

(1) if a fire be not extinguished, it is likely to consume the ship and cargo;
(2) if a stranded vessel be not refloated, she and her cargo will be broken up and lost in subsequent storms which are bound to occur at some time; or

[26] The definition of a general average act in the Marine Insurance Act 1906 (para. A.05, *ante*), seems opposed to the dictum. In *The Gratitudine* (1801) 3 C.Rob. 240, Lord Stowell says that in the cases of extreme necessity when the lives of the crew cannot otherwise be saved, the whole cargo may be thrown overboard, and the ship must contribute its average proportion; but the case which he puts is evidently one in which the object is to save the lives of those on board by preserving the vessel. It may also be pointed out that general average is in many respects analogous to salvage, and that there was no power, until it was given by statute, to remunerate the salvor of life only at the expense of the property. The statement in *Mouses's Case* (1609) 12 Co.Rep. 63 that "everyone ought to bear his loss for the safeguard and life of a man" may also be cited; but it cannot safely be assumed that the court in making it had the question of general average in mind.

[27] [1902] 1 K.B. 734 at 740.

[28] (1891) 46 Fed.Rep. 125; 49 Fed.Rep. 252.

[29] (1867) 14 Allen 300.

(3) if a vessel with a complete machinery breakdown be not salved into a port of refuge, she will drift ashore and become a stranded vessel as in (2).

If a total loss of ship and cargo cannot be envisaged, it is doubtful whether the peril is sufficient to constitute a general average.

In earlier times it used to be suggested that if the quantum of danger was such that, in the absence of a sacrifice, the total loss of all property involved in the adventure was certain, there could be no "sacrifice" of part since this part was *ex hypothesi* already lost. This view has not been accepted by the English courts.[30] If a cargo is on fire, and the fire can only be put out by pouring in water, it has been decided that the damage done by pouring water in is to be replaced as general average.[31]

A Peril, Once Constituted, may Remain in Being even in a Port of Refuge

When a ship is immobilised but in no immediate danger, it is a question of fact whether there is a peril sufficient to support a claim for general average contribution. In *McCall v. Houlder Bros*[32] a vessel carrying perishable cargo had been towed into Las Palmas harbour with a damaged propeller. No greater peril could be suggested than that "if she had remained where she was, she would have rotted away". In the *Law Journal* report of the case, Mathew J. said: A.21

> "It is idle to say that she was not in peril, for she could do nothing but lay where she was ... In my opinion, there existed under the circumstances described a common danger..."

Similar, but not identical, words are to be found in the *Law Times Reports* and *Aspinall. The Times Law Reports* have "... it was idle to think of discharging the cargo ..." *Commercial Cases* (edited by Mr Theobald Mathew) omit these remarks altogether, although the point as to peril was one of the principal issues argued and was essential to the decision. It is submitted that mere inability to proceed further, even with a perishable cargo, is not by itself sufficient peril to support a general average claim.

The Troilus[33] was a case concerned with salvage reward, for services rendered in towing a vessel with a fractured tail-shaft first to the A.22

[30] *Pirie & Co. v. Middle Dock Co.* (1881) 44 L.T. 426 at 430. It has also been rejected in the U.S.: *Barnard v. Adams* (1850) 10 How. 270. However, the question may still arise, namely, whether there can be a sacrifice of some particular item of property involved in the common adventure which is so far damaged or doomed to destruction as to be effectively lost, even if the rest of the adventure is saved: see the commentary of Rules III and IV of the York-Antwerp Rules.

[31] *Stewart v. West India and Pacific S.S. Co.* (1873) L.R. 8 Q.B. 88.

[32] (1897) 66 L.J.Q.B. 408; 13 T.L.R. 280; 2 Com.Cas. 129; 8 Asp.M.C. 252; 76 L.T. 469. The last two are by the same reporter.

[33] [1951] A.C. 820.

quarantine anchorage off Aden, and subsequently to the United Kingdom. The principles of law to be applied were different from those of general average, but the facts afford a good illustration of the test as to when a vessel is in peril. The Admiralty assessors in the Court of Appeal advised that the vessel while off Aden was in "no immediate danger, but in the event of an unusual gale springing up she would certainly be in greater danger than a ship with all her main power available". The assessors in the House of Lords advised that she was in no greater danger than a vessel with motive power available, since she had proper tackle to keep her at anchor. It is submitted that, for general average purposes, the vessel was in peril on the basis of the advice given to the Court of Appeal, but not on the basis of the advice given to the House of Lords.

A.23 In *Orient Mid-East Lines Inc. v. S.S. Orient Transporter*[34] the United States Court of Appeals held that general average does not apply to expenses incurred to remove a ship intentionally grounded in an abandoned ship channel to permit repairs, and that the York-Antwerp Rules 1950 did not do away with the fundamental requirement that a ship be in a position of peril before the law of general average applies.

The facts in that case were that the vessel had completed loading a cargo at Beaumont and because voyage repairs to the boilers had not then been completed, she was taken under the guidance of a pilot to an abandoned ship channel in the Neches River and intentionally grounded on a soft silt bottom to permit repairs to be continued. The anchorage proved unsuitable and it was only with difficulty that the vessel was removed from the silt and mud at a cost of approximately $9,000.

> "The District Court found that the (vessel) was not in a position of peril when resting on the bottom of the Neches River. The facts support this finding. The vessel was far removed from any danger of collision with another ship and did not interfere in any way with navigation. The pilot ... testified that the ship would not have been disturbed by heavy weather."

How Immediate must the Peril be?

A.24 Some accidents are so serious that they undeniably place ship and cargo in *immediate* peril (of being totally lost), for example:

(1) A loaded tanker set ablaze in the Arabian Gulf by a missile attack.
(2) A loaded vessel cast ashore on rocks in a raging storm.

Other accidents may create a situation potentially just as dangerous, but more in the future, rather than the immediate present. The simplest example may be:

[34] (1974) A.M.C. 2593.

(3) A loaded vessel which suddenly loses her propeller, but in fine weather in the open sea.

Clearly there is no immediate danger to ship and cargo, though it will be appreciated that if nothing be done, sooner or later a storm must break and/or the vessel will drift ashore.

In *Vlassopoulos v. The British & Foreign Marine Insce. Co. Ltd*[35] the propeller of the *Makis* fouled some wreckage while on passage from Bordeaux to Cardiff and the vessel was obliged to put into Cherbourg for repairs. Roche J. held that the ship and cargo were in danger and said: **A.25**

> "It is not necessary that the ship should be actually in the grip or even nearly in the grip of the disaster that may arise from a danger. It would be a very bad thing if shipmasters had to wait until that state of things arose in order to justify them doing an act which would be a general average act.
>
> That is all, I think, which need be said with regard to that matter, unless I add this: that 'peril,' which means the same thing as 'danger' is the word used in the general rule (A), just as it is the word used in the Marine Insurance Act, Sec. 66. The word is not 'Immediate peril or danger.' It is sufficient to say that the ship must be in danger, or that the act must be done in order to preserve her from peril. It means, of course, that the peril must be real and not imaginary. It means that it must be substantial and not merely slight or nugatory. It must be a danger."

In other words, it is the *potential* peril or danger which is important, rather than the present (though it must be stressed in the words of Roche J. that the peril "must be real and not imaginary . . . it must be substantial and not merely slight or nugatory").

The facts in the *Makis* case, above, concerned an accident to the propeller, a vital part of the propulsion of any vessel, and on a voyage which—though short—is through relatively hazardous waters. What of situations such as the following: **A.26**

(4) A vessel loaded to the maximum draft to enter a certain port or waterway strikes some object causing a small leak into the forepeak tank, which fills. There is no danger to the ship and cargo at any time while at sea except . . . that her draft is increased and she cannot enter her port of discharge or the waterway en route without grounding?

(5) A vessel suffers some machinery breakdown such that her speed is reduced to seven knots. This is perfectly adequate for safety on her lengthy sea voyage, but inadequate to combat the strong currents in the Bosphorous, the Inland Sea of Japan (or wherever en route to her destination)?

[35] [1929] 1 K.B. 187.

(6) A vessel loses one or both anchors on a voyage to Bhavnagar. She can proceed in perfect safety to this port, but there is no prospect of her being able to lie there in safety to discharge her cargo, for in this particular port two anchors and several shackles of cable must always be used if the vessel is not to be driven ashore?

If the "peril" is so far distant, and preceded by a passage of complete safety, can the shipowner be entitled to call upon the general average system to make cargo interests contribute to the port of refuge expenses or the cost of extra tugs hired to avoid or combat that future peril?

A.27 It is submitted that such extra expenses are properly admissible as general average, provided only that the accident creating the future peril occurred on the current voyage, and while the cargo was on board. (A distinction may be drawn, perhaps, between *sacrifices* and *expenditure*. A sacrifice of the cargo, or of any part of the ship, will generally be made only in times of extreme emergency and imminent danger, and when there is really no other alternative if the common adventure is to be saved. On the other hand, an expenditure (for example the putting into a port of refuge) can often be delayed for some short time while the facilities for repairs or cargo handling at various ports in the area are considered, and the cheapest or most efficient course of action decided upon).[36]

The Peril must be Real and not Imagined

A.28 A sacrifice made in the mistaken—though reasonable—belief that a peril in fact exists is not general average under English or American law, nor under the York-Antwerp Rules. However, where a peril does exist, a mistake on the part of the master as to the precise nature or degree of the danger, or of the action necessary, will not prejudice that sacrifice or expenditure being treated as general average.

Imagined peril

In *Joseph Watson & Son Ltd v. Firemen's Fund Insurance Co. of San Francisco*,[37] the captain saw what he (wrongly) assumed to be smoke issuing from the hold, which indicated to him that there was a fire. Acting on that mistaken assumption, he caused high-pressure steam to be directed into the hold for the purpose of extinguishing the supposed fire, and damaged the cargo therein.

Rowlatt J. held that the damage to the cargo was not a general average loss because the evidence failed to establish that there had been an actual

[36] See, *e.g. Phelps v. Hill* [1891] 1 Q.B. 605, C.A.
[37] [1922] 2 K.B. 355; 38 T.L.R. 752; 12 Ll.L.Rep. 133.

fire in the hold and that, therefore, there had been no peril; he was not prepared to accept that there was a peril in every case where the captain believed it existed.

The facts in the American case of *The West Imboden*[38] were very similar to those prevailing in *Watson v. Firemen's Fund* (above) in that steam and water were injected into the hold when the master mistakenly assumed that there was a fire therein because the deck above the hold was found to be hot, and when rain and heavy seas fell on the deck, it caused vapour and steam to arise. On arrival at destination, no fire was found to have existed, but a steam pipe in the hold was found to be broken near the deck and escaping steam had heated the deck.

In identical fashion, it was held that the damage to the cargo was not be a general average loss.

Mistake as to action necessary

In *The Wordsworth*,[39] the vessel encountered heavy weather and the master erroneously came to the conclusion that a flooded forepeak was due to a hole in the ship forward and below the water-line. Fearing that the collision bulkhead might give way, and considering that it was the only way to save the ship, he opened the sluices of the collision bulkhead, thereby damaging cargo. When the water by this means had been reduced in the forepeak sufficiently to allow persons to go down and examine the inside, it was found that the leak arose from a break in the port hawse pipe and this break was soon repaired. Had the master known that the damage was to the port hawse pipe, he could have repaired the same without opening the sluices. **A.29**

The damage to the cargo was allowed in general average upon the grounds that (as referred to in later cases):

> "There was an actual peril to cargo, the Master being merely mistaken as to its degree." (*West Imboden*)

> "There was peril, for water was coming into the ship, although not in the manner supposed by the Captain, and no one knew what would be the result." (*Watson v. Firemen's Fund*)

In *Corry v. Coulthard*[40] the vessel met with gales and very heavy seas, rolling and straining very heavily, and the mainmast settled down in the ship about four inches, very suddenly slacking up the rigging and allowing the mast to roll about heavily. Being afraid of the heel of the mast working down to the plating and going through the bottom of the ship, the main mast was cut away and this loss was allowed as general average. **A.30**

[38] (1936) A.M.C. 696.
[39] 88 Fed.Rep. 313 (1898).
[40] Unreported. Exch. Div., Dec. 31, 1876, C.A., January 17, 1877. See 3 Asp. M.L.C. 546(n).

It appears that the master was mistaken as to the danger of the mast going through the ship's bottom, but in the Court of Appeal, Cockburn, C.J. held:

> "It is not necessary that the judgment of the master should be borne out by the facts when they come to be examined into.[41]
>
> The question in all this case is, not whether the event shows the wisdom of what was done, but whether, under all the circumstances, it was the exercise of a reasonable, prudent, sound judgment.[42]
>
> He sacrificed the mast because, if it had been allowed to remain where it was, it would in his judgment, have led to the common destruction of mast, ship and cargo."[43]

Although the master was mistaken as to the danger of the mast going through the ship's bottom, there was still a real danger, that is, of the mast lurching out of the ship and causing critical damage: "... whatever be the condition of the mast it was a source of danger to the ship ..."; also, "The jury found that (the master) was right in supposing there was a danger".

Thus the *Corry* case is on all fours with the decision in *The Wordsworth*[44] (also *Montgomery v. Indemnity Mutual Marine Insce Co.*[45]); a real peril existed, unlike the situation in the *Watson* case.[46]

A.31 An interesting case encountered in practice relating to an "imagined" peril concerned a chemical tanker which carried a part cargo of phenol in two of her four stainless steel tanks. Phenol is a relatively weak acid, though it is classified as hazardous whether in liquid or solid form, and is rapidly absorbed through the skin and causes severe burns. Within three days of sailing, it was found that the phenol had inexplicably eaten through certain gasket seals in the tanks and had flooded the adjacent pump-rooms. The cargo was transferred into the other tanks but soon destroyed their gasket seals, with the result that the ship might now be considered to have one continuous and common tank.

The phenol having finally flooded the after pump-room next to the engine-room and accommodation, and considering that it would only be a short time before the phenol had eaten its way through the seals in the engine-room bulkhead, and fearing for the safety of his crew and the ship, the master ordered the whole cargo to be jettisoned.

Subsequent investigation showed that the seals in this particular bulkhead were made of a different material and would have been impervious to the ravages of the phenol, and it can be suggested, therefore, on the grounds of the cases of *Watson v. Firemen's Fund*[47] and

[41] *Ex Shepherd v. Kottgen* (1877) 2 C.P.D. 578 at 583.
[42] Ex 3 Asp.M.L.C. 546(n) at 547.
[43] *Ibid.*
[44] 88 Fed.Rep. 313 (1898).
[45] [1902] 1 K.B. 734.
[46] [1922] 2 K.B. 355; 38 T.L.R. 752; 12 Ll.L.Rep. 133.
[47] [1922] 2 K.B. 355; 38 T.L.T. 752; 12 Ll.L.Rep. 133.

The West Imboden[48] that no real peril existed and that the jettison could not be treated as general average. However, it is submitted that those two cases are easily distinguished in that in neither was there the supposed fire which would have created the peril. In the chemical tanker case, a *real* accident had occurred and the hazardous acid had already broken bounds and escaped from its proper location, and it was only with hindsight that the master was to learn that the phenol would not gain access to the engineroom and accommodation and endanger the crew and the ship. The additional requirement that the sacrifice must be reasonable was clearly satisfied. The master would have been foolhardy to adopt a "wait and see" attitude.

Fear of Peril not Sufficient

In the vast majority of cases, peril can exist only *after* some accident or other extraordinary circumstance has operated and caused damage which impairs the seaworthiness, manoeuvrability, or general ability of the ship to withstand the normal maritime perils. **A.32**

It is not impossible that the ship and her cargo can be in peril, even though presently undamaged, but the impending disaster from which relief is sought by the supposed sacrifice or expenditure must then be immediately imminent and all but inevitable. Anchors can be lost by being dropped in an emergency to avoid a collision[49] and vessels may be intentionally run aground to avoid a collision, but the evidence in such cases should always be examined with even greater care as it is to be questioned whether the supposed sacrifice or expenditure was truly *extraordinary*,[50] of just an ordinary measure taken in the ordinary course of navigation, and one which was part of the shipowner's ordinary obligations under the contract of affreightment. Thus, the expense of moving a vessel out of port or to a typhoon anchorage when extremely bad weather is forecast is an ordinary voyage expense and not general average, though the position may be different if her moorings have already broken and/or other damage has been sustained.

In *Societé Nouvelle d'Armement v. Spillers and Bakers Ltd,*[51] the expenditure in respect of which a claim was made in general average was the engagement of a tug to tow a French sailing ship in June 1915, from Queenstown to Sharpness, so as to minimise the risk of attack by enemy submarines. The evidence did not satisfy the learned judge that on this particular voyage the vessel would be exposed to any exceptional risk of attack, and no submarine was in fact sighted during the towage. On the facts he held that the risk of attack was not, for time of war, an **A.33**

48 (1936) A.M.C. 696.
49 See para. A.66, *post*.
50 See paras. A.56–A.61, *post*. See also *Hamel v. P. & O. S.N. Co.* [1908] 2 K.B. 298, quoted in para. A.68, *post*.
51 [1917] 1 K.B. 865.

extraordinary and abnormal one, and that, although the towage might have minimised the risk, it was impossible to say that it preserved the property in time of peril.

The Peril must Affect all Interests

A.34 A sacrifice or expenditure incurred for the safety of one interest alone can never be general average; the peril sought to be avoided must affect all interests. Thus, if the refrigerating machinery of a reefer ship broke down, a deviation into a port of refuge for repairs could not be treated as general average as it would be solely for the safety of the refrigerated cargo.

Provided that the impending peril does affect all interests, no distinction will be made between any varying degrees of peril to which it might be suggested that the different interests were subject. Thus, if a vessel carrying both refrigerated cargo and, say, pig iron, were to suffer a total machinery breakdown, it is clear that delay and natural deterioration will cause the refrigerated cargo to become a total loss long before the pig iron. However, any general average or salvage services will remove them both from essentially the same risk of total loss by stranding or shipwreck, etc., and on these grounds the salvage or general average expenditure will be apportioned strictly *pro rata* over the values saved.[52]

Practical Examples and Situations to Illustrate the Problem of PERIL

Fire

A.35 Fire continues to be possibly the most alarming of any peril on board ship. Once started, it can quickly spread if unchecked, and on these grounds it can safely be asserted that any fire on board, however small, constitutes a real *peril* and that damage caused in extinguishing it can be treated as a general average sacrifice. (This is not to suggest, of course, that the cumbersome general average system will be brought into action for the damage caused by the bucket of water thrown over the third engineer's bedclothes set alight by smoking in bed!)

Groundings

A.36 Prima facie, any ship aground in a place where she is not intended to be is likely to be in peril, but it is a question of fact, to be decided on

[52] American courts have declined to evaluate different degrees of peril to the various interests: *Willcox v. American Smelting Co.; The Trojan* 210 Fed.Rep. 9 (1913); and see *The St. Paul* (1898) 82 Fed. Rep. 104; 86 Fed.Rep. 340. See also *The M. Vatan* [1990] 1 Lloyd's Rep. 336 and also the further remarks, in para. 6.29, *post*.

the circumstances existing in each particular case, whether or not the vessel is in any real and substantial peril.

When a vessel grounds in the open sea or on an exposed coastline there is seldom any doubt that the vessel is in peril, for even if safe enough at the time, danger must be apprehended should bad weather come on. Difficulties are more likely to arise when the vessel grounds in more protected waters, such as inland seas and lakes, rivers and estuaries, or in ports and harbours. For such guidance as they may offer, the facts and fairly extensive extracts from the judgments in three English legal decisions now follow.

In *Trafalgar Steamship Co. v. British and Foreign Marine Insce Co.*[53] the *Rodney* grounded some distance below Point Indio Lightship after leaving Buenos Aires. Here she remained fast for nearly two hours, her engines being worked ahead and astern to enable the vessel to get off, and ultimately, owing to the rising water, she floated and proceeded on her voyage. The expense of opening up and repairing the damage to the machinery was claimed in general average, but Channell J. ruled that the vessel was not in peril and that the damage was not admissible in general average. **A.37**

> "It seems to be an extremely common thing to go through this soft mud and occasionally to stick, and the evidence is very clear that you will not have any wind that will cause any damage to you from being aground, which will not, some 12 hours, it is said, before that wind comes to you, have raised the water so as to get you off. It seems, therefore, that, although, I suppose, people would generally say that in anything that can be called an open road-stead to be aground is to a certain extent to be in peril, yet in this particular place it rather seems that that is not so; it is a place where the water is shallow, where vessels habitually disregard it; they do not appear to wait until there is a southerly wind to raise the water, and it is not in practice considered to be a danger."

In *Charter Shipping Co. Ltd v. Bowring Jones & Tidy Ltd*[54] the case for the shipowners was that shortly after leaving the quay at Jacksonville the ship ran aground and was for a time, it was alleged, in danger of breaking her back. The engines were run full speed ahead and astern alternately, but that failed to refloat the vessel. She was refloated, however, with the assistance of a tug after being aground for nearly three hours. **A.38**

In his judgment, Roche J. stated:

> "It is said, in the first place, that the vessel was not in a position of peril, that she was in no real danger, that she was in inland waters 20 miles from the sea, and that it was merely a matter of rising water and if necessary, the assistance of a tug to get her off. The danger was not very great, but still I am satisfied that there was a position of peril within the meaning of the rule

[53] *Shipping Gazette*, November 18, 1904.
[54] (1930) 36 Ll.L.Rep. 272.

> (VII of the York-Antwerp Rules 1890); the danger was real and substantial enough to necessitate the use of the engines; and the risk of damage which was undergone, and the damage, if any, which resulted from their use and other circumstances, was damage within that rule of the York-Antwerp Rules."

A.39 In *Daniolos v. Bunge & Co.*,[55] the case for the shipowners was that while the vessel was sailing up the narrow navigable channel in the Randers Fjord on January 7, 1936, the strong ebb current caught her starboard bow and she grounded on her port side near Raaby Odde.

Efforts to refloat her by her own engines proved unsuccessful, and a tug was made fast. She was refloated momentarily, but was immediately caught again by the current and the wind and taken ashore on her starboard side on the north bank of the channel. Another attempt was made to refloat her, but, after moving about 150 yards ahead, she again went firmly aground and remained on the edge of the steep bank on the north side of the channel, being supported by only half her width on the starboard side, which was resting on a hard and uneven bottom of mud and stones.

Though continual efforts to refloat the ship were made, she remained aground until January 11, and was in constant danger of being taken further up the bank and of receiving damage to her bottom and internal structure, and of collision with passing vessels, with consequent loss or damage to her cargo. She was refloated at about 8 a.m. on January 11, the water having risen owing to the wind veering, and she proceeded to Randers, where the cargo was discharged.

Goddard J. decided that the vessel had not been in any real danger and stated:

> "... I cannot find here that there was any real danger to this ship. In determining whether there was real danger I think the first thing one has to look at, and what is more valuable to consider, is the views and conduct of the people who were on the spot at the time. It is not very easy afterwards when considering whether one body of underwriters should be made to contribute, when the only assistance one has in coming to a conclusion is the assistance of experts who point out this and that would never have occurred, without having the evidence of anybody who was there at the time to confirm their views; and when one has that assistance and looks at the actions and conduct and views formed at the time by those who were on the spot, one gets the surest guide.
>
> The first thing that strikes one is this. This happened in an inland waterway where there is no danger of a sea getting up and where there is no danger of any substantial degree of bumping while the ship is on the bottom. She was not against mere soft mud. I do not think that for a moment. I think it would be quite wrong to hold on the evidence which I have heard that she was against soft mud like one knows you find in a great many rivers. I think she was against a soft bank, soft in the sense that it was not a firm, hard bank. Nor do I think that the bottom was mud. There again I do not think it was a very hard bottom, but I think it was the sort of bottom which

[55] (1938) 62 Ll.L.Rep. 65; affirming (1937) 59 Ll.L.R. 175.

> you would expect to find if the bed of the river was chalky, and no doubt it had some flints in it. But when once this ship had come to rest as it did that night against the bank, although during the time she was there the action of the wind pressed her further into the bank, I think that she was in a position really of safety. That she would suffer some damage to her bottom in getting where she was, and that she would suffer some damage to her bottom in getting out from where she was, was only to be expected; but the damage that was in fact done, the damage that was found when she had gone into dry dock—assuming, as I do assume, that every bit of it that was found was done on this occasion—was not of a character which in my judgment exposed the cargo to any danger. The damage to the bilge keel, which is the point that is most insisted on, I think it equally follows that that was done when they were getting the ship out; but I am quite certain nobody every thought for a moment that that ship was ever in a position of danger when she lay in the Randers Fjord."

This decision was affirmed in the Court of Appeal.

A similar array of cases from the courts of the United States, includes *Wilcox, Peck and Hughes v. American Smelting and Refining Co.,*[56] *The Mincio,*[57] *The Edward Rutledge,*[58] and *The National Defender.*[59]

Accidents to machinery, also Miscellaneous

Main engine breakdowns If a vessel is totally immobilised at sea by, for instance, a complete breakdown of the main engine or its crankshaft, or by a breakage of the tailshaft and/or loss of the propeller, and has no other means of propulsion,[60] the common adventure must almost invariably be in *peril*, even if the accident occur in fine weather.[61] The cost of towage and/or salvage into a port of refuge will then unquestionably be treated as general average. **A.40**

Twin-engined vessels. Some vessels are fitted with two (or more) engines for greater speed, manoeuvrability, and reliability. If one of these engines is completely immobilised, the vessel will sometimes put into port for repairs, but can it be said that the common adventure is in *peril*? **A.41**

As a general rule the answer is "no", and it will usually be found that the decision to deviate for repairs was taken for economic reasons only, and that the safety of the vessel and her cargo was not in question. If both engines can propel the vessel at 15 knots, a single engine will usually produce 10 knots, and the deviation is simply to get the benefit of cheaper and/or better repair facilities, and/or to save time on the voyage. Many

[56] 210 Fed.Rep. 89 (1913).
[57] (1936) A.M.C. 1765.
[58] (1954) A.M.C. 2070.
[59] (1969) A.M.C. 1219.
[60] In *Ballantyne v. Mackinnon* (1896) 65 L.J.Q.B. 616, a schooner-rigged steamer ran out of fuel and burned all her spare wood and some part of her fittings and was towed into her destination. In his official deposition, the master stated there was "no damage to our vessel, and we could have proceeded under sail, and we were not in distress".
[61] See para A.24, *ante*.

examples will be found in practice of vessels continuing to trade for six months or more with a single engine.

Similar considerations usually apply to vessels with two main boilers.

A.42 **Turbo charger.** Turbo chargers make use of the exhaust gases from the main engine to provide additional power and/or efficiency, and if a turbo charger sustains damage, it does not automatically mean that the ship and cargo are necessarily in peril. Very often, the turbo charger can be blanked off at sea by the crew and the vessel can proceed at, for example, 60 per cent power and 80 per cent speed in perfect safety.

A.43 **Broken cylinder heads or liners.** Another example of fairly frequent occurrence concerns the putting into port to replace a broken cylinder head or liner in the main engine.

If a main engine were fitted with only two cylinders it can be appreciated that the loss of power from the missing cylinder might render the vessel unfit to encounter the ordinary perils of the seas, and that entry into port for repairs would be justified as general average. However, with, say, a four or six cylinder engine, it is unlikely that the loss of power would be material to the safety of the adventure; the resort to a port for repairs would be largely for the purpose of greater speed and efficiency on the voyage.

It may also be remarked that it is not always essential to put into port for such repairs. In practice, vessels tend to enter port when one is near at hand; if the vessel is far out at sea, the repairs are often accomplished by the crew without shore assistance.

A.44 **Generators.** A vessel may be fitted with three generators, of which only one is required to supply the normal electrical load at sea, and two when in port working cargo. When navigating in restricted or crowded waterways it is sometimes considered prudent to have two generators running in parallel in order to prevent a blackout occurring at an inopportune moment should one machine suffer damage, but in theory one generator should be capable of taking the load. It is seldom that a vessel will put into port for a single generator breakdown but not infrequent if two generators have failed. Prima facie, the third generator should be sufficient for all the vessel's needs on the sea voyage, and if she put into port it could be for fear of a future peril rather than the existence of a present peril. If the accidents which have befallen the two other generators are quite separate and unrelated, it is suggested that the entry into port for repairs does not constitute a general average act. However, the position might be otherwise if, for instance, the two generators broke down as the result of contaminated lubricating oil which has also been used in the third generator. In such a case, a further breakdown might reasonably be anticipated within a short time.

Derricks, cargo pumps, auxiliary boilers, etc. If a vessel is proceeding to a port where there are no discharging or repair facilities and sustains damage to her derricks, cargo pumps, auxiliary boilers for heating oil cargo, or other gear which makes it impossible for her to discharge her cargo at destination, she will probably put into some earlier port for necessary repairs. If the damage did not render the vessel unfit to encounter the ordinary perils of the seas, then the common safety has not been endangered and the port charges cannot be treated as general average. **A.45**

Radar and wireless, etc. Most ocean-going ships are now fitted with wireless, radar, direction finders, loran, and all manner of modern sophisticated aids to navigation. The deck officers and pilots have come to rely and depend on such equipment and if, for instance, the radar mast and all the various antennae sustain damage, repairs will be carried out at the very earliest opportunity—indeed, the vessel may put into an unscheduled port especially for such repairs. Without such equipment in working order, can the common adventure be said to be in *peril*? **A.46**

It has been held by arbitrators that there should be no allowance in general average for the expenses of returning to port to repair the broken wireless equipment, there being no existing peril but only the fear that the vessel might be helpless if a peril arose. This is sound logic, and it is probably true to say that only if the particular voyage in question is so hazardous (Query: something of the order of the legendary "North-West Passage"?) that it would not be possible to attempt it without such equipment can it be said that the common safety of the adventure is imperilled. General average is not concerned with mere greater speed or efficiency on the voyage, or even greater risks; there must be a real and certain substantial peril. A breakdown of such equipment in the majority of cases can be overcome or compensated, and the voyage proceed in perfect safety, by keeping a more careful lookout and reducing speed where appropriate.

Shortage of bunkers. A vessel proceeding west-bound across the North Atlantic in winter may meet with continuous adverse weather and make such little headway that it is thought likely that her bunkers will be exhausted before she reaches destination. Accordingly, she may turn about and run with the wind to a port, say, in Ireland to replenish bunkers. The expenses at that port will be allowed as general average, subject to any question of fault under Rule D. **A.47**

This is a good example of a situation where the peril is both real and substantial but the ship is not in the immediate grip of that peril; she would still have on board a fair supply of bunkers at the time the decision was taken to turn about and make for Ireland. Clearly, it would be ridiculous to deny a general average situation until all the bunkers had been consumed.

A.48 **To survey the damage.** After stranding, a vessel may put into port to obtain a diver's survey or other inspection to ensure that it is safe to proceed on the voyage. If the vessel is permitted to proceed without any repairs at that time, it follows that the common adventure was not in peril and the entry into port was not a general average act.

3. Necessity for a Common Maritime Adventure

A.49 One of the essential features of a general average act is that it must be for the purpose of preserving from peril the property involved in a COMMON MARITIME ADVENTURE.

The doctrine of general average is derived from the maritime law, and there is no authority at common law for extending it to property not engaged in a common maritime adventure in the nature of a voyage.[62] In *Morrison S.S. Co. v. Greystoke Castle*[63] Lord Uthwatt said:

> "The principle involved in general average contribution is peculiar to the law of the sea and extends only to sea risks."

General average does not extend to the transport of goods by land, or by air,[64] nor does it apply to the intentional sacrifice of property on land, for example, to extinguish or contain a conflagration in a town or forest, or even in a dockside warehouse.

A.50 Where a VLCC or other ship is used as a hulk or warehouse to store oil or other goods, the case may be thought more doubtful, but it is submitted that while the vessel is used only as a store and not for transport, there is no maritime adventure common to her and the goods which she contains, and no right of contribution between their respective owners.[65] It is conceivable that, on occasion, salvage services may be rendered to the storeship and her cargo, but this should be treated as

[62] "With regard to salvage, general average, and contribution," said Bowen L.J. in *Falcke v. Scottish Imperial Ins. Co.* (1886) 34 Ch.D. 234 at 248, "the maritime law differs from the common law. This has been so from the time of the Roman law downwards. The maritime law, for the purposes of public policy and for the advantage of trade, imposes in these cases a liability upon the thing saved, a liability which is a special consequence arising out of the character of mercantile enterprises, the nature of sea perils, and the fact that the thing saved was saved under great stress and exceptional circumstances. No similar doctrine applies to things lost upon land, nor to anything except ships or goods in peril at sea." And dealing with a contract for the conveyance of goods by ship and railway, Lush J. said: "Goods may be damaged in their transit in ship or on the railway, but general average contribution can only arise in respect of damage on ship": *Crooks v. Allan* (1879) 5 Q.B.D. 38 at 40.

[63] [1947] A.C. 265 at 310.

[64] See McNair, *Law of the Air* (3rd ed.), Chap. 10. For a case of jettison from a passenger airline on a normal scheduled flight, see *The Times*, March 28, 1960, and *cf. Re California Eastern Airways* U.S. Av.Rep. 327 (1951).

[65] *Cf. European and Australian Co. v. P. & O.* (1866) 14 L.T. 704.

pure salvage and the ancillary allowances and principles of the general average system should not be introduced.

Similar remarks apply to an oil-rig while it is stationary and on the drilling site. There is then no maritime adventure in the accepted sense of that term. The position may be different while the rig is moving or being towed from one place to another—provided also that there is other property on board the rig. It is further submitted that the well being drilled cannot form part of the common maritime adventure; it is not on board the rig and is too remote.

Must more than One Interest be Imperilled?

A further question is whether general average can exist if the ship is the sole property imperilled, that is when no cargo is on board and the vessel is not under charter. **A.51**

The definitions of a general average act provided by the English courts all seem to contemplate that more than one interest must be in peril. Indeed, in *Kemp v. Halliday*,[66] Blackburn J. expressly said: "It is essential that there should be a voluntary sacrifice to preserve more subjects than one." And the statutory definition in section 66(1) of the Marine Insurance Act 1906, speaks of "the property imperilled in the common adventure"; again implying that more than one interest must be concerned.

In the case of *The Brigella*,[67] the vessel being outward bound in ballast to her loading port, so that the only interest at stake was that of the shipowner, Gorell Barnes J. held that port of refuge expenses on this voyage could not be general average, as there could be no contribution. But this decision was expressly disapproved in *Montgomery v. Indemnity Mutual Assurance Co.*,[68] where the mast of *The Airlie* had been cut away in time of peril, the shipowner being also the owner of the cargo on board. The Court of Appeal affirmed the judgment of Mathew J., holding that "a general average act is not affected by the consideration whether there will be a contribution or not". Vaughan Williams L.J., in delivering the judgment of the Court of Appeal, said: **A.52**

> "The object of the maritime law seems to be to give the master of the ship absolute freedom to make whatever sacrifice he thinks best to avert the perils of the sea, without any regard whatsoever to the ownership of the property sacrificed; and, in our judgment, such a sacrifice is a general average act quite independently of unity or diversity of ownership."[69]

[66] (1866) L.R. 1 Q.B. 520.
[67] [1893] P. 189.
[68] [1902] 1 K.B. 734.
[69] [1902] 1 K.B. 740.

A.53 It must accordingly be regarded as settled that contribution is not an essential element in general average; but is it essential that there shall be more than one interest?

So far as the liability of underwriters to indemnify the assured against general average losses is concerned, it is clear from the Marine Insurance Act 1906, that the interests may be in common ownership. Section 66(7) provides that:

> "Where ship, freight, and cargo, or any two of those interests, are owned by the same assured, the liability of the insurer in respect of general average losses or contributions is to be determined as if those subjects were owned by different persons."

The Court of Appeal in *Montgomery v. Indemnity Mutual Marine Assurance Co.,*[70] quoted with approval a portion of the judgment of Story J. in the case of *Potter v. Ocean Assurance Co.,*[71] which definitely suggests that general average is payable where there is only a single interest at stake, and that inasmuch as the expenses may be said to have been incurred as much for the benefit of underwriters as for the shipowner, they are "in the nature of general average". It is to be noted, however, that this was an American decision, and that in the United States it has been held that in the case of a ship in ballast, or even in the case of a yacht, general average is payable. The American view seems to be founded upon the consideration of the liability of underwriters being deemed an interest at stake.[72]

A.54 Whatever may be the law in the United States, it is submitted that in the United Kingdom and under the York-Antwerp Rules, more than one interest must be imperilled if there is to be a general average act. The many definitions of a general average act found in the judgments of the courts, the statutory definition contained in the Marine Insurance Act, as well as the York-Antwerp Rule A definition, all indicate that an essential element of general average is that the act shall be done for the preservation of more than one interest, and it is hard to see how the interest of underwriters can be included for this purpose.[73]

When the loss consists of the incurring of *expenses*, in the case of the ship alone being at risk, the expenses, or some of them, may be

[70] [1902] 1 K.B. 734.

[71] (1837) 3 Sumner 27.

[72] *Dollar v. La Fonciere* 162 Fed.Rep. 563 (1908), following *Potter v. Ocean, etc.*

[73] *Cf. per* Scrutton L.J. in *Foscolo Mango v. Stag Line Ltd.* [1931] 2 K.B. at 60, where in considering the question of a reasonable deviation he said: "I think the interests to be considered must be those of the parties to the adventure in the contract adventure, which may include consideration of the position of underwriters." It is also worthy of note in this connection that in *Oppenheim v. Fry* (1863) 3 B. & S. 873, where hull and machinery of *The Baroness Tecco* were insured, separately valued, with a clause "average payable on the whole or on each as if separately insured", the court clearly indicated that it thought that the expenses of extinguishing a fire might be general average as two interests, separately valued, were preserved. See *per* Blackburn J. at 884 (*obiter*).

recoverable under the "suing and labouring" clause, if this is contained in the policy.[74]

Tug and Tow

The circumstances in which a tug and tow, or a linked flotilla of tug and barges, etc., may constitute a common maritime adventure are discussed under Rule B. **A.55**

4. Necessity for an *Extraordinary* Sacrifice or Expenditure

In order to constitute a general average act, the sacrifice or expenditure must be EXTRAORDINARY in its nature.[75] **A.56**

Ipso facto, any sacrifice of cargo by the master of the ship at a time of peril must be extraordinary. The cargo ought never, under those ordinary circumstances which alone are provided for by the contract of affreightment, to be exposed to risk; that is to say, to a risk beyond that which is common to the entire adventure; and, therefore, in case of exposure to any risk greater than ordinary, as by uncovering the hatches during a gale to throw cargo overboard, such exposure, if followed by loss or damage, is treated as a sacrifice.

The position is rather less certain, however, when a supposed sacrifice of the ship is made, or expenditure incurred. Certain parts of the ship and her tackle or machinery are always, or may be under ordinary circumstances and still more in a gale, exposed to a risk greater than ordinary; as in the case of sails and tackling, which may be liable to greater risk of destruction in a gale than in fair weather, not merely from the stress of the wind, but on account of the greater necessity of carrying sail on the ship, for example to avoid a lee-shore. Some degree of exposure to extraordinary risk, therefore, on the part of the ship's tackling and machinery, may naturally be regarded as no more than the ship's ordinary duty, and not amounting to a sacrifice for which compensation should be made.

[74] Many hull policies contain a clause providing that in the event of the ship being in ballast, and not under charter, general average shall nevertheless be payable generally in accordance with the provisions of the York-Antwerp Rules. Clause 10.3 of the Institute Time Clauses (Hulls) reads as follows: "When the Vessel sails in ballast, not under charter, the provisions of the York-Antwerp Rules, 1994 (excluding Rules XI(d), XX and XXI), shall be applicable, and the voyage for this purpose shall be deemed to continue from the port of place of departure until the arrival of the Vessel at the first port or place thereafter other than a port or place of refuge or a port of place of call for bunkering only. If at any such intermediate port or place there is an abandonment of the adventure originally contemplated the voyage shall thereupon be deemed to be terminated."

[75] Editions of this work prior to the 11th have mentioned this aspect more as an afterthought under the heading, *Miscellaneous*, and placed greater stress on the simple truism that the sacrifice or expenditure must have been made on an extraordinary occasion.

The question must then be asked: "In consideration of the payment of the agreed freight for the voyage, has the cargo owner the right under the contract of affreightment to expect the shipowner to make such 'sacrifice' or incur such expenditure without requiring a supplementary contribution from the cargo owner? Was the sacrifice or expenditure truly extraordinary and out of the usual course, or was it encompassed within the shipowner's obligations under, and performance of, the contract of affreightment?" This point is further illustrated by Rule VII.

The position is best illustrated by a few[76] of the many legal cases from sailing ship days.

Damage by Carrying Press of Sail to Escape from Capture or a Lee-shore

A.57 If a vessel carries a press of sail in order to beat off a lee-shore or to escape from an enemy, and the sails are thereby blown away, the masts sprung, or the hull extraordinarily strained, such loss is in this country considered *not* to be the subject of general average contribution.

In *Covington v. Roberts*[77] the *Nancy* had been captured by a French privateer, but as it blew a gale and the sea ran high the Frenchman could not board her; whereupon the master of the *Nancy*, in order to make her escape, carried an unusual spread of canvas, in consequence of which she was much strained, opened most of her seams, and carried away the head of her mainmast; but succeeded in getting clear away. The owner of the *Nancy* sued his underwriter on ship for this damage, as particular average. The underwriter contended that he was only liable for his share, treating it as a general average, as a loss occasioned by an exertion to save the whole concern; and *Birkley v. Presgrove*[78] was cited in support of this view. But Sir J. Mansfield C.J. said:

> "In the case referred to, there was an article given up for the benefit of the whole concern. A cable was sacrificed. The language of Lawrence J. is, that all loss which arises in consequence of extraordinary sacrifices or expenses incurred for the preservation of the ship and cargo come within the description of general average. This is only a common sea risk. If the weather had been rather better, or the ship stronger, nothing might have happened."[79]

In *Power v. Whitmore*[80] a ship was in imminent danger of being driven ashore during a gale, and in order to avoid this danger was stood out to sea with a press of sail greater than she was able to bear in such weather, with the result that serious damage was sustained to the masts, sails and

[76] But see also *Birkley v. Presgrave* (1801) 1 East 220; *Taylor v. Curtis* (1815) 4 Camp. 337; *Soc. Nouvelle d'Armement v. Spillers & Bakers etc.* [1917] 1 K.B. 865.

[77] (1806) 2 Bos. & P.N.R. 378.

[78] (1801) 1 East 220.

[79] In *The Bona* [1895] P. 125 at 134, Lord Esher said that the court would not be disposed to extend *Covington v. Roberts*.

[80] (1815) 4 M. & S. 141.

the hull itself. It was held, as counsel for the shipowners had admitted in argument[81] that no part of this damage was the subject of general average.

In some countries the position is otherwise, and damage caused by carrying a press of sail is treated as general average. Those countries which reject the allowance usually do so on the grounds that the shipowner is bound under his contract of affreightment to furnish the cargo with all the ordinary means of reaching its destination which are supplied by the ship and her tackling, each part used in its appropriate way, whether it be with greater or less strain put upon it; and this includes, upon occasion, the carrying a press of sail.[82] The sails are not intended for fair weather only. The practice in this country to exclude such claims from general average is ordinarily defended on substantially the same grounds.[83] See also the *old* Rule VI of York-Antwerp Rules, current from 1864 to 1950, but considered obsolete in 1974, though still correct. **A.58**

Damage and Expense in Using Auxiliary Engine

In *Wilson v. Bank of Victoria*,[84] an auxiliary sailing vessel (that is one that normally proceeded under sail and used her engine only when the wind was light, or adverse) struck an iceberg and was dismasted while on voyage from Melbourne to Great Britain and was obliged to put into Rio de Janeiro as a port of refuge under her auxiliary steam power. The cost of repairs being prohibitive, the master effected only temporary repairs at Rio and proceeded to destination under steam, purchasing additional coals at both Rio and Fayal for this purpose. A claim was made for a general average contribution towards the cost of these coals, but disallowed on the grounds that the expenditure was merely the performance of a service owed by the shipowner to the cargo owners under the contract of affreightment. As Blackburn J. said: **A.59**

> "(The measure taken) caused the disbursements for coals to be extraordinarily heavy, but it did not render it an extraordinary disbursement ..."

Somewhat similar considerations applied in the case of *Harrison v. Bank of Australasia*,[85] decided five years later. It concerned a sailing ship, also on voyage from Melbourne to Great Britain, which sprang a leak in a cyclone. The vessel was fitted with a donkey-engine for loading and unloading cargo, hoisting sails, and for pumping the ship. To save **A.60**

[81] *Ibid.* at 146.
[82] *e.g.* Ulrich, *Grosse Haverei*, p. 41.
[83] In the U.S., see 2 Phillips, Ins. 1296; 2 Parsons, Ins. 302; Gourlie, 203.
[84] (1867) L.R. 2 Q.B. 203.
[85] (1872) L.R. 7 Ex. 39.

the vessel from foundering, the donkey-engine was used continuously throughout the voyage and, when the existing supply of bunkers was exhausted, the master was obliged to burn spare spars and ship's stores, and to purchase additional bunkers from a passing steamer. Further, the donkey-engine needed repairs by reason of its excessive use. A claim for a general average contribution from cargo was allowed in respect of the ship's spars and stores, which truly constituted an extraordinary sacrifice of those items, but not for the cost of the coals consumed or of repairing the donkey-engine.

An identical situation was decided in identical fashion in the case of *Robinson v. Price*.[86]

A.61 Such is the meaning of the term *extraordinary* under both English law and the York-Antwerp Rule A. This somewhat firm line was not altogether acceptable to shipowners and commercial interests, and the position is considerably ameliorated in practice by the express terms of some of the numbered Rules of the York-Antwerp Rules which, by reason of the Rule of Interpretation, take precedence over the lettered Rules when the prevailing circumstances of any casualty meet the more specific provisions of the numbered Rules.

But for any general average claim which can be made only under the lettered Rules—and there are many—full force must be given to the word *extraordinary*.

If introduction were needed, this last sentence offers an opportune and suitable location for a section of this work which in editions prior to the Eleventh appeared under the heading:

"INSTANCES NOT YET COVERED BY ENGLISH LEGAL AUTHORITY"

Sacrifices of Ship

A.62 The variety of ship's sacrifices which can occur is of necessity so considerable that many instances are not directly covered by previous decisions of the courts or by any of the specific provisions of the numbered Rules of the York-Antwerp Rules. In such cases average adjusters rely upon the principles underlying the law and practice of general average and upon "custom" (using the word in its popular rather than in its legal sense). The "custom" of average adjusters carries no weight in litigation if the court considers that it conflicts with principle. Nevertheless where no such conflict arises or in case of doubt, there is, as Lowndes pointed out: "a natural tendency—difficult indeed to be reckoned on, since it is naturally stronger in some judges than others—to pay a sort of prima facie respect to such customs, as

[86] (1876) 2 Q.B.D. 91; (1877) 2 Q.B.D. 295.

presumably falling in with the wishes and perhaps requirements of mercantile men."[87]

The Principle

Lowndes stated the principle to be applied in the following terms: **A.63**

> "The principle which underlies most if not all these matters of ordinary practice may be expressed as follows: while it is the duty of the master under his contract to apply each part of his ship and tackling to its proper uses in carrying on his voyage, without regard to the more or less of exposure to danger which the doing so may involve,[88] he is not bound to destroy any of them, nor to abuse any—understanding by this term 'abuse' the using it for purposes for which it was not intended nor constructed, and which, therefore, expose it to an extraordinary risk.[89] If he does so, he does it as general average, *i.e.* under an implied contract with all those whose property he shall bring into safety by so doing, that any loss he thereby incurs shall be made good by the contribution of all."

Examples

Cutting away to clear collision. Speaking generally, when two vessels are in collision, and it becomes necessary for the safety of one of them to clear her by cutting away parts of the rigging which are entangled with that of the other ship, the rigging so cut away is not treated in practice as in a state of wreck and worthless; but an allowance is made in general average for its value at the time when it was cut away. **A.64**

A schooner, drifting in a strong tideway, was carried under the hawse of a ship at anchor and, the ship's bowsprit catching the stay between the two masts of the schooner, the latter was pressed over so as to be in danger of capsizing, to prevent which the schooner's masts were cut away. This was treated as general average.

Two vessels, both at anchor, were in collision, and in attempting to get clear the anchor of one of them was hove up, but found to have hooked the chain of the other; whereupon, to get clear and avoid a second collision, the anchor was slipped. This was treated as general average.

Boat or spars washed adrift. If a boat has been washed to leeward in a gale, and is thereby rendered dangerous to the ship, as for instance by **A.65**

[87] 4th ed., p. 112. "A general practice", says Lord Blackburn, "long continued amongst English adjusters, affords strong ground for thinking that the practice is one which is not in general inconvenient, and it throws a considerable onus on those who impugn it to show that the particular circumstances are such as to render an adherence to the practice in that case against principle": *Svendsen v. Wallace* (1885) 10 A.C. 404 at 416. See also the judgments in *Balmoral S.S. Co. v. Marten* [1902] A.C. 511, as to the desirability of upholding a long-established practice of average adjusters.

[88] See *Covington v. Roberts* (1806) 2 Bos. & P.N.R. 378, para A.57, *ante*.

[89] See *Birkley v. Presgrave* (1801) 1 East 220 (para. A.75, *post*); *The Bona* [1895] P. 125 (para. 7.03, *post*).

keeping her from righting if she is on her beam ends, and is on that account broken up by the crew or thrown overboard, the practice formerly was to disallow the boat as in a state of wreck and valueless. This is clearly wrong. A boat, or spare spars or other articles properly on deck, which are adrift and dangerous, but which if it were safe to wait till the gale should go down could certainly be secured again, are on precisely the same footing as the deals in *Johnson v. Chapman.*[90]

A.66 **Anchors and cables suddenly let go.** An anchor is normally dropped only when the vessel has lost nearly all way, and its sole intended purpose is to *hold* the vessel in a certain position; it is not designed to serve as a *brake.*[91] If, therefore, an anchor is let go without the usual preparations in order to check the vessel and avoid some sudden danger, such as an impending collision or running aground, and in consequence the cable breaks, the loss is in practice treated as general average. However, the full facts relating to any such claim must be carefully ascertained, as it is not unknown for anchor cables to part from accidental or other causes.

A.67 **Anchors and cables slipped in efforts to refloat.** When a vessel runs aground, her anchors will sometimes be carried out and dropped in deep water astern to serve as ground tackle to prevent the vessel riding further up the reef or beach and, at the appropriate time, to heave upon and haul the vessel clear of the strand. At the moment of refloating, it is occasionally necessary to slip the anchors. If they be not recovered, the loss is allowed as general average provided that the vessel was in a position of peril when aground.

A.68 **Anchors and cables slipped in an emergency.** In theory at least, it is possible for a vessel at anchor to slip the anchor and cable to avoid some impending danger such as collision or a typhoon. This is achieved either by punching out the securing pin in one of the joining shackles, thereby releasing the cable and anchor, or by letting the cable run out in the hope that it will break free from its securing on the bulkhead in the chain locker. Failing a breakage, the senhouse slip must be released. It is difficult to visualise either of these measures being adopted in practice for they both can take several minutes to carry out, but when they are performed in the appropriate circumstances of real danger to the common adventure, the loss should, on principle, be allowed as general average.

On the particular facts ruling in *Hamel v. P. & O. Steam Navigation Co.,*[92] Lord Alverstone C.J. decided that the slipping of an anchor

[90] (1865) 19 C.B. (N.S.) 563; para. 1.07, *post.* See also *Rogers v. Mechanics' Ins. Co.* (1841) 1 Storey 604, and cases cited in Gourlie, p. 174.

[91] But an anchor may be so used to enable a vessel to manoeuvre at slow speed with full engine-power.

[92] [1908] 2 K.B. 298; 77 L.J.K.B. 637; 98 L.T. 861; 24 T.L.R. 535; 13 Com. Cas. 270; 11 Asp.M.C. 71.

(afterwards recovered) was not a general average act, but it is submitted that this decision does not necessarily conflict with the principle enunciated in the paragraph above. The following extract is taken from *Commercial Cases*, but the facts and judgment are variously reported in the different reports:

> "... the vessel, within a few minutes after leaving her berth to proceed on her voyage, got into difficulties, and for an hour or thereabouts she was engaged in endeavouring to avoid perils of the river. The vessel swung up in consequence of the tide catching her stern; she was in danger of colliding with a vessel higher up; and she had to slip her anchor to avoid collision with some other craft ... The slipping of the anchor, which was to some extent relied upon, was not a general average act; it was an ordinary measure taken in the ordinary course of navigation—a measure taken to avoid danger, and not a sacrifice of the anchor in the sense in which that word is used in general average cases. Moreover, the anchor was recovered afterwards."

Anchors and cables slipped because foul. Anchors slipped because they become "foul"—that is, held fast by some obstruction under water, as by having caught under a rock or some other anchors or chains, are allowable as general average only when it may reasonably be inferred that the obstruction was of a temporary nature, so that the anchor might have been cleared if it had not been dangerous to wait. If then, after all practicable exertions have been made to raise the anchor, the captain slips the chain in despair of ever recovering it, this is not general average.[93] **A.69**

Jury-rig and analogous cases. A very ancient, general and undisputed custom is that which relates to jury-rig. When a ship's mast or rudder is carried away, and a "jury" or temporary mast or rudder is fitted up at sea as a substitute, the value of the materials cut up or destroyed for the purpose such as spare spars, ropes, chain, or the like, together with any damage done to the hull of the ship by cutting or adapting it to the purpose, or by the action of the jury-materials, is in practice treated as general average. **A.70**

On the same principle spars or ropes cut up at sea to "fish" or secure a mast that is sprung, or to secure boats or spare spars when adrift, or to make a "drag" to get the ship's head round when in a position of danger, or to construct pumping machines, or for any such out-of-the-way purpose which may have the effect of rescuing the ship from danger, are treated as general average. Again, when a ship's anchors have been carried away, and to prevent her running aground it is necessary to moor her in a tideway by a hawser and a kedge and these, being insufficient for such work, part as soon as they are let go, this loss has also been treated as general average.

[93] See Gourlie, pp. 195,196.

This practice is in accordance with the decision in *Birkley v. Presgrave*,[94] so far as the articles thus used are applied to different uses from those for which they were originally intended. This would apply to running-rigging or towing lines cut up for securing a jury rudder; but hardly perhaps to the spare spars, since these are put on board for such purposes only; but in practice no distinction is drawn between them. The entire cost of the jury-rig is treated as general average; not only the spars and ropes cut up and deliberately spoilt for the purpose, but also the jury-sails which are subsequently blown away by reason of their not being adapted to the service to which they are thus provisionally turned, or of their having from any reason been exposed to an unusual risk as, for example, from bending a top gallant sail to do the work of a topsail.

A.71 **Damage done in getting ship clear.** On the same principle, damage done to a ship by the means taken to get her off a shore, or clear of a collision, or otherwise out of a situation of imminent danger, may frequently give rise to a claim for general average; of which the following cases, taken from the ordinary practice of adjusters, are examples.

Damage done to ship's boats. If, after a ship has run aground, one of her boats is launched to carry out a hawser in order to heave her off, or otherwise to assist in floating her, and the boat is swamped or injured in the attempt, this damage is treated as general average; not so, if the boat were got out merely to save the lives of the passengers or crew.[95]

Damage done to ship by efforts to refloat. Damage done to the ship in heaving her afloat, such as hawsers broken, damage to anchors and chains,[96] a windlass or winch strained, stanchions started, or other damage directly caused to the ship's upperworks or bottom by the strain used, is general average. It may sometimes be a little difficult to distinguish between damage caused by having been on the ground, and by pulling off, but where this distinction can properly be drawn, the damage to the bottom caused by the efforts to refloat is clearly allowable as general average.[97]

A.72 **Damage to ship by discharging cargo.** If a ship is damaged in the act of discharging cargo whilst aground or at a port of refuge, as, for instance, where the lighters or craft range against the ship's side, or if the rails or hatches are broken for want of proper appliances or from the necessity of unusual haste, it seems clear that, provided the cost of discharging belongs to general average, this damage should be treated in the same way. In *The Felix*[98] damage to a vessel's propeller by timber jettisoned

[94] (1801) 1 East 220; see also *The Bona* [1895] P. 125.
[95] See, however, the dictum as to sacrifices made in fear of death, para. A.19, *ante*.
[96] *Roberts v. The Ocean Star* (1860) Fed.Cas. 11908.
[97] See also York-Antwerp Rule VII.
[98] (1927) A.M.C. 844.

from on deck for the general safety was allowed in general average, although loss of the timber was disallowed under the York-Antwerp Rules 1890.

Damage to ship by collision with salving vessel. If a tug, coming alongside a ship to render a salvage service, staves in the ship's bulwark, or does such other damage to her upper works as may fairly be regarded as the natural consequence of approaching the vessel at such a time, the damage is, in practice, treated as general average.[99] A.73

Use of rockets, fenders, storm oil, etc., damage to pumps. Rockets or blue lights burnt as signals of distress, or oil carried specially for use as storm-oil, and so used in bad weather, or fenders put out to prevent collision, and smashed, or damage to the pumps caused by the stress of pumping a leaky ship, have not been treated as general average;[1] for that is the very purpose for which such things are carried in the ship. Fire extinguishers are considered in paragraph 3.18, below. A.74

Cutting away a cable. If a cable is cut in order that it may be used for a purpose for which it was not intended and such cutting and use are to meet an emergency which threatens the whole adventure, this is a general average sacrifice. A.75

In *Birkley v. Presgrave*[2] the *Argo*, bound for Sunderland, was, whilst entering that port, caught by a sudden squall, which rendered it necessary to let go the anchor. She was fastened with a warp to the South Pier, in order to secure her from the storm; but the warp soon parted. More cable was then paid away, and the ship was permitted to drive alongside the North Pier, to which she was made fast with hawser ends and towing lines, which were proper ropes, and such as were usually provided and employed for that purpose. Fearing that another ship would be adrift and come down upon the *Argo*, the master cut the cable, and therewith moored the *Argo* to the pier; and this he did for the preservation of the ship and cargo. Whilst they were so fastening her with the cable, the other ropes, through the violence of the storm and by another ship driving down upon the *Argo*, broke.

On these facts, however, the owner of the ship claimed as general average the value of the cable thus cut, and also that of the hawsers and towing lines. At the trial, the counsel for the plaintiff withdrew the demand in respect of the damage to the hawser-ends and towing lines, admitting that these were not claimable, as having only been applied to the ordinary purposes for which such things are provided: but claimed the cable, which had been "appropriated to a different use from what it

[99] *Cf. Australian Coastal Shipping Commission v. Green* [1971] 1 Q.B. 456.

[1] Where pumps were put to an abnormal use, as to pump out water impregnated with acid from the cargo, the damage was allowed in the U.S.: see the 8th ed. of this work, p. 298.

[2] (1801) 1 East 220.

was originally intended for, and which contributed to the preservation of the ship and cargo". This claim was admitted by the court. Lord Kenyon C.J. said:

> "All ordinary loss and damage sustained by the ship, happening immediately from the storm or perils of the seas, must be borne by the shipowners; but all those articles which were made use of by the master and crew upon the particular emergency, and out of the ordinary course, for the benefit of the whole concern, and the other expenses incurred, must be paid proportionably by the defendant as general average."

A.76 **Damage caused by fighting.** Damage so caused is probably not a general average loss, at all events if a ship is specially equipped to fight.

In *Taylor v. Curtis*[3] the ship *Hibernia* on her voyage to St Thomas, was attacked by a privateer. She resisted, and a severe engagement ensued. The privateer was beaten off, and the *Hibernia* delivered her cargo safe to the consignees. A claim as general average was made for damage sustained in her hull and rigging by the enemy's shot, for the cost of curing the seamen's wounds, and for gunpowder and shot expended, Gibbs C.J. decided against the claim.

> "I cannot," he said, "distinguish this from the case of a ship carrying a press of sail to escape from her enemy. That is done voluntarily for the preservation of all; but it has been held that a loss arising from a hazard so incurred is not the subject of general average."[4]

The learned judge intimated, however, a strong opinion that some reward should be given for a gallant resistance, otherwise such resistances would not be made. This case was carried up to the full court, but the decision at Nisi Prius was confirmed. Gibbs C.J. said:

> "The measure of resisting the privateer was for the general benefit, but it was part of the adventure. No particular part of the property was voluntarily sacrificed for the protection of the rest. The losses fell where the fortune of war cast them, and there it seems to me they ought to rest."[5]

A.77 This decision has been much questioned. Damage, says Benecke, which is the consequence of a determination to resist, may be looked upon as damage voluntarily sustained; the defence is intended for the preservation of the whole.[6] The argument that it was the duty of the crew to fight, says Phillips, proves too much; it is their duty to cut away a mast in case of need, or to make any sacrifice that may be requisite for the safety of

[3] (1815) 4 Camp. 337 and on appeal (1816) 6 Taunt. 608.

[4] In 1 Holt's N.P. 193, this judgment is given in somewhat different language. "I do not think this is general average. It was the duty of the sailors to defend the ship from capture in proportion to their means, and within measures of discretion. By so doing all parties have benefited. But in what respect have the captain and crew exceeded the line of their proper duty? What sacrifice have they made which they were not bound to make?"

[5] This passage from the judgment of Gibbs C.J. was cited and applied by Sankey J. in *Société Nouvelle D'Armement v. Spillers & Bakers* [1917] 1 K.B. 865.

[6] Benecke, p. 231.

ship and cargo.[7] It is however, not so easy to resist the argument from analogy with carrying a press of sail. If a ship sails on her voyage provided with guns and ammunition sufficient to resist an enemy, these are provided for that purpose and no other; and the use or expenditure of them, more or less, for their appropriate purpose, is not regarded as the subject of general average. The ship being so equipped, again, is surely a notice to the crew that they are hired to fight in case of need, and not merely to navigate the ship.

Sacrifices of Cargo

A curious case in which a claim was made for damage to cargo was *McCall v. Houlder*.[8] A ship having sustained damage to her propeller, was towed into a port of refuge where the cargo, which was perishable, could not be stored. In order to repair the propeller with the cargo on board she was tipped and, in consequence of the tipping, part of the cargo was damaged by seawater. Mathew J. held that the tipping was resorted to for the preservation of the ship and cargo and was a general average act and that the damage to the cargo being incidental thereto, although not contemplated, was a general average loss. There may, however, be cases where such damage is too remote, being caused by some extraneous and unforeseen event. **A.78**

Cargo damaged by flooding of hold

Damage caused to cargo when the master flooded the hold following an accidental stranding, to steady the vessel upon the rocks to prevent pounding and the consequent break up of the ship, would be treated as general average.[9] **A.79**

Cargo given as salvage

Should cargo be sacrificed by being given in kind as salvage for the entire property, such a sacrifice must, of course, be treated as general average.[10]

[7] Phillips, para. 1310.

[8] (1897) 2 Com.Cas. 129. *Cf. Gage v. Libby* (1867) 14 Allen (Mass.) 261, where wastage of a cargo of ice caused by opening the hold in order to renew a mast at a port of refuge, was allowed in general average.

[9] *Pacific Mail S.S. Co. v. Dupre* 74 Fed.Rep. 250 (1896).

[10] On the same principle, where cargo is voluntarily given up to pirates by way of composition, the sacrifice is a subject for contribution: *Hicks v. Palington* (1590) Moore 297.

Cargo sold or pledged to raise funds

Cargo may also be sacrificed by being sold or pledged in order to raise funds in a port of refuge, when the owners of the ship and cargo are unable or unwilling to supply the sum needed for the purpose of releasing the ship from her obligations at such port and thereby enabling her to proceed on her voyage.

This case, however, is involved in complications which properly belong to a larger subject, namely the treatment of loss and expense incurred in order to raise funds required for general average purposes. This is dealt with under Rule XX.

Partial loss of cargo by putting into port of refuge

A.80 The case of *Anglo-Argentine Live Stock Agency v. Temperley S.S. Co.*[11] provides an unusual example of a sacrifice of cargo. The facts were that the *Edenbridge* took on board in the River Plate a deck cargo of cattle and sheep for Britain, under a contract which provided that the vessel should on no account touch at any Brazilian or European Continental ports before landing her livestock. Soon after sailing she sprang a leak, and as the water could not be kept down, the master put into Bahia, a Brazilian port, for repairs. The consequence was that, by reason of an Order in Council then in force, the cattle could not be landed in Britain and they were taken instead to Antwerp where they realised much lower prices than they would have fetched in Britain. Bigham J. held that the owners of the livestock were entitled to recover in general average the difference in prices as a loss which was the direct and immediate consequence of the general average act. "The moment the vessel touched the Brazilian port", he said, "the plaintiffs' property was *ipso facto* rendered of less value than it was before, because by that act the plaintiffs were deprived of one of their means, and that the best, of realising their property."

Sacrifice of Goods not Included in Bills of Lading or Cargo Manifests

A.81 The question, whether goods which are not shipped as cargo must be contributed for if they are sacrificed, does not appear to be covered by express authority. On the other hand, the rule seems established in practice that any kind of property which is preserved from destruction must contribute unless there be some special reason for exempting it.[12] Arnould stated that the jettison of goods for which there is no bill of

[11] [1899] 2 Q.B. 403.
[12] See para. 17.18, *post*.

lading gives no claim to contribution.[13] He only cited foreign authorities, and probably had in his mind the case of a clandestine shipment in fraud of the shipowner, in which case the disallowance of contribution may well be justified.[14] With this exception, however, there is no valid reason for refusing contribution on the ground that no bill of lading has been given for the goods, if it be proved that they were sacrificed or damaged by a general average act.

Sacrifices of Miscellaneous Property

Passengers' baggage and effects

The question whether passengers are entitled to contribution for the sacrifice of their effects has not been litigated in this country, and instances of such sacrifice seem to have been too rare to give rise to any settled practice. It may be argued that as passengers' baggage is not made to contribute when saved, it ought not to be contributed for when sacrificed. The argument founded on the want of reciprocity does not appear to be convincing. **A.82**

The contrary view was admirably expressed by Brown D.J. in an American case,[15] in which he held that there is a right of contribution for passengers' baggage. His decision on this question, the only one raised on appeal, was affirmed by the Circuit Court of Appeals.[16]

He also came to the conclusion that passengers' baggage in the baggage compartment is liable to contribute, but it is clear that, even if he had formed a different opinion on that part of the case, his decision that passengers' baggage must be contributed for would not have been affected and it is submitted that on this point his judgment is correct.

Crew's effects

It can hardly be doubted that the master and crew are entitled to contribution for the sacrifice of their effects, and their right is generally recognised by the foreign codes. The "reciprocity" argument has little or no weight in their case; and their exemption from contribution may be explained on the ground that they have done their share towards the preservation of the ship by their personal efforts,[17] and also as regards **A.83**

[13] Arnould (2nd ed.), p. 904; but see *British Shipping Laws*, Vol 10; Arnould, *Marine Insurance* (15th ed.) para. 929.

[14] Most of the foreign codes do not allow contribution for the sacrifice of goods, unless the captain has given a bill of lading for them or declared them in the manifest, and one of the authorities cited by Arnould is para. 420 of the French Code de Commerce, which contains a provision to this effect. See also York-Antwerp Rule XIX.

[15] *Heye v. North German Lloyd* 33 Fed.Rep. 60 (1887).

[16] 36 Fed.Rep. 705 (1887). A lengthy extract from the judgment was quoted in para. A.94 of the 11th edition.

[17] *Per* Brown D.J. in *Heye v. North German Lloyd*, n. 15, *supra.*

their wearing apparel on the ground that it may be considered as attached to the person, which is not a contributory interest.[18]

5. Necessity for Reasonableness

A.84 According to the statutory definition and Rule A, the sacrifice or expenditure must have been REASONABLY made. In practice, the word "reasonably" is probably used more as an earnest hope, rather than as a mandatory expectation.

In the case of sacrifice, one hopes, for instance, that it will be the low-valued iron ore in the lower hold, which will be selected for jettison, rather than the valuable general cargo in the 'tweendeck, though by its very stowage and the greater ease with which it can be lifted out of the hold, the valuable general cargo is likely to be the first to be jettisoned. The master, as the person on the spot and in the agony of the moment, should be—and generally is—credited with the benefit of any doubt as to the wisdom of his actions, provided that a real peril exists; hindsight and the superior wisdom of the desk-bound operative should be ignored. Reference may be made to the remarks of Cockburn C.J. in *Corry v. Coulthard*[19] quoted in paragraph A.37, above and of Hobhouse J. in *Corfu Navigation Co. v. Mobil Shipping Co. Ltd*[20] with regard to the reasonableness of the courses of action taken by the respective masters.

A.85 The same principle holds good in the case of expenditure, except that here one may encounter the additional problem that some suppliers of labour and services look upon a casualty as "manna from heaven" and their charges rise accordingly. Thus, a party called upon to contribute to general average expenditure may seek to challenge the claim not only on the grounds that it was unreasonable for the master to adopt the measures which resulted in the expenditure (to which the remarks in paragraph A.84, above apply) but also on the grounds that the amount of the expenditure is itself unreasonable. With regard to the latter point it is clear that contribution can only be recovered in respect of such amount as was reasonably incurred, and that if the master or shipowner agree to pay an excessive sum, contribution can only be recovered in respect of the amount which it would have been reasonable to pay, and not towards the excess.

A.86 Thus, in *Anderson v. Ocean S.S. Co.*[21] the owners of cargo carried on board the *Achilles* refused to pay the full amount of general average

[18] See paras. 17.59 and 17.64, *post*.
[19] Unreported, Exch. Div., December 21, 1876; Court of Appeal, January 17, 1877.
[20] [1991] 2 Lloyd's Rep. 515.
[21] (1884) 10 A.C. 107, H.L., reversing *sub nom. Ocean S.S. Co. v. Anderson* (1883) 13 Q.B.D. 651.

claimed from them in respect of towage expenses, on the grounds that the amount paid by the shipowner to the towage contractor was exorbitant and the shipowner was only bound to pay a reasonable sum (or if he had agreed to pay an exorbitant sum he could not charge the cargo with the excess). In delivering the judgment of the House of Lords, Lord Blackburn said[22]:

> "But I think there is neither reason nor authority for saying that the whole amount which the owners of the ship choose to pay is, as a matter of law, to be charged to general average. And though I quite agree that there is some evidence here that the *Achilles* and her cargo were both in danger, and were both saved by the services of the *Shanghai*, and though I also agree that it is not a question of law whether the amount of the sum charged as a disbursement was exorbitant or not, still I cannot find that any question as to the amount was submitted to the jury."

A new trial was therefore ordered, since no question as the reasonableness of the amount paid had been put to the jury.[23] In *Australian Coastal Shipping Commission v. Green*[24] Lord Denning M.R. summarised the effect of the case as follows:

> "If the master of the *Achilles* agreed to pay an exorbitant charge, such that he ought never, in justice to the cargo owners, to have agreed to, then the excess of the charge (over and above a reasonable charge) would not flow from the general average act, but from the onerous clause which the master had agreed to. The only amount allowable as a 'general average loss' would be a reasonable charge."

It is submitted that, in determining what is a reasonable charge, it is the conduct of the shipowner or master, in all the circumstances and pressures of the casualty, which must be considered, rather than the conduct of the contractor who demanded the charge, and it is irrelevant that in other circumstances the same services might have been acquired at a much lower price. Thus, in *The Gratitudine*[25] the master hypothecated ship and cargo to a moneylender on most onerous terms, but since he had no practical alternative but to accept the contract, the loss under it was held to be general average.

[22] (1884) 10 A.C. 107 at 117.

[23] The shipowner, who had paid £2,691.19.6d. to the towage contractor, contended that this was fixed under the terms of his agreement with the contractor. Upon the first trial, the case proceeded to the House of Lords apparently upon the footing that the jury had determined this question in favour of the shipowner, and all that was lacking was any finding as to the reasonableness of the shipowner's conduct. One the retrial, however, the jury found that there was no binding agreement between the shipowner and contractor which fixed the remuneration, and that the shipowner's obligation was to pay a reasonable sum, which they determined to be £1,500. It was therefore to this reduced sum of £1,500, rather than the £2,691 paid by the shipowner, that cargo was finally held liable to contribute. For the full history of the retrial of this unusually hard-fought case see (1885) 1 T.L.R. 324 at 413 and 615, and (1886) 2 T.L.R. 537 and 859.

[24] [1971] 1 Q.B. 456 at 483. See also *The Gratitudine* 3 Ch. Rob. 240 at 277.

[25] 3 Ch. Rob. 240 at 272–276.

Historical Development and Practice of Rule A

York-Antwerp Rules 1924

A.87 As originally drafted in 1924, Rule A comprised two paragraphs (as it does in 1994), but upon discussion at Stockholm it was considered advisable that the two paragraphs should be separated and constitute individual Rules (A and B). This was reportedly to avoid any misapprehension concerning the treatment of general average losses and expenditure specifically provided for by the numbered Rules but not falling within the definition of general average contained in the first paragraph. [In fact, just such a misapprehension occurred in the *Makis* case.[26]]

York-Antwerp Rules 1950 and 1974.

No change, the two original paragraphs continuing their separate existence as Rules A and B.

York-Antwerp Rules 1994

A.88 To provide houseroom for a newborn infant of a Rule[27] without unduly upsetting the existing "numbering" of the Rules, a marriage of mere convenience took place between the previous Rules A and B, which were now combined as two separate paragraphs in the latest Rule A.

The first paragraph remains with its tried and tested wording, and the second paragraph also survives with only the most minor change to preserve an uniformity of wording within the same Rule. To conform with the use of the word *expenditure* in the first paragraph, the word *expenses* in the second paragraph was similarly expressed as *expenditures*.

First paragraph

A.89 The wording of this paragraph of Rule A is clearly based upon and follows very closely the English statutory definition of a general average act[28] but it may also be of interest to examine some of the definitions which prevailed apart from the Rules under the laws of leading maritime nations:

> BELGIUM. Extraordinary expenses incurred and damage sustained voluntarily for the common good and safety of the ship and cargo, are general average.[29]

[26] *Vlassopoulos v. British & Foreign Marine Insurance Co. Ltd* [1929] 1 K.B.187.
[27] The 1994 Rule B on "Tug and Tow".
[28] See para. A.06, *ante*.
[29] Law of February 10, 1908, Art. 147.

FRANCE. In general, damage voluntarily sustained and expenses incurred after express deliberation, for the common good and safety of the ship and cargo, from their loading and departure to their arrival and discharge.[30]

GERMANY. All damage intentionally done to ship or cargo, or both, by the master or by his orders, for the purpose of rescuing both from a common danger, together with an further damage caused by such measures, and also expenses incurred for the same purpose, are general average.[31]

HOLLAND. In general, all loss or damage intentionally caused from necessity and sustained as a direct consequence thereof, and costs incurred under like circumstances and after requisite consultation, for the purpose of preserving ship and cargo and for their common safety.[32]

ITALY. Expenses and damage directly caused by measures reasonably taken by the master, or by others in his stead, for the safety of the common maritime adventure, are general average and are shared amongst all those concerned in the adventure, whenever the damage voluntarily caused be not the same as would necessarily have happened according to the natural course of events.[33]

JAPAN. General average includes all damage and expense arising from any disposition made by the master in regard to the ship or cargo to save both from a common danger.[34]

SPAIN. Gross or general average consists as a general rule of all losses and expenses which are advisedly incurred to save the ship, her cargo, or both together, from a known and real danger.[35]

SCANDINAVIA. (Denmark, Norway and Sweden). All damage intentionally done to ship and cargo in order to save ship and cargo from any danger threatening both, as well as every other sacrifice made for such purpose and all damage and loss occasioned thereby shall be treated as general average.[36]

UNITED STATES. The requirements to justify general average contribution are:

1. That the ship and cargo should be placed in a common imminent peril.
2. That there should be a voluntary sacrifice of property to avert that peril.
3. That by that sacrifice the safety of the other property should be presently and successfully attained.[37]

The reasons why the Stockholm Conference in 1924 selected the word "intentionally", rather than "voluntarily" to define the general average act have already been described earlier in paragraph A.08, above. **A.90**

[30] Code de Commerce, s. 400.

[31] Commercial Code, s. 700.

[32] Commercial Code, Art. 699 (23).

[33] Code of Navigation 1942, Art. 469.

[34] Commercial Code 1899, amended by the law of May 2, 1911, and again amended by the law of April 15, 1922 (Chap. IV, Art. 641).

[35] Commercial Code 1885, s. 811.

[36] Swedish Maritime Law 1891 (amended June 5, 1936), s. 187. In substance and arrangement the maritime laws of Denmark and Norway are the same as that of Sweden.

[37] Opinion of Story J. in *Columbian Ins. Co. v. Ashby* (1839) 13 Pet. 331 (Sup. Ct., 1839). The definition in *The Star of Hope* 9 Wall. 203 (1869) U.S. Sup. Ct. (para. A.03, *ante*) may be preferable since it contains a reference to expenditure.

Much discussion also ensued on the selection of the proper words to imply that the common safety of the adventure was the only justification for an act being treated as general average. The view has sometimes been expressed that the principle of common safety is peculiarly a British one and that other nations are inclined to widen the scope of general average so as to justify the inclusion as general average of acts performed merely for the benefit of the adventure, without the element of a common peril being present. No one at the conference, however, expressed any desire to widen the definition of general average so as to include in its scope losses or expenses other than those arising from an intention to save the common adventure from a common peril. In the end not only were the words "for the common safety" inserted in the definition, but the principle implied by these words was further emphasised by continuing with the phrase "*for the purpose of preserving from peril* the property involved in a common maritime adventure". However, the numbered Rules contain several instances where those who supported "benefit of the adventure" have prevailed.

A.91 As regards the degree of imminence of the peril to avert which the sacrifice is made, the feeling of the Stockholm Conference was clearly in favour of not restricting the operations of general average only to cases in which the danger was immediate or imminent. This was emphasised by several of the representatives present and it is quite clear that the definition finally agreed upon was intended to imply that although the danger must be such as to threaten the common safety, it is not necessary that it be immediately pending. In so deciding, the Conference took the view which is generally held in all countries. There is not such unanimity, however, concerning a sacrifice made to avoid what is erroneously believed to be a threatening peril.[38]

Rule A

A.92 **There is a general average act when, and only when, any extraordinary sacrifice or expenditure is intentionally and reasonably made or incurred for the common safety for the purpose of preserving from peril the property involved in a common maritime adventure.**

General average sacrifices and expenditures shall be borne by the different contributing interests on the basis hereinafter provided.

[38] Contrast the English case of *Joseph Watson & Sons Ltd v. Firemen's Fund Insurance Co.* [1922] 2 K.B. 355, with the U.S. case of *The Wordsworth* 88 Fed.Rep. 313 (1898): see paras. A.28–A.29, *ante*.

CONSTRUCTION

First Paragraph

"general average act" The five essential features necessary to constitute a general average act [intentional; peril (common safety); common maritime adventure; extraordinary (sacrifice or expenditure); reasonable] have each been discussed earlier, and antecedent references will be quoted again in this short section on the construction of each of these terms.

"when, and only when," In point of law these words seem to add little to the corresponding "where" of section 66(2) of the Marine Insurance Act 1906, so far as English law is concerned; they are no doubt used for the sake of clarity and emphasis, and an attempt to have them removed as mere surplusage in 1994 was defeated.

"extraordinary" See paragraphs A.56 to A.61, above.

"sacrifice or expenditure" A general average act may take the form of either or both: **A.93**

(1) a *sacrifice* of physical property (for example the jettison of cargo and the freight attaching thereto, or the damage to a ship's engines sustained in efforts to refloat after stranding, together with the concomitant commission,[39] interest,[40] and adjustment charges thereon)
(2) an *expenditure* of money for the purchase of services to extricate the vessel and her cargo, *etc.*, from the peril in which they find themselves, for example for the hire of tugs to refloat a stranded vessel, or of lighters and labour to off-load cargo in similar circumstances, or of port or refuge expenses, etc.

This distinction is of no great importance at this stage of our discussions, but it may be recorded that whereas both sacrifices and expenditures are allowed as general average, the value of any *sacrifice* of property "made good" in general average is added to the value of the property arriving at destination and is called upon to contribute to the general average,[41] whereas pure general average *expenditure* does not generally affect the contributory values of the property saved.

"intentionally" See paragraphs A.08 to A.16, above.

[39] See Rule XX.
[40] See Rule XXI.
[41] See para. 17.14, *post*.

A.94 **"reasonably"** See paragraphs A.84 to A.86, above, also the commentary on the Rule Paramount in paragraphs PRE.24 to PRE.25. However, for general average adjustments still subject to the York-Antwerp Rules 1974 (or even 1950 or 1924), it should be noted that the requirement that sacrifices and expenditures should be *reasonably* made or incurred applies solely to those claimable only under the lettered Rules (for example, a jettison of cargo[42] or damage to the bottom of a ship sustained in efforts to refloat when aground and in a position of peril[43] under Rule A, or substituted expenses under Rule F). Claims under the numbered Rules, in the absence of express wording[44] therein requiring it, are not subject to this requirement of reasonableness.

This was decided in the case of the *Alpha*[45], where cargo interests, on the grounds that the actions of the master were unreasonable, denied liability for a claim made under the numbered Rule VII for serious damage to the main and auxiliary machinery of that vessel caused in efforts to refloat from a position of peril.

The catalogue of the master's failings was indeed extensive, and Hobhouse J. found that his "*conduct was not merely unskilful; it was in my judgment unreasonable* . . .". He nevertheless held cargo interests liable for their general average contribution and said:

> "The word *reasonably* is not used in Rule VII . . . Thus, where the vessel is aground and in peril, the test to be satisfied is one of actual intent to refloat, not one of reasonableness. This numbered Rule provides a clear illustration of the York-Antwerp Rules making a specific provision for a specific situation to the exclusion of Rule A."

The judgment was probably technically correct, but it was unwelcome, and accounted for the introduction of the Rule Paramount in 1994.

A.95 **"intentionally and reasonably made or incurred"** Both the adverbs apply to each of the verbs and thus the sacrifice "must be made or expenditure incurred intentionally and made or incurred reasonably".[46]

In *Australian Coastal Shipping Commission v. Green*[47] a tug was hired in time of peril, at a fixed rate of hire but with the indemnity provisions of the United Kingdom Standard Towage Conditions. The Court of Appeal held that the contract made by the shipowners with the tug was a general average act within Rule A. Cairns L.J. said[48]:

[42] See also para. 1.01, *post*.
[43] See also para. 7.08, *post*.
[44] Rule XVIII mentions "*reasonable* cost of repairing" and "*reasonable* depreciation"; Rule X(c) has "including insurance if *reasonably* incurred", while Rules XI(a) and (b) mentions "wages and maintenance of . . . crew *reasonably* incurred". In each case, the inclusion of the words *reasonable* or *reasonably* was almost by chance, or gratuitous.
[45] *Corfu Navigation Co. v. Mobil Shipping Co. Ltd* [1991] 2 Lloyd's Rep. 515.
[46] *Athel Line Ltd v. Liverpool and London War Risks Ins. Assn. Ltd* [1944] K.B. 87 at 93, *per* Tucker J. In *The Seapool* [1934] P. 53 at 64, Langton J. seemed to incline to the view that "intentionally" only applied to "sacrifice . . . made".
[47] [1971] 1 Q.B. 456.
[48] *Ibid.* at 486.

> "I think the definitions make sense, without the introduction of any words that are not there, if one realizes that the incurring of expenditure is something different from the making of expenditure and that expenditure is incurred when a contract is entered into, say, between a shipowner and a tugowner and the contract provides for payments to be made by the shipowner to the tugowner. Thus the making of the contract is the general average act and I think that any payment that falls due under the contract is a direct consequence of it."

It is impossible for the necessary intention to have been formed if the act relied upon was done in obedience to orders from a superior.

> "The rule ... clearly envisages the exercise by someone of his reasoning powers and discretion applied to a particular problem with freedom of choice to decide to act in one out of two or more possible ways, and the language is quite inappropriate to describe the blind and unreasoning obedience of a subordinate to the lawful orders of a superior authority."[49]

Furthermore the intention must be to preserve from peril, not merely to perform the act of sacrifice.[50] The Rule does not specify by whom the sacrifice must be made or expenditure incurred and there is no decision on the point.[51] In the absence of any indication from the wording of the Rule the common law will apply and it is suggested that the actor need not be the master.[52]

"for the common safety" See paragraphs A.17 to A.34, above, and note also that the meaning of these words is really defined by the remainder of the Rule, but they are important because they occur in a number of the other Rules as a shorter and more convenient phrase than "for the purpose of preserving from peril the property involved in a common maritime adventure". It should be noted that the phrase refers to the physical safety of the property and not to the successful conclusion of the voyage,[53] although in *McCall v. Houlder*[54] the distinction seems not to have been very closely observed. A.96

"for the purpose of preserving from peril the property involved in a common maritime adventure." The peril need not be immediate, but it must be real and not imaginary and must be substantial and not merely slight or A.97

[49] *Athel Line Ltd v. Liverpool and London War Risks Ins. Assn. Ltd* [1944] K.B. 87 at 93, *per* Tucker J. who held that extraordinary expenditure incurred in the execution of Admiralty orders was not intentionally incurred within the meaning of the Rule.

[50] *Daniolos v. Bunge & Co. Ltd* (1937) 59 Ll.L. Rep. 175 at 180; affirmed (1938) 62 Ll.L. Rep. 65, C.A.

[51] It was argued but not decided in *Athel Line Ltd v. Liverpool and London War Risks Ins. Assn. Ltd* [1944] K.B. 87; *cf. Australian Coastal Shipping Commission v. Green, supra.*

[52] See discussion of this question, paras. A.10–A.15, above.

[53] Contrast the phrase "For the safe prosecution of the voyage" in Rule X(b).

[54] (1897) 66 L.J.Q.B. 408; 2 Com.Cas. 127. See para. A.21, *ante*.

nugatory.[55] It is probably not enough that the act should be done in order to secure the general safety of all shipping in a given area, even though this includes the common adventure. The act must be specifically designed to secure the particular safety of the particular adventure.[56]

"common maritime adventure" See paragraphs A.49 to A.54, above, also Rule B.

Second Paragraph

A.98 The second paragraph seems to give rise to no problems of construction. In both 1974 and 1994 it was suggested that it was superfluous and in 1994 it was proposed that it should therefore be deleted. However, this received no real support.

"different contributing interests" These are considered when dealing with Rule XVII.

[55] *Vlassopoulous v. British and Foreign Marine Insurance Co. Ltd* [1929] 1 K.B. 187 at 200, *per* Roche J. and *Daniolos v. Bunge & Co. Ltd* (1938) 62 Ll.L.Rep. 65 at 68, C.A. It has been held by arbitrators that there should be no allowance in general average for the expenses of returning to port in order to repair the vessel's wireless apparatus, which had broken down. There was no existing peril, only the fear that the vessel might be helpless if a peril arose.

[56] *Athel Line Ltd v. Liverpool and London War Risks Ins. Assn. Ltd* [1944] K.B. 87 at 95.

Rule B

(Tug and Tow)

English Background and Foreign Law

The commentary on the preceding Rule A dealt at length with the essential features necessary to constitute a general average act, and these included the requirement that there be a COMMON MARITIME ADVENTURE involving more interests than one[1] whose safety was threatened by a situation of peril. **B.01**

A ship and the cargo she carries are necessarily involved in a common adventure, but what of the situation where a tug is towing (or pushing) one or more barges, an oil rig or other craft, on any of which there may or may not be cargo? Are they all engaged in a common adventure, and does a peril affecting one unit of the flotilla involve them all in a common general average?

Clearly the towage contract and/or the conditions of carriage must be closely examined for special provision regarding general average and unusual situations on the voyage, but it is submitted that, unless there be independent commanders on board the various units of a linked flotilla, each capable of making independent decisions and giving effect thereto, all units and the cargoes they carry are engaged in a common maritime adventure which could be subject to a collective general average. However, the more important question of which units should contribute to a general average affecting any one or more of them will depend upon whether the various units, when linked together, are *all* affected and imperilled by the same *common danger* (or peril). Furthermore, in the majority of tug and tow cases the alleged general average act is a disconnection of one or more units of the flotilla, and in such cases it is necessary to consider whether the disconnection is a sacrifice. It should not be so regarded unless the chances of survival of the disconnected unit are lessened, for example by lack of motive power or personnel on board.

Legal decisions on the subject are few in number and of rather doubtful authority. The facts ruling in some of the cases will be quoted, but it may be preferable to start this section with certain guidelines which, it is hoped, are based on sound principle. **B.02**

[1] See para. A.51, *ante*.

1. A single barge under tow is holed and leaking badly after striking a rock or a passing vessel, but the tug is not herself in danger as a result of the incident. Measures taken to save the barge and her cargo will be general average as between those interests, but the tug will not contribute, since she is not imperilled. Even if the tug was imperilled by the accident (for example the barge was sinking in deep water and the tug was in danger of being dragged under) disconnection of the towing line would not be a sacrifice because it would not further reduce the small or non-existent chances of saving the barge.

2. One of a flotilla of barges runs aground in sheltered waters and cannot be freed by the tug, but the tug and the remaining barges are not in danger. Measures taken to save the grounded barge and her cargo will not be contributed to by the tug and the remaining barges. If the grounding occurs in exposed or dangerous waters with the result that the other units are imperilled, and the grounded barge is cast off, it must be considered, before concluding that the disconnection is a sacrifice, whether the grounded barge is in a worse situation as a result.

3. If an oil rig or other large structure is being towed by two or more tugs, an accident to one of those tugs is unlikely to place the other tug(s) or the tow in any peril, and they would not contribute to the general average—if any—on the damaged tug.

4. A complete main engine breakdown on the high seas of the (single) tug is the most likely situation where a common peril affecting the entire flotilla might exist. If the barge or tow can be detached and lie or anchor in safety until the tug has repaired at a port of refuge and returned to resume the voyage, the barge or tow should not be called on to contribute to any general average on the tug. However, if the barge or tow cannot be left in safety unattended and must needs be taken together with the tug to a port of refuge, it would appear correct that the whole flotilla and their cargoes should contribute to the general average expenses incurred.

B.03 5. On occasion, a severe storm and heavy seas could threaten the safety of both the tug and her tow, and the tug may cast the tow adrift, hoping perhaps to pick it up again when the weather abates, but with the prospect that she may not be able then to find the tow and that it may either sink or drift ashore.

From the point of principle, this perhaps is the most difficult situation. If by casting the tow adrift, both units stand an *equally* better chance of surviving the storm, it is submitted that there is no "sacrifice" and that anything which subsequently causes loss to either of them during the temporary suspension of the common adventure is a loss particular to the unit sustaining it, and not to be contributed to as general average by the surviving units or property. However, in the more likely situation where, by reason of its generally greater seagoing qualities, the tug casts the tow adrift with the object of giving itself alone a better chance of survival, leaving the tow to its fate and the likelihood of being swept ashore or lost in the storm, the casting adrift may be likened to a jettison of cargo, and any loss or damage to, or salvage of, the tow should be similarly considered and treated as general average to which the tug should contribute, unless the storm is so severe that whether the barge had remained in tow or been cast adrift she would inevitably have foundered even though the tug survived the barge.

In *The J.P. Donaldson*,[2] a tug which had been towing some sailing barges cast them off in a storm, to save herself from going ashore. The barges went ashore, and were lost with their cargoes. The tug arrived safely. She had been towing on the terms of receiving part of the freight which would have been earned by the barges. A claim for contribution in general average was made against the tug by the owners of the barges. **B.04**

It was held by the Supreme Court of the United States that no contribution was payable. The master of the tug was not in control of the barges in the sense necessary to empower him to make a sacrifice binding tug and barges as a single maritime adventure. In all respects, except that of performing the contract of towage, the barges were under the control of their own masters.

> "The master of the tug having no authority to decide, as between a barge and her cargo, what part shall be sacrificed for the safety of the rest, and thereby to subject what is saved to contribution in general average for what is lost, can surely have no greater authority by abandoning all the barges with their cargoes to subject the tug to a general average contribution."[3]

This case was distinguished by the United States District Court in *S.C. Loveland Co. v. U.S.A.*[4] where the libellant owned both the tug and two barges carrying government cargo. One of the barges was deliberately run on shore after a casualty to prevent it sinking. This measure was in no way directed towards the safety of the tug, the other barge or the cargo in it, but it was held that all should contribute in general average. **B.05**

It is submitted that neither decision is altogether satisfactory; of the two, *S.C. Loveland Co. v. U.S.A.*[5] is the more surprising, since by the time of the sacrifice there was, on the facts, no common danger threatening the whole adventure. But if there is such a danger, it is hard to see why the master of a tug should not be treated, at any rate, for some purposes and for the time being, as in control of tug, barges and cargo.

[2] 167 U.S. 399 (1897)

[3] 167 U.S. 605 (1897). See also *The John Perkins* (1822) Ware (U.S.) 87; 3 Kent Comm. 243n., where the cutting of a cable to prevent a collision with another vessel was not a ground for contribution from that vessel. *Cf.* Phill., s. 1311.

[4] (1963) A.M.C. 260.

[5] (1963) A.M.C. 260.

B.06 In *Northland Navigation Co., Ltd v. Patterson Boiler Works Ltd*[6] a tug towing a loaded barge from Vancouver to Prince Rupert encountered heavy seas which broke over the stern of the tug, flooding the bilge and entering the engine-room. The engine began to shudder and the tug let go the tow line and headed for shelter. Collier J. accepted that "It may well be that the tug and tow were in danger of going down, if the barge had not been let free" and stated, further, that:

> "The casting adrift of the barge, in the knowledge it would inevitably strand or go under, can be characterized as a general average sacrifice."

The barge with her cargo drifted ashore onto rocks, attempts to refloat her proved unsuccessful and the barge was abandoned, but the entire cargo was saved. Until that time when it was decided that the barge herself could not be refloated, the judge held that the expenses of attempting to save both barge and cargo were properly allowable as general average, but expenses subsequent to that time were particular charges on the barge's cargo. He further held that the tug should not contribute to such general average, basing this view on *Walthew v. Mavrojani*[7] in that the common peril had expired and the tug was in safety when the general average expenses were incurred.

With respect, it is submitted that this decision also is highly suspect. This was not a separate general average affecting only the barge and her cargo, and commencing when the barge ran ashore; the real general average act was—as already accepted by the judge—the intentional casting adrift of the barge and her cargo at a time when the tug, plus the barge and her cargo, were in joint danger. The sacrifice made by the master of the tug was the full value of the barge and her cargo, less whatever could be salved from either or both the barge and her cargo. Thus, the general average in this case consisted essentially of the value of the lost barge plus all the expenses incurred in attempting to save the barge and her cargo.[8] The important point to note, however, is that the tug should contribute to the sacrifice of the barge and its cargo, which was made for the joint benefit of the tug and—as it happens—the cargo which was saved.

B.07 The most recent—and again unsatisfactory—legal decision comes from the Norwegian Court of Appeal and concerns the ship *Alppi*,[9] which, pur-

[6] (1983) 2 C.F. 59.

[7] (1870) L.R. 5 Ex. 116: see para 8.13, *post*, for the facts of the case. There is, however, a crucial difference between the two cases, since in *Walthew v. Mavrojani* the discharging of the cargo, which brought about the physical separation of the ship and cargo, was not the direct (or even indirect) cause of the expense subsequently incurred in refloating the ship; this expense, therefore, was neither incurred for the common safety, *nor was it the direct result of an antecedent act which was itself a general average act.*

[8] One sometimes encounters cases where cargo is jettisoned for the common safety but some is found floating and recovered. The allowance in general average is for the full value of that cargo, less its damaged value after recovery and the costs of salvage, etc., on those goods.

[9] *The Alppi v. The Bjorn Eskil* (ND 1989, 397 Eidsiating Appeal Court).

suant to a contract of towage, was in the course of being towed unmanned and in ballast from Norway to Spain. Very heavy weather was encountered in the English Channel and tug and tow were both in danger of being driven ashore. All attempts to tow the *Alppi* away from the shore proved unavailing and the master of the tug decided to cast off the towing line in order to save the tug. The *Alppi* did drive ashore and became a total loss.

A general average adjustment was prepared in Oslo in which the loss of the *Alppi* was treated as general average to which the tug should contribute, and this claim was upheld in the court of first instance. The decision was reversed in the Court of Appeal, however, it being unanimously held that grounds in theory and/or legal usage for such a claim in general average had not been proved, and some stress appearing to be made of the fact that the *Alppi* carried no cargo:

> "Existing literature is primarily aimed at the situation where a ship pushes or tows a barge carrying a cargo. Even then opinions seem to differ whether there is any basis for applying the provisions (of general average). Case law in this area is limited ... Among international judgments, it is ... only the *Loveland*[10] judgment which imposes the payment of a contribution, but then in connection with a barge carrying a cargo."

However, the fact that the *Alppi* was not carrying cargo provides no convincing reason why her loss should not be general average as between those interests (namely her and the tug) which were imperilled. The facts of the case correspond very closely with those outlined in the fifth example given in paragraph B.03, above, and it is submitted that under English law a loss occurring in these circumstances ought to be made good in general average, so long as it can genuinely be said that the tug as well as the tow was imperilled, while linked together.

Historical Development and Practice of Rule B

York-Antwerp Rules 1994

The subject of general average involving a tug and tow was considered of sufficient importance in 1994 to warrant a new lettered Rule of principle thereon, to follow immediately after Rule A. This space being then occupied by a somewhat little-used Rule B, the wording of that Rule B was incorporated in 1994 as the final part of Rule A, thereby leaving the required room for the new Rule B, below. This new wording is based largely on the provisions in Rule XXV of the Rhine Rules (IVR 1979), and before dealing with Rule B itself, it may be useful to consider the Rhine Rule. It is entitled *Convoys* and the relevant first two sections read as follows: **B.08**

[10] *S.C. Loveland Co. v. U.S.A.* (1963) A.M.C. 260.

Rule B

1. For the purpose of this Rule, a convoy is considered to be a group of vessels coupled with each other in such a way that none of the vessels has any freedom of independent movement.
2. When measures are taken to preserve a vessel and/or some or all vessels of such convoy and their cargo from a common peril, Rules I to XXIV shall be applied accordingly. A vessel forming part of a convoy is not in common peril with another vessel of that convoy, if by a mere uncoupling of the connection with such other vessel she can be placed in safety.

In brief: *section 1* defines a *convoy* as consisting of a group of vessels coupled together such that they must travel together, while *section 2* states that if one or more of the vessels in the convoy should be in peril and (general average) measures be taken to preserve them, all the preceding Rhine Rules I to XXIV shall apply to such general average. Probably by way of confirmation that not every unit in the convoy need be involved in the general average, *section 2* then continues with the statement that a vessel forming part of the convoy is not in common peril with the others if by a mere uncoupling of the connection she can be placed in safety.

The Rhine Rule may itself not be perfect, but in its translation into the new Rule B of the York-Antwerp Rules, below, potential areas for argument have been introduced, particularly in the third paragraph.

RULE B

B.09 **There is a common maritime adventure when one or more vessels are towing or pushing another vessel or vessels, provided that they are all involved in commercial activities and not in a salvage operation.**

When measures are taken to preserve the vessels and their cargoes, if any, from a common peril, these Rules shall apply.

A vessel is not in common peril with another vessel or vessels if by simply disconnecting from the other vessel or vessels she is in safety; but if the disconnection is itself a general average act the common maritime adventure continues.

CONSTRUCTION

First Paragraph

B.10 **"common maritime adventure"** See paragraphs A.51 to A.54, above, for general remarks on this expression. Its use here is to secure an internationally uniform approach to the problem of whether and when a tug and tow constitutes a common maritime adventure and to resolve the doubt created by the differing decisions[11] of the courts of those countries which have been called upon to consider the problem. This first paragraph spells out that a linked flotilla of tug(s) and other vessels *will* constitute a common maritime adventure . . .

"... provided that they are all involved in commercial activities and not in a salvage operation." All operations of towage or carriage of goods at sea or in rivers will surely be considered as a commercial activity, as indeed will any salvage operation, and the purpose of this proviso must simply be to ensure that if a vessel with her cargo—if any—is in peril and engages *salvage* assistance or towage, that particular operation shall not constitute yet another common maritime adventure and invite the possibility of a separate general average involving also the salvage vessel within the existing general average.

Second Paragraph

This second paragraph corresponds with the first sentence of section 2 of the Rhine Rule, but instead of referring to "*a vessel and/or some* or all vessels of such convoy", the York-Antwerp Rule refers simply to "*the vessels*", and this use of the definite article and the plural thereby creates the impression that the whole of the common adventure is to be threatened if the York-Antwerp Rules are to apply. **B.11**

In fact, the style of wording used may be capable of a construction covering the situation where only part of the flotilla is in peril, but one could wish that it had been more clearly expressed on lines such as: "When measures are taken to preserve one or more of the vessels and their cargoes, if any, from a peril common to that or those vessels, these Rules shall apply."

"When measures are taken to preserve the vessels and their cargoes, if any, from a common peril, these Rules shall apply." The first paragraph of the Rule having declared that a tug and tow (or linked flotilla of tugs and barges etc.) will generally constitute a common maritime adventure, this second paragraph states that when the constituent parts of that adventure are threatened by a common peril, the York-Antwerp Rules shall apply to any extraordinary sacrifice or expenditure necessarily incurred for their joint preservation.

"these Rules shall apply." These words having something of an *ex cathedra* ring about them, it needs to be stressed that the York-Antwerp Rules will *not* apply unless they are expressly incorporated in the relevant contracts of carriage between any ship or barge in the flotilla and her

[11] The legal decisions are recounted in paras. B.04–B.07, *ante*.

cargo, and, perhaps even more importantly, the contracts of towage between the tug(s) and the individual units of the flotilla.

B.12 The precise wording of the individual towage contract will need close examination, but it will be appreciated that towage contracts frequently contain very wide exemption clauses and indemnities in favour of the tug owner, and it is necessary to consider the effect of these clauses on rights and liabilities in general average. Thus under the United Kingdom Standard Conditions for Towage, except where there has been a personal failure by the tugowner to make the tug seaworthy, (1) the tugowner is exonerated from any liability for damage to the tow; and (2) the hirer must indemnify the tugowner against damage to the tug and all "claims". As observed in the commentary on Rule D,[12] the first of these provisions would not of itself exclude claims in general average for a sacrifice of the tow, but the second provision has the result that any sacrifice or expenditure for the common safety is effectively being made entirely for the benefit of the hirer, who would otherwise bear the full cost of the damage to both tug and tow, and of any claims; and this, it is suggested, is sufficient to exclude any liability of the tugowner in general average. Other towage contracts in widespread use, the International Ocean Towage Agreement, Lump Sum ("Towcon") and Daily Hire ("Towhire") are more even-handed in their provisions, but they stipulate that loss of or damage to the tow or tug respectively are "for the sole account of" the hirer or tugowner respectively "without any recourse", and again this is probably wide enough to exclude recourse in general average. In any event it is hardly to be anticipated that there will be any rush by tugowners to incorporate the York-Antwerp Rules within their contracts of towage.

B.13 **"cargoes, if any,"** The words *if any* were included to overcome the thinking in the Norwegian case of the *Alppi*[13] and to ensure that a general average situation could still arise in appropriate circumstances even though the tow might carry no cargo.

"a common peril" In the context of Rule B, a *common peril* might appear to be one which simultaneously affects all units of the flotilla, and each of them to an equal degree, but it is submitted that it can and should be applied to any one or more of the units in the flotilla and their cargoes.

[12] See, for instance, para. D.11, *post*, and the general rule under English law that a contractual or statutory provision exempting a party from liability will not be construed as referring to a liability to contribute in general average unless it expressly so provides.

[13] See para. B.07, note 9, *ante*.

Third Paragraph

This third paragraph is somewhat badly expressed, and could possibly give rise to different interpretations in everyday practice. It is in two parts, separated by a semi-colon, and the first part corresponds fairly closely with the second sentence of section 2 of the Rhine Rule, while the second part is new. **B.14**

"A vessel is not in common peril with another vessel ... if by simply disconnecting ... she is in safety;" This first part of the third paragraph endeavours to deal with the question whether the various units of a flotilla are in common peril, as required by the second paragraph of the Rule, but does it provide a clear answer?

Upon any disconnection, and by reason of its usually stronger construction and engine power, a tug will almost invariably be better placed to survive any threatening emergency than its generally unmanned and unpowered tows, for whom—unless safely moored in port—any disconnection is likely to place them under some threat of added danger, even in the finest of weather. The tug, then, will usually be the only—and in any case, the greatest—beneficiary of any disconnection, and a superficial reading of this wording might create the impression, therefore, that even when the *whole* of the flotilla, while coupled together, is in danger,[14] the tug can escape any liability to contribute to a potential general average simply by casting off the towlines and creating a *sauve qui peut* situation in which each unit is responsible for its own losses and salvage expenses.

It is almost certain that this was not the intention of the framers of the Rule. It pre-supposes a highly radical and unlikely change in that *peril*, and the particular units of the flotilla which it affects, should be determined in the disconnected state, rather than the normal connected state. (This might be likened to determining peril on a free-standing vessel *after* a jettison!)

No. It is far more likely that the framers of the Rule were simply thinking of situations such as the first three practical examples given earlier in paragraphs B.02 to B.03, above, where there is a peril, but it affects only a single unit of the flotilla and is not common to them all. In such situations, by simply disconnecting the imperilled unit, the other units will continue in safety and there is no sound reason why they should contribute to the cost of any measures taken to preserve the affected unit.

In any case, the paragraph continues with a proviso construed in paragraph B.16, below.

"in safety" These two words in the first leg of the third paragraph may also cause problems of construction. For example, a simple disconnection **B.15**

[14] Such as the *Northland* and *Alppi* cases: see paras. B.06–B.07, *ante*.

of a barge or vessel on fire from another will not automatically place the other in safety. Even though in practice one or other of the units is likely to move or be shifted away in order to avoid an extension of the fire, a strict construction of the wording might require that their continued close proximity to each other be assumed, and a common peril (that is, common to them both) to continue. The provisions of the second paragraph would then require that the non-burning vessel should contribute to any sacrifice or expenditure incurred to extinguish the fire on the burning vessel—the only one that is really in peril.

This would be somewhat ludicrous, for the disconnection and shifting away of the individual units is unlikely ever to constitute a general average act or sacrifice, that is in no way would it worsen the situation on the unit ablaze or lessen its chances of survival.

If the full wording of the Rhine Rule XXV had been used: "... *she can be placed in safety*", this particular problem would not have arisen.

B.16 **"but if the disconnection is itself a general average act"** (This is the proviso referred to above and relating to the wording construed in paragraph B.14). An excellent practical example for this phrase has already been given as Example No. 5 in the earlier paragraph B.03, also in the commentary on *Northland Navigation Co. Ltd v. Patterson Boiler Works Ltd* in paragraph B.06, above, that is that where the tug herself is also in peril while joined to the tow and, in order to save herself, sacrifices the tow by casting it adrift, the tug should contribute to whatever loss and/or damage is sustained by the tow and any cargo she carries, even though it might be said that such loss occurred subsequent to the separation of the tug and her tow; in reality, the separation was itself the general average act, exactly comparable to a jettison.

B.17 **"the common maritime adventure continues."** Although anything but ideal, these words were designed to and should overcome the effect of those particular legal decisions which, on the (erroneous) grounds that the common adventure was then over, have denied any contribution in general average from the tug in respect of losses and expenses sustained by the tows, nominally subsequent to their being cast off by the tug, but effectively as the direct result of the casting off. Clearly, the adventure continues beyond the time of that casting off.

No indication is given as to when the adventure terminates, but assuming that the original adventure is not resumed and completed, it is submitted that for each of the units the adventure ends when they respectively reach a place of safety, but see also the more detailed commentary in Rule G and Rule XVII.

Rule C

Causation, Consequences and Damage to the Environment

General Introduction

Since 1924, when the lettered Rules were first introduced, Rule C has been the provision in the York-Antwerp Rules dealing generally with problems of causation and consequences. As a result of new provisions adopted in 1994, the Rule now also deals with the largely distinct topic of damage to the environment. **C.01**

Causation and Consequences

To what extent must a general average act, whether involving sacrifice or expenditure, be followed to its more or less remote consequences? This question underlies a great many general average questions. Rules II, V, VIII, X, XI, XII and XIV of the York-Antwerp Rules are all concerned in whole or in part with settling disputed problems as to remoteness; so was the great dispute at common law as to port of refuge expenses.[1]

It can never have been intended that every loss which would not or could not have taken place, had the sacrifice been not made, must be replaced by contribution. The cutting away of a mast, for example, while saving the ship and cargo from some imminent danger, may, by retarding the ship's sailing, bring them within the action of some new danger, from which they would otherwise have been free through having reached their destination. Suppose that from this cause she were to fall into an enemy's hands, it could hardly be contended that the loss by capture should be replaced by contribution as a consequence of cutting away the mast.

On the other hand, if all losses and expenses were excluded from consideration unless consciously intended by the master at the time of the act, many consequences which flow naturally and forseeably from the act would have to be disregarded, thus giving rise to an artificial result.

[1] See paras. 10.01 *et seq., post*. In *Svendsen v. Wallace* (1884) 13 Q.B.D. 69 at 84 in the Court of Appeal, Bowen L.J. said that the object of general average contribution was "to indemnify the person making the general average sacrifice against so much of the loss *caused directly thereby* as does not fall to his own proportionate share".

Damage to the Environment

C.02 The growing significance in general average of liabilities and expenses consequent upon actual or threatened environmental damage, in particular oil pollution, led to the introduction of special provisions on the subject in the 1994 Rules. The most important of these provisions, which is contained in the second paragraph of Rule C, is an exclusion from general average of liabilities in respect of damage to the environment. This exclusion, which is best regarded as something distinct from the remainder of Rule C, and potentially inconsistent with it, owes less to principle than to policy, and to the reluctance of insurers of hull and cargo (that is, property) to become insurers of liabilities through the mechanism of the general average system. Until the change effected to the Rule in 1994 there was no reason in English law why liability for damage to the environment should not have been allowed in general average, whether the adjustment was governed by the York-Antwerp Rules or not.[2]

English Law and Background

Causation generally

C.03 The Marine Insurance Act 1906, which has been held to codify the English law, and therefore to apply between the parties to the adventure as well as to claims under policies of marine insurance,[3] provides that the loss to be made good in general average must be "caused by or directly consequential on" the general average act.[4] When a rule of general application, Rule C,[5] was introduced for the first time into the York-Antwerp Rules in 1924, its wording was modelled closely on the Act and it applied the test of "direct consequences". However, the English decisions on questions of causation, including those decided after the introduction of the Marine Insurance Act and of Rule C, have continued to pay great regard to the rather more elaborate tests proposed by Lowndes and by Ulrich.[6]

The tests adopted by Lowndes and Ulrich

C.04 In most of the English cases, where problems of remoteness and

[2] See paras. C.15 and C.26, *post*. However, a questionnaire circulated by A.I.D.E., the results of which were published in their Report of September 1993, revealed that the law of different countries on the point was far from uniform, and the practice of adjusters varied, even where the adjustment was governed by the York-Antwerp Rules.

[3-4] See para. C.09, *post*, and para. 50.02, *post*.

[5] See para. C.16, *post*.

[6] See paras. C.04–C.05, *post*. The position may be different where one of the numbered Rules applies; see para. C.16, *post*.

causation have arisen, two tests have been applied in resolving the problem. The first is that of Lowndes, who referred to the general rule of English law as to remoteness of damage, citing *Mayne on Damages* (3rd ed.), p. 39:

> "The first, and in fact the only inquiry in all these cases is, whether the damage complained of is the natural and reasonable result of the defendant's act; it will assume this character if it can be shewn to be such a consequence as in the ordinary course of things would flow from the act, or, in cases of contract, if it appears to have been contemplated by both parties."[7]

Lowndes continued:

> "Applying this rule more closely to general average, it may be thought that, since we have to determine *quod pro omnibus datum est*, and since giving must always imply an intention to give, what we have here to ascertain must be, what loss at once has in fact occurred, and likewise must be regarded as the natural and reasonable result of the act of sacrifice? Or, in other words, what the shipmaster would naturally, or might reasonably have intended to give for all when he resolved upon the act? If then, upon the act of sacrifice any loss ensues, which the master did not in fact bring before his mind at the time of making the sacrifice, it would have to be considered whether it were a loss of which he naturally might or reasonably ought to have taken account."

The second test is that of the German writer Ulrich[8]: **C.05**

> General average comprises not only the damage purposely done to ship and cargo, but also (1) all damage or expense which was to be foreseen as the natural (immediate) consequence of the first sacrifice, since this unmistakably forms part of that which was *given* for the common safety; (2) all damage or expense which, though not to be foreseen, stands to the sacrifice in relation of effect to cause, or, in other words, was its *necessary* consequence. Not so, however, those losses or expenses which, though they would not have occurred but for the sacrifice, yet, likewise, would not have occurred but for some subsequent accident.

The authorities on English law

In *McCall v. Houlder Bros*[9] (decided under the York-Antwerp Rules 1890), the vessel's propellor was damaged when she struck a bar on leaving the loading port, and she was detained at her next bunkering port, as a port of refuge. As there were no facilities for the storage of the cargo, which was perishable, the vessel was tipped so that repairs to **C.06**

[7] For the modern law on this topic, see *McGregor on Damages* (15th ed.), paras. 133–268. It is at least possible that, the test for general average purposes having crystallised at this stage in the development of the common law, there is now a divergence between remoteness in general average cases and remoteness at common law. *Cf. Australian Coastal Shipping Commission v. Green* [1971] 1 Q.B. 456.

[8] *Grosse-Haverei*, p. 5.

[9] (1897) 2 Com.Cas. 129 at 132. For a comparison of the various reports of this case see para. A.21, *ante*.

the propellor could be carried out. The tipping of the vessel was held to be a general average act. It was later discovered that as a result of the operation, cargo had been damaged by seawater entering the hold through a broken air pipe. The fracture had occurred during the striking of the bar, but was unknown to the master when he decided to tip the vessel. The cargo damage was allowed in general average. Mathew J. said:

> "It was not known what the result of the vessel striking when crossing the bar had been, but it was clear that if any damage had been done to the structure of the ship, the process of setting the ship down by the head might be attended by considerable risk to the cargo. The Master, it seems to me, acted prudently in determining to run that risk ... It was said that the loss was particular average only, because it was not foreseen, and was not, therefore, a voluntary sacrifice. But it is not necessary that a particular loss should have been contemplated, if it be incidental to the general average act."

While Mathew J. did not expressly refer to the test of either Lowndes or Ulrich, his reasoning reflects that of Lowndes, since the risk of damage to the cargo, although not the precise manner in which it occurred, was or ought to have been something the master would take into account in deciding to tip the vessel.[10]

C.07 In *Anglo-Argentine Live Stock Agency v. Temperley S.S. Co.*[11] the vessel had loaded cattle and sheep in the River Plate for conveyance to Britain, under a contract which provided that on no account should the vessel call at any Brazilian or European Continental ports on her way to Britain. In consequence of springing a leak the vessel was forced to put into Bahia in Brazil for repairs. In consequence, by reason of an Order in Council then in force, the cattle could not be landed in Britain and were taken instead to Antwerp, where they were sold for much less than they would have realised in Britain. The loss on sale was held to be allowable in general average as a direct and immediate consequence of the general average act of putting into Bahia. In the course of his judgment, Bigham J. cited the test of Lowndes and Ulrich, and said:

> "These two passages seem to me to express accurately the principles upon which the damages to be made good in general average are to be ascertained ... and applying those principles to the present case, I think that as, when the master of the *Edenbridge* resolved upon the average act, he knew, or ought to have known, that he was sacrificing the advantages which the plaintiffs then possessed by reason of the ship not having touched a Brazilian port, he must be taken to have intended that the value of those advantages

[10] A modern example of the same problem occurs on old ships with wasted and leaky bulkheads; water poured into one hold to extinguish a fire in that hold will frequently find its way into adjacent (or all) holds and damage the cargo therein. It is the practice to allow the damage so caused, leaving it to the injured parties to enforce their remedies for unseaworthiness, if appropriate.

[11] [1899] 2 Q.B. 403 at 410.

> should be made good in general average; and the master's intention is the intention of the parties interested, whose agent he is. I am further of opinion that the damage in question is the necessary consequence of the general average act."

The loss in value was therefore allowed in general average.

In *Austin Friars S.S. Co. v. Spillers and Bakers*[12] the plaintiffs' ship, **C.08**
bound for Sharpness dock with a cargo of maize, stranded just above the dock and was seriously damaged. Refloated with the aid of tugs, she was making water so fast that the master and pilot decided to take her into Sharpness, rather than beaching her further downstream as first intended. Because of the strong ebb tide both master and pilot contemplated (and the pilot actually intended) that the ship would strike the lower pier of the dock, and do some damage. She struck harder than intended and damaged herself to the extent of £1,600 and the pier to the extent of £5,000.

Bailhache J. held that "to put into Sharpness with the knowledge that in doing so the ship would strike the pier was a reasonable and prudent thing to do". On the question of causation he cited the tests of Lowndes and Ulrich, and said they were "admirable guides" to the decision in the case. The shipowner therefore recovered contribution in respect of the damage to the ship and in respect of the liability incurred for the damage to the dock.

The main ground on which the right to contribution was disputed was that there could be no contribution in general average where the act consisted of inflicting damage on the property of a third person, particularly when the damage amounted to a tort. However Bailhache J. held that "the master has implied authority when occasion arises for a general average act to do whatever is necessary and prudent for the preservation of ship and cargo, even if this involves committing a trespass . . .".

In *Anglo Grecian Steam Trading Co. v. Beynon (T.) & Co.*[13] the ship **C.09**
fouled the cable of a buoy while leaving port, as a result of which she lost power and fractured her aft peak. She was therefore in "distinct and considerable" danger. Since she was unable to clear the cable, it was decided to beach her, using tugs, in the centre of a nearby bay. The operation was carried out, but she took the ground rather sooner and rather further to the east than the pilot wished or expected. When the tide rose the tugs were unable to hold her, the tow ropes parted and she was carried onto rocks on the east side of the bay and damaged.

Roche J. held that the initial stranding of the ship was voluntary, and that the decision to beach her was reasonable. He then turned to the question whether the damage was a sufficiently direct or immediate result

[12] [1915] 1 K.B. 833 at 836; affirmed [1915] 3 K.B. 586, C.A.
[13] (1926) 24 Ll.L.Rep. 122.

of the stranding. He held that the chain of causation would have been broken if the vessel's being carried onto the rocks was the result either of a supervening act of negligence or of some accident "not connected with the original beaching". Having held that there was no negligence, he referred to the statement of the law in *Anglo-Argentine Live Stock Agency v. Temperley S.S. Co.,*[14] and the test of Ulrich there cited, and concluded that the loss should be allowed because:

> "although the grounding on the rocks was not at any rate foreseen as either a necessary or even a probable consequence by the pilot, yet it was not a subsequent accident *unconnected with the grounding.*"[15]

In the two cases referred to above, both Bailhache and Roche JJ. regarded the question of remoteness as governed by the provisions of section 66(1) of the Marine Insurance Act.[16]

C.10 In the light of these decisions, it cannot be said that a precise rule has been laid down on remoteness at common law. The decisions have relied on the tests of both Lowndes and Ulrich but without providing any real indication of which is to be preferred. Yet the difference in approach between the two tests is considerable, since Lowndes approaches the problem by seeking to determine what loss the master did or ought to have taken into account, as a guide to presumed intention, whereas Ulrich lays emphasis on the lack of any intervening accidental cause. The tests will not always produce the same result. The Marine Insurance Act, which defines a general average loss as a loss "caused by or directly consequently on a general act", introduces a further complication. At first sight it seems to follow the approach of Ulrich rather than that of Lowndes, yet Bailhache J. in *Austin Friars S.S. Co. v. Spillers and Bakers,*[17] while holding that he was bound to apply the provisions of the Act as a codification of the common law, derived assistance from the test of Lowndes as well as that of Ulrich. And in *Anglo-Grecian Steam Trading Co. v. Beynon (T.) & Co.,*[18] Roche J., also holding that he was bound to apply the provisions of the Act, adopted the statement of the law in *Anglo-Argentine Live Stock Agency v. Temperley S.S. Co.,*[19] which follows Lowndes' approach, as a correct statement of the law.

C.11 As a matter of principle, it is submitted that the test of Lowndes is to be preferred, and particularly its last sentence, which interprets what has

[14] See para. C.07, *ante*.

[15] (1926) 24 Ll.L. Rep. 122 at 127. The references to the York-Antwerp Rules 1924 are mistaken, as Roche J. explained in *Vlassopoulos v. British & Foreign Marine Insurance Co.* [1929] 1 K.B. 187 at 193.

[16] The second of those cases was decided under the York-Antwerp Rules 1890 but these contained no general provision on causation.

[17] [1915] 1 K.B. 833; see para. C.08, *ante*.

[18] (1926) 24 Ll.L.Rep. 122; see para. C.09, *ante*.

[19] [1899] 2 Q.B. 403; see para. C.07, *ante*.

gone before. At the risk of introducing yet a third test, it is suggested that no consequence is too remote if:

(1) The master did in fact expect it to happen; or
(2) he "naturally might or reasonably ought" to have so expected; or
(3) he did appreciate, or naturally might have or reasonably ought to have appreciated, that there was a substantial risk of its happening.[20]

Loss by Delay

English law has been slow to allow loss by delay, mainly on the practical grounds that the loss depends frequently upon the private contractual arrangements of one of the parties to the adventure in some degree, and that it gives rise to considerable difficulties of quantification. Thus in *Anglo-Argentine Live Stock Agency v. Temperley S.S. Co.*, Bigham J. rejected that part of the claim that related to the wages of cattlemen employed by the charterers, and the cost of fodder for the cattle during the period of delay at the port of refuge. After holding that these expenses did not fall within Rule X or XI of the York-Antwerp Rules 1890, he continued: **C.12**

> "But it was said that though these two claims may not be recoverable under the York-Antwerp Rules, they are nevertheless recoverable at common law. I am, however, of opinion that they are not. Everyone concerned in the adventure suffers damage by the delay at the port of refuge. Each cargo-owner is delayed in the use or the sale of his goods. The freight-owner is delayed in getting payment of his freight, and the shipowner is deprived of the use of his ship. Yet none of these cases afford the foundation of any claim in general average according to our common law."

In *The Leitrim*[21] the vessel was delayed at a port of refuge while undergoing general average repairs. The vessel was running under a time charter, which contained a clause providing that in the event of damage occurring which prevented the working of the vessel for more than 24 hours, the hire should cease. The shipowner claimed in general average the loss of time freight through the delay, but the court decided against the claim. The grounds of the decision appear to be: **C.13**

(1) that the loss of hire was an "accidental circumstance peculiar to the shipowner";
(2) that "the loss of time is common to all the parties interested and

[20] "Necessary", "immediate" and "direct" are adjectives which have been used in U.S. decisions: *Columbian Insurance Co. v. Ashby* 13 Pet. 331 (1839); Parsons, *Maritime Law*, p. 304; *The Wordsworth* 88 Fed.Rep. 313 (1898). But a wider rule is sometimes applied: *Norwich & N.Y. Trans. Co. v. Ins. Co. of N.A.* (1903) 118 Fed.Rep. 307; 129 Fed.Rep. 1006; 194 U.S. 637.

[21] [1902] P. 256.

all suffer damage by the delay, so that the damages by loss of time may be considered proportionate to the interests and may be left out of consideration"; and

(3) that great inconvenience could result if losses due to delay had to be assessed, and the practice of adjusters had been to exclude them.

C.14 Both of these cases on loss by delay were decided before the passing of the Marine Insurance Act 1906, but it was held in *Wetherall v. The London Assurance*[22] that the provisions of section 66(1) of the Act did not affect the rules of the common law excluding loss by delay. *The Leitrim* was decided under the York-Antwerp Rules 1890, but since those Rules contained no general provisions equivalent to Rule C the recoverability of the loss caused by delay was governed by English law.

Damage to the Environment

C.15 There is no decision in English law on the question whether liabilities in respect of pollution or other damage to the environment are allowable in general average. However, *Austin Friars SS. Co. v. Spillers and Bakers*[23] establishes that there is no objection to such a claim on the grounds of public policy, and liabilities of this nature may therefore be allowed, so long as they fall within the to the usual requirements of a general average loss, of which the most relevant are likely to be that the liability should be caused by or directly consequential on a general average act, and that it should be reasonably incurred.

Historical Development and Practice of Rule C

C.16 Before 1924 there was no general provision in the Rules dealing with problems of remoteness and causation, although certain of the numbered rules contained provisions relevant to these questions in the particular circumstances to which they applied. The 1994 numbered Rules do likewise,[24] and in those particular circumstances the numbered rules override Rule C to the extent of any inconsistency.[25]

[22] [1931] 2 K.B. 448: see para. C.18, *post*.
[23] [1915] 1 K.B. 833; [1915] 3 K.B. 586, C.A.: see para. C.08, *ante*. See also para. C.26, *post*.
[24] *e.g.* Rules II, V, VIII, X, XI and XIV.
[25] See the Rule of Interpretation.

York-Antwerp Rules 1924

> Only such damages, losses or expenses which are the direct consequence of the general average act shall be allowed as general average.
>
> Damage or loss sustained by the ship or cargo through delay on the voyage, and indirect loss from the same cause, such as demurrage and loss of market, shall not be admitted as general average.

Continental decisions on causation. Although the 1924 version of the Rule accorded with the English common law as it was then understood,[26] decisions had been given in some continental courts which indicated that the consequences of a general average act were not everywhere limited so strictly. C.17

In one case decided in Denmark, a neutral vessel carrying a cargo of fish from Iceland to Fleetwood met with a German submarine, which threatened to sink her is she did not return to Iceland with her cargo. She accordingly did return to Iceland, where the cargo was sold at a great loss. This loss, together with the expenses of the return voyage, were held to be general average. The decision was affirmed in the Supreme Court (1917).

In another case, *The Champlain,*[27] it was decided in the Cour de Cassation, France, that damage to cargo through delay at a port of refuge into which the vessel had put in consequence of sea perils was properly allowable in general average.[28]

The same court decided in the cases of *The Willesden* (1926) and *The Madali* (1934) that demurrage during repairs was allowable in general average under French law.

Decisions on the 1924 Rule C. In *Wetherall v. The London Assurance,*[29] where the ship was damaged by a general average act and repaired after the termination of the adventure, the shipowner argued that the second paragraph of the Rule did not exclude, and by implication permitted, a claim in respect of delay arising *after* the termination of the voyage. The claim was for loss of use of the ship during the period in which permanent repairs were effected. Rowlatt J. held that, even though the Rule did not exclude the claim in respect of delay subsequent to the voyage, it did not by implication permit such a claim, and that, following *The Leitrim,*[30] the loss was irrecoverable. C.18

However, in *The Elini* (1938), the Rennes Court of Appeal held that the loss suffered by the shipowner through delay during repairs of general average damage after the completion of the voyage was not allowable in

[26] See paras. C.03–C.15, *ante*.

[27] *Cie Bateaux à Vapeur du Nord v. Coppin*, Cour de Cassation (Petition Chamber), March 19, 1923.

[28] A similar decision was given in 1927 by the Court of Appeal at Rouen in the case of *La Bourbonnais*, to which the York-Antwerp Rules 1890 applied.

[29] [1931] 2 K.B. 448.

[30] [1902] P. 256: see para. C.13, *ante*.

general average under Rule C, even though under French law such a claim would have been allowed.

York-Antwerp Rules 1950

C.19 As a result of the doubts on the interpretation of the 1924 Rule created by *Wetherall v. The London Assurance*,[31] thc words *on the voyage* in the second paragraph of the Rule were changed to *on the voyage or subsequently*.

York-Antwerp Rules 1974

No change.

York-Antwerp Rules 1994

C.20 The main single issue at the Sydney Conference was the way in which the increasingly important question of pollution liabilities[32] should be dealt with. A number of different views were advanced. The U.S. delegation was in favour of a complete exclusion, by means of a Rule Paramount, of all pollution liabilities and of the costs of clean-up of pollutants. Other countries, and the P. and I. Clubs, took the view that pollution liabilities should be dealt with on the same footing as any other liabilities.[33] A third solution, proposed by the Association of Average Adjusters and A.I.D.E., and supported by the British delegation, favoured a general exclusion of *pollution liabilities* but express allowance of certain of the *costs of avoiding pollution*; it was felt that this held a fair balance between ship and cargo interests, and that it would promote good practice by encouraging the prevention of pollution while excluding from general average liabilities in respect of pollution which had actually occurred.

It was this third solution which was adopted at the Sydney Conference. The general exclusion of pollution liabilities is found in the lettered Rule C; and the express allowances of costs of preventing or minimising pollution are found mainly in Rule XI(d), but also in those provisions of Rule VI which deal with salvage awards enhanced by reason of the salvor's efforts in that regard. By virtue of the Rule of Interpretation these allowances in the numbered Rules will override the general exclusion in Rule C. In addition, in order to prevent claims in respect of pollution costs from arising under any of the other numbered Rules, amendments

[31] [1931] 2 K.B. 448; see para. C.18, *ante*.

[32] For the sake of simplicity we refer in this introductory paragraph to "pollution liabilities". However Rule C itself is in wider terms, and includes within its scope any "damage to the environment". See para. C.31, *post*.

[33] For English law on the subject see para. C.15, *ante*. However there appears to be no uniformity of approach between different countries; see para. C.02, n. 2, *ante*.

have been made to Rules II, V and VIII since it was felt that the provisions of these particular Rules in their 1974 form could have allowed claims in respect of pollution liabilities and expenses.

Apart from the new paragraph dealing with pollution liabilities, certain improvements of a drafting nature have also been made in the Rule. In particular the discrepancy between the apparent scope of the first paragraph (which refers to *losses, damages or expenses*) and the last paragraph (which referred only to *loss or damage*) has been eliminated[34]; and the somewhat misleading reference to loss of market as an example of *indirect loss*[35] has been altered. **C.21**

RULE C

Only such losses, damages or expenses which are the direct consequence of the general average act shall be allowed as general average.

In no case shall there be any allowance in general average for losses, damages or expenses incurred in respect of damage to the environment or in consequence of the escape or release of pollutant substances from the property involved in the common maritime adventure.

Demurrage, loss of market, and any loss or damage sustained or expense incurred by reason of delay, whether on the voyage or subsequently, and any indirect loss whatsoever shall not be admitted as general average.

CONSTRUCTION

First Paragraph

"losses, damages or expenses" This is a comprehensive expression which is clearly intended to include every kind of adverse consequence of a general average act. The effect of the first paragraph of Rule C is therefore that all such consequences will initially be subjected to the same test, namely whether they are a direct consequence of the general average act. If they are a direct consequence, they can be allowed in general average, unless they fall within the specific exclusions of the second or third paragraphs of Rule C, or of any of the numbered Rules. If they are not a direct consequence, they are excluded from any allowance in general average unless they fall within a specific provision of a numbered Rule. **C.22**

[34] See para. C.30, *post*.
[35] See para. C.34, *post*.

C.23 **"the direct consequence of the general average act"** These words are in essence the same as the wording of section 66(1) of the Marine Insurance Act 1906.[36]

The only case in the English Courts in which their interpretation has been considered is *Australian Coastal Shipping Commission v. Green.*[37] In that case the plaintiff shipowners had engaged towage assistance for two of their vessels in distress, *Bulwarra* and *Wangarra*. Each towage contract was on the United Kingdom Standard Towage Conditions, which provided for an indemnity in wide terms in favour of the tug owner. In each case the towing line broke during the towage. *Bulwarra*'s tug became a total loss, and *Wangarra*'s tug was salved and incurred salvage charges, and the tug owners claimed against the plaintiffs under the indemnity provisions. The claim in respect of *Bulwarra* failed, but the plaintiffs incurred expense in defending it. The claim in respect of *Wangarra* succeeded for an indemnity plus legal costs. The plaintiffs now sought to recover the ship's proportion of all of the above sums from their hull insurers, under policies which provided for the adjustment of general average in accordance with the York-Antwerp Rules 1950.

Mocatta J. held that the liability incurred to the owners of the tug by reason of the breaking of the towing line was the direct result of the general average act within the meaning of Rule C, on the grounds that, applying Lowndes' test, it was a liability which the plaintiffs "naturally might, or reasonably ought to have contemplated", and applying Ulrich's test as explained by Roche J. in *Anglo Grecian Steam Trading Co. v. Beynon (T.) & Co.*[38] that the liability to the tug owners consequent upon the breaking of the tow ropes was a possibility which was so connected with the act of engaging the tugs as not to break the chain of causation.[39]

C.24 This decision was upheld in the Court of Appeal, where an authoritative exposition of the Rule is to be found in the judgment of Lord Denning M.R.[40]:

> "At the time when the Rules were made in 1924, all lawyers thought that they could tell the difference between direct and indirect consequences. The distinction had been hallowed by the great authority of Lord Sumner in *Weld-Blundell v. Stephens* [1920] A.C. 956, 983–984. It had been adopted by Parliament in the Indemnity Act 1920 ... Naturally enough, therefore, the framers of the York-Antwerp Rules used it too. But 40 years later the Privy Council poured scorn upon it. It was in *The Wagon Mound* [1961] A.C. 388 when Lord Simonds said, at p. 423, that the test of the direct consequence leads to nowhere but the never-ending and insoluble problem of causation. To add to the confusion, Rule C of the York-Antwerp Rules gives loss of market as a typical instance of indirect loss, following, no doubt, *The Parana* (1877) 2 P.D. 118 whereas in *Czarnikow (C) Ltd. v. Koufos* [1969] 1 A.C.

[36] "Caused by or directly consequential on a general average act".
[37] [1971] 1 Q.B. 456.
[38] (1926) 24 Ll.L.Rep. 122; see para. C.09, *ante*.
[39] [1971] 1 Q.B. 456 at 471.
[40] [1971] 1 Q.B. 481.

350, 385, Lord Reid says that the loss of market there was directly caused by the defendant's breach of contract.

In these circumstances I propose to go back to the concept, as I understood it in 1924, when the York-Antwerp Rules were made. Direct consequences denote those consequences which flow in an unbroken sequence from the act: whereas indirect consequences are those in which the sequence is broken by an intervening or extraneous cause. I realise that this is not very helpful: because the metaphor of breaking the chain of causation means one thing to one man and another thing to another. But still we have to do the best we can with it."

However, Lord Denning then rejected Ulrich's test and turned to foreseeability:[41]

> "If the master, when he does 'the general average act,' ought reasonably to have foreseen that a subsequent accident of the kind might occur—or even that there was a distinct possibility of it—then the subsequent accident does not break the chain of causation ... If, however, there is a subsequent incident which was only a remote possibility, it would be different."

Neither Phillimore L.J. nor Cairns L.J. considered that any problem of causation arose where the expenditure was incurred under a contract which was itself a general average act; but they were prepared to accept the test of Ulrich for cases of sacrifice. All of the judges held that the legal costs incurred by the owners were recoverable, without giving separate consideration to them.

In the light of this decision it appears that the approach of the English courts to general questions of causation under the York-Antwerp Rules will not differ from that adopted in the cases decided before the introduction of Rule C. The effect of the first paragraph of Rule C may be summarised by saying that a consequence is direct if it flows from the general average act without any intervening or extraneous cause; and that if the master ought reasonably to have foreseen such intervening or extraneous cause as a distinct possibility, the result is still a direct consequence of the general average act. **C.25**

Other decisions on causation

In an English arbitration shipowners claimed contribution towards their liability for pollution, resulting from jettison of oil to refloat the vessel, as general average expenditure. The arbitrator found that the shipowners' liability was both a direct and a foreseeable consequence of the jettison, and the claim (which was governed by the York-Antwerp Rules 1950) succeeded. Under the 1994 Rules, however, such a claim would be excluded by the second paragraph of Rule C. **C.26**

In *Federal Commerce and Navigation Ltd v. Eisenerz GmbH,*[42] Rule C

[41] *Ibid.* at 482.
[42] [1970] 2 Lloyd's Rep. 332; [1975] 1 Lloyd's Rep. 105 (S.C. Can.).

was relied on by the party who had suffered loss, in order to show that it was not a general average loss. Damage to cargo occurred during discharge and reloading at a port of refuge. If this had been a necessary consequence of the limited facilities available, the shipowners would have been bound to contribute in general average (Rule XII), but would not have been liable for any greater amount because the fact of a general average loss is a defence to cargo claims.[43] However, it was found that the damage was caused by negligence of the master (amongst others) in failing to supervise the cargo operations. The shipowners could not be heard to say that the master's own negligence should be foreseen as a distinct possibility. So the chain of causation was broken, the loss was not a direct consequence of the general average act, and the cargo owners recovered in full for breach of the contract of carriage.

C.27 In *Sea-Land Service Inc. v. Aetna Insce; The Beauregard*[44] a ship stranded accidentally and the master engaged a tug to tow her off. During the towage operation, the towing line broke, and the vessel, which was beginning to come free, was driven by wind and waves sideways to port as a result of which she sustained bottom damage. The shipowners' claim to have this damage made good in general average failed, because they were unable to prove that the vessel would not have drifted to port and sustained the same damage if no towage had been attempted. However, had they been able to do so the claim would have succeeded. The master did anticipate, or should have anticipated, that the towing line might part, and the damage would therefore have been the direct result of the engagement of the tug.

In *Corfu Navigation v. Mobil Shipping*[45] (York-Antwerp Rules 1974) the claim was for damage to machinery in endeavouring to refloat, but questions of causation were regarded as being governed by Rule C.[46] The claim was resisted on the ground that the master had not prepared adequately for the attempt and had not used proper means to refloat the vessel, and that his unreasonable conduct broke the chain of causation. Rejecting this argument, Hobhouse J. said:

> "The general average act is the refloating attempt involving the running of the engines in such a way as to risk the damage. The damage to the engines was the actual and immediate consequence of that act without the intervention of any other cause; like in the *Australian Coastal Shipping* case, the general average act itself contemplates the loss and there is really no room for the argument that the loss is anything other than the direct consequence of the act."

[43] See paras. 00.62 *et seq., ante.*

[44] [1977] 2 Lloyd's Rep. 84; [1976] A.M.C. 2164 (U.S. Court of Appeals).

[45] [1991] 2 Lloyd's Rep. 515 at 522, the decision which led to the introduction of the Rule Paramount, which would provide a defence to the claim under the 1994 Rules.

[46] See para. PRE.09, *ante*, where the correctness of this view is discussed.

Costs of adjustment

It might be argued that this Rule excludes any allowance in general average of the fees and expenses of an adjuster, since the shipowner is probably not bound to employ an adjuster and may prepare his own average statement.[47] However, he is bound to produce an average statement of some kind (since the York-Antwerp Rules have so provided, at any rate by implication, since 1924)[48] and it is the invariable practice for such costs to be treated as part of the general average under the Rules; it is submitted that the practice is correct. A consequence may be direct, if in the circumstances it will invariably happen, although one of the parties can avoid it if he choose to do so. In the United States a commission of two-and-a-half per cent for settlement and collection is charged to general average and received by the adjuster.[49] **C.28**

Legal costs

It is clear from *Australian Coastal Shipping Commission v. Green*[50] that where a general average act gives rise to legal proceedings which are reasonably prosecuted or defended, the costs so incurred by a party to the adventure are general average.

Second Paragraph

General observations

This paragraph, introduced in 1994, essentially denies any allowance in general average in respect of any of the consequences of *either*: **C.29**

(1) actual or threatened damage to the environment, if caused by the property involved in the common adventure[51]; *or*
(2) the escape or release of pollutant substances from the property involved in the common adventure,

even though these consequences may be the direct result of a general average act. Subject to the exceptions described below, all the consequences of these events are excluded, whether they take the form of damage to property, the costs of cleaning up pollution or making good damage, or liabilities to third parties.

[47] *Wavertree Sailing Ship Co. v. Love* [1897] A.C. 373. See paras. 30.04–30.06, *post*.
[48] *Chandris v. Argo Insurance Co. Ltd.* [1963] 2 Lloyd's Rep. 65.
[49] *Moore-McCormack Lines v. Esso Camden* (1957) A.M.C. 971.
[50] [1971] 1 Q.B. 456: see paras. C.23–C.24, *ante*.
[51] See para. C.32, *post*, as to threatened damage, and the case where the damage to the environment arises from another source.

The new paragraph does not debar the allowance in general average of:

(1) the value of property sacrificed, including oil, chemicals or other pollutant substances, even if the sacrifice causes damage to the environment or involves an escape or release of pollutants, for example a jettison of a cargo of chemicals, or a discharge of bunker oil in order to lighten a ship,
(2) those losses damages and expenses recovery of which is specifically sanctioned by the numbered Rules, namely:
  (a) damage *to the property involved in the common maritime adventure* consequent upon a sacrifice or other general average act, which may still be allowed under Rule II, III or V, and
  (b) certain costs of preventing or minimising damage to the environment, which may be recoverable under Rule XI(d) or Rule VI.

Whilst there is a considerable overlap between *damage to the environment* and *the escape or release of pollutant substances*, the two expressions cover slightly different events, as explained in paragraphs C.31 and C.33, below.

C.30 **"In no case"** Despite the seeming paramountcy to be accorded to any provision commencing with the phrase *in no case*, these powerful words are sufficient only to exclude from general average claims sustainable solely under the provisions of Rule A, such as the example mentioned in paragraph C.26, above, or under any of the other *lettered* rules. As explained in the commentary on the Rule of Interpretation, claims under any of the *numbered* rules are not affected by any of the provisions of Rule C which are inconsistent with them. The words under review simply emphasise that the losses, etc., referred to in this paragraph are excluded even if they are the direct consequence of the general average act.

"losses, damages or expenses" These words are identical to the corresponding wording in the first paragraph of the Rule,[52] and are also intended to be of the same comprehensive nature. The exclusion contained in this paragraph therefore extends not only to physical loss or damage to the environment and to clean-up costs, but also to liabilities[53] incurred

[52] See para. C.22, *ante*.

[53] At the Sydney conference in 1994 the U.S. delegation was concerned that this wording did not, with complete certainty, exclude liabilities. Accordingly they made a formal statement in the plenary session of the Conference as follows:

> "The Delegation of the United States of America understands that the proposed York-Antwerp Rules 1994 exclude allowances in general average in respect of liability in consequence of the escape or release of pollutant substances from the property involved in the common maritime adventure."

The British delegation entertained no such doubts.

to third parties in respect of environmental damage. The original draft considered by the C.M.I. Conference at Sydney contained an express reference to liabilities, but this was deleted at the instigation of hull and cargo insurers.[54]

"in respect of damage to the environment" The expression *damage to the environment* is the same as that used in the International Convention on Salvage 1989,[55] where it is defined as meaning: C.31

> "substantial physical damage to human health or to marine life or resources in coastal or inland waters or areas adjacent thereto, caused by pollution, contamination, fire, explosion or similar major incidents."

The Convention, and its definition of damage to the environment, are expressly referred to in Rule VI(a), and it seems clear that the identical phrase *damage to the environment* used in Rule C is intended to have exactly the same meaning, with the result that it effectively incorporates the definition of the phrase contained in the Salvage Convention. The 1984 C.M.I. Report to I.M.C.O. on the draft Convention has the following comments on the definition:

> "By using the words 'substantial' and 'major' as well as the reference to 'pollution, explosion, contamination, fire' it is intended to make it clear that the definition does not include damage to any particular person or installation. There must be a risk of damage of a more general nature in the area concerned, and it must be a risk of substantial damage.
>
> During the Montreal Conference the words 'to human health or to marine life or resources' were added to exclude further from the concept cases where there may only be a risk of substantial physical damage to other property, *e.g.* warehouses or other buildings ashore.
>
> The use of the words 'coastal or inland waters' serves to make it clear that cases where there is only a risk of damage to the environment on the high seas are excluded. This is felt to be important since there would often be a possibility of speculative and inflated claims based on loose assertions that general environment damage to fishing or other ecology was involved. It must be stressed, however, that damage in coastal waters emanating from a ship in danger on the high seas is not excluded.
>
> As can easily be seen, the definition includes much more than pollution. It is not limited to risk of damage caused by oil or other specific cargoes. The use of the words 'explosion' and 'fire' in particular shows that it is the intention to cover all major incidents comprehensively."

It will therefore be observed that the provisions of Rule C relating to damage to the environment are by no means confined to pollution, and comprise damage resulting from any major incident. However, they do not include the following kinds of damage, whatever may be its cause:

[54] Some hull and cargo insurers, while not disputing that in certain circumstances liabilities would be allowable in general average under the York-Antwerp Rules, were anxious to avoid any express references to liabilities in the Rules, even in a provision excluding them from allowances.

[55] The Convention now has the force of law in England: see the Merchant Shipping Act 1995, s. 224 and Sched. 11.

(1) damage which affects only one person or installation. It follows from this that damage to a single pier, such as occurred in *Austin Friars S.S. Co. v. Spillers and Bakers*[56] would not be excluded by Rule C even if caused by an event which falls within the definition such as explosion or fire;
(2) damage which affects only buildings or installations ashore;
(3) damage which affects only deep-sea waters, without threatening coastal areas.

However where the damage results from the escape or release of a pollutant these situations will fall within the subsequent words of the paragraph, discussed in paragraph C.33, below.

C.32 The words *in respect of* have a wide meaning and include any losses, damages or expenses which are the result of or attributable to damage to the environment arising from the general average act. They may be contrasted with narrower expressions used elsewhere in the Rules, such as *in consequence of* (the expression used later in this paragraph of Rule C, and commented on in paragraph C.33, below). It seems probable that the intention was also to include losses, etc., which are the result of *alleged* or *threatened* damage to the environment, such as might arise if a national authority were to impose a fine on the shipowner in the erroneous belief that damage to the environment had occurred for which he was responsible, or were to insist on the taking of expensive measures in order to avoid damage (or further damage) to the environment. All such cases are therefore prima facie excluded from general average by Rule C, although the great majority of losses and expenses incurred in order to prevent or minimise threatened damage to the environment will fall within the specific provisions of Rule XI(d), and will therefore be allowable.

Although the wording of this part of the Rule does not make it as clear as it might, the Rule was not intended to exclude allowances in cases where the actual or threatened damage to the environment is not attributable to the property involved in the common maritime adventure or from any efforts made to safeguard the same, but to an external source. For example, the expense of measures taken to protect the ship and cargo from the consequences of a conflagration on another vessel or at a shore installation should not be excluded by the Rule, and should therefore be allowable so long as the measures comply with the requirements of Rule A, or of one of the numbered Rules.

C.33 **"or"** This word makes it clear that Rule C excludes from allowances in general average all losses damages and expenses which are *either* "in respect of damage to the environment" *or* "in consequence of the escape

[56] [1915] 1 K.B. 833; [1915] 3 K.B. 586.

or release of pollutant substances from the property involved in the common maritime adventure".

"in consequence of the escape or release of pollutant substances" As explained in paragraph C.31, above, the expression "damage to the environment" does not cover every situation where loss, damage or expense is caused by an escape or release of a pollutant from the ship or cargo, and Rule C therefore contains this further specific provision, the effect of which is to exclude all such losses, etc., from allowance in general average (unless they fall within the terms of one of the numbered Rules). *Escape* covers the case where the pollutant substance is emitted accidentally, and *release* where it is emitted by design. The effect of the words *in consequence of* is that there must have been an actual (that is, not merely an alleged or threatened) escape or release of the pollutant substance if this part of the Rule is to apply. However, if the threatened pollution damage is such as would amount to "damage to the environment" the case would fall within the antecedent provision of the Rule.

"from the property involved in the common maritime adventure." These words serve a dual purpose. In the first place they exclude from the operation of this paragraph of Rule C the case where general average expenses are incurred in consequence of the escape or release of a pollutant substance from another ship, or from a shore installation. Secondly, they make it clear that there must be an escape or release of the pollutant substance beyond the confines of ship and cargo; thus an escape or release of a pollutant from the ship into the cargo or vice versa falls outside the scope of the provision, with the result that the consequent loss or damage may be chargeable to general average. Damage to the outer hull of the ship, caused by an escape or release of her cargo or bunkers is only consistent with an escape or release beyond the confines of the ship and cargo, and is therefore prima facie barred by the Rule. However, such damage will be allowable under Rule II if it is the consequence of a sacrifice and is reasonably incurred.

Third Paragraph

"loss of market" Earlier versions of Rule C referred to loss of market as an example of indirect loss, whereas in English law it is usually regarded as a direct loss,[57] and a loss caused by a fall in the market at the destination is not too remote to be recoverable from a carrier by sea as damages for breach of contract.[58] The wording of the earlier versions could therefore have been interpreted as an indication that the expression **C.34**

[57] See *Australian Coastal Shipping v. Green* [1971] 1 Q.B. 456 at 481, *per* Lord Denning M.R., para, C.24, *ante*.

[58] See *Koufos v. C. Czarnikow* [1969] 1 A.C. 350. See also para. C.04, note 7, *ante*.

direct consequence in Rule C had a particularly narrow meaning, although it seems unlikely that this was actually the intention.[59] The 1994 Rule has eliminated this potential source of misunderstanding; loss of market is now excluded in its own right, and cannot be treated as having any influence on the meaning of *direct consequence.*

There is no authority on the meaning of *loss of market.* It clearly bars recovery of any loss resulting from market fluctuation during a period of delay. Thus if goods shipped specially for the Christmas market are delayed in consequence of a general average act on the voyage, and arrive in January physically sound but of considerably reduced value, the cargo owner has no claim in general average. However, it is submitted that Rule C does not exclude from general average a loss resulting from the goods becoming unsaleable, or less valuable, in the market at their destination, whether as a result of physical damage or as a result of legal or other obstacles. Thus the cargo's loss in value, in *Anglo-Argentine Livestock Agency v. Temperley S.S. Co.*[60] should be allowed under Rule C as it was under English law. That loss in value was not caused by delay, but by the goods becoming subject to the prohibition on import at the intended destination, as a direct result of the general average act.

The exclusion of claims for loss of market does not, of course, mean that the value of the cargo at destination is ignored in calculating the amount to be made good for loss or damage caused by a general average sacrifice. Rule XVI of the York-Antwerp Rules contains detailed provisions for calculating the amount made good, which is based on invoice value at destination.

C.35 **"any loss or damage sustained or expense incurred by reason of delay,"** The exclusion of loss, etc., by delay reflects English law on the subject.[61] Earlier versions of Rule C referred only to *loss or damage* through delay, leaving open the argument that *expense* incurred through delay was not caught by the exclusion.[62] In the 1994 Rule the drafting has been improved and the uncertainty removed, since the words *loss or damage sustained or expense incurred* mirror the language of the first two paragraphs of the Rule (discussed at paragraphs C.22 and C.30, above) and there can thus be no doubt that they are intended to be of equal width.

[59] See *Australian Coastal Shipping v. Green (ibid.)* [1971] 1 Q.B. 456 at 481, and at 487. The point is discussed at para. C.30 of the 11th ed., where this interpretation is rejected.

[60] [1899] 2 Q.B. 403. See para. C.07, *ante.*

[61] See paras. C.12. *et seq., ante.*

[62] On the ground that *expenses* were specifically referred to in the first paragraph of Rule C, but were omitted from the paragraph dealing with loss, etc., by delay. The merits of this argument are discussed at para. C.28 of the 11th. edition, where the view is expressed that, despite the deficiencies in the drafting of the Rule, *expenses* caused by delay did fall within the scope of this paragraph of the Rule, and were therefore excluded from general average.

"whether on the voyage or subsequently," The reason for the introduction of this phrase in 1950 has already been discussed.[63]

"delay" There are cases where it may be difficult to determine whether a loss is caused by a delay or by some other factor, for example: **C.36**

(1) Water used to extinguish a fire puts the refrigerating machinery out of action and the contents are ruined because their temperature rises above that at which they can be stored. Such loss has been allowed.
(2) A vessel puts into a port of refuge loaded down to summer load line. By the time she leaves, winter load lines have come into force and she is obliged to leave part of her cargo. This is seldom allowed.

"any indirect loss whatsoever" This is simply the corollary of the provisions of the first paragraph of the rule, which allows in general average only those losses, damages and expenses which are the *direct consequence* of the general average act. The meaning of that expression is discussed above at paragraph C.23. **C.37**

[63] See para. C.19, *ante*.

RULE D

THE EFFECT OF FAULT

ENGLISH LAW AND BACKGROUND

D.01 In the majority of cases in which a claim for contribution in general average is disputed, the defence raised is that the peril which gave rise to the general average act was caused by the fault of the person claiming contribution, for example the shipowner has failed to exercise due diligence to provide a seaworthy ship. The circumstances in which such a defence will succeed, both at common law and under the York-Antwerp Rules,[1] are here examined. With one possible exception,[2] there is no difference between English law and York-Antwerp Rules in their treatment of the effect of fault.

General Rule in English Law

D.02 If the necessity for a general average act arose as a result[3] of the fault of one of the parties to the adventure,[4] the act retains its general average character and contribution is due between the parties to the adventure, subject to the important exception that the party at fault is not entitled to recover contribution from any other at whose suit the fault was actionable[5] at the time at which the sacrifice or expenditure was made or incurred.[6] The justification for this exception has been attributed to the policy of the courts of avoiding circuity of action[7] and to the principle that a person shall not recover from any other person in respect of the consequences of his own wrong.[8] It has also been suggested that

[1] Rule D: see paras. D.22 *et seq.*, *post*.

[2] Where the liability of the person claiming contribution is limited by statue or by contact: see paras. D.08, D.10, D.31, *post*.

[3] The issue is whether the claimant "has by his own [actionable] fault occasioned the peril which immediately gave rise to the claim"; *Strang Steel & Co. v. A. Scott & Co.* (1889) 14 A.C. 601 at 608, per Lord Watson; and *Pirie & Co. v. Middle Dock Co.* (1881) 44 L.T. 426 at 429. But fault after the peril has arisen may also be relevant: *Eisenerz GmbH v. Federal Commerce & Navigation Co.* [1975] 1 Lloyd's Rep. 105.

[4] *Strang Steel & Co. v. A. Scott & Co.* (1889) 14 A.C. 601 at 609, P.C.; *Louis Dreyfus & Co. v. Tempus Shipping Co.* [1931] A.C. 726 at 747, H.L.

[5] *Schloss v. Heriot* (1863) 14 C.B. (N.S.) 59; *Strang Steel & Co. v. A. Scott & Co.* (*supra*) at 608; *Louis Dreyfus & Co. v. Tempus Shipping Co.* (*supra*) at 738, 747.

[6] *Goulandris Bros. Ltd v. B. Goldman & Sons Ltd* [1958] 1 Q.B. 74 at 104.

[7] *Schloss v. Heriot* (*supra*) at 64.

[8] *Goulandris Bros. Ltd v. B. Goldman & Sons Ltd* (*supra*) at 95.

contribution is irrecoverable because the sacrifice or expenditure by the party at fault is made or incurred for the benefit of that party alone and not for the benefit of the adventure as a whole, since the party at fault would have been liable to the proposed contributor in respect of the loss averted by the general average act.[9] In the ninth edition of the present work this was considered the better view. But (1) it encounters the same objection as the argument based on circuity of action in cases where the wrongdoer would be only partially liable[10]; (2) it is inconsistent with the right of a party not at fault to recover contribution from another party not at fault; and (3) it seems artificial to suppose, on the facts, that the motive was not the preservation of all the property involved.

Actionable Fault

Although the exception is usually expressed in terms of actionable fault,[11] the fault will frequently be actionable only in an artificial sense, if at all, since the general average act may avert the damage in respect of which an action would have lain. Thus if a ship is unseaworthy at the commencement of a voyage, as a result of want of due diligence on the part of her owner, and in consequence the master engages towage assistance to save the vessel and cargo from danger, the engagement of towage assistance will usually prevent any loss or damage to the cargo in respect of which an action could be maintained.[12] However in such a case, if the contract of carriage imposed upon the shipowner the obligation to exercise due diligence to make the ship seaworthy, the cargo owner would have a defence to a claim for contribution. The true test of actionable fault is therefore whether, if the general average act had not been performed with the result that the peril had operated, the person claiming contribution would have been legally liable to the person against whom contribution is claimed for the damage to the property of the latter.[13] A similar approach is adopted in determining whether an exceptions clause prevents the fault from being actionable.[14] **D.03**

[9] *Tempus Shipping Co. v. Louis Dreyfus & Co.* [1931] 1 K.B. 195 at 211, *per* Greer L.J. [1931] A.C. 726 at 742, *per* Lord Warrington (but see Viscount Dunedin at 734).

[10] *The Ettrick* (1881) 6 P.D. 127. See paras. D.08 and D.10, *post.*

[11] See the cases cited in nn. 5, 6, *ante.*

[12] The cargo owner would have a claim in contract for nominal damages, but no tort would have been committed. If, on the other hand, instead of the master engaging a tug under a towage contract, the ship and cargo had been salved and the cargo interests had incurred liability to the salvors, the shipowner would be liable for substantial damages.

[13] See *Louis Dreyfus & Co. v. Tempus Shipping Co. (supra); The Makedonia* [1962] 1 Lloyd's Rep. 316 at 339, 341. Such liability may arise out of the failure to perform the general average act (see paras. 00.56 *et seq., ante*), but liability which would have arisen solely out of such a failure must be ignored for the purpose of applying the test propounded here.

[14] See paras. D.04 *et seq., post.*

Effect of Contractual or Statutory Exemptions from Liability

D.04 The obligations normally undertaken by the carrier and the shipper under the contract of affreightment are described in outline elsewhere,[15] and it is these obligations which must in the first instance be determined in order to ascertain whether the peril which occasioned the general average act was caused by the failure of the party claiming contribution properly to perform his contractual obligations to the party from whom contribution is claimed. Where there is no contract between the parties it must likewise be determined whether the peril arose as a result of a failure by the person claiming contribution to comply with a duty owed to the other party in tort, or as a bailee. The next step is to ascertain whether the failure is actionable, or whether on the other hand it is excused by a statutory provision or (where the relationship between the parties is governed by contract) by the provisions of a contractual exceptions clause. The exempting provisions which may be relevant in determining this question take a number of different forms; they may, for example, (1) prevent any legal responsibility at all from arising in circumstances when it would otherwise arise; or (2) exclude any liability for "loss or damage" arising from a specified cause; or (3) limit liability to a particular sum; or (4) exonerate the shipowner from liability unless suit is brought within a specified period of time. It is desirable to examine these provisions separately for their effect on the existence of actionable fault. For this purpose no distinction in principle need be drawn between contractual and statutory exemptions.[16]

Provisions which prevent any legal responsibility from arising

D.05 It has always been accepted that exceptions clauses of the first category nullify the existence of any actionable fault, for all purposes including general average. In *The Carron Park*[17] a clause stating "neglect or default whatsoever of ... the servants of the shipowner always excepted" was held to prevent the shipowner from being under any responsibility for the entry of water into the holds, as a result of negligence by the ship's engineers in the operation of her valves, and therefore to preserve unaffected by that negligence the shipowner's right to contribution in general average. In the light of *Louis Dreyfus v. Tempus Shipping*[18] it is clear that statutory provisions in similar terms should receive exactly the same effect.

[15] See paras. 00.31 *et seq.*, *ante*.
[16] *Louis Dreyfus v. Tempus Shipping* [1931] A.C. 726.
[17] (1890) 15 P.D. 203. The decision was approved and followed by the Court of Appeal in *Milburn & Co. v. Jamaica Fruit Importing & Trading Co.* [1900] 2 Q.B. 540, where the relevant clause was in similar terms.
[18] [1931] A.C. 726.

Provisions which exclude liability for loss or damage

Until the decision of the House of Lords in *Louis Dreyfus and Co. v. Tempus Shipping Co.*[19] it was not clear whether provisions of this second type had the same effect. In that case, fire broke out on the voyage as a result of the failure to exercise due diligence to make the ship seaworthy, in breach of the contract of carriage. Expenses were incurred at a port of refuge, and the shipowner claimed contribution. Under section 502 of the Merchant Shipping Act 1894, the shipowner was exempt from liability for "loss or damage" caused by fire arising without his actual fault or privity. It was argued by the cargo owners that the shipowner's breach was actionable; the section merely relieved him of certain consequences of his default—namely liability for "loss or damage", and that it had no relevance to a claim for general average. This argument was accepted by Wright J.[20] and Scrutton L.J.,[21] but rejected by the majority of the Court of Appeal and by the House of Lords. Slesser L.J. considered that the correct test was whether any actionable liability would have lain on the party claiming contribution if the sacrifice or expenditure had not been made, and if the property had been lost, and he concluded: "it must be admitted that whatever the shipowner did to save the cargo, if he had not done it no action would have arisen."[22] In the House of Lords, Lord Dunedin considered that "an actionable wrong for which you can recover nothing is a contradiction in terms".[23] **D.06**

The same approach was adopted in *The Makedonia*,[24] where the exceptions clause provided that the deck cargo was "carried ... at the sole risk of the owner of such cargo" and excused the carrier from liability for "loss, damage or delay". The ship, which was unseaworthy, broke down and salvage services were engaged by the owner, who sought to recover in general average the cargo's share of the salvage award. This claim failed with regard to the under-deck cargo, but succeeded with regard to the deck cargo. Dealing with the argument that the exception clause dealt only with physical loss or damage, and not with pecuniary loss, Hewson J. said: "the shipowners were, as I see it, averting a physical loss for which they would not have been liable."[25] A similar decision had already been reached in Australia in *Westfal-Larsen v. Colonial Sugar Refining Co.*,[26] where the clause exempted the shipowner from responsibility for loss of or damage to goods on board, or for delay, unless caused by the personal want of due diligence of the owners or their manager to make the ship seaworthy, or by the personal act or **D.07**

[19] [1931] A.C. 726.
[20] [1930] 1 K.B. 699.
[21] [1931] 1 K.B. 195 at 207–208.
[22] *Ibid.* at 218.
[23] [1931] A.C. 726 at 739.
[24] [1962] P. 190; [1962] 1 Lloyd's Rep. 316 at 339–341.
[25] [1962] 1 Lloyd's Rep. 316 at 341.
[26] [1960] 2 Lloyd's Rep. 206.

omission or default of the owners or their manager. The ship was unseaworthy as a result of the negligence of the ship's engineers in taking on board the wrong type of fuel oil, she broke down on the voyage, and general average expenses were incurred. Neither the owners or their manager were personally at fault, and accordingly it was held by Walsh J. that the effect of the clause was that the cargo owners had no defence to a claim for contribution since "the threatened loss or damage to the goods, or delay in their transport, arose from a cause outside the area of the responsibility of the owners, as defined by the contract".[27]

Provisions which limit liability

D.08 Where the terms of the contract or statute merely limit the amount of the party's liability, as opposed to excluding it, they do not nullify the existence of actionable fault. The result is that, where the adjustment is not governed by the York-Antwerp Rules, nothing can be recovered.[28] For a discussion of the effect of the Rules, see paragraph D.29, below.

Provisions which exclude liability unless suit is brought within a defined period

In general, provisions of this nature will have no effect on the question of actionable fault, for the reasons described in paragraph D.12, below.

The Effect of Certain Specific Provisions

Having considered the general principles, it may be useful to examine the effect of certain widely encountered statutory or contractual provisions.

[27] *Ibid.* at 211. The case concerned the Baltime exceptions clause, which has subsequently been held by the House of Lords to be confined to responsibility for physical loss or damage to the goods, or delay, and to provide no protection against claims for financial loss: see *Tor Line v. Alltrans* [1984] 1 Lloyd's Rep. 123. In that case Lord Roskill expressed the view that *Westfal-Larsen* was wrongly decided, apparently on the ground that Walsh J. had erroneously interpreted the clause as providing protection against claims for financial loss as well as physical loss and damage. It is true that the construction of the clause adopted by Walsh J. leads inevitably to the conclusion that the clause covers financial loss, and therefore can no longer be regarded as sound. However, the reasons for his decision that contribution was recoverable which (in so far as they are relevant to the point under discussion here) are those contained in the passage quoted in the text, are not based on any erroneous belief that the clause provided protection against claims for financial loss, and remain perfectly valid even on the narrower interpretation of the clause adopted by the House of Lords. The *Tor Line* case was not concerned with general average, and none of the relevant authorities on actionable fault are referred to.

[28] There is no direct authority for this proposition, but it is submitted that it follows from *The Ettrick* (1881) 6 P.D. 127, and the equation of statutory with contractual exemptions from liability in *Louis Dreyfus & Co. v. Tempus Shipping Co.* [1931] A.C. 726, H.L.

Effect of section 186 of the Merchant Shipping Act 1995 (fire)

In cases to which this section applies, the shipowner cannot be made liable at the suit of the other interests for loss or damage and accordingly his "fault" is not actionable and he can recover contribution in general average.[29] No distinction is to be made between this section which prevents the recovery of losses from a shipowner and an exceptions clause which negatives a duty which would otherwise rest upon the shipowner.[30] **D.09**

Effect of section 185 of the Merchant Shipping Act 1995 (limitation of liability)

This section gives legal effect to the Convention on Limitation of Liability for Maritime Claims 1976. The Convention by limiting, as opposed to negativing, liability leaves the fault of the shipowner actionable and he is accordingly unable to recover contribution in general average,[31] at any rate where the York-Antwerp Rules do not apply.[32] **D.10**

Article IV, Rules 1 and 2 of the Hague or Hague-Visby Rules

Article IV Rules 1 and 2 of both the Hague and the Hague-Visby Rules confer on the carrier exemption from liability for loss or damage to or in connection with[33] goods arising from a variety of causes. It follows that when the peril which occasions the general average act arises from one of these causes the defence of actionable fault cannot be raised in answer to a claim for contribution. Most of these Hague and Hague-Visby Rule exceptions have no application if the underlying cause of the loss or damage is the negligence of the carrier or of his servants or agents, but some protect the carrier even in the event of negligence by his servants or agents, namely the exception of act, neglect or default in the navigation or the management of the ship,[34] and the exception of fire. **D.11**

[29] See *Louis Dreyfus & Co. v. Tempus Shipping Co.* [1931] A.C. 726, H.L., decided under the equivalent provisions of the Merchant Shipping Act 1894, s. 502.

[30] *Ibid.* at 739, 750.

[31] *The Ettrick* (1881) 6 P.D. 127; *Louis Dreyfus & Co. v. Tempus Shipping Co.* [1931] A.C. 726 at 747, H.L.

[32] As to the York-Antwerp Rules, see para. D.31, *post*.

[33] The Rules simply refer to "loss or damage", but this has been held to mean loss or damage to, or in connection with the carriage of, the goods: see *G.H. Renton & Co. Ltd v. Palmyra Trading Corporation* [1957] A.C. 149; *Adamastos Shipping Co. Ltd v. Anglo-Saxon Petroleum Co. Ltd* [1959] A.C. 133.

[34] See para. 00.44, *ante*.

Article III, Rule 6 of the Hague and the Hague-Visby Rules

D.12 Both the Hague and the Hague-Visby Rules contain examples of the fourth type of exemption clause referred to in paragraph D.04, above, which exonerate the carrier from liability unless suit is brought within a specified time. Thus Article III Rule 6 of the Hague Rules provides that the carrier shall be "discharged from all liability in respect of loss or damage"[35] unless suit is brought within one year of the delivery of the goods or the date when the goods ought to have been delivered. In *Goulandris Bros v. B. Goldman & Sons*[36] it was held that this provision did not prevent a cargo owner from raising actionable fault as a defence to the carrier's claim for contribution, even though he had not brought suit within one year for the purpose of establishing the actionable fault on the part of the carrier. The cargo owner was entitled to wait until an action for contribution was brought against him, whenever that might be, and to raise the defence of actionable fault at that time, because Article III Rule 6 only brings about a discharge of liabilities and not a barring of defences.[37] The case was decided under the York—Antwerp Rules,[38] but the same conclusion will hold good where the claim is governed by English law. It also holds good, it is submitted, where the contract of carriage incorporates the Hague-Visby Rules rather than the Hague Rules,[39] and it will apply *a fortiori* where the time-bar is merely procedural—that is where it bars the remedy rather than extinguishing the liability.

Fault on the Part of the Person from Whom Contribution is Claimed

D.13 We have so far been considering the effect of fault on the part of the person claiming contribution. What is the result in the converse case, where the accident which gave rise to the general average was caused by the fault of the party to the adventure from whom contribution is claimed? Clearly such a party cannot rely on his own fault as a defence to the claim for contribution, but if the fault was actionable at the suit of the person claiming contribution,[40] it will usually be more advantageous to the claimant to seek to recover his entire loss, as damages for breach of contract or in tort, and not merely a contribution towards it in general

[35] See n. 33, *ante*.
[36] [1958] 1 Q.B. 74.
[37] An additional ground for the decision was that "loss or damage" in Art. III, r. 6 did not include a liability to contribute in general average. *Sed quaere*; see para. 00.50, n. 47, and para. D.11, n. 33, *ante*.
[38] Rule D of the York-Antwerp Rules 1950. Subsequent amendments to Rule D have no effect on this conclusion.
[39] The equivalent wording in Art. III, r. 6, of the Hague-Visby Rules is "the carrier shall be discharged from all liability whatsoever in respect of the goods", and whilst this is in some respects rather wider than the provision in the Hague Rules it still only brings about a discharge of liabilities, and not a barring of defence.
[40] See para. D.03, *ante*, as to the meaning of actionable fault.

average. As a result, the claim in general average, although remaining perfectly valid, will often be subsumed in a larger claim for damages.

Thus in *Dixon v. Royal Exchange Shipping Co.*[41] the cargo owners claimed from the shipowner the entire value of cargo jettisoned, as damages on the grounds that the jettison resulted from the shipowner's breach of contract in taking a deck cargo; the shipowner accepted liability for a contribution in general average, but it was held that he was liable for the entire loss. Equally, if a shipowner incurs general average expense as a result of the loading by a shipper of dangerous cargo, without the master's knowledge or consent,[42] the shipowner may recover the entire expense from that shipper and not merely a contribution; and since the fault of the shipper does not deprive the act of its general average character the shipowner may also claim contribution from the owners of any cargo on board at the time of the general average act, the only qualification being that he is not entitled to recover more than once for the same loss. **D.14**

Exceptions Clauses in Favour of the Party from Whom Contribution is Claimed

In determining whether there has been actionable fault on the part of the person from whom contribution is claimed, regard must be had to all the exceptions clauses in the contract in favour of that party, on the principles explained above.[43] **D.15**

If the exempting provision negatives the existence of actionable fault on his part it will, of course, protect him from being held liable in damages in respect of the whole loss on the grounds discussed in paragraphs D.13 and D.14, above. However it does not follow that it will protect him against liability to contribute in general average towards the loss, and in practice it is very unlikely that it will have this effect, since the courts have consistently adopted the approach that a contractual or statutory provision exempting a party from liability will not be construed as referring to a liability to contribute in general average, unless it expressly so provides.

Thus in *Schmidt v. Royal Mail Steamship Co.*,[44] where the bill of lading contained an exception of "fire on board", it was held that this did not prevent the charterer from claiming a general average contribution from the owner in respect of cargo sacrificed in extinguishing the fire. Blackburn **D.16**

[41] [1886] 12 App.Cas. 11. See para. 1.12, *post*. In *Gould v. Oliver* (1840) 2 Man. & Gr. 208 the cargo owner, who had succeeded in a previous action in recovering a general average contribution to the loss of his deckload by jettison, brought a second action to recover his full loss and claimed damages on the grounds that the jettison was caused by bad stowage.

[42] See paras. 00.59 *et seq.*, *ante*.

[43] See paras. D.04–D.10, *ante*.

[44] (1876) 45 L.J.Q.B. 646.

J. expressed the view that: "the office of the bill of lading is to provide for the rights and liabilities of the parties in reference to the contract to carry, and is not concerned with liabilities to contribution in general average." The same conclusion was reached in *Crooks v. Allen*[45] where the provisions of the contract exempted the shipowner from liability "for any damage to any goods which is capable of being covered by insurance", and in *Burton v. English*[46] where the contract provided that a deck load was to be carried "at merchant's risk". In all of these cases the clause in question, whilst it prevented the shipowner from being held liable in damages, was held to have no bearing on his liability in general average.

D.17 In *Greenshields, Cowie & Co. v. Stephen & Sons Ltd*[47] the same approach was adopted towards a statutory provision. A cargo of coal ignited spontaneously as a result of inherent vice. The cargo was sacrificed and the shipowner, in defence to a claim for general average contribution, relied on the implied exception of inherent vice in the contract of carriage, and the statutory exception of fire under section 502 of the Merchant Shipping Act 1894. These arguments were rejected, since the implied exception, while providing a defence to a claim for damage or non-delivery, had no relevance to a claim for contribution, and "the statute is not dealing with general average at all".[48] the result would have been different if there had been a breach of contract in the shipping of the coal, since the loss would then have arisen as a result of the actionable fault of the cargo owner who was claiming contribution. However, the shipowner had agreed to carry the coal with full knowledge of its nature.

Claims for contribution in general average are, by Article III(a), expressly excluded from the scope of the Convention on the Limitation of Liability for Maritime Claims 1976, thus ruling out any argument of the kind raised by the defendant in *Greenshields, Cowie & Co. v. Stephen & Sons Ltd.*

D.18 It follows that if a party wishes to be relieved from the obligation to contribute, he must use express words referring to contribution in general

[45] (1879) 5 Q.B.D. 38.

[46] (1883) 12 Q.B.D. 218.

[47] [1908] A.C. 431.

[48] *Ibid.* at 436, *per* Lord Halsbury. This phrase was relied upon by the cargo owners in their unsuccessful argument in *Louis Dreyfus & Co. v. Tempus Shipping Ltd* (para. D.06, *supra*) as demonstrating that the statutory exception in s. 502 of the Merchant Shipping Act was irrelevant for all purposes of general average. The House of Lords held that the views expressed by Lord Halsbury were confined to the context where the provision was relied upon as a defence to a claim for contribution. There is no inconsistency in approach between the decisions on "actionable fault" and those on the effect of exceptions in favour of the person from whom contribution is claimed. In each case the question is where the loss would have fallen if the sacrifice or expenditure had not been made. In the *Greenshield* case, if the general average act had not been carried out, some of the resulting damage (namely that to the ship) would have been borne by the shipowner, and neither the statute nor the contractual exception of inherent vice would have entitled him to claim that loss from the cargo owner. It would therefore be illogical if those provisions were to protect him against a claim for contribution by the cargo owner.

average. This is sometimes done with regard to deck cargo and dangerous cargo.[49]

Special considerations apply when the exception clause relied on is a contractual time limit for bringing actions. Here a different approach has been adopted by the courts, and the time limit will normally be construed as applying to a claim for general average contribution, at any rate where the obligation to contribute in general average is contractual.[50] The effect of such time limits is considered in more detail below.[51] **D.19**

General Average Resulting From Fault of Cargo

When a claim in general average is resisted on the ground of fault it is usually the fault of the shipowner which is in issue; but this is not always so. For example, cargo which has ignited spontaneously may be jettisoned, or damaged by firefighting operations and the shipowner and other cargo owners may seek to defend a claim for contribution by the owner of the sacrificed cargo on the ground that the sacrifice arose as a result of the fault of the cargo itself. **D.20**

Until the decision in *Greenshields, Cowie & Co. v. Stephen & Sons Ltd*[52] the view was sometimes advanced that in such a case contribution could not be recovered in respect of sacrifice of cargo if it was the inherent vice of the cargo itself which had caused the danger. However, this view has been said to involve "a complete fallacy",[53] and it is now settled beyond argument that exactly the same principle applies in this case as in any other. Contribution can be recovered unless the danger arose as a result of actionable fault on the part of the owner[54] of the cargo sacrificed; it is no defence to the claim merely to show that the damage arose from the inherent vice of the cargo.[55] **D.21**

[49] *e.g.* Art. IV, r. 6 of the Hague Rules (dangerous cargo); see para. 00.60, *ante*.

[50] See paras. 00.19 *et seq.*, *ante*.

[51] Under *Enforcing Rights of Contribution*, paras. 30.71 *et seq.*, *post*.

[52] [1908] A.C. 431, see para. D.17, *ante*.

[53] *Pirie v. Middle Dock Co.* (1881) 4 Asp.M.L.C. 388 at 391, *per* Watkin Williams J.

[54] See paras. 00.58 *et seq.*, *ante*, as to the obligation of the shipper with regard to the nature of the goods shipped, and the question whether those obligations are transferred to a bill of lading holder.

[55] See *Johnson v. Chapman* (1865) 19 C.B. (N.S.) 563; *Pirie v. Middle Dock Co.* (1981) 4 Asp. M.L.C. 388; *Greenshields Cowie v. Stephen* [1908] A.C. 431. Consideration may need to be given in such a case to the separate question whether the cargo was effectively lost anyway. See paras. 3.01 *et seq.*, *post*.

Historical Development and Practice of Rule D

D.22 The 1924 Rule reproduced the Antwerp Rule 1903,[56] with the substitution of the word *fault* for *default.*

The intention of those who drafted the Rule seems to have been to try to separate rights under the contract of affreightment from rights in general average.[57] Logically such a separation must result in rights in general average being unimpaired by any breach of the contract of affreightment, whether or not the claimant be the party in default. In practice the Rule has been interpreted as affirming that the rights in general average of "innocent" parties are unaffected by any breach of the contract of affreightment, but not as improving the common law position of the party in fault. This construction seems to accord with the intentions of the Antwerp Conference of 1903 and the Stockholm Conference of 1924.

York-Antwerp Rules 1924 and York-Antwerp Rules 1950

D.23 The Rule was in the same terms as that set out below, except that it ended *but this shall not prejudice any remedies which may be open against that party for such fault.*

York-Antwerp Rules 1974

In 1974 the final words of the Rule were enlarged so as to provide *but this shall not prejudice any remedies <u>or defences</u> which may be open against <u>or to</u> that party in respect of such fault.* The effect, of this alteration is considered below.[58]

York-Antwerp Rules 1994

D.24 There was no change. A proposal was made[59] to amend the Rule to provide that a party from whom contribution was claimed should be obliged in the first instance to pay the contribution properly assessed on his interest, and only then be entitled to raise the issue of actionable fault, in separate proceedings to recover the amount already paid—"pay first sue later". However, the proposal was strongly criticised by cargo interests as being a serious inroad into the principle, adopted by many national laws, that actionable fault is a *defence* to a claim for contribution,

[56] See para. 00.80, *ante.*

[57] See papers by Kennedy L.J. and T.G. Carver in *The Journal of Comparative Legislation,* Vol. V, p. 221, 224.

[58] See para. D.31, *post.*

[59] By the Association Internationale de Dispacheurs Europeens.

rather than being merely a matter of counterclaim, and no national delegation could be found to support it.

Rule D

Rights to contribution in general average shall not be affected, though the event which gave rise to the sacrifice or expenditure may have been due to the fault of one of the parties to the adventure, but this shall not prejudice any remedies or defences which may be open against or to that party in respect of such fault.

Construction

The object of the rule is to keep all questions of alleged fault outside the average adjustment and to preserve the legal position at the stage of enforcement. The first part of the rule permits an adjustment to be prepared on the assumption that the casualty occurred without the fault of any party to the adventure. The second part of the rule then operates as a proviso to the first, enabling the prima facie rights of the parties derived under the first part to be defeated by the remedies which are preserved by the second part.[60] **D.25**

To illustrate the principles set forth earlier in this consideration of Rule D, a couple of practical and everyday examples may be of value. **D.26**

First, let it be assumed that a shipowner fails to exercise due diligence to provide a seaworthy ship, as the direct result of which the vessel sustains a machinery breakdown, and for the common safety, is obliged to put or be towed into a port of refuge to effect repairs.

A general average situation exists, the shipowner has incurred general average expenditure, and it is therefore perfectly in order for an adjustment to be prepared. However, the cargo are entitled to refuse payment of any general average contribution demanded of them.

If the preparation of the adjustment in such circumstances appears to be a somewhat futile operation, or the bona fides of the adjuster in preparing such an adjustment be questioned, it should be noted that the adjustment will generally be required in any event in order that the shipowner may claim:

(1) The ship's proportion of general average from the hull insurers, whose policies customarily preclude the denial of liability on the grounds of unseaworthiness of the vessel.

[60] *Goulandris Bros Ltd v. B. Goldman & Sons Ltd* [1958] 1 Q.B. 74 at 92–93.

(2) The cargo's proportion of general average from his Protecting and Indemnity Association, if unrecovered from the cargo interests themselves.

Further, the adjuster is concerned only with whether a general average situation exists, and it does not fall within his province or competence to determine and adjudge whether the ship was seaworthy or not, or whether the shipowner has failed to exercise due diligence to provide a seaworthy ship.

D.27 For our second and more complex example, let it be similarly assumed that the shipowner fails to exercise due diligence to provide a seaworthy ship, as the direct result of which the vessel strands and is obliged to jettison cargo and incur expenses admissible as general average within the terms of the York-Antwerp Rules.

A general average adjustment may be prepared showing figures such as the following:

Shipowner's general average expenditure	100,000
Jettison of cargo	900,000
	1,000,000

An owner of cargo delivered in sound condition may be shown liable in the adjustment to pay a general average contribution of 10,000, effectively comprising:

1,000	due to the shipowner in respect of expenditure incurred by him and
9,000	due to the owners of the jettisoned cargo.
10,000	

The cargo interest may legitimately decline to pay the 1,000 nominally due to the shipowner whose fault has brought about the stranding, but he ought and must contribute his 9,000 share of the loss suffered by the innocent owners of the jettisoned cargo.

A collective claim of 900,000 can then be made against the shipowner by all those parties who have suffered or "made good" the loss by jettison of 900,000.

This procedure may again appear ponderous and circuitous, but the cargo interests suffering the loss by jettison will at least recoup their loss with some degree of certainty and within a reasonable period of time, whereas it could take several years to prosecute and recover their direct claim against the shipowner—or he may be without funds or uninsured.

D.28 **"event"** In line with English law, this word refers to the original accident or occurrence which occasioned the sacrifice or expenditure.[61] Fault at subsequent stages may also be relevant, but will not necessarily have the same effect. Thus if the measures adopted to avert the peril are wholly unreasonable there will be no general average act within the definition of Rule A, or within the requirement of the new Rule Paramount,[62] and Rule D will not become relevant at all. If the measures adopted are reasonable but are negligently carried out, Rule C or the rule of English law as to remoteness will normally prevent recovery of any additional loss resulting from the negligence of the person claiming contribution,[63] and where that additional loss has fallen upon another party, the rights of the latter under the contract of carriage in respect of that negligence will be preserved.[64]

"fault" Fault is not defined and its meaning falls to be determined in accordance with the proper law of the contact,[65] or, it is submitted, more correctly in accordance with the law governing the adjustment. As a matter of English law it means a legal wrong which is actionable as between the parties at the time at which the sacrifice or expenditure is made or incurred.[66] **D.29**

"remedies or defences" This is similarly undefined and resort must be had to the appropriate system of law.[67] As a matter of English law the word "remedies" included defences as well as cross claims and the 1950 Rule thus preserved for an innocent party to the adventure the equitable defence that a party at fault cannot recover contribution in respect of the consequences of his own wrong.[68] **D.30**

"open against or to that party" The party in question is the party to the adventure whose fault occasioned the event which gave rise to the general average act. The purpose of the reference to the remedies and defences open *against* that party is obvious, and has been considered above.[69] The reason for expressly preserving the remedies and defences open *to* the party at fault is less apparent. If it is merely to preserve his right to contribution where his fault is not actionable at all it is superfluous, at any rate in English law, since the 1950 Rule clearly had this effect anyway. It is submitted that the addition of the words *or to* in 1974 may well produce the result that a party claiming contribution, **D.31**

[61] *Federal Commerce & Navigation Ltd v. Eisenerz GmbH* [1975] 1 Lloyd's Rep. 105 at 110.

[62] See paras. PRE. 21–PRE. 25 and A.84–A.86, *ante*. The position is the same under English law: see the Marine Insurance Act 1906, s. 66(1), para. A.05, *ante*.

[63] See paras. C.01 *et seq.*, *ante*.

[64] See paras. 00.31 *et seq.*, *ante*.

[65] *Goulandris Bros Ltd v. B. Goldman & Sons Ltd* [1958] 1 Q.B. 74 at 91. *Cf.* paras. 30.32 *et seq.*, *post*.

[66] *Ibid.* at 104.

[67] *Ibid.* at 93.

[68] *Ibid.* at 98, 100.

[69] See paras. D.25, D.29, D.30, *ante*.

even where his fault is actionable, can rely on any limit of liability which would have been open to him if the sacrifice or expenditure had not been made and the property imperilled had been lost, and can claim contribution to any loss in excess of that limit. The expression "remedies or defences" is wide enough to extend to a right to limit liability.[70] In considering whether the remedy or defence is "open in respect of such fault" it is submitted that the same approach should be adopted as in *Louis Dreyfus and Co. v. Tempus Shipping Ltd*[71] and the *The Makedonia,*[72] and that the relevant question is to determine what the liability of the person at fault would have been for the consequent loss or damage of the property imperilled if the sacrifice or expenditure had not been made.

D.32 **"in respect of such fault."** This refers back to the earlier part of the Rule, and to fault which has caused an event giving rise to the sacrifice or expenditure. It does not include fault by one of the parties to the adventure, subsequent to the general average act, which causes independent loss or damage. In this latter case a remedy will generally be afforded by the contract of carriage. The law of general average does not affect that remedy, and Rule D is not needed to preserve it.[73]

D.33 *Deviation.* An unjustifiable deviation is within the meaning of "fault" as a matter of English law. However, it merits separate mention as it gives rise to special rights or remedies, the other party to the contract being entitled to treat the deviation as going to the root of the contract and to declare himself no longer bound by the contract terms.[74] The effect of deviation upon rights to contribution in general average are discussed in the sections on Principles of Carriage by Sea and Enforcing Rights of Contribution.[75]

United States Law

D.34 Rule D does not obviate the necessity for the inclusion of a Jason or similar clause in the contract of carriage. In the absence of such a clause, it is a defence to a claim for general average contribution that the necessity for the general average act arose from the fault of the carrier notwithstanding that he is protected from liability by an exceptions clause.[76]

[70] See *Goulandris Brothers Ltd v. B. Goldman & Sons Ltd* [1958] 1 Q.B. 74 at 100 as to the scope of the word "remedies".
[71] [1931] 1 K.B. 195; [1931] A.C. 726.
[72] [1962] P. 190; [1962] 1 Lloyd's Rep. 316 at 339–341.
[73] *Federal Commerce and Navigation Ltd v. Eisenerz GmbH* [1970] 2 Lloyd's Rep. 332; [1975] 1 Lloyd's Rep. 105. See also para. D.28, *ante*.
[74] *Hain S.S. Co. Ltd v. Tate & Lyle* (1936) 41 Com. Cas. 350 at 354, *per* Lord Atkin.
[75] See paras. 00.35, 00.36, *ante*., and paras. 30.57 *et seq.*, *post*.
[76] See paras. 00.52–00.53, *ante*.

Rule E

Onus of Proof

Historical Development and Practice

Rule E appeared for the first time in the 1924 Rules and remained unaltered until 1994. In its original form it did no more than to provide that the burden of proof lay on the party claiming contribution. In 1994 two paragraphs were added to the Rule, the first of which imposes a time limit of one year for notifying claims to the adjuster, and the second of which imposes a time limit for producing evidence to the adjuster of losses and of contributory values. If these time limits are not complied with, the adjuster is entitled to make his own assessment on the material before him, which can only be challenged on limited grounds. **E.01**

York-Antwerp Rules 1924

In its original form the Rule was as follows: **E.02**

> The onus of proof is upon the party claiming in general average to show that the loss or expense claimed is properly allowable as general average.

York-Antwerp Rules 1950 and 1974

No change, though in 1974 the International Subcommittee of the C.M.I. had proposed a further paragraph reading:

> Thereafter the onus of proof is upon the party refusing to contribute in general average to show that he is not liable to contribute.

This was rejected at the Hamburg Conference, not because it was thought to be incorrect but on the ground that it was unnecessary and might cause confusion.

York-Antwerp Rules 1994

Before the Sydney Conference, concern had been expressed at the length of time sometimes required in order to obtain the relevant information relating to losses and contributory values from the parties to the adventure. In an attempt to speed up this process Rule E was expanded by the addition of new provisions, the effect of which has been **E.03** summarised in paragraph E.01 above.[1] A further proposal[2] with the same object, namely to impose a time limit for commencing proceedings to recover contribution, had received little support and was not put forward at the Conference.

RULE E

The onus of proof is upon the party claiming in general average to show that the loss or expense claimed is properly allowable as general average.

All parties claiming in general average shall give notice in writing to the average adjuster of the loss or expense in respect of which they claim contribution within 12 months of the date of the termination of the common maritime adventure.

Failing such notification, or if within 12 months of a request for the same any of the parties shall fail to supply evidence in support of a notified claim, or particulars of value in respect of a contributory interest, the average adjuster shall be at liberty to estimate the extent of the allowance or the contributory value on the basis of the information available to him, which estimate may be challenged only on the ground that it is manifestly incorrect.

CONSTRUCTION

First Paragraph

General observations.

E.04 This paragraph seems to present no real problems of construction and has been mentioned in only one reported English case.[3] It appears to state a very obvious truth, almost a truism it might seem. However, since national laws may differ on the point, it is no doubt considered desirable that the onus of proof that the loss is properly claimable as general average should be clearly and definitely thrown upon the claimant. So far as concerns English law it does no more than reflect the ordinary rule, that the onus lies upon a claimant to prove the facts necessary to

[1] The British M.L.A. and A.I.D.E. had both prepared drafts, not differing greatly in substance, of recommended additions to the Rule. The International Standing Committee on General Average of C.M.I. then produced its own draft. The Rule in its final form adopts the A.I.D.E. draft for the second paragraph, and the I.S.C. draft, with one significant amendment, for the third paragraph.

[2] As with the proposals actually adopted at Sydney, this proposal also was advanced by the British M.L.A.

[3] *The Seapool* [1934] P. 53 at 61.

support his claim. Once the claimant has established that an allowance is due, if the other parties wish to defeat the claim on the grounds of, for example, fault, the onus shifts to them to do so.

Standard of proof

The paragraph does not mention the *standard* of proof, which may vary from country to country.[4] English law requires that the necessary facts must be proved on the balance of probability; and since the standard of proof is a matter of procedure rather than substance,[5] this standard will be applied in any legal proceedings in the United Kingdom, whatever the standard imposed by the law governing the adjustment. The average adjuster will likewise apply the standard of proof required by the law of the country in which he operates. Equally Rule E is not concerned with *methods* of proof, which are also governed by the rules of evidence of the *lex fori*.[6] The mere production of a general average adjustment is not, in English law, proof of anything,[7] except where the York-Antwerp Rules 1994 apply, and the adjuster has made an estimate of losses or contributory values under the third paragraph of Rule E. But in practice it is almost unknown for the figures in an adjustment to be challenged in court, even if the principles applied are in dispute. **E.05**

To require that the claimant must prove his claim does not mean that he must have direct and precise evidence of every fact upon which it is based. Such evidence is often unobtainable in establishing what occurred during an emergency at sea; a recording angel does not stand by during an emergency jettison making a precise and accurate tally of each separate package or quantity of bulk cargo jettisoned. It is often necessary to reach a solution by drawing inferences from the facts that are definitely established, making use of common sense and experience. **E.06**

The greatest problems with regard to the onus of proof are likely to arise in cases of underwater damage to the bottom of a ship[8] alleged to have been sustained in efforts to refloat after stranding, and the problem can occasionally be exacerbated in these modern times, when ships are regularly drydocked only a intervals of two years or more. Where the balance of probabilities that the bottom damage might have been caused **E.07**

[4] Selmer, *Survival of General Average*, p. 62, instances the marked difference between the laws of Norway and Denmark in the degree of proof required to establish whether damage to the bottom of the ship was sustained in efforts to refloat.

[5] See Dicey and Morris *The Conflict of Laws* (12th ed.), p. 179.

[6] *Ibid.* p. 174.

[7] *Chandris v. Argo Insurance Co.* [1963] 2 Lloyd's Rep. 65 at 76. In the U.S. an adjustment is prima facie proof of quantum, if a general average act has been proved and the contract contains a general average agreement: *The Clydewater* [1967] A.M.C. 1474.

[8] See the further remarks relating to Rule VII in para. 7.10, *post*, and the case of *Sea-Land Service Inc. v. Aetna Insce. Co.* (1976) A.M.C. 2164; [1977] 2 Lloyd's Rep. 84, there referred to; also para. E.04, n.4, *ante*.

either by stranding or by efforts to refloat is *equal*, clearly the onus of proof has not been satisfied and there can be no allowance in general average. This contrasts with the case where it is known (or can be assumed) that a loss or damage is the result of *two* causes. Thus, if a cargo which has been force-discharged at a port of refuge arrives at final destination with shortage of two per cent and the normal shortage is only one per cent, it is reasonable to allow as general average the extra loss of one per cent as being caused by the forced discharge.

Effect on the preparation of an adjustment

E.08 The language of the first paragraph of Rule E might suggest that if a party wishes to claim any loss or expenditure as general average the responsibility is on him to submit his claim to the average adjuster, supported by the necessary evidence, failing which the adjuster should ignore it. The practice is different, and when the shipowner has appointed an average adjuster to adjust what appears prima facie to be a case of general average, the adjuster will take upon himself the responsibility of acting as agent for all the parties to the adventure, seek and collect all the relevant evidence as to the nature of the casualty and the ensuing losses and expenses, and then act as both prosecuting and defence counsel in arguing the merits of each claim, and finally as arbitrator. Thus, if either the shipowner or cargo interests overlook a claim for an expenditure incurred or, say, some loss or damage to cargo caused by a forced discharge, the average adjuster will put in hand the inquiries necessary to elicit the production of the necessary documents to support the claim.

E.09 This practice is implicitly recognised in the second and third paragraphs of Rule E, and it in no way offends against the first paragraph of the Rule, which is concerned with the resolution of disputed claims once the evidence has been presented. But this does not mean that the average adjuster is free to ignore the burden of proof. Once he has collected what evidence he can, he must decide whether the facts necessary to support an allowance are established on the balance of probability. If they are not, or if the probabilities are equal, no allowance should be given.

Construction

E.10 **"the party claiming in general average"** It is submitted that these words include not only those parties who are net creditors in the general average, but also those who have incurred any loss or expense which ought to be the subject of an allowance.

Second Paragraph

"All parties claiming in general average" See paragraph E.10, above. **E.11**

"the average adjuster" See the commentary under the third paragraph of the Rule at paragraph E.14, below.

"the date of the termination of the common maritime adventure." The problems which may arise in identifying the date when the adventure terminates are discussed in the commentary under Rule G.[9] Although the words of Rule E differ from the corresponding expression in Rule G—"the time ... when ... the adventure ends"—there does not appear to be any ground for distinguishing between them.

Third Paragraph

General observations

This part of the Rule reflects the practice described in paragraph E.08, above, that the average adjuster will pursue the question whether a party is entitled to an allowance, and seek to obtain evidence of allowable losses, even where a party has himself advanced no claim, or has failed to put forward any evidence in support of it. Although the obligations imposed by Rule E are directed to the parties to the adventure, it is implicit that the average adjuster has to act properly and promptly in the performance of his duties. In particular, he should: **E.12**

(1) formally request any claimants in general average (and in particular the shipowner) to furnish the necessary documentary evidence in support of their claims;
(2) send a prompt reminder for a copy of the commercial invoice from any cargo interests who have not furnished the same with their valuation form;
(3) whenever there is an indication that a cargo interest has suffered loss or damage make a prompt request that particulars of the same be provided;
(4) in any case where after the lapse of 12 months the evidence supplied is inadequate or inconclusive, promptly proceed to make a fair estimation of the claim or contributory value, as the case may be, and attempt to agree the same on this basis with the party concerned.

The concluding provisions of the paragraph are a significant departure from the English law rule that an adjustment has no legal effect, and

[9] See paras. G.22–G.45, *post*.

certain questions to which this gives rise are discussed in paragraphs E.14 and E.15, below.

Construction

E.13 **"Failing such notification,"** That is the notification required under the provisions of the second paragraph of the Rule, within the 12-month period there laid down.

"evidence in support of a notified claim, or particulars of value in respect of a contributory interest," On the face of it, the evidence and particulars which must be supplied are those requested by the adjuster, however detailed, but there is probably an implied requirement that the adjuster shall act reasonably and in accordance with usual practice in deciding how much information to request.

E.14 **"the average adjuster"** In English law there is no legal requirement that a professional adjuster will be employed; the shipowner is at liberty to produce his own adjustment, as indeed is a cargo owner; consistently with this liberal approach, there is nothing to prevent the cargo owner from employing his own professional adjuster, even if the shipowner also employs one. None of this matters in English law, because nothing in the adjustment binds any of the parties to the adventure.[10] In contrast, where the third paragraph of Rule E applies, it renders the adjustment prima facie binding as regards allowances and contributory values, subject to challenge only on limited grounds, and thus confers a distinct legal status on the adjustment.[11] Two questions therefore arise:

(1) When the Rules apply, is the effect of Rule E to oblige the shipowner[12] to employ a professional adjuster?
(2) Does the third paragraph of Rule E apply only if a professional adjuster is employed?

It is submitted, although with considerable diffidence,[12a] that the answer to the first of these questions is "no", and to the second "yes". The paragraphs which were added to the Rule E in 1994 reflect the almost invariable practice to employ a professional adjuster, and it seems

[10] See *Wavertree Sailing Ship Co. v. Love* [1897] A.C. 373, and the other cases referred to in paras. 30.03–30.04, *post.*

[11] In similar vein, Rule XXII, which confers on "the average adjuster" the power to certify the making of payments on account or refunds out of the special account into which cash deposits have been paid, also seems to be based on the assumption that a professional adjuster will be employed.

[12] If such an obligation is imposed, it can in practice only be on the shipowner, since it is upon him that lies the duty of procuring an adjustment: see n.13, below. See also para. 30.08, *post.*

[12a] It is noteworthy that in 1983, *i.e.* before the provisions under discussion were added to Rule E, the Privy Council regarded it as an open question whether the shipowner was obliged to employ a professional adjuster: see para. 30.06, *post.*

reasonably clear, in the light of their content, that the assumption that this practice will be followed is to be regarded as fundamental to their operation. On the other hand they impose no express requirement that a professional adjuster be employed, and it is not necessary to imply any such requirement. The Rules are perfectly workable in the case where no professional adjuster is employed, even though the new paragraphs of the Rule are inapplicable.

A further question is, who is "*the* average adjuster" in the case where more than one is employed? Since it is upon the shipowner[13] that the duty lies of procuring an adjustment it should follow that the professional adjuster appointed by him is "the average adjuster" for the purpose of the clause, and that an adjuster appointed by any of the other parties to the adventure can only occupy this role if the shipowner makes it clear that he does not wish to engage an adjuster himself, or delays unduly in procuring an adjustment. Once an adjustment has been produced by an adjuster who qualifies as "the average adjuster", as described above, which contains estimates of allowances and contributory values pursuant to the liberty conferred on the adjuster by Rule E, any other adjuster who is subsequently employed will likewise be bound by the estimates of allowances and contributory values adopted in the original adjustment, unless they are manifestly incorrect.[14] **E.15**

It is the practice in some countries for cargo interests to appoint their own co-adjuster, whose function is to assist in obtaining details of losses and contributory values from cargo, and to check, before publication, the adjustment prepared by the shipowner's adjuster.

"shall be at liberty" The adjuster's liberty to make an estimate of allowances or contributory values arises as soon as the relevant 12-month period has expired (that is, 12 months from the termination of the adventure for notifying general average loss or expense, and 12 months from the date of the adjuster's request for furnishing evidence of the loss or expense or particulars of the contributory value). However, the adjuster is not obliged to exercise this liberty immediately. He may allow the parties further time, and take into account information which becomes available to him later, and there are some situations when he should take this course: see paragraph E.18, below. **E.16**

"to estimate the extent of the allowance or the contributory value" The purpose of this phrase is to give the adjuster power to make factual assumptions and estimates of value in order to fill in gaps in the **E.17**

[13] See *Crooks v. Allen* (1895) 5 Q.B.D. 38, para. 30.43, *post.*

[14] The Rule does not preclude the engagement of more than one adjuster, as occurred in *The Bijela*, where successive professional adjustments were drawn up (see the report of the proceedings at first instance at [1992] 1 Lloyd's Rep. 626 at 638). However, if the York-Antwerp Rules 1994 had applied, the second adjusters would have been bound by any such estimates properly made by the original adjusters under Rule E.

information available to him. As this power will only have become exercisable because a party to the adventure has failed to notify a claim, or to supply the information required of him, in accordance with the provisions of the Rule there may be a temptation to make assumptions and draw inferences which are adverse to the interests of that party. However, at any rate so far as concerns estimating contributory values, the Rule contains no justification for adopting this course, and the adjuster must make his estimate even-handedly on the material available. The position is slightly different when it comes to estimating allowable loss and expense. Here the first paragraph of the Rule places the onus of proof upon the party claiming the allowance, and the adjuster should give effect to this when making his estimate under the third paragraph. If, as a result of a party's failure to provide the required information, the adjuster is unable to conclude on the balance of probability that the party has suffered any allowable loss, or a particular item of loss, he should exclude it altogether.

E.18 **"on the basis of the information available to him,"** On the face of it, this means the information available at the time when the adjuster makes his estimate, and the adjuster is entitled to ignore any information subsequently received. However, there is probably an implicit requirement that the adjuster shall keep any estimate which he makes under review, and revise it if appropriate in the light of any relevant new information. Clearly there must come a point of time at which the adjuster becomes entitled to make a final estimate, which he is not obliged to change in the light of subsequent information, and, if the Rule is not to be unworkable, this point must at the latest be the date when the adjustment is published. However, there are good practical reasons for saying that it is reached at an earlier date, namely when the preparation of the adjustment is so far advanced that to alter the amount in question would involve unreasonable delay and expense.

E.19 **"which estimate may be challenged only on the ground that it is manifestly incorrect."** The restriction on the right of challenge affects all parties equally, and it makes no difference whether the challenge is mounted by the party who failed to supply the information or another party. It was recognised at Sydney that this could sometimes operate rather harshly against parties not in default,[15] but it was decided to make the restriction all-embracing in the interests of simplicity and finality.

E.20 Unfortunately the Rule does not make clear at which date, and on the basis of what material, the correctness of the estimate falls to be determined, and this is by no means an easy question. To allow the party in default to challenge the estimate on the basis of new material, which

[15] In both the British M.L.A. and the A.I.D.E. draft proposals the restriction on the right of challenge only applied to the party who had failed to supply the information.

he failed to produce to the adjuster at the proper time, seems to deprive the Rule of some of its intended effect. On the other hand, it could in some cases produce even more objectionable results to refuse to allow innocent parties to produce new evidence, not before available to the adjuster, in support of a challenge mounted by them. Moreover, the choice of the present tense ("*is* manifestly incorrect") tends to support the view that the correctness of the estimate must be judged by reference to matters as they stand at the time of the challenge.[16]

Nevertheless, the Rule poses a substantial obstacle to any party who wishes to challenge the adjuster's estimate. It places the burden of proof on him, and he cannot discharge the burden of proof merely by showing that the estimate is wrong on the balance of probability. He must show that it is *manifestly* wrong, and the effect of this is that if, in the light of all the available information, there remains a reasonable possibility that the estimated amount is correct the challenge will fail, even though it has become apparent that a different amount is more likely to be correct.

Since the purpose of empowering the adjuster to make an estimate is to prevent the completion of the adjustment being held up by lack of factual information, the Rule should not affect the right of a party to challenge the estimate on the ground that the adjuster has taken a wrong view of the law or of the effect of the York-Antwerp Rules.[17] However, the effect of the third paragraph of Rule E is that the onus would lie upon that party to identify the error of law or of interpretation upon which the estimate was based. **E.21**

[16] The I.S.C. draft of the Rule restricted the right of challenge to those cases where the adjuster had acted unreasonably, the effect of which would have been that information not available to him when he made his estimate could not be relied on.

[17] The Rule would not, *e.g.* affect the right of a shipowner to challenge an amount allowed in respect of temporary repairs on the ground that it was based on an erroneous interpretation of Rule XIV. It would not be necessary to show that the interpretation was "manifestly incorrect".

Rule F

Substituted Expenses

F.01 As the name implies, *substituted* expenses are the expenses incurred in respect of a course of action undertaken as an alternative to—or in substitution for—what, prime facie, might be thought of as being the normal or standard means of dealing with a given situation.[1]

For example, if a vessel strands and sustains damage to her bottom which obliges her to put into a port of refuge for the common safety and to effect repairs necessary for the safe prosecution of the voyage, the standard course of action might be thought to consist of discharging the cargo and storing it ashore or in lighters, drydocking and effecting permanent repairs, thereafter reloading the cargo and continuing the voyage. However, some or all of these costly operations can often be avoided in the port of refuge—or the time and expense necessary for them be reduced—to the benefit and advantage of all the parties to the adventure, by the adoption of alternative courses of action such as the following:

(1) Temporary[2] repairs alone may be affected, with the cargo remaining on board;
(2) (a) The vessel may be towed to destination with the cargo on board, and after only minimal repairs; or
    (b) The vessel may purchase bunkers and proceed to destination under engine power, rather than her normal sails;[3]
(3) The cargo may be forwarded to destination by other vessels;
(4) The cargo (particularly if low valued) may be sold, and a replacement cargo purchased on completion of repairs;
(5) Extra blocks and cradles may be installed in the drydock sufficient to support the additional weight of all or part of the cargo while repairs are effected;
(6) Overtime may be worked on repairs or the cargo operations;
(7) Spare parts necessary for the repairs may be transported to the port of refuge by air, rather than by sea.

How should the expenses of these alternative courses of action be dealt

[1] See *Marida Ltd v. Oswal Steel; The Bijela* [1993] 1 Lloyd's Rep. 411 at 421, *per* Hoffmann L.J.

[2] See Rule XIV, which deals exclusively with temporary repairs, a particular or supposed form of substituted expenses.

[3] See *Wilson v. Bank of Victoria* (1867) L.R. 2 Q.B. 203.

with, and to what extent can they be charged to general average, either under English law or the York-Antwerp Rules?

English Law

Under the fundamental principles of English law, as later expressed in section 66 of the Marine Insurance Act 1906[4] (and partly mirrored in Rule A[5] of the York-Antwerp Rules), *any* extraordinary expenditure intentionally and reasonably incurred at a time of peril for the common safety, or directly consequential on a general average act (that is relating to damage caused by a general average act), can be claimed *direct* as general average, and on such occasions the concept of *substituted* expenses is quite unnecessary. **F.02**

It will be noted, however, that in all the practical examples given above in paragraph F.01, the vessel may be assumed to be in a port of refuge and that the expenses under consideration would be incurred with the object of the successful completion of the adventure, rather than the achievement of safety itself, with which alone general average under English law is concerned. Thus, none of the expenses of these operations could be charged directly to general average. But was there another route of entry?

Rightly or wrongly, English practice in the days of wooden sailing vessels always regarded the adventure as remaining in peril until the vessel had arrived in the port of refuge *and completed any necessary discharge of cargo.*[6] Consequently, the cost of discharge was allowable in general average, and this whether the necessity for the discharge arose from the damage which the ship had sustained, or that by the cargo itself. Thereafter, the cost of storage for the cargo was treated as a special charge on the cargo, and the cost of reloading a special charge on the freight. To the extent, therefore, that the undertaking of courses of action in examples (1) to (5) above resulted in the avoidance of any necessary discharge of cargo at the port of refuge, the question arose: could the cost of the operation be considered a substituted expense for those saved costs of discharge, storage, and reloading, plus possible savings in the repair costs to the ship, and could it then be charged to ship, freight and cargo in the same proportions that those interests would have borne the cost of the cargo operations and repairs? **F.03**

[4] See para. A.05, *ante*.
[5] See paras. A.06 or A.01, *ante*.
[6] See para. 10.06, n. 7, *post*.

F.04 The question was considered by Blackburn J. in the case of *Wilson v. Bank of Victoria*[7] and, in the absence of a custom of the trade, he decided that the principle was not tenable at law. The case concerned an auxiliary sailing vessel which struck an iceberg while on voyage from Melbourne to Great Britain and was dismasted and otherwise damaged such that she could no longer sail. She put into Rio de Janeiro as a port of refuge under her auxiliary steam power and, the cost of repairs there being prohibitive, the master effected only temporary repairs at Rio and proceeded to destination under steam, purchasing coals at both Rio and Fayal for this purpose. The shipowner claimed a general average contribution towards the cost of these coals on the grounds—*inter alia*—that they were a substituted expense for the expenses that would have been incurred at Rio if permanent repairs had been effected there, some of which might have been expected to be charged to general average. The claim was denied and Blackburn J. said:

> "... we think that the expenses actually incurred must be apportioned according to the facts that actually happened, and that there is no legal principle on which they can be apportioned according to what might have been the facts if a different course had been pursued.
>
> No case or authority was cited to support the principle contended for, nor are we aware of any. If in any particular trade it has been found convenient to act on this principle, and that has been done to such an extent as to create a custom ... the case would be different; but as it is, the principle proposed is not, we think, tenable at law."[8]

As to reinforce his general refusal to accept the principle of substituted expenses, Blackburn J. had stated earlier in his judgment on the facts of this particular case:

> "We wish to guard against being supposed to sanction the notion that in a case like this the shipowners could have charged the owners of the cargo with part of the expenses of unshipping and warehousing the gold at Rio, supposing the master had under the circumstances adopted that course. Inasmuch as the master could, by the expenditure of a comparatively small sum on temporary repairs and coals, bring the ship and cargo safely home, it was his duty to do so; and, though we do not decide a point which does

[7] (1867) L.R. 2 Q.B. 203.

[8] The fact that English law did not recognise the principle of substituted expenses on the particular facts of *Wilson v. Bank of Victoria* (1867) L.R. 2 Q.B. 203 is not surprising, even on practical or commercial grounds, for the course adopted by the shipowner was largely for his own individual benefit. The vessel was detained in the port of refuge undergoing her slight temporary repairs for only three days, whereas permanent repairs would have taken many months and, further, their cost would probably have exceeded the value of the ship when repaired. Thus, and quite apart from his contractual obligation to prosecute the voyage with all reasonable despatch, thoroughly compelling reasons on his own financial account would have dictated to any reasonable and prudent shipowner—even if no general average situation had been present—that he adopt precisely the same course as was in fact taken. The additional expenses of completing the voyage were thrust upon him by the *accident* of striking the iceberg, and he *sacrificed* or *gave* nothing to cargo beyond his obligations under the contract of affreightment for which the agreed freight had been paid or was payable.

> not arise, we are not to be taken as deciding that his owners would not have been liable to the owners of the cargo if he had not taken this course."

Thus, the question raised earlier of whether the expense of an alternative course of action should be treated in the same manner as would have been applied to the "standard" expenses they replace is answered firmly in the negative.[9] In fact, the supposed alternative or substituted course of action may itself at times be taken to be the standard course of action and, furthermore, one that is thrust upon the shipowner as part of his obligations under the contract of affreightment. **F.05**

As Lowndes himself wrote in 1873:

> "The master's right, not only to enter a port of refuge, but to remain and incur expense there, is strictly limited to the necessity of the case. He must not subject the cargo to delay or expense which it is in his power, with safety to all, to prevent. He has not an absolute right to make a complete repair of the ship at the port of refuge, if a partial or temporary repair will suffice to render her seaworthy to carry the cargo to its destination. Hence, if there be two courses open to him at the port of refuge, by the first of which the ship will be completely repaired, but there will be a long delay or a considerable expense of general average, while by the second this delay or expense will be diminished, and the ship, though incompletely repaired, will be fit to sail on her voyage with her whole cargo, the second course is that which the master if legally bound to adopt. Having done so, he has no right to make a merit of his conduct, and claim compensation from the cargo, on the ground of his having rendered it a service by not having chosen the more expensive course.[10] In such a case, therefore, an adjustment on the basis of 'substituted expenses' would be incorrect."

English Practice

Although in the case of *Wilson v. Bank of Victoria* Blackburn J. had held that the principle of substituted expenses was not tenable at law, he did state that the case would be different if there had been a custom in the trade to apply the principle. No evidence of such a custom was presumably produced during the court hearing, nor did a custom necessarily exist, but one can see the principle of substituted expenses being explored even as early as 1851 by the highly respected L.R. Baily on page 78 of his *General Average*: **F.06**

[9] It should be noted that another case sometimes quoted in support of the substituted expense principle—*Lee v. Southern Insce. Co.* (1870) L.R.5 C.P. 397—is in reality no authority; that case was concerned only with evaluating the measure of indemnity for particular charges on a policy of marine insurance.

[10] If confirmation of this view were necessary, it received it from *e.g.* Earl of Halsbury, L.C. in *Ruabon Steamship Co. v. London Assurance* [1900] A.C. 6, or Bowen L.J. in *Svendsen v. Wallace Bros.* (1885) 10 A.C. 404. There is no rule of (English) law that a person can be called upon for a payment towards the expense of another merely because he may have obtained some benefit from that other person's actions.

> "When such extra expense has been incurred to avoid discharging the cargo, the excess of the expense actually incurred in temporary and permanent repairs, beyond what would have been incurred if the vessel had been permanently repaired at the intermediate port, should be divided as follows:-
>
> Ship, freight and cargo should bear the extra expense in the same proportion that they would have borne the expense for discharging, warehouse rent, and re-shipping, that would have been incurred if the cargo had been discharged; and the residue of the expenses should be paid by the shipowners."

Although there may have been no accepted custom to apply the principle of substituted expenses in 1867 and the case of *Wilson v. Bank of Victoria*[11] it does appear that commercial men favoured the principle, certainly in so far as it applied to towage of a vessel to destination, or the forwarding of her cargo, and they set about creating or evidencing the custom. Richard Lowndes endeavoured to introduce a Rule of Practice on the subject of towage at the semi-annual meeting of the Association of Average Adjusters in November 1870, and although unsuccessful on that occasion, he received the unanimous support of members when in 1876 he persuaded the representative of the Liverpool Underwriters' Association to propose a similar Rule, also one on the forwarding of cargo.

It will be useful now to examine more closely the facts likely to be present in each of the seven examples quoted in paragraph F.01, above, and to see how English practice developed over the years:

F.07 Example (1): Temporary Repairs

This particular example is dealt with more fully in its own individual Rule XIV, and it is sufficient here to state that following the remarks of Blackburn J. in *Wilson v. Bank of Victoria* that "Inasmuch as the master could, by the expenditure of a comparatively small sum on temporary repairs and coals, bring the ship and cargo safely home, it was his duty to do so", English practice (absent the York-Antwerp Rules) has been not to allow the cost of temporary repairs to accidental damage as general average.

F.08 Example (2)(a): Towage to Destination

It is thought that towage to destination would but rarely be considered an obligation under the contract of affreightment, and the subsidiary reasoning in *Wilson v. The Bank of Victoria* which would deny temporary repairs to accidental damage being considered for any allowance in general average may not be applicable here, where a shipowner incurs

[11] (1867) L.R. 2 Q.B. 203.

the expense of having his vessel towed to destination with her cargo to avoid the (generally larger) expenses that would have been incurred to discharge, store and reload the cargo, and effect repairs at the port of refuge. In any case, as recorded in paragraph F.06, above, a "custom of the trade" was established in 1876 when a Rule of Practice on the subject was passed unanimously by the Association of Average Adjusters, and the Rule remains unchanged and in force in 1997:

F14 Towage from a Port of Refuge

> "That if a ship be in a port of refuge at which it is practicable to repair her, and if, in order to save expense, she be towed thence to some other port, then the extra cost of such towage shall be divided in proportion to the saving of expense thereby occasioned to the several parties to the adventure."

The situation envisaged by the Rule of Practice is encountered in practice with some frequency, and a simplified example of its operation might be as follows: **F.09**

A ship with accidental damage is at a port of refuge at which it is possible to repair her, but repair charges are highly expensive and it would cost .... more than if the same repairs were effected at destination.	200,000
Furthermore, those repairs would involve a lengthy detention at the port of refuge and necessitate the discharge, storage, and subsequent reloading of part of the cargo, the whole operation resulting in charges to general average[12] of	400,000
	600,000
The ship is in a fit condition to be towed to destination, and this can be accomplished for a net cost of .... after crediting ordinary voyage expenses saved.	330,000

The extra cost of towage, 330,000, would be treated as a substituted expense and apportioned over the savings to the various parties as follows:

The SHIPOWNER, in respect of the savings in the cost of his repairs	on	200,000	pays	110,000
GENERAL AVERAGE, in respect of the savings in expenses at the port of refuge	on	400,000	pays	220,000
		600,000	pays	330,000

Such a practice seems reasonably fair, though it is to be wondered whether the Rule of Practice would have had such an easy passage in 1876 if, for instance, the savings in the cost of repairs, had been 400,000, that is, sufficient by itself to justify the employment of the tug? Or, by

[12] In fact, under English law and practice, the discharging, storage, and reloading expenses would be charged respectively to General Average and Special Charges on Cargo and on Freight, but for the purpose of the present illustration it is simpler to assume that all these expenses are treated as General Average.

reason of the greater efficiency of the repair yard at destination and the fact that some of the work could be pre-fabricated while the voyage was being progressed, the time actually taken on repairs was considerably reduced, thus enabling the shipowner to earn additional time hire or freights of 400,000?

F.10 Example (2)(b): Using Bunkers for Auxiliary Engine to Proceed to Destination rather than under Sail

As decided in *Wilson v. The Bank of Victoria*[13] the expense of the bunkers to complete the voyage under steam could not be considered for an allowance in general average as a substituted expense. By their contract of affreightment, the owners of a vessel equipped with an auxiliary screw were bound to give the full services of the ship, including the screw, and to make all disbursements necessary for that purpose.

F.11 Example (3): Forwarding Cargo from a Port of Refuge

Not only did commercial men in 1876 consider that the cost of towage from a port of refuge should be treated on a substituted expense basis, but also where cargo was forwarded from a port of refuge to avoid the cost of storing it there. At the same meeting of the Association of Average Adjusters in 1876, the members passed unanimously another Rule of Practice proposed by the Representative of the Liverpool Underwriters' Association (and which remains in force today):

F15 Cargo Forwarded from a Port of Refuge

> "That if a ship be in a port of refuge at which it is practicable to repair her so as to enable her to carry on the whole cargo, but, in order to save expense, the cargo or a portion of it, be transhipped by another vessel, or otherwise forwarded, then the cost of such transhipment (up to the amount of expense saved) shall be divided in proportion to the saving of expense thereby occasioned to the several parties to the adventure."

F.12 The situation envisaged by this Rule of Practice is also encountered in practice with some frequency, and it is worth mentioning that this particular substituted expense will sometimes be greater than the expenses avoided at the port of refuge, the shipowner undertaking the forwarding of the cargo largely to preserve the goodwill of cargo interests (by delivering their cargo much earlier than would otherwise be the case). Up to the expenses avoided at the port of refuge, the substituted expenses will be allowed and treated in like manner, and any excess must be borne by the carrier.

[13] (1867) L.R. 2 Q.B. 203.

As an example, assume that a vessel has severe damage to her bottom and that she is unable to carry the cargo to destination until repaired, and that it is necessary first to discharge the cargo, store it in a warehouse for the lengthy period of repairs, and then reload it. The expenses might be as follows:

Discharging	—	100,000
Storage	—	120,000
Reloading	—	100,000
		320,000

and for the purpose of this illustration it will be assumed that they would be wholly chargeable to general average.[14]

The shipowner will generally be obliged to continue with repairs at the port of refuge but he decides to forward the cargo to destination by another vessel. Whether the cargo be stored at the port of refuge or forwarded by another vessel, the costs of discharging and (re-)loading must still be incurred and it is effectively only the cost of storage, 120,000, which can be avoided. If the net freight on the forwarding vessel (after crediting normal voyage expenses saved to the original vessel) is *less* than 120,000, this net freight will be allowed as a substituted expense for the storage expenses saved. On the other hand, in the event that the net forwarding freight is *greater* than 120,000, only this sum can be allowed in substitution, and the excess must be borne by the shipowner.

There is no obligation on the part of the shipowner under his contract of affreightment to forward the cargo to destination, and Rule of Practice F15 appears fair and reasonable, and unobjectionable.

Example (4): Loss by Sale of Cargo at a Port of Refuge F.13

As an example of a proper and legitimate substituted expense (or loss), every edition of this work since 1873 has instanced the case of a vessel carrying a low-valued cargo such as coals which it was necessary to discharge at a port of refuge. In order to avoid the storage expenses, etc., thereon, the cargo was sometimes sold and a fresh cargo purchased on completion of repairs. The loss on the sale and repurchase was treated as a substitution for the expenditure saved, and divided in the proportions in which that expenditure would have fallen.

The present editors indorse the practice and suggest that the modern counterpart might more frequently be the return of a grain cargo to the original silos after a serious casualty in the loading port, and the reloading of a new cargo of similar grade and quality on completion of repairs. The "handling" charge may be equated with storage.

[14] See para. F.09, n. 12, *ante*.

In 1902 the Association of Average Adjusters introduced a Rule of Practice on the subject:

F16 Cargo Sold at a Port of Refuge

> "That if a ship be in a port of refuge at which it is practicable to repair her so as to enable her to carry on the whole cargo, or such portion of it as is fit to be carried on, but, in order to save expense, the cargo, or a portion of it, be, with the consent of the owners of such cargo, sold at the port of refuge, then the loss by sale including loss of freight on cargo so sold (up to the amount of expense saved) shall be divided in proportion to the saving of expense thereby occasioned to the several parties to the adventure; provided always that the amount so divided shall in no case exceed the cost of transhipment and/or forwarding referred to in the preceding rule of the Association."

F.14 Although the Rule of Practice may may be assumed to cover Lowndes' own example, it appears also to extend the principle to cases where no replacement cargo is purchased, and the original voyage is effectively abandoned. Whether this extension of the principle is justifiable could be open to question, and it can certainly be suggested that the practical application of the Rule could be fraught with difficulties, dependent on whether the freight is at risk or prepaid, and whether the port of refuge is early in the voyage or near the destination.

In fact, any decision to terminate the voyage and sell the cargo can only be made by special agreement between the owners of the ship and the cargo (with the concurrence of their respective insurers), and as it is clear that such agreement will be obtained only after considering and specifying what freight should be paid, and the allowances to be made in general average, it may be that the Rule of Practice is superfluous[15]; the matter would probably be resolved by a special agreement between the parties rather than by the Rule of Practice.

F.15 **Example (5): Drydocking with Cargo on Board**

If a loaded vessel requires to drydock for underwater repairs, it will usually be necessary to discharge all or part of the cargo in order to achieve a weight that both the ship and the drydock can safely bear. However, to avoid the heavy cost of discharging, storing and reloading the cargo, it is sometimes possible to install extra blocks and cradles in the drydock to support the additional weight and to leave the cargo on board.

[15] The facts and figures in the case of *The Minnetonka* (1905) 10 Asp. M.L.C. 142 will be of interest to anyone confronted with such a problem. By chance, the collision occurred one month to the day after Rule of Practice F16 had been passed, and although a thoroughly reasonable and business-like arrangement was made to sell the cargo, it is not entirely clear whether an actual general average adjustment would have been prepared.

The cost of installing the extra blocks and cradles is treated as a substituted expense for, and allocated in the same manner as would have applied to the cost of discharging, storing and reloading the cargo. The practice appears well founded. It has also been accepted (*obiter*) in the United States case of *Browning v. Thebaud.*[16]

Example (6): Overtime Working on Repairs; Example (7): Air Freight **F.16**

Lowndes had no cause to address these particular examples of possible substituted expenses and it will be sensible, therefore, to defer comment upon them until their treatment under York-Antwerp Rule F is discussed later in paragraphs F.30 to F.32 and F.55 to F.59, below, and to conclude this section on English law and practice with one final example of a substituted expenses mentioned by Lowndes:

Example (8): Hire of Hulks and Lighters **F.17**

This particular example is dealt with in an old Custom of Lloyd's dating from 1876 or earlier and now incorporated as a Rule of Practice—F12(f):

> "When the cargo, instead of being sent ashore, is placed on board hulk or lighters during the ship's stay in port, the hulk-hire is divided between general average, cargo, and freight, in such proportions as may place the several contributing interests in nearly the same relative positions as if the cargo had been landed and stored."

Although the Rule treats the hulk-hire on a substituted expense basis, it is highly unlikely that it would ever be called into use in modern times on the practical grounds that, in the experience of the present editors, the place where cargo is stored—whether lighter, warehouse, or on the quay, etc.,—is governed largely by the nature of the particular cargo[17] and the actual facilities which happen to be available in the port of refuge at the time. In that sense, there is very little choice about the matter, or opportunity for substitution, and the hulk or lighter hire would be treated as plain "storage". Modern cargoes can be highly sophisticated, and often in bulk, whereas the Rule envisaged cargo that was generally *packaged* and could be stored in a warehouse.

The almost universal adoption of the York-Antwerp Rules also makes the Rule of Practice virtually obsolete.

[16] 42 Fed.Rep. 796 (1890).

[17] Where shore tanks are unavailable in a port of refuge for the storage of an oil cargo, another tanker will sometimes be chartered and it may then be found that the cargo can be forwarded to destination at less cost than would be incurred if the on-carrying tanker acted merely as a storeship during the repairs.

F.18 Historical Development and Practice of Rule F

*York-Antwerp Rules 1890—The old **Rule X(d)***

A month prior to the International Conference held at Liverpool in August 1890 to produce the York-Antwerp Rules of 1890, the British Association of Average Adjusters had held an Extraordinary General Meeting to consider what proposals they would put forward. One possibility was a new Rule on substituted expenses which would effectively combine the provisions of their own two Rules of Practice F.14[18] and F.15[19] passed in 1876 and dealing with the specific examples of towage to destination and forwarding cargo to destination. However, this was rejected and struck out on the (seconded) objection of the influential member Charles McArthur on the grounds that it did not come within the province of the York-Antwerp Rules and, further, that they were attempting to carry out too much.

Nevertheless, at the Liverpool Conference itself, the same Charles McArthur interrupted the proceedings to move an addition which proposed as a substituted expense the cost of forwarding cargo, alone. This proposal being seconded, McArthur then said that "it had been suggested to him that the rule would be made more complete if it included towage (to destination), and he would be quite willing to accept that suggestion". Those present were also willing and the motion, as amended, was agreed to *nem. con.* as follows:

> "If a ship under average be in a port or place at which it is practicable to repair her, so as to enable her to carry on the whole cargo, and if, in order to save expense, either she is towed thence to some other port or place of repair or to her destination, or the cargo or a portion of it is transhipped by another ship, or otherwise forwarded, then the extra cost of such towage, transhipment and forwarding or any of them (up to the amount of the extra expense saved) shall be payable by the several parties to the adventure in proportion to the extraordinary expense saved."

It would appear that even in 1890 there must have been some doubts as to the complete propriety of the provisions—(towage, at least)—but they were essentially unobjectionable and reasonably fair in that the shipowner was required to contribute to the expenses on the basis of any savings achieved by him in the cost of repairs (something achieved usually in the case of towage only).

F.19 *York-Antwerp Rules 1924—The new **Rule F***

Rule X(d) dealing with just two specific examples of substituted expenses remained unchanged in 1924, but it was supplemented on this

[18] See para. 70.41, *post*, and para. F.08, *ante*.
[19] See para. 70.42, *post*, and para. F.11, *ante*.

occasion with a new lettered Rule F serving as a general statement of the principle of substituted expenses, with wording as follows:

> "Any extra expense incurred in place of another expense which would have been allowable as general average shall be deemed to be general average and so allowed ...[20] but only up to the amount of the general average expense avoided."

As originally proposed by the Drafting Committee, the Rule opened as follows: "Any extra expense *or loss* incurred in place of another expense *or loss* ..." but after discussion, the delegates at the 1924 Conference unanimously agreed to omit the words "or loss". indicating their intention[21] that only *expenses* were to be taken into account, in accordance with the Rule of Practice[22] of average adjusters in this country.

York-Antwerp Rules 1950

Between 1924 and 1950, it is believed that genuine substituted expenses falling to be dealt with under Rule F were charged, in practice, entirely to general average up to the amount of the general average expenses avoided, and without regard to any possible savings to other interests. To the present editors, this appears to be the correct construction to be placed upon the 1924 wording of Rule F. However, an alternative view—that all parties who had benefited by a substituted expense should contribute thereto[23]—may have had its adherents, and this alternative view was expressed as late even as 1948 in the seventh edition[24] of this work. **F.20**

To avoid any possible doubt upon the construction to be given to Rule F, in 1950 the words "without regard to the saving, if any, to other interests" were added in the space ... left in the 1924 Rule quoted above. It was then quite plain that, up to the amount of the general expenses

[20] See para. F.20, *post*.

[21] Although it was most certainly the intention that there should be no allowance in general average for substituted losses incurred in place of another expense or loss which would have been allowable as general average, it is submitted that unless the wording of Rule F expressly prohibits such a substitution there may be grounds (subject to Rule C and the law of the port of destination) for the allowance of certain substituted losses akin to general average sacrifices. *E.g.* an adjustment has been seen where a motor-vessel proceeding in ballast under charter to load cargo was obliged to put into a port of refuge with accidental damage to her main engine. Temporary repairs necessary for the safe prosecution of the voyage were effected but these necessitated the use at all times of diesel oil instead of the usual fuel oil. As the vessel already had on board a complete supply of fuel oil, the extra diesel oil required could only be shipped by shutting out an equivalent weight of cargo. The loss of freight thereon, together with the cost of the temporary repairs, was allowed as general average on a substituted expense basis.

[22] F17. See para. 70.44, *post*.

[23] *E.g.* see the commentary on the English Rules of Practice F14–F15 in paras. F.08–F.09, and F.11–F.12, *ante*.

[24] See pp. 363–364.

avoided, truly substituted expenses were to be charged entirely to general average and that the savings to other interests were to be ignored.

A proposal that the words "or loss" should be added after the third word of the Rule, "expense", was not accepted as it might have led to abuse. It was appreciated that extra losses were incurred occasionally in order to avoid general average expenditure, but it was felt that, in practice, it was better to deal with these substituted losses by a special agreement.

York-Antwerp Rules 1974

F.21 There was no change to Rule F, but the suggestion was again made by one country that the words *or loss* should be added after the word *expense*. Rule X(d), introduced in 1890, was rescinded on this occasion in favour of the principle established by the later Rules F and XIV whereby, if the savings to general average were sufficient, the whole of the substituted expenses were chargeable to general average, and all other savings were ignored.

York-Antwerp Rules 1994

F.22 Only one small change was made on this occasion: the opening phrase "Any *extra* expense" was changed to "Any *additional* expense". This, however, disguises the fact that the whole subject of substituted expenses in general, and temporary repairs[25] in particular, had been the subject of considerable critical discussion (including that in the eleventh edition of this work), in the years and months prior to the Conference at Sydney in October 1994.

There were a number of proposals to curb or limit the scope of interpretation and practical application of the Rule, but perhaps the most authoritative criticism came at an early stage, when the United States Maritime Law Association stated that it was not content with the current status of the treatment of substituted expenses in the lettered and numbered Rules and was giving consideration to a proposal to lead to the restoration of (old) Rule X(d) and the application of its principles to *all* substituted expenses. Subsequently, they put forward the revolutionary proposal that the alternative course against which the substituted expenses actually incurred would be set would need to be *reasonably incurred.* Although both proposals appear to have been withdrawn, the United States Maritime Law Association achieved their ends by securing the passage of their Rule Paramount,[26] the effect of which will be considered below in paragraphs F.38 and F.39.

The regular proposal that provision should be made for substituted

[25] See Rule XIV, *post*.
[26] See para. PRE.22, *ante*.

losses was not pursued, it being feared that it might open the door to abuse, but in any case would expand the scope of general average, something generally unwanted at a time when looks askance were being directed at the whole system.

Rule F

Any additional expense incurred in place of another expense which would have been allowable as general average shall be deemed to be general average and so allowed without regard to the saving, if any, to other interests, but only up to the amount of the general average expense avoided.

Construction

"Any additional expense" The only change to Rule F in 1994 was the substitution of the word *additional* in the phrase under discussion for the previous *extra*, and it was reported that no change in meaning or practice was intended, merely a clarification "*to express what has always been the intention and also is expressed in the French text, which uses the word 'supplémentaire'*". In reality, the change was purposely designed to ensure that the original word *extra* could not be construed or interpreted as *extraordinary*, as had been suggested here in previous editions: **F.23**

> "... it seems that the word *extra* is not used in the sense of additional since no basic expenditure is indicated ... It is submitted that the words are intended to be descriptive of any extra-ordinary expenditure not itself allowable in general average as an extraordinary expenditure under the Rules." (8th to 10th editions)
>
> "For this purpose, it is highly important that the precise meaning of the word *extra* should be analysed. The first thing to note is that it is a derivative and shortened form of the word *extraordinary*[27] and the full length word, perhaps, may heighten our perception of what is intended—*i.e.* something out of the ordinary. The supposed extraordinary course of action and its concomitant expenses must be truly out of the ordinary, and not just an alternative but standard or normal and routine way of accomplishing the task in hand." (11th edition)

This view also received some support from Hoffmann L.J. when he mentioned, *obiter*, in his judgment in *The Bijela*[28] case that:

[27] In 1974 Great Britain suggested that "the wording of this Rule could be improved by substituting *extraordinary* for *extra*", and in 1994 a number of people were in favour of its use in the phrase under discussion.

[28] *Marida Ltd v. Oswal Steel; The Bijela* [1992] 1 Lloyd's Rep. 636; [1993] 1 Lloyd's Rep. 411 at 422.

> "Rule F (of the 1974 Rules) ... contemplates that the owner has taken a course which involves *extraordinary* expense compared with what he would have done if he merely fulfilled his obligations under the contract of affreightment."

We are now enjoined to consider that a substituted expense need no longer be an *extraordinary* expense, but that it should be *additional.* However, if the wording or the Rule still fails to give any indication of what is the basic expenditure to which other expenses will be additional or supplementary, we are left with the question:

Additional to What?

F.24 This question is not easy of answer, more particularly because the basic purpose behind the incurring of any substituted expense is, as was perfectly expressed in the original Rule X(d) dealing with substituted expenses, "*in order to save expense*". Prima facie, a substituted expense *reduces* the overall cost of an operation, and to speak of it as being *additional*—(or extra when used in that same sense)—is somewhat inappropriate, the costs incurred being generally neither additional nor extra, but simply "unusual" and an alternative for some other expense that would, under any of the York-Antwerp Rules, be admissible as general average.

The opening words of the Rule, "*Any additional expense*", followed as they are by "*incurred in place of another expense*", clearly refer to the substituted expense itself, and it would appear that such an expense must be *additional*, either free-standing in its own right (for example the forwarding of cargo instead of storing), or perhaps as some enhanced portion of the same expense (for example overtime on repairs). But additional to what? A number of possibilities exist:

F.25 *(1) Is it sufficient simply that the expense be additional to those for which specific provision has already been made in the numbered Rules of the York-Antwerp Rules, that is, further/other expenses?*

Such an interpretation is undoubtedly correct, but of itself it is quite inadequate. Indeed, with such a limited definition the word *additional* becomes unnecessary and devoid of meaning. Something more stringent must surely have been intended, and the character of the substituted expense be no less a "sacrifice" to the party making it than the expense which it replaces.

(2) Is it sufficient that the expense be additional to what are generally considered to be ordinary voyage expenses? **F.26**

In *Wilson v. The Bank of Victoria*[29] Blackburn J. said:

> "The disaster ... caused the disbursements for coals to be extraordinarily heavy; but it did not render it an extraordinary disbursement."

and although it can be maintained that an enhanced ordinary charge generally remains an ordinary charge, there are occasions when the enhanced portion of such a charge may reasonably be considered as a valid substituted expense. Indeed, if one examines the main examples of substituted expenses quoted in paragraph F.01, above (regardless of whether or not they are acceptable in general average), it will be found that they can all be broadly classified as additional to:

	Ordinary Voyage Expenses	*Normal Repair Costs*
Temporary Repairs		THIS
Towage to Destination	Partly this	Partly this
Forwarding Cargo to Destination	THIS	
Drydocking with Cargo on Board		THIS
Overtime on Repairs		THIS
Air Freight		THIS

It is worthy of record that, in considering as a substituted expense the costs of the two items in the column headed "Ordinary Voyage Expenses", (Towage and Forwarding Cargo to Destination), credit is in practice given for the ordinary voyage expenses saved. Thus, the amount put forward as a claim is *additional* to ordinary or normal, and the definition is worthy of consideration, but it is doubtful whether it is yet adequate or sufficiently precise.

(3) As Hoffmann L.J. inquired, but did not answer, in The Bijela[30]*: "Is it necessary that ... the substituted expense should fall outside (be additional to) the obligations contained in the contract of affreightment?"* **F.27**

Probably as the result of the statement by Blackburn J. in *Wilson v. The Bank of Victoria*[31] that:

> "Inasmuch as the master could, by the expenditure of a comparatively small sum on temporary repairs and coals, bring the ship and cargo safely home, it was his duty to do so;"

[29] (1867) L.R. 2 Q.B. 203.

[30] *Marida Ltd v. Oswal Steel; The Bijela* [1992] 1 Lloyd's Rep. 636; [1993] 1 Lloyd's Rep. 411 at 421, 422.

[31] (1867) L.R. 2 Q.B. 203, see para. F.04, *ante*, and the views of Lowndes to the same effect at para. F.05, *ante*.

it will often be found stated in text books that an expense cannot qualify under Rule F as an extra (additional) or substituted expense if it is one that the shipowner would be obliged to incur under the terms of his contract of affreightment. Such a conclusion appears undoubtedly correct, but might also be more precisely stated as follows:—if the alternative course would have constituted a breach of the contract of affreightment, in that it would unreasonably and unnecessarily have delayed the voyage or cast unwarranted expenditure upon the cargo, the cost of the course actually adopted, as the only course which could be adopted without a breach of contract, cannot generally be considered as a substituted expense and set against the cost of an unjustifiable and unreasonable alternative course. It follows that this requirement is in truth concerned less with the qualities of the actual course than with those of the alternative course, and it is discussed, further, in paragraphs F.36, F.37, below.

F.28 *(4) Is it necessary that the expense be additional to those that would have been incurred if the "standard/normal"*[32] *course of action had been followed?*

If by additional we here mean *greater*, then as a generalisation, and as already mentioned in paragraph F.24, above, this definition is hardly appropriate, for the principle reason for incurring and claiming any substituted expense is that it is *less* than the expense it replaces. However, one can appreciate that if the overall expenditure to complete the voyage and repair the ship be "compartmentalised", it is quite possible that a greater expenditure in one segment may produce savings in another, and it may well be that it is this type of greater expense which can appropriately be comprised within the word *additional.*

However, in order to determine whether any particular expense can justifiably be deemed *additional*, it is clearly necessary first to consider the supposed standard course of action it replaces and to establish that it is one to which a reasonable shipowner would normally give serious thought and be likely to adopt in practice. If such a course would not be adopted by a reasonable shipowner, then the course of action actually undertaken, and purportedly *substituted*, may itself be the *standard* course and the costs accordingly fail to qualify as *additional* under Rule F. In similar fashion, if it is part of a shipowner's fairly regular or routine repairing practice, even when no general average situation is present, to send spare parts abroad by air rather than by sea, and to work overtime on repairs, the practice then becomes the standard, and the nominally increased cost of these operations disappears entirely, and it would be wrong and unfair to the other parties to the adventure to treat them as *additional* under Rule F.

Each of the practical examples of potential substituted expenses listed

[32] See the opening paragraph in para. F.01, *ante*.

in paragraph F.01, above, will be re-examined, in paragraphs F.45 *et seq.*, below, but for the purpose of the present discussion it will be convenient to mention two.

Forwarding of Cargo to Destination[33] **F.29**

A vessel has severe damage to her bottom which must be repaired before she can proceed to destination, and for the purpose of repairs the cargo must be discharged. The standard and normal course of action by any reasonable shipowner, and widely accepted, would then be to store the cargo ashore until repairs had been completed; but to save the cost of that storage, the cargo will on occasion be forwarded to destination. The cost of such forwarding, less the expenses that would have been incurred for the original vessel to complete the voyage, must surely qualify as *additional.*

Overtime Working on Repairs[34] **F.30**

A vessel requires to drydock in a port of refuge for repairs to accidental damage to the bottom, and repairs are estimated to cost a basic 180,000 and take 20 days. However, by working overtime on the repairs at an "additional" cost of 8,000, that is a total of 188,000, the repairs can be accomplished in 14 days, saving six days of detention during which crew wages, port charges and storage of the cargo customarily charged to general average and amounting to 20,000 will be saved.

Is this 8,000 increase in the cost of repairs also to be considered, as was the cost of forwarding, as *additional*?

In accordance with the criterion set out in paragraph F.28, above, it is first necessary to inquire what would be the standard or normal course adopted by a reasonable shipowner in such circumstances. Would he undertake those repairs only in the regular working hours for which the workers receive bare basic rates of pay?

The answer is almost certainly NO, for the basic figures of 180,000 and 188,000 tell only half the story, and the true cost of the repairs would likely have been as follows:

	In Normal Hours	With Overtime
Repairs	180,000	188,000
Drydock Dues and other ancilliary expenses for 20 and 14 days respectively	20,000	14,000
	200,000	202,000

[33] See also paras. F.11, F.12, *ante*, and paras. F.47, F.48, *post*.
[34] See also paras. F.55, F.56, *post*.

The real increase in the cost of repairs by working overtime is only 2,000, and, as a simple matter of plain good housekeeping, any shipowner would be bound to order at least as much overtime working as would be compensated by the savings in drydock dues and other ancilliary repair charges; to do otherwise would in fact be *un*reasonable.

F.31 As stated, only 2,000 of the extra 8,000 cost of working overtime in this example should rank as a candidate for consideration as *additional*. Indeed, even this 2,000 is not unreservedly additional, for the working of overtime is likely to have produced further savings of six days' loss of earnings to the shipowner. However, and as discussed, in paragraph F.41, below, this saving of a *loss*, rather than an expense, is generally to be ignored, though if it be the regular practice of the shipowner to work overtime on repairs even when no general average situation is present, even the 2,000 in the example under discussion may count as normal or standard, rather than an *additional* expense.

Thus, the owner of a passenger or cargo liner running to a regular and advertised schedule to which that vessel makes every endeavour to adhere, will customarily work whatever overtime is necessary on repairs in order to maintain that schedule, and the extra cost of working the overtime should generally be considered as normal and part of the reasonable cost of repairs, rather than as a substituted expense for, for example the wages and maintenance of crew, etc., during any prolonged period of detention for repairs in ordinary working hours.[35]

F.32 Thus, while it can be accepted as a basic concept that the overall cost of setting the ship and cargo again on their voyage can be "compartmentalised" and that increased costs in one segment, in lieu of savings in another, can at times be considered as *additional*, the "repair costs" compartment must be taken as a whole, including all necessary and indispensable ancilliaries such as drydock dues, and that until all compensating savings within the same compartment have been exhausted (for example the drydock dues in the above example), an increased cost can hardly be considered as *additional*. To suggest otherwise would mean that the cost to the shipowner of the repairs to the accidental damage to his ship would be only 194,000, that is, *less* than if carried out in the supposed standard manner, and that he profits quite unfairly at the expense of the general average.

[35] Similar remarks might be made regarding the cost of temporary repairs to a passenger or cargo liner at a port of refuge, but the specific wording of Rule XIV on the subject of temporary repairs precludes any such remarks.

Summary F.33

From the above discussion, an *additional* expense would appear to be an expense incurred in carrying out an operation in a non-standard manner and for which no specific provision is made in the numbered Rules of the York-Antwerp Rules, but which is incurred with the primary (rather than incidental) object of avoiding or reducing some other expense which would properly be admissible in general average under the Rules. It is not a mere enhancement of an ordinary voyage expense which the carrier should bear as an obligation under the contract of affreightment, nor, when the expense relates to repairs of the ship, should it be one which a shipowner would incur as part of his regular repairing procedure even when no general average situation was present. Finally, and supposing an expense to qualify as above, it is not necessarily the whole of that expense which is additional and constituting a substituted expense, but only the extra cost to the party incurring the expense after deducting:

(1) any ordinary voyage expenses which would have been incurred by him, and have been saved thereby, and
(2) any expenses in the same segment of operations (for example repair of the ship) which would have been incurred by him in carrying out the operation in the standard manner, and which have been saved thereby.

"incurred in place of another expense which would have been allowable as general average" For this Rule to have any application there must have been an alternative course of action which, if adopted, would have involved expenditure which could properly be charged to general average. Thus, and assuming repairs to the ship could have been effected at the port of refuge to enable her to continue on voyage to destination with the cargo, the extra cost of: F.34

(1) towage to destination[36]; or
(2) forwarding the cargo[37]; or
(3) drydocking with cargo on board,[38]

might all be considered as substituted expenses incurred in lieu of, for instance, the cost of discharging, storing and reloading the cargo and other detention expenses at the port of refuge, if these would be allowable as general average.

[36] See para. F.08, *ante*, and paras. F.49–F.51, *post*.
[37] See para. F.11, *ante*, and paras. F.47, F.48, *post*.
[38] See para. F.15, *ante*, and para. F.54, *post*.

F.35 **Qualities Required of the Alternative Course**

If the expense of the course actually adopted is to be admissible in general average as a *substituted* expense under the York-Antwerp Rules, there must be a genuine alternative course available whose qualities will fulfil the following requirements:

(1) It should be a natural and logical alternative, such as has already been suggested for the examples immediately above, and not some wild and absurd "invention". As an extreme example, the continuing hire payable on containers at a port of refuge is a loss by delay and excluded by Rule C, but the suggestion has been made that the hire can be charged to general average as a "substituted" expense for the cost of unstuffing the containers and storing the contents in a warehouse. Such a course of action would be so totally unnatural and unreasonable that it does not brook consideration.

(2) The alternative should be *possible*. For example, if suitable repairs of any kind at the port of refuge were quite impossible and there was no alternative other than, say, to tow the vessel to some other port or to her destination, clearly that expense cannot be treated as a "substituted" expense (though it may be allowable as general average under Rules A, X(a), or by agreement).

F.36 (3) The alternative course should not (a) be so costly that, for example the cost of repairs plus any contribution to the general average will mean that the vessel is a commercial total loss, or (b) take so long that the adventure is frustrated. In either of these circumstances conditions (4) and (5) below will normally result in the Rule having no application, but in any event being restricted in its scope since the general average expenditure avoided is likely to be limited to:

(i) storage expenses on the cargo, and
(ii) wages and maintenance of crew, fuel and stores, and port charges only up to the date of completion of discharge.[39]

(4) To adopt the alternative course would not have been in breach of the contact of affreightment.

(5) The alternative course would be reasonable for all the parties to the adventure.

These last two requirements are closely bound up together, and will be dealt with consecutively.

F.37 ***Breach of the contract of affreightment***

A carrier's principal duties under any contract of affreightment in respect of cargo on board are carefully to keep and carry that cargo to

[39] See Rule X(c) and Rule XI(b), *post*.

destination, and to prosecute the voyage with all reasonable despatch. The operation of an accident or other excepted peril may necessitate a resort into a port of refuge and a measure of unavoidable delay, but the overriding duty to prosecute the voyage with reasonable despatch remains, and a shipowner would be in breach of contract if he unreasonably adopted a course which involves the cargo in unnecessary expense, handling or delay. Hoffmann L.J. mused upon this theme when considering a claim for temporary repairs in the case of *The Bijela*[40] when he said (at page 421):

> "This generalised Rule [F] also seems to contemplate that the hypothetical alternative would be a course which the owner was at least legitimately entitled to take."

or at page 422:

> "What if the choice of [*the hypothetical alternative*] was, in terms of expense and delay, so commercially sensible that the duty of the owner under the contract of affreightment was to [*adopt the course actually followed*] and complete the voyage? Rule F would not apply because, as we have seen, it contemplates that the owner has taken a course which involves extraordinary expense compared with what he would have done if her merely fulfilled his obligations under the contract of affreightment."

No. When considered in conjunction with the remarks of Blackburn J. in *Wilson v. Bank of Victoria*[41] quoted (secondly) in paragraph F.04, above, and those of Lowndes himself in paragraph F.05, above, it appears evident that if the alternative course would have resulted in a breach of the contract of affreightment, that alternative course and its cost lose their validity for comparison with the costs of the course actually adopted, and there is no substitution.

It may also be remarked that the grounds on which the claim for temporary repairs under Rule XIV succeeded in the case of *The Bijela*[42] do not apply to Rule F; here there is no wording which requires one to ignore the availability of the course adopted. The one exception in practice is where the course actually adopted is forwarding; since it is a pure option of the shipowner whether to adopt this course or not, he cannot be in breach of contract merely by declining to adopt it.

The requirement of reasonableness F.38

Probably of identical and equal force to the requirement that the alternative course should not amount to a breach of the contract of affreightment are the express provisions in the new Rule Paramount[43] that "*In no case shall there be any allowance for sacrifice or expenditure unless reasonably made or incurred*".

As recorded earlier in paragraph F.22, above, in the preparatory stages preceding the Sydney Conference in 1994 the United States Maritime

[40] *Marida Ltd v. Oswal Steel; The Bijela* [1993] 1 Lloyd's Rep. 411.
[41] (1867) L.R. 2 Q.B. 203.
[42] *Marida Ltd v. Oswal Steel; The Bijela* [1994] 2 Lloyd's Rep. 1.
[43] See para. PRE.22, *ante*.

Law Association had proposed an amendment whereby a substituted expense would qualify for consideration as general average only when the expense of the alternative course of action "*would have been reasonably incurred* and allowable as general average". This proposal was not maintained when the all-embracing Rule Paramount put forward by the same U.S.M.L.A. was accepted at Sydney, for this latter proposal clearly comprises the former.

However, because the original proposal was allowed to lapse and no specific mention is made in the Rule Paramount to the alternative course of action, it may be argued by some that although the Rule requires the costs of the course actually adopted to have been reasonably incurred, no such requirement of reasonableness applies to the hypothetical course of action. It does; indeed, this requirement of reasonableness has probably always existed in respect of claims under any of the lettered Rules by the provisions of Rule A, as was accepted by J.R. Danson when he questioned the practice of adjusters in his address to the Association of Average Adjusters in 1946:

> "It has not . . . been the custom of adjusters to enquire too deeply into the reasonableness or otherwise of the various courses open to the shipowner and it has been their practice to charge the lesser sum to general average under the strict terms of Rule F, *without considering the effect of the overriding wording of Rule A*."

F.39 The problem was also considered in the seventh edition of this work at page 387 when dealing with the old Rule X(d), whose wording permitted substituted expense allowances in general average only when the vessel was in a port at which it was *practicable* to repair her:

> "It may be argued, of course, that if the alternative is extravagantly expensive . . . it would be unreasonable to undertake it, and in fact it would never be seriously contemplated, and therefore it cannot be brought into consideration in applying this Rule. In other words, there would be no course commercially possible for which the towage or transhipment was substituted."

It also received mention in the address of A.B. Dann to the Association of Average Adjusters in 1976:

> "When one is considering substituted expense for allowance in general average one cannot allow expenses substituted for something which, being unreasonable, could not have been allowed in general average at all."

and in subsequent correspondence from the same gentleman:

> "It would be monstrous to allow in general average expenses substituted for something which would not be allowed in general average itself because it was unreasonable. I suspect that sometimes adjusters are guilty of doing this, i.e. not considering critically whether the so called alternative would itself have been allowable."

What is "reasonable" is always a question of fact and, adapting the words of Lord Atkin:[44]

> "The true test seems to be what *course of action* might a prudent person controlling the voyage at the time *adopt*, having in mind all the relevant circumstances existing at the time, including the terms of the contract and the interests of all parties concerned, but without obligation to consider the interests of any one as conclusive".

"and so allowed without regard to the saving, if any, to other interests," It is convenient to construe, first, the concluding words of this phrase. The *other interests* are not those parties to the adventure other than the one who has incurred the additional expense, but the individual and particular interests (as opposed to general average interests) of *any* of the parties to the adventure. Thus, the shipowner may incur an expense of 5,000 which it will be assumed qualifies as *additional* and whereby overall savings are achieved as follows: F.40

(1) *To General Average*	6,000
(2) *To the Shipowner* in respect of:	
(a) the cost of repairing accidental damage to the ship ...	6,000
(b) Loss of earnings (or time-hire)	6,000
(3) *To the Cargo Interests* in respect of deterioration in the condition of their cargo and/or loss of interest on their capital	6,000
	24,000

Turning now to the whole phrase, the 5,000 additional expense incurred by the shipowner being less than the 6,000 savings to general average, the 5,000 can be wholly charged to general average, and the other savings of 18,000 may be disregarded. Let us consider those other savings:

Heads (2)(b) and (3)—Loss of earnings, and deterioration of cargo F.41

Rule F deals with *expenses* alone, not losses,[45] and it is perhaps appropriate, therefore, that any saving achieved by the substituted course of action and/or reduced detention in the port of refuge in loss of earnings to the shipowner, or of deterioration to the cargo, should be disregarded. Further, it may on occasion be possible to say that these losses to the ship and cargo interests will tend to cancel each other out. It is to be noted, however, that although the Rule permits the shipowner's loss of earnings to be consciously ignored, they have such a very strong influence on any operational decision made by him that they will tend to set the pattern for his normal repairing practice. As an example, the

[44] *Stag Line v. Foscola Mango* [1932] A.C. 328; 101 L.J.K.B. 165.
[45] See paras. F.19–F.22, *ante*.

use of air-freight[46] for sending spare parts to a ship abroad is now almost routine, part of the normal and reasonable cost of repairs, and but rarely to be considered as an additional expense. Similar remarks may apply also to the working of overtime on repairs.[47]

F.42 *Head (2)(a)—Saving in cost of repairs to accidental damage*

The only alternative course of action likely to produce a saving in the cost of repairs to the ship and requiring to be considered under Rule F[48] occurs when the ship is towed from the port of refuge to her destination or elsewhere. Unlike the loss of earnings or deterioration of cargo dealt with in paragraph F.41, above, a saving in the cost of repairs is undoubtedly an *expense* to which the wording of the Rule applies and the saving can be ignored provided that the cost of towage qualifies as additional. This problem will be discussed further in paragraphs F.49, F.50, below.

F.43 **"but only up to the the amount of the general average expenses avoided."** The allowance in general average for substituted expenses properly acceptable as general average must clearly not exceed the cost of the alternative expenses which would have been incurred and be chargeable to general average. Thus, if cargo is forwarded to destination at a cost (after crediting normal voyage expenses saved) of 150,000 but the alternative expenses of storing the cargo, etc., at the port of refuge amount only to 120,000, only 120,000 of the forwarding expenses can be charged to general average and the excess of 30,000 will, in the absence of special agreement, be for the account of the party incurring the expenditure—usually the shipowner.[49]

F.44 To conclude the commentary on this phrase it may be remarked that merely because a certain course of action produces a saving in general average expenditure, this does not automatically mean that those savings can be charged to general average. There must be an additional and substituted expense actually incurred against which to set those savings. Thus, if cargo is forwarded from a port of refuge by a sister ship operating on the same liner service, the owner is not entitled to charge a *pro forma* second freight merely to "soak up" the general average savings of storing the cargo.

Unless he is entitled to and does charge the cargo with a second freight, he may put forward for consideration in general average only the additional expenses to which he has been put by the forwarding

[46] See para. F.28, *ante*, and paras. F.58, F.59, *post*.

[47] See paras. F.30, F.31, *ante*, and paras. F.55, F.56, *post*.

[48] Temporary repairs also produce considerable savings in the majority of cases, but these are dealt with under the specific provisions of Rule XIV.

[49] *Lee v. Southern Ins. Co.* (1870) L.R. 5 C.P. 397; 39 L.J.C.P. 218; 22 L.T. 443; 18 W.R. 863.

vessel's extended stay at the port of loading, or her unscheduled call there.

The Practical Examples Re-Considered

The construction of the wording of the Rule having been completed, it will be appropriate again to consider the various practical examples of substituted expenses commonly encountered in practice, (and mentioned in paragraphs F.07, F.16, above, and elsewhere), in the light of the criteria propounded earlier in this Section, and in particular: **F.45**

(1) Is the expense truly *additional*, as required by the Rule?
(2) Would the expense of the alternative course of action be properly chargeable to general average, or might such alternative course constitute a breach of the contract of affreightment in that it would cause *unreasonable* delay or expense to the cargo and thereby wholly or partly debar the expense from admission as general average by the terms of the Rule Paramount?[50]

Example (1): Temporary Repairs **F.46**

Specific provision for dealing with the cost of temporary repairs is made in Rule XIV, and that being a numbered Rule, by reason of the Rule of Interpretation[51] it is unnecessary to consider the subject under the general provisions of this lettered Rule F.

However, were it ever necessary to do so, on the authority of *Wilson v. The Bank of Victoria,*[52] temporary repairs to accidental damage (unless involving a sacrifice of other materials in the ship) would in the great majority of cases be debarred from consideration as a substituted expense on one or both the above grounds.[53]

Example (2)(a): Towage to Destination, and Example (3): Forwarding Cargo from a Port of Refuge **F.47**

From 1890 to 1974 (when the Rule was discarded), both of these examples were the subject of specific provisions in Rule X(d) of the York-Antwerp Rules, as follows:

> "(d) If a ship under average be in a port or place at which it is practicable to repair her, so as to enable her to carry on the whole cargo, and if, in

[50] See para. PRE.22, *ante*.
[51] See para. PRE.04, *ante*.
[52] (1867) L.R. 2 Q.B. 203.
[53] See also paras. 14.01, 14.02, *post*, also "The Cuckoo in the Nest" at para. 14.39, *post*.

order to save expense, either she is towed thence to some other port or place of repair or to her destination, or the cargo or a portion of it is transhipped by another ship, or otherwise forwarded, then the extra cost of such towage, transhipment and forwarding or any of them (up to the amount of the extra expense saved) shall be payable by the several parties to the adventure in proportion to the extraordinary expense saved."

A comparison of this wording with that of the British Rules of Practice F.14[54] and F.15[55] shows that the provisions were all but identical and that the extra expense of towing the vessel or forwarding the cargo to destination (that is after crediting the normal expenses of completing the voyage in the original vessel and under her own power) was payable by the several parties to the adventure in proportion to the extraordinary expenses saved (by each of them).

As a generalisation it may be assumed that in the case of:

F.48 "*Forwarding*" the cargo, the only expense saved will be for storing the cargo at the port of refuge during the period of repairs to the ship, allowable as general average by the terms of Rule X(c), and the effect of Rule F or X(d) will be the same. (See the further remarks and example in paragraphs F.11, F.12, above).

The cost measures up admirably to the criteria set out in paragraph F.45, above:

(1) It will almost invariably qualify as being *additional*, for the shipowner is under no obligation under the terms of the contract of affreightment to forward; he has complete discretion whether to forward. Equally, the forwarding will have no effect on any repairs to the ship, which will continue to be carried out at the port of refuge or nearby, whether the cargo be forwarded or stored.
(2) The cost of the alternative course of action of storing the cargo would be properly chargeable to general average (unless the voyage is frustrated), again because the shipowner has complete discretion whether or not to forward.

F.49 With regard to "*Towage to Destination*", the savings achieved thereby in the port of refuge may include:

(1) detention expenses (crew wages, and daily port charges, etc.)[56];
(2) the cost of discharging, storing and reloading cargo (if necessary to effect repairs to the ship)[57]; and
(3) a reduction in the cost of repairs, if repair charges at destination or elsewhere are cheaper than in the port of refuge.

[54] See para. F.08, *ante*.
[55] See para. F.11, *ante*.
[56] Potentially chargeable to general average under Rules X or XI.
[57] Potentially chargeable to general average under Rules X or XI.

As set out in the example in paragraph F.09, above, if the repairs were to accidental damage, under the old Rule X(d) the shipowner would contribute to the cost of towage in respect of any saving in the cost of his repairs.[58] Under Rule F, however, provided that the cost of towage can be considered an *additional* expense, the wording permits this saving in the cost of repairs to be ignored and the net cost of towage to be charged direct to general average up to the amount of the general average expense avoided.

Whether this cost of towage can be considered as an additional expense depends, perhaps, on whether it can be classified (or compartmentalised) wholly as an expense of completing the *voyage*, or as part of the cost of *repairs*.

For the purpose of this discussion, let it be assumed that the expenses in the port of refuge avoided by the towage consist of:

1. General average (*e.g.* detention expenses and/or costs of discharging, storing and reloading cargo)[59]		200,000
2. Repairs to accidental damage		350,000
and that:		
3. The net cost of towage to destination is	100,000	
Less: Normal expenses of completing the voyage (*e.g.* bunkers saved)	20,000	80,000

Now if the cost of repairs at destination amounts to 400,000 **F.50**
(that is, 50,000 more than in the port of refuge), there could be no doubt that the net cost of towage (80,000) was exclusively a *voyage* expense, that it was wholly *additional*, and, having saved 200,000 of general average expenses in the port of refuge, that it should qualify for admission in general average—as, indeed, might the 50,000 difference in the cost of repairs to the accidental damage itself.

In practice, however, the cost of repairs at destination is rather more likely to be less than at the port of refuge, *e.g.* .... 200,000 showing a saving of 150,000, alone sufficient to justify the shipowner in deciding to defer the repairs and to engage the tugs. The cost of towage thus appears more in the nature of a repair move, and, indeed, were it required, would properly constitute part of the "*reasonable cost of repairs*" within the terms of section 69 of the Marine Insurance Act 1906. Moreover, this cost of towage can hardly be said to represent a *sacrifice* of cash to the shipowner.

[58] In explaining why Rule X(d) should be retained in the 1950 York-Antwerp Rules, it was stated at the Amsterdam Conference:

> "That Rule X(d) is a safeguard for cargo interests. It ensures that a shipowner should not abuse the situation by entering upon a course which is of greater benefit to him than to other interests, and then being able to recover the whole expenses in general average."

[59] Potentially chargeable to general average under Rules X or XI.

Nevertheless, and on the grounds that it cannot be predicated that his decision to tow to destination was taken *exclusively* for the savings in repair costs, and that the particular wording of Rule F ("*without regard to the savings ... to other interests*") permits these repair cost savings to be ignored, the whole cost of towage can be charged to general average up to the amount of the general average expense avoided, subject only to the qualification under the Rule Paramount[60] that:

F.51 The costs associated with the alternative course (generally permanent repairs at the port of refuge), would have been reasonably incurred and allowable as general average. This must depend on the figures and delay involved in any particular case. If the net cost of towage, as in the example above in paragraph F.49, were only 80,000, but the costs of discharging, storing and reloading the cargo, etc., at the port of refuge 500,000, and the extra delay of two months, such alternative course might well be considered unreasonable and a breach of the contract of affreightment; if the costs were only 120,000 and the extra delay a mere couple of weeks, the conclusion might be otherwise.

F.52 **Example (2)(b): Using Bunkers for Auxiliary Engine rather than Proceeding under Sail**

This situation is not likely to be encountered in modern practice, but its present day equivalent "*Using more expensive bunkers*", was considered by an A.I.D.E. Working Group which produced a Discussion Paper on York-Antwerp Rules F and XIV at York in September 1989. In Section c(ii) they instanced:

> "... a case where, in order to save general average detention expenses whilst waiting for the delivery of engine parts, the vessel is permitted to proceed using diesel oil instead of I.F.O. which would normally be consumed by the main engines, (and) it is only the difference between the cost of the diesel and I.F.O. which is to be taken into consideration" (as a substituted expense).

The report provoked considerable discussion at York and the extra cost of the diesel oil over the I.F.O. was not unreservedly accepted as a genuine substituted expense. However, and even assuming the extra cost of the fuel were considered *additional*, the alternative course of action would need to be most carefully considered to ensure that it would not be unreasonable and constitute a breach of the contract of carriage, thereby rendering the cost inadmissible as general average.

[60] See para. PRE.22, *ante*.

Example (4): Loss by Sale of Cargo at a Port of Refuge F.53

A loss by sale on a cargo sold at a port of refuge to avoid the greater expense of storing it, etc., during the period of repairs may be, in appropriate circumstances, a proper subject for an allowance in general average, but as Rule F was intended to deal with substituted *expenses*, not losses, and any sale of cargo can take place only by special agreement of the cargo owners and the shipowners (plus their respective insurers) it is suggested that such special agreement should also make reference, *inter alia*, to whether any part of the loss by sale should be the subject of general average.

Example (5): Drydocking with Cargo on Board F.54

The cost of pumping out a drydock on two occasions to install and remove extra blocks and cradles sufficient to support the additional weight of a vessel with her cargo still on board must undoubtedly be an *additional* expense; the normal practice of most shipowners is to drydock their vessels in a ballast condition, and any additional cost when cargo is on board cannot readily be considered as a normal part of the "reasonable cost of repairs" in terms of section 69 of the Marine Insurance Act 1906.

However, the additional cost of drydocking with cargo on board will usually be relatively insignificant when compared with the costs avoided of the alternative course of discharging, storing and reloading the cargo (for example 3,000 versus 200,000, and possibly delaying the adventure by an extra week). On such figures, and even allowing for the extra risk of drydocking with cargo on board, the alternative course would appear to be unjustifiable, unreasonable, and its cost should accordingly not be made good in general average. This means, as a matter of strict principle, that the cost of the course adopted (for example 3,000) ought not to be charged to general average.

Bearing in mind, however, that almost the only object in incurring this additional expense will be to reduce the "general average" expenditure otherwise to be expected, and that no other worthwhile benefits whatever would accrue to any of the parties to the adventure, the editors feel bound to express a certain sympathy for the existing practice and that this particular substituted expense should continue to gain admission to general average.

Example (6): (1) Overtime Working on Repairs or other Operations F.55

When any job of work is undertaken in "overtime" hours, at night, weekends, or on national holidays, there will generally be an *extra* cost as compared with the cost of the work in normal hours, the labour probably receiving "time and a half" or "double-time" for their efforts. If the work be emergency temporary repairs or discharging of cargo, the extra cost of the overtime working will be treated as part of the reasonable cost of the operation itself and charged direct to general average. However, if the overtime be ordered simply to speed up the time to be taken on, for instance, repairs to accidental damage in a port of refuge, can the extra cost of working that overtime be treated as a substituted expense and charged to general average up to the saving in other expenses (for example crew wages and maintenance) that would have been incurred and allowed to general average during the extra detention that would have resulted if repairs had been carried out in normal working hours?

How does this extra cost of working overtime measure up to the criteria set down in paragraph F.45, above? (1) Is the expense truly *additional?*, and (2) might the alternative course of action cause unreasonable delay and expense and the cost, therefore, be inadmissible as general average?

There should rarely be any difficulty with the *second* condition. If the work were carried out in normal working hours, there would obviously be additional delay and an increase in those charges accruing on a daily basis, but neither the delay nor the expense of the alternative course is ever likely to be considered unreasonable. Thus, if the extra cost of working overtime can satisfy the *first* condition and be considered an *additional* expense, it will be properly chargeable to general average (up to the savings in general average achieved).

F.56 This particular problem—a difficult one—has already been addressed in paragraphs F.30, F.31, above, and reference is requested to the views expressed therein. However, these are in contrast to the working practice of average adjusters in general, who, in the interests of uniformity, will follow the expressed Opinions of the Advisory Committee of the Association of Average Adjusters on a problem first posed by Lloyd's in 1954. It concerned the working of overtime on repairs to accidental damage in drydock, and it appeared that before considering the allowance to be made in general average, some adjusters deducted from the cost of the overtime the cost of the drydock dues, etc., saved, while others considered the whole of the overtime should be treated as general average up to the general average expense avoided. In reply, the Advisory Committee were:

> "... of the opinion that the cost of the overtime represents an extra expense incurred within the terms of Rule F and, as such, forms a first charge on the general average saving without regard to the savings, if any, to other interests, e.g. dry-dock dues."

This Opinion being considered somewhat suspect, the problem was reposed in 1989 and the Advisory Committee then reported that it:

"... has been unanimously agreed that no amendment to the previous Committee's Opinion is necessary.

... neither has any evidence been given of any divergence in practice since the previous Opinion was delivered."

With the semi-authority of the 1954 Report, it is un-surprising that in 1989 all members of the A.A.A. were following the same practice, but it is perhaps surprising that an *Advisory* Committee should not give some serious consideration to the principles involved in the problem. To the extent that the working of such overtime:

(1) can be considered as part of the *reasonable cost of repairs*[61] in that it produces compensating savings in drydock dues and/or other ancilliary expenses forming an indispensable part of the repairs, or

(2) would be ordered by the shipowner as part of his normal repairing practice,

the cost cannot be considered as an additional expense within Rule F.

Example (6): (2) Overtime of Crew **F.57**

By reason of the 24-hours-a-day nature of life on board ship and the progressive reduction in the acceptable number of hours in a working week, a considerable amount of "regular" overtime is paid to sailors acting as nightwatchmen, to engineers on generator watches, and to catering staff preparing early, late, and weekend meals. As stated in paragraph 11.35, below, "regular" overtime is treated in practice as an integral part of the crew's wages and accordingly allowed direct to general average when the basic wages are so allowable. Overtime paid to crew for work on repairs to damage caused by sacrifice (or, indeed, for work on any general average operation) is also probably allowable direct to general average without reference to Rule F.

However, overtime paid to crew for work on repairs to damage caused by accident or other extraordinary circumstance can only be considered for an allowance in general average in precisely the same manner and subject to the same criteria as overtime of shore repairers dealt with under paragraphs F.55, F.56, immediately above. And where the ship-owner makes use of the enforced stay of his vessel at a port of refuge by setting the crew to work on some considerable maintenance or upkeep programme (such as overhauling a boiler, painting the accommodation or stripping down a generator), general average should never be burdened with any part of the overtime paid to the crew for this particular work. This was the basic intention behind the old Rule XI(d),[62] introduced in

[61] See the Marine Insurance Act 1906, s. 69(1).

[62] "XI(d) When overtime is paid to the master, officers or crew for maintenance of the ship or repairs, the cost of which is not allowable in general average, such overtime shall be allowed in general average only up to the saving in expense which would have been incurred and admitted as general average, had such overtime had been incurred."

1950 but rescinded in 1994, essentially to make room for the second leg of the "pollution compromise" now appearing in Rule C. There was a suggestion that the old Rule (XI)(d) had been open to abuse, but if so, that abuse can no doubt still be practiced under this Rule F.

F.58 Example (7): Air Freight

The practical difficulty of distinguishing between expenses which some will consider to be "additional", but others as perfectly normal and routine, is perhaps best highlighted by the differing treatment accorded the cost of sending machinery parts, etc., to a port of refuge by air, rather than by sea.

In *Western Canada Steamship Co. Ltd v. Canadian Commercial Corporation,*[63] shipowners recovered contribution towards the expense of flying by a specially chartered Halifax bomber a new tailshaft from Wales to Singapore, in so far as it exceeded the freight for such a voyage by sea, on the ground that port of refuge expenses in a larger amount were thereby saved, and would otherwise have been allowed in general average. The defendants' contention that such an expense was usual and not "additional" was rejected.

Judgment in the above case was given in 1960 and related to events which took place in 1947. Since that time the carriage of goods by air has increased more than a hundred fold[64] and what was at one time unusual and exceptional must by now be considered commonplace and regarded as the rule. If such a stage has been reached, the cost of air transport must be treated as part of the reasonable cost of repairs and should no longer be considered as a substituted expense for sea or other transport.

In 1947 it was the general practice in Britain to treat the extra cost of sending *any* shipment by air as a substituted expense for the general average expenses saved, and an example before us from that time is in respect of a case of engine spares valued at 300 being air-freighted from England to New Zealand for 550, whereas they could have been sent by sea for 20. The increased cost of 530 was charged to general average, but with hindsight one wonders just how many *thousands* in extra freight or hire would have been earned in the enormous time saved thereby! The shipowner would undoubtedly have sent those spares by air even if there had been no cargo on board, and even at that time he would have considered the air freight as part of the reasonable cost of repairs.

[63] [1960] 2 Lloyd's Rep. 313; SCR 632.

[64] I.C.A.O. Statistics of World Air Transport (excluding China and U.S.S.R.) shown in freight ton miles.

1945	45 millions
1949	390 millions
1959	1,330 millions
1969	7,080 millions
1986	29,596 millions (including China and U.S.S.R.)

By 1960 most members of the British Association of Average Adjusters had also recognised the true nature of the expenses of air freight, but in that year their United States counterpart passed a Rule of Practice whereby the supposed extra cost of air freight should be allowed as general average, and in 1969 confirmed that in their opinion the Rule was correct both in principle and practice. It is to be noted that when an almost identical Rule of Practice was put before the British Association of Average Adjusters in 1970, only one person voted in favour of the proposal. **F.59**

A sub-committee of the *Association Internationale de Dispacheurs Europeens*, reporting in 1969 on the simplification of the York-Antwerp Rules, suggested that air freight on engine parts by scheduled flights was now quite a normal means of transport and should be treated as part of the cost of repairs and not as a substituted expense, but that this stage had not then been reached with charter flights. By 1997, even charter flights are probably a normal and routine means of transporting larger parts.

Not until 1991 did the United States Association change their Rule of Practice, but they then swept the stable really clean and, moreover, issued such a sound exposition on the proper treatment of air freight on chartered aircraft that we gratefully copy it with their kind permission:

"Rule XXI—Air Freight

"The cost of ordinary air freight on repair parts shall be allowed as part of the reasonable cost of repairs. **F.60**

The cost of any extraordinary shipments by air, such as chartered aircraft or similar means, shall be dealt with by the Adjuster considering (1) the reasons for such shipment and/or (2) the savings resulting therefrom. The Adjuster shall insert a note in the average statement in explanation of the allowances or charges made."

and in explanation of the second paragraph:

"The word 'extraordinary' primarily refers to shipment by chartered airplane. The circumstances envisaged are:

1) The size of the part is such that it will not fit on regular schedule airplanes at tariff rates. If the cost of the chartered airplane is reasonably incurred, then the cost of the shipment follows the cost of repairs, e.g. Particular Average, General Average or Owners.
   One example of what might be regarded as not reasonable is when it is know for some time that an oversized part is required at a scheduled repair port, and that the part could have been shipped by sea well in advance of that time.
2) The part could have been shipped by ordinary airfreight, but some saving results from the use of a chartered airplane. For example, if the repair port is remote and the shipment would require three changes of airplane, resulting in seven days of transit, while a chartered airplane would deliver the part in two days, there has been a saving of five days. The Adjuster would determine the saving involved in G.A., and/or P.A. and explain the saving in the note following the invoice."

RULE G

G.01 The *numbered* Rules of the York-Antwerp Rules each have a title—or heading—giving some indication of the subject-matter they cover, but for reasons unknown, the *lettered* Rules are not similarly identified with the general principles they cover. If some heading is to be found for Rule G, it might be:

WHERE AND WHEN GENERAL AVERAGE LOSSES ARE TO BE VALUED, AND CONTRIBUTORY VALUES ASSESSED

G.02 The basic answer to all these questions might sensibly be deduced by considering the likely position in those early times when the general average distribution system first evolved, when merchants travelled with their cargoes for the whole voyage on board the ship. In the absence of an alternative prior agreement between all the parties to the adventure, it is reasonable to assume that any necessary general average adjustment would have been prepared:

(1) Only when the parties were about to disperse, that is, on safe arrival at the intended destination (or some other place where the adventure was abandoned).
(2) On the basis of the values of the properties at that time and place, both for the assessment of contributory values and for making good any general average sacrifices.
(3) In accordance with the law applicable at that place.

Although the merchants may no longer travel with the ship today, the answers are still very much the same—the law and values at destination govern everything—and the only likely difference is that the appointed adjuster may exercise his professional skills from his own regular place of business, rather than necessarily at the place where the adventure terminates. However, the subject is considerably more complex than is suggested by the bald principle outlined above, and it is necessary to consider these same questions in rather greater detail.

Rule G is concerned only with the *valuation* of the property involved in the common adventure; the Rule specifically leaves open the question of the *place* at which the adjustment is to be prepared and the *law* of the adjustment. These latter topics are dealt with separately in Section 5, and particularly paragraphs 30.01–30.35, below.

English Law and Background

The Time and Place of Valuation

In any adjustment there are two sets of values to be considered. First there is that of the general average loss which is to be made good and secondly there is the contributory value of each contributing interest, and it is worth stressing here that only by assessing the allowance in general average for property sacrificed on precisely the same basis as contributory values are calculated—at the termination of the adventure—can the supremely equitable aims of the general average system be achieved whereby it should be financially immaterial to any party to the adventure whether his goods or property were sacrificed, or those of another. **G.03**

If the general average loss consists of extraordinary expenditure its "value" is determined at the time when it is incurred and paid. If, however, the general average loss consists of a sacrifice, the thing sacrificed may be worth £*x* at the time of the sacrifice but nevertheless it may be shown that, had there been no sacrifice, its market value would have risen or fallen as the voyage proceeded or indeed that it would have become valueless by the time the vessel reached the port of destination or the place at which the voyage was abandoned. Again a contributing interest may be worth £*y* at the time of the general average loss but, because of subsequent accident or the effects of the peril to avert which the loss was incurred, when it reaches the port of destination it also may be of greatly reduced value or be worthless. It will thus be seen that the time and place as at which, and thus the state of facts real or assumed upon which, the adjustment is made is of the greatest importance.

Sacrifices

Where the general average loss consists of a sacrifice it is generally agreed that the state of facts, real in the case of contributing interests and assumed in the case of the thing sacrificed, which forms the basis of the adjustment is that existing at the termination of the adventure. This will be the date of discharge at the port of destination unless the voyage is wholly broken up earlier, in which case it will be the date when the voyage was broken up. This is decided by *Fletcher v. Alexander*,[1] in which a ship bound from Liverpool to Calcutta with a cargo consisting entirely of salt stranded on a sandbank. In order to refloat, a very large portion of the salt was thrown overboard and she was then towed off the bank and brought back to Liverpool in a leaky state. Of the salt not **G.04**

[1] (1868) L.R. 3 C.P. 375.

jettisoned, the greater part was either washed out by sea-water or so damaged as not to be fit for reshipment.

Bovill C.J. referred to the valuation of the contributing interests in the following terms:

> "If after jettison or the matter which is the subject of general average has arisen, the remainder of the goods are totally lost, and so no benefit accrues to the owners of the other goods from the jettison, no contribution can be claimed. The whole law on the subject is founded on the principle that the loss to the individual whose goods are sacrificed for the benefit of the rest is to be compensated according to the loss sustained on the one hand and the benefit derived on the other."[2]

Of the valuation of the thing sacrificed, he said:

> "It is clear that the value of the goods at the time of the jettison is not to be taken as the test, because, if the whole adventure is afterwards brought to an end by the loss of ship and cargo, there will be no contribution at all. The rules as to contribution and adjustment seem to me to depend upon the probable state of things at, and to have reference to, the time and place of adjustment,[3] that is to say, when and where the adjustment ought to take place ... In the present case, it is almost a matter of certainty that, if the salt which was jettisoned had remained on board, it could not have reached the port of adjustment, Liverpool, in a sound state. What, then, is the loss which the owner has sustained by the jettison? The only loss I can suggest is the value of the salt if it had arrived in an unsound state."[4]

Thus, although property may have been in sound condition when it was jettisoned or otherwise sacrificed, the allowance in general average will not be for the full sound value if it can confidently be asserted that such property would have suffered loss or damage during the remainder of the voyage subsequent to the sacrifice. The allowance for property sacrificed must be subjected to the same vicissitudes of the continuing voyage as were suffered by the properties which arrived at destination, and reduced accordingly.

Expenditure

G.05 For many years there was a dispute between the writers of textbooks as to whether the same rule applied to expenditure. However, it is thought that this controversy may now be allowed to subside, and the answer taken to be laid down by Sankey J. in 1921, which has not since been overturned.[5] In the case of expenditure, as with sacrifices, contributory values are assessed at the termination of the adventure; if

[2] *Ibid.* at 382.

[3] In this and other early reported cases, the phrase *place of adjustment* equates with termination of the adventure. The matter is discussed further at para. 30.02, *post*.

[4] (1868) L.R. 3 C.P. 375 at 383.

[5] *Chellew v. Royal Commission on the Sugar Supply* [1921] 2 K.B. 627; [1922] 1 K.B. 12.

none of the interests survive, there is no contribution.[6] Where the York-Antwerp Rules apply, there can be no doubt that this is the result.[7]

Historical Development and Practice of Rule G

York-Antwerp Rules 1924 **G.06**

Detailed provisions relating to the assessment of contributory values and amounts made good for general average losses had appeared in the *numbered* Rules of the York-Antwerp Rules from their very advent in 1860, and those same provisions were expressed in briefer and even more general terms in Rule G, introduced in 1924 as part of the new set of *lettered* Rules setting out the fundamental principles of general average. Rule G then read:

> General average shall be adjusted as regards both loss and contribution upon the basis of values at the time and place when and where the adventure ends.
>
> This rule shall not affect the determination of the place at which the average statement is to be made up.

The *first paragraph* was thoroughly innocuous in that it merely expressed what was generally accepted worldwide and was purposely silent on what practitioners really required, that is some pronouncement or working rule on the vexed question of when and where the adventure ended on those increasingly common occasions when the vessel had on board cargo for a number of ports of discharge.

A Draft Code of General Average prepared in 1914 by Mr H.C. Dowdall K.C. had proposed that: **G.07**

> Section 5.(1) General average shall be adjusted as regards both loss and contribution upon the basis of values at the first port of discharge after the general average act occurs, or at any earlier place at which the voyage may be broken up. Such port or place is hereinafter called the place of adjustment.
>
> (2)...
>
> (3) The provisions of this section shall not affect the determination of the place at which the average statement is to be made up.

However, as the more generally accepted practice in this country and the Continent was to adjust general average as regards both loss and

[6] The contrary view, championed by Lowndes, is discussed at length in the 10th edition, paras. 345 *et seq.* The point was left open by the Court of Appeal in the *Chellew* case: see [1922] 1 K.B. 12 at 20, *per* Scrutton L.J. See also *The Mary Thomas* [1894] P. 108; *Green Star Shipping v. The London Assurance* [1933] 1 K.B. 378 at 390; *Morrison S.S. Co. Ltd v. Greystoke Castle* [1947] A.C. 265 at 285, 312.

[7] See para. G.20, *post*. See also the *Chellew* case in the Court of Appeal, and *Green Star Shipping v. The London Assurance* (see n. 6, *ante*).

contribution upon the basis of values at the port of destination of the part of the cargo concerned, and in respect of the ship at the *last* port to which any of the cargo on board at the time of the general average act was consigned, the central proposal in the Draft Code to adopt the *first* port of discharge as the termination of the adventure was not generally acceptable. In fact, it will be noted that Rule G opts neither for the first or last port of discharge, leaving the matter quite open, but the Rule does follow exactly the opening and concluding words of the Draft Code of 1914.

The *second paragraph* of Rule G was in accordance with and gave contractual effect to the decision of the Privy Council in the case of *Wavertree Sailing Ship Co. v. Love.*[8]

G.08 **The applicable law and practice.** The lack of any reference in Rule G to the law and practice which should apply to the adjustment of any general average was an important omission; the subject had previously even merited a Rule of its own—Rule XVIII of the York-Antwerp Rules 1890.[9] Although the practice was well settled that adjustments should be prepared in accordance with the law and practice obtaining at the termination of the adventure, the difficulty was to determine or agree on every occasion precisely where the adventure did end, and this, together with the (unfulfilled) anticipation that because the York-Antwerp Rules were by 1924 a fairly comprehensive and self-contained set of Rules "it should be a matter of indifference at which port the adventure was deemed to be terminated",[10] probably accounts for the omission in the 1924 Rules.

York-Antwerp Rules 1950 and 1974.

No change.

G.09 **York-Antwerp Rules 1994.**

The existing wording of Rule G was again retained unaltered, but a further two paragraphs were added which constituted what previously had been popularly known as a *Non-Separation Agreement* and the *Bigham Clause.* These had customarily been used on an *ad hoc* basis and attached to the individual general average security documents on those occasions when cargo was forwarded to destination by other vessels from a port of refuge, but this need to make special and time-consuming arrangements with each of the cargo interests should now generally

[8] [1897] A.C. 373. See para, 30.04, *post.*
[9] See para. 60.63, *post.*
[10] See *The York-Antwerp Rules* (by G.R. Rudolf, 1926) p. 61.

be obviated by their incorporation within the York-Antwerp Rules themselves:

> When a ship is at any port or place in circumstances which would give rise to an allowance in general average under the provisions of Rules X and XI, and the cargo or part thereof is forwarded to destination by other means, rights and liabilities in general average shall, subject to cargo interests being notified if practicable, remain as nearly as possible the same as they would have been in the absence of such forwarding, as if the adventure had continued in the original ship for so long as justifiable under the contract of affreightment and the applicable law.
>
> The proportion attaching to cargo of the allowances made in general average by reason of applying the third paragraph of this Rule shall not exceed the cost which would have been borne by the owners of cargo if the cargo had been forwarded at their expense.

This is a convenient place to describe the function of Non-Separation Agreements.

Non-Separation Agreements

Background

If the cargo is forwarded to destination—even in continuation of the voyage—it is probably true to say that the *common* adventure ceases when the original carrying vessel and her cargo part company,[11] and that all allowances in general average to the shipowner under Rule XI(b) for crew wages, bunkers, and daily port charges during repairs will cease at that time. Certainly, the cargo cannot be called upon to contribute to general average expenses incurred after leaving the ship.[12] **G.10**

Except in those cases where the voyage by the original vessel has been frustrated, it would seem unfair that the shipowner should suffer these disallowances and possibly bear also part of the cost of the forwarding when, by that forwarding, the cargo interests receive the distinct advantage of a much earlier delivery of their cargo than would otherwise have been the case, plus the additional benefit of being required to contribute only to a reduced general average, that is, one that has been saved the above mentioned allowances under Rule XI(b) for crew wages, etc., and also the cost of storing the cargo allowable under Rule X(c).

Standard Non-Separation Agreement

Accordingly, it has been the custom for over a century[13] to ask cargo interests, in return for the forwarding of their cargo and an earlier delivery, to agree to contribute to a general average adjusted as though **G.11**

[11] See para. G.41, *post*.
[12] *Royal Mail S.P. Co. v. English Bank of Rio* (1887) 19 Q.B.D. 362.
[13] See also Rule of Practice F15 (para. 70.42, *post*) adopted in 1876.

their cargo had remained at the port of refuge during the repairs to the ship, and been carried to destination in the original carrying vessel.

This is achieved by incorporating what is termed a *Non-Separation Agreement* into the Average Bond and General Average Guarantee signed by the consignees and the cargo insurers, respectively. The wording of the Agreement can be tailor-made, to suit any particular circumstances, but a Standard Form of Non-Separation Agreement has been in use in the British market since 1967:

> It is agreed that in the event of the vessel's cargo or part thereof being forwarded to original destination by other vessel, vessels or conveyances, rights and liabilities in General Average shall not be affected by such forwarding, it being the intention to place the parties concerned as nearly as possible in the same position in this respect as they would have been in the absence of such forwarding and with the adventure continuing by the original vessel for so long as justifiable under the law applicable or under the Contract of Affreightment.
>
> The basis of contribution to General Average of the property involved shall be the values on delivery at original destination unless sold or otherwise disposed of short of that destination, but where none of her cargo is carried forward in the vessel she shall contribute on the basis of her actual value on the date she completes discharge of her cargo.

Interpretation of the Agreement

G.12 The object of the Agreement is to place the parties to the adventure in the same position with regard to their rights and liabilities in general average as if the cargo had been justifiably[14] retained at the port of refuge and carried to destination in the original carrying vessel after repairs.[15] Thus, and assuming that the delay for repairs was not sufficient to frustrate the adventure and the contract of carriage, the effect of the Agreement would be:

(1) The wages and maintenance of the crew, bunkers consumed and daily port charges throughout the detention undergoing repairs at the port of refuge would be allowable as general average under Rule XI(b).

(2) The *extra* cost of forwarding the cargo (that is, the actual costs incurred less those expenses which would have been incurred by the original vessel herself to complete the voyage in respect of crew wages, etc., bunkers, port charges and discharging costs at destination—if payable by the carrier) would be charged to general

[14] See paras. G.13, G.14, *post*.

[15] The Drafting Committee for the 1924 York-Antwerp Rules had proposed that a final clause should be added to the old Rule X(d):

> "Where the cargo or a portion of it is forwarded to destination as above, such cargo shall remain liable to contribute to the general average as if it had not been forwarded."

but the Stockholm Conference did not accept the proposal, considering the matter best left to individual special agreements.

average under Rule F as a substituted expense for any necessary cost of storing the cargo at the port of refuge allowable under Rule X(c).

If the savings to general average are insufficient, the excess and unsaved cost of forwarding will be borne by the shipowner.

(3) The contributory values of the property will be:

For the cargo: calculated in the normal way as per Rule XVII on delivery at the original destination, unless sold or otherwise disposed of short of that destination.

For the ship (and bunkers, etc.): calculated in the normal way as per Rule XVII but on the date on which the ship completes discharge of her cargo (at the port of refuge, assuming the whole cargo to be forwarded).

Where the damage to the ship and the repairs necessary to prosecute the voyage are such that the parties to the contract of carriage are legally entitled to say that the voyage has been frustrated and should be abandoned, the strict legal position may be different.

Where the delay would frustrate the adventure

Suppose that the cargo is perishable, or for a seasonal market, or the port of refuge is reasonably close to destination, and the time required to repair the ship is very lengthy (for example six months), when a delay of only some weeks would frustrate the contract. **G.13**

If such a situation were clearly recognisable at the outset, the shipowner would not be entitled to retain the cargo and require it to contribute to general average detention expenses for the full six months. He must either make early arrangements to forward the cargo to destination at his own expense, or he must abandon the voyage and offer delivery of the cargo at the port of refuge, leaving the cargo interests to make alternative arrangements for their cargo and/or to bear any expenses of forwarding. The latter course may be the legal and commercial solution for the shipowner if his freight was prepaid, the former, if the freight is at risk to him and the forwarding can be accomplished at less cost than the freight to be earned.

Clearly, the cargo must contribute to any general average losses and expenses incurred up to the completion of discharge, but nothing thereafter.

However, the circumstances ruling in any casualty situation are rarely so clear-cut, and whether or not the voyage is frustrated can often be determined only at a later stage when it is possible to make a reasonably reliable estimate as to whether the amount of delay or expense is so great **G.14** that the adventure is frustrated.[16] In the meantime, the cargo may have been forwarded in good faith subject to the above standard form of Non-Separation Agreement.

The effect of the standard form is that the allowances for which it provides will cease when the delay to the ship at the port of refuge is sufficient to frustrate the contract, and the agreement is so worded that it probably modifies the common law rule that frustration may occur as a result of prospective delay.[17] For example, if a delay of two months is required to frustrate the contract, the allowances will continue until the two months have expired even though it may be possible at an earlier date to predict with the necessary degree of certainty that the delay will exceed the two months.

Bigham Clause

G.15 For the greater protection of cargo interests fearful of what they may be undertaking when signing a Non-Separation Agreement, it is a common practice in the United States to include what is commonly known as the *Bigham Clause*:

> It is understood that the amount charged to cargo under this agreement shall not exceed what it would have cost the cargo owners if cargo was delivered to them at . . . (port of refuge) and forwarded by them to destination.

In other words, cargo interests cannot be called upon to contribute towards "general average" expenditure incurred during an extended period of repairs more than it would have cost them to forward the cargo themselves from the port of refuge to destination. The Clause is a sensible addition to the Non-Separation Agreement from the point of view of the cargo interests and it calls into question whether the cargo interests have the right, if they consider that it will be cheaper for them to take delivery of their cargo at the port of refuge rather than contribute to any continuing general average expenses incurred after the discharge of their cargo, to refuse to sign a Non-Separation Agreement in any form, but to insist upon taking delivery at the port of refuge and to pay there the freight and any other charges due upon the goods. Under the laws of Canada and of the United States it is clear that the cargo owner has this right.

G.16 Thus in *Ellerman Lines v. Gibbs Nathaniel (Canada); The City of Colombo*[18] the vessel, while on a voyage from Cochin to Toronto, was detained for 69 days for repairs at Montreal, only 350 miles from

[16] See para. 00.40, *ante*.
[17] *Ibid.*
[18] (1986) 26 D.L.R. (4th) 161; (1986) A.M.C. 2217. See also *The Julia Blake* 107 U.S. 418 (1882); *The Domingo de Larrinaga* (1928) A.M.C. 64.

Toronto.[19] It was held that the owners of the Toronto cargo were under no obligation to allow the shipowner to retain and carry their cargo to Toronto in the original ship, after repairs, but were entitled to delivery at any port where the vessel put in, on payment of full freight and of any other charges due upon the cargo.

Whilst there is no English authority on the point, the decision has much to recommend it. Undoubtedly the shipowner is entitled to keep possession of the goods for a reasonable time for the purpose of earning his freight, for as Sir James Hannen said in *The Blenheim*[20]: **G.17**

> "The shipowner has a lien on the cargo for the purpose of enabling him to earn his freight, and the cargo owner is not entitled to insist on delivery of the cargo without payment of freight before the completion of the voyage on which the freight is to be earned."

But, having paid the freight, and any extra expenses incurred by the shipowner in making a special discharge of the cargo, and furnishing security in respect of general average sacrifices and expenditures incurred up to the time of taking delivery, any cargo owner should be entitled to demand delivery of his cargo at an intermediate port of call and a termination of his liability to contribute to continuing general average expenses.

Rule G

General average shall be adjusted as regards both loss and contribution upon the basis of values at the time and place when and where the adventure ends. **G.18**

This rule shall not affect the determination of the place at which the average statement is to be made up.

When a ship is at any port or place in circumstances which would give rise to an allowance in general average under the provisions of Rules X and XI, and the cargo or part thereof is forwarded to destination by other means, rights and liabilities in general average shall, subject to cargo interests being notified if practicable, remain as nearly as possible the same as they would have been in the absence of such forwarding, as if the adventure had continued in the original ship for so long as justifiable under the contract of affreightment and the applicable law.

[19] The delay was such that it might have given rise to the frustration of the adventure, but the issue of frustration was not raised.

[20] (1885) 10 P.D. 167; 54 L.J.P. 81; 5 Asp. M.C. 522.

The proportion attaching to cargo of the allowances made in general average by reason of applying the third paragraph of this Rule shall not exceed the cost which would have been borne by the owners of cargo if the cargo had been forwarded at their expense.

G.19 The first two paragraphs of Rule G, a *lettered* Rule, are concerned only with general principles and, by reason of the Rule of Interpretation,[21] must yield to the specific provisions of the *numbered* Rules XVI and XVII in the event of any conflict. The purpose of these two paragraphs is to set the scene and define in general terms at what time and place the values of the properties in a common maritime adventure and at risk at the time of a general average act should be assessed, for the purpose of calculating both the allowance to be made in general average for any property sacrificed, and also the values on which the property saved should be called upon to contribute to such sacrifice or to any general average expenditure.

CONSTRUCTION

First Paragraph

G.20 **"as regards both loss and contribution"** The effect of the first sentence of the rule is that:

(1) the amount to be made good in respect of any general average loss, whether consisting of sacrifice or of expenditure, and
(2) the amount of contribution due from the other interests,

are assessed on the basis of the actual value of those interests, and the notional value[22] of any property sacrificed, at the end of the adventure.

This Rule, together with Rule XVII therefore resolves the doubt which existed at common law[23] as to whether in the case of general average expenditure contributory values fall to be assessed as at the time and place of the expenditure or whether, as in the case of sacrifices, these values must be assessed as at the termination of the adventure. Thus, a person incurring general average expenditure runs the risk of loss arising out of a subsequent change in the values of the contributing interests as a result, for example, of a casualty[24]; and the contributing interests

[21] See para. PRE.04, *ante*.
[22] See paras. G.03, G.04, *ante*.
[23] See para. G.05, *ante*.
[24] See *Chellew v. Royal Commission on the Sugar Supply* [1921] 2 K.B. 627; [1922] 1 K.B. 12, C.A.

themselves run the risk of the contribution of some being increased by a casualty affecting the value of the remainder.[25]

"loss" In this Rule the word is used in contradistinction to "contribution", and includes "loss", "damage" and "expense", although in other Rules it is to be contrasted with damage (for example Rules II, III, and IV). The word is apt to cover expenditure as well as sacrifice[26], and it might therefore be thought that expenditure, like sacrifice, is to be valued not when it is made, but at the time when the adventure ends. It is submitted however that such a view is erroneous, since the Rule merely provides that loss shall be adjusted "*upon the basis* of values at the time and place when the adventure ends", but not that it shall be itself valued at that time and place. The "values" referred to in the Rule are those of the property at risk in the common adventure,[27] and these values have no relevance to the valuation of expenditure, which therefore falls to be valued at the time when it was made, as it does under English law.[28] In practice, since expenditure is not at risk in the adventure, the correct time and place for its valuation will only be of practical importance in connection with rates of exchange. So far as concerns these, expenditure is to be exchanged at the rate prevailing on the date when the expenditure was made.[29] G.21

"upon the basis of values at the time and place when and where the adventure ends." As previously mentioned, the Rule is deficient in that it fails to define when and where the adventure ends.[30] A similar difficulty exists at common law.[31] A solution to the problem is not assisted by the fact that the Rule expresses the noun *adventure* in the singular, thereby possibly creating the impression that, however complex the voyage, there is only one single adventure, and which editors since the eighth edition have submitted must be the "*common* maritime adventure" referred to in Rule A. G.22

This may well be the case where a single shipment of cargo is carried to a single port of discharge, but less obviously so where the vessel loads a number of shipments at various ports of loading for two or more ports of discharge, possibly even with some transhipment cargo under

[25] See *Green Star Shipping v. The London Assurance* [1933] 1 K.B. 378. See para. G.29, *post*.

[26] "A general average *loss* includes a general average expenditure as well as a general average sacrifice" (Marine Insurance Act 1906, s. 66(1)).

[27] Namely the notional value of property sacrificed and the actual values of other property: see paras. G.03, G.04, *ante*.

[28] See para. G.03, *ante*.

[29] See paras. 40.04, 40.24, *post*.

[30] For the Rule of Practice governing the ascertainment of the end of the adventure for purposes of insurance claims where the vessel is in ballast, see para. 70.12 (Rule B26), *post*.

[31] See paras. G.06, G.07, *ante*.

"through" bills of lading. In any such situation it might more accurately reflect the situation to state that there are *several* commercial adventures at risk, with different termini and of different lengths, but that for *part* of those lengths they and the ship all coincide and are common. This section of the overall voyage can undoubtedly be considered as a common maritime adventure.

G.23 Rule A is concerned only with defining a general average *act*, something which occurs at or during a limited period of the overall voyage and which affects and must be shared by all those separate adventurers who happen to be bound up with the ship at the particular time of the general average act. Rule G addresses a quite separate issue, the evaluation of the general average losses and of the properties which shall continue thereto, and the present editors submit that for this purpose of evaluating the individual general average losses and contributory values, there may be *several* adventures which, in the absence of an earlier abandonment of the voyage, will each terminate at their several destinations. As a basic concept, the relevant maritime adventures for cargo and freight will generally end when their community of interest *with the ship* separates on partition and discharge[32] from the ship at the different ports of discharge, and that for the ship ends on completion of discharge at the final port of discharge.

Potential difficulties in defining the precise termination of the adventure in individual circumstances will be discussed in greater detail as indicated below.

TERMINATION OF THE ADVENTURE

G.24

	Paragraph
(A) Where the voyage is to a single destination and is wholly performed.	G.25
(B) Where the voyage is to two or more ports of destination.	G.26–G.30
(C) Where the scheduled voyage involves the forwarding of cargo from a transhipment port under a through bill of lading.	G.31
(D) Where the intended voyage is justifiably and wholly abandoned at a port short of destination(s).	G.32–G.35
(E) Where the voyage is successfully completed by the ship and some of the cargo, but other cargo is justifiably left behind at a port of refuge.	G.36–G.40
(F) Where the cargo is forwarded from a port of refuge by other vessels, possibly in conjunction with (D) or (E) above:	

[32] The practice is to take the last day of discharge at each of the ports of discharge, this being the relevant date under Rule XVI (see para. 16.18, *post*) until 1974.

(1) By the shipowner, in continuation of the voyage to earn a freight payable only on right delivery at destination, or
(2) By or on behalf of the cargo interests, at their expense or,
(3) Under a Non-Separation Agreement. G.41–G.45

A. Where the voyage is to a single destination and is wholly performed **G.25**

No problems are anticipated in the straightforward situation where the vessel is bound for a single port of discharge and, together with such cargo as has not been lost or destroyed by a general average sacrifice, she arrives there successfully. In the absence of alternative provisions in the contract of affreightment, the law and practice applicable at that destination governs the adjustment, and general average losses and contributory values are both to be assessed on the basis of the values ruling at that place and at the time of discharge (in practice, on the last day of discharge for all the cargo).

B. Where the voyage is two or more ports of destination **G.26**

If a vessel incurs general average expenditure or makes a general average sacrifice when carrying cargo for two or more ports of discharge, does the adventure end at the first port, or at the second (or final) port of discharge? This problem has been touched upon earlier in paragraphs G.22 and G.23, but the principle involved is of sufficient importance and financial consequence that a more detailed study is warranted here.

To illustrate the problem in simple form, let it be assumed that on a voyage to ports A and B the ship and cargoes A and B are each worth 1,000,000, and that during the early part of the voyage a jettison of cargo is made valued at 300,000 or 10 per cent of the total contributory values (including amounts made good). The voyage to port A is successfully completed thereafter without further incident, but the ship and cargo B are totally lost before arrival at port B.

Let the jettison of 300,000 be exclusively of cargo for port A. The interests of cargo A will be best served by suggesting that port A is the termination of that adventure which is common to all the contributors, and that the subsequent portion of the voyage is a matter with which cargo A has no concern. Thus, the general average would be apportioned on values as at A and, effectively, ship and cargo B should contribute their due proportion of say 200,000 towards cargo A's loss of 300,000.

To this view it must be objected, certainly so far as cargo B is concerned, that the voyage is not yet over and that it may perish on the second stage to port B. To assess their value for contribution at A is to fly in the face of the rule that there can be no contribution unless there is benefit, and the extent of that benefit can only be assessed on arrival at B. Further, how can cargo A exercise any lien on or enforce contribution from the ship and cargo B at port A?

Let the jettison of 300,000 be exclusively of cargo for port B. On this occasion, it will suit cargo A to do a *volte-face* and protest if it be similarly suggested that the common adventure ends on the completion of discharge of their cargo at A, and that they should thereupon become liable immediately to pay their due portion of 100,000 towards cargo B's loss of 300,000. They will rightly maintain that if (as in fact happened), the ship and remaining cargo B were lost before arrival at B, cargo B would have lost or sacrificed nothing by the earlier jettison, for that jettisoned cargo would similarly have been totally lost, and, accordingly, that nothing is to be made good in general average.

G.27 In the absence of any contrary law ruling at port A, it is submitted that for the purpose of Rule G there are *two* adventures involved here with different terminii, but united and common at the time of the jettison: one for cargo A, which ended on completion of discharge at port A, and another for the ship and cargo B, which would have terminated for both on completion of discharge at port B but did in fact terminate on their prior loss at sea. Rights of contribution to general average can be enforced only at the place where any adventure ends,[33] and while port A was the appropriate place to exercise these for cargo A, not until their safe arrival at port B could the ship and cargo B be required to contribute towards any general average *sacrifice* sustained by them. Their rights to any general average *expenditure* incurred by them, however, survive the total loss and would be payable wholly by surviving cargo A.

G.28 If we return now to cargo A, its adventure terminates on completion of discharge at port A and it cannot be called upon to contribute to any subsequent salvage or general average suffered by the ship and cargo B after leaving port A. It will be obliged to provide proper general average security before delivery at port A, but although its contributory value and the amount of its own sacrifice can be quantified fairly immediately, its obligation to contribute to any losses sustained by the ship and cargo B and its rights to receive anything from them are obviously deferred until their own adventure has been successfully completed—or lost. Thus, the final stage of the adventure to port B remains of considerable interest to cargo A, and in accordance with the view expressed elsewhere in this series,[34] the adventure does not terminate at the first port of discharge, but continues in part until the last port of discharge of the cargo on board at the time of the general average act. It may be added that in most cases the shippers of cargo for port A will appreciate that the vessel

[33] See paras. 30.36 *et seq., post.*

[34] *British Shipping Laws*, Vol. 3: Carver, *Carriage by Sea* (13th ed.), paras. 1451–1452. For a fuller discussion see the 12th ed., paras. 945–947. See also *British Shipping Laws*, Vol. 10: Arnould, *Marine Insurance*, para. 992.

is also destined for port B, and that cargo has been or may in the future be loaded for that port. In liner service this is common, and the shipowner discloses it in his advertisements.

It is appropriate here to record the facts of a case which supports the view that the common adventure does not cease at the first port at which any of the cargo is discharged, (except as regards the cargo discharged there), but continues in part until the last port of discharge. In the case of *Green Star Shipping Co. Ltd v. The London Assurance*,[35] the vessel was loading at New York when fire broke out in the holds, in consequence of which general average expenditure was incurred by the shipowners. Cargo valued at $18,000 was discharged and not reloaded. The vessel duly sailed from New York with the remainder of the cargo but was involved in a collision and sank. The salved value of ship and cargo, excluding the cargo discharged at New York, was about $142,000 but general average expenditure resulting from the collision amounted to $180,000. **G.29**

Roche J. held that[36]:

> "This 18,000 dollars worth of cargo was the only property in the adventure which was available for the purpose of contribution in the first general average, because the expenditure occasioned by the second general average, the collision, fell to be deducted from the values of ship and cargo (see York-Antwerp Rule XVII)[37] for the purposes of the adjustment of the first general average. After this deduction was made the values of the rest of the cargo and of the ship were nil."

Later in his judgment he reverted to the matter thus[38]:

> "The cargo which went on from New York was reduced in value by the collision and second general average from about 19,000 dollars to nothing. Had there been no collision the full contribution recoverable from cargo in respect of the first general average (fire) would have been recovered. But if the cargo which went on to meet with the collision had not met with that collision and been thereby reduced in value, the cargo which remained at New York would not have been liable to make contribution up to 100 per cent., as it in fact did in the circumstances as altered by the collision."

It is possible that Roche J. considered that the appropriate sound values for ship and all the cargo were New York values, on the basis that the common adventure ended there, Rule XVII providing for the deduction of charges incurred even after the end of the adventure. **G.30**

[35] [1933] 1 K.B. 378. The case was decided under the York-Antwerp Rules 1890 but there is no difference between the Rules and English law on the point.

[36] *Ibid.* at 382.

[37] Of the 1890 Rules which provided that: "The contribution to a general average shall be made upon the actual values of the property at the end of the adventure ... deduction also being made from the value of the property of all charges incurred in respect thereof subsequently to the general average." The 1890 Rules, however, contained no equivalent of Rule G or of the Rule of Interpretation.

[38] [1933] 1 K.B. 378 at 385.

However, this seems unlikely in view of the way in which he expresses himself in the second passage quoted above, and it can hardly be correct to take the physical condition of the goods at one port but to deduct charges incurred up to a subsequent port. It seems more probable that the ship and the cargo reloaded were valued at their actual destination. The case may therefore be regarded as authority for the view that, at any rate where the York-Antwerp Rules apply, the adventure continues in part until the last port of discharge.

G.31 *C. Where the scheduled voyage involves the forwarding of cargo from a transhipment port under a through bill of lading*

In the absence of any specific provisions in the bill of lading, the common adventure as regards the cargo transhipped ends at the transhipment port and the cargo becomes legally liable there and then to contribute to any earlier general average, and on its value in the condition in which it is at that time and place, regardless of what may happen to it on any subsequent stage of its scheduled transport.

However, on practical and commercial grounds, it will usually be found difficult for the shipowner to hold up the cargo at the transhipment port and exercise his lien there and collect general average security at what, for the cargo, is but an intermediate port. In the circumstances, it is likely that the shipowner will permit the cargo to go forward to final destination in the normal way, but taking steps to ensure that the cargo is not released at final destination until the proper general average formalities have been fulfilled.

For practical convenience, as stated in paragraph 17.26, below, the contributory value will be assessed on the value of the cargo at its final destination, except that damage known to have occurred subsequent to leaving the original vessel will not be deducted. However, with even greater practical considerations in mind, particularly the possibility of the cargo being totally lost on the second leg of its voyage, it might be wise to insure the safe arrival of the cargo by a policy covering the average disbursements[39] and adopt as the contributory value the actual value, if any, at final destination.

G.32 *D. Where the intended voyage is wholly abandoned at a port short of destination(s)*

In *Fletcher v. Alexander*,[40] the facts of which are set out in paragraph G.04, the vessel returned to the loading port after stranding and the voyage was there abandoned. The owners of the jettisoned salt refused to furnish a substitute cargo, and when the ship was repaired, her owner

[39] The insurance of average disbursements is discussed, paras. 20.17–20.21, *post*.
[40] (1868) L.R. 3 C.P. 375.

took in a fresh cargo of salt on his own account, and sent it to Calcutta, where it arrived, and was sold at a profit.

On behalf of the owner of the salt it was contended (so far as is here material) that he was entitled to the sum which the jettisoned salt would have produced had it been carried in the ship to Calcutta; and, since the event proved that in that case it would have been sold at a profit, as the second cargo was, he was entitled to such profit. As a consequence of this contention, it was argued that Calcutta was the proper place, and the date of the ship's arrival there the proper time, for adjusting the general average.

Bovill C.J. held that, although in general the port of destination was the proper place for adjusting a general average, yet, when the voyage was broken up, and the adventure brought to an end at some other place, the average should be adjusted there. Thus, if at some intermediate port the entire voyage is wholly abandoned owing to an excepted peril, general average losses and contributory values are both to be assessed on the basis of the values of the property at that place. For example, in respect of:

Cargo sold at the port of refuge. G.33

(1) *Damaged solely by an accidental cause.* The contributory value will be the net sale proceeds of the cargo after deducting any charges incurred to achieve such proceeds (for example reconditioning charges).

(2) *Damaged solely by a general average sacrifice.*
  (a) The contributory value will be the net sale proceeds, as before, plus any amount made good in general average.
  (b) The amount made good will be assessed by deducting the net sale proceeds from the sound value at the port of refuge, which in the normal case is likely to be the sound value at the scheduled destination, less the estimated cost of getting the cargo there.

Cargo forwarded to original destination. Cargo interests may well decide to forward sound or moderately damaged cargo to the scheduled destination in the anticipation that its value there is likely to be greater than any sale proceeds at the port of refuge, but as stated earlier, general average losses and contributory values ought both to be assessed on the values at the place where the voyage was abandoned and general average security presumably obtained. G.34

In practice, this will be achieved by adopting the actual sound or damaged values as at the scheduled destination, but deducting therefrom such charges as were incurred to achieve those destination values (for example the forwarding freight). Loss or damage from any new cause known to have occurred during the forwarding passage must clearly be added back to the actual values at destination, but any natural extension of existing damage may reasonably be ignored or treated as a *quid pro quo* for the likely higher values at intended destination as compared with sale proceeds at the port of refuge.

G.35 The preceding remarks under this head D. are predicated on the assumption that an *accident* caused the voyage to be justifiably abandoned; in the unusual event that a general average *sacrifice* dictated the abandonment of the voyage (for example a voluntary stranding from which the vessel could not be refloated), general average allowances and contributory values should be based on values at the intended destination(s), on the grounds that the loss of the value at destination was a direct result of the general average act.

G.36 *E. Where the voyage is successfully completed by the ship and some of the cargo, but other cargo is justifiably left behind at a port of refuge*

Such a situation occurred in the case of *Hill v. Wilson.*[41] As more fully recorded in paragraph 30.17, below, the *Virago* stranded during the course of a voyage from Riga to Hull with a general cargo, and, after jettisoning a small part of the cargo, was got off and towed into Copenhagen. There the cargo was discharged, much of it sold, some of it forwarded to destination, and, after repairs, the vessel completed the voyage with the remainder of the cargo.

The matter at issue was simply whether English or Danish law should govern the adjustment of the general average, and Lindley J. decided that English law was applicable, both for the ship and the cargo, including that left behind and sold at Copenhagen. He was not concerned with the amounts to be made good in general average or with contributory values, but on the particular facts of case, where it may reasonably be assumed that the damage to the cargo necessarily sold at Copenhagen was of *accidental* origin, there seems little doubt that such cargo should contribute on its net sale proceeds at Copenhagen, while the cargo forwarded in other vessels or carried to destination by the *Virago* would contribute on its value at final destination, Hull.

With regard to the cargo jettisoned, the amount to be made good in general average should be based on the likely condition in which the cargo would, but for the jettison, have arrived at Copenhagen: (1) if badly damaged and requiring to be sold at Copenhagen, on its value at that port, or (2) if sound, or in fit condition to be carried to Hull, on its value there.

G.37 The facts in *Hill v. Wilson*[42] having served as one practical example, this and other practical situations will now be considered with greater precision, essentially under the York-Antwerp Rules. Under this head E.

[41] (1879) 4 C.P.D. 329.
[42] *Ibid.*

these examples will all relate to where the cargo is *sold* at the port of refuge, while examples involving the *forwarding* of cargo to destination will be dealt with below under head F.

Where the cargo is sold at the port of refuge. *(1) Damaged solely by an accidental cause.* Provided that the discharge was not for the common safety, or the cargo be left behind as some form of general average sacrifice (dealt with under head (3), below): G.38

(a) As regards the cargo discharged and sold, both the common adventure and the voyage itself obviously terminate at the port of refuge.
(b) The cargo is not liable for any general average expenses or losses sustained subsequent to its discharge.
(c) The shipowner's general average lien must be exercised at the port of refuge, but will be at least partly subject to the safe arrival of the other property at the scheduled destinations.
(d) The contributory value will be the net sale proceeds of the cargo after deducting any charges incurred to achieve such proceeds (for example reconditioning expenses).

(2) Damaged solely by a general average sacrifice. G.39

(a) For the *net sale proceeds*, the common adventure and the voyage itself terminate at the port of refuge, and the proceeds do not contribute to any general average expenses or losses sustained subsequent to the discharge of cargo. If a general average lien needs to be exercised, it is at the port of refuge.
(b) The *amount made good* effectively travels with the ship and other cargo to the intended destination. Thus, the common adventure continues and the amount made good is subject to the same vicissitudes as are suffered by the other properties.[43] However, assuming that no further casualties are encountered
    (i) The amount made good in general average will be the sound c.i.f. invoice value at the scheduled destination, less the net sale proceeds at the port of refuge.
    (ii) The contributory value, to include the amount made good, will be the sound c.i.f. invoice value.

(3) Sound or damaged from any cause, but the sale necessitated by some form of general average sacrifice. The guiding principle to be borne in mind whenever cargo is left behind at a port of refuge as the direct result of a general average act or sacrifice is that the owner should be placed in the same position as he would have been in if his cargo had remained G.40

[43] See para. 17.31, n. 19a, *post*; also Report No 34 of the Advisory Committee of the Association of Average Adjusters.

on board or been reloaded on the original vessel and carried on to the intended destination.

An example is given, in paragraph 15.04, below, of an outbreak of fire in the cargo of a vessel already loaded down to her marks being extinguished by the use of water, all of which cannot be pumped out, and necessitating the discharge of an equivalent weight of cargo to enable the vessel to continue on voyage. It is there stated that the loss of any freight thereon at risk to the carrier will be made good as general average, and it follows that if that same freight has been prepaid "lost or not lost" by the cargo interests, this prepaid freight element in the value of their cargo may also be sacrificed when the cargo is left behind and should be made good in general average, even when the sole cause of any damage to the cargo itself is of accidental origin.

In similar fashion, burning and other sound or water damaged cargo may be discharged as part of a concerted plan for the common safety during fire extinguishing operations, and if this cargo be left behind, it will often constitute an effective general average sacrifice of the prepaid freight at least, even on cargo damaged by accident. (Other examples spring to mind.) In such cases:

(a) The termination of the adventure will be as in head (2)(a), above.
(b) The amount made good as general average will depend on individual circumstances.
(c) The contributory value will be the net sale proceeds plus any amount made good.

G.41 *F. Where the cargo is forwarded from a port of refuge by other vessels*

A vessel may enter a port of refuge and, on survey, be found to be a constructive total loss, or requiring repairs which will take so long as to destroy the commercial purpose of the voyage. In either situation the adventure is potentially frustrated[44] and, if the cargo be sound or in such condition as to warrant forwarding to destination the shipowner must elect within a reasonable time:

(1) to exercise his implied right of transhipment[45] and to complete the contract voyage in another bottom at his own expense in order to earn freight still at risk; or
(2) to abandon the voyage and leave it to the cargo interests to make their own arrangements for forwarding goods to destination, or himself make the forwarding arrangements as agent for the cargo interests and at their expense.

In all of these circumstances the adventure terminates, as regards the

[44] See paras. 00.37 *et seq.*, *ante*, as to the circumstances in which the adventure is frustrated.
[45] See para. 00.41, *ante*.

ship, when the cargo has been discharged at the port of refuge.[46] But so far as concerns the transhipped cargo, does the adventure terminate at the port of refuge or does it continue until arrival at the scheduled destination?

In principle the answer to this question is clear enough. It involves drawing a distinction between (1) the case where the shipowner, in the exercise of a liberty conferred upon him and in order to earn his freight, tranships and forwards the cargo in continuation of the voyage and at his own expense, and (2) the case where the cargo is forwarded by the cargo interests, or by the shipowner acting as their agent and looking to them for reimbursement of the costs of forwarding: **G.42**

(a) *In continuation of the voyage.* In this case it can hardly be said that the voyage is broken up. There is simply the substitution by the shipowner of one bottom for another under circumstances entitling him to make such substitution. The contract, and therefore the adventure which is constituted by it, still subsists: all rights under it, including the right of lien for, and recovery of, general average on delivery of the cargo to the consignee, still remain in force. In this case, therefore, it is submitted that the proper place for adjustment is the port of destination.[47]

(b) *Forwarding by or on behalf of cargo owners.* In this case, unlike that where the shipowner tranships in continuation of the voyage, the voyage has been broken up at the place of transhipment. This then is the proper place for adjustment. The shipowner will usually hold the cargo at the port of refuge until proper general average security has been furnished, but if he does defer his rights until arrival he may instead forward the goods under a bill of lading taken out in his own name, in which case he will be able to exercise a lien on them at the destination. However, even in that case, it is submitted that the voyage still terminates at the port of refuge.

Which of these two courses the shipowner will adopt is likely to depend upon whether the costs of completing the voyage at his expense exceed any freight still at risk, and whether in the shipowner's view the adventure has been frustrated, thereby entitling him to abandon the voyage at the port of refuge. But the crucial distinction between the two cases is that in the first case, where the transhipment is in continuation of the voyage, the shipowner will bear the costs of forwarding, being remunerated for carriage to the scheduled destination by the contract freight originally agreed,[48] whereas in the second case the cargo bears the expenses, and if **G.43**

[46] See para. G.10, *post*.

[47] *Cf. Barnard v. Adams* (1850) 10 How. 270 at 307; *McLoon v. Cummings* (1873) 73 Penn. St.Rep. 98; *Bradley v. Cargo of Lumber* (1886) 29 Fed.Rep. 648.

[48] In certain limited circumstances the cost of forwarding cargo is allowed in general average as a substituted expense: see paras. F.11, F.12, F.48, *ante*.

the shipowner pays them in the first instance, he does so merely as a financing exercise, and is entitled to be reimbursed.

G.44 In practice, however, the distinction is not always easy to draw because one party to the adventure (normally the shipowner) may pay the costs in the first instance but claim to recover them from the other party; and at the time of the adjustment it may still be in dispute who is liable to pay the costs. In such cases it is generally true to say that forwarding should be regarded as being in continuation of the voyage unless:

(1) there has been some express notice of abandonment of the voyage by the shipowner, or some conduct which shows clearly that he regards the voyage as terminated at the port of refuge, and
(2) the abandonment is either agreed to by the cargo interests or is justified by the frustration of the adventure[49] or by the express terms of the contract of carriage.

On occasion the cargo is forwarded (or carried forward) under the terms of a special agreement which may, for example, require the shipowner to fund the forwarding expenses but oblige the cargo owners to reimburse him if the contract was justifiably terminated at the port of refuge, for example on the grounds of frustration, and an example of such an agreement appears at the end of this section on Rule G.

G.45 *Where the cargo is forwarded from a port of refuge by other vessels under a Non-Separation Agreement*

The customary termination of any adventure takes place when ship and cargo part company, that is, usually on discharge at the scheduled destination(s), or at some earlier port or place where the voyage is abandoned. Occasionally, however, ship and cargo will part company at a port of refuge and the cargo be forwarded to destination by other vessels in circumstances where the voyage is not frustrated, and essentially for the convenience of cargo interests in terms of an earlier delivery than if detained at the port of refuge until the original carrying vessel was capable of resuming the voyage.

In such a situation, and with the object of preventing the normal termination of the adventure and the consequent cessation of continuing general average allowances to the shipowner, the York-Antwerp Rules since 1994 provide that the adventure continues (beyond the separation of ship and cargo): (1) for the *Ship*—under Rule G "*for so long as justifiable under the contract of affreightment and the applicable law*", and (2) for the *Cargo*—under Rule XVII, effectively "*until delivery at original destination*".

[49] See paras. 00.37 *et seq.*, *ante*.

Second Paragraph

"This rule shall not affect the determination of the place at which the average statement is to be made up." This second paragraph reproduces what was held to be the common law in *Wavertree Sailing Ship Co. v. Love*[50] and its purpose is presumably to make it clear that the Rule does not affect the determination of either the law governing the adjustment[51] of the place where the adjustment is actually prepared.[52] **G.46**

Third Paragraph

This paragraph essentially reproduces the first paragraph of the Standard Form of Non-Separation Agreement in use in the British market since 1967, the *Background and Interpretation* of which is dealt with at length, in paragraphs G.10 to G.14, above. **G.47**

"When a ship is at any port or place" See commentary in paragraph 10.34, below.

"in circumstances which would give rise to an allowance in general average under the provisions of Rules X and XI," The circumstances which would give rise to an allowance in general average under the provisions of Rules X and XI are best recorded with an extract from Rule XI(b):

> "When a ship shall have entered or been detained in any port or place in consequence of accident, sacrifice or other extraordinary circumstances which render that necessary for the common safety, or to enable damage to the ship caused by sacrifice or accident to be repaired, if the repairs were necessary for the safe prosecution of the voyage ..."

A construction of these various phrases is given in paragraph 11.26, with further references to paragraphs 10.33 to 10.36 and 10.49, below, and paragraph A.96, above. The general average allowances referred to include the cost of cargo operations in Rules X(a) and (b), and crew wages and maintenance, fuel and stores consumed, and port charges under Rule XI(b).

"and the cargo or part thereof is forwarded to destination by other means," Although forwarding will customarily be carried out by another *ship*, if the port of refuge is close to the scheduled destination the cargo may be forwarded by lighters, or by rail, etc. Although unstated, it would appear reasonable to assume that the forwarding must have been **G.48**

[50] [1897] A.C. 373: see paras. 30.03 *et seq., post.*
[51] See paras. 30.08 *et seq., post.*
[52] See paras. 30.03 *et seq., post.*

undertaken by the shipowner at his expense for the general provisions of this Non-Separation Agreement to apply.

"subject to cargo interests being notified if practicable,"[53] Non-Separation Agreements were customarily agreed and signed in the appropriate circumstances only *after* a casualty, and it is understandable that some slight reservations might be felt in certain quarters about the wisdom of contractually giving away that agreement, or right to object, *in advance*. This particular phrase was insisted upon by the United States delegation at Sydney in 1994. They feared—probably unnecessarily—that the incorporation of the Non-Separation Agreement within the York-Antwerp Rules might override the decision in the *City of Colombo*[54] case and that by including this phrase cargo interests would be given the opportunity to object to the forwarding, or the continuing general average allowances, if considered appropriate.[55] It was appreciated, however, that such notification may not always be practicable, particularly with multi-bill of lading shipments by container vessels.

G.49 **"rights and liabilities in general average shall ... remain as nearly as possible the same as they would have been in the absence of such forwarding,"** As stated in paragraph G.12, above, the object of a Non-Separation Agreement is to place the parties to the adventure in the same position with regard to their rights and liabilities in general average as if the cargo had been justifiably retained at the port of refuge and carried to destination in the original carrying vessel after repairs. The rights in general average will be the continuing daily allowances to the shipowner under Rules X and XI, and the liabilities for all parties will be to contribute to the general average on the basis of their values as set out in the third paragraph of Rule XVII.

"as if the adventure had continued in the original ship" This phrase forms an integral part of and reinforces the idea expressed in the immediately preceding wording that, contrary to the fact that ship and cargo have actually parted company, the adventure should be deemed to continue.

"for so long as justifiable under the contract of affreightment and the applicable law." This is a thoroughly important phrase designed to serve as the first of two limitations on the length of time during which daily general average allowances can continue to be made to

[53] This phrase is dealt with out of order and appears in the space ... in the next following phrase for construction.

[54] *Ellerman Lines v. Gibbs Nathaniel (Canada)* (1986) A.M.C. 2217.

[55] Whether the U.S. delegations were aware of it is unknown, but it is interesting to record that in *Shoe v. Craig* (1912) 194 Fed. Rep. 678, where a vessel was towed to destination without consulting the cargo, in spite of the fact that their office was only a few blocks away from that of the shipowner, the judge noted this position and stated that: "I do not believe that a substituted expense is ever allowable in general average unless all parties in interest have first agreed to it."

the shipowner. Reference is here requested to the full commentary in paragraphs G.13, G.14, above, and particularly the remarks that if a delay of two months is required to frustrate the contract, the allowances can probably continue until the two months have expired even though it may be possible at an earlier date to predict with the necessary degree of certainty that the delay will exceed the two months.

Fourth Paragraph

"The proportion attaching to cargo of the allowances made in general average by reason of applying the third paragraph of this Rule shall not exceed the cost which would have been borne by the owners of cargo if the cargo had been forwarded at their expense." This paragraph is essentially the old Bigham Clause commented on in paragraphs G.15 to G.17, above, and constitutes the second limitation on the continuing daily general average allowances which can be made under the Non-Separation Agreement. Cargo interests cannot be called upon to contribute towards "general average" expenditure incurred during an extended period of repairs more than it would cost to forward the cargo themselves from the port of refuge to destination. G.50

Example of a Special Agreement for the On-Carriage of Cargo[56] G.51

(First relate the facts of the case)

The Shipowners contend that the adventure to Le Havre, Rotterdam and Hamburg is frustrated at Las Palmas and have given notice to that effect to the various Cargo Interests. However, the Cargo Interests have expressed the wish that the cargo shall be carried from Las Palmas to Rotterdam in the damaged vessel "   " and the Classification Society has given a Certificate of Seaworthiness for this particular passage in tow as a dead ship with the cargo onboard.

In the circumstances it is agreed:

(a) The cargo shall be deemed to have been delivered at Las Palmas and Cargo Underwriters shall provide an Underwriters' Guarantee to the Shipowners as security for the cargo's contribution to general average and special charges and shall provide their own security to the salvors.

(b) The Shipowners shall work the ship in tow from Las Palmas to Rotterdam, the expenses of so doing, including the cost of towage, and all the ship's expenses and port charges and discharging expenses, to be for account of the Cargo Underwriters.

(c) The Shipowners to finance the expenses under (b) and to be reimbursed with advancing commission of 2 percent and interest at   percent per annum by Cargo Underwriters on presentation of their statement of expenses with vouchers in support. On reimbursement, the Shipowners to provide Cargo Underwriters with a Guarantee to cover the event of it being established subsequently that abandonment of the adventure at Las Palmas was not justifiable.

[56] See para. G.44, *ante*.

(d) Ship Underwriters agree to the vessel being towed and that any action of the Shipowners in working the ship to Rotterdam shall not be considered a waiver or revocation of the notice of abandonment.

(e) The P & I Association agree that the entry of the vessel in the Association shall be continued until completion of discharge of cargo at Rotterdam, such entry and proportion of Club calls if apportionable to be for account of the concerned as interest may appear.

(f) Cargo Underwriters on behalf of Cargo Owners agree that Cargo to be carried from Las Palmas to Rotterdam at Cargo Owners' sole risk, the Shipowners not to be responsible for unseaworthiness or for loss or damage from any cause whatsoever, including negligence, and that all cargo—sound or damaged—to be discharged from vessel.

(g) In the event of it being established subsequently that abandonment of the adventure at Las Palmas was not justifiable, the general average shall be adjusted in the normal manner in accordance with York-Antwerp Rules as provided by the contract of afreightment, and the cost of towage from Las Palmas to Rotterdam, less any expenses saved, shall be allowed in general average.

For Information: An insurance on average disbursements, salvage, and special charges has been effected for account of the concerned as interest may appear. This insurance is for the period of time vessel and cargo at Las Palmas and it is understood that the insurance will be continued for the voyage in tow to Rotterdam and will be extended to cover the cost of towage and ship's expenses.

Rule I

Jettison of Cargo

Jettison is the classic and supreme example of a general average sacrifice; it is almost the central core of the whole general average system and at no time in any of the maritime nations of the world has there ever been any doubt or dispute that *underdeck* cargo thrown overboard at a time of peril for the common safety should be made good in general average. So widely held and applied has been this basic concept that, either by oversight or because it was thought to be stating the obvious and unnecessary, the York-Antwerp Rules have never made any *specific* provision for such an allowance! **1.01**

Thus, losses by jettison must in practice be claimed under the general provisions and basic principles of Rule A and it is there, perhaps, that the subject should be treated. However, during the litigious nineteenth century there was very considerable dispute concerning the jettison of cargo carried *on deck*, and as Rule I was originally framed to deal with this vexed topic, this is a convenient place to deal with the whole subject of jettison.

English Law and Background

The first reference to contribution towards jettison recorded in our law books occurred in 1285 in the reign of Edward I.[1] The second is given in Coke's Reports, as occurring in the sixth year of King James I's reign, under the title of *Mouse's Case*.[2] **1.02**

The modern law concerning the master's right to jettison cargo in case of imminent danger begins with the case of *The Gratitudine*[3] in 1801, where Lord Stowell gave judgment as follows:

> "It must unavoidably be admitted that in some cases he [the master] must exercise the discretion of an authorized agent over the cargo, as well in the prosecution of the voyage at sea, as in intermediate ports, into which he may be compelled to enter. The case of throwing overboard parts of the cargo at sea, is of that kind. Nothing can be better settled than that the master has a right to exercise this power in case of imminent danger. He may select what article he pleases; he may determine what quantity; no

[1] See para. 00.17, *ante*.
[2] (1609) 12 Co.Rep. 63.
[3] (1801) 3 C. Rob. 240.

proportion is limited; a fourth, a moiety, three-fourths, nay, in cases of extreme necessity, when the lives of the crew cannot otherwise be saved,[4] it never can be maintained that he might not throw the whole cargo overboard. The only obligation will be, that the ship should contribute its average proportion."

1.03 As the passage cited above shows, jettison has two important aspects. First, it entitles the owner of cargo thrown overboard to contribution in general average from the property saved. Secondly, it provides a defence to the shipowner against any claim by the owner of the cargo lost for failure to carry it safely to its destination.[5] In each case the jettison must be such as to qualify as a general average act, that is, the goods must be thrown overboard, not accidentally carried away by heavy weather, and this must be reasonably done in order to preserve the vessel and the remainder of the cargo from a loss threatening the whole adventure. Thus, where the master of a vessel which was about to be attacked threw a quantity of dollars into the sea merely to prevent it falling into enemy hands, and not for the preservation of the property involved in the common adventure, no right to contribution in general average could arise.[6] Likewise, in each case the consequences of jettison may differ if the need for it was caused by fault of one of the parties to the adventure.[7] But the principle remains that the master of a ship is entitled to jettison cargo in circumstances of necessity and if he does so, his owners have a defence to a claim for the loss of the cargo but are subject to a liability to contribute in general average.

Jettison of Deckload

The rule in the case of deckload

1.04 To the rule that jettison is general average there is one ancient and well-established exception: goods carried on a ship's deck if thrown overboard are, generally speaking, not made good by contribution, although if saved they must contribute like anything else. The reason is that a ship's deck is generally an improper place for cargo.[8] Where this

[4] As to sacrifices made "in fear of death", see para. A.18, *ante*.

[5] This is further considered at para. 00.62, *ante*.

[6] *Butler v. Wildman* (1820) 3 B. & Ald. 398.

[7] See para. D.02, *ante*.

[8] "According to the rules of maritime law, the placing of goods upon the deck of a sea-going ship is improper stowage, because they are hindrances to the safe navigation of the vessel; and their jettison is therefore regarded, in a question with the other shippers of cargo, as a justifiable riddance of incumbrances which ought never to have been there, and not as a sacrifice for the common safety": *per* Lord Watson, *Strang v. Scott* [1889] 14 A.C. 601 at 609.

The carrying of cargo on deck is absolutely forbidden by many old sea laws: *e.g.* by the decrees of the Hanseatic League (A.D. 1477) 2 Pard. 483; by the old law of Genoa (A.D. 1441) 4 Pard. 463; by the Ordonnance of Louis XIV, para. 13. The Hague Rules except from the definition of "goods", cargo which by the contract of carriage is stated as being carried on deck, and is so carried (Art. I(c)).

is not so, as in some coasting[9] and other trades where the carrying of deck loads is justified by custom, or if all parties have agreed that cargo shall be carried on deck, the exception is not applicable.

Former practice in England

The practice in this country, followed by adjusters for years, was to exclude from the benefit of general average all cargo carried on deck; if carried without the shipper's consent, the loss by jettison or accident was made to fall on the shipowner; if with his consent, the loss from either of these causes fell on the shipper. **1.05**

The party liable, shipowner or shipper as the case might be, usually protected himself by insurance. Even where there was a well-known usage of trade to carry deckloads, as in the case of the North American and Baltic timber trades, the same rule was followed.

This practice was disturbed in the year 1837 by the decision of the Court of Common Pleas in *Gould v. Oliver*,[10] but a succession of important legal decisions given over the next half-century gradually clarified and resolved the position to that set out in paragraph 1.04, above, and followed today. A short summary of the leading cases between 1837 and 1889 now follows. **1.06**

In *Gould v. Oliver* a deckload of timber was jettisoned for the common safety on a voyage from Quebec to London, and it was admitted on both sides that it was the custom of the trade between those ports to carry a portion of the timber on deck. After a full review of the authorities, Tindall C.J. decided that the jettison of the deckload was properly admissible in general average.[11]

In *Milward v. Hibbert*[12] it was decided that the underwriters on ship were liable to contribute, as general average, for a jettison of pigs from Ireland to London, carried on deck in accordance with the custom of the trade.

In *Johnson v. Chapman*[13] part of the deck cargo of deals was necessarily jettisoned during the voyage from Quebec and the shipowner resisted the cargo-owner's claim for a general average contribution to the loss on the grounds that the deals were already in a state of wreck when jettisoned, **1.07**

[9] *Cf.* the passage in the judgment of the Court of Appeal in *Wright v. Marwood* (1881) 7 Q.B.D. 62, which suggests a more general right to contribution in the case of coasting voyages. See also *per* Walton J. in *Appollinaris Co. v. Nord Deutsche Ins. Co.* [1904] 1 K.B. 252 at 259.

[10] (1837) 4 Bing. N.C. 134.

[11] This decision was not accepted at Lloyd's and amongst the British adjusters as final, and there ensued some further unsatisfactory litigation and a change of practice ("general contribution"), which may be pronounced even more unsatisfactory. See 10th ed., para. 109.

[12] (1842) 3 Q.B. 120.

[13] (1865) 19 C.B. (N.S.) 563; 35 L.J.C.P. 23.

but not on the grounds that the cargo was carried on deck. Willes J. decided in favour of the cargo-owner's claim, but the important part of his judgment—in the present context—was that here was a charterparty contract with a single shipper which expressly provided for a full cargo, including a deckload.

> "... it is not necessary to refer to any custom affecting the voyage, because, according to the contract between the parties, there was to be a deck cargo. Then, immediately you find that the deck cargo is within the contemplation of the parties, you must deal with it as if shipping a deck cargo was lawful. When you have established that it is a deck cargo, lawfully there by the contract of the parties, it becomes subject to the rule of general average."

1.08 In *Wright v. Marwood*[14] there was again a contract with the shipper specifying that his cargo of 100 head of cattle from New York to Portsmouth in England were to be carried on deck, but on this occasion the vessel was a general ship carrying the goods of various parties. The cattle were jettisoned for the common safety and, on the authority of *Johnson v. Chapman*, the loss was held at the original trial to be general average. In the Court of Appeal, however, it was held that there was no right of contribution, even from the shipowner, by whom the goods were carried on deck, and the earlier case was distinguished on the grounds that the present vessel was a general ship carrying the goods of various parties.

> "... whatever may be the agreement between deck cargo and shipowner, the other cargo owners are no parties to it, nor bound to inquire into it, or notice it, as they are bound to take notice of a custom."

It may also be mentioned that no evidence was given at the original trial of any custom allowing cattle to be carried as deck cargo, and the judgment of the Court of Appeal states "that there is no custom alleged bearing upon the case".

1.09 In *Burton v. English*[15] the sole question for determination was whether the words in the charterparty "at merchant's risk" excluded the liability to contribute for the jettison of deck cargo. (It did not; for a fuller account of the case, see paragraph 1.13, below). It was not disputed that but for this clause the liability would have arisen, as there was a custom of the trade to carry timber on deck from the Baltic to London, and the ship was chartered to carry a full cargo.

1.10 In what might be considered to be the final clarification of English law on the subject of deck-load jettison, Lord Watson, in delivering the

[14] (1881) 7 Q.B.D. 62.
[15] (1883) 10 Q.B.D. 426; 12 Q.B.D. 218.

advice of the Privy Council in *Strang v. Scott*,[16] said that the exception (to allow as general average) in the case of deck cargo does not apply either:

> "(1) In those cases where, according to the established custom of navigation, such cargoes are permitted, or
> (2) In any case where the other owners of cargo have consented that the goods jettisoned should be carried on the deck of the ship."

He thus accepts the principle that there is a right to contribution when all the parties to the adventure have agreed to the carriage of a deck cargo, for example, by a provision in the bill of lading that: "The carrier shall have liberty to carry livestock and/or cargo on deck."

If this be the correct principle, the case where there are only two parties who have expressly contracted for a deck cargo is an *a fortiori* one.[17]

What is a custom of the trade?

To constitute a custom of the trade to carry cargo on deck, much more is required than the occasional or even frequent carrying of deckloads. There must be a practice so general and universal in the trade that everyone in that trade must be taken to know that his goods will or may probably be put on deck. It must also be consistent with the express terms of the contract of affreightment. **1.11**

Cotton, for example, in earlier times, used often to be carried on the decks of steamers between ports in the United States and Great Britain. This was done, sometimes by express agreement with the shippers, sometimes without the shipper's consent or even knowledge, the shipowner in the latter case, according to the general understanding for many years, taking the risk upon himself.

In *Dixon v. Royal Exchange Shipping Co.*[18] an attempt was made to establish that the practice set out above amounted to a custom of the trade such as would enable the jettison of a deckload to be treated as a general average act. Action was brought by the owner of the deckload against the shipowner for the full value of the deckload on the grounds that the shipowner was in breach of his contract by stowing the cotton on deck; the shipowner contended that he was not liable for more than his share of the loss, treated as general average. The case went to the **1.12**

[16] (1889) 14 A.C. 601 at 609. Lord Watson's judgment was referred to by Lord Dunedin in the House of Lords in 1931 as an "authoritative statement" of the law, though it is true that this was on another point, namely, on the right of a person to claim contribution where the necessity had arisen through his own default: see *Louis Dreyfus & Co. v. Tempus Shipping Co.* [1931] A.C. 726 at 735.

[17] See *The Freda* 226 Fed. Rep. 551 (1920).

[18] Court of Appeal, May 18, 1885; affirmed in House of Lords (1886) 12 A.C. 11. A similar decision was given by the Court of Appeal in *Newell v. Royal Exchange Shipping Co.* (1885) 33 W.R. 868.

Court of Appeal, and was there decided against the shipowner. Brett M.R. (afterwards Lord Esher) said:

> "It is suggested that there is a practice which it must be taken that they knew. Now the only practice which it can be taken in law that they impliedly knew (that is, taken that they knew, although they did not) is a general practice; so general and universal in the trade and at the port from which these goods were taken, that everybody who ships cotton on board a ship at New Orleans for England must be taken to know that his goods probably will, or may probably be put on deck ... To say that there is a practice, or to say that there is a frequent practice, is only to say that it is sometimes done, leaving it open that as often, or oftener, it is not done. Such evidence as that is not evidence to go to a jury, upon which they would be justified in finding a general usage."

Effect of special clauses

1.13 Where cargo is carried on deck under a custom of the trade a jettison of it must be treated as general average, notwithstanding a clause in the charterparty declaring that the deckload is to be "at merchant's risk".[19]

In *Burton v. English*[20] the ship was chartered to carry a full cargo of timber from a port in the Baltic for London, and the charterparty contained the clause; "The steamer to be provided with a deckload, if required, at full freight, but at merchant's risk." It was proved that there was a custom or usage in such voyages to carry a deckload of timber. In the Queen's Bench Division it was decided that the words "at merchants risk" exempted the shipowner from liability to contribute towards the loss of deck cargo lawfully jettisoned.

The reasons given by Cave J. who delivered the judgment of the Queen's Bench Division (Cave and Day JJ.), were, in substance, that there was no reason why the shipowner should not, if he pleased, introduce the bill of lading clauses modifying the rights to general average; and that it was difficult to attach any other meaning to the words "at shipper's risk" than that the shipper was to take the risk of jettison, since the shipowner was already protected by the general terms of the charterparty. This judgment, however, was reversed in the Court of Appeal. The grounds on which the learned judge went are even more deserving of attention than the decision itself.

Brett M.R. said[21]:

> "By what law does the right arise to general average contribution? ... It is not as a matter of contract, but in consequence of a common danger, where natural justice requires that all should contribute to indemnify for the loss of property which is sacrificed by one in order that the whole adventure may be saved. If this be so, the liability to contribute does not arise out of any contract at all, and is not covered by the stipulation in the charterparty

[19] See *Svenssons v. Cliffe* [1932] 1 K.B. 490 for the meaning of the words "at charterers' risk".

[20] (1883) 10 Q.B.D. 426; 12 Q.B.D. 218.

[21] (1883) 12 Q.B.D. 218 at 219–221.

> on which the defendants rely. I therefore disagree with the decision of the Divisional Court in this case ... The acts of the captain with reference to properly or improperly jettisoning part of the cargo are not both done by him in the same capacity; one is done by him as the agent of the cargo-owner, and the other as the servant of the shipowner. For these reasons I think that the liability to general average contribution is not covered by any words of the contract in the charterparty, and consequently that the defendants are liable."

The law in the United States is the same. In *Nicaraguan Lumber Co. v. Moody*[22] the bills of lading included a clause provided for "all lumber loaded on deck at shipper's risk", but it was held that this did not preclude the cargo owner from recovering a loss by jettison for the common safety as general average.

It may also be mentioned that in *Wright v. Marwood*[23] the cattle were shipped under a bill of lading with the clause: "Not accountable for mortality or for any accident or injury of any kind or nature whatever." but no notice was taken of this clause throughout the arguments and judgment in the case.

Practice of adjusters

As a matter of practice, jettison of deck cargo is not treated by adjusters as general average in this country, unless the carriage of a deck cargo on the particular voyage is sanctioned by custom. The rule (No. F1) of the Association of Average Adjusters dealing with this point is as follows: **1.14**

> The jettison of a deckload carried according to the usage of trade and not in violation of the contracts of affreightment is general average.
>
> There is an exception to this rule in the case of cargoes of cotton, tallow, acids and some other goods.[24]

The practice, therefore, is in accordance with the view expressed by Lowndes on this subject.[25] It is, however, important to remember that should an adjustment be challenged in the courts, the law as determined by the authorities will prevail over the practice of adjusters, unless, of course, the parties have contracted to contribute in general average in accordance with the practice of adjusters.[26]

[22] (1954) A.M.C. 658.

[23] (1881) 7 Q.B.D. 62.

[24] The rule of the Average Adjusters' Association of the U.S. in dealing with this subject is as follows: "Where cargo consisting of one kind of goods is, in accordance with a custom of trade, carried on and under deck, that portion of the cargo loaded on deck shall be subject to the same rules of adjustment in case of jettison, or expenses incurred, as if the same were laden under deck." See also Gourlie, pp. 86–87. Specific provision is made in the codes of some European countries relating to jettison of deckload.

[25] See 9th ed. of this work, para. 116.

[26] See, *e.g. Stewart v. West India and Pacific S.S. Co.* (1873) L.R. 8 Q.B. 88.

1.15 The reason for the rule which disallows contribution for the jettison of deck cargo can hardly apply to an inland voyage by river or canal; for on such a voyage it is difficult to suppose that the deck is an improper place for cargo.[27] Therefore, even without evidence of custom, it is apprehended that in the unlikely event of a jettison of deck cargo on such a voyage for the general safety there will be a right to contribution.

Bulk cargo pumped or baled out

1.16 Where part of a cargo of wheat had been pumped into the sea by the ship's pumps, working in the ordinary way to keep down a leak, it was held that that was not a general average loss.[28]

But where water is baled out of a ship, in an extraordinary manner, for the general safety and under such conditions that some of the cargo is necessarily thrown out with it, this is in practice treated as a jettison. The same rule is applied in the United States when, as happens on the Great Lakes, cargo such as grain is deliberately pumped overboard by salvage pumps to lighten the vessel.

Jettison of ship's stores

1.17 A jettison of ship's stores is treated as on the same footing with a jettison of cargo.[29]

The practice of adjusters here introduces a distinction analogous to that of deck and under-deck cargo. Many ships are lumbered with all kinds of useless articles on deck, which increase the risk and are sure to be thrown overboard on the first approach of danger. To guard against the abuse of this practice, the rule in this country, as in Germany and many other states, is that no jettison of ship's materials off the upper deck is treated as general average unless it be of such articles as are necessary for the navigation of the ship and, therefore, are carried on deck in conformity with the custom of the trade. Boats, studding-sails and their gear, spare spars, anchors, are examples of articles properly carried on deck; water-casks, provisions, spare sails, cables, ought not to be. Hawsers in coasting trades or for short voyages may properly be on deck, though for a long voyage they should be got below as soon as they are dry.

[27] See the judgment of Walton J. in *Apollinaris Co. v. Nord Deutsche Ins. Co.* [1904] 1 K.B. 252.

[28] *Hills v. London Assurance Co.* (1839) 9 L.J. Ex. 25; 5 M. & W. 569.

[29] *Price v. Noble* (1811) 4 Taunt. 123 (guns, two anchors, two chains and other stores from the middle deck). Such sacrifices demand close scrutiny: *The Santa Ana Maria* 49 Fed. Rep. 878 (1892).

HISTORICAL DEVELOPMENT AND PRACTICE OF RULE I

York Rules 1864 **1.18**

At no time has there ever been any doubt in any of the maritime nations that a jettison of cargo from underdeck was properly allowable as general average.[30] With regard to the jettison of a deckload, however (and even if in earlier times such loss had been as universally disallowed) the situation was changing and becoming less settled in 1864. Certainly in the timber trades, at least, ships were being constructed expressly to carry large deckloads and their greater safety had been tacitly recognised in Britain by the repeal of earlier Acts of Parliament[31] prohibiting the carriage of deckloads of timber by any ship clearing out of any British port in North America, or in Honduras, for any port in the United Kingdom between September 1 and May 1. In certain other trades, for example cotton, livestock, tallow, tar and rosin, it was becoming increasingly frequent for part of such cargoes to be shipped on deck, though not so invariably as to constitute what would be termed a recognised custom of the trade.

In the United States, where there was a considerable timber trade with up to one-third of the cargo being shipped on deck, there was no case law on the subject, but a uniform practice was applied excluding from general average the jettison of any deckload. In the European countries it is believed that the same practice was followed except, possibly, on short coastal voyages where the law permitted the carriage of deckloads.

In an attempt to secure world wide uniformity, the following Rule was passed at the 1864 Conference at York: **1.19**

Rule I. Jettison of Deck Cargo

> A jettison of timber or deals, or any other description of wood cargo, carried on the deck of a ship in pursuance of a general custom of the trade in which the ship is then engaged, shall be made good as general average, in like manner as if such cargo had been jettisoned from below deck.
>
> No jettison of deck cargo, other than timber or deals, or other wood cargo, so carried as aforesaid, shall be made good as general average.
>
> Every structure not built in with the frame of the vessel shall be considered to be a part of the deck of the vessel.

The final voting of 18–2 in favour of the first paragraph of the Rule belies the true sentiments of many of the delegates; 8 of the 20 delegates had earlier voted in favour of an amendment excluding any allowance in general average for the jettison of deckloads, and one or two of those who voted in favour of an allowance for timber did so only on the

[30] See para. 1.01, *ante*.
[31] 8 & 9 Vict., c. 93, ss. 24–26; 16 & 17 Vict., c. 107.

grounds of convenience and in recognition of the fact that timber was, and would be, regularly carried on deck. Some saw the introduction of timber as being the "thin end of the wedge" and, indeed, proposals were made at the 1864 Conference to make tar, cotton, tallow, cattle and coastal voyages subject to the same provisions, but these proposals were defeated.

The wording of the Rule itself calls for no explanation other than, possibly, the last paragraph, which was an endeavour to define what constituted the "deck". The wording would exclude cargo in most types of deckhouses, but was sufficient to cover cargo carried in the poop. In practice, a great deal of silk and other light valuable cargo was stowed there.

1.20 *York-Antwerp Rules 1877*

The 1877 Conference was held at Antwerp and European delegates attended in much greater force than at York. Their opinions held sway, and by 26 votes to 10 the 1846 Rule was completely reversed and the following substituted:

Rule I. Jettison of Deck Cargo

> No jettison of deck cargo shall be made good as general average. Every structure not built in with the frame of the vessel shall be considered to be a part of the deck of the vessel.

1.21 *York-Antwerp Rules 1890*

The 1890 Conference was at Liverpool and the British Association of Average Adjusters was primarily responsible for drawing up proposed amendments for the new Rules. In the intervening years English law on deckload jettison had been clarified considerably, and cases such as:

Johnson v. Chapman[32]
Wright v. Marwood[33]
Burton v. English[34]
Strang v. Scott[35]

had decided that the jettison of a deckload carried in accordance with a recognised custom of the trade, and not in violation of the contract of affreightment, was general average as between *all* the parties to the adventure.

English law and commercial practice having overtaken the York-Antwerp Rules, Rule I needed to be reconsidered if it was to be kept *en*

[32] (1865) 19 C.B. (N.S.) 563. See para. 1.07, *ante*.
[33] (1881) 7 Q.B.D. 62. See para. 1.08, *ante*.
[34] (1883) 12 Q.B.D. 218. See para. 1.09, *ante*.
[35] (1889) 14 A.C. 601. See para. 1.10, *ante*.

rapport with current requirements. The British Association proposed, *inter alia*, that:

> "A jettison of wood, tar, and resin, or any of them, carried on deck in accordance with a general custom of the trade, when not in violation of the contract of affreightment, shall be made good as general average if the jettison be made for the common safety."

This proposal was withdrawn, however, in deference to the wishes of the European delegates, who were unanimously opposed to the new Rule. The previous 1877 Rule was reaffirmed, and contracts of affreightment in the timber trade continued, increasingly, to be drawn up with provisions for the York-Antwerp Rules, but excluding the word "No" in Rule I.[36]

York-Antwerp Rules 1924 **1.22**

This increasing practice influenced the drafting Committee for the 1924 Rules to add to the old Rule the words: "unless such cargo is carried in accordance with the recognised custom of the trade" and to delete the word "deck" from both the title and the text. This amendment was accepted by the Stockholm Conference, if with a certain continuing reluctance on the part of some of the European delegates.

A considerable discussion took place at the Stockholm Conference with regard to the definition of a deck contained in the old Rule. In the end it was decided to omit any reference to the deck. Many technical objections were raised as to the wording and the view eventually prevailed that any definition was unnecessary and that it should be left to be decided as a matter of fact in each case as it arose whether the place of stowage, be it technically on deck or under deck, was a place sanctioned by the custom of the particular trade as a proper place for the carriage of the cargo jettisoned.

In the form finally agreed, the Rule read as follows:

> *Rule I.—Jettison of Cargo*
>
> No jettison of cargo shall be made good as general average, unless such cargo is carried in accordance with the recognised custom of the trade.

York-Antwerp Rules 1950 and 1974 **1.23**

No change, but it may be recorded that the President's Report and Draft Text for the 1974 Rules published by the *Comité Maritime Internationale* in February 1973 stated:

[36] See *e.g. De Hart v. Compania Anomina "Aurora"* [1903] 1 K.B. 109; [1903] 2 K.B. 503; 8 Com. Cas. 42, 314.

"*Note*: No provision was made for containers because it was felt that generally a custom to carry containers on deck was already held to exist,[37] and that in any event a provision covering containers as such would probably not be sufficient to cover technological developments in the future."

By 1997 the custom must be firmly established.

York-Antwerp Rules 1994

No change, but a proposal was made, but received little support, that:

Jettison of cargo, wherever stowed, shall be made good as general average when made for the common safety.

RULE I

JETTISON OF CARGO

1.24 **No jettison of cargo shall be made good as general average, unless such cargo is carried in accordance with the recognised custom of the trade.**

CONSTRUCTION

"cargo" It is submitted that "cargo" in this and throughout the Rules means property in the possession of the shipowner under a contract of affreightment, including containers and commercial vehicles, whether loaded or not. It also includes mails and motor-cars carried in the vessel on which the owners are passengers, and passengers' luggage provided that it is not retained in the possession of the passenger, for example for use on the voyage.[38]

1.25 **"unless it is carried in accordance with the recognised custom of the trade."** Previous editions of the work have recorded that the construction of this Rule has not been debated in the courts and that the

[37] But see *Du Pont de Nemours International v. Mormacvega* [1972] A.M.C. 2366; [1973] 1 Lloyd's Rep. 267, affirmed [1974] 1 Lloyd's Rep. 296, in which the shipowners' assertion that in 1967 there was a custom in the shipping industry of carrying containers on deck and that a bill of lading not claused for deck shipment would be presumed to have been issued subject to the custom was not upheld; the custom was not sufficiently ancient.

[38] By the express terms of Rule XVII mails, passengers' luggage, personal effects, and accompanied private motor vehicles do not contribute in general average: see para. 17.61, *post*.

exact scope of this particular exception is difficult to determine and may well be surprisingly narrow. In practice, it is believed that the words are interpreted in the light of the remarks of Brett M.R. in *Dixon v. Royal Exchange Shipping Co.*[39]:

> "... a general practice; so general and universal in the trade and at the port from which these goods were taken, that everybody who ships (cotton) on board a ship at (New Orleans) for (England) must be taken to know that his goods probably will, or may probably be put on deck..."

"carried" It is submitted that this refers more to the manner rather than the fact of carriage—in fact, that it is equivalent to "stowed". Goods carried by sea are of such infinite variety that it would otherwise be possible to argue in very many cases that so few goods of the particular description have ever been carried on the particular route that there is no recognised custom to carry them at all. If, however, "carried" means "stowed", it is possible to contend that all goods of certain broad categories are or may be carried on deck, and that other goods, again described in very broad categories, will or should always be carried in the hold.

"recognised custom" These words prompt the inquiries "Recognised by whom?" and "What is a custom?" It is submitted that no formal recognition by the courts or by trade bodies is necessary, and that the word "custom" does not bear the restricted meaning attaching to custom in the strict legal sense. Each case will have to be judged on its own facts, but it is suggested that the right approach is to consider whether a person familiar with the trade would, upon being apprised of the method of stowage adopted, comment "That is an unusual stowage". See also paragraphs 1.11, 1.12, above. **1.26**

"trade" This word has to be construed in relation both to the type of goods being carried in the vessel and to the route upon which she is trading.

The idea which lies behind the Rule and which must form the basis of its construction is that no party to the adventure should be asked to contribute towards a loss by jettison of goods which are peculiarly liable to be jettisoned, for example deck cargo, unless the cargo was carried in accordance with the custom of the trade and the party had reason to expect the presence of such goods by reason of the construction or trade of the vessel.[40] However, the words must be given their natural meaning, and the exception contained in the Rule cannot be extended to allow contribution towards a jettison of cargo carried in an unusual manner but in a manner sanctioned by the contract of affreightment, and this remains so even where the whole cargo is in one ownership. Furthermore,

[39] Court of Appeal, May 18, 1885; affirmed in House of Lords (1886) 12 A.C. 11.
[40] *Strang v. Scott* (1889) 14 A.C. 601 at 609.

the operation of the first part of the Rule cannot be confined to deck load, however defined, although jettison of under-deck cargo is universally admitted to be the classic example of a general average sacrifice. On the other hand, it will be much easier to prove that under-deck cargo is "carried in accordance with the recognised custom of the trade". It should be added that as a result of the inclusion of the Rule of Interpretation, contribution is not recoverable under Rule A if it is barred by this Rule.

The burden of proving that the exception applies and contribution is recoverable lies, by the terms of Rule E, on the claimant.

Rule II

Loss or Damage by Sacrifices for the Common Safety

English Law and Background

Damage Incidental to Jettison of Cargo

Damage which is incidental to a jettison, so that the jettison cannot reasonably be made without incurring it, must be regarded as part of the loss by jettison and included in the general average: for example holes cut in the deck, or bulkheads or bulwarks stove in, in order to get at the cargo or throw it over. So if goods are damaged by reason of the opening of the hatches to throw cargo overboard, from seas which break over the deck, all such damage is properly and in practice made the subject of general average, being the necessary consequence of the measure for the common safety. This rule is as old as the Roman law, and may be regarded as universally accepted,[1] even though the practice was at one time otherwise.[2] The same principle applies to damage done by chafing or breakage of packages, or otherwise from the derangement of stowage consequent on a jettison: for example if the cargo consisted of barrels, well secured in their places while the hold was full, but which could not be prevented from shifting after a portion of the cargo had been thrown out; or if goods were lost or damaged in consequence of having been brought on deck in order to get access to less valuable goods for the purpose of jettison.[3] **2.01**

[1] *The Brig Mary* (1842) 1 Sprague 17. Damage done to cargo by water going down a hole made in the deck from cutting away a mast has been treated in the American courts on the same principle as general average: *Maggrath v. Church* (1803) 1 Caines 176; Phillips, para. 1286.

See also *Abbott on Merchant Shipping* (5th ed.), p. 136, which was adopted by Cresswell J. in *Hallett v. Wigram* (1850) 9 C.B. at 608: "From the rule thus established by the Rhodians, various corollaries have been deduced. Thus, if in the act of jettison, or in order to accomplish it, other goods in the ship are broken, damaged or destroyed, the value of these also must be included in the general contribution."

[2] See para. 2.03, *post*.

[3] Benecke, p. 213.

Damage from Sacrifice of Ship

2.02 Damage done to cargo, in consequence of cutting away of a mast, or other general average sacrifice of some part of a ship—as, for example, if the mast when cut away breaks below the partners so that water gets down through the opening and wets the goods[4]; or if a similar mischance occurs, as is very likely, in cutting away an iron mast, which is hollow and has openings below through which seas shipped on deck may reach the cargo—is evidently allowable as general average. It is perfectly analogous to damage occasioned by seas shipped while the hatches are open for jettison.

Historical Development and Practice of Rule II

2.03 *Glasgow Resolutions 1860*

There being differences of opinion on the treatment of losses to cargo by chafage and breakage consequent upon the stowage being deranged after a jettison, a Resolution was passed at the Glasgow Conference as follows:

> (3) That the damage done to cargo by chafing and breakage, resulting from a jettison of part of the remainder of the cargo, ought not to be allowed in general average.

At this particular time the belief was widely—if mistakenly—held that, in principle, an allowance could not be made in general average unless the property in respect of which the claim arose had been *selected* to be damaged for the general benefit; further, it was considered that such loss was only a remote and uncertain consequence of the jettison. On practical grounds, it was thought wise to exclude such losses to prevent all damage sustained during the voyage from being claimed as resulting from the jettison.

2.04 *York Rules 1864*

Before 1860, damage done by water going down the hatches whilst a jettison was in progress was allowed as general average.[5] Whilst admitting, in principle, that this was correct, it was suggested in the preliminary discussions prior to the Conference of York in 1864 that such claims should also be excluded on account of the difficulty of proving the real cause of damage.

[4] See n.1, *ante*.
[5] See, *e.g.* Benecke (1824), p. 178 or Baily (1851), p. 47.

This suggestion met with considerable opposition, it being argued that proof of the cause of damage would not be so difficult as to warrant a deviation from a just principle.

The result was that the whole subject of damage consequent upon a jettison was considered afresh, and at the York Conference in 1864 the previous Glasgow Resolution was reversed and a new first paragraph added affirming the allowance of damage by water going down the hatches during a jettison. The Rule was as follows:

Rule II. Damage by Jettison

> Damage done to goods or merchandise by water which unavoidably goes down a ship's hatches opened, or other opening made, for the purpose of making a jettison shall be made good as general average, in case the loss by jettison is so made good.
>
> Damage done by breakage or chafing, or otherwise from derangement of stowage consequent upon a jettison, shall be made good as general average.

York-Antwerp Rules 1877 **2.05**

The two paragraphs of the Rule were brought into accord by the addition at the end of the second paragraph of the concluding words of the first paragraph: "in case the loss by jettison is so made good".

York-Antwerp Rules 1890 **2.06**

The 1877 and earlier editions of Rule II made no mention of damage to ship, and other cases of damage to cargo which arose in practice (for example a mast might be cut away for the common safety and, in falling, tear a hole in the deck through which water might gain access to the cargo[6]). These losses, also, were customarily allowed as general average, but to avoid any possible doubt there might be on the matter, the Rule was completely recast in 1890 to make it rather more general in its provisions:

Rule II. Damage by Jettison and Sacrifice for the Common Safety

> Damage done to a ship and cargo, or either of them, by or in consequence of a sacrifice made for the common safety, and by water which goes down a ship's hatches opened or other opening made for the purpose of making a jettison for the common safety, shall be made good as general average.

York-Antwerp Rules 1924 **2.07**

With the introduction of the lettered Rules (and, in particular, Rules A and C) in 1924, there was no longer any real need for this Rule II. However, it was thought preferable by those drafting the 1924 Rules to

[6] See paras. 2.01, n. 1, and 2.02, *ante*.

leave the old Rules undisturbed as much as possible, well known as they were to the business community, and only to effect such amendments or deletions as appeared to be absolutely necessary to bring them into harmony with modern conditions. This being so, the 1890 Rule was left unaltered.

York-Antwerp Rules 1950 and 1974

No change.

York-Antwerp Rules 1994

2.08 The changes in 1890 may have made the provisions of the Rule more general in their application, but they were still limited to sacrificial damage done to the *ship* and *cargo* alone. Purely as a minor "tidying-up" operation, and to ensure that any other properties on board (for example freight and time-charterers' bunkers) should also be covered by the Rule, an early proposal for amendments in 1994 included one that Rule II should open with the simple and generalised statement that:

> Loss or damage caused in consequence of a sacrifice...

However, when the far more important new provisions in Rule C to exclude any allowance for environmental damage consequent on the escape or release of pollutant substances from the ship were subsequently being considered, it was realised that this exclusion in the *lettered* Rule C would be ineffectual and capable of being overridden[7]—by the proposed amendment, above, for the *numbered* Rule II.

To prevent such a "back door" circumvention of the provisions of Rule C, additional wording was incorporated within the amendment for Rule II (and also in Rules V and VIII) to limit any allowances thereunder for loss or damage in consequence of a sacrifice to:

> *the property involved in the common maritime adventure*

thereby ruling out the possibility of allowances for external environmental damage.

The title of the Rule was also amended on this occasion.

[7] See Rule of Interpretation, para. PRE.04, *ante*.

Rule II 2.09

Loss or Damage by Sacrifices for the Common Safety

Loss of or damage to the property involved in the common maritime adventure by or in consequence of a sacrifice made for the common safety, and by water which goes down a ship's hatches opened or other opening made for the purpose of making a jettison for the common safety, shall be made good as general average.

Construction

The Rule deals with three different cases of loss or damage to any of the property involved in the common maritime adventure, namely: (1) by a sacrifice (for example to the ship's propeller by a log jettisoned for the common safety); (2) in consequence of a sacrifice (for example by chafage or breakage of packages consequent on the derangement of stowage resulting from a jettison); and (3) the special case of water going down an opening made for the purpose of a jettison, that is, a specific example of head (2).

"the property involved in the common maritime adventure" This expression was added to the wording of the Rule in 1994 in substitution for the previous and more limited *ship and cargo*. To the extent that loss of or damage to *any* of the property involved in the common maritime adventure (for example freight and time-charterers' bunkers, in addition) may now be made good under the Rule, the new wording is wider in its coverage. However, its prime purpose is limiting, and to prevent any allowance being made good in general average, via the back-door—as it were—of any *numbered* Rule, for damage to the environment in consequence of the escape or release of pollutant substances from the ship by a general average act, when such a loss is intended to be universally excluded by the provisions of the *lettered* Rule C.[8]

"sacrifice" See commentary in paragraph A.93, above or paragraph 50.04, below.

"for the common safety," See commentary in paragraph A.96, above. 2.10

It should be noted that loss of or damage to the property involved in the common maritime adventure in consequence of a sacrifice for the

[8] For an explanation concerning the greater importance of the numbered Rules as compared with the lettered Rules, see the Rule of Interpretation, para. PRE.04, *ante*.

common safety is recoverable even if the original sacrifice itself is irrecoverable because of the provisions of Rule I. This is illustrated by a decision given in the United States District Court (Southern District of New York).[9]

The *S.S. Felix* shipped a cargo of mahogany and cedar logs, partly on deck, at Belize for carriage to New York, under a bill of lading which contained a clause providing that general average should be adjusted according to the York-Antwerp Rules 1890. During the voyage the vessel stranded and it became necessary to jettison part of the deck cargo in order to lighten her. In doing so, damage was caused to the hull and equipment of the steamer and a log which had been jettisoned became jammed between the propeller and the stern frame, stopped the engines and damaged one of the propeller blades, damage being also caused to the engines in endeavouring to clear the log from the propeller. It was held that all this damage, both to hull and machinery, was allowable in general average in accordance with the terms of Rule II, notwithstanding the fact that the jettison of the deck cargo was not allowable in general average under Rule I.[10]

[9] *Ove Lange, Trustee v. George D. Emery & Co. and Insurance Co. of North America* (Unreported), January 1926.

[10] Rule I of the 1877 and 1890 Rules excluded any contribution in respect of jettison of deck cargo. For text of that Rule see para. 1.20, *ante*.

Rule III

Extinguishing Fire on Shipboard

English Law and Background

If a ship is on fire and the fire is quenched by pouring water into the hold, or by scuttling the ship in shallow water, or by filling the hold with steam, the damage done by this means to the ship, cargo, or freight is properly the subject of general average contribution. In broad terms, this is the law and practice of all countries and it was only with regard to extinguishing damage caused to such portions of the ship and bulk cargo, or to such separate packages of cargo, as were or had been on fire, that there was until 1974 a possible divergence of opinion.[1] **3.01**

Former Practice of Adjusters

Damage to cargo done by the means used to extinguish a fire was probably treated as general average in this country until at least the 1820s, but a contrary practice was then established, possibly initiated by Stevens. In the fourth edition of his *Essay on Average* published in 1822 he gave it as his opinion that such damage should be treated as general average.[2] He suggested a doubt, however, in saying: **3.02**

> "When claimed as a general average, it is objected to on the ground that the damage done to the goods is secondary and accidental, and not primary and intentional (as in cutting away a mast, etc.), which it ought to be to establish such a claim."[3]

This perhaps meant that the water was poured in for the purpose of quenching the fire and not of wetting the goods, and was not aimed at any particular package. On whatever ground it may have rested, however, we find that the practice of excluding such claims from contribution was completely established before the year 1851. Baily spoke of it as a settled rule.[4]

[1] See para. 3.10, *post*.
[2] And see, to the same effect, Benecke, p. 243.
[3] Stevens, *Average* (4th ed.), p. 243.
[4] Baily, *General Average*, p. 60.

Manley Hopkins[5] considered the practice to be wrong, though he was prepared to accept that it might be advisable to pursue it solely on the grounds of expediency, and with the proviso that the practice was not justified by a defence which was shown to be fallacious.

3.03 Until the year 1873 then, the practice of adjusters in case of fire was this: if a hole was cut in a ship's deck, in order to pour water down it to flood the cargo and quench the fire, the cost of repairing the deck was replaced in general average, but the damage done to the goods by the water poured down was not replaced. If a hole was cut in a ship's side in order to scuttle the ship for the same purpose, the damage done to the ship by cutting the hole was allowed as general average, but the damage done to the ship and goods by the water that flowed in through the hole was not allowed. This practice held good only until it was challenged in *Stewart v. West India and Pacific S.S. Co.*[6]

In that case a parcel of 180 serons of bark had been shipped at Santa Martha on board the steamer *Venezuelan*, bound for London, under a bill of lading containing the clause, "average, if any, to be adjusted according to British custom". While the *Venezuelan* was at Santa Martha, loaded and about to sail, a fire broke out in her forehold, which was only extinguished by pouring in water down the hatchways, and through holes cut in the deck, and by cutting a hole in the side of the ship and filling her fore-compartment with water. By the water thus poured or let into the ship, 152 of the 180 serons of bark were destroyed. The owner of it claimed contribution from the shipowner, as general average. The question was tried on an agreed case, in which it was admitted that if these measures had not been taken, the remaining cargo would in all probability have been destroyed, and the ship most seriously damaged, if not rendered a total wreck. It was admitted also that "it has been the practice of British average adjusters, in adjusting losses, to treat a loss occasioned by water in the manner above described as not a general loss".

3.04 The judgment of the Court of Queen's Bench was delivered by Quain J. who said:

> "The first question argued before us was, whether the loss in question was a loss which properly formed the subject of a general average contribution, according to the law of England ... On these facts we are clearly of opinion that the loss was, according to the general law, properly the subject of a general average contribution. It was a voluntary and intentional sacrifice of the bark, made under pressure of imminent danger, and for the benefit, and with a view to secure the safety, of the whole adventure then at risk."

Accordingly, he held that, if the case depended wholly on the common law applicable to general average losses, the plaintiffs would be entitled

[5] Manley Hopkins, *Handbook on Average* (1857), p. 38.
[6] (1873) L.R. 8 Q.B. 88.

to recover. However, as the parties had agreed to make the custom of British average adjusters a part of their contract, the case had to be decided in accordance with the custom, and judgment was given for the defendants.

Quain J. concluded his judgment with the remark:

> "It is to be hoped, however, that in future there will be no difference between law and custom on this point, and that average adjusters will act on the law as now declared, and that bills of lading will also be framed in accordance with it."

Practice Altered

The effect of this decision was such as might have been expected. The practice at once disappeared. The Association of Average Adjusters, at their 1873 annual meeting, passed a resolution: "That damage done by water poured down a ship's hold to extinguish a fire be treated as general average."[7] **3.05**

However, the principle established by the court does not appear to have been accepted unreservedly by average adjusters, for the Rule of Practice was passed only by 11 votes to six and a modifying Rule[8] was introduced the following year. Nor may the decision have been accepted by shipowners, merchants and underwriters, for *Stewart v. West India and Pacific S.S. Co.* was carried to the Exchequer Chamber[9] and a number of further cases were fought up to 1908. In each one of these cases the principle was reiterated by the court that damage caused by means used to extinguish a fire was properly the subject of a general average allowance.

In 1874 *Achard v. Ring*[10] was tried at Nisi Prius to determine whether there existed a custom at Lloyd's excluding from general average, damage to cargo by scuttling (or voluntary stranding) to put out a fire: **3.06**

> "It is quite clear", said Cockburn C.J., "that this [alleged] custom is in opposition to, and in derogation of, the law of the land relating to insurance, and to the matter of average as between the shipowner and the owner of the goods. It would be general average according to the law of the land but for this custom, and therefore the custom militates against, and derogates from, the law of the land, and where a person sets up a custom of that sort in derogation of the law, he is bound to prove it, and to prove it fully to the satisfaction of the jury."

The jury found that the custom was not made out.

[7] Rule F2. See App. 3, para. 70.29, *post*.

[8] The modifying Rule is quoted, para. 3.10, *post*; it was rescinded in 1974 and wording identical with Rule III of the York-Antwerp Rules 1974, substituted in its place.

[9] (1873) L.R. 8 Q.B. 362.

[10] (1874) 31 L.T. (N.S.) 647; 2 Asp. M.C. 423.

3.07 In *Pirie v. Middle Dock Co.*[11] a fire had broken out on board the ship *Attila* bound for Singapore with a cargo of coals, owing, as was admitted, to the spontaneous combustion of the coal. Water was poured into the cargo continuously for three days and the ship was taken into Batavia for safety, where the fire was quenched. Owing to the damaged state of the coal from the sea water, it was found necessary to sell the whole of it at Batavia. The result was that the shipowner lost his freight, while the owner of the coals, receiving the proceeds freight free, suffered no loss, but on the contrary made a profit by the mishap. The shipowner thereupon claimed from him, as general average, contribution towards this loss of freight, occasioned by the means taken to extinguish the fire. The owner of the coals disputed his liability. Watkin Williams J. gave judgment in favour of the shipowner's claim. The question, he said, was to be tested by applying the maxim of the Rhodian law, *Omnium contributione sarciatur quod pro omnibus datum est.* As to the objection, that the fire arose from spontaneous combustion, that is, from the fault of the cargo, it was to be observed that the present claim was not made on behalf of the owner of the cargo, but, on the contrary, was by the shipowner upon him, so that the fault of the cargo was no answer. The learned judge, after a careful examination of the authorities and principles by which the question must be governed, arrived at the conclusion that the danger affected the whole, ship as well as cargo, and that the operation was successful in saving the ship and a large part of the cargo, while it caused the destruction of the freight; consequently, that the freight, being given for all, must be replaced by contribution.[12]

3.08 In *Whitecross Wire Co. v. Savill*,[13] the whole matter was argued afresh in the Court of Appeal unhampered by precedent. The iron ship, *Himalaya*, bound for Wellington, New Zealand, had arrived at that port, and had landed the greater portion of her cargo, when a fire broke out on board, which was extinguished by pouring water into her hold. Among other portions of the cargo damaged by the water poured in was a quantity of iron wire belonging to the plaintiffs. The owners of the wire made a claim on the shipowners for contribution towards their damage, as general average, and Pollock B. gave judgment in their favour. This was appealed against. The judgment of the court was unanimous against the appeal.

> "It must be shown", said Lord Coleridge,[14] "that an imminent peril existed, and that the master deliberately and for the sake of preserving the adventure sacrificed that in respect of which contribution is claimed ... I am unable to come to the conclusion that this is not a case of general average; the facts seem to me to fall within the definition of a general average act ... No authority is against our decision."

[11] (1881) 44 L.T. 426; Asp. M.C. 388.
[12] *Cf. Nimick v. Holmes* (1855) 25 Penns.Rep. 366; *Crockett v. Dodge* (1835) 3 Fairf. 190.
[13] (1882) 8 Q.B.D. 653; *cf. Garrels v. Behr & Mathew* (1933) 47 Ll.L. Rep. 219.
[14] (1882) 8 Q.B.D. 653 at 659.

Brett L.J. said[15]: 3.09

> "If there is an imminent danger, and if the captain sacrifices part in order to save the rest of the adventure, a claim for a general average contribution arises ... here the captain intentionally inundated the cargo and thereby necessarily damaged it by water ... All the circumstances seem to me to exist which constitute a general average loss."

If any doubt could possibly have remained after these decisions as to the right to recover in general average for the damage done by pouring water into the hold to extinguish a fire, it was set at rest by the judgment of the House of Lords in *Greenshields v. Stephens*[16]: and the same principle obviously applies in the case of other reasonable steps, such as scuttling,[17] taken for the same purpose.

Damage to Packages Already on Fire

As previously mentioned,[18] at their 1873 meeting and following the decision in *Stewart v. West India & Pacific S.S. Co.*,[19] the Association of Average Adjusters passed a Rule of Practice: 3.10

> "That damage done by water poured down a ship's hold to extinguish a fire be treated as general average."[20]

This was next year modified by another, namely:

> "That goods in a ship which is on fire, or the cargo of which is on fire, affected by water voluntarily used to extinguish such fire, shall not be the subject of general average if the packages so affected be themselves on fire at the time the water was thrown upon them."[21]

This latter Rule was passed without discussion and it is not now possible to deduce with certainty the reasons which prompted the Rule. Lowndes wrote in the 1888 edition of this work:

[15] *Ibid.* at 662.

[16] [1908] A.C. 431; *cf. Pacific Mail S.S. Co.* 74 Fed.Rep. 564 (1896).

[17] So held in *Papayanni v. Grampian S.S. Co.* (1896) 1 Com.Cas. 448; and *Achard v. Ring*, para. 3.06, *ante*.

[18] See para. 3.05, *ante*.

[19] (1873) L.R. 8 Q.B. 88.

[20] Rule F2. See App. 3, para. 70.29, *post*.

[21] The Rule (F3) was rescinded in 1974 and wording identical with Rule III of the York-Antwerp Rules 1974, substituted in its place (see App. 3, para. 70.30, *post*) packages which were on fire at the time the water was thrown upon them are no longer excluded from an allowance in general average.

> "It is based on the argument of common sense, that the water which in the same act damages and saves a package already kindled cannot be said to do that package, on the whole, any harm."[22]

This view was questioned in all subsequent editions.

The loss by fire of the rest of the cargo might have been inevitable if the water had not been poured over it; and the argument that the water had on the whole done no harm might equally well have been advanced in such a case with regard to that part of the cargo. If the package which had been on fire retained some value, and the damage done by the water could be separated from that done by the fire,[23] it seems more in accordance with principle to allow the former. This view was supported by a passage in Channell J.'s judgment in the case of *Greenshields v. Stephens.*[24] Referring to Rule III of the York-Antwerp Rules 1890,[25] the learned judge said:

> "That exception that no compensation shall be made for damage to such portions of the ship and cargo or separate packages as have been on fire, seems to me to mean that in those cases the portions that have been on fire are to be treated as wreck, as it is called, in this case, that is to say, it is something the value of which is already gone, and which cannot, therefore, be considered to be sacrificed for the general good; but, of course, if there were not this rule, there would be a question in each case of fact whether in the particular case the damage had gone to the extent in which you could say it was wreck within the meaning of that word. If it is, there is no sacrifice."

The above remarks relating to *damage to packages already on fire* are now of historical interest only. At their annual meeting in 1974 the Association of Average Adjusters rescinded the Rules of Practice denying any allowance in general average for damages to packages which were already on fire at the time the water was thrown upon them, and substituted for it the wording[26] of Rule III of the York-Antwerp Rules 1974.

[22] The rule observed in practice in the U.S. is the same: Gourlie, *General Average*, p. 157. And in the case of *Slater v. Hayward Rubber Co.* (1857) 26 Conn. 128, it was held that where goods on fire are jettisoned, no contribution in general average is due. See also the case of *Crockett v. Dodge* (1835) 3 Fairf. 190, where a vessel was scuttled in order to extinguish a fire in her cargo of lime. The lime was destroyed in consequence of the scuttling, but the ship was saved. It was held that no contribution was due in respect of the lime because the lime was already doomed. If the lime had not been doomed, contribution would have been payable (*The Rapid Transit* 52 Fed.Rep. 320 (1893); see also *Columbian Ins. Co. v. Ashby* (1839) 13 Pet. 331 at 340). In *Greenshields v. Stephens* [1908] 1 K.B. 51, the Court of Appeal rejected the contention that all the contents of one hold constituted only a single "portion" of a bulk cargo, and the judgment was affirmed [1908] A.C. 431.

[23] In an American case, where it was impossible to distinguish between the damage done by smoke and that done by steam turned into the hold to extinguish the fire, it was held that a claim for contribution had not been made out: *Reliance Mar. Ins. Co. v. N.Y. & C. Mail S.S. Co.* 77 Fed. Rep. 317 (1896).

[24] *Shipping Gazette*, December 29, 1906.

[25] See para. 3.22, *post*.

[26] Rule F3. See App. 3, para. 70.30, *post*.

Smoke Damage

In the (say) 10/15 years prior to 1974, an increasing number of claims were put forward in general average for damage to cargo caused by the *extra* smoke allegedly generated by modern methods of extinguishing fires. As smoke is a natural product of combustion (fire), damage caused thereby should be treated, prima facie, as accidental in origin and not the subject of any allowance in general average. However, there was a divergence of practice among adjusters. **3.11**

When Lowndes first wrote this work, the only effective means of fighting a fire was with water, but the damage so caused to a valuable general cargo could be extremely costly. Today, many ships carry supplies of carbon dioxide gas with which to suppress a fire, and water is used only as a last resort. Carbon dioxide is an inert gas which does not interact with other substances and it cannot, therefore, cause damage to even the most delicate and susceptible cargo (though cases have been encountered in practice where its cooling effect has created a vacuum in containers whereby the containers themselves suffer buckling damage). For this reason, its use is vastly to be preferred to the indiscriminate application of water to flood an affected hold. Even if it cannot always extinguish a fire completely, carbon dioxide will often keep an outbreak under control for weeks on end until, say, the arrival at destination where professional fire-fighting services are available.

However, this manner of fighting or controlling fires almost certainly results in more smoke damage to cargo than used to be the case when water was applied more promptly. Of itself, the carbon dioxide does not produce smoke, but it can aggravate the formation of smoke, by reducing the degree and intensity of combustion, for example from a fiercely flaming conflagration to a smouldering affair.[27] Further, and assuming an effective sealing of the hold has been made, the air pressure will be greater and smoke may be forced further into the packages than it might otherwise be.

If, then, damage caused by water used to extinguish a fire is treated as general average, should not any *increased* damage by smoke be similarly allowed?

There is no case law on the subject in this country, but the courts of the United States have decided against such claims in the case of *Reliance* **3.12**

[27] An excellent example drawn from practice was as follows: during the course of discharging a cargo of groundnuts at Rotterdam, a docker started a fire when he foolishly searched for his lost hook with a lighted match. The flames spread over the fatty bags at enormous speed and the dockers ran for their lives. The crew failed to extinguish the blaze with foam extinguishers and the fire assumed such proportions that the master ordered the hatches to be closed and sealed. Carbon dioxide gas was then injected for several days and eventually succeeded in extinguishing the fire. However, the whole of the cargo in the hold was very seriously damaged by smoke; if the hold had been flooded (and there was no nautical reason why it should not have been) there would have been considerable damage to cargo by water, but very little smoke.

Marine Ins. Co. v. New York & Cuba Mail S.S. Co.[28] In this case fire broke out in a cargo of hemp on board the *Seneca*. The hatches were closed, live steam from the boilers was let into the 'tween decks for about seven hours, and the ship put back to Cuba where part of the cargo was discharged into lighters and the ship then submerged. The insurers of sixty-four bales of tobacco claimed compensation in general average for damage to the tobacco by smoke driven into the compartment for the purpose of extinguishing the fire. The evidence was contrary and inconclusive whether the tobacco was damaged by smoke, and District Judge Brown held that a general average claims was not allowable for damage done through the undesigned and unavoidable spread of fire or smoke in the proper efforts to extinguish them. In the course of his judgment he said:

> "Here not only is there very great doubt whether the tobacco was tainted by smoke at all, but if it was, the smoke was an incident of the fire, and caused by the fire, and not by the act of man ... If the smothering of the fire by closing the ship's hatches, or by forcing water or steam upon the fire, temporarily increased the smoke, the fire was none the less the true and original cause of all the smoke, and hence of all the damage it may have done; and this damage, if there was any such damage, must be classed with fire damage, as particular average and not as general average, because done by smoke alone, as an incident of the fire, and not by the steam voluntarily employed to extinguish it ... Often the first efforts to extinguish a fire give it breath and extend the flames or smoke to articles before untouched. That is an unavoidable result of the endeavour to put out the fire. But damage thus arising is not a voluntary sacrifice giving rise to a general average claim. And similar is the damage arising from any unavoidable spread of smoke by the use of steam ... The fire, as the original cause of the smoke, must be treated as a whole, and as including whatever damage may arise from the fire or the smoke during all proper efforts made to extinguish them ... I cannot find any support for the contention that the spread of fire or smoke damage incidental to proper efforts to extinguish the fire, gives rise to general average demands ... Only when the damage is done by the agency employed to extinguish the fire, as in the case of water damage, can the damage be deemed a voluntary sacrifice ..."

3.13 This judgment was affirmed on appeal but, seemingly, on grounds of practical expediency rather than principle. Shipman J. said:

> "We are of opinion that more damage was caused to the tobacco by the pressure of steam, which carried smoke or its contents, than would have been caused if no steam had been introduced into the lower 'tween decks ... We have, therefore, in this case, an ordinary and extraordinary smoke damage; and no one can tell how much is ordinary, and how much is extraordinary. Under such circumstances, it is unnecessary to consider what might or might not be a proper rule of adjustment in a case where such ordinary and extraordinary damages were susceptible of a separation, and, severally, of exact ascertainment."[29]

[28] (1896) 70 Fed.Rep. 262; 77 Fed.Rep. 317; 165 U.S. 720.

[29] In *Starlight Trading Inc. v. Mitsui O.S.K. Lines Ltd* (1974) a U.S. court allowed general average on smoke damage caused by fire fighting with CO_2.

On these grounds of practical expediency, Rule III of the York-Antwerp Rules 1974, for the first time specifically excluded any compensation for damage by smoke or heat however caused, and the Association of Average Adjusters adopted the same wording for their own Rule of Practice[30] in 1974. The absolute exclusion of damage by *smoke* however caused was retained in the York-Antwerp Rules 1994, but modified for damage by *heat*.[31]

Complex Fire Extinguishing Operations

Reference has already been made to the use in modern times of carbon dioxide gas to suppress a fire,[32] or to keep it under control, possibly until arrival at destination, where professional fire-fighting services will be available. This delayed-action method of extinguishing fires not only produces greater claims for smoke damage,[33] but also creates other general average problems which can best be likened to those dealt with under "Complex Salvage Operations".[34] An imaginary example, based on a number of cases seen in practice, may illustrate the problem. **3.14**

A vessel loaded a full cargo of copra and tapioca products in Indonesian ports for the lengthy voyage via the Cape to Rotterdam and Hamburg. The cargo for Hamburg was stowed at the bottom of each of the vessel's five holds and the cargo for the first port of discharge, Rotterdam, was stowed above. Whilst still in the southern hemisphere, the cargo in No. 2 hold spontaneously ignited; the hold was sealed, large quantities of carbon dioxide gas were injected and the vessel put into Cape Town as a port of refuge. For a further 10 days carbon dioxide was injected into the hold and the temperature dropped sufficiently for the attending surveyors to consider it safe for the vessel to proceed on her voyage.

Some few days before arrival at Rotterdam, the cargo in No. 2 hold again heated and the fire reasserted itself. A common peril threatened the whole adventure but the fire was again suppressed with carbon dioxide gas and the following course of action was decided upon and carried out. At Rotterdam No. 2 hold was left unopened (although it contained cargo for that port) and only the Rotterdam cargo in the other four holds was discharged. The vessel then proceeded to Hamburg and No. 2 hold was again kept sealed whilst the cargo in Nos. 1 and 3 holds was completely discharged (stability requirements dictated that the after holds, Nos. 4 and 5, should not be discharged). Only then were the hatches on No. 2 hold lifted. The influx of fresh air caused the fire to erupt and within minutes there was a great conflagration which was extinguished only by flooding the hold.

[30] Rule F3. See para. 70.30, *post*.
[31] See para. 3.25, *post*.
[32] See para. 3.11, *ante*.
[33] *Ibid.*
[34] See paras. 8.05 *et seq.*, *post*.

Which interests should contribute to the general average damage caused by the flooding of No. 2 hold?

3.15 There may be those who, with a strong natural sense of equity, would contend that the whole of the cargo originally shipped should contribute towards the general average damage caused by flooding No. 2 hold. In support of their view they might maintain that:

(1) The whole of the cargo was on board when the fire reasserted itself and imperilled the common adventure a few days before arrival at Rotterdam; further, that the whole of the cargo was on board when the first steps were taken to extinguish the fire, that is, the injection of carbon dioxide gas into the hold.
(2) The whole course of action, both fire fighting and discharge, was planned at the outset as one continuous operation and carried out as such.
(3) In *Reliance Marine Ins. Co. v. New York & Cuba Mail Steamship Co.*[35] cargo removed from a ship before it was scuttled to extinguish a fire was nevertheless found liable to contribute towards the general average caused by the scuttling.
(4) The alternative view produces a ludicrous result in that the more cargo that is discharged before the final flooding of the hold is undertaken, the greater will be the burden and general average contribution falling on those interests that do contribute.

However, and in spite of a seemingly inequitable result, it is submitted that the correct view is that the general average damage in No. 2 hold should be borne only by the ship and such cargo as was on board at the time when the hold was flooded.

(5) There was nothing exceptional about the method adopted to fight the fire and shippers of cargo have the right to expect that a carrier will prosecute the voyage as cheaply and efficiently as possible.
(6) The fire fighting and discharge may have been planned as one continuous operation, but the discharging of Nos. 1, 3, 4 and 5 holds was not undertaken with the object of, nor did it in any way assist in saving or benefiting the ship and cargo in No. 2 hold.
(7) The cargo was discharged in the normal way at destination under the contract of affreightment, unlike the case of *Reliance Marine Ins. Co. v. New York & Cuba Mail Steamship Co.* Further, in that case, the discharge was for the common benefit in the sense that a valuable shipment of tobacco would have been destroyed by the scuttling, thereby increasing the total amount of the general average allowances. In the present case, the discharge was exclusively for the benefit of the particular cargo interests concerned and the case

[35] (1896) 70 Fed.Rep. 262; 77 Fed.Rep. 317; 165 U.S. 720.

of *Royal Mail Steam Packet Co. v. English Bank of Rio*[36] is more in point.

(8) The alternative view would lead to strange results if consistently applied. For instance, a vessel may be involved in a serious collision just outside her port of discharge, which then becomes a port of refuge for all cargo other than that destined for that port. It would not be suggested that the cargo for that port should contribute to temporary repairs necessary to complete the voyage, or to detention expenses.

However, the cargo for Rotterdam in No. 2 hold over-carried to Hamburg should not be called upon to pay a general average contribution greater than would have been demanded if the fire had been extinguished at the proper port of destination for this cargo, that is, Rotterdam.

Increased Cost of Discharging Cargo at Destination after a Fire

It is customary for stevedores to claim "dirty money" or other enhanced rates of pay if called upon to discharge a cargo which has been damaged, say by fire and subsequent flooding of the hold. Or, a cargo of grain which has been similarly damaged may have to be discharged by grab, rather than elevator, again at extra cost. In practice, the extra cost of discharging is generally considered to be the direct and natural result of the fire and/or the flooding of the hold and, in so far as the extra cost relates to cargo damaged by a general average sacrifice, it is allowed as general average, for example: **3.16**

Actual cost of discharge		10,000
Less: Normal cost		4,000
Extra cost		6,000
Whereof: Attributable to cargo damaged by		
Fire	3,500	
Water	2,500	
	6,000	

The extra cost (2,500) of discharging the cargo damaged by water used to extinguish the fire would be allowed as general average.

[36] (1887) 19 Q.B.D. 362.

Increased Cost of Discharging Cargo at Destination during a Fire

3.17 When a vessel arrives at destination with a fire in the cargo, the cost of discharging may be considerably increased. In order to get at the seat of the fire with the least possible delay, the discharge may take place in overtime hours or the men be paid danger money; or a smouldering cargo of fishmeal, instead of being discharged steadily tier by tier, may be attacked with grabs; or a cargo may be hastily discharged on to a dock wall and require additional handling and transport to the warehouse. Provided that the extra cost was incurred in order to extinguish the fire as quickly as possible and exclusively for the common safety of ship and cargo, it is allowed as general average.

Cost of Refilling Fire Extinguishers, etc., After Use

3.18 It is difficult to justify on established legal grounds the allowance in general average of the cost of refilling foam fire extinguishers and carbon dioxide gas cylinders.[37] They have been used for the very purpose for which they were intended. However, it is the invariable practice to allow the cost of refilling. The Association of Average Adjusters of the United States even have a rule of practice on the subject:

> "RULE XIX. Fire Extinguishers. The cost of replacing gas or any commodity used in efforts to extinguish a fire on board a vessel shall be allowed in general average even though the gas or commodity was on board the vessel at the time the fire was discovered."

In similar fashion, on purely practical grounds it is customary to allow as general average the cost of putting into port specially to replenish stocks of carbon dioxide gas etc. previously used to extinguish a fire; also to allow wages and maintenance of crew during extra detention at a port of refuge while waiting for carbon dioxide gas cylinders to be refilled.

HISTORICAL DEVELOPMENT AND PRACTICE OF RULE III

Glasgow Resolutions 1860

3.19 The second resolution put before the International Conference at Glasgow in 1860 was:

[37] *E.g. Harrison v. Bank of Australasia* (1872) L.R. 7 Exch. 39; *Robinson v. Price* (1876) 2 Q.B.D. 91.

> "That the damage done to ship, cargo, and freight, in extinguishing fire, shall be allowed in General Average."

and this was passed by a majority of 22–6 after very little discussion.

In the printed version of the Rules published soon after the Conference, there is a note under Rule 2:

> "This, it will be observed, includes the damage done by water to property which was actually on fire at the time when the water extinguished that fire."

It is suggested that this note may not necessarily have been intended to be explanatory or directive, but, rather, to draw attention to what was thought by some of the delegates to be a fault in the wording of the Rule.

York Rules 1864 **3.20**

Such discussion as took place on this occasion was concerned only with the form of wording of the Rule, and the final version, passed unanimously, was as follows:

> "Damage done to a ship and cargo, or either of them, by water or otherwise, in extinguishing a fire on board the ship, shall be general average."

It may be noted that the Rule makes no mention of "freight", and it was the intention of the Conference to deal with freight in a more general way in the Bill that might be brought before Parliament.

York-Antwerp Rules 1877 **3.21**

The 1864 Rule was confirmed at Antwerp in 1877, but with additional wording proposed by Richard Lowndes:

> ". . . except that no compensation be made for damage done by water to packages which have been on fire."

The Association of Average Adjusters had passed a British Rule of Practice of similar effect in 1874[38] and, no doubt, were pleased to see their views accepted by 36 votes to 4 at the International Conference. It is difficult to believe that Lowndes had any particular motive in his choice of the words *which have been on fire*, rather than the words in the British Rule: *on fire at the time the water was thrown upon them*, but their effect was, of course, quite different.[39]

[38] The Rule is quoted para. 3.10, *ante*.
[39] This distinction was relevant only up to and including the 1950 edition of the Rule.

3.22 *York-Antwerp Rules 1890*

The alterations made in the Rule at the Liverpool Conference in 1890 were largely of a clarifying nature. In the first, *positive*, part of the Rule were added the words: "including damage by beaching or scuttling a burning ship" although they may not have been strictly necessary.

In the second, *negative*, part of the Rule were added: "such portions of the ship and bulk cargo." There existed, almost certainly, a school of thought which maintained that if any part of a bulk cargo was on fire, no allowance could be made in general average for damage caused by water or otherwise to any other part of the bulk cargo in that particular hold. The additional wording in the Rule was intended to resolve this problem, but clearly failed to do so, as evidenced by the need to fight the case of *Greenshields Cowie & Co. v. Stephens & Sons.*[40]

> "Damage done to a ship and cargo, or either of them, by water or otherwise, including damage by beaching or scuttling a burning ship, in extinguishing a fire on board the ship, shall be made good as general average; except that no compensation shall be made for damage to such portions of the ship and bulk cargo, or to such separate packages of cargo, as have been on fire."

3.23 *York-Antwerp Rules 1924 and York-Antwerp Rules 1950*

No change made in the Rule, either in 1924 or 1950, but on each occasion the point had been raised that the exception in the second half of the Rule should be deleted. In its report[41] prior to the Amsterdam Conference in 1949, the Drafting Committee agreed that it was "illogical not to allow in general average damage sustained through extinguishing operations to such portions of the ship and cargo as have been on fire", but, for a reason which bears no close examination, recommended that the Rule should be left in its then existing form.

3.24 *York-Antwerp Rules 1974*

One radical alteration and an important addition were made to this Rule at the Hamburg Conference in 1974.

The previous exclusion in the second half of the Rule that no compensation should be made for damage "to such portions of the ship and bulk cargo, or to such separate packages of cargo, as have been on fire" was deleted, thus facilitating considerably the work of both the cargo surveyor and the average adjuster. As Mr N. G. Hudson said in his address to the Association of Average Adjusters in 1973:

> "The cargo surveyor will not need to make a separation of water damaged cargo into parcels suffering water damage only and those which have additionally been touched by fire. The other parties to the adventure will

[40] [1908] 1 K.B. 51, C.A.
[41] International Maritime Committee Bulletin, No. 104, p. 111.

> not now have to pay for the additional labour cost involved in making this separation, nor if it has been overlooked, will the average adjuster have to rely on guesswork. Nor will it be necessary to explore the realm of semantics to decide what is a 'portion' of a bulk cargo, or whether there is a distinction between a package which is 'charred' and one which is 'scorched.' Everyone will benefit by this real and practical simplification."

A new provision was also added to the Rule to exclude any allowance in general for damage by smoke or heat, however caused.

The vexed subject of smoke damage and the increasing number of claims being put forward for such damage as the result of modern methods of extinguishing fires is discussed earlier[42] in this work; it was resolved in 1974 and uniformity of practice achieved by the addition to the Rule of the words: "except that no compensation shall be made for damage *by smoke or heat however caused.*"

York-Antwerp Rules 1994 **3.25**

At an early stage of the proceedings leading to the 1994 Rules, the Netherlands Maritime Law Association drew attention to the fact that the exclusion of any compensation in general average for damage *by smoke or heat however caused* introduced in 1974 worked unfairly if the heat or smoke damage was attributable to general average measures. However, as the 1974 exclusion was purposely introduced on the grounds of practical expediency alone, the Netherlands did not press further with any proposals they might have had for change.

At a later stage of the proceedings, a somewhat similar point was made by the United States delegation and this achieved greater success. It concerned refrigerated cargoes, which were likely to suffer deterioration if it proved necessary to turn off the refrigerating equipment in order to extinguish a fire, or the refrigerating equipment was put out of action by water used to extinguish a fire—a general average act. The damage to the cargo from this cause would be the direct consequence of the general average act, but, rightly or wrongly, it had been argued that no allowance in general average could be made on the grounds that the deterioration was the consequence of *heat however caused*, as excluded by the Rule.

The United States Maritime Law Association proposed, therefore, that the exclusion of damage by *heat however caused* should be modified to exclude only damage by *heat of the fire*, and this was accepted at Sydney.

[42] See para. 3.11, *ante*.

RULE III

EXTINGUISHING FIRE ON SHIPBOARD

3.26 **Damage done to a ship and cargo, or either of them, by water or otherwise, including damage by beaching or scuttling a burning ship, in extinguishing a fire on board the ship, shall be made good as general average; except that no compensation shall be made for damage by smoke however caused or by heat of the fire.**

CONSTRUCTION

3.27 **"damage"** The word is used in contradistinction to "loss", and cargo which is *lost* by water used to extinguish a fire (for example sugar) may, more properly, be recoverable under the lettered Rules rather than under Rule III. Similarly, if cargo is jettisoned because part of it is on fire, the loss—if it is recoverable at all (see *Slater v. Hayward Rubber Co.*[43]), should be claimed under the lettered Rules.

"ship and cargo" For a commentary on "cargo" see Rule I.[44] Damage caused by the means used to extinguish a fire to property not carried under a contract of affreightment will be made good under the lettered Rules, as will damage to crew's clothing while fighting a fire. Loss of freight will be claimed under Rule XV.

"by water or otherwise" The word "otherwise" is understood to comprise those other means of extinguishing fires such as steam, carbon dioxide gas, and foam, etc.

"extinguishing" Contribution under this Rule is confined to damage done in extinguishing an existing fire, as opposed to damage done in preventing a fire, for example by pouring water on a bulk cargo which is heating dangerously and will otherwise ignite. Damage done as a result of preventive measures might, however, be recoverable under the lettered Rules.

3.28 **"fire"** To constitute fire there must be actual ignition, that is visible flames, a ruddy glow, or incandescence. "Mere *heating* which has not

[43] (1857) 26 Conn. 128.
[44] See para. 1.24, *ante*.

arrived at the stage of incandescence or ignition is not within the specific word 'fire' ".[45]

"no compensation shall be made for damage by smoke however caused or by heat of the fire" Damage caused by *smoke*, whether naturally resulting from the fire itself or whether enhanced by the use of CO_2 gas or other modern methods of extinguishing a fire, is hereby excluded from compensation in general average absolutely on the grounds of practical expediency, as recounted in paragraphs 3.11 to 3.13 and 3.25, above.

To the extent that damage caused by *heat* resulting from the fire itself can be separated from that resulting directly from the means used to extinguish the fire, the former is excluded from general average and the latter allowed.

[45] *Tempus Shipping Co. v. Louis Dreyus & Co.* [1930] 1 K.B. 699 at 708; *Harris v. Poland* [1941] 1 K.B. 462.

Rule IV

Cutting Away Wreck

English Law and Background

4.01 A class of case which at one time gave rise to much difference of opinion consists in the cutting away of ship's materials when they are in what is called a state of wreck.

When a ship's mast had been carried away, and was held fast alongside, with the yards, sails, and rigging, and this wreck, beating against the ship's side, threatened to stave it in, and thus endangered ship and cargo, supposing that in such a case the master, instead of waiting to try how much he could save of this "wreck", for the common safety cut it all away, was any part of this loss properly the subject of general average?

4.02 Emerigon,[1] and other foreign writers, held that an allowance should in such cases be made, as general average, for so much as the articles thus sacrificed, in their actual condition, may reasonably be taken to be worth. And this was always the rule in many foreign countries. In this country and the United States, however, a contrary practice prevailed until it was disapproved in the latter part of the nineteenth century by a series of legal cases decided in both[2] countries. At this present time, therefore, the law and practice in most countries is the same and, but for the York-Antwerp Rules, favours an allowance in general average of the damaged value of any wreck cut away for the common safety if that wreck would have survived the storm (or other emergency). However, the contrary practice of British and American average adjusters was incorporated into the York-Antwerp Rules from their inception in 1860 and remains to this day, for the soundest of practical reasons.[3] To the extent that the York-Antwerp Rules are now of almost universal application, the law on this subject is of less practical importance than when Lowndes himself prepared the first four editions of this work.

[1] *Assurances*, c. 12, para. 41; p. 422 of Boulay-Paty's ed.

[2] In the U.S., *The Margarethe Blanca* (1882) 12 Fed.Rep. 728; 14 Fed. 59; *The Mary Gibbs* (1884) 22 Fed.Rep. 463. A working scale for such allowances was prepared by Captain F. A. Martin on behalf of the New York Board of Underwriters.

[3] See York-Antwerp Rule IV, para. 4.14, *post*.

Principle Established by Decided Cases

The principle may be expressed thus: whatever, when cut away or parted from for the common safety, is already "in a state of wreck", is not admissible as general average. That is "in a state of wreck" which is in such a state that, even if it had not been thus cut away or parted from, and though the ship and cargo had nevertheless escaped the danger, that thing would certainly have perished or become of no value. It is not enough that it would perhaps or very likely have perished: on the other hand, it is not necessary that its perishing should be demonstrably certain; but if, according to the ordinary course of human events, no expectation could be entertained that it could be saved (a matter on which the judgment of experts may be called in), then it must be treated as "in a state of wreck" or of no value. **4.03**

Cases on State of Wreck

In *Johnson v. Chapman*[4] (the facts of which have already been considered in paragraph 1.07, above) Willes J. said: **4.04**

> "The cargo appears to have broken away, appears to have got loose on deck; it was not washed overboard; it had not become valueless; it was not spoiled with water; and if the weather had been fine it would have been restowed, and it might have come on and been just as valuable except getting a little wetting with salt water. It was in fact once restowed, or part of it, during the voyage, so that it clearly was not in a state of wreck, in the sense of having become lost property, which they could not recover, or make use of if they recovered it."

In arriving at this conclusion Willes J. gave an example of what truly constituted a state of wreck: **4.05**

> "If a mast were sprung and a part of it were to go overboard with a quantity of spars and sails attached to it hanging on by a stay which must give way in a minute or two, whilst in the meantime, by battering against the side of the vessel, it adds to the danger, and if the stay were cut to let it go at once, it would be very difficult to say that that was anything more than wreck. A lawyer could not lay it down as a matter of pure law that all cumber cut loose is wreck. But what I say is, if it was virtually lost, if not recoverable, if the act of cutting the rope was only hastening the moment at which it would be lost, you would properly call that wreck, and you would not say it was general average. The reason given is, because you cannot keep it. There is no intentional sacrifice in cutting it away. You must lose it, and the losing it a minute or two sooner can make all the difference of its doing great injury or not; but you cannot help losing it."

[4] (1865) 19 C.B. (N.S.) 563 at 582; 35 L.J.C.P. 23 at 28.

4.06 Three cases have been tried in our courts in which the attempt was made to exclude from general average the value of a mast cut away while still *in situ*, on the ground that by reason of previous damage to it or its supports the mast had been rendered of no value and virtually a wreck.

The first of these, *Corry v. Coulthard*,[5] is unfortunately not reported, but from the references to it in the case next cited we may gather that the mast, an iron one, having become loose, the master, fearing that if it broke it would go through the bottom of the ship, cut it away. The question having been raised whether this was general average, the judge, Cleasby B. directed the jury that the question turned on whether "if the weather had moderated, the mast could possibly have been saved". The jury found for the plaintiff, that is, in favour of general average. The case was carried up to the Court of Appeal, on the question of misdirection: but the court unanimously pronounced that the question had been rightly put to the jury. Brett L.J. said:

> "You do not mean to say that it was so valueless that a man, in a calm, would have thrown it overboard: it was worth money ... Wreck means rubbish, I suppose."

4.07 In *Shepherd v. Kottgen*,[6] the barque *Rollo* met with a heavy gale, and portions of the rigging gave way, owing to which the mainmast began to lurch violently, so that the crew feared it would rip up the decks and endanger the ship's safety. To prevent this, the master, after vainly attempting to secure the mast, cut it away. At the trial, Manisty J. put the question to the jury in the following form: "Are you of opinion that that mast was virtually a wreck and valueless and gone at the time it went over?" The jury found that the mast was a wreck; and, to a further question from the learned judge, "Do you find whether it was hopelessly lost?" they answered "Yes". On this the judgment was given against general average.

In the Divisional Court[7] the judgment was set aside upon the ground that the question should have been put to the jury in the same form as in *Corry v. Coulthard*.[8] The Court of Appeal,[9] whilst it adopted and concurred with the law as laid down in the Divisional Court, differed from it in thinking that the law as laid down to the jury by Manisty J. amounted to the same thing and restored the original judgment.

4.08 Bramwell L.J. said:

> "Where the thing destroyed has some peculiar condition attached to it, so that it will be lost whether the whole adventure is saved or not, then its destruction cannot be deemed a sacrifice. I think that this proposition applies

[5] Heard in Exch. Div., December 21, 1876, and in the Court of Appeal, January 17, 1877; mentioned in *Shepherd v. Kottgen* (1877) 2 C.P.D. 578 at 583.

[6] (1872) 2 C.P.D. 578 at 583.

[7] (1877) 2 C.P.D. 578.

[8] *Supra*.

[9] (1877) 2 C.P.D. 585.

to the present facts. The mast was in such a state that it must have been lost, whether the vessel got safely to port or not. Consequently there was no sacrifice of it when it was cut away, and the plaintiffs have no claim for contribution."

Brett L.J. said:

> "Now, consistently with the decision of this court in *Corry v. Coulthard*,[10] and in accordance, as it seems to me, with what was intimated by the court in that case, the following proposition may be stated: If anything on board a ship, which is cut or cast away because it is endangering the whole adventure, is in such a state or condition that it must itself certainly be lost, although the rest of the adventure should be saved without the cutting or casting away, then the destruction of the thing gives no claim for general average. Or the proposition may be stated in the following terms: where, whether the act relied upon as the act of sacrifice had been done or not, the thing in respect of which contribution is claimed would, by reason of its own state or condition, have been of no value whatever, or would have been certainly or absolutely lost to the owner, although the rest of the adventure had been saved, there is nothing lost to the owner by the act, and therefore there is nothing sacrificed, that is to say, there is no sacrifice."[11]

Cotton L.J. said:

> "'Hopelessly lost' must mean 'impossible to be saved.' In the language of everyday life a thing is impossible when, according to the ordinary course of human events, no expectation can be entertained that it will happen ... Where the thing said to have been voluntarily abandoned or destroyed is in such a state, by reason of a peril peculiar to itself, that if the act of supposed sacrifice had not been done, it would have very shortly been destroyed, without the rest of the common adventure being lost, the act of slightly hastening the moment of loss, is not an act of sacrifice which enables the owner of the thing to claim contribution."

In *Montgomery v. Indemnity Mutual Marine Ins. Co.*,[12] the facts were that the *Airlie* encountered bad weather, in which she rolled and lurched violently. The mainmast, which was made of iron, and hollow, settled down, and the master, fearing that it would break and fall on the deck and cause the loss of the vessel, cut away the windward rigging, after which the mast fell on the side and was cut adrift. It was afterwards found that the mast had been in no greater peril than the rest of the adventure. It had broken across about 12 inches from the keelson. The upper portion had crushed into the lower in telescope fashion and rested securely on the keelson. Mathew J. said: **4.09**

[10] See para. 4.06, *ante*.

[11] *Cf.* the judgment of Bigham J. in the case of *Iredale v. China Traders' Insce. Co.* [1899] 2 Q.B. 356 at 360, where he suggests *obiter* that whether the thing sacrificed is in a state of wreck has to be ascertained subjectively in the light of the facts known at the time of the sacrifice. It is submitted that this is not correct and that the true test is whether the thing sacrificed was in fact in a state of wreck, to be ascertained in the light of all the facts known at the time of making the adjustment.

[12] [1901] 1 Q.B. 147.

"The mast was not in such a condition that it must have been lost whether the rest of the adventure had been saved or not. It could not be said that the mast had no value, or that it was impossible to be saved. There was a chance of saving it, and that chance was thrown away for the safety of the whole adventure. The master would seem to have exercised his judgment reasonably, and it was not necessary that his views should be borne out by the facts when they came to be afterwards examined. For the defendants reliance was placed on the case of *Shepherd v. Kottgen*,[13] where the mast was cut away, but was held to have been already lost. There it appeared that the rigging had been loosened in the storm, and that all that was done was to anticipate by a few minutes an inevitable loss. The mast of the *Airlie* before the rigging was cut was firmly upheld, and could have stood and been saved if the master had not ordered it to be cut away. Upon the question of fact I am of opinion that there was a general average sacrifice."[14]

Proposed Rules of Practice

4.10 The principle to be extracted from these decisions has been set out above.[15] Lowndes proposed that this principle should be applied to particular cases in the form of a set of *working* rules for which reference may be made to the 4th/9th editions of this work.

Historical Development and Practice of Rule IV

4.11 *Glasgow Resolutions 1860*

If a ship's mast carried away in a gale, but was held fast alongside by the rigging and that rigging was cut away in order to get rid of the mast because it threatened to stave in the ship's side and endanger the ship and cargo, it was the custom in most foreign countries in 1860 to allow as general average the value, in their then damaged condition, of the lost mast, spars, sails and rigging. Nevertheless, all but two of the delegates at the 1860 Conference at Glasgow voted in favour of the Resolution (No.5):

"That the loss sustained by cutting away the wreck of masts accidentally broken ought not to be allowed in general average."

[13] (1877) 2 C.P.D. 578.

[14] *Cf. May v. Keystone Yellow Pine Co.* 117 Fed.Rep. 287 (1902), where the rudder of a ship, partly torn loose in a gale, was cut away to prevent it from beating a hole in the ship. But for the storm it could have been replaced in position; and its value in its damaged condition was allowed in general average.

[15] See para. 4.03, *ante*.

This resolution was based on the inveterate practice[16] of British and American adjusters. Even if the theoretical grounds for the practice would be considered unsound today, they carried some weight in 1860, and the practical difficulties of placing a value in their then damaged condition on the sacrificed mast, spars, sails and rigging were probably sufficient to sway the voting in favour of the Resolution.

York Rules 1864 **4.12**

The wording of the 1860 Resolution was amended slightly in 1864 and carried by a large majority, three votes only being given against it.

> "Loss or damage caused by cutting away the wreck or remains of spars, or of other things which have previously been carried away by sea-peril, shall not be made good as general average."

York-Antwerp Rules 1877, York-Antwerp Rules 1890, York-Antwerp Rules 1924 and York-Antwerp Rules 1950

No change.

York-Antwerp Rules 1974 **4.13**

The wording of the 1864 Rule survived unchanged for 110 years; but as it related essentially to sailing ships, the question was raised when considering any necessary revision for the 1974 Rules whether the Rule was obsolete and should be deleted. No strong opinions were expressed one way or another and the view prevailed, as expressed by the President of the International Sub-Committee:

> "... that the Rule does serve some function in a limited number of cases and, perhaps more important, it serves to express a principle which is nowhere else expressed in the Rules."

Accordingly, a modernised text omitting any reference to spars was passed at the Hamburg Conference in 1974:

> "Loss or damage sustained by cutting away wreck or parts of the ship which have been previously carried away or are effectively lost by accident shall not be made good as general average."

[16] Stevens (1816), p. 18, considered that the situation in which these articles were placed by the breaking of the mast rendered them of no value whatever. Benecke (1824), p. 185, denied that the articles were valueless, but, having recourse to his favourite doctrine that where there was no choice there could be no sacrifice, considered that, generally speaking, it would be impossible to work the vessel without cutting away the broken mast and the rigging in which it was entangled, so that this act was not optional but dictated by necessity, and consequently was not a sacrifice. Baily (1851), pp. 33–34, considered that no allowance could be made in general average for the sacrifice of an article which was itself the immediate cause of the danger necessitating the sacrifice.

4.14 **York-Antwerp Rules 1994**

No change, but the suggestion was again made that the Rule was anachronistic with modern ships and should be deleted. The United States Maritime Law Association indorsed this view and proposed to fill the ensuing void with:

> "When the ship, cargo or other property on board the ship sustains a combination of sacrificial damage and damage which is not general average, the amount to be made good in general average under any of these Rules shall not exceed the increase in net repair or replacement costs resulting from the sacrificial damage."

The wording may not have been perfect, but here was an eminently sound and sensible proposal based on the same fundamental principle that what has already been lost by accident cannot be sacrificed. Unfortunately, the opinion was expressed that the proposed was devoid of practical benefit and it was rejected.

The type of problem which the proposal would have addressed is considered in paragraphs 18.13 to 18.15, below.

Rule IV

Cutting Away Wreck

Loss or damage sustained by cutting away wreck or parts of the ship which have been previously carried away or are effectively lost by accident shall not be made good as general average.

Construction

4.15 It is submitted that both the original and current versions of Rule IV are rules of practical convenience rather than of principle. It is no doubt correct that there can be no sacrifice of that which is already valueless.[17] But the Rule extends this principle. There may be great practical difficulties in determining:

(1) whether, for instance, a mast or spars (or other part of the ship) previously carried away in a storm but still lying alongside the ship attached by the rigging were "hopelessly lost" or might have survived the storm had they not been cut away, and

[17] See paras. 4.01–4.10, *ante*.

(2) if they had so survived, what their likely value would have been in damaged condition.

These are solved by assuming that any part of the ship which has previously been carried away by accident shall be considered to be valueless when cut away from the common safety, and not the subject of any general average allowance.

"loss or damage" The wording of the Rule as a whole is less than perfect, and a difficulty arises from the introduction of the word "damage". It is possible to visualise, for instance, that a broken mast on an auxiliary sailing vessel might be cut away for the common safety, and, before clearing the vessel, cause damage to the propeller. The loss of the mast is plainly excluded by the wording of the Rule. The propeller was not itself previously harmed, by accident or otherwise. Is the damage to it to be excluded, because it was sustained through cutting away the mast? It is submitted that the loss or damage referred to are the financial consequences to the shipowner solely through cutting away the wreck or parts of the ship, and that the damage to the propeller is not excluded. This accords with principle.[18] **4.16**

"wreck" See paragraphs 4.04 to 4.09, above.

[18] *E.g.* see *Ove Lange, Trustee v. George D. Emery & Co. and Insurance Co. of North America* (unreported), January 1926, the facts of which are recorded at para. 2.10, *ante*.

Rule V

Voluntary Stranding

Law and Background

5.01 When a ship is voluntarily run upon a sandbank, or scuttled, or purposely sunk in shallow water, in order to escape the pursuit of an enemy or the imminent danger of being dashed to pieces on rocks, or sinking in deep water, or to extinguish a fire on board, and if the ship or the cargo suffers damage by reason of that measure, is such damage properly the subject of general average? The answer which would first occur to perhaps everyone to whom this should come as a perfectly new question would probably be, without hesitation, in the affirmative. Such damage is the result of a measure, out of the ordinary course, taken for the common safety and to avert an imminent peril, and involving a sacrifice, namely the danger of almost certain injury to the bottom of the ship, and considerable risk to the cargo in the lower hold, from leakage caused by the shock below. It is the substitution of a danger affecting mainly, if not exclusively, the lower portion of the ship and cargo for a danger of total loss, that is, a danger affecting all parts equally. In this sense it is the sacrifice of a part for the benefit of the remainder. Accordingly, the rule in almost every country is to treat such damage, at all events when the ship is got off again, as general average.

English Law

5.02 It is surprising that no case has ever come before the courts of this country involving the voluntary stranding of a vessel and depending for a decision on English law, unencumbered by the York-Antwerp Rules. The chance of such a case being brought for trial must now be considered extremely remote for the following reasons:

(1) The almost universal use of the York-Antwerp Rules, with their specific provision[1] on the subject, makes unnecessary any decision upon the basic principles.

[1] Rule V, para. 5.18, *post*.

(2) Driving ashore (whether voluntarily, or by accident) is no longer the common occurrence that it was in sailing ship days.

This lack of binding authority led to there being, at least throughout the nineteenth century, a considerable difference of opinion amongst adjusters and amongst the writers of textbooks; in fact, it is probable that more discussion took place and more was written on the subject of voluntary stranding than on any other single example of a general average sacrifice. Reference is requested to any of the 1st/9th editions of this work for a full account of the varying viewpoints held, as the present editors propose not to repeat those arguments at length for the reasons expressed above. In addition there used to be a Custom of Lloyd's excluding from general average all damage to ship and cargo resulting from a voluntary stranding except such damage as was done by beaching or scuttling a burning ship to extinguish a fire. Whilst this Custom remained in being, any British adjuster was bound to attach considerable weight to the Custom, even if he was not obliged to follow it blindly, and it was partly to refute this old and possibly invalid Custom that previous editions of this work were designed. This reason no longer applies, for in 1968 the Association of Average Adjusters rescinded the old Custom and substituted wording identical with the then current (1950) Rule V of the York-Antwerp Rules, to be followed in 1996 with the 1974 wording of Rule V of the York-Antwerp Rules[2]: **5.03**

> "When a ship is intentionally run on shore for the common safety, whether or not she might have been driven on shore, the consequent loss or damage shall be allowed in general average."

As stated earlier, there is little or no decided case law in this country on the subject of voluntary stranding, though Abbott, *Shipping* (in the last edition published (in 1827) in Lord Tenderden's lifetime), laid down that: **5.04**

> "damage voluntarily done to a ship by ... running it on a rock, shallow, or strand to avoid the danger of a storm or of an enemy, and the expense of recovering the ship from this latter situation ... are to be sustained by a general contribution."[3]

There is no doubt that the great current of authority sets that way. The *Consolado del Mare*, Roccus, Targa, Emerigon, Abbott, are cited by Arnould, who concludes: "there is no rule more clearly established than this by the uniform course of maritime law and usage."[4]

[2] Rule F4, para. 70.31, *post*.
[3] 5th ed., p. 349.
[4] Arnould, *Insurance* (2nd ed.), p. 915. See also 16th ed., para. 943.

Law in the United States

5.05 The law in the United States is better defined, and from the many cases which have come before the courts of that country it is possible to deduce the governing principles.

1. Even if the ship must inevitably ground somewhere, and the only act of volition consists of selecting a place for grounding where she will suffer least, this is enough: the damage done is general average.

5.06 In *Sims v. Gurney*,[5] tried in the Supreme Court of Pennsylvania, the ship *Woodrop Sims* was lying at anchor in a bay when a violent gale came on, and one of her chains parted. The master then asked the pilot what was to be done in case the remaining chain should part, to which he answered "If the chain does part, I can do nothing with her but run her ashore to the eastward". The chain did part, whereupon two sails were set, and an attempt was made to fetch out to sea; but this proved impracticable, and she was run up the bay again. The master said to the pilot: "As we must go ashore somewhere, had we not better put her on Cape May?" The pilot said he would try. She was with difficulty run ashore on Cape May, and was eventually, after the storm abated, got off, though with damage to the hull by grounding. At the trial the pilot stated that his motive for running the ship ashore on Cape May was to get the most convenient place to save the ship, crew, and property; that if her course had not been changed she must have gone on Egg Island Flats; that all the men in existence could not have prevented her going on shore—if not run ashore she must have drifted ashore; and that when he put her head towards Cape May, he had not an idea she would go there, and told Captain Heath so at the time.

The court was unanimously of opinion that the damage must be so treated. Tilghman C.J. said:

> "It is said for the defendants that the ship must have gone ashore somewhere, and it made no difference where that shore was; that there was no advantage in taking the course that was taken, and that the ship was exposed to no greater danger than she would have been if the course had not been altered. It is not necessary that the ship should be exposed to greater danger than she would have been, to make a case of general average. It is sufficient if a *certain loss* is incurred for the common benefit."

5.07 A similar case was that of *Barnard v. Adams*,[6] where the Supreme Court allowed a claim in general average notwithstanding the fact that it was admitted that a stranding at one place or another was inevitable.

The judgment of the majority of the court was given by Grier J.:

[5] 4 Binney's Penns. Rep. 513.
[6] (1850) 10 Howard's S.C. Rep. 270 at 286.

"The assertion, so much relied on in the argument that if the peril be inevitable there can be no contribution, seems, when more carefully stated, to be this: that, if the common peril was of such a nature that the *jactus*, or thing cast away to preserve the rest, would have perished anyhow, or perished *inevitably*, even if it had not been selected to suffer in place of the whole, there can be no contribution. If this be the meaning of the proposition, and we can discover no other, it is a denial of the whole doctrine upon which the claim for general average has its foundation. For the master of the ship would not be justified in casting a part of the cargo into the sea, or slipping his anchor, or cutting away his masts, or stranding his vessel, unless compelled to it by the necessity of the case, in order to save ship and cargo, or one of them, from an imminent peril which threatened their common destruction. The necessity of the case must compel him to choose between the loss of the whole and part; and, however metaphysicians may stumble at the assertion, it is this forced choice which is necessary to justify the master in making a sacrifice (as it is called) of a part for the whole ... If the case does not show that the jettison was *indispensable*, in order to escape the common peril, the master would himself be liable for the loss consequent thereof..."

The learned judge illustrated this by the case of a jettison, and added:

"But suppose the ship cannot be saved by casting the cargo into the sea, but the cargo, which is of far greater value, can be saved by casting the vessel on the land, or stranding her, ... the imminent destruction of the whole has been evaded, as a whole, and part saved, by transferring the whole peril to another part."

2. The consequences need not be those which were intended by the master provided that the subsequent stranding is the result of the action of those in command; if while the master is running the ship for one point on the strand, she takes the ground on another, that loss is general average. **5.08**

This principle is well illustrated by a number of American cases,[7] also the English case of *Anglo-Grecian Steam Trading Co. Ltd v. T. Beynon & Co.*[8] in which Roche J. said:

"It is said ... that the ship was not intentionally run on shore. Now that depends on this. On the facts as I have found them it was intended to beach her and she did take the beach during the operation of beaching her; but she took the beach before the person in control of the operation expected she would ... I hold that there was an intentional beaching, none the less because the actual taking of the ground ... occurred sooner than anticipated and not precisely in that place of the beach area which was expected and desired. Of course the pilot did not intend to put her on the rocks, neither do I find that he put her on the rocks. She got on the rocks because, after getting on the beach, by the operation of natural causes, she was moved from the place she took on the beach towards the rocks and on to the rocks."

[7] *Rea v. Cutler* (1846) 1 Sprague, 135; *Sturgess v. Cary* (1854) 2 Curtis, Cir. Ct. 59; *The Star of Hope* (1869) 9 Wall 203; *Norwich & N. Y. Transport Co. v. Ins. Co. of North America* (1902) 118 Fed.Rep. 307.

[8] (1926) 24 Ll.L. Rep. 122 at 125.

5.09 *3. A voluntary stranding is equally the subject of general average, whether the stranded ship is afterwards saved and repaired, or is totally lost by the stranding.*

In *Columbian Ins. Co. v. Ashby* (1839)[9] the brig *Hope*, going down Chesapeake Bay, found the weather too bad to proceed to sea, and bore away for a projecting headland in the Bay, called Sewell's Point, where she anchored. On the second and following day the gale increased in violence; the brig dragged her anchors from time to time, till finally she struck on the shoals, and her head swinging round brought her broadside to the wind and a heavy sea. In this situation the captain, finding no possible chance of saving the ship and cargo, and preserving the lives of the crew, slipped his cables and ran the brig ashore as high up the beach as possible, where, after the storm, she was left high and dry, and there was no possibility of getting her off. The cargo was saved.

The unanimous opinion of the court, that this loss was the subject of general average, was delivered by Mr. Justice Story, who stated:

> "The intention is not to destroy the ship, but to place her in less peril, if possible, as well as the cargo. The act is hazardous to the ship and cargo, but is done to escape from a more pressing danger; it is done for the common safety; and if the salvation of the cargo is accomplished thereby, it is difficult to perceive why, because from inevitable calamity the damage has exceeded the expectation or intention of the parties, the whole sacrifice should be borne by the shipowner, when he has thereby accomplished the safety of the cargo."

5.10 *4. Stranding must be consequence of intentional act.*

If the master does not intend to strand the vessel there can, of course, be no claim in general average on the basis of a voluntary stranding.

By way of illustration, in *Walker v. U.S. Ins. Co.*,[10] where the captain cut his cable and hoisted sail with the intention of running out to sea, but this failing, by reason of the sail being blown away, the ship became ungovernable and was drifted ashore, this was pronounced not to be a voluntary stranding.

> "An accidental loss", said Gibson J., "which happens in an endeavour to bring about a very different event, is not a subject of compensation ... If there were in fact an intention to run the vessel ashore, there was no act done in pursuance of it, for the vessel became ungovernable the instant the cables were cut, and was driven on the rocks exclusively by the agency of the wind and the waves."

9 (1839) 13 Pet. 343. In *Iredale v. China Traders' Ins. Co.* [1899] 2 Q.B. 356 at 363, Bingham J. said that he believed English law on the point to be the same as that laid down in this case.

10 (1824) 11 Sarg. & Rawle's Penns. Rep. 61 at 65.

Similarly if there was an intention to strand, but, because of the force of the elements or for some other reason, the master is unable to influence the course of the vessel any subsequent stranding will not be a voluntary stranding. 5.11

This is illustrated by *Shoe v. Low Moor Iron Co.*[11] In that case the ship was dragging her anchor and was bound to go ashore; the master slipped her cable and voluntarily stranded her, but (it was found) in substantially the same place and with the same results as would have followed from the dragging. It was held that this was not a case for general average.

Conclusions

To sum up, in the United States, the law now seems to be that although *some* stranding was inevitable, the loss is allowable in general average (*Barnard v. Adams*),[12] but that if the *same* stranding was inevitable, it is not (*Shoe v. Low Moor Iron Co.*).[13] Or, as was stated in *Phillips on Insurance*: 5.12

> "On the whole, then, if the intentional stranding is, under the particular circumstances, the direct result of voluntary agency, rather than of the action of the elements, and the actual stranding is another than the one impending, and not merely an incidental and inconsiderable modification of it, the case is one for general average."[14]

Historical Development and Practice of Rule V

Glasgow Resolutions 1860 5.13

At the International Conference held at Glasgow in 1860 the principle appears to have been generally accepted by those delegates who spoke that damage done to a ship and her cargo by a voluntary stranding was properly allowable as general average. However, it was the opinion of L. R. Baily, undoubtedly the most respected and persuasive delegate present (and at this time the senior partner of Richard Lowndes), that in this particular instance it was better to depart from sound principle and adopt a practical rule which excluded from general average any loss caused by voluntary stranding.

> "The practical difficulties are so great that however correct in theory it may be to allow such damages, I would in practice reject them from general

[11] 49 Fed.Rep. 252 (1891).
[12] (1850) 10 Howard's S.C. Rep. 270. *Cf. Norwich & N. Y. Trans. Co. v. Ins. Co. of N.A.* (1903) 118 Fed.Rep. 307; (1904) 129 Fed. 1006; 194 U.S.637.
[13] 49 Fed.Rep. 252 (1891).
[14] Phillips, *Insurance*, p. 1313.

> average; for when a ship is run ashore, much water is already in her, and she and her cargo have both sustained much damage previously. By running her on shore these injuries may be increased; but who in the world is to say what that increase is? Is it not better to waive your principle, and make a practical rule to prevent litigation?"

Accordingly, Baily put forward the resolution:

> "That the damage done to ship, cargo, and freight, by running a ship on shore ... shall not be allowed in General Average."

In this form, the resolution was perfectly clear and unambiguous, and generally acceptable as a working rule to those present, but it flew in the teeth of the principles upon which general average was founded and, as Judge Marvin (United States) said, they should not give up a good principle when they might avoid the inconvenience. Further discussion ensued and a number of amendments were proposed which on practical grounds would exclude from general average any damage caused by voluntary stranding without denying the basic principle that such damage might properly be admissible as general average.

Finally, the following Resolution proposed by Lord Neaves was passed:

> "That, as a general rule in the case of the stranding of a vessel in the course of her voyage, the loss or damage to ship, cargo, or freight shall not be the subject of general average, but without prejudice to such a claim in exceptional cases, upon clear proof of special facts."

5.14 *York Rules 1864*

As in so many cases where a rule has been agreed only after considerable argument and compromise, the 1860 Glasgow Resolution on voluntary stranding was decidedly vague in its wording, and one can imagine that almost every case of voluntary stranding was capable of being construed as an "exceptional case" to be allowed in general average. After the 1860 Glasgow Conference, a number of reports and questionnaires were circulated amongst the delegates and a more specific and tighter wording was put forward for discussion at the International Conference held at York in 1864. It was proposed that damage caused by a voluntary stranding should be allowed as general average only if the stranding was to avoid capture or foundering.

In the discussion which followed, the same points raised at the 1860 Conference were again stressed, namely that by the specific laws of some countries, also on the grounds of general principle, damage caused by voluntary stranding was allowable as general average; however, the practical difficulties of carrying out the principle, and the abuses and frauds to which it was open, made it preferable to limit allowances in general average to the minimum.

It was finally agreed to accept the wording of L. R. Baily, as follows:

> "When a ship is intentionally run on shore because she is sinking or driving on shore or rocks, no damage caused to the ship, the cargo and the freight, or any or either of them, by such intentional running on shore, shall be made good as general average."

This Rule had the merit of being clear and unambiguous and it removed from general average those cases of voluntary stranding most likely to offer opportunities for fraud and abuse, but it suffered from the defect that, to those not aware of the background, it might appear that these two instances of voluntary stranding were not allowable in general average on principle. This was not necessarily so, even in Britain, where for the previous forty years or more no allowances had been made in general average for cases of voluntary stranding. As the Chairman, Sir Fitzroy Kelly (afterwards Lord Chief Baron of the Exchequer) said at the 1864 Conference:

> "The law of England, as it then stood, that where an injury had been *bona fide* done, whether to ship, freight or cargo, by the voluntary act of the master, in order to prevent some greater calamity, then the consequences whatever they might be, would belong to general average. On this principle, the law, as regards voluntary strandings, would be the same in England as in the United States."

York-Antwerp Rules 1877

The existing 1864 York Rule was unanimously confirmed at the Conference at Antwerp in 1877.

York-Antwerp Rules 1890 **5.15**

The only change in Rule V intended at the Conference at Liverpool in 1890 was the insignificant addition of the words "loss or" before the word "damage" (to read "no loss or damage").

Charles McArthur considered that the Rule might be further clarified by additional wording on two subjects:

(1) The Rule in 1877 form mentioned only those situations where damage caused by voluntary stranding was excluded from general average; it failed to provide for those positive situations where the damage could be made good. It may have been that silence gave consent, and that it was the intention of those who framed the earlier Rule that all those cases not expressly excepted should be treated as general average; if so, it was better to express it. For those countries (and he instanced France, Germany, Italy, Holland, Sweden, Norway, Denmark, Russia, Spain, Portugal, the United States, and the Argentine Republic) which had codes providing for voluntary stranding, there was no problem but in Britain, at

least, there was an old custom[15] not yet overruled and still considered to be binding in practice.

(2) The words "driving on shore or on rocks" required greater definition. In the 4th edition of this work, Richard Lowndes stated at page 137 concerning the 1877 Rule:

> "It was understood, I believe, that this rule was only applicable to a stranding *in extremis*, when a loss was inevitable, and it may be read in this sense; but the vagueness of the terms used is to be regretted."

MacArthur, therefore, proposed the following amendment:

> "When a ship is intentionally run on shore, and the circumstances are such that if that course were not adopted, she would inevitably sink or drive on shore or on rocks, no loss or damage caused to the ship, cargo, and freight, or any of them by such intentional running on shore shall be made good as general average. But in all other cases where a ship is intentionally run on shore for the common safety, the consequent loss or damage shall be allowed as general average."

This was carried *nem con.*

5.16 *York-Antwerp Rules 1924*

At the Stockholm Conference in 1924, at the suggestion of the Association of Average Adjusters, it was unanimously agreed that the words "sink or" should be deleted from the 1890 Rule. There now remained but a single exception to the allowance in general average of loss or damage caused by voluntary stranding: where the ship would inevitably drive on shore or on rocks if that course was not adopted.

York-Antwerp Rules 1950

The words "but loss or damage incurred in refloating such a ship shall be allowed as general average" were added to the first paragraph of the Rule in 1950 to clarify a point on which there was no dispute in practice, but on which the wording of the 1924 Rule was open to the opposite construction.

> "When a ship is intentionally run on shore, and the circumstances are such that if that course were not adopted she would inevitably drive on shore or on rocks, no loss or damage caused to the ship, cargo and freight or any of them by such intentional running on shore shall be made good as general average, but loss or damage incurred in refloating such a ship shall be allowed as general average.

[15] The custom of Lloyd's excludes from general average all damage to ship or cargo resulting from a voluntary stranding. This rule does not necessarily exclude such damage as is done by beaching or scuttling a burning vessel to extinguish the fire.

In all other cases where a ship is intentionally run on shore for the common safety, the consequent loss or damage shall be allowed as general average."

York-Antwerp Rules 1974 5.17

In their replies to the questionnaire circulated by the *Comité Maritime International* in 1970, National Associations were practically unanimous in suggesting that Rule V should not be changed. However, the West German Association considered that difficulties[16] would be removed and some simplification achieved if it were no longer necessary to differentiate between those cases of voluntary stranding, where the vessel would inevitably drive on shore or on rocks, and other cases of voluntary stranding. This view found favour and the new 1974 Rule allowing loss or damage caused by running a ship on shore for the common safety in all circumstances was passed at the Hamburg Conference without comment.

It probably reflects the law of most countries on the subject and also sound principle.

York-Antwerp Rules 1994 5.18

As previously recorded in paragraphs C.20 and 2.08, above, important new provisions were introduced in 1994 to Rule C to exclude any allowance in general average for environmental damage consequent on the escape or release of pollutant substances from the property involved in the common maritime adventure. By reason of the Rule of Interpretation, the provisions of the *lettered* Rule C would be subservient to any contrary provisions in any of the *numbered* Rules, and if the provisions of Rule C were always to retain their force, it was essential that potentially contrary provisions such as existed in Rules II, V and VIII should be neutralised.

The 1974 Rule V permitted the allowance in general average of *any* loss or damage consequent upon a voluntary stranding for the common safety, but limiting wording added in 1994 will ensure that the only loss or damage allowable in general average from a voluntary stranding will be that caused *to the property involved in the common maritime adventure*, that is, the ship and cargo, etc., and not to local beaches and fishing grounds, etc.

[16] The difficulty would be in determining under the 1950 Rule whether a ship would "inevitably" drive on shore or on rocks. It is believed that one of the reasons why "sinking" was removed from the 1924 Rule was this same difficulty in determining whether a vessel would "inevitably" have sunk; the matter could have been only one of conjecture.

Rule V

Voluntary Stranding

When a ship is intentionally run on shore for the common safety, whether or not she might have been driven on shore, the consequent loss or damage to the property involved in the common maritime adventure shall be allowed in general average.

Construction

5.19 **"intentionally"** For comments on the general meaning of the word, see under Rule A.[17] The relevant intention is an intention to run on shore, not to run on shore at a precisely defined spot, though it must be stressed that conditions must exist which make it possible for the master or those on board to carry out that intention and exercise some control over the manoeuvre and to run the vessel ashore at some spot other than that on which the elements would have driven her.[18]

In *Anglo–Grecian Steam Trading Co. Ltd v. Beynon & Co.*[19] it was intended to put the vessel ashore at a defined point in the centre of Whitmore Bay, but the vessel touched the ground sooner and more to the eastward than had been intended or expected. Roche J. held[20] that under the 1890 Rule: "there was an intentional beaching none the less because the actual taking of the ground, which after all must be a matter of some uncertainty, occurred sooner than was anticipated and not precisely in that place of the beach area which was expected and desired."

With the advent of the Rule Paramount[21] in 1994, it may be appropriate to record a further extract from the judgment of Roche J.:

> "... it is necessary for the plaintiffs to satisfy me and for me to be satisfied that the vessel was *reasonably* and intentionally run on shore."

5.20 **"run on shore"** These words are equivalent to "stranded"[22] and mean going with the bottom on the shore. They do not cover running the vessel against the side of structures or objects attached to the shore, the vessel being still afloat, although damage so caused may be a sacrifice or

[17] See particularly para. A.08, *ante*.
[18] See para. 5.10, *ante*.
[19] (1926) 24 Ll.L.R. 122. See also the American cases quoted in para. 5.08, n. 7, *ante*.
[20] *Ibid.* at 125.
[21] See para. PRE.22, *ante*.
[22] For the meaning of "stranded", see *Dobson v. Bolton* (1799) 1 Park, *Ins.* 239; *C'Dougle v. Royal Exch. Ass. Co.* (1816) 4 Camp. 283; 4 M. & S. 503; *Wells v. Hopwood* (1832) 3 B. & Ad. 20.

extraordinary expenditure within the meaning of Rule A.

In *The Seapool*[23] the vessel was intentionally run broadside against a pier with the object of using the pier as a lever to get the head of the ship into such a position that she could steam out to sea in a gale when her anchor had dragged, her port cable had parted and she was in great peril. As a result, the vessel was severely damaged and her owners became liable to pay and paid for the damage to the pier. Langton J. held that this was not a loss which fell within the terms of Rule V but that it was covered by Rule A as an extraordinary sacrifice. So far as Rule V is concerned he said that[24]:

> "On the other side, however, it was contended that 'stranding' is a well-known term. It is a term which occurs both in Continental law and in English law and it has a well ascertained meaning. 'Stranding' means going with the bottom on the shore and for my part I have always so understood it. I find it difficult to imagine that anybody could consciously have used language such as this if they had intended to include running a ship against the end of a pier, while the bottom of the ship was clear of the ground. It is true that some colour may be lent to the argument by the fact that in this particular case the ship appears to have bumped upon the ground whilst she was lying against the end of the pier, but, apart from that—which seems to me an extraneous circumstance—I see very little colour in this argument at all."

Damage by Emergency Docking

In similar fashion, when a ship, having lost her anchors, or being very leaky, so that it is dangerous to remain in the river or roadstead, is run into a dock when it would under ordinary circumstances have been improper to do so and is damaged by striking against the pier in entering it, the damage both to ship and pier should be treated as general average[25] under Rule A. **5.21**

In *Austin Friars S.S. Co. Ltd v. Spillers & Bakers Ltd*,[26] the steamship *Winchester*, bound for Sharpness dock, stranded in the Severn near to the dock, and when she was got off was so seriously damaged and making so much water, that her master and the pilot decided (reasonably and prudently it was found) to take her at once into the dock, although in consequence of the strong ebb tide they expected that she would strike the pier and suffer some damage. She did collide with the pier and was not only damaged, but also did damage to thc pier. Bailhache J. and the Court of Appeal held that the owners of the ship were entitled to a contribution in general average from the cargo owners in respect both

[23] [1934] P. 53. So far as the damage to the pier is concerned, it should have been regarded rather as an extraordinary expenditure.

[24] (1934) P. 53 at 62.

[25] Similarly it might be an extraordinary use of the ship to enter a narrow channel, and risk damage by grounding, in order to avoid a peril at sea.

[26] [1915] 1 K.B. 833; [1915] 3 K.B. 586, C.A.

of the damage to the ship and of their liability to compensate the dock authorities for the damage to the pier, the loss being in each case the direct consequence of the act of putting into the dock, which in the circumstances was a general average act.

It will be noticed that Sharpness dock was the ship's place of discharge, but she would not have been taken into the dock in that state of the tide but for the purpose of averting greater damage to the whole adventure. For that purpose, said the Court of Appeal, there was in the circumstances no difference between a port of refuge and a port of discharge.

5.22 **"for the common safety"** See under Rule A.[27]

"consequent loss or damage" Rule C limits that which may be made good in general average to the direct consequences of a general average act, but, in the light of the Rule of Interpretation, this limitation does not affect the numbered Rules. Indirect loss and damage may, therefore, be recoverable under this part of the Rule, a fear expressed by the Drafting Committee for the 1950 Rules,[28] although it is thought that in practice the word "consequent" is construed restrictively and comprising only the "direct" loss or damage caused by a voluntary stranding.[29]

Whether wages and maintenance of crew can be allowed whilst the vessel is intentionally stranded is dealt with in paragraph 11.09, below.

"to the property involved in the common maritime adventure" As recorded in paragraph 5.18, above, this expression was added in 1994 to ensure that if, for instance, the cargo tanks of an oil tanker (or the bunker tanks of any vessel) became ruptured as the result of a voluntary stranding for the common safety, the only allowance in general average would be for the resulting loss of oil and damage to the ship, that is, the property involved in the common maritime adventure. Any claim for damage to the environment caused by the leaking oil or for any expense incurred by a party to the adventure consequent on such damage, although a direct result of the voluntary stranding, would be excluded by the provisions of Rule C.[30]

27 See particularly paras. A.17 *et seq.*, *ante*.

28 International Maritime Committee, Bulletin No. 104, p. 111.

29 The French Association of Average Adjusters has resolved that wages and provisions of the crew, after the termination of the voyage but during repairs the cost of which is allowed in general average under this Rule, are also to be allowed in general average.

30 See particularly paras. C.29–C.33, *ante*.

Rule VI

Salvage Remuneration

English Law and Practice

In simple terms, salvage is the payment made for the rescue of property from loss at sea, but the law relating to the subject can be exceedingly complex, deserving in the *British Shipping Law* series of a whole volume to itself (Kennedy, *Law of Salvage*), a full chapter in Carver, *Carriage by Sea*, and large sections in other volumes such as Arnould and Temperley. It is to these other works, or to paragraphs 243–257 of the tenth edition of the present work, that interested readers are referred for a comprehensive survey of the subject. **6.01**

In the present section on English law, and in the context of York-Antwerp Rule VI on Salvage Remuneration, we are primarily concerned with, and limit our attention to, whether—or in what circumstances—salvage is or should be treated as general average.

When maritime property has suffered some accident on the high seas and is in peril, efforts will generally be made to rescue that property from the continuing danger it faces. Those efforts will have essentially but a single object in view—to save the property—but English law as codified by the Marine Insurance Act 1906, will classify the cost of the rescue operations under one of the following three headings: **6.02**

Salvage charges	Section 65
General average	Section 66
Sue and labour (or particular) charges	Section 78

depending on the circumstances in which the services were performed, by whom, the nature of their employment, and the rights of the various parties against each other, etc.

Sue and labour charges is a term peculiar to marine insurance, and means expenses incurred by the assured or his "factors, servants or assigns", exclusively for the purpose of saving his own property from loss by a peril insured against; where several interests are imperilled and the expense is incurred for the *common* benefit, such expenses cannot be sue and labour charges. As such, sue and labour charges can be dismissed from the present discussion.

6.03 *General average*, as will be appreciated already from the commentary on Rule A, relates to the saving conjointly of the property involved in a common maritime adventure, and for the purposes of English law a general average act is defined by section 66(2) of the Marine Insurance Act 1906, to include:

> "... any extraordinary ... expenditure ... voluntarily and reasonably ... incurred in time of peril for the purpose of preserving the property imperilled in the common adventure."

Salvage charges are defined by section 65(2) of the same Act as meaning:

> "... the charges recoverable under maritime law by a salvor independently of contract. They do not include the expenses of services in the nature of salvage rendered by the assured or his agents, or any person employed for hire by them ..."

6.04 We must now compare and contrast salvage charges with general average as defined in the Marine Insurance Act, and for this purpose let it be assumed that a vessel has suffered a main engine breakdown or other casualty on the high seas whereby both she and her cargo are in peril, and that their rescue is accomplished by tugs operating on three differing bases:

(1) Depending on the vessel's location and weather conditions, etc., the master or his owners may be able to engage towage assistance to a nearby port or to destination on the basis of an ordinary contract for hire of work and labour, either for a fixed sum or at so much per hour or day. Such a contract creates no maritime lien, and the contractor can look for payment only to the party employing him. Accordingly, the expenses incurred for the tugs will constitute a simple general average expenditure[1]; the services may be *in the nature of salvage* but as they are *rendered by ... any person employed for hire*, the expense cannot qualify as salvage charges within the definition of section 65(2) of the Marine Insurance Act 1906.

(2) The situation is considerably more serious, and, having sent out radio distress messages, the crew have abandoned ship or been taken off for their own safety. A tug which has picked up the distress signals subsequently takes the vessel in tow to a nearby port and thereby qualifies for an award of salvage which will constitute salvage charges, pure and simple. No contract has been made with the tug, no voluntary act made by the master, and the award, therefore, cannot qualify as general average under English law.

[1] *Anderson v. Ocean S.S. Co.* (1884) 10 App.Cas. 107; 54 L.J.Q.B. 192; *The Raisby* (1885) 10 P.D. 114; 53 L.T. 56.

(3) The situation is as in head (1) above, but on this occasion the tugs are prepared to assist only on the basis of a salvage contract such as Lloyd's Open Form,[2] and the master accepts and signs the contract.

In signing the salvage contract, it is sometimes suggested that the master is taking the award of salvage out of the realms of salvage charges *(recoverable under maritime law by a salvor independently of contract*[3]*)*, and performing a general average act in that he is *voluntarily incurring an extraordinary expenditure in time of peril for the purpose of preserving the property imperilled in the common adventure.*[4] On neither count is the suggestion legally correct.[5] **6.05**

The fact that a contract for salvage services is almost invariably entered into today by the salvage contractor and the master or other representatives of the property to be salved does not necessarily take the award or payment out of the legal classification of salvage charges when, as is usual, the contract itself preserves the essential ingredients of salvage, that is:

(1) Payment of any award to be contingent or conditional upon the successful salving of some of the property.
(2) The salvor to have a maritime lien upon the salved property to secure his award.
(3) Liability to pay the salvage award not to be the responsibility of any one party, nor even a joint affair; liability to pay to be

[2] See para. 80.07, *post.*
[3] Marine Insurance Act 1906, s. 65(2).
[4] *Ibid.*
[5] In *Australian Coastal Shipping Commission v. Green* [1971] 1 Q.B. 456 at 480, it was said that "if the tug had rendered salvage services on the usual terms of 'no cure—no pay', the contract would undoubtedly have been a 'general average act'". This was not essential to the decision as the case concerned contracts under the terms of the totally different U.K. Standard Towage Conditions (a hiring agreement), and the precise point had not been argued. The authority of the view expressed is further diminished because it seems to have been assumed that this hypothetical "no cure no pay" contract would have been on terms which (unlike Lloyd's Open Form) rendered the shipowner alone liable to the contractor, as opposed to each interest incurring its own separate liability (see para. 6.06, *post*).

In *Amerada Hess Corpn v. "Mobil Apex"* (1979) A.M.C. 2406, following an explosion and fire, two tugs had towed the vessel away from the dock with the consent of the master and the claim for salvage services was settled by the shipowner for $40,000. The cargo interests had argued that salvage services performed by a volunteer, not under contract, could never satisfy Rule A of the York-Antwerp Rules 1950 which is in terms almost indistinguishable from the Marine Insurance Act 1906, s. 66(2). The U.S. Court of Appeals held that this expenditure fell within Rule A, but the case is unsatisfactory because it is unclear whether the court took the view that the shipowner had accepted the towage on the terms that he was to be personally liable for the entire cost. If he did, the payment was undoubtedly general average, on any view of the law (see para. 6.04, *ante*). If he did not, it is unclear why, or with what authority, the shipowner had settled the cargo interests' share of the liability. Following on from this failure, the judgment contains no discussion of the crucial question whether services accepted on terms that each interest is individually liable for the value of the services rendered to that interest can give rise to expenditure *for the common safety.*

individual to each and every one of the owners of the salved property.

Lloyd's Open Form of Salvage Contract "No Cure—No Pay" (under the terms of which, or similar, the majority of salvage services are undertaken) designedly preserves all these essential ingredients in the title and in clauses 1(b), 6 and 16, subject to one special exception.[6]

Where the Marine Insurance Act defines "salvage charges" as meaning "... the charges recoverable under maritime law by a salvor independently of contract", it does not require that the salvage services should be performed without a contract, but is simply re-stating the far more fundamental concept that the right to an award of salvage is independent of whether there was a contract or not.[7]

6.06 It is also to be noted that in engaging the services of the tugs on a *salvage* basis, the master was not performing a general average act, for he was not thereby sacrificing or committing the property or purses of just one or a few of the parties to the adventure to suffer an immediate loss which would then need to be shared by all the parties benefited on a *pro rata* basis via the general average distribution system. In engaging the tugs on a salvage basis, the master was committing each and every one of the parties to the adventure with a liability to settle directly with the salvors for their own individual proportion of any award, and the general average distribution system does not need to be called in aid for any re-allocation of the award.

Even in those cases where a shipowner may give salvage security for the whole of the salved property and pay the whole of the salvage award, this does not translate the payment into a general average expenditure. The shipowner makes that payment only as an *agent*[8] for those other interests and he is legally entitled to recover the cargo's proportion independently of general average principles, as money paid to the use of the cargo owner, and regardless of whether the property is totally lost subsequent to leaving the port or place where the salvage services terminated and before arrival at final destination.

6.07 Having endeavoured to demonstrate the distinction—however fine—which exists in English law between general average and salvage charges, we come now to the more important question of whether that distinction is of any practical or commercial consequence, that is, can or should salvage charges be treated in practice as general average? The answer

[6] See App. 4, para. 80.07, *post*. The exception to the "no cure no pay" principle is the special compensation which may become payable by the shipowner under the International Convention on Salvage 1989, Art. 14 (see para. 6.15, *post*), the provisions of which are incorporated into LOF 1990 and LOF 1995.

[7] *The Hestia* (1895) 64 L.J. 82; 72 L.T. 364; 7 Asp.M.C. 599.

[8] *E.g.* see clause 16 of Lloyd's Open Form of Salvage Agreement, App. 4, para. 80.07, *post*.

must clearly depend upon the circumstances ruling in any individual case, but when the values of the property at the time and place where the salvage services end, and on which a single salvage award is assessed, are the same as, or closely correspond with the values assessed at destination for general average purposes, it is generally immaterial to the parties to the common adventure whether the salvage charges be treated separately as such, or merged with and as general average. Indeed, on such occasions, and on the grounds of general convenience and simplicity, there is much to be said in favour of treating a global salvage award and all associated legal costs as general average, and apportioning them pro rata over the general average contributory values at destination.

Only when the salved values at the time and place where the salvage services terminate are materially different from those at destination (for example by reason of fluctuations in the market values of the ship and cargo, or by reason of subsequent damage to any of the property between the port where the salvage services terminate and the destination), or where the ship and cargo interests settle separately with the salvors for differing awards, would there be any need to differentiate between the two classes of expenditure and apportion them separately and over differing values. On such occasions, it would clearly be material to the parties to the adventure to recognise the separate legal identities of salvage charges and general average under English law and to preserve the distinction. As will be seen below[9], however, where the York-Antwerp Rules are applicable this distinction is nullified. **6.08**

Earlier Practice of Adjusters

In the mid-nineteenth century, when many of the strands of the law on general average and on salvage had been formulated but had not yet been woven into a single thread, it is conjectured that British average adjusters probably followed the practice outlined in paragraph 6.08, above. Lowndes wrote in 1873 that: **6.09**

> "As jettison is regarded as the type or simplest form of general average sacrifice, so salvage, it has been said, may be regarded as the type of a general average expenditure. This, however, is only from one point of view. Salvage is always an extraordinary expense, and is always incurred in order to rescue the thing salved from danger: in these respects it is the perfect form of general average expenditure; but it is not always incurred for the common safety of ship and cargo."

However, an equal authority in London—Manley Hopkins—may have been more certain of the true position when he wrote in 1868 on page 63 of his *Handbook of Average*:

[9] See paras. 6.23 *et. seq.*, *post*.

> "When salvage services to a ship and cargo are paid for in one sum, in accordance with a previous agreement or a subsequent compromise, by an award of referees ... or by the decision of the Admiralty Court, that amount is frequently allowed to form an item of the general average contribution, and is divided on the same values as the other common expenses. But if special valuations of ship, goods, and freight were made by or for the arbitrators ... it is the better plan to adhere to those valuations in dividing the salvage."

The strands of the law on salvage became yet more clearly defined following the decision in 1885 in *The Raisby*[10] and from that date until about 1927 it is reasonably certain that British adjusters, in contrast with those in most other countries, drew a clear distinction between salvage and general average and treated them separately. Salvage was apportioned over the values at the place where the salvage services terminated, as adopted at the salvage proceedings, and the proportion of salvage attributable to each interest simply formed a deduction to be applied in arriving at the contributory value of that interest for apportioning the general average proper.

6.10 This distinction became a little costly, however, following the introduction in the York-Antwerp Rules of 1924 of an allowance of two per cent commission and five per cent interest on disbursements which were allowed as *general average*. Adjustments prepared in the United States or on the European Continent would show an allowance for commission and interest on salvage awards, but not so in Britain.

To remedy this apparent anomaly, in 1926 a Special Committee of the Association of Average Adjusters was formed, including representatives of underwriters and shipowners. They recommended a Rule of Practice stating:

> "That in the application of Rules XXI and XXII of York-Antwerp Rules, 1924, no distinction shall be drawn in practice between General Average Expenses and Expenses for Salvage Services rendered by Agreement ..."

and this was passed unanimously in 1927 and confirmed in 1928 without discussion.

The purpose of the Rule was clearly to ensure that commission and interest should be allowable on salvage awards in general, but it did not direct that salvage should be charged to general average and re-apportioned over the general average contributory values.

Thus, for the next 15 years there was a "multiformity" of practice among British adjusters; some treated salvage as general average, while others continued to keep it quite separate but nevertheless allowed commission and interest thereon.

This situation was remedied in 1942 and 1943 by rescinding the old Rule of Practice and adopting a new one stating that:

[10] *Cardiff Steamship Co. v. Barwick* (1885) 54 L.J. 65; 53 L.T. 56; 5 Asp.M.C. 473.

> "Expenses for salvage services rendered by or accepted under Agreement shall in practice be treated as General Average ..."

With the introduction of the new Rule of Practice C1 in 1942–1943, uniformity of practice among British adjusters was achieved, and, moreover, they were in line with the rest of the world. At the same time, it must be pointed out that the British Rules of Practice are not mandatory or binding on members, and it was always open for any adjuster to depart from the provisions of the Rule in appropriate circumstances, and some invariably did so in those cases where ship and cargo negotiated separate and differential salvage awards.

Historical Development and Practice of Rule VI

It is believed that in all maritime countries other than the United Kingdom, salvage (at any rate under contract) was invariably treated as general average and, with other general average expenses and allowances, apportioned over the values which arrived at destination. In this country, however, it was possible to draw a number of legal distinctions[11] between general average and salvage and the practice of British adjusters was not uniform.[12] **6.11**

The first attempt to introduce a rule dealing with salvage into the York-Antwerp Rules was at the Conference in Liverpool for the 1890 Rules, when the British Association of Average Adjusters proposed a Rule:

> "Payment for salvage services rendered to a stranded or otherwise disabled ship shall be dealt with as general average; except that payment for salvage services assessed by legal process on specific values shall be charged directly to the interests specified."

The proposal was withdrawn, however, following strong criticism from T. G. Carver and Charles McArthur.

In 1942 a Rule of Practice on the subject was introduced as follows:

C1: Salvage Services rendered under an Agreement

> "Expenses for salvage services rendered by or accepted under agreement shall in practice be treated as general average provided that such expenses were incurred for the common safety within the meaning of Rule "A" of the York-Antwerp Rules 1924 or York-Antwerp Rules 1950."

[11] This subject is discussed in paras. 6.02–6.06, *ante*. See also the address of the Chairman of the Association of Average Adjusters, 1973, pp. 28–29, and 1988, pp. 10–17.

[12] See paras. 6.09–6.10, *ante*.

Nevertheless British adjusters on a few isolated occasions still felt obliged to differentiate between general average and salvage, and apportion them separately and over different values.

6.12 *York-Antwerp Rules 1974*

To overcome these difficulties, and to ensure greater international uniformity, the following provision was introduced in 1974 as Rule VI[13]:

> Expenditure incurred by the parties to the adventure on account of salvage, whether under contract or otherwise, shall be allowed in general average to the extent that the salvage operations were undertaken for the purpose of preserving from peril the property involved in the common maritime adventure.

This provision made it clear that under the York-Antwerp Rules there was to be no distinction in principle between salvage, whether performed under a contract or not, and general average. However, salvage expenditure was only allowable *to the extent that the salvage operations were undertaken for the purpose of preserving from peril the property involved in the common maritime adventure*, and this limitation soon gave rise to problems when salvage awards began to reflect measures taken by the salvors to minimise pollution.

6.13 *Salvage awards enhanced by the avoidance of pollution*

(a) Lloyd's Standard Form of Salvage Agreement 1980. This form (LOF 1980) stated in Clause 1(a)

> The Contractor (*salvor*) further agrees to use his best endeavours to prevent the escape of oil from the vessel while performing the service of salving the subject vessel and/or her cargo bunkers and stores.

and in their assessment of any salvage award under this form Lloyd's Arbitrators would take into account this additional obligation on the part of salvors and their skill and efforts in complying with it.

The element of enhancement in any award of salvage on the grounds of the salvors' skill and efforts in avoiding pollution was quite clearly outside the scope of the words in Rule VI "for the purpose of preserving ... the property involved in the common maritime adventure" as the only properties really being preserved from pollution were the local beaches and fishing grounds, etc. The element of enhancement should therefore have been excluded from general average, and have fallen on the shipowner alone and his various forms of insurance. However, in

[13] Rule VI in previous editions of the York-Antwerp Rules had dealt with an entirely different subject—*Carrying Press of Sail*—but this was considered obsolete in 1974 and abolished. The various texts of the old Rule VI from 1864 to 1950 are set out in paras. 60.23 and 60.44, *post*.

practice, the position was different, and on pure grounds of commercial expediency the *whole* of any enhanced award was generally charged to general average when the dominant purpose of any salvage operation was to save property. Indeed, before the issue of LOF 1980, London market insurers and the International Group of P. & I. Associations had issued a joint statement (or "Funding Agreement") in the following terms[14]:

> "In order that the revision of Lloyd's Open Form can proceed as quickly as possible, the International Group of P. & I. Clubs for their part and The Institute of London Underwriters and Lloyd's Underwriters Association for their part confirm the following:
> ... (2) The Underwriters will continue to accept that Salvage Awards are recoverable by ship, cargo and freight under the existing forms of policies for those interests, notwithstanding that such Awards may have been enhanced to take account of measures taken to prevent the escape of oil from the ship."

The decisions of these leading sections of the international insurance market are widely followed in other parts of the world and it was sensible that average adjusters should give effect to them in their general average adjustments. It was always open to any uninsured cargo interest to dispute his liability for the element of enhancement in any salvage award, though it must be mentioned that Lloyd's arbitrators do not specify[15] in their awards the extent of any enhancement, and would be extremely reluctant to do so.

A second innovation introduced by LOF 1980[16] was that when the vessel to which salvage services were rendered was a tanker wholly or partly laden with oil, and the salvage was wholly or partly unsuccessful, or could not be completed, for reasons occurring without the fault of the salvor, the salvor was entitled to be awarded his expenses, plus a discretionary increment of up to 15 per cent, to the extent that the sum in question exceeded the amount recoverable under the ordinary salvage award. 6.14

The shipowner alone was liable to the salvor for any sums awarded under this special provision.

(b) The International Salvage Convention 1989. This Convention, which was resolved upon at the International Conference on Salvage held in London in April 1989, adopts and in many respects extends both of the 6.15

[14] For the funding agreement relating to LOF 1990, see paras. 6.33–6.34, *post*.

[15] It is believed that the American Institute of Marine Underwriters would have liked (in 1985) to have it made mandatory that arbitrators should identify that portion of their award which relates to the skill and efforts of the salvors in preventing or minimising damage to the environment. In England the practice remains as stated above, and extends to awards under the 1989 Salvage Convention and Lloyd's Open Form 1990 and 1995; see paras. 6.32 *et seq.*, *post*.

[16] Cl. 1(c).

above anti-pollution elements of the 1980 Lloyd's Open Form. First, under Article 13, paragraph 1(b) of the Convention it is expressly provided that the skill and efforts of the salvors in preventing or minimising damage to the environment[17] shall be taken into account in fixing the amount of the award. Secondly, Article 14 of the Convention provides for special compensation to be payable by the shipowner to the salvor if the vessel or its cargo threatened damage to the environment and the amount of the salvor's remuneration under Article 13 is not at least equal to the amount of special compensation. The basic amount of special compensation is equal to the expenses incurred by the salvor but, if the salvage operations have actually prevented or minimised damage to the environment, a discretionary increment of up to 30 per cent, or in exceptional cases up to 100 per cent, may be awarded to the salvor.

Both of these provisions are in most respects[18] wider than those of LOF 1980, since they apply to threats to the environment by "pollution, contamination, fire, explosion or other major incident",[19] whereas the anti-pollution provisions of LOF 1980 apply only to endeavours to prevent the escape of oil, and the special compensation provisions of clause 1(c) apply only where the subject vessel is a tanker wholly or partly laden with oil.

The Salvage Convention did not acquire the force of law in England until 1995, but many of its important features were incorporated into Lloyd's Open Form 1990 and thus applied by contract to many salvages.[20]

6.16 *York-Antwerp Rules 1974 as amended 1990*

In order to deal with the problems caused by the 1989 Salvage Convention the Rule was expanded, following a special conference of the Comité Maritime International held in Paris in June 1990, by the addition of two new paragraphs, the first of which allowed in general average the element of enhancement of the award for the salvor's efforts in avoiding or minimising damage to the environment, and the second of which excluded from general average any special compensation payable under Article 14 of the 1989 Convention, or under any similar provision. In addition, some changes in wording were made to the first paragraph of the 1974 Rule, as follows:

(1) *on account of salvage* was replaced by *in the nature of salvage*;
(2) *to the extent that* was replaced by *provided that*;
(3) *undertaken* was replaced by *carried out*.

[17] "Damage to the environment" is defined in Art. 1(d) of the Convention: see para. C.31, *ante*.

[18] The Salvage Convention is narrower in one respect, namely that it will only apply if there is a threat of damage "in coastal or inland waters or areas adjacent thereto": see *ibid.* Art. 1(d).

[19] See *ibid.* Art. 1(d).

[20] See para. 6.33, *post*.

The main purpose of these changes was to reflect the fact that the allowance of the element of enhancement of the award under Article 13 paragraph 1(b) of the Convention was inconsistent with the 1974 version of Rule VI.[21] The effect of the new phraseology is considered in more detail below.

York-Antwerp Rules 1994 **6.17**

No changes were made on this occasion to the wording adopted in 1990, but a number were suggested. Of these the subject of differential settlements and costs, and whether they should be brought into the general apportionment,[22] was the most important. It is in this area that the major disagreements arise, and there is a gulf which is difficult to bridge between those who feel that material inequity is worked by Rule VI when it obliges otherwise advantageous individual settlements to be "cast into the general average pot", and those who regard it as an imperfect but nevertheless practical tool to give effect to the community of interest that underlies the notion of general average.

Rule VI

Salvage Remuneration

(a) Expenditure incurred by the parties to the adventure in the nature of salvage, whether under contract or otherwise, shall be allowed in general average provided that the salvage operations were carried out for the purpose of preserving from peril the property involved in the common maritime adventure.

Expenditure allowed in general average shall include any salvage remuneration in which the skill and efforts of the salvors in preventing or minimising damage to the environment such as is referred to in Article 13 paragraph 1(b) of the International Convention on Salvage, 1989 have been taken into account.

(b) Special compensation payable to a salvor by the shipowner under Article 14 of the said Convention to the extent specified in paragraph 4 of that Article or under any other provision similar in substance shall not be allowed in general average.

[21] See para. 6.13, *ante*.
[22] This subject is discussed at paras. 6.23–6.25, *post*.

Construction

Rule VI (a), First Paragraph

6.18 **"Expenditure ... in the nature of salvage,"** The change in wording from the 1974 Rule (*expenditure on account of salvage*) is probably superfluous since the words which follow[23] make it clear that the Rule is not confined to salvage charges in the strict sense.[24] However the new wording is more accurate, certainly so far as English law is concerned.

Since the new wording lacks the rather expansive phrase of the 1974 Rule, *on account of salvage*, it can be said that it applies only to expenditure on services which are themselves in the nature of salvage, or strictly incidental thereto, and does not apply to all consequential expenses, such as legal costs in attempting to resist or reduce a salvage claim.[25]

"by the parties to the adventure" When, as sometimes occurs, the insurers of ship or cargo organise and make all arrangements for salvage and pay all or part of a salvage award direct to the salvors, the amount of that payment is nevertheless treated as general average, even though insurers can hardly be termed "parties to the adventure".

6.19 **"salvage, whether under contract"** The original text put forward for discussion at the Hamburg Conference in 1974 was "salvage, whether under maritime law or under contract". At the last moment difficulty arose over the French text since there is no equivalent in French jurisprudence for the expression *maritime law*, whilst the word *loi* on its own offended those who favour accurate translation. This apart, there is no problem in comprehending the English words *salvage under contract*, which comprise all contracts of any classification, whether they be strictly for *salvage charges*, or merely for *services in the nature of salvage*, both as detailed in section 65(2) of the Marine Insurance Act 1906, and discussed earlier in paragraphs 6.02 to 6.06, above.

6.20 **"... or otherwise,"** These words comprise all those awards of salvage made under maritime law where *no* contract has been entered into with the salvors, for example because the ship has already been abandoned by her entire crew. Prior to the introduction of Rule VI in 1974, the award for salvage services in such circumstances would not have been treated as general average in the United Kingdom or the United States,

[23] *I.e.* the phrase "whether under contract or otherwise": see paras. 6.19–6.20, *post*.

[24] For the English definition of "salvage charges", see para. 6.03, *ante*. The Marine Insurance Act 1906 draws a clear distinction between "salvage charges" and "charges in the nature of salvage", incurred by the assured under contract (s. 65(2)). Rule VI is clearly intended to apply to all such charges.

[25] See paras. 6.24, 6.25, *post*.

at least, on the grounds that the services would have been rendered on a pure volunteer basis and with the representatives of the ship and cargo not being in any position to make an "intentional" sacrifice or expenditure within the terms of Rule A.

The position is now changed and, by the express terms of Rule VI, the absence of an actual contract for salvage services does not affect the issue and any award is to be treated as general average and apportioned over the values at final destination rather than those at the time and place where the salvage services terminated. Commission and interest under Rules XX and XXI are also allowable when the salvage is treated as general average.

An exception to this provision might occur in those rare cases where the ship and her cargo are a true "derelict", that is, abandoned by the crew and by the owners of the property, without hope on their part of recovering it and without intention of returning to it. The "common maritime adventure" might then be said to be at an end, in which case any salvage award would probably be treated as a particular charge on the property salved.

"shall be allowed in general average" The salvage expenses allowable as **6.21**
general average under the terms of this Rule are, in practice, the *net* expenses after crediting any voyage expenses saved under the contract of carriage by reason of the salvage services.

Expenses saved to be credited

Thus, where a vessel is towed to (or towards) her destination, it will usually be found that the shipowner (or time-charterer) has been saved the cost of bunkers that would normally have been consumed on the main engine, and credit for this must clearly be given against the cost of the towage itself.

Although there is no express provision[26] in the Rule to this effect, it is one of the fundamental principles of the equitable system of general average that none of the parties to the adventure ought to make a "profit" from the general average act, and it is to be noted that the United States Association of Average Adjusters has a Rule of Practice (No. V) on this subject adopted in 1902:

> "Where salvage services are rendered to a vessel, or she becomes disabled and is necessarily towed to her port of destination, and the expenses of such towage are allowable in general average, there shall be credited against the allowance such ordinary expenses as would have been incurred, but have been saved by the salvage or towage services."

Commenting on this Rule of Practice in his admirable textbook *Marine*

[26] Probably the result only of an oversight; the fundamental principle receives express provision in, *e.g.* Rules VIII, IX and XV and 1950 Rule X(d).

Insurance & General Average in the United States, the late Leslie J. Buglass states:

> "However, in applying this rule it is the practice of average adjusters to offset the saving in voyage expenses (usually fuel and stores etc ...) by the extra wages, etc., of the crew incurred as a result of the enhanced duration of the voyage due to the vessel being under tow."

This same practice was repeated here in paragraph 6.16 of the eleventh edition with tacit approval, and it was also indorsed by the Advisory Committee of the Association of Average Adjusters in their Report No. 43 dated September 29, 1992. However, on a more mature consideration, it is now submitted that the practice is wrong in principle when the need for the towage was the result of *accidental* damage.

The saving of the bunkers that would normally have been consumed in the main engine to accomplish the same distance as under tow is the natural and direct result of the towage alone, and their value must clearly be credited to general average when the cost of the towage is so allowed.

The supposed "extra" wages, etc., of the crew incurred during a "slow-speed" towage, however, in no way result from the towage—indeed, but for the towage they would no doubt be larger—but simply from the original accidental engine breakdown or other incident which necessitated the towage.

6.22 A similar need to credit savings can arise, for instance, where cargo is discharged during salvage operations and, for convenience or other reasons, it is on-carried by that other vessel to destination as part of the salvage services. On the authority of cases such as *Guthrie v. Northern China Ins. Co. Ltd*[27] and *The Winson*,[28] the cargo interests will receive their cargo free of any freight which might have been payable on delivery at destination by the original carrying vessel. The freight thus saved ought to be credited to the general average and debited to those cargo interests who escaped payment of the normal freight.

The values over which salvage expenses allowable as general average under the terms of this Rule will be apportioned are the net arrived values of the property at destination in accordance with Rule XVII[29] and, to the extent that these values differ from the values at the termination of the salvage services, the salved values assessed by the court or by an arbitrator will be ignored.

6.23 *Differential salvage awards, settlements and costs*

It sometimes happens that ship and cargo interests will be separately represented at any salvage proceedings and that they will make separate

[27] (1902) 7 Com.Cas. 130.

[28] [1982] 1 Lloyd's Rep. 117 at 123.

[29] The situation where differential awards might be made because ship and cargo are rescued from different risks is discussed at para. 6.29, *post*.

settlements with the salvors whereby, for instance, the ship interests may pay a five per cent award and the cargo interests pay six per cent. The benefit or prejudice of these separate settlements will be lost to the individual parties as the aggregate of these payments for salvage must now be charged to general average and re-apportioned on a pro-rata basis.[30] This view was adopted in the Tenth Edition of this work as the proper construction of the 1974 Rules, and was indorsed in 1983 by the Advisory Committee of the Association of Average Adjusters in its Report No. 40. The Committee was:

> "... unanimously of the opinion that Rule VI is mandatory as between the parties to a Contract of Affreightment providing for adjustment of General Average according to York-Antwerp Rules 1974. The Committee accordingly takes the view that subject to the overall requirement of reasonableness in the amounts claimed by parties to the adventure, differential expenditure, including costs, on account of the salvage should be allowed in General Average and apportioned as such."

The Report was received by insurers with no great acclaim or popularity, but it is difficult to see how the Advisory Committee could have come to any other conclusion when the parties to the adventure had mutually agreed in their contract of affreightment to the provisions of the York-Antwerp Rules 1974. Indeed it is debatable whether the 1974 Rules even imposed a requirement of reasonableness, a deficiency now remedied.[31] Nevertheless—and more particularly in the present age when there is an increasing tendency for the various interests to provide separate security to salvors and to have separate legal representation at the salvage arbitration—the Rule does give rise to some strange anomalies.

Although the wording of the Rule makes no reference to the legal **6.24**
costs associated with the salvage proceedings, or other expenses of collecting and giving salvage security, these are also treated in practice as general average and apportioned as such. These ancillary expenses can at times appear even more anomalous than the occasional differential awards arising from one individual party settling with salvors before the Arbitration, or making a separate Appeal. As examples:

(1) The separate legal costs of a minor interest, such as time-charterer, in respect of his bunkers can be totally disproportionate to those incurred by the ship or by the cargo interests.
(2) One party may appeal against an award, unsuccessfully, and be condemned to pay the whole costs of the appeal.
(3) While a simple letter of undertaking from an important and affluent corporation may be adequate and acceptable security to salvors,

[30] American case law already provided for this method of adjustment: *The Jason* 162 Fed.Rep. 56 (1908); 175 Fed.Rep. 414 (1910).

[31] See para. 6.25, *post*.

> other less credit-worthy interests may need to incur the considerable and continuing expense of a bank guarantee, or bail fees and insurance thereon, plus the fees and expenses of an agent in London.

Yet all these expenses and results of the personal decisions or circumstances of individual interests are thrown back in the general average melting pot and apportioned over contributory values!

The only exceptions to the above practice are:

(a) Increased legal costs incurred as the result of delay on the part of any of the parties in posting salvage security.
(b) Additional interest charged by reason of late payment by any of the parties of their proportion of the salvage award.

These "avoidable" expenses are charged to the individual parties responsible for the delay, though in practice interest up to the seven per cent rate allowable under Rule XXI can be equitably charged to general average from the date on which the salvage award should have been paid.

6.25 The practice referred to in the previous paragraph was no doubt justifiable under the 1974 Rule, since legal costs and similar ancillary expenditure fell within the terms of the Rule itself, being *expenditure on account of salvage.*[32] However, expenses of this kind can hardly be said to fall within the expression used in the 1990 and 1994 Rule, *expenditure in the nature of salvage*. It follows that they can only be recovered under Rule C, and accordingly that any additional expenses caused by a failure to act reasonably and promptly will not be recoverable since they would not be the direct consequence of the general average act.[33] Under the 1994 Rules, the Rule Paramount makes reasonableness an overriding requirement in any event, and the requirement therefore extends even to those expenditures which do fall within the express terms of Rule VI, such as a settlement figure agreed with and paid to the salvors, or even to the salvage award itself.

Determining the reasonableness of conduct which has resulted in differential awards, settlements and costs may present the adjuster with considerable difficulty. The mere fact that one interest has settled at a slightly lower figure than another does not of itself lead to the conclusion that the latter has acted unreasonably, but where the discrepancies in the amounts paid or the costs incurred are very substantial the party putting forward the larger claim should be asked to justify the reasonableness of his conduct. Moreover, just as a settlement figure may be unreasonable, so in some circumstances may a refusal to settle. Thus a

[32] See para. 6.12, *ante*.
[33] See paras. C.23–C.25, C.28, *ante*.

party who has had a large salvage award made against him, when he ought reasonably to have settled the earlier claim, should not recover in full.

"provided that the salvage operations were carried out for the purpose of preserving from peril the property involved in the common maritime adventure." In broad terms, Rule VI provides that salvage awards and expenditure shall be treated as and allowed in general average. As a general observation, the words *provided that* seem to indicate that a salvage operation must be judged as a whole, according to its primary purpose, in determining whether it was carried out *for the purpose of preserving from peril the property involved in the common adventure*. There is no room for the approach, which might have been justified under the 1974 Rule, of dividing up the costs of a single operation according to how much of the operation fell strictly within the subsequent words. On the other hand, the position under the 1974 Rule is partly restored by the replacement of *undertaken* by *carried out*. This change makes it clear that the purpose of the operations should not merely be judged when they were first embarked upon, but kept under review as they proceed. If there comes a point at which it can properly be said that a separate stage of the operations, not falling within the subsequent words of the Rule, is being carried out, the operations will no longer fall within Rule VI. This section of the Rule thus serves as a restraining influence on the automatic charging to general average of all or any expense which may be put forward or masquerade as "salvage." The following specific points may be worthy of consideration: 6.26

(a) *The property involved in the common adventure must have been in peril.* This is an obvious *sine qua non*, and in accordance with the general provisions of Rule A, but one can think of examples where a salvage contract either has been—or might be—entered into where the property was not in any real peril, and perhaps merely to save delay, for example: 6.27

> *Ballantyne v. Mackinnon*,[34] where a schooner-rigged steamer ran out of fuel and was "salved" into her destination but, as the master stated in his official deposition: "There was no damage to our vessel, and we could have proceeded under sail ..."
>
> *Trafalgar Steamship Co. v. British & Foreign Marine Insurance Co.*[35] where a ship grounded in the River Plate and was in no danger, as any wind which might cause damage would previously have raised the water sufficiently to get her off the ground.

[34] (1896) 65 L.J.Q.B. 616.
[35] *Shipping Gazette*, November 18, 1904.

(b) *Salvage awards enhanced by the avoidance of pollution.* We have already observed[36] the difficulties caused by the 1974 Rule in cases where salvage awards were enhanced by the salvor's efforts in avoiding pollution or damage to the environment. These problems are now dealt with specifically in the succeeding paragraphs of the 1994 Rule.[37]

6.28 (c) *Some salvage services go beyond the extrication from peril of the salved property.* With the object of preserving the highest possible salved values and increasing the services and expense they can parade before the arbitrator, it sometimes appears in practice that salvors are performing services which go beyond the mere extrication from peril of the salved property, that is, after the property has been brought to safety in port and could be returned to its respective owners.

Examples of these additional services which spring to mind include the following:

(1) The engine room of a loaded vessel is flooded by accident and she is immobilised and in some peril. Salvors may stop the leak, pump out the engine room, and tow the vessel to a safe berth—all proper salvage, to which ship and cargo should contribute. But if the salvors now continue to perform the valuable service of de-watering and preserving all the flooded machinery, is it reasonable that any enhanced award for this service (which is really in the nature of a repair of accidental damage) should be contributed by cargo interests?

(2) Cargo may similarly be reconditioned by salvors after damage by accident; should not the owners of the particular cargo concerned pay this extra cost?

(3) A vessel carrying a deck cargo of timber is improperly stowed and, on leaving port and reaching the open sea, takes on a severe list such that the deck lashings and stanchions break and some of the cargo is lost into the sea. Salvors beach the vessel, bring lighters alongside and transfer sufficient deck cargo to correct the list, and then tow the vessel back to port where she and her cargo are in perfect safety.

The "additional" services performed and expenses incurred by the salvors include:

(a) Payment of all inward port charges for the vessel.
(b) Payment of all the expenses of discharging the remaining shifted deck cargo.
(c) Payment of the local boatmen and other people who collected much of the deck cargo which had fallen overboard.

Can it be right that all these expenses should be treated at generous "salvage" rates and apportioned as general average? It may be

[36] See paras. 6.13–6.15, *ante*.
[37] See paras. 6.32 *et seq.*, *post*.

> questioned whether the payments to the independent boatmen who brought in the timber which had fallen overboard should more properly have been settled by the shipowner and debited as special charges to the owners of the particular cargo concerned,[38] and whether the cost of discharging the remaining shifted deck cargo should have been borne by the shipowner himself as it was necessary only for the purpose of restowing properly and is thereby excluded from general average by the terms of Rule X(b).[39]

It is to be submitted that the words of Rule VI(a) require it to be demonstrated, at each separate stage of the operations, that the operations were being carried out for the purpose of preserving from peril the property involved in the common adventure. Once this purpose has been achieved, it would seem that any further operations cannot fall within Rule VI,[40] nor under the similar wording of Rule A.

More difficult is the situation where different interests reach the point of safety at different times. For example, cargo may be removed and taken to safety before a grounded ship is refloated. Whether or not the cost of refloating the ship should be charged to general average will depend upon whether the removal of the cargo and the refloating can be regarded as a continuous salvage operation, a topic discussed in more detail under Rule VIII.[41]

(d) *Rescue from different risks.* Occasionally ship and cargo are rescued **6.29**
from different risks, as distinct from different degrees of risk. Thus, a vessel which has sustained a machinery breakdown may require to engage the services of a single tug to tow her to a port of refuge for the common safety. If, however, she has on board a perishable cargo of fruit, the services of a second and even third tug may be engaged to expedite the voyage in order that the cargo does not perish before arrival. In these circumstances, should the cost of all the tugs be allowed in general average, or should the cost of the second and third tugs be charged to cargo and freight alone?

There is a decision of the Admiralty Court[42] to the effect that in such circumstances a salvage award may depart from the normal principle of rateable contribution in proportion to salved values, although the decision has been widely criticised and is seldom followed.[43] But whatever may

[38] On the question of salvage operations performed after ship and cargo have become separated, see further paras. 6.30 and 8.05–8.19, *post*.

[39] See para. 10.45, *post*.

[40] See para. 6.26, *ante*.

[41] See paras. 8.05–8.18, *post*.

[42] *The Velox* [1906] P. 263, where a disabled ship with a cargo of fresh fish was towed to her destination, by a single salving vessel, and non-proportionate awards were made against ship and cargo.

[43] On the grounds that the approach which it adopts is contrary to established practice, and impossible to apply fairly or consistently: see *The M. Vatan* [1990] 1 Lloyd's Rep. 336; Kennedy, *Law of Salvage*, paras. 1192–1195; Brice, *Maritime Law of Salvage*, paras. 4.28–4.30. The criticisms appear soundly based. The distinction sometimes drawn between the

be the right approach under the law of salvage, the changed wording of Rule VI (*provided that* instead of *to the extent that*) seems to require that, in the example given, the cost of all three tugs must be allowed in general average. So long as all of the interests remain imperilled, and the operations are carried out for the purpose of preserving them from peril, the cost of the operation falls within the Rule, which provides no justification for adjustment based on differing kinds of degrees of risk, or expenditure. One possible way of avoiding this conclusion, on the facts of our example, would be to say that the second and third tugs were engaged on a separate operation, to which Rule VI did not apply at all, but apart from its artificiality[44] this approach still faces the difficulty that the second and third tugs are in fact salving the ship as well as the cargo, whether or not they would have been engaged if the cargo were not perishable.

6.30 The situation is rather different when ship and cargo have become separated when the salvage operations in question are performed. Here, the operations carried out on each interest will usually be truly separate, rather than a single operation performed for the general benefit. Thus, a vessel carrying a timber cargo partly on deck may develop a severe list whereby the deck lashings are broken and part of the deck cargo lost overboard. Salvage services rendered to the ship and her remaining cargo will obviously be treated as general average, but payments made for recovering timber washed ashore or collected by local fishing vessels or other craft should be borne exclusively by the particular cargo rescued.

This situation must be distinguished from:

(1) the case where the cargo, instead of being washed overboard accidentally, is *jettisoned* for the common safety; here one would allow as general average the full value of the cargo jettisoned, less its recovered value after deducting any salvage expenditure thereon;
(2) those cases, discussed in the commentary on Rule VIII, where the cargo is *intentionally discharged* from the ship, as part of a complex salvage operation, to enable the ship to be salved and the voyage to be prosecuted.

situation where the salved interests are exposed to different *degrees* of risk (where it is never suggested that the ordinary rule of rateable contribution should be departed from) and the situation where they are exposed to different *kinds* of risk is artificial. The expense attributable to the predicament of one particular interest will frequently be very difficult to identify, and even in a case as apparently clear-cut as the example given above it cannot be said that the shipowner derives no benefit from the second and third tugs. The duration and risk of the towage is reduced, as will be the cost of the first tug; the ship will be repaired sooner and able to earn freight; and the cargo will doubtless arrive with a greater value on which to contribute.

[44] If, instead of three tugs, one very powerful (and more expensive) tug were engaged, the argument that part of the expense of towage was the expense of a separate operation could not even be contemplated.

(e) *Life salvage.* Apart from statute, the saving of life at sea attracts no right to salvage unless associated with the saving of property. However, where salvors succeed in saving both life and property, the amount awarded to them for the salving of the property is traditionally increased to take into account their skills and efforts in saving life.[45] It is not the practice of salvage arbitrators in this country to quantify the increase in the amount of the award attributable to the saving of life, and the full amount of the award is payable rateably by the salved property interests, in the usual way. Similarly, where the salvage expenditure falls to be treated as general average (as under Rule VI) the practice is that the entire amount of the salvage award is included in the general average, without reduction to reflect the fact that the award in part remunerates the salvors for operations other than the preservation from peril of the property involved in the common adventure. 6.31

The Merchant Shipping Act 1894 imposed a statutory liability to pay salvage remuneration for the saving of life alone.[46] This liability, which was imposed on the owners of the ship, her cargo and apparel was, like other salvage remuneration, payable rateably by these interests in proportion to the value of the property which survived.[47] However, whilst liability for salvage under the Act could not exceed the value of the property which survived,[48] the purpose of the award was solely to remunerate the salvors for their efforts in saving life; it was unnecessary that the property should have survived by the efforts of the life salvors, or even that the life salvors should have made any efforts to salve the property.[49] For this reason salvage payable under the Act is not admissible in general average.[50]

Rule VI (a), Second Paragraph 6.32

"damage to the environment" This phrase is probably intended to bear the same meaning as under the 1989 Salvage Convention, where it is so defined as to exclude any case where the only risk is of deep-sea pollution which does not affect coastal or inland waters.[51] The same definition is imported into the 1990 and 1995[52] Lloyd's Open Forms. For this reason, when the vessel to be salvaged is a tanker laden with oil which is not in coastal waters, salvors occasionally insist on being engaged under LOF

[45] This practice is confirmed in numerous decisions, see, *e.g. The Fusilier* (1865) 3 Moo. P.C. (N.S.) 51. It is also embodied in the International Convention on Salvage 1989, Art. 13 para. 1(e).

[46] Merchant Shipping Act 1894, s. 544, repealed by the Merchant Shipping Act 1994.

[47] *The Fusilier* (1865) 3 Moo. P.C. (N.S.) 51 at 55.

[48] Where the value of the property is insufficient there was a discretion to award payment out of the Merchant Marine Fund.

[49] *The Cairo* (1874) L.R. 4 A.& E. 184.

[50] Salvage payable by virtue of a similar statute in the U.S. is treated as general average.

[51] See para. C.31, *ante*.

[52] See App. 4, para. 80.07, *post*.

1980[53] rather than LOF 1990 or 1995, with the effect considered in the next paragraph.

6.33 **"such as is referred to in Article 13 paragraph 1(b) of the International Convention on Salvage, 1989"** The provisions of that Article relating to enhanced awards for preventing or minimising damage to the environment have already been explained in outline. The Convention is incorporated into the 1990 and 1995[54] versions of Lloyd's Open Form, with the result that Article 13 paragraph 1(b) applies to any salvage performed on those terms. Moreover, by virtue of section 224 of the Merchant Shipping Act 1995, the Convention now has the force of law in the United Kingdom and governs salvage operations commenced after January 1, 1995. A Funding Agreement made in January 1991 between the International Group of P. and I. Clubs and London Market Insurers provides that the insurers will pay any award under LOF 1990, even though the award may be enhanced by the salvor's efforts in avoiding or minimising damage to the environment.[55]

The only further point which need be made is that the phrase *such as is referred to in Article 13, paragraph 1(b) of the International Convention on Salvage* indicates that an award may fall within Rule VI(a) even if it is not actually made under the Convention itself, so long as the element of enhancement is made in respect of preventing or minimising *damage to the environment* falling within the scope of that phrase as defined in the Convention.[56] If the award is made under LOF 1990 or 1995 this requirement will automatically be satisfied, since the arbitrator will apply the provisions of the Convention in fixing the amount of the salvors remuneration. However, if the award is made under LOF 1980 with its rather different provisions the same result will not necessarily follow, particularly if the salved vessel is in mid-ocean.[57]

6.34 **Rule VI (b)**

"Special compensation ... under Article 14 of the said Convention" See paragraph 6.15, above. The Funding Agreement referred to in the previous paragraph provides that the P. and I. Clubs will take responsibility for Special Compensation awarded under Article 14.

[53] See paras. 6.13, 6.14, *ante*.

[54] See App. 4, para. 80.07, *post*.

[55] The Agreement extends to the case where the contract of affreightment incorporates the York-Antwerp Rules 1974. For the purposes of the Agreement, references in the contract or the policy to the 1974 Rules take effect as if the reference were to the 1974 Rules as amended in 1990.

[56] See para. C.31, *ante*.

[57] Because in such a case the salvor might be entitled to an enhanced award under LOF 1980, to which he would not have been entitled under the Convention: see para. 6.32, *ante*.

"to the extent specified in paragraph 4 of that Article" Where special compensation is earned under Article 14 of the 1989 Salvage Convention, the amount will be assessed at between 100 and 200 per cent of the salvors expenses, although the Article seems to envisage that only in the most exceptional circumstances should it exceed 130 per cent. The shipowner alone is liable for this special compensation, but Article 14 paragraph 4 stipulates that the special compensation is only payable to the extent that the amount so assessed exceeds the amount awarded under paragraph 13. The purpose of the words under review is to make it clear that it is only this excess amount which is excluded from general average. All amounts payable under Article 13 are included even though they may be enhanced by measures taken to avoid pollution.

"or under any provision similar in substance" An example of such a provision is clause 1(c) of LOF 1980, the effect of which is described above.[58]

[58] See para. 6.14, *ante*.

Rule VII

Damage to Machinery and Boilers

English Law and Background

7.01 When dealing with Rule A[1] and the conditions which needed to be present in order to constitute a general average act, it was stated that the sacrifice or expenditure must be *extraordinary* in its nature. A number of legal cases were quoted[2] to demonstrate that even though the adventure might be in some danger (for example, of the vessel being driven ashore in a gale), while the vessel remained *afloat*, cargo interests have a right under the contract of affreightment to expect the full use of the vessel's sails or engine to extricate herself from that danger without being called upon to contribute to any damage caused by carrying a press of sail[3] or by straining the engine.

Damage by Setting Sail to Force Ship off Ground

7.02 Although no allowance in general average is made in this country for damage caused by carrying a press of sail when the ship is *afloat*, the situation is quite different when the ship is *aground* and in a position of peril. The Customs of Lloyd's, as collected in 1874,[4] provide that:

> "Sails damaged by being set, or kept set to force a ship off the ground, or to drive her higher up the ground for the common safety, are general average."

On this subject, Lowndes wrote:

> "If indeed the ship is in a position in which the setting of sails at all must be regarded as something unusual, and which would be improper but for

[1] See particularly para. A.56, *ante*.

[2] *Covington v. Roberts* (1806) 2 Bos. & P.N.R. 378; *Power v. Whitmore* (1815) 4 M. & S. 141; *Wilson v. Bank of Victoria* (1867) L.R. 2 Q.B. 203; *Harrison v. Bank of Australasia* (1872) L.R. 7 Ex. 39.

[3] From 1860 to 1974, when it was deleted on the grounds of obsolescence, the York-Antwerp Rule had always included a Rule denying any allowance in general average for damage to ship or cargo by carrying a press of sail when the vessel was afloat; see the various forms of the old Rule VI, paras. 60.23, 60.44, *post*.

[4] Now Rule of Practice F6, para. 70.33, *post*.

emergency, the case may perhaps be otherwise. When a ship is aground, for example, and at tide times sails are set on her in the hope of forcing her off the bank, by which means she is got afloat, but the sails are blown to pieces, this loss in practice is treated as general average. On account of the greater resistance offered by a ship that is aground, this may be considered as an abusing of the sails, or applying them to a purpose for which they were not intended."

Damage to Engines used to Refloat

When a steamer or motor vessel is aground in a position of peril and the engines are set or kept going in order to back her off or over the ground, the machinery may be strained, bearings overheat, or the propeller strike the ground and sustain damage, etc. Damage done in this manner is analogous to and indistinguishable from the loss of sails blown away when set in order to force a ship off the ground and is likewise treated as general average. **7.03**

In *The Bona*,[5] the question arose whether the act of working a vessel's engines for the purpose of getting her off a strand, on which she was hard and fast, was a general average act. The consequent damage to the engines had been allowed in general average, under Rule VII of the York-Antwerp Rules 1890, which formed part of the contract; and the actual question in the case was whether the coal consumed in working the engines should also be allowed. This was considered to depend upon whether the use of the engines was, at law, a general average sacrifice. If that was true, the coal formed part of the sacrifice. The Court of Appeal affirming Sir Francis Jeune P. held that it was true. Lord Esher M.R. said the question depended on:

> "Whether the engines were used not only under unusual circumstances, but in an unusual and abnormal manner ... The manoeuvre which this captain determined to follow, knowing that it was a dangerous manoeuvre to the property of his owners, was to use the engines so as to force the ship off the ground ... That is not using the ship and her equipment in the ordinary way. It is putting them to an abnormal use intentionally, knowing the risk, for the purpose of saving the ship and cargo from the imminent danger in which they were."[6]

[5] [1895] P. 125; *cf. Trafalgar S.S. Co. v. British and Foreign Mar. Ins. Co.* (para. 6.26, *ante*); *The Mincio* (1936) A.M.C. 1765; *Willcox v. American Smelting Co.*; *The Trojan* 210 Fed. Rep. 89 (1913). In *Walford de Baerdemaecker v. Galindez* (1897) 2 Com.Cas. 127, damage done to the boilers of a steamship through using cannel coal, which was part of the cargo, in an emergency, when the supply of bunker coal had been exhausted, was allowed in general average. *Cf.* also *Charter S.S. Co. Ltd v. Bowring Jones & Tidy Ltd* (1930) 36 Ll.L.Rep. 272. In this case trouble experienced with engines and boilers subsequent to a stranding, was claimed as general average arising through working engines to refloat and it was held that a small part of the damage to engines was so caused and therefore claimable, but that no part of the boiler trouble so arose.

[6] [1895] P. 125 at 138.

Historical Development and Practice of Rule VII

7.04 *York-Antwerp Rules 1890*

The British Association of Average Adjusters were largely responsible for drafting the proposed Rules put forward for discussion at the International Conference at Liverpool in 1890, and, they having passed a domestic Rule of Practice on this very subject only a few months previously, it is not surprising that the following Rule was introduced and agreed in 1890:

Damage to Engines in Refloating A Ship

"Damage caused to machinery and boilers of a ship which is ashore and in a position of peril, in endeavouring to refloat, shall be allowed in general average when shown to have arisen from an actual intention to float the ship for the common safety at the risk of such damage."

7.05 *York-Antwerp Rules 1924*

The Drafting Committee for the 1924 Rules suggested amending the 1890 Rule to read:

Damage by Use of Machinery

"Damage done to a ship or cargo and caused by the use for the common safety of the machinery and boilers of a ship which is ashore and in a position of peril shall be allowed in general average;..."

The important difference between the suggested new wording and the existing wording of the 1890 Rule was, of course, that the new wording would not have limited the damage to be made good in general average to that sustained only by the machinery and boilers, but would extend to any damage done to the ship and her cargo by using the machinery when aground in efforts to refloat. It would have covered, for example, injury to the hull by excessive vibration of the engines,[7] or to the cargo by leakage of water through plates started by the same vibration. There is nothing objectionable in principle to such allowances, but in practice it can be difficult to distinguish between such damage caused by the stranding itself and that caused by the subsequent working of engines. For these practical reasons, and also the possibility that the proposed new Rule would be construed to admit in general average the damage done to the bottom of a ship when being forced off the ground by the use of her engines, some of the delegates at the Stockholm Conference

[7] *Cf. Compania de Nav. Olazarri v. Merchants Marine Ins. Co. Ltd* (1905, unreported), where damage to a ship through straining of the hull caused by the working of the engines in the endeavour to refloat her when stranded was held to be general average. Such damage is very rarely allowed in the U.S.

objected to the new Rule and it was decided to retain the wording of the 1890 Rule as the first part of the 1924 Rule.

It must here be remarked that the members were probably mistaken in believing that they had achieved their object, since damage to the bottom, etc., would often have been covered by Rule A. Unless there is an express or implied exclusion of any particular damage in a numbered Rule, it is always open to any injured party to rest his claim under the general provisions of the lettered Rules.

Some difference of opinion was revealed in the discussion on the last clause of the draft rule put forward:

> "but where a ship is afloat no loss or damage caused by working the machinery and boilers shall be made good as general average."

It was evidently the view of some of the delegates present that when damage was caused to a vessel's engines by being strained when in imminent danger of running ashore, this should be treated as general average. In the end, however, the limitation imposed by the final clause in the draft rule was passed unanimously.

York-Antwerp Rules 1950 **7.06**

As stated above, a second section dealing with damage caused by working the machinery and boilers when afloat was added to Rule VII at the 1924 Conference at Stockholm, but the original 1890 title ("Damage to Engines in Refloating a Ship") was retained unaltered, although it was not entirely apt to cover the new wording. The titles form part of the Rules, to which the parties have by contract agreed and may therefore be used as an aid to interpreting what is stated in the Rules where the latter is ambiguous or unclear; but, where the meaning of the Rules is clear, it cannot be altered by the title. Nevertheless, it was found in practice that in certain countries the title was being used to override and defeat the detailed wording of the Rule itself. It was contended, from the title, that the Rule applied only to damage to engines *in refloating*, and that an allowance for damage to machinery and boilers while the vessel was afloat was not prohibited if the vessel had not been ashore. To avoid this form of interpretation, the title of Rule VII was amended in 1950 to "Damage to Machinery and Boilers".

A further amendment in 1950 consisted of the addition of the following italicised words in the second part of the Rule:

> "but where a ship is afloat no loss or damage caused by working the machinery and boilers, *including loss or damage due to compounding of engines or such measures*, shall *in any circumstances* be made good as general average."

These additional words were necessary because in the courts of Italy, at least, it had been held that "compounding of engines" (effectively, the cutting out of one of the cylinders, or altering a triple or quadruple expansion steam engine in such a way as to admit steam directly to some or all of the intermediate or low pressure cylinders instead of feeding it successively from one cylinder to another) was not working the engines:

> "Damage caused to machinery and boilers of a ship which is ashore and in a position of peril, in endeavouring to refloat, shall be allowed in general average when shown to have arisen from an actual intention to float the ship for the common safety at the risk of such damage; but where a ship is afloat no loss or damage caused by working the machinery and boilers, including loss or damage due to compounding of engines or such measures, shall in any circumstances be made good as general average."

7.07 *York-Antwerp Rules 1974*

Two alterations of some note were made in this Rule in 1974:

(1) The words "including loss or damage due to compounding of engines or such measures" were deleted for the reasons that:
  (a) Compounding can be done only on steam-engines, and they becoming obsolete, compounding of engines was of very infrequent occurrence.
  (b) The French text of the 1950 Rule (*y comprise la perte ou avarie due à un forcement de machines ou une mesure de ce genre*) did not exactly correspond with the English text and needed harmonising even if the provision had been retained.

(2) Two changes were made affecting the machinery and boilers to which the Rule applied.
  (a) The word "any" was added in the positive part of the Rule ("Damage caused to ... machinery and boilers") to ensure that, for instance, damage to auxiliary machinery, boilers and pumps, etc., caused in efforts to refloat a ship which is ashore and in a position of peril could be allowed in general average.
  (b) The word "propelling" was added in the second, negative, section of the Rule ("no loss or damage caused by working the ... machinery and boilers"), thereby confirming the expressed opinion of the Drafting Committee of the 1950 Rules[8] and enabling an allowance to be made in general average for loss or damage to auxiliary machinery, boilers and pumps etc. caused by a general average act when the vessel was afloat.

[8] The Drafting Committee for the 1950 Rules reported: "In the discussions both in the International Commission and in the Drafting Committee consideration has been given to defining what is meant by "machinery" and it has been found impossible to find any clear definition. The Drafting Committee therefore feels that it should state in its report that what is meant is the main engines and the propelling machinery of a vessel and not machinery such as pumps even though these form part of the main engines."

York-Antwerp Rules 1994

No change, but the correct—if unwelcome—decision in the case of the *Alpha*[9] concerning Rule VII prompted the United States Maritime Law Association to propose the highly important new Rule Paramount requiring sacrifices and expenditures to be *reasonably* made or incurred before any allowance in general average could be made under any of the York-Antwerp Rules. **7.08**

Rule VII

Damage to Machinery and Boilers

Damage caused to any machinery and boilers of a ship which is ashore and in a position of peril, in endeavouring to refloat, shall be allowed in general average when shown to have arisen from an actual intention to float the ship for the common safety at the risk of such damage; but where a ship is afloat no loss or damage caused by working the propelling machinery and boilers shall in any circumstances be made good as general average.

Construction

"Damage caused to any machinery and boilers" Although the wording of the first part of this Rule is expressed in positive terms, the Rule as a whole is effectively negative in character. Allowances which can be made in general average under this Rule are strictly limited to the damage caused: **7.09**

to machinery and boilers
by working the propelling machinery and boilers

in efforts to refloat a ship which is ashore and in a position of peril.

Any other loss or damage caused by the efforts to refloat is recoverable, if at all, under the lettered Rule A. Examples of such other loss or damage include:

(1) The extra bunkers and stores consumed whilst working the machinery in actual efforts to refloat (but not the normal consumption

[9] *Corfu Navigation Co. v. Mobil Shipping Co. Ltd* [1991] 2 Lloyd's Rep. 515. See para. PRE-21, *ante*, for an account of this case.

by auxiliary engines, etc., for supplying domestic light, heat and power whilst aground).[10]

(2) Damage to hull by excessive vibration of the engines, or to the cargo by leakage of water through plates started by the same vibration.

(3) Damage to the bottom of the ship caused by forcing or hauling her off or over the ground. The principles involved are admirably stated by a book published in the United States.[11]

> "In respect of damages to the hull below the water line the legal presumption is, except in cases of voluntary stranding, that they were accidentally caused, and it is only upon evidence removing this presumption that consideration can be had as to whether they were sustained as a natural consequence of the measures taken to float the vessel.
>
> The damage may not have been designed or foreseen by the master, but if it was a natural result of these measures it is regarded as an incident to them and, as such, partakes of their voluntary character, but a mere surmise or supposition that it was sustained in "getting off" rather than in "getting on" or by the accidental pounding of the vessel on the bottom while stranded, is insufficient to warrant allowance in general average.
>
> A careful investigation of all the circumstances is necessary, the nature of the damage being usually determined from the evidence given by the master and by the opinion of disinterested experts."

7.10 Thus, there is no doubt in principle that damage caused to the bottom by efforts to refloat a vessel which is ashore and in a position of peril is properly allowable as general average. The real difficulty in practice is for the shipowner to demonstrate with some degree of certainty that not only did the damage occur *during* the refloating operations, but that it was actually caused by or the result of the particular method or means used to refloat, rather than just a natural consequence of the grounding itself; also that it would not have occurred even if no attempt to refloat had been made. Rule E provides that the onus of proof is upon the party claiming in general average, and this onus is not necessarily discharged merely because some attending surveyor expresses the opinion in his report that such and such damage was attributable to efforts to refloat. (On the subject of bottom damage, see particularly paragraph E.07, above.)

An interesting case from the United States courts where the shipowner was unable to discharge this burden of proof occurred in *Sea-Land Services Inc. v. Aetna Insce. Co.*[12] where the vessel grounded with her forefoot in the rubble of the breakwater when entering Rio Haina in very rough weather. A tug pulled for 10 minutes and the vessel was beginning to move when the towline broke, whereafter the wind and waves pushed the vessel to a slightly new position where she sustained considerable additional damage to the bottom. The shipowner maintained

[10] See *The Bona* ([1895] P. 125) at para. 7.03, *ante*.
[11] E. W. Congdon, *General Average* (1913), pp. 74–75.
[12] (1976) A.M.C. 2164; [1977] 2 Lloyd's Rep. 84.

that the vessel's bow was so firmly embedded when she first ran aground that, but for the movement started by the tug when the towline broke, the vessel could not have swung into the new position.

As a matter of pure fact, the District Court Judge found (and the Court of Appeals confirmed by a majority) that it was more likely than not that the ship would have shifted by wind and current to roughly the new position regardless of whether the tow had been attempted, and the claim in general average for refloating damage was accordingly denied. As a matter of principle, the standard was "whether the towing materially increased the possibility of the shift from A to B".

(4) Damage caused in endeavouring to drive a ship higher up the ground, or to keep her on a rock.

"ashore" The word "stranded" appeared in the original draft for this Rule prepared in 1890 by the Association of Average Adjusters, but because it had a well-defined and narrow meaning in this country, it was purposely discarded in favour of the word "ashore". Strictly, even the word "ashore" must mean that the vessel has grounded on the shore, but it is suggested that it would be construed as if it read "aground" and would thus include grounding upon a permanently submerged bar or reef or, possibly, submerged rocks. **7.11**

"in a position of peril" It is a condition precedent that the vessel should be in a position of peril before any allowance can be made under this Rule and further reference is requested to the specific examples on groundings given in Rule A.[13]

"when shown" By the provisions of Rule E, the burden of proof lies upon the claimant. **7.12**

"actual intention to float the ship ... at the risk of such damage;" As will be appreciated from the account of the historical development of this Rule given in paragraphs 7.04, 7.05, above, these words were almost certainly intended in 1890 to be extremely restrictive and to limit the scope of the Rule to a case in which the master actually contemplated damage to machinery and boilers as a possible result of his actions in endeavouring to refloat the ship, and to exclude a claim if he did not actually foresee such damage even if he ought to have done so. It is also evident that this same approach would be expected in respect of, for instance, damage to the bottom of the ship caused by efforts to refloat. However, and as stated in all editions of this work since 1955, an actual contemplation of all reasonably foreseeable damage will no doubt be held to have been shown on very little evidence, unless and until evidence is given to rebut the presumption.

[13] See paras. A.36–A.39, *ante*.

This view is confirmed by *Australian Coastal Shipping Commission v. Green*[14] in which Lord Denning, M.R. stated:

> "If the master, when he does a 'general average act' ought reasonably to have foreseen that a subsequent accident of the kind (the tow-rope parted and fouled the tug's propeller) might occur—or even that there was a distinct possibility of it—then the subsequent accident does not break the chain of causation. The loss or damage is the direct consequence of the original general average act."

and also by *Sea-Land Services Inc. v. Aetna Insurance Co.*,[15] in which the United States Court of Appeals similarly agreed that in their case the master did or should have anticipated that the towline might part.

Further discussion on this matter is provided in Rule C, and particularly in paragraphs C.02 to C.11 and C.21, C.22, above, all supporting the general view that *actual contemplation* of damage is not necessary. The wording of Rule VII may in theory be stricter, but in practice any difference is more apparent than real.

7.13 **"for the common safety"** See commentary under Rule A,[16] and also the discussion of complex salvage operations in paragraphs 8.05 *et seq.*, below.

"but where a ship is afloat..." As a result of the inclusion of the Rule of Interpretation, the second part of this Rule will be decisive against any claim to contribution in respect of loss or damage to machinery or boilers falling within its terms, even if such contribution would otherwise have been recoverable under the lettered Rules.

"no loss or damage caused by working the propelling machinery and boilers" It should be noticed that this exclusion is not limited to loss or damage to machinery and boilers (as the title to the Rule would suggest) but applies to any kind of loss or damage caused by *working* the machinery and boilers whilst the ship is afloat.

The word *working* is intended in practice to cover any and every use of the machinery or boilers, even if that use might better be considered an abuse of their normal functioning.

[14] [1971] 1 Q.B. 456; 1 Lloyd's Rep. 16, C.A.
[15] (1976) A.M.C. 2164; [1977] 2 Lloyd's Rep. 84.
[16] See paras. A.17 *et seq.*, *ante*.

Rule VIII

Expenses Lightening a Ship When Ashore and Consequent Damage

English Practice and Background

The expense of a forced discharge and the attendant loss or damage to cargo, etc., requires consideration under two separate classifications: **8.01**

(1) Where the discharge takes place at a time of peril when a ship is ashore.
(2) Where the discharge takes place in the comparative safety of a port of refuge.

We are here concerned only with the first mentioned situation, and reference should be made to Rules X(b) and (c) and XII for the treatment to be accorded to the expenses and attendant losses and damages at a port of refuge.

If, in order to refloat a vessel which is aground and in a position of peril, cargo is discharged onto the beach or into lighters, the cost of discharge has been universally allowed as general average since time immemorial. In similar fashion, loss or damage sustained by the cargo whilst being discharged, or whilst on the beach or in the lighters, has also been always treated as general average.[1]

On the subject of loss or damage to the cargo, there are circumstances in which the discharging of cargo can scarcely be distinguished from a jettison. For example, if a ship is stranded she may be in extreme danger unless she can be lightened sufficiently to float her off by the next rise of tide; for which purpose a portion of the cargo may be thrown out, perhaps upon the sand or beach, not intending its destruction but with the hope that it may be fetched into safety by carts or boats from the shore. Or it may be that the only way in which the cargo can be put ashore is by dragging it through surf, or floating it in rafts. Again, it **8.02**

[1] There is a sentence in the Roman law (Dig. lib. XIV. tit. 2, f.4) (see para. 60.06, *post*) to the effect that if, to lighten a stranded ship, a part of the cargo is put into a boat or lighter, and if the boat and goods on board are lost before reaching the shore, the loss of the goods is allowable as general average, as in the case of jettison—"*proinde tanquam si jactura facta esset*". This is simply one example of the more general rule stated in the text.

may have to be landed through heavy rains, with no means of protection, or the only place where it can be deposited may be a bank of mud. In cases of this kind, where exposure of the cargo to great risk or even certainty of damage is deliberately adopted to avert the greater evil of extreme danger to the entire property, all damage or loss of cargo which occurs in consequence of such exposure, and in spite of reasonable care to prevent it, is clearly the subject of general average. It is perfectly analogous to damage by water going down when the hatches are open for jettison, or when water is poured upon the cargo to extinguish a fire; that is to say, this or that particular damage was not intended or aimed at, but, for the common safety, a measure was resorted to which naturally and indeed inevitably produced these results.[2] It must be pointed out that what is here said is only applicable where the discharge itself is properly a general average act. In cases of wreck, where the cargo is discharged really or principally for its own preservation, there is no ground for claiming as general average the damage it may sustain in the process. Nor, indeed, in such cases is the expense of discharging properly to be treated as general average.

8.03 With regard to the *expense* of lightening the ship when ashore, as stated in paragraph 8.02, above, this has always been accepted as general average when the ship and cargo were in peril. As Lord Campbell stated in *Job v. Langton*[3]:

> "Although the stranding was fortuitous, all expenses incurred from the misadventure till all the cargo had been discharged confessedly constituted general average."

Thus far, and in the context of the title of Rule VIII, we are concerned only with the expenses of lightening the ship as a necessary preliminary to refloating the ship herself (together with any cargo remaining on board). Although the expense of refloating should more properly be dealt with under Rule A, it is probably convenient to continue with the subject here.

8.04 Prima facie, it would be logical to assume that the succeeding expense of refloating the vessel which is stranded and in a position of peril should be as readily admissible in general average as is the cost of discharging the cargo to facilitate that operation and which preceded it. In fact, the situation under English law (though not necessarily under English practice) is less straightforward and we are in the next place to consider, more precisely, in what circumstances the expenses of refloating a stranded ship and her cargo are to be treated as general average. Further, and of equal importance, when those expenses are treated as general average, which interests should contribute towards them.

[2] See *McCall v. Houlder* (1897) 2 Com.Cas. 129.
[3] (1856) 6 E. & B. 779.

Complex Salvage Operations

The operations by which a ship and cargo are rescued from a situation of peril may be divided into three classes: **8.05**

(1) Those which throughout deal with the property as a whole, and, in saving any part, save all at once; as, for example, when a loaded ship is towed off a sandbank. These expenses are always treated as general average.
(2) Those which consist in the rescuing of portions of the property, disconnectedly, so that the saving of one portion has no reference to, and does not assist in, the saving of another portion; such as the recovery of goods or ship's materials strewn along a beach, or floating about at sea, after the ship has broken up. These expenses are never treated as general average, but charged individually to the separate interests salved.
(3) Those which have for their object the saving of the whole property, or so much of it as can be saved, not all at once, but by a series of distinct operations, each of which has or may have the twofold effect of immediately rescuing from danger one portion of the property, and of facilitating the eventual recovery of the remainder; as when, a ship being ashore, and her floating uncertain, some of the cargo is first taken out, and it then becomes possible to tow her off when she has been lightened. These last may be called "*complex salvage operations*", although it is not the salvage operations themselves which are necessarily so complex, but rather the legal problems at issue.

The leading cases on complex salvage operations are reported below. When studying them, it should be borne in mind that these decisions were properly governed by the very strict views on general average which have always been maintained by the courts of this country, including the following: **8.06**

(1) That general average is at an end when *physical safety* has been attained (as contrasted with some other countries, where the more liberal theories of *common benefit* and *completion of the adventure* hold sway).
(2) That when ship and cargo part company (as when cargo is discharged in order to lighten a vessel for refloating), the previous community of interest is likely to be severed and that expenses incurred thereafter are more for the individual benefit of a particular interest, than for the common adventure.

On the basis of these two principles, the preponderant view of English legal decisions is that, where cargo is removed from a stranded vessel and placed in a position of safety ashore, in the absence of exceptional circumstances such cargo cannot be called upon to contribute towards the expenses of refloating the vessel (and any cargo remaining on board) incurred subsequent to its removal.

8.07 However, this strict assessment by the English courts of the legal rights and responsibilities of the various parties in complex salvage situations has never been wholly acceptable to commercial interests, particularly those whose business is of an international character. It seemed inequitable to them, where a salvage operation was planned and carried out as one continuous operation and with no dramatic changes in the condition of the stranded property, that cargo landed safely ashore should escape contribution towards the subsequent expenses incurred in refloating the ship and any cargo still remaining on board. In many cases the cargo discharged would owe its good fortune and immunity merely to the fact that it was stowed near the hatches, or in holds where its removal would be most efficacious in refloating the ship, and this was felt to be wrong. Other anomalies present themselves.

In practice, therefore, there has been a tendency to ignore certain aspects of the decisions which follow and, except in *sauve qui peut* cases and situations such as occurred in *Royal Mail Steam Packet Co. v. English Bank of Rio*,[4] to treat the whole cost of complex salvage operations as general average, at any rate up to the point of time when the safety of all the property at risk has been attained. These divergencies from the strict legal position are noted below in connection with each of the cases considered.

The authorities

8.08 In *Job v. Langton*,[5] the barque *Snowdon*, on a voyage from Liverpool to St. John's, Newfoundland, ran ashore in Malahide Bay, on the coast of Ireland. The vessel at low water was high and dry; and it became necessary to discharge the whole of the cargo and the ballast before she was got off. After the cargo was discharged and placed in store in Dublin, the vessel was got off at considerable cost, with the aid of a steam-tug, and by cutting a channel for her. She was then towed to Liverpool and repaired. The cargo was, in order to save its market, sent on by another vessel; but, by agreement, the question before the court was to be determined as if the *Snowdon*, after being repaired, had carried on her cargo. The question was, whether the expenses incurred in getting off the ship and taking her to Liverpool to repair, after the entire cargo was discharged, were chargeable to general average, or to particular average on the ship alone. Lord Campbell, delivering the judgment of the Court

[4] (1887) 19 Q.B.D. 362. See para. 8.15, *post*.
[5] (1856) 6 E. & B. 779.

of Queen's Bench, pronounced that the expenses were not chargeable to general average, but to the ship alone.

He said[6]: **8.09**

> "The expenses, to constitute general average, must therefore be brought within the second category, 'extraordinary expenses incurred for the joint benefit of ship and cargo ...' Although the stranding was fortuitous, all expenses incurred from the misadventure till all the cargo had been discharged confessedly constituted general average. But how can it be said that the subsequent expenses in getting off the ship and taking her to Liverpool for repair were of the same character? The employment of the steam-tug, and the cutting of the channel by which the ship was rescued cannot, as was contended for, be part of the same operation as the unloading of the cargo; for the case expressly finds that 'the steam-tug did no work at the ship until after the cargo was landed, and the coals and ballast taken out of her.' We therefore, do not see how these expenses are to be distinguished from the expenses of repairing the ship when she had been brought to Liverpool, which, it is admitted, must fall exclusively on the owner of the ship or the underwriter on the ship, as particular average. If the owner of the ship was to earn the stipulated freight by carrying the cargo to Newfoundland, it was his duty to repair her and to carry her to a place where she might be repaired..."

The decision in *Job v. Langton*[7] is unquestionably correct, but it is suggested that, in modern practice, all the expenses incurred in refloating the ship and towing her to Liverpool would be allowed as general average.

In *Moran v. Jones*,[8] tried in the same court in the following year, *Job v. Langton* was distinguished. The ship *Tribune*, shortly after sailing from Liverpool to Callao, ran aground on East Hoyle Bank. She was in ballast, under charter to fetch a cargo from the Chinchas on which the freight was at risk; but she had on board, by the charterer's permission, a small quantity of goods belonging to other parties. Two days after she ran ashore, the weather being more moderate, assistance was procured from Liverpool, and men were employed saving from alongside the wreck of the ship's foremast which had been cut away, the materials of the ship, and the goods, all of which were sent in lighters to Liverpool. Afterwards, a stream anchor was carried out, the ship was scuttled [*sic*], about 300 tons of ballast were thrown overboard, and then the ship, being kept free by pumping, floated. She was then towed by two steamers back to Liverpool, and there repaired. The question raised was, whether the sum of £643, which had been expended after the cargo was taken out, for the purpose of floating the ship and bringing her to Liverpool for repair, should be treated as general average. **8.10**

[6] *Ibid.* at 790.
[7] [1887] 19 Q.B.D. 362.
[8] (1857) 7 E. & B. 523.

8.11 Lord Campbell said[9]:

> "In the case we never doubted that the defendant, as underwriter on the freight was liable for a contribution to general average in respect of the sum of £643, the expenses incurred in order to get the ship off from the bank on which she was stranded, whether the goods were or were not liable to contribute to this portion of the loss. It is admitted that the ship could not have been got off and completed her voyage unless these various expenses had been incurred. Therefore, without these expenses, there would have been a total loss of the freight, amounting to the sum of £6,750...
>
> But the sum for which this defendant is liable will depend, to a certain degree, upon the question whether, under the circumstances stated, these goods are to contribute in respect of the £643. And upon this question likewise we are bound to give our opinion. The goods had been taken from the ship and put on board a lighter before these expenses were incurred; and if this had been a separate operation by which they were intended to be saved for the benefit of the owners of the goods, we should have thought (as in *Job v. Langton*[10]) that the goods were not liable to contribute to the expenses subsequently incurred. Looking, however, to the facts stated in this special case, it seems to us that the act of putting the goods in the lighter was only part of one continuous operation, *viz.* getting the ship off the bank on which she was stranded, and sending her to Liverpool, where she might be repaired with a view to prosecute the original adventure. When she got to Liverpool, the operation of saving her from shipwreck was completed, and the whole expense of the repairs fell upon the owner as owner, and must be borne by him in that capacity, or by the underwriters on the ship: but the expenses of the continuous operation, for the common benefit of ship, goods and freight, are the subject of a general average. In *Job v. Langton*,[11] we considered that the goods had been saved by a distinct and completed operation, and that afterwards a new operation began which could not be properly distinguished from the repairs done to the ship to enable her to pursue the voyage ... But in the case on which we have now to adjudicate, the goods were put into a lighter by the master of the ship, along with materials of the ship saved from the wreck and they remained in the custody and under the control of the master till the ship was repaired, when they were reloaded in the ship and carried forward, without any interference by the owner of the goods, to their destined port. Unless it had been intended that an operation should be undertaken and completed by which both ship and goods should be rescued from the peril to which they were exposed nothing might have been done and the goods might have perished. Because the goods happened to be saved in the earliest part of the operation, this can be no sufficient reason for saying that they ought not to contribute to all the expenses of the operation which contemplated the benefit of all the interests imperilled by the stranding..."

8.12 In holding that the landing of the goods and the salving of the ship were parts of a continuous operation, the court in *Moran v. Jones*[12] was, to some extent at least, influenced by the fact that the whole series of operations was necessary to enable the adventure to be successfully prosecuted; a circumstance which, as has been pointed out, does not

[9] *Ibid.* at 532.
[10] (1856) 6 E. & B. 779.
[11] *Ibid.*
[12] (1857) 7 E. & B. 523.

according to English law make the operation as a whole general average. It is very questionable whether, on the particular facts of the case, the judgment in *Moran v. Jones* can be supported.[13] Nevertheless, and accepting that the decision is of doubtful worth, the general sentiments expressed by Lord Campbell (and particularly the phrase "one continuous operation") are more attractive to commercial interests and most adjusters, and the case is preferred in practice to *Job v. Langton.*[14]

The third of these cases, *Walthew v. Mavrojani,*[15] was that of the ship *Southern Belle*, which, while lying at Calcutta laden with a cargo of linseed for London, was driven from her moorings by a cyclone and left fast aground on a mud-bank. A survey was held on her, and it was recommended that the cargo and ballast should be discharged, and the ship dismantled, it being in the surveyor's opinion otherwise impossible to remove the ship from the strand. By October 19, the whole of the cargo was safely warehoused in Calcutta. On that day a surveyor examined the ship and advised that she would not float without extraordinary means being employed to get her off the strand. Tenders having been invited, a firm at Calcutta contracted with the plaintiff's agents to float the ship; but on November 24, their efforts having proved unavailing, they declared their inability to perform the contract and abandoned the attempt. The plaintiff's agents then made a fresh contract with Messrs. Burns & Co. for £2,300 to float the ship, and they, by constructing an embankment round the vessel, so as to form a dock which they afterwards filled with water, succeeded on December 31, in floating her. Thereafter, the ship was repaired and reloaded with the cargo, which was delivered at destination. **8.13**

Here the question was raised, whether this £2,300 was the subject of general average. In the Court of Exchequer it was held not to be so, but this was appealed against.

[13] See the remarks of Bovill C.J., in *Walthew v. Mavrojani* (1870) L.R. 5 Exch. 116 at 122, on *Moran v. Jones.*

"I take it to be settled now", said Wills J. in *Royal Mail Steam Packet Co. v. English Bank of Rio* (1887) 19 Q.B.D. 370, "that the circumstances which impose a liability in the nature of general average must be such as to imperil the *safety* of ship and cargo and not merely such as to impede the successful prosecution of the particular voyage. I take it also to be settled that if the cargo as a whole be landed and in safety, the expenses of getting the ship afloat incurred thereafter are not general average: *Job v. Langton*, a case with which *Moran v. Jones* has been supposed to conflict, but which does not seem to me, so far as principles are concerned, to be open to that observation. It is the decisions, if anything, which are at variance, not the principles upon which they are based." And Grantham J. said, *ibid.* at 377: "As that case (*i.e. Moran v. Jones*) has not been since followed, even if it has not been overruled, we could not act upon that decision unless the facts were absolutely identical."

In *Svendsen v. Wallace* (1884) 13 Q.B.D. 80, Brett M.R. said that, in his opinion, *Moran v. Jones* could not be supported; Bowen L.J. said (at 93): "The inferences of fact drawn by the Court of Queen's Bench may or may not have been correct, but the decision has reference only to the special facts of the case."

[14] (1856) 6 E. & B. 779.

[15] (1870) L.R. 5 Exch. 116.

The decision of the court was unanimous that the expense should not be general average. Bovill C.J. said[16]:

> "Whereas to ground a claim for general average there must be a danger, actual or impending, common to both ship and cargo, here the cargo was safe and the ship only in peril; it was indifferent to the owners of the cargo whether the ship floated or not, and there was therefore no sacrifice made, or extraordinary expense incurred, to save both ship and cargo, or for the common benefit of both."

8.14 The judgment in this case is faultless and unchallengeable. However, on the basis that the doctrine of "completion of the adventure" is preferred by commercial interests, it is submitted that, in practice, the costs of refloating the vessel would now be allowed as general average.

8.15 In *Royal Mail Steam Packet Co. v. English Bank of Rio*,[17] the *Tagus*, on a voyage from Rio de Janeiro to Southampton, having on board specie of the value of £125,000, partly belonging to the defendants, and a general cargo, ran aground on an island near Bahia and lay in a dangerous position. The weather being bad, the master landed the specie on the next day on the island, afterwards jettisoned some of the cargo, and with the assistance of several tugs got the ship off the ground. After the specie was landed, it was taken to Bahia and forwarded in another vessel; but the parties agreed that for the purpose of ascertaining whether any general average contribution was due from the defendants it should be treated as having been carried by the plaintiffs in the *Tagus* to Southampton.

The plaintiffs claimed a contribution from the defendants in respect both of the jettison, the expense of floating the ship, and the cost of landing the specie and conveying it to Bahia; and a special case having been stated, their counsel argued before a Divisional Court that the specie was landed on the island, and sent on to Bahia, as part of a continuous salvage operation, undertaken for the common preservation of ship, cargo and freight, of which the jettison and the employment of the tugs formed another part. The court held, however, that the landing of the specie was not part of the general average act, and that the specie was not bound to contribute to the expense of getting the ship off the shore.

8.16 Wills J. after reviewing the authorities, said[18]:

> "Cases, no doubt, may occur in which it may be difficult to say whether the purpose for which the goods are removed is that of lightening the ship or of saving the goods, and there will no doubt from time to time be instances in which it is impossible to separate the one purpose from the other. 'The mere fact that the cargo is unladen, although it is done in part for the

[16] *Ibid.* at 124.
[17] [1887] 19 Q.B.D. 362.
[18] *Ibid.* at 374.

purpose of saving the goods, yet if it is also done for the purpose of lightening the vessel and as a means of causing her to float, and of saving her from the common peril will not necessarily divest the transaction of its character as an act performed for the joint benefit of ship and cargo': *McAndrews v. Thatcher*[19] in the Supreme Court of the United States. It is impossible with reference to such a matter to lay down any right or inflexible rule. The question will be one of circumstance and degree, and each case must depend upon its own facts ... The whole of the specie in this case weighed, we are told, about a ton and a half. The *Tagus* is a vessel of some 3,000 tons burthen. The ease to the vessel could be nothing at all. The combined value and smallness of total weight would be certain in any case to save the specie from jettison. Its value and the facility with which it could be got ashore would be certain, in any case where it was possible to land it, to save it from being left on board, and I cannot doubt that its removal was carried out, not in any sense or degree as a means of securing the common safety of ship and cargo, but simply for the purpose of saving the specie itself. I think, therefore, that when the general average loss was incurred, in whatever sense, restricted or enlarged, that phrase can be properly used, it had ceased to be at risk, that upon no reasonable view of the facts can its removal be considered as a part of the means taken for saving any common adventure. I am consequently of opinion that it is not liable, using the words of the special case, 'to contribute to the jettison or to any of the expenses of getting the ship off the ground incurred after it was landed.'"[20]

Practice and the law are here *ad idem*.

In *Kemp v. Halliday*,[21] the *Chebucto* encountered heavy gales when on voyage from Liverpool to Rio de Janeiro with a general cargo and it became necessary for the common safety to cut away all forward and to put into Falmouth as a port of refuge. Part of the cargo was discharged ashore and repairs were commenced, but before these had been completed, a hurricane caused the ship with that part of the cargo still on board to sink at her moorings. The ship and cargo were raised together as a single operation and, in order to determine the main point at issue (that is, whether the ship was a constructive total loss) the court had 8.17

[19] (1865) 3 Wallace 347 at 370. But English law may differ from that of the U.S. on this point. In the 8th ed. of this work the following propositions were submitted as the result of three American cases: when a vessel strands near her destination and her cargo is discharged and delivered at destination by lighters, or other similar means, the salvage and other extraordinary expenses up to the time of delivery of the cargo are general average, and the subsequent expenses of floating the ship are chargeable to the ship unless she is floated without much expense or delay after the cargo has been delivered. In the latter event all the extraordinary expenses are to be treated as general average. See *McAndrews v. Thatcher* 3 Wall 347 (1865); *The Julie Blake* 107 U.S. 418 (1882); *L'Amerique* 35 Fed.Rep. 835 (1888). If the casualty occurs short of destination, and the cargo is reloaded, or intended to be reloaded, all the expenses are treated as general average: *N.Y. and Cuba Mail S.S. Co. v. Reliance Marine Ins. Co.* 70 Fed.Rep. 262 (1895); (1896) 77 Fed.Rep. 317; 165 U.S. 720; *The Joseph Farwell* 31 Fed.Rep. 844 (1887). When the services have not been continuous, expenses incurred after a separation of interests are not general average: *Pacific Mail S.S. Co. v. N.Y.H. and R. Mining Co.* 69 Fed.Rep. 414 (1895); 74 Fed.Rep. 564 (1896).

[20] For cases where specie has been held liable to contribute, see *The St Paul* 82 Fed.Rep. 340 (1898); *The Mullhouse* Fed.Cas. 9910 (1859).

[21] (1865) 6 B. & S. 723; 34 L.J.Q.B. 233.

first to decide whether the expense of raising the ship and cargo was general average.

8.18 Blackburn J. decided that the expense of this operation was general average chargeable to the ship and that portion of the cargo on board, but "not as against the part that was safe". He then continued with the remarks for which the case is generally remembered:

> "I do not mean to say that in every case where a ship with a cargo is submerged, and the two are in fact raised together by one operation, the expenditure incurred must necessarily be for the common preservation of both. I think it is in every case a question of fact whether it was so; and if the cargo could easily and cheaply be taken out of the ship, and saved by itself, it would not be proper to charge it with any portion of the joint operation; which in that case would not be incurred for the preservation of the cargo."[22]

This case presents no difficulties and practice and the law are as one. No average adjuster would contemplate charging to the cargo safely ashore any proportion of the expense of raising the ship and other cargo, for the simple reason that the expense resulted from a *new and separate accident* which did not imperil the cargo ashore and was in no way connected with the original accident.

For interest: it is believed that cargo insurers seldom take advantage of the *obiter* remarks of Blackburn J. quoted above, and have always been prepared to pay the full *pro rata* share of general average expenses attaching to cargo remaining on board during a general average act.

Further removal of cargo

8.19 It is to be remembered that we have been speaking only, thus far, of the expenses of removing the ship and cargo, from the strand or bottom, to the nearest place of actual safety. This very often is only the first portion of the extraordinary expenditure which the accident has necessitated. The cargo may be in safety, but on rocks, or on a beach above high-water mark, or on open fields, it is at all events safe from perils of the seas.[23] It may be of little or no value, however, in that position; it must be removed either to a market or to a port of shipment for its own or some other market. Here we come upon a fresh set of complications. Who is to bear the expense of this removal from a place of bare actual or physical safety to one of mercantile safety? Shall this be treated as general average, as a charge on the specific cargo saved, or on the freight, or on the cargo and freight conjointly?

[22] (1865) 6 B. & S. 723; 34 L.J.Q.B. 233 at 243.

[23] It may, however, be necessary to remove the cargo to another place for shelter, or to be conditioned. In this case the place mentioned in the text would not be considered a place of safety: *Rose v. Bank of Australasia* [1894] A.C. 687.

It is submitted that the expense of the further removal of the cargo to a place of mercantile safety falls to be dealt with in accordance with whether or not the expense of the preliminary stage in the saving of the cargo was or was not a general average expenditure.

Freight earned by substituted ship

If the ship is not floated or raised, or is found not capable of repair so as to carry the cargo, and the shipowner avails himself of his privilege of substituting another ship and sends it to the nearest port to fetch the goods, it seems obvious that the same principle should apply: the cost of bringing the goods to the port should be a charge on the cargo and freight, and the cost of loading the goods should be a charge on the freight alone.[24] **8.20**

Agency fees to shipowners and/or their managers

When the ship has gone ashore, or some other maritime disaster has happened which imperils the whole adventure, the shipowner is bound to use his best endeavours in the interest of all parties concerned. There is, however, no rigid rule of law that he is bound to do everything himself; and in a proper case he may employ experienced persons to act for the benefit of all parties, and charge their remuneration as a general average expenditure.[25] **8.21**

In addition to the financial expenditure involved in any general average situation, the shipowner will probably expend a considerable amount of extra time and trouble organising salvage assistance, arranging repairs and the discharge and reloading of cargo at a port of refuge, etc., and the question arises: is he entitled to any remuneration for this extra time and trouble? In general terms, the answer is that he is entitled to his actual out-of-pocket expenses such as travel and cables, but not to any remuneration. Rule of Practice No. A3 of the Association of Average Adjusters provides as follows:

Agency Commission and Agency

> "That, in practice, neither commission (excepting bank commission) nor any charge by way of agency or remuneration for trouble is allowed to the shipowner in average, except in respect of services rendered on behalf of cargo when such services are not involved in the contract of affreightment."

[24] The question which has just been considered was raised in *Rose v. Bank of Australasia* [1894] A.C. 687; but under the circumstances of the case it was unnecessary in the House of Lords to decide it.

[25] *Rose v. Bank of Australasia* [1894] A.C. 687, disapproving *Schuster v. Fletcher* (1878) 3 Q.B.D. 418. The House of Lords also held that he was entitled to charge against the cargo owners the commission paid to a merchant for arranging the sale of unidentified portions of the cargo as having acted reasonably in the particular circumstances, and Lord Herschell considered ([1894] A.C. 687 at 697) that there might be circumstances under which he might even charge for his own services.

8.22 It frequently occurs that the registered owner of a vessel will leave the day-to-day operation of his vessel to a firm of ship managers who may be recompensed on a fee or commission basis. If the ship managers are entitled under the terms of their agreement to make a special charge for extra services rendered in a general average situation, is that charge properly admissible in general average?

The position is by no means clear, but some guidance may be obtained from *Rose v. Bank of Australasia.*[26] In that case, the *Sir Walter Raleigh* stranded on the coast of France near Cap Gris Nez when on a voyage to the United Kingdom with a general cargo. The owner of the ship operated from Aberdeen and, therefore, he instructed a firm in London with experience in salvage operations and disasters of this kind to take all necessary steps in his interest and the interest of others concerned in the adventure. This firm proceeded at once to do what they could to save the ship and cargo and sent one of their men to the scene of the disaster and arranged for a local firm to do the best possible to save the cargo. For these services the London firm was to get £750 and the French firm was to receive a percentage of the value of the cargo salved; this proved to amount to £1,500. The ship ultimately proved to be a total loss but the cargo was discharged, carried to the top of the cliff and later carted to Boulogne. A quantity of seawater-damaged cargo was attended to and spread out to prevent deterioration, and ultimately it was forwarded to London. These two payments of £750 and £1,500 were charged—in part, at least—to general average, and the cargo interests disputed liability. Certainly with regard to the £750 it was alleged that these services were a matter for the shipowner himself and that it merely represented the discharge of a duty incumbent upon him. If he chose to employ others to do this job it must be treated as if he had done it himself.

8.23 The House of Lords decided that both amounts were properly allowable and Herschell L.C. said:

> "There is no doubt that when a disaster of this kind happens the ship-owner is bound to use his best endeavours in the interest of all concerned; but whether he is to do anything himself, and what he ought to do himself without making a charge for it, must, it seems to me, depend upon the circumstances of the case; there can be no rigid rule of law laid down with regard to it. It would in some cases, as it strikes me, be most unreasonable not to allow the shipowner to employ others to do the work, whilst in other cases it would be most unreasonable that he should, or that if he did he should make any charge in respect of it ... I quite concede that a shipowner owes a duty to all interested; that he cannot throw the expense of doing what he ought to do himself upon some other interests because he chooses to employ somebody else. Whilst conceding that, it appears to me clear that there are many cases where the employment of others is a reasonable and

[26] [1894] A.C. 687. In *The Westport (No. 3)* [1966] 1 Lloyd's Rep. 342, an agent's remuneration was held to be recoverable by him as a "disbursement" within the Administration of Justice Act 1956, s. 1(1).

> right course to take; and where by such employment extraordinary expenditure is incurred for the general benefit, I am at a loss to see why it may not be distributed over those who receive the benefit."

The expense to the owner of sending a special agent to a port of distress has been allowed in American cases, when such procedure was reasonable and the agent's services were for the general benefit.[27] **8.24**

HISTORICAL DEVELOPMENT AND PRACTICE OF RULE VIII

York-Antwerp Rules 1890 **8.25**

For the reason that the cost of discharging cargo, etc., from a vessel which was aground and in a position of peril, and any attendant loss or damage to the cargo, has always and universally been allowed as general average, the following Rule was accepted without discussion when first introduced in 1890:

> "When a ship is ashore and, in order to float her, cargo, bunker coals and ship's stores, or any of them are discharged, the extra cost of lightening, lighter hire and re-shipping (if incurred), and the loss or damage sustained thereby, shall be admitted as general average."

Although this wording contained no explicit provision that the ship and cargo should be in a position of peril before the cost of discharging cargo, etc., could be allowed as general average, it can confidently be asserted that this omission was but an oversight on the part of those who framed the Rules and that this condition precedent would never have been far from their minds. Nevertheless, the omission did not go unnoticed, and the courts of Holland, at least, in applying this rule held[28] that it was not necessary that the ship should be in peril; it was sufficient merely that she be ashore in order to charge the cost of discharging, etc., to general average.

York-Antwerp Rules 1924 **8.26**

This defect in the 1890 Rule was remedied at Stockholm in 1924 by introducing the necessity for the discharge to be done "as a general average act". The definition of a general average act contained in Rule A preserves to the full the necessity of the common safety being involved and the element of peril being present.

[27] *Hobson v. Lord* 92 U.S. 397 (1875); *Besse v. Hecht* 85 Fed.Rep. 677 (1898); *The Eliza Lines* 102 Fed.Rep. 184 (1900); also *Rose v. Bank of Australasia* [1894] A.C. 687.
[28] The cases are reported in the 5th ed. of this work, p. 596 and in the 6th ed., p. 608.

York-Antwerp Rules 1950

No change.

York-Antwerp Rules 1994

8.27 No changes to this particular Rule were anticipated in the preliminary discussions for the 1994 Rules but, following the introduction on this occasion of the major new provisions in Rule C[29] to prevent the allowance in general average of any liabilities to third parties resulting from the escape or release of pollutant substances from the property involved in the common maritime adventure, it became essential to make changes here and in Rules II and V to ensure that the then existing provisions in those *numbered* Rules could not circumvent and override[30] the fundamental new principle set forth in the *lettered* Rule C.

The 1974 wording of Rule VIII covered "... *the loss or damage sustained*" (by discharging, etc.) and this wording would generally have been considered sufficiently wide to permit the allowance in general average of third-party claims arising from damage to the environment caused by, for instance, a loss of oil from a broken pipeline during discharging operations from a stranded tanker in efforts to refloat.

New and precise wording was introduced in 1994 to make it clear that loss or damage only "*to the property involved in the common maritime adventure*" was allowable.

Rule VIII

Expenses Lightening a Ship when Ashore, and Consequent Damage

When a ship is ashore and cargo and ship's fuel and stores or any of them are discharged as a general average act, the extra cost of lightening, lighter hire and re-shipping (if incurred), and any loss or damage to the property involved in the common maritime adventure in consequence thereof, shall be admitted as general average.

[29] See paras. C.29 *et seq.*, *ante*.
[30] See the Rule of Interpretation para PRE.04, *ante*.

Construction

"ashore" See commentary on Rule VII.[31] 8.28

"cargo" See commentary on Rule I.[32]

"discharged" The first draft of this Rule, submitted to an Extraordinary General Meeting of the Association of Average Adjusters prior to the Liverpool Conference in 1890, used the words "discharged into lighters". The words "into lighters" were struck out in order to ensure that the provisions of the Rule should apply also to a discharge direct on to the beach.

"general average act" This phrase is defined by Rule A.

"extra cost" If the cargo, etc., is reshipped, the whole cost of the operation will constitute "extra" cost. The word "extra" assumes importance more particularly when the discharge takes place at or near the intended port of destination. If, for any reason, the cargo is not reshipped into the original carrying vessel (for example because the cargo would customarily have been discharged into lighters, craft or other vessels) it would be manifestly unjust that the carrier or other parties should be relieved of the normal expenses of discharging and lighter hire, etc., merely because the ship was ashore. In such a case, it is only the increase in cost which is admissible in general average.

"to the property involved in the common maritime adventure" As explained earlier in paragraph 8.27, above, these words were added in 1994 to ensure that loss or damage only to the property itself involved in the common maritime adventure consequent upon a forced discharge while ashore could be allowed in general average. 8.29

Thus, any loss of oil from a broken pipeline during discharging operations from a stranded tanker in efforts to refloat from a position of peril would be allowable as general average under this Rule, also any resulting contamination of the ship or other cargo, but damage to the environment—unmentioned here—is now outside the scope of Rule VIII, and any attempt to recover it under the lettered Rules will be defeated by the provisions added to Rule C in 1994.

A side-effect of the words under discussion is that all liabilities for loss of or damage to the property of third parties now fall outside the Rule, whether or not the liability is in respect of damage to the environment or in consequence of the escape or release of pollutant substances. It follows that all such liabilities must now be claimed under Rule C, and

[31] See para. 7.11, *ante*.
[32] See para. 1.24, *ante*.

subject to the provisions of that Rule, which may be more restrictive than those of Rule VIII (see the discussion below under "**in consequence**").

8.30 **"in consequence"** This might be freely translated as "*caused by*" or "*as a result*", but the term is undoubtedly sufficiently wide to include both direct and indirect consequences. Rule C may require any loss, etc., to be the *direct* consequence of the general average act, but, in the light of the Rule of Interpretation this limitation does not affect the numbered Rules.

"thereof" This relates:

(1) In general—	To the discharge as a general average act.
(2) In particular—	To the act of lightening from the ship ashore, plus the period in the lighter, in so far as these are extra to any normal lightening.
	To the period while on the beach or on shore.
	To the act of re-shipping, if incurred.

Thus, *any* loss or damage to cargo, fuel and/or stores from an external cause sustained during the operations or intervening period just mentioned may be allowed in general average. This is perfectly in accordance with the fundamental principles of general average; if by reason of a general average act (the forced discharge), cargo, etc., is exposed to increased risks over and above those it would expect to encounter if it had remained undisturbed on board ship, the resulting loss or damage should be borne by all the properties involved in the common maritime adventure.

Rule IX

Cargo, Ship's Materials and Stores used for Fuel

English Law and Background

When sail gave way to steam there were bound to be occasions at sea when the ship's bunkers were exhausted—or about to become so—and, for the common safety, it was necessary to burn cargo or ship's materials in the furnaces. **9.01**

The use of *cargo* for nominally ship's purposes at a time of peril very clearly constitutes an extraordinary sacrifice which is properly allowable as general average, (see paragraph A.56, above) but the position with regard to a supposed sacrifice of the ship's materials was rather less certain. Was such "sacrifice" truly extraordinary and out of the usual course, or was it comprised within the shipowner's obligations under and performance of the contract of affreightment? The question was resolved in 1872 by the decision in *Harrison v. Bank of Australasia*,[1] in which it was held that spare spars, planks, and other ship's materials used upon emergency for fuel for the ship's engines to avert some danger and when there has been no original insufficiency in the supply of bunkers, are the subject of general average. The facts of the case are recorded in paragraph A.60, above.

In the subsequent case of *Robinson v. Price*,[2] a question substantially the same was decided in the Court of Appeal. The ship *John Baring*, bound with timber from Quebec for London, was supplied with a donkey-engine adapted for the loading and discharge of cargo and ballast and also for pumping the ship, to aid the ship's hand pumps, when required. At the time of sailing the ship had five tons of coal on board, which was admitted to be a sufficient supply of fuel for all purposes of the ship while at sea, other than pumping, for a much longer voyage than that from Quebec to London. While at sea the ship fell in with bad weather, and sprang so bad a leak that she could hardly be kept free by constant pumping. For this purpose it presently became necessary to have the pumps worked by the donkey-engine, and as the supply of coal threatened to run short, the captain ordered some of the ship's spare spars, and a portion of the cargo, to be used with the coal to keep up the fire of the

[1] (1872) L.R. 7 Ex. 39.
[2] (1876) 2 Q.B.D. 91.

donkey-engine; by which means the ship was eventually brought safe into port. The questions for the court were whether the burning of the spare spars and whether the burning of the cargo, were to be made good as general average.

9.02 The judgment of the court was delivered by Lush J. who said:

> "The circumstances under which the ship's spars and the cargo were used as fuel for the donkey-engine satisfy all the conditions of a general average claim. The peril was imminent; the sacrifice voluntary, in the sense of being an act of will on the part of the master; it was, in the emergency, necessary in order to save the ship from sinking, and was, of course, made with a view to the safety of the whole adventure—ship, freight, and cargo. Prima facie, therefore, the case of the plaintiff is made out. But it was objected that, as the ship was furnished with a donkey-engine, adapted and intended, in the case of need, for pumping as well as for loading and discharging the cargo, the owner was bound to provide sufficient fuel for its use; that if this had been done the resort to the spars and cargo would not have been required; that it was not done and, therefore, the use of the spars and cargo was not a necessity brought about by the perils of the sea, but a necessity occasioned by his own default.
>
> Although we cannot accede to the proposition in its terms, we entirely accede to the principle which underlies it. We think that a shipper of cargo is entitled, in time of peril, to the benefit not only of the best services of the crew, in order to save his goods, but of the use of all the appliances for that purpose with which the ship is provided. It follows that, where a ship is fitted up with auxiliary steam pumping power, it is the duty of the owner to make some provision for supplying the engine with fuel. Not that he is bound to have on board enough for every possible emergency, but he is bound to have a reasonable supply, having regard to the nature of the voyage, the season of the year, the quality of the cargo, the condition of the ship, and what experience has shewn to be prudent to provide against under those conditions. If he fails to do so, he cannot call upon the owners of cargo to contribute towards that reasonable supply. That would be to make them pay for that which he ought to have provided at his own expense. If, under such circumstances, the opportunity occurs during a time of peril of buying coals from a passing steamer, we think it clear that he could not charge their cost as an extraordinary expenditure entitling him to general average.
>
> That statement of the case not being so explicit as it might have been upon this point, we thought it right to send it back to the learned counsel who settled it between the parties, to find from the evidence he had taken one way or the other upon this question. He has returned it to us, with a statement as follows: 'I find that the *John Baring*, when she left Quebec, had on board a reasonable supply of coal for the donkey-engine for pumping purposes.' This finding concludes the defendants. The prima facie claim to general average contributions is not displaced by any default on the part of the owner, and our judgment must be for the plaintiff."

9.03 This decision was affirmed upon appeal.[3] Lord Coleridge said: "In my opinion the judgment of the Queen's Bench Division was perfectly right. The facts are now stated so distinctly as to preclude all argument. It is

[3] (1877) 2 Q.B.D. 295.

impossible to say that under the circumstances this sacrifice of the spars and cargo was not general average." Bramwell and Brett L.JJ. concurred.

There seems to be no distinction in point of principle between burning cargo to feed a ship's donkey-engine, and burning it to feed the ordinary working engines of a steamer.

What is Sufficient Supply of Fuel?

There is "no obligation cast upon the shipowner to have more than a reasonable and ordinary supply of fuel on board, having regard to the character of the voyage and the character of the weather that was to be expected".[4] Account must be taken *inter alia* of the distance to be covered to destination or the next intended bunkering port; the distance expected to be covered each day, having regard to the weather likely to be encountered at that particular season of the year, the state of cleanliness of the vessel's bottom, and the condition of the engines and/or boilers; the anticipated daily consumption of fuel at the expected speed of the vessel. With these factors in mind, the required quantity of bunkers can be calculated but, to the sum so produced, must be added a reasonable margin[5] to cover emergencies according to what prudent owners usually do in the particular trade. **9.04**

Thus in *E. B. Aaby's Rederi v. Union of India (No. 2)*[6] Donaldson J. said that the supply of fuel should be "sufficient to get the vessel to the next bunkering port in all reasonably forseeable circumstances". In that case the voyage was from Portland to Bombay via Yokohama as an intended bunkering port. It was common ground between the parties that a reserve of 25 per cent over the anticipated consumption was sufficient, and Donaldson J. expressed the view that in calculating the margin a further allowance should be made for adverse winds and currents expected on the voyage, as well as unpumpable fuel and possible error in calculating the quantity of fuel on board. The appropriate reserve will vary from voyage to voyage, and on a westward crossing of the North Atlantic in winter would probably be at least 33 per cent. Equally

[4] *Per* Keating J., *Shand v. Ash*, Mitchell's Mar. Reg. 1872, 242.

[5] The U.S. cases' of *Hurlburt v. Turnure* 81 Fed.Rep. 208 (1897) and *The Abbazia* 127 Fed.Rep. 495 (1904), may offer some guidance as to what constitutes a "reasonable margin". The first of these cases is also worth recording for its decision on a point which may not have come before the British courts. A steamship bound from a Cuban port to New York had but $9\frac{1}{2}$ days' supply of coal, whereas the customary supply was for 10 days. Ordinarily, the voyage would have taken eight days, but she encountered a hurricane which delayed her so that she was obliged, from lack of coal, to put into Newport News, and also the loss of ship's materials and cargo during the time the coal she ought to have taken would have lasted, but that the remainder of the loss was a general average charge.

[6] [1976] 2 Lloyd's Rep. 714; affirmed [1978] Lloyd's Rep. 351. The shipowners' claim was for the costs of towage into Yokohama. Since Rule IX does not apply to such a case it fell to be determined under the lettered Rules, and the claim was defeated because the shipowners failed to establish that they had exercised due diligence to provide an adequate supply of the correct type of fuel.

on a short voyage the reserve expressed as a percentage of the anticipated consumption will be considerably greater.

9.05 If it is necessary for purposes of bunkering to divide a voyage into "stages", the vessel must load a reasonably sufficient quantity of fuel at the commencement of each "stage" in order to comply with the warranty of seaworthiness.[7] *Semble* the vessel must load sufficient fuel to enable her to reach the intended bunkering port where the next stage is to begin; the fact that in the course of the voyage there may be an opportunity to rebunker at another port will not satisfy the warranty.[8]

Problems occasionally arise when a grade of fuel is supplied which is unsuitable for the vessel, and which causes increased consumption.[9] In such circumstances it seems clear enough that the shipowner must demonstrate that the quality as well as the quantity of fuel was satisfactory.

In order that the interested parties may make an assessment of the adequacy or otherwise of the supply of fuel, the Association of Average Adjusters have the following Rule of Practice:

B9 Claims arising out of Deficiency of Fuel

> "That in adjusting general average arising out of deficiency of fuel, the facts on which the general average is based shall be set forth in the adjustment, including the material dates and distances, and particulars of fuel supplies and consumption."

Historical Development and Practice of Rule IX

9.06 *York-Antwerp Rules 1890*

The following Rule, proposed by the Association of Average Adjusters, was unanimously accepted at the Conference at Liverpool in 1890:

Cargo, Ship's Materials and Stores Burnt for Fuel

> "Cargo, ship's materials and stores, or any of them, necessarily burnt for fuel for the common safety at a time of peril, shall be admitted as general average, when and only when an ample supply of fuel had been provided; but the estimated quantity of coals that would have been consumed, calculated at the price current at the ship's last port of departure at the date of her leaving shall be charged to the shipowner and credited to the general average."

[7] *The Vortigern* [1899] P. 140, C.A.; *Greenock S.S. Co. v. Maritime Ins. Co.* [1903] 2 K.B. 657, C.A.

[8] *Timm & Son v. Northumbrian Shipping Co.* [1939] A.C. 397.

[9] *E.g. E. B. Aaby's Rederi v. Union of India* (see para. 9.03, *ante*).

It will be noted that an allowance in general average was conditional upon an ample supply of fuel having been provided for the voyage and, further, that the value of the "coals" that would normally have been consumed should be credited to the general average and charged to the shipowner.

York-Antwerp Rules 1924 **9.07**

At the Stockholm Conference in 1924, three changes were made in the Rule:

(1) The word "cargo", which was the first word on the 1890 Rule (and of the title) was deleted in order that the cargo-owner's right to contribution should not depend upon the adequacy of the original supply of fuel, a matter with which he would not normally be concerned. Thenceforth, if cargo was burnt as fuel for the common safety at a time of peril, the value of that cargo would be allowable as general average under the lettered Rule A, and regardless of whether or not an ample supply of fuel had been provided.
(2) The more comprehensive word "fuel" was substituted for "coals" in order that the Rule should be kept up-to-date and apply to the more advanced oil-fired ships.
(3) Lastly, words were omitted which indicated that the sum to be credited to the general average in respect of the value of the fuel that would have been consumed should automatically be debited to the shipowner. This latter amendment was prompted by the consideration that it is sometimes the charterer who is responsible for the cost of supplying the fuel for the voyage.

York-Antwerp Rules 1950 and 1974

No change.

York-Antwerp Rules 1994

In that the 1974 Rule IX dealt only with ship's materials and stores burnt for fuel, and that it would generally be impossible to burn such solid items in the diesel or turbine marine engines in fairly universal use today, there were suggestions from a few countries that Rule IX might be deleted. Having regard to the fact that only in the case of tankers loaded with an oil cargo was there now likely to be an alternative source of fuel available on board, and that the sacrifice of such cargo was already covered by Rule A, it would probably have been sensible to have adopted the suggestion to delete the Rule. **9.08**

In fact, the Rule has been retained, but *cargo* has been re-introduced and made subject to its provisions. More unfortunately, the sound proposals by the United States Maritime Law Association:

(1) that general average should in all cases continue to be credited with the value of the fuel that would normally have been consumed, and
(2) that allowances for ship's materials and stores could only be made when an ample supply of fuel had been provided,

were not pursued at the Sydney Conference. Instead the Conference adopted an early proposal of the British Maritime Law Association, under which (a) where *cargo* was used as fuel the general average received no credit for the value of the fuel saved; and (b) the requirement of an ample supply of fuel was omitted altogether.

Rule IX

Cargo, Ship's Materials and Stores used for Fuel

Cargo, ship's materials and stores, or any of them, necessarily used for fuel for the common safety at a time of peril, shall be admitted as general average, but when such an allowance is made for the cost of ship's materials and stores the general average shall be credited with the estimated cost of the fuel which would otherwise have been consumed in prosecuting the intended voyage.

Construction

9.09 **"Cargo"** As submitted in paragraph 1.24, above, this means property in the possession of the shipowner and/or charterer under a contract of affreightment.

"ship's materials and stores" These words are nowhere defined, but they clearly do not include cargo even if owned by the shipowner. Nor, it is submitted, do they include one type of fuel instead of another. (For instance, a motor vessel which customarily uses fuel oil whilst at sea and the more expensive diesel oil only whilst manoeuvring, may exhaust or be unable to use her supply of fuel oil and be compelled to use diesel oil to continue the voyage. The extra cost involved would not be admissible in general average; in any case, it could hardly be contended that the adventure was "in peril" whilst an alternative supply of bunkers remained.)

Under all previous versions of this Rule, allowances in general average in respect of ship's materials and stores could be made "*when and only when an ample supply of fuel had been provided*". The effect of these words was to override Rule D and to make it a condition precedent to a claim under the Rule that the ship was seaworthy, so far as the provision of fuel was concerned, at the beginning of the relevant stage of the voyage, irrespective of whether under the contract of carriage the shipowner was under any liability for unseaworthiness or failure to use due diligence to make the ship seaworthy. Furthermore, the words "only when" prevented any such claim being made under the lettered Rules. **9.10**

The omission of these words in the current 1994 version of Rule IX clearly absolves the average adjuster from any necessity or obligation to investigate the sufficiency or otherwise of the quantity of fuel originally supplied (and as to which see paragraph 9.04, above). This onus now passes to the cargo interests called upon to contribute to the general average charges and is to be highly deprecated, even if the change may appear to be sanctioned by Rule D. Cargo interests should not be obliged to do their own detective work and then contest payment on such questionable allowances; far better that the adjustment should never be prepared with its attendant costs.

If the omission was on the ground that, if it is the duty of the charterer to provide and pay for the fuel, it is unreasonable that the shipowner should be deprived of his right to claim contribution simply because the supply of fuel was inadequate, this seems to ignore the fact that even if it be the charterer's duty to provide and pay for fuel, it remains the master's duty to ensure that he has such a supply before he sails[10] and the shipowner is responsible for the master's failure to do so.[11]

"for the common safety" See commentary under Rule A.[12] **9.11**

"at a time of peril" For the purposes of Rule A and the other Rules which refer to "the common safety", the peril must be real but it need not be immediate. It may have been intended in 1890, by the emphatic use of the twin expressions "for the common safety" and "at a time of peril", to make it necessary for the ship to be in the grip of the peril before this Rule could apply, but it is submitted that in modern times the words do not have so drastic an effect. In practice, the words "at a time of peril" are considered not to modify the ordinary meaning of "for the common safety".

This particular problem was raised at the Stockholm Conference in 1924 when one delegate questioned at what time a state of peril began and the master became entitled to burn the cargo or ship's stores. Was it only when the very last drop of fuel had been exhausted? It was his

[10] *Park v. Duncan* (1898) 25 R. 528, Ct. of Sess.
[11] *McIver v. Tate* [1903] 1 K.B. 382.
[12] See paras. A.17 *et seq.*, *ante*.

opinion—and it appears the sensible approach—that a "time of peril" would commence at a much earlier stage if the cargo and/or ship's stores, etc., were such that they would not burn alone, but only in conjunction[13] with the ship's bunkers.

For the sake of completeness, it may be mentioned that a state of peril would be deemed to exist when the ship's own supply of fuel had been consumed, even though the cargo was itself "fuel".

9.12 **"the general average shall be credited with the estimated cost of the fuel which would otherwise have been consumed..."** It is entirely appropriate and in accordance with equitable principles that a credit should be given to general average when general average has been charged with something which should properly be provided by the ship interests, whether shipowner or charterer. The Rule, however, provides that this credit shall be given only in those infrequent cases where ship's materials and stores may be used, and not in the more likely situation where cargo is consumed. If this gives an immediate impression of being a concession to the cargo, in that the whole of its value will be made good, the reality is that the "no credit" provision is an unwarranted gift to the party responsible for paying for normal bunker consumption, as the following hypothetical example will show:

A loaded tanker is obliged to use part of the oil cargo when her own bunkers are exhausted. The value of the cargo consumed is 10,000, chargeable to general average, and the cost of the normal bunkers saved would be 8,000.

	Contributory Value		*General Average*
SHIP	40%	liable for	4,000
CARGO	60%	"	6,000
	100%	liable for	10,000

Financial Result

SHIP	liable for 4,000 but saves 8,000	= PROFIT	of 4,000
CARGO	liable for 6,000	= LOSS	of 6,000

9.13 These calculations assume that the *Shipowner* is responsible for providing the bunkers. When a *Time Charterer* is responsible for the supply, the overall Financial Result will be that the cargo is still condemned to suffer a loss of 6,000, essentially to subsidise the normal running expenses of the ship interests, and on this occasion the Time Charterer profits to

[13] In his *Handbook of Average*, Manley Hopkins records a remarkable case in 1856 of a steamer being driven to burn 150 pigs for fuel. Clearly these would not burn alone and without some coal to support combustion.

the extent of 8,000 (the cost of the bunkers saved), and the Shipowner loses 4,000 (his general average contribution).

The equitable principles of general average can only be served by an adjustment on the following lines:

	General Average	Debit: SHIP Interests
Value of Cargo consumed as Fuel	10,000	
Credit: Estimated cost of Fuel which would otherwise have been consumed	8,000	8,000
NET	2,000	

Apportioned

SHIP—	40%	pays	800 .		800
CARGO—	60%	pays	1,200 . .	1,200	
	100%	pays	2,000		
				1,200	8,800

Financial Result

CARGO receives value of cargo consumed		10,000
Less: Proportion G.A., as above		1,200
Net: Receives		8,800
SHIP pays, as above	8,800	

Rule X

Expenses at Port of Refuge, etc.

English Law and Practice

10.01 *In contrast to the situation relating to most other of the York-Antwerp Rules, English law and practice on the subject of Port of Refuge Expenses played little or no part in the development of Rule X; in fact, it might be truer to state that any contribution it made was of a negative character in that English mercantile interests may have been only too willing to escape from the somewhat complex and not entirely logical provisions of English law and practice.*

Except, therefore, for those few cases where a general average may still have to be adjusted in accordance with English law and practice, the following paragraphs 10.02 to 10.25 are not required reading.

10.02 Next to salvage charges, or the expenditure incurred in saving a ship and cargo from wreck, raising them when sunk, floating them when stranded, or otherwise rescuing them from imminent total loss, if not even before these in importance, on account of its greater frequency, comes the expenditure incurred by entering a port of refuge to repair damage.[1] This step on the part of the master is always one of grave responsibility. If taken without sufficient justification it may constitute a deviation with unfortunate consequences for the shipowner.[2] However, there are occasions on which the safety of the ship and cargo, and the lives of all on board, may make it imperative for the master to take this step. When resolved on, it is a measure involving sacrifice—the sacrifice of time and money. At first sight, therefore, it would seem that the act of putting into a port of refuge, if justifiable, must fall within the definition of an act of general average. On the other hand, it might be argued, and certainly used to be, that when the ship has been damaged by an accident so as to have been rendered unseaworthy, it immediately becomes the duty of the shipowner to take measures at his own expense, to restore her to a seaworthy condition in which the voyage can be

[1] Not all the cases on this topic involve deviating to an unscheduled port. See *Hobson v. Lord* 92 U.S. 397 (1875) (detention at port of call); *May v. Keystone Yellow Pine Co.* 117 Fed.Rep. 287 (1902) (delay at sea); *The Brig Mary* (1842) 1 Sprague 17; Fed.Cas. 9188.

[2] As to the effect of deviation on the contract of affreightment and on the right of the shipowner and cargo owner respectively to claim general average contribution, see the discussion on those questions; paras. 00.35–00.36 and 00.47, *ante*.

continued. If so, can it be said that the master's act in bearing up for the nearest place where the ship can be repaired is any more than the performance of the shipowner's duty?

This question gave rise to very considerable controversy throughout most of the nineteenth century, culminating in the bringing of two important test actions before the courts.[3] The decisions given in those two cases were not received with wholehearted satisfaction (Lowndes referred to them as "bundle of contradictions"), but they did enable the Association of Average Adjusters to revise and frame a number of Rules of Practice which ensured uniformity of practice amongst British adjusters on this most complex of subjects. The most important of these Rules are quoted immediately below, leaving until later a review and discussion of the situation leading up to the legal cases and the cases themselves. This order is adopted for the reason that, whereas the issues involved were of the utmost practical importance at the time the actions were fought, they are now of little more than academic interest having regard to the almost universal adoption of the York-Antwerp Rules. **10.03**

Rules of Practice

F8 Resort to Port of Refuge for General Average Repairs: Treatment of the Charges Incurred

"That when a ship puts into a port in consequence of damage which is itself the subject of general average, and sails thence with her original cargo, or a part of it, the outward as well as the inward port charges shall be treated as general average; and when cargo is discharged for the purpose of repairing such damage, the warehouse rent and reloading of the same shall, as well as the discharge, be treated as general average (See *Atwood v. Sellar.*)" **10.04**

F9 Resort to Port of Refuge on Account of Particular Average Repairs: Treatment of the Charges Incurred

"That when a ship puts into a port of refuge in consequences of damage which is itself the subject of particular average (or not of general average) and when the cargo has been discharged in consequence of such damage, the inward port charges and the cost of discharging the cargo shall be general average, the warehouse rent of cargo shall be a particular charge on cargo, and the cost of reloading and outward port charges shall be a particular charge on freight. (See *Svendsen v. Wallace.*)"

(Other Rules of Practice relating to the treatment of expenses at a port of refuge are quoted below.[4])

[3] *Atwood v. Sellar* (1880) 5 Q.B.D. 286; *Svendsen v. Wallace* (1885) 10 A.C. 404.

[4] F10 Treatment of Costs of Storage and Reloading at Port of Refuge.

That when the cargo is discharged for the purpose of repairing, re-conditioning, or diminishing damage to ship or cargo which is itself the subject of general average, the cost of storage on it and of reloading it shall be treated as general average, equally with the cost of discharging it.

Practice of average adjusters prior to 1879

10.05 The practice was as follows:

In most countries except Great Britain the entire expense incurred by putting into a port to repair was (as it still is) treated as general average: that is to say, the pilotage and port-charges going into the port and coming out; the cost of discharging the cargo, whether for its own safety or that of the ship, or both, for example if the ship were leaky and the cargo damaged; or to repair the ship, for example to lighten her and enable her to enter a dry dock; the warehouse rent of the cargo so discharged, and the cost of reloading it.[5] On the other hand, the cost of repairing the ship at the port of refuge was not so treated.[6] This was

F11 INSURANCE ON CARGO DISCHARGED UNDER AVERAGE.

That in practice, where the cost of insurance has been reasonably incurred by the shipowner, or his agents, on cargo discharged under average, such cost shall be treated as part of the cost of storage.

F12 EXPENSES AT A PORT OF REFUGE (CUSTOM OF LLOYD'S, AMENDED, 1890–91).

When a ship puts into a port of refuge on account of accident and not in consequence of damage which is itself the subject of general average, then on the assumption that the ship was seaworthy at the commencement of the voyage, the Custom of Lloyd's is as follows:

(a) All costs of towage, pilotage, harbour dues, and other extraordinary expenses incurred in order to bring the ship and cargo into a place of safety, are general average. Under the term "extraordinary expenses" are not included wages or victuals of crew, coals, or engine stores, or demurrage.

(b) The cost of discharging the cargo, whether for the common safety, or to repair the ship, together with the cost of conveying it to the warehouse, is general average. The cost of discharging the cargo on account of damage to it resulting from its own *vice propre*, is chargeable to the owners of the cargo.

(c) The warehouse rent, or other expenses which take the place of warehouse rent, of the cargo when so discharged is, except as under, a special charge on the cargo.

(d) The cost of reloading the cargo, and the outward port charges incurred through leaving the port of refuge, are, when the discharge of cargo falls in general average, a special charge on freight.

(e) The expenses referred to in clause (d) are charged to the party who runs the risk of freight—that is, wholly to the charterer—if the whole freight has been prepaid; and, if part only, then in the proportion which the part prepaid bears to the whole freight.

(f) When the cargo, instead of being sent ashore, is placed on board hulk or lighters during the ship's stay in port, the hulk-hire is divided between general average, cargo, and freight, in such proportions as may place the several contributing interests in nearly the same relative positions as if the cargo had been landed and stored.

F13 TREATMENT OF COSTS OF EXTRAORDINARY DISCHARGE.

That no distinction be drawn in practice between discharging cargo for the common safety of ship and cargo, and discharging it for the purpose of effecting at an intermediate port or ports of refuge repairs necessary for the prosecution of the voyage.

F18 TREATMENT OF DAMAGE TO CARGO CAUSED BY DISCHARGE, STORING, AND RELOADING.

That damage necessarily done to cargo by discharging, storing, and reloading it, be treated as general average when, and only when, the cost of those measures respectively is so treated.

[5] As to fuel, see Gourlie, p. 243.

[6] Temporary repairs at an intermediate port (where permanent repairs cannot be made), if necessary to enable the ship to proceed on her voyage, are treated as general average in the United States: *Hobson v. Lord* 92 U.S. 397 (1875); *Bowring v. Thebaud* 42 Fed.Rep. 796 (1890); *The Star of Hope* 17 Wall. 651 (1873); *Phillips on Insurance* (5th ed.), para. 1500.

dealt with as general average only if the damage were occasioned by a sacrifice for the common safety, but not otherwise. This item was not treated as a part of the sacrifice involved in bearing up for the port of refuge, since the ship must have been repaired sooner or later. With some unimportant exceptions, this may be not to have been the universal rule over the European Continent and in North and South America.

In Britain, for a long period, the same rule prevailed in practice. But about the beginning of the nineteenth century a practice grew up amongst British adjusters, which amounted to this, that so much only of the expense of putting into port to repair should be treated as general average as was incurred up to the time when the ship and cargo were placed out of danger. That is to say the pilotage and port charges incurred in going into the port of refuge and the expense of discharging the cargo, whether for safety or to repair[7] the ship, were treated as general average; but all subsequent expenses were allotted to the particular interests immediately concerned: the warehouse rent of the cargo was made a specific charge on the cargo, and the expenses of setting forth again on the voyage (for example the cost of re-loading the cargo, and the outward pilotage and port charges) were treated as a specific charge on freight.[8] **10.06**

This treatment was applied indiscriminately to all cases of putting into a port of refuge, no matter whether the damage to the ship which occasioned the putting in had been the result of an accident or of a sacrifice for the common safety, such as the cutting away of a mast.

Eventually, after holding its ground for almost a century, the practice was assailed, and it is interesting to record that Richard Lowndes was the protagonist. In his early career he was the staunchest advocate of the British practice (at the conference leading to the York Rules of 1864 he was the only delegate to urge its retention) and he continued to support the practice strongly in the first two editions of this work. By 1874, however, he was beginning to entertain doubts as to the correctness of his earlier views and, by the time the third edition was published, the *volte-face* was complete. **10.07**

His new views were based, not on the theory of "completion of the adventure", but rather on the principle that when a master decides to put into a port of refuge, he effectively decides at the same time to leave that port after repairs. In similar fashion, a decision to discharge the cargo necessarily entailed its subsequent reloading, etc. From 1876

[7] The expense of discharging the cargo at a port of refuge in order to effect repairs was invariably charged to general average, even when the ship and cargo were in perfect safety in the port. To a modern eye, this practice hardly appears to accord with the theory that the general average terminated as soon as physical safety had been attained, but it should be remembered that in the times when the practice originated ships were built of wood and that, as a general rule when the cargo had to be discharged, it was usually because the ship was leaking and matters of this kind were best regulated by simple rules of thumb.

[8] The beginning of this practice may be seen in some of the earlier editions of *Stevens on Average*, and in Benecke.

onwards, Lowndes gave effect to these new views in his business practice, but, in the first instance, limited their application to those cases where the necessity to put into a port of refuge arose from a general average sacrifice as opposed to an accidental cause. His adjustments were "after more or less of discussion, passed by underwriters",[9] but eventually one such case came before the courts.

The Authorities

Atwood v. Sellar[10]

10.08 The ship *Sullivan Sawin*, on a voyage in the year 1877 from Savannah to Liverpool, met with a gale in which, for the general safety, the master was compelled to cut away her fore-topmast and this in its fall did such damage to her hull that the master was obliged to put into Charleston to repair it, for which purpose he had to discharge a portion of the cargo and to place it in a warehouse. After repairing, this cargo was reladen and the vessel then completed her voyage to Liverpool. The case (which was an agreed case stated by an arbitrator) then set forth the practice of adjusters, which, it was stated, had been for the last 70 or 80 years (and then was) in all such cases, whether the putting in were as in that case the result of a sacrifice or of a mere accident, to allow in general average the expense of going into port and discharging the cargo, but to treat the warehouse rent as a special charge on the cargo and the reloading, together with the outward port charges, as a special charge on the freight.

The plaintiffs in this case claimed that the whole of the expenses above enumerated should be treated as general average. The defendants contended that they were only liable to pay in conformity with the practice.

10.09 In the Queen's Bench Division,[11] judgment was given by a majority of the court,[12] in favour of the plaintiffs.

Cockburn C.J.[13] began by considering what, independently of the practice of average adjusters, was the principle or rule of law applicable to this case. That the expenses in question (those of quitting the port, and of warehousing and reshipping the cargo) should, according to legal principles, be made the subject of general average, appeared to him to flow necessarily from the fundamental principle on which the whole doctrine of general average rests; namely, that all loss which arises from extraordinary sacrifices made, or expenses incurred, for the preservation of the ship and cargo, must be borne proportionately by all who are interested.

[9] 3rd ed., p. 107.
[10] (1879) 4 Q.B.D. 342.
[11] (1879) 4 Q.B.D. 342.
[12] Cockburn C.J. and Mellor J.; Manisty J. dissenting.
[13] (1879) 4 Q.B.D. 342 at 354.

"It is admitted on all hands that the expenses of entering the port of refuge should be carried to general average. Logically, it would seem to follow that, as the coming out of port is—at least where the common adventure is intended to be, and is, further prosecuted—the necessary consequence of going in, the expenses incidental to the later stage of the proceedings should stand on the same footing as the former."

In the Court of Appeal[14] the case was argued before Bramwell, Baggallay, and Thesiger L.JJ., and the Court of Appeal unanimously confirmed the judgment of the Queen's Bench Division. Their judgment was delivered by Thesiger L.J. who stated: **10.10**

"The going into port, the unloading, warehousing, and reloading of the cargo and the coming out of port, are at all events part of one act or operation contemplated, resolved upon, and carried through for the common safety and benefit and properly to be regarded as continuous. The shipowner is at least entitled to reship the goods and prosecute his voyage with them; and the expenses necessary for that purpose, being *ex hypothesi* consequent upon a damage voluntarily incurred for the general advantage, should legitimately be the subject of general average contribution, or to use the language of Lord Tenterden in his work on shipping, 'if the damage to be repaired be in itself an object of contribution, it seems reasonable that all expenses necessary, although collateral to the reparation, should also be objects of contribution; the accessory should follow the nature of its principal.'"

After carefully reviewing the previous decisions and dicta, Thesiger L.J. concluded:

"The result of this review of the authorities is to confirm the opinion which, apart from authority, we entertain and have already expressed upon the question submitted to us. The practice, then, of the average adjusters, as stated in the special case, appears to us to be neither founded upon true principles, nor to be in accordance with the views of the textwriters, and, so far as there is case authority upon the matter, it appears to us to be opposed to legal decisions."

The effect of the decision of the Court of Appeal in *Atwood v. Sellar* may be summarised as follows: **10.11**

In circumstances in which a vessel goes into a port of refuge in order to repair damage caused by a general average sacrifice, the expenses necessarily involved in so doing are a general average expenditure. This is certainly true of the expenses going in: for example pilotage, towage and harbour dues, etc. Also it is true of the necessary expenses of leaving the port of refuge provided that the acts of going into and coming out of the port can fairly be treated as: "parts of one act or operation contemplated, resolved upon and carried through for the common safety and benefit and properly to be regarded as continuous."[15]

This decision was regarded as conclusive on the question immediately

[14] (1880) 5 Q.B.D. 286.
[15] (1880) 5 Q.B.D. 286 at 290, *per* Thesiger L.J.

before the courts, where the ship had put into port on account of a sacrifice, and no attempt was made to carry the case up to the House of Lords. It was not so clear, however, whether the change in practice was to stop here, or whether it should be extended to the case of putting into a port of refuge on account of *accidental* damage, as contended by Lowndes in the third edition of this work.[16] With the usual courage of his convictions, and with the tacit approval of the marine insurance market in Liverpool (but not London), Lowndes changed his practice and allowed as general average the costs of entering and leaving port, and of discharging, warehousing and reloading cargo, even in those cases where the necessity to seek a port of refuge arose from accidental damage. As anticipated, this changed practice was challenged in the courts.

Svendsen v. Wallace

10.12 Having got a fair and straightforward case where the facts were simple, the advocates of the Custom of Lloyd's, as defendants representing the cargo, resisted the claim made on them for their share, as general average, of the items in dispute; namely, the cost of warehousing and reloading the cargo and of the expenses of quitting the port to resume the voyage. This they did on the twofold plea: first, of custom and secondly, of principle. Their first plea was that there was a certain ancient and well-known custom amongst shipowners, shippers and consignees of cargo, assured, underwriters and average adjusters, applicable to voyages from Rangoon to Liverpool (this being the voyage in the case) in virtue of which, when a ship puts into a port of refuge to repair accidental damage to the ship, the cost of warehousing the cargo (meaning the warehouse rent) was chargeable as a particular charge upon the cargo; and the expense of reloading it and the outward port charges and pilotage to sea were chargeable as a particular charge on the freight. Secondly, they pleaded that, independently of the custom, this mode of treating the expenses in question was right in principle.

10.13 The facts were these: The ship *Olaf Trygvason*, owned in Norway, on a voyage with a cargo of rice from Rangoon for Liverpool, sprang a dangerous leak in bad weather, which obliged the captain, for the safety of ship and cargo, to put into Rangoon for repair. When in port the cargo was necessarily landed in order to repair the ship and also, as was pointed out in the House of Lords, but not till then, for the common safety[17]: it was warehoused, and after the ship had been repaired it was re-shipped.

At Guildhall and in the Queen's Bench Division, the first plea relating to custom was dismissed, both courts holding that there was no reasonable evidence of a usage controlling the contract.

[16] At pp. 109, 110.

[17] Even in port, the vessel was making $10\frac{1}{2}$ inches of water per hour.

The next step, therefore, was to obtain the judgment of Lopes J. on the question of whether the practice referred to was right in principle. As to this the learned judge, after hearing the arguments, decided against the defendants. He was bound, he said, by the decision in *Atwood v. Sellar* for he could see no practical distinction between the two cases.

> "The putting into a port of refuge, if necessary, is an act of voluntary sacrifice, undertaken for the common benefit of the adventure, ship, cargo, and freight, and I think every expense consequent upon it, incurred to enable the ship afterwards to proceed safely on her voyage with her cargo so as to earn the freight, is incurred for the common benefit of the adventure, and is chargeable to general average."[18]

A majority decision in the Court of Appeal reversed Lopes J. Brett M.R. regarded the expenses subsequent to entry and unloading as disconnected from the going in; the proximate motive in warehousing cargo being quite detached from any question of preservation or safety of the ship, and the proximate motive in coming out being the intention to proceed with the voyage, not that of escaping from danger. He continued: **10.14**

> "When the cargo is landed, it may or may not, according to its own nature, or the circumstances of the locality, require to be warehoused or otherwise protected. It may, in consequence of partial damage already suffered, or from its own nature, require for its own safety to be manipulated, as, for instance, to be unpacked or dried; but such acts cannot possibly be necessary for the safety or preservation of the ship. She is at that moment safe or unsafe; but these acts cannot contribute in any way to her safety if she is unsafe. They cannot be said to be a part of the act of going into port to repair; they have no reference to the act of repairing, or of putting the ship into a position in which she can be repaired. They are, therefore, not within the principle. The repairing of the ship has nothing to do with the safety of the cargo. It is done in respect of the ship alone. The reloading of the cargo and the outward expenses are expenses of acts done when both ship and cargo are safe from existing danger, and are, therefore, not within the rule. They cannot be said to be a part of the act of placing the ship in a position to be repaired. Unless, therefore, we are bound by authority to hold otherwise, I am of opinion that, according to the law of England, when a ship is obliged, for the safety of ship and cargo, to go into and goes into a port of distress in order to repair damage done by sea peril, the expenses of going into the port are general average expenses; that if it is necessary for the safety of both ship and cargo to unload the cargo, or if it is necessary to unload the cargo in order to repair the ship, though it is not necessary for the safety of the cargo, the expense of unloading the cargo is a general average expense; but if the unloading of the cargo is not for either of these causes the expense of unloading is not a general average expense. I am of opinion, in the same way and in the same case, that the expenses of warehousing, guarding, or manipulating the cargo, of repairing the ship, of reloading the cargo, of taking the ship out of port, of the charges of going out of port, are not general average expenses."[19]

[18] (1883) 11 Q.B.D. 616 at 617.
[19] (1884) 13 Q.B.D. 69 at 77.

10.15 Distinguishing *Atwood v. Sellar*, Brett M.R. said:

> "The real ground of the decision was, I think, that where the putting into port for repairs is the necessary consequence of a previous general average sacrifice, the law of England is as elastic in respect of the subsequent acts done and expenses incurred in the port as the American and other laws are stated to be in all cases of a ship necessarily putting into a port of distress to repair. And for that proposition there were, before the decision in *Atwood v. Sellar*,[20] many weighty dicta by English writers of authority and English judges, but all which dicta threw a distinction between the going into a port of distress in consequence of a voluntary sacrifice, and of putting into port in consequence of a particular average damage. I adopt that distinction because I do not think that we are bound in the present case by the decision in *Atwood v. Sellar*,[21] and the propriety of that decision, with reference to the facts on which it was decided, we are not at liberty to question."[22]

Baggallay L.J. dissented exclusively on the ground that the decision in *Atwood v. Sellar*, which he considered to be right, obliged them in consistency to decide the present case in the same way.

10.16 This decision was affirmed in the House of Lords,[23] Lord Blackburn saying[24]:

> "I do not think it necessary to inquire what would be the proper course if the seeking the port of refuge had been solely for the purpose of doing repairs, the cargo not being in any danger. Such a case may perhaps sometimes, though rarely, occur. Nor do I think it necessary to inquire what would be the proper course if the ship and cargo were both safe in the harbour of refuge, and the unloading of the cargo was entirely for the purpose of facilitating the repairs. Such a case seems more likely to happen than that first supposed. I think, on examining the two adjustments, and exercising the power which I have assumed to be given, there can be no doubt that the cargo on board the ship, leaking to the extent which she did, was not safe even in harbour until the ship was so far lightened that she could be taken into dry dock. Should the expense of reloading her, after the repairs were made, be charged to freight, the goods having been taken out under such circumstances? I think it should."[25]

10.17 In his judgment, therefore, the cargo owners were not chargeable with a general average contribution in respect of reshipping the cargo; the further question of the expenses coming out he expressly left undecided. These expenses were small and enough had already been paid to cover them. Lord Blackburn also discussed and criticised *Atwood v. Sellar*[26] and in view of his observations it is probably doubtful if the decision of

[20] (1880) 5 Q.B.D. 286.
[21] *Ibid.*
[22] (1884) 13 Q.B.D. 69 at 79.
[23] (1885) 10 A.C. 404.
[24] (1885) 10 A.C. 404 at 416.
[25] *A fortiori*, in the second case put by Lord Blackburn, namely where the unloading is solely for the purpose of repairing particular average to the ship, the cost of reloading cannot be general average.
[26] (1879) 4 Q.B.D. 342

the Court of Appeal in that case can be regarded as an entirely satisfactory authority. Lords Watson and Fitzgerald concurred, but gave no reasons.

Principles to be deduced

It is submitted that the resolutions of the Association of Average Adjusters accurately state the law subject to the following reservations: **10.18**

(1) *Atwood v. Sellar* is only to be relied upon as authority for the proposition that the cost of discharging, warehousing and reloading is to be treated as general average if such cost, on the facts of the particular case, can be said to have been incurred for the preservation of both ship and cargo and that therefore such cost is of its own right an extraordinary expenditure of a general average nature or is necessarily incident to a general average act.

(2) *Svendsen v. Wallace* is not to be relied upon as authority for the proposition that where the cost of reloading and outward port charges are a particular charge on freight, such charge falls on the cargo owner if, and to the extent that, freight is prepaid and non-returnable.[27] None of the judgments expressly deals with this point and as the freight was partly prepaid in this case, such a proposition seems inconsistent with the speech of Lord Blackburn, who said that if: "the cost of reshipping is properly charged to freight the defendants [cargo-owners] are not liable to pay any part of it."[28] Rule F9, read literally, accurately summarises the decision in the case so far as the incidence of the cost of reloading cargo is concerned. The difficulty arises over what is meant by "freight". It is clear from the arguments and the speeches that the rival contentions were (a) that the expense was incurred for the common benefit and should be treated as general average expenditure, and (b) that it was necessarily incurred by the shipowner in order to fulfil his contract.[29] The fact that freight is or is not absolutely prepaid has no bearing upon a shipowner's obligations under a contract of carriage and only affects the incidence of the loss of freight if the voyage is frustrated. It should therefore have no bearing on the incidence of the cost of reloading, which, unlike the cost of storage ashore, is, in the absence of contractual provisions to the contrary, an obligation of the shipowner. A consideration of where the risk of loss lies is peculiar to general average and should not be imported into a realm which *ex hypothesi* is not general average. Furthermore, if one is to look at the incidence of the risk of losing the freight, and if (as *Svendsen v.* **10.19**

[27] *Cf.* Rules of Practice, Nos. F9 and F12, App. 3, paras. 70.36 and 70.39, *post*.
[28] (1885) 10 A.C. 404 at 416.
[29] *Ibid.* at 417.

Wallace affirms) it is the duty of the shipowner to reload the cargo, freight or at least an equivalent amount is at the risk of the shipowner, for if he failed to reload and on-carry the cargo, he could not rely upon the fact that the freight had been prepaid as a defence to an action by the cargo owner for damages for such failure. Such damages would probably be the cost of reloading together with the freight paid by the cargo owner to the person who in fact carried the cargo for the remaining part of the voyage.

This case is also no authority for the proposition that the inward port charges and the cost of discharging cargo are in every case general average expenditures, irrespective of whether or not the vessel put into a port of refuge for the preservation of both ship and cargo. This is made clear by the decision in *Hamel v. P. & O. S.N. Co.*,[30] although it related to damage during discharge and not to the cost of such discharge.

10.20 In that case a ship, having through perils of navigation sustained injuries which prevented her from proceeding upon her voyage, put back into port for repairs. To enable her to be repaired it was necessary to unload the cargo, during which process the cargo was damaged. The cargo was at no time in any danger and Alverstone C.J. held that the cargo owners were not entitled to contribution in general average from the owners of the ship on the grounds that:

> "if the consequence of a peril of the sea is merely to render one part of the venture abortive, merely to render the ship unfit to proceed or the cargo unfit to be carried further on the voyage, acts done merely to make the ship fit to proceed or done merely to make the cargo fit to be carried further on the voyage are not general average acts and do not afford ground for a general average contribution."

Application of the Principle

Where is point of safety?

10.21 What is the precise point at which the general average is to cease, on the ground that a state of safety has been attained? What is to be considered as a state of safety?

Even in the pursuit of safety, the master is not at liberty wholly to neglect his ultimate purpose of completing the voyage. Supposing there are two ports of refuge which he has to choose between, the first nearer and cheaper to enter, so far as regards the mere cost of going in, than the second, but the first a place at which the ship cannot be repaired, while at the second she can; the second is that which he ought, if

[30] [1908] 2 K.B. 298.

practicable, to select. Were he not to do so, he might even be committing a deviation. He is bound to pursue the direct course of his voyage, unless driven from it by necessity; in which case, he must depart from it no further than is requisite in order that he may resume his voyage with safety. The liberty thus given to depart from the direct course is really given only as a means towards eventually completing his voyage. He is bound so to shape his course towards the place of destination as to obtain that combination of directness, dispatch and safety, which on the whole is best adapted to the completion of his undertaking. Hence, if he carries the ship to a place where she cannot be repaired, when he might with prudence have gone to a place where she could, he has not performed his duty.

As a rule, then, the "place of safety" to which the master may take the ship at the charge of the general average is the nearest port at which she can be repaired. The term "nearest" must be understood not with reference to mere mileage; it is that port which, on the whole, in the actual circumstances of the ship, is the fittest place for repairing; convenience and cheapness being fairly balanced against the advantages of mere nearness.[31]

Cost of towage to a place of repair

It sometimes happens that such a port can only be reached in two stages. The ship may have to be brought to anchor in a sheltered roadstead, in order to wait for a tug to tow her to the repairing port. In this roadstead she may be in a sort of temporary safety; she might even lie there for ever without danger. Still, as this is a place to which the captain would not be justified in going, except as a step towards entering a proper harbour for repairing, and as, consequently, entering the roadstead can only be regarded as one part of a larger entire operation, the cost of towing the ship from the roadstead to the port is admitted into general average.[32] **10.22**

Expenses at port of refuge

Cost of pumping. When the port of refuge at which the ship is to be repaired has been reached, it is not always the case that the ship and cargo are at that moment in safety. The ship may be leaky, and may require pumping to keep her afloat. The cost of labourers hired for this purpose, while the cargo remains on board, is properly admitted into general average.[33] **10.23**

[31] See *Phelps v. Hill* [1891] 1 Q.B. 605, C.A.

[32] As to when salvage services cease by reason of the vessel having reached a place of safety, see *The Troilus* [1951] A.C. 820. See also *China Pacific v. Food Corpn. of India* [1982] A.C. 939 at 956.

[33] *Birkley v. Presgrave* (1801) 1 East 220.

Discharging cargo. With regard to the discharging of the cargo, it is hardly necessary to add anything to what has been already set down. No question arises if it is discharged for the common safety. If the cargo is not itself in danger and is discharged merely to enable the ship to be repaired, the cost of discharge had always been treated as a general average expense, but it is impossible to justify this course unless on the facts such discharge can be said to be directly caused by an antecedent general average act. This seems scarcely possible if the common danger has been averted. The only other possible justification is that the practice has become inveterate.[34] When the discharge is for the exclusive benefit of the cargo or some part of it, for example when cargo has been accidentally wetted by sea-water, and must be landed in order to be opened out and dried, the practice is to treat the cost of discharging, not as general average, but as a special charge on cargo.

10.24 **Reloading charges.** These have been discussed above.[35] The practice is that they are charged either to general average or as a special charge on freight, according to whether or not the putting into port was a consequence of damage, itself the subject of general average.[36]

One of the Customs of Lloyd's[37] provides that, when treated as a special charge on freight, the reloading charges:

> "are charged to the party who runs the risk of freight—that is, wholly to the charterer—if the whole freight has been prepaid; and, if part only, then in the proportion which the part prepaid bears to the whole freight."

It is submitted that this Custom is wholly indefensible on any rational or legal ground, and that the whole of any special charge on freight should be borne by the carrier, regardless of whether any part of the freight has been prepaid.

10.25 **Expenses consequent upon putting into port of refuge to restow cargo.** It is not uncommon for deck cargoes of timber to shift in heavy weather, thereby causing the vessel to list and with the possibility of capsizing. Or an under-deck cargo of ore concentrates may liquefy and turn into slurry and similarly endanger the vessel's stability and the common adventure. In such situations the vessel will often be obliged to put into a port of refuge for the common safety and to discharge or restow the cargo for the safe prosecution of the voyage.

There seems to be no decision of the courts on how the expenses incurred at the port of refuge are to be dealt with, but it is submitted that the correct practice is as follows:

[34] See para. 10.06, n. 7, *ante*; *Svendsen v. Wallace* (1884) 13 Q.B.D. 69 at 87, *per* Bowen L.J.; Rule of Practice F12(b), para. 70.39, *post*.

[35] See paras. 10.02–10.20, *ante*.

[36] See Rules of Practice F8 and F9, App. 3, paras. 70.35–70.36, *post*.

[37] See Rule of Practice F12(3), App. 3, para. 70.39, *post*.

Entry charges. On the assumption that the common safety of the adventure was imperilled, the entry charges are allowed as general average.

Discharging or restowing expenses. If, even in the comparative shelter of the port, there is still some danger of the vessel capsizing, the cost of discharging or restowing only as much cargo as is necessary to secure stability and safety is also allowed as general average. In the vast majority of cases, however, safety will have been attained on entry into the port, and the cost of discharging or restowing cargo will then be treated as a special charge to be borne by the carrier.

Storage charges ashore. If incurred, they are treated as a special charge on cargo.

Reloading (if any) and outward charges. These are treated as a special charge to be borne by the carrier.

The submissions made above are all subject to the qualification that if the shifting of cargo is a consequence of a breach by the shipowner or charterer of his obligations under his contract of carriage, the whole expense falls to be borne by him.

Historical Development and Practice of Rule X(a)

Glasgow Resolutions 1860 **10.26**

At the International Conference at Glasgow in 1860, the complex treatment of port of refuge expenses by British average adjusters[38] was set aside in favour of the "completion of the adventure" theory practised elsewhere in the world, and the following Resolution was passed by 24 votes to 5:

> "(6) That the expense of warehouse rent at a port of refuge on cargo necessarily discharged there, the expense of re-shipping it, and the outward port charges at that port, ought to be allowed in general average."

It was deemed unnecessary to make provision for dealing with inward port charges and the expense of discharging cargo as these were universally allowed as general average.

York Rules 1864 **10.27**

On this occasion, the wording of the Rule was much improved and made more precise, but its provisions were still directed exclusively to the cost

[38] See para. 10.06, *ante*.

of storing and reloading cargo and the outward port charges, it being taken for granted that the inward port charges and cost of discharging would be universally allowed as general average in the appropriate circumstances.

The first sentence of the Rule was passed unanimously, the only discussion taking place on the last sentence, which was added as an amendment by L. R. Baily.

Rule VII. Port of Refuge Expenses

> "When a ship shall have entered a port of refuge under such circumstances that the expenses of entering the port are admissible as general average, and when she shall have sailed thence with her original cargo or a part of it, the corresponding expenses of leaving such port shall likewise be so admitted as general average; and whenever the cost of discharging cargo at such port is admissible as general average, the cost of reloading and stowing such cargo on board the said ship, together with all storage charges on such cargo, shall likewise be so admitted. Except that any portion of the cargo left at such port of refuge, on account of its being unfit to be carried forward, or on account of the unfitness or inability of the ship to carry it, shall not be called on to contribute to such general average."

10.28 *York-Antwerp Rules 1877*

At the Conference at Antwerp in 1877, the 1864 Rule was re-affirmed in its main provisions, but the final sentence was expunged after considerable discussion. This discussion is not reported but from one of the reports issued prior to the Conference it may be conjectured that it proceeded on the basis that as any portions of cargo which had been left behind in a port of refuge had equally benefited with the rest by putting into a port of refuge they should not be exempted from contribution to general average.

It was made quite clear at the 1864 Conference that cargo left behind at a port of refuge would not be exempted from contribution to the inward port charges and the cost of discharge and previous sacrifices and expenses, that is, those from which it derived benefit, and one may wonder whether the 1877 delegates fully appreciated this fact and that the Rule did not deal with those particular earlier losses and expenses, but applied only to the cost of storage, reloading and outward port charges, etc.

10.29 *York-Antwerp Rules 1890*

The 1877 Rule made no attempt to define what was a port of refuge, nor did it make provision for expenses incurred as the result of an accident which occurred in a port of refuge, for example during the course of loading cargo, or when sailing but before having left the confines of the port. Only if a vessel entered a port as a port of refuge could the old Rule apply.

These two main deficiencies were remedied at the International Conference at Liverpool in 1890 and specific mention was at last made that inward port charges should be admissible as general average. The wording of the Rule was changed to the form we know it today and the Rule was sub-divided into three sections (a, b and c) to deal individually with the various charges incurred at a port of refuge. Rule X(a) deals only with inward and outward port charges:

> "When a ship shall have entered a port or place of refuge, or shall have returned to her port or place of loading, in consequence of accident, sacrifice, or other extraordinary circumstances which render that necessary for the common safety, the expenses of entering such port or place shall be admitted as general average; and when she shall have sailed thence with her original cargo, or a part of it, the corresponding expenses of leaving such port or place, consequent upon such entry or return, shall likewise be admitted as general average."

York-Antwerp Rules 1924

No change.

York-Antwerp Rules 1950 **10.30**

The Rule of 1890 and 1924 was continued unchanged, but on this occasion a second paragraph was added to give recognition and authority to a practice which was already followed to a very large extent throughout the world, but on which at one time there had been some diversity of opinion, particularly in England.[39]

If, for the common safety, a vessel was obliged to put into a port of refuge at which there were no repair facilities, it would usually be necessary—after the immediate emergency was over—to move the vessel to another port where repairs could be carried out. In practical terms, both ports might be considered to be "ports of refuge", but it was argued, and with some reason, that if the vessel and her cargo were already in safety at the first port of refuge, it could hardly be suggested that the move to the second port was for the common safety, the only grounds for allowing the inward and outward port changes under the York-Antwerp Rules.

The practical view prevailed and the second paragraph was added in 1950:

> "When a ship is at any port or place of refuge and is necessarily removed to another port or place because repairs cannot be carried out in the first port or place, the provisions of this Rule shall be applied to the second port or place as if it were a port or place of refuge. The provisions of Rule XI shall be applied to the prolongation of the voyage occasioned by such removal."

[39] See Rule of Practice No. C3, para. 70.26, *post*.

The intention of the Conference was that the expenses incurred in proceeding to and entering "the second port or place", of detention there and of sailing thence to the point of deviation from the intended voyage or an equivalent point should be treated in the same manner as those incurred in relation to the first port. The Conference did not intend any distinction to be drawn between ports of refuge, loading and call. The practice of average adjusters gives effect to these intentions.[40]

York-Antwerp Rules 1974

10.31 In making the addition to this Rule at the 1950 Conference, it appears to have been overlooked that when a vessel required to move from one port of refuge to another because repairs could not be carried out at the first port, she would often be disabled and in need of towage assistance to the second port. As the numbered Rules of the York-Antwerp Rules have to be construed strictly, this omission concerning the cost of towage gave rise to numerous arguments in practice, it being contended (as with the 1924 Rule) that if the vessel and cargo were already in safety at the first port of refuge, the cost of towage was not for the common safety and should be treated as part of the cost of repairs.

This strict construction of the Rule was not in keeping with the true intention, and the situation was made clear in 1974 by the addition of the words:

> "and the cost of such removal including temporary repairs and towage shall be admitted as general average."

10.32 York-Antwerp Rules 1994

No change of any substance in practical effect, but two commas previously appearing after *place of refuge* and *extraordinary circumstances* in lines 1 and 3 of the first paragraph were deleted on this occasion. The purpose of this was to make it clear that the requirements imposed by the subsequent words of the Rule (*in consequence of accident . . . for the common safety*) applied equally to both a port or place of refuge and a port or place of loading, and thus to resolve a problem of construction mentioned in footnote 46 of paragraph 10.35 in the eleventh edition.

The second paragraph of the rule remains unchanged, but a number of delegates had proposed that temporary repairs and towage costs incurred in moving a vessel from one port of refuge at which repairs could not be effected to another should follow the cost of the repairs

[40] See also Rule of Practice No. C3, para. 70.26, *post*. Another Rule of Practice (No. C.4, para. 70.27, *post*) provides that a ship shall be deemed to be at a port or place of refuge, within the second paragraph, when the wages and maintenance of her master, officers and crew during any extra period of detention there would be admissible in general average under Rule XI.

carried out at the second port, rather than be charged automatically to general average. On this matter see also paragraphs 14.14 *et seq.*, below.

Rule X(a)

Expenses at Port of Refuge, etc

(a) When a ship shall have entered a port or place of refuge or shall have returned to her port or place of loading in consequence of accident, sacrifice or other extraordinary circumstances which render that necessary for the common safety, the expenses of entering such port or place shall be admitted as general average; and when she shall have sailed thence with her original cargo, or a part of it, the corresponding expenses of leaving such port or place consequent upon such entry or return shall likewise be admitted as general average.

When a ship is at any port or place of refuge and is necessarily removed to another port or place because repairs cannot be carried out in the first port or place, the provisions of this Rule shall be applied to the second port or place as if it were a port or place of refuge and the cost of such removal including temporary repairs and towage shall be admitted as general average. The provisions of Rule XI shall be applied to the prolongation of the voyage occasioned by such removal.

Construction

First Paragraph

The broad intention of the first paragraph of this sub-rule is clear, namely: that where, solely for the common safety, a ship puts into any port or place, or, having left the confines of a loading port, puts back to the loading port, the expenses of entering or returning to that port or place shall be allowed in general average. Further, that if she sails thence in continuation of the common adventure, the expenses of leaving that port or place shall similarly be allowable. **10.33**

"shall have entered" These words apply when a vessel puts into a port of refuge from the sea or other waters outside the confines of the port, as opposed to putting back to a port of loading before having left its confines.

10.34 **"port or place"** The 8th/10th editions of this work construed only the word "place", submitting that, in the words of Scrutton L.J.[41]:

> "'place' following 'port' must be interpreted as *ejusdem generis* with 'port' as a locality having some or many of the characteristics of a port."

If the word "port" conjures up a vision of quays, wharves, warehouses and dock cranes, this might carry the inference that a deviation into and detention in some "place" such as a sheltered bay having none of these characteristics was not a proper subject for any allowances in general average. Nothing could be further from the truth!

The words "*port or place*" are better construed, not in isolation, but as part of the complete phrase from which they are taken: "port or place *of refuge*". The word "refuge" governs "port or place" and signifies the *purpose*[42] of the resort to the port or place and, indeed, is one of the essential characteristics of a port. As Lord Herschell said in the House of Lords in *Hunter v. Northern Marine Insurance Co.*[43]:

> "It appears to me that you must then consider what are commonly understood to be the characteristics of a port ... a port is a place where a vessel can lie in a position of more or less shelter from the elements ..."

Where an undamaged vessel seeks shelter in a protected bay merely *to avoid* a threatened storm or gale, this can never constitute a general average act, but if some accident or misfortune has already been suffered which places the ship and her cargo in peril, it matters not whether the vessel puts into a proper port or a mere *place* of refuge to secure the common safety. Indeed, in this modern age it is often impossible for mammoth tankers and bulk carriers to enter many of the ports of the world when they are in trouble, and they are then obliged to put into sheltered bays and anchorages in order to carry out repairs or other measures necessary to prosecute their voyages in safety.

This distinction between "port" and "place" is usually of little consequence in the context of this Rule X(a) as it is unlikely that any charges will be incurred for the use of a "place" of refuge, but the point becomes material when considering allowances for crew wages, etc., under Rule XI(a).[44]

It may be remarked that American adjusters have long interpreted "port or place" to include a sheltered bay or anchorage.

10.35 **"of refuge"** These words import the qualification that the presence of the ship in the port or place is "for the purpose of preserving from peril

[41] *Humber Conservancy Board v. Federated Coal & Shipping Co.* (1927) 29 Ll.L. Rep. 177 at 179, a case concerning a claim for pilotage dues under the Pilotage Act 1913, which were chargeable if the vessel made use of "any port". However, the Act incorporated the Merchant Shipping Act, which defined a *port* as including a *place*.

[42] *Maritime Insurance Co. v. Alianza Co.* [1907] 2 K.B. 660.

[43] (1888) 13 A.C. 717 at 726.

[44] See para. 11.05, *post*.

the property involved in a common maritime adventure".[45]

If a ship is obliged to enter a port for the common safety, but it so happens that she would in any event have entered that port as a port of call, can she be said to have entered a port of refuge? It is suggested that the port of call becomes a port of refuge but that "the expenses of entering such a port or place" are only so much of the total expenses as exceed the cost of entering the port as a port of call.

"or shall have returned to her port or place of loading" Reference is requested to the remarks in paragraph 10.29, above.

"in consequence of..." See paragraph 10.32, above.

"accident" It is suggested that the word involves some element of suddenness, the unforeseen and the fortuitous, but an accident is easier to recognise than to define. Thus, abnormal wear of machinery would not of itself be an accident although sudden breakage of machinery, even if due to normal wear and tear, might well be. In such a case the consequence may be an accident, though the cause was not.[46]

"sacrifice" See commentary in paragraph A.93 above and paragraph 50.04, below.

"other extraordinary circumstances" If there be a genus which includes **10.36** "accident" and "sacrifice" these words will be construed *ejusdem generis*, but in any event it is suggested that they should be construed strictly and full weight given to the adjective. Examples of such circumstances are serious depletion of the crew by an epidemic on board, a shortage of bunkers, drunken football supporters running amok on a ferry, or (an unusual case encountered in practice) where the master is murdered and the assailant is unknown and still at large. Further, the term might be construed to cover such situations as, for instance, where bearings slowly overheat and a serious breakdown can be expected within a short time unless precautionary repairs are carried out.

"for the common safety" For a full and comprehensive commentary on these important words, see paragraphs A17 *et seq.*, above, in Rule A.

"expenses of entering such port" If port dues for the whole or a part of **10.37** the time during which the vessel remains in port are payable on entry, these are part of the expenses of entering the port, but any other port dues fall to be considered under Rule XI(b).[47] It is submitted that damage suffered in entering port would not be an expense within this Rule,

[45] *Cf.* Rule A.
[46] See also the *Makis* decision on this word in Rule X(b) (para. 10.50, *post*), *Mills v. Smith* [1964] 1 Q.B. 30; and *R. v. Morris* [1972] 1 W.L.R. 728.
[47] See para. 11.23, *post*.

though it might give rise to a claim for contribution under the lettered Rules.

The "expenses of entering such port" are usually construed in practice to include the cost of reaching a berth within the port. This construction is important when dealing with a case such as the following: a ship may put into a port of refuge with machinery trouble, but only as far as the anchorage, it being thought that repairs can be accomplished there. On opening up, however, the damage is found to be more extensive than was expected, or shore cranes or other facilities are required, and the vessel will then shift to a berth within the port. It can be argued with good reason that the cost of this move should be dealt with in the same manner as the cost of the repairs, but in practice the cost of the move will be treated as the "expense of entering such port" and allowed as general average.

10.38 **"and when she shall have sailed thence with her original cargo, or a part of it,..."** Introduced in 1864, these words are perfectly adequate for those countries which admit a general average situation only when a vessel has cargo on board. However, for the benefit of those countries following the English legal system, which contemplates a general average situation even when the vessel is in ballast but under charter,[48] the words might with convenience be translated as *when she shall have sailed thence in continuance of her original voyage*. This probably reflects the precise intention of the framers of the Rule and would also be appropriate to those hull insurance conditions which accept a general average even when the vessel is in ballast and *not* under charter.

"corresponding expenses" Where a ship put back to her port of loading and, whilst she was there detained, ice formed in the river through which she had to proceed to sea, Bigham J. held, obiter,[49] that the shipowner could not recover contribution in respect of the expense of cutting a passage through the ice, as the expenses contemplated by the Rule were "the ordinary expenses of leaving the place of loading 'corresponding' to the expenses of entering such place". This seems a somewhat narrow construction to put upon the words. It is suggested that what is meant is that if the expense of getting to point A in a harbour is, and is allowed as, the expense of entering the port, but the expense of getting from point A to point B within the harbour is not such an expense, then, in the reverse direction, the expense of sailing outward from point A will be so allowed even if it greatly exceeds the corresponding expense of entry.

[48] See paras. 17.47–17.49, *post*.
[49] *Westall v. Carter* (1898) 3 Com.Cas. 112 at 114 (1890 Rules).

Second Paragraph

The broad intention[50] of this paragraph is clear, namely: if a ship is necessarily removed from a port or place of refuge at which repairs are impossible to another port or place in order that repairs may be effected, the second port or place shall also be treated as a port of refuge to which all the provisions of Rules X and XI will apply. Further, the cost of moving to the other port, including any necessary temporary repairs and towage, plus crew wages, etc., and bunkers, shall also be allowed as general average. **10.39**

"necessarily removed ... because repairs cannot be carried out" It is suggested that the repairs contemplated are those necessary to complete the voyage, which may or may not be permanent repairs. If it is possible, in a commercial sense, to effect such repairs, the paragraph will not apply. In *Marida v. Oswal Steel; The Bijela*[51] Hobhouse J. held that the paragraph did not apply if either temporary or permanent repairs were possible at the first port of refuge, and on the wording of the paragraph this conclusion seems inevitable.

"necessarily removed to another port" The other port to which the vessel is removed for repairs should be a *necessary* choice and, if only by reason of the new Rule Paramount, that choice should be reasonable to *all* the parties to the adventure. Cases are occasionally encountered in practice where the repairs necessary to complete the voyage might have been effected at a "neighbouring" port but, perhaps because the cargo has been forwarded under a Non-Separation Agreement,[52] the vessel then proceeds even on a trans-Atlantic or trans-Pacific voyage simply to secure the most advantageous repair charges. The costs of proceeding to such a repair port, or during any resulting over-extended delay, will but rarely be admitted as general average.

"the provisions of this Rule shall be applied to the second port..." This Rule X deals, effectively, only with the cost of:

(1) entering and leaving a port of refuge;
(2) discharging cargo; or
(3) storing and reloading cargo;

[50] See also paras. 10.30–10.31, *ante*.

[51] [1992] 1 Lloyd's Rep. 636 at 644. The decision was upheld in the Court of Appeal ([1993] 1 Lloyd's Rep. 411, Hoffmann L.J. dissenting) but reversed in the House of Lord ([1994] 1 Lloyd's Rep. 1), but in neither of those tribunals did the point under the second paragraph of Rule X(a) arise directly for decision. In the House of Lords the views of Hobhouse J. on the point are referred to without criticism, and it is submitted that his decision on the second paragraph of Rule X(a) remains valid. The case is discussed in more detail in connection with Rule XIV, para. 14.33 *et seq.*, *post.*

[52] See Rule G, *ante.*

and, whilst it might have made the matter clearer if Rule XI had also been expression mentioned, there can be no doubt that the port charges and crew wages, etc., incurred during the detention *at* the second port of refuge are independently recoverable under the provisions of Rule XI(b), which applies to any port or place, whether it be a first or second port of refuge.

10.40 **"the provisions of Rule XI shall be applied to the prolongation of the voyage occasioned by such removal."** Rule XI provides, *inter alia*, for the allowance in general average of crew wages, etc., and fuel and stores consumed during the periods:

(1) deviating into and out of a port of refuge; or
(2) detained in a port of refuge.

Both periods might naturally be construed as a "prolongation of the voyage", but in the particular context and development of the York-Antwerp Rules, the term "prolongation of the voyage" applies particularly to period (1) above.[53]

The important point to note is that the wages and maintenance of the crew and any fuel and stores consumed during any deviation to and from the second port of refuge are allowable as general average.

Historical Development and Practice of Rule X(b)

10.41 *Glasgow Resolutions 1860, York Rules 1864 and York-Antwerp Rules 1877*

These are considered under Rule X(a)[54] as the Rule was not then divided.

York-Antwerp Rules 1890

The 1877 Rule VII had stated that:

> "Whenever the cost of discharging cargo ... is admissible as general average, the cost of reloading and stowing such cargo ... shall likewise be so admitted."

but it failed to provide under what circumstances the discharge of the cargo should be admitted as general average. This was remedied at the International Conference at Liverpool in 1890 as follows:

[53] See also para. 11.08, *post*.
[54] See paras. 10.26–10.28, *ante*.

Rule X(b)

"The cost of discharging cargo from a ship, whether at a port or place of loading, call or refuge, shall be admitted as general average, when the discharge was necessary for the common safety or to enable damage to the ship, caused by sacrifice or accident during the voyage, to be repaired, if the repairs were necessary for the safe prosecution of the voyage."

York-Antwerp Rules 1924 **10.42**

The amendments made on this occasion consisted of allowing the cost of "handling on board" as well as of actual discharging, and of extending the allowance to the cost of handling and discharging, not only cargo, but fuel and stores as well. Before 1924 a certain difference in practice, at any rate in this country, had existed regarding the treatment of the cost of moving cargo from one hold to another or on to deck, without an actual discharge overside, in order to effect repairs; also of the cost of handling or discharging fuel or stores, neither of which were mentioned in the old rule. These difficulties were removed by the amendments made at that time.

A further amendment to the 1890 Rule was the deletion of the words "during the voyage" appearing in that Rule after the words "sacrifice or accident". These words were left out both by the Committee of the Association of Average Adjusters in their proposals for revision of the 1890 Rules and also by the Drafting Committee appointed by the International Law Association. The intention of the omission of these words was to include within the scope of the Rule cases in which a vessel has sustained damage which is entirely unsuspected at the time of her arrival at a port of loading, and it is not until her draught is increased by reasons of loading cargo that the damage becomes apparent (for example by water entering a hold; this incursion of water would constitute an "accident" within the meaning of the York-Antwerp Rules). In such circumstances, if cargo has to be discharged in order to effect repairs necessary for the safe prosecution of the voyage, and a claim is made by the shipowner for general average contribution, it would, of course, be open to the owner of the cargo called upon to contribute to exercise any rights of defence or counterclaim which he may have under the contract of affreightment.

Rule X(b)

"The cost of handling on board or discharging cargo, fuel or stores, whether at a port or place of loading, call or refuge, shall be admitted as general average when the handling or discharge was necessary for the common safety or to enable damage to the ship caused by sacrifice or accident to be repaired, if the repairs were necessary for the safe prosecution of the voyage."

York-Antwerp Rules 1950

No change.

York-Antwerp Rules 1974

10.43 The existing 1950 Rule was retained unaltered on this occasion but certain new wording was added at the end of the Rule to deny general average allowances in two specific instances:

> "(i) ... except in cases where the damage is discovered at a port or place of loading or call without any accident or other extraordinary circumstance connected with such damage having taken place during the voyage."

An example of the situation envisaged by this wording might be as follows: while a vessel is in a port loading cargo, or at a port of call, the opportunity is taken to open up the main engine for routine survey and inspection and a crack is discovered in the crankshaft for which repairs necessary for the safe prosecution of the voyage are essential. As there has been no sudden breakage or breakdown (which in itself would constitute an "accident"[55] within the meaning of the York-Antwerp Rules), there will now be no allowance in general average for any discharge, etc., of cargo unless it can reasonably be shown that the fracture owed its origin to some "accident"[56] or other extraordinary circumstance"[57] having taken place during the current voyage.

10.44

> "(ii) The cost of handling on board or discharging cargo, fuel or stores shall not be admissible as general average when incurred solely for the purpose of re-stowage due to shifting during the voyage unless such re-stowage is necessary for the common safety."

It is not uncommon for cargoes (particularly deck cargoes of timber) to shift in heavy weather, and for the carrying vessel to put into a port of refuge for the common safety and to re-stow the cargo. Whilst the cost of entering and leaving the port of refuge in such circumstances is admissible as general average, the cost of re-stowing is so allowed only if the common safety is at risk even in the port, that is, if the vessel may still capsize in the port unless the list is righted. In the majority of cases the vessel and her shifted cargo are in no danger within the port and the re-stowage is carried out essentially for the "safe prosecution of the voyage".[58]

Although there were no words in the York-Antwerp Rules 1950 to permit the allowance in general average of the cost of discharging or handling cargo except when necessary for the common safety, or to

[55] See para. 10.35, *ante*.
[56] *Ibid.*
[57] See para. 10.36, *ante*.
[58] See para. 10.49, *post*.

enable damage to the ship caused by sacrifice or accident to be repaired, if the repairs were necessary for the safe prosecution of the voyage, it is believed that in certain parts of the world, and notably on the West Coast of the United States, the Rules were construed on a less than strict basis and that the cost of re-stowing shifted cargoes was treated as general average.

To make the matter clear beyond doubt, express wording, as above, was introduced in 1974.

It may here be remarked that wages and maintenance of crew, etc. during detention of a vessel to re-stow cargo which has shifted were customarily allowed as general average under the 1950 Rules and the framers of the 1974 Rules accordingly felt that no special provision on this subject was needed in Rule XI(b) of the 1974 Rules. The matter was again raised in 1994 and reference may be made to paragraph 10.65, below.

York-Antwerp Rules 1994 10.45

No change, but there were proposals to reverse the thoroughly sound provisions of 1974 that the cost of restowing a shifted cargo should be chargeable to general average only when necessary for the *common safety*. It was suggested that at the end of the second paragraph should be added *or for the safe prosecution of the voyage*, an expression which would have permitted the allowance in general average of the cost of restowing almost every shifted cargo. This proposal was sensibly not accepted by the International Sub-Committee.

Rule X(b)

(b) The cost of handling on board or discharging cargo, fuel or stores whether at a port or place of loading, call or refuge, shall be admitted as general average, when the handling or discharging was necessary for the common safety or to enable damage to the ship caused by sacrifice or accident to be repaired, if the repairs were necessary for the safe prosecution of the voyage, except in cases where the damage to the ship is discovered at a port or place of loading or call without any accident or other extraordinary circumstance connected with such damage having taken place during the voyage.

The cost of handling on board or discharging cargo, fuel or stores shall not be admissible as general average when incurred solely for the purpose of restowage due to shifting during the voyage, unless such restowage is necessary for the common safety.

CONSTRUCTION

10.46 In its positive provisions, this sub-rule deals with the cost of handling or discharging cargo, fuel and stores in two distinct sets of circumstances, namely: (1) where necessary for the common safety (which would be a general average act at common law), and (2) to enable damage caused by sacrifice or accident to be repaired, if the repairs were necessary for the safe prosecution of the voyage (which would *not* be a general average act either at common law or under Rule A unless incurred as a direct consequence of a general average act, for example, for the repair of damage to the ship caused by general average sacrifice).

10.47 **"The cost of handling on board"** As already mentioned, this expression relates to the situation where cargo, fuel or stores need to be shifted for the common safety or to effect repairs necessary for the safe prosecution of the voyage, but where it is not necessary that they be discharged ashore from the vessel.

"or discharging" The word "discharge" means simply to relieve a vessel of her cargo, fuel or stores, that is, to get them out of the vessel. This definition is important when dealing, for instance, with the cost of discharging worthless cargo, to which further reference will be made in paragraphs 10.73 *et seq.*, below. The word cannot be construed and extended to include also transporting to a dumping site.

"cargo" See under Rule I.[59]

10.48 **"for the common safety"** See commentary under Rule A. In that commentary, the following quotation was given from the judgment of Roche J. in the case of *Vlassopoulos v. British and Foreign Marine Insurance Co. Ltd*[60]:

> "It is not necessary that the ship should be actually in the grip or even nearly in the grip of the disaster that may arise from a danger."

In a sense, the learned Judge was there laying down the *minimum* requirements for the degree of peril necessary to put the "common safety" at risk and thereby justifying the allowance in general average of the costs of entering a port of refuge.

In the context of the present Rule relating to expenses incurred when the vessel is within the comparative safety of a port of refuge, it is clear that the same words "common safety" must relate to a situation of the utmost gravity, that is, when ship and cargo are truly in the "grip of a

[59] See para. 1.24, *ante*.
[60] [1929] 1 K.B. 187.

disaster". Examples of situations where the discharge or shifting of cargo, etc., might be necessary for the common safety are set out below:

> *Where the ship is holed and making water.* Clearly, the discharge will save such cargo as is removed from the ship and, on occasion, the draught of the ship may thereby be reduced so that the hole is brought above the waterline.
>
> *Where the ship or cargo is on fire.* The discharge or shifting of cargo will preserve that particular cargo, may reduce the ultimate conflagration by removing combustible material from the sphere of the fire, and enable the firemen to attack the seat of the fire more easily.

At this stage, it is appropriate to deal with that other condition which justifies the allowance in general average of the cost of discharging cargo, etc., at a port of refuge, namely "*to enable damage to the ship ... to be repaired, if the repairs were ...*".

"necessary for the safe prosecution of the voyage" This expression looks 10.49
to a time in the future when the common safety will be endangered if the voyage continues. It is a notable example of the occasions where those who supported completion of the adventure as the basis of general average prevailed over those who supported the common safety concept. The degree of *damage* to the ship necessary to meet the requirements of the expression is the same as—and no less than—would be necessary to endanger the "common safety" of the adventure if the vessel were at sea.

For example, a vessel may lose her propeller at sea and thereby be rendered unfit to encounter the ordinary perils of the sea. A resort to a port of refuge will be justified for the "common safety", but once within a port where repairs can be effected, safety will have been attained, and some alternative expression is required if (as was intended by the early framers of the Rules) general average allowances are to continue. The alternative expression chosen was "necessary for the safe prosecution of the voyage", and it merely provides for a situation in port which, if the ship were at sea, would endanger the "common safety". It does not introduce yet another, lower, standard of damage which will permit general average allowances to be made under this or other of the York-Antwerp Rules.

"sacrifice or accident" These words presumably have the same meanings 10.50
as in sub-rule (a).[61] It will be noticed that the words "extraordinary circumstances"[62] are omitted so that if such circumstances (as opposed to sacrifice or accident) necessitate putting into a port of refuge for repairs, the expenses of entering the port, and the corresponding expenses

[61] See para. 10.35, *ante*.
[62] *Cf.* Rule X(a), para. 10.36, *ante*.

of leaving will be allowed in general average, but the cost of handling and discharging the cargo will not be allowed unless such handing or discharging were necessary for the common safety. An example of a case which would be within sub-rule (a) but not (b) is that of a ship whose main shaft is out of alignment on sailing with the result that the bearings slowly overheat and the ship is obliged to put into a port of refuge for the common safety, but is safe as soon as she is within the port.

In *Vlassopoulos v. British and Foreign Marine Insurance Co.*[63] (the *Makis* case), Roche J. construed "accident" in the sub-rule as being confined to accidents which involved a threat to the common safety, but this decision was influenced by the fact that (as Roche J. held) under the 1924 Rules the lettered Rules governed the interpretation of the numbered Rules. With the inclusion of the Rule of Interpretation, this decision is no longer applicable.

10.51 **"except in cases where the damage to the ship is discovered at a port or place of loading or call without any accident or other extraordinary circumstances connected with such damage having taken place during the voyage."** These words were added to the sub-rule in 1974, on which occasion some effort was made to reduce the incidence of general average cases by increasing the stringency of the criteria by which it should be determined whether a general average situation exists. It was felt that the outstanding candidate for exclusion was the "port of call" type general average where damage was merely *discovered* at a port of loading or of call without any accident or other extraordinary circumstance having taken place during the voyage.

Two examples already mentioned may serve as a guide to the practice probably intended to be established.

(1) Concurrently with the loading of cargo, the opportunity is taken to open up the main engine for routine survey and inspection, and a crack is discovered in the crankshaft for which repairs necessary for the safe prosecution of the voyage are essential. The crack has progressed gradually over a lengthy period and its origin antedates the commencement of the current voyage.[64]

[63] [1929] 1 K.B. 187 at 201.

[64] The Drafting Committee considered it unnecessary to define the extent of "voyage" for the purpose of this Rule as the functions mentioned were sufficiently general to make such a definition otiose, that is to say, that if provision had been made for allowance of costs of "handling on board", there was no further need to provide that "voyage" begins at the commencement of loading.

On the grounds that the Drafting Committee intended that the voyage begins only at the commencement of loading, and that there should be a community of interests at the *time* of *the accident*, it is submitted that:

(1) Where a vessel sails in ballast from A under charter to load at B and sustains damage during the passage which is discovered only during or after loading the cargo at B, but before leaving B, there is NO general average unless some "new accident" has occurred such as suggested in the main text above.

(2) Where the vessel loads at A and B and damage sustained during the passage from A to B is discovered during or after loading cargo at B, but before leaving B, there

No allowances can now be made in general average for discharging cargo, etc., or for detention expenses at the port.

(2) At some date prior to the commencement of the current voyage[64a] a crack is caused in the ship's side plating which passes completely unnoticed. On loading cargo, however, the ship's draught increases and water pours through the crack into the hold, necessitating the discharge of cargo in order to carry out repairs necessary for the safe prosecution of the voyage.

Although the crack itself was sustained before the commencement of the voyage, what might be termed a new accident has intervened with the cargo on board (the incursion of sea water), and the cost of discharging cargo, etc., and other detention expenses at the port can be treated as general average. The shipowner's right to claim contribution *from the cargo* would again be subject to any defence or counterclaim of the cargo owner for breach of the contract of affreightment, for example breach of any absolute warranty of seaworthiness or of the Hague Rules duty to use due diligence to make the ship seaworthy. However, provided a general average situation can be established under the York-Antwerp Rules, the shipowner should be able to recover the total general average from his underwriters or Protecting and Indemnity Association, subject to the conditions of insurance or of entry.

"The cost of handling on board or discharging cargo, fuel or stores shall not be admissible as general average when incurred solely for the purpose of restowage due to shifting during the voyage," As stated above,[65] this second paragraph of the sub-rule was added in 1974 to emphasise that where cargo, fuel or stores had shifted during the voyage and the sole object of the handling on board or discharge was to restow properly and to correct the vessel's trim and stability for the safe prosecution of the voyage, the cost would not be admissible as general average. Where, however, the handling or discharge was also necessary (1) because the common safety was at risk even within the comparative shelter of the port of refuge, or (2) to enable damage to the ship caused by sacrifice or accident to be repaired, if the repairs were necessary for the safe prosecution of the voyage, the cost of handling on board or discharging **10.52**

is an acceptable general average for the ship and cargo A (other than for the cost of discharging, etc., cargo loaded at B). But should cargo B be brought in to contribute to such general average, even if it can deny liability and allege a breach of the contract of affreightment?

On the basis outlined in (1) above, no general average exists vis-a-vis cargo B, and it would appear appropriate, therefore, to exclude the value of cargo B from contribution.

(3) Where the vessel loads at A and B and damage sustained during the passage from A to B is discovered after leaving B, all property on board at the time of any deviation to a port of refuge must be brought in to contribute, but cargo B may plead a breach of the contract of affreightment.

[64A] See n.64, *supra*.

[65] See para. 10.44, *ante*.

only as much cargo as was necessary for either of these purposes would be recoverable under the positive provisions of the first paragraph of the sub-rule.

10.53 **"unless such restowage is necessary for the common safety."** In the light of the commentary in the previous paragraph these words are possibly superfluous, but they may serve to emphasise that the cost of restowing a shifted cargo, etc., *is* allowable as general average when necessary for the common safety. (It must be reiterated that the cost is also allowable when the handling or discharge is necessary for repairs for the safe prosecution of the voyage.)

10.54 Difficult problems with regard to the cost of discharging cargo can arise when the voyage either is, or might be, lawfully abandoned[66] at a port of refuge. If the discharge is necessary for the common safety, the cost is always allowable as general average, but where the discharge is only for the purpose of repairs that would have been necessary for the safe prosecution of the voyage, and that voyage is not prosecuted, it is submitted that the cost should fall on the cargo interests alone,[67] subject to any express provision in the contract of affreightment. This applies even in those cases where no formal declaration of the abandonment of the voyage is made, and also to those cases where no decision to abandon could be taken until the discharge had been wholly or partly carried out.

It has been argued that, because Rules X(c) and XI(b) provide for the allowance in general average of certain storage charges and wages, etc., of crew until the completion of discharge even though the voyage has been abandoned previously, the cost of discharge itself must be allowable. This argument is untenable, however equitable it may appear. It is well recognised that the numbered Rules fall to be construed strictly, and there are special reasons why wages and maintenance of crew, etc., are allowed after the abandonment of the voyage which have no application to the cost of discharge.

Historical Development and Practice of Rule X(c)

10.55 This sub-rule deals essentially with the costs of (1) storage, and (2) reloading of cargo discharged at a port of refuge. Under the laws of almost all countries, the cost of both operations were charged in appropriate circumstances to general average, but in this country the practice[68] was to charge the costs of storage and reloading as special charges on cargo and freight, respectively.

[66] For the circumstances in which the shipowner is entitled to abandon the voyage, see para. 10.65, *post*, and paras. 00.37 *et seq.*, *ante*.

[67] *Medina Princess* [1965] 1 Lloyd's Rep. 361 at 522.

[68] See para. 10.06, *ante*.

To secure international uniformity, the costs of both operations were made the subject of general average from the very first international conference at Glasgow in 1860. The wording of the Glasgow Resolution 1860, the York Rule 1864, and the York-Antwerp Rule 1877 has already been discussed.[69]

York-Antwerp Rules 1890 **10.56**

It was on this occasion that the single Rule entitled "Expenses at Port of Refuge etc.," was sub-divided into three sections, of which Rule X(c) read as follows:

> "Whenever the cost of discharging cargo from a ship is admissible as general average, the cost of re-loading and storing such cargo on board the said ship, together with all storage charges on such cargo, shall likewise be so admitted. But when the ship is condemned or does not proceed on her original voyage, no storage expenses incurred after the date of the ship's condemnation or of the abandonment of the voyage shall be admitted as general average."

The first sentence was almost identical with the wording in the 1877 Rule, and although the second sentence was new, it was probably nothing more than a re-statement of the existing practice.

York-Antwerp Rules 1924.

Rule X(c)

> "Whenever the cost of handling or discharging cargo, fuel or stores is admissible as general average, the cost of reloading and stowing such cargo, fuel or stores on board the ship, together with all storage charges (including fire insurance, if incurred) on such cargo, fuel or stores, shall likewise be so admitted. But when the ship is condemned or does not proceed on her original voyage, no storage expenses incurred after the date of the ship's condemnation or of the abandonment of the voyage shall be admitted as general average. In the event of the condemnation of the ship or the abandonment of the voyage before completion of discharge of cargo, storage expenses, as above, shall be admitted as general average up to date of completion of discharge." **10.57**

Under the 1890 Rules this sub-rule related only to the cost of storage and reloading *cargo*. In the 1924 Rules an amendment was introduced (as was done in the case of sub-rule (b)) extending this sub-rule to cover such costs in relation to fuel and stores. Two other amendments were made in the first sentence of the sub-rule. First, the word "stowing" was substituted for the misleading expression "storing" ("storing such cargo on board the said ship"). The second amendment consisted of including the cost of fire insurance (if incurred) as one of the charges of storage

[69] See paras. 10.26–10.28, *ante*.

ashore. This had long formed a contentious question among average adjusters in this country. Marine underwriters, at whose risk the goods still remain although temporarily parted from the ship, would be responsible in the great majority of cases for a loss by fire ashore, and they had not infrequently expressed the view that they did not always desire such risk to be specially covered. However, the problem before an average adjuster was usually not whether to advise such insurance to be effected (although this also frequently arose), but how to treat the cost when it had been incurred. It was argued on the one hand that as a loss by fire sustained by cargo stored on the quay or in a warehouse at a port of refuge did not form the subject of an allowance under general average, the cost of insuring it against such a risk could not logically be allowed in general average, and those who advocated this view accordingly treated the charge as falling wholly on the cargo so insured. On the other hand, it was argued that as it was only reasonable in the majority of cases to insure the cargo against fire while it was subjected to that risk ashore, the cost of insurance should be regarded as part of the cost of storage and treated accordingly. Not infrequently also the storage charges included fire insurance premiums, and it was difficult in such a case to distinguish, either in actual cost or in method of treatment, between the cost of fire insurance and that of storage. A further consideration, which was by no means negligible where the goods discharged and stored consisted of a large number of packages of general cargo belonging to many different merchants, was that the task of calculating the proportion of the fire insurance premium falling on each might be onerous and costly, hardly justified by the amount involved, and adding unnecessarily to the complications of the adjustment.

In 1925 the Association of Average Adjusters passed the following Rule of Practice to much the same effect:

> "19A. That in practice, where the cost of fire insurance has been reasonably incurred by the shipowner, or his agents, on cargo discharged under average, such cost shall be treated as part of the cost of storage."[70]

10.58 The last of the 1924 amendments consisted of adding the third sentence of the sub-rule, extending the allowance of storage expenses ashore until all the cargo was discharged, even though at that date the ship had been condemned or the voyage abandoned. Although the amount of money at issue is probably small, there appears to be no sound reason why general average should be burdened with this extra charge, which should properly be borne by the cargo interests themselves. Further, it only encourages the untenable assertion that, because storage charges may be allowed after the ship's condemnation or the abandonment of the voyage and up to the completion of discharge, the cost of discharging the cargo ought similarly to be allowed. It must be stressed that once the voyage has been abandoned or the ship condemned, the cost of discharging

[70] Now Rule of Practice F11; amended in 1968 by deleting the word "fire".

cargo can be treated as general average only if necessary for the common safety.

York-Antwerp Rules 1950 **10.59**

The 1950 version of the sub-rule was the same as that of 1924 save that for the words "(including fire insurance, if incurred)" were substituted "(including insurance, if reasonably incurred)", thus permitting the allowance of premiums for reasonable but wider insurances where, for instance, cargo was discharged into lighters rather than into a warehouse.

One objection to the deletion of the word "fire" was that it might foster the idea that the shipowner was under some duty to effect insurances against all manner of extraneous risks. To counter this suggestion it was proposed at the Amsterdam Conference that it be minuted that the intention was not to impose any duty of effecting insurance upon the shipowner and that no such obligation should rest upon him.

It is clear beyond doubt that the carrier, as bailee of the cargo, must take all necessary steps to ensure that cargo discharged ashore at a port of refuge is properly kept and cared for, in so far as the facilities of the port permit, but, as was stated at the Amsterdam Conference, the carrier is under no duty or obligation to effect wide insurances on the cargo discharged ashore. It is even possible to argue that the carrier is under no duty to place *any* insurances on the cargo, on the grounds that:

(1) In the majority of cases, the cargo will have been insured for the whole voyage by the owners of that cargo, and those prior insurances continue to provide cover during a forced discharge at a port of refuge.
(2) In those cases where the cargo is not insured for the voyage, its owners must be deemed to accept also those additional—but usually lesser—risks to be encountered whilst in storage at a port of refuge.

10.60 However, and having regard to the decision in the United States courts of *The Mormacmar*,[71] the carrier will probably be wise to cover for the benefit of the owners of cargo those risks which, although foreseeable as possibilities, are unlikely (for example fire in a warehouse), but if they do occur, would not give rise to a claim in general average for the resultant loss or damage. Where there is any real degree of risk of loss or damage arising from a forced discharge (for example where port facilities are inadequate and cargo is necessarily stored on the quayside under old and damaged tarpaulins), readily foreseeable losses such as storm damage and pilferage would be generally admissible in general

[71] (1947) A.M.C. 1611; (1956) A.M.C. 1028.

average and there would be no point in incurring heavy insurance costs to cover such risks.

In *The Mormacmar*[72] cargo discharged ashore into a warehouse at a port of refuge was destroyed by fire, and no insurances on the cargo whilst ashore were placed by the carrier. It was held by Medina D.J. that:

> "The respondents ... were trustees of the goods thus placed ashore and their duty to keep and care for[73] the goods necessarily included, under the circumstances, the duty to place insurance against the risk of fire, collapse of structures and rising of navigable water."

York-Antwerp Rules 1974

On this occasion, the wording of the sub-rule was rearranged for greater clarity, but no changes in previous practice were intended or made.

York-Antwerp Rules 1994

The 1974 wording was left unchanged on this occasion but a probably unnecessary and therefore confusing addition was made at the end of the first paragraph:

> "The provisions of Rule XI shall be applied to the extra period of detention occasioned by such reloading or restowing."

The effect of this addition will be discussed below in paragraph 10.65.

10.61 RULE X(c)

(c) Whenever the cost of handling or discharging cargo, fuel or stores is admissible as general average, the costs of storage, including insurance if reasonably incurred, reloading and stowing of such cargo, fuel or stores shall likewise be admitted as general average. The provisions of Rule XI shall be applied to the extra period of detention occasioned by such reloading or restowing.

But when the ship is condemned or does not proceed on her original voyage, storage expenses shall be admitted as general average only up to the date of the ship's condemnation or of the abandonment of the voyage or up to the date of completion of discharge of cargo if the condemnation or abandonment takes place before that date.

[72] (1947) A.M.C. 1611.
[73] Carriage of Goods by Sea Act (46 U.S. Code, s. 1303(2)).

CONSTRUCTION

This sub-rule is complementary to the sub-rule (b) above. Between them they provide a complete code for the treatment of the cost of handling on board, discharging, reloading and stowing cargo, fuel and stores on board the ship, and of storage ashore, whether the adventure be terminated at the port or placed concerned or continued therefrom. **10.62**

"Whenever the cost of handling or discharging cargo, fuel or stores is admissible as general average," If a claim is to be admissible under this sub-rule the facts must be such that a claim for the costs of handling or discharging cargo, etc., can be substantiated under sub-rule (b).[74]

"the costs of storage," The word "storage" comprises both:

(1) The action of *transporting* cargo fuel or stores to a warehouse or other place of storage, and **10.63**
(2) The period during which the property remains in store and for which rent or hire will be charged.

On occasion, cargo which has been discharged for the common safety or to enable repairs to be effected to the ship which are necessary for the safe prosecution of the voyage, is not reloaded for various reasons. The cost of storage on such cargo is invariably allowed as general average up to the time when the vessel resumes her voyage, but thereafter its treatment will depend upon individual circumstances. If the cargo is left behind merely because it has been damaged by accidental causes, the cost of storage after the vessel has sailed will be treated as a special charge on cargo. If, however, the cargo is not reloaded for reasons directly caused by a general average act, for example: (a) the cargo was damaged by a general average sacrifice; (b) the ship cannot reload the cargo because she is already down to her marks owing to flooding of the holds to extinguish a fire; (c) water used to extinguish a fire renders part of the cargo dangerous and liable to combust spontaneously, and the master decides upon a less tight stowage, necessitating the leaving behind of part cargo (even if sound, or damaged by accidental causes); the cost of storage for a reasonable time will still be allowed as general average.

"including insurance, if reasonably incurred," Insurances under this part of the sub-rule are not limited to the risks of fire alone; other appropriate and reasonable risks may be insured against.[75] **10.64**

[74] See para. 10.45, *ante*.
[75] See paras. 10.59, 10.60, *ante*. See also Wilson, *The Insurance of Average Disbursements & Other Subsidiary Interests Following a Marine Casualty* (1988), published by the Association of Average Adjusters.

In *Marine Insurance & General Average in the United States*, Leslie J. Buglass states:

> "It is highly desirable that any cargo discharged from the vessel should be insured against shore perils (including fire) and, if it is stored on lighters, also have effective marine insurance. The amount to be insured is the estimated value of the cargo in its sound or damaged condition, as the case may be. Such insurance should also contain a clause to the effect that it take precedence over any other insurance effected on the goods because such insurance is for the benefit of the owners of the goods or the original insurers. Sometimes, such insurances also incorporate a clause stipulating that in the event of damage to goods, the general average has first lien (on the proceeds of any claim under the insurance) for any unpaid salvage and/or general average or special charges."

10.65 **"The provisions of Rule XI shall be applied to the extra period of detention occasioned by such reloading or *re*stowing."** This sentence was added in 1994 at the suggestion of the United States Maritime Law Association and received the support of the International Sub-Committee, they reporting that it was felt to be a clarification of the then present practice and not an extension of general average.

One can accept that the new addition is not an extension of general average, because it is likely to be interpreted as merely giving formal effect to an existing practice, but its claim to be a clarification is less easy to justify. Rule XI(b) permits the allowance in general average of:

> Crew wages and maintenance incurred,
> Fuel and stores consumed, and
> Port charges incurred,

during the extra period of detention in a port of refuge until the ship shall or should have been made ready to proceed on her voyage. In practice, the ship's readiness to proceed has always been construed as referring to her readiness as a laden ship—that is, with previously discharged cargo reloaded and stowed. However, as stated in paragraph 11.29, below, it is the condition of the ship alone which will govern how long the extra period of detention shall run, and it could be suggested that this period will end as soon as the ship has completed her repairs and, accordingly, could sail from port.

To prevent such a construction, it is not inappropriate that additional wording should be incorporated within the Rules to ensure that the extra period of detention includes the time spent reloading and stowing a previously discharged cargo.

However, the particular location in which the new wording appears—as part of the first paragraph of Rule X(c), rather than in Rule XI—is somewhat ill-chosen and could be argued to reduce the circumstances in which crew, etc., expenses are allowable under Rule XI(b). The present Rule X(c) permits the allowance in general average of the costs of reloading and stowing a previously discharged cargo only when the cost of that previous discharge is so admissible. Thus, if, in accordance with Rule X(b), the cost of handling or discharging a shifted cargo is not chargeable to general average, and therefore neither is the restowage under X(c), the natural inference to be drawn from the use here of the wording "*such reloading or restowing*" might be that neither can the concomitant crew wages and detention expenses be allowed. This, however, was not the intention.

"when the ship is condemned" This may arise when the ship has suffered such damage by excepted perils that repairs would be commercially impossible, and the shipowner is in consequence discharged from his obligation to repair her and continue the voyage.[76] **10.66**

"or does not proceed on her original voyage," Even where the ship is not condemned, it may be impracticable for her to proceed upon her original voyage. For example, the delay during the necessary repairs may be so great as to frustrate the contract of carriage; or the extent of the damage and the repair facilities at the port of refuge may be such that the only practicable course is to abandon the voyage or tranship the cargo, and take the original ship in ballast to another port for repairs. The circumstances in which matters of this nature will entitle the shipowner to abandon the voyage are dealt with in Section 2 of this work,[77] where it is also noted that the shipowner has the right to tranship the cargo, if he so wishes.

However, in the application of the second paragraph of Rule X(c) it appears to matter not whether the shipowner is justified in abandoning the voyage. On the wording of the Rule, the only relevant consideration is whether or not the vessel proceeds on the original voyage. Thus if, for good reason or bad, the shipowner decides not to continue the voyage from the port of refuge, storage charges will cease to qualify as general average expenditure from the date of abandonment or, if later, of the completion of discharge. If the shipowner wrongfully abandons the voyage he will be liable in damages and the provisions of Rule D will apply.

So long as the shipowner is justified in abandoning the voyage at the port of refuge, he will be entitled to recover in full from the cargo owner any storage charges which he incurs thereafter on the cargo, not as general average, but in quasi-contract.[78] However, it seems unlikely that this right would extend to entitle the shipowner to recover the expense of destroying or disposing of worthless cargo; such remedies as the shipowner has to recover these expenses are discussed below.[79]

[76] See *Assicurazioni Generali v. Bessie Morris S.S. Co.* [1892] 1 Q.B. 571; [1892] 2 Q.B. 652, *Kulukundis v. Norwich Union* [1937] 1 K.B. 1; see para. 00.39, *ante.*

[77] See paras. 00.37 *et seq., ante.*

[78] See *China Pacific v. Food Corporation of India* [1982] A.C. 939 at 960; *Notara v. Henderson* (1872) L.R. 7 Q.B. 225.

[79] See paras. 10.73 *et seq., post.*

10.67 **"storage expenses"** The second paragraph of Rule X(c) makes no mention of the other expenses, apart from storage, referred to in the first paragraph of the Rule—that is, insurance, reloading and stowage. However the intention appears to be that insurance charges should be dealt with in the same way as storage charges and, if reasonably incurred, allowed up to the same date, and that once storage charges have ceased to qualify for contribution in general average, any subsequent reloading and stowage expenses involved in forwarding the cargo from the port of refuge will also be disallowed. Where cargo has to be left at the port of refuge because it has been damaged as a result of a general average sacrifice, any storage expenses reasonably incurred will be allowed under Rule XVI or under the lettered Rules.

10.68 **"the date of the ship's condemnation or of the abandonment of the voyage"** It is suggested that the date is not that of the casualty or frustrating event but:

(1) in the case of the ship's condemnation, the date upon which it is ascertained that the ship is commercially irreparable[80];
(2) in the case of abandonment of the voyage, the date upon which
  (a) it is ascertained that the voyage is frustrated,[81] or
  (b) the parties agree to abandon the voyage, or
  (c) the shipowner gives notice that he is abandoning the voyage, or
  (d) the decision is taken to tranship the cargo[82]
  whichever is earlier.

10.69 It is submitted that "the abandonment of the voyage" in Rule X(c) includes the case where the decision is taken to tranship, even when the transhipment is in continuation of the voyage.[83] This interpretation reflects the earlier phrase—"when the ship ... does not proceed on her original voyage", which clearly includes the case where the *original* ship does not proceed on the voyage. It would also reflect the usual practice in cases of transhipment, which is to treat cargo handling expenses at the port of refuge as a particular charge on freight, except in so far as they fall to be made good in general average as a substituted expense.

10.70 **"up to the date of completion of discharge"** It is suggested that these words should be read as including that date.

"cargo" See commentary on Rule I.[84]

The Rule does not provide for the case where part of the cargo is sold

[80] See para. 10.65, *ante*.
[81] See paras. 00.37 *et seq.*, *ante*.
[82] See para. 10.69, *infra*.
[83] See paras. G.16 *et seq.*, *ante*.
[84] See para. 1.24, *ante*.

or disposed of at the port of refuge. For the method of adjustment in such a case reference should be made to paragraphs 16.28 and 17.84 to 17.87, below.

Historical Development and Practice of Rule X(d)

This sub-Rule, abolished in 1974, related to two specific forms of substituted expenses (towage to another port of repair or to destination, and the forwarding of cargo), and was the first York-Antwerp Rule on the subject of substituted expenses. It was introduced in 1890 and remained unchanged in the 1924 and 1950 editions of the York-Antwerp Rules, but was abandoned in 1974 for the reason that it was then considered that all forms of substituted expenses (other than temporary repairs) should be treated in identical fashion in accordance with the provisions of Rule F,[85] introduced in 1924. **10.71**

Rule X(d) read as follows:

> "(d) If a ship under average be in a port or place at which it is practicable to repair her, so as to enable her to carry on the whole cargo, and if, in order to save expense, either she is towed thence to some other port or place of repair or to her destination, or the cargo or a portion of it is transhipped by another ship, or otherwise forwarded, then the extra cost of such towage, transhipment and forwarding, or any of them (up to the amount of the extra expense saved) shall be payable by the several parties to the adventure in proportion to the extraordinary expense saved."

and was an almost word for word combination of two British Rules of Practice, Nos. F14[86] and F15,[87] introduced in 1876 and commented upon in this work in paragraphs F.08, F.09 and F.11, F.12, above.

The essential difference between the treatment of these two forms of substituted expenses under the old Rule X(d) and the current Rule F was that under Rule X(d) the substituted expenses were payable by the several parties to the adventure in proportion to the expenses saved *to each of them*, and which would usually include savings to the shipowner in respect of the cost of repairs to the ship. Under Rule F, if the savings to general average expenditure are sufficient, the whole of the substituted expenses are charged to general average, and other savings (for example in the cost of repairs) are ignored. **10.72**

Clearly, Rule X(d) was far more equitable and considerate of the interests of cargo than the subsequent Rules F and XIV dealing with substituted expenses, and in the early proceedings for the 1994 Rules the

[85] See para. F.21, *ante*.
[86] See para. 70.41, *post*.
[87] See para. 70.42, *post*.

United States Maritime Law Association proposed the reintroduction of Rule X(d).

Discharging and Disposal of Worthless Cargo

10.73 This is a convenient place to introduce a subject first dealt with in the eleventh edition of this work and, perhaps because it often involves considerable sums of money, one on which there exists a divergence of practice amongst average adjusters in different parts of the world.

Cargo may be damaged and rendered worthless by *accident* (fire, stranding, collision, etc.) or by general average *sacrifice* (for example water used to extinguish a fire), but in this section will be considered only the case where the cargo is damaged by an accidental cause.

The typical situation occurs when a loaded vessel is involved in a serious collision whereby the shell plating is breached and one or more of the holds is flooded and tidal, submerging all or most of the cargo therein. If that cargo is thereby rendered worthless, who is to bear the cost of discharging and dumping it?

There is little doubt that when such an accident occurs shortly before arrival at destination, and the vessel is able to proceed or be towed there, the whole cost of this highly expensive operation will fall upon the shipowner or carrier alone, and he must look to his Protecting and Indemnity Association to recover any additional costs.

10.74 But what of the situation where the vessel puts into a port of refuge and, in order to carry out repairs necessary for the safe prosecution of the voyage (but NOT for the common safety), it is necessary to discharge the whole of the cargo from the affected hold? Is the position any different? Is general average to bear all or any part of such operations as discharging from the ship, temporary storage ashore, separating "sound" from worthless cargo, loading into trucks or barges, and transporting to a dumping site?

In his *Marine Insurance and General Average in the United States*, that knowledgeable and highly regarded adjuster, Buglass, states on page 239 that:

> "Sometimes cargo which has been discharged in order to effect repairs is damaged to such an extent as to be worthless and has to be dumped at the port of refuge. Under American practice, any expenses incurred in dumping such cargo at the port of refuge is allowed in general average. The entire operation of discharging the cargo, storing it and either reloading it into the vessel or dumping it if worthless, is considered to be one continuous general average act, and the entire cost is treated accordingly."

The words "American practice" might be construed to mean the practice applies only when there is no provision in the contract of affreightment for general average to be adjusted in accordance with York-Antwerp Rules, but there is reason to suppose that this same practice is applied even when the York-Antwerp Rules govern the situation, and not only in the United States. If this be so, can the practice be justified, and on what grounds?

Consider the following practice examples.

Case A **10.75**

A mixed general cargo of bags, bales, boxes, crates, and drums, etc., is largely submerged in the affected hold. It is discharged ashore, transported to a warehouse, and there sorted and separated into categories such as:

(1) fit to be reloaded after repairs to the ship;
(2) fit to be reloaded into the original or a following vessel after reconditioning;
(3) severely damaged, and to be sold locally; and
(4) worthless, and to be dumped

It is submitted that the various expenses should be dealt with as follows:

Discharging. As general average in accordance with Rule X(b),[88] the discharge being necessary in order to carry out repairs to the ship necessary for the safe prosecution of the voyage. The fact that some of the cargo may be worthless does not affect the issue.

Transporting to warehouse. As general average in accordance with Rule X(c)[89] as part of the cost of "storage" (putting into store).

Sorting and separating. As special charges on the cargo involved, this being exclusively for the benefit of that cargo, and of no concern to the general average, the damage being the result of an accident.

Reconditioning. As special charges on the particular cargo involved.

Dumping. These charges will have to be paid in the first instance by the shipowner (as "father of the adventure") and although he might wish and endeavour to recover the same from the owners of the cargo dumped, it is commercially unlikely that they will respond for such charges and the shipowner will be obliged to bear them himself and recover from his P. and I. Club.

Warehouse rent (storage). As general average in accordance with Rule X(c)[90] up to the time when the ship leaves port after repairs; thereafter, the rent will be a special charge on the cargo still being reconditioned.

[88] See para. 10.74, *ante.*
[89] See para. 10.63, *ante.*
[90] *Ibid.*

(It is assumed that the worthless cargo will already have been dumped.)

Reloading

(a) *Into the original vessel.* As general average in accordance with Rule X(c).[91]
(b) *Into a following vessel.* As special charges on the cargo concerned. It is probable that the cost of reloading into another vessel will be no more than the charge that would have been incurred in reloading into the original vessel and which would have been allowed as general average, but one must take facts as one finds them, and the fact is that the common adventure is over for the cargo left behind when the original vessel leaves the port of refuge, and it contributes on its value at that port.

10.76 **Case B**

The submerged cargo in the affected hold is recognised at a very early stage to be worthless and requiring dumping. However, and with ecological problems in mind, the local authorities take about a month to approve a suitable site for the dumping. Accordingly, the worthless cargo is discharged into barges and stored there until final arrangements can be made concerning the dumping. The worthless cargo is then transferred to trucks and transported to the dumping site.

The ship completes repairs and sails from the port of refuge before the dumping takes place.

It is submitted that the various expenses should be dealt with as follows:

Discharging into barges. As general average in accordance with Rule X(b)[92] the discharge being necessary in order to carry out repairs to the ship necessary for the safe prosecution of the voyage, and even though it is known at the time that the cargo is worthless.

Barge hire. From a commonsense point of view, this charge is part of the cost of disposing of the worthless cargo, but as the numbered rules of the York-Antwerp Rules must be construed strictly, the barge hire counts as "storage" and, up to the time the original vessel leaves the port of refuge on completion of repairs, it can be allowed as general average in accordance with Rule X(c).[93]

Dumping. The barge hire subsequent to the original vessel leaving the port of refuge, the cost of discharging from the barges and loading into

[91] See para. 10.61, *ante*.
[92] See para. 10.47, *ante*.
[93] See para. 10.63, *ante*.

the trucks, and the transport to and discharge at the dumping site, will all fall on the shipowner and/or P. and I. Club.

Case C **10.77**

The vessel carries a bulk cargo of phosphate and is allowed to enter the port of refuge only after she has been beached and a great timber patch built on her side. In order to carry out repairs necessary for the safe prosecution of the voyage, it is necessary to discharge the entire cargo and it is recognised that the cargo in the affected hold is worthless and requires dumping.

The cargo is discharged into lorries, the sound being transported to a storage area and the worthless to a dumping site. The transport costs, whether to the storage area or to the dumping site, are identical.

It is submitted that the various expenses should be dealt with as follows:

Discharging. As general average in accordance with Rule X(b).[94]

Transporting to dumping site. As cost of disposing of worthless cargo, payable by the shipowner and/or his P. and I. Club.

The fact that it costs no more to transport the worthless cargo to a dumping site than to a storage area is no reason to expect general average to bear that cost. It is not a substituted expense, for there is never any reason to do anything other than dump the cargo, and while the word "storage" in Rule X(c)[95] comprises the cost of transporting to a "store", a dumping site can in no way be construed as being a "store".

Case D **10.78**

The vessel carries a bulk cargo of grain products and it is recognised that the cargo remaining in the affected hold is worthless. Authority is given for this damaged cargo to be discharged into barges and dumped about 10 miles out to sea. Attempts are first made to pump out this cargo afloat, but it has tended to cake and solidify, with the result that the operation proves so difficult that, eventually, the vessel drydocks, the damaged shell plating is removed, and the worthless cargo is bulldozed from the hold into the drydock, loaded onto a conveyor belt and discharged to the dumping barge alongside.

It is submitted that the various expenses should be dealt with as follows:

[94] See para. 10.47, *ante*.
[95] See para. 10.63, *ante*.

Afloat:

Hire of pumps, etc., for discharging. As general average in accordance with Rule X(b),[96] the discharge being necessary in order to carry out repairs necessary for the safe prosecution of the voyage.

Hire of barges. As costs of disposing of worthless cargo, and payable by the shipowner and/or his P. and I. Club.

The purpose of the barge is to transport the worthless cargo to the dumping ground, and not to "store" the cargo as in Case B.

In drydock:

Drydocking, dues, and removal of damaged plating. As particular average on ship, except that any extra drydock dues incurred over and above the normal period of repairs can be considered as costs of discharge and allowed as general average in accordance with Rule X(b).[97] The drydock has been stemmed solely for repairs, and the damaged shell plating has to be removed for permanent repairs to the collision damage.

Hire of bulldozers, etc. As part of the costs of discharge and allowed as general average.

Hire of conveyor belt (payloader). It has already been suggested in paragraph 10.47, above, that the word "discharge" means simply to relieve the vessel of her cargo, that is, to get it out of the vessel. The present cost of transferring the worthless cargo from the drydock bottom to the dumping barge might, therefore, be considered as something other than "discharge". However, on this occasion it appears legitimate to consider it as a substituted expense for the more difficult and expensive operation of pumping out the cargo afloat, already attempted and partly effected. Accordingly, it is submitted that this charge should be treated as "discharging" and allowed as general average

Hire of barges. As costs of disposal of worthless cargo, as above.

10.79 Case E

The vessel carries a bulk cargo of wheat, and part of the sound cargo in the unaffected holds is discharged into barges, transferred to a grain elevator, and subsequently reloaded after repairs. The damaged cargo in the affected hold is discharged into trucks and transported to a landfill and dumped.

[96] See para. 10.47, *ante*.
[97] *Ibid.*

It is submitted that the various expenses should be dealt with as follows:

Discharge whether into barges or trucks. As general average in accordance with Rule X(b),[98] the discharge being necessary in order to carry out repairs necessary for the safe prosecution of the voyage.

Hire of barges. As general average in accordance with Rule X(c)[99] the barges being used to transport the cargo to a store.

Hire of trucks. As costs of disposal of worthless cargo, and payable by the shipowner and/or his P. and I. Club.

Credit: Expenses Saved at Destination

In each of the above Cases A/E it has been suggested that the cost of discharging the cargo from the ship at the port of refuge should be allowed as general average. There can be no dispute with regard to that portion of the cargo which is reloaded into the original carrying vessel after repairs, but what of the worthless cargo which is dumped, or the damaged cargo which is sold at the port of refuge or forwarded by other vessels after reconditioning? Can it be suggested that this cargo is at "destination" and that the charges fall, therefore, on the carrier if he is responsible for discharging the cargo at destination, or on the cargo interests themselves under, for example a "free in and out" contract? **10.80**

It is submitted that the correct answer is that the discharge takes place at an unintended port—a port of refuge—and that the cost is properly allowable as general average in accordance with a strict construction of the wording of Rule X(b).[1] However, in accordance with general principles which are spelled out, for instance, in Rules VIII, IX and XV and the 1950 Rule X(d),[2] credit must always be given to general average for any expense saved as the result of an operation which itself has been charged to general average. Thus, it is submitted that the estimated cost of discharging that worthless cargo, etc., at its intended destination should be credited to general average, and in its actual damaged state, rather than in sound condition.

The net result would appear to be that general average should only bear any part of the costs of discharging worthless cargo, etc., if it can be shown those costs are greater at the port of refuge than they would have been at the intended port of discharge, for example because labour rates and other charges are higher.

[98] See para. 10.47, *ante*.
[99] See para. 10.63, *ante*.
[1] See para. 10.47, *ante*.
[2] See para. 10.71, *ante*.

Rule X

Replacement Cargo

10.81 Yet another problem worthy of mention, and which could present itself in both Cases D and E above, concerns the likely need to obtain a new cargo or solid ballast to stow in the empty hold from which the cargo has been washed out after the collision, or is dumped in the port of refuge.

It will be appreciated that a ship may not be sufficiently strong to withstand a storm and heavy seas if one hold—particularly in the centre of the ship—is completely empty; she might break in two unless the cargo is evenly spread throughout her length. But the grain cargo remaining in the ship cannot simply be part transferred to an empty hold, for international regulations require that a bulk cargo of "liquid" grain must fill any hold in which it is carried to avoid it shifting in heavy weather and possibly causing the ship to list and capsize.

It is possible, therefore, that the shipowner may find it necessary to incur considerable extra expense to:

(1) bag 25 per cent of the cargo to stow on top of the bulk grain, or
(2) purchase a suitable amount of solid ballast to put in the empty hold, and dispose of it after the voyage, or
(3) seek an additional part cargo for the empty hold.

Such additional expenses will be for the sole purpose of prosecuting the original voyage in safety, but there is no York-Antwerp Rule—lettered or numbered—which will admit those expenses as general average. There is no peril affecting the ship and cargo while they remain in the port of refuge, and the expenses must therefore constitute simply an additional voyage expense to the shipowner caused by an accident. Although not relevant to the subject of general average, these expenses might be recoverable from the insurers on freight, but only if the freight is at risk.

Rule XI

Wages and Maintenance of Crew and other Expenses Bearing up for and in a Port of Refuge, etc.

English Law and Practice

Wages and maintenance of crew during the detention *at* a port of refuge were allowable as general average under the law of many countries, some of whom also admitted the wages and maintenance of crew whilst *at sea*, bearing up for a port of refuge and regaining position after leaving the port. In neither set of circumstances, however, has it ever been the practice in the United Kingdom[1] to allow such crew wages, etc. **11.01**

Two reasons are offered for the English rule. The first is, that the general average is terminated so soon as the port of refuge is reached, so that the expenses in question, it is contended, do not really form part of the cost of the general average operation, but of the delay in port in order to repair, which, in the case at least of accidental damage, falls within the shipowner's duty under his contract. The second reason is based on the principle, that, to constitute general average, an expenditure must be extraordinary in its kind, not the mere augmentation of an ordinary expenditure. The services of the crew during the whole voyage are due to the cargo, being, like the use of the ship itself, purchased by the engagement to pay freight. The shipowner must take the chance of a longer or shorter voyage.

Lowndes continued with: **11.02**

> "The English rule has been sanctioned by a series of decisions in our courts, which, though unsatisfactory enough as regards the reasons on which they are based, having for the most part been given at a time when the subject of general average was little understood, must now, it is presumed, be regarded as of binding authority."

[1] U.S. case law on the subject includes *Campbell v. Alknomac* (1798) Bee 124; Fed.Cas. 2350; *Star of Hope* 9 Wall. 203 (1869); *Hobson v. Lord* 92 U.S. 397 (1875). The allowance ceases when the voyage is abandoned, or the vessel is ready to resume her voyage: *The Joseph Farwell* 31 Fed.Rep. 844 (1887).

and in a footnote set out some of these decisions.[2] Nevertheless, it is clear that the point is still open for argument.[3]

To return to Lowndes' own text:

"It would certainly have been more satisfactory if we could say that the arguments in favour of the allowance of wages and provisions had been laid before, and at least listened to by, the judges of the English courts. There is really something to be said in support of a practice which is of great antiquity, and very general amongst seafaring communities.

Let us confine ourselves to the case of a ship which has put into port to repair damage which is itself the subject of general average.

The shipowner contends that he is entitled to an indemnity for his loss of the ship's employment during the detention caused by the sacrifice made for the common safety. If he is entitled to a complete compensation for such loss, this ingredient in it is too important to be let out of sight. His right to compensation for loss of time is recognised by the courts when it is a question of damages under a collision suit. In such a case he received compensation for it, under the name of demurrage.

But, it may objected, if the claim is for demurrage, why limit this to the cost of keeping the crew? Why not also bring in the loss of time? The answer is: The shipowner's loss of time is balanced by a corresponding loss on the part of the owners of the cargo. The delay is or may be prejudicial to the latter in two ways: they may lose their market—but against this may be set the chance of a rise in the market during the delay; they also lose the interest, during the delay, on the cost of their merchandise. This loss of interest bears the same proportion to the value of the goods which the shipowners's loss, by being deprived of the use of the ship, bears to the value of the ship. At any rate, if not always precisely the same, these two losses may not unfairly be set off against one another.[4] If insurance be left out of sight, it makes little or no difference, as between the owners of cargo and the owner of the ship, whether both these losses are brought in, or both left out. But, over and above this loss of time, the shipowner has to bear an additional burden by having to pay and maintain his crew, who would be paid off at the end of the voyage. He is not really compensated for the sacrifice which necessitated the delay, unless this outlay is made good to him.

If, then, at any future time the courts should lay down the principle that, when there is a delay caused by a sacrifice, the loss thereby occasioned is to be completely compensated in general average, it may become necessary to reconsider the present rule as to the crew's wages and provisions. It is by no means improbable that in this respect a distinction may be drawn between the case of putting into port to repair accidental damage, and that in which the putting in has been necessitated by a sacrifice for the common safety.

At present, however, we do not seem to be ripe for such a change; the exclusion from general average of the crew's wages, during the delay[5] in the

[2] 4th ed., p. 240, n. (z). The case most directly in point is *Power v. Whitmore* (1815) 4 M. & S. 141, in which Lord Ellenborough thus briefly dismissed the claim: "General average must lay its foundation in a sacrifice of a part for the sake of the rest; but here was no sacrifice of any part by the master, but only of his time and patience."

[3] See *Atwood v. Sellar* [1880] 5 Q.B.D. 286 at 291, C.A.; and *The Leitrim* [1902] P. 256 at 268.

[4] This argument is supported by the decision of Barnes J. in *The Leitrim* [1902] P. 256, which was followed and applied by Rowlatt J. in *Wetherall (J.H.) & Co. v. The London Assurance* [1931] 2 K.B. 448. See also *Anglo-Argentine Live Stock Agency v. Temperley S.S. Co.* [1899] 2 Q.B. 403 at 412.

[5] See *Anglo-Argentine Live Stock Agency v. Temperley S.S. Co.* [1899] 2 Q.B. 403.

> course of a voyage not terminated by wreck, must be taken to be a settled rule."

Historical Development and Practice of Rule XI(a)

York-Antwerp Rules 1924 11.03

Wages and maintenance of crew during the detention *at* a port of refuge were allowable as general average under the laws of many countries (though not Britain), and it is not surprising that the York-Antwerp Rules have made similar provision[6] since 1860. There was less international uniformity, however, with regard to the treatment of wages and maintenance of crew whilst *at sea*, bearing up for a port of refuge and regaining position after leaving the port, and it was not until 1924 that a Rule on this subject was introduced.

Rule XX. Expenses Bearing up for Port, etc.

> "Fuel and stores consumed, and wages and maintenance of master, officers and crew incurred, during the prolongation of the voyage occasioned by a ship entering a port or place of refuge or returning to her port or place of loading shall be admitted as general average when the expenses of entering such port or place are allowable in general average in accordance with Rule X(a)."

If the expenses of entering a port of refuge were to be allowed as general average in accordance with Rule X(a),[7] it was only logical that there should also be allowed the—often considerably greater—expenses of bearing up for that port of refuge and subsequently regaining position.

York-Antwerp Rules 1950 11.04

The new rule on wages, etc., introduced in 1924 was numbered XX, and was inconveniently separated from the original but continuing Rule XI on the same subject. In 1950, the opportunity was taken to combine the two rules in one Rule XI. The only other changes were that: (1) the words "wages and maintenance", etc., were placed before the words "fuel and stores"; and (2) an over-cautious draftsman introduced the word "reasonably" in the second line.

York-Antwerp Rules 1974

No change.

[6] See Rule XI(b) para. 11.11, *post*.
[7] See para. 10.32, *ante*.

11.05 **York-Antwerp Rules 1994**

No change.

RULE XI(a)

WAGES AND MAINTENANCE OF CREW AND OTHER EXPENSES BEARING UP FOR AND IN A PORT OF REFUGE ETC.

Wages and maintenance of master, officers and crew reasonably incurred and fuel and stores consumed during the prolongation of the voyage occasioned by a ship entering a port or place of refuge or returning to her port or place of loading shall be admitted as general average when the expenses of entering such port or place are allowable in general average in accordance with Rule X(a).

CONSTRUCTION

11.06 **"wages"** These are defined by sub-rule (c).[8]

"maintenance" This word is construed to include not only the cost of food and drink supplied for the crew, but also the cost of laundering, bedding, etc. If it is necessary for the crew or part of them to be housed ashore at a port of refuge, either because of some immediate danger to the ship or because their own accommodation has been damaged and rendered uninhabitable, it would include the cost of lodging.[9]

"crew" This does not include "cattlemen",[10] or presumably a supercargo, because they are not under command of the master, are not in the service of the shipowner, and do not sign the ship's articles. In the case of passenger vessels and cruise liners it includes all those stewards and other personnel employed solely to serve and attend upon the passengers, provided that they are engaged under articles or entered in the master's portage bill.

Some vessels now have two regular crews, only one of which will be on board ship at any time. The wages of the "working" crew alone can

[8] See para. 11.36, *post*.

[9] See *Board of Trade v. Anglo-American Oil Co.* (1911) 16 Com.Cas. 151, where maintenance of a distressed seaman under the Merchant Shipping Act 1906, s. 41(1) was held to mean his board and lodging. See also the Opinion No. 22 of the Advisory Committee of the Association of Average Adjusters.

[10] See *Anglo-Argentine Live Stock Agency v. Temperley S.S. Co.* [1899] 2 Q.B. 403.

be considered for allowance under the Rule, but it is clear that the "leave pay" considered as "wages" under Rule XI(c) will be substantial.

"fuel" This includes all fuel consumed in the main engine, auxiliary machinery, and galley. **11.07**

"stores" In earlier times this word may have been construed to cover only lubricating oils, grease, and waste, etc., consumed in the necessary running and maintenance of engines in the engine room, but this limited construction no longer applies. The Advisory Committee of the Association of Average Adjusters gave it as their opinion (No. 21) that:

> "... there is no difference of practice between the adjusters of the United States and the adjusters in this country which is to allow under the York-Antwerp Rules for such *deck, engine room or steward's stores* as may be consumed during the vessel's detention, and which are not covered by allowances elsewhere provided for in the York-Antwerp Rules."

"the prolongation of the voyage" This phrase relates to the extra period spent *at sea* during a vessel's resort to and from a port of refuge. The period commences from the moment of deviation from the intended route, ceases temporarily on the ship's arrival at the port of refuge, resumes when she leaves that port, and ends finally when the original point of deviation—or course—has been regained. In the common case where the ship sails from the port of refuge on a direct course for her destination and does not pass the original point of deviation, account must obviously be taken and credit given for the unperformed leg of the voyage (AB in the diagram below). **11.08**

In this same common case, and particularly where the vessel is disabled and proceeds at slow speed into the port of refuge, but after repairs is able to resume the voyage at normal full speed, a variety of methods for calculating the precise extent of this "prolongation of the voyage" present themselves, and there is no international uniformity of practice amongst adjusters.

This was accepted by an A.I.D.E. Working Group in a Report prior to the meetings at Sydney at which the York-Antwerp Rules 1994 were promulgated. A majority of members of the Working Group favoured a re-drafting of Rule XI(a) to clarify exactly what was intended, but, unfortunately, no text was offered to meet this perceived need for clarification, with the result that no change in the wording was made in 1994 and average adjusters are seemingly left free to pursue their own individual interpretations of the meaning of the phrase.

For the purpose of illustrating some of the possible methods of calculating this "prolongation of the voyage", a typical—if extreme—example will be adopted, with the vessel limping or being towed from point "A" into the port of refuge "X" at five knots, and after repairs

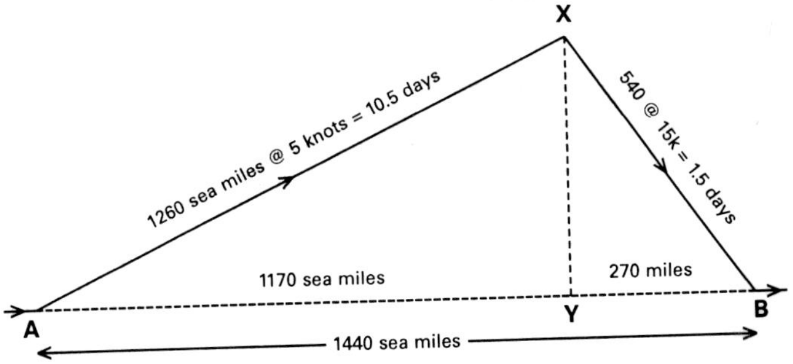

Prolongation of Voyage - Calculation Diagram

there resuming the voyage to point "B" and onward at her normal speed of 15 knots.

In the last two editions of this work it was submitted that the practice was to calculate the *extra distance* covered by the deviation and to allow crew wages, etc., during the time taken to cover that extra distance, *commencing with the original point of deviation*. Thus: the extra distance is AX (1,260) plus XB (540) = 1,800, less the normal AB (1,400) equals 360 miles, commencing at point "A" and, accordingly, at five knots, taking three days, during which the cost of the crew wages and the bunkers actually consumed can be charged to general average.

As a simple rule of thumb, this practice has much to commend it—it is far more reasonable than the "Time Only" method 1 detailed below[11]—

[11] **Methods of Calculating the Prolongation of the Voyage:**

1. *The "Time Only" Method.* This adopts the actual times taken on legs AX and XB and gives credit for leg AB at normal full speed; *i.e.*

10.5 + 1.5 = 12 days less 4 = **8 days.**

This method is patently wrong and unfair in cases of *accidental* damage in that it charges to general average the whole loss by delay due to slow-steaming on the passage (AX) to the port of refuge while effectively progressing at least part of the scheduled voyage. (It will be appreciated that, for instance, if a vessel is obliged to put into a scheduled port of call as a port of refuge, NO allowance of crew wages, etc., would be permissible: see para 11.10, *post*). The assumption for the time credit of only 4 days at normal full speed when the vessel is incapable of such speed is also highly suspect.

We now return to the more commendable methods which confine their attention to the *extra distance* steamed of 360 sea miles, but apply differing factors to translate this extra distance into a period of time.

2. *The "Original Lowndes" Method* described in the text (as above), produces **3 days**.
3. *The "Lowndes Converse" Method.* Whereas the original Lowndes Method 2, above, places this 360 miles immediately on the commencement of the deviation at point "A", *i.e.* at 5 knots and, therefore, taking 3 days, the converse would be to say that the true deviation does not commence until the scheduled or normal 1440 miles from A to B has been accomplished. Thus, the 360 miles is sited at the end of the 15 knot passage XB and, therefore, takes only **1 day**.
4. *The "Normal Speed" Method* assumes that any reductions in speed resulting from an *accidental* cause should be ignored completely, and that the vessel at all times proceeded at her normal pre-accident speed. In the quoted example, at a uniform normal speed of 15 knots the allowances in general average would be AX + XB less AB, *i.e.* 3.5 days plus 1.5 days = 5 days, less the normal 4 days, equals **1 day** for both crew wages and bunkers consumed at full speed.

but it cannot be denied that it is still somewhat over-generous in that the shipowner receives some compensation in general average for a delay occasioned essentially by the reduction in speed resulting from an *accident*, the consequences of which ought not to be made good in general average. The separate delays occasioned by the putting into the

Although in the particular example given, this method produces the same **1 day** as Method 3, it differs from Method 3 in that if the vessel *turned back* to a port of call as a port of refuge, the passages to and from that port would be assumed under Method 4 to be both at 15 knots, whereas under Method 3 the two passages would be taken at their actual speeds.

5. *The "Average" Method.* This Method effectively places the extra 360 miles partly on each of the passages to and from the port of refuge, as follows:

AX	=	1,260	sea miles taking	10.5 days
XB	=	540	,, ,, ,,	1.5 ,,
		1,800	sea miles taking	12.0 days
Extra Distance		360	sea miles in ppn	**2.4 days**

6. *The "NGH" Method.* In his book *The York/Antwerp Rules*, Mr N.G. Hudson favours a method which also places the extra 360 miles on both passages, to and from the port of refuge, but in a different manner. On the diagram above, a perpendicular is dropped from the apex "X" to line AB, bisecting it at point "Y" such that (in this case) AY will equal 1170 miles and YB will equal 270 miles. The division of the 360 miles then proceeds as follows:

AX	=	1,260 sea miles, less	AY	1,170	=	90 miles @ 5k	=	.75 day
XB	=	540 ,, ,, ,,	YB	270	=	270 ,, @ 15k	=	.75 ,,
		1,800 sea miles, less		1,440	=	360 miles	=	**1.5 days**

This method, like the *"Average" Method 5*, is essentially a compromise between the *"Original Lowndes" Method 2* and the *"Lowndes Converse" Method 3*, but it may be worthy of record that if the direction of the voyage is reversed, whereas the *"Average" Method 5* gives a reasonably logical and lesser prolongation of **1.6 days** on an overall reduced delay, the *"NGH" Method* produces a surprising increased allowance of **2.5 days**, as below:

BY	=	270 miles @ 5k	=	2.25 days
YA	=	90 ,, @ 15k	=	.25 ,,
		360 miles		2.50 days

7. *The "Towage" Method.* In contrast to the previous examples where the vessel proceeded into the port of refuge under her own power, it will now be assumed that following, say, a complete engine breakdown from an accidental cause, the vessel is towed at 5 knots into the port of refuge.

For the purpose of illustration it will be best to put representative figures to the various items under consideration: the daily costs are: crew wages, etc., 500; bunkers consumed at 100 per ton—20 tons on main engine at full speed; 1 ton on generators, etc., whether at full speed or under tow; and the towage 100,000.

Towage—1,260 sea miles @ 5 knots = 10.5 days			100,000
Credit: Bunkers saved on main engine:			
Should steam	1,440 sea miles	(A − B)	
Did steam	540 ,, ,,	(X − B)	
Saved	900 sea miles		
@ 15 knots = 2.5 days = 50 tons @ 100			5,000
			95,000
Crew Wages, etc., per "Average" Method 5—2.4 days (say)			1,200
Bunkers—2.4 days			240
		Total Allowances	96,440

port of refuge and those consequent upon accident ought really to be kept apart and their costs more properly borne by the appropriate parties.

A number of possible methods for calculating the prolongation of the voyage occasioned by a ship entering a port or place of refuge are listed in the footnote 11, below. The editors have given serious consideration to each of these but are of the view that none can claim to be incontrovertibly perfect. In the circumstances, and until there can be some international agreement on the matter, they favour Method 5, below, the "Average" Method.

It is convenient to state here that the combined allowances for wages and maintenance of crew made under Rule XI(a) and (b) are calculated in this country to the nearest half-day,[12] but in the United States to the nearest whole day.[13] Thus, a total allowance of 80 hours would count as three and a half days in this country, but only three days in the United States.

Allowances Commence only from Moment of Deviation

11.09 No allowance can be made in general average for wages and maintenance of crew, etc., until a vessel makes a positive move and deviation towards a port of refuge. Thus:

(1) A vessel involved in a collision may anchor immediately pending a diver's inspection or the arrival of tugs, but not until she commences to weigh anchor and head towards a port of refuge can the allowance of wages and maintenance of crew, etc., commence.
(2) A vessel may sustain severe damages in a gale making it imperative that she put into a port of refuge. However, if she is quite unable to turn about for fear of broaching to, no allowance of wages and maintenance of crew, etc., can commence until the weather moderates and she is able to head in the general direction of the port of refuge.
(3) Not until a vessel refloats from an accidental stranding can the allowance of wages and maintenance of crew, etc., commence, (though payments to crew for overtime worked in jettisoning or discharging cargo, or other efforts to refloat, can be allowed as general average, also the fuel and stores consumed in working the winches and in actual efforts to refloat—assuming the vessel to be in peril).

If a collision or other accident renders it necessary to put the vessel ashore to prevent her sinking, or because the authorities refuse entry

[12] Opinion No. 5 of the Advisory Committee of the Association of Average Adjusters.
[13] Rule of Practice XVIII of the Association of Average Adjusters of the United States.

into the port of refuge, proper, until temporary repairs have been effected, crew wages, etc., will generally be allowable while the vessel is "voluntarily stranded". It will be necessary to demonstrate only that the vessel and her cargo were in peril, that she has deviated from her intended voyage, and that the stranding place is a "place of refuge" within the meaning outlined in paragraph 10.34, below.

"port or place of refuge" If a ship can be said to have entered a port or place of refuge when, for the common safety, she enters a port which she would in any event have entered as a port of call,[14] there is no prolongation of the voyage within the meaning of this sub-rule. **11.10**

It occasionally happens that a vessel aground and in peril will discharge part of her cargo into lighters, which may then be towed to some nearly safe anchorage or port. After refloating, the vessel deviates to that anchorage or port solely to reload the cargo. Although not strictly within the rule, the wages and maintenance of the crew, etc., during any deviation and whilst reloading cargo are customarily allowed in general average.

"when the expenses of entering such port or place are allowable in general average in accordance with Rule X(a)." This sub-rule can operate only when the expenses of entering the port or place are allowable under Rule X(a), that is, "in consequence of accident, sacrifice or other extraordinary circumstances, which render that necessary for the common safety".

Historical Development and Practice of Rule XI(b)

Glasgow Resolutions 1860 **11.11**

In most countries other than England, wages and maintenance of crew during the detention at a port of refuge were allowable as general average. This majority view prevailed at the International Conference at Glasgow in 1860 and the following Resolution was passed:

> "(8). That the wages and provisions for the ship's crew ought to be allowed to the shipowner in general average, from the date the ship reaches a port of refuge in distress until the date on which she leaves it."

York Rules 1864 **11.12**

The general principle that wages and maintenance of crew at a port of refuge should be made good as general average, as stated in the first sentence of the rule quoted below, was accepted unanimously by the delegates to the York Conference in 1864. A proposal that there should

[14] See Commentary under Rule X(a), para. 10.35, *ante*. See also para. 10.34, *ante*, for meaning of "port or place".

be no allowance for wages and maintenance if the ship was condemned at the port of refuge was, however, strongly contested. The general view was that wages and maintenance should be allowed up to the date of the ship's condemnation, but in deference to the British viewpoint, the proposal was deleted and the problem left as an open question.

The second sentence of the Rule was added after the reported discussion, no doubt to conform with an identical provision in Rule VII (now Rule X(a)).[15]

> "When a ship shall have entered a port of refuge under the circumstances defined in Rule VII, the wages and cost of maintenance of the master and mariners, from the time of entering such port until the ship shall have been made ready to proceed upon her voyage shall be made good as general average. Except that any portion of the cargo left at such port of refuge on account of its being unfit to be carried forward, or on account of the unfitness or inability of the ship to carry it, shall not be called on to contribute to such general average."

11.13 *York-Antwerp Rules 1877*

On this occasion, the first sentence of the 1864 Rule was affirmed unchanged, but the second sentence was deleted to correspond with an identical deletion from Rule VII (now Rule X(a))[16]:

> "When a ship shall have entered a port of refuge under the circumstances defined in Rule VII, the wages and cost of maintenance of the master and mariners, from time of entering such port until the ship shall have been made ready to proceed upon her voyage, shall be made good as general average."

11.14 *York-Antwerp Rules 1890*

Apart from renumbering the Rule and greater precision in the wording used, no material changes were made on this occasion, but an extra sentence was added to provide for the situation where the ship was condemned or the voyage abandoned. This had been left as an open question by the framers of the 1864 Rules:

> "When a ship shall have entered or been detained in any port or place under the circumstances, or for the purposes of the repairs, mentioned in Rule X, the wages, payable to the master, officers and crew together with the cost of maintenance of the same, during the extra period of detention in such port or place until the ship shall or should have been made ready to proceed upon her voyage, shall be admitted as general average. But when the ship is condemned or does not proceed on her original voyage, the wages and maintenance of the master, officers and crew, incurred after the date of the ship's condemnation or of the abandonment of the voyage, shall not be admitted as general average."

[15] See para. 10.27, *ante*.
[16] See para. 10.28, *ante*.

York-Antwerp Rules 1924 **11.15**

The 1890 Rule was affirmed unchanged, but a new sentence was added at the Stockholm Conference providing (consistently with Rule X(c)) that the allowance of wages and maintenance should continue, in the event of condemnation of the ship or abandonment of the voyage, until completion of discharge of cargo.

> "In the event of the condemnation of the ship or the abandonment of the voyage before completion of discharge of cargo, wages and maintenance of crew, as above, shall be admitted as general average up to the date of completion of discharge."

It was supposed that, without this provision, the owner of a ship which had been condemned might be tempted to discharge the crew in order to save expense, and that this course would not be to the advantage of the cargo, having regard to the possibility among other things of a sudden outbreak of fire on board.

Another innovation in 1924 was Rule XX, providing for the allowance in general average of fuel and stores consumed during the extra detention in a port or place of refuge, thus belatedly recognising that steam (and motorships) had ousted sail. Wages and maintenance of crew during the same period had been allowable under the Rules since 1860.[17] **11.16**

Rule XX (second paragraph)

> "Fuel and stores consumed during extra detention in a port or place of loading, call or refuge shall also be allowed in general average for the period during which wages and maintenance of master, officers and crew are allowed in terms of Rule XI, except such fuel and stores as are consumed in effecting repairs not allowable in general average."

York-Antwerp Rules 1950 **11.17**

The whole of the 1924 Rule XI became the first paragraph of the 1950 Rule XI(b) and, whilst there was no change in the substance of the Rule, there were improvements in the drafting. The 1924 Rule referred to the vessel entering or being detained in any port or place under the circumstances or for the purpose of the repairs mentioned in Rule X, but these words did not make it clear to which sub-sections of Rule X reference was intended. Clarification was achieved by spelling out in the 1950 Rule that wages, etc., were allowable when the vessel had entered or been detained in any port or place in consequence of accident, sacrifice or other extraordinary circumstances which rendered that necessary for the common safety, or to enable damage to the ship caused by sacrifice

[17] See para. 11.11, *ante*.

or accident to be repaired, if the repairs were necessary for the safe prosecution of the voyage.

11.18 "(b) When a ship shall have entered or been detained in any port or place in consequence of accident, sacrifice or other extraordinary circumstances which render that necessary for the common safety, or to enable damage to the ship caused by sacrifice or accident to be repaired, if the repairs were necessary for the safe prosecution of the voyage, the wages and maintenance of the master, officers and crew reasonably incurred during the extra period of detention in such port or place until the ship shall or should have been made ready to proceed upon her voyage, shall be admitted in general average. When the ship is condemned or does not proceed on her original voyage, the extra period of detention shall be deemed not to extend beyond the date of the ship's condemnation or of the abandonment of the voyage or, if discharge of charge is not then completed, beyond the date of completion of discharge."

11.19 The opportunity was also taken in 1950 to incorporate within Rule XI(b) part of the old and inconveniently situated Rule XX dealing with the allied subject of fuel and stores consumed at a port of refuge.

"Fuel and stores consumed during the extra period of detention shall be admitted as general average, except such fuel and stores as are consumed in effecting repairs not allowable in general average."

11.20 Another new paragraph was added to this sub-rule in 1950. In accordance with an Opinion of the Advisory Committee of the Association of Average Adjusters issued in 1944, the practice in the United Kingdom was to treat port charges incurred during the extra period of detention of a ship (that is, beyond the period permitted by the initial charge payable on entering the port), in the same manner as the cost of the operations being undertaken during the period for which such dues were charged.

This did not accord with the practice in other countries, in most, if not in all, of which such dues were invariably allowed in general average in full. But it became apparent during the discussions of the British Maritime Law Association's Sub-Committee that British underwriters were not prepared to agree to the allowance of port charges on a basis other than that of the British practice, and they proposed the wording in the current Rule:

"Port charges incurred during the extra period of detention shall likewise be admitted as general average except such charges as are incurred solely by reason of repairs not allowable in general average."

11.21 A different wording was put forward for discussion at the Amsterdam Conference, but British underwriters again offered as an amendment their own wording and this was accepted by the Conference without discussion.[18]

The wording of the final form of this paragraph left much to be desired and it is a fact that average adjusters abroad interpreted the new rule as being a confirmation of their old practice, while British adjusters again began to differ in their treatment of "daily" port charges until 1955. It was then agreed, on a strict interpretation of the wording, and in the interests of international uniformity, to follow the practice adopted in other countries.

York-Antwerp Rules 1974 **11.22**

In conformity with the changes made concurrently in Rule X(b), an important new paragraph was added to this sub-rule in 1974 to deny general average allowances in those cases where damages were merely *discovered* at a port of loading or of call without any accident or other extraordinary circumstances connected with such damage having taken place during the voyage. (An example of the situation envisaged by the new wording is given in paragraph 10.51, above). Some minor changes were also made in the wording of the sub-rule relating to condemnation of the ship and abandonment of the voyage, but in all other respects the 1950 sub-rule remained unaltered.

York-Antwerp Rules 1994

No changes of any real consequence were made on this occasion, but:

(1) The framers of the additions and minor changes made in 1974 had made mention of crew wages, etc., and fuel and stores consumed, but overlooked the concomitant port charges that would be incurred. This oversight has now been remedied and, for ease of reference, the additional wordings are printed in italics in the full text of the sub-Rule copied in the next paragraph.
(2) The five paragraphs of the Rule were re-arranged in what is thought to be a more logical order.

Rule XI(b)

When a ship shall have entered or been detained in any port or place in consequence of accident, sacrifice or other extraordinary circumstances which render that necessary for the common safety, or **11.23**

[18] See para. 11.32, *post*, also the annual report for 1955 of the Association of Average Adjusters.

to enable damage to the ship caused by sacrifice or accident to be repaired, if the repairs were necessary for the safe prosecution of the voyage, the wages and maintenance of the master, officers and crew reasonably incurred during the extra period of detention in such port or place until the ship shall or should have been made ready to proceed upon her voyage, shall be admitted in general average.

Fuel and stores consumed during the extra period of detention shall be admitted as general average, except such fuel and stores as are consumed in effecting repairs not allowable in general average.

Port charges incurred during the extra period of detention shall likewise be admitted as general average except such charges as are incurred solely by reason of repairs not allowable in general average.

Provided that when damage to the ship is discovered at a port or place of loading or call without any accident or other extraordinary circumstance connected with such damage having taken place during the voyage, then the wages and maintenance of master, officers and crew and fuel and stores consumed *and port charges incurred* during the extra detention for repairs to damages so discovered shall not be admissible as general average, even if the repairs are necessary for the safe prosecution of the voyage.

When the ship is condemned or does not proceed on her original voyage, *the* wages and maintenance of the master, officers and crew and fuel and stores consumed *and port charges* shall be admitted as general average only up to the ship's condemnation or of the abandonment of the voyage or up to the date of completion of discharge of cargo if the condemnation or abandonment takes place before that date.

Construction

11.24 Whereas the previous sub-rule XI(a) provides for the period while *at sea* proceeding to or from a port of refuge, the present sub-rule XI(b) deals with the period spent *within* any port or place (of refuge) and permits the allowance in general average of:

(1) wages and maintenance of crew;
(2) fuel and stores consumed; and
(3) port charges incurred;

during the extra period of detention in the port when the ship shall have:

(a) **"entered"** in consequence of accident, sacrifice or other extraordinary circumstances which render that necessary for the common safety. (Estimated to cover 98 per cent of all cases);

(b) been **"detained"** in consequence of accident, sacrifice or other extraordinary circumstances which render that necessary for the common safety. (Estimated to cover one per cent of all cases. For example a serious collision in the port causes severe leakage, or a fire in the cargo threatens the common safety even within the port);

(c) been **"detained"** to enable damage to the ship caused by sacrifice or accident to be repaired, if the repairs were necessary for the safe prosecution of the voyage. (Estimated to cover one per cent of all cases. For example, some accident to the ship occurs in the port which in no way threatens the common safety while within the port, but which requires repair before the voyage can be safely prosecuted).

Thus, the scope of this sub-rule is undoubtedly very wide, but there are a few situations where wages and maintenance of crew, etc., during any extra detention would not be allowed as general average, for example: **11.25**

(1) To recondition damaged cargo, whether the damage be from accidental cause or by general average sacrifice.

(2) To rectify some defect in the ship which constitutes neither accident[19] nor sacrifice,[20] but merely an extraordinary circumstance[21] (for example overheated bearings, or a slowly extending fracture in a crankshaft), if the work is done at a port of loading or of call at which the vessel has called in the normal course of her voyage. See also the commentary on Rule X(b).[22]

(3) Where a vessel has been ordered *out* of port for the safety of the port (for example in fear of an explosion on board ship).

(4) During the extra time it may take to discharge damaged cargo at its intended destination, even though the damage may be caused by, for example, flooding the hold for the common safety.

First Paragraph

"shall have entered" See commentary on Rule X(a).[23] **11.26**

"any port or place" These words are clearly wide enough to cover the port of loading whether or not the ship had sailed and returned thereto, a port of call, a port of refuge and a port to which the ship has removed from a port of loading, call or refuge for repairs.[24]

[19] See para. 10.35, *ante*.
[20] See para. 2.10, *ante*.
[21] See para. 10.36, *ante*.
[22] See para. 10.50, *ante*.
[23] See para. 10.33, *ante*.
[24] See also commentary under Rule X(a) para. 10.33, *ante*.

"accident, sacrifice or other extraordinary circumstances" See commentary on Rule X(a).[25]

"the common safety" See commentary on Rule A.[26]

"necessary for the safe prosecution of the voyage." See commentary on Rule X(b).[27] "The voyage" is the voyage which is the common maritime adventure, and detention during repairs postponed until after the voyage (including repairs at the discharging part) is outside the scope of this sub-rule.[28] It is submitted that permanent repairs may not be necessary for the safe prosecution of the voyage if temporary repairs can be effected more speedily; but this is really a question of fact to be determined in each case.

11.27 **"wages"** These are defined by sub-rule (c).[29]

"maintenance" See commentary on Rule XI(a).[30]

"crew" See commentary on Rule XI(a).[31]

"reasonably" This word was first introduced in the 1950 edition of this sub-rule, probably to give effect to the suggestion by the Scandinavian Committees that the duty to discharge part of the crew, if practicable, should not be entirely overlooked. When an extended stay in a port of refuge is to be expected, it is sometimes found that part of the crew will be signed off and repatriated, and a new crew engaged when the vessel is ready to resume her voyage. In such circumstances, the wages, etc., of the crew whilst on board ship are allowed in general average, also the cost of signing off, repatriation and re-engagement, up to the wages, etc., saved thereby.

11.28 **"extra period of detention"** Where a ship puts into a port of refuge and is there detained for the reasons specified in the sub-rule, the cost of wages, etc., during the whole period of detention will usually be admissible in general average. The word "extra" is not, however, mere surplusage but will take effect in such cases as detention at a port of call, in which case crew wages, etc., will be admissible only during the extra period of detention beyond what is required to fulfil the purpose of her scheduled call at the port.

[25] See paras. 10.35–10.36, *ante*.
[26] See para. A.96, *ante*.
[27] See para. 10.49, *ante*.
[28] *Wetherall (J. H.) & Co. v. The London Assurance* [1931] 2 K.B. 448. The adventure continues until discharge is completed, even if the voyage ends earlier: *Whitecross Wire Co. v. Savill* (1882) 8 Q.B.D. 653.
[29] See para. 11.36, *post*.
[30] See para. 11.06, *ante*.
[31] See para. 11.06, *ante*.

Very complex questions can arise when, for instance, fire breaks out in the cargo of a ship at one of her ports of discharge and an "extra period of detention" thereby results to the ship. It is not intended to raise, or answer, all the many questions that can arise in practice, but one on which much discussion has taken place concerns the period during which the fire continues to burn. As the Chairman of the United States Association of Average Adjusters said in his annual address in 1962:

> "It is considered by some that the detention period should commence at the time the fire is extinguished while others are of the view that the full period of time during which efforts are being made to extinguish the fire should be included in General Average."

It is submitted that the latter view is correct and that the vessel has been "detained . . . in consequence of accident . . . which render(s) that necessary for the common safety" within the meaning of the sub-rule. The practice in the United States is to commence allowances under the sub-rule from the time of the first act to extinguish the fire.

"until the ship shall or should have been made ready to proceed upon her voyage" It is to be stressed that it is the condition of the ship alone which will govern how long the "extra period of detention" in the port of refuge shall run; the fact that damaged cargo may still be in the course of being reconditioned when the ship is ready to sail, or that cargo interests (or the ship) have not yet provided salvage security, will not enable the period during which crew wages, etc., are allowed to be extended. **11.29**

It is also to be noted that the use of the word "should" provides that the extra period of detention may end before the ship is actually able or ready to proceed upon her voyage. This will be the case if it is found that the repairing of the ship was unnecessarily protracted[32] or that repairs falling outside the scope of the Rule have added to the period of detention. Once the ship has been made ready to proceed upon her voyage, the expenses of any extra period of detention resulting from an inability to sail owing to:

Fog or gales, will not be admissible in general average on the grounds that weather conditions are generally variable and irregular, and a similar delay might just as easily occur at sea on the voyage itself. **11.30**

Ice conditions may be allowable provided that it can be shown that such ice conditions were to be expected and were, or ought to have been,

[32] other than by a strike of repair workmen during the repairs. In the case of the *HMS "London"* (1914) T.LR. 196, where repairs were extended in time owing to a strike, the learned President stated that: "In the ordinary course of business industrial disputes may and do occur, and strikes ensue. Business men in the ordinary course assume this . . .".

within the contemplation of the master when he decided to put into the port of refuge.

A strike of pilots or tugs might also be allowable, depending upon circumstances. Strikes being less accurately predictable than ice conditions, but not so uncommon in modern times and in certain countries with troubled labour relations as to be beyond the bounds of forseeability.

Waiting for convoy (in war-time), was not admissible in general average, but the practice might be questioned if convoys sailed on known dates or at regular intervals.

Second Paragraph

11.31 **"Fuel and stores"** See commentary on Rule XI(a).[33]

"except such fuel and stores as are consumed in effecting repairs not allowable in general average." A ship in port consumes power to provide lighting and heating for crew, refrigeration and ventilation of cargo holds, etc.; the cost of all fuel and stores consumed for these routine ship's purposes during the extra detention is chargeable direct to general average. However, if additional fuel and stores are consumed in shifting a vessel to a dry dock or other repair berth, or to provide extra lighting, for repairs not allowable in general average, the cost of this additional fuel and stores is not allowable as general average.

Third Paragraph

11.32 **"port charges"** It is difficult to give an exhaustive list of what are comprised in "port charges" but the words certainly include port and dock dues payable on a day to day basis and may also include the cost of gangway watchmen, launch hire and garbage removal, etc., and perhaps also charges for steam, water and electricity supplied from ashore for use on ordinary ship's purposes during the extra period of detention.

"except such charges as are incurred solely by reason of repairs not allowable in general average." These words raise a nice problem of causation in some cases. Suppose that a ship meets with an accident and puts into a port of refuge for the common safety, but is out of danger once she is in port. Suppose also that repairs must be effected for the safe prosecution of the voyage and that it is decided to effect permanent repairs. Whilst the vessel is so detained port charges are incurred on a day to day basis, but in addition charges are payable for the use of a dry dock to enable the work of repair to be done. Are either the day to day or the dry dock charges "incurred solely by reason of repairs not

[33] See para. 11.07, *ante*.

allowable in general average"? It is suggested that the dry dock charges are clearly excluded by this exception. So far as the day to day charges are concerned, they are incurred by reason of the detention. But how does the detention arise? Does it arise solely by reason of the repairs? Or does it arise by reason of the unfitness of the vessel to resume the voyage unless and until the repairs are completed? It is suggested that the courts would hold that the cause of these day to day charges was the detention but that, if this be wrong, they would hold that the cause was the unseaworthiness of the ship. Thus on either view the day to day charges would be outside the exception and so would be admitted as general average.

Fourth Paragraph

"Provided that when damage to the ship is discovered at a port or place of loading or call without any accident or other extraordinary circumstances connected with such damage having taken place during the voyage," See commentary on Rule X(b).[34] 11.33

Fifth Paragraph

"When the ship is condemned or does not proceed on her original voyage," See commentary on Rule X(c).[35] 11.34

"the date of the ship's condemnation or of the abandonment of the voyage" See commentary on Rule X(c).[36]

Historical Development and Practice of Rule XI(c)

York-Antwerp Rules 1950 11.35

With the ending of the Second World War a great change in labour relations and working conditions was set in motion, many countries including legislation to create a "welfare" state with social security, etc., while notionally shorter working hours on board a ship in fact meant the payment of considerably more overtime to the crew.

This resulted in some doubt as to really what was comprised within the term *wages* in Rule XI and practice varied with regard to payments for compulsory social insurance, pension funds and crew overtime, etc.

[34] See paras. 10.43 and 10.51, *ante*.
[35] See para. 10.65, *ante*.
[36] See para. 10.68, *ante*.

This was resolved in 1950 with the introduction of sub-rule (c), a definition of the term *wages*. Henceforth, *all* such payments would be treated as wages whether imposed by law upon the shipowners or made under the articles of employment, and the sub-rule has remained unchanged ever since.[37]

York-Antwerp Rules 1994

RULE XI(c)

11.36 **For the purpose of this and the other Rules wages shall include all payments made to or for the benefit of the master, officers and crew, whether such payments be imposed by law upon the shipowners or be made under the terms or articles of employment.**

CONSTRUCTION

No problem of construction appears to arise on this part of the Rule and the wording has not yet been considered by the English courts.

Although given in a different context, the following definition of wages by the Advisory Committee of the Association of Average Adjusters is apt for general average purposes:

> "The term 'wages' comprises the gross amount of all those payments made by the Shipowners to the members of the crew on a monthly, weekly or other periodic basis including leave pay, overseas allowance, etc. and the employer's contribution to State and other Insurance and/or Pension Schemes which relate to those payments, and also payments of overtime to the crew in pursuance of their normal watchkeeping and/or other duties which may loosely be termed regular overtime."

Examples of "regular overtime" include sailors acting as night-watchmen, engineers on generator watches, and catering staff preparing early, late, and weekend meals, all resulting from the 24-hours-a-day nature of life on board ship and the progressive reduction in the acceptable number of hours in a working week.

It is not uncommon today for a shipowner to arrange with a crewing agent to provide an entire or part crew for his vessel, often from another country. Obviously the agents charge for the various services they

[37] A parallel sub-rule (d) relating to crew overtime was also introduced in 1950, but this was subsequently regarded as superfluous and deleted in 1994. The wording of this sub-rule (d), and a commentary thereon, appears in paras. 11.36, 11.37 of the 11th ed.

perform, and it is submitted that their agency charges cannot be considered as "wages" for allowance under Rule XI, they being neither "payments made to (n)or for the benefit of the master, officers and crew".

Historical Development and Practice of Rule XI(d)

(Rule XI(d) deals with the cost of measures to prevent or minimise damage to the environment)

English Law and Practice

Just as liability for actual pollution or environmental damage may in certain circumstances be allowed in general average in English law,[38] so may the costs of taking measures to avoid or minimise such damage. Nevertheless, the avoidance of pollution or environmental damage, however laudable, is not in itself an objective which gives rise to a claim in general average, and it follows that in principle the costs of avoidance measures are not as such allowable in English law, even if they are carried out as part of an operation performed for the common safety; they are only allowable if they are a *necessary part*, or a *direct consequence*, of such an operation. The position is the same under the pre-1990 versions of the York-Antwerp Rules. In practice, however, the cost of such measures was often allowed in general average in all the above circumstances, particularly when the operation of which they formed part was undertaken by salvors acting on a "no cure no pay" basis and the salvage award was increased as a result of the salvors' skill and efforts in preventing or minimising pollution.[39] In 1990 this practice with regard to salvage was sanctioned under the York-Antwerp Rules by the amendment effected to Rule VI.[40] **11.37**

York-Antwerp Rules 1994

Rule XI(d) forms part of the "pollution compromise" adopted at the 1994 CMI Conference at Sydney, the basic feature of which was to exclude from general average liabilities and clean-up costs in connection with pollution which had actually occurred, but to admit certain of the costs of avoidance measures. Rule XI(d) was selected as the vehicle for the provisions which allow the costs of these avoidance measures, Rule **11.38**

[38] See para. C.15, *ante*.
[39] See para. 6.13, *ante*.
[40] See para. 6.16, *ante*.

XI(d) of the 1974 Rules (which dealt with crew overtime during repairs at a port of refuge) having been deleted on the grounds that it was superfluous. However, in contrast with the other sections of Rule XI, the new Rule XI(d) is by no means confined to expenses incurred at or in entering a port of refuge, and its provisions would no doubt have been considered worthy of a separate rule of their own but for a natural reluctance to add to or alter the numbering of the Rules.

The general exclusion of losses and expenses relating to pollution or damage to the environment is contained in the second paragraph of Rule C, and the overall intention is that unless such costs are recoverable under Rule XI(d) or the second paragraph of Rule VI(a) they are excluded altogether from general average.

11.39 RULE XI(d)

The cost of measures undertaken to prevent or minimise damage to the environment shall be allowed in general average when incurred in any or all of the following circumstances:

(i) as part of an operation performed for the common safety which, had it been undertaken by a party outside the common maritime adventure, would have entitled such party to a salvage reward;

(ii) as a condition of entry into or departure from any port or place in the circumstances prescribed in Rule X(a);

(iii) as a condition of remaining at any port or place in the circumstances prescribed in Rule XI(b), provided that when there is an actual escape or release of pollutant substances the cost of any additional measures required on that account to prevent or minimise pollution or environmental damage shall not be allowed as general average;

(iv) necessarily in connection with the discharging, storing or reloading of cargo whenever the cost of those operations is admissible as general average.

CONSTRUCTION

11.40 **"to prevent or minimise"** The wording is the same as that used in the International Convention on Salvage 1989[41]. The inclusion of a reference to *minimising* damage to the environment makes it clear that the allowances granted by the Rule do not cease to apply as soon as some

[41] Art. 8, para. 1(b), which imposes on salvors a duty "to exercise due care to prevent or minimise damage to the environment". Art. 13, para. 1(b) requires that their skill and efforts in that regard must be taken into account in fixing their remuneration.

environmental damage has occurred, but the Rule does require a clear distinction to be drawn between the costs of avoiding further damage, and expenses in respect of damage already incurred. It is no fault of the draughtsman of the Rule that the distinction will sometimes be difficult to draw. For example, the costs of minimising the amount of a pollutant substance which escapes is clearly within the Rule even though some has already escaped and caused damage to the environment, as are the costs of limiting the area over which the escaped pollutant is able to disperse.[42] But assume that the pollutant has already contaminated a coastline. Can the costs of a clean-up operation be allowed? If the operation is undertaken by or on behalf of the shipowner, if it will reduce "damage to the environment",[43] and if it is undertaken in the circumstances described in one of the sub-paragraphs of the Rule, the costs could be argued to fall within the words of the Rule. However, it was definitely not the intention of the framers of the Rule that such clean-up costs should ever be allowed, even when the shipowner was required to give a guarantee in respect of clean-up costs as a condition of entering or remaining in a port of refuge (see sub-paragraphs (ii) and (iii) below).

"damage to the environment" Again the words are the same as those of the 1989 Salvage Convention, and their effect has been discussed in the context of Rule C.[44] It will be noted that the opening provisions of Rule XI(d), unlike Rule C, contain no additional reference to "the escape or release of pollutant substances". It follows that the actual or threatened escape or release of a pollutant does not of itself bring Rule XI(d) into play, and it must in each case be determined whether the result of the escape or release would be "damage to the environment". In the specific cases referred to in sub-paragraphs (ii) to (iv) of the Rule, this requirement will be fulfilled when the actual or threatened pollution is sufficiently major to cause substantial damage to human health or to marine life or resources. However, in the case of a deep-sea salvage operation, which would otherwise fall within Rule XI(d)(i), even a major escape or release of pollutant substances may give rise to no actual or threatened damage to the environment,[45] with the consequence that the costs of preventing or minimising the escape do not fall within Rule XI(d) and cannot be recovered. **11.41**

[42] However, where the claim is made under sub-para. (iii) costs of this nature are not allowable; see paras. 11.47—11.48, *post*.

[43] See the definition of "damage to the environment" in the 1989 Salvage Convention: see para. C.31, *ante*.

[44] See para. C.31, *ante*.

[45] *I.e.* because there is no threat of damage which affects "coastal or inland waters or areas adjacent thereto": see the definition of "damage to the environment" set out in para. C.31, *ante*.

Sub-paragraph (i)

11.42 **"as part of an operation performed for the common safety"** The purpose of sub-paragraph (i) is to ensure that a party to the adventure who carries out salvage operations for the common safety, or who hires a contractor to perform the operations at a fixed price or rate, can recover in general average the costs of those measures for preventing or avoiding damage to the environment which, had they been performed by a salvor working on a "no cure no pay" basis, would have entitled him to an enhanced award under the 1989 Salvage Convention.[46] Under the Convention the salvor owes a duty to the owners of ship and cargo to exercise due care to prevent or minimise such damage, and his skill and efforts in so doing are taken into account in fixing the reward; Rule VI then provides that the full amount of the award shall be allowed in general average. Against this background it would clearly be illogical that a shipowner who performed the operations himself, or hired a contractor to do so, should not be able to recover the costs of those measures for preventing or minimising environmental damage which formed part of the operations. If he were unable to do so, a shipowner would be encouraged to engage salvors on a "no cure no pay" basis, which would usually mean that cargo's liability would in the end be greater.

The sub-paragraph does not impose any requirement such as probably exists under English law[47] to the effect that the preventive measures should be a necessary part of, or directly caused by, the operation performed for the common safety. It simply requires that they should be *part of* that operation. This clearly covers the case where the measures in question are taken to prevent the salvage operations themselves from causing environmental damage, and it probably includes every other case where the measures can properly be regarded as ancillary to the operation being performed for the common safety. The latter must always be the predominant purpose of the operation as a whole.

The expression *for the common safety* is the same as that used in Rule A, and its meaning is discussed in the context of that Rule.[48]

11.43 **"which ... would have entitled such party to a salvage reward;"** Under the Salvage Convention 1989, which has been incorporated into English law,[49] the right to a salvage award arises when "salvage operations which have had a useful result" have been rendered.[50] "Salvage operations" are widely defined as:

[46] However, the Rule contains no specific requirement that the claimant's efforts in preventing or minimising environmental damage should be such as would merit an enhanced reward under the Salvage Convention: see para. 11.43, *post*.

[47] See para. 11.37, *ante*.

[48] See paras. A.17 *et seq.*, *ante*.

[49] See the Merchant Shipping Act 1995, s. 224.

[50] Salvage Convention 1989, Art. 12 para. 1.

> "any act or activity undertaken to assist a vessel or any other property in danger in navigable waters or in any other waters whatsoever."[51]

These requirements will usually be fulfilled in any general average situation, and it will be remembered that Rule XI(d)(i) itself requires that the operations should have been undertaken for the common safety. However the requirement that the operations should have had a useful result may sometimes be of practical significance. Rule XI(d)(i) contemplates that the outcome of the salvage operation must be such that, if the operation had been performed by a salvor outside the common maritime adventure, it would have entitled him to a reward under Article 13 of the Convention. Thus if the property is not saved, or if the operations referred to in the opening words of Rule XI(d) did not contribute to its preservation, there can be no claim under XI(d)(i).[52] It is not sufficient that the operations should have given rise to a right to special compensation under Article 14 of the Convention, since this does not, it is submitted, amount to a "salvage reward". Just as special compensation under Article 14 is excluded from Rule VI,[53] so it falls outside the scope of Rule XI(d)(i).

Once it is established that the operation in question would, if undertaken by a party outside the common maritime adventure, have entitled him to an award under Article 13 of the Salvage Convention, the actual costs of the measures undertaken as part of the operation to prevent or minimise environmental damage are allowable in general average. The Rule does not require the adjuster to consider the amount by which, if the salvage operation had been undertaken by a stranger to the adventure, the award would have been enhanced under the provisions of Article 13 paragraph 1(b) of the Convention, or even to consider whether it would have been enhanced at all.

"had it been undertaken by a party outside the common maritime adventure;" The reason for the insertion of these words is the rule that a person who is under a pre-existing duty to render services for the purpose of safeguarding the property cannot claim a salvage reward.[54] For obvious reasons, in determining whether a party to the adventure is entitled to an allowance under sub-paragraph (i), this rule is to be disregarded.

[51] *Ibid.* Art. 1 para. (a).

[52] The principle which normally prevails in general average, outside the context of Rule XI(d)(i), is rather different. So long as the sacrifice or expenditure was reasonably made or incurred *for the purpose* of preserving the property from a common peril, and so long as some property is preserved (in the absence of which there would be no contributing interests), contribution is due. It is unnecessary to inquire whether the sacrifice or expenditure in question was instrumental in preserving the property.

[53] See Rule VI(b).

[54] The 1989 Salvage Convention gives effect to this rule by Art.17, which provides: "No payment is due under the provisions of this Convention unless the services rendered exceed what can reasonably be considered as due performance of a contract entered into before the danger arose."

Sub-paragraph (ii)

11.44 **"as a condition of entry into or departure from any port or place"** The purpose of sub-paragraph (ii) is to allow in general average the cost of those measures which must be undertaken, by reason of the requirements of local law, or of the legally constituted port or other authorities, if the ship is to be allowed to enter or leave the port or place. The distinction between these costs and the costs of measures undertaken as a condition of remaining at the port is discussed at paragraph 11.45, below.

Even if the authorities or the local law require a particular measure to be adopted in relation to environmental damage, the cost of that measure will only be allowable if it falls within the opening words of the Rule—that is, if it is undertaken to *prevent or minimise* damage to the environment, the scope of which expression is discussed above at paragraph 11.40. For example, if the authorities require the shipowner to give a guarantee covering (1) liability to third parties in respect of pollution damage, or (2) clean-up costs,[55] the costs of so doing will not be recoverable.

"in the circumstances prescribed in Rule X(a);" Rule X(a), the commentary on which will be found at paragraphs 10.33 to 10.40, above, essentially provides that the costs of entering and leaving a port of refuge shall be allowed in general average when, but only when, it was necessary to enter the port *for the common safety.*

Sub-paragraph (iii)

11.45 **"as a condition of remaining at any port or place"** Whereas sub-paragraph (ii) deals with costs when incurred as a condition of *entry or departure*, sub-paragraph (iii) deals with costs incurred as a condition of *remaining* at a port or place. However, there are other significant differences, discussed below, in the scope of sub-paragraphs (ii) and (iii), and it is therefore important to distinguish correctly between these two categories of costs. This may be less easy than at first appears. Suppose that a ship which is leaking oil wishes to enter port, and the port authorities stipulate that the ship will only be allowed to enter the port if booms are placed around immediately she has entered and are kept in place so long as she remains in the port. Is the undertaking of this measure, and the incurring of the consequent cost, a condition of entry, on the ground that it was imposed before the ship was allowed into the port, or is it a condition of remaining at the port, on the ground that the measures themselves are to be taken after rather than before the ship arrives in the port? If the latter, would it make any difference if the port authority required the shipowner to hire the booms, or to furnish a

[55] Clean-up costs are intended to be excluded from the scope of Rule XI(d): see para. 11.40, *ante*.

guarantee covering the costs of hiring and installing them before the ship was allowed to enter? Whilst the question is not free from difficulty, it is submitted that the former view is correct. The natural interpretation of the language of the Rule is simply that the undertaking of the measure and the resulting incurring of the cost must be something which is required of the shipowner (or another party to the adventure) if the ship is to be permitted to enter the port or place of refuge. The Rule contains no express requirement that the measures must be carried out in advance of entry, and there seems no good reason to imply such a requirement. Nevertheless, it seems clear that some limitation must be imposed on the expenses recoverable under sub-paragraph (ii). The scheme of Rule XI(d) is that any expenses incurred at a port or place in respect of a period after the common safety has been achieved, and where the delay is merely to enable repairs necessary for the safe prosecution of the voyage to be carried out, should be dealt with solely under sub-paragraph (iii) and subject to the restriction contained in that paragraph. It follows such costs should not be allowed under sub-paragraph (ii), even if the requirement in question was imposed, as a condition of entry, for the entire period of the ship's stay.

It is of course essential in all cases that the measures required by the authorities should relate to preventing or minimising damage to the environment. The cost of complying with any requirement that goes beyond this is not allowable.[56]

"in the circumstances prescribed in Rule XI(b),"[57] Rule XI(b), the commentary on which is at paragraphs 11.11 to 11.34, above, provides that crew wages and certain other expenses shall be allowed in general average during detention at any port or place where the detention is necessary either *for the common safety* or to enable repairs necessary *for the safe prosecution of the voyage* to be effected. It follows that, unlike sub-paragraph (ii), this sub-paragraph is not confined to those cases where the anti-environmental damage measures were imposed as a condition of an operation performed for the common safety, and in a few isolated cases it may apply even when the ship and cargo have never been in peril.[58] The logic of this distinction is not particularly clear, and it could lead to cases where the cost of complying with anti-pollution requirements necessary to enable the ship to enter a port would be disallowed, but the **11.46**

[56] See paras. 11.40, 11.44, *ante*.

[57] Some confusion arose, at the Sydney Conference and subsequently, concerning the identity of the Rule which was intended to be referred to in sub-paragraph (iii) of Rule XI(d). In its original draft form (Rule XI(d) is based on a draft submitted by the British M.L.A., which received the recommendation of the International Standing Committee of C.M.I.), this sub-paragraph referred to Rule XI(b); the draft which was before the Plenary Session of the Conference, when it voted to adopt the York-Antwerp Rules 1994, referred to Rule X(a), as did the C.M.I. Newsletter No. 3 of 1994; the first official C.M.I. publication of the Rules referred to Rule X(b), but C.M.I. later published an amendment which changed the reference from Rule X(b) to XI(b). In the version of the Rules published in the 1994 C.M.I. Yearbook the reference is to Rule XI(b).

[58] See para. 11.24, *ante*.

cost of complying with requirements necessary to enable her to remain there would be allowed.

11.47 **"provided that when there is an actual escape or release of pollutant substances the cost of any additional measures required on that account to prevent or minimise pollution or environmental damage shall not be allowed as general average;"** The effect, if not the purpose, of this proviso is largely self-explanatory. Whenever there is an actual escape or release of pollutant substances it excludes from any claim under sub-paragraph (iii) the cost of any measures over and above those which would be required anyway, as a precaution, even if there had been no actual escape. Thus it will exclude the costs of additional measures taken to minimise the amount of pollutant which escapes, or the area over which it spreads, even though these costs fall within the scope of the opening words of Rule XI(d).[59] The cost of those precautionary measures which would have been required anyway even if there were no escape or release will continue to be allowed, so long as these measures did actually continue to be required and the costs in question were actually incurred.

11.48 The phrase *escape or release* is the same as that used in Rule C, and it probably also contemplates that there should be an escape or release beyond the confines of the property involved in the common maritime adventure.[60] The proviso was probably intended to deal with the case where the escape or release first began after the ship had entered the port or place, but it is not expressly confined to that situation and there is no reason why it should not apply whenever there is an escape or release which begins or continues after arrival. However, where the escape has begun before the ship enters the port or place, the likelihood is that the authorities will impose all their anti-pollution requirements as a condition of entry, and in these circumstances those costs incurred in respect of the period before the common safety has been achieved will be recoverable under sub-paragraph (ii),[61] which contains no similar proviso.

It may sometimes be difficult, when an actual escape or release occurs, to identify which additional measures are to be regarded as having been *required on that account* within the meaning of the proviso. Clearly this phrase includes any extra measures required to be undertaken in order to deal with the actual escape or release, such as stopping the spread of a pollutant which has already escaped. However it probably does not include the cost of measures of a precautionary nature, required by the authorities merely in case the escape or release should recur, even though those measures would go beyond those which the authorities would have required if no escape or release had previously occurred.

[59] See para. 11.40, *ante*.
[60] See para. C.33, *ante*.
[61] See para. 11.45, *ante*.

As already mentioned, the purpose of this proviso, which has no counterpart in sub-paragraph (ii), is not particularly clear. If it is necessary for the common safety that the ship remains at the port or place of refuge why should not the allowances in general average for the costs of complying with anti-pollution requirements be as generous under sub-paragraph (iii) as under sub-paragraph (ii)? It is of course true that sub-paragraph (iii) extends to cases where the common safety is not imperilled, and it may therefore have been thought desirable to make the allowances more restrictive than those available under sub-paragraph (ii); the draughtsman may have envisaged that those costs of remaining at the port or place where that was necessary for the common safety would always be recoverable under sub-paragraph (i) or sub-paragraph (ii). However, it cannot be regarded as certain that this will invariably be the case. **11.49**

Sub-paragraph (iv)

"necessarily in connection with the discharging, storing or reloading of cargo" The requirement that the costs to which this sub-paragraph relates must be *necessarily* incurred is fairly stringent, but would probably be satisfied whenever the costs are reasonably incurred in taking those measures to prevent or minimise damage to the environment: **11.50**

(1) which are insisted on by (a) the legally constituted authorities at the port or place in question, or (b) commercial enterprises such as stevedores and warehousemen without whose co-operation the discharge, storing and re-loading of the cargo cannot be achieved;
(2) which any reasonably prudent person would take in the circumstances of the case.

"whenever the cost of those operations is admissible as general average." The cost of discharging cargo at a port or place of refuge is admissible in general average under the provisions of Rule X(b)[62] when necessary for the common safety, alternatively to enable damage to the ship to be repaired, if the repairs were necessary for the safe prosecution of the voyage. And whenever the cost of discharging is so allowable, the cost of storing and reloading such cargo is admissible under Rule X(c).[63] Similar charges to lighten a vessel when ashore are admissible as general average in the terms of Rule VIII.

[62] See paras. 10.45–10.54, *ante*.
[63] See paras. 10.61–10.70, *ante*.

RULE XII

DAMAGE TO CARGO IN DISCHARGING, ETC.

Note: *By reason of the fact that Rule VIII deals, inter alia, with damage to cargo when discharged from a ship ashore,the prime intention of this Rule XII is to deal with the situation where the discharge takes place in a port of refuge.*

ENGLISH PRACTICE AND BACKGROUND

12.01 When cargo is discharged from a ship under such circumstances that the act of discharging it is a general average act, or an extraordinary act performed for the common preservation of ship and cargo, and when such discharging necessarily[1] entails damage or partial loss to the cargo, such damage or loss falls within the definition of general average, and in practice is so treated.[2]

Thus, when a ship, being in a leaky state or needing repairs, is for the common safety taken into a port of refuge and it is necessary to discharge the cargo there, then, if the discharging is for the common safety of all, and is on this, or indeed any other, ground properly treated as a general average act, any damage or loss of cargo which necessarily follows from so discharging it is properly to be treated as general average loss.[3] It is otherwise where the cargo is not in danger but has to be discharged to enable the ship to be repaired after sustaining a particular average loss.[4]

A British Rule of Practice on the subject in force from 1886 until 1996 (when the wording of the 1994 York-Antwerp Rule XII was substituted), read as follows:

[1] As to when the cargo is negligently damaged in the course of discharge, see *Federal Commerce and Navigation Co. Ltd v. Eisenerz GmbH* [1970] 2 Lloyd's Rep. 332; [1975] 1 Lloyd's Rep. 105; para. 12.11, n. 15, *post*.

[2] Thus, a loss of cargo in barges, into which it had been discharged to enable the vessel to make a port of refuge, should be allowed as general average. See Abbott (5th ed.), p. 346, cited with approval by Cresswell J. in *Hallett v. Wigram* (1850) 9 C.B. 580 at 608, and by Mathew J. in *McCall v. Houlder* (1897) 2 Com.Cas. 129 at 132. See also *per* Wills J. in *Royal Mail Steam Packet Co. v. English Bank of Rio* (1887) 19 Q.B.D. 362 at 372, and the American cases *Hennew v. Monroe*, 8 Martin, La., 227 (IV. 449; O.S. 1826); *Lewis v. Williams* 1 Hall, N.Y. 430 (1820); Gourlie, 213; *Heyliger v. N.Y.F. Ins. Co.* 11 Johns. R. 85 (1814).

[3] But not damage or deterioration which would have occurred if the cargo had remained on board: *Spafford v. Dodge* (1817) 14 Mass. 65; Gourlie. 214.

[4] *Hamel v. P. & O. Steam Nav. Co.* [1908] 2 K.B. 298, Lord Alverstone C.J.

F18 Treatment of Damage to Cargo caused by Discharge, Storing and Reloading.

> "That damage necessarily done to cargo by discharging, storing, and reloading it, be treated as general average when, and only when the cost of those measures respectively is so treated."

Why Damage should Follow Discharging

It is not, perhaps, at first sight obvious why the discharging of cargo in a port of refuge should necessarily lead to its being damaged. There are three principal reasons: (1) the cargo may have to be discharged with unusual haste, as when the ship is leaky; or (2) in a place where it is not usual to unload so large ships or cargoes of that kind, so that there are not the proper appliances; or, (3) the cargo may be of such a nature, for example coal, that it cannot be landed without suffering loss by breakage or the like, so that to discharge it at a port of refuge, in addition to the port of destination, is simply doubling the ordinary wastage. In any of these cases, what the discharging actually costs is the money outlay *plus* the inevitable damage to cargo. Allowance is also made in practice for cargo pilfered during a forced discharge, so far as such loss might reasonably be anticipated. Damage to cargo merely through delay at a port of refuge is not, however, allowed, whether it be left on the vessel or stored on shore, nor is a loss by fire or other accident while the cargo is stored, made good.[5] **12.02**

HISTORICAL DEVELOPMENT AND PRACTICE OF RULE XII

Glasgow Resolutions 1860 **12.03**

The practice in this country in 1860 was to allow in general average any loss or damage to cargo caused by a forced discharge for the common safety whilst the vessel was at sea or ashore, but until 1883 to exclude such loss or damage if the discharge took place at a port of refuge in the manner customary at that port.[6] This British practice applicable to a forced discharge at a port of refuge was accepted by 19 votes to 6 at the International Conference at Glasgow in 1860:

> "(4) That the damage done to cargo, and the loss of it and the freight on it, resulting from discharging it at a port of refuge in the way usual in that port with ships not in distress, ought not to be allowed in general average."

[5] The dictum to the contrary in *The Brig Mary* (1842) 1 Sprague 17 is not followed by American adjusters.

[6] See the textbooks of the period, or the Custom of Lloyd's: *V.—Damage to Cargo in Discharging*. Damage done to cargo by discharging it at a port of refuge, in the manner and under the circumstances customary at that port, is not allowed as general average.

12.04 *York Rules 1864*

No change was made in the effect of the earlier Glasgow Resolution but its wording was rearranged:

> "(IX) Damage done to cargo by discharging it at a port of refuge shall not be admissible as general average in case such cargo shall have been discharged at the place and in the manner customary at that port with ships not in distress."

York-Antwerp Rules 1877

No change, but it is believed that opposition to the Rule was mounting.

12.05 *York-Antwerp Rules 1890*

Probably as the result of the decisions in the cases of *Atwood v. Sellar*[7] and *Svendsen v. Wallace*[8] the practice of British average adjusters changed between 1877 and 1890. In 1883 the Association of Average Adjusters introduced a Rule of Practice to the effect that whenever the cost of discharging cargo was general average, all loss or damage necessarily arising to cargo therefrom should also be allowed in general average, and in 1886 this was extended to cover damage done by "discharging, storing and reloading".[9]

It is not surprising, therefore, that at the International Conference held at Liverpool in 1890 the York-Antwerp Rule was amended to reflect this progress.

The first draft put forward in 1890 had opened with:

> "Damage done to, or loss of cargo by discharging, stor*age*, reloading and stowing..."

but this was considered too wide and notice was given that the word *storage* would cause difficulty (almost certainly on the grounds that it was likely to be construed as covering losses sustained *during* the period of storage). It is very clear from the discussion that the only losses intended to be made good as general average were those *necessarily* sustained in the *act of handling* the cargo, that is, when putting it out of the ship, into the warehouse, or back into the ship. Loss or damage sustained during the period of storage (even an almost inevitable loss) was not covered, and the word *storage* first suggested was changed to *storing*, and *necessarily caused in the act of* was inserted before the various cargo operations.

[7] (1880) 5 Q.B.D. 286.
[8] (1885) 10 A.C. 404.
[9] Rule of Practice F18. See para. 70.45, *post*.

"(XII) Damage done to or loss of cargo necessarily caused in the act of discharging, storing, reloading and stowing, shall be made good as general average when and only when the cost of those measures respectively is admitted as general average."

York-Antwerp Rules 1924 12.06

Minor changes to the wording were introduced on this occasion:

(1) The insertion of the words "fuel or stores" after the word "cargo" and of the word "handling" before the words "discharging, storing", so that the Rule should correspond with the alterations then being made in Rule X(b) under which "the cost of handling on board or discharging cargo, fuel or stores" at a port of refuge was to be allowed as general average.

(2) The omission of the word "necessarily" before the word "caused". The phrase "necessarily caused" had been found difficult of construction and it was thought that the wording adopted in 1924 indicated with sufficient precision what damage or loss was allowable as general average. (In practice, the deletion of the word *necessarily* meant that loss or damage from any cause whatever occurring during the act of handling the cargo would be chargeable to general average. The merits or otherwise of this widening of the allowances under Rule XII is discussed in paragraphs 12.12 and 12.13, below.

York-Antwerp Rules 1950 12.07

No change, but a discussion took place on a most important matter of principle.

Prior to the International Conference at Amsterdam, the Belgian Committee had pointed out that they considered the existing wording of Rule XII too restrictive in that it covered loss or damage to cargo caused only in the *act* of handling, etc. They instanced the case of refrigerated cargo being discharged at a port of refuge at which no refrigerated storage facilities existed. The master knew perfectly well that such cargo must suffer damage as the result of the forced discharge and they considered that this damage should be allowed as general average. They proposed, therefore, that the words: "caused in the act of handling, etc.," should be replaced by: "in consequence of handling, etc."

The International Committee were sympathetic to this view and decided to amend the Rule in the manner required. The Drafting Committee gave expression to the idea in an alternative form of wording "caused by[10] handling, etc.," but, as it was open to abuse, felt some doubt as to

[10] At the Conference itself, the Belgian delegation proposed that the wording should be "*directly* caused by" in the hope that it would avoid some of the abuses which the wording might otherwise allow. It would restrict the allowance to those cases in which goods would not have suffered from the delay of the vessel but for being discharged into an inefficient store.

the advisability of making any amendment and recommended that the question should be discussed at the Amsterdam Conference.

Considerable discussion ensued and the pertinent question raised: What was the cause of damage sustained in such circumstances by perishable cargo? Was it the act of handling, etc., or was it decay or deterioration? If damage by delay were to be allowed under Rule XII, it would conflict with the general principle laid down in Rule C.

Having regard to the difficulty of amending the Rule in any agreed form and the difficulty of choosing the right words to express any possible amendment, the Conference eventually decided to revert to and retain the existing wording of the 1890/1924 Rule.

York-Antwerp Rules 1974

No change.

12.08 York-Antwerp Rules 1994

Where those in 1950 feared to tread, their successors in 1994 plunged boldly and introduced the previously desired change. The opening words of the 1924/1974 Rule:

> "Damage to or loss of cargo ... *caused in the act of* handling, discharging, storing, reloading and stowing..."

were amended to:

> "Damage to or loss of cargo ... *sustained in consequence of their* handling, discharging, storing, reloading and stowing..."

This was reported to be merely a minor drafting amendment, and the International Sub-Committee felt that it would work in the interests of clarity and uniformity, but usage alone will determine whether this proves to be the case. The intentions behind the change are unclear. It was first put forward to make the Rule include *consequential loss and damage*, an apparent extension which, for instance, might have included (as desired in 1950) deterioration damage to refrigerated cargo discharged at a port of refuge at which no refrigerated storage facilities existed. By mid-1994, however, when insurers issued their "no expansion" (of general average) edict, the amendment was reported to be of a limiting nature, required because the existing *caused in the act of* was considered to be too wide and including loss or damage not necessarily the natural consequence of the discharging, etc., but the result of some extraneous cause such as negligence of stevedores.[11] Those who adopted this view considered that

[11] *e.g.* as in *Federal Commerce and Navigation Co. v. Eisenerz GmbH* [1970] 2 Lloyd's Rep. 332; [1975] 1 Lloyd's Rep. 105.

it should be necessary to establish a causal connection between the handling, etc., and the damage sustained.

Rule XII

Damage to Cargo in Discharging, etc.

Damage to or loss of cargo, fuel or stores sustained in consequence of their handling, discharging, storing, reloading and stowing shall be made good as general average, when and only when the cost of those measures respectively is admitted as general average.

Construction

"cargo" See commentary under Rule I.[12] **12.09**

"in consequence of". (This phrase requiring a more extensive commentary than normal, it will be dealt with after the various cargo operations to which it refers. See paragraph 12.11, below.)

"handling" Although this word might be construed to comprise the complete range of cargo movements mentioned in the Rule, there is no doubt that when introduced in 1924, (see paragraphs 12.06, also 10.42, above), this single word was clearly intended as an abbreviation for the phrase *handling on board* in Rule X(b), that is, it related to the situation where cargo, etc., was moved from one compartment of the ship to another, or on to deck, without an actual discharge overside. **12.10**

"discharging" By custom, the operation of discharging includes also the transit to the warehouse or other place where the cargo, etc., is stored.[13]

"storing" As related in paragraph 12.05, above, this word was intended to cover only the operation of placing and stacking the cargo, etc., in the warehouse or other place of storage. In everyday use it is, of course, perfectly capable of bearing the construction that it covers the whole period in store, but the original intention to exclude this period should not be entirely overlooked. (See also paragraphs 12.14 to 12.16, below.)

[12] See para 1.24, *ante*.
[13] See Rule of Practice F12(b) in para. 70.39, *post*.

"reloading" By tradition[14] and analogy with *discharging*, above, this term will include the unstacking and return conveyance of the cargo etc. from the warehouse to the ship, its transfer on board, and also its...

"... stowing" on board the ship.

12.11 **"in consequence of"** Introduced in 1994, these words replaced the previous "*caused in the act of*", an expression almost incapable of being misconstrued and which imposed no express requirement that the loss or damage sustained during the mentioned cargo operations should be such as would have been contemplated or foreseen as likely to occur.[15]

The new wording does introduce this concept of *consequences* and will accordingly be less easy to construe in practice, more particularly because it omits to define whether the consequences be limited to direct, or include also indirect:

> "Direct consequences", said Lord Denning in the case of *Australian Coastal Commission v. Green,*[16] "denote those consequences which flow in an unbroken sequence from the act: whereas indirect consequences are those in which the sequence is broken by an intervening or extraneous cause."

Simple examples of both types of losses have already been given in paragraph 12.02, above (for example the almost inevitable breakage or loss sustained in any handling of a coal or other bulk cargo as a direct loss, and a loss by fire ashore as an indirect loss). It appears probable that the framers of the Rule intended that, to be treated as general average, any loss or damage should be the direct consequence of the cargo handling operations detailed below, but this is by no means certain, and it may be appropriate, therefore, to consider what common sense and sound principle would suggest is appropriate.

[14] Under earlier English practice, the cost of discharging and conveyance to the warehouse was general average, the warehouse rent was a special charge on the cargo itself, and the relocating expenses, etc., were a special charge on the freight.

[15] In spite of the Canadian decision to opposite effect in the case of *Federal Commerce and Navigation Co. v. Eisenerz GmbH* [1970] 2 Lloyd's Rep. 332; [1975] 1 Lloyd's Rep. 105. In that case the *Oak Hill* discharged and reloaded cargo at Levis as a port of refuge. During these operations two grades of pig-iron became intermingled and damaged. It was found that this was due to negligence of the stevedores and of the master, who had failed to supervise their work. The charterers claimed damages, and the owners pleaded that they were liable for no more than a contribution in general average under Rule XII of the York-Antwerp Rules 1950.

The Supreme Court of Canada held that the damage could only be general average if it was a direct consequence of the general average act, and that as the master could not be allowed to foresee his own negligence this test was not satisfied. Hence the charterers' claim for the whole loss succeeded. It is submitted that the court's reasoning is not wholly satisfactory, although it led to the correct conclusion. The damage was general average within the 1950 Rule XII, whether or not it was within Rule C, for the Rule of Interpretation so provides. But since there was fault on the part of the owners, in the negligence of their master, they could not rely on the general average act as a defence to the charterers' claim for the whole loss.

[16] [1971] 1 Q.B. 456 at 481.

On those occasions when, as provided by Rules X(b) and X(c), the operations of handling on board, discharging, storing, reloading and stowing cargo, fuel or stores are to be considered as general average acts and their cost to be charged to general average, the owners of such shifted cargo, etc., have an equal right to expect that if their property is thereby exposed to *greater* risks than would be expected if it remained undisturbed on board the ship, and those greater risks operate, either during the handling operations themselves *or whilst stored ashore*, the loss or damage sustained thereby should similarly be allowed as general average, either under Rule XII itself, or Rules A and C. 12.12

Losses During Cargo Handling Operations 12.13

The risks attendant upon the active processes of cargo handling, etc., are wholly avoided if the goods remain undisturbed in the ship, and it follows that even if the goods should be *un*necessarily lost or damaged during discharging operations, etc., as the result of negligence of stevedores, that loss should be allowed as general average. For what they may be worth, all rights of recourse against any party responsible for a loss admitted in general average must accrue to the general average itself, but there should never be any doubt that the merchant or other party initially suffering the loss should have a prime right to compensation in general average from his fellow adventurers for that loss.

The following examples of loss or damage covered by the Rule may be mentioned:

(1) total loss of or damage to packages dropped into the sea, on to the quay, or into the hold during discharge or reloading operations;
(2) loss of contents from bags burst, or barrels strained, by the rough handling of stevedores at the port of refuge;
(3) rain or weather damage to baled goods or steel pipes whilst being transported to the warehouse.

Losses During the Period of Storage 12.14

The risks attendant upon the passive condition of storage are always present to some degree, whether the goods are aboard or ashore—indeed, they may even be reduced while ashore—and different considerations apply. If cargo, etc., is discharged at a port of refuge into what is thought to be suitable and adequate storage and some unexpected accident occurs, for example:

— a fire in the warehouse;
— the roof of the warehouse is torn off by a hurricane;
— a lighter is cast from its moorings in a gale and sunk;

the consequent loss or damage to the cargo would not normally be made good in general average for the reason that, whilst it is always possible to envisage that such events *may* happen, the chances of their actual occurrence are somewhat remote and it is unlikely that they would be seriously taken into account by the master when considering the discharge.[17]

However, if the facilities for storage at the port of refuge are known to be insufficient or inadequate, the possibility of damage would be fairly within the contemplation of the master and it is, and should, accordingly, be allowed as general average, either under Rules XII or C, for example:

— weather and dirt damage to cargo stored in the open;
— damage by rain through the defective roof of an ancient warehouse;
— similar damage to goods in a lighter through worn and inadequate tarpaulins;

and, of course,

— a certain amount of pilferage of food, drink, and other valuable small goods is almost inevitable in any warehouse, whatever its condition.

12.15 A topic on which some difference of opinion may exist concerns the deterioration which a perishable or frozen cargo may sustain as the result of a forced discharge, for example:

— a cargo of apples may be bruised by rough handling and in consequence the fruit go rotten.

Provided that this damage may fairly be attributable to the actual handling, it should be allowed in full.

— A cargo of new potatoes may sustain little or no damage by the forced discharge, but the detention may cause the potatoes to become a little soft and lose their "scraping" qualities.

This is a loss by delay and should not be allowed.[18] It is probable that the same loss would have occurred even if the potatoes had remained in the vessel and had not been discharged.

12.16 — A cargo of frozen meat may be discharged at a port of refuge where there are no, or inadequate, refrigerated storage facilities.

[17] An insurance against this class of accident is frequently arranged at the time of the discharge and the premium charged to general average. Any claims on the policy, however, would be paid to the owners of the cargo.

[18] See Rule C.

Deterioration of the meat is inevitable and, provided that the ship's own refrigerating machinery is functioning efficiently, there is no good reason why such loss should not be treated as general average. Indeed, one of the reasons for the 1994 change may well have been to resolve the previous agonising over this problem from 1950 recorded in paragraph 12.07, above.

"only when the cost of those measures respectively is admitted as general average." Claims for loss of or damage to cargo, etc., sustained in consequence of handling on board or discharging, etc., are allowable under this Rule only when the cost of those various measures is admissible in general average. The circumstances in which such cost is allowable are as follows: 12.17

Handling on board and discharging, under Rule X(b), when necessary for the common safety or to enable damage to the ship caused by sacrifice or accident to be repaired, if the repairs were necessary for the safe prosecution of the voyage.

Storing, reloading and stowing, under Rule X(c), when the handling or discharging (as above) was admissible in general average.

RULE XIII

DEDUCTIONS FROM COST OF REPAIRS

ENGLISH LAW AND BACKGROUND

13.01 When any part of a ship's hull, gear, or machinery, etc., is sacrificed for the common safety, and when the ship is afterwards repaired, the sum allowable in general average as compensation for this damage is the reasonable[1] cost of repairs, with an appropriate deduction for the advantage—if any—which the owner derives from having new work in place of old.[2]

Deductions "new for old"

13.02 By an ancient and widespread custom prevailing amongst almost all maritime countries, the deduction from the cost of repairs was fixed at one-third of the cost of repairs, with certain equally well-defined exceptions. No deduction was made during a vessel's first voyage[3] (and in the days of sail, this could often take a year); anchors were allowed in full, while chain cables were subject to a deduction of one-sixth only; and unbroached stores, such as coils of rope taken from a store-room, or spare sails which had never been bent, were allowed without deduction.

These customary deductions, "new for old", may have been appropriate in the days of wooden sailing ships, but with the introduction of the more durable iron and steel ships, and machinery in place of sails, it was considered that a deduction of one-third from the cost of repairs was unnecessarily severe on shipowners. In 1884, therefore, the Association of Average Adjusters appointed a special committee to make inquiry into the subject. In accordance with their recommendations, a detailed Rule of Practice[4] was introduced, and this has been amended from time to time to accord with the latest developments in shipbuilding, and in 1974 in the interests of simplification.

[1] For an indication of the considerations which apply when construing the term "reasonable cost of repairs", see the commentary, para. 18.10, *post*, on Rule XVIII of the York-Antwerp Rules 1974.

[2] The notion of betterment causes difficulty in other branches of the law: see *Harbutt's Plasticine Ltd v. Wayne Tank and Pump Co. Ltd* [1970] 1 Q.B. 447.

[3] *Pirie v. Steel* (1837) 2 M. & Rob. 49; 8 C. & P. 200.

[4] F19, see para. 70.46, *post*.

Historical Development and Practice of Rule XIII

York-Antwerp Rules 1890 13.03

A Rule on the subject of deductions from the cost of repairs, "new for old", was first introduced into the York-Antwerp Rules at the Conference held in Liverpool in 1890, and the wording followed very closely that of the British Rule of Practice passed by the Association of Average Adjusters in 1887.

The technical advances and developments made over the years in the shipbuilding industry were matched by appropriate amendments in the Rule in 1924 and 1950, but, as in all its editions the Rule was essentially *technical* in its provisions, none of the lengthy wordings is quoted here, but they may be referred to in the Appendices of the 7th/11th editions of this work.

York-Antwerp Rules 1974 13.04

With a view to simplifying the process of general average adjustment, a complete and radical change was suggested for Rule XIII in 1974: that no deductions "new for old" should be made from the cost of any repairs allowable in general average.

Although the principle that some deduction should be made from the cost of repairs to represent the theoretical betterment of the ship by reason of new material replacing old is eminently sound and unassailable, it was doubted whether, in modern practice, the extra work of assessing the deductions was entirely justified or worthwhile, more particularly as the 1950 and earlier Rules on this subject suffered from the defects common to rule-of-thumb methods of applying principles, and were somewhat arbitrary in their provisions. The deductions might be justified where expendable items such as sails, rigging and ropes, etc., were concerned, but it was generally illusory to assume that even the oldest vessel was in any way improved, or that any benefit which could be realised in cash was conferred upon the shipowner, by, say, the fitting of a new strake of plating; the vessel would still end her useful trading life and be sent to the breakers' yard at much the same time as she would normally have done. Accordingly, the following wording was put forward for discussion at the Hamburg Conference in 1974:

> "No deductions 'new for old' shall be made from the cost of permanent or temporary repairs to the ship in any circumstances.
>
> There shall be no allowance in general average in any circumstance for cleaning and painting of bottom."

Contrary to what might have been expected from the replies by the National Associations to the questionnaire circulated by the Comité 13.05

Maritime International in 1970, the proposal to abolish deductions "new for old" was most strenuously resisted by a number of countries. A counter-proposal, based upon a recommendation made at the 1967 Assembly of A.I.D.E., was put forward by a number of delegations. The voting at the working session of the Hamburg Conference showed a majority of 11 to 8 in favour of the abolition of deductions "new for old". However, the proposal was raised again at a plenary session of the Conference in the form of an amendment proposed by Sweden. The result of a vote, taken on the "abolition" text first, as being the most radical, was a 12 to 12 tie, so that it failed. The amendment was then put to the vote and passed in preference to the retention of the 1950 text.

York-Antwerp Rules 1994

13.06 No change, but it is worthy of record that:

(1) The abolition of deductions "new for old" was again briefly considered, but the principle being sound,[5] and the simplified deductions of the 1974 Rule causing no difficulties in practical application, it was decided to retain the first section of the Rule unchanged.
(2) There appeared to be general agreement that the last two paragraphs of the Rule (dealing with drydock dues and cleaning and painting of bottom, etc.) should be transferred to and form part of Rule XVIII, but this eminently sensible suggestion foundered at Sydney, as related in paragraph 18.09, below.

Rule XIII

Deductions from Cost of Repairs

Repairs to be allowed in general average shall not be subject to deductions in respect of "new for old" where old material or parts are replaced by new unless the ship is over fifteen years old in which case there shall be a deduction of one third. The deductions shall be regulated by the age of the ship from the December 31 of the year of completion of construction to the date of the general average act, except for insulation, life and similar boats, communications and

[5] Even if the renewal of a strake of plating may not extend the life and increase the value of an old vessel, the renewal of a main engine or similar most certainly does, and the recent case of the 22-year old *Alpha* is a reminder that such examples can occur: *Corfu Navigation Co. v. Mobil Shipping Co. Ltd* [1991] 2 Lloyd's Rep. 52.

navigational apparatus and equipment, machinery and boilers for which deductions shall be regulated by the age of the particular parts to which they apply. The deductions shall be made only from the cost of the new material or parts when finished and ready to be installed in the ship.

No deductions shall be made in respect of provisions, stores, anchors and chain cables.

Drydock and slipway dues and costs of shifting the ship shall be allowed in full.

The costs of cleaning, painting or coating of bottom shall not be allowed in general average unless the bottom has been painted or coated within the twelve months preceding the date of the general average act in which case one half of such costs shall be allowed.

CONSTRUCTION

Whether the cost of repairing damage or replacing loss to the ship, her machinery or gear is in principle allowable in general average falls to be decided under the lettered Rules or under Rules II, III, IV, V, VII, IX, or XIV. If the cost is so allowable under any of these Rules, other than Rule XIV, Rule XVIII read with this Rule regulates the amount to be allowed in general average. In cases falling within Rule XIV, no deductions "new for old" are made. **13.07**

In very broad terms, no deductions "new for old" are made from the cost of repairs allowable as general average until the ship is over 15 years old, when a deduction of one-third is made only from the cost of the new material or parts in their finished state when ready to be installed in the ship.

"life and similar boats" It is suggested that by "similar boats" is meant boats similarly carried on board during passage, for example launch, cutter, gig, etc., and not merely boats carried for a purpose analogous to that of a life-boat.

"cost of the new material or parts when finished and ready to be installed in the ship." Deductions are confined to the cost of the new material, the cost of manufacturing the new article from the new material, the cost of such final preparation of the new material or the new article as may be necessary for fitting, and such local transportation costs as occur upon the repairers' or manufacturers' premises or in the drydock or yard. Although possibly not in accordance with a strict construction of the Rule, in practice no deduction is made from the cost of transporting, for instance, a new propeller, tailshaft, or other machinery part from specialist manufacturers to the repair yard.[6]

Credit for Scrap Materials

13.08 In Britain, at least, the practice has existed for a century or more to make deductions "new for old" from the gross cost of new materials or parts, that is, *before* dealing with any credit received for the old materials sold or taken over as scrap. This practice was criticised as being inequitable by the Chairman in his address to the Association of Average Adjusters in 1963[7] and he instanced the case of a new bronze propeller costing £6,000 with a credit of £2,000 for the scrap propeller, and where a difference of £667 can result in the net amount allowed in general average. However, having regard to the many other arbitrary results that inevitably flow from a rule-of-thumb such as Rule XIII, it is to be doubted whether any great weight should be attached to this criticism; it is more important that the practice should be uniform rather than that it should be unassailably correct.

"stores" It is difficult if not impossible to devise an accurate definition of this word in its context, but it was formally recorded at the Stockholm Conference in 1924 that the word was intended to include hawsers, ropes, and sheets. In practice it is probably construed also to include such other expendable items as paints, oils, tools and (in view of its deletion from the previous 1950 Rule) "gear".

13.09 **"Drydock and slipway dues and costs of shifting the ship shall be allowed in full."** This sentence means only that any allowance in general average under Rule XVIII for the cost of drydocking and dues, etc., incurred to repair damage caused by sacrifice shall not be subject to deductions "new for old"; it does not mean that the whole cost of drydocking and dues is necessarily chargeable to general average irrespective of what other work or repairs may be carried out in the drydock concurrently.[8]

[6] This problem was mentioned by Mr E. W. Reading at the Amsterdam Conference (p. 481) for the 1950 Rules: "For the purpose of record, if I may go on Sir, we have discussed in the Drafting Committee the difficulty that arises in connection with this Rule, particularly in the case of modern motor vessels, when heavy machinery parts have to be sent out from the builder to a vessel that has had an accident abroad. A new shaft may cost £1,500 to make; it may cost a further £1,500 to send it to the port at which the ship is detained. The deduction, we have thought, should not be made from that cost of transportation. Quite obviously if one ship has had an accident in her home port the repair will have cost £1,500; but if a similar ship in the same fleet has the same accident 3,000 miles away, and the repair plus transportation has cost £3,000, the value is not increased by £3,000. The enhancement in value must in fact be the same in the case of both ships, but it is, I think, impossible to find words which would ensure that that deduction from the cost of transportation was made only when the transportation was exceptional."

[7] A.A.A. 1963 Report, p. 5.

[8] For a fuller commentary on this subject, see paras. 18.12–18.14, *post*.

"The costs of cleaning, painting or coating of bottom shall not be allowed in general average unless the bottom has been painted or coated within the 12 months preceding the date of the general average act in which case one half of such costs shall be allowed." As this Rule XIII deals only with "*Deductions* from Cost of Repairs" and is in any case subservient or subject to Rule XVIII, there can be no doubt that this particular section of Rule XIII is badly worded and might have been better expressed on lines such as the following: **13.10**

> "The costs of cleaning, painting or coating of those parts of the bottom *damaged by a general average act* shall be subject to a deduction of one-half, except that when the bottom has not been painted or coated within the 12 months preceding the date of the general average act, no allowance shall be made."

In its present form, this 1974 wording is open to a construction quite opposed to the equitable principles of general average, and with the highly expensive "grit-blasting" taking the place of the old-fashioned "scraping", cargo interests could find themselves severely prejudiced.

For example, a vessel may strand for her full length and, quite apart from any damaged plating, the whole of the bottom paint may be removed, scored or scuffed by the stranding alone—an *accident*. In principle, none of the costs of grit-blasting or repainting should be charged to general average, but it is conceivable that 50 per cent of such costs might be charged to general average under the existing wording if, for instance, the propeller or other underwater part was damaged by refloating operations.

Another area for doubt which could be resolved by precise wording concerns the cost of supplying and applying new anti-fouling paint to replace that destroyed *only* by exposure to the atmosphere during the period in drydock necessary for the repair of damage caused by a general average act. For example, a vessel may strand without damage, but the efforts to refloat cause damage to the propeller, and exposure to the atmosphere during the period of drydocking necessary for the propeller repairs may destroy the qualities of the anti-fouling paint. It is probably correct to say that the paint has not been destroyed by a general average act (the refloating operations) but by *delay*, to be excluded by the terms of Rule C. However, if there are specific provisions in a numbered rule (as there may be here), those provisions override the general provisions of a lettered Rule in accordance with the Rule of Interpretation. **13.11**

Postscript for 1997. The remarks above in paragraphs 13.10 and 13.11, above, are still applicable today, but the 1974 provisions of the Rule themselves regarding bottom painting are a relic of earlier times and often inappropriate to modern high duty painting systems. The following may be of interest: **13.12**

Until, say, the 1970s, most ships drydocked about once every year for routine maintenance and "scraping and painting" of bottom. As the water was gradually let out of the drydock, men on rafts scraped off the weeds and barnacles, also any loose paint, rust and scale. Bare patches of steel were touched up with primer, followed by a full coat of anti-corrosive to protect against the natural corrosive action of salt water, and then a full coat of anti-fouling to arrest the attachment of seaweed and other marine growths. The whole process was relatively unsophisticated, cheap, and took place generally during the first and last day in drydock.

Reasonably appropriate to this unsophisticated process were the rule of thumb provisions of Rule XIII in the 1890, 1924 and 1950 York-Antwerp Rules, which basically provided that: "*No painting bottom to be allowed if the bottom has not been painted within six months previous to the date of the accident.*" (How much of the cost was to be allowed if the bottom had been painted within the previous six months was unspecified, and was no doubt discretionary, but hull insurance conditions almost invariably excluded any claim whatever for bottom painting.)

Today, due to increased sea pollution and a general desire on the part of shipowners to extend the periods of trading between drydockings, the modern approach to painting the bottom is far more sophisticated—and highly expensive!

Before a modern high duty paint system can be applied successfully, it is essential that the steel plate be blast cleaned to bare metal to SA2 or SA2.5 standards, an operation which may cost in the region of £5 or more per square metre. Three coats of primer/anti-corrosive are then usually applied to the bare metal and these may have a life of eight years or more. The final coat of anti-fouling will usually be renewed at every drydocking, but this may now be at intervals of even three years.

New provisions are very necessary for this section of Rule XIII and it is to be regretted that no change whatever was made at Sydney in 1994.

RULE XIV

TEMPORARY REPAIRS

ENGLISH LAW AND BACKGROUND

Repairs carried out to a ship may be either complete and of a permanent character, or they may be of a *temporary* nature only, sufficient to enable the remaining voyage to be prosecuted in safety, but of no lasting benefit to the ship and requiring to be removed at destination or elsewhere and replaced with full permanent repairs. **14.01**

Temporary repairs reasonably effected to damage caused by a general average *sacrifice* (for example by a voluntary stranding[1]) cause no problem; the cost of such repairs follows the nature of the damage itself and is charged to general average.

For temporary repairs to damage caused by *accident*, the position under English law is, with one exception, precisely the same; the cost of the temporary repairs similarly follows the nature of the damage itself and is borne wholly by the shipowner or his insurers as *particular* average. The exception is when those temporary repairs are made at a time of peril, for the common safety, and involve the *sacrifice* of property on board ship intended for some other purpose, thereby constituting a general average act and justifying in its own right the allowance in general average of the value of the property sacrificed. Thus, crew's mattresses, etc., stuffed into torn plating to stem a leak following a collision, or, as still recorded in paragraph A.70, above, in Lowndes' own wording:

> "A very ancient, general, and undisputed custom ... relates to jury-rig. When a ship's mast or rudder is carried away and a 'jury' or temporary mast or rudder is fitted up at sea as a substitute, the value of the materials cut up or destroyed for the purpose ... (is) in practice treated as general average."

With regard to temporary repairs of *accidental* damage effected, not at a time of peril, but in the safety of a port of refuge, various reasons may be put forward for the decision to effect only temporary repairs, for example:

[1] See paras. 5.01 *et seq.*, *ante*.

(1) Repair facilities in the port of refuge may not exist—or be inadequate—for full permanent repairs.
(2) Repair costs at the port of refuge may be much higher than at destination or elsewhere.
(3) Temporary repairs may be effected with the cargo remaining on board, whereas permanent repairs would require a costly discharge of the cargo.
(4) Temporary repairs may be effected in much less time than permanent, thereby saving delay and expense.

For all or any of these reasons, can the cost of the temporary repairs be charged to general average, either wholly or in part?

14.02 As already stated earlier, English law is quite unequivocal in its answer to this question: by the terms of his contract of affreightment, and unless otherwise excused, the shipowner is obliged to maintain his vessel at all times in a fit condition to carry the cargo to its destination, and to prosecute that voyage with all reasonable despatch. It follows that in respect of damage sustained by an accidental cause, the shipowner himself must bear the full cost of any repairs—whether temporary or permanent—and, further, that he may not always be entitled to effect permanent repairs when temporary repairs can be carried out with much less delay and are adequate for the vessel to continue her voyage in safety.

With one possible aberration in 1815, the position has been ever thus. In Roman times, a vessel bound for Ostia suffered considerably by storm; her mast, yard and some other furniture were burnt by lightning. She put into Hippo, and after having speedily provided what was requisite, she completed her voyage and delivered her cargo in good condition. A question arose whether the proprietors of the cargo ought to contribute to the repairs of the vessel, and this was decided in the negative because the expenses had been incurred "rather to fit out the ship than to preserve the cargo".[2]

In more recent times, Bovill C.J. stated in *Walthew v. Mavrojani*[3]:

> "There is no doubt that the expense of all repairs to the vessel rendered necessary by the ordinary perils of navigation, and which are required to enable it to prosecute the voyage and complete the adventure, must be borne by the owner. He has undertaken, subject to the usual exceptions, to carry the cargo to its destination and there deliver it, and therefore the costs of repairs are expenses incurred for the benefit of the ship alone and cannot be treated as the subject of general average."

[2] L. 6 de leg. Rhod.—see para. 60.07, *post*, with the particular translation above by Hoffmann L.J. in *Marida Ltd v. Oswal Steel; The Bijela* [1993] 1 Lloyd's Rep. 411 at 420.
[3] (1870) L.R. 5 Ex. 116.

and in *Wilson v. Bank of Victoria*[4] Blackburn J. had said:

> "Inasmuch as the master could, by the expenditure of a comparatively small sum on temporary repairs and coals, bring the ship and cargo safely home, it was his duty to do so;..."

Even more recently, in 1992 in the *Bijela*[5] Hobhouse J. said:

> "... the prima facie position is that the expenses of [temporary] repair were particular average expenses incurred by the shipowner in the course of fulfilling their contractual obligations under the contracts of carriage."

It is worthy of record that the cost of the temporary repairs in the *Wilson* case above was not even claimed, although Lowndes recorded in 1873 that previously to the decision in that case in 1867 there had been a tendency to look with favour on such claims. If this be so, it seems likely that the practice was of recent origin and applied only in certain very limited situations. In the second edition of his *General Average* published in 1856, Lowndes' senior partner (and an even greater lion), Lawrence R. Baily, wrote: **14.03**

> "To avoid the expense that would result from discharging cargo at a port of refuge, a vessel is sometimes repaired there in a temporary manner.
>
> When the sum of the cost of such temporary repairs, and the cost of the repairs effected subsequently in a proper manner, is greater than the cost would have been for repairing the vessel in a proper manner at the port of refuge, the excess of the expense actually incurred in temporary and proper repairs over the expense which would have been incurred for repairing the vessel in a proper manner at the port of refuge, should ... be charged to general average."

These remarks constitute the only intelligent construction that can be placed in support of the decision in the case of *Plummer v. Wildman*,[6] the legal aberration referred to earlier, and the remarks have some equitable merit even today and when considering the provisions of Rule XIV of the York-Antwerp Rules.

The facts in *Plummer v. Wildman* were as follows: the ship *Cambridge* sailed from Kingston with a cargo of sugars and rum for London, and a day or two later was in collision with a brig whereby her false stern and knees were broken and the master was in consequence obliged to cut away part of the rigging of her bowsprit, and to return to Kingston to repair the damage sustained by the accident and the cutting away. Upon her return the cargo was necessarily relanded and warehoused in order that such temporary repairs might be done as would enable her to prosecute her voyage. Permanent repairs were effected on the vessel's **14.04**

[4] (1867) L.R. 2 Q.B. 203. This case also features strongly in the English law section on Rule F—Substituted Expenses: see paras. F.04 *et seq.*, *ante*.

[5] *Marida Ltd v. Oswal Steel; The Bijela* [1992] 1 Lloyd's Rep. 637.

[6] (1815) 3 M. & S. 486.

arrival in London and this cost was not included in the claim for contribution.

The combined judgments of Lord Ellenborough C.J., Le Blanc and Bayley J.J., as reported, occupy no more than a page in this present volume, but it is possible to deduce from the language used that an allowance might be made in general average in respect of the cost of temporary repairs to accidental damage sufficient only "to enable the ship to prosecute her voyage home, and were afterwards of no benefit to the ship". Nevertheless, such a deduction was not drawn by the contemporary writers *Stevens* (1816)[7] or *Benecke* (1824),[8] nor by any writer since, and *Plummer v. Wildman*[9] must today be considered either to be overruled, or not to be an authority for the rule deduced from it.[10]

Historical Development and Practice of Rule XIV

14.05 *York-Antwerp Rules 1890*

Deductions "new for old" are made from the cost of repairs to damage caused by general average sacrifice to represent the supposed betterment or improvement in the value of the ship by reason of having new parts in place of old. By their very nature, however, temporary repairs make no improvement to the ship and will be removed on some later occasion when the damage is properly repaired. In consequence, no deductions "new for old" should be made from the cost of temporary repairs and a Rule to this effect was introduced in 1890 as follows:

> "No deductions 'new for old' shall be made from the cost of temporary repairs of damage allowable as general average."

It should be noted, however, that in the 1890 Rules there was no provision to show in what circumstances temporary repairs could be allowed as general average and it is to be assumed that only temporary repairs of damage caused by general average sacrifice, or themselves involving a general average sacrifice, would have been allowed.

14.06 In 1892 the Assembly of the Association for the Reform and Codification of the Law of Nations was held in Genoa and, among other

[7] *Essay on Average*: "It is surprising that any discussion should have taken place on this subject, or that there could ever have been any doubt that the owner of the ship was bound to keep his ship in repair."

[8] *Marine Insurance*: "But the repairs done to a vessel are always a benefit to her, and I doubt whether, according to the above distinction, any part of those repairs which in themselves are of the nature of a particular average, can ever be construed into a general average."

[9] (1815) 3 M. & S. 486.

[10] Fuller views on this case are expressed in para. 952 of Arnould, *Law of Marine Insurance and Average* in the British Shipping Law series.

things, it took over the study of the York-Antwerp Rules as modified by the Liverpool Conference in 1890. The Italian Delegation, headed by Professor Francesco Berlingieri (grandfather of the President *ad honorem* of C.M.I. in 1995) submitted the wording of a proposed new rule which might be freely translated as follows:

> "Temporary repairs of particular average damage carried out in a port of refuge shall exceptionally be considered as general average when the vessel is in such a condition as to be unable, unless effecting such repairs, to continue the voyage and permanent repairs are not possible or would require so long a time or so heavy an expense as to jeopardise the completion of the adventure.
>
> From the general average should be deducted the benefit of the temporary repairs when making the permanent repairs."

Professor Berlingieri, in his *Le Regole di York Anversa 1924* (2nd edition, 1927) states that, as a matter of principle, it cannot be doubted that repairs of particular average damages, no matter how effected, can but be considered as particular average, and it was made clear that the proposal was based neither on Italian legislation (the Code of Commerce 1882 ruling at the time does not mention temporary repairs), nor on any then known foreign law, but was inspired by the customs of trade, in which the concept of substituted expenses was already established.

Further proposals for reform were made prior to the First World War (see paragraphs 00.82 to 00.86, above) by Judge Dowdall Q.C., and one of the proposals included as Item 2(d) of Schedule 1 to an *avant projet* presented to the Madrid Conference of the International Law Association in 1913 was that the cost of temporary repairs, together with towage and forwarding expenses, should be allowed as general average on a substituted expense basis. **14.07**

No record has been found from whence may have come the objection to the allowance in general average of temporary repairs to accidental damage, but when the *avant projet* was amended and printed in the spring of 1914 as a *Draft Code Relating to General Average*, although towage and forwarding charges remained to be dealt with on a substituted expense basis, the reference to temporary repairs had been deliberately omitted. As Judge Dowdall told members of the Association of Average Adjusters at an Extraordinary General Meeting on July 17, 1914:

> "The Code as drafted treated temporary repairs of general average as general average, and temporary repairs of particular average as particular average."

York-Antwerp Rules 1924 **14.08**

The question of the proper treatment of temporary repairs at a port of refuge was one upon which much difference of opinion existed among the jurists of various nations. In this country the question had been settled by the decision in *Wilson v. Bank of Victoria*,[11] and at any rate so far as temporary repairs of particular average damage were concerned, no allowance in general average was possible except where a sacrifice was made.

The practice in foreign countries relating to the treatment of the cost of temporary repairs to accidental damage at a port of refuge has been reported in the various editions of *Rudolf* or *Lowndes & Rudolf* since 1926 essentially as follows: in the United States, reasonable temporary repairs of damage arising from excepted perils, made at some intermediate port, where permanent repairs could not be made, if necessary to remove the disability of the ship to proceed on her voyage, were regarded as general average. Such repairs had to be purely temporary in their nature and must serve no permanent purpose. Temporary repairs made solely to save the excessive cost of permanent repairs were not general average. When permanent repairs could be made at a port of refuge, but at a large expense, and it would necessitate the discharge of cargo and the incurring of heavy general average expenses, and, perhaps, serious damage to cargo in handling, it was the practice to treat the temporary repairs as general average. In Italy also the practice was to allow purely temporary repairs of particular average damage as a general average provided permanent repairs were not possible or practicable. In other countries, (Germany, Holland and Scandinavia for example) the cost of temporary repairs of particular average damage was allowed as general average if by effecting such repairs greater general average expenses were saved.

14.09 These varying practices may have been precisely as reported, but it may be questioned whether these practices were correctly based on any sound legal authority in the countries concerned. For instance, in the United States the supposed authorities were reported to be:

The Star of Hope 9 Wall. 203 (1869) (rather than 17 Wall. 651),
Hobson v. Lord 92 U.S. 397, (1875),
Bowring v. Thebaud 42 Fed. 796 (1890),
Phillips on Insurance (5th ed.), sec. 1500.

to which one might add ex *Congdon* on *General Average*

Shoe v. Craig 189 Fed. 227 (1911).

A reading of these cases, however, will disclose that even if the subject of temporary repairs is mentioned, the facts in the cases did not involve temporary repairs, or such repairs were to damage caused by general average sacrifice—a very different matter. Thus, no real authority can be adduced from these cases on this particular subject, and others might be

[11] (1867) L.R. 2 Q.B. 203.

quoted to counter them (for example *The Queen* 28 Fed.Rep. 755 (1886) and *Fowler v. Rathbones* 12 Wall. 117 (1870)).

Phillips on *Insurance* was an excellent and authoritative American work, but the 5th edition was published as long ago as 1867 and was beset by the fact that any principles on this subject had to be deduced from the early American case of *Brooks v. Oriental Insurance Co.* 7. Pick. 259 (1828), where a valiant attempt had been made to understand and follow the doubtful decision in the English case of *Plummer v. Wildman.*[12]

Germany. In 1881 the Hanseatic Supreme Court had given judgment in the case of the *Prince Eugene*, and a reported summary of the case shows that the facts and the judgment correspond almost precisely with our own leading case on the subject of *Wilson v. Bank of Victoria.*[13] **14.10**

Holland. Here also, as quoted on page 586 of the sixth edition of *Lowndes* by a decision of the Court of Appeal at The Hague on April 26, 1918, N.J. 1918, "The cost of preliminary repairs in a port of refuge is not allowed as general average. Of the theory of 'substituted expenses' no trace can be found in the law."

France and Belgium. The great French authority, *Rodière*, in paragraph 434 dealing with temporary repairs of accidental damage, states that:

> "D'après la loi francçaise, le problème ne se poserait pas et cette réparation provisoire resterait avarie particulière."

The position is the same in Belgium.

With a diversity in the laws and practice of the different countries, a Rule on the subject was desirable, and at the Stockholm Conference in 1924 the draft Rule suggested by the Association of Average Adjusters was accepted almost word for word. For the first time in the history of the Rules a definite provision was introduced dealing with this vexed question: **14.11**

> "Where temporary repairs are effected to a ship at a port of loading, call or refuge, for the common safety, or of damage caused by general average sacrifice, the cost of such repairs shall be admitted as general average; but where temporary repairs of accidental damage are effected merely to enable the adventure to be completed, the cost of such repairs shall be admitted as general average ... only up to the saving in expense which would have been incurred and allowed in general average had such repairs not been effected there.
>
> No deductions 'new for old' shall be made from the cost of temporary repairs allowable as general average."

[12] (1815) M. & S. 486.
[13] (1867) L.R. 2 Q.B. 203.

14.12 *York-Antwerp Rules 1950*

In the United Kingdom, at least, the 1924 Rule attracted two schools of thought in respect of the cost of "temporary repairs of accidental damage effected merely to enable the adventure to be completed":

(1) That the cost should be a first charge on the savings to general average alone.
(2) That the cost should be apportioned over *all* savings. If temporary repairs were undertaken at a port of refuge with the ancillary benefit in mind of a saving, for instance, in the cost of permanent repairs, it could hardly be said that the temporary repairs were effected *merely* to enable the adventure to be completed, and it was only equitable to apportion the cost over all savings.

Having confirmed that foreign adjusters adopted the first view above, the Association of Average Adjusters passed a Uniformity Resolution[14] in 1928 giving effect to this view. Thereafter, a uniform interpretation of Rule XIV was applied throughout the world, but it was thought wise in the 1950 Rules to remove all possible doubt on this matter by adding the words "without regard to the saving, if any, to other interests, but" in the space ... left in the 1924 Rule quoted above.

14.13 *York-Antwerp Rules 1974*

As stated above, extra wording was added to the Rule in 1950 to make it clear that the cost of temporary repairs to accidental damage should be a first charge on savings to general average alone, even if, in effecting those temporary repairs, the shipowner might be actuated by some motive in addition to the mere completion of the adventure (for example a saving in the cost of permanent repairs). However, the draftsmen of the 1950 Rule had left the word *merely* in the phrase:

> "Where temporary repairs of accidental damage are effected *merely* to enable the adventure to be completed..."

There is little doubt that the word *merely* was intended solely to contrast the provisions of the second paragraph with the first limb of the first paragraph (where the repairs must be necessary for the common safety), but the word may have created some difficulty in construction.

For the sake of clarity in general application, in 1974 the words *in order* were substituted for the word *merely*. Even if this substitution did not overcome every problem, there was no doubt in practice that, if *one* of the reasons for effecting temporary repairs was to enable the adventure to be completed, the second paragraph would apply. The repairs must,

[14] See App. 3. para. 70.50, *post*.

of course, have been necessary for this purpose, and no more than was necessary to complete the voyage.

York-Antwerp Rules 1994

In the event, "No Change" was made to the wording of this Rule, but the second paragraph, dealing with the allowance in general average of the cost of temporary repairs to *accidental* damage, probably excited more attention and criticism in the years leading up to 1994 than any other section of the York-Antwerp Rules. This attention was no doubt fuelled by the passage through the British courts of the celebrated case of the *Bijela.*[15] **14.14**

Suggestions for reform in 1994 included:

(1) the deletion of this second paragraph altogether (coupled with the proposal for Rule X(a) that temporary repairs should not be charged direct to general average, but follow the treatment of the permanent repairs);
(2) that in no circumstances should the cost of temporary repairs be admitted as general average except where such repairs involved an extraordinary sacrifice of any of the property engaged in the common maritime adventure;
(3) that temporary repairs of accidental damage should be allowable in general average only if permanent repairs would have been practicable at the port at which the temporary repairs were effected.

None of these suggestions was accepted and Rule XIV thus remains in 1994 precisely as before, but in its practical application it could be subject to two potential changes.

(a) the view previously and widely held that temporary repairs to accidental damage could be charged to general average only when facilities for permanent repairs existed at the same port of refuge, was disproved in the case of the *Bijela*[16];
(b) Rule XIV is now subject to the new Rule Paramount[17] and the requirement of reasonableness imposed thereby.

These two potential changes will be discussed below in paragraphs 14.36 and 14.33 respectively.

[15] *Marida Ltd v. Oswal Steel; The Bijela* [1992] 1 Lloyd's Rep. 636; [1993] 1 Lloyd's Rep. 411; [1994] 2 Lloyd's Rep. 1.
[16] *Ibid.*
[17] See para. PRE.22, *ante*.

Rule XIV

Temporary Repairs

14.15 **Where temporary repairs are effected to a ship at a port of loading, call or refuge, for the common safety, or of damage caused by general average sacrifice, the cost of such repairs shall be admitted as general average.**

Where temporary repairs of accidental damage are effected in order to enable the adventure to be completed, the cost of such repairs shall be admitted as general average without regard to the saving, if any, to other interests, but only up to the saving in expense which would have been incurred and allowed in general average if such repairs had not been effected there.

No deductions "new for old" shall be made from the cost of temporary repairs allowable as general average.

Construction

General Observations

14.16 The first two paragraphs of the Rule provide for the allowance in general average of the cost of temporary repairs carried out in a port of loading, call or refuge, and falling within two main categories:

First paragraph—Temporary repairs:

(a) For the common safety (for example the plugging of a hole in the ship's shell plating to prevent her sinking within the port).
(b) To damage caused by a general average sacrifice (for example by a voluntary stranding,[18] or efforts to refloat,[19] etc.).

The cost of such temporary repairs is charged direct to general average and this will be in accordance with the law and practice of probably all countries.

14.17 *Second paragraph*—This deals with the cost of temporary repairs to *accidental* damage which are not necessary for the common safety within the port (as in *First paragraph* above), but are necessary in order to

[18] See Rules V, VII respectively.
[19] *Ibid.*

enable the continuing voyage to be prosecuted and completed[20] in safety.

The intention of the Rule seems clear: that the cost of such temporary repairs to accidental damage should be treated as general average on a substituted expense basis. Thus, if, instead of temporary repairs, permanent repairs had been carried out in the port and these would have taken longer to effect than temporary, and/or would involve the discharge of cargo, the cost of the temporary repairs should be compared with the alternative cost of the daily port charges and crew wages, etc., which would have been incurred during the extra detention for permanent repairs, and/or the cost of discharging, storing and reloading the cargo necessary for permanent repairs. Such alternative expenses might generally be expected to be charged to general average under Rules X and XI and, up to these general average expenses avoided, the cost of the temporary repairs to accidental damage should be charged to general average.

First Paragraph

"temporary repairs" The finer points of construction on the term "temporary repairs" are associated with the second paragraph of this Rule; see later paragraphs 14.20 to 14.23. **14.18**

"port of loading, call or refuge," The first paragraph of this Rule deals only with temporary repairs effected at a port of loading, call or refuge for the common safety, or of damage caused by general average sacrifice. Temporary repairs, of course, are frequently carried out *at sea*, and the cost may similarly be allowed as general average under the lettered Rules.

When temporary repairs to damage caused by general average sacrifice are carried out *at destination* the cost may also be allowed as general average, but the adjuster will then need to satisfy himself that it was reasonable to carry out only temporary repairs. If facilities for permanent repairs do not exist at the port of destination, or if permanent repairs can be effected more cheaply at some other port, it would clearly be reasonable to allow the cost, but it might be otherwise if such repairs are done solely for the convenience of the shipowner.

"for the common safety," See the general commentary on Rule A[21] but, **14.19**
for greater relevance to situations where the vessel is already within the comparative safety of a port of refuge, see the commentary in paragraph

[20] The provisions of the second paragraph of the Rule apply only to those cases where the temporary repairs enable the vessel to proceed direct to her destination. When a ship is at any port or place of refuge at which permanent repairs cannot be carried out, and she is necessarily removed to another port or place of refuge, the cost of any temporary repairs necessary for that *removal* can be allowed direct to general average under the terms of the second paragraph of Rule X(a) and without regard to savings.

[21] See paras. A.17 *et seq., ante.*

10.48, above. For temporary repairs to be necessary *for the common safety* when the vessel is in port, they must have been required to combat some truly dire emergency such as a danger of sinking at the berth.

"damage caused by general average sacrifice," If damage is caused to the ship by a general average act or sacrifice, for example in extinguishing a fire on board,[22] by a voluntary stranding,[23] or in efforts to refloat,[24] etc., the cost of any necessary temporary repairs to such damage at a port of refuge is charged direct to general average without conditions such as are expressed in the second paragraph of the Rule for repairs to accidental damage.

Second Paragraph

14.20 **"temporary repairs"**

How Long is "Temporary"?

One of the original theories behind the allowance in general average of the cost of temporary repairs was that they were of no *lasting benefit*,[25] they were undertaken merely to enable the vessel to proceed on her voyage; at the end they would be taken out and the damage fully and permanently repaired. Today, however, those temporary repairs, even though no stronger than necessary to complete the immediate voyage, may enable the vessel to continue trading for a prolonged period, say until her next annual or special survey. In the discussions preceding the York-Antwerp Rules 1950 the French delegation proposed that if permanent repairs were not effected within six months of the completion of the adventure, only 50 per cent of the cost of temporary repairs should be made good in general average. This proposal did not find favour with the other delegates, it being argued that the period was too short and that it was sometimes not possible to obtain a licence to do permanent repairs or, alternatively, to find a suitable shipyard willing to undertake the work. And if the suggested period of six months were extended, say, to two or three years, general average adjustments would be held up.

In similar discussions preceding the 1994 Rules, an Italian proposal that no allowance in general average should be made unless permanent repairs were carried out within a "reasonable time" was indorsed by the United States Maritime Law Association, but with a specific limit of six

[22] See Rule III.
[23] See Rule V.
[24] See Rule VIII.
[25] *Plummer v. Wildman* (1815) 3 M. & S. 486. Among the early proposals for the new 1994 York-Antwerp Rules was a set of definitions by A.I.D.E., one of which stated that: "... the expression '*temporary repairs*' shall mean such repairs as confer *no lasting material benefit* to the ship." It was not proceeded with, but temporary repairs usually confer very real *material benefit* on the ship.

months[26] after the completion of the voyage. These proposals were rejected.

The practice, therefore, and however unreasonable, with temporary repairs of accidental damage undertaken merely to enable the adventure to be completed, is likely to be that it matters not if the vessel continues trading with her "temporary" repairs; provided that sufficient general average expenses are saved by not effecting permanent repairs at the port of refuge, the whole cost of the temporary repairs will be allowed as general average.

However, certain important considerations must be borne in mind:

(1) The temporary repairs which can be considered for an allowance in general average are only those which are necessary to complete the *current* cargo voyage. If the temporary repairs are designedly stronger, and with the object of enabling the vessel to continue trading beyond the termination of the current voyage, clearly the shipowner must bear the cost of the extra stiffeners or strengthening. **14.21**

(2) The original theory of "no lasting benefit" cannot be totally ignored, that is, there is the implication that the temporary repairs will be removed and full permanent repairs undertaken on some future occasion. Thus, if temporary repairs are carried out in the expectation that full permanent repairs are unlikely ever to be effected, the "temporary" repairs must themselves be considered as *permanent*. This is highly relevant in the case of elderly vessels at a time of an acute shipping depression such as the mid-1980s. If in the particular economic climate prevailing at the time of the accident the shipowner would not give consideration to permanent repairs because temporary repairs would suffice for the expected life of the ship, there is no real "substitution" of expense. **14.22**

An extreme example of this situation occurs where a vessel is proceeding on her last voyage to the breakers' yard and sustains accidental damage which obliges her to put into a port of refuge for repairs. The repairs undertaken will obviously be limited to the very minimum necessary for the vessel to arrive at the breakers' yard and should all be considered as *permanent*. The fact that, in the case of a newish ship, the (say) damaged plating would be renewed, does not translate our (for example) cement box and doublers into a temporary repair.

[26] It may be of interest to record that this period of six months' use for temporary repairs was considered to be "of some benefit to the ship" in the early American case of *Brooks v. Oriental Insurance Co.* 7 Pick 259 (1828), when Putnam J. endeavoured to follow what he thought to be English law as declared in *Plummer v. Wildman* (1815) 3 M. & S. 486. In his case a schooner sustained damages on two occasions about six months apart which were temporarily repaired at the time and permanent repairs to both effected on the vessel's return home to Salem immediately following the second temporary repairs. The cost of the second temporary repairs was allowed as general average, but not of those for the earlier accident, which "were of some benefit to the ship".

14.23 Occasional difficulties may arise in practice in deciding whether certain repairs undertaken on grounds of simple economy but of uncertain durability should be treated as temporary or permanent. For instance, a fractured bedplate may be repaired by the Metalock process, or new tips may be brazed into the damaged blades of a bronze alloy propeller. A new bedplate or propeller might be the ideal permanent repair, but possibly an unnecessarily expensive one. It is usually considered that if these alternative repairs survive for six months or so, it is probable that they will last as long as the original bedplate or propeller. It is submitted, therefore, that such repairs should be considered as permanent unless they fail in service.

Fitting of spare propellers

14.24 In a report by the Advisory Committee of the Association of Average Adjusters dated December 13, 1937, the Committee expressed their view that:

> "Where a vessel has lost her propeller, the cost of replacing this at a port of refuge with a spare propeller is, in the absence of exceptional circumstances, a temporary repair within the meaning of Rule XIV."

It may be remarked that the Committee were considering a case where the working manganese propeller had been replaced with a spare cast-iron propeller; for technical reasons, cast iron propellers are rarely encountered in modern times.

Temporary repairs are a general average expense and not a sacrifice

14.25 In another report of the same Committee dated February 10, 1942, the view was expressed that temporary repairs of accidental damage allowed as general average under Rule XIV should be regarded as a general average expense, and not a sacrifice. Hence the cost should not be treated as an amount made good to be included in the value of the ship for contribution.

Removal of temporary repairs

14.26 If the cost of effecting temporary repairs is allowable in general average under any of the provisions of Rule XIV, it follows that the cost of removing those same repairs (if any) falls to be dealt with under the same provision.

Abortive temporary repairs

14.27 A number of cases have been encountered in practice where temporary repairs to accidental damage have been attempted at a port of refuge in order to save general average detention, but have failed, necessitating the effecting of permanent repairs. On the theory that the cost of temporary repairs should be chargeable to general average because they are of no value to the ship, it might be equitable to allow the cost in general average in such cases. However, the Rule is quite explicit on this point, and as, in fact, the temporary repairs effected no savings to general average, their cost cannot be allowed.

"accidental damage" In this second paragraph of Rule XIV, the temporary repairs under consideration are those to *accidental damage*, necessary in order to enable the voyage to be completed, but not for the common safety. The meaning of the term "accident" has been considered in paragraph 10.35, above, but a further example may be appropriate here. **14.28**

An elderly vessel springs a leak in her plating during heavy weather and puts into a port of refuge for temporary repairs. On a close inspection of the damage, the Classification Surveyor discovers that the surrounding plating and repairs are thoroughly wasted and insists on far more extensive repairs than are strictly necessary to restore the vessel to her pre-accident condition. The split plating itself would probably be regarded as *accidental damage* (even though resulting from general debility) and the temporary repairs thereto considered for an allowance in general average. The additional repairs required by the surveyor, however, would be in respect of pure wear and tear and would not be considered for any allowance. Nor would the crew wages, etc., during any extra detention for such wear and tear repairs, or the cost of discharging, etc., any additional cargo to gain access to the wear and tear repairs.

"port of loading, call or refuge" These words appear in the first paragraph of Rule XIV, but not in the second, and it is suggested that this omissions was unintended and that the wording of the second paragraph should apply only to temporary repairs of accidental damage carried out at a port of loading, call or refuge.[27] **14.29**

Temporary repairs in a roadstead, etc.

However, the omission presents a useful opportunity to introduce the subject of temporary repairs to accidental damage effected elsewhere than within the shelter and safety of a port, an increasingly common occurrence with the mammoth vessels in service today. For example, a very large bulk carrier may load a precisely calculated maximum quantity of cargo which enables her to leave the loading port only when the tide is at peak height, and then with just a few inches of water beneath her

[27] In the *Bijela* (*Marida Ltd v. Oswal Steel* [1993] 1 Lloyd's Rep. 411 at 416) Neill L.J. accepted that: "the temporary repairs covered by the second paragraph are those effected at a port of loading, call or refuge".

bottom. If any miscalculation is made in navigation or timing, the vessel may strand and rupture her bottom and the pumps be unable to cope with the inflow of water. With her increased draft, there will be no possibility of returning to the loading port, and temporary repairs necessary before the vessel can proceed elsewhere may need to be carried out at an anchorage, open roadstead, or in some nearby bay.

Carried out within the shelter and safety of a port, those same repairs might be considered as being only "*necessary for the safe prosecution of the voyage*"[28] (or "*to enable the adventure to be completed*"). However, and depending on the precise location and its exposure to wind, tides, and passing ships, those repairs may now be necessary for the "*common safety*",[29] and, if capable of being considered as an "extraordinary sacrifice or expenditure" within the meaning of Rule A,[30] be treated as general average.

14.30 *Temporary repairs at destination*

On occasion, it may be necessary to carry out temporary repairs at destination to accidental damage before it is possible to discharge the cargo, and whether this cost can be charged to general average raises a problem, often of considerable monetary interest. It most frequently arises with tankers carrying cargoes of crude oil, which can only be discharged at a temperature of at least 135°F. Steam for heating and discharging the cargo is often provided by auxiliary boilers, and if they suffer damage it is generally impossible to discharge the cargo by any means other than repairing one or more of the boilers. Circumstances may differ and there is as yet no authoritative answer to this problem; but in no case yet encountered in practice has any allowance in general average been justified.

"in order to enable the adventure to be completed," See the commentary in paragraph 14.13, above. The expression may also be considered as a less precise alternative to "necessary for the safe prosecution of the voyage" appearing elsewhere in the Rules and construed in paragraph 10.49, above.

14.31 **"without regard to the saving, if any, to other interests,"** (Although construed in the order in which it appears in the Rule, this particular phrase might more sensibly be reserved until after "*but only up to the saving in expense* ..." dealt with below in paragraph 14.32, below.

If, instead of effecting permanent repairs at a port of refuge, temporary repairs alone are carried out, assumed savings to general average may result, while the shipowner may be able to save on the cost of permanent

[28] See para. 10.49, *ante*.
[29] See paras. A.17–A.34, *ante*.
[30] See paras. A.56 *et seq.*, *ante*.

repairs effected at a cheaper port of repair, or a shorter period off-hire for his vessel, and the cargo interests may benefit by an earlier delivery of their cargo at destination.

If savings to general average can be shown, the cost of temporary repairs to accidental damage will be a first charge against the savings to general average alone, and not apportioned over *all* savings effected. (See also paragraphs 14.12 and F.40, above).

"but only up to the saving in expense which would have been incurred and allowed in general average if such repairs had not been effected there." As stated in paragraph 14.17, above, the intention of this section of the Rule seems clear: that the cost of temporary repairs to accidental damage should not be looked upon as a simple repair charge, but be treated on a "substituted expense" basis, that is, as a substitution for those alternative and larger expenses which would have been charged to general average if (in 99 cases out of 100) *permanent* repairs had instead been effected in the port of refuge. Permanent repairs would generally have taken *longer* than the temporary repairs and, if the damage was to the bottom of the ship, they might also have necessitated the discharging, storing and reloading of the cargo. The port charges and crew wages, etc., during the additional detention, and the costs of any discharging, storing and reloading of cargo, are normally allowable as general average under Rules X(b), X(c) and XI(b) and, up to the amount of these additional and alternative expenses avoided by effecting only temporary repairs, the cost of the temporary repairs should in practice be charged to general average. **14.32**

Whether the precise wording used in Rule XIV adequately and clearly expressed this intention was queried here from the eighth edition onwards. Allowances under Rules X(b), X(c) and XI(b), for port charges, crew wages and cargo operations are all subject to the requirement that the repairs were "*necessary for the safe prosecution of the voyage*", and although the temporary repairs will generally fulfil this criterion, it is self-evident that if those temporary repairs were sufficient to prosecute the voyage in safety, permanent repairs could not possible be necessary for that purpose (or were greater than was necessary for that purpose). On this basis, the additional port charges, crew wages, and cargo operations would not have justified any allowance in general average, and there could be no "*saving in expense which would have been ... allowed in general average*" against which to set the cost of the temporary repairs.

This particular quandary was resolved, and the construction placed upon the wording of Rule XIV by adjusters worldwide for the previous 70 years confirmed, in the case of *Marida Ltd v. Oswal Steel; The Bijela.*[31] **14.33**

[31] *Marida Ltd v. Oswal Steel; The Bijela* [1992] 1 Lloyd's Rep. 636; [1993] 1 Lloyd's Rep. 411; [1994] 2 Lloyd's Rep. 1.

In that case, the vessel grounded very shortly after leaving her loading port of Providence, Rhode Island, thereby sustaining considerable damage to her bottom and leakage into the double bottom tanks. She put into Jamestown as a port of refuge (a port at which permanent repairs were impossible), effected temporary repairs afloat, thereafter resuming her voyage and delivering the cargo of shredded scrap at Kandla in India and then proceeding to Singapore for permanent repairs.

Final judgment was given in the House of Lords, overruling the decisions of the courts below, and Lord Lloyd of Berwick pointed to the concluding words of the second paragraph of Rule XIV and said:

> "The second paragraph of Rule XIV obliges us to suppose that the temporary repairs had not been effected at Jamestown. What then would have happened? The answer is simple. She would have gone into dry-dock in New York. Was the discharge of the cargo necessary to enable the damage to the ship to be repaired in dry-dock? The answer is clearly yes. Were those repairs necessary to enable the vessel to proceed safely to (destination), always assuming that she had not already been repaired in Jamestown? The answer, again, is clearly yes."

The rationale of this judgment means that when one is obliged to ignore the course actually adopted of temporary repairs, the next most reasonable alternative course then becomes and must be deemed *necessary*, as required for the hypothetical allowances under Rules X(b) and XI(b) against which the cost of the temporary repairs will be set. Further, when the alternative course takes on this mantle of necessity, *a fortiori* it must also be assumed to be *reasonable*, as required by the new Rule Paramount,[32] and not such as could amount to a breach of the contract of carriage.

14.34 The only limitation to this general premise might occur in those situations where the adoption of the standard alternative course of permanent repairs would entitle the parties to the adventure to abandon the voyage, that is, for the reason that:

(1) it would be so costly that, for example the cost of repairs plus any contribution to the general average would mean that the vessel was a commercial total loss; or
(2) it would take so long that the adventure would be frustrated.

Faced with such alternatives, one must endeavour to answer the question posed by Lord Lloyd in his judgment, quoted above: "*What then would have happened?*"

It must surely be accepted that the reasonable course then to adopt would be to abandon the voyage, whereupon it is to be noted that all general average allowances cease effectively on the date of that abandonment and that there would thus be no—or insufficient—allow-

[32] See para. PRE.22, *ante*.

ances against which to set the cost of the temporary repairs effected. It is submitted that the shipowner, not actually having exercised his option to forward the cargo in another vessel, is not entitled to rely upon the general average allowances which might have been available if that option had been exercised.[33]

It may also be added that although a real-life abandonment of the voyage might result in the cargo interests being obliged to pay a second freight or other comparable charges to get their cargo to destination, these additional charges cannot be invoked to increase any allowance for the cost of temporary repairs, since Rule XIV permits only the "saving in expenses which would have been ... allowed in general average" to be taken into account.

It should be noted that in *The Bijela* Hoffmann L.J., who delivered a dissenting judgment in the Court of Appeal, took the view that for the purpose of determining what general average expenses had been saved by the temporary repairs it was necessary to assume that the temporary repairs *could not* have been carried out.[34] However, the House of Lords, although agreeing with Hoffmann L.J. in the result, expressly declined to adopt this part of his reasoning. Thus immediately after the passage quoted in paragraph 14.33, above, Lord Lloyd continued: **14.35**

> "It is not necessary to assume that the vessel *could not* have been repaired at Jamestown in order to give effect to the two rules [rules X and XIV]. It is only necessary to assume that she was not so repaired, as r. XIV requires."

The more limited assumption made by the House of Lords will not, it is submitted, satisfy the requirements of the second paragraph of Rule X(a), which extends the port of refuge allowances of Rule X to a second port of refuge to which the ship is necessarily removed *because repairs cannot be carried out in the first port or place*[35]. It follows that, in determining what adventure expenses have been saved by the temporary repairs, expenses which would have been incurred at a second port or place of refuge cannot be taken into account, unless the expenses at that port or place qualify for allowances on some independent ground, for example that the port or place in question was a port or place of loading or of call.[36] In *The Bijela* itself the port of refuge expenses saved by the

[33] See Rule G, para. G.41, *ante*.

[34] [1993] 1 Lloyd's Rep. 411 at 423.

[35] One of the grounds on which Hobhouse J. rejected the claim ([1992] 1 Lloyd's Rep. 637 at 644) was that, since repairs could be carried out at Jamestown, the requirements of the second paragraph of Rule X(a) were not satisfied. Hoffmann L.J. ([1993] 1 Lloyd's Rep. 411 at 424) held that they were satisfied because it was necessary to assume that the temporary repairs at Jamestown were not an available option. The House of Lords, for the reasons set out at the end of para. 14.34, *ante*, found it unnecessary to express any view on the point.

[36] See the first paragraph of Rule X(a) (see para. 10.32, *ante*), and Rule X(b) (see para. 10.45, *ante*).

temporary repairs (and in excess of the cost of the temporary repairs) would have been incurred at the port of loading, Providence, where the cargo would have been discharged and stored before the ship proceeded to New York for repairs. It was therefore unnecessary for the shipowner to rely on the second paragraph of Rule X(a) in order to establish that the expenses saved would have been allowable in general average.

Where permanent repairs impossible at the port of refuge

14.36 Vessels which sustain severe damage may, on occasion, be obliged for the common safety to put into ports of refuge at which facilities do not exist for the carrying out of permanent repairs (for example a drydock for repairs to the bottom). Temporary repairs may then be the only option, sometimes sufficient to enable the vessel to prosecute the whole voyage in safety, at other times adequate only to enable the vessel to reach another and better-equipped port of refuge.

In the latter case, the cost of any temporary repairs for a *necessary* removal to the second port of refuge can be charged direct to general average in accordance with the second paragraph of Rule X(a).[37] With regard to the case where temporary repairs to accidental damage enable the vessel to proceed to destination, it was the fairly general practice of average adjusters worldwide prior to the first legal action in the case of *The Bijela*[38] to consider that if the temporary repairs were effected at a port of refuge at which there were no facilities for carrying out permanent repairs, there was no alternative but to do this class of repairs and there was no substitution of expense. Accordingly, there could be no allowance in general average for the cost of the temporary repairs.[39]

This practice was followed by the adjusters first employed to adjust the case of *The Bijela*,[40] where substantial temporary repairs sufficient to enable the adventure to be safely completed were effected at a port of refuge at which permanent repairs were impossible. The legal action was finally decided in the House of Lords on other grounds, but purely as a matter of construction, in the Court of Appeal Neill L.J. was of the opinion that there was "*no obligation on the owners to show that the permanent repairs could have been carried out at the port where the temporary repairs were effected*", a view also indorsed by Hoffmann L.J. Attempts to have the earlier practice reinstated by special wording in the 1994 Rule XIV were rejected, and the practice will clearly no longer be followed.

[37] See para. 10.39, *ante*.

[38] *Marida Ltd v. Oswal Steel; The Bijela* [1992] 1 Lloyd's Rep. 637; [1993] 1 Lloyd's Rep. 411; [1994] 2 Lloyd's Rep. 1.

[39] The practice would have originated as an inherited "carry-over" from the earliest Rule X(d) on substituted expenses, which opened with the words "If a ship under average be in a port or place at *which it is practicable to her* ...". See also under para. 14.31 and its lengthy footnote 32 in the 11th edition.

[40] See n. 38, *ante*.

A Case in a Hundred **14.37**

It was stated earlier in paragraph 14.32, above, that in *99 cases out of 100* the cost of temporary repairs to accidental damage will be allowed as general average in substitution for those alternative and larger expenses which would have been charged to general average if, instead, permanent repairs had been effected as the port of refuge. An example of that hundredth case, taken from practice, concerned a ship bound from a South American port to Rotterdam which experienced trouble with broken tailshaft coupling bolts when 2/300 miles south-west of Falmouth. Permanent repairs would require the vessel to drydock, and the vessel might have proceeded to a port of refuge where there were drydock facilities, or she might have accepted salvage services from the salvage tugs tailing her in anticipation of a breakdown. Instead, and on the grounds of pure economy, the vessel proceeded at slow speed into Brixham (where there was no drydock) to obtain shore labour for temporary repairs to enable her to continue to destination.

Here the cost of temporary repairs was set against the prospective salvage award payable to the tugs, and the example is perhaps doubly interesting in that:

(1) The standard alternative in the "99 cases" is the effecting of permanent repairs which must be *necessary for the safe prosecution of the voyage*, a necessity which can be assumed only on the hypothesis that the temporary repairs had not been effected. In contrast, the alternative in this hundredth case was a salvage service rendered at sea when the *common maritime adventure was in peril*, a condition which needed no assumption; it was a fact.
(2) If, as they were invited to do, cargo interests in *The Bijela*[41] case had been able to provide such an example for their lordships' consideration, might the case have been decided differently? There is more than the faintest suggestion in the judgments of Lord Lloyd in the House of Lords and of Hoffman L.J. in the Court of Appeal that they reached their conclusions in order to give *some* business efficacy to the second paragraph of Rule XIV, which on the basis of the standard 99 examples put before them they thought would otherwise have been devoid of all practical effect.

"there." The second paragraph of the Rule omits to state where the temporary repairs under discussion must have been effected; but it would be reasonable to assume that it must be at a port of loading, call or refuge where alternative general average expenses can be incurred, and **14.38**

[41] *Marida Ltd v. Oswal Steel; The Bijela* [1992] 1 Lloyd's Rep. 637; [1993] 1 Lloyd's Rep. 411; [1994] 2 Lloyd's Rep. 1.

not at sea. (The draft Rule submitted by the Danish Committee for the York-Antwerp Rules 1950 made special mention of this point.)

"deductions 'new for old'" See Rule XIII.

"THE CUCKOO IN THE NEST"

14.39 The case of *The Bijela*,[42] dealing with the cost of temporary repairs to accidental damage under Rule XIV, became a *cause célèbre* during its passage through the courts in the early 1990s, thereby earning for itself more than 20 references in this present edition. Perhaps its most memorable and perceptive remark came from Hoffmann L.J. (as he then was) in the Court of Appeal, when he said (at page 422):

> "This Rule ... is something of a cuckoo in the otherwise tidy nest of the substitution principle as exemplified by the old Rule X(d) and Rule F."

Insofar as it relates to the cost of temporary repairs to accidental damage, Rule XIV is, indeed, a thoroughly unwelcome intruder into the professedly equitable principles of general average, for it is almost indisputable that in the absence of the Rule, and in the words of Mann L.J. in *The Bijela*[43]:

> "... the cost of such (temporary) repairs rests with the owner as being part of the ordinary expenses of performing his duty to convey the cargo to its destination. The expense is thus *particular* average."

14.40 The reality of the matter in practice is that there is but rarely any true substitution of one expense for another when temporary repairs are effected to accidental damage; the alternative course is largely fanciful and would seldom be adopted by any prudent shipowner. Given the choice, he will almost invariably carry out temporary repairs,[44] deferring the permanent repairs to a time and place convenient for his own personal financial benefit, as in *The Bijela*[45] case itself. The cost of the temporary repairs rarely involves the shipowner in any financial *sacrifice* whatever, an essential feature of any true general average loss.

However, as was finally decided by the House of Lords, the particular wording of Rule XIV did permit the allowance in general average of this basically particular average expense. Exception cannot be taken to the decision itself, but must be reserved for the particular wording of the Rule and those responsible in 1994 for considering it appropriate to continue with that same wording unchanged. The House of Lords may have confirmed the practitioners' previous

[42] *Marida Ltd v. Oswal Steel; The Bijela* [1992] 1 Lloyd's Rep. 637; [1993] 1 Lloyd's Rep. 411; [1994] 2 Lloyd's Rep. 1.

[43] *Ibid.*

[44] *E.g. Marc Rich and Co. A.G. v. Bishop Rock Marine Co. Ltd; The Nicholas H* [1992] 2 Lloyd's Rep. 481, where the Classification Surveyor at first ordered permanent repairs to be effected, at which the owners "baulked" and persuaded the surveyor that only temporary repairs were necessary. These failed, and the vessel and her cargo were lost.

[45] See n. 42, *ante*.

interpretation of the wording of the Rule, but that can hardly be taken as an indorsement of the provisions of the Rule itself, which, in so far as they relate to the cost of temporary repairs of accidental damage, are entirely unprincipled.

One important feature of *The Bijela* which is to be regretted, however, is that the courts were dealing with a case with wholly exceptional facts, in that the time taken to effect the temporary repairs was as long as would have been required if, instead, the vessel had proceeded from the port of refuge to New York for permanent repairs. It follows that in the unlikely event that the shipowner had elected to adopt this alternative course, it would not have delayed the voyage and thereby raised the possibility of a breach of the contract of carriage. The usual position is that the alternative courses (for example permanent repairs) will frequently involve so much extra delay and/or expense that they would amount to a breach of the contract of affreightment, and therefore cannot be considered as a course of action for which temporary repairs are a substitute. (Where this is not the case, the shipowner is perfectly entitled to effect permanent repairs.) **14.41**

The reasoning of the House of Lords requires one to ignore the possibility of temporary repairs in deciding whether the alternative was a breach of the contract, but their Lordships might have been much more reluctant to adopt this reasoning in a case where the alternative would have clearly been wholly unreasonable, as in the great majority of cases.

Rule XV

Loss of Freight

English Law and Background

When is Loss of Freight made Good?

15.01 Freight is one of the properties involved in the common maritime adventure. Thus a loss of freight at the risk of the carrier[1] falls to be made good in general average in the same circumstances as loss or damage to ship or cargo, namely when the carrier's right to receive freight is intentionally sacrificed by a general average act.

Examples of a sacrifice of freight are given in the succeeding paragraphs, but the ultimate question is always whether, as a direct result of a general average act, the carrier has been deprived of the right to receive the freight or a part of it. For this purpose it is necessary to have regard to the effect of the contract of affreightment, and some of the more important points may be summarised here.[2]

(1) If freight is not at the risk of the carrier at the time of the general average act,[3] there can be no sacrifice of freight as such, since the freight will be payable whether or not the cargo reaches the destination. The risk has passed to the cargo owner and the freight is treated as an additional element in the value of the cargo,[4] for the purposes of computing both the contributory value of the cargo (see paragraphs 17.26 and 17.28, below) and the amount made good on a sacrifice of the cargo (see paragraph 16.29, below).

(2) Since freight is payable without deduction on damaged cargo, provided it retains its commercial identity,[5] there can be no sacrifice of freight where cargo is merely damaged as a result of a general average act.

[1] See *infra* as to freight at the risk of the cargo owner. For the meaning of "carrier" in this context see para. 15.02, *post*.

[2] See also para. 17.42, *post*.

[3] See para. 17.42, *post*, as to whether freight is at the risk of the carrier or of the cargo owner.

[4] *Cf. Maldonado v. British and Foreign Marine Insce. Co.* 182 Fed.Rep. 744 (1910), and see para. 17.41, *post*.

[5] See paras. 17.40–17.42, *post*.

(3) If freight is payable on a lump sum basis, or on the intake quantity, there can be no sacrifice of freight by, for example, a jettison of part of the cargo.[6]

(4) In the absence of contrary agreement, freight is payable only on delivery at the scheduled destination, and the carrier is not entitled to a proportion of the freight if he delivers the cargo short of destination.[7]

In the commentary on Rule XVII will be found a description of the various types of freight contract, and a discussion of the circumstances in which freight is at the risk of the carrier.[8] It is also important to bear in mind that, in determining whether freight is at the risk of the carrier, and in computing the value of the freight, it is the immediate contract with the cargo owner alone which is relevant.[9] If freight is not at carrier's risk under that contract it neither contributes nor is it made good, regardless of whether it is at a charterer's risk or at the shipowner's risk under an antecedent contract. On the other hand, if freight *is* at carrier's risk under the immediate contract with the cargo owner, the carrier under an antecedent contract may be entitled to share in any amount made good, in the same way as he would have been liable to participate in making contribution upon that freight.[10] For example: **15.02**

Shipowner A charters his ship to B	@	£5 per ton, at risk
B puts it on the berth	@	£6 per ton, at risk
The amount made good will be:		£6[11] per ton
Of which: B's share is		£1[12] per ton
Shipowner's share		£5[13] per ton
		£6
If the Shipowner had chartered to B (so that B was making a loss of £1 per ton)	@	£7 per ton
The amount made good will still be		£6[14] per ton
Of which: B's share		nil
Shipowner's share		£6[15] per ton

[6] See para. 15.03, *post.* See para. 16.34, *post,* for the effect of a lump sum freight term on the amount made good for sacrifice of cargo.

[7] But see *British Shipping Laws,* Vol. III: Carver, *Carriage by Sea* (13th ed.), paras. 1685–1690. The courts will sometimes imply an agreement to pay *pro rata* freight.

[8] See paras. 17.40–17.42, *post.*

[9] See paras. 17.41–17.42, *post,* for the application of the same rule to contribution in respect of freight.

[10] *Ibid.*

[11] Less any expenses saved; see para. 15.18, *post.*

[12] *Ibid.*

[13] *Ibid.*

[14] *Ibid.*

[15] *Ibid.*

Time charter hire, since it accrues continuously while the ship is on hire, is never at risk in the same way as voyage freight, and is therefore not treated as a separate interest for the purpose of general average.[16]

EXAMPLES OF FREIGHT LOSSES

15.03 (1) *By jettison or total destruction of cargo*

If the value of cargo jettisoned or otherwise destroyed by sacrifice is itself made good in general average, the loss to the carrier[17] of the freight due on that cargo must similarly be made good provided that the original voyage is successfully completed.

(2) *By loss of specie*

If cargo loses its specie and ceases to be merchantable, by reason, for instance, of water used to extinguish a fire, the loss to the carrier of the freight thereon can be made good as general average.

15.04 (3) *By the necessity to discharge and leave behind some of the cargo at a port of refuge*

(A) An outbreak of fire in the cargo of a vessel already loaded down to her marks may be extinguished at a port of refuge by the use of water. If her cargo absorbs the water and it cannot all be pumped out, an equivalent weight of cargo will require to be discharged and left behind at the port of refuge. The loss of freight thereon will be made good as general average.

(B) A vessel loaded down to her summer loadline may put into a port of refuge and, when ready to resume her voyage, find that winter loadlines are applicable. Accordingly, she will be obliged to reduce her draft by discharging and leaving behind some of the cargo. The loss of freight thereon will not be made good as general average, arising as it does from delay.

[16] See para. 17.53, *post*. The situation will rarely arise in which the owner of time-charter hire will be entitled to share in the amount made good on voyage freight, since a sacrifice of cargo will normally cause no loss of hire.

[17] Freight is occasionally payable at destination on a lump sum basis, or on the "intake" quantity. Provided that a worthwhile quantity of cargo is delivered at destination, the whole freight is payable and the carrier suffers no loss by a jettison or other sacrifice. For a fuller account and example, see para. 16.34, *post*.

(4) *By abandonment of the voyage* **15.05**

A voyage may be abandoned short of destination for various reasons, of which the following are examples:

(A) (i) the SHIP may be so damaged as to be a commercial total loss[18] and not worth repairing;
(ii) though worth repairing, the time required for those repairs necessary to enable the ship to continue the voyage may be so long that the voyage is frustrated; or
(iii) in either case, if the expenses of transhipping the cargo and forwarding it to destination would be greater than the FREIGHT at risk.

(B) The CARGO may be so damaged as to be not fit to be carried to destination.

The damage giving rise to any of the above situations in this head (4) may be caused by:

(a) accident;
(b) sacrifice; or
(c) a combination of them both.

Where the voyage is abandoned, the carrier will lose the freight at risk and it remains to be seen in what circumstances the loss can be made good in general average:

COMMERCIAL TOTAL LOSS OF THE SHIP (head (4) (A) (i) above) **15.06**

(a) *By accident alone*

Clearly there can be no allowance in general average for any loss of freight from such a cause.

(b) *By sacrifice alone*

It is difficult to visualise a situation in practice where a sacrifice does not follow some previous accident to the ship, but if such a situation did arise, the resulting loss of freight would be allowable in general average.

(c) *By combination of both accident and sacrifice*

A typical example might occur where the estimated cost of repairing damage caused by stranding and by efforts to refloat would together

[18] Where the estimated cost of repairs would exceed the difference between the sound and scrap values of the ship.

amount to more than was worth spending on the vessel. It is suggested that the ratio of the damages one to another—whether it be 1:3 or 3:1—has no direct bearing on whether the loss of freight at risk can be allowed as general average.

The crucial factor is whether, but for the refloating (or sacrifice) damage, the vessel would have been worth repairing and, further, whether those repairs could have been effected within a time that would not cause the voyage to be frustrated. If the answer to both these questions is YES, the proximate cause of the loss of freight would appear to be the damage caused by sacrifice, and the freight should be made good in general average.

15.07 *FRUSTRATION OF THE VOYAGE BY TIME (head (4) (A) (ii) above)*

If repairs to the ship (whether of general average damage or not), though worth effecting, would take so long that the voyage is frustrated, the loss of freight would be the result of *delay* and excluded by the terms of Rule C.

15.08 *COMMERCIAL TOTAL LOSS OF THE CARGO (head (4) (B) above)*

(that is, where the cargo is so damaged as to be not fit—or worth reconditioning—for carriage to destination)

(a) *By accident alone*

There can be no claim in general average for the freight lost. In *Iredale & Porter v. China Traders Insurance Co. Ltd*[19] a vessel on voyage from Cardiff to Esquimalt was obliged to put into a port of refuge in the River Plate owing to the dangerous overheating of her cargo of coals. It was found that none of the cargo could with safety be forwarded to destination and it was accordingly sold at the port of refuge. A claim in general average by the shipowner for his loss of freight was disallowed, it being held that owing to the condition of the cargo, the freight was already lost when the vessel put into the port of refuge.

(b) *By sacrifice alone*

Sound cargo may be rendered unfit for carriage to destination by a general average sacrifice, for example the use of water to extinguish a fire in other cargo in the ship. The loss of freight to the carrier caused by such a sacrifice should be made good in general average.

In *Pirie v. Middle Dock Co.*[20] fire broke out in a cargo of coals and this was extinguished by pouring a large quantity of water into the hold.

[19] [1900] 2 Q.B. 515.
[20] (1881) 44 L.T. 426; 4 Asp. M.C. 3788.

The vessel put into a port of refuge and the whole cargo was discharged there and sold, it being found that a considerable portion of the cargo was completely charred and burnt, and the remainder so damaged by saturation with water that it was practically impossible to forward it to its destination. The shipowner thereby lost his freight, and it was held that on that portion of the cargo which was not within the immediate reach of the fire and which was too much damaged by water to be forwarded to its destination, the freight should be made good in general average.

(c) *By combination of both accident and sacrifice* **15.09**

It is possible for two separate causes to operate on the same portion of cargo and for the combined effect to produce a total loss or loss of specie of that cargo whereby the carrier will lose his freight. For example, let us again take a cargo of coals, the whole of which has heated dangerously and on part of which water has been poured as a general average sacrifice.

The damage to that part of the cargo damaged by both heating and water may well be allocated 50 : 50 (or other proportion) to each cause, but by reason of the fact that freight is payable either in full or not at all (see paragraph 15.02, above) the loss of freight must be attributed wholly either to the heating or to the water damage. If, but for the use of the water, the cargo could have been economically made fit for further carriage to the intended destination, the loss of freight can be allowed as general average. However, if as in the *Iredale*[21] case the coals would be sold even with only the damage by heating, no allowance for freight can be made good in general average. The water will have caused no loss of freight.

Amount to Be Made Good for Freight Lost **15.10**

Normal voyage expenses saved to be credited

Where the carrier sustains a loss of freight as the result of a general average sacrifice, the amount to be made good is the gross freight lost, less those expenses which the carrier would have incurred to earn such freight, but which in consequence of the sacrifice, he escapes.[22]

In the case of the whole voyage being abandoned short of destination, those expenses will include the wages and maintenance of the crew and the bunkers that would have been consumed in prosecuting the remainder

[21] See n. 19, *ante*.

[22] See also Rule of Practice, No. F20, para. 70.47, *post*. See also *Nathl. Hooper* (1839) 3 Sumner 543; *Mutual Ins. Co. v. Cargo Brig George* (1845) Olcott 89. Rule of Practice, No. 14, of the Average Adjusters Association of the U.S. provides for deduction of the expenses saved through not earning the freight.

of the voyage until final completion of discharge of cargo, plus the port charges and discharging expenses, etc., to be incurred at the port(s) of destination, and canal dues en route, if any. Where only part of the freight is lost (for example by jettison) and the vessel herself continues to destination, the only expenses likely to be saved are the cost of discharging the (jettisoned) cargo, as it is seldom that other voyage expenses will in any way be reduced by reason of the sacrifice.

Freight on cargo taken to fill up

15.11 If, after a jettison, the ship puts into a port of refuge, and there takes in fresh cargo in the space left vacant through the jettison, editions of this work prior to the tenth have stated that the new freight thus earned must go in diminution of the shipowner's claim for loss of freight unless that new cargo might equally have been received on board even if there had been no jettison.[23]

It would probably be more correct to state that the new freight thus earned (less the extra expenses incurred to earn it) should go in diminution of the *total general average*, and that regardless of whether the shipowner's original freight was at risk or not.

15.12 In the United States case of the *Rosamond*,[24] a deck cargo of timber was jettisoned for the common safety and the vessel put into a port of refuge for repairs. Thereafter, she secured a new deck cargo and an additional freight. The freight on the original deck cargo had been prepaid absolutely, and the shipowner could have been in the happy position of earning two freights on the same voyage. Further, the value of the original deck cargo jettisoned did not fall to be made good in general average.[25] The Circuit Court of Appeals held:

(1) It would be inequitable to permit the vessel to benefit by the freight on the new deck cargo without giving proper allowance to underdeck cargo for such new freight.
(2) The net new freight and not the gross new freight should be apportioned between the interests to the extent of the general average expense.
(3) If the net new freight exceeds the general average expense, then there has in fact been no loss and no contribution is due from anyone, but if the general average expense exceeds the net new freight, then only the amount of the excess should be apportioned among the contributing interests.

[23] Baily, *General Average*, p. 134.
[24] (1940) A.M.C. 195.
[25] The bill of lading incorporated the York-Antwerp Rules 1890, Rule 1 of which stated: "No jettison of deck cargo shall be made good as general average."

The Court commented:

> "We think fairness requires a holding in such a case at this with its peculiar facts that: If the net new freight exceeds the general average expense, then there has in fact been no loss and no contribution is due from anyone; if the general average expense exceeds the amount of the net new freight, then only the amount of the excess should be apportioned among the contributing interests. We arrive at this result because the event causing the loss also enabled the ship to carry new cargo. Were it not for the event, such new cargo would not have been obtained. It is only right, we think, that the ship's profit be restricted to the amount of the excess of the net new freight over the general average expense."

Historical Development and Practice of Rule XV

York Rules 1864 15.13

A jettison or similar sacrifice of cargo carries with it the loss to the carrier of any freight payable at destination on the cargo sacrificed. This simple truth was given formal expression in Rule XI at the International Conference at York in 1864 and passed unanimously:

> In every case in which a sacrifice of cargo is made good as general average, the loss of freight, if any, which is caused by such loss of cargo, shall likewise be so made good.

York-Antwerp Rules 1877

No change.

York-Antwerp Rules 1890 15.14

A possible lacuna in the 1864 Rule was revealed in 1881 by the decision in the case of *Pirie v. Middle Dock Co.*[26] A cargo of coals was necessarily sold at a port of refuge in consequence of damage by water used to extinguish a fire; the shipowner thereby lost the freight that would have been payable on delivery at destination and it was held that this loss should be made good in general average. As the cargo owner received his coals freight-free and suffered no loss as the result of the general average act (in fact he made an unexpected profit) nothing was made good in general average for the damage to the cargo.

Under the existing York-Antwerp Rule it might have been possible to argue that an allowance in general average for loss of freight was conditional upon an allowance being made for the cargo itself, and to avoid this situation, the Rule was amended as follows and unanimously agreed at the International Conference at Liverpool in 1890:

[26] (1881) 44 L.T. 426.

Loss of freight arising from damage to or loss of cargo shall be made good as general average, either when caused by a general average act, or when the damage to or loss of cargo is so made good.

15.15 *York-Antwerp Rules 1924*

On this occasion the existing 1890 Rule was retained unchanged but, at the suggestion of the Association of Average Adjusters, a second paragraph was added[27] of identical effect to one of their own Rules of Practice[28] passed in 1894.

York-Antwerp Rules 1950 and 1974

No change.

York-Antwerp Rules 1994

No change.

Rule XV

Loss of Freight

15.16 **Loss of freight arising from damage to or loss of cargo shall be made good as general average, either when caused by a general average act, or when the damage to or loss of cargo is so made good.**

Deduction shall be made from the amount of gross freight lost, of the charges which the owner thereof would have incurred to earn such freight, but has, in consequence of the sacrifice, not incurred.

Construction

(The provisions of Rule XV follow and are in total accord with English law and practice, and reference to the preceding paragraphs 15.01–15.12, above, is requested for a more detailed analysis and examples.)

[27] It may also be remarked that a third paragraph relating to new freight earned on goods carried in lieu of goods sacrificed was suggested, but not approved. This subject is dealt with paras. 15.11–15.12, *ante*.

[28] No. F20. See para. 70.47, *post*.

"freight" See paragraph 15.01, above, and paragraphs 17.40 *et seq.*, below, for the meaning of freight in this context. 15.17

"arising from damage to or loss of cargo" Rule XV deals only with loss of freight arising from damage to or loss of *cargo*. Loss of freight arising out of damage to or loss of the *ship* is not made good under this Rule, although it may be made good under the lettered Rules.

"Deduction shall be made ... not incurred." It is manifestly right that the allowance in general average to the owner of freight sacrificed should be limited to the actual loss he has sustained and this can only be arrived at by allowing him the net freight, after deduction of the charges he would have had to pay to earn it. Such charges are limited, of course, to those which have not been incurred in consequence of the sacrifice, for example the estimated cost of discharging at destination. They do not extend to the wages and maintenance of the crew or port charges paid during the remainder of the voyage, unless in some exceptional case these charges have been saved in whole or in part by reason of the sacrifice (see also paragraph 15.10, above). 15.18

Where freight is *not* at risk to the carrier, similar savings in the costs that would have been incurred to discharge the cargo jettisoned may be made by him, but in practice these savings are ignored. General average aims to provide a partial indemnity against losses, not to enforce the sharing of profits; and a general average adjustment must not place a person in a worse position than he would have been in if the adventure, instead of being saved, had been totally lost at the time of the general average act.

As to the deduction of freight or hire payable by the carrier under an antecedent charter, see paragraph 15.02, above.

Rule XVI

Amount to be Made Good for Cargo Lost or Damaged by Sacrifice

English Law and Practice

16.01 *Note: For the benefit of readers of this section on English law and practice, it is well to stress at the outset that claims in general average for loss of or damage to cargo according to English law are based on* **market** *values on the last day of discharge at the port(s) of destination, or other place where the adventure ends. However, claims under Rule XVI of the York-Antwerp Rules 1974 et seq. are based on the* **invoice** *values to the receivers, and sometimes in accordance with differing principles, and there can thus be marked differences in the ultimate allowances under the two systems. Since general average adjustments prepared in accordance with English practice might now represent less than one per cent of the total, the early paragraphs (16.01 to 16.12, below) should be regarded more as a historical survey of the subject.*

The changes made in 1974 to Rules XVI and XVII of the York-Antwerp Rules were designed for simplicity in operation, rather than for the soundness of their principles, and further remarks on this aspect are made in paragraph 17.08, below.

16.02 The basic principle which regulates the amount to be made good for loss of or damage to cargo caused by a general average sacrifice is that the owner of the goods is to be so compensated that:

(1) he shall be in the same position as if, not his goods, but those of some other person had been thus sacrificed, or (what amounts to the same thing)
(2) it will be financially immaterial to him whether his cargo was sacrificed or delivered in similar condition to the cargo of the other interested parties.

To give full effect to this principle, interest ought to be allowed to the owner of cargo sacrificed from the time of the termination of the adventure until he actually receives the amount made good to him. Otherwise he is not put on an equality with those other owners of cargo who receive their cargo when the vessel arrives. In practice, however, such interest is never allowed in this country.[1]

Amounts Allowable when Voyage Completed

In case of total loss of part cargo

Whenever there has been a general average sacrifice of cargo and the ship reaches her intended port of destination with at least part of her cargo, the amount of the loss to be made good in general average for a total loss of part of the cargo is always[2] based upon the net market value of the goods: that is to say, the sum which the goods would have been worth, or would have fetched if, immediately upon delivery[3] to the consignee, he had sold them in the market, deducting therefrom all those expenses which he would have incurred subsequent to the general average act to realise that sum, and which he escapes if the goods are totally lost. Hence, the freight must be deducted if it is payable only on right delivery at destination: so must the expenses of landing the cargo and, in appropriate circumstances, any duty or sale charges. Expenses incurred *before* the general average act (such as the cost of marine insurance), or payable whether or not the ship and/or cargo arrive at destination, are not deducted. **16.03**

In the case of non-delivery, either of a number of packages or of a whole consignment, the amount to be allowed as general average is the net market value of the cargo short-delivered, calculated as above. In the case of goods arriving at destination in a totally worthless condition, the amount to be allowed is also the net market value, calculated as above, plus the charges—if any—incurred by the consignee in dumping the cargo.

[1] See Rule of Practice No. A2, para. 70.02, *post*; *cf.* Rule XXI, York-Antwerp Rules. In the U.S. such interest is allowed: *The Brig Mary* 1 Sprague 17 (1842). See also paras. 21.01–21.04, *post*.

[2] It is, however, said, that if jewels or other valuables are described in the bill of lading as articles of inferior value, they are to be contributed for as of such inferior value. See Benecke, p. 294; Arnould (2nd ed.), p. 947; *British Shipping Laws*, Vol. 10: Arnould, *Marine Insurance* (16th ed.), para. 979; Code de Com. Art. 418; *cf. Lebeau v. Gen. Steam Nav. Co.* (1872) L.R. 8 C.P. 88. So also, according to the Laws of Wisby and some of the older writers, if valuables are packed in a box without any intimation to the master of their value, they shall be contributed for only upon the value of the box, or of the goods the master might reasonably suppose it to contain. See Arnould, *ubi supra*. Phillips, however, considers that if the omission to give notice of the contents of the box was not due to the fault or negligence of the shipper, the contribution should be for their value: Phillips, para. 1372. See also Rule XIX of the York-Antwerp Rules.

[3] In practice, the last day of discharge is the date customarily adopted. In the case of certain commodities (such as wool) which are only sold at stated intervals, the practice is to adopt the values as determined at the next following sale.

Net market value

16.04 The net market value at the last day of discharge is in all cases the basis of compensation. The expression "net market value" assumes that there is a *market* at the destination for the particular goods sacrificed. This will usually be the case with basic commodities for which there is a wide need and demand, but in the case of goods or manufactured products imported for a particular need, there may be no general market. It is then generally found appropriate to adopt both for the purpose of compensation and for contribution the *invoice* price with an addition of say 10 per cent to represent the net market value.

Basic commodities (for example grain) are often bought and sold many times during the course of a voyage at varying prices which reflect the general market value on the particular date of sale, and the fact that the particular receiver of the goods at destination may have paid a higher or lower price than the eventual market value on the last day of discharge is disregarded; it is the latter which is made the basis of both compensation and contribution.[4]

When goods delivered damaged

16.05 Where cargo is delivered at destination in damaged condition, the amount to be allowed as general average is as follows:

(1) When the cargo is sold, the general practice among adjusters (according to the eighth and ninth editions of this work) was to allow the difference between the sound market value of the goods on the date of their sale and the amount they actually realised. Prima facie, this was an exception to the general rule that the relevant date for comparison purposes is the last day of discharge, and it is submitted that (particularly having regard to the change in practice brought about by the York-Antwerp Rules 1950[5]) modern practice would be to allow the difference between the sound market value of the goods on the last day of discharge and the amount they actually realise.

(2) When the cargo is accepted by the consignee in its damaged condition:

(a) if it requires repair or reconditioning, the amount to be allowed is the actual cost of repair or reconditioning, plus, if the cargo is even then in less than sound condition, a further sum to represent the depreciation in value;

[4] This, which had for many years been the practice amongst adjusters, was confirmed by the Court of Appeal in *Rodocanachi v. Milburn* (1886) Q.B.D. 67 at 76. This was an action against the shipowner for non-delivery, but the principles laid down by Lord Esher M.R. are equally applicable to the case of general average. See *per* Gorell Barnes J. in *The Leitrim* [1902] P. 256 at 267.

[5] *Cf.* Rule XVI, see para. 16.19, *post.*

(b) it frequently occurs that a surveyor acting on behalf of the general average interests, or on behalf of cargo underwriters, will agree with the consignees a measure of depreciation to represent the damage. If that depreciation is expressed as a flat sum per package, or on the whole consignment, that sum is the amount to be allowed as general average. If, however, the agreed depreciation is expressed as a percentage (and this is usually the case), the amount to be allowed as general average is the sum that results from the application of that percentage to—almost invariably—the *gross* sound market value of the goods on the last day of discharge. The reason why the percentage is applied to the gross sound market value rather than the net, is that, in agreeing on that percentage depreciation, the consignee and the surveyor will both be thinking in terms of the saleable value at destination, and this will include freight and landing charges paid at destination. As an example, a cargo of grain might have the following value:

Gross Sound Market Value	£20,000
Less: freight and landing charges	8,000
Net Sound Market Value	£12,000

If the surveyor agrees a depreciation of 10 per cent it is almost certain that he will have based this figure on the expectation that the grain could only be sold in its damaged condition for £18,000, that is a loss of £2,000. To allow in general average only 10 per cent of the net sound market value, that is £1,200, would not give a proper indemnity to the consignee.

It is convenient here to mention briefly a problem encountered on rare occasions in practice. Were the surveyor to agree a depreciation of, say, 80 per cent on the above consignment of grain, or were it to be sold for £4,000, the loss to the merchant in either case would be £16,000, and this is the sum which is allowable as general average, even though it exceeds the contributory value of £12,000. This particular problem will again be mentioned in paragraph 16.31, below, when dealing with Rule XVI.

Exception where goods replaced at port of loading

Where the vessel returns to her port of loading as a port of refuge, or puts into some other nearby port and sacrificed goods are replaced there, the amount allowed in practice is the actual cost of replacing them.[6] **16.06**

[6] Gourlie, p. 480.

Amounts Allowable when Voyage Terminated Short of Destination

When the voyage is terminated short of destination for both ship *and* cargo, either by the wreck of the ship or some other justifiable cause, the allowance in general average for cargo sacrifices must be regulated by the value of the cargo at the time and place where the voyage was abandoned, though it must be recognised that if the damaged goods either were, or would have been, forwarded to their original destination, the value at the place where the voyage was abandoned is the value at the original destination, *less* the cost of getting them there, and that amounts made good should be based on original destination value.

Subsequent total loss of ship and cargo

16.07 On the authority of *Chellew v. Royal Commission on the Sugar Supply*,[7] when a sacrifice is followed by a total loss of ship and cargo, there is of course no allowance in general average. When a jettison is followed by a wreck with partial salvage, the sum allowable is so much as presumably would have been saved had the jettisoned goods been left on board and shared the fortunes of the remainder.

Reduction in value for actual or notional damage

16.08 If the goods jettisoned had previously been damaged, or if, though not damaged at the time, it can confidently be asserted that, had they remained on shipboard with the rest of the cargo, they must inevitably have suffered damage before reaching their destination, the amount to be made good is to be reduced to their value in the damaged state.[8]

In carrying out this principle, it is to be borne in mind that the owner of goods jettisoned has a prima facie claim to their value in a sound state; consequently, the burden of proof rests with those who wish to admit a lower value; and the allowance should not be reduced except upon reasonably clear evidence that the damage either actually existed, or, if in the future, that it was almost inevitable. In practice when the goods were sound at the time of jettison, and when other cargo arrives partly sound and partly damaged, so that it is uncertain whether the goods jettisoned would have been damaged or not, they are treated as if sound.[9]

[7] [1922] 1 K.B. 12.

[8] *E.g. Fletcher v. Alexander* (1868) L.R. 3 C.P. 375. On the same principle, if the goods jettisoned were subject to leakage or breakage, allowance ought to be made for the ordinary leakage or breakage in estimating their value: 2 Phillips, paras. 1366; *British Shipping Laws*, Vol. 10: Arnould, *Marine Insurance* (16th ed.), paras. 979. No deduction should be made solely on account of the peril existing at the time of the sacrifice: *Rogers v. Mechanics Ins. Co.* (1842) 2 Story 173.

[9] Baily, *General Average*, p. 137n.

Reduction in amount made good to achieve equality

To give effect to the cardinal principle that the owner of cargo sacrificed shall be placed in the same position as if, not his goods, but those of some other person had been sacrificed, it is necessary in the adjustment to contrive certain reductions in the amounts effectively allowable in general average such that they should be subject to and reflect the same vicissitudes of the continuing voyage as were suffered by those goods which were saved by the general average act. Thus: **16.09**

(1) *Reduction for actual or notional damage*

As outlined in the previous paragraph 16.08, if all the cargo in the same compartment of the ship arrives at destination in a damaged condition, it is reasonable to assume that the sacrificed goods would have arrived similarly damaged and the general average allowance must be based accordingly.

(2) *Amount made good must contribute; also hypothetical salvage* **16.10**

Any amount made good in general average in respect of property sacrificed must be brought in as a contributing interest rateably with the property preserved, and this will again be referred to with a figured example in paragraph 17.14, below, when dealing with Rule XVII. However, this is a convenient opportunity to offer an identical and parallel example where—under English law alone—salvage is or might be treated separately and apart from general average ("hypothetical" salvage).

Assume that a vessel and her cargo are stranded in a position of peril and that, in order to refloat, salvage services are engaged and that cargo B with a value of 1,000 is jettisoned. An award of salvage of 25 per cent—750 is made on the values of the properties saved, that is:

Ship	on	1,000	pays	250
Cargo A	on	1,000	,,	250
Cargo B	on	—	,,	—
Cargo C	on	1,000	,,	250
		3,000	pays	750

To make good in general average the whole of the value of 1,000 to the owners of jettisoned cargo B would be totally inequitable and place them in a particularly favoured position, especially as they also escape any liability for salvage. Accordingly, this position is remedied in any general average adjustment prepared in accordance with English law in the following manner:

16.11 The amount to be allowed in general average in respect of the jettison of Cargo B 1,000
would be reduced by the hypothetical amount of salvage to which the other salved property was subject, *i.e.* 25 per cent = 250
Amount to be allowed in general average 750

This sum would be apportioned as follows (Cargo B also being required to contribute):

Ship on arrived value	1,000		
Less: ppn. salvage	250		
	750	pays	187.50
Cargo A (as for Ship)	750	,,	187.50
Cargo B (on amount made good)	750	,,	187.50
Cargo C (as for Ship)	750	,,	187.50
	3,000	pays	750.00

The overall financial result to each of the parties to the adventure is that the shipowner and merchants A and C each have salved property worth		1,000.00
Less: ppns. salvage	250.00	
general average	187.50	
	437.50	437.50
		562.50
whereas merchant B receives the general average contributions payable by the shipowner and merchants A and C, *i.e.*:	187.50 × 3 =	562.50

Equality of sacrifice has thus been preserved.

16.12 (3) *Second general averages*

In similar fashion, if a second general average sacrifice or expenditure is made or incurred during the remaining part of the voyage, the amount made good in respect of property sacrificed in the first general average must contribute also to the second general average. (A figured example showing the general principle is given in paragraph 17.82, below.)

Historical Development and Practice of Rule XVI

16.13 *York-Antwerp Rules 1877*

The only new Rule introduced at the Antwerp Conference in 1877 was the relatively simple and straightforward statement that:

> "The value to be allowed for goods sacrificed shall be that value which the owner would have received if such goods had not been sacrificed."

As such, it was accepted unanimously.

York-Antwerp Rules 1890 16.14

Having regard to the provisions of the then current Rule on contributory values,[10] it appears reasonably clear that allowances under the 1877 Rule for cargo sacrifices were intended to be based on market values at the termination of the adventure. However, the wording of the Rule was not altogether certain on this point and was capable of being construed to give the owner of sacrificed cargo the price for which he had sold it under a forward contract. For greater precision on this matter, and to ensure that any allowance was based on market values, the wording was altered in 1890 as follows:

> "The amount to be made good as general average for damage or loss of goods sacrificed shall be the loss which the owner of the goods has sustained thereby, based on the market values at the date of the arrival of the vessel or at the termination of the adventure."

York-Antwerp Rules 1924 16.15

In the 1924 revision the words "where this ends at a place other than the original destination" were added at the suggestion of the Association of Average Adjusters, the intention being to indicate that a premature termination of the adventure was referred to. A more important amendment consisted of the addition of a second paragraph which read:

> "Where goods so damaged are sold after arrival, the loss to be made good in general average shall be calculated by applying to the sound value on the date of arrival of the vessel the percentage of loss resulting from a comparison of the proceeds with the sound value on date of sale."

Prior to the 1924 amendment of the Rule there were three main methods of ascertaining the allowance to be made in general average in respect of the goods sold, although it cannot be said that any of these were, or could be, consistently applied, as so much depended on the particular circumstances of the case.

Provided that there was no change in the market value of the goods between the last day of discharge[11] and the date on which they were sold, it was immaterial which of the three methods was employed—they would all give an identical result for the amount to be allowed in general average. However, when a change in market values did take place, wide 16.16

[10] See para. 17.04, *post*.

[11] Although the Rule specified the "date of arrival of the vessel" the practice was to adopt the sound value on last day of discharge in preference to that on date or arrival of the vessel, this being justified on the grounds that, even if the goods had arrived sound, some time would have been occupied in discharging the goods and preparing them for sale and that therefore the values on the last date of discharge had a greater relevance in assessing the loss. A similar practice existed with regard to the first paragraph of the Rule.

differences in the amounts to be made good in general average could arise, as demonstrated below[12]:

	On a *rising* Market	On a *falling* Market
Sound value on last day of discharge	100	100
Sound value on date of sale	120	80
Proceeds realised	90	60
Method 1		
Sound value on last day of discharge	100	100
Less: Proceeds realised	90	60
Allow as general average	10	40
Method 2		
Sound value on date of sale	120	80
Less: Proceeds realised	90	60
Allow as general average	30	20
Method 3		
Sound value on date of sale	120	80
Less: Proceeds realised	90	60
	30	20
=	25%	25%
Allow 25 per cent of sound value on last day of discharge	25	25

16.17 International uniformity was desirable on such an important matter and Method 3 (above) was adopted at the Stockholm Conference in 1924 by 24 votes to 8 of those present and voting. This method was very familiar to anyone conversant with the calculation of cargo claims under a contract of marine insurance, and it was claimed by the advocates of this method that it provided a perfect solution of the many difficulties inherent in the other methods. It is also of interest to note that the proper interpretation of this Rule XVI in the 1890 Rules came before the French courts in the case of *Sprunt & Sons v. Cap. Mal and French Government* ("*Seine*"), where in respect of bales of cotton sold in damaged condition at destination, general average allowances had been made on the basis of Method 1 (that is the difference between the sound value upon the last day of landing and the proceeds actually realised). However, the market had risen considerably in the interval between the last day of landing and the date of sale, and the consignees objected, claiming that they were entitled to a greater allowance under either of Methods 2 or

[12] For a more complete discussion on the three methods and their respective merits and demerits, reference is requested to the 7th to 9th editions of this work.

3. The adjustment was upheld in the Tribunal of Commerce of Havre and by the Court of Appeal at Rouen, but on further appeal to the Cour de Cassation, this court in a judgment of July 7, 1932, held in favour of Method 3 (*réglement par quotité*).

York-Antwerp Rules 1950 **16.18**

As revised in 1950, the Rule read as follows:

> "The amount to be made good as general average for damage to or loss of goods sacrificed shall be the loss which the owner of the goods has sustained thereby, based on the market values at the last day of discharge of the vessel or at the termination of the adventure where this ends at a place other than the original destination.
>
> Where the goods so damaged are sold and the amount of the damage has not been otherwise agreed, the loss to be made good in general average shall be the difference between the net proceeds of sale and the net sound value at the last day of discharge of the vessel or at the termination of the adventure where this ends at a place other than the original destination."

So far as the first paragraph of the Rule was concerned, the only amendment was the substitution of "the last day of discharge of the vessel" for "the date of the arrival of the vessel", thus giving validity to what had always been the practice. The justification for the adoption of the later date was that it approximated more closely to the date upon which the owner could have sold his goods had they arrived in a sound condition.

The second paragraph was completely redrafted and Method 3 discussed above (*réglement par quotité*) was abandoned in favour of Method 1 (value on last day of discharge less proceeds of sale). This was done at the request of the United States, which had never accepted the 1924 Rule XVI and customarily excluded it when providing for York-Antwerp Rules in contracts of affreightment. Under Method 1, market fluctuations between the last day of discharge and the date of sale would influence the amount to be allowed in general average for damage to cargo, but it was the only method which would provide the owner of cargo sold damaged with an allowance in general average which, together with the actual sale proceeds, would amount to the sum he would have received for the goods but for the sacrifice, namely, the sound value on the last day of discharge. Although general average would bear the whole burden of these market fluctuations, it was felt that the owner of the damaged goods could claim with some justification that an additional loss by a market fluctuation due to a delayed sale was just as much a consequence of the sacrifice as the loss directly attributable to the damage itself.

In redrafting the second paragraph, the last day of discharge of the vessel was again adopted rather than the date of arrival.

16.19 *York-Antwerp Rules 1974*

The principles of the previous Rule remained unchanged in 1974, but important amendments to the wording were necessary to correspond with the radical new provisions introduced at this time in Rule XVII[13] relating to contributory values. The value shown in the commercial invoice rendered to the receiver of the cargo at the time of discharge was henceforth to be adopted as (or in place of) the "market value at the last day of discharge".

16.20 **York-Antwerp Rules 1994**

No change, but to give contractual recognition and authority to a commonly adopted working practice it had been proposed here, and also in Rule XVII, to amend the expression "*at the time of discharge*" (from the vessel suffering the general average) to "*at the time of delivery under the contract of carriage*" (at the ultimate destination of the goods). The reasons for the proposed change, and the effects—if any—of its defeat, will be discussed below in paragraphs 16.23 to 16.28, below.

Rule XVI

Amount to be Made Good for Cargo Lost or Damaged by Sacrifice

The amount to be made good as general average for damage to or loss of cargo sacrificed shall be the loss which has been sustained thereby based on the value at the time of discharge, ascertained from the commercial invoice rendered to the receiver or if there is no such invoice from the shipped value. The value at the time of discharge shall include the cost of insurance and freight except insofar as such freight is at the risk of interests other than the cargo.

When cargo so damaged is sold and the amount of the damage has not been otherwise agreed, the loss to be made good in general average shall be the difference between the net proceeds of sale and the net sound value as computed in the first paragraph of this Rule.

[13] See para. 17.08, *post*.

First Paragraph

CONSTRUCTION

The first paragraph enunciates the general principle to be applied in ascertaining the amount to be made good in general average for damage to or loss of goods sacrificed and the second paragraph lays down the method to be adopted in a particular case, namely when damaged goods are sold and the amount of damage has not been otherwise agreed. Whether or not the owner of the goods is entitled to have his loss made good in general average at all is a question which falls to be decided under other Rules, that is, Rules A, C, D, E, I, II, III, V, VIII, IX, XII, and XIX. 16.21

First Paragraph

"The amount to be made good as general average for damage to or loss of cargo sacrificed shall be the loss which has been sustained thereby . . ." The basic principle set forth in paragraph 16.02, above, that the owner of goods sacrificed should be so compensated that he shall be in the same position as if, not his goods, but those of some other person had been thus sacrificed is here preserved in the opening wording of the Rule, also the principle set out in Rule IV that there can be no sacrifice of what is already irrevocably lost. However, as will be recorded shortly, an indemnity based on fluctuating *market* values was changed in 1974 on the grounds of practical simplicity to an indemnity on an "agreed value" basis related to *invoice* values. 16.22

". . . based on the value at the time of discharge . . .". Although unstated, it is well understood that the discharge referred to is from the vessel suffering the general average, also that this discharge is the termination of the *common* adventure[14] for the cargo concerned.

TRANSHIPMENT CARGO 16.23

In practice, and more particularly since the advent of containerisation, this discharge may be merely one staging post in the particular adventure on which the cargo is engaged, and it may not yet have reached its final scheduled destination. The cargo could be due for transhipment by another ocean-going vessel to a more distant seaport, and thence even

[14] The *termination of the adventure* is not precisely defined either in Rule G, or here in Rule XVI or Rule XVII, but see, for instance, the more extended wording of this Rule XVI prior to 1974: ". . . based on the market values at the last day of discharge of the vessel or at the termination of the adventure where this ends at a place *other than the original destination.*" See also the discussion in paras. G.24 *et seq.*, *ante*.

by road, rail or barge for delivery to the consignee at some inland destination. Upon its discharge from the vessel suffering the general average, such cargo may justifiably regard itself to be still in transit and its own particular adventure to be continuing, but, in conformity with fundamental principles, the Rule specifies that any claim in general average for loss or damage to such cargo shall be "*based on the* (its) *value at the time of discharge*" from the vessel suffering the general average.

Thus:

(1) If cargo damaged by the general average act continues its journey to ultimate destination, any subsequent accident causing additional loss or damage will not reduce the value on which it contributes, nor extinguish to any degree the allowance to be made in the general average per the original carrying vessel.

(2) As the calculation of any claims in general average for loss of or damage to cargo almost invariably requires a consideration of both sound and damaged values of the cargo concerned, it would appear evident that these values must similarly both be assessed as at this *time of discharge* from the vessel suffering the general average.

Calculation of Claims with Transhipment Cargoes

16.24 The *sound value* (at least) of the damaged cargo at the time of discharge is, by the express provision of the Rule since 1974 to be "*ascertained from the commercial invoice rendered to the receiver*". (See also paragraph 16.29, below). If, as is likely, the complete transit to ultimate destination be covered by a single "through" bill of lading or contract of carriage, and the commercial invoice shows a single c.i.f. or c.& f. price which includes all the prepaid freight(s), handling charges and—where appropriate—insurance costs for the complete journey, it is that single invoice price which represents and is to be adopted as the sound value of the cargo concerned, most certainly if the freights and other ancillary charges are prepaid and non-returnable ship and/or cargo "lost or not lost". Deduction from the ultimate destination invoice price of either the known or the notional costs of forwarding the cargo to that ultimate destination from the port at which it was originally discharged is justified only in those cases where such charges have not been prepaid on a non-returnable basis and would be saved to the consignee if the ship or cargo were to be lost or abandoned prior to delivery at the ultimate destination. As is stated later in the Rule (see also paragraph 17.29, below): "*The value at the time of discharge shall include the cost of insurance and freight except insofar as such freight is at the risk of interests other than the cargo.*"

16.25 The *damaged value* at the time of discharge (or, to be more precise, the value of the lost or damaged cargo), may or may not be ascertained from the commercial invoice. If, for instance, it has been jettisoned, it will have *no* value; if it be sold in damaged condition, the actual net proceeds of sale will generally be adopted as the damaged value as per the second paragraph of the Rule. (See also the commentary in paragraph 16.30, below). The important point, as stated earlier, is that the value of the loss or damage is crystallised at the time of discharge from the vessel suffering the general average, and damage sustained thereafter from a subsequent accident cannot be taken into account.

The fact that the loss or damage should effectively be valued on discharge from the vessel suffering the general average does not mean that a detailed survey of all the cargo discharged must be carried out at that port. In practice, seriously damaged cargo may well be detained and either sold or reconditioned there, but where it is thought sensible to forward the cargo to its intended destination in the normal way, it will be equally sensible in calculating the general average allowances to adopt the degrees of damage assessed by the surveyors at that destination, even if it might be suggested that there has been some natural progression of the original damage during the final stages of the voyage.

Ever since multimodal transport became common, simplicity and practical considerations have usually dictated that average adjusters should adopt practices such as are outlined above,[15] but to give them greater authority and recognition, and to avoid any doubts which might be attributed to what might be termed a "pre-1974 approach", it had been proposed at Sydney in 1994 that the expression "*at the time of discharge*" (from the vessel suffering the general average), here and also in the parallel Rule XVII, be amended to "*at the time of delivery under the contract of carriage*" (at the ultimate destination of the goods). **16.26**

A number of the delegates at Sydney, however, were critical of the proposal, possibly sensing that under Rule XVII an increased proportion of the general average might thereby be cast upon the cargo interests, or that general average was being "dragged ashore" and extended to land transit, and three attempts to secure its passage in varying formats were all defeated.

The proposed new wording would undoubtedly have had the effect of making general average allowances to lost or damaged cargo dependent on safe arrival at its ultimate destination, and cargo contributory values in general subject to the results of accidents on land, but in reality, none of the concerns expressed at Sydney was justified on the grounds that general average would be *expanded*. However, the failure of the proposed alterations in the wording of the Rules might create the impression that average adjusters should change their pre-1994 practice of basing claims and contributory values on the ultimate destination invoice price, and require them to discover or estimate the actual costs relating to the later **16.27**

[15] See, for instance, the 1981 Resolution of A.I.D.E.

stages of the voyage and deduct these from the ultimate destination price to arrive at a notional *value at the time of discharge* from the vessel suffering the general average. At the time of writing, negotiations may be in hand with underwriting interests in Britain and the United States to secure a market agreement to the continuance of the practice of adopting ultimate destination prices, but this is strictly unnecessary, as indicated in the earlier commentary on this Rule.

16.28 For the purpose of demonstrating that sound principle *demands* that the ultimate destination invoice values must be adopted as the sound value in the calculation of any claim for loss or damage to cargo admissible in general average, two examples will be given in which it will be assumed that the c.i.f. invoice price at final destination is 10,500, and that if that price could be projected back to the port of discharge, it would be 10,000. These examples demonstrate that only when ultimate destination values are adopted can a full and proper indemnity be provided to the suffering cargo interest.

(1) A consignment of paper is delivered at ultimate destination with 50 per cent depreciation for damage caused by water used to extinguish a fire, and the consignee obviously suffers a loss of 50% × 10,500 = 5,250, and not the notional 5,000 assessable on supposed values at the earlier port of discharge.
(2) The same consignment is jettisoned for the common safety. Again, the loss suffered by the consignee will clearly be the full 10,500 ultimate destination price he has paid unless he is able to obtain any recovery from the carriers or cargo handlers for their unperformed services.

16.29 "... based on the value) **... ascertained from the commercial invoice"** See commentary under Rule XVII in paragraph 17.25, below.

"... rendered to the receiver ..." See commentary under Rule XVII in paragraph 17.27, below.

"... if there is no such invoice from the shipped value." See commentary under Rule XVII, in paragraph 17.27, below, and note that when dealing with the allowances in general average permitted by this Rule XVI, in the case of:

(1) *goods shipped "on consignment"*, a "shipped" value is not necessarily the equivalent of an f.o.b. invoice value, which latter would include an element of profit to the shipper/exporter;
(2) *personal and household goods*, the value of those goods is but rarely increased by the amount of the freight payable for transporting them.

"The value ... shall include the cost of insurance and freight except insofar as such freight is at the risk of interests other than the cargo." See commentary under Rule XVII in paragraph 17.28, below.

Second Paragraph

"When cargo so damaged is sold ..." The provisions of the second paragraph apply only to those cases where damaged cargo is sold and... **16.30**

"... the amount of the damage has not been otherwise agreed ...," in which case the claim will be dealt with under the provisions of the first paragraph of the Rule. In practice the damage is very often agreed as a percentage of the sound value of the goods, or at so much per unit of weight or measurement, the percentage or amount having been recommended by cargo surveyors who have inspected the damaged cargo.

"... the loss to be made good ... shall be the difference between the net proceeds of sale and the net sound value as computed in the first paragraph of this Rule." In calculating the amount to be allowed as general average in terms of the second paragraph of the Rule, the basic idea of Method 1[16] (sound value less proceeds) has been preserved in the 1994 Rule and the term "net proceeds of sale" still means the actual gross proceeds of sale less the expenses of making the cargo ready for sale and of the sale (for example the cost of sorting, repacking, transportation, selling commission, etc.). However, the term "net sound value" is no longer based on market values, but is ascertained or computed from the invoice to the receiver in accordance with the provisions of the first paragraph of the Rule. Thus, and as mentioned earlier, one is comparing unlike terms, that is a "market" value with an "invoice" value, but this particular anomaly was knowingly and purposely intended by the framers of the current Rule. However, and for the benefit of younger readers unfamiliar with the practical application of the previous 1950 Rule XVI,[17] it must now be mentioned that a further and unintended comparison of unlike terms which would appear to be required on occasion by the specific wording of the Rule is not applied in practice. This particular anomaly which was carried over from the 1950 Rule is that when the goods are sold at destination the term "net proceeds of sale" will almost invariably include *freight* (whether prepaid or payable at destination), whereas the term "net sound value" will *exclude* freight on those occasions when it is "at the risk of interests other than the cargo".[18]

[16] Described in para. 16.16, *ante*.
[17] See para. 16.18, *ante*.
[18] See para. 17.28, *post*.

16.31 Thus, if goods with an f.o.b. invoice value of 7,500 and on which freight of 2,500 was payable only on right delivery at destination arrived in damaged condition and were sold for net proceeds of 6,000, the loss to be allowed in general average in accordance with a strict construction of the wording would be only:

Net Sound Value (*i.e.* f.o.b.)	7,500
Deduct: Net Proceeds of Sale	6,000
	1,500

However, this would be manifestly unfair to the receiver who has had to pay freight of 2,500 to achieve his net sale proceeds of 6,000, and in practice the loss is (and was under the 1950 wording) calculated by a comparison of *like* values, that is:

Net Sound Value (as before)		7,500
Deduct: Net Proceeds of Sale	6,000	
Less: Freight	2,500	
	3,500	3,500
	Loss	4,000

In similar fashion, if goods arriving at destination in damaged conditions are sold in a "duty paid" condition, the allowance in general average should be assessed by a comparison of *like* values, that is:

Sound c.i.f. invoice value		10,000
Add: Normal duty at 25%	2,500	
Less: Refund by Customs	1,000	
Duty Paid	1,500	1,500
		11,500
Deduct: Net Proceeds of Sale		5,000
	Loss	6,500

Calculation of Claims

16.32 There should be no difficulty in dealing with claims for cargo jettisoned or destroyed by a general average act; the value which the cargo lost would have had upon discharge[19] is to be ascertained from the commercial invoice—although it will not in all cases be the same as the invoice price. However, there can be problems when cargo is delivered in a damaged condition, and particularly if it is sold. The following examples are given, relating to a shipment of 100 bales with an invoice price of 10,000 on c.i.f. terms, or 7,500 on f.o.b. terms.

[19] See paras. 16.22 *et seq.*, *ante*, for a discussion on the expression "*value at the time of discharge*".

On c.i.f. terms (10,000)

(1) *The 100 bales are delivered at destination damaged to the extent of 20 per cent.*

(a) If the market is *rising* (for example sound value 12,500) it will profit the receiver to agree a 20 per cent depreciation with a surveyor to ensure that an allowance is made in general average of 20 per cent of 10,000 = 2,000.

Were he to sell the cargo for, say, 80 per cent of 12,500 = 10,000, there would be nothing to make good in general average.

(b) If the market is *falling* (for example sound value 8,000) it will profit the receiver to sell the cargo and ensure that no percentage depreciation is agreed with a surveyor. If the cargo were sold to produce a 20 per cent depreciation (that is 6,400) the allowance in general average would be:

Invoice value	10,000
Less: proceeds	6,400
	3,600

On f.o.b. terms (7,500)

(2) *The 100 bales are delivered damaged at destination and a depreciation of 20 per cent is agreed with the surveyor.* **16.33**

It is suggested that the 20 per cent depreciation is likely to have been assessed on a landed value basis (that is inclusive of freight), and that, therefore, the 20 per cent depreciation should be applied, not to the f.o.b. price of 7,500 but to the notional c.i.f. value of 10,000 to produce an allowance in general average of 2,000.

(This problem already existed under the 1950 Rules and was dealt with in the manner outlined. It was discussed further in paragraph 16.05, above.)

(3) *The 100 bales are delivered at destination damaged to the extent of 20 per cent, and are sold for:*

(a) 10,000 when the sound value is 12,500

As stated in Example (1)(a), it will profit the receiver to agree a 20 per cent depreciation with a surveyor, failing which no allowance in general average can be made. Further, and as stated in Example (2), it is suggested that the 20 per cent depreciation should be applied, not to the f.o.b. price of 7,500, but to the notional c.i.f. value to produce an allowance in general average of 2,000.

(b) 6,400 when the sound value is 8,000

As stated in Example (1)(b), it will profit the receiver to sell the goods for 6,400 and, as the price paid will effectively include a freight constituent of 2,500, the allowance in general average should again be assessed on a c.i.f. basis, that is:

Notional c.i.f. price	10,000
Less: proceeds	6,400
	3,600

16.34 One further small problem received judicial consideration in the United States courts in the case of *Christie v. Davis Coal & Coke Co.*[20] Particularly in the bulk oil trade one occasionally finds that freight is at risk to the carrier but, provided any worthwhile quantity of cargo is delivered at destination, payable in full on the "intake" quantity. Thus, and for example, 1000 tons of cargo might be shipped with:

an f.o.b. invoice value of	80 per ton =	80,000
and freight at risk of	20 per ton =	20,000
	100	100,000

If 300 tons of the cargo were to be jettisoned, the cargo interests would be obliged to pay the full freight of 20,000, and in valuing the cargo jettisoned for allowance in general average, it is necessary to take into account not only the f.o.b. value of 80 per ton but also the proportion of the freight paid of 20 per ton, that is a total allowance of 30,000.[21]

[20] 95 Fed.Rep. 837 (1899).

[21] It could be suggested that the contributory values to be calculated in accordance with Rule XVII of the York-Antwerp Rules 1974 would be as follows:

CARGO—700 tons delivered at f.o.b. invoice value 80		= 56,000
	Add: Made Good	30,000
		86,000
FREIGHT—At Risk and Earned (less costs of earning same)		20,000
		106,000

However, on the "principle of the cake" set forth in para. 17.92, *post*, this is clearly wrong as the combined contributory values of cargo and freight cannot exceed 100,000.

In fact, the cargo will contribute only on the f.o.b. element of 300 × 80 = 24,000 of the total amount made good of 30,000, the shipowner (or carrier) continuing to bear the contribution attaching to the *full* freight at his risk of 20,000. This problem, is very similar to that of the time-charterers' bunkers mentioned in para. 17.38, *post*, but an easier way of confirming the correctness of the contributory values would be to calculate them in accordance with English law or the 1950 Rules, *i.e.*:

CARGO—700 tons delivered at landed value 100		= 70,000
	Add: Made Good	30,000
		100,000
	Deduct: Freight	20,000
		80,000
FREIGHT—At Risk and Earned (less costs of earning same)		20,000
	Combined Contributory Values	100,000

Rule XVII

Contributory Values (also Contributing Interests)

Once it has been established that a general average loss has occurred and the amount to be made good has been determined, the following questions arise: **17.01**

(1) Which of the properties associated with the SHIP, her passengers and crew, her FREIGHT or earnings, also the CARGO, should contribute to the general average?
(2) On what basis should the contributory values be calculated for those interests called upon to contribute?

This is such an important and lengthy topic that a slightly different presentation has been adopted when dealing with Rule XVII, this with the object of making the general principles easier to understand, and to ensure that all the material on any individual property or contributing interest appears in one continuous section. For ready reference, the subject-matter of this section is as follows:

Historical Development and Practice of Rule XVII

Glasgow Resolutions 1860

17.02 Contributory values were assessed in the mid-nineteenth century by a variety of methods in which sound reason does not always appear to have played a great part. For instance, in France and Holland ship and freight contributed on only 50 per cent of their respective values, while in Hamburg, Sweden and Denmark cargo was made to contribute on its invoice value regardless of loss or damage sustained during the voyage. The situation was not much better in England.

An attempt to secure international uniformity was made at the Glasgow Conference in 1860 with the passing of the following Resolutions:

> (9) That when the amount of expenses is less than the value of the property finally saved, the contributing values of ship, freight, and cargo, ought to be their values to the owners of them respectively, at the termination of the adventure.
>
> (10) That, when the amount of expenses is greater than the value of the property saved, the proceeds of the property so saved ought to be applied towards those expenses, and the excess of the expenses over the proceeds ought to be apportioned as if the whole property had finally reached its destination.
>
> (11) That, in fixing the value of the freight, the wages and port charges up to the date of the general average act ought not to be deducted, and the wages and port charges after that date ought to be deducted from the gross freight at the risk of the shipowner.

Although Resolutions Nos. 9 and 11 were sound in principle, the same cannot be said of No. 10, having regard to the decision in 1922 of *Chellew v. Royal Commission on the Sugar Supply.*[1]

York Rules 1864

17.03 The following changes in the Glasgow Resolutions were made at York in 1864.

Resolution No. 10 relating to general average expenses in excess of the contributory values was withdrawn in the face of strenuous opposition from Continental delegates.

The sound principle established by Resolution No. 11 was changed in favour of an arbitrary provision that the contributory value of freight should be three-fifths of the amount at risk. This measure was adopted in order to avoid certain practical difficulties arising from the varying liability of the shipowner to pay crew wages under different national laws.

The substance was then combined into a single Rule and couched in clear language which was to serve as the framework of the Rule on contributory values for the next 110 years.

[1] [1922] 1 K.B. 12.

> "The contribution to general average shall be made upon the actual values of the property at the termination of the adventure, to which shall be added the amount made good as general average for property sacrificed; deduction being made from the shipowner's freight and passage-money at risk of two-fifths of such freight, in lieu of crew's wages, port charges, and all other deductions; deduction being also made from the value of the property of all charges incurred in respect thereof subsequently to the arising of the claim to general average."

York-Antwerp Rules 1877

The decision taken in 1864 to adopt an arbitrary contributory value for freight of three-fifths of the amount at risk was unanimously reversed in 1877 and a return made to principle with the following words: **17.04**

> "... deduction being made from the shipowner's freight and passage-money at risk, of such port charges and crew's wages as would not have been incurred had the ship and cargo been totally lost at the date of the general average act or sacrifice;"

No alteration was made to the remainder of the Rule.

York-Antwerp Rules 1890

An oversight in previous editions of the Rule was remedied at the International Conference held at Liverpool in 1890. **17.05**

From the shipowner's freight and passage money at risk were deducted such port charges and crew's wages as would not have been incurred had the ship and cargo been totally lost at the date of the general average act or sacrifice, and from the value of property in general were deducted all charges incurred in respect thereof subsequently to the general average act. In so far as those port charges, crew's wages, and other charges were made good in general average, it was essential for sound principle that the amounts so made good should also contribute to the general average, and to rectify this earlier omission, suitable wording was added in the appropriate places in 1890.

A further paragraph relating to passengers' luggage was also added at the end of the Rule in 1890. This was prompted by the decision in the United States courts of *Heye v. North German Lloyd*[2] in which it was held that, except for apparel and other articles taken for use on the voyage, passengers' baggage stored in the baggage compartment was liable to contribute in general average. The delegates to the Conference recognised that considerable inconvenience and ill-will would arise if general average security were demanded from the large number of passengers travelling by sea in 1890 and it was unanimously agreed that passengers' luggage and personal effects not shipped under bill of lading

[2] 33 Fed.Rep. 60 (1887); 36 Fed.Rep. 705 (1888).

should be exempted from contribution. The 1890 Rule now read as follows:

> "The contribution to a general average shall be made upon the actual values of the property at the termination of the adventure to which shall be added the amount made good as general average for property sacrificed; deduction being made from the shipowner's freight and passage-money at risk, of such port charges and crew's wages as would not have been incurred had the ship and cargo been totally lost at the date of the general average act or sacrifice, and have not been allowed as general average; deduction being also made from the value of the property of all charges incurred in respect thereof subsequently to the general average act, except such charges as are allowed in general average.
>
> Passengers' luggage and personal effects, not shipped under bill of lading, shall not contribute to general average."

Considerable discussion also took place on a proposal of similar effect to the Glasgow Resolution No. 10 of 1860, but this was eventually withdrawn.

York-Antwerp Rules 1924

17.06 The following amendments to the Rule were made in 1924:

(1) The word "net" inserted before the word "values", so as to read, "the contribution to a general average shall be made upon the actual net values of the property, etc."
(2) The words "if not already included" inserted after the provision that amounts made good in general average shall be added to the actual net values, in order to correct an anomaly in the 1890 Rule revealed by the case of *The Strathdon*,[3] in which the cost of general average repairs had been brought in *twice* to contribute to the general average.
(3) The omission of the word "port" before the words "charges and crew's wages", in the provision dealing with the deductions to be made from freight and passage money at risk, in order to permit

[3] 94 Fed.Rep. 206 (1899); 101 Fed.Rep. 600 (1900); though the case is not reported on the point dealt with. A fire broke out on board the vessel, which was extinguished by the use of water. She was forced to put into a port of refuge, where repairs were effected, after which she duly completed her voyage. In the adjustment of the general average the vessel's value for contribution was ascertained by deducting from the sound value at destination, the cost of repairs effected at the port of refuge in so far as they were not allowed as general average. On the matter coming before the court, however, it was held that the true interpretation of Rule XVII of the 1890 Rules was that the vessel should contribute on her actual value at the termination of the adventure, which in this case (the vessel having been repaired before arrival) was her sound value on her arrival. To this value the amount made good for general average repairs was to be added and from the total thus arrived at there should be deducted (in accordance with the final sentence of the first paragraph of the Rule) the total cost of the repairs effected at the port of refuge except such as had been allowed in general average. The result of this method of assessment of the value was, of course, that the cost of the general average repairs was brought in twice to contribute to the general average.

the deduction of the cost of bunkers and stores bought (and consumed) after the general average act.

(4) The words"in earning the freight" added to qualify the description of the charges to be deducted from the amount of freight at risk.

(5) The omission of the superfluous words "or sacrifice" in the old rule, after the words "at the date of the general average act".

In order to bring about uniformity in the treatment of ulterior freight the Drafting Committee for the 1924 Rules put forward the following paragraph for inclusion in Rule XVII:

> "When a ship is in ballast, but under charter, the ship and the freight (computed as above) earned under the charter, shall contribute to general average."

Exception was taken to this proposal by several of the Continental delegates present at the Stockholm Conference, as perhaps might have been expected, as only the United Kingdom recognises such freight as a contributory interest, and this proposal was rejected by a considerable majority.

Two other additions to the Rule were proposed, of similar effect to the original Glasgow Resolution No. 10, but neither of these suggestions was put forward by the Drafting Committee for the consideration of the Stockholm Conference as there was little reason to suppose that either of them would find favour with the majority of the delegates present.

York-Antwerp Rules 1950

No change, but at the time of the drafting of the 1950 Rules, the **17.07**
Netherlands proposed that mails and time-charter hire should be included in the second paragraph of the Rule and so excluded from any liability to contribute. This proposal was subsequently withdrawn.

York-Antwerp Rules 1974

Simplification in the processes of preparing an adjustment was the **17.08**
objective governing most of the changes made in the Rules in 1974, and the greatest single contribution to that objective were the radical new provisions in Rule XVII relating to contributory values

(1) In respect of CARGO, and stripped of all detail, the fundamental change was that instead of being based on fluctuating free-market values, the contributory value of cargo was now to be based on the invoice price to the receiver (essentially on c.i.f. or f.o.b. terms, depending on whether or not the freight was at risk to the carrier) at the time of discharge, with no percentage addition for anticipated profit.

The intended simplification was undoubtedly achieved in those (say 95 per cent of) cases where cargo was delivered at destination in sound condition, and it is also probably true to state that cargo interests in general benefited in that they often contributed on a lesser value than formerly, in that no addition for profit was made to the invoice value of the cargo. However, in the case of cargo delivered *damaged*, whether by accidental cause or by general average sacrifice, the calculations became more complicated, and certain anomalies crept into the actual allowances in general average for damage by sacrifice by reason of the occasional comparisons required by Rules XVI and XVII of unlike and dissimilar values—that is, invoice values and real market values as evidenced by sale proceeds. The equitable nature of the general average system would normally require a comparison of like with like.

(2) In respect of SHIP, the contributory value was now to be based on her "free" market value, ignoring the beneficial or detrimental effect of any demise or time charterparty to which the ship might be committed. This change was in the interests of international uniformity.

A further suggestion that freight should contribute on a "forfeit" basis was not proceeded with as it would often have led to unreasonable results not justified by the insignificant simplification achieved.

York-Antwerp Rules 1994

17.09 The Rule passed in 1974 remained essentially unchanged, but certain additions were made on this occasion:

(1) At the end of the second paragraph was added wording which will prevent awards which fall upon the shipowner for special compensation under Article 14 of the International Convention on Salvage 1989 being treated as an "extra charge" in terms of Rule XVII and thereby reducing the contributory value of the ship. York-Antwerp Rule VI(b)[4] specifically states that such compensation shall not be allowed in general average, and that provision would have been partly frustrated if, by reducing the contributory value of the ship, the ship thereby paid a lesser proportion of the admissible general average.

(2) Consequent on the introduction in 1994 of a Non-Separation Agreement in Rule G,[5] a new third paragraph was necessary here in Rule XVII to provide for the basis of assessing contributory values when cargo was forwarded to destination.

(3) The final paragraph of the 1974 Rule excepted from contribution to general average passengers' luggage and personal effects not shipped under bill of lading. On practical grounds, these exceptions have been extended in 1994 to comprise "*mails, passengers' luggage, personal effects and accompanied private motor vehicles*".

[4] See para. 6.34, *ante*.
[5] See paras. G.09–G.14, *ante*.

A fourth set of changes had been proposed, identical for both Rules XVI and XVII, to amend the expression "*at the time of discharge*" (from the vessel suffering the general average) to "*at the time of delivery under the contract of carriage*" (at the ultimate destination of the goods). This suggestion was to give contractual recognition and authority to a working practice already commonly adopted, but it was strenuously opposed and defeated at Sydney in October 1974, and in this respect Rule XVII remains in its 1974 format. The reasons for the proposed change, and the effects—if any—of its defeat, are discussed earlier in paragraphs 16.23 to 16.28, above.

Rule XVII

Contributory Values

The contribution to a general average shall be made upon the actual net values of the property at the termination of the adventure except that the value of cargo shall be the value at the time of discharge, ascertained from the commercial invoice rendered to the receiver or if there is no such invoice from the shipped value. The value of the cargo shall include the cost of insurance and freight unless and insofar as such freight is at the risk of interests other than the cargo, deducting therefrom any loss or damage suffered by the cargo prior to or at the time of discharge. The value of the ship shall be assessed without taking into account the beneficial or detrimental effect of any demise or time charterparty to which the ship may be committed. 17.10

To these values shall be added the amount made good as general average for property sacrificed, if not already included, deduction being made from the freight and passage money at risk of such charges and crew's wages as would not have been incurred in earning the freight had the ship and cargo been totally lost at the date of the general average act and have not been allowed as general average; deduction being also made from the value of the property of all extra charges incurred in respect thereof subsequently to the general average act, except such charges as are allowed in general average or fall upon the ship by virtue of an award for special compensation under Art. 14 of the International Convention on Salvage, 1989 or under any other provision similar in substance.

In the circumstances envisaged in the third paragraph of Rule G, the cargo and other property shall contribute on the basis of its value upon delivery at original destination unless sold or otherwise disposed of short of that destination, and the ship shall contribute upon its actual net value at the time of completion of discharge of cargo.

Where cargo is sold short of destination, however, it shall contribute

upon the actual net proceeds of sale, with the addition of any amount made good as general average.

Mails, passengers' luggage, personal effects and accompanied private motor vehicles shall not contribute in general average.

17.11 With numerous grafts and additions to a basic text over a period of all but 125 years, it is hardly surprising that the present wording of the Rule should be a cumbersome mixture of occasionally duplicated general principles and specific exceptions, presented with little semblance of any logical order. Practitioners however, are accustomed to the wording and few problems are encountered in practice.

Before proceeding to construe the precise text of the current Rule, it will be worthwhile setting out what are the general and fundamental principles which govern the assessment of contributory values. The first and most important thing to state is that on the principle that it should be financially immaterial to a man whether his own property is sacrificed, or that belonging to someone else, it follows that the basis of calculating the contributory value of property which is saved is exactly the same as that adopted for calculating the amount to be made good in general average for property sacrificed. Thus, just as in computing the amount to be made good it must be determined what has been the true loss to the owner of property sacrificed, so in ascertaining the contributory values upon which contribution shall be based it is necessary to determine which owners of property have benefited, and to what extent, by a safe arrival.

17.12 The next and self-evident principle to state is that only those interests which were on board the ship or at risk at the time of the general average act can be called upon to contribute, and then only provided that success attends the continuing adventure and that some property with value arrives at its intended destination or some other place where the adventure is abandoned. A general average becomes "crystallised" and enforceable only on safe arrival at destination, and a prior total loss of the adventure before such arrival renders null and of no effect any earlier general average.[6]

This is evidenced in broad terms by Rule G:

> "General average shall be adjusted as regards both loss and contribution upon the basis of values at the time and place when and where the adventure ends."

Thus, and to the extent that any property suffers further loss or damage during the remainder of the voyage subsequent to the general average act, its contributory value will be reduced to the value it has in the actual condition in which it arrives at destination.

[6] *Chellew v. Royal Commission on the Sugar Supply* [1922] 1 K.B. 12.

A further principle must now be applied; the arrived value of properties at destination must be reduced by all those charges incurred subsequent to the general average act in order to realise that destination value and which would have been avoided if, instead of being saved by the general average act, the property had at that time been totally lost. Thus, and for example: **17.13**

(1) If cargo has a destination value of	100,000
but this includes a freight payable only on right delivery at destination of	20,000
The contributory value of the cargo will be	80,000
(2) If the shipowner has freight at risk to him payable only on right delivery of the cargo at destination (as above) of	20,000
but in order to earn that freight he must incur voyage expenses subsequent to the general average act of	8,000
The contributory value of the freight will be	12,000
(3) If the ship has an arrived destination value of	1,000,000
but the shipowner has already carried out full permanent repairs to the damage giving rise to the general average of	100,000
The contributory value of the ship will be	900,000

In other words, destination values must be converted (reduced) to the equivalent values of the property immediately following the accident which gave rise to the general average, in the same way that the present value of an obligation to pay 1,000 in one year's time when interest rates are 10 per cent per annum is only 909.

In practice, charges incurred subsequent to the general average act which are themselves allowable as general average are not deducted from the destination values to arrive at the contributory values, for the reasons expressed in the succeeding paragraph; if general average charges were first deducted, they would then have to be added back as amounts "made good".

The final principle to apply in arriving at the contributory values of the property is that to the sums produced thus far must be added any amount made good in general average for loss of or damage to the property, or for expenses incurred in respect of that property. **17.14**

As a simple proof of this requirement, assume that if a voyage had been successfully concluded without accident, the values at destination would have been:

Ship	1,000
Cargo A	1,000
Cargo B	1,000
Cargo C	1,000
	4,000

Let it also be assumed that Cargo B is jettisoned for the common safety. A general average of 1,000 falls to be apportioned, and if this were between only those parties whose property arrived, the figures would be:

Ship on	1,000	pays	334
Cargo A on	1,000	"	333
Cargo B on	—	"	—
Cargo C on	1,000	"	333
	3,000	pays	1,000

The financial result of such an apportionment would be that the shipowner and merchants A and C would have property with an effective value of 667, whereas merchant B would have cash amounting to 1,000.

This is so clearly inequitable that merchant B is also made to contribute to the general average on the amount of the loss nominally made good to him in general average, that is:

Ship on	1,000	pays	250
Cargo A on	1,000	"	250
Cargo B on	1,000	is liable for	250
Cargo C on	1,000	pays	250
	4,000	pays	1,000

The equitable result now is that each of the parties to the adventure reaches destination with property or cash in the sum of 750.

17.15 The fundamental principles set forth above in paragraphs 17.11 to 17.14 might be summarised and paraphrased into "rule" form as follows:

"general average sacrifices and expenses shall be borne by...
... the ship and other properties on board at the time of the general average act...
... in proportion to their actual values at the termination of the adventure
... after deducting therefrom all charges incurred subsequent to the general average act (other than those allowed as general average) which would not have been incurred if the adventure had been totally lost at the date of the general average act...
... to which values shall be added the amount made good for property sacrificed, if not already included."

We now construe the current Rule XVII, but dealing first with the *general* principles enunciated at intervals throughout the Rule, and concluding with those particular provisions which relate specifically to:

Cargo
Ship
Freight and Passage Money
Mails, Passengers' Luggage, Personal Effects, and Accompanied Private Motor Vehicles

Remarks of a general nature concerning English and/or foreign law and practice will precede the specific provisions of Rule XVII for each of these particular properties.

Construction

General Principles

"The contribution to a general average shall be made upon the actual net values of the property at the termination of the adventure" This provision is in accordance with the fundamental principles outlined in paragraphs 17.12, 17.13, above, and the only words to which particular attention need be drawn are: 17.16

"contribution" Technically, a general average contribution is the sum paid by or to any individual party to the adventure *after* taking into account any loss or expense borne by him and allowed in the general average. However, practitioners are well aware that what is intended is that the total general average shall be *apportioned* (over the actual net values).

"actual net values" It is submitted that the word "actual" excludes any consideration of claims which the owner may have against persons who are not parties to the adventure for damage to the property, for example collision damage[7] subsequent to and independent of the general average act. 17.17

In certain cases, parties to the adventure other than the owner of the damaged property may have their own right of action against the wrongdoer, as in *Morrison S.S. Co. v. Greystoke Castle (Cargo Owners)*.[8] In the United States it has been held that, since the owner of sacrificed cargo has a maritime lien over the carrying vessel for the contribution due to him, he is entitled to share pro-rata in any sums recovered by the owners of the carrying vessel against a colliding vessel as damages for loss of or damage to the carrying vessel.[9]

[7] See also paras 50.123 *et seq., post.*
[8] [1947] A.C. 265: see para.50.123, *post.*
[9] *Armour v. Green Star Shipping Co.* (1930) 37 Ll. L. R. 178 (District Ct.); (1931) 39 Ll. L. R. 199 (Circuit Ct. of Appeals). See para. G.29, *ante*, for the circumstances out of which the claim arose. English law does not recognise a maritime lien for general average contribution.

17.18 **"the property"** Lowndes wrote that:

> "The ship, the cargo, and the freight, constitute, generally speaking, the whole of the property on shipboard liable to contribute to general average. Should there be any kind of property, not coming under any of these heads, which is preserved from destruction by a general average act, this likewise must contribute, unless there be some special reason for exempting it. ... If there be anything else on shipboard, not constituting merchandise in the proper sense of the word, yet possessing a substantial value, it ought to contribute. For example, the unconsumed stores of a troop ship,[10] or those laid in by a passenger charterer[11]; planks or other materials used as dunnage, or covering boards, or for the construction of temporary bulkheads for cargo, or the like, should properly be brought in as contributing. It is only the small value of such articles which occasions their being, in practice, frequently disregarded."

This rule laid down by Lowndes, that any kind of property saved by a general average act must contribute in the absence of special reasons for exemption, is based on the fundamental principle of general average.[12]

Many of the various properties forming part of a common maritime adventure which may be encountered in practice are listed below and dealt with seriatim in succeeding sections, as indicated, but as broad concepts (and in the context in which they are considered in this chapter):

	Paragraphs
The SHIP	17.32–17.39
comprises her hull and machinery, and those items of equipment travelling more or less permanently with her from voyage to voyage, such as:	
Wireless and navigational equipment	17.71
Consumable provisions and stores to sustain those on board	17.73
The bunkers to propel the vessel	17.38
Other properties associated with the ship include:	
Munitions	17.72
The lives of the passengers and crew	17.62
Personal effects of master, officers and crew	17.64
Wages of master, officers and crew	17.63
Bottomry bonds	17.75

[10] Government stores in a transport are liable to general average. See *British Shipping Laws*, Vol. 10: Arnould, *Marine Insurance* (16th. ed.), para. 973. So determined in the U.S.: *United States v. Wilder* 3 Sumner, U.S. 308 (1838).

[11] Arnould (4th ed.), p. 793.

[12] Magens (Vol. 1, p. 62), and Stevens (p. 44) maintained that "what pays no freight pays no average"; but the latter author inconsistently allowed (p. 45) that this rule should not be construed literally: "or it would be very unjust that the master, or owner, or any other person who had goods on board, should not contribute, merely because he pays no freight for the carriage of them." By goods he meant "the wares or cargo for sale, laden on board the ship".

	Paragraphs
The CARGO	17.23–17.31
comprises the lading of the ship, or what she carries on a temporary basis for the purpose of being transported for a specific voyage from A to B, (and whether owned by merchants, charterers, shipowner, master or crew, or passengers), whereby the ship earns money for her owners and operators. For the purpose of this survey, CARGO includes:	
Merchandise (goods) in general, and livestock etc.	
Mails, Passengers Luggage, Personal Effects and Accompanied Private Motor Vehicles	17.58–17.61
Lorries and their cargo	17.65
Containers	17.66
Bullion and specie	17.67
Jewels and other valuables	17.68
Bank notes and securities	17.69
Shops and banks, and their stock on liners	17.70
Respondentia bonds	17.75

The FREIGHT	17.40–17.57
comprises any earnings of the Ship, whether as:	
Bill of lading freight	
Voyage charter party freight	
Time charter hire, or	17.52
Passage money	17.54

Which of these properties contribute to general average and which do not (whether on legal grounds or those of practical expediency), and whether the provisions of the York-Antwerp Rules govern those that do contribute, is discussed in the appropriate sections.

"at the termination of the adventure" This highly important phrase, relevant to Rules G, XVI and XVII, receives no precise definition in the York-Antwerp Rules, but some of the problem areas associated with the phrase are discussed at length in paragraphs G.22 *et seq.*, and also in paragraphs 16.23 to 16.28, above. In practice, however: (1) If a complete cargo is being carried to a single port of destination, the adventure terminates upon completion of discharge at the destination or upon the earlier abandonment of the voyage. (2) If parts of the cargo are consigned to several different ports of destination, in the absence of an earlier termination of the whole voyage, the ship is valued at the last port of discharge of any part of the cargo on board at the time of the general average act, and each part of the cargo (and any freight at risk thereon) at its own respective port of discharge from the ship. This includes cargo shipped under a "through" bill of lading for further on-carriage whether by sea and/or land. **17.19**

If the ship is in ballast and under charter, and the adjustment is being prepared for purposes of a claim on an English policy of marine insurance,

Rule of Practice B.26[13] *will apply and the adventure will be deemed to terminate:*

(a) upon completion of discharge at the final port of discharge of the cargo carried under the charter, if the vessel is under a voyage charter entered into by the shipowner before the general average act;
(b) at the first loading port upon the commencement of loading cargo, if the vessel is under a time charter.

Adjustment to values of ship and cargo

17.20 **"To these values shall be added the amount made good as general average for property sacrificed, if not already included, . . . "** The provision that any amount made good in general average must also contribute to the general average is one of the fundamental principles of general average, the reasons for which have already been explained with a figured example in paragraph 17.14, above.

The final words—*if not already included*—were added in 1924 for the reason mentioned in paragraph 17.06, above, and relate to those cases where the general average sacrifice has already been repaired before the termination of the adventure: for example the ship may have suffered a general average sacrifice which has been repaired at a port of refuge. In such cases the amount made good is already included in the actual net value of the property at the termination of the adventure and does not have to be added to that value.

17.21 **". . . deduction being also made from the value of the property of all extra charges incurred in respect thereof subsequently to the general average act, except such charges as are allowed in general average"** This wording encompasses another of the fundamental principles to be observed in assessing the contributory value of any property, and a number of simple figured examples were given in paragraph 17.13, above. From the *actual net values . . . at the termination of the adventure* must be deducted all those charges incurred subsequent to the general average act in order to realise that destination value and which would not have been incurred if, instead of being saved by the general average act, the property had at that time been totally lost.

The concluding words *except such charges as are allowed in general average* dispense with the need to deduct such of those charges incurred subsequent to the general average act as are themselves allowed as general average. If they were deducted, sound principle would require them to be treated as "made good" and added back again as per the Rule wording analysed in the previous paragraph 17.20 that is:

[13] See para. 70.12, *post*.

Freight at risk to shipowner	20,000
Less: Voyage expenses subsequent to the general average act	8,000
Contributory value of freight	12,000

The "voyage" expenses" in the example are expenses which have not been allowed as general average, but if crew wages incurred during a detention at a port of refuge of 1,000 were also to be deducted as "charges subsequent to the general average act", the calculation of the contributory value would have to proceed as follows:

Freight at risk to shipowner	20,000
Less: Voyage expenses subsequent to the general average act (8,000 + 1,000)	9,000
	11,000
Add: Made good (in general average)	1,000
Contributory value (as before)	12,000

One last point worthy of mention: the word *extra* in "all extra charges" was added only in 1974 and might conceivably be considered to confuse the general issues, rather than clarify. In arriving at any contributory value it is legitimate and proper to deduct *all* reasonable charges necessarily incurred subsequent to the general average act to realise the value at destination—whether *normal and routine* (for example the ordinary "voyage" expenses in the example immediately above) or *extra*. **17.22**

It is believed that the word *extra* was added in 1974 particularly to cope with a potential problem anticipated with the valuation of cargo. Prior to 1974 the assessment of cargo values often started with their *landed* market values, from which needed to be deducted freight (unless prepaid and non-returnable), landing and warehousing charges, duty, and brokerage, etc. With the radical changes in 1974 to bare invoice values, these particular deductions could no longer be made, but *extra* charges (for example by reason of damage) might so fall to be deducted.

Specific Provisions

CARGO—ENGLISH LAW AND PRACTICE

Cargo contributes on its actual or assumed landed *market* values on the last day of discharge at destination or other place where the adventure ends. In practice, market values are adopted for all those basic commodities regularly traded on the Exchanges of the world, such as grain, coffee, cotton, rubber, oil, etc., but in the case of manufactured products (where a similar "market" might not exist) it is the general custom in **17.23** respect of goods delivered at their intended destination to base the contributory value on the c.i.f. invoice value to the receiver of the goods, plus say 10 per cent[14] for assumed profit.

If the goods are damaged as at the last day of discharge, the damaged value forms the basis of contribution, but damage sustained from a new cause subsequent to the discharge from the vessel (the subject of the general average) should properly be ignored.

17.24 From the above values are deducted such expenses as the cargo owner has incurred to realise that value and which he would escape if the adventure had been totally lost at the time of the general average act. These expenses might include freight (unless prepaid and/or payable "lost or not lost"), landing and warehousing charges, duty and brokerage. Particular charges attaching to the cargo which would not be incurred if the adventure had been totally lost at the time of the general average act are also deducted.[15]

(Additional information can be found in paragraphs 416 to 418 of the tenth edition.)

CARGO AND YORK-ANTWERP RULE XVII

Construction

First Paragraph

17.25 **"except that the value of cargo ..."** The opening word indicates that the contributory value of cargo is to be assessed in a manner which may differ from the general provisions of the Rule dealt with earlier.

"... shall be the value at the time of discharge ..." However, the basic principle that contributory values shall be based on the condition and arrived values at the time and place when and where the adventure ends, in accordance with Rule G, and the opening words of Rule XVII is preserved thus far.

"... ascertained from the commercial invoice ..." These words contain the most important single alteration in the Rules in 1974,[16] and simplification of the task of adjusting general average was the predominant motive of the Hamburg Conference.

[14] In *Mormacsaga v. Crelinston Fruit Co.* (1969) A.M.C. 1621, the court added 15 per cent when assessing the value of cargo not replaceable locally.

[15] *The Eliza Lines* (1900–2) 102 Fed.Rep. 184; 114 Fed. Rep. 307.

[16] See para. 17.08, *ante*.

Instead of the earlier practice of generally basing the contributory values of:

(1) *basic commodities* on the wholesale market value of those commodities on the last day of discharge, such that the several receivers of, for instance, grade RSS 1 rubber would contribute on identical values, or
(2) *manufactured products* on the invoice prior to the receiver, usually with a percentage addition for assumed profit,

contributory values in both categories are now based on the invoice price to the receiver, without the addition of any profit margin. In so far as the various receivers of the identical grade RSS 1 rubber in category (1) are concerned, they now contribute on the differing prices disclosed by their individual invoices.

It should be noticed that the invoice must be a commercial one; it must state a price payable on a genuine sale. If it does not, it should be disregarded.

Transhipment cargo

For transhipment cargo carried under a "through" bill of lading or contract of carriage for further transport after its discharge from the vessel suffering the general average, although its own particular adventure may yet be continuing, the *common* maritime adventure terminates on the present discharge and such cargo must contribute on its value and in its condition at that time. This value, however, will still be "*ascertained from the commercial invoice rendered to the receiver*", and if that invoice be on a c.i.f. ultimate destination basis, with all the freights, transport, handling charges and insurance, etc., for the complete journey prepaid and non-returnable ship and/or cargo "lost or not lost", the value at the intermediate port of discharge will—if sound—be precisely the same as at the ultimate destination. No deduction from the ultimate destination c.i.f. invoice price should be made for the notional expense of getting the cargo from the (first) port of discharge to the ultimate destination. **17.26**

Account must clearly be taken of loss or damage already present on discharge from the vessel suffering the general average, but additional loss or damage sustained thereafter from a new cause will not reduce the value on which such cargo contributes.

(A more extensive commentary on the problems with transhipment cargo appears in paragraphs 16.23 to 16.28, above.)

"... rendered to the receiver" Some goods, particularly basic commodities, are often bought and sold many times during the course of a voyage, and invoices will obviously be prepared to substantiate each individual sale. The particular invoice which is most likely to record the **17.27**

value at the termination of the adventure is the invoice rendered to the actual receiver of the goods and the Rule provides accordingly.

The adoption of invoice values undoubtedly simplifies adjustments, but invoices themselves are not without their problems. Various deductions from the basic price are frequently made and it is not necessarily the final price quoted on the invoice which should always be taken for contribution purposes. Some of the more common deductions are as follows:

"Less 5 per cent to Commission Agent"	—	Do not deduct
"Less 2 per cent Cash Discount"	—	Deduct
"Less 4 per cent for Ordinary Loss"	—	Deduct
"Less 2 per cent Advertising Allowance"	—	Do not deduct
"Less $2\frac{1}{2}$ per cent for Letter of Credit"	—	Deduct
"Less 5 per cent Quantity Rebate"	—	Deduct

"if there is no such invoice from the shipped value." Some goods are shipped without an invoice being rendered to the receiver (for example personal and household effects, goods sold "on consignment", and possibly government and foreign aid cargoes). In such cases, the adjuster must assess the contributory value as best he can from the shipped value.

17.28 **"The value of the cargo shall include ...":**

(a) "... the cost of insurance ..." The use of the expression "*cost* of insurance" suggests that where the cargo is not insured, the contributory value should be assessed (subject to the following remarks on freight) on c. & f. or f.o.b. terms.

(b) "... and freight unless and insofar as such freight is at the risk[17] of interests other than the cargo," Freight will form part of the contributory value of the cargo to the extent that it is at risk to the cargo at the time of the general average act, either by reason of it having been pre-paid on non-returnable conditions, or being payable subsequently on "lost or not lost" conditions. The words **"insofar as"** cover those cases where the freight is partly prepaid and partly at carrier's risk, the partly prepaid portion only being included in the contributory value of the cargo.

17.29 **"deducting therefrom any loss or damage suffered by the cargo prior to or at the time of discharge."** The value of any loss or damage suffered by the cargo prior to or at the time of discharge must clearly be deducted in accordance with general principle, and, having regard to the basis of valuation set out in the earlier part of the Rule, it is submitted that the loss or damage must similarly be valued on the "invoice" basis. Thus

[17] The party to whom the freight is at risk is discussed in paras. 17.42–17.44, *post*.

cargo sold at destination in damaged condition by the receiver will not contribute on the actual sale proceeds; it will be necessary to ascertain what would have been the value in sound condition, calculate the percentage depreciation, and deduct this percentage from the invoice value.

This last sentence is best illustrated by example, and using the same facts and figures as is paragraph 16.32, above, that a shipment of 100 bales with a c.i.f. invoice price of 10,000 delivered at destination damaged to the extent of 20 per cent. If the market is rising (for example, sound value 12,500) and the cargo is damaged by *accidental* causes and sold for 10,000, it would appear quite illogical to adopt that damaged value of 10,000 as the contributory value when similar cargo in *sound* condition will contribute on the same c.i.f. value of 10,000. The wording of the Rule requires that the contributory value shall be based upon and

"***ascertained*** *from the commercial invoice*", *i.e.*	10,000
but "*deducting therefrom any loss or damage*", *i.e.*	
20 per cent	2,000
Contributory Value	8,000

17.30 Although perhaps more relevant to the construction of Rule XVI, it is interesting and convenient here to calculate the allowance in general average and the contributory value for the same consignment with an arrived sound value of 12,500 where the damage has been caused by general average sacrifice. As stated in paragraph 16.32, above, if the receiver agrees a depreciation of 20 per cent with the surveyor, the allowance in general average would be calculated by applying this 20 per cent depreciation to the invoice value of 10,000, that is 2,000.

The contributory value would be assessed as:

Invoice value	10,000
Less: damage	2,000
	8,000
Add: made good	2,000
Contributory value	10,000

On the other hand, if as per Rule XVI, the "*cargo so damaged is sold and the amount of the damage has not been otherwise agreed*", nothing will be made good in general average as there is NO "*difference between the net proceeds of sale* (10,000) *and the net sound value* ..... (10,000)". The contributory value, accordingly, will be assessed as:

Invoice value	10,000
Less: damage	2,000
	8,000
Add: made good	—
Contributory value	8,000

Third Paragraph

17.30a **"In the circumstances envisaged in the third paragraph of Rule G, the cargo ... shall contribute on the basis of its value upon delivery at original destination unless sold or otherwise disposed of short of that destination,"** The "*third paragraph of Rule G*", introduced in 1994, constitutes the first half of what was popularly known as a Non-Separation Agreement,[18] and the second half of the Agreement, relating to the valuation of the various properties, was clearly more appropriately sited here in Rule XVII than in Rule G.[19] The wording under discussion provides that cargo forwarded from a port of refuge by other vessels in circumstances entitling the shipowner to retain the cargo there during repairs shall contribute to the continuing general average on the basis of its value, *not* when it left the ship at the port of refuge, but "*upon delivery at original destination unless sold or otherwise disposed of short of destination*".

Fourth Paragraph

17.31 **"Where cargo is sold short of destination, however, it shall contribute upon the actual net proceeds of sale, ..."** This particular paragraph was added in 1974 at the request of the British delegation to legislate for a problem[19a] encountered in practice, as detaild in Report No. 34 of the Advisory Committee of the Association of Average Adjusters dated May 7, 1968. The wording makes an exception to the general provision that cargo shall contribute on the basis of the value shown in the commercial invoice rendered to the receiver in the case of cargo sold short of destination. The actual net proceeds of sale, plus **any amount made good as general average** will be the contributory value.

Where the voyage is justifiably and wholly abandoned at a place short of the scheduled destination, cargo which is undamaged or not requiring to be sold at that place will often be forwarded to its intended destination.

[18] For a description, see paras. G.10–G.17, *ante*.

[19] There was the further advantage that any provision concerning valuations in the *lettered* Rule G might, by reason of the Rule of Interpretation, have been overridden by any conflicting basis of valuation detailed in the *numbered* Rule XVII.

[19a] The problem appears to have been particularly concerned with whether cargo sold short of destination should contribute to expenses incurred at the port of refuge, or subsequently, which were general average essentially for the reason that they were necessary for the safe prosecution of a voyage in which the particular cargo sold would have no interest. It is doubtful whether the new wording in Rule XVII addresses this problem but, prima facie, any amount to be made good in general average does have a continuing interest in the safe prosecution of the voyage (failing which it will not be made good!). Accordingly, it is submitted that the amount to be made good should effectively suffer all the vicissitudes to which the other property is subject, and contribute to the *whole* of any general averages, etc., but that the net sale proceeds should not so contribute. Whether the difference in ultimate contribution will warrant the extra cost of preparing the more complex adjustment must depend on the particular circumstances of any individual case.

The contributory value should then be assessed in the normal way from its destination invoice price, deducting therefrom all charges incurred by the cargo interests themselves subsequent to the abandonment to get their cargo to the intended destination.

If the voyage is abandoned at or near the port of loading and the cargo returned to the shippers, the contributory value should be an "ex factory" type price, but calculated backwards from the original destination invoice, and again deducting therefrom all charges incurred by the cargo interests themselves subsequent to the abandonment to return the cargo to their factory or other premises.

In both the above situations, the cargo is effectively being valued at the place where the voyage was abandoned and the adventure ended, but based or *ascertained from the commercial invoice.*[19b]

SHIP—ENGLISH LAW AND PRACTICE

The ship contributes upon her value at the completion of discharge at **17.32**
the final port of destination, or other place where the adventure ends, and in that condition—whether sound or damaged—in which she then finds herself. From this value should be deducted the cost of any repairs already carried out subsequent to the general average act, and to this value should be added any sum made good in general average for damage to the ship.

The general principle having been set forth, it must now be stated that unless the ship has actually been sold at the time and place when and where the adventure ends, thereby placing a fairly precise and unarguable value upon her,[20] the problem of placing a fair and reasonable valuation upon a ship is beset with difficulties.[21] This is not necessarily of any great consequence when the amount or the percentage of general average is fairly small, but it does become important when the general average is large and represents a substantial percentage of the contributory values.

In the great majority of cases, the ship will not have been sold, and it is then necessary to assess as best possible what was the likely value of

[19b] See para. 17.25, *ante.*

[20] *Bell v. Smith* (1806) 2 Johnson R. 98.

[21] An interesting case where the vessel was actually sold illustrates the occasional extremes in values which can be encountered and the difficulties of assessing a true and fair contributory value for a ship.

A Panamanian flag vessel on a voyage from the U.S. to Europe was obliged to put into an east coast U.S. port with severe damage, estimated to cost $4,000,000 to repair. Her sound value on an "international" basis was $6,000,000, resulting in a contributory value of $2,000,000. However, as she had been damaged in U.S. waters, she became eligible under the U.S. Wreck Act for import to the U.S. flag and operation in U.S. coastwise trading and, as such, she was sold in her *damaged* condition for $10,000,000. This was adopted as the contributory value.

(See also other problems with regard to the valuation of a ship in paras. 17.77–17.81, *post.*)

the ship in her actual condition at the termination of the adventure (thereafter deducting the cost of any repairs effected subsequent to the general average act and adding any amount made good). In practice it is seldom that a ship valuer will actually inspect the ship at that time and place, and it is customary to seek an opinion of the sound[22] value of the vessel at that time from a recognised ship valuer, and to deduct from this value the cost of repairing all damage carried by the vessel to arrive at a damaged value.

17.33 It is also necessary to define those constituent parts of the ship which will be included in the global value assessed by the ship valuer (in the same way that, when buying a house, it is well understood that this does not include the furniture, curtains and carpets, etc., unless expressly mentioned). Using the definition contained in Rule of Construction No. 15 of the Marine Insurance Act 1906, as a starting point, the term "ship" includes the hull, materials and outfit, stores and provisions for the officers and crew, the ordinary fittings requisite for the trade in which she is engaged, the main engine, the generators and other auxiliary machinery. It does not include, for instance, the bunkers, unbroached stores and spare gear, etc., which are usually paid for separately by the purchaser of any vessel, nor does it include property on board the ship belonging to other parties, for example wireless and navigational equipment (sometimes hired) or containers.

17.34 To determine the sound value of a ship is not easy. On principle, a merchant-ship being simply a machine for earning freights, the real value to her owner of a ship in sound condition is the present capitalised value of all her future earnings, so long as she can be used as a ship, after deduction of her working expenses, to which must be added the present value of the sum for which she may eventually be sold to be broken up. But, as the data for such a calculation do not exist, we have to adopt other tests, by way of approximation. One such test is the market value of such a ship in sound condition. This represents the current opinions of shipowners on the point and can be adopted when there is a sufficiently extensive market for ships of the kind. In the case of ships of a peculiar build, or exceptional size, or having qualities which specially adapt them to a limited trade, the value in the market may not come near to the real value. In such a case it may be necessary to take account of the first cost, to make a deduction for age and wear and tear, and to allow, likewise, for changes which have taken place in the cost of materials or the price of labour since the ship was built and which may have decreased or, more probably, increased her value, and for later improvements in construction which may diminish her value.

[22] The term "sound" is a relative one, and will take account of the routine maintenance and upkeep work likely to be necessary, having regard to the time elapsed since the last annual drydocking and special survey. For this reason, the cost of normal wear and tear repairs is not deducted from the sound value.

Long-Term Time Charters

Ship finance is a highly complex subject in this modern age, and many vessels are now operated under long-term charters which can affect their market values. The majority of these chartering arrangements are straightforward business transactions between parties at arm's length, whilst others have as part of their objective the securing of tax or other advantages offered by different countries. The assessment of market values in such cases presented considerable problems under adjustments prepared *only* in accordance with English law. **17.35**

The effect of a long-term time charter on the value of a ship for salvage purposes has been the subject of two cases fought in the Admiralty Court of this country.

In *The San Onofre*,[23] the vessel was committed to a time charter which had several years to run at a relatively disadvantageous rate of hire. The President, Sir Samuel Evans, held that the contractual arrangements between the owners and the charterers were immaterial and must be disregarded, and he adopted the (higher) free-market value of the vessel.

In a later case, *The Castor*[24] the vessel was similarly subject to a time charter which had several years to run, but this particular charter was more profitable than could have been secured at the time. In following *The Harmonides*[25] and similar collision cases, the President, Lord Merrivale, said: **17.36**

> "It seems to me inconsistent with authority, and wrong in principle to exclude from consideration the earning power of the *Castor* under the charterparty, under which, so long as it subsists, she could alone earn money for her owners."

Accordingly, he valued the vessel at a higher figure than her free-market value.

Lord Merrivale was able to find grounds to distinguish the case of *The Castor* from *The San Onofre*, but they do appear to conflict and it may be that one of the cases would now be decided differently.[26]

In the United States, a case was heard in the Circuit Court of Appeals where the facts were similar to *The San Onofre*.[27] In *The Kia Ora*,[28] circuit Judge Woods said: **17.37**

> "Free on the market at the time she was stranded, her market value would have been $3,000,000; but the fact that she was under requisition of the

[23] [1917] P. 96.
[24] [1932] P. 142.
[25] [1903] P. 5.
[26] *E.g.* see the discussions in Kennedy's *Law of Salvage* (5th ed.), paras. 1050–1059 in the British Shipping Laws Series.
[27] [1917] P. 96.
[28] 252 Fed.Rep. 507 (1918).

> British government reduced her market value to $1,772,600. It seems clear that her real value, as properly found by the District Court, was her value under the actual conditions of requisition, not what would have been her value with that condition removed."

Many other countries take no account of the beneficial or detrimental effect of a vessel's long term charter engagements.

Fortunately, this matter has now been resolved by special provisions introduced into Rule XVII in 1974 that **"the value of the ship shall be assessed without taking into account the beneficial or detrimental effect of any demise or time charterparty to which the ship may be committed."**

To summarise, no inflexible rule can be laid down beyond this: the principle is, the ship is to be valued at that sum for which the owner as a reasonable man would be willing to sell her, and this sum must be ascertained by the adjuster as well as he can.[29]

Rule B24 of the Association of Average Adjusters provides:

> *"Contributory Value of Ship*
>
> That in any adjustment of general average there shall be set forth the certificate on which the contributory value of the ship is based, or if there be no such certificate, the information adopted in lieu thereof, and any amount made good shall be specified."

Ship's Bunkers

17.38 Whether owned by the shipowner or by a time-charterer, ship's bunkers remaining on board the vessel at the completion of the adventure and which were on board at the time of the general average act should contribute as a separate interest to any general average. They contribute on their value at the time and place where the adventure ends, plus any amount made good in general average for bunkers previously consumed (or sacrificed) during any resort to a port of refuge, etc.

Where the vessel is engaged under time charter and, as is customary under such charters, the time charterer provides the bunkers, it has always been the practice to treat these bunkers as a separate contributing interest. It is only recently (1980s), however, that this same practice has been introduced where the bunkers are the property of the shipowner. Previously, the bunkers were ignored or deemed to be comprised within the value of the ship itself, but the shipping depression of the 1980s with its low values for ships but high cost of bunkers makes the new practice necessary. (It should be noted that the reported sale prices of ships, on which sound values for general average purposes will be based, are customarily exclusive of bunkers and unbroached stores, etc.)

[29] See *African Steamship Co. v. Swanzy* (1956) 2 K. & J. 660; *Grainger v. Martin* (1862) 4 B. & S. 9. See also *The Harmonides* [1903] P. 1.

It should also be recorded that when a vessel is engaged under time charter, she is generally placed "off-hire" during any time lost as the result of, for instance, a general average deviation and detention, and the bunkers consumed during that period are debited by the time-charterer to the shipowner. Any amount "made good" in general average for bunkers consumed during this period is accordingly credited to the party out-of-pocket for the expense—that is the shipowner. However, the bunkers still remain the property of the time-charterer and it is he who will be called upon to pay the general average contribution attaching to the amount made good. This practice was confirmed by the Advisory Committee of the Association of Average Adjusters in their Report No. 37, dated April 15, 1977.

THE SHIP AND YORK-ANTWERP RULE XVII

In any general average subject to the York-Antwerp Rules the contributory value of the ship is assessed in accordance with the fundamental principles outlined in paragraphs 17.11 to 17.15, above, and the general remarks in paragraph 17.32, above, that is, it contributes on its net sale proceeds or *free* market value at the time and place when and where the adventure ends. From this value is deducted the cost of any repairs already carried out subsequent to the general average act, and any sum made good in general average for damage to the ship is added. **17.39**

The only special provisions in Rule XVII relating particular to the ship are that:

(End of First Paragraph) **17.39a**

"The value of the ship shall be assessed without taking into account the beneficial or detrimental effect of any demise or time charterparty to which the ship may be committed." This proposal to assess the contributory value of a ship free of charter commitments was made by the Norwegian delegation in the interests of international uniformity and was carried by a large majority at the Hamburg Conference in 1974. A discussion on the reason for this provision has already been given in paragraphs 17.35 to 17.37, above.

It is to be noted that it is only the beneficial or detrimental effect of any demise or time charterparty which is to be ignored, and not the charterparty itself. Thus, if on the strength of a long-term freight or hire contract a ship were to be designed and built for a lifetime of service in a single specialised trade, outside which she would have, perhaps, only a scrap value, her value for general average purposes should be assessed as a going concern (see paragraph 17.34, above), and not on a scrap-value basis.

It is also to be noted that:

(1) The beneficial or detrimental effect on the value of a ship secured by existing fixtures on a *voyage* basis for voyages subsequent to that on which the general average occurred would also be ignored in practice.

(2) In salvage cases, the courts and arbitrators of any country may still take account of the effect of these time charterparties in valuing the salved property and assess their awards accordingly. Any distribution they decide on must be reviewed in the general average adjustment, and the total award for salvage be apportioned in accordance with Rule VI over the contributory values determined in the manner provided by this Rule XVII.

17.39b *(End of Second Paragraph)*

"(except such charges as . . .) fall upon the ship by virtue of an award for special compensation under Art. 14 of the International Convention on Salvage, 1989 or under any other provision similar in substance." Article 14 of the International Convention on Salvage provides that where the value of the property salved is insufficient to provide an adequate reward to salvors for their services, but those services have prevented or minimised damage to the environment, special compensation shall be paid by the shipowner to the salvors. It is specifically provided in Rule VI(b) of the York-Antwerp Rules that such special compensation shall *not* be allowed in general average, but that provision would effectively be partly circumvented if such compensation were to rank, as it normally would, as an "extra charge" against the ship and form a deduction from its contributory value, thereby casting an increased proportion of the admissible general average on the cargo.

To prevent such a situation, the wording under discussion was added to Rule XVII in 1994 to deny the right for any award for special compensation under the International Convention on Salvage (or similar provisions) to rank as a deduction from the contributory value of the ship.

17.39c *(Third Paragraph)*

"In the circumstances envisaged in the third paragraph of Rule G, . . . the ship shall contribute upon its actual net value at the time of completion of discharge of cargo." (at the port of refuge). See the commentary in paragraph 17.30a, above, relating to *Cargo*; this is the comparable addition relating to the *Ship*, and is self-explanatory.

FREIGHT

General Remarks

The term "freight" is a compendious one capable of many meanings but in its simplest form it is the remuneration payable for the carriage of goods by sea in a ship. It is sufficiently wide to comprise the payment made under a bill of lading or a voyage charterparty, or the hire paid under a time charterparty[30]; it can also include the profit derivable by a shipowner from the employment of his ship to carry his own goods or movables, but it does not include passage money.[31] Freight may be at risk to the carrier and payable only upon right delivery at destination, or it may be pre-paid absolutely, ship and/or cargo lost or not lost, or it may be partly pre-paid and partly at risk. On a voyage basis, it may be charged on the tonnage or volume of cargo loaded, or even on a lump-sum basis, and, in the case of time charters, on the vessel's deadweight cargo-carrying capacity at a rate per ton per month. **17.40**

The variations are endless, and it is not uncommon to find that a ship is operating under several forms of freight contract at one and the same time. For instance, a shipowner may hire his vessel to a charterer on a time basis; the time charterer may sublet the vessel on a voyage charterparty basis; and the sub-charterer may operate the vessel "on the berth" and issue bills of lading under some of which the freight is pre-paid absolutely, whilst others may provide for freight to be payable only on right delivery.

Having regard to these many types of freight and the manner in which it is paid, it will be appreciated that the subject of when freight should contribute to general average and on what value is most complex. **17.41**

However, before dealing with the complexities it may be helpful to state the general principles.

Where freight at risk to the carrier

As a separate interest in its own right, freight contributes in general average when, and only when, it is at risk to the carrier at the time of the general average act, and is earned or made good.

Where freight pre-paid[32]

Where the freight has been earned by the time of the general average

[30] See paras. 17.52 *et seq., post.*
[31] Marine Insurance Act 1906, s. 90.
[32] The word "pre-paid" is used in the text as a shorthand expression to describe any freight which is not at the risk of the carrier at the time of the general average act. As to the circumstances in which freight is at the risk of the carrier, see para. 17.42., *post.*

act it does not contribute as a separate interest, but is treated as part of the value of the goods, with the result that it is the cargo owner who will effectively bear the contribution.[33] This was decided in *Frayes v. Worms*[34] where it was held that the charterer, who was also the owner of the goods at the time of the general average act, was liable to contribute in respect of pre-paid freight, because, in the words of Byles J. "in substance the goods are augmented in value by the pre-payment he has made".[35] The modern approach, exemplified by the York-Antwerp Rules, is simply to treat pre-paid freight as an element in the value of the cargo rather than as a contributing interest.

When vessel engaged under several freight contracts

Where the vessel is operating under more than one freight engagement, the question whether, and the amount on which, freight contributes (or is contributed for) is governed by the terms of that contract which is most immediate to the cargo owners themselves.

If the immediate contract between the carrier and the cargo provides for the freight to be pre-paid, any antecedent charter arrangements will be ignored for general average contribution purposes and, for instance, the shipowner would not be required to contribute to a general average in respect of freight at risk to him and payable by a charterer only on right delivery. The only relevance of antecedent charters is that, where freight is at risk to the carrier under the immediate contract with the cargo owners, and is therefore a contributing interest, the shipowner would be obliged to participate in the contribution, in respect of charterparty freight at risk to him, as illustrated in paragraph 17.94, below.

When is Freight at the Risk of the Carrier?

17.42 As will be clear from the above, it is essential to determine whether freight is at the risk of the carrier or of the cargo owner at the time of the general average act. For a full discussion of this subject reference should be made to the works on carriage by sea.[36] However, the principles may be summarised as follows:

(1) The basic rule is that freight is earned and payable only on right and true delivery[37] of the cargo. Thus it is effectively at the carrier's risk throughout the adventure.

[33] Because he will contribute on the arrived value of the goods, without deduction of freight: see para. 17.28, *ante*.

[34] (1865) 19 C.B. (N.S.) 159.

[35] *Ibid.* at 177.

[36] *E.g. British Shipping Laws* (13th ed.) Vol. 2: Carver, *Carriage by Sea*, paras. 1661–1702.

[37] For the meaning of this phrase see text head (3) below.

(2) The rule is frequently modified by express terms of the bill of lading or charterparty which advance the date at which freight (or part of it) is *earned*, and/or the date at which it is *payable* (for example a term that freight shall be deemed earned on signing bills of lading, and payable 10 days after signature). Whilst the question is always one of the interpretation of the contract as a whole, it will generally be true to say that once the date arrives at which freight is *either* earned *or* payable[38] it will cease to be at the risk of the carrier, and will thereafter be an element in the value of the goods for the purpose of general average. Thus in the example given immediately above, freight will cease to be at the risk of the carrier as soon as the bills of lading are issued, although not payable for a further 10 days.

(3) Freight is payable in full even if the cargo is damaged on delivery, provided that it retains its "specie" or commercial identity.[39] This rule is unaffected by a term providing for payment "on right and true delivery", which is taken to mean delivery to the right person and at the right place. Thus so long as the goods retain their commercial identity freight will contribute in full.

We may now proceed to consider in more detail the circumstances in which freight contributes in general average under various types of freight engagement, and the contributory value of such freights.

[38] For the general principle see *Allison v. Bristol Marine Insurance* (1879) 1 App. Cas. 209. Many of the older cases discuss the question whether a prepayment is a mere loan to the carrier, and thus repayable if the freight is not earned by delivery of the cargo, or is a true (or "absolute") payment of freight, in which case the risk is transferred to the cargo owner. A pre-payment will be regarded as falling into the former category only if the terms of the contract indicate that it remains at carrier's risk, or if there is nothing in the contract to indicate that the pre-payment is a payment of or on account of *freight*. The present editors have not encountered any modern form of bill of lading or charterparty where a provision for pre-payment could be construed as amounting merely to a loan.

For modern applications of the rule see: *Compania Naviera General S.A. V. Kerametal* [1981] 2 Lloyd's Rep. 559; [1983] 1 Lloyd's Rep. 373, C.A. "Freight non-returnable cargo and/or vessel lost or not lost . . . to be paid . . . 75 per cent within five days after the master signed bills of lading and the balance on right and true delivery." Vessel and cargo lost in a storm within five days of signing bills of lading. *Held*: no freight payable.

Vagres Cia Maritima v. Nissho Iwai [1988] 2 Lloyd's Rep. 330. "Freight deemed earned as cargo loaded," 95 per cent to be paid in advance and balance after completion of discharge. Vessel and cargo lost after cargo loaded and advance freight paid. *Held*: balance was payable although discharge never took place.

Bank of Boston v. European Grain & Shipping [1989] 2 W.L.R. 440. "Freight deemed earned on signing bills of lading," payable five days after surrender of the bills. After signing the bills, but (probably) before freight became payable, the carrier wrongfully abandoned the voyage. *Held*: freight was earned and payable.

[39] See *Dakin v. Oxley* (1864) 15 C.B. (N.S.) 646; *Asfar v. Blundell* [1896] 1 Q.B. 123; *Montedison v. Icroma* [1980] 1 Lloyd's Rep. 91.

When Cargo on Board

If wholly pre-paid

17.43 If the freight has been wholly pre-paid,[40] then the risk in that freight rests not with the carrier but with the owner of the cargo. As such, the freight becomes merged in the value of the cargo and does not contribute as a separate entity.

If wholly at carrier's risk

If the payment of freight, whether under a bill of lading or voyage charterparty, is made conditional upon the arrival and delivery of cargo at destination, it is clear that the rescuing of the ship and cargo from total loss confers upon the carrier an advantage to the extent of the amount of freight that is at risk and earned, less those expenses incurred subsequent to the general average act to earn that freight and which he would have escaped if the adventure had been totally lost. This difference represents the contributory value of the freight in such a case.[41]

If partly pre-paid and partly at risk

17.44 As already mentioned,[42] freight for any voyage may be partly pre-paid[43] and partly at risk. Thus, in the case of a general cargo, some of the bills of lading may evidence that the freight has been wholly pre-paid and/or is payable "ship and/or cargo lost or not lost", while other bills of lading may evidence that the freight is payable only on right delivery at destination. In the case of a voyage charterparty, part of the freight may be pre-paid, with the balance at risk to the carrier, and the situation may be the same even under individual bills of lading, for example 90 per cent may be payable within seven days of signing the bill of lading and the balance on right delivery at destination, etc.

Whenever any *part* of the freight is at risk, only that part of the freight contributes to any general average, and its contributory value is calculated by deducting the *full* expenses of earning the *whole* freight, as detailed in paragraph 17.45 and—in appropriate cases—paragraph 17.50, below.

Deductions from freight earned

17.45 These may comprise the cost of:

[40] See para. 17.41, n. 32, *ante*.
[41] See *per* Gorell Barnes J. in *The Brigella* [1893] P. 189 at 196.
[42] See para. 17.40, *ante*, and the cases referred to in para. 17.42, *ante*.
[43] See para. 17.41, n. 32, *ante*.

(1) crew's wages[44] and other benefits from the time of the general average act until completion of discharge at the final port of destination or other port where the voyage is abandoned;
(2) provisions for the crew purchased subsequent to the general average act and consumed before the termination of the adventure as in head (1) above;
(3) bunkers and stores purchased subsequent to the general average act and consumed before the termination of the adventure as in head (1) above (the cost of bunkers may include, on occasion, a proportion of the port charges at the bunkering port);
(4) canal dues, light dues, pilots, tugs and other port charges at all ports of call necessary for the current cargo voyage and until the termination of the adventure as in head (1) above. (The cost of entering a last port of discharge forms a proper deduction from the contributory value of the freight, but not the cost of leaving that port);
(5) discharging cargo at the various ports of discharge, unless payable by the cargo interests under an f.i.o. contract;

except such of the above charges as have been allowed as general average.

The Rule of Practice of the Association of Average Adjusters dealing in general terms with the contributory value of freight is Rule F22, as follows: **17.46**

"*Contributory Value of Freight*

That freight at the risk of the shipowner shall contribute to general average upon its gross amount, deducting such charges and crew's wages as would not have been incurred in earning the freight had the ship and cargo been totally lost at the date of the general average act and have not been allowed as general average."

When the Vessel is in Ballast

Under voyage charterparty

It is universally accepted that freight which is at risk to the carrier shall contribute to a general average occurring when the cargo is on board, but there is no such unanimity with regard to the freight due to be earned and contracted for under the terms of a voyage charterparty **17.47**

[44] By statute the wages of a seaman may continue to be payable for a time despite the wreck or loss of a ship (see the Merchant Shipping (International Labour Conventions) Act 1925, s. 1, and the Merchant Shipping Act 1970, s. 15). It could be argued that, as the shipowner does not necessarily escape payment of crew's wages by reason of the total loss of his vessel, those wages should not be deducted in arriving at the contributory value of the freight. Such an argument, however, would be considered uncommercial and the practice is, without exception, as stated above.

whilst the vessel is proceeding in ballast to the loading port. In most countries, such freight is ignored[45] as a contributing interest to any general average (if a general average situation be admitted at all), or assumed to be comprised within the value of the ship. However, in those countries where English law applies, provided that the vessel has broken ground and is proceeding on the voyage described in the charterparty, the freight earned under the terms of that contract will be brought in as a separate contributing interest to any general average occurring on a preliminary ballast passage to the loading port.

English law

17.48 In the case of *S.S. Carisbrook Co. v. London and Provincial Marine Insurance Co.*,[46] the facts were that a vessel was chartered to proceed from England to Savannah, and there, having discharged her cargo (if any), to load a cargo of cotton and proceed therewith to Liverpool, Manchester or Bremen. She sailed in ballast from Fleetwood to Savannah, and in the course of the voyage a general average sacrifice was made. She subsequently arrived at Savannah, loaded her cargo, and earned her freight by completing the voyage. The shipowners having sued the underwriters on the ship for a particular average loss, the underwriters contended that the shipowners were liable to contribute as in general average[47] in respect of the chartered freight, and both Matthew J. and the Court of Appeal held on the authority of *Williams v. London Assurance Co.*,[48] that their contention was well founded. In the course of his judgment, Collins M.R. said[49]:

> "Looking at the matter in point of principle, and apart from authority, it would seem to me that the freight should be one of the contributories in such a case as this. The vessel in a round charter such as this is earning the only freight that is payable from the moment it breaks ground down to the time it delivers the cargo at the ultimate port; it is in process of earning that just as much before the goods are put on board as afterwards."

The earlier authorities on which the *Carisbrook* case was based were *Williams v. London Assurance Co.* and *The Progress*,[50] to which extended coverage was given in paragraphs 427 to 428 of the tenth edition of this work.

[45] Chartered freight does not contribute in the United States if there was no cargo on board: see Rule of Practice, No. 14 and *cf. The Brig Mary* (1842) 1 Sprague 17. There is a resolution of the French Association of Average Adjusters to the like effect.

[46] [1901] 2 K.B. 861; [1902] 2 K.B. 681, C.A.

[47] Where the interests at risk are owned by the same person, so that there is no contribution, losses in the nature of general average must nevertheless be adjusted between him and his insurers as if the interests were owned by different parties. *Montgomery v. Indemnity Mutual Marine Ins. Co.* [1902] 1 K.B. 734, C.A.; Marine Insurance Act 1906, s. 66(7).

[48] (1813) 1 M. & S. 318.

[49] [1902] 2 K.B. 681 at 690.

[50] (1810) 1 Edw. A.R. 210.

The effect of these legal decisions is summed up in Rule of Practice B26 of the Association of Average Adjusters, part of which reads as follows: **17.49**

> *"Vessel in Ballast and under Charter: Contributing Interests*
>
> For the purpose of ascertaining the liability of Underwriters on British[51] policies of insurance, the following provisions shall apply:
>
> When a vessel is proceeding in ballast to load under a voyage charter entered into by the shipowner before the general average act, the interests contributing to the general average shall be the vessel, such items of stores and equipment as belong to parties other than the owners of the vessel (*e.g.* bunkers, wireless installation and navigational instruments) and the freight earned under the voyage charter computed in the usual way after deduction of contingent expenses subsequent to the general average act. Failing a prior termination of the adventure, the place where the adventure shall be deemed to end and at which the values for contribution to general average shall be calculated is the final port of discharge of the cargo carried under the charter but in the event of the prior loss of the vessel and freight, or either of them, the general average shall attach to any surviving interest or interests including freight advanced at the loading port deducting therefrom contingent expenses subsequent to the general average act."

Deductions from freight earned

For the purpose of calculating the contributory value of freight to a general average occurring when the vessel is proceeding in ballast to a loading port under the terms of a voyage charterparty, all those expenses borne by the carrier detailed in paragraph 17.45, above, may be deducted, and also: **17.50**

(6) the cost of loading the cargo and all port charges entering, leaving, and at the port(s) of loading.

Future chartered freight

In his endeavours to secure profitable employment for his ship, it frequently occurs that an owner will fix his vessel to load cargoes for one or more voyages subsequent to that on which she is currently engaged. Although contracted for, the freights earned on these subsequent voyages are not brought in as separate entities to contribute to any general average occurring on the current voyage. The Rule of Practice of the Association of Average Adjusters on this subject is B27, as follows: **17.51**

> *"Chartered Freight (Ulterior): Contribution to General Average*
>
> That when at the time of a general average act the vessel has on board cargo shipped under charterparty or bills of lading, and is also under a separate charter to load another cargo after the cargo then in course of

[51] It must be stressed that the Rule applies only to claims on British policies of insurance.

carriage has been discharged, the ulterior chartered freight shall not contribute to the general average."

It is submitted that this Rule of Practice reflects the law[52] and is correct in principle, although inconsistent with the judgment in *Norson v. Jones*,[53] for ulterior freight is not a party to the common adventure in respect of which general average is to be adjusted. In this respect it can be distinguished from the homeward freight of a round voyage which does of course contribute.[54] The only occasion upon which it might be taken into account under adjustments prepared in accordance with English law, and that only indirectly, is if the value of the ship is increased by having future fixtures at a rate of freight above the market rate. Where the adjustment is governed by the York-Antwerp Rules, as mentioned in paragraph 17.39, above, it is submitted that these future fixtures would be ignored.

Time Charters

17.52 By custom, freight has always been considered to be payable on a voyage basis, but many vessels are engaged on a long-term or time basis (for example six or 12 months; seven or 15 years) and payment is made on a daily or monthly hire bass, regardless of whether the vessel is in ballast or loaded, the quantity of cargo carried, or the nature or number of voyages undertaken during the period of the time charter. The essential feature of any time charter for this purpose is that payment—or hire—is earned on a daily or monthly basis; so that a charter for a round voyage at so much per month would be treated as a time charter. But a charter for 12 months, to perform as many voyages as possible and with freight payable on a voyage basis, would be treated as a voyage charter, and freight for subsequent voyages thereunder as ulterior freight within the principle stated above.

[52] *E.g.* the remarks of: (1) Lord Stowell in *The Progress* (1810) 1 Edw. A.R. 210, "If there had been two distinct voyages, as is sometimes the case in charterparties, distinguishing the outward from the homeward voyage, the case would have assumed a different aspect." (2) Collins M.R. in *S.S. Carisbrook Co. v. London and Provincial Marine Insurance Co.* [1902] 2 K.B. 681, C.A., "No doubt there are differences of convenience when there is a cargo carried to the intermediate port as distinguished from the case where no cargo is carried to the intermediate port, and if cargo is carried under a charter which entitles the ship to a freight at the intermediate port, one can easily understand why the average adjusters should make a difference and limit the contribution in respect of such an average sacrifice, on what I may call the first part of the voyage, to the freight which was to be earned at the first port where the cargo was to be discharged."

[53] (1857) 7 E. & B. 523.

[54] See para. 17.47, *ante*.

Time-charter hire

If a vessel is time-chartered for a number of years, to be at the absolute disposal of the charterer, and the charterer employs her to make a series of voyages, carrying perhaps 20 different cargoes in the time, is the total hire under the charter to contribute to a general average that may occur on, say, the first of these voyages? **17.53**

This is a case in which it is difficult to separate the freight from the value of the ship. The value of this vessel to her owner is made up of two ingredients—the freight he is to receive for the period during which she has been hired, and the value now of a vessel which is not to come into his possession for any purpose of profit, until the end of the charter period.[55]

For this reason, time-charter hire due to a shipowner, or time-chartered owner, is not treated as a contributing interest in its own right, although shipowner and disponent owner may be obliged to participate in making any contribution in respect of voyage freights under a bill of lading or sub-charterparty.[56]

Voyage freights when vessel under time charter

The practice with regard to voyage freights, when the ship is operating under a time charter, is as follows.

When cargo on board. In accordance with the principles already set out[57] the time charterer (or, where the vessel is sub-chartered, the sub-charterer who is the party to the immediate contract with cargo interests) will contribute on freight due to him from the cargo interests and at risk. Contribution will be calculated in the manner set out in paragraph 17.45, above, and will be sub-divided between the parties in the manner illustrated in paragraph 17.94, below.

When in ballast. The rule[58] under English law that freight becomes a contributing interest from the moment that the vessel breaks ground on the approach voyage provided for in the charter does not apply in practice when the vessel is operating under a time charterparty. In such a case, therefore, neither the time-charter hire nor any voyage freight in the course of being earned by the time charterer is brought in to contribute to the general average as a separate entity. This is laid down as part of Rule B26 of the Association of Average Adjusters:

> "... When a vessel is proceeding in ballast under a time charter alone or a time charter and a voyage charter entered into by the time charterer, the

[55] See para. 17.34, *ante*.
[56] See para. 17.94, *post*.
[57] See paras. 17.41–17.43, *ante*.
[58] See paras. 17.47–17.49, *ante*.

general average shall attach to the vessel and such items of stores and equipment as are indicated above. Failing a prior termination of the adventure, the adventure shall be deemed to end and the values for contribution to general average calculated at the first loading port upon the commencement of loading cargo. ... In practice neither time charter hire, as such, nor time charterer's voyage freight shall contribute to general average."

Passage Money

17.54 Passage money, being usually paid in advance and not liable to be refunded if the ship is lost, is not made to contribute; but in cases where coolies or pilgrims were carried at so much a head payable on arrival, the passage money was in English practice, said Lowndes, made to contribute.[59]

FREIGHT AND YORK-ANTWERP RULE XVII

17.55 Rule XVII (second paragraph) deals with freight in the following terms:

> **"deduction being made from the freight and passage money at risk of such charges and crew's wages as would not have been incurred in earning the freight had the ship and cargo been totally lost at the date of the general average."**

This provision is exclusively concerned with the contributing value of freight, rather than with defining the circumstances in which freight contributes at all. It follows that the latter question will depend upon the law governing the adjustment, and when English law applies the position will be as described in paragraphs 17.40 to 17.54, above. Thus, for example:

(1) Freight will universally be called upon to contribute as a separate entity to general average when it is in respect of cargo already on board ship at the time of the general average act, and is at risk to the carrier. Whether freight at risk to the carrier under a voyage charter party will be brought in to contribute to a general average occurring while the vessel is proceeding *in ballast* to a loading port will depend on the law and practice governing the adjustment.[60] In places where English law prevails or is followed, such freight will contribute; in others such as the United States and France, it will not.

[59] 4th ed. App. O, p. 636.
[60] See paras. 30.02 *et seq.*, *post.*

(2) Where the vessel is operating under a time charter, the liability to contribute will be as described in paragraphs 17.52, 17.53, above.

"... the freight and passage money at risk ..." The wording reflects the principle, already stated in paragraph 17.41, above, that it is only freight at risk to the carrier at the time of the general average that is a contributing interest. **17.56**

As mentioned in paragraph 17.40, above, a ship may be operating under numerous forms of freight contract at one and the same time, but in any chain of contracts it is the freight payment terms in the contract which is most immediate to the cargo owners themselves which will govern whether that freight should contribute to a general average. If the freight under that "final" contract is pre-paid, it will not be called upon to contribute and any freights or time-charter hire at risk to earlier operators in the chain will be ignored; they are *res inter alios acta*. However, if that final freight is at risk to the carrier and brought in to contribute, there may be a sub-division of the contributory value between the various operators in the chain as detailed in the example in paragraph 17.94, below.

It will be noted that passage money is also mentioned, but this is rarely at risk (see paragraph 17.54, above).

"deduction being made ... of such charges and crew's wages as would not have been incurred in earning the freight had the ship and cargo been totally lost at the date of the general average act and have not been allowed as general average." This wording is a mere re-statement of a fundamental principle in assessing any contributory value, as discussed earlier in paragraph 17.13. The types of charges likely to be deductible, and the English Rule of Practice F22, are set out in paragraphs 17.45, 17.46, above. **17.57**

MAILS, PASSENGERS' LUGGAGE, PERSONAL EFFECTS, AND ACCOMPANIED PRIVATE MOTOR VEHICLES

General Remarks **17.58**

The concluding fifth paragraph of Rule XVII[61] makes special provision exempting these particular properties from liability to contribute to any general average, but in the absence of such provision, the position under English law (if any) and the commercial practice would generally be as follows.

[61] See para. 17.61, *post*.

Mails

On principle, there seems to be no reason why articles of pecuniary value carried by post should not contribute, and there is no English authority to prevent the collection of general average contributions from mails. However, it is believed that in practice articles carried under a mail contract have never been made to contribute. A sufficient reason for the exemption of ordinary correspondence is that letters cannot have a definite pecuniary value. On principle, indeed, there seems to be no reason why articles of pecuniary value carried by post should not contribute, though it is unlikely that the mail contract will include agreement to the application of the York-Antwerp Rules. There are also almost insuperable practical difficulties in the way of enforcing a lien on, and valuing, mails and tracing the owners.[62] In practice, the appropriate allowance in general average is made for loss of or damage to mails by a general average act and the amount so made good is brought in as a contributory factor, but no contribution is customarily levied on mails, not so lost or damaged. However, if the circumstances warrant it and the amount justifies the trouble involved, there is no English authority to prevent the collection of general average contributions from mails.

17.59 **Passengers' Luggage and Personal Effects**

If the doctrine that only goods put on board as merchandise are liable to contribute is accepted as the rule of English law,[63] it follows that all the effects of a passenger are exempt[64]; and the general practice in this country seems to have been to exempt them. If passengers' effects were to be held liable to contribution, the liability would be restricted to such effects as are stowed in the baggage compartment, thus exempting the property which the passenger retains in his own care for use on the

[62] The editors of the 7th ed. were informed that in one case the postal authorities in South Africa, fearing that a claim for general average made by the shipowners might be pressed, exacted deposits from the receivers of registered parcels; but the shipowners did not pursue the claim further.

In the German courts in the case of *The Goeben* (judgment of R.G. 1913), it was held that mail matter was not liable to contribute on the grounds that the secrecy of the post was inviolate, and also because of the practical difficulty of enforcing a lien. (The Cour de Cassation in France expressed a similar opinion on May 4, 1957). However, it does not necessarily follow that loss of or damage to articles carried by mail caused by a general average act may not form the subject of compensation in general average under German law. This decision gives an indication of the construction which would be put upon the Rules by a German court, but would not necessarily be followed by an English court.

[63] *Brown v. Stapyleton* (1827) 4 Bing. 119; 12 J. B. Moore 334, quoted in para. 17.73, *post*.

[64] See Abbott (5th ed.), p. 356; Stevens, p. 44. Benecke, however, maintained (p. 308) that passengers ought to contribute for their trunks and luggage, and Beawes ((6th ed.), p. 243) limited the exemption to apparel in use.

voyage, and which, in this sense, is attached to his person.[65] Yet there are practical objections even to this limited responsibility. It must often be difficult, if not impossible, at the time of disembarkation to obtain a proper valuation of the effects of each passenger to fix the amount of his contribution, and to enforce payment or exact security for the claim; and after the passengers have left the ship and dispersed, a right of action only enforceable by a number of separate law-suits, most of them for trifling amounts, would be an illusory remedy. Thus the right to contribution from passengers would in most cases probably resolve itself into a claim for damages against the shipowner, for failing to enforce the right on behalf of the party whose property has been sacrificed.[66]

The question whether passengers' effects are liable to contribute has never arisen in the English courts, but it was litigated in the United States in *Heye v. North German Lloyd*,[67] the action being brought against the shipowners by a passenger whose luggage had been damaged in extinguishing a fire in the baggage compartment, for damages for their failure to enforce the right of contribution against either the cargo or the other passenger's baggage. Brown D.J., in a learned and exhaustive judgment, declared it to be a universal rule that there is contribution for a sacrifice of passengers' effects. Reciprocity, he said, was the rule in general average; but it was not an indispensable part of the principle, and there might be special reasons why a class of articles that share in the common benefit might not be called on to contribute, even though they were to be contributed for. Nevertheless, he came to the conclusion that the passengers' baggage was liable to contribute, with the exception of the apparel and other articles taken with them for use on the voyage. Even if the practice not to detain and hold baggage for a general average adjustment were so long settled and acted on as to form an implied condition upon which passengers embark, he maintained that it would not relieve the passenger from the obligation to contribute. The editors may, however, point out that if there be no lien on the baggage for general average, and the party whose property has been sacrificed has only a right of action against the individual passengers, he will certainly fail to obtain a contribution from many of them, and his position will be worse than if they were totally exempt, and contribution were only levied upon the ship and cargo.[68]

It is submitted that the real test of, and solution to, the question is to

[65] In *The Willem III* (1871) L.R. 3 A. & E. 487, Sir Robert Phillimore held that the wearing apparel of passengers and other effects carried by them for their daily personal use were not liable to pay salvage; and it was admitted that wares or merchandise belonging to them were liable to contribute.

Lord Justice Kennedy considered (*Civil Salvage* (2nd ed.), p. 59) that there was no legal principle for the exemption, from payment of salvage, of such luggage and valuables as are not in daily use and are in the custody of the ship. (*Cf.* (4th ed.), p. 383.)

[66] See para. 30.42, *post*.

[67] 33 Fed.Rep. 60 (1887); on appeal 36 Fed.Rep. 705 (1888).

[68] On appeal the only question raised was whether the damaged baggage had to be contributed for, and on this point the judgment of the District Judge was unanimously affirmed: 36 Fed.Rep. 705.

be found in the proper answer to the further question whether the articles are (1) carried as "goods" under a contract of affreightment, or (2) carried as incidental to a contract for the carriage of a passenger.[69] In (1) the goods contribute and receive in the ordinary way; in (2) the articles do not contribute, but probably receive contribution if damaged by a general average act.

17.60 Passengers' Accompanied Private Motor Vehicles

The accompanying "luggage" of a passenger today will often include a car—and even a caravan—for his personal use and transportation after disembarking from the ship. These private motor vehicles can have considerable value, and this will clearly be taken into account in any award to salvors. On principle, there is no reason why such vehicles should not be called upon to contribute to any general average, but as a matter of general commercial practice passengers are rarely, if ever, called upon to contribute to any general average in respect of their accompanied cars and caravans. The delay, inconvenience and ill-will which would result if passengers were obliged to complete general average formalities before being allowed to drive from the ship and/or port of destination would generally far outweigh the value of any contribution paid by them.

It is believed that most "tickets" for the carriage of passengers' cars and caravans make no provisions regarding general average, and whilst this does not preclude the levying of a general average contribution, any adjustment would have to be prepared in accordance with the law of destination; the York-Antwerp Rules could have no application. Shipowners customarily extend their insurances on the ship[70] to cover the *whole* of any general average up to a substantial sum (for example £100,000) and, further, to pay the proportion of any salvage and/or general average attaching to the cars and caravans, if required.

Under the new 1994 York-Antwerp Rules the owners of accompanied private motor vehicles have been freed from the requirement to contribute to any general average, and the notional contribution which could be said to apply to such property will now be shared by the ship and any other commercial property on board. As stated above, that contribution would previously have been borne in practice by the shipowner alone.

[69] *Cf. per* Day J. in *R. v. Judge of City of London Court* (1883) 12 Q.B.D. 115.

[70] For interest, it is believed that the normal motor insurance provided for cars and commercial vehicles covers only "land" risks, with no "marine" cover for salvage or general average. The cargoes on the lorries are usually insured for "marine" risks.

MAILS AND PASSENGERS' LUGGAGE, ETC.
AND YORK-ANTWERP RULE XVII

"Mails, passengers' luggage, personal effects and accompanied private motor vehicles shall not contribute in general average." 17.61

"Mails," These comprise letters and packages, etc., consigned by the official postal services or by a private enterprise carrier as part of a general consignment entrusted to that carrier by the public at large.

"passengers' luggage, personal effects" The belongings of a passenger contained in suitcases and bags, etc., plus those of his smaller possessions of a personal nature frequently worn, used or carried around, are comprised within these two terms. The previous qualification in Rule XVII that such property was "*not shipped under bill of loading*" having been removed in 1994, it is now immaterial whether the luggage, etc., was for use on the voyage or not. However, the terms are insufficient to comprise accompanied personal property such as a container-load of furniture and household goods being transported to a new home, which therefore remain liable to contribute to any general average.

"accompanied private motor vehicles" It is submitted that the freedom from liability to contribute to a general average is intended to apply also to a caravan without motive power, provided only that it is accompanied by its towing vehicle and passengers.

The fact that the owners of the various properties detailed in this section of the Rule are freed from any requirement to contribute in general average carries no reciprocal denial of the right of those owners to claim a contribution towards any general average loss or damage suffered by their property, for example by water used to extinguish a fire.[71] Nevertheless, and although unresolved by the Rule, it is submitted that whatever amount is made good in general average for loss or damage to mails and passengers' luggage, etc., should contribute to that general average.

MISCELLANEOUS OTHER PROPERTIES

Lives of the Passengers and Crew

The lives which are preserved by the general average act are not 17.62

[71] Unless the passenger ticket or conditions of carriage provide otherwise. These sometimes provide that baggage and personal effects not shipped under bill of lading shall neither contribute nor be contributed for in general average.

brought in to contribute; by reason, it has been said, of the impossibility of assessing them at a pecuniary value.[72]

Wages of Master, Officers and Crew

17.63 The wages of the crew are referred to in many commercial codes, but always to exclude them from contribution, and this has been the long established custom in England also. In point of fact, this is a right not depending on custom, for since the Merchant Shipping Act of 1854,[73] their wages are no longer at risk to the crew and dependent on the successful completion of the voyage of the earning of freight.

Personal Effects of the Master, Officers and Crew

17.64 By custom and inveterate practice, these are never brought in to contribute to any general average and, indeed, if passengers are expressly exempted from any such liability in respect of *their* luggage and personal effects,[74] the officers and crew must have an even better claim to such exemption. As Brown D.J. said in *Heye v. North German Lloyd*[75]:

> "... the clothes of seamen ... do not contribute, though they are paid for if sacrificed. The reasons assigned ... in order that they may not hesitate in sacrificing what is necessary through any fear of personal loss, but on account of their necessary exertion in connection with the special peril."

Commercial Vehicles and their Loads

17.65 As a matter of general commercial practice, it is believed that most ferry operators release even the commercial vehicles and their loads without formality when the general average is of only moderate amount, but they reserve the right to detain them if, for example substantial salvage services have been rendered.

Whether the York-Antwerp Rules will apply is dependent on whether the Rules have been incorporated into the contract of carriage.

Containers

17.66 The conventional "break-bulk" cargo carrier has been increasingly supplanted in the liner trade in recent years by the specialised con-

[72] *Park on Insurance* (8th ed.), p. 293.
[73] 17 & 18 Vict., c. 104, para. 183.
[74] See para. 17.61, *ante*.
[75] 33 Fed.Rep. 60 (1887).

tainership carrying as many as 3,000 separate containers. The containers themselves form no part of the ship's permanent equipment and, whether owned by the shipping line, or by other firms such as road haulage contractors or leasing companies, contribute as a separate interest. The York-Antwerp Rules will apply if the containers are carried subject to a contract providing for the Rules. Having regard to the large number of containers carried on board, their different types, ages, and condition of depreciation, the assessment of contributory values is a matter of some difficulty.

In a Report dated August 29, 1975, the Advisory Committee of the Association of Average Adjusters considered that the method most correct in principle was to adopt the current replacement cost, less depreciation for age, etc. However, on grounds of simplicity, they suggested that insured values could well be adopted, and this method can undoubtedly be commended where the total general average represents only a small percentage of the contributory values. However, when the general average is substantial, the additional work involved in applying correct principle will clearly be warranted, and inquiries should be made to discover exactly how many containers of each type and category were on board (whether loaded or empty), and their individual ages. This information can be obtained from the identification marks and number on any container (for example MOLU 2345678 might be a 20 foot corrugated steel non-refrigerated container built in 1981). The European Association of General Average Adjusters and/or the Syndicat des Sociétés Françaises d'Assurances Maritimes et de Transports occasionally publish the current values in new condition of the various types and sizes of containers, together with their annual rates of depreciation, and this can be very helpful.

Bullion and Specie

By reason of its small bulk and great value, bullion or specie can often be removed to safety with comparative ease in a number of general average situations. In addition, its virtual indestructibility and immunity to damage means that there will often be good prospects for its recovery after a disaster, even from a sunken vessel. **17.67**

It has been suggested,[76] therefore, that bullion and specie are not subject to quite the same degree of risk or peril in any general average situation as are the ship and other parts of the cargo on board. Nevertheless, if on board ship throughout any general average situation, bullion and specie contribute on their full value, and the balance of authority is firmly against any special treatment in their favour.[77]

[76] *E.g. The Emma* (1844) 2 W.Rob. 315.

[77] *The Longford* (1881) 6 P.D. 60, an approach favoured in *The "M. Vatan"* [1990] 1 Lloyd's Rep. 336.

Jewels and Other Valuables

17.68 Jewels, precious stones and other small articles of great value, if shipped as cargo, must contribute.[78] When such articles are brought on board by a passenger as part of his effects, the extent to which they are exempted from contribution is variously stated by the textwriters.[79] If the correct rule be that only goods shipped as merchandise are liable to contribute,[80] there is no necessity to consider specially the case of jewels and other valuables. If, however, this be not the rule of English law, it seems obvious that valuables which are stowed away as part of a passenger's luggage ought to be treated in the same way as his other effects in the baggage compartment. Jewellery and other valuables which he retains in his own care for use or ornament during the voyage ought, it is submitted, to be exempt on the analogy of wearing apparel in use. It may be urged with some show of reason that other valuables which the passenger keeps in his own care ought to contribute, especially if he carries them for purposes of trade. Yet the practice not to exact contribution in respect of valuables in the passenger's own care, partly due, perhaps, to the difficulty of ascertaining their existence without resort to inquisitorial methods of an extreme kind, may be supported on the ground that they do not run the same risks as merchandise or luggage in the hold. For they can usually be saved with the person, and therefore incur no greater danger than the passengers themselves.

Bank Notes and Securities

17.69 Phillips is of opinion that bank notes ought not to contribute, as they "are not so properly actual property, to the amount promised to be paid, as the evidence of demands, which evidence may be supplied by others in case of their being lost".[81] Arnould, on the other hand, following Weskett, considered that they ought to contribute, on the ground that they are convertible into money, and are saved by the sacrifice from

[78] 1 Park (8th ed.), p. 293; *Peters v. Miligan* (1787) *ibid.* p. 296; *per* Park J. in *Brown v. Stapyleton*, para. 17.73, *post.*

[79] Beawes (6th ed.), p. 243 says that money and jewels must contribute, and only exempts apparel in use. On the principle that what pays no freight, pays no average, Magens (Vol. 1, p. 62), and Stevens (p. 44) exempt the jewellery as well as the apparel of passengers. Abbott ((5th ed.), p. 356), says that jewels or other things belonging to the persons of passengers or crew, and taken on board for their private use and not for traffic, do not contribute. Arnould (Vol. 2 (2nd ed.), p. 936) states that all small articles of value contribute, unless carried about the person, or forming part of the wearing apparel, but see *British Shipping Laws*, Vol. 10: Arnould, *Marine Insurance* (16th ed.), para. 972. Marshall ((4th ed.), p. 432), exempts jewels or ornaments when belonging to the persons of the people on board.

[80] See para. 17.73, *post.*

[81] 2 Phillips, para. 1397.

becoming valueless.[82] In practice, bank notes, when shipped as cargo, contribute on their paper and printing costs; but if, for example, they are stolen by salvors and presented, they are contributed for, and contribute, on their face value. Circulated bank notes in the shops, casinos, and banks on board passenger liners should similarly contribute on their face value though if there be no contract of affreightment their liability may need be governed by the law of destination rather than the York-Antwerp Rules. It is submitted that no other instrument or security ought to be made to contribute, the loss of which does not necessarily put an end to the obligation which it creates. Although at common law, according to the weight of authority, an action could not have been maintained on a bill or note which had been lost or destroyed, relief could have been obtained in equity when there was no remedy at common law[83] and now by statute in an action on a bill of exchange or other negotiable instrument the defendant will be prevented from setting up the loss of the instrument if a satisfactory indemnity be given him against other claims.[84]

Shops and Banks on Board Ship

The stock and cash in the shops on board ship, and the circulated cash or other valuables in the bank, are also brought in to contribute to general average; however, the liability may need be governed by the law of destination rather than the York-Antwerp Rules. **17.70**

Wireless and Navigational Equipment

Some forms of specialised equipment, for example wireless equipment, are often owned by persons other than the shipowner. If such equipment is at the risk of its owners, they and not the shipowner will be liable to contribute in general average but they will only be liable to make, or entitled to receive contribution in accordance with the (generally wider) **17.71**

[82] Arnould, Vol. 2 (2nd ed.), p. 936, but the editors of the *British Shipping Laws*, Vols. 9 & 10: Arnould, *Marine Insurance* (16th ed.), take a different view: see para. 973; Weskett, tit. Contrib. No. 1.

[83] See *Hansard v. Robinson* (1827) 7 B & C. 90; *Ramuz v. Crowe* (1847) 1 Exch. 167; *Crowe v. Clay* (1854) 9 Exch. 604; Chitty, *Bills* (11th ed.), p. 191.

[84] Bills of Exchange Act 1882, ss.70, 89; *King v. Zimmerman* (1871) L.R. 6 C.P. 466; see also s. 69 of that Act. No case has yet come to the editors' notice of a consignment of trading stamps; but see *Building and Civil Engineering Holidays Scheme v. Post Office* [1966] 1 Q.B. 247.

provisions of the York-Antwerp Rules in the event of their having agreed to general average being so adjusted.[85]

Munitions Carried for the Defence of the Ship

17.72 These are property for the purposes of the Rule, but they are usually Government property, and it is unlikely that the owners will have agreed to an adjustment under the Rules. In the Second World War liability to contribute or to be paid contribution in respect of such property was excluded by special agreement.

Provisions and Stores

17.73 As already recorded in paragraph 17.18, above, Lowndes wrote that "the unconsumed stores of a troop ship, or those laid in by a passenger charterer ... should properly be brought in as contributing", and it is submitted that this must be correct in principle, and also in practice if the value of the stores unconsumed at the end of the voyage is sufficient to warrant the contribution. Nevertheless, the matter was decided otherwise in the case of *Brown v. Stapyleton.*[86]

The question in that case was whether provisions, and victualling stores, shipped by the defendants on a vessel which they had chartered for the conveyance of convicts to Australia, intended for the use of the convicts, but unconsumed at the time of the general average act, were liable to contribute. The Court of Common Pleas held that the claim could not be supported.

Best C.J.:

> "It is not every object of value which has been held liable to a contribution for average, but only such stores as are termed *merces. Merces* has never

[85] The following Agreement made in 1937, is in force between the Institute of London Underwriters, Lloyd's Underwriters' Association, Liverpool Underwriters' Association, Chamber of Shipping of the United Kingdom, Liverpool Steamship Owners' Association of Underwriters and Insurance Brokers of Glasgow, and the principal wireless telegraph companies:

> "It is agreed that in cases of general average, wireless apparatus, submarine signalling outfit, gyroscopic compasses and other similar equipment, which is not the property of the shipowners, shall only be brought in to contribute when the proportion of general average attaching thereto amounts to £40 or over.
>
> Where the proportion of general average attaching thereto does not amount to £40, the total general average shall be apportioned over the values excluding such equipment.
>
> Where the adjustment as between ship and cargo is based in whole or in part on York-Antwerp Rules, wireless apparatus, etc., as above shall contribute, where liable under this agreement, according to York-Antwerp Rules.
>
> Where, however, the wireless apparatus, etc., is the property of the shipowner, it will be included in the total value of the ship.
>
> This agreement shall be communicated to the Association of Average Adjusters with the request that all their members shall give effect to it in the preparation of adjustments."

[86] (1827) 4 Bing. 119; 12 J. B. Moore, 334.

been held to extend to provisions, but includes only the cargo put on board for the purposes of commerce; and the practice shows that this has been the understanding of all times. Magens, Molloy, Stevens, and other writers, all expound the word 'merces' in this way; all in terms exclude provisions. They concur in saying that things of light weight, but of considerable value, must contribute, if they belong to the cargo, but not if they belong to the passengers. Provisions are laid in for the passengers, and must be esteemed to belong to them."

Bingham's report of the judgment of Park J. leaves it doubtful whether the learned judge agreed unreservedly with the rule laid down by the Chief Justice; but Moore's report makes it clear that he assented to the proposition that only goods which are shipped as merchandise are liable to contribute. **17.74**

Moore:

> "Provisions have always been held to be excepted from the rule of contribution, which only applies to merchandise put on board for the purpose of traffic. In the term *merchandise* is included jewels and articles of like nature, not being the wearing apparel or ornaments of the passengers, but the subject of traffic."[87]

If the claim to contribution had been allowed, it would have been based only on the value of the stores unconsumed at the end of the voyage.

Bottomry and Respondentia Bonds

Money advanced under such bonds is not repayable if the ship or, as the case may be, the cargo is lost during the voyage, and the right to repayment is thus at risk to the lenders. By the law of England, however, such bonds do not contribute to general average.[88] It is also doubtful whether such bonds would constitute "property" within the meaning of Rule XVII. **17.75**

Even if such bonds would be brought in to contribute by the laws of any other country, in no way can they *increase* the total contributory values of the property saved. To the extent that the bond may contribute, the value of the ship (or cargo) must be reduced by an identical amount.

[87] (1827) 12 J. B. Moore, p. 338. Phillips (Vol. 2, para. 1399) said that the assumption in this case that only goods which are *merces* contribute, is erroneous, or at least very questionable.

[88] In *Joyce v. Williamson* (1782) 3 Doug. 164, Lord Mansfield said: "It is clear that, by the law of England, there is neither average nor salvage upon a bottomry bond." In commenting on this case, Park said: "A lender on bottomry or at *respondentia* is neither entitled to the benefit of salvage nor liable to contribute in a case of general average." In *Walpole v. Ewer* (2 Park, Insce., 8th ed., 898) Lord Kenyon is reported to have said: "By the law of England, a lender under *respondentia* is not liable to average losses."

It is interesting to note that in 1876 a resolution was proposed at the annual meeting of the Association of Average Adjusters to the effect that a loan made under a bottomry bond should contribute to a subsequent general average, but the resolution was lost.

Miscellaneous Problems with Contributory Values, etc.

17.76 **(Ship)**

(General)

SHIP

Where the Sound Value of a Ship to her Owner must be Higher than the Reported Sound Value

17.77 Problems of some financial consequence can arise with the contributory value of a ship when the shipowner elects to carry out repairs even though the vessel would appear to be a commercial total loss on the basis of her estimated values in sound condition and as scrap. An example presented for the consideration of the Advisory Committee of the Association of Average Adjusters in 1981/1982 will demonstrate the position:

Estimated sound value of vessel	on completion of the adventure	1,000,000
Estimated net proceeds of sale as scrap		250,000
		750,000

		forward:	750,000
Actual cost of repairs effected to damage caused by:			
Accident	(Stranding)	375,000	
Sacrifice	(Refloating)	900,000	
		1,275,000 >	750,000

Prima facie, the ship was not worth repairing, and unless it can be shown that some unusual or exceptional circumstances prevailed (for example part repairs already effected and unexpected damage revealed only on drydocking or opening up; or violent fluctuation in exchange rates affecting the expected cost of repairs), it must be assumed that the estimated sound value of the ship of 1,000,000 is suspect, and that the true value to the shipowner was much greater. On the basis that it was reasonable for the shipowner to effect repairs, the ship must have been worth to him in sound condition a minimum of:

Estimated scrap value	250,000
Repairs effected	1,275,000
Sound Value	1,525,000

Thus, the Advisory Committee were able to reach an unanimous opinion that the correct contributory value was:

Estimated scrap value	250,000
Add: made good	900,000
	1,150,000

Or, put in another way, to correspond with the normal method adopted on more routine cases:

Sound value (as above)	1,525,000
Deduct: repairs	1,275,000
	250,000
Add: made good	900,000
	1,150,000

But the Contributory Value of a Ship can be Less than her Scrap Value

If the previous example may give the impression that the contributory value of the ship should never drop below her net scrap value, it must be stated that this can happen on occasion without the sound value assessed by an experienced ship valuer being in the least suspect. Assume, for example, a vessel with unchallengeable values as follows: **17.78**

Sound	1,000,000
Scrap	500,000

The vessel sustains severe accidental damage during the early part of a voyage and this is fully repaired at a port of refuge for 400,000. Having left the port of refuge, she has the misfortune to suffer another severe accident, repairs to which are effected at destination, again for 400,000.

Applying the fundamental principles set out in paragraphs 17.11 to 17.14, above, and in the precise wording of Rule XVII, below, the contributory value of the ship should be assessed at 200,000 (that is less than her scrap value of 500,000) and calculated as follows:

"Actual net value ... at the termination of the adventure" ... (i.e. Sound Value 1,000,000 less second repairs 400,000)	600,000
"Deduction being also made from the value of the property of all extra charges incurred in respect thereof subsequently to the general average act" .... (*i.e.* The first repairs at the port of refuge)	400,000
Contributory value	200,000

This is the only benefit conferred on the owner of the ship by the first general average act; had the ship been totally lost at that time (of the first accident), the shipowner would have lost his ship worth, sound 1,000,000

but would have saved the cost of repairing the

First damage	400,000	
Second damage	400,000	
	800,000	800,000
		200,000

If neither of the two damages had been repaired before arrival at destination, the contributory value could not be less than her arrived and scrap value of 500,000, for it would not then be reasonable to effect *any* repairs, but in the particular circumstances of the example above, the repairs on both occasions would be reasonably effected as their individual costs of 400,000 were less than the difference between the sound and scrap values.

Occasional Further Adjustments to Ship Values in Respect of Place of Valuation and Duration of Repairs

17.79 It has already been stated[89] that, except where the ship has actually been sold at the time and place when and where the adventure ends, the placing of a fair and reasonable valuation upon a ship is no easy task. A recognised and professional ship valuer will usually be appointed to

[89] See para. 17.32, *ante*.

give his opinion of the *sound* value of the ship at the appropriate time and place, but his estimate can only be a matter of personal opinion and it is by no means certain that any other professional ship valuer would arrive at the same conclusion. From this sound value is deducted the cost of all damage sustained by the vessel in order to arrive at her likely *damaged* value for contribution purposes.

In the vast majority of general average cases, where the amount or percentage of the general average is not large, this simple approach produces a very fair measure of justice. However, where the damage caused by the accident giving rise to the general average is of such severity that the repairs may take, for instance, six months, and the general average represent 50 per cent of the contributory values, some further adjustments to the "normal" damaged value (as above) may properly be considered.

The place where the ship is valued **17.80**

When the ship valuers are asked to estimate the sound value of a ship at a given time and place, one suspects that they all take account of the *time* of valuation, but they may not all consider the effect of the *place* of valuation. Yet this factor can occasionally have an important bearing on the valuation of a ship.

As an example, take the case of a VLCC generally on service between the Arabian Gulf to Japan.

If the adventure ended (by abandonment of her voyage) at a port reasonably near the Arabian Gulf, such as Karachi, with repairs being carried out in that port, the vessel will be nicely "spot" and well situated to secure a next cargo and freight at minimal cost when repaired.

Contrast the position where the adventure ends on completion of discharge of a cargo in Japan; as compared with Karachi, the vessel would be less valuable there by about the notional cost of the ballast passage from Japan to the Arabian Gulf, for example:

3200 tons Fuel oil @ 100 per ton	$ 320,000
Crew wages and maintenance, etc., say...................	30,000
	$ 350,000

The duration of the repairs **17.81**

Let it be assumed that a vessel will be under repair and out of commission for six months. This will clearly affect the price that any prospective purchaser would be willing to pay for her, for if two vessels were for sale, identical in every respect except that one can be traded immediately and the other only in six months' time, it is reasonably obvious that a lesser price will be paid for the lame duck. It is submitted, therefore, that where a lengthy period of repairs is involved, this is a factor which should be taken into consideration when assessing her value in damaged condition.

The point might also be raised that ship values can change dramatically in six months, and for illustration purposes it is believed that the value of VLCCs such as in the previous example dropped in value by up to one third in a period of six months during 1980. Nevertheless, it must be reiterated that for general average purposes the value of the vessel must be assessed as at the time of the termination of the adventure, and not on the basis of reported sales of similar vessels six months later when the repairs were completed.

Even assuming a static ship sale market during a six months period under repair, any prospective purchaser of such a damaged vessel would surely take into account interest at current rates on the purchase price and his subsequent outlay on repairs in assessing the price he was willing to pay for that damaged vessel.

If, for example, a similar vessel in sound condition might change hands at 10,000,000, the sort of calculations which would be likely to run through the mind of a prospective purchaser might include the following:

Notional present sound value of vessel		10,000,000
Deduct: repair costs (3 equal instalments payable in 2, 4 and 6 months		6,000,000
		4,000,000
Deduct: Interest at 12 per cent p.a. on repair cost instalments:		
2,000,000 for 4 months	80,000	
2,000,000 for 2 months	40,000	
	120,000	120,000
		3,880,000
Present purchase price 100/106 per cent		3,660,377

Set out in an alternative manner to build up to that anticipated sound value of 10,000,000 in six months' time:

Present purchase price, as above	3,660,377
Interest thereon for six months @ 12 per cent p.a.	219,623
Repair costs	6,000,000
Interest on progress payments for repair	120,000
	10,000,000

GENERAL

Double General Averages

17.82 On occasion, the properties involved in a common maritime adventure may have the misfortune to be involved in *two* (or more) general averages on the same voyage. The contributory values for each general average will be calculated separately, and in accordance with the general principles outlined in paragraphs 17.11 to 17.14, above, or the precise wording of Rule XVII (paragraph 17.21, above). In practical terms, this means that the contributory values for the *second* general average must be calculated first, and the proportion of that second general average deducted in arriving at the contributory values for the first general average. This on the principle that if the adventure had been totally lost at the time of the first general average, the expenses of the second general average would have been avoided.

As a simple example, let it be assumed that a

SHIP with a sound value of	6,000,000
loads CARGO for a Port A worth	7,000,000
and for Port B worth	5,000,000
Total Sound Values	18,000,000

General Average No. 1. Whilst proceeding to Port A, the vessel sustains a complete main engine breakdown and is salved into a port of refuge where repairs to the ship costing 400,000 are effected. The total of the salvage and other general average expenses amounts to	780,000
General Average No. 2. Having discharged her cargo at A and resumed the voyage to B, the vessel is involved in a collision whereby the ship sustains damage costing 600,000 to repair, and the cargo in one of the holds damage to the extent of 400,000. The total of the salvage and other general average expenses amounts to	1,000,000

GENERAL AVERAGE NO. 2 APPORTIONED

SHIP on sound value		6,000,000		
Less: Damage No. 2		600,000		
		5,400,000	pays	540,000
CARGO B on sound value	5,000,000			
Less: Damage	400,000			
	4,600,000	4,600,000	pays	460,000
		10,000,000	pays	1,000,000
			=	10 per cent.

GENERAL AVERAGE NO. 1 APPORTIONED

SHIP on "Net" destination value (as above)		5,400,000		
Less: Damage No. 1	400,000			
Ppn. 2nd G.A. (as above)	540,000			
	940,000	940,000		
		4,460,000	pays	223,000
CARGO A on sound value		7,000,000	pays	350,000
CARGO B on destination value (as above)	4,600,000			
Less: Ppn. 2nd G.A. (as above)	460,000			
	4,140,000	4,140,000	pays	207,000
		15,600,000	pays	780,000
				= 5 per cent

17.83 *Important Note*: Solely for the purpose of demonstrating the principle, the *whole* of the proportions of the second general average have been deducted from the damaged values of the ship and cargo B in order to arrive at their contributory values for the first general average. In practice, however, correct principle requires that only the proportions of the second general average, *excluding commission and interest*, should be deducted. These particular items are really book-keeping devices to achieve a greater equality of sacrifice between the parties to the adventure, and do not affect the *values* of the properties. It would be wrong for cargo A to pay a varying proportion of the first general average, dependent simply on whether it took a short or long time to prepare the adjustment.

"One And a Half" General Averages

17.84 This expression, if not in common use, is here used to describe a general average situation arising from a *single* accident, but where the port of refuge happens to be the intended destination for part of the cargo. How should the contributory values be calculated?

In the following example, extreme figures are adopted to highlight the difference which can result if too simplistic an approach is adopted.

A vessel loaded with cargo for ports A and B is involved in a serious collision shortly before arrival at port A and she is salved into that port. Cargo for port A is discharged in the normal way, whereafter the vessel is detained undergoing repairs necessary for the safe prosecution of the voyage to port B.

The award for salvage and costs, etc., amounts to	1,200,000
The port of refuge general average expenses to	400,000
Total general average	1,600,000

Cargo A must clearly contribute to the salvage award, etc., but it does not contribute to general average expenses incurred after it has been discharged, and with the object of completing a voyage in which it has no interest. These port of refuge expenses fall solely upon the ship and cargo B.

The simple (but incorrect) method of preparing the adjustment would be as follows: **17.85**

	GENERAL AVERAGE Payable by	
	ALL INTERESTS	SHIP AND CARGO B
Salvage award and costs etc. ...	1,200,000	
Port of refuge expenses		400,000
	1,200,000	400,000

		APPORTIONED		TOTAL
SHIP on	600,000 pays	360,000 +	240,000 =	600,000
CARGO B on	400,000 pays	240,000 +	160,00 =	400,000
	1,000,000 pays	600,000 +	400,000 =	1,000,000
CARGO A on	1,000,000 pays	600,000	— =	600,000
	2,000,000	1,200,000 +	400,000 =	1,600,000

It is submitted that general averages of this type should be apportioned in the same manner as "double" general averages (as in paragraph 17.82, above), as follows: **17.86**

PORT OF REFUGE EXPENSES APPORTIONED

SHIP on	600,000	pays	240,000
CARGO B on	400,000	pays	160,000
	1,000,000	pays	400,000

SALVAGE AWARD, ETC., APPORTIONED

SHIP on		600,000		
Less: Ppn. port of refuge expenses (as above)		240,000		
		360,000	pays	270,000
CARGO A on		1,000,000	pays	750,000
CARGO B on	400,000			
Less: Ppn. port of refuge expenses (as above)	160,000			
	240,000	240,000	pays	180,000
		1,600,000	pays	1,200,000

17.87 It will be noted that cargo A pays 750,000 (or 75 per cent of its value) under the second method, but only 600,000 (or 60 per cent) under the first method. Logic and equity must be called in aid of the second method, in addition to any fundamental principle of general average or precise wording of Rule XVII.

The salved values on which the award would be based must be assessed on the termination of the salvage services at port A. In respect of

CARGO A, this is clearly its destination value of		....	1,000,000
CARGO B, this is its value at its own destination ..		400,000	
Less: The cost of getting it there, *i.e.* the proportion of the port of refuge expenses		160,000	
		240,000	240,000
THE SHIP, this will be its sound value, *e.g.*		1,200,000	
Less: The costs incurred in restoring it to that condition, *i.e.*:			
Repairs	600,000		
Plus: The proportion of the port of refuge expenses	240,000		
	840,000	840,000	
		360,000	360,000
	Total Salved Values		1,600,000

On the basis of these salved values, cargo A should pay 750,000, and there is no sound or logical reason why it should pay any less, such as by the first method.[90]

[90] The subject of "*One and a Half General Averages*" dealt with in paras. 17.84–17.87, *ante*, was introduced in the 11th ed. for the reason that the practice for calculating contributory values in such cases was not uniform. In 1992 Lloyd's Claims Office asked the Advisory Committee of the Association of Average Adjusters to consider the problem and, by a majority, in their Report the Committee considered that the first (simplistic) method set out in para. 17,85, *ante*, was to be preferred, *i.e. Lowndes* was wrong.

This majority conclusion of the Committee might have been acceptable if it had been reached on grounds of commercial utility, or of simplicity, but the Committee imagined that they had reached their conclusion on grounds of correct principle, and in this they were mistaken. This can easily be demonstrated by assuming that in the example given in para 17.84, *ante*.

1. The shipowner had justifiably abandoned the voyage immediately on delivery at the port of refuge by the salvors. The general average would then consist solely of the salvage award and costs, etc., of 1,200,000 and, for instance, cargo B would not contribute thereto

The exclusion of small contributory values

Although it is a fundamental principle of general average that all properties saved should contribute to the general average sacrifices and expenses incurred in proportion to their values at the termination of the adventure, commercial good sense dictates that properties with small values should be exempted from the requirement to contribute if the contribution they would pay is less than the costs which would be incurred to obtain general average security from them, assess the value, and finally collect the contribution when the adjustment is issued. There **17.88**

on its *final* destination value of 400,000 (as maintained by the Advisory Committee), but on its value at the port of refuge where the voyage was abandoned, *i.e.* 400,000 *less* whatever was the cost of getting it from there to its intended destination.
2. Alternatively, that there had been no salvage operations and that the general average consisted solely of the port of refuge expenses of 400,000 which might normally be expected to be apportioned as in the example:

SHIP	on	600,000	pays	240,000
CARGO	on	400,000	pays	160,000
		1,0000,000	pays	400,000

Let it be additionally assumed, however, as in the *City of Colombo* case (*Ellerman Lines v. Gibbs National (Canada)*) (1986) A.M.C. 2217) that the port of refuge was Montreal and that half the cargo valued at 200,000 was destined for nearby Toronto. Rather than suffer an extended delay and contribute 80,000 towards the expenses, the cargo owners elect at an early stage of that delay—and when only 40,000 had been expended—to take delivery of their cargo at Montreal and arrange its forwarding at a cost of 20,000.

The total general expenses of 400,000 must clearly be allocated:

To:	Ship and ALL Cargo	40,000
	Ship and Cargo Remaining on Board	360,000
		400,000

but what are the respective contributory values?

The cargo forwarded by its owners to destination contributes only to the 40,000 portion of the general average, and on its value at Montreal, *i.e.* Toronto value of 200,000 less 20,000 cost of getting there.

The ship and cargo remaining on board contribute to both portions of the general average; in respect of the 360,000 portion of the general average undoubtedly on their destination values of 600,000 and 200,000 respectively (paying 270,000 and 90,000 respectively), but are these same values applicable also to the 40,000 portion of the general average, as the Advisory Committee would have us believe?

It must surely be accepted that this 360,000 is nothing other than the *cost of getting the ship and remaining cargo to destination*, an exact parallel to the forwarding expenses of 20,000 incurred by the other cargo, and like them, forming a proper deduction from the contributory values of the properties.

Thus, the 40,000 portion of the general average should properly be apportioned:

SHIP	on	600,000	−270,000	=	330,000	pays	21,290
FORWARDED CARGO	on	200,000	− 20,000	=	180,000	pays	11,613
REMAINING CARGO	on	200,000	− 90,000	=	110,000	pays	7,097
					620,000	pays	40,000

Under this method the forwarded cargo pays 11,613 compared with the 7,347 which would be considered appropriate by the Advisory Committee. Even apart from pure principle, this is not an inequitable result when it is remembered that this particular cargo has saved nearly 50,000 by forwarding, thereby thrusting a similar sum to be borne as general average by the other interests.

is no point in spending an additional 100 to collect a contribution of 10—or, indeed, any sum less than 100. It is for this reason that there is an Agreement with the principal wireless telegraph companies that their wireless or other navigational equipment on board ships will not be brought in to contribute to any general average unless the contribution due amounts to £40 or more[91] (and in modern practice, more likely £100). Such exemption from the requirement to contribute is financially beneficial to *all* the contributing interests.

The problem rarely arises in the bulk cargo trades where there are likely to be only one or a few cargo owners, but it may often fall to be considered in the liner trade with a general cargo shipped under a multitude of bills of lading, and with a total general average of only moderate amount.[92] In practice, what happens is that in the days immediately following the casualty giving rise to a general average act, the adjusters will make a very provisional assessment of the total general average and the likely total contributory values, and calculate the likely rate of contribution. If, for instance, this works out to say two per cent of the total contributory values and they also consider (purely for example) that it costs $100 to collect general average security and the eventual contribution from any individual bill of lading consignment, it would be uneconomic to collect security from those small consignments with values of less than $5,000, and the necessary instructions can be sent to the ship's agents at the various ports of destination to release such cargo without general average formality. If the adjusters considered that the general average contribution was in the region of five per cent, the minimum value called upon to contribute would be $2,000.

Negative contributory values

17.89 In broad terms, and as stated in paragraph 17.18, above, all property which is saved by a general average act must contribute to that general average on its actual net value at the termination of the adventure, less those charges incurred subsequent to the general average act in order to realise that value and which would have been avoided if, instead of being saved by the general average act, the property had at that time been totally lost.

If the charges incurred subsequent to a general average act by any individual property exceed its net value at the termination of the adventure, it is clear that that property cannot be called upon to contribute to the general average. However, as that property would have been financially better off if, instead of being saved, the adventure had been

[91] See para. 17.71, n. 85, *ante*.

[92] In fact, a number of shipowners in the liner trade arrange for special provisions to be incorporated in the policies of insurance covering their vessels that, when required to do so, hull insurers will pay the *whole* of any general average up to a specified sum. Such a clause is to be commended in that it avoids much unjustified work and trouble to all concerned.

totally lost, it may be questioned whether that property should be assessed at a negative contributory value and be paid a general average contribution as part compensation for the expenses it has incurred. The problem is best illustrated by example.

If delivered in sound condition, the contributory value of a consignment of cargo would be as follows: **17.90**

Gross arrived value	100
Less: Freight payable on delivery	40
Contributory value	60

As the result of a stranding during the voyage, that same cargo sustains very serious damage by seawater but is delivered in specie, thereby entitling the carrier to his full freight.

The cargo is sold in damaged condition for	25
Less: Freight payable on delivery	40
	NIL or (15)?

It is submitted that the true contributory value of the cargo is minus 15, and that it should be paid a contribution at the same percentage rate shown due in the adjustment from those properties which arrived with positive values. This may be understood more easily if it is appreciated that the sale proceeds of the cargo 25

represents the *combined* contributory value of both the cargo and the freight thereon. It follows, therefore, that the shipowner should contribute on his freight at risk and earned 40

and that the cargo should receive contribution on .... (15)
25

It would benefit unnecessarily the other contributing interests to ignore completely the negative contributory value of the cargo and merely show the shipowner due to pay contribution on his freight earned of 40.

In similar fashion, if the damage to that same cargo had been caused by a general average act (for example, water used to extinguish a fire), the amount made good would be the loss sustained by the merchant, whether based on net or gross values, that is: **17.91**

			Net Value	Gross Value
Gross sound arrived value			100	100
Less: freight			40	
			60	
Less: sale proceeds	25			25
Less: freight	40			
	(15)		(15)	
Loss sustained by the merchant			75	75
and the contributory value would be:				
Net arrived damaged value				(15)
Add: made good				75
				60

It must be admitted that there is neither legal precedent nor established practice to support a claim to contribution based on negative contributory value, and that this particular topic has received nothing but friendly chaffing since it appeared in the tenth edition. However, such a claim is totally consistent with principle and the material worthy of reprinting. The editors will welcome any constructive criticism to demonstrate any flaw in the theory, and meanwhile refer interested readers also to paragraph 17.92, below, "The Principle of the Cake".

Contributory Values—The Principle of the "Cake"

17.92 The preceding subject of negative contributory values is really a corollary of a principle believed not to have been mentioned prior to the eleventh edition of this work: that the total contributory values of ship, cargo, freight, and any other properties involved in a common maritime adventure may be likened to a "cake", and that however you may slice that cake, the sum of the component slices, slabs and chunks must come to the total size of the original cake. Until any parts of it are eaten, the overall size of the cake remains constant and unvariable, and it is submitted that this is a natural, logical and unassailable proposition.

The same is true of any *part* of the cake. If a slab representing the cargo is cut from the whole cake, that particular slab may be sub-divided into further slices, but together they constitute the original slab. Thus, in the first example given in paragraph 17.90, above, a particular slice of the sound cargo had an agreed value at destination of 100, but this had been further sliced and shared between the:

Shipowner, in respect of the freight payment at destination	40
Merchant, in respect of the residual value	60
	100

Similarly, in the second example in paragraph 17.90, above, an identical slice of cargo (except that it was damaged) had an indisputable value of 25, for that was the price for which it was sold at destination. Again, this 25 must be further sliced and shared between the:

Shipowner, in respect of the freight payable at destination	40
Merchant, in respect of the residual value (or liability)	(15)
	25

It runs entirely counter to sound principle to adopt a value for the	
Merchant of	Nil
and for the *Shipowner* in respect of his freight	40
	40

and it would be even worse, and transgress equitable principles to give the benefit of the "lost" 15 to the shipowner and require him to contribute in respect of his earned freight of 40 on a reduced value of only 25.

Contingent expenses of earning the freight

We return to the general principle and the whole cake, and submit a further corollary: where freight is pre-paid absolutely and constitutes an inseparable and indivisible part of the cargo value, the expenses incurred by the shipowner or operator of the vessel in fulfilment of the contract to carry the cargo to its destination subsequent to the general average act, and which would have been avoided if the adventure had at that time been totally lost, *constitute a proper deduction from the value of the ship, or of the charterers' property.* **17.93**

Using hypothetical figures for the purpose of example, there may be a tendency in practice to value the total cake on the following bases, depending on whether the freight is at risk, or pre-paid absolutely.

			FREIGHT	
			AT RISK	PREPAID
SHIP			2,000,000	2,000,000
CARGO	F.O.B.	1,600,000	1,600,000	
	Freight	400,000		
	C. & F.	2,000,000	....	2,000,000
FREIGHT at risk		400,000		
Less: Contingent Expenses		50,000		
		350,000	350,000	–
			3,950,000	4,000,000

On the stated principle that the total cake cannot vary in size, and that in this particular example it weighed in at 3,950,000, it follows that where the freight was pre-paid absolutely, the contingent expenses of 50,000 incurred subsequent to the general average act to earn the freight must properly be deducted from the value of the:

> *Ship*;[93] if wholly incurred by the shipowner, and also the *Time Charterers' Bunkers or Other Property*, if partly incurred by a time charterer.[94] If this results in a negative contributory value ... so be it!

Freight contributory value—subdivision between shipowner and time charterer.

17.94 If voyage freight at risk to the time charterer contributes to a general average, the contributory value of that freight will be calculated to arrive at the identical result that would have been achieved if the freight had been at risk to the shipowner, but that contributory value will then be apportioned[95] between the time charterer and the shipowner in proportion to their respective interests in the freight. For example:

Gross voyage freight at risk and earned			100,000
Deduct: Wages of crew		5,000	
Bunkers purchased	25,000		
Less: unconsumed	20,000		
		5,000	
Port charges and cost of discharging cargo		10,000	
			20,000
Contributory value of freight			80,000

Sub-divided[96]

The Time Charterer contributes on gross voyage freight earned		100,000
Deduct: Bunkers used (as above)	5,000	
forward:	5,000	100,000

[93] In *The Pantanassa* [1970] 1 Lloyd's Rep. 153, freight was payable at destination *per* the bills of lading, but pre-paid according to the voyage charterparty. The salvors accepted that the very substantial expenses incurred to earn the freight after the casualty were a proper deduction from one or other of the freight or the ship.

[94] Sub-division to be made in accordance with the principles shown in para. 17.94, *post*.

[95] Unless the time charterparty provides (as does the *Baltime* Charter): "Hire not to contribute to general average", in which case the time charterer pays the contribution attaching to the whole of the freight.

(It may be remarked that the above footnote and example first appeared in the 10th ed. of this work and were considered "correct and just" by the Advisory Committee of the Association of Average Adjusters in their Report No. 38 dated August 8, 1977.)

[96] Under the usual terms of a time charterparty, the time-charterer is responsible for providing the bunkers and paying for all port charges and cargo expenses, etc., while the shipowner pays and feeds the crew.

forward:	5,000	100,000
Port charges and cost of discharging cargo	10,000	
Time hire payable to shipowner after general average act	25,000	
		40,000
Time charterer contributes on		60,000
The Shipowner contributes on time hire	25,000	
Deduct: Wages of crew	5,000	
Shipowner contributes on		20,000
Contributory value of freight (as before)		80,000

Similar principles will apply where the freight is payable to a voyage charterer. They will also apply, in those cases where more than one charterparty is interposed between the cargo owners and the shipowner, in calculating the amount to be contributed by each charterer.

General average in excess of 100 per cent of the contributory values

On some rare occasions, total general average expenses and allowances can exceed the contributory values, and the question then arises: **17.95**

> "Can any party to the adventure be legally required to pay a general average contribution in excess of 100 per cent, of the contributory value of their property?"

In accordance with the provisions of Rule G and the opening words of this Rule XVII (*The contribution to a general average shall be made upon the actual net values of the property at the termination of the adventure* ...), it is clear that no contribution can be exacted from an interest which has no contributory value at the termination of the adventure. It is also clear that if, as in *Chellew v. Royal Commission on the Sugar Supply*,[97] all the property is totally lost during the voyage, those who have financed any earlier general average expenditure must bear it alone and no contribution is due from other interests. What of the position, however, where *some* property is saved by a general average act and a general average adjustment needs to be prepared? If, for instance, general average expenditure of 10,000 has been incurred by the shipowner, but property to the value of only 1,000 has been saved, can the owner of that property be called upon to pay the whole of the 10,000?

Ordinary common sense and commercial logic dictate that the answer must be "No", for the owner of that property would clearly prefer that his property had been totally lost, rather than that he should be "taxed" with a liability in excess of its value. In *Green Star Shipping Co. v. The* **17.96**

[97] [1921] 2 K.B. 627; [1922] 1 K.B. 12, C.A.
The same view seems to have been taken by the House of Lords in *Morrison S.S. Co. Ltd v. Greystoke Castle* [1947] A.C. 265 at 285, 312.

London Assurance[98] Roche J based his judgment on the assumption that contribution in general average could not exceed the contributory value and said:

> "The salved value of the cargo was rather over 26,000 dollars. The owners of that cargo are liable to make contribution up to its full value and the [shipowners] have received this contribution amounting to 26,249 dollars. Apart from this they have not received and are not entitled to receive any further contribution from owners of cargo."

Although the assumption of Roche J. may have been based on the law of Philadelphia, it can certainly be stated that the law of a number of countries specifically states that a general average contribution cannot exceed the contributory value; it is also to be doubted whether any country which has no specific law on the subject could logically arrive at any other conclusion.

17.97 However, and although this basic principle is widely accepted almost as a truism, it is submitted that it applies only to the *capital* items of any general average, whether sacrifice, expenditure, or adjustment charges, etc.

The same common sense and commercial logic which dictate the basic principle must surely also sustain the view that *interest* is payable in addition on the debt or contribution, and broadly from the time of the expenditure or sacrifice by the creditor until at least the time when the general average adjustment is issued.

Interest is a legal and equitable right, admirably explained by Lord Wright in *Riches v. Westminster Bank Ltd*[99]:

> "The essence of interest is that it is a payment which becomes due because the creditor has not had his money at the due date. It may be regarded as representing the profit he might have made if he had had the use of the money, or conversely the loss he suffered because he had not that use. The general idea is that he is entitled to compensation for the deprivation."

Or by Brandon J. in "*The Mecca*"[1]:

> "In my view the purpose, and the sole purpose, of awarding interest, whether in an action for damages or a limitation action ... is to compensate for the fact that the damages are paid late."

The period during which interest accrues must surely follow the provisions of Rule XXI or the remarks of Megaw J. in *Chandris v. Argo Insurance Co. Ltd*[2]:

[98] [1933] 1 K.B. 378 at 383.
[99] [1947] A.C. 390 at 400. See also Dr Lushington's remarks in "*The Aalia*" (1864) 5 N.R. 164.
[1] [1968] 2 Lloyd's Rep. 27.
[2] [1963] 2 Lloyd's Rep. 65.

> "In my judgment (and I think this is borne out by the authority of the House of Lords in decisions which I shall mention later) ... the right to receive, and the liability to pay, contribution arise on the occurrence of the loss. ... That liability arises as soon as the general average loss has occurred, if it involves contribution. It is not postponed until the amount of the contribution is, or can be assessed."

With regard to the question of whether interest is comprised within, or allowable in addition to, an imposed maximum liability (for example a limitation fund in a collision action), the remarks of Brandon J. quoted above are sufficient evidence that interest is payable *in addition* to the limitation fund itself.

The infrequency with which the problem is encountered does not warrant that too much space or time be spent on the subject, but the following suggestions are offered as a practical and commercial approach in those cases where the total general average is likely to exceed the contributory values: **17.98**

(1) The adjustment should be limited to general average *expenditure* alone (as was probably intended by Glasgow Resolution No. 10 in 1860, and the proposals in 1890 and 1924), and general average *sacrifices* of property should be excluded and ignored. The extra work and costs involved of adjusting the sacrifices will generally be totally unwarranted and uneconomic because the amounts made good (exclusive of interest) will simply increase the contributory values by an identical amount and pay 100 per cent—or more.
(2) The *capital* items of the general average should be limited to 100 per cent of the total contributory values, with the necessary reductions being applied exclusively to the net creditors of the general average, they being the parties obliged to suffer at the hands of the debtors, who cannot be compelled to pay more than a basic 100 per cent of their contributory values.
(3) Interest at seven per cent per annum[3] should be allowed on the reduced general average in the normal way, but no two per cent commission.[4]

[3] See Rule XXI.
[4] See Rule XX.

Rule XVIII

Damage to Ship

English Law and Background

When the Ship is Repaired

18.01 As previously stated in paragraph 13.01, above, when discussing Rule XIII, when any part of a ship's hull, gear, or machinery, etc., is sacrificed for the common safety, and when the ship is afterwards repaired, the sum allowable in general average as compensation for this damage is the reasonable[1] cost of repairs, with an appropriate deduction for the advantage—if any—which the owner derives from having new work in place of old.[2]

When the Ship is not Repaired

18.02 When the injury to the ship, whether caused by the sacrifice alone, or by that conjointly with accidental damage, is so extensive that she is not worth repairing and is therefore sold, the allowance in general average is not necessarily the estimated cost of replacing the articles sacrificed. We are in that case to inquire whether or not the sacrifice was that which caused the loss of the ship. If the accidental damage, apart from the sacrifice, would have sufficed to condemn the ship, all that can be allowed by way of compensation for the sacrifice is the difference between the sum which the ship would have fetched, other things remaining the same, had the sacrifice not been made and the sum which she actually fetched. This difference is all which the shipowner has really lost by the sacrifice. If, on the other hand, it is the damage done by the sacrifice which has turned the scale, that is to say, if the ship, in spite of all her previous accidental damage, would have been worth repairing and would have

[1] For an indication of the considerations which apply when construing the term "reasonable cost of repairs", see the commentary, para. 18.10, *post*. By a Rule of Practice (No. A.4) it is the duty of the adjuster in adjusting particular average on a ship, or general average which includes repairs, to satisfy himself that such reasonable and usual precautions have been taken to keep down the cost of repairs as a prudent shipowner would have taken if uninsured. See also Rule of Practice No. A.5 (machinery), paras. 70.05, *post*.

[2] See Rule XIII, *ante*.

been repaired but for her masts having been cut away, or some similar sacrifice made for the general safety, then the amount allowable in general average for this sacrifice is the value of the ship before the damage—with her net freight, in case this be lost by the sale of the ship—minus the estimated cost of repairing the accidental damage and the net proceeds of the sale; this difference being, in the case supposed, the measure of the shipowner's actual loss through the sacrifice.

The above remarks (which have appeared since the first edition in **18.03**
1873) were applied in the decision in the case of *Henderson v. Shankland*[3] where a vessel on voyage from Chittagong to Dundee encountered heavy weather and sustained considerable damage. The heavy weather continuing and the vessel being on her beam ends, the mainmast and foremast were cut away. She was subsequently towed into Calcutta, where it was ascertained that the cost of repairing her would exceed her repaired value and she was accordingly condemned as a constructive total loss and sold.

An adjustment was prepared on the instructions of the shipowners, in which the allowance for general average damage was calculated by estimating the cost of repairing the general and particular average damage separately, which came to 63 per cent and 37 per cent respectively. The loss shown by deducting the net proceeds from the sound value was then divided *pro rata* to these percentages and 63 per cent allowed in general average.[4]

The court decided, however, that the proper method of adjustment was first to ascertain the value of the ship immediately after the particular average damage and before the general average sacrifice, by deducting the estimated cost of particular average repairs from the sound value, and then deducting from the result so obtained the proceeds realised by the sale of the wreck.

As an example: **18.04**

Sound (repaired) value of ship		1,000,000
Estimated cost of repairing:		
Accidental damage	800,000	
General average damage	250,000	
	1,050,000>	1,000,000

The ship is clearly a constructive total loss and not worth repairing, and if she can be sold for scrap for say 120,000, only 80,000 of the estimated cost of repairing the general average damage (250,000) can be charged to general average, calculated as follows:

[3] [1896] 1 Q.B. 525.

[4] According to L. J. Buglass *Marine Insurance and General Average in the United States* (p. 212), some American adjusters use this method when there is an actual or commercial total loss of the ship and the York-Antwerp Rules do not apply.

Sound (repaired) value of ship		1,000,000
Deduct:		
Estimated cost of repairing accidental damage	800,000	
Sale proceeds of ship	120,000	
	920,000	920,000
Allow as general average		80,000

18.05 When the injury to the ship caused by sacrifice is less extensive, and the ship is worth repairing but the damage has not been repaired by the time the general average adjustment is ready to issue, the practice is to allow the reasonable depreciation in the value of the vessel by reason of the sacrifice, but not exceeding the estimated cost of repairs.

Historical Development and Practice of Rule XVIII

18.06 *York-Antwerp Rules 1924 and 1950*

This Rule appeared for the first time in the 1924 Rules,[5] the only amendment in the 1950 Rules being the substitution of "subject to deduction in accordance with Rule XIII" for "deductions being made as above (Rule XIII) when old material is replaced by new".

> "The amount to be allowed as general average for damage or loss to the ship, her machinery and/or gear when repaired or replaced shall be the actual reasonable cost of repairing or replacing such damage or loss, subject to deduction in accordance with Rule XIII. When not repaired, the reasonable depreciation shall be allowed, not exceeding the estimated cost of repairs.
>
> Where there is an actual or constructive total loss of the ship the amount to be allowed as general average for damage or loss to the ship caused by a general average act shall be the estimated sound value of the ship after deducting therefrom the estimated cost of repairing damage which is not general average and the proceeds of sale, if any."

The Rule appears to have been based on English law and practice, with which it was in complete accord; the first paragraph of the Rule closely followed the provisions of section 69 of the Marine Insurance

[5] Rule XVIII of the 1890 Rules dealt with a different subject-matter.

Act 1906,[6] for the ascertainment of the liability of underwriters under a marine policy in the event of a partial loss of a ship, and the second paragraph of the Rule was in accordance with the decision in *Henderson v. Shankland.*[7]

York-Antwerp Rules 1974 **18.07**

No change whatever was made in the general provisions and intention of the Rule in 1974 but the layout and some of the wording was altered in order to define more clearly and to secure greater uniformity of practice on two particular points:

(1) The words "constructive total loss" in the second paragraph of the 1950 Rule were not defined, and as this expression had varying legal meanings in different jurisdictions,[8] one meaning was selected and the words "constructive total loss" were changed in 1974 to: "When the cost of repairs of the damage would exceed the value of the ship when repaired."
(2) There were occasional differences in practice under the 1950 Rules where damage to the vessel was, in fact, repaired, but where the figures would demonstrate that the vessel was a commercial[9] total loss.

[6] "69.—Where a ship is damaged, but is not totally lost, the measure of indemnity, subject to any express provision in the policy, is as follows:

(1) Where the ship has been repaired, the assured is entitled to the reasonable cost of repairs, less the customary deductions, but not exceeding the sum insured in respect of any one casualty.
(2) Where the ship has only been partially repaired, the assured is entitled to the reasonable cost of such repairs, computed as above, and also to be indemnified for the reasonable depreciation, if any, arising from the unrepaired damage, provided that the aggregate amount shall not exceed the cost of repairing the whole damage, computed as above.
(3) Where the ship has not been repaired, and has not been sold in her damaged state during the risk, the assured is entitled to be indemnified for the reasonable depreciation arising from the unrepaired damage, but not exceeding the reasonable cost of repairing such damage, computed as above."

[7] [1896] 1 Q.B. 525. See also para. 18.03, *ante*.

[8] In the U.K. the term is statutorily defined in the Marine Insurance Act 1906, s. 60, part of which reads as follows: "In particular there is a constructive total loss ... In the case of damage to a ship, where she is so damaged by a peril insured against that the cost of repairing the damage would exceed the value of the ship when repaired." It is thought that in the U.S.A. there is a constructive total loss if the damage exceeds 50 per cent of the repaired value (*Wood v. Lincoln and Kennebeck Ins. Co.* 6 Mass. R. 479 (1810), and *Peele v. Merch. Ins. Co.* 3 Mason 27 (1822), and in France if the damage amounts to 75 per cent of the value.

[9] *I.e.* where the estimated cost of repairing the damage would not exceed the value of the ship when repaired, but where, on commercial grounds, a prudent shipowner would choose to scrap his vessel rather than repair, *e.g.*:

The following figures may illustrate the problem:

Actual cost of repairing:		
Accidental damage	75,000	
General average damage	15,000	
Estimated scrap value of vessel	25,000	
Estimated value of vessel when repaired		100,000
	115,000>	100,000

18.08 Because the cost of repairing the accidental damage (75,000) plus the estimated scrap value of the wreck (25,000) were alone equal to the repaired value of the vessel, some adjusters used to make no allowance in general average for the cost of repairing the damage caused by sacrifice. On the other hand, the majority maintained that, provided the shipowner acted reasonably, and repairs were in fact carried out, the cost of those repairs fell to be dealt with under the first paragraph of the Rule. Only in those cases where the vessel was an actual total loss, or where she was sold for scrap because the estimates demonstrated that she was a commercial total loss, did the second paragraph apply.

By separating the provisions of the 1974 Rule into two sections: "(a) when repaired or replaced; (b) when not repaired or replaced", it was made clear that the previous majority view should now prevail.

It should also be noted that this earlier problem was resolved in that if the shipowner does elect to carry out repair to his vessel even though she is an apparent commercial total loss on the basis of her estimated values in sound condition and as scrap, the repaired value of the vessel to the shipowner would be assumed to be 115,000 in the example above, rather than the 100,000 estimated by the ship valuer. This subject is further discussed in paragraph 17.77, above, when dealing with Rule XVII.

18.09 York-Antwerp Rules 1994

Proposals for change of some importance to both sections (a) and (b) of the Rule had been put forward, but, in the event, none was accepted at Sydney.

With regard to section (a), the logical proposal that the last two paragraphs of Rule XIII dealing with the charges for drydocking and

Estimated cost of repairs	60,000	
Scrap value	40,000	
Sound (repaired) value		75,000
	100,000	75,000

The estimated cost of repairs does not exceed the repaired value, but it is doubtful whether a reasonable shipowner would repair that ship at a cost of 60,000 if for a mere 35,000 in addition to the scrap proceeds he could purchase another vessel of fairly similar size and age.

for cleaning and painting of bottom should be transferred to and form part of the present Rule XVIII had received fairly widespread support. Both paragraphs were sadly in need of revision and up-dating to include also gas-freeing and tank-cleaning, but the most important reason why no agreement could be obtained on the necessary revisions was the issue of apportionment of the charges where repairs of both general and particular average damage were effected concurrently. Further remarks on this topic will be made in the ensuing text on section (a) of the Rule.

With regard to section (b) of the Rule dealing with the amount to be charged to general average when the vessel is an actual or commercial total loss from a combination of both accidental and sacrificial damages, A.I.D.E. had earlier recommended that the *Henderson v. Shankland*[10] formula be abandoned in favour of a proportional division. This would always have had the effect of increasing general average allowances to the shipowner and, because any increase in the general average system was to be avoided in 1994 if possible, no national delegation adopted this unprincipled suggestion and the matter was not debated at Sydney.

Rule XVIII

Damage to Ship

The amount to be allowed as general average for damage or loss to the ship, her machinery and/or gear caused by a general average act shall be as follows:

(a) When repaired or replaced, the actual reasonable cost of repairing or replacing such damage or loss, subject to deduction in accordance with Rule XIII;

(b) When not repaired or replaced, the reasonable depreciation arising from such damage or loss, but not exceeding the estimated cost of repairs. But where the ship is an actual total loss or when the cost of repairs of the damage would exceed the value of the ship when repaired, the amount to be allowed as general average shall be the difference between the estimated sound value of the ship after deducting therefrom the estimated cost of repairing damage which is not general average and the value of the ship in her damaged state which may be measured by the net proceeds of sale, if any.

[10] [1896] 1 Q.B. 525.

CONSTRUCTION

Section (a)

"the actual reasonable cost of repairing ... such damage..." When any part of the ship's hull, machinery or gear is sacrificed for the common safety, and when the ship is afterwards repaired the sum allowance as compensation for this damage is the actual reasonable cost of repairing it, with the appropriate deduction—if any—in accordance with Rule XIII to represent the advantage which the owner derives from having new material in place of old.

The cost of repairing such damage must be taken to be the cost of repairing it at the time and place where it ought to be repaired. Should it be necessary for the ship, after the sacrifice, to go into some port of refuge, and there repair this damage, the reasonable cost of repairing at that place, however expensive it may be, is the sum allowable. Otherwise, the cost of repairing at the place of destination, and at the time of the ship's arrival, is to be taken, provided the repair either is or ought to be effected then and there. It may happen, however, that from motives of economy, the repairs are deferred until the vessel reaches some cheaper place, in which case, under ordinary circumstances, the sum allowable must be reduced to the actual cost at the place selected for the purpose. These rules are founded on the principle that the owner is entitled to no more than compensation for his actual loss, and that he is bound to do what is reasonable to make that loss as light as may be.

18.11 If the damage to the ship caused by general average sacrifice does not affect the seaworthiness of the vessel, repairs may be deferred until some more convenient opportunity, even until the vessel undergoes her next quadrennial special survey. If, at that time, inflation has resulted in an increase in the cost of repairs, it may be necessary (certainly with ships not engaged in a liner service and running to a regular and advertised schedule) to reduce the allowance in general average to the cost that would have been incurred if the repairs had been effected at the first reasonable opportunity. In practice, this is often construed as the first routine drydocking or overhaul after the casualty.

Charges for drydocking, tank cleaning and gas freeing

18.12 As a preliminary to the effecting of repairs to any ship, it may often be necessary to place the vessel in drydock, and/or to clean and render gas-free her bunker or cargo tanks. The charges for such measures will generally be regarded as forming part of the cost of those repairs, and the question then arises: "How should the charges be treated when the measures are necessary not only for the purpose of effecting repairs to damage caused by a general average sacrifice, but also—as is usual—for repairs to accidental damage and other upkeep maintenance work effected *concurrently*?"

As a typical example of this everyday and costly situation, an oil tanker may strand and her bottom thereby sustain damage by the stranding itself, also by the efforts to refloat. Repairs to both classes of damage necessitate tank-cleaning, gas-freeing and drydocking, and the work is effected concurrently with other repairs on shipowner's or charterer's account, and even to other accidental damage, all of which require the same services (but for differing periods as indicated in the column headings below).

The British practice for allocating these charges is likely to be on the following lines:

		Stranding Damage (12 days)	*General Average Damage* (4 days)	*Owners' Work* (4 days)
(1) *Where the vessel drydocks especially for repairs after the stranding*				
Entry and leaving charges	2,000	1,000	1,000	–
Dues for 4 days	2,400	1,200	1,200	–
Dues for 8 days	4,800	4,800	–	–
12 days	9,200	7,000	2,200	–
Tank-Cleaning and Gas-Freeing	15,800	7,900	7,900	–
	25,000	14,900	10,100	–
(2) *Where the repairs are deferred to a routine overall*				
Entry and leaving charges	2,000	500	500	1,000
Dues for 4 days	2,400	600	600	1,200
Dues for 8 days	4,800	4,800	–	–
12 days	9,200	5,900	1,100	2,200
Tank-Cleaning and Gas-Freeing	15,800	3,950	3,950	7,900
	25,000	9,850	5,050	10,100

The grounds for such a practice might be attributed to the decision of the House of Lords in the case of *The Vancouver*,[11] but that was a case concerned only with a claim on a marine insurance policy, and the decision itself is questionable and was effectively overruled by the House of Lords in *The Carslogie*.[12]

[11] *Marine Insurance Co. Ltd v. China Transpacific SS. Co. Ltd* (1886) 11 A.C. 573.
[12] [1951] 2 Lloyd's Rep. 441.

18.13 The practice abroad varies from country to country and possibly from adjuster to adjuster, but it may confidently be asserted that *some* proportion of these common charges will always be allocated to any damage caused by a general average sacrifice.

Can any of the varying practices be indorsed as correct?

If one starts with the fundamental principle that general average is concerned with the sharing of *losses*, and that no-one should make a profit from the system, it is suggested that the only true solution to this problem should be governed by the answer to a further question:

> "*What* **additional** *expenditure has been thrust upon the shipowner in respect of drydocking, tank-cleaning or gas-freeing by reason of the general average sacrifice damage to his ship? (I.e., what is his loss*?)"

By the terms of Rule E, the onus is upon the claimant to show that the "loss or expense" is properly allowable as general average, and this surely pre-supposes that the shipowner must first demonstrate that any particular expense truly constitutes a loss to him.

In reality, it is probably fair to say that in nine cases out of 10 the charges incurred in respect of drydocking, tank-cleaning and gas-freeing would be *precisely the same* whether or not the general average sacrifice damage were repaired at the same time. The fixed costs of entering and leaving the drydock, or of tank-cleaning and gas-freeing, will usually be pre-empted by—and should be borne by—the earlier accidental stranding damage, and only if the overall period of repairs has been *extended* by reason of the sacrificial damage should any part of the daily charges for the drydock, etc., be charged to general average.

This principle has existed from time immemorial, and is recorded by Baily in his *General Average*, published in 1851:

> "When, therefore, irrespective of the extreme peril to avoid which the general average act was performed, the same loss would have been sustained or the same expense have been incurred as results from the general average act, there is no claim for general average."

18.14 It was for this reason that two members of an A.I.D.E. Working Group on the Rule, proposed that:

> "In determining the reasonable cost of repair or replacement, when damage caused by a general average act is repaired concurrently with other damage and both require the use of a drydock &/or that the tanks of the vessel be cleaned &/or gas freed, the costs of entering and leaving the drydock, together with any necessary drydock dues, tank cleaning or gas freeing, shall be allowed as general average only to the extent that the damage caused by a general average act has increased such costs as would have been incurred to repair the other damage on its own."

On a more official basis, and as recorded in paragraph 4.14, above, the United States Maritime Law Association proposed to fairly similar effect that Rule IV should be deleted and replaced with provisions of a general character:

> "When the ship, cargo or other property on board the ship sustains a combination of sacrificial damage and damage which is not general average, the amount to be made good in general average under any of these Rules shall not exceed the increase in net repair or replacement costs resulting from the sacrificial damage."

Unfortunately, the expressed opinion of the International Sub-Committee was that this "proposal was devoid of any practical benefit. There was no support for this proposal", and the thoroughly sound principles of the proposed changes were rejected, thereby leaving a void and preserving the previous freedom to adjust such charges at will.

Costs of cleaning, painting or coating of bottom **18.15**

If any part of the coatings on the bottom of a ship be damaged directly by a general average act, such as a voluntary stranding, or by efforts to refloat from a position of peril, the cost of repainting the damaged area ought properly to be dealt with on the principle enunciated above of establishing as nearly as possible the real amount of the loss—if any—sustained by the owner. Thus, if the paintwork was already damaged by an accidental grounding which would necessitate its renewal, or if the damaged paintwork was not renewed until a time at which it would normally have been renewed, the shipowner clearly sustains no loss by the apparent damage from the general average act, and no allowance in general average should be made. At the other end of the spectrum, if the bottom had been painted only a month before the general average act and was otherwise undamaged, the whole cost of repainting the area damaged by the general average act should be allowable if effected soon after the damage.

To provide for these and intermediate situations we have only the suspect and generally inadequate provisions in the final paragraph of Rule XIII.[13]

Cost of opening up for examination—no damage found **18.16**

Another practical problem worthy of mention is whether, if no damage be found, the cost of opening up machinery or other parts to check whether damage may have been caused by general average sacrifice (for example in efforts to refloat) can be charged to general average. There is an English law case relating to cargo insurance, *Lysaght v. Coleman*[14] from which it might be possible to argue that there can be no allowance for the cost of opening up if no damage be found, but it is submitted that this particular decision has no application to general average.

[13] See paras. 13.10–13.12, *ante*.
[14] [1895] 1 Q.B. 49, C.A.

Accordingly, if it is reasonable to open up any representative bearing or cylinder (but not necessarily all), or to draw the tailshaft, etc., to examine for possible damage by general average sacrifice, the reasonable cost may be charged to general average even if no damage be found. The only proviso is that the opening up must be solely and specially for that purpose; if the bearing, cylinder, or tailshaft, etc., would in any event have been opened up or drawn at that time for classification or other purposes, the shipowner sustains no financial loss and there can be no allowance in general average.

Section (b)

18.17 **"when not repaired, . . ."** The Rule does not state at what date the ship has to be unrepaired, if this sentence is to apply. Three possibilities exist. The relevant date may be:

(1) That of the adjustment, though it is suggested that if the repairs had not been completed by the time the adjuster was ready to issue his adjustment, but were likely to be effected on some future occasion, he would almost certainly allow the *estimated* cost of repairing the damage (less the customary deductions), rather than, or in substitution for, the more nebulous "reasonable depreciation".

(2) That favourite of the courts, "a reasonable time".

(3) The termination of the adventure, on the ground that the right to contribution has then accrued and cannot be defeated.[15] In practice, however, it is submitted that this particular date would be adopted only in those rare cases where the vessel is totally lost after the termination of the adventure and with the general average damage still unrepaired. It is, of course, possible to argue that the shipowner has sustained no loss at the time of the total loss from his earlier general average sacrifice, but, on the analogy of comparable marine insurance cases, the shipowner's claim in general average for the unrepaired damage would appear to be well founded.

18.18 **"the reasonable depreciation"** No guidance is given on how this shall be assessed. The failure to do so in this sentence is peculiar, but it is suggested that it is without significance, and that the reasonable depreciation is the reduction in the sale value of the vessel represented by the unrepaired general average damage, but not exceeding the estimated cost of repairs, *less* any appropriate deduction under Rule XIII.

In practice, it is suggested that reasonable depreciation is adopted as the basis for ascertaining the amount to be allowed as general average in the following circumstances:

[15] See para. 30.38, *post*.

(1) When, so far as can be foreseen, the vessel is unlikely to be repaired in full, or at all. For instance, an old vessel destined shortly for the breakers' yard may sustain general average damage to her shell plating. If that damage does not affect the seaworthiness of the vessel, it may well remain unrepaired. The price paid by the shipbreakers is unlikely to be affected by the existence of the damage and, in such circumstances, the reasonable depreciation would appear to be *nil.*

(2) When the vessel is totally lost after the termination of the adventure with the damage still unrepaired (as mentioned in paragraph 18.17, above).

(3) When the vessel is sold for future trading in her damaged condition. In such a case, the loss by sale resulting from the unrepaired damage will usually reflect the "reasonable depreciation". An example, drawn from practice, may illustrate the point. The cost of repairing damage to the bottom of a ship by general average sacrifice was estimated by an expert surveyor at £11,000; the vessel was sold for future trading for £7,000 less than her true sound value and this £7,000 the adjuster allowed as the "reasonable depreciation". It may be remarked that where the vessel is sold, no deductions "new for old" need be taken into consideration. An actual sale provides positive evidence of the true loss caused by the sacrifice, whereas Rule XIII provides but an arbitrary means of arriving at a similar, but less certain figure.

The above three examples relate to comparatively minor damage which **18.19**
does not affect the ability of the vessel to continue trading for some time. However, it may also be necessary to found a claim for "reasonable depreciation" when a major damage results in the decision to scrap the vessel. The estimated cost of repairs may be less than the value of the ship when repaired (see paragraph 18.20, below) but greater than any prudent owner would spend, taking into account also the value of the vessel as scrap. Thus:

Sound (repaired) value of ship		1,000,000
Estimated cost of repairing:		
Accidental damage	700,000	
General average damage	250,000	
	950,000<	1,000,000
Scrap value of ship	120,000	
	1,070,000>	1,000,000

No commercial man would spend 950,000 to repair a ship with a sound value of 1,000,000 when for 880,000 plus his scrap proceeds of 120,000 he can purchase a similar vessel to the one damaged.

On figures as in the above example, the reasonable depreciation caused by the general average damage would be calculated as follows:

Sound (repaired) value of ship	1,000,000
Deduct: Estimated cost of repairing accidental damage .	700,000
Pre-general average value	300,000
Deduct: Sale proceeds of ship	120,000
Reasonable depreciation to be allowed as general average	180,000

18.20 **"when the cost of repairs of the damage would exceed the value of the ship when repaired,"** This wording was substituted in 1974 for the previous "constructive total loss", and is effectively the British statutory definition[16] of that term. When the cost of repairs would exceed the value of the ship when repaired, or when the ship is an actual total loss, the amount to be allowed as general average is:

> **"the difference between the estimated sound value of the ship after deducting therefrom the estimated cost of repairing damage which is not general average and the value of the ship in her damaged state which may be measured by the net proceeds of sale, if any."**

This provision is based on the decision in the English courts of *Henderson v. Shankland*,[17] of which the facts—and a practical example—were given in paragraphs 18.03, 18.04, above.

18.21 For the sake of completeness, this commentary on Rule XVIII ends with the mention of an injustice which a shipowner will occasionally suffer owing to the strict construction which must be given to the numbered Rules. Fortunately, the number of cases in which the situation arises is fairly small,[18] and it was for this reason that the matter was not taken further when the York-Antwerp Rules were revised in 1950, 1974 and again in 1994.

A vessel may become a commercial total loss and the sale proceeds of the wreck be reduced owing to the lack of equipment such as anchors and cables which were sacrificed as a general average act. There is no good or sound reason why this loss should not be made good in general average except that Rule XVIII does not permit it, for example:

Estimated sound value			50,000
Estimated cost of repairing accidental damage		40,000	
Normal proceeds of sale	20,000		
Less: sacrificed anchors, etc.	1,000		
Actual proceeds of sale	19,000	19,000	
		59,000	59,000
Allowance in General Average			Nil

[16] Marine Insurance Act 1906, s. 60(2)(ii).

[17] [1896] 1 Q.B. 525.

[18] The number of cases may be small but the editors have seen one, at least, where the amount involved was substantial. The normal scrap value of a vessel would have been about $130,000 but, owing to potential hazards and liabilities created by a general average sacrifice, she could only be sold for a token payment of about 10c.

RULE XIX

UNDECLARED OR WRONGFULLY DECLARED CARGO

ENGLISH LAW AND BACKGROUND

None known, but see paragraph A.81, above.

HISTORICAL DEVELOPMENT AND PRACTICE OF RULE XIX

This Rule appeared for the first time in the 1924 Rules and is reproduced verbatim in the 1950, 1974 and 1994 Rules. It embodies a principle which appears in the laws of many countries, especially in the great majority of those possessing a Commercial Code, which in itself is an argument in favour of its inclusion in rules intended for international use, though the occasions upon which it is invoked are infrequent. The provision that damage or loss to "goods loaded without the knowledge of the shipowner or his agent" shall not be allowed in general average agrees with the usual practice of excluding from the benefits of general average such goods as do not appear on the ship's manifest or for which no bill of lading has been issued. The addition of "goods wilfully misdescribed at time of shipment" is justifiable upon the practical ground that if valuable goods, such as platinum, are shipped as (say) tinware, they will not be accorded the careful stowage and treatment which their real value would deserve and may be sacrificed without much consideration. It would be highly inequitable in such a case if the owner, who has probably wilfully misdescribed them in order to obtain a low rate of freight, should be entitled to receive compensation in general average at their correct value. The penalty inflicted by Rule XIX is severe in that it excludes such goods from receiving any compensation in general average at all. Where goods, however, are properly described on shipment but a value is declared which is lower than their real value, the second paragraph of the Rule permits compensation but only at the declared value. Whether the goods have been concealed or misdescribed or their value has been wilfully misdeclared, they remain liable to contribute on their true value, which is perfectly just, for that value has been saved by the general average act. **19.01**

RULE XIX

UNDECLARED OR WRONGFULLY DECLARED CARGO

19.02 **Damage or loss caused to goods loaded without the knowledge of the shipowner or his agent or to goods wilfully misdescribed at time of shipment shall not be allowed as general average, but such goods shall remain liable to contribute, if saved.**

Damage or loss caused to goods which have been wrongfully declared on shipment at a value which is lower than their real value shall be contributed for at the declared value, but such goods shall contribute upon their actual value.

CONSTRUCTION

Second paragraph

19.03 **"contributed for at the declared value,"** If goods of a value of £100 are declared on shipment to have a value of £50 and are totally lost the amount allowed in general average will be £50. It is suggested that if such goods are damaged so that their value is reduced to £60, a proportionate part of the loss, that is, $\frac{50}{100} \times (100 - 60) = £20$, will be allowed in general average.

RULE XX

PROVISION OF FUNDS

ENGLISH LAW AND BACKGROUND

On principle, as the entire business of raising funds for general average, like general average itself, belongs to that reserved portion of the contract of affreightment for which no man is directly responsible, it would seem obvious that the liability to supply the funds is a mere appurtenance to the liability to pay the general average, and should fall conjointly on all. **20.01**

Historical

In those old times when the merchants sailed with the ships, an ingenious arrangement was in common use, whereby these merchants, often having on board large sums of money, proceeds of former or materials for future ventures, or in any case having at hand goods by the sale of which money could be raised, were the ordinary financiers on any emergency, being bound in case of need to supply the master with either money or goods for sale. They were repaid and secured in the same method as in the case of jettison; that is to say, if the ship arrived, they were put on a par with their co-adventurers by a prompt and secure repayment, but if she perished on the voyage, they got nothing beyond the consolation that they were no worse off than if they had lent or sold nothing.[1] **20.02**

[1] *Consolado*, Ch. 61 (106). "Again, the merchant is bound towards the master of the ship (*senyor de la nau*) that if the merchant have money, and if they are in a place where the master has need of supply or things necessary for the ship, the merchant must lend it to him, so far as the sailing-master (*notxer*) and the other merchants shall agree that he ought to do. And on this account all the part-owners (*personers*) who shall be in the ship, and the lenders (*prestadors*), must all bind themselves to the said merchant. But if the master of the ship, or the part-owners, or the lenders, shall find any man who will lend to them, the aforesaid merchant is not bound to lend anything" (2 Pard. 109).

Ch. 62 (107). "Again, further, if the master of the ship shall be in need of money, and cannot obtain enough as aforesaid, and is in a desert place, and if the said money is necessary for the dispatch of the ship, and if the said merchants have not money, they are bound to sell of their merchandise to dispatch the ship; and no lender or part-owner can say anything or make opposition until the said merchants shall have been paid, excepting the wages of the mariners. It is, however, to be understood that the merchant shall see and make sure that which he lends is for the dispatch of the ship and necessary for her" (2 Pard. 110).

When the merchants began to live ashore, the authority of the master was so far extended that he had power to do for the merchants that which they would presumably have done, or have been obliged to do, had they been there: that is, in the case of necessity, when no money was to be had from the shipowner, or when the master or shipowner were unknown in the port and could obtain no personal credit, the master was empowered:

(1) In the first instance, to hypothecate, the ship and the freight by means of a bottomry bond. If the security offered by the ship and the freight was insufficient,
(2) To hypothecate[2] also the cargo by means of a *respondentia* bond.
(3) In the last resort, and only when all other means of raising the necessary funds had failed, to sell as much of the cargo[3] as was required.

20.03 It would take too long here to enter into a full discussion of the law of bottomry[4] or of these forced sales but one or two points may be mentioned.

The expense of the bottomry or *respondentia* bond, or the loss on sale of the cargo, was charged eventually to those parties who were liable to pay for the expenses which necessitated the loan or sale. If the expenses at the port of refuge were wholly recoverable as general average, the loss would be recovered in the same way[5]; if, as commonly used to occur, the expenses were chargeable partly as general average, partly specifically on the cargo and freight, and partly to the shipowner, the bottomry premium or loss by sale was divided rateably between those interests in the proportion that they bore to the expenses themselves.

Bottomry and *Respondentia* Bonds

20.04 The master's right to raise money by a bottomry loan on the ship and freight comes into force only when he has exhausted all ordinary means

[2] In *The Gaetano and Maria* (1882) 7 P.D. 137 at 145, Brett L.J. said: "This authority of the master of the ship to hypothecate the ship or cargo is peculiar. . . . It arises from the necessity of things; it arises from the obligation of the shipowner and the master to carry the goods from one country to another, and from its being inevitable from the nature of things that the ship and cargo may at some time or other be in a strange port where the captain may be without means, and where the shipowner may have no credit because he is not known there, that for the safety of all concerned and for the carrying out of the ultimate object of the whole adventure, there must be a power in the master not only to hypothecate the ship, but the cargo."

[3] *The Gratitudine* (1801) 3 C.Rob. 240.: *Australasian S.N. Co. v. Morse* (1872) L.R. 4 P.C. 222, and other cases.

[4] For such a discussion, see Franck, *De Bodmeriâ; British Shipping Laws*, Vol. 3: Carver, *Carriage by Sea* (12th ed.), paras. 775–785; and *The James W. Elwell* [1921] P. 351. In practice bottomry is believed to be obsolete.

[5] *The Constancia* (1846) 4 Not. of Cas. 677; *The Gratitudine* (1801) 3 C.Rob. 240.

of obtaining the necessary funds, that is when no money is to be had by applying to the shipowner, or by pledging his personal credit or that of the shipowner. It has from very old times been requisite that the shipowner should first be communicated with whenever it was possible to do so without unduly delaying the voyage.

Only if the security offered by the ship and freight is insufficient to attract the funds necessary at the port of refuge is the master permitted to hypothecate the cargo in addition, and it is a legal requirement that the owners of the cargo be first communicated with; no bond on cargo is valid if this precaution has been neglected.

Should the loan not be repaid on the due date at destination, the lender has a maritime lien upon the property charged which can be enforced by proceedings *in rem* in the Admiralty Court. If necessary, the property pledged can be sold, but only if the proceeds of the ship and freight are insufficient to repay the loan will any part of the cargo be used to satisfy the balance, and then only if the cargo was included in the bond.

Forced Sale of Goods at Port of Refuge

As stated earlier,[6] where cargo was sold at an intermediate port in order to raise funds to pay for repairs or other expenses necessary to enable the voyage to be prosecuted, any loss by sale sustained by the owner of that cargo was added to the cost of those repairs or other necessary expenses and dealt with in the same manner as the principal sums themselves. **20.05**

The amount of that loss by sale would usually be quantified by deducting the net proceeds at the port of refuge from the sum the goods would have fetched at destination (after payment of any freight, etc., due there). If the ship was lost before arrival at destination, however, the cargo owner could nevertheless claim the net proceeds realised by his cargo at the port of refuge. This was decided in *Atkinson v. Stephens*,[7] where, in the course of the argument, Alderson B. said:

> "The owner of the goods is entitled to the amount which they actually fetch, although the vessel does not arrive; but if she does, then he is entitled to [the sum] which such goods would fetch in the market."

On occasion, and largely because any freight due at destination would no longer be payable on cargo sold at a port of refuge,[8] it was possible for the cargo owner to make an unexpected profit from the sale because

[6] See para. 20.03., *ante*.
[7] (1852) 7 Exch. 567.
[8] Nor is freight *pro rata itineris* due on the cargo sold at the intermediate port: *Hopper v. Burness* (1876) 1 C.P.D. 137.

he was entitled to the whole of the net proceeds of sale, even though they exceeded what he would have obtained at destination.

20.06 In *Richardson v. Nourse*[9] the question was, whether the owner of goods sold in Mauritius to pay for repairs to the ship and other port of refuge expenses was entitled to their net value at the port of destination, or to their actual proceeds, the latter being the larger sum of the two. Three arbitrators, to whom the matter had been referred, had pronounced that the owner was entitled to the larger sum; and the court, on being appealed to, refused to disturb their award.

In the course of his judgment, Abbott C.J. said:

> "I cannot say that their decision was wrong; for by holding that the owner of a ship may lose but that he can never gain, by such a sale as this, we shall furnish the strongest possible inducement to him to take care that all the goods are conveyed to their place of destination."

Whenever cargo was sold at an intermediate port to raise funds and the shipowner thereby lost the freight that would have been payable at destination on the cargo sold, his loss of freight would similarly be added to the principal sums expended at the intermediate port and dealt with accordingly.[10]

Cost of Raising Funds in Modern Times

20.07 The section thus far is but an edited version of what Lowndes himself wrote more than a century ago on the subject of raising funds. What he wrote was, and remains, an accurate statement of the law on the subject, but it must be recorded that modern means of communication and the facility to remit funds from one country to another by telegraphic transfer make it quite unnecessary to raise funds at an intermediate port by such archaic and expensive means. In the experience of the present editors, the raising of funds by means of a bottomry bond or the selling of part of the cargo has never been encountered. However, there always exists the possibility that a shipowner totally without funds or credit, even in his own place of business, may one day need to resort to this extremely short-term[11] form of finance so that the subject cannot be entirely omitted from this work.

In modern times, therefore, it would appear that the meaning of the term *cost of raising funds*, in practice, is limited to the actual charges made by a bank for *remitting* funds, but excluding interest.[12]

[9] (1819) 3 B. & Ald. 237.
[10] E.g. *Pirie v. Middle Dock Co.* (1881) 44 L.T. 426.
[11] Bottomry bonds are—or were—almost invariably repayable within three days of arrival at destination.
[12] See also para. 21.01, *post*.

Historical Development and Practice of Rule XX

Mercantile men have always recognised that the ability and willingness to advance funds on behalf of third parties merited the payment of an advancing commission, and general average disbursements—"for which no man is directly responsible"[13]—are no exception to this rule. In Germany, for example, a commission of one per cent was allowed on general average disbursements; in Belgium, two per cent and in the United States, 2.5 per cent. In this country, however, the practice was *not* to allow a commission for advancing funds, and this practice dated possibly from the time of *Schuster v. Fletcher*.[14] **20.08**

When the York-Antwerp Rules came to be revised in 1924 a demand was made that the practice of foreign countries should be introduced and embodied in the Rules.

York-Antwerp Rules 1924

Rule XXI, Provisions of Funds

> A commission of 2 per cent, on general average disbursements (...[15]) shall be allowed in general average, but when the funds are not provided by any of the contributing interests, the necessary cost of obtaining the funds required by means of a bottomry bond or otherwise, or the loss sustained by owners of goods sold for the purpose, shall be allowed in general average.
>
> The cost of insuring money advanced to pay for general average disbursements shall also be allowed in general average.[16]

York-Antwerp Rules 1950 **20.09**

A period of cheap money prevailed at the time when the 1924 Rules were revised, and various suggestions were put forward to limit the amount charged to general average for advancing commission. One suggestion was to reduce the rate to one per cent while another was that commission should be allowed only on those disbursements incurred (which presumably meant paid) before the end of the voyage. In somewhat haphazard fashion it was agreed to adopt the proposal of the United States sub-committee to retain the rate of commission and the

[13] See also para. 20.01, *ante*.

[14] (1878) 3 Q.B.D. 418.

[15] Additional wording placed here in 1950.

[16] See also Rules of Practice of the Association of Average Adjusters:

No. A2. "That, in practice, interest and commission for advancing funds are only allowable in average when, proper and necessary steps having been taken to make a collection on account, an out-of-pocket expense for interest and/or commission for advancing funds is reasonably incurred."

No. A3. "That, in practice, neither commission (excepting bank commission) nor any charge by way of agency or remuneration for trouble is allowed to the shipowner in average, except in respect of services rendered on behalf of cargo when such services are not involved in the contract of affreightment."

existing wording of the Rule, but in the space above (...) to add wording to exclude commission on wages and maintenance of master, officers and crew (regarded as the enhancement of ordinary voyage expenses, and not as extraordinary expenses for this purpose) and on fuel and stores not replaced during the voyage.

York-Antwerp Rules 1974

No change.

20.10 York-Antwerp Rules 1994

An early proposal that *all* general average disbursements should attract the two per cent commission was regarded by the insurance community as another example of the unwanted expansion of the general average system, and was accordingly withdrawn at the Sydney Conference. Other proposals which did succeed were essentially "modernising" drafting refinements: reference to the ancient system of raising funds by means of a bottomry bond was deleted, as also were the words "*money advanced to pay for*" in the final paragraph.

Rule XX

Provision of Funds

A commission of 2 per cent. on general average disbursements, other than the wages and maintenance of master, officers and crew and fuel and stores not replaced during the voyage, shall be allowed in general average.

The capital loss sustained by the owners of goods sold for the purpose of raising funds to defray general average disbursements shall be allowed in general average.

The cost of insuring general average disbursements shall also be admitted in general average.

Construction

First Paragraph

20.11 **"commission"** The two per cent commission allowed by this Rule is a "flat" allowance credited to those (whether parties to the adventure, their insurers or the deposit funds) who advance funds to settle accounts which are allowable as general average. It is not in the nature of a rate of interest, that is, two per cent is earned on payment and regardless of the length of time between disbursement of the funds by the original payor and reimbursement to him by other parties to the adventure or by his own underwriters. So much is clear from the wording of the Rule, particularly if it is compared with Rule XXI.

The two per cent commission referred to in the previous paragraph is the modern equivalent of the variable premium payable on arrival at destination to the lender of money obtained abroad by means of a bottomry bond, all reference to which was deleted when Rule XX was amended in 1994. As far as is known, money is no longer raised on the security of a bottomry bond,[17] but in the event of this form of finance being used, the premium on that part of the borrowed funds used to settle general average disbursements at the port of refuge would still be allowed as general average. Although the money would have been raised on the security of the ship and freight (and, occasionally, the cargo), in practice the money would not be regarded as being provided by the interests whose property was pledged, thereby entitling them, in addition, to the flat two per cent commission. Nor would two per cent commission be allowed to the parties on repayment of the bottomry loan.

"general average disbursements," The commission is allowed on all general average disbursements other than "the wages and maintenance of master, officers and crew and fuel and stores not replaced during the voyage" and certain other exceptions discussed below. **20.12**

The term "general average disbursements" is not synonymous with "general average expenditure", which is of much more limited application:[18] General average disbursements embrace any general average sacrifice or expenditure which, at the time of issuing the adjustment, is represented by an actual outlay of cash. Thus, if cargo damaged by a general average sacrifice is accepted by the consignee with a percentage allowance for depreciation, no commission is allowed; but if that same damage is repaired by the outlay of cash on reconditioning, the expense incurred would attract a two per cent commission. The position is the same with general average damage to ship: if repaired, two per cent commission is allowed on the cost of repairs charged to general average, but if unrepaired, no commission is payable.

Salvage awards payable under the terms of a contract such as Lloyd's Standard Form of Salvage Agreement[19] were in practice treated as general average disbursements attracting two per cent commission provided that the services were engaged for the purpose of saving a common adventure. **20.13**

[17] See para. 20.04, *ante*.
[18] See para. 50.03, *post*.
[19] See para. 80.07, *post*.

This is now confirmed by Rule VI which extends to salvage whether under contract or otherwise.

It has been suggested that the fact that an account has not been paid, that is, disbursement has not yet been made by the date of the adjustment, is no reason for disallowing the commission if a liability has been incurred which will in due course have to be discharged, but that there was no settled practice in this respect.

If it be recognised that the commission is earned only by advancing funds, and not by a mere guarantee to pay, it will be readily understood that commission cannot be charged on items unpaid at the date of the adjustment. Those outstanding accounts may well be settled from general average contributions or other payments made by other parties.

20.14 **"other than the wages and maintenance[20] of master, officers and crew..."** Commission is not allowed on wages and maintenance of master, officers and crew for the reason explained in paragraph 20.09, above, and this regardless of whether the crew are "replaced during the voyage". (These particular words govern only "fuel and stores".)

Although it might be contended that as commission is not allowable on wages, etc., of crew, neither should it be allowed on other expenses charged to general average on a substituted expense basis and in lieu of wages, etc., this is not the practice. An exclusion, such as this, may not be construed more widely than its actual wording, and commission is allowed on the substituted expenses.

"... and fuel and stores not replaced during the voyage," Commission is allowed on fuel and stores only when they are replaced during the voyage. The position is the same with time-chartered vessels, but the commission is credited to the time-charterer only if he does not debit the shipowner with the cost of the bunkers consumed whilst off-hire (for example during a general average deviation and detention). If, as is customary, the ship owner is debited with the cost of bunkers consumed during an off-hire period, the commission (if any) is credited to the shipowner.

Second Paragraph

20.15 **"The capital loss sustained by the owner of goods sold for the purpose of raising funds to defray general average disbursements shall be allowed in general average."** All reference to the archaic method of raising funds by means of a bottomry bond was deleted from the Rule in 1994, yet mention of the even less likely sale of cargo for the same purpose was surprisingly retained! As recorded more fully in paragraphs 20.02 to

[20] For definitions of the words "wages" and "maintenance" see paras. 11.36 and 11.06, *ante*.

20.06, above, it is only as an absolutely last resort, when all other means of raising funds have failed (including the prior requirement to hypothecate the ship and freight, and then the cargo itself), that the master is empowered to sell the cargo. Even then it is a legal requirement that he must first communicate with the owners of the cargo, unless it is impossible to do so.

In the absence of more specific conditions then imposed by the forced seller, the loss to be allowed in general average in terms of the Rule is limited to the capital loss sustained by the owner of the goods, (that is based essentially on bare *c.i.f.* invoice values), and only in so far as the funds realised are used to settle general average disbursements. As the funds realised by sale are the absolute property of the owner of the goods, he is of course entitled to two per cent commission on those funds used to settle general average disbursements.

Third Paragraph

"The cost of insuring general average disbursements shall also be allowed **20.16**
in general average." It is an almost universal practice to effect insurance on money advanced for general average disbursements, for if a total loss of ship and cargo should occur after the making of general average disbursements, or should the ship or cargo be reduced in value by a subsequent accident so as to be worth less than the amount of general average expenses, it would be impossible in practice to recover the whole of the general average from the interests concerned. It has certainly been the practice in this country, and probably in all others, to allow the cost of such insurance in general average, and the rule in this respect, therefore, embodies a custom prevalent throughout the world.

The cost of insurance is only allowable when the general average disbursements have been financed by a contributing interest. There is no reason for the borrowers to insure money raised on bottomry or *respondentia* as the *loan* is not repayable unless the property pledged arrives safely at destination.(The lender customarily insures his advance and charges the premium in his own bottomry premium.)

The proceeds of cargo sold for the purpose of raising funds should be insured, however, as these proceeds are repayable regardless of the safe arrival at destination of the ship and other cargo.

The Insurance of General Average Disbursements

General average expenses incurred at a port of refuge are customarily **20.17**
financed by the shipowner, and in order that he may recover the proportion of those expenses attaching to the cargo interests, the shipowner is granted a lien on and may hold the cargo until satisfactory

security has been provided by them to meet their proper contribution. However, that lien can be exercised only on arrival *at destination*, and if the ship and cargo were to become a total loss between the port of refuge and the final destination, the shipowner will be unable to recover any part of his general average expenditure from the cargo interests.

A graphic example occurred in the case of *Chellew v. Royal Commission on the Sugar Supply*[21] where, during the course of a voyage from Cuba to Europe, the *Penlee* encountered a hurricane and sustained damage which obliged her to put into Horta as a general average act. Upon completion of the repairs, the vessel resumed her voyage from Horta, but a few days later she and her cargo of sugar were totally destroyed by fire. The shipowners sought to recover from the cargo interests their proportion of the general average expenses incurred at Horta, but this claim was denied. In the course of his judgment in the Court of Appeal, Scrutton L.J. said:

> "The person incurring the expenditure runs a risk of loss which he can cover by insurance of his interest in the arrival of the interests on which he has a lien for contribution to his expenditure."

(Such an insurable interest in the general average expenses payable by cargo interests had previously been confirmed in 1849 by Lord Denman, C.J. in *Briggs v. The Merchant Traders' Ship Loan and Assurance Association*.[22]

20.18 In point of fact, and assuming the ship to be already fully insured with conditions such as the Institute Time Clauses, Hulls, if the ship and cargo were totally lost between the port of refuge and the destination as the result of some new accident, the shipowner would be entitled on the principle of "successive losses"[23] to recover from his hull insurers the *whole* of the general average expenses already incurred by him, *plus* the subsequent total loss. However, as general average has a prior existence independent from insurance, it is probably reasonable that he who advances general average expenses on behalf of other parties should insure against the possibility of failing to recover the proportion of those expenses attaching to the other parties. (See also the only other recorded English legal decision concerning the insurance of average disbursements, *Green Star Shipping Co. Ltd v. London Assurance*,[24] where only the proportion of general average expenses attaching to the cargo had been insured).

[21] [1922] 1 K.B. 12; 91 L.J.K.B. 58; 126 L.T. 103; 27 Com.Cas. 1; 37 T.L.R. 903; 15 Asp.M.L.C. 393; 8 Ll.L.R. 305.

[22] (1849) 13 Q.B. 167; 18 L.J.Q.B. 178; 13 Jur 787; 78 R.R. 341.

[23] Marine Insurance Act 1906, s. 77. (The same principle attaches, of course, to insurances on cargo, and would protect the cargo interests if they had advanced general average expenditure or had provided separate security to salvors and paid their own proportion of any salvage award.)

[24] [1933] 1 K.B. 378; 145 L.T. 180; 36 ComCas.258; 43 Ll.L.R. 523; 39 Ll.L.R. 213.

In current practice, it is generally found that the *full* general average expenses are insured, and not merely the proportion of those expenses attaching to the cargo. The justification for this, one must suppose, is that no-one likes to see an expenditure of money rendered worthless and abortive by a subsequent total loss of the property the expenditure was designed to save.

It is also generally found in current practice that the extent of the insurance cover is considerably increased in that the general average disbursements are covered not only against the risk of total loss, but also against the risks of any loss or damage to the ship, cargo or freight, etc., which *reduces* its value during the remainder of the voyage. The justification for such an extended insurance is that it helps to preserve the original anticipated percentage of general average contribution. Thus, if the anticipated contributory values were: **20.19**

SHIP	500,000
CARGO	500,000
	1,000,000

and the general average expenses 100,000, the contribution would be 10 per cent. However, if for instance the ship were to strike a quaywall when arriving at destination and sustain damage costing 200,000 to repair, the contributory values would be reduced to:

SHIP	300,000
CARGO	500,000
	800,000

and the general average of 100,000 would now represent 12.5 per cent of the contributory values. Instead of paying 10 per cent × 500,000 = 50,000, cargo interests would be called upon to pay 12.5 per cent = 62,500.

Such an increase would be avoided if the average disbursement of 100,000 were insured on "full" conditions.[25] The insurance policy would cover the proportion of general average attaching to the reduction in the value of the property (200,000) and—effectively—constitute another contributing interest. The general average might now be considered to be apportioned as follows: **20.20**

SHIP	300,000	pays	30,000
POLICY	200,000	pays	20,000
CARGO	500,000	pays	50,000
	1,000,000	pays	100,000

[25] In May 1987 two new sets of Average Disbursement Clauses agreed by the Association of Average Adjusters and the Institute of London Underwriters were issued. The (A) set is on "full" conditions and effectively covers that proportion of the general average expenses insured attaching to *any* reduction in the value of the contributing interests. The (B) set is on "limited" conditions and a claim can arise only when the values of the property at destination are less than the amount of the disbursements insured.

and it will be noted that the general average contribution attaching to the cargo interests returns to the originally expected figure of 50,000.

20.21 In practice, the indemnity provided by the "full" conditions is usually rather less complete than as set out in the simple example above, for it is not the *total* general average that is insured, but only those expenses and losses which are represented by an outlay of *money* at the port of refuge and/or short of destination. Thus, claims allowable in general average for, for example jettison or other sacrifice of cargo, or for repairs to general average damage to the ship carried out at destination or subsequently, do not represent any outlay of money that needs protecting during the remainder of the voyage, and they are accordingly not declared on the insurance. (Such claims for jettison of cargo, or for general average repairs to ship at destination, are only *contingent* claims in general average, allowable only if some part of the property survives and there is a successful conclusion of the adventure).[26]

[26] For a fuller discussion on the subject of the Insurance of Average Disbursements (also the Insurance of Other Subsidiary Interests following a Casualty), see the booklet by D.J. Wilson published by the Association of Average Adjusters in 1988.

Rule XXI

Interest on Losses Made Good in General Average

English Law and Practice

With the almost universal adoption in contracts of affreightment of the York-Antwerp Rules, very few general average adjustments are prepared today which are subject only to English law.[1] In the few such adjustments seen by the present editors, commission for advancing funds and interest on outlays and losses have never been encountered, and this practice probably derives from the Rule of Practice A2 of the Association of Average Adjusters: **21.01**

Interest and Commission for Advancing Funds

> "That, in practice, interest and commission for advancing funds are only allowable in average when, proper and necessary steps have been taken to make a collection on account, an out-of-pocket expense for interest and/or commission for advancing funds is reasonably incurred."

Although this Rule[2] does not deny that commission and interest may be allowable, it does appear to limit any allowance to an actual out-of-pocket expense paid to a bank or some other financier in respect of a specific advance related exclusively to the average expenses in question, and then only if steps have been taken to obtain collections on account from, presumably, hull underwriters and/or cargo interests.

The Rule seems to be unduly narrow in its outlook and disregards the fact that money, whether provided by one of the parties to the adventure, or by others, is often a scarce and expensive commodity and its use should be paid for. The present editors prefer the views of Lowndes himself in: **21.02**

[1] In *E. B. Aaby's Rederi A/S v. Union of India* [1974] 3 W.L.R. 269, H.L., commission and interest were the only points of distinction between a claim for general average contribution which was, and one which was not, based on the York-Antwerp Rules.

[2] For a history of this Rule, interested readers are referred to the annual reports of the Association of Average Adjusters: 1878, pp. 18 *et seq.*; 1879, pp. 30 *et seq.*; 1880, pp. 28 *et seq.*; 1905, pp. 56 *et seq.*; 1906, pp. 21 *et seq.*; 1907, pp. 46 *et seq.*

First to third editions:

"If the disbursements have been in the first instance paid by the shipowner, and cannot be refunded to him until after some lapse of time, is the owner entitled to charge interest on his outlay? Custom, founded probably on obsolete notions about usury, is against this: (*a*) but it may be doubted whether such a custom, which is plainly opposed to the true principle of general average, would be held binding in a Court of Law. The person who makes the advance for the sake of all ought certainly to be compensated for the use of his money. In the United States[3] more rational practice prevails.

(*a*) This custom is subject to one exception. If the shipowner advances money which he is not bound to advance, he may charge interest like any one else. He is not bound to pay salvage on cargo; the cargo being directly liable to the salvor. He is not bound to remit money to a foreign port, by sending out a letter of credit, or cash, in anticipation of the completion of the accounts; although he would be bound to accept the master's draft on him, when the accounts are closed. In many cases a bottomry premium is saved by such remittance, and it is then customary to allow interest or a commission to the owner. This whole subject, however, is at present in an unsatisfactory condition."

Fourth to seventh editions:

"The expenses of doing this, including a rate of interest just sufficient to place all parties in a position of ultimate equality, so that no one should either wish, or shun, to advance more than his share, should be charged as a pendant to the capital expenditure itself."

21.03 Or the opinion of T. E. Scrutton, K.C. and J. A. Hamilton, K.C. given in about 1904:

"1. We are of opinion that, where a shipowner makes disbursements and finds funds for general average expenditure ..., his outlay should ... be treated as a sacrifice of the use of money, which he would otherwise have employed profitably elsewhere, and in principle, such sacrifice should be made good by an allowance of interest in general average. We know of no rule which requires a shipowner to possess and furnish gratuitously the funds required at a port of refuge, and the cases upon a master's authority to raise money on bottomry indicate the contrary.

2. We do not think that interest can be allowed to a consignee of goods sacrificed until after the arrival of the ship at the port of delivery, because in his case the goods, while on the voyage, are not interest bearing to him, and he makes no sacrifice of the employment of his money elsewhere during that time.

3. After the vessel's arrival at its port of destination, and pending the adjustment and collection of the contribution, we think that, in principle, interest

[3] A commission of $2\frac{1}{2}$ per cent is in practice allowed in the U.S., together with interest at the legal rate prevailing at the place of adjustment: *Simms v. Willing* 8 Serg. & R. 103 (1822). Commission is also allowed for collecting and settling the general average: *Barnard v. Adams* (1850) 10 How. 270; *Sturgess v. Cary* (1854) 2 Curt. 59. U.S. Interest is also allowed beyond the date of issuing any general average statement up to the estimated date when settlement will be effected (*e.g.* two or three months).

may be allowed both to shipowner and cargo owner, though the point is more doubtful than the two previous ones. It may be said that there is no element of maritime sacrifice in waiting till a complicated adjustment can be completed, but there seems nothing unbusinesslike in interest up to the time when the amount of reimbursement is first determined in fact, and not merely determinable in theory, being allowed to a co-adventurer, who has laid out his money for the common good, and the contrary would work hardship. The shipowner, at any rate, should, it seems, have interest on his outlays till the date of the average statement, when contributions first become ascertained debts, if not till actual payment. Similarly, the cargo owner should have interest on the arrived value of goods sacrificed to the same date, though possibly it should not commence till such a time has elapsed after arrival as would be requisite, in ordinary course, to sell and obtain payment for the goods. To the shipowner, in respect of materials sacrificed and damage done to the ship for general average purposes, interest should not begin to run till the corresponding replacements or repairs have been paid for."

The views quoted above were expressed in the context of the common law rule which in general excluded any award of interest by way of damages or compensation for late payment.[4] That rule has been affirmed by the House of Lords,[5] but there are two important exceptions to it: **21.04**

(1) Under a long-standing practice of the Admiralty Court, interest was awarded in damage actions, and it has recently been recognised[6] that this power extends to all claims within the Admiralty jurisdiction of the High Court, which include claims for general average contribution.
(2) Since 1934 there has existed a statutory power which, in its current form[7] entitles the court or arbitrator to award interest on any sums claimed in the proceedings from the date when the cause of action arose until the day of judgment, or of payment if earlier,[8] at such rate as the tribunal thinks fit.

By virtue of these powers, which are almost invariably exercised in favour of the claimant,[9] the court or arbitrator would be entitled to award interest from the date of the sacrifice or expenditure until judgment for, or earlier payment of, the amount stated in the adjustment. However, one important limitation is that no interest can be awarded in any

[4] *London Chatham & Dover Railway Co. v. South Eastern Railway Co.* [1893] A.C. 429.
[5] *President of India v. La Pintada Cia.* [1975] A.C. 104.
[6] *Ibid.* at 121. See also *The Aldora* [1975] Q.B. 748.
[7] Supreme Court Act 1981, s. 35A, County Courts Act 1984, s. 69.
[8] The court or arbitrator cannot award interest for any period after the judgment or award until payment, but interest runs automatically on a judgment or award at a rate fixed by Statutory Instrument (since 1993 eight per cent). Equally there is no power to award interest for any period during which interest already runs.
[9] The award of interest is made simply on the basis that the successful claimant has been out of pocket. Interest is normally refused only on some exceptional ground, such as culpable delay by the claimant which has caused prejudice to the defendant.

proceedings on principal sums paid before the proceedings were commenced.[10]

If a person from whom contribution is due delays in making payment but nevertheless pays before proceedings against him are commenced, he will escape liability for interest, except such as may properly be awarded against him under the principles mentioned in paragraph 21.02, above, or under Rule XXI of York-Antwerp Rules.

Historical Development and Practice of Rule XXI

21.05 *York-Antwerp Rules 1924*

It is one of the fundamental principles of general average that it should be financially immaterial to the parties to the adventure, upon adjustment, whose property or purse was selected to suffer for the general benefit. It is obvious, therefore, that unless interest be allowed, the full extent of the loss suffered by the owner of property sacrificed or by the disburser of general average expenditure is not made good to him. The owner of goods jettisoned, for example, is not put on an equality with the shipowner or the other cargo owners if the value of the jettisoned cargo is alone made good to him in the adjustment, settlement under which may take place years after the arrival of the vessel. The shipowner who has made general average disbursements is not fully compensated if, having spent the money long before he receives contributions from the other interests, he only receives in general average the bare expenditure. In both these instances, selected as typical, the allowance of interest is essential to achieve a true equality of sacrifice between the parties.

21.06 It had long been the practice in many countries to allow interest on general average sacrifices and expenditures, but the custom in this country was otherwise.[11] To remedy this obvious and unnecessary discrepancy a new York-Antwerp Rule, based on a draft[12] proposed by the Association of Average Adjusters, was introduced at the Stockholm Conference in 1924:

[10] *See President of India v. La Pintada Cia.* (*supra*) where the limitations of the statutory power were criticised by Lords Scarman and Roskill. For the limits on the Admiralty jurisdiction to award interest see at 119–121, *per* Lord Brandon.

[11] See Rule of Practice A2 quoted, in para. 21.01, *ante*.

[12] The "Draft International Code for General Average" intended for discussion by the International Law Association at a meeting which would have been held at The Hague in September 1914 also included a proposal that: "Interest at the current rate shall be paid on all loss, damage or expense from the time of accrual or date of payment to the date of adjustment."

Rule XXII. Interest on Losses made good in General Average

> "Interest shall be allowed on expenditure, sacrifices and allowances charged to general average at the legal rate per annum prevailing at the final port of destination at which the adventure ends, or where there is no recognised legal rate, at the rate of 5 per cent, per annum, until the date of the general average statement, due allowance being made for any interim reimbursement from the contributory interests or from the general average deposit fund."

The reported discussion shows that the delegates would have preferred a standard rate of interest to the "legal" rate proposed, but, the discussion turning on whether the standard rate should be five or six per cent, the matter was resolved by the simpler expedient of passing the Rule in its proposed form.

York-Antwerp Rules 1950 **21.07**

The 1950 Rule reproduced Rule XXII of the 1924 Rules with the omission of the words "at the legal rate per annum prevailing at the final port of destination, or where there is no recognised legal rate ...," thus providing for a uniform rate of five per cent irrespective of whether or not there can be said to be some different legal rate of interest at the final port of destination. The amendment gave effect to a resolution adopted by the International Law Association at its Conference in Brussels in September, 1948. The reason for the resolution was that interested parties, in particular underwriters, took the view that "legal rates" of up to eight per cent or even 10 per cent which prevailed in some parts of the world were exorbitant in light of the cheap money policies of that year.

It was further shown that there was no "recognised legal rate" in England, nor in the majority of the main importing countries, and that profits (or losses) not warranted by the reason behind the Rule were being made. An example quoted was of a British ship bound for "Ruritania", where the legal rate of interest might be 10 per cent per annum. Although the owner might (at that time) be able to finance his general average disbursements for five per cent, he would nevertheless receive credit in accordance with the Rule at 10 per cent.

The reporting Committee unhesitatingly expressed the view that no case could be made out for retaining in the Rule the reference to legal rate of interest at the port of destination, and that the fixing of a definite rate of interest to be applied in all cases would more accurately give effect to the principles underlying the concept of general average.

York-Antwerp Rules 1974 **21.08**

The rate of interest was increased from five to seven per cent. As had been pointed out by the British Maritime Law Association, any arbitrarily fixed rate of interest will sometimes be too high, and sometimes too low.

At the time of the Hamburg Conference in 1974, world interest rates generally exceeded seven per cent; they have since been very much higher, subsiding from their peaks in say 1982/83, but except in countries such as Japan and Switzerland with very strong currencies, seldom below the regulation seven per cent.

21.09 York-Antwerp Rules 1994

The provisions of this Rule aroused a fair measure of interest and discussion for the revisions which took place in 1994, but the eventual changes were small: (1) the rate of interest to be allowed on losses made good in general average would continue after 1994 at the same existing rate of seven per cent per annum, but (2) the period during which interest would be earned would be extended by three months, to run from the date of issue of the general average adjustment. The reason for this latter amendment is set out in the commentary in paragraph 21.11, below.

Other proposals for the Rule were designed to resolve the complex problems associated with rates of exchange and the currency of the adjustment, but these failed to secure any agreement, and the Rule therefore remains silent on the subject. The alternative proposals are discussed in the commentary in Section 6 at paragraphs 40.49 *et seq.*, below.

Rule XXI

Interest on Losses Made Good in General Average

Interest shall be allowed on expenditure, sacrifices and allowances in general average at the rate of 7 per cent per annum, until three months after the date of issue of the general average adjustment, due allowance being made for any payment on account by the contributory interests or from the general average deposit fund.

Construction

21.10 Although this Rule determines when the allowance of interest shall cease (three months after the date of issue of the general average adjustment), it does not state on what date interest begins to accrue. Resort can legitimately be had therefore to the object of the Rule which is to ensure full and fair compensation to any interest which has suffered in the common cause, and to the practice of average adjusters.

It is impossible to provide for every individual circumstance, but it is believed that the general practice is to commence the allowance of interest on:

(1) *General average expenditure* (or any sacrifice or allowance represented by an actual outlay of cash)—from the date of payment.
(2) *Cargo claims*—from the last day of discharge.

"expenditure, sacrifices and allowances" The word "allowances" occurs only in this Rule, and is more apt to describe the shipowner's right to contribution in respect of fuel and stores consumed [Rule XI(a) and (b)] and the cargo owner's right to contribution under Rule XX in respect of goods sold to raise funds than "expenditure" or "sacrifice". The three words between them cover all forms of claim in general average.

"until three months after the date of issue of the general average adjustment," Allowances for interest on losses made good in general average under the previous 1924, 1950, and 1974 Rules continued only until the date on which the average adjuster completed and issued his adjustment, and no interest accrued during the period thereafter and until settlement of the various contributions due. **21.11**

Perhaps until about the early 1970s, when money was "cheap", when general average deposits were more frequently provided as security, and when debit balances under the adjustment were settled far more promptly, no real injustice was caused to any of the parties to the adventure by this loss of interest during the period between the date of issuing the adjustment and settlement thereunder.

However, possibly due to the very high rates of interest prevailing in later years, there has been a very marked tendency on the part of many debtors under any general average adjustment to decline or delay payment of their contributions for as long as possible and for any excuse. This resulted in the creditors under the adjustment being kept out of their money for lengthy periods and *without compensating interest* during the delay, and was the reason for adopting the new wording, the meaning of which is self-explanatory.

The English statute and case law on the awarded of interest after the issue of the adjustment is referred to in paragraph 21.04, above. **21.12**

It is the practice of English courts and arbitrators, in the exercise of their statutory powers, to award interest at a commercial rate, which might well exceed the seven per cent allowed under the Rule. However, the creditor cannot take advantage of this possibly more favourable rate and claim statutory interest from the date of the sacrifice or expenditure, as the statutory power to award interest does not apply during a period in which the claimant has a contractual right to interest,[13] such as is conferred by Rule XXI. It follows that statutory interest can only be

[13] Supreme Court Act 1981, s. 35A(4); County Courts Act 1984, s. 69(4).

awarded from the date on which the interest ceases to accrue under Rule XXI. The fact that the right to interest under the Rule ceases after three months from the publication of the adjustment should not provide any reason for the court or arbitrator to refuse to exercise its discretion to award interest thereafter.

The statute does not sanction the awarding of interest upon interest, with the result that any interest to which the claimant had become entitled under this Rule would have to be left out of account in computing statutory interest.

21.13 **"due allowance being made for any payment on account..."** In practice[14] effect is given to this part of the Rule by crediting the contributory interests concerned with the full amount of interest allowable to them under the earlier words of the Rule, and then debiting them with interest on the amount of the payment on account for the period between such payment and three months after the date of the general average statement, and crediting a like amount to the source of the funds from which the payment on account was made, for example deposit fund or contributory interests (or their underwriters) as the case may be. The alternative—a straightforward reduction in the amount of interest credited to a party—might work an injustice, since the saving in interest would benefit the parties to the adventure in proportion to their liability in general average, whereas the funds which made the interim payment possible may have been provided by the parties in quite different proportions, or even by only one of the parties. The Rule makes no provision for interim reimbursement from other sources, for example as damages from a colliding vessel, and the treatment of interest in such a case is best explained by example.

A shipowner incurs general average expenditure of 150,000 consequent upon a collision for which the other vessel is two-thirds to blame. One year after the expenditure was incurred, a recovery is effected from the colliding vessel of:

$\frac{2}{3} \times 150,000$	100,000
Interest for 1 year @ 12 per cent	12,000
	112,000

and the general average adjustment is issued six months thereafter showing the following figures:

General average expenditure		150,000
Interest @ 7 per cent for 1 year on	150,000	10,500
Credit: Recovery	100,000	
and for 9[15] months on	50,000	2,625
	forward:	163,125

[14] The same practice prevails in the U.S.
[15] Six, plus three months after the adjustment.

	forward:	163,125
Credit: Recovery	100,000	(100,000)
Interest 1 year @ 12 per cent	12,000	(7,000)[16]
	112,000	
Net General Average		56,125

[16] General average cannot be credited with interest at a greater rate than is allowable under Rule XXI, *i.e.* seven per cent.

Rule XXII

Treatment of Cash Deposits

Note: The Collection of cash deposits forms but one small part of the overall general average security and enforcement system; for a complete survey, reference is requested to the chapter on Recovery of General Average at paragraphs 30.01 et seq., below.

Historical Development and Practice

22.01 *York-Antwerp Rules 1924*

Prior to 1924 there was considerable diversity of practice in the treatment of cash deposits collected from cargo interests, which was not always satisfactory to the depositors. In some countries the deposits were retained in the shipowners' own banking accounts, or in their businesses, and cases occurred of the deposits being lost if the shipowners became bankrupt before completion of the adjustment. For the greater protection of depositors and also in the interests of uniformity, the Association of Average Adjusters proposed a new Rule in accordance with the practice in this country and based to a large extent on the wording of the then current Lloyd's Average Bond,[1] a document itself designed to be fair to all parties.

Rule XXIII. Treatment of Cash Deposits

> "Where cash deposits have been collected in respect of cargo's liability for general average, salvage or special charges, such deposits shall be paid into a special account, earning interest where possible, in the joint names of two trustees (one to be nominated on behalf of the shipowner and the other on behalf of the depositors) in a bank to be approved by such trustees. The sum so deposited, together with accrued interest, if any, shall be held as security for and upon trust for payment to the parties entitled thereto of the general average, salvage or special charges payable by the cargo in respect to which the deposits have been collected. The trustees shall have power to make payments on account or refunds of deposits which may be certified to in writing by the average adjuster. Such deposits and payments or refunds shall be without prejudice to the ultimate liability of the parties."

[1] See App. 3, paras. 1101–1104 in the 10th ed. of this work. The present Lloyd's Average Bond (App. 4, para. 80.02, *post*, makes no reference to deposits).

York-Antwerp Rules 1950 **22.02**

Because it conflicted with the anti-trust laws in certain States, Rule XXIII of the York-Antwerp Rules 1924 was never acceptable in the United States, and contracts of affreightment were often worded: "General average to be adjusted in accordance with York-Antwerp Rules 1924, Rules 1/15 and 17/22 inclusive . . ." thereby excluding the application of this particular Rule. To overcome this objection the Rule was amended in 1950, all words being omitted from which it might be inferred that the deposit account was in the nature of a trust. The alteration did not affect the liability of the two representatives to deal with the deposits in accordance with their mandate, but, as noted below, it did alter the procedure to be adopted if they were in doubt concerning the rights of the parties to the deposit funds.

Another minor addition to the Rule was that deposits were to be paid *without any delay* into the special bank account, and Rule XXIII was renumbered XXII.

York-Antwerp Rules 1974

No change.

York-Antwerp Rules 1994

No change.

Rule XXII

Treatment of Cash Deposits

Where cash deposits have been collected in respect of cargo's liability for general average, salvage or special charges, such deposits shall be paid without any delay into a special account in the joint names of a representative nominated on behalf of the shipowner and a representative nominated on behalf of the depositors in a bank to be approved by both. The sum so deposited, together with accrued interest, if any, shall be held as security for payment to the parties entitled thereto of the general average, salvage or special charges payable by cargo in respect of which the deposits have been collected. Payments on account or refunds of deposits may be made if certified to in writing by the average adjuster. Such deposits and payments or refunds shall be without prejudice to the ultimate liability of the parties. **22.03**

Construction

22.04 This Rule is largely enabling in character. Thus, it does not direct that the cargo owner shall provide a deposit to secure the payment of cargo's liability in general average or for salvage or special charges. Whether the cargo owner can be compelled to pay such a deposit depends upon the law of the place where the cargo owner seeks to take delivery. In England, the shipowner can exercise his lien on the cargo until its owner either pays what is demanded as contribution or pays a deposit or otherwise provides reasonable security for payment of what may be due.[2] On the other hand, it does provide what shall be done with any deposits which are in fact paid, and ensures that the interests of the cargo owner are fully protected against the risk of misapplication by a financially embarrassed shipowner.

The representatives of the depositor and the shipowner are required by the Rule to approve a bank into which the deposit shall be paid. Unless they jointly instruct the bank otherwise or there is some requirement of local law to the contrary, the deposit will presumably be retained by the bank in the currency in which it is made.[3]

22.05 **"Where cash deposits have been collected ... in a bank to be approved by both."** The first sentence of the Rule is of a procedural nature only and self-explanatory; no analysis is thought to be necessary. Once the deposit has been paid to the carrier or to his agent, the carrier falls under the obligation imposed by the Rule to open the special account and to pay in the money, and is responsible if the money is lost before that time.

"The sum so deposited ... shall be held as security ..." It is perhaps worth stating that the principle security provided by the consignee in order to obtain delivery of his cargo and release from the shipowners'

[2] See paras. 30.02 *et seq., post*. An interesting case (*Francis H. Legget & Co. v. Italia America Shipping Corporation* (1926) A.M.C. 1670) arising out of a demand for a general average deposit in accordance with a special clause in the bill of lading was decided in the U.S. Circuit of Appeals. The clause referred to read as follows:

> "All consignees agree to deposit with the Shipowning Company or its Agency the amount requested by the said Company as a guarantee for the contribution which they may be called to pay in the Average Adjustment."

General average expenses were incurred on the voyage and upon arrival of the vessel at New York the ship's agents at that port demanded that a cash deposit should be made with them. The consignees refused to do this, but offered either to deposit cash with a New York bank as trustee or to provide a bond of any surety company which the ship's agents might choose to designate.

It was held that the clause in the bill of lading was unreasonable, and that the consignees were entitled to delivery of their goods in exchange for either a bond for a reasonable amount with satisfactory sureties or a cash deposit lodged with a trustee.

[3] In the U.S. it has been decided, under the 1924 Rule, that a shipowner need only account for the deposit in the currency in which it was collected: *The Motormar* (1954) A.M.C. 870.

lien is, in fact, the undertaking he gives when signing an average bond and agreeing "to pay the proper proportion of any salvage and/or general average ...". When a general average deposit is paid, the deposit is nominally only a collateral security to the principal undertaking in the average bond, to be cashed only if the consignee fails to honour any proper demand for the general average contribution (or a payment on account thereof, as also provided in the average bond). It is not an advance payment, as such, of the contribution ultimately found to be due.

In practical terms, this distinction may appear over-fine, but it could be important, for instance, if the trustees of the deposit funds chose to exchange the deposits[4] into some other currency without first seeking the consent of the depositors. (Compare Examples 1 and 2 in paragraph 22.09, below.)

"Payments on account or refunds of deposits may be made if certified to in writing by the average adjuster." The above wording is emphatic and unequivocal and appears almost to place the ordering and control of the deposit funds in the hands of the average adjuster, rather than the "trustees".[5] Such confidence in the adjuster may well be merited and justified, but in these litigious times it will be a wise precaution—if cargo deposit funds are to be paid to the shipowner—for the average adjuster and/or the representative nominated on behalf of the depositors (cargo) to consult first with some of the major cargo interests to check that they have no sound reason to dispute liability for the general average. 22.06

Payments on account from the deposit funds to those cargo interests whose property has been sacrificed, or refunds of deposits where (1) the original estimates on which the deposits were based subsequently prove to be excessive, or (2) a deposit was taken when general average damage to that cargo will make it a creditor of the general average,[6] can safely be left to the discretion of the adjusters.

This Rule and Rule E contain the only provisions in the York-Antwerp Rules which refer to *the average adjuster* and authorise him to make certain decisions which are binding on the parties. The question what is meant by *the average adjuster* in this context is considered in paragraphs E.14 and 15, above.

[4] In the German case of *Worms and Co. v. Deutsche Levante Linie* (1924) the Supreme Court confirmed the decision of two lower courts that a deposit paid in Rumanian Lei should be returned to the depositors for its full amount, less the general average contribution due in German Marks (a depreciated currency).

[5] The pre-1977 form of Lloyd's Average Bond on which Rule XXII was based used to provide:

> "AND IT IS HEREBY DECLARED AND AGREED than any payment ... on account which shall be made by the Trustees ... in pursuance of any Certificate ... given by the said Adjusters ... shall discharge such Trustees from all liability in respect of the amounts so paid and it shall not be necessary for them to inquire into the correctness of the Statement or Certificate."

[6] *The Norway* (1865) Br. & L. 404 at 411, P.C.

22.07 **"Such deposits and payments or refunds shall be without prejudice to the ultimate liability of the parties."** The payment of a general average deposit by a cargo owner or insurer is made simply to obtain the release of the cargo from the shipowners' lien.[7] The above words clearly indicate that the payment of the deposit can in no way be construed as an admission by the depositor that a general average situation exists, or prevent him—at any later stage—from challenging any of the allowances made by the adjuster in the general average adjustment, or challenging liability (wholly or in part) if he can demonstrate that "*the event which gave rise to the sacrifice or expenditure may have been due to the fault of one of the parties to the adventure.*" (Rule D).

A similar situation exists if a refund of part or the whole of a deposit is refunded to the depositor; this cannot be construed as an admission by the shipowner that a general average situation did not exist.[8]

Nor is the position altered if the depositor permits payments to be made ex the deposit, either to settle his alleged proportion of any salvage award, or to make a payment on account to other parties to the adventure who have financed large average expenditures or sustained large sacrifices. However, problems of some financial consequence might arise if, for instance, payments from the deposit funds were made without seeking the prior approval of some of the major depositors when the deposits are in one currency, but the liability is in another, and exchange rates have moved. The situation is best explained by example, and for this purpose the same currencies and rates of exchange are adopted as elsewhere[9] when dealing with problems of rates of exchange.

Examples

22.08 *Common Facts.* An American shipowner carrying a Japanese cargo incurs salvage services and port of refuge expenses in Yen, which he settles in his own operating currency of U.S. Dollars @ $1.00 = Y 250.

Provisional estimates of the total general average and contributory values suggest a contribution in the region of seven or eight per cent of

[7] The pre-1977 form of Lloyd's Average Bond on which Rule XXII was based used to provide:

> "PROVIDED ALWAYS that the deposits ... shall be treated as payments made without prejudice and without admitting liability in respect of the said alleged salvage and/or general average ... and as though the same had been made by the Depositors respectively for the purpose only of obtaining delivery of their goods..."

[8] The pre-1977 form of Lloyd's Average Bond on which Rule XXII was based used to provide:

> "... and in like manner all amounts returned by the Trustees to the Depositors shall be received by the latter respectively without prejudice to any claim which the Master or Owner of the said Ship may have against them respectively."

[9] See paras. 40.02 and 40.33 *et seq., post.*

the contributory values, and general average, deposits at the rate of 10 per cent are required.

Japanese Consignee "A", with cargo worth Y 25,000,000 (@ 250 = $100,000), is required to pay a 10 per cent deposit of . . . . Y 2,500,000.

The general average adjustment is shown in the shipowners' operating currency of U.S. Dollars and the final contribution is eight per cent. Consignee "A" is therefore called upon to pay . . . . $ 8,000

The rate of exchange ruling at the time of the adjustment and settlement is . . . . $ 1.00 = Y 125

Example 1—Deposit Retained in **Yen.** **22.09**

		Debit		Credit
Consignee "A"—	Wants his Deposit			Y 2,500,000
	Pays General Average	$ 8,000		
		@ 125	=	1,000,000
	Net: HE RECEIVES			Y 1,500,000

Example 2—Deposit Exchanged into **Dollars.**
(@ 250 = $ 10,000)

		Debit		Credit
Consignee "A"—	Wants his Deposit			$ 10,000
	Pays General Average	$ 8,000		8,000
	Net: HE RECEIVES			$ 2,000
		@ 125	=	Y 250,000

Note: On the assumption that the deposit is merely security for payment of a future liability, it is submitted that the holders of the deposit funds have no right to transfer those deposits into any other currency—even the currency of the liability—except with the prior permission of the depositors, or if the bill of lading, contract of affreightment, or average bond expressly permits it.[10] The fact that the deposit may be in a "weak" currency does not alter the position, even if it should encourage the

[10] The concluding part of a common American bill of lading clause (the first part is quoted in para. 40.15, *post* reads as follows:

> "Such cash deposit as the Carrier or his agents may deem sufficient as additional security for the contribution of the goods and for any salvage and special charges thereon, shall, if required, be made by the goods, shippers, consignees, or owners of the goods to the Carrier before delivery. Such deposit shall, at the option of the Carrier, be payable in United States money, and may be remitted to the adjuster. When so remitted the deposit shall be held in a special account at the place of adjustment in the name of the adjuster pending settlement of the General Average and refunds or credit balances, if any, shall be paid in United States money."

holders of the deposit funds to seek the necessary permission to make the exchange.

Accordingly, it is submitted that unless Consignee "A" gave consent to the exchange of his deposit into U.S. Dollars, under Example 2 he has the right to sue for the Y 1,250,000 lost to him by the exchange.

22.10 *Example 3*—Deposit Retained in **Yen.**
—Payment on Account taken of \$ 5,000 @ 200 = Y 1,000,000

	Debit		*Credit*
Consignee "A"—Wants his Deposit			Y 2,500,000
Liable for General Average	\$ 8,000		
Less: Payment on Account	5,000	=	1,000,000
			Y 1,500,000
Balance to Pay	\$ 3,000		
	@ 125	=	375,000
Net: HE RECEIVES			Y 1,125,000

Note: Unless Consignee "A" gave consent to the payment on account taken from his deposit, it is presumably possible for him to base a case for a refund of Y 1,500,000 (as in Example 1) on the grounds that his *ultimate liability* for general average is \$ 8,000 and, in terms of Rule XXII, any "*payments* (on account) ... *shall be without prejudice to the ultimate liability*." It is submitted[11] that this is not correct in practice (particularly when the deposit is being used to finance the Consignee's own proportion of a salvage award), and that *ultimate liability* refers to an overall liability to contribute to general average, rather than for a precise sum, but the point is of sufficient importance to make the strong recommendation that a clause dealing with matters of rates of exchange in general average should be incorporated in every bill of lading, contract of affreightment, or the average agreement itself. Failing this, the prior consent of at least some of the major cargo interests will always need to be obtained before any exchange, or use, can be made of deposits funds.

[11] For the sake of completeness, reference might be made to the case of *Noreuro Traders Ltd v. E. Hardy & Co.* (1923) 16 Ll.L.Rep. 319, where the rates of exchange applicable to payments on account was a problem touched upon, but that case is today of doubtful authority and, in any case, was not concerned with general average deposits.

SECTION 5

DETERMINING THE PLACE AND LAW OF THE ADJUSTMENT AND ENFORCING RIGHTS OF CONTRIBUTION

The topics discussed in this Section are (1) the place of and the law governing the adjustment, and (2) the means by which each interest may recover contribution to which it is entitled from the other parties to the adventure. 30.01

In truth the determination of the law governing the adjustment is concerned more with substantive rights in general average than with the means of enforcing those rights, and it could be said to merit a section of its own. The two topics are discussed in the same section partly for convenience, and partly because they are to some extent related. For example, the question of which courts or other tribunals have jurisdiction over disputes concerning general average may depend on the law governing the adjustment, and many general average clauses, the interpretation of which is discussed in this section, deal both with substantive rights and with the means of determining disputes and recovering payment.

1. THE PLACE AND LAW OF THE ADJUSTMENT

The Meaning of the "Place of Adjustment"

In many of the reported cases,[1] phrases such as "the place of adjustment" are used to describe the place where the adventure ends, that being the place: 30.02

(1) at which the interests involved in the common adventure are to be valued,
(2) whose law and practice is to be adopted in the adjustment,
(3) where rights of contribution are enforced, and
(4) whose courts would be resorted to in the event of a dispute.

The phrase "place of adjustment" also suggests that the adjustment itself should be prepared at the same place; but to this extent it is misleading, as demonstrated below.

[1] *E.g. Simonds v. White* (1824) 2 B. & C. 805, see para. 30.10, *post*.

In this part of Section 5 we deal first with the question where the adjustment should be prepared, and then with the more important question of the law governing the adjustment and the effect of contractual provisions regarding general average. The valuation of contributing interests is dealt with under Rule G and Rule XVII, and questions of enforcement under part 2 of this Section.

At what place should the adjustment be prepared?

30.03 The basic answer to this question is that there is no requirement imposed by law that the adjustment be prepared at any particular place. The York-Antwerp Rules are also silent on the question. Accordingly, so long as the correct governing law is selected in its preparation, it matters not where the adjustment is prepared nor where the adjuster carries on business, does his calculations or publishes the adjustment. As Blackburn J. is reported to have observed in *Mavro v. Ocean Marine Ins. Co.*[2]: "it does not matter who stated the average, whether a Turk or a Frenchman or the arbitrator in England."

30.04 The leading case on the subject is *Wavertree Sailing Ship v. Love*[3] in which it was contended that the shipowner was bound to have an average statement drawn up by an average adjuster at the port of discharge. The voyage had ended at Sydney, New South Wales, and the cargo interests had entered into a bond by which they undertook to furnish particulars of the value of their goods for the purpose of enabling general average to be "ascertained and adjusted in the usual manner". The shipowners employed a Liverpool firm of adjusters, there being no difference between the law of England and the law of New South Wales relating to general average. The Privy Council rejected the argument of the cargo interests that the shipowner was obliged to employ an adjuster at Sydney. Lord Herschell said:

> "The shipowner was not bound to employ a member of any particular class of persons or indeed to employ any one at all. He might if he pleased make out his own average statement, and he may do the same at the present time if so minded. If he engages the services of an average stater, it is merely as a matter of business convenience on his part. The average stater is not engaged, nor does he act on behalf of any of the other parties concerned, nor does his statement bind them."[4]

[2] (1875) 32 L.T. 743 at 745; 2 Asp. M.L.C. 590 at 592. The expression is omitted from the report in L.R. 10.C.P. 414.

[3] [1897] A.C. 373.

[4] *Ibid.* at 380. See also *The Santa Anna Maria* 49 Fed.Rep. 878 (1892); *The Alpine* 23 Fed.Rep. 815 (1884); *Chandris v. Argo Insurance Co. Ltd* [1963] 2 Lloyd's Rep. 65; *Union of India v. E.B. Aaby's Rederi A/S* [1974] 3 W.L.R. 269. It is, however, possible for all interests jointly to instruct an average adjuster and also to agree to be bound by his adjustments. In such a case the adjuster is in the position of an arbitrator and is not liable for negligence: *Tharsis Sulphur and Copper Co. Ltd v. Loftus* (1872) L.R. 8 C.P.1; and see now the Arbitration Act 1996, s. 29, for the immunity of an arbitrator, unless acting in bad faith. However, if the adjuster is to have the status of an arbitrator or quasi-arbitrator,

Lord Herschell then referred to the phrase "adjustment at the usual and proper place", which Abbot C.J. (Lord Tenterden) had used in *Simonds v. White*,[5] and continued:

> "In their Lordships' opinion, however, these words do not refer to the preparation of an average statement, but to the actual settlement and adjustment of the general average contributions. The preparation of a general average statement which does not bind the shipper is not 'the adjustment' of general average. In order to understand Lord Tenterden's language it is necessary to bear in mind what would happen if all parties stood on their rights. The shipowner would hold the goods until he obtained the general average contribution to which they were subject. If the owner of the goods disputed his claim, he would appeal to the tribunals of the country to obtain possession of them on payment of what was due. These tribunals would have to determine whether the owner of the goods was entitled to them and what payment he must make to release them. It would naturally follow, as Lord Tenterden said, that the parties must be understood as consenting to the adjustment according to the law there administered."[6]

As this decision showed, the importance of the place of adjustment is that it determines not where the adjuster's work is to be done, but what system of law and practice is to be applied and which tribunals should have jurisdiction over disputes relating to general average. Many firms of average adjusters have offices or correspondents in other countries, but there is no reason in law why an adjustment governed by the law of one country should not be prepared in another. **30.05**

Although the actual decision in the case would no doubt be followed today, Lord Herschell's observations on the meaning of the "adjustment" of general average must be treated with some caution, particularly in the interpretation of contractual provisions regarding the adjustment of general average, for the reasons given in paragraph 30.07, below.

Although Lord Herschell's judgment does not expressly address the question whether there is any legal obligation on the shipowner to produce any average statement at all, his language strongly suggests that he recognises such an obligation to exist, and *Crooks v. Allen*[7] also **30.06**

and thus enjoy the immunity, it is essential that "there should be a formulated dispute between at least two parties which his decision is required to resolve. It is not enough that the parties who may be affected by the decision have opposed interests—still less that the decision is on a matter which is not agreed between them.": see *Arenson v. Arenson* [1977] A.C. 405 at 424. See also *Sutcliffe v, Thackrah* [1974] A.C. 727. In some European countries the adjuster's position is equivalent to that of a judge of first instance, and his decision binding on the parties unless appealed against.

In the light of Lord Herschell's remarks it may be doubted whether the adjuster owes any duty of care except to the party who engages him. However, since adjustments prepared by professional adjusters are in practice normally accepted and acted upon by the other interests, and since there is a sufficiently close proximity between the adjuster and those other interests, he would probably be held to owe to them a duty of care, at any rate in relation to statements of fact contained in the adjustment, in cases where he is not acting as an arbitrator: *cf. Smith v. Eric S. Bush* [1990] 1 A.C. 831.

[5] (1824) 2 B. & C. 805 at 813. See para. 30.10, *post*.

[6] [1897] A.C. 373 at 381.

[7] (1879) 5 QBD 38; 49 L.J.Q.B. 201.

provides support for the view that a statement must be prepared.

In *Chandris v. Argo Insurance Co. Ltd*[8] it was held that a contract incorporating the York-Antwerp Rules 1924, by implication, provided that an average statement should be produced in support of a claim for general average contribution, but not that a professional average adjuster must be employed. This is, however, the usual practice,[9] and the Lloyd's form of Average Bond and Guarantee probably requires the employment of a professional adjuster.[10] Moreover in 1983 the Privy Council, without expressing any view on the matter, raised the question whether changes in mercantile practice which had taken place since the *Wavertree* case now made it necessary to imply a term into the contract of affreightment that the shipowner would procure an average adjustment and statement to be prepared by a professional average adjuster.[11] Changes to the York-Antwerp Rules in 1994 add force to the argument that, when the Rules apply, the implication of such a term may be necessary.[12]

30.07 A number of further observations should be made about the decision in *Wavertree Sailing Ship v. Love.*[13]

(1) Although Lord Herschell talks only in terms of a statement prepared by the shipowner or his agent not being binding on the other parties to the adventure, it is clear from *Marida v. Oswal Steel; The Bijela*[14] that an average statement is not, as such, binding even on the party who orders its preparation.
(2) Where the York-Antwerp Rules 1994 apply, Rule E stipulates that estimates of allowances and contributory values made by the average adjuster may in some circumstances be binding on the parties, and thus provides a limited exception to the rule that the statement is not binding.
(3) The case illustrates the ambiguity in the word "adjustment". As used by Lord Herschell in the passage quoted above it means the determination, in a manner binding on the parties, of rights and liabilities in general average. Technically that is the correct meaning of the word. On the other hand, the word is frequently used to

[8] [1963] 2 Lloyd's Rep. 65.
[9] *Ibid.* at 76.
[10] See para. 30.22, *post.*
[11] *Castle Insurance Co. v. Hong Kong Islands Shipping Co.* [1984] A.C. 226 at 237.
[12] *I.e.* the provisions added to Rule E in 1994: see para. E.14, *ante.*
[13] [1897] A.C. 373.
[14] [1992] 1 Lloyd's Rep. 656. The shipowner engaged a firm of adjusters to prepare a general average statement. Being dissatisfied with the statement which they produced, he then engaged another firm of adjusters, who produced a statement which was more favourable to him, and which was held by the House of Lords ([1994] 2 Lloyd's Rep. 1; see para. 14.33, *ante*) to be correct. It was never suggested that the shipowner was bound by the first statement, and in principle this appears correct. In the absence of special circumstances giving rise to an estoppel there would seem to be no reason why a party who, or whose agent, produces a statement should not withdraw it or contend that it is wrong.

describe the task normally undertaken by an average adjuster, that is to say the collection of information and the production of a document which states the adjuster's conclusions as to the amounts to be paid to and contributed by the parties to the adventure in general average, albeit that the statement does not (at any rate under English law) bind any of the parties. Often the word is used simply to describe the document itself. The production of a non-binding statement of the parties' rights and liabilities is, of course, precisely what Lord Herschell insisted "is *not* 'the adjustment' of general average", and there can be no doubt that it would be more accurately described as the "statement" of general average.[15] Equally there can be no doubt that in modern times the word "adjustment" is far more commonly used in this latter sense. The subject is discussed further at paragraphs 30.20 to 30.22, below, in connection with the interpretation of contractual general average clauses, where it will be seen that the modern authorities have taken a rather different view of the meaning of the word from that adopted in the *Wavertree* case.

The Law Governing the Adjustment

The traditional view, supported by all the English authorities on the point, is that the adjustment of general average between the various parties to the adventure is, in the absence of agreement to the contrary, governed by the law of the place at which the voyage terminates.[16] This place, as already observed, is called the place of adjustment. It seems unlikely, at any rate where the contract of carriage contains no express choice of governing law for the contract as a whole,[17] that the validity of this traditional view has been affected by the Contracts (Applicable Law) Act 1990, which enacts the 1980 Rome Convention on the Law Applicable to Contractual Obligations. Whenever the obligation to contribute is contractual,[18] the provisions of the Convention will apply in determining the governing law, and the basic rule laid down in the Convention, in the absence of a choice of the governing law by the **30.08**

[15] See the first passage quoted in para. 30.04, *ante*, where Lord Herschell uses the word "statement" to describe this process. See also Rule G and Rule XXI of the York-Antwerp Rules, where the same word is used to describe the document itself.

[16] See the cases referred to in paras. 30.10–30.11 and 30.16–30.17, *post*. See also Dicey and Morris *The Conflict of Laws* (10th ed.), Rule 159 (the current (12th) edition does not deal with general average); *British Shipping Laws*, Vol. 2: Carver, Carriage by Sea (13th ed.), para. 1453; Arnould, *Law of Marine Insurance* (16th ed.), Vol. 2, para. 992. Previous editions of this work, as well as the majority of the decisions under English law, refer to the termination of the "voyage" whereas the York-Antwerp Rules, in the context of contributory values, refer to the "end" (Rule G) or "termination" (Rule XVII) of the "adventure". However, this difference in terminology does not appear to have any practical significance.

[17] As to the case where there is such a clause, see para. 30.24, *post*.

[18] See Art. 1.1; and see paras. 00.19–00.30, *ante*, as to when the obligation is contractual.

parties themselves,[19] is that the contract is governed by the law of the country with which it is most closely connected.[20] However, the Convention qualifies this basic rule by providing that "a severable part of the contract which has a closer connection with another country may by way of exception be governed by the law of that other country", and there are sufficient reasons for regarding the obligation to contribute in general average as a severable part of the contract of affreightment, and as having its closest connection with the place where the adventure ends.[21] The presumptions laid down by the Convention as to the country with which the contract is most closely connected seem inapplicable to the obligation to contribute in general average.[22]

30.09 This rule causes no difficulty where all the cargo on board at the time of the general average act is destined for the same port, and where the voyage to that port is actually completed, but problems arise where the voyage is broken up short of the original destination, and where the cargo is destined for different ports. The various circumstances are considered below under the same headings as those employed in the discussion, under Rule G, of the place of valuation of the properties involved in the common maritime adventure. The place of valuation, as we have seen, also depends on the place where the adventure ends, and the problems to which it gives rise are therefore very similar to those involved in determining the law governing the adjustment. However,

[19] For the case where the parties themselves choose the governing law see Art. 3.1, para. 30.24, *post*.

[20] Art. 4.1.

[21] The reasons for treating general average as a severable part of the contract of carriage are, it is submitted, clear enough; it is usually provided for (if at all) by its own separate contractual clause or clauses, and in the absence of those clauses it would fall outside the purview of the contract; and it may, and often will, involve interests other than the two parties to the contract of carriage. Perhaps less clear-cut, under modern mercantile conditions, is the proposition that the adjustment of general average is most closely connected with the country where the adventure ends. The traditional justification for this view is that, because the common property is situate there when the lien comes to be enforced, disputed claims for contribution must be resolved by the courts, and therefore by the law, of that country. Since in modern practice the lien is almost invariably given up in exchange for a bond, guarantee or deposit, and any disputes about liability will arise long after the goods have been released, the relevance of this view may be questioned. However, if the parties are unable to reach agreement on the matter of security, the traditional view of the importance of the place where the adventure ends retains its validity in the last resort. Moreover, it is hallowed by tradition, and there is no sign that the mercantile community regards it as obsolete. For example, the general average provisions of the Institute Time Clauses are based on the assumption that, in the absence of agreement, the adjustment will be governed by the law of the place where the adventure ends.

[22] *I.e.* the general presumption contained in Art. 4.2 and the special presumption relating to contracts of carriage contained in Art. 4.4. It is uncertain whether these presumptions apply at all to a severable part of the contract, but, if they do, it would seem that they must be applied to the severed part (see Plender: *The European Contracts Convention*, para. 6.08). In these circumstances, Art. 4.2 is inapplicable because there is no characteristic performance of the severable part of the contract, each party being merely obliged to pay his share of the general average loss (see Art. 4.5); and Art. 4.4 is inapplicable because the severable agreement to contribute in general average is not "a contract for the carriage of goods", or "a contract which has as its main purpose the carriage of goods".

they are not identical, and those relating to the place of valuation are essentially more complicated. The rules stated below are, of course, subject to variation by express agreement between the parties.[23]

The York-Antwerp Rules contain no provisions which determine the law or place of adjustment, or which define the place at which the adventure ends.[24] Where the Rules apply, the role of the governing law and practice will clearly be of far less importance than in the rare cases where the Rules are not incorporated. However, as explained in paragraphs PRE.01 and PRE.05, above, the law and practice governing the adjustment may still have a part to play.

Where the voyage is to a single destination and is wholly performed

In this case the relevant place is the port of destination and the law **30.10**
to be applied is that of that port.

In *Simonds v. White*,[25] an English shipper and owner of cargo, carried from Gibraltar to St Petersburg under a bill of lading governed by English law, had been compelled at St Petersburg, in order to obtain possession of his goods, to pay a sum of money as contribution towards general average, resulting from the ship having been obliged to put into a port of refuge on the voyage. This contribution, it was admitted, was assessed correctly according to the law of Russia, but amounted to a larger sum than the merchant would have been liable for had the average been adjusted according to English law. The ship was owned in this country, and the merchant sued the shipowner for the amount which he had thus been compelled to pay in excess of his liability under English law.

Abbott C.J., in delivering the judgment of the court, said that there was one point upon which the laws of all maritime states were agreed, namely, that the place at which a general average should be adjusted was the place of the ship's destination or delivery of the cargo. He continued:

> "The shipper of goods tacitly, if not expressly, assents to general average as a known maritime usage, which may, according to the events of the voyage, be either beneficial or disadvantageous to him. And by assenting to general average he must be understood to assent also to its adjustment at the usual and proper place; and to all this it seems to us to be only an obvious consequence to add that he must be understood to consent also to its adjustment according to the usage and law of the place at which the adjustment is to be made."

[23] See paras. 30.19 *et seq.*, *post*.

[24] Rule XVIII of the York-Antwerp Rules 1890 (see para. 60.63, *post*) made provision to the effect that any matter not dealt with by the Rules should be determined according to the law and practice which would have governed the adjustment if the contract of affreightment had not incorporated the Rules. So far as it went this was unexceptionable, in fact almost a truism, but since the Rule gave no positive guidance in identifying the relevant law and practice it was of little or no practical significance, and in 1924 it was abandoned.

[25] (1824) 2 B. & C. 805.

For these reasons it was determined that, as between the shipowner and the owner of cargo, the adjustment, being admittedly correct according to the law of Russia, must be regarded as final.[26]

30.11 In *Lloyd v. Guibert*,[27] the Court of Exchequer Chamber, while laying down that for many purposes the law of the flag must be resorted to, in order to determine the rights under a contract of affreightment, expressly stated that this was not the rule for general average:

> "The adjustment of a general average at the port of discharge, according to the law prevailing there, is binding upon the shipowner and the merchant, as they must be taken to have assented to adjustment being made at the usual and proper place, and, as a consequence, according to the law of that place."

Where the voyage is to two or more ports of destination

30.12 The problems which arise where cargoes destined for different ports are on board at the time of a general average act concern mainly the ascertainment of contributory values and of the amount of loss to be made good, and are dealt with under Rule G. In this section we are concerned with the effect which the delivery of cargo at different ports will have on the law governing the adjustment, but the problems are related, since they each involve an aspect of the place of adjustment.[28]

There is no direct authority on the law which governs the adjustment in such a case. Effectively there are three possibilities:

(1) the law of the *first* port of discharge of any cargo on board at the time of the general average governs the entire adjustment;
(2) the law of the *last* port of discharge governs;
(3) the law of the place where each parcel of cargo is discharged governs the adjustment between that cargo (and any freight at risk thereon) and ship, but liabilities between cargoes for different destinations will be governed by the law of the place where the *debtor* cargo is discharged.

30.13 Neither of the first two possibilities is entirely practicable, and the favoured solution is the third. The reasoning adopted in *Simonds v. White*[29] and *Wavertree Sailing Ship Co. v. Love*[30] is that the law of the place where the adventure ends governs the adjustment of general average, because it is at that place that the property is situated and the lien[31] will be exercised, and it is to the courts of that place that the

[26] See also *Dalglish v. Davidson* (1824) 5 Dowl. & Ryl. 6; *Wavertree Sailing Ship Co. v. Love* [1897] A.C. 373 (see para. 30.04, *ante*).
[27] (1865) L.R. 1 Q.B. 115.
[28] See paras. G.02 and 30.02, *ante*.
[29] (1824) 2 B. & C. 805.
[30] [1897] A.C. 373.
[31] See paras. 30.36 *et seq.*, *post*, as to the right of lien.

parties must resort if there are disputes. This reasoning would suggest that the law of each country where cargo is discharged should apply to the adjustment of any general average contributions due from the owners of the cargo discharged there.

This is in line with the practice adopted in determining the place or places at which contributory interests should be valued, and with *Green Star Shipping v. The London Assurance*,[32] and it is submitted that it is probably correct, despite the inconvenience involved in preparing an adjustment in accordance with several systems of law.[33] The adjustment would need to be prepared in the manner adopted in the case cited by Lowndes:

> The steamer *Sarnia*, having on board cargo, partly destined for Halifax in Nova Scotia and partly for Portland in the United States, met with an accident which obliged her to put back into Liverpool, where her cargo was discharged, for repairs; after which she proceeded and delivered her cargo at both ports without further mishap. The adjustment of general average, as between ship, freight and cargo, was prepared by adjusters from Halifax and the United States, associated together. They drew up a joint statement containing two columns for general average, one headed "Halifax", and the other "Portland"; and they certified that the amounts shown in the first column were the amounts payable according to British law and should be paid by the owners of the cargo delivered at Halifax, and the amounts shown in the second were according to American law and should be paid by the owners of the cargo delivered at Portland. And this was acted on.

Using hypothetical figures, and on the assumption that all expenses had been financed by the shipowner, the adjustment might have looked as follows: **30.14**

	GENERAL AVERAGE	
	HALIFAX	PORTLAND
Cost of:		
Entering Port of Refuge	5,000	5,000
Discharging Cargo	10,000	10,000
Storing Cargo	—	5,000
Reloading Cargo	—	10,000
Outward Port Charges	—	2,500
Commission and Interest	—	1,500
	15,000	34,000

APPORTIONED

SHIP	30%		
HALIFAX CARGO	30%	Pays 4,500	
PORTLAND CARGO	40%	Pays	13,600
	100%		

[32] [1933] 1 K.B. 378.

[33] Similar problems arise if the various contracts of affreightment make provision for the adjustment of general average, but subject to different codes: See paras. 30.26 *et seq.*, *post.*

The position would be far more complex[34] were sacrifices of cargo also to be involved, and it cannot be stressed too strongly that shipowners and charterers should endeavour to ensure that all time and voyage charter-parties and bills of lading in force at any one time on the same ship should make *identical* provisions for the adjustment of general average.

Where the scheduled voyage involves the forwarding of cargo from a transhipment port under a through bill of lading

30.15 This is another situation which is not covered by authority, but it is submitted that, in line with the views expressed in paragraph G.31, above, the common adventure ends at the port of transhipment, and the on-carriage in another vessel is disregarded. It follows that the adjustment is governed by the law of the port of transhipment.

Where the intended voyage is justifiably and wholly abandoned at a port short of destination(s)

30.16 If at some intermediate port or place owing to an excepted peril the voyage is, by agreement or by necessity, wholly broken up and ship and cargo finally part company, the place of adjustment is that at which the voyage is broken up and the relevant law is the law of that place.

In *Fletcher v. Alexander*,[35] the facts of which are set out in paragraph G.04, above, the vessel returned to the loading port after stranding, and the voyage was there abandoned. Bovill C.J. held that, although in general the port of destination was the proper place for adjusting a general average, yet, when the voyage was broken up, and the adventure brought to an end at some other place, the average should be adjusted there, and by the law which there prevailed.

The same view is adopted in *Mavro v. Ocean Marine Ins. Co.*[36] where Cockburn C.J. said:

> "The adjustment must be made at the port of destination, if it be reached, but if the voyage is interrupted by some supervening cause, which necessitates or justifies its termination at some intermediate place, that place is the proper place of adjustment."[37]

Where the voyage is successfully completed by the ship and some of the cargo, but other cargo is justifiably left behind at a port of refuge

30.17 In both *Fletcher v. Alexander*[38] and *Mavro v. Ocean Marine Ins. Co.*[39] the entire voyage was abandoned at the port of refuge, which was

[34] See the further example given, in paras. 30.29 *et seq., post.*
[35] (1868) L.R. 3 C.P. 375.
[36] (1874) L.R. 9 C.P. 595; L.R. 10 C.P. 414.
[37] L.R. 10 C.P. 414 at 416.
[38] See n. 35, *supra.*
[39] See n. 36, *supra.*

therefore held to be the proper place of adjustment. What of the case where part of the cargo is left at the port of refuge, but the remainder is carried to the port of destination in the original vessel? This fell to be decided in *Hill v. Wilson*[40] in which the *Virago* sailed from Riga with a general cargo, bound for Hull, and was stranded and injured, but after jettisoning a small part of the cargo was got off and towed into Copenhagen, where the cargo was discharged and the ship was repaired at large expense. A small quantity of cargo was forwarded to the destination by sister ships, but the whole of the goods belonging to the plaintiffs, being damaged, were sold, as was admittedly proper, at Copenhagen: the ship, with a portion of her original cargo belonging to other shippers, proceeded on her voyage and arrived at Hull. The plaintiffs claimed the proceeds of sale less such charges and general average expenses as the defendant shipowner might be entitled to deduct under English law. The shipowners claimed that, as between themselves and the plaintiffs, the voyage ended at Copenhagen, and that general average as between them must be adjusted at, and by the law of Copenhagen, which was more favourable to the shipowners than the law of England, as giving them a *pro rata* freight and in other respects. The portion of cargo sold at Copenhagen amounted to about seven-eighths of the whole.

It seems to have been common ground that liability for *pro rata* freight was to be determined by the law governing the adjustment.[41] Lindley J. stated that if the Danish adjustment was to be binding upon the plaintiffs, the shipowners would have to establish:

(1) that the voyage actually terminated at Copenhagen; and
(2) that it terminated there by agreement or by necessity.

Dealing with the first point, he continued[42]:

> "With respect to 90 tons of the original cargo, there was no termination whatever of the voyage at that port, but only a suspension of it whilst the ship was under repair. The plaintiffs' goods were no doubt sold at Copenhagen, and as to them the voyage obviously terminated there: but this of itself cannot make an average adjustment there binding on the plaintiffs, as will be seen at once by supposing all the rest of the cargo to have been brought home in the *Virago* after a short detention for repairs."

The case therefore seems to be authority for the view that where some of the cargo is carried on in the original vessel to the port of destination, the law applied at that port will govern the entire adjustment, both as regards the cargo left behind at the port of refuge, and the cargo forwarded by sister ships. For the reasons given in the next paragraph it

[40] (1879) 4 C.P.D. 329.
[41] But see para. 30.33, *post*.
[42] (1879) 4 C.P.D. 329 at 334.

is submitted that the result would be the same even if all the cargo carried on to Hull had been forwarded in other vessels rather than carried in the *Virago*, so long as the forwarding was in continuation of the voyage.

Where the cargo is forwarded from a port of refuge by other vessels

30.18 When the ship is at the port of refuge it may be found that she is a commercial total loss, or that she cannot be repaired without delay which would frustrate the adventure. In such a case the shipowner has a right to tranship the cargo at the port of refuge and to forward it to destination by another vessel or vessels. This right is discussed in detail in paragraphs G.41 to G.44, above, where it is also explained that transhipment and forwarding may be effected in either of two ways:

(1) *in continuation of the voyage, that is under arrangements made by the shipowner and at his risk and expense.* In this case the adventure continues, and the law of the place of destination will therefore apply; or
(2) *under arrangements made by or on behalf of cargo interests and at their risk and expense.* In this case there is a breaking up of the common adventure at the port of refuge, whose law will therefore govern the adjustment.

Hill v. Wilson makes it clear that it is only a *total* abandonment of the voyage at the port of refuge that will have the effect that the law of the port of refuge governs the adjustment, and consequently if any of the cargo is forwarded in continuation of the voyage the law of the scheduled destination will govern the whole adjustment, even though the remaining cargo is sold at the port of refuge or forwarded at the expense of cargo interests.

The non-separation provisions of Rule G do not appear to affect the above conclusions.

Contractual Provisions Governing the Adjustment

30.19 It is not unusual for the bill of lading or charterparty to contain a clause which makes express provision for the place of or the law governing general average, often combined with the incorporation of the York-Antwerp Rules. Clauses which specify the law which is to govern the adjustment, or which provide for adjustment according to the York-Antwerp Rules do not appear to have given rise to problems in practice, but the interpretation of those clauses which purport to specify the *place* of general average has proved more difficult. The effect of the more common provisions is discussed here, and the impact of contractual time limits on claims in general average is dealt with at the end of this section.

Clauses which specify the place of general average

Clauses of this nature most commonly provide that general average shall be "adjusted" or "settled" at a particular place; sometimes a more comprehensive phrase is used, such as "adjusted, stated and settled", sometimes an even more elliptical one, such as "general average, if any, in London".[43] Whilst some of these clauses contain additional provisions which explain their meaning, many are not conspicuous for their clarity and provide no unambiguous answer to many potential questions. Is the effect of such a clause to specify: (1) the place where the appointed average adjuster is to carry on business, do his calculations, or produce his adjustment; (2) the place whose tribunals are to have jurisdiction over any disputes regarding general average; (3) the place whose law and practice is to govern the adjustment; and/or (4) the place where security must be provided and contribution must be paid? **30.20**

It is impossible to lay down any fixed rules for resolving these questions, since the result will depend on the terms of the clause as a whole, and may be affected by other terms of the contract of affreightment, such as the presence of an arbitration clause.[44] Nevertheless, there are a number of comments which may usefully be made: **30.21**

(1) As a general rule, clauses which specify the place of general average have the effect that the adjustment of general average will be governed by the law and practice of the specified place.[45]
(2) The purpose of clauses specifying a place for adjustment or settlement of general average may be presumed to be the selection of a single law and practice to govern the adjustment. Not surprisingly, it does not appear that it has ever been suggested that such clauses, without more, also have the effect that losses and contributions are to be assessed by reference to the values at that place.
(3) "*Adjusted*". In *Sameon v. Petrofina*,[46] where the clause stipulated that general average should be "adjusted" in London, Langley J. expressed the view that "the word adjusted is normally to be taken as referring to the process of assessment of rights of contribution in a non-binding manner", and he held that the clause did not amount to an agreement that London should be the place of payment, or that the English courts should have jurisdiction over disputes relating to general average. The decision is difficult to reconcile with some of the reasoning, although not the actual

[43] See cl. 29 of the Sugar Charterparty.
[44] See para. 30.23, *post*.
[45] See *Wavertree Sailing Ship Co. v. Love* [1897] A.C. 373 at 381; *Union of India v. E.B. Aaby's Rederi* [1975] A.C. 797 at 808–809, 811, 817; *Sameon v. Petrofina* (Commercial Court, March 13, 1996; unreported).
[46] See n. 45, *ante*.

result, in *Wavertree Sailing Ship Co. v. Love*,[47] and reflects the ambiguity already referred to in the meaning of the word "adjustment". It should be noted, however, that the Privy Council has also declined to follow the views expressed on this topic in the *Wavertree* case.[48]

(4) "*Settled*". It was held in *Alma Shipping Corp. v. Union of India*[49] that a clause providing that general average was to be "settled" in London meant that the adjustment was to be prepared in London, but did not provide for a forum for settlement of disputes. The same decision was reached by the House of Lords in *Union of India v. E.B. Aaby's Rederi.*[50] The question whether the specified place for settlement was also the place for payment of contributions did not arise in those cases, but Lord Dilhorne[51] was of the opinion that the clause did impose an obligation to make payment at the specified place, and Lord Salmon also inclined to this view.[52]

Other general average clauses

30.22 As already indicated, clauses which provide that the adjustment shall be governed by the York-Antwerp Rules, or by a specified system of law and practice, do not appear to have given rise to disputes. In the absence of clear words to that effect, clauses specifying a place or mode of adjustment will not affect the general rule in English law that the statement produced by the average adjuster is not binding on the parties.[53] In the case of particular average it has been held that even where the contract calls for an adjustment by a named adjuster his adjustment is not binding.[54]

The provision in the Lloyd's Average Bond that the consignee should furnish particulars of the value of the cargo "in order that ... General Average may be ascertained and adjusted in the usual manner" fell to be considered by the Privy Council in *Wavertree Sailing Ship Co. v. Love*[55] and *Castle Insurance Co. v. Hong Kong Islands Shipping Co.*[56] In the former case, as was noted in paragraph 30.04, above, it was held that the clause did not require the appointment of an adjuster at the port of destination, since the phrase "adjusted in the usual manner"

[47] See n. 45, *ante*, and paras. 30.04 *et seq.*, *ante*.

[48] *Castle Insurance Co. v. Hong Kong Islands Shipping Co.* [1984] A.C. 226: see para. 30.22, *post*.

[49] [1971] 2 Lloyd's Rep. 494 at 501.

[50] [1975] A.C. 797.

[51] *Ibid.* at 815.

[52] *Ibid.* at 817.

[53] See the cases cited in n. 10, *ante*, and *Castle Insurance Co. v. Hong Kong Islands Shipping Co.* [1984] A.C. 226 at 238. The rule is by no means universal. In some countries (Sweden for example) an adjustment is binding in the absence of an appeal to the court within a specified period of time.

[54] See *Attaleia v. Bimeh Iran* [1993] 2 Lloyd's Rep. 497.

[55] [1897] A.C. 373.

[56] [1984] A.C. 226.

referred to the determination in a manner binding on the parties of disputed rights and liabilities rather than the process of preparing a non-binding average statement. However, in the latter case the Privy Council, while not questioning the correctness of the actual decision in the *Wavertree* case, was of the view that the phrase refers to the usual procedure of appointing an average adjuster to prepare the (non-binding) average statement; and they also appear to have been of the view that the clause requires the appointment of a professional adjuster, that being the normal practice.[57]

Other aspects of the Lloyd's bonds are considered later in this section.

Arbitration clauses and general average

Where the contract of affreightment contains an arbitration clause in the usual form, disputed claims for contribution in general average will fall within the scope of the clause, even though the contract contains a clause dealing specifically with the settlement of general average.[58] The courts are reluctant to impute to the parties the intention that there should be one procedure for determining disputed claims in general average, and a different procedure for determining all other disputed claims,[59] and it follows that the presence of an arbitration clause in the contract weighs against interpreting a general average clause as providing an agreed machinery for determining disputed claims. Similar considerations would apply in the case of an exclusive jurisdiction clause. **30.23**

However where, in order to procure the release of the shipowner's lien over the cargo or for some other sufficient consideration, a party to the contract has entered into a fresh agreement to pay general average, such as a Lloyd's Average Bond or a letter of undertaking, an arbitration clause in the original contract of affreightment will not apply to a claim under the fresh agreement.[60]

Choice of law governing the contract of carriage

The cases discussed earlier in this section[61] establish that the adjustment of general average is separated from the law governing the contract of carriage as a whole, and is ruled by the law of the port of destination. Does the same result follow where there is an express choice of law in **30.24**

[57] *Ibid.* at 240.

[58] *Alma Shipping Corp. v. Union of India* [1971] 2 Lloyd's Rep. 491 ("any dispute arising under this charter"); *Union of India v. E.B. Aaby's Rederi* [1975] A.C. 797 ("all disputes ... arising out of this contract"). The result would be otherwise if the general average clause clearly provided its own separate machinery for determining disputed claims in general average.

[59] See *Swiss Bank Corp. v. Novorossiysk Shipping* [1995] 1 Lloyd's Rep. 202 at 206; *c.f. The Ioanna* [1978] 1 Lloyd's Rep. 238.

[60] *Union of India v. E.B. Aaby's Rederi* [1975] A.C. 797.

[61] See paras. 30.10 *et seq., ante*. See in particular *Simonds v. White* (1824) 2 B. & C. 805 and *Lloyd v. Guibert* (1865) L.R. 1 Q.B. 115.

the contract of carriage, not, by its terms, extending to general average? For example a bill of lading may provide (1) that the contract shall be governed by the law of France, and (2) that general average shall be adjusted in London. In such a case it is submitted that English law and practice apply to the adjustment of general average, and this will be so whether or not the obligation to contribute is contractual, since English law allows the parties to select different laws to govern different parts of their contract.[62] But what if stipulation (1) alone is included, and (2) omitted, but the port of discharge is in England? Previous editions of this work have adopted the view that this case was indistinguishable from *Lloyd v. Guibert*,[63] so that again the adjustment of general average would be governed by English law and practice. However, *Lloyd v. Guibert* was not really dealing with the case of an express choice of law, and as a matter of construction there seem good reasons for holding that a choice of governing law will prima facie cover all aspects of the contract, including the obligation to contribute in general average, where that is contractual.[64]

30.25 In *Schothorst and Schuitema v. Franz Dauter GmbH*[65] the view was expressed that an average bond which contained no express choice of law was governed by the proper law of the contract of carriage rather than by the law of adjustment. One of the issues which arose in the case was whether a claim for contribution in general average made under a Lloyd's average bond was a claim to enforce a contract governed by English law for the purposes of Order 11 of the Rules of the Supreme Court. Kerr J. rejected a submission that the bond was governed by Belgian law because the voyage ended at Antwerp, and took the view[66] that it incorporated English law by reference to the contract of carriage. The judge did not, however, say that the adjustment (which had been prepared in Rotterdam) should be completed in accordance with English law and practice as to questions of general average; and it is submitted

[62] See the Rome Convention on the law applicable to contractual obligations, Art. 3.1.

[63] (1865) L.R. 1 Q.B. 115.

[64] This is the approach which has been adopted in the cases on the applicability of arbitration clauses to claims in general average; see para. 30.23, *ante*. The question is ultimately one of construction, but where the wording of the clause is wide enough to apply to all aspects of the contract, and there is nothing in the other provisions of the contract, construed in the context of the surrounding circumstances, to indicate that it was not intended to apply to general average, it should be allowed to take effect according to its terms. The matter must now be considered in the light of the Rome Convention (see para. 30.08, *ante*). Whilst the Convention does not make specific provision for interpreting the scope of choice of law clauses, Art. 3.1 supports the view that if there is an express choice of law which is, on the face of it, wide enough to cover the adjustment of general average, and if the contract contains no other terms which cut down its scope, it will take effect according to its terms, unless it can be demonstrated with reasonable certainty from the circumstances of the case that the parties did not intend that it should apply to general average. In the ordinary case, it is difficult to see how this could be demonstrated with the required degree of certainty.

[65] [1973] 2 Lloyd's Rep. 91. *Cf. Armar Shipping v. Caisse Algerienne* [1981] 1 W.L.R. 207, and see para. 30.63, *post*.

[66] The submission was withdrawn, and the view expressed *obiter*.

that as to such matters Belgian law was appropriate, there being no express choice of law in the contract of carriage.[67]

Conflicting Provisions Regarding General Average

If the contracts of affreightment contain *no* specific provisions regarding the adjustment of general average (as might have been the case when Lowndes was active), any adjustment would be prepared in accordance with the law(s) of the port(s) of destination, and in paragraph 30.13, above, a simple example was given of a Lowndes' adjustment relating to general average expenditure incurred by the shipowner alone, and with the cargo destined for Halifax, N.S. and Portland, United States. The total amount of the general average varied in accordance with the differing laws of the United Kingdom and the United States, with the result that the shipowner might have received from the Halifax cargo a general average contribution of say one per cent of its value, whereas the Portland cargo might have paid two and one-half per cent. In similar fashion, if the general average had consisted solely of a general average sacrifice of the cargo for one of those ports of destination, the owner of the cargo sacrificed might receive from the cargo destined to the other port either more or less than he would expect under the law of the country where his own cargo was discharged. In either case this profit or loss would be just the "luck of the draw" and would lie where it fell—so long as there were *no* provisions in the contract of affreightment regarding the adjustment of general average. **30.26**

Is the position the same where *specific* provisions regarding the adjustment of general average are incorporated in the contracts of affreightment, but the shipowner fails to ensure that his contracts with each of the cargo owners contain *identical* provisions? For example, some of the bills of lading may incorporate the 1974 Rules and some the 1994 Rules, or other provisions; or the bills of lading may contain differing provisions relating to the place or law of adjustment. In such a situation problems similar to those mentioned in paragraph 30.13, above, will arise and, if there are material differences between the provisions, it will be necessary to prepare an adjustment in accordance with more than one legal régime. However, there is a further question, namely whether the shipowner or carrier who incorporates into his contract of carriage with any particular cargo owner a provision that general average shall be adjusted in a particular manner, impliedly agrees with that cargo owner to contract in similar terms with all the other cargo interests. **30.27**

[67] Whilst not entirely clear from the report, it appears that the contract of carriage was governed by English law by implication rather than by express choice.

30.28 There is no authority on this question,[68] but it is submitted that a clause in a bill of lading such as "general average to be adjusted in accordance with the York-Antwerp Rules, 1994" imports that it should be so adjusted and settled as though all the interests had agreed thereto and not merely the shipowner and that bill of lading holder.[69] From this it follows that there is an implied (if not express) term of the nature already mentioned. As will be seen in the example which follows, it is the shipowner or carrier[70] who will usually be the sufferer if settlements from or to cargo interests whose bills of lading contain no or other provisions regarding general average are on a different basis.

30.29 The correct approach is best illustrated by a figured example. (It should perhaps be pointed out that the extreme figures used in the example serve only to illustrate the principle to follow, and are hardly representative of the very minor changes effected in Rule III of the 1994 York-Antwerp Rules. The figures were appropriate, however, in the 11th edition, when general average allowances under the widely different terms of Rule III in the 1950 and 1974 versions of the York-Antwerp Rules were being considered.)[71]

A vessel loads cargo in India and Egypt for Ruritania. The cargo from India is shipped under bills of lading providing for general average to be adjusted in accordance with the York-Antwerp Rules 1994, whereas the Egyptian cargo is subject to the York-Antwerp Rules 1974.

Fire breaks out in the cargo after leaving Egypt and considerable damage is caused by water used to extinguish the fire. This damage would warrant allowances in general average as follows:

[68] But see *U.S. Shipping Board v. R. Durrell & Co. Ltd* [1923] 2 K.B. 739, where it was held that a shipowner does not undertake that all other bills of lading relating to cargo carried on the same voyage shall contain the same provisions as to demurrage. However, the grounds for the decision would seem inapplicable to provisions regarding general average.

[69] The shipowner undoubtedly acquires *authority*, under such a provision, to contract on similar terms with the remaining cargo owners. Otherwise the owner of cargo carried under a bill of lading incorporating the 1994 Rules could insist that general average should be adjusted under the common law as between him and the remaining cargo owners, even if the latter cargo was also carried under bills of lading incorporating the 1994 Rules. This is obviously absurd. For other types of bills of lading clauses which create direct rights and obligations between the bill of lading holders *inter se*, see *Grange v. Taylor* (1904) 9 Com.Cas. 223 and *Berry, Barclay v. Louis Dreyfus* (1929) 35 Ll.L. Rep. 173. The question whether the shipowner was *obliged* to contract in similar terms with all the bill of lading holders did not arise in those cases. See also *The Satanita* [1897] A.C. 59.

[70] The party liable under the implied term is the party liable to cargo under the bill of lading contract—*i.e.* normally the shipowner but occasionally the charterer. Where it is the shipowner who is liable to cargo, but the charterer was responsible for the form of the bills of lading, the shipowner may be entitled to an indemnity: see *British Shipping Laws*, Vol. II: Carver, *Carriage by Sea* (13th ed.), paras. 704–719, 737–739.

[71] See paras. 3.23–3.24, *ante*.

	General Average per:		
	YAR 1974	YAR 1994	Ruritanian Law
Extinguishing water damage	80,000	200,000	150,000

It is suggested that, there being no agreement to the contrary binding all the parties to the adventure, the proper course is to prepare an adjustment under the law of the destination, which will govern the rights of the parties initially, and then to see what modifications are necessary in order to give effect to the special agreement of those parties who have agreed to the same set of Rules.

(1) Assuming first that the Indian cargo has suffered the damage, an adjustment under Ruritanian law could be as follows: **30.30**

	Ppn. GA	Credit Made Good	Balance	
			To Pay	To Receive
Ship— 30% liable for	45,000	—	45,000	—
Indian cargo— 30% liable for	45,000	150,000	—	105,000
Egyptian cargo— 40% liable for	60,000	—	60,000	—
100% liable for	150,000	150,000	105,000	105,000

However, ship and Indian cargo have agreed to adjustment under York-Antwerp Rules 1994, namely:

	Ppn. GA	Credit Made Good	Balance	
			To Pay	To Receive
Ship— 30%[72] liable for	60,000	—	60,000	—
Indian cargo— 30% liable for	60,000	200,000	—	140,000
Egyptian cargo— 40% liable for	80,000	—	80,000	—
100% liable for	200,000	200,000	140,000	140,000

[72] Note that these contributory values would almost certainly be different under the 1994 Rules, but, to avoid complicating the issue even further, the same proportions are used for Ruritanian law, the 1994 Rules and the 1974 Rules.

The Egyptian cargo is not affected by the latter adjustment, not having agreed to York-Antwerp Rules 1994. The relevant features of the adjustment are (i) the amount payable by the ship to Indian cargo, which replaces the amount payable under Ruritanian law and (ii) the total contribution of 140,000 to which the Indian cargo is entitled under York-Antwerp Rules 1994; and which is relevant to the operation of the implied term.

No further adjustment is necessary under York-Antwerp Rules 1974, to which ship and Egyptian cargo have agreed, since no rights or liabilities in general average arise *inter se*. However, for the purpose of giving effect to the implied term, it is necessary to note that while under York-Antwerp Rules 1974, the liability of the Egyptian cargo would be only 32,000 (40 per cent of 80,000) it is actually liable to pay 60,000 under Ruritanian law.

The overall result is therefore:

(a) In general average the Indian cargo is entitled to:

60,000	from ship
60,000	from Egyptian cargo
120,000	

(b) The carriers' liability in damages for breach of the implied term is:

to Indian cargo	(140,000 − 120,000)	20,000
to Egyptian cargo	(60,000 − 32,000)	28,000
		48,000[73]

30.31 (2) Assume next that it is the Egyptian cargo which sustains the damage. Under Ruritanian law the adjustment would be:

	Ppn. GA	Credit Made Good	Balance	
			To Pay	To Receive
Ship— 30% liable for	45,000	—	45,000	—
Indian cargo— 30% liable for	45,000	—	45,000	—
Egyptian cargo— 40% liable for	60,000	150,000	—	90,000
100% liable for	150,000	150,000	90,000	90,000

[73] In a simple case the same overall result may be reached by starting with an adjustment in accordance with the provisions binding on the party incurring the loss (York-Antwerp Rules 1994), requiring the remaining cargo interests to pay in accordance with their own contracts with the shipowner, and calling upon the shipowner to pay the entire balance (140,000 − 32,000 = 60,000 + 48,000). However, this does not elucidate the true legal position, and the difference will be material if one party is insolvent, if the party liable under the implied term is not the shipowner, or in ascertaining rights against insurers.

However, ship and Egyptian cargo have agreed to adjustment under York-Antwerp Rules 1974, namely:

	Ppn. GA	Credit Made Good	Balance To Pay	Balance To Receive
Ship— 30% liable for	24,000	—	24,000	—
Indian cargo— 30% liable for	24,000	—	24,000	—
Egyptian cargo— 40% liable for	32,000	80,000	—	48,000
100% liable for	80,000	80,000	48,000	48,000

As already noted in paragraph 30.30, above, the Indian cargo is not affected by the latter adjustment, but the amount payable by the ship is governed by this adjustment rather than by the Ruritanian law adjustment.

Also to be noted is that in this case, unlike that where the Indian cargo sustained the damage, no loss has been suffered by either cargo interest as a result of the breach of the implied term. Indian cargo is better off than if the Egyptian bill of lading had incorporated York-Antwerp Rules 1994, and Egyptian cargo is better off than if the Indian bill of lading had incorporated York-Antwerp Rules 1974.

The overall result is therefore:

(a) In general average the Egyptian cargo is entitled to:
24,000 from Ship
45,000 from Indian cargo
69,000

(b) The carrier's liability in damages for breach of the implied term is nil.

The Role of the Law Governing the Adjustment

We have already seen[74] that there may be a difference between the law governing the contract of carriage in general and the law governing general average. Normally this gives rise to little difficulty in practice; for example, few people would doubt that the question whether freight had become payable was governed by the proper law of the contract of carriage, whereas the method of valuing the contributing interests was governed by the law of the adjustment. However, it may be difficult in some instances to determine whether a particular problem should be **30.32**

[74] See paras. 30.08, 30.24–30.25, *ante*.

characterised as one of contract or of general average; such as the interpretation of the words "at merchant's risk" in *Burton v. English*.[75]

30.33 There is, strangely enough, no discussion of the problem in any of the decided cases. For example, in *Hill v. Wilson*[76] it was assumed that the question whether the shipowner was entitled to *pro rata* freight was a matter for the law governing the adjustment, although if the same question arose today it would almost certainly be regarded as a matter to be governed by the proper law of the contract of carriage as a whole. As a matter of principle, it is submitted that since the interpretation and effect of the contract is, in general, governed by its proper law,[77] that law should be applied to all such questions other than those concerned exclusively with general average. Thus the question whether fault is actionable, or whether freight has been earned or is still at risk, are questions which can and normally will arise quite independently of any claim for general average, and should therefore be governed by the law governing the contract of carriage, even when they arise in the context of a claim for contribution. In *Drew Brown v. The Orient Trader*,[78] the question whether a statutory exception of fire protected the carrier against liability for a fire which broke out after a deviation was treated as a question to be answered by reference to the proper law of the contract.

30.34 Equally, it is submitted that questions such as that which arose in *Burton v. English*[79] are to be determined under the proper law of the contract of carriage, since the effect of a clause such as "at merchant's risk" may have to be considered in a number of different situations, and it would be illogical that it should receive one interpretation in the context of a general average claim and a different interpretation in any other context.

30.35 On the other hand, the question whether fault which is not actionable is a defence to a claim for general average, and the nature of the remedies or defences open to a party against whom contribution is claimed,[80] should be a matter for the law governing the adjustment. For example, if a contract of carriage governed by United States law provided for general average to be adjusted in London in accordance with English law, and contained an exception of negligent navigation, it would be irrelevant whether the contract contained a *Jason Clause* or a *New Jason*

[75] (1883) 12 Q.B.D. 218.
[76] (1879) 4 C.P.D. 329. See para. 30.17, *ante*.
[77] See the Contracts (Applicable Law) Act 1990, Sched. I, art. 10.1.
[78] [1972] 1 Lloyd's Rep. 35; [1973] 2 Lloyd's Rep. 174.
[79] See n. 75, *ante*.
[80] *Cf. Goulandris v. B. Goldman & Sons* [1958] 1 Q.B. 74, and see paras. D.29–D.31, *ante*.

Clause[81] and contribution could be recovered even though the peril was brought about by negligent navigation of the ship.

2. Enforcing Rights of Contribution

(A.) Enforcement by Lien

Shipowner's Common Law Lien

The shipowner has, at common law, a lien on the cargo while in his possession or in that of his servants as a carrier, not only for the freight, but also for the cargo's share of general average.[82] The enforcement of this lien is made the more necessary for a shipowner from the circumstance that a mere consignee of cargo, not being the owner at the time of the sacrifice or expenditure, is not liable for general average in the absence of agreement.[83] **30.36**

The lien, by contrast, is a possessory lien, exercisable over the cargo without regard to the question whether the consignee is under any personal liability to contribute.[84]

Procedure in exercising the lien

Under the ordinary rules of the common law relating to the exercise of possessory liens, the person who is entitled to exercise the lien has a right to demand immediate payment of the amount for which the lien subsists, and need not content himself with security; but conversely he is obliged, at the time when he exercises his lien, to quantify his demand correctly, or at any rate to give to the owner of the goods sufficient particulars from which the latter can ascertain and tender the correct amount. If the lienor fails to follow this procedure his continued detention of the goods becomes unlawful, and the lien is therefore lost.[85] **30.37**

[81] As to the origin and effect of Jason and New Jason clauses, see paras. 00.51–00.53, *ante*.

[82] "It is a possessory lien at common law, by virtue of which he (the master or owner of the ship) is entitled to hold the goods till his lien be satisfied": *per* Lord Kingsdown, in *Cargo ex Galam* (1863) Br. & L. 167 at 182. The same lien which the master has for general average, he has likewise for special or particular charges on cargo incurred during the transit: *Hingston v. Wendt* (1876) 1 Q.B.D. 367.

[83] See paras. 30.54 *et seq., post*.

[84] *Castle Insurance Co. v. Hong Kong Shipping Co.* [1984] A.C. 226, P.C. See para. 30.39, *post*.

[85] See *Albemarle Supply Co. v. Hind* [1928] 1 K.B. 307, applying *Scarfe v. Morgan* (1838) 4 M & W 270, *Dirks v. Richards* (1842) 4 M & G 574, *Huth v. Lamport* (1886) 16 Q.B.D. 735 and *Ramsey v. North Eastern Railway* (1863) 14 C.B.N.S. 641. Even if the person exercising the lien does give sufficient particulars, the goods owner will be excused from tendering the correct amount if the former makes it clear that he will not part with possession of the goods until his excessive demand is met in full. See the cases cited above and para. 30.40, *post*.

30.38 This right of lien would therefore entitle the shipowner to insist on payment of the general average by the consignees before delivery of their goods, were he at that point of time in a position to state the amount of his claim. This, however, is seldom or never the case, since the amount of contribution depends upon the value of the goods, which usually cannot be ascertained until they have been landed, and their condition examined. Nor are the details of general average expenditure, or the value of the ship, always immediately known. In practice, therefore, this right of lien can only be used as a means for enforcing the giving of satisfactory security or other equivalent to a payment before delivery.[86]

The usual form of security required will invariably include the signing of an average bond[87] by the receiver of the goods whereby he undertakes to pay the proper proportion of any salvage and/or general average and/or other charges attaching to the goods, and also to provide the information necessary to value the cargo and any loss or damage thereto. As collateral security, the receiver will also be required to furnish *either*:

(1) A cash deposit,[88] more particularly in those cases where:
   (a) The cargo is uninsured, or where a general average guarantee offered by insurers is considered unsuitable.
   (b) The amount of the general average is substantial and the shipowner has given salvage security on behalf of the cargo and/or expects to need ready cash to make payments on account before the general average adjustment is completed to those parties to the adventure who have sustained large losses or expenditures.

(2) An unlimited guarantee[89] from his insurers, whereby they guarantee (and generally make) the due payment of the proportion of the general average and other charges attaching to the cargo.

30.39 A bank guarantee is sometimes accepted in lieu of a general average deposit but this can be an expensive undertaking and the bank charges are not admissible in general average. The practice was described as follows in *Castle Insurance Co. v. Hong Kong Islands Shipping Co.*[90]:

> "There attaches to all cargo that has been preserved in consequence of a general average sacrifice or expenditure a lien in favour of those concerned in ship or cargo who have sustained a general average loss. The lien attaches to the preserved cargo at the time when the sacrifice is made or the liability to the expenditure incurred. The lien is a possessory lien and it is the duty of the master of the vessel to exercise the lien at the time of discharge of

[86] The practice is recognised by law in the U.S.: *Wellman v. Morse* 76 Fed.Rep. 563 (1896).

[87] For typical form of bond, see App. 4, para. 80.02, *post*.

[88] For typical form of deposit receipt, see App. 4, para. 80.06, *post*. Rule of Practice, No. B36, para. 70.22, *post*, deals with interest on deposits. Rule XXII of the York-Antwerp Rules regulates the terms on which deposits are held.

[89] For typical form of guarantee, see App. 4, para. 80.04, *post*.

[90] [1984] A.C. 226.

> the preserved cargo in such a way as will provide equivalent security for contributions towards general average sacrifices made or expenditure incurred not only by those concerned in the ship but also by those concerned in cargo in respect of which a net general average loss has been sustained. The lien, being a possessory one and not a maritime lien, is exercisable only against the consignee, but it is exercisable whether or not the consignee was owner of the consignment at the time of the general average sacrifice or expenditure that gave rise to the lien: a fact of which the shipowner may well be unaware. At the time of discharge the sum for which the lien is security (save in the simplest cases, which do not include that of a general ship) is unquantifiable until after there has been an average adjustment. Indeed in the case of some consignees of cargo that has been preserved in part only or damaged in consequence of a general average loss, so far from being liable to a net general average contribution they may eventually turn out to be entitled to a net payment in general average. The disadvantages and legal complications which would result from the master's actually withholding delivery to its consignee of cargo preserved by general average acts are conveniently set out in Lowndes & Rudolf, *General Average and York-Antwerp Rules* (*British Shipping Laws*, vol. 7), 10th ed. (1975), para. 453 and need not be repeated here. In practice what happens is what happened in the instant case; the master, acting on behalf of the shipowner and of any persons interested in cargo who will be found on the adjustment to be entitled to a net general average payment, release the preserved cargo to the consignees upon the execution by each consignee of an average bond in one or other of Lloyd's standard forms accompanied, in the comparatively rare cases of cargo that is uninsured or underinsured, by a deposit in a bank in joint names of money as security or, more usually, by a letter of guarantee from the insurer of the cargo."[91]

It is clear from this case that, where the shipowner seeks security for his claim rather than immediate payment, he will not be required to quantify his claim precisely, or to give particulars from which the cargo owner is able to do so.[92] The information which the shipowner who exercises his lien for the purpose of obtaining security is required to give is considered in more detail below.[93]

Limitations against abuse

Since the correct sum for which the lien is security is normally unquantifiable at the time of discharge, it is possible that the shipowner might abuse his power of lien by demanding payment (or deposit by way of security) of an excessive sum, or by insisting on unreasonable terms relating to the security. Against this eventuality the law provides the following safeguards: **30.40**

(1) The shipowner who insists on outright payment, rather than security, does so at his peril if he exaggerates his claim and fails

[91] [1984] A.C. 226 at 234, *per* Lord Diplock delivering the judgment of the Privy Council.
[92] As he is required to do if he demands outright payment. See para. 30.37, *ante*.
[93] See para. 30.40 and n. 91, *post*.

30.40
cont.

to give the necessary particulars from which the consignee can ascertain the correct amount to tender.[94]

(2) Where outright payment is demanded, the consignee of goods can always obtain a right to the delivery of his goods, and, consequently, a right of action for damages, if they are not delivered, by tendering to the shipowner or captain a sum sufficient to meet his rightful demand. The duty of determining the amount to be tendered is thus cast upon the consignee, unless indeed the shipowner or master shall have made his demand in such a manner as to imply a resolution on his part to take no smaller sum.[95] Unless the consignee employs the procedure described in sub-paragraph (4) below the tender must be by way of outright payment.[96]

In practice, for the reasons already described in paragraph 30.38, above, outright payment is rarely, if ever,[97] demanded or tendered.

(3) In the usual case, where the shipowner detains the goods for the purpose of obtaining security, rather than actual payment, he is obliged to accept security which is reasonable both in its form and in the amount of any deposit which is demanded[98] and if he refuses a reasonable offer of security, or makes it plain that he will accept nothing other than the unreasonable security which he demands, the lien is discharged.[99] Where the York-Antwerp Rules apply, the consignee is entitled to insist that any deposit paid by him shall be held on the terms laid down in Rule XXII. The consignee is entitled to such information as will enable him to ascertain whether the amount of any deposit claimed is reasonable, and any failure to provide such information is a breach of the contract of carriage.[1]

[94] See para. 30.37, *ante*.

[95] As to the law with regard to the making of tenders in cases of disputed liability, see the cases referred to in para. 30.37, n. 85, *ante*. See also *Allen v. Smith* (1862) 12 C.B.(N.S.) 638; affirmed (1863) 9 Jur.(N.S.) 1248, Ex.Ch.; *Ashmole v. Wainwright* (1842) 2 Q.B. 837; *Nicholson v. Chapman* (1793) 2 H.Bl. 254; *Kerford v. Mondel* (1859) 28 L.J. Exch. 303; *The Norway*, in (1865) Br. & L. 404 at 410–411, P.C.; *per* Lord Blackburn in *Anderson v. Ocean S.S. Co.* (1884) 10 App. Cas. 107 at 115; *Huth v. Lamport* (1885–86) 16 Q.B.D. 442 at 735, para. 30.48, *post*.

[96] See *Huth v. Lamport* (*supra*) *per* Lord Esher at 736. The point was left open by Lindley L.J. and by Mathew J.

[97] One of the editors recollects a "quayside" adjustment of a small general average, which left all parties very contented with the result.

[98] *Huth v. Lamport* (*supra*).

[99] See para. 30.37, *ante*. As to what is reasonable security see *post*, paras. 30.48 *et seq.*, *post*.

[1] *The Norway* (1864) Br. & L. 377 at 397–398. In that case Dr Lushington held that it was the duty of the master, when he demands a deposit for general average, to furnish the consignee "with some memorandum from an average adjuster as to the probable amount of contribution from the cargo for the general average". The reference to "an average adjuster" conflicts, however, with the opinion of the Judicial Committee of the Privy Council in *Wavertree Sailing Ship Co. v. Love* [1897] A.C. 373, where it was stated that if the shipowner employed an average adjuster it was "as a matter of business convenience on his part". It is suggested that the view of the Judicial Committee underestimates the skill required in drawing up a complex adjustment. *Cf. Chandris v. Argo Insurance Co. Ltd* [1963] 2 Lloyd's Rep. 65; *E.B. Aaby's Rederi A/S v. Union of India* [1973] 1 Lloyd's Rep. 509, C.A.; [1974] 3 W.L.R. 269, H.L.; *Castle Insurance Co. v. Hong Kong Islands Shipping Co.* [1984] A.C. 226 at 237.

(4) The consignee can sue the shipowner in conversion, whereupon the shipowner will set up his lien by way of defence and the consignee can apply to the court under Order 29, Rule 6[2] of the Rules of the Supreme Court for the delivery up of his cargo upon his paying into court—*not* to the shipowner—a sum equal to that in respect of which the lien is claimed and some further sum to cover interest and costs if the court so directs. The advantage of this procedure is obvious in any case in which the solvency of the shipowner is in doubt and the shipowner demands outright payment, or security in the form of a deposit to be held to his order. However there is little purpose in applying for such an order, and the court would be unlikely to grant the application, where the shipowner is content that the sum demanded of the consignee should be held in joint names, for example in accordance with the provisions of Rule XXII of the York-Antwerp Rules.

(5) Although the consignee whose goods have been jettisoned or sold abroad has, at common law, no security against the ship corresponding to the shipowner's right of lien, yet if the shipowner exerts his right of lien to enforce from the former a deposit for general average, he is bound to set against the sum he demands, and place to the credit of the consignee, the amount of any claim which the latter may rightfully have upon the ship, in respect of a jettison or other sacrifice of goods.[3]

(6) At common law, and except so far as this rule has been modified by statute,[4] the shipowner who enforces a right of lien must do so at his own expense. If he were to land and store the goods, or deposit them with a wharfinger, his position at common law was that, even if he did not by such an act lose that possession of the goods on which his right of lien depended, at any rate the expense he was put to in storing and retaining the goods could not be recovered from the consignee.[5] This position may, however, be modified by contract. A shipowner need not land cargo on which he has a lien in order to stop demurrage accruing, provided

[2] Ord. 29, r. 6 provides: "Where the plaintiff, or the defendant by way of counterclaim, claims the recovery of specific property (other than land) and the party from whom recovery is sought does not dispute the title of the party making the claim but claims to retain the property by virtue of a lien or otherwise as security for any sum of money, the court, at any time after the claim to be so entitled appears from the pleadings (if any) or by affidavit or otherwise to its satisfaction, may order that the party seeking to recover the property be at liberty to pay into court, to abide the event of the action, the amount of money in respect of which the security is claimed and such further sum (if any) for interest and costs as the court may direct and that, upon such payment being made, the property claimed be given up to the party claiming it ..." An analogous procedure is available in the U.S.

[3] *The Norway* in (1865) Br. & L. 404, 3 Moo. P.C. (N.S.) 245, P.C.

[4] See para. 30.41, *post*.

[5] See *Somes v. British Empire Shipping Co.* (1858–60) E.B. & E. 353 at 367, Ex.Ch.; 8 H.L.Cas. 338. At common law, the right of lien does not in general carry with it a right to sell the articles retained: *Thames Ironworks Co. v. The Patent Derrick Co.* (1860) 1 J. & H. 93.

that the exercise of the lien by retaining the goods on board is reasonable.[6]

Statutory extension of the lien

30.41 So far as concerns goods carried to the United Kingdom the common law rules relating to the landing of goods under lien, and the expenses of exercising the lien, are extensively modified by sections 492 to 501 of the Merchant Shipping Act 1894.[7] These sections provide that, at the time when any goods are landed from any ship and placed in the custody of any person as wharf or warehouse owner, the shipowner may give notice in writing to the wharf or warehouse owner requiring him to retain the goods subject to the claim for freight or other charges; which notice the wharf or warehouse owner is bound to act upon, under the penalty of being himself liable for any loss resulting from his omission. When such a notice has been served, the owner of the goods can only obtain delivery by depositing with the warehouse owner a sum equal to that demanded. This deposit is to be paid over to the shipowner in satisfaction of his claim, unless, within fifteen days after making it, the consignee or representative of the cargo shall give to the warehouse owner notice in writing to retain either the whole, or such portion as he asserts to be in excess of his admitted liability. After receiving such a notice, the warehouse owner is at once to communicate it to the shipowner, who must then, within 30 days, institute proceedings (in the form of an action or arbitration)[8] to enforce his disputed claim; or else the deposit, or that portion of it which is not admitted to be due, is to be returned by the warehouse owner to the party who made it. And it is specially provided in the Act that the warehouse rent and the expenses of the wharfinger, while the goods are detained under this right of lien, shall be a charge upon the goods.[9]

If the consignee of the goods shall make no deposit, the warehouseman or wharfinger is to detain the goods for 90 days, and at the expiration of that time (or sooner, if the goods are perishable), is to sell them, and to apply the proceeds, first in payment of his own charges, and secondly in satisfaction of the shipowner's lien, after which the balance is to be paid to the consignee.

[6] *Lyle & Co. v. Cardiff* (1899) 5 Com.Cas. 87; *Smailes v. Hans Dessen & Co.* (1906) 12 Com.Cas. 117. It would seem that in some cases, if the consignee refuses to take delivery of the goods or to satisfy the lien on them, a master might be justified in carrying the goods back to the port of shipment, and there enforcing his lien against the shipper, on the principle that one who has a lien on goods may do what is reasonable to enforce it, and, if he cannot do so on the spot without incurring expense, may carry the goods to some place where he can: *Edwards v. Southgate* (1862) 10 W.R. 528.

[7] 57 & 58 Vict., c. 60.

[8] Arbitration Act 1996, Sched. 3, para. 1.

[9] As to the working of the warehousing provisions of this Act, see *Miedbrodt v. Fitzsimon* (1875) L.R. 6 P.C. 306; *Smailes v. Hans Dessen & Co.* (1905–06) 11 Com.Cas. 74; 12 Com.Cas. 117, C.A. For the position when goods are warehoused otherwise than under the Act, see *Dennis v. Cork S.S. Co.* [1913] 2 K.B. 393.

Remedy of Cargo Owner

Such are the remedies available to the owner of the ship. The owner of goods sacrificed for all is not in so advantageous a position simply because, not being in possession like the shipowner, he can have no direct right of lien.[10] However, as the shipowner can and must exercise a lien on the cargo for a sum sufficient to satisfy not only his own claim to contribution (for example for general average expenditure that he has incurred, or loss of freight) but also that of the unfortunate cargo owner, the latter can exercise a lien, albeit indirectly. If the shipowner fails to exercise his lien by requiring payment or the giving of reasonable security for payment before delivering the surviving cargo, he will be liable in damages to the owner of the sacrificed cargo. **30.42**

Cases which establish these propositions

In *Crooks v. Allan*[11] the *Sardinian* took fire at sea, which made it necessary, in order to protect the whole from destruction, to flood the cargo with water, thus occasioning a general average loss to the plaintiff's goods. The ship returned to Liverpool, and there the shipowners, conceiving they were not liable to contribute to the damage to the cargo because of the terms of the bills of lading[12] and not proposing themselves to make any claim upon the cargo, took no steps as to collecting a general average, but simply discharged the damaged cargo and handed it over to the Liverpool Salvage Association[13] to be distributed and disposed of as might be most for the benefit of the parties concerned. The plaintiffs brought an action in which they asserted that it was a breach of duty by the shipowners first to fail to obtain security in the usual form from the owners of other cargo, and secondly not to inform the owners of the sacrificed cargo of the identity of the other contributing interests, and of their contributing values. **30.43**

Lush J., after dealing with another point, said:

> "The next question is whether a shipowner is bound to exercise the power he is invested with, when a general average loss has arisen, and to afford the means in his power for adjusting the general average claims and liabilities, and secure their payment to the parties entitled. It seems strange that such a point has not been formally decided in this country. It has been decided

[10] In the U.S. the owner of goods sacrificed has a lien, enforceable in Admiralty, against the vessel and other interests for the amount due to him. In England he can in effect obtain security from the shipowner by commencing an Admiralty action *in rem*: see paras. 30.64, 30.66, *post*.

[11] (1879) 5 Q.B.D. 38; 49 L.J.Q.B. 201.

[12] The court ruled against the shipowners on this point; see para. D.16, *ante*.

[13] An association, formed by the underwriters of that city, to organise a system of concerted action in case of wreck or maritime disaster, so as to minimise the loss by providing machinery for disposing of the property saved to the best advantage, sending out agents to ships in distress and other analogous methods. There is another similar institution in London.

> in America in favour of the shipper. I am not aware that it has ever been judicially questioned here, and I can only account for the absence of direct authority by supposing that the universal practice has been accepted as proof of the obligation. It is clear that the shipowner has a lien for general average on the whole of the cargo liable to contribution, and can require, before he parts with it, security for its due payment. In early times the master, when he had jettisoned part of the cargo to save the whole adventure, took and rendered contribution in kind. The ordinary course now is, and has been for a very long time, for the shipowner to require before he delivers the cargo, an average bond or agreement for the payment of what shall be found due from each shipper for his proportion of the loss. He is the only person who has the power to require this security.
>
> The right to detain for average contribution is derived from the civil law, which also imposes on the master of the ship the duty of having the contribution settled, and of collecting the amount, and the usage has always been substantially in accordance with this law, and has become part of the common law of the land.
>
> I am therefore of opinion, ... that he [the shipowner] is liable to this action for not having taken the necessary steps for procuring an adjustment of the general average and securing its payment."[14]

As a result of this decision the shipowners collected and gave the requisite information, and caused an adjustment of general average to be drawn up, which was settled by all parties concerned, including the shipowners and their underwriters, without further question.

30.44 The decision in *Crooks v. Allen*[15] that it was the master's duty to enforce the lien for general average contribution against each of the other cargo owners for the benefit of the owner of the goods sacrificed, was affirmed by the Privy Council in *Strang v. Scott*,[16] where it was stated that the master was the agent of the owner of sacrificed cargo for the purposes of exercising the lien, and was applied in *Nobel's Explosives Co. v. Rea*,[17] where the shipowners were held liable in damages to the owners of goods jettisoned for delivering the other cargo without taking security from the consignees. The rule has also been recognised in *Hain SS Co. Ltd v. Tate & Lyle*,[18] *Morrison SS Co. Ltd v. Greystoke Castle*[19] and in *Castle Insurance Co. Ltd v. Hong Kong Islands Shipping Co.*[20] and

[14] (1879) 5 Q.B.D. 38 at 41.

[15] (1879) 5 Q.B.D. 38.

[16] (1889) 14 App. Cas. 601.

[17] (1897) 2 Com.Cas. 293. There was no evidence that the contribution was irrecoverable from the other cargo owners, and the decision effectively imposes on the shipowner who fails to obtain security for the other interests an obligation to pay the contribution due from those interests.

[18] (1934) 39 Com.Cas. 259 at 281, *per* Greer L.J.; approved in the House of Lords (1936) 41 Com.Cas. 350 at 356, *per* Lord Atkin.

[19] [1947] A.C. 265 at 283.

[20] [1984] A.C. 226 at 234. See para. 30.39, *ante*. See also *The Santa Ana* 154 Fed.Rep. 800 (1907).

may be regarded as settled law. In so far as *Hallet v. Bousfield*[21] is a decision to the contrary, it must be regarded as having been wrongly decided.

The shipowner's exercise of his lien for the benefit of the owner of sacrificed cargo will only secure the contribution owed by other cargo owners, since the shipowner is under no obligation imposed by law to provide security for his own contribution. However the cargo owner can in effect obtain security in respect of the shipowner's contribution by commencing an Admiralty action *in rem* and arresting the ship or a sister ship.[22] **30.45**

The other aspect of the decision in *Crooks v. Allen*,[23] that it was the shipowner's duty not only to obtain security from the consignees of other cargo, but also to procure an adjustment of general average, has not arisen for decision in any subsequent case. Normally the shipowner has incurred expense himself, and is therefore willing to undertake the task voluntarily. **30.46**

Average Bonds or Agreements

Since the shipowner's lien is almost invariably exercised for the purpose of obtaining security rather than actual payment, the question which next arises is what form that security should take. The usual procedure, as indicated in *Castle Insurance Co. v. Hong Kong Islands Shipping Co.*,[24] is for the shipowner to accept an average bond under which the consignee agrees to pay the amount of general average chargeable on the goods delivered to him, and undertakes to furnish correct particulars of the value of the goods; where required the consignee secures his obligations under the bond either by providing a cash deposit, or by procuring a guarantee of the cargo insurers. Alternatively, cargo owners and insurers may enter into a tripartite agreement with the shipowner. The Lloyd's forms of such agreements are set out in Appendix 4.[25] However, it is open to the parties to make their own formal or informal agreement as **30.47**

[21] (1811) 18 Ves. 187, a case in which Lord Eldon refused an injunction to restrain the shipowner from delivering the cargo without obtaining security for the plaintiff's claim. In commenting on this case in *Strang v. Scott* (1889) 14 App. Cas. 601, Lord Watson observed (at 606): "Courts of equity are chary of granting injunctions which may lead to inconvenient results; and it does not follow from *Hallett v. Bousfield* that a master might not be restrained from making delivery of the cargo, at the instance of all or most of those entitled to contribution, without taking security for their claims."

[22] See para. 30.66, *post*. In the U.S. the owner of goods sacrificed has a lien, enforceable in Admiralty, against the vessel and other interests for the amount due to him.

[23] See n. 15, *supra*.

[24] [1984] A.C. 226 at 234, see para. 30.39, *ante*. See also *Crooks v. Allen*, para. 30.43, *ante*.

[25] See paras. 80.02 *et seq.*, *post*.

they please.[26] In such a case, the shipowner who demands security must not be unreasonable in his demands either as to the form or the amount of security, or as to the terms upon which it is held.[27]

Reasonable security

30.48 What is reasonable depends upon the circumstances of each case, but a demand for the deposit of a sum larger in amount than that of any anticipated contribution, or that the deposit shall be paid to the shipowner or his agent, or that the contribution shall be determined by some person appointed by the shipowner without recourse to a legal tribunal is unreasonable.

In *Huth v. Lamport*[28] the then existing Liverpool form of Average Agreement was challenged and held by Mathew and Smith J.J., and by the Court of Appeal, to be unreasonable.

Lord Esher said[29]:

> "If the shipowner requires the consignee to enter into a bond in particular terms, the question arises whether the bond is unreasonable, and if part of what is insisted upon is unreasonable, the whole instrument is unreasonable. That the bond is unreasonable, considered as one which the master may impose on the consignee, is, I think, clear. First, it makes the shipowner's average adjuster an arbitrator, and that is unreasonable. Then there is a peculiar kind of appeal from the decision of the average adjuster, which prevents the parties from taking the opinion of a legal tribunal. Further, the terms of the deposit are unreasonable, inasmuch as it requires a deposit in the joint names of the representative of the shipowner and the average adjuster. Then as to the mode in which payments are to be made out of the deposit. The average adjuster of the shipowner is to be the judge, and what purports to be a deposit is to be drawn upon for such disbursements as these two, without the consent of the depositor, think ought to be paid to the shipowner. For these different reasons the bond is one which, I think, the Liverpool shipowners have no right to impose upon the owner of any cargo which arrives there."

Earlier in his judgment he criticised the terms of the bond on the additional ground that it entitled the shipowner to draw from the deposit the whole amount of disbursements made by him, although it might turn out on the final settlement that a substantial part of those disbursements fell to be borne by him as his share of the general average.

30.49 Where the shipowner is obliged to obtain security for the benefit of the owner of sacrificed cargo, as well as obtaining it for his own benefit, the security must not only be reasonable as regards the consignees who are asked to provide it, but the shipowner is also obliged to ensure that

[26] As in *Union of India v. E.B. Aaby's Rederi* [1975] A.C. 797.
[27] See para. 30.48, *post*.
[28] (1885) 16 Q.B.D. 442; (1886) 16 Q.B.D. 735.
[29] (1886) 16 Q.B.D. 735 at 737.

it provides reasonable protection to the owner of the sacrificed cargo, a question considered in more detail below.[30]

Guarantees

Security for the payment of the cargo's contribution to general average is today customarily provided by a guarantee[31] given by the underwriters of the cargo rather than by a deposit. This method has proved a very convenient one in the majority of cases, especially to the cargo owner, because he is not called upon to make a cash deposit.[32] **30.50**

The question remains to be considered, whether a shipowner who accepts a guarantee, instead of requiring a deposit, fulfils his duty to the cargo owner to whom a general average contribution is owing. In one respect a guarantee can never be as good a security as a deposit of money, for it may become inadequate or even valueless through the insolvency of the guarantor. It may therefore be argued that a shipowner fails in his duty to the cargo owner, if he agrees to substitute a guarantee for a deposit. It must, however, be remembered that in another respect a guarantee of the whole amount of the contribution may be a better security than a deposit; for the amount of the contribution is uncertain at the time when the security is given, and there is a possibility that it will exceed the deposit, especially where the currency of the deposit differs from the currency of the adjustment.[33] **30.51**

It is submitted that the shipowner fulfils his obligation if he obtains such security for the payment of the contribution as a prudent man would be content to take for his own benefit.[34] The guarantee of the Corporation of Lloyd's[35] or that of a bank[36] or insurance company of high standing would normally satisfy this test.

There can be no doubt that a guarantee for a part only of the contribution would be an insufficient security.

There is, however, a practice in cases where the general average is of

[30] See para. 30.51, *post*.

[31] For forms of guarantee see App. 4, paras. 80.04–80.05, *post*.

[32] See paras. 30.52 *et seq*., *post*. See also para. 30.38, *ante*, to the circumstances in which such deposits are normally required.

[33] For the currency in which deposits are to be held, see para. 22.09, *ante*.

[34] The judgments of Mathew J. and Lindley L.J. in *Huth v. Lamport* (para. 30.48, *ante*) suggest that the shipowner's duty is to take reasonable security. Even a trustee is not expected, save in the investment of the trust funds, to take greater precautions in managing trust affairs than an ordinary prudent man of business would take in managing similar affairs of his own: *per* Lord Blackburn, in *Speight v. Gaunt* (1883) 9 App. Cas. 1 at 19; *per* Lord Watson, in *Learoyd v. Whiteley* (1887) 12 App. Cas. 727 at 733.

[35] Those forms which have been officially adopted by the Committee of Lloyd's are set out in App. 4, paras. 80.04, *et seq*., *post*.

[36] Provided that the guarantee is not of limited duration. Some banks will not give a guarantee lasting for more than one year, although they will usually renew it. Unless the bank is *obliged* to renew the guarantee from year to year, this would, it is suggested, be insufficient.

a minor nature and there are a great many cargo interests, to take security only from the larger of them. Alternatively in such a case it may be suggested to the ship's insurers that they should pay the whole loss, to avoid disproportionate expense in collecting contributions.

Cash Deposits

30.52 Cash deposits are normally required in the circumstances already described in paragraph 30.38, above.

As has already been seen, it is a breach of contract by the shipowner to use his lien so as to demand a deposit which exceeds the maximum amount for which the consignee could realistically be liable to contribute, or so as to seek to impose unreasonable terms as to the manner in which the deposit is held.[37] The York-Antwerp Rules, where they apply, govern the terms upon which the deposit is held.[38]

30.53 It is the usual practice of the consignees of the cargo, when they have been obliged to make a cash deposit in order to obtain delivery of their goods, to claim the amount of the deposit from their insurers, who generally agree to reimburse them this amount in whole or in part, according as to whether the goods are fully or only partly insured. The assured then hand over to the insurers the receipt given for the deposit, sometimes accompanied by a formal assignment to the insurers of their interest in the deposit, up to the amount provided by the insurers.

It may also be remarked that the receipt customarily given to the depositor is a special Lloyd's form of General Average Deposit Receipt.[39] These receipts are transferable documents of title, which entitle any holder to present the same and claim the refund eventually found to be due. Unless special arrangements are made when the insurers reimburse their assured for the deposit paid, the whole of the bank interest earned on the deposit will be paid to the holder of the Deposit Receipt, regardless of the period for which each party has been out of pocket for the amount of the deposit.[40]

(B) Enforcement by Action

Shipowner's Right to Sue

30.54 The shipowner is entitled to sue to recover contribution from the owners of surviving cargo. If the ownership of the cargo remains

[37] See paras. 30.40, 30.48, *ante*.
[38] Rule XXII, *ante*.
[39] See para. 80.06, *post*.
[40] See Rule of Practice B36, para. 70.22, *post*.

unchanged throughout the voyage there is no difficulty in identifying the proper defendant. If, however, there is a change in ownership, the person liable is the owner of the cargo at the time of the sacrifice or expenditure, although the liability may be retained by the shipper, or passed on to subsequent assignees of the goods, by appropriate contractual stipulations.[41] Thus in *Walford de Baerdemaecker v. Galindez*[42] it was held that the special terms of the bills of lading imposed the obligation to contribute on the shippers alone, irrespective of the ownership of the goods at the time of the sacrifice. In *Castle Insurance v. Hong Kong Shipping Co.*[43] it was held that a clause in a bill of lading which provided "General Average shall be adjusted, stated and settled according to York-Antwerp Rules 1950" imposed upon the consignee or indorsee of the bill of lading a contractual obligation to pay any general average contribution on the cargo shipped under that bill of lading.

30.55 An unauthorised deviation, unless waived by the bill of lading holder, would prevent the shipowner from enforcing the bill of lading holder's *contractual* liability to contribute as a party to the bill of lading contract.[44] Whether it will also prevent him from claiming contribution under the general law has been discussed in paragraph 00.36, above.

Enforcing an average agreement

30.56 Where the shipowner has obtained security in the form of an average agreement or bond, he will of course be entitled to enforce the liability to contribute against the parties to the agreement in accordance with its terms.[45] The Lloyd's average bond imposes upon those consignees who sign it the obligation to pay:

> "the proper proportion of any salvage and/or general average and/or special charges which may hereafter be ascertained to be due from the goods or the shippers or owners thereof under an adjustment prepared in accordance with the provisions of the contract of affreightment governing the carriage of the goods or, failing any such provision, in accordance with the law and practice of the place where the common maritime adventure ended and which is payable in respect of the goods by the shippers or owners thereof."

Under an agreement in these terms general average will be payable provided that it was properly chargeable against the owner of the consignment at the time of the general average; and the amount due is

[41] *Hain S.S. Co. v. Tate & Lyle* (1936) 41 Com.Cas. 350 at 356, *per* Lord Atkin; *Morrison S.S. Co. v. Greystoke Castle* [1947] A.C. 265; *Castle Insurance Co. v. Hong Kong Islands Shipping Co.* [1984] 1 A.C. 226 at 233–234, para. 00.29, *ante*.

[42] (1897) 2 Com.Cas. 137.

[43] [1984] 1 A.C. 226 at 235.

[44] *Scaife v. Tobin* (1832) 3 B. & Ad. 523; *Hain S.S. Co. v. Tate & Lyle* (*supra*). For the liability in these circumstances of a consignee who has signed an average bond, see paras. 30.57 *et seq.*, *post*.

[45] See para. 30.47, *ante*. For the effect of such agreements upon the limitation period, see para. 30.74, *post*.

to be calculated in accordance with the terms of the contract between the latter and the shipowner. The previous form of Lloyd's average bond[46] was to the same effect, although less clear in its terms.[47]

It seems probable that no liability arises under the bond until an adjustment has been published,[48] but the bond does not have the effect that the adjustment is binding on the parties.[49]

Effect of deviation or actionable fault on liability under the bond

30.57 The concluding words of the Lloyd's average bond, "and which is payable ..." preserve the right of the signatory to rely on actionable fault as a defence to a claim under the bond,[50] but it remains to consider (1) what is the effect of deviation on liability under the bond, and (2) at whose suit must the fault be actionable if it is to provide the signatory with a defence.

In *Hain SS Co. v. Tate & Lyle*[51] the ship deviated before the general average occurred but the deviation was waived by the charterer, who was the owner of the goods at the time of the general average act. The bills of lading were subsequently indorsed to the receivers, who obtained delivery upon entering into a Lloyd's average bond. In these circumstances the House of Lords held that although the consignees, who had not waived the deviation, had been discharged by the deviation from any liability under the bills of lading, they were nevertheless liable under the bond since the deviation would have provided no defence to a claim against those who owned the cargo at the time of the general average.

30.58 It must be kept in mind that in *Hain SS. Co. v. Tate & Lyle* the ship had returned to her proper route before the general average occurred and the court did not regard the accident as having been caused by the deviation.[52] The case therefore did not raise the same questions as arise where the consignee who enters into the average agreement contends that the event which gave rise to the general average was caused by the

[46] See 10th ed., paras. 1101 *et seq.* for the previous form.

[47] *Hain S.S. Co. v. Tate & Lyle*, para. 30.57, *post.* See also *Castle Insurance Co. v. Hong Kong Islands Shipping Co.* [1984] 1 A.C. 226, para. 00.28, *ante*, and para. 30.39, *ante*. In *Thompson v. Micks, Lambert & Co.* (1933) 39 Com.Cas. 40, the consignee was held liable under the previous form of Lloyd's average bond to pay general average in accordance with the York-Antwerp Rules, which were incorporated into the contract between the shipowner and the cargo owner, although the consignee had never become a party to that contract. His argument that the bond, by referring to adjustment "in the usual manner", required an adjustment under the law of the destination rather than the Rules, was rejected.

[48] See para. 30.74, *post*.

[49] *State Trading Corporation of India v. Doyle Carriers* [1991] 2 Lloyd's Rep. 55.

[50] *Ibid.* at 62.

[51] (1936) 41 Com.Cas. 350.

[52] Despite the remarks of Lord Wright *ibid.*, at 361, which probably refer to the situation which would have existed if the charterers had *not* affirmed the contract, and the responsibility of the shipowner as a common carrier were in issue: see *British Shipping Laws*, Vol. 3: Carver, *Carriage by Sea* (13th ed.), para. 1202.

actionable fault of the shipowner.[53] In such a case it is submitted that the general approach described in paragraph 30.57, above, holds good, and that if the consignee can establish that the event which gave rise to the general average was caused by fault which is actionable at the suit of the party who was the owner at the time of the cargo, contribution is not payable under the agreement.[54]

What of the case where the shipowner's fault is not actionable by the owner of the cargo at the time of the general average, but is actionable by the consignee who enters into the average agreement? Such a situation could arise where the charterparty confers on the shipowner wider exemptions from liability than the bill of lading and the charterer, who owns the cargo at the time of the general average, subsequently indorses the bill of lading to the consignee who takes delivery upon entering into an average agreement. In such a case it seems clear that the consignee, although prima facie liable in terms of the agreement, can rely on the shipowner's breach of the bill of lading contract in order to defeat the claim by circuity of action.[55] **30.59**

Charterer's liability to contribute

If the charterer is the owner of a freight at risk, contribution on freight may be recovered from him in accordance with the terms of the charter, or of any average agreement entered into by him. However, in the absence of agreement to the contrary, a charterer as such is not liable to pay cargo's contribution upon cargo not owned by him. Although there is no direct authority on the point, it is submitted that a clause such as that under consideration in *Castle Insurance Co. v. Hong Kong Islands Shipping Co.*[56] which simply provides for the method of adjustment and settlement, would not, when incorporated into a charterparty, amount to a contractual agreement on the part of the charterer to pay general average assessed on cargo owned by another. The purposes of such a clause is primarily to agree the terms upon which cargo owner should contribute, the charterer being obliged to procure that such terms are incorporated in the bills of lading. In some forms of charterparty, such as the Gencom, this is put beyond doubt, since the liability to contribute **30.60**

[53] See paras. D.01 *et seq.*, *ante*, as to the effect of actionable fault.

[54] It could be argued that the terms of Rule D lead to the opposite conclusion, and that the only relevant consideration is whether the fault is actionable at the suit of the person who entered into the average agreement. The latter, if not a bill of lading holder, may have no cause of action in contract or tort in respect of any fault by the shipowner: see *Leigh & Sillavan v. Aliakmon Shipping* [1986] A.C. 785.

[55] In *Hain S.S. Co. v. Tate & Lyle* (para. 30.57, *ante*) the consignee did not contend that the general average was to avert a loss for which the shipowner, as common carrier, would have been liable to the consignee, thus providing the consignee with a defence on the grounds of actionable fault. This would have given rise to the question whether, the bill of lading contract having been abrogated, the shipowner owed the duties of a common carrier to anyone except the owner of the goods at the time.

[56] [1984] 1 A.C. 226; para. 30.54, *ante*.

is expressly imposed upon the proprietors of the cargo.

A charterer who owns the cargo, and who has obtained delivery of his goods over which the shipowner was asserting a lien, is bound to pay general average in accordance with the terms of the charter, and is not entitled to rely upon a cesser clause in the charter.[57]

Cargo Owner's Right to Sue

30.61 The cargo owner may sue (1) the shipowner in respect of contributions in respect of ship and, sometimes, freight; (2) other cargo-owners.[58] In the case of a collision as a result of which he has become liable to contribute in general average, the cargo owner may also recover from the owners of the other colliding ship a part of the contribution which he has been compelled to pay directly proportional to the extent of the responsibility of that ship for the collision.[59]

Charterer's Right to Sue

30.62 Where the charterer is the owner of freight at risk which has been sacrificed by a general average act, he will have rights of suit against the other parties to the adventure similar to those of the owner of sacrificed cargo. It seems unlikely, however, that a charterer who did not have a possessory interest in the cargo could successfully claim to recover, from the owners of a colliding ship, any general average contribution which he had become liable to pay on freight.[60]

Jurisdiction

High Court

30.63 The general jurisdiction of the High Court is limited only by the need to effect service on the defendant in accordance with the Rules of the Supreme Court or the E.E.C. Convention on Jurisdiction and the

[57] *Marvigor Cia. Naviera S.A. v. Romano Export State Company for Foreign Trade* [1977] 2 Lloyd's Rep. 280.

[58] *Dobson v. Wilson* (1813) 3 Camp. 480. In that case the master had sold part of the cargo to procure his release from prison for debt. It was held that the goods had not been sacrificed for the safety of the ship and the residue of the cargo.

[59] *Morrison v. Greystoke Castle* [1947] A.C. 265. See also paras. 50.123 *et seq., post.*

[60] Because of the rules governing the recoverability of financial loss in tort, the charterer has no cause of action in tort in respect of loss of freight (see *Elliott Steam Tug v. Shipping Controller* [1922] 1 K.B. 127; *Candlewood Corp. v. Mitsui* [1986] A.C. 1) and it is difficult to see how he could have any greater rights in respect of contribution on freight saved. However, in *The Okehampton* [1913] P. 173, it was held that a charterer who had received the cargo from the shipper, placed it on board and issued a bill of lading in his own name was in possession of the cargo and therefore entitled to claim damages in tort for loss of freight thereon.

Enforcement of Judgments in Civil and Commercial Matters.[61] Both the Rules of the Supreme Court and the Convention permit service out of the jurisdiction where the parties have agreed that the English courts shall have jurisdiction to determine the dispute.[62] Whether or not service out of the jurisdiction is permissible in other cases may depend on whether the law of the adjustment, or the law governing any bond or guarantee which the action is brought to enforce, is English law,[63] or whether payment is to be made in England.[64]

The law governing the adjustment and the place where contributions are to be settled has already been discussed when dealing with *The Place and Law of the Adjustment* in paragraphs 30.02 *et seq.*, above. So far as concerns average bonds, there is little clear authority on the law which governs them, or the place where payment under them is to be made, and the Lloyd's average bond contains no express provision on these matters. In *Schothorst and Schuitema v. Franz Dauter*[65] Kerr J. expressed the view that the average bond should derive its proper law from the law governing the contract of carriage as a whole rather than the law governing the adjustment. It is submitted, however, that an average bond is rather more closely connected with the law governing the adjustment than that governing the contract of carriage, and in *Armar Shipping v. Caisse Algerienne*[66] the views of Kerr J. were not adopted. However, on the facts of the latter case the Court of Appeal declined to hold that the proper law of the bond was the same as the law of the adjustment, since the bill of lading contract (to which the defendant was not a party) conferred upon the carrier a right to select the place of adjustment, and the selection had not been made when the bond was executed; the proper law of the bond could not "float" until the selection had been made, but must be ascertainable when the contract was formed.

The Admiralty jurisdiction of the High Court is currently derived from section 20(2) of the Supreme Court Act 1981, and includes: **30.64**

[61] See R.S.C. Ords. 10 and 11. Where the defendant is domiciled in a Contracting State as defined by the Civil Jurisdiction and Judgments Act 1982, jurisdiction is governed by the Act, which gives effect to the provisions of the E.E.C. Convention on Jurisdiction and the Enforcement of Judgments in Civil and Commercial Matters.

[62] See R.S.C. Ord. 11, r. 1(1)(d)(iv) and the Convention, Art. 17.

[63] R.S.C., Ord. 11, r. 1(1)(d)(iii)—contract governed by English law. The Convention contains no equivalent provision. Under R.S.C. the jurisdiction extends to a claim to enforce a quasi-contractual claim (see *Rousou's Trustee v. Rousou* [1955] 3 All E.R. 486) and therefore, it is suggested, to a claim in general average where the obligation to contribute is not contractual. Where the obligation to contribute *is* contractual, it is submitted that the court can exercise jurisdiction under this sub-rule, whatever the proper law of the contract of carriage as a whole, so long as the law of adjustment is English. *Sed quaere*: see *Armar Shipping v. Caisse Algerienne* [1981] 1 W.L.R. 207 at 212, [1980] 2 Lloyd's Rep. 450 at 456.

[64] R.S.C. Ord. 11, r. 1(1)(e)—breach of contract within the jurisdiction; Convention, Art. 5.1—place of performance of the obligation in question.

[65] [1973] 2 Lloyd's Rep. 91.

[66] [1981] 1 W.L.R. 207, [1980] 2 Lloyd's Rep. 450.

(g) any claim for loss of or damage to goods carried in a ship;
(h) any claim arising out of any agreement relating to the carriage of goods in a ship or to the use or hire of a ship;
(j) any claim in the nature of salvage...;
(q) any claim arising out of an act which is or is claimed to be a general average act.

This jurisdiction is exercisable *in rem* in accordance with the conditions set out in section 21(4) of the Act, as outlined in paragraph 30.66, below.

County courts

30.65 Until 1991 the general jurisdiction of the county courts in claims in contract or tort was limited, in the absence of agreement to the contrary, to cases where the debt, demand or damage claimed did not exceed £5,000. In 1991 the financial limit on the general jurisdiction of the court was abolished, but a limit of £5,000 still applies where the court is exercising its admiralty jurisdiction, as defined in section 27(1) of the County Courts Act 1984.[67] Unlike the equivalent statutory provision which defines the admiralty jurisdiction of the High Court,[68] section 27(1) makes no specific reference to claims in general average, but it does include all of the other types of claim referred to in paragraph 30.64, above, and it follows that, except in most unusual circumstances,[69] a claim in general average will fall within the admiralty jurisdiction of the county court, as a "claim arising out of any agreement relating to the carriage of goods in a ship or to the use or hire of a ship", and will therefore be subject to the £5,000 limit. The limit will not apply if the parties have made a written agreement to submit the dispute to a specified county court.

Proceedings in rem and arrest

30.66 The admiralty jurisdiction of both the High Court and the county court is exercisable *in rem* in accordance with the relevant statutory provisions.[70] Whilst these are too complicated to discuss in detail here, their effect in relation to claims in general average is, broadly speaking, as follows:

[67] The abolition was effected by the High Court and County Courts Jurisdiction Order 1991, S.I. 1991 No. 724 (made under the Courts and Legal Services Act 1990), art. 2(8) and Sched. 1. Art 12(b) preserves the limit in relation to proceedings under the county courts' admiralty jurisdiction. The limit of £5,000 (modified in the case of salvage claims) is contained in the County Courts Act 1984, s. 27(2).

[68] *I.e.* the Supreme Court Act 1981, s. 20(2): para. 30.64, *ante*.

[69] See paras. 00.19—00.30, *ante*, as to the circumstances in which a claim in general average can be said to arise out of the contract of carriage.

[70] For the High Court see the Supreme Court Act 1981, s. 21(4), and for the county court, see the County Courts Act 1984, s. 28(4).

(1) an action for contribution due from the shipowner may be pursued *in rem* against:
   (a) the ship in connection with which the claim arose, provided that it is still owned by him at the time when the action is commenced; or
   (b) any other ship owned by him at the time when the action is commenced;
(2) an action for contribution due from the charterer may be pursued *in rem* against any ship owned by him at the time when the action is commenced;
(3) an action for contribution due from a cargo owner, not being the shipowner or charterer, cannot be pursued by an action *in rem*.

The main advantage of an action *in rem*, where the claimant is unsecured or inadequately secured, is that he may arrest the vessel against which the action is brought and thus obtain security for his claim.

Jurisdiction in the United States

Cases involving questions of general average may come within the jurisdiction of either the District Courts of the United States (Federal Courts), or the State Courts. The District Courts, however, have exclusive jurisdiction in Admiralty, and proceedings *in rem* against vessels and in salvage cases are necessarily brought before them. The owner of goods sacrificed has, in the United States, a lien on the vessel and other interests for the amount due to him. Since the United States District Courts in Admiralty by their process *in rem* afford the most convenient means of enforcing this right, and of enforcing the shipowner's lien on the cargo, it is by the District Courts that almost all cases involving general average are now heard. **30.67**

Arbitration

Parties to a dispute may of course refer it to arbitration once it has arisen, and this gives rise to no specific problems in connection with general average. However, where the contract of carriage contains an arbitration agreement, for example in relation to all disputes arising under or out of it, and a claim for general average contribution is disputed, it is necessary to decide whether the dispute so arises. This has already been considered in connection with the case of *Union of India v. E.B. Aaby's Rederi*.[71] **30.68**

[71] [1975] A.C. 797; para. 00.27, *ante*. See also para. 30.23, *ante*.

Responsibility for Collecting Contributions

30.69 We have seen that the shipowner is responsible for obtaining security for the cargo owner's claims in general average and for procuring an adjustment.[72] The reason why it has been held that he is under these duties is that the cargo owner is usually in no position to take these steps himself. But does the shipowner's responsibility extend to the actual collection of general average contributions from the other interests? Whilst there is no authority on the point there would seem to be no valid reason for imposing on him this burden, which could be very onerous, provided that he has taken proper steps to obtain security.[73] If this is correct, it follows that any party who is a creditor in the general average is responsible for taking the necessary steps, at his own expense, to enforce payment. The one limited exception to this is that where the shipowner has obtained security in a form which gives him alone the legal right to enforce it,[74] he must be under an obligation to allow the cargo owner to bring proceedings in his name to enforce the security, against a suitable indemnity in respect of the costs.

In practice, because of his familiarity with the case, his possession of all the general average security and claims documents and his previous dealings with many of the parties involved, the average adjuster is usually entrusted in the first instance with the collection and settlement of all cargo debit and credit balances shown due in the adjustment. His fees for these services will be charged to general average in the adjustment itself.

30.70 It follows from the above that, provided that the shipowner has taken proper steps to obtain security, the risk that contribution may be irrecoverable from one or more of the parties to the adventure, for example by reason of insolvency or exchange controls or other legal or practical obstacles, falls on those parties to whom the lost contribution is due, that is those parties whose property has been sacrificed or who

[72] See paras. 30.42–30.46, *ante*.

[73] It was held in *Nobel's Explosives v. Rea* (1897) 2 Com.Cas. 293 (para. 30.44, *ante*) that a shipowner who fails to take proper steps to obtain security for the benefit of the cargo owner is liable in damages to the cargo owner, but the case does not support the proposition that the shipowner is under any further obligations with regard to the collection of contributions due to the cargo owner.

[74] The Lloyd's average bond appears to fall into this category, since the promise of payment is, on the face of it, made solely to the shipowner. On the other hand the promise of payment is not expressly confined to the sums due to the shipowner in respect of his own losses, and having regard to the shipowner's well-established obligation to obtain security for the claims of cargo owners, it is submitted that it extends to these losses as well as his own. It is possible that the shipowner would be held to have entered into the bond as agent on behalf of those cargo owners who were creditors in the general average, in which case the latter would have the right to sue on the bond in their own names as principals. However it seems more likely that the shipowner would be regarded as having entered into the bond as trustee for those persons, in which case proceedings to enforce a cargo owner's claim would have to be brought in the shipowner's name, although at the cargo owner's expense.

have incurred general average expenditure, and *pro rata* to the general average allowances credited to each of them. No further contribution can be levied against those parties who have paid their full proportion of the general average.

Limitation of Action

Two separate issues need to be considered in the context of limitation of actions. The first is the date at which the cause of action accrues for the purpose of the Limitation Act,[75] and the second is the period of limitation. **30.71**

Accrual of the cause of action

Claims under policies of insurance. The question of when time starts to run for the purpose of the Limitation Act[76] in relation to a claim for contribution was considered by the English courts, for the first time so far as can be discovered, in *Chandris v. Argo Insurance Co. Ltd.*[77] In that case the defendants relied on the statute as a defence to a claim by their assured for indemnity against liability to contribute in general average. The plaintiffs contended that their liability arose on the issue and publication of an adjustment, the defendants that it arose when sacrifices were made or expenditure incurred, or alternatively on the termination of the adventure. **30.72**

Megaw J. held (1) that by reason of the terms of the policy, and of the York-Antwerp Rules 1924, incorporated therein, the parties had contemplated and provided that an average statement should be produced (but not that it should be binding upon them), but (2) that the publication of an adjustment had not been made a condition precedent to the existence of a cause of action, and (3) that in the absence of an express term to that effect, liability to contribute arose when a sacrifice was made or expenditure incurred. The decision on the third point was based in part on *Noreuro Traders Ltd v. E. Hardy & Co.*[78] and dicta in *Tate & Lyle Ltd v. Hain Steamship Co. Ltd*[79] and *Morrison Steamship Co. Ltd v. Greystoke Castle*,[80] and in part on section 66(3) of the Marine Insurance Act 1906.[81]

[75] The Limitation Act 1980, replacing the Limitation Act 1939.
[76] *Ibid.*
[77] [1963] 2 Lloyd's Rep. 65.
[78] (1923) 16 Ll.L.Rep. 320.
[79] (1934) 151 L.T. 249, reversed *sub nom. Hain Steamship Co. Ltd v. Tate & Lyle Ltd* (1936) 41 Com.Cas. 350.
[80] [1947] A.C. 265 at 283, 312.
[81] 6 Edw. 7, c. 41

30.73 **Claims between the parties to the adventure.** In *Schothorst and Schuitema v. Franz Dauter GmbH*[82] it was argued that the position was different as between the parties to an adventure, and that in their case time started to run on the publication of an adjustment. Kerr J. rejected this argument, holding that the reasoning of Megaw J. applied equally to a claim for general average contribution made by one party to the adventure against another party to the adventure, so that time began to run at the date of the general average sacrifice or expenditure.

The same conclusion was reached in *Castle Insurance Co. v. Hong Kong Shipping Co.*,[83] where the Privy Council held that the shipowner's claim under the bills of lading[84] for contribution from cargo arose when the sacrifice was made or the expenditure incurred. It made no difference that the bills of lading contemplated that an adjustment would be prepared in accordance with the York-Antwerp Rules.

It should be noted that a cause of action can only be said to accrue in a somewhat artificial manner before the adventure has terminated, since only then can it be known what property is to contribute and what its value is. But the accrual of a cause of action is in any event an artificial conception, as a number of cases have shown in other branches of the law.[85]

30.74 **Claims under average agreements.** Where the defendant has entered into a bond, guarantee or other form of undertaking whereby he agrees to pay such general average as may be legally due, the undertaking creates a fresh cause of action, in respect of which time cannot begin to run until the undertaking is given.[86] However, it does not follow that time will necessarily begin to run at that date, since the terms of the undertaking may, expressly or by implication, provide that the publication of an adjustment shall be a condition precedent to the making of any claim thereunder. Thus in *Castle Insurance Co. v. Hong Kong Islands Shipping Co.*[87] it was held that the Lloyd's bond executed by the consignees, and the average guarantees executed by the insurers of the cargo made it clear by implication that the claim was not to arise until the adjustment had been completed. There can in practice be few forms of undertaking which would give rise to a different interpretation, since one of the forms of guarantee merely contained a promise to pay "any contribution which may be legally chargeable".

[82] [1973] 2 Lloyd's Rep. 91.

[83] [1984] 1 A.C. 226.

[84] The opposite conclusion was reached in relation to the shipowner's alternative claim under the average bonds and guarantees; see para. 30.74, *post*.

[85] *E.g. Central Electricity Generating Board v. Halifax Corporation* [1963] A.C. 785.

[86] *Union of India v. E.B. Aaby's Rederi* [1975] A.C. 797.

[87] *Ibid.* The contrary view expressed by Kerr J. in *Schothorst and Schuitema v. Franz Dauter* [1973] 2 Lloyd's Rep. 91 at 97 was disapproved.

The period of limitation

Where the claim for contribution is founded on contract, the Limitation Act 1980 provides that the limitation period is six years from the date of the accrual of the cause of action.[88] It has been held that a clause in a bill of lading which provides for adjustment or settlement of general average in accordance with the York-Antwerp Rules imposes a contractual obligation to contribute[89] and a similar conclusion has been reached where the claim for contribution arose between shipowner and charterer, and the charterparty contained a similar clause.[90] It follows that, since such clauses are almost universally incorporated into charterparties and bills of lading, there will be few cases where the six-year time limit does not apply, and in such circumstances it is not open to the parties to seek to avoid the limitation period by advancing the claim under the mercantile law independently of the contract.[91] **30.75**

In the exceptional case where the claim for contribution is not governed by contract, it is an open question whether the court would hold that the claim was sufficiently analogous to a claim founded on contract to attract the provisions of section 5 of the Limitation Act, or whether the claim would be time-barred only in the event of laches.[92]

Contractual limitation periods

Where a contractual provision stipulates a special time limit for claims under or arising out of the contract, it is a question of construction of the contract as a whole whether the clause extends to claims for general average contribution. Where a charterparty imposed a 12-month time limit from arrival at the port of discharge for claims under the charter, and contained a clause providing for adjustment in accordance with the York-Antwerp Rules, it was held that the claim arose under the charter and was therefore time-barred.[93] However, where the defendant has entered into a separate undertaking to contribute to general average, the time limit contained in the contract of affreightment would not protect him against a claim on the undertaking.[94] **30.76**

In principle it would seem that, where the relevant contract of affreightment incorporates the Hague-Visby Rules, a claim by a cargo owner against the carrier for contribution towards a sacrifice of the cargo would fall within the provisions of Article III Rule 6 and become time-

[88] Limitation Act 1980, s. 5. The exemption from the provisions of the Act, previously accorded by the Limitation Act 1939 to claims which could be pursued by an admiralty action *in rem*, was abolished in the 1980 Act.

[89] *Castle Insurance Co. v. Hong Kong Shipping Co.* [1984] A.C. 226.

[90–91] *Union of India v. E.B. Aaby's Rederi* [1975] A.C. 797. See also *Alma Shipping Corp. v. Union of India* [1971] 2 Lloyd's Rep. 494; para. 00.27, *ante*.

[92] See paras. 00.19 *et seq*, *ante*, as to the basis of the right to contribution. And see *Halsbury's Laws* (4th ed.), Vol. 28, para. 661; *Goff and Jones: Law of Restitution* (4th ed.), p. 772; *Re Diplock* [1948] Ch. 465.

[93] *Alma Shipping Corp. v. Union of India* (*supra*).

[94] *Union of India v. E.B. Aaby's Rederi* (*supra*).

barred after a year.[95] The inconvenience of such a result requires no elaboration.

United States

30.77 The courts of the United States have held that the cause of action accrues at the termination of the adventure, though the alternative which they had to consider was the publication of an adjustment, and not the date of a sacrifice or expenditure.[96]

The fact that the defendant, in order to obtain the release of his cargo, has entered into an undertaking to pay general average, does not extend the time limit.[97] However, there is no statute of limitations directly applicable to a claim for general average, and the claim will be barred only by laches.

[95] In *Goulandris v. Goldman* [1958] 1 Q.B. 74, Pearson J. appears to have envisaged that the rather narrower provisions of Art. III, r. 6 of the unamended Hague Rules would have applied to such a case.

[96] *The Logan* (1936) A.M.C. 993; *Transpacific S.S. Co. v. Marine Office of America* (1957) A.M.C. 1070.

[97] *Argyll Shipping Co. v. Hanover Insce. Co.* [1968] A.M.C. 2195; *The Beatrice* [1975] 1 Lloyd's Rep. 220.

SECTION 6

THE CURRENCY OF THE ADJUSTMENT

RATES OF EXCHANGE AND THE PROBLEM OF SET-OFF

When a general average occurs on any international voyage, problems of considerable financial consequence can arise if the rates of exchange alter between the time of the general average act and the date of settlement under the general average adjustment. **40.01**

Devaluation or revaluation of any currency inevitably and inescapably brings profit or loss in its wake, and it is clearly important that these profits and losses should fall on the proper parties. They cannot be allowed to alight by mere chance, nor by a shrewd selection of the currency to be adopted in the adjustment or the dates on which exchange rates are applied; the matter must be governed by some convention, even if that convention seems arbitrary to those whose interest it offends and reasonable only to those whom it suits. It is important that the parties to the adventure should know their strict legal rights and responsibilities.

To illustrate the problem, and in recognition of the fact that even a major currency such as the United States Dollar could halve in value within the space of two years against the Japanese Yen, our example shall concern an American-owned ship which incurs a general average expenditure of $100,000 to which the Japanese-owned cargo should contribute 60 per cent. **40.02**

The rates of exchange current:

At the time of the general average expenditure	$ 1.00 = Y 250
When the adjustment is issued	$ 1.00 = Y 125

If the adjustment is drawn up in **Yen**. (@ 250)	= Y 25,000,000
The shipowner would receive from cargo interests 60 per cent	= Y 15,000,000
Converted @ 125, this would produce	$ 120,000
As the shipowner requires to balance his books only	60,000
He would make a PROFIT of	$ 60,000

If the adjustment is drawn up in **Dollars** *i.e.*	$ 100,000
The shipowner would receive from cargo interests 60 per cent	$ 60,000
which precisely balances his books, but...	
By reason of the great appreciation in the value of the Yen, at 125 this would cost only	Y 7,500,00
Instead of, as in the previous example	15,000,000
showing a SAVING to cargo interests of	Y 7,500,000

What then, are the legal principles and practice which now govern the situation?

English Law Before 1974

40.03 Until 1974 English law and practice on claims involving foreign currency was governed by a rule whose origins could be traced to decisions in the sixteenth century or earlier.[1] The first limb of the rule was that the English court could only give judgment in sterling, and the second limb was that the rate of exchange to be applied in converting any foreign currency into sterling was the rate prevailing at the date when the cause of action arose. Judgment would be given in sterling, months or years later, by which time rates of exchange might have moved, resulting in either a profit or loss in his own currency to the claimant.

This rule, which came to be known as the "breach-date-sterling rule" was firmly settled by decisions of the House of Lords[2] and applied to claims for damages in tort[3] or for breach of contract[4] and to claims to recover debts, even when the debt was expressed in a foreign currency.[5]

40.04 In *Noreuro Traders Ltd v. E. Hardy & Co.*[6] the same rule was held to be applicable to a claim for general average contribution. In that case the voyage, which ended at Antwerp, was completed immediately before the outbreak of the First World War, but the adjustment, which was in Belgian francs, was not completed until 1921. One issue between the parties concerned the rates of exchange to be applied in converting the ultimate liability in francs into sterling for purposes of an English

[1] For the history of the rule see the judgments of Lord Wilberforce and Lord Cross in the House of Lords in *Miliangos v. George Frank Textiles Ltd* [1976] A.C. 443 at 466–467, 491–495, [1976] 1 Lloyd's Rep. 201 at 209, 225–9.
[2] See nn. 3, 5, *infra.*
[3] *The Volturno* [1921] 2 A.C. 544, H.L.
[4] See, *e.g. De Fernando v. Simon Smits* [1920] 3 K.B. 409.
[5] *Re United Railways of Havana and Regla Warehouses* [1961] A.C. 1007.
[6] (1923) 16 Ll.L.Rep. 319.

judgment.[7] On this point Rowlatt J. decided in favour of the pre-war rate of exchange.[8]

The effect of the breach-date-sterling rule was that the chance of profit or the risk of loss rested entirely with the foreign claimant or creditor, if sterling fluctuated against his own currency. At the time when major world currencies were based on the gold standard this would normally be of little or no financial consequence; and in those cases where there were appreciable fluctuations the rule tended to work to the advantage of the claimant, since sterling was in general a strong currency. However, in the final years of this legal régime, not only had the gold standard disappeared, but sterling tended to be weak, with the result that foreign claimants showed a declining interest in availing themselves of the renowned British justice when it produced judgments (and settlements) in depreciated sterling. **40.05**

In these circumstances, the breach-date-sterling rule began to be called into question, and by a series of decisions between 1974 and 1979 it was effectively swept aside.[9]

The Modern English Law

The modern law on currency and rates of exchange is embodied in three decisions of the House of Lords concerning debt, damages in tort and damages for breach of contract.

(1) Debt

In *Miliangos v. George Frank (Textiles) Ltd*[10] the plaintiffs claimed payment for a quantity of polyester yarn sold to the defendants under a contract in which the price was expressed in Swiss francs. The proper law of the contract was Swiss law and the money of account and of payment was Swiss francs. **40.06**

It was held (Lord Simon of Glaisdale dissenting) that the rule adopted by the House of Lords in earlier cases that an English court could not

[7] The other issue was the rate of exchange to be applied in converting the payments on account, as to which, see para. 22.09, *ante*.

[8] It is not clear from the judgment whether Rowlatt J. regarded the correct date for conversion as being the date of the sacrifice or expenditure or the date when the voyage terminated. The former seems more likely—see also para. 40.24, n. 41, *post*.

[9] *I.e.* the three decisions of the House of Lords referred to in the next following paragraphs, which were preceded by two important decisions of the Court of Appeal: in *Jugoslovenska Oceanska Plovidba v. Castle Investment Co.* [1974] Q.B. 292, it was held that English arbitrators had power to make an award in a foreign currency; in *Schorsch Meier v. Hennin* [1975] Q.B. 416, a revolutionary case, it was held that where the claim was for a foreign currency debt judgment could be given in the currency of the debt.

[10] [1976] A.C. 443, [1976] 1 Lloyd's Rep. 201.

give judgment for payment of a sum of foreign currency could not be justified and must be abandoned,[11] and that the plaintiffs were entitled to judgment in Swiss francs.

(2) Damages in Tort

40.07 In *The Despina R*[12] the plaintiffs' ship was damaged in collision for which the other ship was 85 per cent to blame. The plaintiffs had incurred expenses for repairs, etc., in Chinese R.M.B., Japanese yen and United States dollars, but had settled these various expenses in their operating currency of United States dollars.

It was unanimously held that, given the new ability of an English court to give judgments in a foreign currency, to give a judgment in the currency in which the loss was sustained (that is, United States dollars) produced a juster result than one which fixed the plaintiff with a sum in sterling taken at the rates of exchange ruling at the date of the breach or of the loss.

(3) Damages for breach of contract

40.08 *The Folias*[13] concerned a claim for damage to a cargo of onions owing to the failure of the vessel's refrigerating machinery and for which the shipowner was responsible. The Brazilian receivers of the cargo had rendered their claim to the charterers of the vessel in Brazilian cruzeiros and this had been settled by them by purchase of the necessary Brazilian cruzeiros with French francs. In turn, they presented their claim against the shipowners in French francs.

It was unanimously held that, in contractual as in other cases, a judgment could be given in a currency other than sterling, and that according to the normal principle of *restitutio in integrum*, the charterers' recoverable loss was the sum of French francs which they had expended, rather than Brazilian cruzeiros.

40.09 The purpose underlying these decisions was described as follows by Lord Wilberforce in *Miliangos v. Frank*,[14] in the context of a claim in debt:

[11] In *Miliangos v. Frank* the House of Lords exercised its discretion under its 1966 Practice Direction to depart from the decision in *In Re United Railways of Havana and Regla Warehouses*; and in *The Despina R* and *The Folias* (*intra*) the House of Lords took the view that *The Volturno*, and the decisions on damages for breach of contract, (see para. 40.03, *ante*) turned entirely upon the old rule which required a judgment to be in sterling, and therefore as being of no application once that rule had been abolished.

[12] [1979] A.C. 685, [1979] 1 Lloyd's Rep. 1.

[13] *Ibid.*

[14] [1976] A.C. 443 at 465; [1976] 1 Lloyd's Rep. 201 at 208.

> "I do not for myself think it doubtful that, in a case such as the present, justice demands that the creditor should not suffer from fluctuations in the value of sterling. His contract has nothing to do with sterling: he has bargained for his own currency and only his own currency."

and in *The Despina R*,[15] in the context of a damages claim:

> "... to give a judgment in the currency in which the loss was sustained produces a juster result than one which fixes the plaintiff with a sum in sterling taken at the date of the breach or of the loss. ... To fix such a plaintiff with sterling commits him to the risk of changes in the value of a currency with which he has no connection: to award him a sum in the currency of the expenditure or loss, or that in which he bears the expenditure or loss, gives him exactly what he has lost and commits him only to the risk of changes in the value of that currency, or those currencies, which are either his currency or those which he has chosen to use."

From a practical point of view the major effect has been to remove from the *creditor* the risk of profit or loss on exchange fluctuation (unless he has bargained for a currency of account other than his own currency). The profits and losses themselves are totally unavoidable, but they now fall upon the *debtor*, unless his own currency happens to be that in which the claim is calculated. A recent decision of the House of Lords[16] provides a vivid illustration of how great these profits or losses may be.

The modern law may be summarised as embodying two principles. **40.10**
The first is that where the parties have agreed, expressly or by implication, on a currency which shall be used as a measure of the obligation—"the currency of the contract"—the courts will give judgment in that currency; the second is that where there is no currency of the contract the damage should be calculated, and judgment given, in the currency in which the loss was felt by the claimant, or "which most truly expresses his loss".[17] The determination of that currency, and the rates of exchange for converting other currencies are considered in more detail below.

Application of the Modern Law to General Average

None of the three cases upon which the modern law is founded was **40.11**
concerned with general average, and it may be objected that general average differs from debt in that there is normally no specified currency of account, and from damages in that the right of recovery does not arise out of any breach of duty. However, in the case where the parties

[15] [1979] A.C. 685 at 696–697, [1979] 1 Lloyd's Rep. 1 at 5.

[16] *The Texaco Melbourne* [1994] 1 Lloyd's Rep. 473: see para. 40.28, *post*. In that case the debtor *profited* from the fluctuation.

[17] *Per* Lord Wilberforce in *The Folias* [1979] A.C. 701, [1979] 1 Lloyd's Rep. 1 at 8. See para. 40.22, *post*.

have agreed upon a currency of account for general average, the situation cannot be distinguished from *Miliangos*[18] and there can be no doubt that the court would apply the same rule. Even in those cases where there is no agreement, it is illogical to have a special rule for general average which differs from the rules applicable to any other monetary claims. The principle of *restitutio in integrum*, upon which the decision of the House of Lords in *The Despina R* and *The Folias*[19] is based, is no less applicable to general average than to damages, and it should therefore prevail in the absence of any binding practice to the contrary.[20] It follows that the ordinary rules of law summarised in the previous paragraph should apply equally to general average.

40.12 Nevertheless, general average will often give rise to currency problems which are more complicated than those which arise in other areas, and the cases decided since 1975 scarcely provide comprehensive answers to many of these problems. In what currencies should the adjustment be prepared? At what dates should disbursements, the amount to be made good for sacrifices, and contributory values, be exchanged? Upon what dates should the competing claims of the different parties to the adventure be set off against each other? How are payments on account and cash deposits to be treated? If a claim for contribution has to be enforced by action or arbitration, can it be based on the currency amount shown in the adjustment?

40.13 We shall attempt to answer these questions later in this section.[21] However, it can be said at the outset that one undoubted effect of the abolition of the rule that the English court must give judgment in sterling is that, where the adjustment is governed by English law, there will now be no difference between the currency in which the adjustment should be prepared and the currency in which the judgment will be recovered if the claim is enforced by proceedings in England. The adjuster ought to give effect to the principles set out in paragraph 40.10, above and, if he does so correctly, the court will give judgment in the currency of the adjustment.

Even where the adjustment is governed by foreign law[22] there is no reason why the English court should not give judgment in the currency of the adjustment, provided that the adjuster has correctly applied the foreign law in selecting that currency. The situation which arose in *Noreuro Traders v. E. Hardy & Co.*[23] where it was accepted that the

[18] [1976] A.C. 443, [1976] 1 Lloyd's Rep. 201.

[19] [1979] A.C. 685, [1979] 1 Lloyd's Rep. 1.

[20] No uniform practice of average adjusters has yet emerged, see para. 40.20, n. 32, *post*.

[21] The treatment of payments on account and cash deposits is dealt with in paras. 22.09–22.10, *ante*.

[22] The selection of the currency in which the adjustment should be made is determined by the substantive law governing the obligation—see *The Folias* [1979] A.C. 685 at 700. In general average this is the law governing the adjustment.

[23] (1923) 16 Ll.L.R. 319, para. 40.04, *ante*.

adjustment fell to be made in Belgian francs but all the losses had to be re-converted from francs into sterling at the rate prevailing on the date when they were incurred, or on the date when the adventure terminated,[24] is a thing of the past.

Determining the Currency of Adjustment

We shall now consider in more detail the currency or currencies in which the adjustment should be prepared, and the exchange rates which should be used when conversion from one currency to another is necessary. As Lord Wilberforce stated in *The Folias*[25]: **40.14**

> "The first step must be to see whether, expressly or by implication, the contract provides an answer to the currency question. This may lead to selection of the 'currency of the contract.'"

Express provision for currency of adjustment

For reasons which will become painfully clear from Examples 4 and 5 later in this section,[26] *it cannot be too strongly recommended that every bill of lading and charterparty should include special provisions specifying a single currency in which any general average adjustment is to be prepared and settled, for example*: **40.15**

> "General Average shall be adjusted, stated and settled at [ ] according to York-Antwerp Rules of 1974 ... In such adjustment, disbursements in foreign currencies shall be exchanged into [ ] money at the rate prevailing on the dates made and allowances for damage to cargo claimed in foreign currency shall be converted at the rate prevailing on the last day of discharge at the port or place of final discharge of such damaged cargo from the ship."

There is no legal objection to such a contractual provision in English law, and, provided that the specified currency is an accepted international trading currency, or bears some relationship to the particular trade on which the vessel is engaged, such a provision should be commercially acceptable, and this would resolve the many problems and arguments which currently occur where no such currency provision is made.

Some clauses confer upon the shipowner the option to select the currency of the adjustment. There is no reason in English law why such a clause should not be enforceable, but the courts would undoubtedly be reluctant to allow the option to be used so as to enable the shipowner to engage in a free currency speculation at the expense of the other **40.16**

[24] It is not clear in the report of the case which date was adopted. See also para. 40.04, *ante* and para. 40.24, n. 41, *post*.
[25] [1979] A.C. 685 at 700, [1979] 1 Lloyd's Rep. 1 at 7.
[26] See paras. 40.42–40.48, *post*.

parties to the adventure. It would therefore be likely to be held that the option was to be exercised very promptly upon the making of the sacrifice or the expenditure, and that the selection by the shipowner of a currency which had no connection with the loss was an invalid exercise of the option.

40.17 Where the contract makes provision for a specific currency, all expenditure and sacrifices should be converted into that currency for the purposes of the adjustment, with the result that the adjustment will be in a single currency. The dates on which, subject to any special terms of the contract, other currencies are to be converted into the currency of the contract are considered below.[27]

Implied currency of the adjustment

40.18 In the absence of a clause expressly specifying the currency of the contract for general average purposes, can any particular currency of the contract be implied?

There are a number of possibilities, namely,

(1) the currency in which other payments under the contract, such as freight, are expressed,
(2) where there is an express choice of the law governing the adjustment, the currency of the country whose law governs the adjustment, and
(3) the currency of the country or countries where the adventure ends.

The first possibility may be dismissed, for as Lord Wilberforce said in *The Folias*[28]:

> "In the present case the fact that U.S. dollars have been named as the currency in which payments in respect of hire and other contractual payments are to be made, provides no necessary or indeed plausible reason why damages for breach of the contract should be paid in that currency. The terms of other contracts may lead to a similar conclusion."

Equally, the second possibility has little to recommend it. The losses suffered in the general average may have little or no connection with the country whose law is chosen and there is no reason why a choice of law, or a choice of place, for the adjustment should be treated as an indication that the parties intended that the currency of that country should be

[27] See para. 40.24, *post*.

[28] [1979] A.C. 685 at 701. [1979] 1 Lloyd's Rep. 1 at 8. The observations to the contrary in *Jugoslavenska Oceanska Plovidba v. Castle Investment Co.* [1974] Q.B. 292 at 298 can no longer be regarded as sound. For a case in which it was held, applying *The Folias*, that a provision in a charterparty that the cost of overtime should be shared between owners and charterers imported no choice of the currency in which overtime expenses were incurred: see *Food Corporation of India v. Carras* [1980] 2 Lloyd's Rep. 577.

used. In *The Folias*[29] the parties had expressly chosen English law and arbitration; but that was not considered to indicate an intention to choose English currency for payment of damages.

The third possibility deserves more serious consideration. Before 1974 it was generally considered that, because general average was historically settled at destination, and it was there that the shipowner could exercise his lien, the currency or currencies of the ports of destination, or where the adventure ended, should be adopted. This viewpoint derived some support from Rule G of the York-Antwerp Rules, reflecting the common law, which provides that: **40.19**

> "General average shall be adjusted as regards both loss and contribution upon the basis of values at the time and place when and where the adventure ends."

It also followed the viewpoint accepted in *Noreuro Traders Ltd v. E. Hardy & Co.*[30] that on a voyage to Antwerp, the general average adjustment fell to be made in Belgian francs, and in *The Arkansas*[31] (a case where the bill of lading incorporated the York-Antwerp Rules) where the District Court Judge said:

> "inasmuch as adjustment is always made in the currency of the place where the voyage terminates..."

Against this argument ranks the fact that the place where the adventure ends may be fortuitous, and even where it ends at the contractual destination, the currency of that country may have little connection with the losses suffered, particularly those suffered by the shipowner. Nor is the currency of the destination likely to lead to greater simplicity in adjustment, since the great majority of general averages consists simply of expenditure by the shipowner alone, whereas there may be ports of discharge in several different countries. The practice of preparing the adjustment in the currency of the place of destination, although widespread before 1974 and certainly correct as the law then stood, was not universal, nor of particularly long standing.[32] Moreover, it must be remembered that although the great majority of awards were settled in the currency of the adjustment, under the breach-date-sterling rule the currency of the adjustment would have no ultimate significance in determining the currency in which the claim was calculated, so long as it was necessary to bring proceedings to enforce it.[33] **40.20**

[29] [1979] A.C. 685, [1979] 1 Lloyd's Rep. 1.
[30] (1923) 16 LL.L.Rep. 319 at 320.
[31] (1929) A.M.C. 581.
[32] See the 10th ed. of this work, paras. 1142 *et seq.* The practice there described of preparing the adjustment in the shipowner's currency was widespread until 1914, when it was gradually replaced, on the grounds of legal accuracy, by the currency of the destination.
[33] See para. 40.04, *ante*.

40.21 On the whole, it seems preferable to recognise that a historical viewpoint will provide no solution to the problem. Therefore, while one cannot rule out the possibility that the currency of the place where the adventure ends might be held to be an implied choice of currency, the present editors adhere to the view first expressed in the tenth edition[34] that there will normally be no currency of the contract for general average purposes except where a currency of adjustment has been expressly agreed upon.

The currency in which the loss was felt by the claimant

40.22 In the absence of any express or implied currency of the contract for general average, we return to the views expressed by Lord Wilberforce in *The Folias*[35]:

> "If then the contract fails to provide a decisive interpretation, the damage should be calculated in the currency in which the loss was felt by the Plaintiff or 'which most truly expresses his loss.' "

Further clarification is afforded by Lord Wilberforce in *The Despina R*,[36] starting with the passage in which he describes the two main alternatives:

> "The first is to take the currency in which the expense or loss was immediately sustained. This I shall call 'the expenditure currency.' The second is to take the currency in which the loss was effectively felt or borne by the plaintiff, having regard to the currency in which he generally operates or with which he has the closest connection—this I shall call 'the plaintiff's currency.' "[37]

Lord Wilberforce then rejects "the expenditure currency" in favour of "the plaintiff's currency":

> "My Lords, in my opinion, this question can be solved by applying the normal principles ... of *restitutio in integrum* and that of the reasonable foreseeability[38] of the damage sustained. It appears to me that a plaintiff, who normally conducts his business through a particular currency, and who, when other currencies are immediately involved, uses his own currency to obtain those currencies, can reasonably say that the loss he sustains is to be measured not by the immediate currencies in which the loss first emerges but by the amount of his own currency, which in the normal course of operation, he uses to obtain those currencies. This is the currency in which his loss is felt, and is the currency which it is reasonably foreseeable he will have to spend."[39]

[34] 10th ed. (1975), para. 471, anticipating the approach in *The Folias*.
[35] [1979] A.C. 685 at 701, [1979] 1 Lloyd's Rep. 1 at 8.
[36] *Ibid.*
[37] *Ibid.* at 696, and at 4–5.
[38] See para. 40.25, n. 46, *post*, as to the reference to reasonable foreseeability.
[39] [1979] A.C. 685 at 697, [1979] 1 Lloyd's Rep. 1 at 5.

Returning to "the plaintiff's currency", he observes:

> "I should refer to the definition I have used of this expression and emphasise that it does not suggest the use of a personal currency attached, like nationality, to a plaintiff, but a currency which he is able to show is that in which he normally conducts trading operations."[40]

Thus, we arrive at the conclusion that: **40.23**

(1) Where a currency for general average purposes has been *expressed* in the bill of lading or contract of affreightment, the general average sacrifices and expenditures of the various parties to the adventure should be exchanged into that single currency of the contract, and settlement between the parties effected in that currency.
(2) In the absence of an expressed currency of the contract, no particular currency can generally be implied, but the general average sacrifices and expenditures of the various parties to the adventure should be shown in the operating currencies of those who have sustained the sacrifices and financed the expenditures, that is the currency in which they each feel their loss.

How settlement should take place between the parties will be discussed later.

Rates of Exchange

In each case, the court and the adjuster should seek to give effect to the principle of *restitutio in integrum*, and this will normally involve adopting the rate prevailing on the date(s) when the loss was felt by the claimant.[41] As a general rule these dates will be as follows: **40.24**

> **In the case of expenditures**—on the various dates when the accounts were paid or, when the payment is made through an agent, when the agent was placed in funds.[42]

[40] *Ibid.*, at 698, and at 6.

[41] Under the pre-1974 law it was uncertain whether the rate of exchange for conversion to sterling should be that at the date of the sacrifice or the expenditure or that at the date when the adventure ended (see para. 40.04, *ante*). The latter date has been adopted by the courts in the U.S.A. for the purpose of selecting a rate of exchange (*Det Forenede Dampskibsselskabet v. Insurance Co. of North America* A.M.C. 1453 (1928), A.M.C. 581 (1929)). The former is that supported by the English cases on when a cause of action arises for the purposes of limitation. However, such refinements no longer seem relevant, since the decisions in *The Despina R* and *The Folias* do not require the rate of exchange at the date of accrual of the cause of action to be adopted.

[42] See *Food Corporation of India v. Carras* [1980] 2 Lloyd's Rep. 577. Where the adjustment is made in the operating currency of the claimant there will frequently be no need to undertake any exchange exercise; it will merely be necessary to ascertain how much of his own operating currency the claimant has expended. This was the case in *The Despina R* and *The Folias*.

In the case of cargo sacrifices—on the date of the last day of discharge at each of the ports of discharge.[43]

Adjustment charges and agency fees, etc.—payable only when the adjustment has been issued, should be exchanged at the rates of exchange ruling at the date of completion of the adjustment.

Commission and interest—where allowable, are calculated on the principal sum in the currencies of the adjustment and cause no exchange problems.

Ascertaining the Currency in which the Claimants' Loss is Felt

40.25 The old cast-iron certainty which existed under the breach-date-sterling rule has been replaced by a degree of uncertainty as to what constitutes the appropriate currency, and this uncertainty was recognised by Lord Wilberforce himself[44]:

> "Finally it is said (and this argument would apply equally if the expenditure currency were taken) that uncertainty will take the place of certainty under the present rule. Undoubtedly the present (sterling-breach-date) rule produces certainty—but it is often simpler to produce an unjust rule than a just one. The question is whether, in order to produce a just or juster rule, too high a price has to be paid in terms of certainty."

Undoubtedly, as Lord Wilberforce had stated earlier in his judgment[45]:

> "The plaintiff has to prove his loss: if he wishes to present his claim in his own currency, the burden is on him to show to the satisfaction of the tribunal that his operations are conducted in that currency and that in fact it was his currency that was used, in a normal manner, to meet the expenditure for which he claims or that his loss can only be appropriately measured in that currency (this would apply in the case of a total loss of a vessel which cannot be dealt with by the "expenditure" method). The same answer can be given to the objection that some companies, particularly large multi-national companies, maintain accounts and operate in several currencies. Here again it is for the plaintiff to satisfy the court or arbitrators that the use of the particular currency was in the course of normal operations of that company and was reasonably foreseeable."[46]

Nevertheless, to any internationally minded person or trader who thinks

[43] On the grounds of practical expediency, and because the precise date on which a consignee may have paid for his cargo is rarely known—whether, *e.g.* on shipment, or 90 days after landing, etc.—the last day of discharge is recommended for a common approach in exchanging the currency of the commercial invoice rendered to the receivers into his operating currency.

[44] [1979] A.C. 698, [1979] 1 Lloyd's Rep. 6.

[45] *Ibid.*

[46] Lord Wilberforce is here referring to the test of remoteness in the tort of negligence. In general average the question will be whether the loss was the direct consequence of the general average act (see paras. C.01 *et seq.*, *ante*). It is submitted that, as a general rule, a claimant's right to recover general average contribution calculated in his operating currency will not be affected by Rule C of the York Antwerp Rules (or by the common law relating to remoteness).

and operates in a number of world currencies, it is not difficult to appreciate the ease with which a claim can be presented and seemingly substantiated in some particular (favourable) currency. It may not be beyond the authority of a court, with its power to order discovery and its rules of evidence, to investigate and refute the use of a particular currency, but an employed average adjuster is hardly in the same strong position.

Two collision cases demonstrate the difficulty of determining what, in fact, was the relevant currency in which the plaintiff truly felt his loss. In *The Lash Atlantico*[47] the managers of the vessel operated in United States dollars (as did the managers of *The Despina R*), but the owners produced their annual balance sheet in Greek drachmas and the accounts rendered by the managers to the owners were expressed in drachmas. **40.26**

The Registrar awarded damages in United States dollars, the Admiralty Court in Greek drachmas, and the Court of Appeal in United States dollars.

In *The Transoceanica Francesca*,[48] the Italian owners first presented their claim in Italian lire but amended this subsequently to United States dollars. In support of this latter, more favourable, currency the owners were able to point out that the vessel was operating under a long-term charterparty under which the hire was paid in United States dollars, and that they maintained a United States dollar bank account into which all the earnings of the vessel were paid, and from which all trading expenses were disbursed—including the cost of repairs in the subject collision claim. However, the decision of the Registrar and of the Admiralty Court was that the United States dollar account was a mere "buffer", or convenient dollar float, and that the real profits or losses on the trading of the vessel were converted into, and felt in, Italian lire. **40.27**

The approach in *The Transoceanica Francesca*[49] is entirely in accordance with the principles of *restitutio in integrum* upon which *The Despina R*[50] and *The Folias*[51] are based, and a similar approach was adopted by the House of Lords in *The Texaco Melbourne*[52]. Thus the adoption of **40.28**

[47] [1985] 2 Lloyd's Rep. 464; [1987] 2 Lloyd's Rep. 114, C.A.

[48] [1987] 2 Lloyd's Rep. 155.

[49] *Ibid.*

[50] [1979] A.C. 685, [1979] 1 Lloyd's Rep. 1.

[51] *Ibid.*

[52] [1992] 1 Lloyd's Rep. 303; [1993] 1 Lloyd's Rep. 471, C.A.; [1994] 1 Lloyd's Rep. 473, H.L. The claim was for non-delivery of a cargo of oil at the Ghanaian port of Takoradi. The plaintiff oil company carried on business in Ghana and maintained its bank accounts in Ghanaian cedis; if the cargo had been duly delivered the plaintiffs would have sold it and received payment in cedis. Although the plaintiffs conducted all their international oil trading operations in U.S. dollars, exchange control regulations prevented them from maintaining funds in dollars, and the necessary dollar funds were provided by their bank for each operation. In these circumstances the House of Lords had little difficulty in holding that the plaintiffs had felt their loss in cedis. The decision supports the view that in identifying the currency in which the loss is felt the most important factor is the currency in which the plaintiff maintains his funds rather than that in which operations are conducted or in which the loss is immediately suffered. The House of Lords rejected the argument

the immediate operating currency is not appropriate where it is shown that the loss was really felt in another currency. *The Lash Atlantico*[53] is to be explained on the basis that although the accounts and the balance sheet were expressed in drachmas, there was no evidence that any payments were made in that currency, or that funds were held in that currency by the owners.

40.29 As a simple generalisation, it will generally be true that, for example a British shipowner feels his loss in sterling, a German shipowner in deutschmarks, and cargo interests in the national currency of the country of the port of destination. In the case of cargo, however, this is always subject to the usual inquiry whether the local national currency in fact represents the true loss sustained by the party concerned. In some countries where the value of the local currency is ravaged by continuous galloping inflation and used only for immediate daily domestic purchases, trading operations even between locals may customarily be conducted, and funds held, in an international currency such as the United States dollar. In such a case, the place of business of the claimant may provide little guidance in ascertaining the currency in which his loss is truly felt. If there is no adequate evidence as to the currency in which the loss was felt the correct conclusion may be that it was felt in the currency in which it immediately arose—"the expenditure currency".[54]

40.30 Certain passages in the judgments of the House of Lords in *The Despina R*[55] might be taken to support the view that the claimant may advance his claim either in the currency in which he felt the loss or in sterling at his option. However, this approach would be inconsistent with the general principles upon which *The Despina R*[56] and *The Folias*[57] are based, and difficult to reconcile with subsequent decisions in which those

that because the international oil trade is conducted in dollars, and if the plaintiffs had bought a substitute cargo they would have paid for it in dollars, the loss was to be measured in dollars. If the plaintiffs had bought a replacement cargo they would have sold it for cedis or converted the proceeds of sale into cedis.

The case also makes it clear that the approach laid down in *The Despina R* and *The Folias* will be applied however great is the fluctuation in currency values. At the date when the cargo should have been delivered there were 2.75 cedis to the dollar; at the date of judgment there were 375. Thus the damages recovered by the plaintiff represented, at the date of judgment, less than one per cent of the value of the original cargo, and the liability of the defendants, who presumably kept their funds in dollars, was virtually extinguished.

[53] See n. 47, *ante*.

[54] See *The Despina R* [1979] A.C. 685 at 698, [1979] 1 Lloyd's Rep. 1 at 6, *per* Lord Wilberforce. Such an approach should not be adopted too readily where the currency in which the loss was immediately felt is much stronger than the national currency of the claimant and there is incomplete evidence about his operating currency. Lord Wilberforce appears to envisage that it will always be in the interests of the claimant to provide full information about his operating currency (see the passage cited at para. 40.25, *ante*) but there are cases where this may not be so.

[55] In particular the opening section of the passage quoted, para. 40.25, *ante*: "If he wishes to present his claim in his own currency . . .".

[56] [1979] A.C. 685, [1979] 1 Lloyd's Rep. 1.

[57] *Ibid.*

principles have been applied.[58] The court and the adjuster should always seek to give recovery of the claim in the currency which, on the evidence before it, best reflects the claimant's loss.

Contributory values

In any general average adjustment, and regardless of the number of currencies in which the general average allowances may need to be shown, contributory values must necessarily be shown *in a single currency* for the purpose of apportioning the total general average. It matters not which currency is chosen: it may be that of any one of the destinations, or even, for convenience, the currency of a port of shipment, or an international trading currency such as the United States dollar. However, any necessary exchange into that currency should be made at the rate prevailing—for cargo on the last day of discharge at each individual port of discharge, and for the ship at the rate ruling on the last day of discharge at the final port of discharge. **40.31**

The Question of "Set-Off"

When general average sacrifices and/or expenditures are incurred by both ship and cargo interests, and those losses are felt in different currencies, it is clearly necessary to strike a balance between the respective claims in some common currency—in practice, the currency of the creditor. The question then arises whether those claims should be exchanged into the common currency at the rates of exchange ruling: **40.32**

(1) when the losses were sustained;
(2) when the adjustment is issued;
(3) at the date of judgment or agreement on liability and quantum; or
(4) when payment is made.

Lord Russel of Killowen mentioned this problem in his judgment in the House of Lords in the collision action of *The Despina R.*[59]

> "I have not overlooked the arguments advanced based upon complications involved in departure from *The Volturno* in fields such as set-off, counter-claim, limitation of liability, insolvency. They do not arise in this case, and should not be incapable of just solutions when they do arise. I do not propose to advance hypothetical solutions."

Would that a "just solution" can be found and applied by the courts which produces the same degree of certainty in the fields of set-off and counterclaim as existed prior to 1974!

[58] See in particular *The Texaco Melbourne, supra.*
[59] [1979] A.C. 685 at 704, [1979] 1 Lloyd's Rep. 1 at 10.

40.33 Two simple examples will illustrate the problem, and for this purpose it will be convenient to adopt the same currencies and rates of exchange used throughout this section.

£0.75 = $1.00 = Y250 at the time of loss or expenditure.
$1.00 = Y125 at the time when claims agreed.

Example 1

An American and a Japanese vessel collide in the English Channel and both sustain serious damage which obliges them to put into Falmouth for repairs. Both vessels are equally at fault and repairs and other expenses to each vessel cost £300,000 and this is settled by the:

American owner @ £0.75 = $ 1.00 = $ 400,000
Japanese owner @ £0.75 = Y 250 = Y 100,000,000

Example 2

A Japanese vessel carrying an American cargo with a value identical to that of the ship strands in a position of peril and engages the services of salvage tugs to refloat. An award of £600,000 is made and, both ship and cargo having provided separate salvage security, they each pay £300,000 settled as follows:

American cargo @ £0.75 = $ 1.00 = $ 400,000
Japanese ship @ £0.75 = Y 250 = Y 100,000,000

40.34 If the respective claims of the parties in both Examples 1 and 2 are set-off against each other and exchanged (1) *at the time of loss or when the expenditure was incurred*, it will be readily appreciated that no money changes hands as each party has already borne his precise and proper share of 50 per cent of the total damage, or salvage award. This would be the situation under the old breach-date-sterling rule. However, if the respective claims were to be maintained in their settlement currencies and set-off against each other only (2) *when the claims were agreed and/or a general average adjustment was issued*, the financial position of the parties would be totally different. The value of the claims would then be:

American claim— $ 400,000 @ 125 = Y 50,000,000
Japanese claim —Y 100,000,000 @ 125 = $ 800,000

The claim of the Japanese ship is now double the value of that of the American cargo and it can be/has been suggested that the American should pay to the Japanese 50 per cent of the difference between their respective claims, whether for collision damages or as a general average contribution, that is Y25,000,000 @ 125 = $200,000.

Support for method (2), that is, maintaining the respective claims in their settlement currencies and setting them off against each other only when the claims have been agreed and/or a general average adjustment has been issued, can be found in current English case law in collision actions and the continental *systéme des masses* for general average. 40.35

Set-off in collision actions

When giving judgment in 1977 in the court of first instance in *The Despina R*,[60] Brandon J. addressed himself to this problem of set-off of the respective claims and gave it as his provisional view, and without the benefit of argument, that this set-off should effectively take place at the date of judgment ("date on which the amount of the two liabilities are established by agreement or decision") rather than at the time of loss. The Court of Appeal in that case also suggested that a solution to these special problems could be found such as Brandon J. provisionally offered.[61]

In *The Transoceanica Francesca*[62] Brandon J.'s view was adopted and the respective claims of the two vessels were exchanged at rates ruling on the date on which the amount of both liabilities was finally agreed. Thus the Italian plaintiff, whose lire claim exceeded the defendant's (United States dollar) claim if exchanged at the time of the collision, but fell short of the defendant's claim if exchanged at the date when both claims had been agreed,[63] found himself transformed from a creditor into a debtor.[64]

Set-off in general average in English law

While there is no direct authority on the point, it is submitted that in the adjustment of general average under English law the competing claims should be set off against each other at the date *when the losses were sustained*, and that the practice in collision actions should not be followed. The legal, practical and commercial arguments in favour of this course, some of which are mentioned below, are overwhelming. 40.36

[60] [1978] Q.B. 396 at 415.

[61] *Ibid.* at 437.

[62] [1987] 2 Lloyd's Rep. 155.

[63] There appears to have been no complete agreement on quantum, since the appropriate currency in which the claim was to be calculated remained in dispute until determined by the Court (para. 40.27, *ante*). The agreement, referred to in the report, which determined the date of set-off, was presumably an agreement on all the individual items, subject to the currency argument.

[64] For conflicting views on the merits of this approach see J. A. Knott, "The Wealth-time Continuum Revisited: Set-off in Marine Collison Claims", *Lloyd's Maritime & Commercial Law Quarterly*, May 1981, and D. J. Wilson, "Rates of Exchange Revisited", *Hull Claims Analysis*, Vol. 4, Issue 12, p. 174.

(1) Both-to-blame collision cases do not fall within the ordinary categories of cross-claims in respect of which a set-off arises.[65] By contrast, where general average losses are suffered by several contributing interests on a single common adventure, the claims to have those losses made good in general average give rise to set-off in the true sense; no party is entitled to advance a claim in respect of his losses without giving credit for the losses suffered by the other parties to the adventure, and the only claim which can be recovered by proceedings is for the balance of the general average account.[66]

(2) Since there is no recoverable claim except for the balance of account, it would be wholly illogical and uncommercial that the vagaries of currency fluctuations should operate upon the full amount of each party's loss, when he has no right in law to bring proceedings to recover his full loss, and has in fact already recouped himself in whole or in part, by means of the extinction or reduction of his own liability to contribute. That liability arises at the time of the loss or, at any rate, at the termination of the adventure[67] and it can make no difference that it has not been quantified or agreed upon at that date.

(3) The effect of the old breach-date-sterling rule was that set-offs took place at the date when the losses were sustained, or the cause of action arose. Any currency fluctuations would only operate on the net *balance* payable by the debtor.[68] None of the reasons for changing that rule demands any change in the previous law relating to the date when set-off takes effect; in fact the principle of *restitutio in integrum* requires that on this point the law should remain unchanged.

(4) Under English law the adjustment is not binding on the parties. Therefore if set-off is only to take effect at the date of judgment or agreement, the time for effecting set-off would not have arrived by the date of the completion of the adjustment. Thus the adjuster would be unable to fulfill his traditional role of stating the balance actually payable.

40.37 In the examples which follow, the parties' losses are expressed in their operating currency, and in Examples 3, 4, and 5, which involve set-off, the necessary currency conversion is effected at the rates of exchange ruling at the time of the loss.

[65] As to the latter, see *Hanak v. Green* [1958] 2 Q.B. 9.

[66] See the judgment of the Privy Council in *Grant v. Norway* 3 Moo.N.S. 245 at 267–269, *per* Knight-Bruce L.J.

[67] See *Chandris v. Argo Insurance Co.* [1963] 2 Lloyd's Rep. 65 and para. 40.24, n. 41, *ante*.

[68] The same will be the case where the contract of affreightment contains a currency clause for general average claims (see paras. 40.15–40.17, *ante*).

EXAMPLES

Note: *The following examples will gradually build in greater complexities, but common features throughout will be that:* **40.38**

(1) The SHIP is Japanese, and the Owners feel their loss in Japanese Yen. (Y 25,000,000—worth at the time of loss $100,000).
(2) The CARGO is generally destined for the United States and the Owners feel any loss in U.S. Dollars (usually U.S.$100,000—worth at the time of loss Y 25,000,000).
(3) The RATES OF EXCHANGE will be:

$1.00 = Y 250 at the time of the expenditure or loss.
$1.00 = Y 125 at the time of settlement under the Adjustment.

(4) The CONTRIBUTORY VALUES will be:

SHIP —	$ 4,000,000
CARGO—	6,000,000
	$10,000,000

EXAMPLE 1 **40.39**

Port of Refuge Expenses by Shipowner only . . . . Y 25,000,000

Note: *The Adjustment to be prepared in the currency of the Creditor—The Shipowner—i.e. Yen.*

APPORTIONED

SHIP —	$ 4,000,000	pays	Y 10,000,000	
CARGO—	6,000,000	pays	15,000,000	(Cost @ 125 = $120,000)
	$10,000,000	pays	Y 25,000,000	

EXAMPLE 2 **40.40**

Jettison of Cargo only $100,000

Note: *The Adjustment to be prepared in the currency of the Creditor—the Cargo Owner—i.e. Dollars.*

APPORTIONED

SHIP —	$ 4,000,000	pays	$ 40,000	(Cost @ 125 = Y 5,000,000)
CARGO—	6,000,000	pays	60,000	
	$10,000,000	pays	$100,000	

40.41 *EXAMPLE 3*

Port of Refuge Expenses by Shipowner ....Y 25,000,000
Jettison of Cargo $100,000

Note: The Shipowner has spent Y 25,000,000 @ 250 = $100,000
Equivalent to $2\frac{1}{2}$ per cent of Contributory Value of Ship ($4,000,000)
The Cargo has lost $100,000
Equivalent to 1.66 per cent of Contributory Value of Cargo ($6,000,000)

It follows that the Cargo will be a Debtor to the Ship and the Adjustment should be prepared in Yen. *i.e.*

Port of Refuge Expenses by Shipowner		Y 25,000,000
Jettison of Cargo	$100,000 @ 250[69]	25,000,000
		Y 50,000,000

APPORTIONMENT AND SETTLEMENT

			Credit Own Loss	*Balance To Receive*	*To Pay*
SHIP	$4,000,000 pays	Y 20,000,000	Y 25,000,000	Y 5,000,000	—
CARGO	6,000,000 pays	30,000,000	25,000,000[70]	—	Y 5,000,000
	10,000,000 pays	Y 50,000,000	Y 50,000,000	Y 5,000,000	Y 5,000,000
					@ 125 = $40,000

40.42 *EXAMPLE 4*

The losses are the same as for Example 3, *i.e.*:

Port of Refuge Expenses by Shipowner ....Y 25,000,000
Jettison of Cargo $100,000

but the cargo is consigned to two separate receivers, of whom:

"A" with Cargo worth $1,000,000 sustains the whole of the jettison
"B" with Cargo worth 5,000,000 sustains no loss
$6,000,000

A preliminary calculation will disclose that the respective degrees of loss suffered by the parties are as follows:

[69] The cargo owners' loss of $100,000 is converted into Yen at the rate of exchange prevailing at the date when the loss was incurred, *i.e.* $1.00–Y 250. (See paras. 40.32 *et seq.*, and particularly para. 40.36, *ante*.
[70] See n. 69, *ante*).

SHIP ($100,000) —$2\frac{1}{2}$ per cent of Contributory Value ($4,000,000)
CARGO "A" ($100,000)—10 per cent of Contributory Value ($1,000,000)
CARGO "B" —NIL per cent of Contributory Value

It follows, therefore that:

The SHIP —is a Debtor to "A", but a Creditor of "B"
CARGO "A"—is a Creditor of both Ship and "B"
CARGO "B"—is a Debtor to both Ship and "A"

There being Creditors in *two* currencies, the Adjustment must be prepared in both those currencies, *i.e.*: 40.43

		Yen	*U.S. $*
Port of Refuge Expenses	Y 25,000,000 @ 250	Y 25,000,000	$100,000
Jettison of Cargo	$100,000 @ 250	25,000,000	100,000
		Y 50,000,000	$200,000

APPORTIONED

SHIP—	$4,000,000	Pays Y 20,000,000	$ 80,000
CARGO "A"	1,000,000	Pays 5,000,000	20,000
CARGO "B"	5,000,000	Pays 25,000,000	100,000
	10,000,000	Pays Y 50,000,000	$200,000

FINANCIAL SETTLEMENT 40.44

		SHIP (40 per cent)	CARGO "A" (10 per cent)	CARGO "B" (50 per cent)
Shipowner v. Cargo "A" (In $ as "A" the Net Creditor)				
S/O liable "A"—40 per cent × $100,000 =	$40,000			
"A" liable S/O—10 per cent × $100,000 =	10,000			
NET: Shipowner Pays "A"	$30,000	$30,000 @ 125 = Y 3,750,000	($30,000)	
Shipowner v. Cargo "B" (In Yen as Shipowner the Creditor)				
"B" liable S/O—50 per cent × Y 25M =	Y 12,500,000	(12,500,000)		Y 12,500,000 @ 125 = $100,000
Cargo "A" v. Cargo "B" (In $ as "A" the Creditor)				
"B" liable "A"—50 per cent × $100,000 =	$50,000		($50,000)	50,000
		Receives (Y 8,750,000)	Receives ($80,000)	Pays $150,000

40.45 *EXAMPLE 5*

Note: *The basic principles for adjusting and settling a general average adjustment have already been set forth in previous examples, and there is no real need to study the present example. It merely introduces a third currency—the Canadian Dollar—and more cargo interests, purely as an illustration of the complex problems facing any adjuster (and at which even a computer might baulk?) called upon to prepare a multi-bill of lading general average adjustment with cargo destined for several countries.*

The losses are the same as for Example 3, *i.e.*:

Port of Refuge Expenses by Shipowner	Y 25,000,000
Jettison of Cargo	$100,000

but the Cargo is consigned to a number of receivers in both the United States and Canada, of whom:

United States	Cargo "A" value	US $ 500,000	Jettison	US $ 50,000
	Cargo "B" value	1,500,000	Sound	
	Cargo "C" value	3,000,000	Sound	
Canadian	Cargo "D" value	200,000	Jettison C$75,000 =	50,000
	Cargo "E" value	800,000	Sound	
		US $6,000,000		US $ 100,000

THE RATES OF EXCHANGE current at the times of:

(1) The Loss —U.S. $1.00 = Y 250 = Can $1.50
(2) The Adjustment—U.S. $1.00 = Y 125 = Can $1.20

40.46 A preliminary calculation will disclose that the respective degrees of loss suffered by the parties are as follows:

SHIP—	($100,000)—2½ per cent of Contributory Value ($4,000,000)
CARGO "A"—	($50,000)—10 per cent of Contributory Value ($500,000)
CARGO "D"—	($50,000)—25 per cent of Contributory Value ($200,000)
CARGO "B", "C" & "E"—	NIL per cent of Contributory Value

It follows, therefore, that:

The SHIP—	is a debtor to A and D, but a creditor of B, C and E
CARGO "A"—	is a debtor to D, but a creditor of SHIP, B, C and E
CARGO "D"—	is a Creditor of all other interests.
CARGO "B", "C" & "E"—	are Debtors to all other interests.

There being Creditors in *three* currencies, the Adjustment must be prepared in those three currencies, *i.e.* 40.47

	Yen	*U.S. $*	*Can $*
Port of Refuge Expenses Y 25M @ 250/1/1.50	Y 25,000,000	$100,000	C$150,000
Jettison of CARGO "A" U.S.$ 50 K @ 250/1/1.50	12,500,000	50,000	75,000
Jettison of CARGO "D" C$ 75 K @ 250/1/1.50	12,500,000	50,000	75,000
	Y 50,000,000	$200,000	C$300,000

APPORTIONED

SHIP	$4,000,000	pays	Y 20,000,000	$80,000	C$120,000
CARGO "A"	500,000	pays	2,500,000	10,000	15,000
CARGO "B"	1,500,000	pays	7,500,000	30,000	45,000
CARGO "C"	3,000,000	pays	15,000,000	60,000	90,000
CARGO "D"	200,000	pays	1,000,000	4,000	6,000
CARGO "E"	800,000	pays	4,000,000	16,000	24,000
	$10,000,000	pays	Y 50,000,000	$200,000	C$300,000

40.48

FINANCIAL SETTLEMENT

	JAPANESE	UNITED STATES		CANADIAN	
	SHIP (40%)	CGO "A" (5%)	CGO "B" & "C" (45%)	CGO "D" (2%)	CGO "E" (8%)
Shipowner v. Cargo "A" S/O liable A—40 per cent × 50K = $20K A liable S/O—5% × 100K = 5 *Net*: S/O pays "A" $15K	$15,000 @ 125 = Y1.875M	($15,000)			
Shipowner v. Cargo "B" & "C" Cgo. liable S/O—45% × Y25M = Y11.25M	(11.250)		Y11.250M @ 125 = $90,000		
Shipowner v. Cargo "D" S/O liable D—40% × C$75K = 30K D liable S/O—2% × C$150K = 3 *Net*: S/O pays "D" C$27K	C$27,000 @ 125/1.20 = 2.812			(C$27,000)	
Shipowner v. Cargo "E" Cgo. liable S/O—8% × Y25M = Y2M	(2.000)				Y2m @ 125/1.20 = C$19,200
Cargo "A" v. Cargo "B" & C B & C liable A—45% × $50K = $22.5K		(22,500)	22,500		
Cargo "A" v. Cargo "D" A liable D—5% × C$75K = C$3,750 D liable A—2% × C$75K = 1,500 *Net*: "A" pays "D" C$2,250		C$2,250 @ 1.20 = 1,875		(2,250)	
Cargo "A" v. Cargo "E" E liable A—8% × U.S.$ 50K = U.S. 4K		(4,000)			US $4,000 @ 1.20 = 4,800
Cargo "D" v. Cargo "B & C" B & C liable D—45% × C$75K = C$33,750			(C$33,750) @ 1.20 = 28,125	(33,750)	
Cargo "D" v. Cargo "E" E liable D—8% × C$75K = C$6,000				(6,000)	6,000
	Receives (Y.8,562,500)	Receives ($39,625)	Pays $140,625	Receives (C$69,000)	Pays C$30,000

Whereof:
B—$ 46,875
C—$ 93,750
$140,625

Proposals for the York-Antwerp Rules 1994

A lost opportunity was that the problems of currencies and rates of exchange might have been resolved by the new York-Antwerp Rules 1994. The International Sub-Committee was, in principle, in favour of introducing additional wording into Rule XXI to regulate these matters and the British Maritime Law Association submitted a draft wording[71] which provided that, except where the parties had already agreed that the adjustment should be prepared in a specific currency, it should be prepared in SDRs. **40.49**

Special Drawing Rights (SDRs)

The SDR is a unit of account created by the International Monetary Fund purely as an official reserve asset and comprising a "basket" of the currencies of the five member countries of the IMF with the largest exports of goods and services during the five-year period preceding any revision, weighted to reflect broadly their relative importance in international trade and finance. The overall effect of adopting SDRs as a unit of account is that it smooths out some of the extremes of fluctuation between any two of the five individual currencies. For example, whereas between July 1991 and February 1995 the Yen appreciated by 42 per cent against the U.S. Dollar, it was only 25 per cent via the medium of the SDR.

Although the use of SDRs would be a far from perfect vehicle[72] for resolving every problem regarding profits and losses on rates of exchange in general average adjustments, it would provide some certainty and uniformity on methods to be employed, and greatly simplify the adjusters' work on cases such as in Example 5, above.

[71] "Unless the parties have agreed that the adjustment shall be prepared in a specific currency, the adjustment shall be prepared in Special Drawing Rights (SDRs). For this purpose the conributory values and the amounts made good for general average sacrifice (other than disbursements) shall be converted into SDRs or the specified currency at the rate of exchange prevailing at the termination of the adventure, and disbursements shall be so converted at the rate of exchange prevailing on the dates when payment was made. The final balances calculated shall be paid to the creditors in the currency of their choice at the rate of exchange prevailing on the date of settlement. Where no official SDR exchange rate is quoted for any currency, conversion to and from SDRs shall be made by reference to United States dollars. Interest shall be allowed on expenditure, sacrifices and allowances from the date of conversion, as set out in the preceding paragraph, until three months after the date of issue of the adjustment. When the adjustment has been prepared in SDRs, the rate of interest shall be the rate published by IMF ruling on the date of termination of the adventure; otherwise the rate of interest shall be . . .".

[72] *E.g.*, it might be thought inappropriate to inflict SDRs on the participants in a coastal voyage, or where both ship and cargo operate in the same currency. For instance, an American merchant requiring a U.S.$40,000 contribution from the American shipowner in June 1991 would receive U.S.$45,449 in February 1995 if adjusted via the medium of SDRs.

A.I.D.E. alternative text

40.50 Members of A.I.D.E., however, were unenthusiastic about the use of SDRs and put forward an alternative text[73] with the adjustment being:

> "prepared in such currency or currencies as may be equitable in the interests of the parties, having regard to the currencies in which the major claimants in general average have sustained financial loss."

This certainly gives the impression of being based on English legal precedents, but the subject of rates of exchange should never be left to be determined by any individual on grounds of supposed *equity*; the claims of both parties in any dispute on matters of exchange have equal validity! Far better to have a clear, firm and undisputed method for regulating these matters.

In the event, no agreement could be reached at Sydney in October 1994 on how best this important topic could be incorporated within the York-Antwerp Rules, with the result that those Rules remain—as before—silent on the matter of rates of exchange.

The effect of adopting SDRs

40.51 For the benefit of interested readers, and to show the effect of the use of the SDR, the earlier Examples 1, 2 and 5 in paragraphs 40.38 to 40.40 and 40.45 to 40.48, above will now be re-worked in SDRs, valued as at end June 1991 and end February 1995[74]; contributory values and other common features remain as before.

[73] "Unless the parties have agreed that the adjustment shall be prepared in a specific currency, the adjustment shall be prepared in such currency or currencies as may be equitable in the interests of the parties, having regard to the currencies in which the major claimants in general average have sustained financial loss. For this purpose the contributory values and the amounts made good for general average sacrifice (other than disbursements) shall be converted into the currencies of the adjustment at the rate of exchange prevailing on the last day of discharge at the final port of destination, or at the termination of the adventure when this occurs at a port or place other than the final port of destination, and disbursements shall be so converted at the rate of exchange prevailing on the dates when payment was made. . . ."

[74]

	As at End June 1991		*As at End Feb. 1995*		
Currency in SDR Basket	Approx. Rate Exch	U.S. $ Equilnt	Approx. Rate Exch	U.S. $ Equivlnt	%age Change
U.S. $ .572	1.00	0.572	1.00	0.572	Nil
DM .453	1.81	0.250	1.46	0.310	+24
Y 31.8	138	0.230	97	0.328	+42
Fr.Fr. .8	6.14	0.130	5.15	0.155	+19
£0.0812	1.62	0.132	1.58	0.128	−2
	SDR 1.00	=$1.314	SDR 1.00	=$1.493	−11
		or DM2.378		or DM 2.18	+9
		Y 181.33		Y 144.82	+25
		Fr. 8.07		Fr. 7.69	+5
		£0.811		£0.945	−14

EXAMPLE 1A **40.52**

Port of Refuge Expenses by Shipowner only	Y 13,800,000		SDR 76,104	(At 181.33)
Whereof: Wanted from Cargo—60%	Y 8,280,000			
Liability of Cargo	*Per English Law*		*In SDRs*	
Proportion GA attaching to Cargo—60%	Y 8,280,000		SDR 45,662	
Cost to Cargo to Settle (At 97)	$85,361	>	$68,174	(At 1.493)
Shipowner Receives	Y 8,280,000	>	Y 6,661,858	(At 144.82)

Notes: *With SDRs a "weak" debtor pays less than he ought, and a "strong" creditor receives less than he requires.*

EXAMPLE 2A **40.53**

Jettison of Cargo only	$100,000		SDR 76,104	(At 1.314)
Whereof: Wanted from Shipowner—40%	$ 40,000			
Liability of Shipowner	*Per English Law*		*In SDRs*	
Proportion GA attaching to Ship—40%	$ 40,000		SDR 30,442	
Cost to Shipowner to Settle (At 97)	Y 3,880,000	<	Y 4,408,553	(At 144.82)
Cargo Owner Receives	$ 40,000	<	$ 45,449	

Notes: *With SDRs a "strong" debtor pays more than he ought, and a "weak" creditor receives more than he requires to balance his books.*

EXAMPLE 5A **40.54**

The Rates of Exchange current at the time of the:

(1) Loss in 6.'91	US$1.00 = Y 138 = Can $1.14	=	SDR 0.761
(2) Adjustment in 2.'95	US$1.00 = Y 97 = Can $1.40	=	SDR 0.670

The losses are as follows:

Port of Refuge Expenses by Shipowner	Y 13,800,000	=	SDR 76,104
Jettison of U.S. Cargo "A"	U.S. $50,000	=	38,052
Jettison of Can. Cargo "D"	Can $57,000	=	38,052
			SDR 152,208

	Contrib Value (Per Cent)	Ppn. G.A. (SDRs)	CREDIT Own Loss (SDRs)	BALANCE To Pay (SDRs)	To Receive (SDRs)
Japanese SHIP	40	60,883	76,104		15,221
US CARGO "A"	5	7,610	38,052		30,442
"B"	15	22,831		22,831	
"C"	30	45,663		45,663	
Can CARGO "D"	2	3,044	38,052		35,008
"E"	8	12,177		12,177	
	100	152,208	152,208	80,671	80,671

COMPARISON OF AMOUNTS PAID/RECEIVED
IN NATIONAL CURRENCIES

		(SDRs)	With SDRs	Eng. Law System
Japanese SHIP	receives	15,221 × 144.82	Y 2,204,305	Y 4,437,257
US CARGO "A"	receives	30,442 × 1.493	US$ 45,450	US$ 40,279
"B"	pays	22,831 × 1.493	US$ 34,087	US$ 34,947
"C"	pays	45,663 × 1.493	US$ 68,175	US$ 69,895
Can CARGO "D"	receives	35,008 × 2.09	C$ 73,167	C$ 52,440
"E"	pays	12,177 × 2.09	C$ 25,450	C$ 26,094

Note: *An analysis or comparison of the financial effect of preparing Example 5A in SDRs is less easy than with Examples 1A and 2A by reason of the introduction of losses in* three *currencies and the supplanting of the U.S. dollar as the weak currency by the weaker Canadian dollar. However, the basic concept that "weak" debtors pay less than they ought remains true, if less marked than previously. That "weak" creditors receive more than required to balance their books is particularly noticeable in the case of the Canadian Cargo "D", a creditor receiving C$73,167 of depreciated currency to make good his 1991 loss of only C$57,000. "Strong" creditors continue to receive less than they ought, and it will be noted that the Japanese shipowner receives only Y2,204,305 when he might expect Y4,437,257 under the English system. (As against this, if the whole adjustment had been prepared in his own currency, he would have received only Y2,760,000.)*

Overall Conclusions

40.55 This section has endeavoured to demonstrate the difference in the financial consequences between a general average adjustment prepared in accordance with English legal precedents and one prepared under the alternative projected system using the neutral Special Drawing Rights (SDRs) as the unit of account.

In the absence of their own preferred solution of specific provisions in the contract of affreightment, the editors' comments on the other two systems are as follows:

The "English" System

The system based on English legal precedents requires adjustments to be prepared in the operating currency of the *creditor* of the general average, and this is basically unobjectionable, except possibly to those whose currency is particularly "weak", whereupon they are faced with making more costly payments to creditors in their own depreciated currency. Those parties to the adventure with a "strong" currency will undoubtedly welcome adjustments prepared in accordance with the "English" system. **40.56**

Ignoring the profits and losses mentioned in the previous paragraph, and inherent in any system, the particular disadvantages from which the English system might be suggested to suffer are as follows:

(1) It is occasionally difficult to establish what is the currency in which the shipowner or other creditor of the general average feels his loss (for example see the case of the *Transoceanica Francesca*[75] quoted in paragraph 40.27, above).

(2) In perhaps 90 per cent of all cases, the shipowner finances the whole of the general average expenditure, etc., and the adjustment need be prepared in only a single currency. Whether this be the shipowner's operating currency, SDRs, or a currency specified in the contract of affreightment, the work of the adjuster will be effectively the same. However, in the remaining 10 per cent of cases, (and these are likely to be the largest, and involve far more money), where cargo interests suffer general average sacrifices of their cargo, or are called upon to finance their own proportions of salvage awards, etc., the English system becomes extremely complex and difficult to apply in practice. Indeed, it may be so troublesome that most adjusters will throw up their hands in horror and find reason to opt for some expedient such as adopting just one of the currencies involved.

(3) If interest on general average allowances continues under the new 1994 Rule XXI for three months beyond the date of issue of the adjustment in recognition of the fact that settlement thereunder is likely to take place no earlier, how can anyone possibly forecast so far ahead at what rates of exchange settlements of the various

[75] [1987] 2 Lloyd's Rep. 155.

debit and credit balances under the adjustment should take place? This problem cannot arise when SDRs or any specified single currency is used.

The SDR System

40.57 The figures in and Notes following Examples 1A, 2A, and 5A prompt the immediate suggestion that nationals with currently "weak" currencies would welcome with open arms the adoption of the SDR system; as debtors they pay less and as creditors they receive more of their own currency. Conversely, nationals with a currently "strong" currency would wish to avoid the use of SDRs, for they pay more as debtors and receive less as creditors in their own currency.

However, few currencies remain for ever strong—or weak.[76] The strongest currency will one day peak and then become a weak currency in relation to the others, and perhaps the philosophy of swings and roundabouts should not be overlooked.

In any case, consider, for instance, the apparent anomaly of the Canadian merchant "D" in Example 5A who, even after being debited with a proportion of general average of Say Can $6,362, still receives under the SDR system a contribution from the other parties to the adventure of Can $73,167 in respect of his loss by jettison of only Can $57,000. This looks ridiculous, but is it so very unfair? What does either amount represent in, say, Canadian wheat or Japanese cars at the respective times?

The SDR, being a "basket" of currencies, softens the harsh effects of violent fluctuations in rates of exchange between individual currencies and, unless the co-adventurers share the same currency, probably achieves a more equitable result between the co-adventurers on any voyage than would their individual currencies.

[76] Even sterling, generally a "weak" currency, climbed from 83.7 to 96.1 on the Sterling Index between May and December 1996!

SECTION 7

GENERAL AVERAGE AND INSURANCE

1. RIGHTS OF RECOVERY ON POLICIES FOR GENERAL AVERAGE LOSSES

As related in previous Sections of this work, general average originated probably some 2,500 years ago as an equitable and international "law of the sea" for the purpose of sharing on a rateable basis between all the parties to a common adventure those sacrifices and expenses voluntarily made or incurred at a time of peril by just one or a few of the parties, for the joint benefit of all. As such, it was (and remains) an extremely limited and primitive form of *mutual* insurance in respect of the risks to be encountered on any maritime voyage. **50.01**

Marine insurance proper (and the earliest form of any insurance was *marine*) was first developed some 2,000 years later, in the thirteenth and fourteenth centuries, and although general average continued its totally separate existence, it was natural that one of the risks sought to be covered by those early policies[1] was the possibility of the assured being called upon to pay a general average contribution towards the voluntary sacrifices and expenses incurred by other parties to the adventure, or of suffering those same losses himself.

In this Section will be discussed the rights of any party insured by a typical policy of marine insurance governed by English law, covering ship, cargo or freight, etc., to recover on such a policy for:

(1) Loss of or damage to the property insured caused by a general average *sacrifice*.
(2) General average *expenditure* incurred by the assured for the common benefit.
(3) General average *contributions* payable by the assured to other parties to the adventure.
(4) General average *deposits* paid as security for those contributions.

[1] The archaic wording in the early policies of insurance was preserved almost unchanged and in continuous use until 1983 in the Lloyd's S.G. and kindred policy forms. In fact, the only specific reference to general average in such a policy was the expression in the Memorandum "... warranted, free from average, unless general, ..." but in *Hall v. Janson* (1855) 4 E. & B. 500; 24 L.J.Q.B. 97, Lord Campbell was able to confirm that by this phrase: "the underwriters ... expressly, absolutely, and universally undertake to pay general average however large or however minute the amount may be."

50.02 These various headings of claim will be considered in detail later in this Section, but for a better understanding of the text and of the examples given, it will be sensible first to define some of the expressions frequently used:

A general average *loss*, as defined by section 66(1) of the Marine Insurance Act 1906 "is a loss caused by or directly consequential on a general average act.[2] It includes a general average *expenditure* as well as a general average *sacrifice*."

50.03 A general average *expenditure* is simply the expenditure or outlay of money in order to purchase services or facilities which will relieve the property in the common adventure from the peril in which it finds itself, for example the hire of labour and lighters to discharge cargo from a vessel ashore, the hire of tugs to tow the vessel to a port of refuge, or the expenses of entering a port of refuge.

50.04 A general average *sacrifice*, even though it must be subsequently quantified in money terms in any general average adjustment, in the first instance comprises or is constituted by the intentional causing of loss or damage to one or more of the physical properties at risk in the common adventure—ship, cargo or freight, etc., for example the jettison of cargo and the freight attaching thereto, or the damage to machinery of a stranded vessel caused in efforts to refloat.

Commission, interest, and adjustment charges, where applicable, will follow the treatment of the capital sums on which they are based and will constitute sacrifice or expenditure, as appropriate.

50.05 A general average *contribution* as defined by section 66(3) of the Marine Insurance Act 1906,[3] is the sum payable:

(1) *By* any party to the adventure after setting off against his rateable proportion of the total general average any credit due for sacrifices or expenditures incurred by him.
(2) *To* any party to the adventure in respect of general average sacrifices or expenditures incurred by him, after setting off his own liability to contribute to the total general average.

50.06 The term is not synonymous with "*Proportion of general average*", which denotes the rateable proportion of the total general average for which any contributing interest is liable before crediting any general average allowances due to him in the adjustment.

A figured example may assist in appreciating the distinctions between

[2] A general average act is defined by the Marine Insurance Act 1906, s. 66(2) and given extensive coverage (*ante*) when dealing with Rule A of the York-Antwerp Rules.

[3] "Where there is a general average loss, the party on whom it falls is entitled, subject to the conditions imposed by maritime law, to a rateable contribution from the other parties interested, and such contribution is called a general average contribution."

these various terms, essential if one is to understand the differing legal rights of an assured when making a claim for any particular form of general average loss on a policy of marine insurance.

A vessel strands in a position of peril and, in order to refloat, is obliged to engage salvage services, (each party paying their own proportion of the award), to jettison cargo, to work the ship's engines, and subsequently to put into a port of refuge for the common safety.

The general average is made up of the following: 50.07

			General average
SHIPOWNER'S	Sacrifice—Refloating damage to machinery		30,000
	Expenditure—In the port of refuge		25,000
	Salvage payment		100,000
			155,000
CARGO A'S	Expenditure—Salvage payment		100,000
CARGO B'S	Sacrifice—Jettison	250,000	
	Expenditure—Salvage payment	75,000	325,000
CARGO C'S	Expenditure—Salvage payment		100,000
			680,000

APPORTIONMENT AND SETTLEMENT 50.08

	Contributory Value		Ppn. G.A.	Credit Allowance in G.A.	CONTRIBUTION To Pay	CONTRIBUTION To Receive
SHIP—Sound Value	1,200,000					
Less: Damage	230,000					
	970,000					
Add Made Good	30,000					
	1,000,000	liable for	170,000	155,000	15,000	—
CARGO A—Value	1,000,000	liable for	170,000	100,000	70,000	—
CARGO B—Value (incl. Jettison)	1,000,000	liable for	170,000	325,000	—	155,000
CARGO D—Value	1,000,000	liable for	170,000	100,000	70,000	—
	4,000,000	liable for	680,000	680,000	155,000	155,000

The *proportion of general average* attaching to each of the contributing interests is a uniform 170,000, but the *contributions* payable by ship, and cargos A and C are 15,000, 70,000 and 70,000 respectively (totalling 155,000), while the contribution receivable by cargo B is 155,000.

The individual rights of the owners of ship, cargo and freight for the various forms of general average losses will be studied below, but before discussing the precise *amount* of any claim, it is necessary to consider 50.09

whether there is any claim at all for general average on any particular form of policy.

Under section 66(2) of the Marine Insurance Act 1906, a general average act will be constituted whenever:

> "... any extraordinary sacrifice or expenditure is voluntarily made or incurred in time of peril...".

and the peril may arise from any cause whatever, whereas a policy of marine insurance generally covers the property insured against the risk of loss or damage only from certain specified perils.

The initial accident or occurrence creating the peril may, in terms of the policy, be specifically covered or excluded, or unmentioned, and the peril which the general average act seeks to avoid may similarly be covered, excluded, or unmentioned in the policy. In determining whether a claim for general average arises on any particular policy, the governing factor is the *peril sought to be avoided*, as provided by section 66(6) of the Marine Insurance Act 1906:

> "In the absence of express stipulation, the insurer is not liable for any general average loss or contribution where the loss was not incurred for the purpose of avoiding, or in connection with the avoidance of, a peril insured against."

50.10 In the majority of cases in practice, the accident which gives rise to the peril (for example fire) is the same peril which the general average act seeks to avoid (destruction by fire), and where, as is usual, fire is one of the perils insured against by the policy, both the damage caused by the fire, and the sacrifices made and the expenditures incurred to extinguish that fire, will be recoverable on the same policy. However, less straightforward cases can occur, and the following examples may assist in understanding the doctrine set forth in the above section 66(6) of the Act:

(1) A vessel and her cargo may be in peril arising from a complete main engine breakdown at sea, the result of pure wear and tear. The expense of repairing that damage to the main engine is most unlikely to be recoverable on the hull policy, but if the engine breakdown was likely to result in the risk of loss by the vessel drifting ashore, or by heavy weather or collision (all insured perils), the general average losses or expenses would be recoverable.

(2) In *Pyman S.S. Co. Ltd v. Admiralty*[4] the propeller shaft of a vessel broke in the North Sea during the First World War. A heavy gale was blowing at the time and there was an added danger that the vessel might drift on to an enemy minefield. Salvage services were rendered, and the arbitrator apportioned his award as to 75 per

[4] [1918] 1 K.B. 480; [1919] 1 K.B. 49; 14 Asp. M.L.C. 171 at 364; 34 T.L.R. 174; 35 T.L.R. 79.

cent marine and 25 per cent war, and this was upheld in the Court of King's Bench and the Court of Appeal. The cause of the breakage of the propeller shaft is irrelevant to the question of liability for the ensuing general average.

(3) A vessel struck a mine shortly after the end of the Second World War, sustaining very severe damage and incurring substantial general average expenditure. The whole claim was settled by the war risk insurers. About a year after the extensive repairs, the main engine crankshaft broke in mid-ocean and the damage was reasonably attributed to the earlier striking of the mine and the cost of repairs settled by the war risk insurers. The general average expenses, however, being incurred to avoid the perils of drifting ashore or on rocks, or of loss by heavy weather, were chargeable to the marine insurers on risk at the time of the breakage of the crankshaft.

The various sets of Institute Clauses conform with or depart from the provisions of section 66(6) of the Marine Insurance Act as follows: **50.11**

Institute Time (or Voyage) Clauses, Hulls and Institute Time (or Voyage) Clauses, Freight

These all include the wording:

> "No claim under this Clause ... shall in any case be allowed where the loss was not incurred to avoid or in connection with the avoidance of a peril insured against."

and thus correspond precisely with the provisions of section 66(6) of the Marine Insurance Act.

Institute Cargo Clauses (A), (B), or (C)

These all include the wording:

> "This insurance covers general average and salvage charges, adjusted or determined according to the contract of affreightment and/or the governing law and practice, incurred to avoid or in connection with the avoidance of loss from any cause except those excluded by Clauses 4, 5, 6 and 7 or elsewhere in this insurance."

and by the inclusion of the words "... loss *from any cause* except ...," effectively introduce general average, *per se*, as a separate insured peril in the case of the (B) and (C) class Cargo Clause, which otherwise offer cover against limited specified risks only. In the case of the (A) Clauses covering "all risks", the effect is identical with the provisions of section 66(6) of the Act.

One further practical example, additional to those given in paragraph 50.10, above, may be appropriate here. Fire breaks out in the cargo of a vessel as the result of inherent vice of the cargo, and the whole adventure is thereby placed in considerable peril and general average sacrifices and expenditures are made to save the common adventure.

Clause 4.4 of the Institute Cargo Clauses excludes:

> "loss damage or expense caused by inherent vice of the subject-matter insured."

and there can therefore be no claim upon the policy covering the cargo giving rise to the fire, either for loss or damage thereto—whether caused by the fire or the means used to extinguish it—or for any general average contribution which it may be called upon to pay.

50.12 Having disposed of the preliminaries, and assuming that the policy of insurance covers the loss which the general average act sought to avoid, or covers general average *per se*, we may now proceed to study the rights of any assured to recover from his insurers in respect of any general average sacrifice or expenditure falling directly upon him, or in respect of any general average contribution or deposit he is obliged to pay towards the general average losses sustained by the other parties to the common adventure.

(A) GENERAL AVERAGE SACRIFICE

(Loss of or damage to the property insured caused by)

Section 66(4) of the Marine Insurance Act 1906 provides:

> "Subject to any express provision in the policy, ... in the case of a general average **sacrifice** he, [the assured] may recover ... from the insurer in respect of the whole loss without having enforced his right of contribution from the other parties liable to contribute."

Thus, the assured may proceed directly and immediately against the insurers for the *whole* of his loss, and on payment, insurers are thereby subrogated[5] to the general average contributions eventually recovered from the other parties to the adventure when the general average adjustment has been prepared and settled.

[5] Marine Insurance Act 1906, s. 79. Rights of subrogation are dealt with, *post*, in paras. 50.49–50.58, *post*. It is also worthy of record that:

(1) Although an assured shipowner may generally proceed directly and immediately against his insurers for the *whole* of his loss, if he prejudices their rights of subrogation by omitting to collect general average security from cargo interests, the insurers may be entitled to deny liability for such proportion of the sacrifice damage to the ship as would have attached to the cargo.

(2) Where an assured shipowner proceeds first against cargo interests for their due contribution to damage to the ship caused by general average sacrifice, but fails to recover that contribution on grounds such as a breach of the contract of carriage, he may still proceed against his insurers for the *whole* of the ship sacrifice.

This basic right had been re-established in 1868 by the case of *Dickenson v. Jardine*[6] where goods were jettisoned under circumstances which entitled the plaintiff to a general average contribution from the owners of the ship and other cargo. The goods were insured by a policy which included jettison among the perils insured against and the plaintiff sued the insurers for the whole amount insured without having first collected the contributions to which he was entitled from the other parties to the adventure. It was held that he was so entitled to recover, and that the liability of insurers could not be varied by an alleged custom in London between merchants and insurers to hold the latter liable only for the share of the loss cast upon the owner of jettisoned goods in the general average adjustment. Having settled the loss, the insurers were entitled to stand in the place of the assured and were subrogated to the general average contributions recovered from the other parties to the adventure. **50.13**

Thus, the initial claim on any policy of marine insurance for loss of or damage to the property insured by a general average sacrifice is calculated in precisely the same manner and on the same established principles as though the loss were from an *accidental* cause, that is on a particular average or total loss basis, and whether the loss is to ship, cargo or freight, etc.

These insurance principles for calculating claims may produce either a greater or lesser sum than the allowance which will be made in general average in accordance with the provisions of the contract of affreightment, particularly in the case of the insurance of cargo, and some simple examples now follow to illustrate the direct claims[7] upon the policies compared with the allowances in general average. (In practice, the examples will be more complex than shown, but the basic principles should become apparent.) The rights of subrogation attaching thereto will be dealt with subsequently in paragraphs 50.49 to 50.58, below. **50.14**

Cargo

(In the two examples below, the cargo is assumed to have an invoice value of 10,000 and to be insured subject to the Institute Cargo Clauses for: Case A—12,000, so valued
Case B—8,000, so valued)

[6] (1868) L.R. 3 C.P. 639.

[7] It is possible for a policy of marine insurance to be valued or unvalued, and for the sum insured to be less than the insured or insurable value. These variables can affect the amount of a *claim* upon the policy, but for the sake of simplicity and brevity it will be assumed in the text and examples throughout this section that:

SHIP and CARGO are insured by *valued* policies and that the sum insured is the full insured value;

FREIGHT is insured by an *unvalued* policy, with varying sums insured.

50.15 (1) *In the event of a total loss*, for example by jettison.

The allowance in general average per Rule XVI of the York-Antwerp Rules 1994 will be based upon the invoice value, that is 10,000.

The measure of indemnity,[8] in accordance with section 68(1) of the Marine Insurance Act 1906 "is the sum fixed by the policy", that is:

Case A — 12,000
Case B — 8,000

50.16 (2) *In the event of a partial loss*, for example by the jettison of 50 per cent of the cargo insured, or of damage to the complete consignment by water used to extinguish a fire, assessed at 50 per cent of the value.

The allowance in general average per Rule XVI of the York-Antwerp Rules 1994 will be based upon the invoice value, that is, 50 per cent of 10,000 = 5,000.

The measure of indemnity, in accordance with section 71(1) or (3) of the Marine Insurance Act 1906 is 50 per cent of the insured value of the goods, that is:

Case A—50% × 12,000 = 6,000
Case B—50% × 8,000 = 4,000

The insurers' rights of subrogation when the general average adjustment is completed and issued say two years later, will be considered in paragraphs 50.54, 50.55, below.

Ship

(In the example below, the ship is assumed to have a sound market value of 5,000,000 and to be insured subject to the Institute Time Clauses, Hulls 1.11.95 for: Case A—6,000,000, so valued
Case B—4,000,000, so valued.)

50.17 The claim upon a policy of marine insurance for damage to a ship caused by a general average sacrifice is governed by the provisions of section 69 of the Marine Insurance Act 1906,[9] as refined by any special

[8] The Marine Insurance Act 1906, s. 67, defines the extent of the liability of the insurer for loss in the following terms:

"(1) The sum which the assured can recover in respect of a loss on a policy by which he is insured, in the case of an unvalued policy to the full extent of the insurable value, or, in the case of a valued policy to the full extent of the value fixed by the policy, is called the measure of indemnity.

(2) Where there is a loss recoverable under the policy, the insurer, or each insurer if there be more than one, is liable for such proportion of the measure of indemnity as the amount of his subscription bears to the value of the policy in the case of a valued policy, or to the insurable value in the case of an unvalued policy."

[9] See para. 18.06, n. 6, *ante*.

conditions in the policy. In practice, and ignoring any "deductible" or "excess" stipulated in the policy, the assured generally recovers from his insurers the actual and reasonable cost of repairing the damage, in full, without deductions "new for old", and regardless of the insured value of the ship other than as a limiting factor on the maximum claim payable.

In the event of damage, for example, to the propeller and main engine by efforts to refloat after stranding. **50.18**

The allowance in general average per Rule XVIII of the York-Antwerp Rules 1994 will be the "actual reasonable cost of repairing ... such damage...."

damage...."		100,000
subject to deductions "new for old" in accordance with Rule XIII	(say)	5,000
		95,000

The measure of indemnity, in accordance with section 69(1) of the Marine Insurance Act 1906 will be "the reasonable cost of the repairs, less the customary deductions" (that is also 95,000), but by reason of Clause 14 of the Institute Time Clauses, Hulls, which states that "claims payable without deduction new for old", the claim will be for:

Case A — 100,000
and also Case B — 100,000

Freight

(In the example below, the vessel is assumed to be carrying 10,000 tons of cargo on which the freight is at risk to the shipowner and payable only on right delivery of the cargo at destination at the rate of 100 per ton, that is 1,000,000. This is insured by an unvalued policy subject to the Institute Time Clauses, Freight, 1.11.95 for:

Case A — 1,200,000
Case B — 800,000

1000 tons of cargo are jettisoned at a time of peril.)

The allowance in general average in accordance with Rule XV of the York-Antwerp Rules 1994 will be for the "gross freight lost" 100,000 **50.19**

Deduct: "charges which the owner thereof would have incurred to earn such freight, but has, in consequence of the sacrifice, not incurred." (e.g. discharging expenses) . say	5,000
	95,000

The measure of indemnity, in accordance with section 70 of the Marine Insurance Act 1906 will be: "such proportion ... of the insurable value ... as the proportion of the freight lost by the assured bears to the whole freight at the risk of the assured under the policy."

50.20 The insurable value of the freight may be assumed to be:

Gross freight at risk—10,000 tons @ 100 = ...		1,000,000
Add: charges of insurance	say	3,000
		1,003,000

The claims on the respective policies would be, therefore:

Case A—1,000/10,000 × 1,003,000 = ...	100,300
except that Clause 13(1) of the Institute Time Clauses, Freight limits any claim to "the gross freight actually lost", *i.e.*	100,000
Case B—If total insurable value 1,003,000 pays 100,300 Then sum insured 800,000 pays in proportion ..	80,000

(B) GENERAL AVERAGE EXPENDITURE

(Incurred by the assured)

50.21 Section 66(4) of the Marine Insurance Act 1906 provides:

> "Subject to any express provision in the policy, where the assured has incurred a general average **expenditure**, he may recover from the insurer in respect of the proportion of the loss which falls upon him;..."

Unlike a policy claim for general average sacrifice, where the assured can recover the *whole* of his loss immediately and directly from insurers, in the case of general average expenditure he can recover only the proportion which falls upon him. As an example if the shipowner has financed the whole of any general average expenditure (100,000), and the value of his ship represents 25 per cent of the total contributory values, he can usually proceed directly against his insurers for only 25 per cent of his general average expenditure, that is, 25,000. He must either wait until the general average adjustment has been completed and settled before recovering the balance of 75 per cent from cargo and other contributing interests, or seek payments on account from those other contributing interests in accordance with the terms of their general average guarantee, or from any general average deposit funds.

50.22 However, where the cargo or other contributing interests have sustained general average sacrifices of their property, or have financed part of the general average (for example by settling their own proportion of any salvage award), it follows that the "proportion of the loss (general average expenditure) which falls upon him"[10] will not be the above-mentioned 25,000, but a rather different sum. For instance, if the shipowner has incurred general average expenditure amounting, as before, to 100,000 but the cargo sacrifices or expenditures amount to 200,000

Total general average 300,000

The proportion attaching to ship—25 per cent is .... 75,000 and it follows that the shipowner has the right to base his initial claim upon the insurers in respect of his own general average expenditure of 100,000 on a revised figure of 75,000.

Underinsurance

The party who has financed a general average expenditure (or paid salvage charges) is limited in his recovery from insurers not only to the "proportion of the loss which falls upon him"[11] but even that sum may be further reduced if the property is insured for less than its real worth—or that on which the contributory value is based in accordance with the York-Antwerp Rules or other applicable law. **50.23**

Section 73 of the Marine Insurance Act 1906 provides:

> "(1) Subject to any express provision in the policy, where the assured has paid, or is liable for, any general average contribution, the measure of indemnity is the full amount of such contribution, if the subject-matter liable to contribution is insured for its full contributory value; but, if such subject-matter be not insured for its full contributory value, or if only part of it be insured, the indemnity payable by the insurer must be reduced in proportion to the under insurance, and where there has been a particular average loss which constitutes a deduction from the contributory value, and for which the insurer is liable, that amount must be deducted from the insured value in order to ascertain what the insurer is liable to contribute.
>
> (2) Where the insurer is liable for salvage charges the extent of his liability must be determined on the like principle."

We are here discussing general average *expenditure*, and it may be noted that the above section 73 of the Act mentions only general average *contribution*. However, it is well understood that section 73 applies *mutatis mutandis* to general average expenditure in accordance with the provisions of section 75(1) of the Marine Insurance Act 1906:

> "Where there has been a loss in respect of any subject-matter not expressly provided for in the foregoing provisions of this Act, the measure of indemnity

[10] Marine Insurance Act 1906, s. 66(4).
[11] Marine Insurance Act 1906, s. 66(4).

shall be ascertained, as nearly as may be, in accordance with those provisions, in so far as applicable to the particular case."

50.24 A simple example will illustrate the basic principle set forth in section 73 of the Act. In *S.S. Balmoral Co. v. Marten*[12] decided in 1902, the *Balmoral* incurred general average expenditure and salvage services and her salved and contributory value was established at £40,000. She was insured by a valued policy for £33,000 and the House of Lords, affirming previous decisions of the Court of Appeal and of Bigham J., held that the insurers were liable for 33/40ths of the general average and salvage expenditure.

This decision merely indorsed established English practice dating back to at least 1755 when Magens[13] wrote:

> "Whatever is paid in contribution, by the excess of the contributory value over the value in the policy, is paid by the assured; but for whatever is paid on a contributory value not exceeding the value in the policy, the assured is indemnified on the proportion insured."

It is possible that the only reason for taking the case through to our highest court may have been that the same problem had been brought on a number of occasions before the courts of the various states of the United States with divergent decisions, but tending overall to burden the insurers with the *whole* contribution where, as in the *Balmoral* case, the agreed insured value had been fully subscribed by the insurers.[14]

50.25 The terms of section 73 of the Marine Insurance Act undoubtedly give effect to the *Balmoral* decision; furthermore, by incorporating a great deal of the wording of the Custom of Lloyd's on the subject (adopted by the Association of Average Adjusters as a British Rule of Practice in 1876),[15] they appear also to indorse the more refined English practice of that time:

> "If the ship or cargo be insured for more than its contributory value, the underwriter pays what is assessed on the contributory value. But where insured for less than the contributory value, the underwriter pays on the insured value; and when there has been a particular average for damage which forms a deduction from the contributory value of the ship that must be deducted from the insured value to find upon what the underwriter contributes.
>
> This rule does not apply to foreign adjustments, when the basis of contribution is something other than the net value of the thing insured."

[12] [1902] A.C. 511.

[13] 1 Magens 245 case XIX.

[14] See *Phillips on Insurance*, s. 1410, published in 1867 and copied with subsequent U.S. case law up to 1914 in Gow, *Sea Insurance*, pp. 165–166.

It may also be remarked that American insurers adopt the English approach by including special wording in their policy wordings to counteract the effect of any contrary decisions of the American courts.

[15] Now forming the first section of Rule B33; see para. 70.19, *post*.

It may be noted that the adjusters' Rule of Practice refers on a number of occasions to the simple expression "contributory value", (as does the quotation from Magens in paragraph 50.24, above, and all other old text books), whereas section 73 of the Marine Insurance Act quoted in paragraph 50.23, above, on two occasions uses the expression "*full* contributory value". Is there any significance in the use of this alternative expression?

The problem may best be highlighted by a figured example which will also serve to illustrate the equitable principle set forth in the Rule of Practice and section 73 of the Act regarding the deduction from the insured value of "particular average" for which the insurer is liable. In any general average adjustment, one is likely to find that the general average has been apportioned over contributory values shown and calculated in a manner such as the following: **50.26**

SHIP		FREIGHT	
Sound Value	1,000,000	Gross Freight at risk and earned	1,000,000
Deduct: Damage	200,000[16]	*Deduct*: Contingent Expenses	200,000[17]
Contributory Value	800,000	Contributory Value	800,000

The "contributory value" in each case is undoubtedly 800,000, but is the "full contributory value" that same 800,000, or is it the sound or gross value of 1,000,000? Assuming that the ship or the freight were insured by a valued policy for 800,000, in the former case it would mean that the insurers were liable for the whole proportion of any general average expenditure shown due, but in the latter case for perhaps only 80 per cent.

In paragraph 908 of the tenth edition of this work it was submitted: **50.27**

> "... that 'full contributory value' means the value upon which the interest contributes [800,000], even if that be less than the sound value [1,000,000] at the termination of the adventure."

and the present editors whole-heartedly indorse the broad concept of this view on the following grounds:

(1) The wording of section 73 of the Act support this construction, even if the editors of our sister-volume, Arnould, *Law of Marine Insurance and Average*,[18] while accepting that the meaning of the term "full contributory value" is not free from doubt, conclude that the words denote the *maximum* potential contributory value [1,000,000]. Their figured examples produce exceedingly harsh

[16] See para. 17.13, *ante*.
[17] *Ibid.*
[18] 16th ed., para. 1007.

results which seemingly penalise the assured *twice* for any under-insurance, and are demonstrably in error.

(2) As was stated in the Introduction to the First Edition of Digest quoted in Chalmers', *Marine Insurance Act 1906*: "The object of that Bill was to reproduce as accurately as possible the existing law, without making any attempt to amend it."

(3) The known market practice which existed prior to the passing of the Marine Insurance Act in 1906 has been consistently followed—and accepted without demur—ever since.

50.28 We now revert to the figured examples in paragraph 50.26, above, and will endeavour to explain the practical application to the insured value (in the case of a valued policy) of the deductions of 200,000 made from the sound or gross values of 1,000,000 in arriving at the net contributory values of 800,000.

Taking first the FREIGHT, with a gross sum at risk and earned of 1,000,000, the deductions of 200,000 will almost invariably comprise simply the routine voyage expenses incurred by the shipowner to earn that freight subsequent to the general average act. The insurers of the freight will in no way be liable for these expenses, and it is perfectly equitable, therefore, that an insured value of 800,000 should pay the full general average contribution attaching to the net contributory value of 800,000.

50.29 In the case of the SHIP, however, with a sound value of 1,000,000, the deductions (for damage) of 200,000 probably comprise items for which the insurers may be liable, for example as particular average. In such a case, it would be manifestly inequitable that an insured value of 800,000 should respond for the *whole* of any general average expenditure attributable to a net contributory value of 800,000. This was recognised in the old Custom of Lloyd's and indorsed by the Marine Insurance Act by providing that, to the extent that the insurers were liable for any particular average deductions made in arriving at the contributory value, those same deductions should also be made from the insured value when assessing any degree of under-insurance. Thus, and assuming for the sake of example a proportion of general average expenditure of 80,000, where the insurers are liable to pay:

(1) *The whole of the deductions of 200,000*

If contributory value 800,000 pays 80,000.

Then insured value	800,000	
Less Damage CLAIM	200,000	
	600,000	pays in proportion 60,000

(2) *None of the deductions of 200,000* (for example on an F.P.A. policy)

If contributory value 800,000 pays 80,000

Then insured value	800,000	
Less Damage CLAIM	—	
	800,000	pays in full 80,000

(3) *120,000 ex the deductions of 200,000* (for example by reason of a large policy deductible, or because some of the damage was not caused by insured perils).

If contributory value 800,000 pays 80,000

Then insured value	800,000	
Less Damage CLAIM	120,000	
	680,000	pays in proportion 68,000

Note: The old Custom of Lloyd's and the Marine Insurance Act both make reference only to the deduction of *particular average* from the insured value, but the insurers could be liable for other expenses which have constituted deductions in arriving at the net contributory value of any property, for example general average thirds "new for old", or salvage when treated separately and not directly as general average. Accordingly, and to achieve a greater equity in the assessment of any degree of under-insurance, the Association of Average Adjusters added in 1922 a second section to their Rule of Practice B33: **50.30**

> "That in practice, in applying the above rule for the purpose of ascertaining the liability of underwriters for contribution to general average and salvage charges, deduction shall be made from the insured value of all losses and charges for which underwriters are liable and which have been deducted in arriving at the contributory value."

which substitutes *all losses and charges* for the more narrow *particular average* in the Act and the first section of their Rule.

It is also important to stress that the above examples are based on the assumption that the policy is a *valued* one for 800,000 and with a sum insured of 800,000. The position would be quite different were the policy *unvalued*, but with a sum insured of 800,000. It is a surprising fact that although the Marine Insurance Act in sections 68, 70 and 71 makes specific provision for the measure of indemnity in respect of both valued and unvalued policies covering total loss, generally, and partial losses of freight and cargo, it mentions only *valued* policies in section 73 concerning general average contributions, (and nothing in section 69 concerning partial loss of ship!). Nevertheless, it is perfectly easy to deduce the **50.31** correct principles to apply in the case of unvalued policies from other sections of the Act.

50.32 For sound commercial reasons (*inter alia* to avoid the necessity of assessing the sound value in all but general average situations), a ship is invariably insured by a *valued* policy. In the unlikely event that the ship were insured by an unvalued policy with a sum insured of 800,000 when her true value (at the commencement of the risk) was 1,000,000, it is submitted that the claim in Example (1) of paragraph 50.29, above, should be dealt with as follows:

For particular average and general average thirds—		200,000
Recoverable: 800/1000ths		160,000

For general average expenditure—80,000

If contributory value 800,000 pays 80,000

Then sum insured	800,000	
Less Damage CLAIM	160,000	
	640,000 pays in proportion	64,000
		224,000

50.33 Unlike an insurance on ship, freight is almost invariably insured by means of an *unvalued* policy (for the reason, *inter alia*, that many varying freights will be earned in a twelve-month, the amount of any freight is easily quantifiable, and the standard freight clauses limit any loss to the gross freight lost but otherwise provide a very adequate indemnity).

In order to calculate the liability of the insurers of a freight insured by an unvalued policy for 800,000 where the gross amount at risk and earned was 1,000,000, but the contributory value 800,000 (see paragraph 50.26, above), and assuming a proportion of general average expenditure of 80,000 attaching thereto, it is necessary to have regard to a number of the provisions of the Marine Insurance Act:

Section 81 relating to the effect of under-insurance states that:

> "Where the assured is insured for an amount less than the insurable value ... he is deemed to be his own insurer in respect of the uninsured balance."

The insurable value of the freight, as provided by section 16(2):

> "... is the gross amount of the freight at risk of the assured, plus the charges of insurance."

(*i.e.*	1,000,000
Plus insurance premium .... say	3,000
	1,003,000)

By section 67(2) of the Act:

> "... the insurer ... is liable for such proportion of the measure of indemnity as the amount of his subscription bears to the ... insurable value in the case of an unvalued policy."

Thus, the claim for the proportion of general average expenditure of 80,000 attaching to freight should be dealt with as follows:

If insurable value 1,003,000 pays 80,000
Then sum insured 800,000 pays in proportion 63,809

This last example would accord with the practice of all British adjusters as their interpretation of the final section of their Rule of Practice B33, added in 1926: **50.34**

> "In adjusting the liability of underwriters on freight for general average contribution and salvage charges, effect shall be given to Section 73 of the Marine Insurance Act, 1906, by comparing the gross and not the net amount of freight at risk with the insured value in the case of a valued policy or the insurable value in the case of an unvalued policy."

Regrettably, the wording is far from perfect in respect of the unvalued policies generally found in practice, and with regard to valued policies, where the wording is clear, the practice would be wrong, inconsistent with the accepted practice on ship policies, and encouraging and supportive of the erroneous views on the matter expounded in *Arnould.*

To complete this section on the rights of an assured to recover for general average expenditure, one final example is given for CARGO: **50.35**

(The cargo is assumed to have an invoice or market value of 100,000 and to be insured subject to the Institute Cargo Clauses for:

Case A—120,000, so valued
Case B—80,000, so valued

Salvage services are rendered to the vessel and her cargo and the owners of the above cargo are obliged to settle direct with salvors for their proportion of the total award, that is 10,000.)

This sum of 10,000 is the "proportion of the loss which falls upon him" in accordance with section 66(4) of the Marine Insurance Act 1906 and the claim upon insurers will therefore be based on the full sum of 10,000.

In Case A—where the value of the property is fully insured, the measure of indemnity will be the actual amount of (and no more than) the sum paid of 10,000.

In Case B—where the value of the property is under-insured, the measure of indemnity "must be reduced in proportion to the under-insurance",[19] that is to 80,000/100,000 × 10,000 = 8,000.

(Had the insured property also suffered damage by accidental cause and the insurers paid a particular average claim, some further calculations would be necessary to comply with the last lines of section 73(1) of the Marine Insurance Act 1906 such as are explained in paragraphs 50.29, 50.30, above, but by reason of the principles applied in calculating claims on cargo insurance policies, the proportion of the salvage award or general average expenditure recoverable from insurers will almost invariably be 80 per cent in Case B.)

(C) General Average Contributions

(payable to other parties to the adventure)

50.36 The rights of an assured to recover from his insurers in respect of general average contributions payable to other parties to the adventure are governed by the following provisions of the Marine Insurance Act 1906:

Section 66(5):

> "Subject to any express provision in the policy, where the assured has paid, or is liable to pay, a general average contribution in respect of the subject insured, he may recover therefor from the insurer."

together with section 73, the full text of which was quoted in paragraph 50.23, above.

50.37 The term general average *contribution* has been defined earlier in paragraph 50.05 and attention drawn with words and a figured example in paragraphs 50.06 to 50.08, above, to the fact that although the amount of a general average contribution may often be the same as the *proportion of general average* shown in a general average adjustment as attaching to a particular property, the terms are not synonymous.

However, in those simple cases where the amount of the contribution is identical with the proportion of general average (that is because the particular property has not suffered loss or damage by a general average sacrifice, or because the owner of the property has not incurred a general average expenditure), the rights of the assured to recover from the insurers of his ship, cargo or freight, etc., are precisely the same as for

[19] Marine Insurance Act 1906, s. 73(1).

general average expenditure, and reference may therefore be directed to what has been written in paragraphs 50.21 to 50.35, above. It may also be worthy of record, even if reasonably self-evident, that a contribution paid towards the *sacrifice* of another party to the adventure is treated *vis-à-vis* the paying contributor in the same manner as general average *expenditure*, and not in the preferential manner associated with an insurance claim in respect of a general average sacrifice to his own property.

The situation can be mathematically more complex where an insured party is called upon to pay a general average contribution which is for a different sum than the proportion of general average shown in the general average adjustment as attaching to his property, and two examples now follow to illustrate the problem. **50.38**

Cargo

A general average adjustment shows figures such as the following in respect of an individual cargo interest with an invoice or market value of 10,000:

Arrived value	9,000			
Add: Made Good	1,000			
	10,000	liable for **proportion general average**		5,000
Credit: Amount made good in general average for:				
Sacrifice damage to property			1,000	
Salvage payment			1,800	2,800
		Balance to Pay (= **Contribution**)		2,200

Adopting the same insured values as used in earlier examples of:

Case A—12,000
Case B— 8,000

the positions are as follows:

In Case A—where the cargo is fully insured, the measure of indemnity will be for the full general average contribution of 2,200 (in addition to the earlier claims presumed paid by insurers in respect of the: **50.39**

Sacrifice—10 per cent × 12,000 =	1,200
Salvage payment	1,800
	3,000)

50.40 *In Case B*—where the cargo is under-insured, in simple practical terms the measure of indemnity for the general average contribution of 2,200 may well be calculable by a straight comparison of the insured and contributory values, that is:

If contributory value 10,000 pays contribution 2,200	
Then insured value 8,000 pays in proportion	1,760

However, the proper approach (and this applies even in Case A) must be to examine and re-assess the rights of the assured against his insurers to recover for each constituent part of his claim for damage, salvage, and the eventual general average contribution, and from the combined total to deduct such sums—if any—which have already been paid by the insurers.

Thus, the final claim on a policy subject to the Institute Cargo Clauses might well be calculated as follows:

Sacrifice—10 per cent ×	8,000		800
Salvage—If salved value	9,000 pays 1,800		
Then insured value	8,000		
Less: claim paid	800		
	7,200 pays in proportion		1,440
Contribution —If contributory value 10,000 pays 2,200			
Then insured value	8,000 pays in proportion		1,760
	Total Liability		4,000
Credit: Previous payments for Sacrifice		800	
Salvage		1,440	cr.
		2,240	2,240
	Balance to Pay		1,760

It will be noted that the total liability of 4,000 happens to be 8,000/10,000ths of the proportion of general average attaching to the cargo of 5,000, but this would not apply in Case A. It will also be noted that the insurers in this example have previously paid the precisely correct claims for sacrifice and salvage, but these payments might have been for different amounts—or not at all. The matter might also be rendered more complex by the addition of interest on general average allowances.

Ship

50.41 A general average adjustment might show figures such as the following in respect of the ship:

Sound Value		5,000,000		
Less: Damage—P.A.	1,000,000			
G.A.	200,000	1,200,000		
		3,800,000		
Add: Made Good		200,000		
		4,000,000	liable for ppn. G.A.	1,000,000

Credit: Amounts Made Good in General Average		
Sacrifice damage	200,000	cr.
Expenditure by Shipowner	500,000	700,000
Balance to Pay (= **Contribution**)		300,000

Adopting the same insured values for the ship as used in earlier examples of: **50.42**

Case A	—	6,000,000
Case B	—	4,000,000

and assuming the ship to be insured subject to the Institute Time Clauses, Hulls, 1.11.95, but ignoring any deductible:

In Case A—where the ship is fully insured, it can safely be said that the measure of indemnity for the general average contribution of 300,000 will be the full sum of 300,000, but that calculations such as are shown below in Case B will nevertheless need to be made.

50.43 *In Case B*—where the ship is under-insured, the final general average contribution payable to other parties to the adventure of 300,000 will never be looked at in isolation; as with Cargo Case B, above, an overall adjustment must be prepared dealing with each constituent part of the shipowner's claim against his insurers and account taken of any earlier payments on account made by them. For the above example, and assuming that the contributory value of the ship represents 50 per cent of the total contributory values, the overall measure of indemnity would be assessed as follows:

Particular Average				1,000,000
General Average, proportion attaching to Ship 1,000,000				
Whereof: Sacrifice 50% ×	200,000	=	100,000	100,000
Expenditure 50% ×	1,800,000	=	900,000	
	2,000,000	=	1,000,000	

Proportion G.A. Expenditure/Contribution, as above, 900,000

If Contributory Value 4,000,000 pays 900,000

Then Insured Value	4,000,000		
Less: P.A.	1,000,000		
	3,000,000	pays in proportion	675,000
		Measure of Indemnity	1,775,000

Credit: Payments on Account in respect of:

Particular Average	say	850,000		
General Average Sacrifice		170,000		
Expenditure		400,000		
	say	1,420,000		1,420,000
			Balance to Pay	355,000

In practice, the figures will be rendered more complex by the addition of interest on general average allowances, but the balance to pay of 355,000 has no real or direct connection with the final general average contribution of 300,000 payable to the other parties to the adventure, and is dependant entirely on what sums have previously been advanced by insurers on account of their eventual liability.

(D) GENERAL AVERAGE DEPOSITS

(paid as security for general average contributions)

50.44 The circumstances in which a general average deposit may be required, as security for the general average contribution which will eventually be ascertained to be due, have been set forth earlier in paragraph 30.04. Whether the insurers under a typical marine insurance policy are under any legal obligation to reimburse to their assured the deposit paid by them is a question which has not been satisfactorily resolved. In *Brandeis v. Economic Insce. Co.*[20] the assured, under a cargo policy containing a foreign adjustment clause,[21] paid a deposit in order to secure his general average contribution and to obtain the release of his goods. No adjustment was ever prepared, and the assured sought to recover the deposit from the insurers. Bailhache J. expressed the view that the deposit would

[20] [1922] 11 Ll.L.Rep. 42.
[21] See paras. 50.71 *et seq.*, *post*.

ordinarily be recoverable under the policy, but in the particular case the claim failed because of the foreign adjustment clause, which in effect made a foreign adjustment a condition precedent to liability. This reasoning cannot be regarded as wholly satisfactory, since even under the ordinary form of policy the contributions against which the policy ultimately provides the indemnity (under section 66(5) of the Marine Insurance Act) must be the rateable contribution defined by section 66(3), rather than a deposit demanded in order to secure an unquantified liability to contribute. It may well be that the concept of indemnity, which lies at the heart of an insurance policy, also entitles the assured to be held harmless against any reasonable demand for security, which he must in practice comply with in order to obtain his goods. But if this is so, it is difficult to see why the presence of a foreign adjustment clause should deprive the assured of this entitlement.

In practice, whatever be the strict rights of the assured under the policy, it is the practice of cargo insurers to reimburse the amount of the deposit to their assured provided that: **50.45**

(1) The sum insured and the insured value of the goods are at least equal to the invoice value[22] (failing which a proportional reduction will be made); and
(2) The deposit is not excessive, and is properly held[23] (for example in accordance with Rule XXII of the York-Antwerp Rules).

2. Rights of Recovery Where Common Ownership

Section 66(7) of the Marine Insurance Act provides: **50.46**

> "Where ship, freight and cargo, or any two of those interests, are owned by the same assured, the liability of the insurer in respect of general average losses and contributions is to be determined as if those subjects were owned by different persons."

This subsection appears to be intended to codify the decision in *Montgomery v. Indemnity Mutual Marine Insce Co.*,[24] in which it was held by Matthew J. and the Court of Appeal that the fact that all the contributory interests were in the same ownership did not prevent a sacrifice of part of the ship from being a general average act. Section

[22] When the York-Antwerp Rules 1974 or 1994 are applicable.

[23] See *Salvage Association v. Suzuki* (1929) 35 Ll.L.Rep. 45. In *Brandeis v. Economic Ins. Co.* (*supra*) the insurers declined to follow the practice of reimbursing the deposit because they regarded the terms upon which the deposit was paid (*i.e.* not into joint names, and with no security for its return) as unreasonable and imprudent.

[24] [1901] 1 K.B. 147; [1902] 1 K.B. 734. In Chalmer's *Marine Insurance Act 1906* (7th ed.), p. 105, this is said to have been the intention of the subsection, which was twice altered during the passage of the Bill through Parliament.

66(7) now places this beyond argument, at any rate so far as concerns the relationship between insurer and insured.

The section gives rise to no difficulty with regard to expenditure or contribution, since in these cases, quite apart from any question of common ownership, the insured can claim only his own proportion of expenditure, or the contribution for which he is liable. Thus in the case of expenditure by a common owner of ship and cargo, the common owner can claim the ship's proportion from the hull insurers (the Act requiring one to assume that he could recover cargo's contribution from himself in his capacity as cargo owner) and may recover cargo's contribution from the insurers of the cargo. However, in the case of sacrifices there is a difficulty, for here, as has already been noted,[25] where no question of common ownership is involved the insured is entitled to claim in full from the insurer, and need not reduce his claim by the amount of contributions which he is entitled to receive. Does the same rule apply where there is common ownership of the contributory interests? At first sight section 66(7) might suggest that it does. However in *Montgomery v. Indemnity Mutual Marine Insce Co.*[26] the Court of Appeal held, reversing Matthew J. on this point, that the common owner, in claiming from hull underwriters the loss caused by the sacrifice, had to give credit for cargo's contribution "because the shipowner already has in his own pocket his contribution as cargo owner". It seems open to doubt whether this aspect of the decision is codified by section 66(7). Nevertheless, in practice the insurer of property sacrificed is treated as entitled to credit for contributions due from other interests in the same ownership, and it is submitted that this practice would be reconciled with section 66(7) on the grounds that the Court of Appeal rightly treated a contribution due in respect of an interest in common ownership on the same footing as a contribution actually paid, and that the insured would therefore have to give credit for it, just as he would if the contribution had been paid to him by the owner of an interest in different ownership.

3. Rights of Insurers on Payment

Subrogation

50.47 Having settled any claim for general average, whether sacrifice, expenditure, contribution or deposit, the insurer is entitled to "stand in the

[25] See para. 50.12, *ante*.
[26] [1902] 1 K.B. 734.

shoes" of the assured and, in the words of section 79(2) of the Marine Insurance Act 1906:

> "... is thereupon subrogated to all rights and remedies of the assured in and in respect of the subject-matter insured as from the time of the casualty causing the loss, in so far as the assured has been indemnified...."[27]

Those rights and remedies may be against:

(1) The other parties to the common adventure in so far as they are liable to contribute to any general average loss or expenditure sustained by the owner of the insured property greater than his own rateable proportion of the total general average, and for which the insurer has already made settlement with the assured.

(2) Any other party to the common adventure whose actionable fault has resulted in the situation giving rise to the general average (for example the owner of a ship which has made an unjustifiable deviation, or who has failed to exercise due diligence to provide a seaworthy ship). The claim against such offending party would be for the whole loss, in so far as the insurer has already made settlement with the assured. **50.48**

(3) Any other party outside the common adventure whose actionable fault has given rise to the general average situation (for example the owner of another vessel which by negligent navigation has collided with our own vessel). The claim against such offending party would be for the whole or such proportion of the whole loss as corresponds with the degree of blame attaching to the other vessel, and in so far as the insurer has already made settlement with his insured.

In the context of this present section it is proposed to consider only the first classification, that is rights against the other parties to the adventure and without regard to fault.

Item (1) General average ***sacrifice***

50.49 As stated in paragraph 50.12, above, an assured may proceed directly and immediately against his insurers for the *whole* of any loss caused by general average sacrifice, and the insurers are thereby subrogated to the general average contributions eventually received from the other parties

[27] Lest it be thought that the editors have overlooked s. 79(1) of the Act dealing with cases "Where the insurer pays for a total loss" and giving him additional rights entitling him "... to take over the interest of the assured in whatever may remain of the subject-matter so paid for", it is to be noted that the right to recover from third parties (*i.e.* the other contributing interests) passes to the insurer, not under the principle of abandonment outlined above, but only under the more limited principle of subrogation applying to claims for both total and partial loss, and under which the insurer can make no windfall profit, his subrogation rights being limited to 20 shillings in the pound on what he has paid (*Attorney-General v. Glen Line Ltd* [1930] 37 Lloyd's Rep. 55; 36 Com.Cas. 1; 46 T.L.R. 451).

to the adventure when the general average adjustment has been prepared and settled.

Thus, and to take the first example given in paragraph 50.15, above, where cargo with an invoice value of 10,000 was totally lost by jettison, the insurers by a policy subject to the Institute Cargo Clauses and with a sum insured and insured value:

In Case A—of 12,000, were immediately liable to pay the assured	12,000
In Case B—of 8,000, were immediately liable to pay the assured	8,000

In the general average adjustment, the allowance in general average (in accordance with the York-Antwerp Rules, 1994) would be for the invoice value of	10,000
and, assuming that the total general average represented 20 per cent of the overall contributory values, this particular cargo interest would be debited with a proportion of general average amounting to	2,000
Net general average contributions receivable from other parties to the adventure	8,000

50.50 To how much of this contribution received of 8,000 are the insurers entitled?

In Case A—where insurers have settled a loss of 12,000, there is no problem; the assured has already been fully indemnified for his loss and the insurers are entitled to the whole of the recovery of 8,000.

In Case B—where insurers have settled a loss of 8,000, the matter will be resolved on the following equitable basis:

		CREDIT	
		INSURERS	ASSURED
Credit: Amount Made Good	10,000		
To Insurers: Up to the amount settled		8,000	
To Assured: The Balance			2,000
Debit: Proportion General Average	2,000		
To Insurers: If C.V. 10,000 liable for 2,000 Insd. V. 8,000 pays in ppn.		(1,600)	
To Assured: The balance			(400)
General Average Contribution Received	8,000	6,400	1,600

Viewed from a strictly legal standpoint, such a solution is probably wrong, and, up to the amount settled by insurers (8,000), they are entitled to the whole of the recovery (8,000) received here from third parties. Section 27(3) of the Marine Insurance Act 1906 provides that: **50.51**

> "Subject to the provisions of this Act, and in the absence of fraud, the value fixed by the policy is, as between the insurer and assured, conclusive of the insurable value of the subject intended to be insured, whether the loss be total or partial."

In Case B, the assured has insured his goods for an agreed value of only 8,000, he has received that full sum in settlement of his claim, and, consequently, has no sound legal argument to participate in any recovery from third parties of 8,000 or less.

This is borne out by the case of *Boag v. Standard Marine Insce. Co. Ltd*[28] where (and to use the figures in our example above) the assured **50.52**

had first insured his goods for	8,000
but, with market values rising, had later effected a policy with different insurers, and without the knowledge of the original insurers, covering "increased value" for	2,000
	10,000

The goods were jettisoned, and the allowance in the general average adjustment was for the full market value of	10,000
Less: Proportion of general average attaching thereto	2,000
Net Recovery	8,000

It was held that the original insurers for 8,000 were entitled to the whole of the net recovery of 8,000, and the "increased value" insurers[29] to nothing. The insured merchant was in no way concerned in the action, or in the recovery, he having collected the full value of his cargo (10,000) from the two sets of insurers.

The *Boag* case follows established legal precedent and must be considered sound in principle, but strong support for the equitable approach adopted in practice (and accepted by insurers with murmurs only at 10-year intervals) is to be found from the alleged market custom in the mid-nineteenth century, as evidenced by the case of *Dickenson v. Jardine*,[30] the facts of which are recounted in paragraph 50.13, above. **50.53**

It is clear that the insurers of those days endeavoured *not* to settle immediately their direct liability on the policy for the whole of a general average sacrifice, but required the assured first to "send round the hat"

[28] (1937) 57 Ll.L.Rep. 83; 42 Com.Cas. 214.
[29] In many of the "trade" insurance clauses, provision is now made whereby the original insured value is deemed to be increased to the total amount insured at the time of loss, thereby enabling increased value insurers to participate in any recovery.
[30] (1868) L.R. 3 C.P. 639.

to the other parties to the adventure, and thereafter to claim from insurers only in respect of the proportion of general average attaching to the insured cargo. Again using the figures from our example above, it may thus be surmised that the assured would first collect the 8,000 contributions due from his co-adventurers and then proceed to his insurers for their liability in respect of the proportion of the loss falling upon him of 2,000.

Such liability would no doubt have been settled on the following basis:

If contributory value 10,000 pays proportion general average	2,000
Then insured value 8,000 pays in proportion	1,600

thus producing the identical result to that adopted in modern everyday practice, as set out above in paragraph 50.50. One may also refer to the judgment of Willes J. In *Dickenson v. Jardine*[31]:

> "The result is that the owner has two remedies: one for the whole value of the goods against the underwriter; the other for a contribution in case the vessel arrives safely in port: *and he may avail himself of which he pleases*, though he cannot retain the proceeds of both so as to be repaid the value of his loss twice over."

50.54 Identical legal principles and customary practice apply to a case of *partial* loss or damage to insured property by a general average sacrifice, such as our earlier second example in paragraph 50.16, where cargo with an invoice value of 10,000 was partly jettisoned to the extent of 50 per cent, or was damaged by water used to extinguish a fire to the extent of 50 per cent, and was insured by a policy subject to the Institute Cargo Clauses for 12,000 or 8,000.

Insurers were immediately liable to pay

In *Case A* 50 per cent of 12,000 = 6,000
In *Case B* 50 per cent of 8,000 = 4,000

In the general average adjustment the allowance in general average (in accordance with the York-Antwerp Rules 1974) would be for 50 per cent of the invoice value of 10,000, *i.e*	5,000
and, again assuming a 20 per cent rateable proportion of general average, this particular cargo would be debited with a proportion of general average of 20 per cent of 10,000 (including amount made good)	2,000
Net general average contributions receivable from other parties to the adventure	3,000

[31] *Ibid.*

In Case A—where insurers have settled a loss of 6,000, they would be entitled to the whole recovery of 3,000. 50.55

In Case B—where insurers have settled a loss of 4,000, sound legal principles might suggest that they were also entitled to the whole recovery of 3,000, but customary practice will apportion this sum on the following equitable basis:

		CREDIT	
		INSURERS	ASSURED
Credit: Amount Made Good	5,000		
To Insurers: Up to the amount settled		4,000	
To Assured: The Balance			1,000
Debit: Proportion general average (As in Example in paragraph 50.50)	2,000	(1,600)	(400)
General Average Contribution Received	3,000	2,400	600

Interest on amounts made good. To complete this section on the subrogation rights of insurers to amounts made good in general average for loss or damage to the property insured by general average sacrifice, it is necessary to consider also their rights to the interest which will be allowed on the principal sums in accordance with Rule XXI of the York-Antwerp Rules 1994. 50.56

Such interest is apportioned in practice in accordance with Rule of Practice No. B37 of the Association of Average Adjusters:

> *"Apportionment of Interest on Amounts Made Good*
>
> That in practice (in the absence of express agreement between the parties concerned) interest allowed on amounts made good shall be apportioned between assured and underwriters, taking into account the sums paid by underwriters and the dates when such payments were made, notwithstanding that by the addition of interest, the underwriter may receive a larger sum than he has paid."

This equitable basis for the apportionment of the interest has also been questioned at times by insurers, but has been pronounced legally correct in an opinion given in 1955 by the then Eustace Roskill Q.C.[32]

[32] See Opinion No. 23 of the Opinions of the Advisory Committee of the Association of Average Adjusters. A similar approach was adopted in *H. Cousins & Co. v. D. & C. Carriers* [1971] 2 Q.B. 230 at 242–243, where the question arose as to the apportionment between insured and insurers of interest on a subrogated claim awarded by the court under its statutory powers.

50.57 To illustrate the principle of the apportionment we revert to Case B in our first example of the total loss by jettison and the allowance in general average of

general average of	10,000
There would also be allowed interest at 7 per cent per annum from the date on which the goods would have been discharged at destination (say January 1, 1996) until three months after the date on which the adjustment was issued (say January 1, 1998), or	1,400
Total Allowance in General Average	11,400
Deduct: Proportion general average (20 per cent) attaching to 10,000	2,000
General Average Contributions received from other parties to the adventure	9,400

The goods were insured only for 8,000, which sum was settled in full by insurers on say April 1, 1996.

50.58 The apportionment would be as follows:

		CREDIT	
		INSURERS	ASSURED
Credit: Amount Made Good	10,000	8,000	2,000
		(as before)	
Interest thereon from 1.1.96 to 1.1.98	1,400		
To Insurers: On 8,000 from 1.4.96 to 1.1.98		980	
To Assured: On 8,000 from 1.1.96 to 1.4.96			140
and On 2,000 from 1.1.96 to 1.1.98			250
	11,400	8,980	2,420
Debit: Proportion general average (as before)	2,000	1,600	400
	9,400	7,380	2,020

Item (2) General average ***contributions*** *and item (3) General average* ***expenditure***

50.59 Rights of subrogation will seldom exist *vis-à-vis* the other parties to the adventure in respect of either general average contributions or expenditure, for the reason that the immediate liability of insurers is only for the actual contribution or the proportion of the general average expenditure falling upon the assured, and it is unlikely, therefore, that they will have over-settled on their eventual liability.

*Item (4) General average **deposits***

As previously stated, there is no clear and certain liability on the part of insurers to reimburse their assureds for general average deposits paid to secure the release of their goods from the shipowner's lien, but it is the common practice to do so. **50.60**

General average deposits will usually be for an amount estimated to be slightly in excess of the eventual general average contribution required, and as by the terms of Rule XXII of the York-Antwerp Rules 1994 such deposits will be banked in a special account and customarily earn interest, there should generally be some refund due to the holders of the general average deposit receipt when the adjustment has been issued, and after satisfying the liability to contribute to the general average or other charges.

Lloyd's Form of General Average Deposit Receipt[33] contains wording at the foot:

> "N.B.—The refund, if any, will be made only to the bearer of, and in exchange for, this Receipt, and will be the whole balance of the deposit after satisfying the General Average and/or Salvage and/or Charges, without deduction or set off of any other claims of the Shipowner against the Shipper or Consignee."

and unless the average adjusters have been notified by the insurers that only part of the deposit has been refunded to the assured, they will be obliged to return the whole balance of the deposit to the holder of the receipt.

Further, and in accordance with Rule of Practice No. B36 of the Association of Average Adjusters: **50.61**

> "*Interest on Deposits*
>
> That, unless otherwise expressly provided, the interest accrued on deposits on account of salvage and/or general average and/or particular and/or other charges, or on the balance of such deposits after payments on account, if any, have been made, shall be credited to the depositor or those to whom his rights in respect of the deposits have been transferred."

the whole of the bank interest earned on the deposit will be credited to the holder of the deposit receipt (the insurer) regardless of the date on which he refunded the deposit to the assured. Thus, the transfer of the

[33] See para. 80.06, *post*.

deposit receipt to the insurers may be likened to the purchase today by a bank of a bill of exchange payable in 90 days or other period of time.

4. Rates of Exchange

50.62 The currency (or currencies) in which a general average adjustment should be prepared and in which settlement of the general average contributions takes place between the various parties to the common adventure is discussed at length in Section 6, earlier, and in paragraph 40.23 we arrive at the conclusion that:

(1) Where a currency for general average purposes has been *expressed* in the bill of lading or contract of affreightment, the general average sacrifices and expenditures of the various parties to the adventure should be exchanged into that single currency of the contract, and settlement between the parties effected in that currency.
(2) In the absence of an expressed currency of the contract, no particular currency can generally be implied, but the general average sacrifices and expenditures of the various parties to the adventure should be shown in the *operating* currencies of those who have sustained the sacrifices and financed the expenditures, that is, the currency/ies in which they feel their loss.

50.63 Where, as is often the case, the general average consists solely of expenditure incurred by the shipowner, the adjustment will be prepared, and settlement take place, in the currency in which he feels his loss (for example see Example 1 in paragraph 40.39, above).

Where the owners of both ship and cargo have sustained general average losses, and in different currencies, their respective claims in general average must be set off against their general average liabilities to each other, and the adjustment will be prepared, and settlement made:

(1) In the currency of the net creditor, if there be only one creditor (or more than one creditor, but all in the same currency), for example see Example 3 in paragraph 40.41, above.
(2) In the several currencies of the various net creditors where there are a number of creditors who feel their loss in different currencies, for example see Example 4 in paragraph 40.42 or Example 5 in paragraph 40.45, above.

50.64 Regardless of the currency/ies in which a general average adjustment is prepared and settled, or in which a general average sacrifice or expenditure is incurred, any claim upon a policy of marine insurance must be expressed in the currency of the policy, that is, that in which the property was insured; this is the currency of the contract. It follows that conversions from one or more "foreign" currencies into the currency of the policy will often need to be made, and, as for the preparation of the general average adjustment itself,[34] certain rules must be laid down for the appropriate dates on which (and the consequent rates of exchange at which) these conversions are to be made.

Cargo

Policy claims for general average sacrifice, that is, physical loss of or damage to the cargo, are generally calculated by direct reference to the currency of the policy itself (that is, the currency in which the goods are insured) and conversion problems with rates of exchange should seldom arise. However, in the case of general average expenditure, or general average sacrifices represented by an expenditure of cash (for example repair or reconditioning charges), contributions and deposits, the expenditure may often be in a currency other than that of the policy, and a conversion will need to be made. **50.65**

A policy of marine insurance being one of *indemnity*, any necessary exchanges are made at the rate(s) ruling on the date(s) when payment was made by the assured, and, assuming the goods to be insured for their full value, the policy claim reimburses him precisely[35] for the amount(s) he has expended, or produces an equivalent value if the goods were insured in a currency other than that in which he directly feels his loss.

Subrogation

Where cargo has been sacrificed, the owner will often receive a net general average contribution from the other parties to the adventure, and, for the purpose of subrogating the insurers in respect of any direct claim previously paid by them, the general average contribution if in another currency will need exchanging into the currency of the policy at the rate ruling on the date when the contribution was received. **50.66**

Adopting—and adapting—figures previously used in paragraphs 50.15 and 50.49 to 50.52, above, let it be assumed that goods with an invoice value of $10,000 are shipped from the United States to Japan and insured for $8,000. As a general average act, the goods are jettisoned during the voyage and the insurers pay promptly a total loss of the sum insured of $8,000. In the general average adjustment, and on the principles outlined in Section 6, above, the allowance for this jettison is likely to be the

[34] See para. 40.01, *ante*.

[35] Unlike the shipowner, who often finances general average expenditure on behalf of *all* the contributing interests, a cargo owner is rarely called upon to advance more than "the proportion of the loss (expenditure) falling upon him" as per the Marine Insurance Act 1906, s. 66(4).

invoice value of $10,000, but expressed in Yen and at the rate of exchange ruling on the last day of discharge at the intended destination of $1.00 = Y250, that is:

	Y2,500,000
Less: Proportion General Average	500,000
Net General Average Contribution Received	Y2,000,000
Worth, at time of receipt, @ Y125 = $1.00	$16,000

50.67 Although the insurers settled a total loss and are entitled in terms of section 79(1) of the Marine Insurance Act 1906:

> "... to take over the interest of the insured in whatever may remain of the subject-matter so paid for, ..."

and thereby make a profit on a few isolated occasions, in this particular instance nothing remains of the subject-matter insured, and the rights of the insurers against the other parties to the adventure are those of subrogation and extend only, per section 79(2) of the Marine Insurance Act 1906, "in so far as the assured has been indemnified", that is $8,000.

In fact, and in accordance with the practice stated in paragraph 50.50, above, the net general average contribution received of Y2,000,000 = $16,000 would be apportioned as follows (ignoring interest):

		CREDIT	
		INSURERS	ASSURED
Credit: Amount Made Good	Y2,500,000 = $20,000	$8,000[36]	$12,000
Debit: Proportion General Average	500,000 = $4,000	(3,200)	(800)
	Y2,000,000 = $16,000	$4,800	$11,200

Ship

50.68 As stated earlier, the majority of general average cases consist solely of expenditure by the shipowner, and in such cases the adjustment will generally be prepared in the operating currency of the shipowner. If, as is frequently the case, he also insures his vessel in that same operating currency, the claim on the policy for the ship's proportion of the total general average should be a straightforward affair and present no problems with regard to rates of exchange.

[36] Limited to the original claim paid of $8,000—*Yorkshire Insce. Co. Ltd v. Nisbet Shipping Co. Ltd* [1961] 2 All E.R. 487.

On those occasions when, perhaps on the insistence of the mortgagees or for other reasons, the ship has been insured in a currency other than the shipowner's operating currency, it will be necessary to exchange each item of the shipowner's claim in the general average adjustment into the currency of the policy at the published rates of exchange ruling on the various dates when the shipowner settled each item. The proportion attaching to the ship of this total general average in the currency of the policy now forms the basis of the insurance claim.

Where the general average also includes sacrifices of cargo and those sacrifices are at a greater rate than the general average losses incurred by the shipowner, the general average is likely to be prepared and settled in the currency/ies of the cargo creditors, and the shipowner will be shown as a net debtor to (some of) the other contributing interests and be called upon to pay a general average contribution. The claim on his policy will then be based on: **50.69**

(1) The *whole* of his own general average losses, exchanged into the currency of the policy where necessary at the rates ruling on the various dates when he settled the expenses.
(2) The amount of his net contribution to the cargo interests exchanged into the currency of the policy at the rate ruling on the date of settlement of the contribution.

An illustration may be helpful: the ship is insured in U.S.$ and the adjustment is prepared in Yen, with rates of exchange of $1.00 = Y250 at the time of the general average, and $1.00 = Y125 when the adjustment is issued and the contribution paid. **50.70**

The General Average Adjustment

				General Average
Shipowner's	Expenses at port of refuge	$80,000	@ 250 =	Y20,000,000
	Adjustment charges	20,000	@ 125 =	2,500,000
		$100,000		Y22,500,000
Cargo	Sacrifices	200,000	@ 250 =	50,000,000
		$300,000		Y72,500,000

Apportionment and Settlement

	GENERAL AVERAGE	CREDIT ALLOWANCE IN G.A.	BALANCE TO PAY	BALANCE TO RECEIVE
SHIP — 50% pays	Y36,250,000	22,500,000	13,750,000	—
CARGO — 50% pays	36,250,000	50,000,000	—	13,750,000
100% pays	Y72,500,000	72,500,000	13,750,000	13,750,000
			@ 125 = $110,000	

Claim on Ship Policy (If fully insured)

Ship's proportion General Average			Y36,250,000
Whereof: Own expenses	Y22,500,000	= $100,000	
Contributions to Cargo	13,750,000	= 110,000	
	Y36,250,000	= $210,000	

5. Foreign General Average Clauses

(Liability of Insurers for General Average adjusted in accordance with a foreign law)

50.71 We have already observed that English marine insurance law, as codified in the Marine Insurance Act, contains its own definitions of a general average act, and of general average losses and contributions,[37] and that these definitions will apply between the parties to the adventure, where the general average is to be adjusted in accordance with English law.[38]

In practice, however, it is most unlikely that between the parties to the adventure general average will fall to be adjusted in accordance with the definitions in the Act; in a typical case it will, by contract between the parties, fall to be adjusted in accordance with the York-Antwerp Rules, and as to matters not provided for by the Rules (or where the Rules are not incorporated in the contract) it will be governed by the law of the place where the adventure ends.[39] The differences may be considerable, for example with regard to expenses incurred at a port of refuge after the vessel's arrival there which are allowable under the York-Antwerp Rules, and under a number of foreign laws, but not under English law.[40]

It is manifestly convenient that the liability of insurers in respect of general average should be adjusted in the same manner as the liability of the parties to the adventure, and modern insurance policies almost invariably contain express provisions in order to achieve this end. The effect of the Institute Clauses is discussed later in paragraphs 50.83 *et seq.* It is desirable, however, to view the problem historically, and we shall therefore consider it in three stages:

(1) Where the policy contains no provisions on the matter.
(2) The "foreign adjustment clause".
(3) Modern provisions—the Institute Clauses.

[37] See s. 66(1), (2) and (3): see paras. A.05 and 50.05, n. 3, *ante*.
[38] See para. A.05, *ante*.
[39] See paras. G.24 *et seq.*, *ante*.
[40] See the commentary on Rules X and XI, *ante*.

Where No Provisions in the Policy

The authorities provide no clear or comprehensive answer to the question whether the insurer under a policy governed by English law, and containing no special provisions on the subject, is bound by any general average adjustment prepared in accordance with a foreign law by which the parties themselves are bound. It is submitted, however, that the law is correctly stated in the judgment of Brett J. in *Harris v. Scaramanga*,[41] and that such a policy will indemnify the assured against general average losses and contributions ascertained and computed in accordance with the law of the place where the adventure ends, provided that they were incurred in connection with the avoidance of a loss by a peril insured against. **50.72**

The facts of *Harris v. Scaramanga*[42] were that the shipowners, in order to finance expenditure incurred at two ports of refuge for the repair of heavy weather damage suffered on the voyage, had raised money by a bottomry bond on ship, cargo and freight. On arrival at the destination, Bremen, the cargo owner was compelled to pay not only the cargo's proportion of the bottomry debt (for which cargo insurers admitted liability) but also, since the shipowner was insolvent, the proportion attributable to ship and freight. This latter sum had been correctly treated as general average in an average adjustment prepared at Bremen, but the cargo insurers refused to pay it, on the grounds that it was not general average in English law, and that it was caused not by an insured peril but by the shipowner's insolvency. It was held that, by virtue of the foreign adjustment clause in the policy, the insurers were liable, but Brett J. first considered what the position would be in the absence of any special provisions: **50.73**

> "The next point to be determined is, whether, under such circumstances, underwriters of an ordinary English policy would be liable. That raises the question as to how far underwriters of such a policy on an insured voyage to terminate at a foreign port are bound by a foreign general average adjustment made at that port of destination. Now, I think it is clearly established that, upon such a policy, English underwriters are bound by the foreign adjustment as an adjustment, if made according to the law of the country in which it was made. They are bound although the contributions are apportioned between the different interests in a manner different from the English mode, or though matters are brought into or omitted from general average which would not be so treated in England. ... But I think that, according to English and American law, the underwriter of a policy in the ordinary form is not liable to indemnify against any general average loss or contribution, whether it be general according to the law of his own country or according to the law of the foreign country in which the voyage terminates, or whether the adjustment be made according to his domestic or to the foreign law, if the general average loss be not incurred, or the **50.74**

[41] (1872) L.R. 7 C.P. 481.
[42] *Ibid.*

general average contribution be not made, in order to avert loss by a peril insured against."[43]

50.75 The requirement mentioned at the end of the passage quoted above, namely that the loss must be incurred in order to avert a loss by insured perils, is perhaps less easy to apply than appears at first sight. It seems that so long as the initial general average act (for example putting into a port of refuge) was done in order to avert a loss by insured perils, then all those consequential losses and expenses which ordinarily arise (for example storage charges, or crew wages), and which the law of the destination may treat as general average, will be recoverable from the insurer, even though they would likely be disallowed under English law on the grounds that they were too indirect a consequence, or that the point of safety had been reached. On the other hand, losses and expenses which result from some new intervening event, breaking the chain of causation (for example the insolvency of the shipowner) would not be recoverable unless the intervening event was itself an insured peril.[44]

50.76 To summarise the position, where no reference to the adjustment of general average is made in the contract of affreightment or in the policy of insurance, any necessary general average adjustment must be prepared and allowances made in accordance with the law and practice of the port of destination or other place where the adventure ends, and if the adjustment has been correctly prepared in accordance with that law and practice:

(1) each of the parties to the adventure is legally bound to make settlement in accordance with the adjustment, and
(2) the insurers of ship, cargo or freight, etc., are liable to indemnify their respective assureds for any general average losses or contribution payable under such an adjustment, so long as they were incurred in connection with the avoidance of a loss by an insured peril, in the sense described above,

even though the general average allowances or method of apportionment may differ from what would have been the case if the adjustment had been prepared in accordance with English law and practice. For example:

Sacrifice

50.77 If goods "warranted free of particular average" are lost or damaged, and such loss or damage would in England be treated as particular

[43] *Ibid.* at 495–496. The remaining members of the court (Bovill C.J. and Keating J.) expressed no view on the effect of a foreign law on a policy containing no special provision.

[44] While the judgments do not expressly deal with the point, it seems unlikely that the claim in *Harris v. Scaramanga* would have succeeded in the absence of the foreign adjustment clause (*e.g.* see *Greer v. Poole* (1880) 49 L.J.Q.B. 463; 5 Q.B.D. 272; 4 Asp. M.C. 300.) The modern Institute Cargo Clauses expressly exclude losses "arising from insolvency or financial default" of the vessel's owners or operators, etc.

average, and therefore unrecoverable on the policy, the insurers are nevertheless liable for the whole loss if the "foreign" average adjuster properly treats it as general average under the law and practice of the port of destination or other place where the adventure ends.[45] (In practice, and unless the adjuster advises at an early stage that the loss will be admitted as general average, the actual claim is more likely to be only the *balance* of the claim after receiving contributions thereto from the other parties to the adventure.)

Expenditure

If the foreign adjuster properly admits as general average the wages and maintenance of crew at a port of refuge, but such expenses would be treated in England simply as a loss by delay and not recoverable on a policy or admissible as general average, the English insurer of an English shipowner is nevertheless obliged to indemnify him for the proportion of those crew wages attributable to the ship. **50.78**

Contribution

Contribution will be recoverable, if calculated in accordance with the law of the destination, even though the contribution differs from that under English law, always provided that the losses contributed for were incurred in connection with the avoidance of a peril insured against. **50.79**

The "Foreign Adjustment" Clause

A typical "foreign adjustment" clause[46] would simply provide "general average payable per foreign statement", and the insurers would be bound by the foreign statement actually drawn up (provided it is drawn up in good faith, and at the place where the adventure ends),[47] it not being open to the insurers (or the assured) to contend that the statement was wrong or that it did not accurately reflect the relevant foreign law.[48] **50.80**

For a fuller discussion of these clauses the reader is referred to Arnould's *Law of Marine Insurance* (16th ed.), paragraphs 997–999. Here we shall merely note their main features: **50.81**

[45] So held in *Mavro v. Ocean Mar. Ins. Co.* (1874) L.R. 9 C.P. 595, but under the terms of a clause in the policy covering "general average as per foreign statement".

[46] *De Hart v. Compania Aurora* [1903] 2 K.B. 503 at 509.

[47] *The Brigella* [1893] P. 189; *Mavro v. Ocean Marine Ins. Co.* (1874) L.R. 9 C.P. 595; 10 C.P. 414.

[48] In *De Hart v. Compania Aurora* [1903] 2 K.B. 503, C.A., where the clause provided "General Average payable according to foreign statement *if so made up*", it was held that the statement was conclusive and binding. However in that case, and in all others on the foreign adjustment clause, it had been proved or admitted that the statement correctly applied the relevant law.

(1) If no statement was drawn up, there was no claim under the policy.[49]

(2) The clause was construed as creating a distinct and separate obligation, and thus losses treated as general average in the foreign statement were recoverable even if not caused by a peril insured against.[50]

(3) The clause did not prevent the insurer from relying on a specific *exclusion* in the policy. For example, if the policy excluded capture, the insurer would not be liable in respect of a general average loss incurred to prevent a loss by capture.

50.82 (4) However, the foreign statement might be conclusive as to whether the loss fell within an exception. Thus in *Mavro v. Ocean Marine*,[51] where the foreign statement treated damage to cargo as general average, it was not open to the insurer to argue that under English law it was particular average and therefore excluded by an f.p.a. warranty. In *The Mary Thomas*[52] a similar rule was applied for the benefit of the insurer. The shipowner had incurred expenses in consequence of a stranding on the voyage, and these expenses were treated as general average in the adjustment drawn up at the destination (Rotterdam). The insurers of the ship accepted liability for the ship's proportion of the expenses, as shown in the adjustment, but for no more,[53] and the shipowner's attempts to recover from cargo the latter's proportion failed because the stranding was caused by the fault of his servants. The shipowner then claimed the full amount of the expenses from insurers on the grounds that the were, under English law, particular average. It was held, however, that the foreign statement, which was correct by Dutch law, was conclusive as to what was general average and what was particular average.

(5) The foreign statement was binding as to the contributing interests, and the interests to be contributed for.[54]

[49] *Brandeis v. Economic Ins. Co.* (1922) 11 Ll.L.Rep. 42. See para. 50.44, *ante*. To overcome this problem the clause sometimes provided "General average payable per foreign statement *if made up*".

[50] *Harris v. Scaramanga* (*supra*).

[51] (1874) L.R. 9 C.P. 595; 10 C.P. 414.

[52] [1894] P. 108.

[53] See paras. 50.21 *et seq.*, *ante* as to the proportion of general average expenses for which the insurer is liable.

[54] *De Hart v. Compania Aurora* [1903] 1 K.B. 109; [1903] 2 K.B. 503 (Belgian Statement showing contribution due to owners of jettisoned deckload. . . . Under Belgian law, jettison of deckload was not made good in general average unless the contract of affreightment specifically provided that it should be made good, as did the contract in the instant case. Insurers of ship held liable for ship's proportion of the loss.)

Modern Provisions—the Institute Clauses

As noted in paragraph 50.71, above, modern policies almost invariably contain specific provisions designed (subject to certain limits[55]) to equate the liability of the insurer under the policy in respect of general average with that of the assured *vis-à-vis* the other parties to the adventure. The relevant provisions of the Institute Clauses are here analysed, and for reasons which will become apparent it is necessary to draw a distinction between insurances on ship or freight, and insurances on cargo. **50.83**

Insurances on ship or freight

The standard Institute Clauses on Hulls and on Freight, whether for voyage or time, include the following clause: **50.84**

> "Adjustment to be according to the law and practice obtaining at the place where the adventure ends, as if the contract of affreightment contained no special terms upon the subject[56]; but where the contract of affreightment so provides the adjustment shall be according to the York-Antwerp Rules."

As the wording makes clear, the insurers are not prepared to allow their liability to be governed by any provisions in the contract of affreightment other than provisions for the application of unmodified York-Antwerp Rules or the law and practice of the place where the adventure ends. The effect of the clause is that if the contract of affreightment provides for the adjustment of general average in accordance with the York-Antwerp Rules (of any vintage), insurers will accept liability for the proportion of general average attaching to the ship or freight in accordance with those York-Antwerp Rules, in plain unmodified form; in all other circumstances, their liability shall be governed by a general average adjustment drawn up in accordance with the law and practice (on general average alone) of the place where the adventure ends. For ease of understanding, this is now set out in tabular form:

General Average Provisions in contract of affreightment	Insurers' Liability to be Governed by
1) None	Law and practice of place where the adventure ends.
2) Law and practice of the place where the adventure ends.	Law and practice of the place where the adventure ends.

[55] See para. 50.84, *post*.
[56] This phrase was introduced in order to avoid the result in *De Hart v. Compania Aurora*, para. 50.82, n. 54, *ante*.

General Average Provisions in contract of affreightment	**Insurers' Liability to be Governed by**
3) Law and practice of the place where the adventure ends, in any modified or extended form.	Law and practice of place where the adventure ends, alone, and ignoring any modification.
4) York-Antwerp Rules	York-Antwerp Rules
5) York-Antwerp Rules in any modified or extended form.	York-Antwerp Rules in plain form, and ignoring any modification.
6) Any other code of general average	Law and practice of place where the adventure ends.
	Provided that, in each case, the liability of insurers shall not exceed the proportion of general average actually due from the insured

Cargo insurances

50.86 Cargo insurers are well aware that the shippers of general cargo seldom have the opportunity to exercise any influence on the terms of any provision regarding general average in the contract of affreightment, and the standard Institute Cargo Clauses accordingly place no restrictions on the liability of insurers for any general average loss properly adjusted in accordance with the general average provisions in the contract of affreightment, whatever they may be. The wording of the relevant clause (No. 2) is as follows:

> "This insurance covers general average and salvage charges adjusted or determined according to the contract of affreightment and/or the governing law and practice..."

Thus, cargo insurers accept liability for general average as adjusted in accordance with *any* provisions regarding general average in the contract of affreightment, subject only to the general exception previously dealt with in paragraphs 50.09 to 50.11, above, that the general average should not have been:

> "... incurred to avoid or in connection with the avoidance of loss ... excluded ... in this insurance."

Effect of the Institute Clauses

50.87 There are no decided cases in which the current provisions of the Institute Clauses relating to general average have been construed by the courts, but the following observations on their interpretation may be made:

(1) They do not affect the ordinary principle that the insurer is not liable for general average when the sacrifice or expenditure was made or incurred in connection with the avoidance of a peril expressly excluded by the policy.[57]
(2) Subject to any express provisions in the policy (such as are contained in the Institute Cargo Clauses[58]) they do not override the general rule that the insurer is only liable for a general average loss where the loss was incurred for the purpose of avoiding, or in connection with the avoidance of a peril insured against. However, whether a loss falls within this category may fall to be determined by the law of the place where the adventure ends, or by the relevant provisions of the contract of affreightment.[59]

6. Excess Liabilities

For a variety of reasons, the insured value of a vessel in a policy covering her Hull and Machinery, etc., may on occasion be less than her real sound market value. In spite of such under-insurance, however, the measure of indemnity in respect of claims for damage to the ship caused by accident (particular average) or by general average sacrifice will be the full cost of repairs,[60] up to a limit of the insured value. The only headings of general average claim which will suffer and be reduced by reason of any under-insurance are general average expenditure and contributions, and to the extent as explained earlier in paragraphs 50.23 to 50.43, and, in so far as concerns the ship, more particularly paragraphs 50.24, 50.29 and 50.41 to 50.43, above. **50.88**

Additional insurance cover to meet all or part of any claim for general average expenditure unrecoverable on the Hull and Machinery policy can be provided by a separate policy covering Excess Liabilities on conditions such as the Institute Time Clauses, Hulls—Excess Liabilities, or the Institute Time Clauses, Hulls—Disbursements and Increased Value (Total Loss only, including Excess Liabilities), the current editions of which are both dated 1.11.95, and include the following wording:

> **General Average, Salvage and Salvage Charges** recoverable under the insurances on hull and machinery but not recoverable in full by reason of the difference between the insured value of the Vessel as stated therein (or

[57] The Institute Cargo Clauses expressly affirm this principle (see para. 50.86, *ante*).
[58] See para. 50.86, *ante*.
[59] See paras. 50.75, 50.82, *ante*; and see paras. 50.84–50.86, *ante*, as to what provisions of the contract of affreightment are relevant between insurer and insured under the Institute Clauses
[60] Marine Insurance Act 1906, ss. 66(4), 69.

any reduced value arising from the deduction therefrom in process of adjustment of any claim which law or practice or the terms of the insurances covering hull and machinery may have required) and the value of the Vessel adopted for the purpose of contribution to general average, salvage or salvage charges, the liability under this insurance being for such proportion of the amount not recoverable as the amount insured hereunder bears to the said difference or to the total sum insured against excess liabilities if it exceed such difference.

50.89 An example to illustrate the operation of this clause may best be provided with some of the figures used in the example given earlier in paragraphs 50.41 and 50.43, where:

The sound market value of the vessel at the termination of the adventure was	5,000,000
the insured value	4,000,000
and where Hull insurers were liable for a claim for particular average damage to the ship of	1,000,000

The proportion of general average expenditure and/or contribution attaching to the ship was	900,000
and the claim therefor on the Hull and Machinery policy was shown as follows:	

If Contributory Value	4,000,000	pays 900,000	
Then Insured Value	4,000,000		
Less: Particular Average	1,000,000		
	3,000,000	pays in proportion	675,000
		SHORTFALL	225,000

If a policy has been effected to cover Excess Liabilities for:

(a) 500,000 or
(b) 1,000,000

the respective claims will be calculated as follows:

If Contributory Value	4,000,000[61]	pays G.A. expenditure	900,000
and Hull policy on net insured value of	3,000,000	,, ,,	675,000
Difference	1,000,000	pays ,,	225,000
Insured for: (a)	500,000	pays in proportion	112,500
(b)	1,000,000	pays in full	225,000

[61] Effectively:

Effectively:	Sound Value	5,000,000
	Less: Particular average	1,000,000
		4,000,000

Order in which Headings of Claim to be Marshalled

A problem of only rare occurrence which can affect the claim on a policy covering Excess Liabilities concerns the order in which the various headings of claim on a policy covering the Hull and Machinery of a vessel must be marshalled when they collectively exceed the insured value of that policy. **50.90**

For example, a vessel may be insured for 4,000,000, so valued, and sustain very severe damage which the owner nevertheless elects to repair. Ignoring any "excess" customarily applied to any claim on a Hull policy, the various headings of claim against the policy (calculations are shown later) might be:

General Average	sacrifice	—	360,000
	thirds	—	100,000
	expenditure	—	90,000
Particular Average		—	3,500,000
			4,050,000

This sum being in excess of the insured value of 4,000,000, some part of the claim must be reduced by 50,000 and the question arises: which is it to be? In accordance with an opinion given by F. D. Mackinnon (later Mackinnon L.J.), the claim on the Hull and Machinery policy must be marshalled in the following order: **50.91**

Particular Average
General Average sacrifice
thirds
expenditure

Thus, it is the claim for general average expenditure which must be reduced, with a resulting increase in the claim on any policy covering Excess Liabilities.

Example

A vessel is insured as follows: **50.92**

4,000,000	on Hull and Machinery, so valued, subject to the Institute Time Clauses, Hulls, 1.11.95 (No excess)
1,000,000	on Increased Value, so valued, subject to the Institute Time Clauses, Hulls—Disbursements and Increased Value (Total Loss only, including Excess Liabilities) 1.11.95
5,000,000	

Her sound value at the time of the accident is 6,000,000, and an adjustment is prepared showing the following figures:

		P.A.	General Average		
			⅓rd off	Thirds Deducted	In full
Repairs to SHIP	4,200,000	3,500,000	300,000		400,000
Less: Thirds "new for old"			100,000	100,000	
			200,000	....	200,000
G.A. Expenditure	900,000				900,000
	5,100,000	3,500,000	—	100,000	1,500,000

50.93 GENERAL AVERAGE APPORTIONED

SHIP	Sound Value	6,000,000		
	Less: Damage	4,200,000		
		1,800,000		
	Add: Made Good	600,000		
		2,400,000	pays	900,000
CARGO—Net Value		1,600,000	pays	600,000
		4,000,000	pays	1,500,000

50.94 CLAIM ON HULL AND MACHINERY POLICY

1) Particular Average				3,500,000
2) General Average Sacrifice—60% × 600,000				360,000
3) General Average Thirds Deducted				100,000
4) General Average Expenditure—60% ×	900,000		= 540,000	
If Contributory Value	2,400,000	pays	540,000	
Then Insured Value	4,000,000			
Deduct: All losses and charges for which insurers are liable and which have been deducted in arriving at the contributory value (*i.e.* Particular Average and Thirds)	3,600,000	pays		
	400,000	in ppn.	90,000	
	Limited by Insured Value to			40,000
				4,000,000

50.95 CLAIM ON EXCESS LIABILITIES POLICY

If Contributory Value	2,400,000	pays G.A. Expenditure	540,000
And Hull Policy on net insured value	400,000	"	40,000
Difference	2,000,000	pays G.A. Expenditure	500,000
Policy for	1,000,000	pays in proportion	250,000

7. Losses in Excess of the Insured Value

Where the subject-matter insured is totally lost by an insured peril, section 68 of the Marine Insurance Act 1906[62] provides that the measure of indemnity is the sum for which the property was insured, and, in the absence of any express provisions in the policy, this is the maximum liability of the insurers[63] in respect of any one accident. However, even in respect of a single accident it is possible for the total damage sustained and expenses incurred to exceed the sum insured, and it is always possible that during the course of any one voyage the ship and her cargo may meet with two or more accidents, producing a similar financial result. Consideration will now be given to some representative situations and the liability of ship and cargo insurers under standard insurance conditions to respond for these substantial losses. **50.96**

General Average Followed by Total Loss from New Cause

In *Chellew v. Royal Commission on the Sugar Supply*[64] the *Penlee* sustained damage in a hurricane and put into Horta as a port of refuge. Upon completion of repairs she resumed her voyage but a few days later she and her cargo were totally destroyed by fire. **50.97**

As explained previously in paragraph 20.17, the cargo were held not to be liable for any part of the general average expenses incurred at Horta, the whole of these consequently falling upon the shipowner.

On the grounds that the total loss arose from a new and separate accident, and that general average expenditure incurred and settled constitutes a partial loss which has "been repaired or otherwise made good", in accordance with section 77 of the Marine Insurance Act 1906[65] making provision for successive losses, the shipowner would be entitled to recover from his hull insurers:

(1) The *whole* of the general average expenses, being the "proportion of the loss which falls upon him" as stated in section 66(4) of the

[62] "Subject to the provisions of this Act, and to any express provision in the policy, where there is a total loss of the subject-matter insured,—

(1) If the policy be a valued policy, the measure of indemnity is the sum fixed by the policy."

[63] *E.g. Aitchison v. Lohre* (1879) 4 A.C. 755; 4 Asp. M.L.C. 168.

[64] [1922] 1 K.B. 12.

[65] "(1) Unless the policy otherwise provides, and subject to the provisions of this Act, the insurer is liable for successive losses, even though the total amount of such losses may exceed the sum insured.

(2) Where, under the same policy, a partial loss, which has not been repaired or otherwise made good, is followed by a total loss, the assured can only recover in respect of the total loss:

Provided that nothing in this section shall affect the liability of the insurer under the suing and labouring clause."

Marine Insurance Act and as explained by *Green Star Shipping Co. Ltd v. London Assurance.*[66]

(2) The sum insured in respect of the subsequent total loss.

Although in the above example the cargo interests sustained no more than a bare total loss, had they been obliged, for instance, to provide separate security to salvors at the port of refuge, they similarly would be entitled to recover from their insurers both the salvage payment and the subsequent total loss.

General Average Followed by Total Loss from Same Cause

50.98 To illustrate this particular situation, let it be assumed that a loaded vessel strands in a position of peril and sustains damage to her bottom which is temporarily repaired at a port of refuge after refloating. During the ensuing continuation of the voyage, and without the intervention of any new cause, the temporary repairs fail and the ship and her cargo sink and are lost.

As in the first example, the shipowner would be unable to recover from the cargo interests any contribution to the general average expenses incurred by him at the port of refuge, and his claim upon his insurers in respect of this double loss from a single accident might normally be expected to be limited to the sum insured. However, and in the absence of any insurance on average disbursements,[67] the shipowner should be able to recover what might reasonably have been expected to be the ship's proportion of those general average expenses under Clause 11.5/6 of the Institute Time Clauses, Hulls:

> 11.5 When a claim for total loss of the Vessel is admitted under this insurance and expenses have been reasonably incurred in saving or attempting to save the Vessel and other property and there are no proceeds, or the expenses exceed the proceeds, then this insurance shall bear its pro rata share of such proportion of the expenses, or of the expenses in excess of the proceeds, as the case may be, as may reasonably be regarded as having been incurred in respect of the Vessel . . .; but if the Vessel be insured for less than its sound value at the time of the occurrence giving rise to the expenditure, the amount recoverable under this clause shall be reduced in proportion to the under-insurance.
>
> 11.6 The sum recoverable under this Clause 11 shall be in addition to the loss otherwise recoverable under this insurance but shall in no circumstances exceed the amount insured under this insurance in respect of the Vessel.

50.99 These clauses also have particular application in situations such as the following:

[66] [1933] 1 K.B. 378; 39 Ll.L.Rep. 213; 36 Com.Cas. 258; 18 Asp. M.L.C. 225.

[67] See paras. 20.17–20.21, *ante*.

(1) Where a salvage tug is willing to proceed to the assistance of a distressed vessel and her cargo only on the basis of a guaranteed daily hire, and the ship and her cargo sink and are totally lost before the arrival of the tug.
(2) Where expenses are incurred in attempts to refloat and save a ship and her cargo ashore on rocks, but bad weather causes the vessel to break up and be lost together with her cargo.

From the expenses incurred must be deducted the proceeds or value of any property saved, whether ship or cargo, and of the balance the ship insurers will pay:

> "... its pro rata share ... as may reasonably be regarded as having been incurred in respect of the vessel ...; ... reduced in proportion to the under-insurance."

Although the clause gives no precise guide, it is submitted that the abortive salvage expenses—or the excess over any proceeds—should be apportioned over the approximate values of the property sought to be saved, and in the condition in which it was likely to be saved.

This approach was adopted in the Canadian case *Ultramar Canada Inc. v. Mutual Marine Office Inc.*,[68] under the very similar provisions of the equivalent clause in the American Institute Clauses. It was also held in that case that the clause applied even though one of the purposes for which the expense was incurred was the avoidance of pollution, rather than the saving of insured property.[69]

Where no Total Loss, but Loss and Expenses Exceed the Insured Value

In *Aitchison v. Lohre*[70] the *Crimea* encountered heavy weather and sustained severe damage and was in danger of sinking. She was rescued by a steamer which was awarded £800 salvage, and afterwards repaired. Even after deducting thirds "new for old", the cost of repairs exceeded the insured value, and the shipowner endeavoured to recover the salvage award in addition under the sue and labour clause. The insurers were held liable for the cost of repairs up to the sum insured, but not for any part of the salvage expenses. As Lord Blackburn said in the House of Lords: **50.100**

[68] [1995] 1 F.C. 341 (Fed. Ct. Can., Trial Division).

[69] This in itself is no doubt correct, but it leads on to the question whether, for the purpose of giving effect to the clause, any of the expenses should be apportioned to the avoidance of pollution rather than to the salving of property. In the *Ultramar* case all of the expenses were apportioned between hull and cargo and none to the avoidance of pollution, and this seems questionable. It was also held that in assessing the values of the different properties any amount made good in general average in respect of a sacrifice should be added to the value of the interest which had suffered the sacrifice. It is submitted, however, that there is no good reason for adopting this course.

[70] (1879) 4 A.C. 755; 4 Asp. M.L.C. 168.

"I think that general average and salvage do not come within either the words or the object of the suing and labouring clause. ... the object (of the clause) is to encourage exertion on the part of the assured; not to provide an additional remedy for the recovery by the assured, of indemnity for a loss which was by the maritime law a consequence of the peril."

The principle established is now codified in section 78(2) of the Marine Insurance Act 1906:

"General average losses and contributions and salvage charges, as defined by this Act, are not recoverable under the suing and labouring clause."

8. Vessels in Ballast and Not Under Charter

50.101 In order to constitute a general average act under English law, it is essential that there be a *common* adventure, that is, that more than one interest should be at risk on the voyage and that any extraordinary sacrifice or expenditure made or incurred at a time of peril should be for the purpose of saving the joint property.

Thus, it is impossible for a ship proceeding in ballast and not under charter to sustain a *general average* loss. Were she, for example, to run aground in a position of peril, the cost of refloating her would be claimable from insurers as salvage, salvage charges, or sue and labour charges; and damage to the ship caused in efforts to refloat would be treated as particular average. In other words, the major expenses arising from the casualty would still be recoverable under most policies of insurance, but the shipowner would not be able to claim in respect of certain expenses arising from delay but customarily treated as general average, such as the wages and maintenance of the crew and bunkers consumed on ordinary ship's purposes during any extra detention at a port of refuge.

50.102 To remedy this situation, and to put the shipowner in much the same position as he would be in if the vessel had cargo on board, or were engaged under a charter, English-type insurance conditions such as the Institute Time Clauses, Hulls, include the following clause:

10.3 When the Vessel sails in ballast, not under charter, the provisions of the York-Antwerp Rules, 1994 (excluding Rules XI(d), XX and XXI) shall be applicable, and the voyage for this purpose shall be deemed to continue from the port of place of departure until the arrival of the Vessel at the first port or place thereafter other than a port or place of refuge or a port or place of call for bunkering only. If at any such intermediate port or place there is an abandonment of the adventure originally contemplated the voyage shall thereupon be deemed to be terminated.

It can now be assumed that a proper "general average" arises in the appropriate circumstances, and that allowances should be made in accordance with the York-Antwerp Rules 1994, other than Rules XX and XXI, which grant an additional 2 per cent commission on most general average disbursements, and interest at 7 per cent per annum on all general average losses. Rule XI(d) relates to the cost of measures undertaken to prevent or minimise damage to the environment.

Such a clause is unnecessary in the United States as the result of the surprising decision in the case of *Potter v. Ocean Ins. Co.*[71] that the liability of the insurers was an additional interest at risk on any voyage.

9. Liability of Hull Insurers where Differing Codes of General Average

On occasion, bills of lading will be issued to shippers of cargo on the same voyage with differing provisions regarding the adjustment of general average. If the allowances in general average under the differing codes would be materially different, it will be necessary to prepare the general average adjustment with two (or more) separate columns showing the differing general average allowances, and with separate apportionments. 50.103

This subject has already been touched upon in paragraphs 30.13, 30.14, above, and a hypothetical example given where a shipowner had financed the whole of the general average in respect of a vessel bound for Halifax, N.S., and Portland in the United States.

		General Average	
		Halifax	Portland
Cost of:			
	Entering port of refuge	5,000	5,000
	Discharging cargo	10,000	10,000
	Storing cargo	—	5,000
	Reloading cargo	—	10,000
	Outward port charges	—	2,500
	Commission and Interest	—	1,500
		15,000	34,000
Halifax cargo	—30% pays	4,500	—
Portland cargo	—40% pays	—	13,600
Ship	—30% bears	?4,500	?10,200
		15,000	34,000

Assuming standard cargo insurance conditions and the value fully covered by insurance, the insurers of the cargo will be liable to indemnify their assureds for the general average contributions properly charged to them respectively of 4,500 to the Halifax cargo, and 13,600 to the Portland cargo. 50.104

[71] (1837) 216 Fed. Rep. 303; 3 Sumner 27.

What is the position, however, of the insurers of the ship? They cannot be called upon to pay *both* proportions of general average attaching to the ship of 4,500 and 10,200, for the same expenses are essentially duplicated in both general average columns. The correct solution is to claim a part of each "contribution" corresponding to the proportion of the total value of the cargo represented by the cargo subject to that same particular code of general average, that is:

$\frac{30}{70}$ths of the ship's ppn. G.A.— 4,500—per Halifax adjustment	=	1,929
$\frac{40}{70}$ths of the ship's ppn. G.A.—10,200—per Portland adjustment	=	5,828
$\frac{70}{70}$ths Claim on Hull Insurers		7,757

For the purpose of claiming general average "contributions" from the insurers of any freight that may be at risk, similar (but not necessarily identical) principles can be applied.

10. Insurers' Liability for Unrepaired General Average Damage

50.105 A ship insured for a period of 12 months from January 1, may sustain damage by a general average sacrifice on February 1, but repairs be deferred. During the course of a subsequent voyage, but within the currency of the same policy, the vessel is totally lost on November 1.

In accordance with the comments in paragraph 18.17, above, it is conceivable that the reasonable depreciation in the value of the vessel arising from such unrepaired damage may be treated as general average in any average adjustment. The shipowner might then reasonably expect to recover from the cargo and other contributing interests the proportions of such depreciation attaching to their property, but in accordance with the provisions of section 77(2) of the Marine Insurance Act 1906,[72] he cannot recover from his own hull insurers the proportion of the depreciation attaching to the ship.

11. Constructive Total Loss

Extent to which General Average may be taken into Account for Demonstrating Constructive Total Loss of Ship

50.106 The subject of constructive total loss is one of great complexity, and

[72] "Where, under the same policy, a partial loss, which has not been repaired or otherwise made good, is followed by a total loss, the assured can only recover in respect of the total loss:

Provided that nothing in this section shall affect the liability of the insurer under the suing and labouring clause."

for a thorough review, interested readers are referred to the almost 90 pages of text in the British Shipping Law Series, *Arnould on Marine Insurance*. In this present volume, however, it is necessary to refer only to the relatively limited extent to which general average may be taken into account for the purpose of demonstrating a constructive total loss on a policy of marine insurance covering a *ship*.

Section 60(2) of the Marine Insurance Act 1906 provides that:

> In particular, there is a constructive total loss—
>
> . . .
>
> (ii) In the case of damage to a ship, where she is so damaged by a peril insured against, that the cost of repairing the damage would exceed the value of the ship when repaired.
>
> In estimating the cost of repairs, no deduction is to be made in respect of general average contributions to those repairs payable by other interests, but account is to be taken of the expense of future salvage operations and of any future general average contributions to which the ship would be liable if repaired.

In essence, the Marine Insurance Act requires that in order to demonstrate a constructive total loss, the estimated cost of repairs should exceed the *repaired* (or sound) value of the ship, but in everyday practice, while maintaining the general principles set forth in the Act, standard insurance conditions such as the Institute Hull Clauses, 1.11.95, substitute the *insured* value of the vessel for the repaired value, that is: **50.107**

> "19.1 In ascertaining whether the Vessel is a constructive total loss, the insured value shall be taken as the repaired value...
>
> 19.2 No claim for constructive total loss based upon the cost of recovery and/or repair of the Vessel shall be recoverable hereunder unless such cost would exceed the insured value."

In the examples which follow, it will be assumed that the vessel is insured for an agreed value of 1,000,000 and that the cargo on board would contribute 50 per cent towards any general average sacrifice or expenditure.

(1) Estimated cost of repairs to ship— **50.108**

Particular Average	800,000
General Average	300,000
	1,100,000

Although the vessel might be repaired at a net cost to the shipowner of 950,000 after crediting the 150,000 contribution payable towards the general average repairs by the cargo interests, section 60 of the Act makes it clear that:

> "In estimating the cost of repairs, no deduction is to be made in respect of general average contributions payable by other interests."

Thus, the vessel is a constructive total loss, and the Act recognises that, regardless of who may be paying for the repairs, it is totally non-commercial to spend 1,100,000 on repairs to a vessel worth only 1,000,000. (Identical considerations would apply to a vessel damaged in a collision for which the "other" vessel was responsible.)

50.109 (2) Estimated cost of:

Repairs to ship—Particular Average	800,000
Refloating vessel (or jettison of cargo)—General Average	300,000
	1,100,000

In this instance, the vessel is *not* a constructive total loss, for the Act provides:

> "... but account is to be taken of the expense of future salvage operations and of any future general average contributions to which the ship would be liable if repaired;"

that is, it is only the ship's proportion of the shipowner's general average expenditure, or the shipowner's contribution to the general average sacrifice or expenditure of the cargo which may be taken into account. This also is thoroughly commercial in its outlook.

50.110 (3) Estimated cost of:

Repairs to ship—	Particular Average		800,000
	General Average	150,000	
Refloating vessel—	General Average	150,000	300,000
			1,100,000

Prima facie, and following the principles set forth in the first two examples, it might be thought that a constructive total loss could be demonstrated, with the ranking items:

Estimated cost of:		
Repairs to ship—	Particular Average	800,000
	General Average	150,000
Refloating vessel—	50% of 150,000	75,000
		1,025,000

In fact, the vessel is *not* a constructive total loss because the ranking items would be only:

Estimated cost of:			
Repairs to ship—	Particular Average		800,000
	General Average		150,000
Refloating vessel—	50% of 150,000	75,000	
Less: Set-off to general average ship repairs payable by cargo—50% of 150,000		75,000	
		—	—
			950,000

(The above proposition may more readily be understood and proved by substituting a jettison of cargo of 150,000 for the refloating expenses to be incurred by the shipowner of 150,000. There would then be no "future general average contribution" payable between the ship and cargo interests, and 950,000 is the full but only cost which would fall upon the shipowner and which should rank in assessing whether a constructive total loss can be demonstrated.)

Future Salvage Operations

In defining what constitutes one particular class of constructive total loss for a ship, section 60(2)(ii) of the Marine Insurance Act 1906 states that: **50.111**

> "In estimating the cost of repairs ... account is to be taken of the expense of *future* salvage operations...."

It appears that there is some debate as to the particular time-base from which the salvage operations are to be regarded as future; is it that of the casualty, or of the tendering of notice of abandonment? Or, expressed in more pointed form: "Can the cost of salvage operations incurred after a casualty, but before the tendering of notice of abandonment to the insurers, be used in the assessment of whether a vessel is a constructive total loss?"

On the grounds of plain commercial common-sense, the present editors are firmly of opinion that the relevant date must and can only be that of the tendering of notice of abandonment (in practice, the same date as a writ is assumed to be issued). However, because on occasion the liability for great sums of money can depend upon the correct solution to this problem, it will be wise to substantiate their conclusion by dealing with the matter at some length.

The problem is best illustrated by a figured example, and because in practice the establishing of a constructive total loss on a policy covering the hull and machinery of a ship generally unlocks an additional recovery of perhaps 25 per cent of the ship valuation insured on subsidiary **50.112** interests such as freight, disbursements, and increased value, etc., we must complicate the basic figures by including these insurances on subsidiary interests:

A vessel with a sound value of 1,000,000 is insured by policies as follows:

1,000,000 on	Hull and Machinery, so valued, subject to the Institute Time Clauses, Hull, 1.11.95
250,000 on	Increased Value and Excess Liabilities, etc., subject to the Institute Time Clauses, Hulls—Disbursements and Increased Value (Total Loss only, including Excess Liabilities) 1.11.95
1,250,000	

The vessel is driven ashore in a storm while in ballast and is refloated at a cost of	350,000
On being drydocked, the damage to the vessel is found to be severe and the cost of repairs is estimated at	750,000
	1,100,000

50.113 It is now only too clear that the ship was in fact both a commercial and a constructive total loss at the time of the casualty, and that it would have been financially more beneficial to have left her in her stranding place and not to have spent a single penny upon her. What, however, is the position of the various insurers if notice of abandonment is tendered to them only after the expenses of refloating have been incurred and the damage properly surveyed in the drydock? Can the shipowner include the 350,000 previously expended on refloating operations to establish a constructive total loss?

If he is so entitled, and can thereby demonstrate a constructive total loss, his total recovery would be:

The sum insured on—Hull and Machinery, etc.	1,000,000
Increased Value	250,000
Plus: The costs of refloating (Sue and Labour charges)	350,000
	1,600,000

50.114 Alternatively, if the cost of the refloating operations cannot be taken into account because they had already been incurred and were not *future* to the tendering of notice of abandonment, the shipowner would be unable to demonstrate a constructive total loss and would be obliged to treat the loss as partial, keep his vessel, and effect repairs (or claim for unrepaired damage). His claim would then be limited to one on the Hull and Machinery policy alone, and for:

The costs of refloating (Sue and Labour charges)	350,000
Cost of repairs (or unrepaired damage)	750,000
	1,100,000

The difference in the respective claims is no less than 500,000, quite sufficient to encourage and warrant a second school of thought on this problem!

As stated earlier, the editors conclude that the word *future* relates to the tendering of notice of abandonment to the insurers, and in support of their views they offer the following observations:

(1) There are no reported cases in England in which it has been expressly decided that account may be taken of expenses which have been incurred following the casualty but prior to the notice of abandonment, but the converse was held in the case of *Hall v. Hayman*,[73] decided only six years after the passing of the Marine Insurance Act. The facts in that case were that the vessel had been driven ashore on November 16, and sufficient notice of abandonment was given to underwriters on December 9. Bray J. said: **50.115**

> "I have got to see whether on the 9th December the cost of the repairs, as stated in the Act, including those items which are mentioned in the Act, would or would not exceed the value when repaired. *I cannot take into consideration anything that was done before* ... Therefore I cannot allow 1830 dollars"

Between these dates expenses of 1,830 dollars were incurred in attempts to salve the vessel.

It may also be noted that even the counsel for the plaintiff shipowner had previously conceded that if these expenses had been incurred by the shipowner, he could not have claimed them as part of the repairs, "because they were not future salvage operations".

It appears clear that in 1912 no-one doubted that the word "future" related to the tendering of notice of abandonment, and that any alternative theory has developed only since that time.

(2) Ignoring for the moment any considerations of insurance, and adopting the "prudent uninsured owner" test, the whole essence of the particular form of commercial total loss under discussion is that the ship, though not destroyed, is in such a condition that the owner reasonably considers her at the time to have lost all monetary worth,[74] that is that the future expenditure likely to be required if the ship is to be recovered and repaired would exceed her value when repaired, and that to spend anything further upon her would be improvident and simply to "throw good money after bad". **50.116**

Thus, in our example in paragraph 50.112, above, where, having spent 350,000 to refloat his vessel and finding on drydocking that a further

[73] [1912] 2 K.B. 5; 17 Com.Cas. 81; 12 Asp. M.L.C. 158; 28 T.L.R. 171

[74] In *Moss v. Smith* (1850) 19 L.J.C.P. 225, Maule J. gave a nutshell definition of the term when he said:

> "A man may be said to have lost a shilling when he has dropped it into deep water, though it might be possible by some very expensive contrivance to recover it."

750,000 would be required to repair her, it can hardly be suggested that the owner would at this stage consider his vessel to be a commercial total loss and abandon her. He would undoubtedly regret his earlier refloating expenditure of 350,000 and recognise that he would have been financially better off to have left the vessel on the strand, but as a thoroughly commercial man, he would write off the 350,000 to experience and continue with the repairs at a cost of 750,000 in order to have a vessel worth 1,000,000.

The vessel may indeed have been a commercial total loss at the time of the accident, but she was no longer such when refloated and placed in drydock; she then had a monetary worth of approximately 250,000 and was worth repairing.

50.117 A commercial total loss can be evaluated and determined only on a basis which looks ever forward and ignores expenses already incurred; it is illogical and unreasonable to adopt a "hindsight" approach.

The Marine Insurance Act is similarly commercial in its provisions, and every single phrase used in section 60 to define a constructive total loss looks only to *future* expenditure, not to that already incurred. So, if in our example the shipowner were to tender notice of abandonment only when the vessel was surveyed in drydock, he would be unable[75] to demonstrate a constructive total loss and his claim would be on the hull and machinery policy alone, and for 1,100,000 as set out in paragraph 50.114, above.

50.118 (3) The Marine Insurance Act is a remarkable example of fine draftsmanship and it is inconceivable that the drafters would have used the word *future* in the expression "expense of future salvage operations"[76] if the cost of salvage operations undertaken at any time subsequent to the casualty could be taken into consideration when assessing whether a constructive total loss could be proved; some time base other than the date of the casualty is clearly indicated, for otherwise the word "future" would be otiose and mere surplusage. The salvage expenses can hardly be incurred *prior* to the casualty.

50.119 (4) In fact, and on the grounds of logic, legal precedent,[77] business

[75] The alternative view, taken to its logical but absurd conclusion, might permit the shipowner to tender notice of abandonment and claim as for a constructive total loss when, repairs having already been effected, the shipowner finds that the total cost of salvage and repairs amounts to 1,000,001.

[76] The *expense of future salvage operations* under, say, a Lloyd's form of Salvage Agreement remains *future*—even though the salvage operations themselves may have been completed—until such time as security is provided to the salvors. Until then it is always possible to abandon the salved property to the salvors.

[77] *E.g. Ruys v. Royal Exchange Assce. Corp.* [1897] 2 Q.B. 135; 2 Com.Cas. 201; 8 Asp. M.L.C. 294. During a war between Italy and Abyssinia, a vessel with a cargo of munitions for Abyssinia was captured by an Italian cruiser on August 8, 1896. Notice of abandonment was tendered to the war-risk underwriters on August 14, and a writ issued on August 21. At the time of the trial, peace had been declared and the vessel had been returned to her

expediency and established custom of at least two centuries' standing, where the assured elects to claim as for a constructive total loss, such claim falls to be assessed and governed by the state of facts ruling on the date when, having received news of the accident and reliable information from his master, agent, and local experts that the cost of recovering and repairing the vessel would likely exceed the insured value, the assured decides to claim on a constructive total loss basis and *tenders notice of abandonment* to his insurers (and they agree to place him in the same position as if a writ had been issued against them).

The tendering of notice of abandonment by the assured to his insurers is peculiar to marine insurance alone[78] and is deemed to be such a highly important element in the satisfactory operation of the business that it is made a condition precedent to the filing of a claim for constructive total loss.[79] Section 62 of the Marine Insurance Act 1906 states that:

> (1) Subject to the provisions of this section, where the assured elects to abandon the subject-matter insured to the insurer he must give notice of abandonment. If he fails to do so the loss can only be treated as a partial loss.

A state of affairs sufficient to constitute a constructive total loss in terms of section 60 of the Act may exist[80] independently of whether the assured elects to claim on such a basis, but unless he does tender notice of abandonment to his insurers at an appropriate time, the loss can only be treated as a partial loss.

The purpose of tendering notice of abandonment, and the requirement in section 63(2) of the Marine Insurance Act that it be given "with reasonable diligence after receipt of reliable information of the loss" is to ensure that the insurers receive early notice that a very serious loss has occurred, and at a stage where they can obtain some benefit from the notice and can: **50.120**

(1) Take—or recommend the assured to take—such steps as may be deemed prudent to preserve the property or mitigate the loss, or
(2) Avoid further wasteful expenditure (and their liability therefor) by accepting that the vessel is, in fact, a constructive total loss.

owners, but it was held by the court that the assured's rights under the policy were governed by the circumstances existing at the date of issuing the writ, unaffected by any change which may have taken place between that time and the date of trial.

[78] The requirement concerning *notice* of abandonment is quite separate and distinct from the general principle of *abandonment* common to all forms of insurance based on indemnity, whereby there must be an abandonment on the part of the person claiming for a total loss of all his rights in respect of the property for which he receives indemnity (and in the case of marine insurance enshrined in the Marine Insurance Act, s. 79).

[79] Except "where at the time when the assured receives information of the loss there would be no possibility of benefit to the insurer if notice were given to him", or where notice is waived by the insurer (s. 62(7), (8) of the Marine Insurance Act).

[80] *E.g.* See *Robinson v. Petros M. Nomikos* [1939] A.C. 371; 43 Com.Cas. 109; 61 Ll.L.Rep. 105.

50.121 From the assured's point of view, the tendering of notice of abandonment at the earliest possible time after receipt of reliable information concerning the loss ensures that if, as is usual, the insurers decline to accept that the vessel is a constructive total loss but agree to place the assured in the same position as if he had issued a writ against them, the assured can undoubtedly include any reasonable expenditure incurred subsequent to the notice for the purpose of proving his constructive total loss, and if he does so prove his loss, recover the subsequent expenditure in addition to the payments for total loss. Thus, in our example in paragraph 50.112, above, if the assured reasonably considered that the vessel was a constructive total loss and gave notice of abandonment while his vessel was still aground, and the insurers put him to the test and only accepted that a constructive total loss had been demonstrated after the vessel had been surveyed in drydock, he would recover the sums insured under all his policies, *plus* the 350,000 refloating expenses, as set out in paragraph 50.113, above.

50.122 (5) As against our own conclusions of the position in English law, it must be recorded that the courts of the United States adopt the alternative view that expenses incurred prior to the tendering of notice of abandonment may be included in the computation for the purpose of demonstrating a constructive total loss.[81] However, these decisions are hardly indorsed by American business interests. They adopt a commercial approach and have countered the effect of the court decisions by wording in lines 138/139 of the American Institute Hull Clauses (June 2, 1977):

> "... but expenses incurred prior to tender of abandonment shall not be considered if such are to be claimed separately under the Sue and Labor clause."

The assured is thus presented with the choice of claiming (in our own example under discussion):

(a)	Refloating Expenses	350,000
	Repairs (or unrepaired damage)	750,000
		1,100,000
or (b)	Sum insured on policies covering	
	Hull and Machinery, etc.	1,000,000
	Increased Value	250,000
		1,250,000
	(but losing his refloating expenses and giving up his vessel to the insurers)	

whichever suits him best in the circumstances of his own particular case.

[81] See *Bradie v. Maryland Ins. Co.* 37 U.S. 378 (1838); *Young v. Union Ins. Co.* 24 Fed. Rep. 279 (1885); *Cia. Mar Astra v. Archdale* (1954) A.M.C. 1674; [1954] 2 Ll.L.Rep. 469; *Northern Barge Line v. Royal Ins. Co.* (1974) A.M.C. 136.

12. Collision

Cargo Interests have Direct Right of Claim against Wrongdoing Vessel for General Average Contributions Paid to Carrying Vessel

*(**Note:** This particular topic is not directly concerned with INSURANCE, but is most conveniently dealt with in this Section.)*

A collision between two vessels will frequently result in the need for one or both vessels to incur general average sacrifices and expenditures and these will be apportioned between ship and cargo, etc., in the customary manner. Assuming that the "other" vessel is wholly or partly to blame for the collision, what are the respective rights of the ship and cargo interests in a common maritime adventure to claim against that other vessel for such general average sacrifices and expenditure, or the general average contributions that may have been paid by the various parties to the adventure? In particular, do the cargo interests have the right to sue the wrongdoing vessel direct for general average contributions paid to the owner of the carrying vessel? **50.123**

In 1891 it was held in the case of *The Marpessa*[82] that cargo interests had no such right to claim direct against the other vessel for general average contributions paid to the carrying vessel, it being considered that the immediate cause of such contributions was not the collision, but the contract of carriage between the ship and cargo. This decision applied only to general average contributions, and cargo interests were not precluded from proceeding directly against the other vessel for physical *loss or damage* to their property directly sustained in the collision, or by a general average sacrifice of their cargo immediately thereafter. Equally, the cargo interests were not necessarily placed in the position that they had been obliged to pay a general average contribution with no means whatever to recover the same; in his own claim for damages against the other vessel, the owner of the carrying vessel would include the *whole* of the general average expenses, etc., and any recovery would be apportioned subsequently between the ship and cargo interests. Nevertheless, and as the example below will demonstrate, the financial results to the cargo interests could be materially different were they to have the right to claim directly against the colliding vessel. **50.124**

In 1947 this right was recognised when *The Marpessa*[83] was overruled by the House of Lords (Viscount Simon and Lord Simonds dissenting) in the case of *Morrison Steamship Co. v. Greystoke Castle*; *The Cheldale*.[84] **50.125**

[82] [1891] P. 403.
[83] *Ibid.*
[84] [1947] A.C. 265; 80 Ll.L.Rep. 55.

The extract from Lord Porter's judgment quoted in paragraph 00.26, above, may be sufficient to provide the core reason for their Lordships' decision, but the essential fact is that henceforth it was established that cargo interests had the right to recover in their own name, as damages from the owners of a colliding vessel, in respect of any general average contribution paid to the owners of the carrying vessel.

50.126 Where both vessels are at fault for the collision, under what might be termed *The Marpessa*[85] régime, if the carrying vessel included in its claim against the other vessel the *whole* of the general average expenditure, the cargo interests could find on occasion that they failed to recover any part of the general average contribution they paid to the owner of the carrying vessel. Their own claim simply served as a set-off for the owner of the carrying vessel against his own collision liability to the other vessel, benefiting both shipowners, but not the cargo. This would occur particularly where the claims against the carrying vessel were so large that the owner limited liability (as happened in the *Greystoke Castle*[86] case).

An example may assist:

Vessels A and B collide and are held to be equally at fault.

Vessel A incurs general average expenditure of	200,000
of which Cargo A pays 60% =	120,000

Cargo A might expect, therefore, to recover from the owner of Vessel B 50% of 120,000 =	60,000

50.127 Under *The Marpessa*[87] régime, the respective claims of the two vessels would be, say:

Claim of Vessel A

Particular Average and Demurrage	—	600,000
General Average (100%)	—	200,000
		800,000

Claim of Vessel B, which sank as the result of the collision, in ballast,and without loss of life:

Sound Value	8,000,000

[85] [1891] P. 403.
[86] [1947] A.C. 265; 80 Ll.L.Rep. 55.
[87] See n. 85, *supra*.

A single liability settlement between the two vessels might proceed as follows:

A liable to B for 50% of 8,000,000 =	4,000,000
B liable to A for 50% of 800,000 =	400,000
Net, A liable to B for	3,600,000
Limited to	2,000,000

There is no recovery from vessel B, and vessel A having limited liability, there can be no application of the "cross liabilities" principle under standard insurance conditions such as the Institute Time Clauses, Hulls, 1.11.95.

Under the post-*Greystoke Castle*[88] principle, the claim of shipowner A against B would be reduced to: **50.128**

Particular Average and Demurrage	—	600,000
General Average (200,000 − 120,000)	—	80,000
		680,000

but he would still end up by limiting liability and paying B 2,000,000.

Cargo A, however, would recover from B 50 per cent of the general average contribution of 120,000 they had paid to shipowner A, that is, 60,000.

Other side effects or corollaries arising from the *Greystoke Castle*[89] decision included the following: **50.129**

(1) The general average contribution claimable from the wrongdoing vessel would include sundry charges and allowances, previously unclaimable, such as commission and interest allowable under Rules XX and XXI of the York-Antwerp Rules, the fees and charges of the ship's agents collecting general average security, and of the average adjusters preparing the adjustment, etc.

As a matter of *interest*, it may be remarked that in 1947 the standard rate of interest allowed by the courts on actions for damages was 4 per cent per annum, and the then 5 per cent allowed under the York-Antwerp Rules was considered a worthwhile bonus. A generation later, however, when the York-Antwerp Rules gave 7 per cent per annum, but commercial rates of interest were often 15 per cent or more, and sanctioned by the courts, it often became more profitable to revert to presenting collision

[88] [1947] A.C. 265; 80 Ll.L.Rep. 55.
[89] *Ibid.*

claims under the previous *Marpessa*[90] system, and file a claim against the wrongdoer for the actual port of refuge expenses, etc., plus commercial rates of interest, rather than for general average contributions to those expenses.

(2) If cargo interests were entitled to claim general average contributions from the other vessel, it followed—if with rather less certainty—that the shipowner also could include in his claim against the other vessel expenses such as the average adjusters' fees and expenses.

[90] [1891] P. 403. As mentioned above, many claims against colliding vessels are still presented on a *Marpessa* basis, with the owner of the carrying vessel claiming for himself and on behalf of the cargo interests the *whole* of any general average expenditure, including adjustment charges, etc., but with interest at commercial rates, rather than as under the York-Antwerp Rules. Provided that neither vessel has limited liability, this method will generally result in the cargo interests recovering their full entitlement from the other vessel.

The only point to which they should pay attention and protect themselves if possible concerns the matter of legal and adjustment costs. Under the *Greystoke Castle* principle, the costs of recovering a simple general average contribution should be minimal, for the degree of liability attaching to the other vessel has already been determined, as has the amount of the general average contribution paid to the owner of the carrying vessel. Under the *Marpessa* method, however, it is not impossible that cargo interests could find themselves contributing unnecessarily on a pro rata basis to many of the heavy costs incurred by the shipowner for determining liability for the collision, and for apportioning the recovery.

APPENDICES

Appendix 1

THE ROMAN CIVIL LAW

Those portions of the Digest and Institutes of Justinian which bear on the subject of general average are brought together in a convenient form, and illustrated by copious notes, in the first volume of M. Pardessus's "Collection de Lois Maritimes", from which the following extracts are taken.)

Section 1.

WHAT LOSSES ARE THE SUBJECT OF GENERAL AVERAGE

1. Lege Rhodiâ cavetur, "ut, si levandae navis gratiâ jactus mercium factus est, omnium contributione sarciatur quod pro omnibus datum est."

60.01 1. The Rhodian law decrees that, if goods are thrown overboard to lighten a ship, all shall make good by contribution that which has been given for all (*a*).

2. Si conservatis mercibus deterior facta sit navis, aut si quid exarmaverit, nulla facienda est collatio, quia dissimilis earum rerum causa sit, quae navis gratiâ parentur, et earum pro quibus mercedem aliquis acceperit: nam et si faber incudem vel malleum fregerit, non imputaretur ei qui locaverit opus: sed, si voluntate vectorum, vel propter aliquem metum, id detrimentum factum sit, hoc ipsum sarciri oportet.

60.02 2. If, the goods being preserved, the ship suffers damage or loses any of her tackling, there shall be no contribution, there being no distinction between things provided for the use of the ship and other things for which a man receives hire or payment: for, if a smith breaks his anvil or hammer, he cannot charge it against the person who employed him on the work. But if it is by the will of the passengers (*b*), or on account of some danger, that this damage was done, this must be made good (*c*).

3. Cùm arbor, aut aliud navis instrumentum, removendi communis periculi causâ, dejectum est, contributio debetur.

60.03 3. When a mast or other appurtenance of the ship is cut down for the sake of removing a common danger, contribution is due (*d*).

4. Arbore caesâ, ut navis cum mercibus liberari possit, aequitas contributionis habebit locum.

60.04 4. When a mast is cut, that the ship with the goods may escape, the equity of contribution shall come in (*e*).

5. Si navis à piratis redempta sit, Servius, Ofilius, Labeo, omnes conferre debere aiunt. Quod verò praedones abstulerint, eum perdere cujus fuerit; nec conferendum ei qui suas merces redemerit.

60.05 5. If a ship has been ransomed from pirates, Servius, Ofilius, Labeo, all agree that there should be a contribution. But what the robbers have taken away, he must lose whose property it was; nor shall there be a contribution for him who has ransomed goods of his own (*f*).

(*a*) Dig. Lib. 14, Tit. 2, Fr. 1; 1 Pard. 104. M. Pardessus is of opinion that this sentence contains all that the Romans really borrowed from the Rhodians (Vol. 1, p. 23), and that the Rhodians in turn borrowed it from the Phoenicians (Vol. 1, Intra. xxix.).

(*b*) "Vectores" may be translated passengers or merchants on board. The context shows that there were sometimes "vectores sine sarcinâ", passengers who had no wares; but this was probably exceptional. (See 1 Pard. 105, n. 3.)

(*c*) Dig. Lib. 14, Tit. 2, Fr. 2, para. 1; 1 Pard. 105.

(*d*) 1 Pard. 107.

(*e*) Fr. 5, para. 1; Pard. 108.

(*f*) Fr. 2, para. 3; 1 Pard. 106.

60.06 6. Navis onustae levandae causâ, quia intrare flumen vel portum non potuerat cum onere, si quaedam merces in scapham trajectae sunt, ne aut extra flumen periclitetur, aut in ipso ostio vel portu, eaque scapha submersa est, ratio haberi debet inter eos qui in nave merces salvas habent, cum his qui in scaphâ perdiderunt, proinde tanquam si jactura facta esset. ... Contrà, si scapha cum parte mercium salva est, navis periit, ratio haberi non debet eorum qui in navi perdiderunt, quia jactus in tributum nave salvâ venit.

6. If, for the purpose of lightening a laden ship, because she cannot enter a river or haven with her cargo on board, some of the goods are transhipped in a lighter, to avert danger either from remaining outside or in the harbour or port itself, and if the lighter is sunk, a contribution shall be made between those who have their goods safe in the ship, and those who have lost theirs in the lighter, just as if there had been a jettison.

If, on the other hand, the lighter with a part of the goods is saved, and the ship perishes, there shall not be a contribution towards the loss of those in the ship, on the plea that a jettison would have been contributed for if the ship had been saved (*g*).

... Quid enim interest, jactatas res meas amiserim, an nudatas deteriores habere coeperim? Nam sicut ei qui perdiderit subvenitur, ita et ei subveniri oportet qui deteriores propter jactum res habere coeperit.

... What difference does it make, whether by a jettison I lose my goods, or by an exposure of them for the purpose I receive them damaged? As he who loses them is compensated, so compensation should be made to him who receives his goods damaged by reason of the jettison (*h*).

60.07 7. Navis adversâ tempestate depressa, ictu fulminis deustis armamentis et arbore et antennâ, Hipponem delata est, ibique tumultuariis armamentis ad praesens comparatis, Ostiam navigavit et onus integrum pertulit. Quaesitum est an hi quorum onus fuit, nautae pro damno conferre debeant. Respondit non debere: hic enim sumptus instruendae magis navis quam conservandarum mercium gratiâ factus est.

7. A ship damaged in a storm, her mast and yards having been struck by lightning, was taken into Hippo, and having there been equipped for the occasion with temporary spars and gear, performed her voyage to Ostia and delivered her cargo undamaged. The question was raised whether the owners of the cargo should contribute towards the shipowner's loss: and it was determined that they should not: for these expenses were incurred rather for the purpose of refitting the ship than of preserving the cargo (*i*).

60.08 8. Cum depressa navis aut dejecta esset, quod quisque ex ea suum servasset, sibi servare respondit, tanquam ex incendio.

8. When a ship is sunk or wrecked, whatever of his own property each owner may have saved, he shall keep for himself, as if rescued from a fire (*k*).

Section 2.

COMPUTATION OF LOSSES AND CONTRIBUTING INTERESTS

60.09 9. Portio autem pro aestimatione rerum quae salvae sunt, et earum quae amissae sunt, praestari debet: nec ad rem pertinet, si hae quae amissat sunt pluris venire poterunt, quoniam detrimenti, non lucri, fit praestatio. Sed in his rebus quarum nomine conferendum est, aestimatio debet haberi, non quanti emptae sint, sed quanti venire possunt.

9. An apportionment is to be made according to the valuation of the property saved and of that sacrificed: nor does it affect the case if that which was sacrificed might have been sold at a profit, since the compensation is made for loss sustained, not for expected gain. But for the contributing values the estimate is to be taken, not on what they cost, but on what they might have been sold for (*l*).

(*g*) Fr. 4; 1 Pard. 107.
(*h*) Fr. 4, para. 2; 1 Pard. 108.
(*i*) Fr. 6; 1 Pard. 108.
(*k*) Fr. 7; 1 Pard. 108.
(*l*) Fr. 2, para. 4; 1 Pard. 106.

10. Amissae navis damnum collationis consortio non sarcitur per eos qui merces suas naufragio liberaverunt; nam hujus aequitatem tunc admitti placuit, cùm jactus remedio caeteris in communi periculo, salvâ nave, consultum est.

10. If a ship is cast away, the loss shall not be borne by a contribution on the part of those who have rescued their goods from the shipwreck; for this equitable right is only admissible when a jettison has been purposely made for rescuing the remainder in a common danger, and when the ship is saved (*m*). **60.10**

11. Cùm jactus de nave factus est, et alicujus res quae in navi remanserunt deteriores factae sunt, videndum an conferre cogendus sit, quia non debet duplici damno onerari, et collationis, et quòd res deteriores factae sunt. Sed defendendum est, hunc conferre debere pretio praesente rerum: itaque, verbi gratiâ, si vicenûm merces duorum fuerunt, et alterius aspargine decem esse coeperunt, ille cujus res integrae sunt, pro viginti conferat, hic pro decem.

11. When a jettison has been made from a ship, and some of the goods remaining in the ship are damaged, it is to be considered whether the owner of those goods shall be compelled to contribute, seeing that he should not be burdened with a double loss, both of the contribution and of the damage done to his goods. The right view is, that he should contribute upon the present value of his goods: thus, for example, if two men had goods each worth twenty, and one by wetting was brought to the value of ten, he whose goods are sound should contribute on twenty, the other on ten. **60.11**

Potest tamen dici etiam illa sententia, distinguentibus nobis deteriores ex qua causa factae sunt; id est, utrùm propter jacta nudatis rebus damnum secutum est, an verò alia ex causa, veluti quod alicubi jacebant merces in angulo aliquo, et unda penetravit; tunc enim conferre debebit: an ex priore causa, collationis onus pati non debet, quia jactus etiam hunc laesit. Adhuc numquid et si aspargine propter jactum res deteriores factae sunt? Sed distinctio subtilior adhibenda est, quid plus sit in damno, an in collatione: si, verbi gratiâ, hae res viginti fuerunt, et collatio quidem facit decem, damnum autem duo; deducto hoc quod damnum passus est, reliquum conferre debeat? Quid ergò, si plus in damno erit quàm in collatione, utputa decem aureis res deteriores factae sunt, duo autem collationis sunt? Indubitatè utrumque onus pati non debet. Sed hic videamus num et ipsi conferre operteat: quid enim interest, &c.

In giving this judgment, however, a distinction should be made according to the cause of the deterioration; that is, whether the damage to the goods arose from their having been exposed on account of the jettison, or from some other cause, such as, that the goods were stowed in some corner where the water penetrated: in the latter case, they should contribute; in the former case they should be relieved from this burden, since their owner is himself a sufferer by the jettison. Again, how if it is by wetting on account of the jettison that the goods were damaged? Here a more subtle distinction is to be drawn, as to which is most, the damage or the contribution. If, for instance, these goods were worth twenty, and the contribution would make ten, but the damage two; deducting from this value the amount of the damage, should the remainder contribute? How, again, if the damage is more than the contribution: suppose the goods to be deteriorated by ten pounds, while the contribution is two? Undoubtedly the owner ought not to bear both burdens. But here we have to see whether contribution should not be made *to him*: for what difference does it make, &c. (No. 6, *ante*) (*n*).

12. Si navis quae in tempestate jactu mercium unius mercatoris levata est, in alio loco submersa est, et aliquorum mercatorum merces per urinatores extractae sunt datâ

12. If a ship, which in a tempest has been relieved by the jettison of one man's goods, shall afterwards in another place be sunk, and the goods of some merchants are **60.12**

(*m*) Fr. 5; 1 Pard. 108.

(*n*) Fr. 4, para. 2; 1 Pard. 108. The distinctions here suggested seem to indicate that the simple remedy for all these difficulties now universal, namely the bringing in the amount made good as a contributor, had not at this time suggested itself.

mercede, rationem haberi debere ejus cujus merces in navigatione levandae navis causâ jactae sunt, ab his qui postea sua per urinatores servaverunt, Sabinus aeque respondit: eorum verò qui ita servaverunt, invicem rationem haberi non debere ab eo qui in navigatione jactum fecit, si quaedam ex his mercibus per urinatores extractae sunt; eorum enim merces non possunt videri servandae navis causâ jactae esse, quae periit.

brought up by divers for a stated reward, it is rightly held by Sabinus that he whose goods were jettisoned to save the ship is entitled to contribution from those who afterwards recovered theirs by means of divers: but, on the other hand, that there shall be no contribution from him whose goods had been jettisoned towards those whose goods were rescued by the divers; for these last goods cannot be said to have been cast out for the sake of preserving the ship which perished (*o*).

60.13 13. Cum in eadem nave varia mercium genera complures mercatores coëgissent, praetereaque multi vectores servi liberique in ea navigarent, tempestate gravi ortâ, necessariò jactura facta erat. Quaesita deinde sunt haec: an omnes jacturam praestare oporteat; et si qui tales merces imposuissent quibus navis non oneraretur, velut gemmas, margaritas, et quae portio praestanda est; et an etiam pro liberis capitibus dari oporteat, et qua actione ea res expediri possit. Placuit, omnes quorum interfuisset jacturam fieri conferre oportere, quia id tributum ob servatam rem deberent, itaque dominum etiam navis pro portione obligatum esse; jacturae summam pro rerum pretio distribui oportet; corporum liberorum aestimationem nullam fieri posse; ex conducto dominos rerum amissarum cum nautâ, id est, cum magistro, acturos. Itidem agitatum est an etiam vestimentorum cujusque et annulorum aestimationem fieri oporteat; et omnium visum est, nisi si qua consumendi causâ imposita forent, quo in numero essent cibaria, eò magis, quòd, si quando ea defecerint in navigationem, quod quisque haberet in commune conferret.

13. Where in the same ship a number of merchants had shipped various kinds of goods, and also many passengers, slaves and free, were on board, a violent storm having arisen, it was necessary to make a jettison. Hereupon the following questions arose: whether all should take part in the contribution? whether those who had on board such goods as were no burden to the ship, as gems or pearls, should contribute, and if so, in what proportions; whether the lives even of freemen should be taken account of; and in what form of action the matter should be settled? It was determined, that all to whose interest it was that the jettison should be made should contribute, because they owed this ransom on account of their property preserved; therefore that the master of the ship was likewise bound for his proportion; that the amount of the jettison should be distributed rateably on the value of the property; that freemen's lives could have no value set upon them; that the owners of the goods cast over must proceed against the master of the ship *ex conducto* (*p*). At the same time it was discussed whether the wearing apparel and rings of those on board were to be valued; and it was determined that everything should, except such things as were put on board in order to be consumed, under which head came provisions; and this so much the more because, in case of deficiency while at sea, whatever each one had was brought into the common stock (*q*).

60.14 14. Servorum quoque qui in mare perierunt, non magis aestimatio facienda est, quam si qui aegri in nave decesserint, aut aliqui sese praecipitaverint.

14. As for slaves who perished in the sea, no greater valuation is to be set on them than if they had died of disease on shipboard, or had thrown themselves into the sea (*r*).

60.15 15. Si res quae jactae sunt apparuerint, exoneratur collatio: quòd si jam contributio

15. If goods which have been jettisoned are recovered, the contribution is dis-

(*o*) Fr. 4, para. 1; 1 Pard. 107.
(*p*) See note (*u*), *post*.
(*q*) Fr. 2, para. 2; 1 Pard. 105–106.
(*r*) Fr. 2, para. 5; 1 Pard. 106.

facta sit, tunc hi qui solverint agent ex locato cum magistro, ut is ex conducto experiatur, et quod exegerit reddat.

Res autem jacta domini manet, nec fit apprehendentis, quia pro derelicto non habetur.

charged: but if the contribution has already been made, then those who have paid it may proceed *ex locato* against the master, that he may take his course *ex conducto*, and refund what he had demanded (*s*).

The goods jettisoned however remain the property of their first owners, for they are not to be treated as derelict (*t*).

Section 3.

REMEDIES AND MODE OF PROCEDURE

16. Si, laborante nave, jactus factus est, amissarum mercium domini, si mercedes vehendas locaverant, ex locato cum magistro navis agere debent; is deinde, cum reliquis, quorum merces salvae sunt, ex conducto, ut detrimentum pro portione communicetur, agere potest. Servius quidem respondit, ex locato agere cum magistro navis debere, ut caeterorum vectorum merces retineat, donec portionem damni praestent. Imò, etsi retineat merces magister, ultrò ex locato habiturus est actionem cum vectoribus: quid enim si vectores sint qui nullas sarcinas habeant? Planè commodius est, si sint, retinere eas. At si non, [et] totam navem conduxerit, ex conducto aget, sicut vectores qui loca in nave conduxerunt: aequissimum enim est commune detrimentum fieri eorum qui, propter amissas res aliorum, consecuti sunt ut merces suas salvas haberent.

16. If, when the ship is labouring, a jettison has been made, the owners of the goods sacrificed, if they have been shipped for carriage, should proceed *ex locato* against the master; who can then proceed against the others, whose goods are safe, *ex conducto* (*u*), that the loss may be distributed proportionally. Servius, however, is of opinion that they should proceed *ex locato* against the master of the ship, that he may retain the goods of the other merchants, until they have paid their share of the loss. Yes, but though the master may retain the goods, there must likewise be a right of action against the merchants (*vectores*: see note (*b*), p. 419), *ex locato* (*x*): for how if there are merchants who have no goods on board? Clearly it is more convenient, if there are any, to retain them. But if not, and if he has freighted the whole ship, let him proceed *ex conducto*, as on passengers who have hired places in a ship: for it is most equitable that the loss should fall in common amongst those who, by means of the sacrifice of other persons' property, have succeeded in obtaining their own in safety. **60.16**

17. Si quis ex vectoribus solvendo non est, hoc detrimentum magistri navis non erit: nec enim fortunas cujusque nauta excutere debet.

17. If any of the merchants is insolvent, this loss must not fall on the captain; for a sailor cannot be expected to hunt out each man's stability. **60.17**

(*s*) Fr. 2, para. 7; 1 Pard. 107.

(*t*) Fr. 2, para. 8; 1 Pard. 107; see also Fr. 8; 1 Pard. 109.

(*u*) *Locator* is he who lets his ship, or room in it, on hire; *conductor*, he who engages to pay for the use; hence the *actio ex locato*, is a suit against the master or owner of the ship, to enforce the obligations undertaken by him in letting his ship; the *actio ex conducto* is by the master against the merchants, to enforce the duties which this contract imposes upon them. (Sandars, Inst. Just. 457.)

(*x*) This apparently should be *ex conducto*. Instances of this confusion, says Pardessus, are not uncommon in the Roman law. (1, 105, n. 2.)

APPENDIX 2A

GLASGOW RESOLUTIONS (1860), YORK RULES (1864) and YORK-ANTWERP RULES (1877)

Glasgow Resolutions (1860)	York Rules (1864)	York-Antwerp Rules (1877)	
	Rule I. Jettison of Deck Cargo A jettison of timber or deals, or any other description of wood cargo, carried on the deck of a ship in pursuance of a general custom of the trade in which the ship is then engaged, shall be made good as general average, in like manner as if such cargo had been jettisoned from below deck. No jettison of deck cargo, other than timber or deals, or other wood cargo, so carried as aforesaid, shall be made good as general average. Every structure not built in with the frame of the vessel shall be considered to be a part of the deck of the vessel.	**Rule I. Jettison of Deck Cargo** No jettison of deck cargo shall be made good as general average. Every structure not built in with the frame of the vessel shall be considered to be a part of the deck of the vessel.	**60.18**
(3). That the damage done to cargo by chafing and breakage, resulting from a jettison of part of the remainder of the cargo, ought not to be allowed in general average.	**Rule II. Damage by Jettison** Damage done to goods or merchandise by water which unavoidably goes down a ship's hatches opened, or other opening made, for the purpose of making a jettison shall be made good as general average, in case the loss by jettison is so made good. Damage done by breakage or chafing, or otherwise from derangement of stowage consequent upon a jettison, shall be made good as general average.	**Rule II. Damage by Jettison** Damage done to goods or merchandise by water which unavoidably goes down a ship's hatches opened, or other opening made, for the purpose of making a jettison shall be made good as general average, in case the loss by jettison is so made good. Damage done by breakage and chafing, or otherwise from derangement of stowage consequent upon a jettison, shall be made good as general average, in case the loss by jettison is so made good.	**60.19**

	Glasgow Resolutions (1860)	York Rules (1864)	York-Antwerp Rules (1877)
60.20		**Rule III. Extinguishing Fire on Shipboard**	**Rule III. Extinguishing Fire on Shipboard**
	(2). That the damage done to ship, cargo and freight in extinguishing a fire, ought to be allowed in general average.	Damage done to a ship and cargo, or either of them, by water or otherwise, in extinguishing a fire on board the ship, shall be general average.	Damage done to a ship, and cargo, or either of them by water or otherwise, in extinguishing a fire on board the ship, shall be general average; except that no compensation be made for damage done by water to packages which have been on fire.
60.21		**Rule IV. Cutting away Wreck**	**Rule IV. Cutting away Wreck**
	(5). That the loss sustained by cutting away the wreck of masts accidentally broken ought not to be allowed in general average.	Loss or damage caused by cutting away the wreck or remains of spars, or of other things which have previously been carried away by sea-peril, shall not be made good as general average.	Loss or damage caused by cutting away the wreck or remains of spars, or of other things which have previously been carried away by sea-peril, shall not be made good as general average.
60.22		**Rule V. Voluntary Stranding**	**Rule V. Voluntary Stranding**
	(1). That, as a general rule in the case of the voluntary stranding of a vessel in the course of her voyage, the loss or damage to ship, cargo, or freight, ought not to be the subject of general average, but without prejudice to such a claim in exceptional cases upon clear proof of special facts.	When a ship is intentionally run on shore because she is sinking or driving on shore or rocks, no damage caused to the ship, the cargo and the freight, or any or either of them, by such intentional running on shore, shall be made good as general average.	When a ship is intentionally run on shore because she is sinking or driving on shore or rocks, no damage caused to the ship, the cargo and the freight, or any or either of them, by such intentional running on shore, shall be made good as general average.
60.23		**Rule VI. Carrying a Press of Sail**	**Rule VI. Carrying a Press of Sail**
	(7). That the damage done to ship, cargo and freight, by carrying a press of sail, ought not to be allowed in general average.	Damage occasioned to a ship or cargo by carrying a press of sail shall not be made good as general average.	Damage occasioned to a ship or cargo by carrying a press of sail shall not be made good as general average.
60.24		**Rule VII. Port of Refuge Expenses**	**Rule VII. Port of Refuge Expenses**
	(6). That the expense of warehouse rent at a port of refuge on cargo necessarily discharged there, the expense of re-shipping it, and the outward port charges at that port, ought to be	When a ship shall have entered a port of refuge under such circumstances that the expenses of entering the port are admissible as general average, and when she shall have sailed thence with her original cargo or a	When a ship shall have entered a port of refuge under such circumstances that the expenses of entering the port are admissible as general average, and when she shall have sailed thence with her original cargo or a

Glasgow Resolutions (1860)	York Rules (1864)	York-Antwerp Rules (1877)	
allowed in general average.	part of it, the corresponding expenses of leaving such port shall likewise be so admitted as general average; and whenever the cost of discharging cargo at such port is admissible as general average, the cost of reloading and stowing such cargo on board the said ship, together with all storage charges on such cargo, shall likewise be so admitted. Except that any portion of the cargo left at such port of refuge, on account of its being unfit to be carried forward, or on account of the unfitness or inability of the ship to carry it, shall not be called on to contribute to such general average.	part of it, the corresponding expenses of leaving such port shall likewise be admitted as general average; and, whenever the cost of discharging cargo at such port is admissible as general average, the cost of reloading and stowing such cargo on board the said ship, together with all storage charges on such cargo, shall likewise be so admitted.	
	Rule VIII. Wages and Maintenance of Crew in Port of Refuge	**Rule VIII. Wages and Maintenance of Crew in Port of Refuge**	**60.25**
(8). That the wages and provisions for the ship's crew ought to be allowed to the shipowner in general average, from the date the ship reaches a port of refuge in distress until the date on which she leaves it.	When a ship shall have entered a port of refuge under the circumstances defined in Rule VII, the wages and cost of maintenance of the master and mariners, from the time of entering such port until the ship shall have been made ready to proceed upon her voyage, shall be made good as general average. Except that any portion of the cargo left at such port of refuge on account of its being unfit to be carried forward, or on account of the unfitness or inability of the ship to carry it, shall not be called on to contribute to such general average.	When a ship shall have entered a port of refuge under the circumstances defined in Rule VII, the wages and cost of maintenance of the master and mariners, from the time of entering such port until the ship shall have been made ready to proceed upon her voyage, shall be made good as general average.	
	Rule IX. Damage to Cargo in Discharging	**Rule IX. Damage to Cargo in Discharging**	**60.26**
(4). That the damage done to cargo, and the loss of it, and of the freight on it, resulting from discharging it at a port of refuge in the way usual in that port with ships not in distress, ought	Damage done to cargo by discharging it at a port of refuge shall not be admissible as general average in case such cargo shall have been discharged at the place and in the manner cus-	Damage done to cargo by discharging it at a port of refuge shall not be admissible as general average in case such cargo shall have been discharged at the place and in the manner cus-	

	Glasgow Resolutions (1860)	York Rules (1864)	York-Antwerp Rules (1877)
	not to be allowed in general average.	tomary at that port with ships not in distress.	tomary at that port with ships not in distress.
60.27		**Rule X. Contributory Values**	**Rule X. Contributory Values**
	(9). That when the amount of expenses is less than the value of the property finally saved, the contributing values of ship, freight, and cargo, ought to be their values to the owners of them respectively, at the termination of the adventure. (10). That, when the amount of expenses is greater than the value of the property saved, the proceeds of the property so saved ought to be applied towards those expenses, and the excess of the expenses over the proceeds ought to be apportioned as if the whole property had finally reached its destination. (11). That, in fixing the value of the freight, the wages and port charges up to the date of the general average act ought not to be deducted, and the wages and port charges after that date ought to be deducted from the gross freight at the risk of the shipowner.	The contributions to a general average shall be made upon the actual values of the property at the termination of the adventure, to which shall be added the amount made good as general average for property sacrificed; deduction being made from the shipowner's freight and passage-money at risk of two-fifths of such freight, in lieu of crew's wages, port charges, and all other deductions; deduction being also made from the value of the property of all charges incurred in respect thereof subsequently to the arising of the claim to general average.	The contribution to a general average shall be made upon the actual values of the property at the termination of the adventure, to which shall be added the amount made good as general average for property sacrificed; deduction being made from the shipowner's freight and passage-money at risk, of such port charges and crew's wages as would not have been incurred had the ship and cargo been totally lost at the date of the general average act or sacrifice; deduction being also made from the value of the property of all charges incurred in respect thereof subsequently to the arising of the claim to general average.
60.28		**Rule XI. Loss of Freight** In every case in which a sacrifice of cargo is made good as general average, the loss of freight, if any, which is caused by such loss of cargo, shall likewise be so made good.	**Rule XI. Loss of Freight** In every case in which a sacrifice of cargo is made good as general average, the loss of freight, if any, which is caused by such loss of cargo shall likewise be so made good.
60.29			**Rule XII. Amount to be made good for Cargo** The value to be allowed for goods sacrificed shall be that value which the owner would have received if such goods had not been sacrificed.

Appendix 2B

YORK-ANTWERP RULES OF 1890, 1924, 1950, 1974 (and AS AMENDED 1990), and 1994

Together with references to earlier Rules of 1860, 1864 & 1877 in Appendix 2A

	Rules of 1860, 1864 and 1877	York-Antwerp Rules (1890)	York-Antwerp Rules (1924)
60.30			
60.31			
60.32A			**Rule A** There is a general average act when, and only when, any extraordinary sacrifice or expenditure is intentionally and reasonably made or incurred for the common safety for the purpose of preserving from peril the property involved in a common maritime adventure.
60.32B			**Rule B** General average sacrifices and expenses shall be borne by the different contributing interests on the basis hereinafter provided.
60.33			

York-Antwerp Rules (1950)	York-Antwerp Rules (1974)	York-Antwerp Rules (1994)†
Rule of Interpretation In the adjustment of general average the following lettered and numbered Rules shall apply to the exclusion of any Law and Practice inconsistent therewith. Except as provided by the numbered Rules, general average shall be adjusted according to the lettered Rules.	**Rule of Interpretation** In the adjustment of general average the following lettered and numbered Rules shall apply to the exclusion of any Law and Practice inconsistent therewith. Except as provided by the numbered Rules, general average shall be adjusted according to the lettered Rules.	**Rule of Interpretation** In the adjustment of general average the following lettered and numbered Rules shall apply to the exclusion of any Law and Practice inconsistent therewith. Except as provided by *the Rule Paramount and* the numbered Rules, general average shall be adjusted according to the lettered Rules.
		Rule Paramount *In no case shall there be any allowance for sacrifice or expenditure unless reasonably made or incurred.*
Rule A There is a general average act when, and only when, any extraordinary sacrifice or expenditure is intentionally and reasonably made or incurred for the common safety for the purpose of preserving from peril the property involved in a common maritime adventure.	**Rule A** There is a general average act when, and only when, any extraordinary sacrifice or expenditure is intentionally and reasonably made or incurred for the common safety for the purpose of preserving from peril the property involved in a common maritime adventure.	**Rule A** There is a general average act when, and only when, any extraordinary sacrifice or expenditure is intentionally and reasonably made or incurred for the common safety for the purpose of preserving from peril the property involved in a common maritime adventure.
Rule B General average sacrifices and expenses shall be borne by the different contributing interests on the basis hereinafter provided.	**Rule B** General average sacrifices and expenses shall be borne by the different contributing interests on the basis hereinafter provided.	*General average sacrifices and expenditures shall be borne by the different contributing interests on the basis hereinafter provided.*
		Rule B *There is a common maritime adventure when one or more vessels are towing or pushing another vessel or vessels, provided that they are all involved in commercial activities and not in a salvage operation.* *When measures are taken to preserve the vessels and their cargoes, if any, from a common peril, these Rules shall apply.* *A vessel is not in common peril with another vessel or*

† Where the 1994 Rules differ from the 1974 Rules, the 1994 Rules are printed in italics.

	Rules of 1860, 1864 and 1877	York-Antwerp Rules (1890)	York-Antwerp Rules (1924)
60.34			**Rule C** Only such losses, damages or expenses which are the direct consequence of the general average act shall be allowed as general average. Damage or loss sustained by the ship or cargo through delay on the voyage, and indirect loss from the same cause, such as demurrage and loss of market, shall not be admitted as general average.
60.35			**Rule D** Rights to contribution in general average shall not be affected, though the event which gave rise to the sacrifice or expenditure may have been due to the fault of one of the parties to the adventure; but this shall not prejudice any remedies which may be open against that party for such fault.
60.36			**Rule E** The onus of proof is upon the party claiming in general average to show that the loss or expense claimed is properly allowable as general average.

York-Antwerp Rules (1950)	York-Antwerp Rules (1974)	York-Antwerp Rules (1994)
		vessels if by simply disconnecting from the other vessel or vessels she is in safety; but if the disconnection is itself a general average act the common maritime adventure continues.
Rule C Only such losses, damages or expenses which are the direct consequence of the general average act shall be allowed as general average. Loss or damage sustained by the ship or cargo through delay, whether on the voyage or subsequently, such as demurrage, and any indirect loss whatsoever, such as loss of market, shall not be admitted as general average.	**Rule C** Only such losses, damages or expenses which are the direct consequence of the general average act shall be allowed as general average. Loss or damage sustained by the ship or cargo through delay, whether on the voyage or subsequently, such as demurrage, and any indirect loss whatsoever, such as loss of market, shall not be admitted as general average.	**Rule C** Only such losses, damages or expenses which are the direct consequence of the general average act shall be allowed as general average. *In no case shall there be any allowance in general average for losses, damages or expenses incurred in respect of damage to the environment or in consequence of the escape or release of pollutant substances from the property involved in the common maritime adventure.* *Demurrage, loss of market, and any loss or damage sustained or expense incurred by reason of delay, whether on the voyage or subsequently, and any indirect loss whatsoever, shall not be admitted as general average.*
Rule D Rights to contribution in general average shall not be affected, though the event which gave rise to the sacrifice or expenditure may have been due to the fault of one of the parties to the adventure; but this shall not prejudice any remedies which may be open against that party for such fault.	**Rule D** Rights to contribution in general average shall not be affected, though the event which gave rise to the sacrifice or expenditure may have been due to the fault of one of the parties to the adventure, but this shall not prejudice any remedies or defences which may be open against or to that party in respect of such fault.	**Rule D** Rights to contribution in general average shall not be affected, though the event which gave rise to the sacrifice or expenditure may have been due to the fault of one of the parties to the adventure, but this shall not prejudice any remedies or defences which may be open against or to that party in respect of such fault.
Rule E The onus of proof is upon the party claiming in general average to show that the loss or expense claimed is properly allowable as general average.	**Rule E** The onus of proof is upon the party claiming in general average to show that the loss or expense claimed is properly allowable as general average.	**Rule E** The onus of proof is upon the party claiming in general average to show that the loss or expense claimed is properly allowable as general average. *All parties claiming in*

Rules of 1860, 1864 and 1877	York-Antwerp Rules (1890)	York-Antwerp Rules (1924)
		Rule F Any extra expense incurred in place of another expense which would have been allowable as general average shall be deemed to be general average and so allowed, but only up to the amount of the general average expense avoided.
		Rule G General average shall be adjusted as regards both loss and contribution upon the basis of values at the time and place when and where the adventure ends. This rule shall not affect the determination of the place at which the average statement is to be made up.

60.37 (Rule F)

60.38 (Rule G)

York-Antwerp Rules (1950)	York-Antwerp Rules (1974)	York-Antwerp Rules (1994)
		general average shall give notice in writing to the average adjuster of the loss or expense in respect of which they claim contribution within 12 months of the date of the termination of the common maritime adventure. *Failing such notification, or if within 12 months of a request for the same any of the parties shall fail to supply evidence in support of a notified claim, or particulars of value in respect of a contributory interest, the average adjuster shall be at liberty to estimate the extent of the allowance or the contributory value on the basis of the information available to him, which estimate may be challenged only on the ground that it is manifestly incorrect.*
Rule F Any extra expense incurred in place of another expense which would have been allowable as general average shall be deemed to be general average and so allowed without regard to the saving, if any, to other interests, but only up to the amount of the general average expense avoided.	**Rule F** Any extra expense incurred in place of another expense which would have been allowable as general average shall be deemed to be general average and so allowed without regard to the saving, if any, to other interests, but only up to the amount of the general average expense avoided.	**Rule F** Any *additional* expense incurred in place of another expense which would have been allowable as general average shall be deemed to be general average and so allowed without regard to the saving, if any, to other interests, but only up to the amount of the general average expense avoided.
Rule G General average shall be adjusted as regards both loss and contribution upon the basis of values at the time and place when and where the adventure ends. This rule shall not affect the determination of the place at which the average statement is to be made up.	**Rule G** General average shall be adjusted as regards both loss and contribution upon the basis of values at the time and place when and where the adventure ends. This rule shall not affect the determination of the place at which the average statement is to be made up.	**Rule G** General average shall be adjusted as regards both loss and contribution upon the basis of values at the time and place when and where the adventure ends. This rule shall not affect the determination of the place at which the average statement is to be made up. *When a ship is at any port or place in circumstances which would give rise to an allowance in general average under the provisions of Rules X and XI, and the cargo or part thereof is forwarded to destination by other means,*

	Rules of 1860, 1864 and 1877	York-Antwerp Rules (1890)	York-Antwerp Rules (1924)
60.39	See para. 60.18, above.	**Rule I. Jettison of Deck Cargo** No jettison of deck cargo shall be made good as general average. Every structure not built in with the frame of the vessel shall be considered to be a part of the deck of the vessel.	**Rule I. Jettison of Cargo** No jettison of cargo shall be made good as general average, unless such cargo is carried in accordance with the recognised custom of the trade.
60.40	See para. 60.19, above.	**Rule II. Damage by Jettison and Sacrifice for the Common Safety** Damage done to a ship and cargo, or either of them, by or in consequence of a sacrifice made for the common safety, and by water which goes down a ship's hatches opened or other opening made for the purpose of making a jettison for the common safety, shall be made good as general average.	**Rule II. Damage by Jettison and Sacrifice for the Common Safety** Damage done to a ship and cargo, or either of them, by or in consequence of a sacrifice made for the common safety, and by water which goes down a ship's hatches opened or other opening made for the purpose of making a jettison for the common safety, shall be made good as general average.
60.41	See para. 60.20, above.	**Rule III. Extinguishing Fire on Shipboard** Damage done to a ship and cargo, or either of them, by water or otherwise, including damage by beaching or scuttling a burning	**Rule III. Extinguishing Fire on Shipboard** Damage done to a ship and cargo, or either of them, by water or otherwise, including damage by beaching or scuttling a burning

York-Antwerp Rules (1950)	York-Antwerp Rules (1974)	York-Antwerp Rules (1994)
		rights and liabilities in general average shall, subject to cargo interests being notified if practicable, remain as nearly as possible the same as they would have been in the absence of such forwarding, as if the adventure had continued in the original ship for so long as justifiable under the contract of affreightment and the applicable law. *The proportion attaching to cargo of the allowances made in general average by reason of applying the third paragraph of this Rule shall not exceed the cost which would have been borne by the owners of cargo if the cargo had been forwarded at their expense.*
Rule I. Jettison of Cargo No jettison of cargo shall be made good as general average, unless such cargo is carried in accordance with the recognised custom of the trade.	**Rule I. Jettison of Cargo** No jettison of cargo shall be made good as general average, unless such cargo is carried in accordance with the recognised custom of the trade.	**Rule I. Jettison of Cargo** No jettison of cargo shall be made good as general average, unless such cargo is carried in accordance with the recognised custom of the trade.
Rule II. Damage by Jettison and Sacrifice for the Common Safety Damage done to a ship and cargo, or either of them, by or in consequence of a sacrifice made for the common safety, and by water which goes down a ship's hatches opened or other opening made for the purpose of making a jettison for the common safety, shall be made good as general average.	**Rule II. Damage by Jettison and Sacrifice for the Common Safety** Damage done to a ship and cargo, or either of them, by or in consequence of a sacrifice made for the common safety, and by water which goes down a ship's hatches opened or other opening made for the purpose of making a jettison for the common safety, shall be made good as general average.	**Rule II. *Loss or Damage by Sacrifices* for the Common Safety** *Loss of or damage to the property involved in the common maritime adventure* by or in consequence of a sacrifice made for the common safety, and by water which goes down a ship's hatches opened or other opening made for the purpose of making a jettison for the common safety, shall be made good as general average.
Rule III. Extinguishing Fire on Shipboard Damage done to a ship and cargo, or either of them, by water or otherwise, including damage by beaching or scuttling a burning	**Rule III. Extinguishing Fire on Shipboard** Damage done to a ship and cargo, or either of them, by water or otherwise, including damage by beaching or scuttling a burning	**Rule III. Extinguishing Fire on Shipboard** Damage done to a ship and cargo, or either of them, by water or otherwise, including damage by beaching or scuttling a burning

	Rules of 1860, 1864 and 1877	York-Antwerp Rules (1890)	York-Antwerp Rules (1924)
		ship, in extinguishing a fire on board the ship, shall be made good as general average; except that no compensation shall be made for damage to such portions of the ship and bulk cargo, or to such separate packages of cargo, as have been on fire.	ship, in extinguishing a fire on board the ship, shall be made good as general average; except that no compensation shall be made for damage to such portions of the ship and bulk cargo, or to such separate packages of cargo, as have been on fire.
60.42	See para. 60.21, above.	**Rule IV. Cutting away Wreck** Loss or damage caused by cutting away the wreck or remains of spars, or of other things which have previously been carried away by sea-peril, shall not be made good as general average.	**Rule IV. Cutting away Wreck** Loss or damage caused by cutting away the wreck or remains of spars, or of other things which have previously been carried away by sea-peril, shall not be made good as general average.
60.43	See para. 60.22, above.	**Rule V. Voluntary Stranding** When a ship is intentionally run on shore, and the circumstances are such that if that course were not adopted, she would inevitably sink or drive on shore or on rocks, no loss or damage caused to the ship, cargo and freight, or any of them by such intentional running on shore shall be made good as general average. But in all other cases where a ship is intentionally run on shore for the common safety, the consequent loss or damage shall be allowed as general average.	**Rule V. Voluntary Stranding** When a ship is intentionally run on shore, and the circumstances are such that if that course were not adopted, she would inevitably drive on shore or on rocks, no loss or damage caused to the ship, cargo and freight, or any of them by such intentional running on shore shall be made good as general average. But in all other cases where a ship is intentionally run on shore for the common safety, the consequent loss or damage shall be allowed as general average.
60.44	See para. 60.23, above.	**Rule VI. Carrying Press of Sail. Damage to or Loss of Sails** Damage to or loss of sails and spars, or either of them, caused by forcing a ship off the ground or by driving her higher up the ground, for the common safety, shall be made good as general average; but where a ship is afloat, no loss or damage	**Rule VI. Carrying Press of Sail. Damage to or Loss of Sails** Damage to or loss of sails and spars, or either of them, caused by forcing a ship off the ground or by driving her higher up the ground, for the common safety, shall be made good as general average; but where a ship is afloat, no loss or damage

York-Antwerp Rules (1950)	York-Antwerp Rules (1974)	York-Antwerp Rules (1994)
ship, in extinguishing a fire on board the ship, shall be made good as general average; except that no compensation shall be made for damage to such portions of the ship and bulk cargo, or to such separate packages of cargo, as have been on fire.	ship, in extinguishing a fire on board the ship, shall be made good as general average; except that no compensation shall be made for damage by smoke or heat however caused.	ship, in extinguishing a fire on board the ship, shall be made good as general average; except that no compensation shall be made for damage by smoke however caused *or by heat of the fire*.
Rule IV. Cutting away Wreck Loss or damage caused by cutting away the wreck or remains of spars, or of other things which have previously been carried away by sea-peril, shall not be made good as general average.	**Rule IV. Cutting away Wreck** Loss or damage sustained by cutting away wreck or parts of the ship which have been previously carried away or are effectively lost by accident shall not be made good as general average.	**Rule IV. Cutting away Wreck** Loss or damage sustained by cutting away wreck or parts of the ship which have been previously carried away or are effectively lost by accident shall not be made good as general average.
Rule V. Voluntary Stranding When a ship is intentionally run on shore, and the circumstances are such that if that course were not adopted, she would inevitably drive on shore or on rocks, no loss or damage caused to the ship, cargo and freight, or any of them by such intentional running on shore shall be made good as general average, but loss or damage incurred in refloating such a ship shall be allowed as general average. In all other cases where a ship is intentionally run on shore for the common safety, the consequent loss or damage shall be allowed as general average.	**Rule V. Voluntary Stranding** When a ship is intentionally run on shore for the common safety, whether or not she might have been driven on shore, the consequent loss or damage shall be allowed in general average.	**Rule V. Voluntary Stranding** When a ship is intentionally run on shore for the common safety, whether or not she might have been driven on shore, the consequent loss or damage *to the property involved in the common maritime adventure* shall be allowed in general average.
Rule VI. Carrying Press of Sail. Damage to or Loss of Sails Damage to or loss of sails and spars, or either of them, caused by forcing a ship off the ground or by driving her higher up the ground, for the common safety, shall be made good as general average; but where a ship is afloat, no loss or damage	**Rule VI. Salvage Remuneration** Expenditure incurred by the parties to the adventure on account of salvage, whether under contract or otherwise, shall be allowed in general average to the extent that the salvage operations were undertaken for the purpose of preserving from peril the property	**Rule VI. Salvage Remuneration** (a) Expenditure incurred by the parties to the adventure in the nature of salvage, whether under contract or otherwise, shall be allowed in general average provided that the salvage operations were carried out for the purpose of preserving from peril the property involved

	Rules of 1860, 1864 and 1877	York-Antwerp Rules (1890)	York-Antwerp Rules (1924)
60.45		caused to the ship, cargo and freight, or any of them, by carrying a press of sail, shall be made good as general average.	caused to the ship, cargo and freight, or any of them, by carrying a press of sail, shall be made good as general average.
60.46		**Rule VII. Damage to Engines in Refloating a Ship** Damage caused to machinery and boilers of a ship, which is ashore and in a position of peril, in endeavouring to refloat, shall be allowed in general average, when shown to have arisen from an actual intention to float the ship for the common safety at the risk of such damage.	**Rule VII. Damage to Engines in Refloating a Ship** Damage caused to machinery and boilers of a ship, which is ashore and in a position of peril, in endeavouring to refloat, shall be allowed in general average, when shown to have arisen from an actual intention to float the ship for the common safety at the risk of such damage; but where a ship is afloat no loss or damage caused by working the machinery and boilers shall be made good as general average.

York-Antwerp Rules (1950)	York-Antwerp Rules (1974)	York-Antwerp Rules (1994)
caused to the ship, cargo and freight, or any of them, by carrying a press of sail, shall be made good as general average.	involved in the common maritime adventure. **York-Antwerp Rules (1974) as Amended 1990** *(a) Expenditure incurred by the parties to the adventure in the nature of salvage, whether under contract or otherwise, shall be allowed in general average provided that the salvage operations were carried out for the purpose of preserving from peril the property involved in the common maritime adventure.* *Expenditure allowed in general average shall include any salvage remuneration in which the skill and efforts of the salvors in preventing or minimizing damage to the environment such as is referred to in Art. 13 paragraph 1(b) of the International Convention on Salvage, 1989 have been taken into account.* *(b) Special compensation payable to a salvor by the shipowner under Art. 14 of the said Convention to the extent specified in paragraph 4 of that Article or under any other provisions similar in substance shall not be allowed in general average.*	in the common maritime adventure. Expenditure allowed in general average shall include any salvage remuneration in which the skill and efforts of the salvors in preventing or minimizing damage to the environment such as is referred to in Art. 13 paragraph 1(b) of the International Convention on Salvage, 1989 have been taken into account. (b) Special compensation payable to a salvor by the shipowner under Art. 14 of the said Convention to the extent specified in paragraph 4 of that Article or under any other provisions similar in substance shall not be allowed in general average.
Rule VII. Damage to Machinery and Boilers Damage caused to machinery and boilers of a ship, which is ashore and in a position of peril, in endeavouring to refloat, shall be allowed in general average when shown to have arisen from an actual intention to float the ship for the common safety at the risk of such damage; but where a ship is afloat no loss or damage caused by working the machinery and boilers, including loss or damage due to compounding of engines or such measures, shall in any circumstances	**Rule VII. Damage to Machinery and Boilers** Damage caused to any machinery and boilers of a ship which is ashore and in a position of peril, in endeavouring to refloat, shall be allowed in general average when shown to have arisen from an actual intention to float the ship for the common safety at the risk of such damage; but where a ship is afloat no loss or damage caused by working the propelling machinery and boilers shall in any circumstances be made good as general average.	**Rule VII. Damage to Machinery and Boilers** Damage caused to any machinery and boilers of a ship which is ashore and in a position of peril, in endeavouring to refloat, shall be allowed in general average when shown to have arisen from an actual intention to float the ship for the common safety at the risk of such damage; but where a ship is afloat no loss or damage caused by working the propelling machinery and boilers shall in any circumstances be made good as general average.

	Rules of 1860, 1864 and 1877	York-Antwerp Rules (1890)	York-Antwerp Rules (1924)
60.47		**Rule VIII. Expenses Lightening a Ship when Ashore, and Consequent Damage** When a ship is ashore and, in order to float her, cargo, bunker coals and ship's stores, or any of them are discharged, the extra cost of lightening, lighter hire and re-shipping (if incurred), and the loss or damage sustained thereby, shall be admitted as general average.	**Rule VIII. Expenses Lightening a Ship when Ashore, and Consequent Damage** When a ship is ashore and cargo and ship's fuel and stores or any of them are discharged as a general average act, the extra cost of lightening, lighter hire and re-shipping (if incurred), and the loss or damage sustained thereby, shall be admitted as general average.
60.48		**Rule IX. Cargo, Ship's Materials and Stores Burnt for Fuel** Cargo, ship's materials and stores, or any of them, necessarily burnt for fuel for the common safety at a time of peril, shall be admitted as general average, when and only when an ample supply of fuel had been provided; but the estimated quantity of coals that would have been consumed, calculated at the price current at the ship's last port of departure at the date of her leaving, shall be charged to the ship-owner and credited to the general average.	**Rule IX. Ship's Materials and Stores Burnt for Fuel** Ship's materials and stores, or any of them, necessarily burnt for fuel for the common safety at a time of peril, shall be admitted as general average, when and only when an ample supply of fuel had been provided; but the estimated quantity of fuel that would have been consumed, calculated at the price current at the ship's last port of departure at the date of her leaving, shall be credited to the general average.
60.49	See para. 60.24, above.	**Rule X. Expenses at Port of Refuge, etc.** (a) When a ship shall have entered a port or place of refuge, or shall have returned to her port or place of loading, in consequence of accident, sacrifice, or other extraordinary circumstances, which render that necessary for the common safety, the expenses of entering such port or place shall be admitted as general average; and when she shall have sailed thence with her original	**Rule X. Expenses at Port of Refuge, etc.** (a) When a ship shall have entered a port or place of refuge, or shall have returned to her port or place of loading, in consequence of accident, sacrifice or other extraordinary circumstances, which render that necessary for the common safety, the expenses of entering such port or place shall be admitted as general average; and when she shall have sailed thence with her original

York-Antwerp Rules (1950)	York-Antwerp Rules (1974)	York-Antwerp Rules (1994)
be made good as general average.		
Rule VIII. Expenses Lightening a Ship when Ashore, and Consequent Damage When a ship is ashore and cargo and ship's fuel and stores or any of them are discharged as a general average act, the extra cost of lightening, lighter hire and re-shipping (if incurred), and the loss or damage sustained thereby, shall be admitted as general average.	**Rule VIII. Expenses Lightening a Ship when Ashore, and Consequent Damage** When a ship is ashore and cargo and ship's fuel and stores or any of them are discharged as a general average act, the extra cost of lightening, lighter hire and re-shipping (if incurred), and the loss or damage sustained thereby, shall be admitted as general average.	**Rule VIII. Expenses Lightening a Ship when Ashore, and Consequent Damage** When a ship is ashore and cargo and ship's fuel and stores or any of them are discharged as a general average act, the extra cost of lightening, lighter hire and re-shipping (if incurred), and *any* loss or damage *to the property involved in the common maritime adventure in consequence thereof,* shall be admitted as general average.
Rule IX. Ship's Materials and Stores Burnt for Fuel Ship's materials and stores, or any of them, necessarily burnt for fuel for the common safety at a time of peril, shall be admitted as general average, when and only when an ample supply of fuel had been provided; but the estimated quantity of fuel that would have been consumed, calculated at the price current at the ship's last port of departure at the date of her leaving, shall be credited to the general average.	**Rule IX. Ship's Materials and Stores Burnt for Fuel** Ship's materials and stores, or any of them, necessarily burnt for fuel for the common safety at a time of peril, shall be admitted as general average, when and only when an ample supply of fuel had been provided; but the estimated quantity of fuel that would have been consumed, calculated at the price current at the ship's last port of departure at the date of her leaving, shall be credited to the general average.	**Rule IX. *Cargo,* Ship's Materials and Stores Burnt for Fuel** *Cargo,* ship's materials and stores, or any of them, necessarily *used* for fuel for the common safety at a time of peril, shall be admitted as general average, *but when such an allowance is made for the cost of ship's materials and stores the general average shall be credited with the estimated cost of the fuel which would otherwise have been consumed in prosecuting the intended voyage.*
Rule X. Expenses at Port of Refuge, etc. (a) When a ship shall have entered a port or place of refuge, or shall have returned to her port or place of loading, in consequence of accident, sacrifice or other extraordinary circumstances, which render that necessary for the common safety, the expenses of entering such port or place shall be admitted as general average; and when she shall have sailed thence with her original	**Rule X. Expenses at Port of Refuge, etc.** (a) When a ship shall have entered a port or place of refuge, or shall have returned to her port or place of loading, in consequence of accident, sacrifice or other extraordinary circumstances, which render that necessary for the common safety, the expenses of entering such port or place shall be admitted as general average; and when she shall have sailed thence with her original	**Rule X. Expenses at Port of Refuge, etc.** (a) When a ship shall have entered a port or place of refuge, or shall have returned to her port or place of loading, in consequence of accident, sacrifice or other extraordinary circumstances, which render that necessary for the common safety, the expenses of entering such port or place shall be admitted as general average; and when she shall have sailed thence with her original

	Rules of 1860, 1864 and 1877	York-Antwerp Rules (1890)	York-Antwerp Rules (1924)
		cargo, or a part of it, the corresponding expenses of leaving such port or place consequent upon such entry or return, shall likewise be admitted as general average.	cargo, or a part of it, the corresponding expenses of leaving such port or place consequent upon such entry or return shall likewise be admitted as general average.
60.50		(b) The cost of discharging cargo from a ship, whether at a port or place of loading, call or refuge, shall be admitted as general average, when the discharge was necessary for the common safety or to enable damage to the ship, caused by sacrifice or accident during the voyage, to be repaired, if the repairs were necessary for the safe prosecution of the voyage.	(b) The cost of handling on board or discharging cargo, fuel or stores, whether at a port or place of loading, call or refuge, shall be admitted as general average when the handling or discharge was necessary for the common safety or to enable damage to the ship caused by sacrifice or accident to be repaired, if the repairs were necessary for the safe prosecution of the voyage.

York-Antwerp Rules (1950)	**York-Antwerp Rules (1974)**	**York-Antwerp Rules (1994)**
cargo, or a part of it, the corresponding expenses of leaving such port or place consequent upon such entry or return shall likewise be admitted as general average. When a ship is at any port or place of refuge and is necessarily removed to another port or place because repairs cannot be carried out in the first port or place, the provisions of this Rule shall be applied to the second port or place as if it were a port or place of refuge. The provisions of Rule XI shall be applied to the prolongation of the voyage occasioned by such removal.	cargo, or a part of it, the corresponding expenses of leaving such port or place consequent upon such entry or return shall likewise be admitted as general average. When a ship is at any port or place of refuge and is necessarily removed to another port or place because repairs cannot be carried out in the first port or place, the provisions of this Rule shall be applied to the second port or place as if it were a port or place of refuge and the cost of such removal including temporary repairs and towage shall be admitted as general average. The provisions of Rule XI shall be applied to the prolongation of the voyage occasioned by such removal.	cargo, or a part of it, the corresponding expenses of leaving such port or place consequent upon such entry or return shall likewise be admitted as general average. When a ship is at any port or place of refuge and is necessarily removed to another port or place because repairs cannot be carried out in the first port or place, the provisions of this Rule shall be applied to the second port or place as if it were a port or place of refuge and the cost of such removal including temporary repairs and towage shall be admitted as general average. The provisions of Rule XI shall be applied to the prolongation of the voyage occasioned by such removal.
(b) The cost of handling on board or discharging cargo, fuel or stores whether at a port or place of loading, call or refuge, shall be admitted as general average when the handling or discharge was necessary for the common safety or to enable damage to the ship caused by sacrifice or accident to be repaired, if the repairs were necessary for the safe prosecution of the voyage.	(b) The cost of handling on board or discharging cargo, fuel or stores whether at a port or place of loading, call or refuge, shall be admitted as general average, when the handling or discharge was necessary for the common safety or to enable damage to the ship caused by sacrifice or accident to be repaired, if the repairs were necessary for the safe prosecution of the voyage, except in cases where the damage to the ship is discovered at a port or place of loading or call without any accident or other extraordinary circumstances connected with such damage having taken place during the voyage. The cost of handling on board or discharging cargo, fuel or stores shall not be admissible as general average when incurred solely for the purpose of restowage due to shifting during the voyage, unless such restowage is necessary for the common safety.	(b) The cost of handling on board or discharging cargo, fuel or stores whether at a port or place of loading, call or refuge, shall be admitted as general average, when the handling or discharge was necessary for the common safety or to enable damage to the ship caused by sacrifice or accident to be repaired, if the repairs were necessary for the safe prosecution of the voyage, except in cases where the damage to the ship is discovered at a port or place of loading or call without any accident or other extraordinary circumstances connected with such damage having taken place during the voyage. The cost of handling on board or discharging cargo, fuel or stores shall not be admissible as general average when incurred solely for the purpose of restowage due to shifting during the voyage, unless such restowage is necessary for the common safety.

	Rules of 1860, 1864 and 1877	York-Antwerp Rules (1890)	York-Antwerp Rules (1924)
60.51	See para. 60.24, above.	(c) Whenever the cost of discharging cargo from a ship is admissible as general average, the cost of reloading and storing such cargo on board the said ship, together with all storage charges on such cargo, shall likewise be so admitted. But when the ship is condemned or does not proceed on her original voyage, no storage expenses incurred after the date of the ship's condemnation or of the abandonment of the voyage shall be admitted as general average.	(c) Whenever the cost of handling or discharging cargo, fuel or stores is admissible as general average, the cost of reloading and stowing such cargo, fuel or stores on board the ship, together with all storage charges (including fire insurance, if incurred) on such cargo, fuel or stores, shall likewise be so admitted. But when the ship is condemned or does not proceed on her original voyage, no storage expenses incurred after the date of the ship's condemnation or of the abandonment of the voyage shall be admitted as general average. In the event of the condemnation of the ship or the abandonment of the voyage before completion of discharge of cargo, storage expenses, as above, shall be admitted as general average up to date of completion of discharge.
60.52		(d) If a ship under average be in a port or place at which it is practicable to repair her, so as to enable her to carry on the whole cargo, and if, in order to save expenses, either she is towed thence to some other port or place of repair or to her destination, or the cargo or a portion of it is transhipped by another ship, or otherwise forwarded, then the extra cost of such towage, transhipment, and forwarding, or any of them (up to the amount of the extra expense saved) shall be payable by the several parties to the adventure in proportion to the extraordinary expense saved.	(d) If a ship under average be in a port or place at which it is practicable to repair her, so as to enable her to carry on the whole cargo, and if, in order to save expenses, either she is towed thence to some other port or place of repair or to her destination, or the cargo or a portion of it is transhipped by another ship, or otherwise forwarded, then the extra cost of such towage, transhipment and forwarding, or any of them (up to the amount of the extra expense saved) shall be payable by the several parties to the adventure in proportion to the extraordinary expense saved.
60.53		**Rule XI. Wages and Maintenance of Crew in Port of Refuge, etc.**	**Rule XI. Wages and Maintenance of Crew in Port of Refuge, etc.** (For corresponding provision, see Rule XX, *infra.*)

York-Antwerp Rules (1950)	York-Antwerp Rules (1974)	York-Antwerp Rules (1994)
(c) Whenever the cost of handling or discharging cargo, fuel or stores is admissible as general average, the cost of reloading and stowing such cargo, fuel or stores on board the ship, together with all storage charges (including insurance, if reasonably incurred) on such cargo, fuel or stores, shall likewise be so admitted. But when the ship is condemned or does not proceed on her original voyage, no storage expenses incurred after the date of the ship's condemnation or of the abandonment of the voyage shall be admitted as general average. In the event of the condemnation of the ship or the abandonment of the voyage before completion of discharge of cargo, storage expenses, as above, shall be admitted as general average up to the date of completion of discharge. (d) If a ship under average be in a port or place at which it is practicable to repair her, so as to enable her to carry on the whole cargo, and if, in order to save expense, either she is towed thence to some other port or place of repair or to her destination, or the cargo or a portion of it is transhipped by another ship, or otherwise forwarded, then the extra cost of such towage, transhipment and forwarding, or any of them (up to the amount of the extra expense saved) shall be payable by the several parties to the adventure in proportion to the extraordinary expense saved.	(c) Whenever the cost of handling or discharging cargo, fuel or stores is admissible as general average, the costs of storage, including insurance if reasonably incurred, reloading and stowing of such cargo, fuel or stores shall likewise be admitted as general average. But when the ship is condemned or does not proceed on her original voyage, storage expenses shall be admitted as general average only up to the date of the ship's condemnation or of the abandonment of the voyage or up to the date of completion of discharge of cargo if the condemnation or abandonment takes place before that date.	(c) Whenever the cost of handling or discharging cargo, fuel or stores is admissible as general average, the costs of storage, including insurance if reasonably incurred, reloading and stowing of such cargo, fuel or stores shall likewise be admitted as general average. *The provisions of Rule XI shall be applied to the extra period of detention occasioned by such reloading or restowing.* But when the ship is condemned or does not proceed on her original voyage, storage expenses shall be admitted as general average only up to the date of the ship's condemnation or of the abandonment of the voyage or up to the date of completion of discharge of cargo if the condemnation or abandonment takes place before that date.
Rule XI. Wages and Maintenance of Crew and other Expenses bearing up for and in a Port of Refuge, etc. (a) Wages and maintenance of master, officers	**Rule XI. Wages and Maintenance of Crew and other Expenses bearing up for and in a Port of Refuge, etc.** (a) Wages and maintenance of master, officers	**Rule XI. Wages and Maintenance of Crew and other Expenses bearing up for and in a Port of Refuge, etc.** (a) Wages and maintenance of master, officers

	Rules of 1860, 1864 and 1877	York-Antwerp Rules (1890)	York-Antwerp Rules (1924)
60.54	See para. 60.25, above.	When a ship shall have entered or been detained in any port or place under the circumstances, or for the purposes of the repairs, mentioned in Rule X, the wages, payable to the master, officers and crew together with the cost of maintenance of the same, during the extra period of detention in such port or place until the ship shall or should have been made ready to proceed upon her voyage, shall be admitted as general average. But when the ship is condemned or does not proceed on her original voyage, the wages and maintenance of the master, officers and crew, incurred after the date of the ship's condemnation or of the abandonment of the voyage, shall not be admitted as general average.	When a ship shall have entered or been detained in any port or place under the circumstances, or for the purposes of repairs mentioned in Rule X, the wages payable to the master, officers and crew, together with the cost of maintenance of the same, during the extra period of detention in such port or place until the ship shall or should have been made ready to proceed upon her voyage, shall be admitted as general average. But when the ship is condemned or does not proceed on her original voyage, the wages and maintenance of the master, officers and crew, incurred after the date of the ship's condemnation or of the abandonment of the voyage, shall not be admitted as general average. In the event of the condemnation of the ship or the abandonment of the voyage before completion of discharge of cargo, wages and maintenance of crew, as above, shall be admitted as general average up to the date of completion of discharge.

York-Antwerp Rules (1950)	York-Antwerp Rules (1974)	York-Antwerp Rules (1994)
and crew reasonably incurred and fuel and stores consumed during the prolongation of the voyage occasioned by a ship entering a port or place of refuge or returning to her port or place of loading shall be admitted as general average when the expenses of entering such port or place are allowable in general average in accordance with Rule X (a). (b) When a ship shall have entered or been detained in any port or place in consequence of accident, sacrifice or other extraordinary circumstances which render that necessary for the common safety, or to enable damage to the ship caused by sacrifice or accident to be repaired, if the repairs were necessary for the safe prosecution of the voyage, the wages and maintenance of the master, officers and crew reasonably incurred during the extra period of detention in such port or place until the ship shall or should have been made ready to proceed upon her voyage, shall be admitted in general average. When the ship is condemned or does not proceed on her original voyage, the extra period of detention shall be deemed not to extend beyond the date of the ship's condemnation or of the abandonment of the voyage or, if discharge of cargo is not then completed, beyond the date of completion of discharge.	and crew reasonably incurred and fuel and stores consumed during the prolongation of the voyage occasioned by a ship entering a port or place of refuge or returning to her port or place of loading shall be admitted as general average when the expenses of entering such port or place are allowable in general average in accordance with Rule X (a). (b) When a ship shall have entered or been detained in any port or place in consequence of accident, sacrifice or other extraordinary circumstances which render that necessary for the common safety, or to enable damage to the ship caused by sacrifice or accident to be repaired, if the repairs were necessary for the safe prosecution of the voyage, the wages and maintenance of the master, officers and crew reasonably incurred during the extra period of detention in such port or place until the ship shall or should have been made ready to proceed upon her voyage, shall be admitted in general average. Provided that when damage to the ship is discovered at a port or place of loading or call without any accident or other extraordinary circumstance connected with such damage having taken place during the voyage, then the wages and maintenance of master, officers and crew and fuel and stores consumed during the extra detention for repairs to damages so discovered shall not be admissible as general average, even if the repairs are necessary for the safe prosecution of the voyage. When the ship is condemned or does not proceed on her original voyage,	and crew reasonably incurred and fuel and stores consumed during the prolongation of the voyage occasioned by a ship entering a port or place of refuge or returning to her port or place of loading shall be admitted as general average when the expenses of entering such port or place are allowable in general average in accordance with Rule X (a). (b) When a ship shall have entered or been detained in any port or place in consequence of accident, sacrifice or other extraordinary circumstances which render that necessary for the common safety, or to enable damage to the ship caused by sacrifice or accident to be repaired, if the repairs were necessary for the safe prosecution of the voyage, the wages and maintenance of the master, officers and crew reasonably incurred during the extra period of detention in such port or place until the ship shall or should have been made ready to proceed upon her voyage, shall be admitted in general average. Fuel and stores consumed during the extra period of detention shall be admitted as general average, except such fuel and stores as are consumed in effecting repairs not allowable in general average. Port charges incurred during the extra period of detention shall likewise be admitted as general average except such charges as are incurred solely by reason of repairs not allowable in general average. Provided that when damage to the ship is discovered at a port or place of loading or call without any accident or other extraordinary circumstance con-

Rules of 1860, 1864 and 1877	York-Antwerp Rules (1890)	York-Antwerp Rules (1924)

60.55

60.56

York-Antwerp Rules (1950)	York-Antwerp Rules (1974)	York-Antwerp Rules (1994)
	wages and maintenance of the master, officers and crew and fuel and stores consumed shall be admitted as general average only up to the date of the ship's condemnation or of the abandonment of the voyage or up to the date of completion of discharge of cargo if the condemnation or abandonment takes place before that date.	nected with such damage having taken place during the voyage, then the wages and maintenance of master, officers and crew and fuel and stores consumed *and port charges incurred* during the extra detention for repairs to damages so discovered shall not be admissible as general average, even if the repairs are necessary for the safe prosecution of the voyage.
Fuel and stores consumed during the extra period of detention shall be admitted as general average, except such fuel and stores as are consumed in effecting repairs not allowable in general average. Port charges incurred during the extra period of detention shall likewise be admitted as general average except such charges as are incurred solely by reason of repairs not allowable in general average.	Fuel and stores consumed during the extra period of detention shall be admitted as general average, except such fuel and stores as are consumed in effecting repairs not allowable in general average. Port charges incurred during the extra period of detention shall likewise be admitted as general average except such charges as are incurred solely by reason of repairs not allowable in general average.	When the ship is condemned or does not proceed on her original voyage, *the* wages and maintenance of the master, officers and crew and fuel and stores consumed *and port charges* shall be admitted as general average only up to the date of the ship's condemnation or of the abandonment of the voyage or up to the date of completion of discharge of cargo if the condemnation or abandonment takes place before that date.
(c) For the purpose of this and the other Rules wages shall include all payments made to or for the benefit of the master, officers and crew, whether such payments be imposed by law upon the shipowners or be made under the terms or articles of employment.	(c) For the purpose of this and the other Rules wages shall include all payments made to or for the benefit of the master, officers and crew, whether such payments be imposed by law upon the shipowners or be made under the terms or articles of employment.	(c) For the purpose of this and the other Rules wages shall include all payments made to or for the benefit of the master, officers and crew, whether such payments be imposed by law upon the shipowners or be made under the terms or articles of employment.
(d) When overtime is paid to the master, officers or crew for maintenance of the ship or repairs, the cost of which is not allowable in general average, such overtime shall be allowed in general average only up to the saving in expense which would have been incurred and admitted as general average, had such overtime not been incurred.	(d) When overtime is paid to the master, officers or crew for maintenance of the ship or repairs, the cost of which is not allowable in general average, such overtime shall be allowed in general average only up to the saving in expense which would have been incurred and admitted as general average, had such overtime not been incurred.	(d) *The cost of measures undertaken to prevent or minimise damage to the environment shall be allowed in general average when incurred in any or all of the following circumstances:* *(i) as part of an operation performed for the common safety which, had it been undertaken by a party outside the common maritime adventure, would have entitled such party to a salvage reward;* *(ii) as a condition of entry into or departure from any port or place in*

	Rules of 1860, 1864 and 1877	York-Antwerp Rules (1890)	York-Antwerp Rules (1924)
60.57	See para. 60.26, above.	**Rule XII. Damage to Cargo in Discharging, etc.** Damage done to or loss of cargo necessarily caused in the act of discharging, storing, reloading and stowing, shall be made good as general average when and only when the cost of those measures respectively is admitted as general average.	**Rule XII. Damage to Cargo in Discharging, etc.** Damage to or loss of cargo, fuel or stores caused in the act of handling, discharging, storing, reloading and stowing shall be made good as general average, when and only when the cost of those measures respectively is admitted as general average.
60.58		**Rule XIII. Deductions from Cost of Repairs** In adjusting claims for general average, repairs to be allowed in general average shall be subject to the following deductions in respect of "new for old", viz.: In the case of iron or steel ships, from date of original register to the date of accident: (*Reference is requested to any of the 7th/11th editions of this work for precise details of the deductions made.*)	**Rule XIII. Deductions from Cost of Repairs** In adjusting claims for general average, repairs to be allowed in general average shall be subject to the following deductions in respect of "new for old", viz.: In the case of iron or steel ships, from date of original register to the date of accident: (*Reference is requested to any of the 7th/11th editions of this work for precise details of the deductions made.*)

York-Antwerp Rules (1950)	York-Antwerp Rules (1974)	York-Antwerp Rules (1994)
		the circumstances prescribed in Rule X (a); *(iii) as a condition of remaining at any port or place in the circumstances prescribed in Rule X (a), provided that when there is an actual escape or release of pollutant substances the cost of any additional measures required on that account to prevent or minimise pollution or environmental damage shall not be allowed as general average;* *(iv) necessarily in connection with the discharging, storing or reloading of cargo whenever the cost of those operations is admissible as general average.*
Rule XII. Damage to Cargo in Discharging, etc. Damage to or loss of cargo, fuel or stores caused in the act of handling, discharging, storing, reloading and stowing shall be made good as general average, when and only when the cost of those measures respectively is admitted as general average.	**Rule XII. Damage to Cargo in Discharging, etc.** Damage to or loss of cargo, fuel or stores caused in the act of handling, discharging, storing, reloading and stowing shall be made good as general average, when and only when the cost of those measures respectively is admitted as general average.	**Rule XII. Damage to Cargo in Discharging, etc.** Damage to or loss of cargo, fuel or stores *sustained in consequence* of *their* handling, discharging, storing, reloading and stowing shall be made good as general average, when and only when the cost of those measures respectively is admitted as general average.
Rule XIII. Deductions from Cost of Repairs In adjusting claims for general average, repairs to be allowed in general average shall be subject to deductions in respect of "new for old" according to the following rules, where old material or parts are replaced by new. The deductions to be regulated by the age of the ship from date of original register to the date of accident, except for provisions and stores, insulation, life- and similar boats, gyro compass equipment, wireless, direction finding, echo sounding and similar appar-	**Rule XIII. Deductions from Cost of Repairs** Repairs to be allowed in general average shall not be subject to deductions in respect of "new for old" where old material or parts are replaced by new unless the ship is over fifteen years old in which case there shall be a deduction of one third. The deductions shall be regulated by the age of the ship from the 31st December of the year of completion of construction to the date of the general average act, except for insulation, life and similar boats, communications and navigational apparatus and	**Rule XIII. Deductions from Cost of Repairs** Repairs to be allowed in general average shall not be subject to deductions in respect of "new for old" where old material or parts are replaced by new unless the ship is over fifteen years old in which case there shall be a deduction of one third. The deductions shall be regulated by the age of the ship from the 31st December of the year of completion of construction to the date of the general average act, except for insulation, life and similar boats, communications and navigational apparatus and

	Rules of 1860, 1864 and 1877	York-Antwerp Rules (1890)	York-Antwerp Rules (1924)
60.59		**Rule XIV. Temporary Repairs** No deductions "new for old" shall be made from the cost of temporary repairs of damage allowable as general average.	**Rule XIV. Temporary Repairs** Where temporary repairs are effected to a ship at a port of loading, call or refuge, for the common safety, or of damage caused by general average sacrifice, the cost of such repairs shall be admitted as general average; but where temporary repairs of accidental damage are effected merely to enable the adventure to be completed, the cost of such repairs shall be admitted as general average only up to the saving in expense which would have been incurred and allowed in general average had such repairs not been effected there. No deductions "new for old" shall be made from the cost of temporary repairs allowable as general average.

York-Antwerp Rules (1950)	York-Antwerp Rules (1974)	York-Antwerp Rules (1994)
atus, machinery and boilers for which the deductions shall be regulated by the age of the particular parts to which they apply. No deduction to be made in respect of provisions, stores and gear which have not been in use. The deductions shall be made from the cost of new material or parts, including labour and establishment charges, but excluding cost of opening up. Drydock and slipway dues and costs of shifting the ship shall be allowed in full. No cleaning and painting of bottom to be allowed, if the bottom has not been painted within six months previous to the date of the accident. *(Reference is requested to any of the 7th/11th editions of this work for precise details of the deductions made.)*	equipment, machinery and boilers for which the deductions shall be regulated by the age of the particular parts to which they apply. The deductions shall be made only from the cost of the new material or parts when finished and ready to be installed in the ship. No deduction shall be made in respect of provisions, stores, anchors and chain cables. Drydock and slipway dues and costs of shifting the ship shall be allowed in full. The costs of cleaning, painting or coating of bottom shall not be allowed in general average unless the bottom has been painted or coated within the twelve months preceding the date of the general average act in which case one half of such costs shall be allowed.	equipment, machinery and boilers for which the deductions shall be regulated by the age of the particular parts to which they apply. The deductions shall be made only from the cost of the new material or parts when finished and ready to be installed in the ship. No deduction shall be made in respect of provisions, stores, anchors and chain cables. Drydock and slipway dues and costs of shifting the ship shall be allowed in full. The costs of cleaning, painting or coating of bottom shall not be allowed in general average unless the bottom has been painted or coated within the twelve months preceding the date of the general average act in which case one half of such costs shall be allowed.
Rule XIV. Temporary Repairs Where temporary repairs are effected to a ship at a port of loading, call or refuge, for the common safety, or of damage caused by general average sacrifice, the cost of such repairs shall be admitted as general average. Where temporary repairs of accidental damage are effected merely to enable the adventure to be completed, the cost of such repairs shall be admitted as general average without regard to the saving, if any, to other interests, but only up to the saving in expense which would have been incurred and allowed in general average if such repairs had not been effected there. No deductions "new for old" shall be made from the cost of temporary repairs	**Rule XIV. Temporary Repairs** Where temporary repairs are effected to a ship at a port of loading, call or refuge, for the common safety, or of damage caused by general average sacrifice, the cost of such repairs shall be admitted as general average. Where temporary repairs of accidental damage are effected in order to enable the adventure to be completed, the cost of such repairs shall be admitted as general average without regard to the saving, if any, to other interests, but only up to the saving in expense which would have been incurred and allowed in general average if such repairs had not been effected there. No deductions "new for old" shall be made from the	**Rule XIV. Temporary Repairs** Where temporary repairs are effected to a ship at a port of loading, call or refuge, for the common safety, or of damage caused by general average sacrifice, the cost of such repairs shall be admitted as general average. Where temporary repairs of accidental damage are effected in order to enable the adventure to be completed, the cost of such repairs shall be admitted as general average without regard to the saving, if any, to other interests, but only up to the saving in expense which would have been incurred and allowed in general average if such repairs had not been effected there. No deductions "new for old" shall be made from the

	Rules of 1860, 1864 and 1877	York-Antwerp Rules (1890)	York-Antwerp Rules (1924)
60.60	See para. 60.28, above.	**Rule XV. Loss of Freight** Loss of freight arising from damage to or loss of cargo shall be made good as general average, either when caused by a general average act, or when the damage to or loss of cargo is so made good.	**Rule XV. Loss of Freight** Loss of freight arising from damage to or loss of cargo shall be made good as general average, either when caused by a general average act, or when the damage to or loss of cargo is so made good. Deduction shall be made from the amount of gross freight lost, of the charges which the owner thereof would have incurred to earn such freight, but has, in consequence of the sacrifice, not incurred.
60.61	See para. 60.29, above.	**Rule XVI. Amount to be made good for Cargo Lost or Damaged by Sacrifice** The amount to be made good as general average for damage or loss of goods sacrificed shall be the loss which the owner of the goods has sustained thereby, based on the market values at the date of the arrival of the vessel or at the termination of the adventure.	**Rule XVI. Amount to be made good for Cargo Lost or Damaged by Sacrifice** The amount to be made good as general average for damage to or loss of goods sacrificed shall be the loss which the owner of the goods has sustained thereby, based on the market values at the date of the arrival of the vessel or at the termination of the adventure where this ends at a place other than the original destination. Where goods so damaged are sold after arrival, the loss to be made good in general average shall be calculated by applying to the sound value on the date of arrival of the vessel the percentage of loss resulting from a comparison of the proceeds with the sound value on date of sale.
60.62	See para. 60.27, above.	**Rule XVII. Contributory Values** The contribution to a general average shall be	**Rule XVII. Contributory Values** The contribution to a general average shall be

York-Antwerp Rules (1950)	York-Antwerp Rules (1974)	York-Antwerp Rules (1994)
allowable as general average.	cost of temporary repairs allowable as general average.	cost of temporary repairs allowable as general average.
Rule XV. Loss of Freight Loss of freight arising from damage to or loss of cargo shall be made good as general average, either when caused by a general average act, or when the damage to or loss of cargo is so made good. Deduction shall be made from the amount of gross freight lost, of the charges which the owner thereof would have incurred to earn such freight, but has, in consequence of the sacrifice, not incurred.	**Rule XV. Loss of Freight** Loss of freight arising from damage to or loss of cargo shall be made good as general average, either when caused by a general average act, or when the damage to or loss of cargo is so made good. Deduction shall be made from the amount of gross freight lost, of the charges which the owner thereof would have incurred to earn such freight, but has, in consequence of the sacrifice, not incurred.	**Rule XV. Loss of Freight** Loss of freight arising from damage to or loss of cargo shall be made good as general average, either when caused by a general average act, or when the damage to or loss of cargo is so made good. Deduction shall be made from the amount of gross freight lost, of the charges which the owner thereof would have incurred to earn such freight, but has, in consequence of the sacrifice, not incurred.
Rule XVI. Amount to be made good for Cargo Lost or Damaged by Sacrifice The amount to be made good as general average for damage to or loss of goods sacrificed shall be the loss which the owner of the goods has sustained thereby, based on the market values at the last day of discharge of the vessel or at the termination of the adventure where this ends at a place other than the original destination. Where goods so damaged are sold and the amount of the damage has not been otherwise agreed, the loss to be made good in general average shall be the difference between the net proceeds of sale and the net sound value at the last day of discharge of the vessel or at the termination of the adventure where this ends at a place other than the original destination.	**Rule XVI. Amount to be made good for Cargo Lost or Damaged by Sacrifice** The amount to be made good as general average for damage to or loss of cargo sacrificed shall be the loss which has been sustained thereby, based on the value at the time of discharge, ascertained from the commercial invoice rendered to the receiver or if there is no such invoice from the shipped value. The value at the time of discharge shall include the cost of insurance and freight except in so far as such freight is at the risk of interests other than the cargo. Where cargo so damaged is sold and the amount of the damage has not been otherwise agreed, the loss to be made good in general average shall be the difference between the net proceeds of sale and the net sound value as computed in the first paragraph of this Rule.	**Rule XVI. Amount to be made good for Cargo Lost or Damaged by Sacrifice** The amount to be made good as general average for damage to or loss of cargo sacrificed shall be the loss which has been sustained thereby, based on the value at the time of discharge, ascertained from the commercial invoice rendered to the receiver or if there is no such invoice from the shipped value. The value at the time of discharge shall include the cost of insurance and freight except in so far as such freight is at the risk of interests other than the cargo. Where cargo so damaged is sold and the amount of the damage has not been otherwise agreed, the loss to be made good in general average shall be the difference between the net proceeds of sale and the net sound value as computed in the first paragraph of this Rule.
Rule XVII. Contributory Values The contribution to a general average shall be	**Rule XVII. Contributory Values** The contribution to a general average shall be	**Rule XVII. Contributory Values** The contribution to a general average shall be

Rules of 1860, 1864 and 1877	York-Antwerp Rules (1890)	York-Antwerp Rules (1924)
	made upon the actual values of the property at the termination of the adventure, to which shall be added the amount made good as general average for property sacrificed; deduction being made from the shipowner's freight and passage-money at risk, of such port charges and crew's wages as would not have been incurred had the ship and cargo been totally lost at the date of the general average act or sacrifice, and have not been allowed as general average; deduction being also made from the value of the property of all charges incurred in respect thereof subsequently to the general average act, except such charges as are allowed in general average. Passengers' luggage and personal effects, not shipped under bill of lading, shall not contribute in general average.	made upon the actual net values of the property at the termination of the adventure, to which values shall be added the amount made good as general average for property sacrificed, if not already included, deduction being made from the shipowner's freight and passage-money at risk, of such charges and crew's wages as would not have been incurred in earning the freight had the ship and cargo been totally lost at the date of the general average act and have not been allowed as general average; deduction being also made from the value of the property, of all charges incurred in respect thereof subsequently to the general average act, except such charges as are allowed in general average. Passengers' luggage and personal effects not shipped under bill of lading shall not contribute in general average.

York-Antwerp Rules (1950)	York-Antwerp Rules (1974)	York-Antwerp Rules (1994)
made upon the actual net values of the property at the termination of the adventure, to which values shall be added the amount made good as general average for property sacrificed, if not already included, deduction being made from the shipowner's freight and passage money at risk, of such charges and crew's wages as would not have been incurred in earning the freight had the ship and cargo been totally lost at the date of the general average act and have not been allowed as general average; deductions being also made from the value of the property of all charges incurred in respect thereof subsequently to the general average act, except such charges as are allowed in general average. Passengers' luggage and personal effects not shipped under bill of lading shall not contribute in general average.	made upon the actual net values of the property at the termination of the adventure except that the value of cargo shall be the value at the time of discharge, ascertained from the commercial invoice rendered to the receiver or if there is no such invoice from the shipped value. The value of the cargo shall include the cost of insurance and freight unless and insofar as such freight is at the risk of interests other than the cargo, deducting therefrom any loss or damage suffered by the cargo prior to or at the time of discharge. The value of the ship shall be assessed without taking into account the beneficial or detrimental effect of any demise or time charterparty to which the ship may be committed. To these values shall be added the amount made good as general average for property sacrificed, if not already included, deduction being made from the freight and passage money at risk of such charges and crew's wages as would not have been incurred in earning the freight had the ship and cargo been totally lost at the date of the general average act and have not been allowed as general average; deduction being also made from the value of the property of all extra charges incurred in respect thereof subsequently to the general average act, except such charges as are allowed in general average. Where cargo is sold short of destination, however, it shall contribute upon the actual net proceeds of sale, with the addition of any amount made good as general average. Passengers' luggage and personal effects not shipped under bill of lading shall not	made upon the actual net values of the property at the termination of the adventure except that the value of cargo shall be the value at the time of discharge, ascertained from the commercial invoice rendered to the receiver or if there is no such invoice from the shipped value. The value of the cargo shall include the cost of insurance and freight unless and insofar as such freight is at the risk of interests other than the cargo, deducting therefrom any loss or damage suffered by the cargo prior to or at the time of discharge. The value of the ship shall be assessed without taking into account the beneficial or detrimental effect of any demise or time charterparty to which the ship may be committed. To these values shall be added the amount made good as general average for property sacrificed, if not already included, deduction being made from the freight and passage money at risk of such charges and crew's wages as would not have been incurred in earning the freight had the ship and cargo been totally lost at the date of the general average act and have not been allowed as general average; deduction being also made from the value of the property of all extra charges incurred in respect thereof subsequently to the general average act, except such charges as are allowed in general average *or fall upon the ship by virtue of an award for special compensation under Art. 14 of the International Convention on Salvage, 1989 or under any other provision similar in substance.* *In the circumstances envisaged in the third paragraph of Rule G, the cargo and*

	Rules of 1860, 1864 and 1877	York-Antwerp Rules (1890)	York-Antwerp Rules (1924)
60.63		**Rule XVIII. Adjustment** Except as provided in the foregoing rules, the adjustment shall be drawn up in accordance with the law and practice that would have governed the adjustment had the contract of affreightment not contained a clause to pay general average according to these rules.	(No corresponding rule.)
60.64			**Rule XVIII. Damage to Ship** The amount to be allowed as general average for damage or loss to the ship, her machinery and/or gear when repaired or replaced shall be the actual reasonable cost of repairing or replacing such damage or loss, deductions being made as above (Rule XIII) when old material is replaced by new. When not repaired, the reasonable depreciation shall be allowed, not exceeding the estimated cost of repairs. Where there is an actual or constructive total loss of the ship the amount to be allowed as general average for damage or loss to the ship caused by a general

York-Antwerp Rules (1950)	York-Antwerp Rules (1974)	York-Antwerp Rules (1994)
	contribute in general average.	*other property shall contribute on the basis of its value upon delivery at original destination unless sold or otherwise disposed of short of that destination, and the ship shall contribute upon its actual net value at the time of completion of discharge of cargo.* Where cargo is sold short of destination, however, it shall contribute upon the actual net proceeds of sale, with the addition of any amount made good as general average. *Mails, passengers' luggage, personal effects and accompanied private motor vehicles shall not contribute in general average.*
(No corresponding rule.)	(No corresponding rule.)	(No corresponding rule.)
Rule XVIII. Damage to Ship The amount to be allowed as general average for damage or loss to the ship, her machinery and/or gear when repaired or replaced shall be the actual reasonable cost of repairing or replacing such damage or loss, subject to deduction in accordance with Rule XIII. When not repaired, the reasonable depreciation shall be allowed, not exceeding the estimated cost of repairs. Where there is an actual or constructive total loss of the ship the amount to be allowed as general average for damage or loss to the ship caused by a general average act shall be the esti-	**Rule XVIII. Damage to Ship** The amount to be allowed as general average for damage or loss to the ship, her machinery and/or gear caused by a general average act shall be as follows: (a) When repaired or replaced, The actual reasonable cost of repairing or replacing such damage or loss, subject to deductions in accordance with Rule XIII; (b) When not repaired or replaced, The reasonable depreciation arising from such damage or loss, but not exceeding the estimated cost of repairs. But where the ship is an actual total loss or when the cost of repairs	**Rule XVIII. Damage to Ship** The amount to be allowed as general average for damage or loss to the ship, her machinery and/or gear caused by a general average act shall be as follows: (a) When repaired or replaced, The actual reasonable cost of repairing or replacing such damage or loss, subject to deductions in accordance with Rule XIII; (b) When not repaired or replaced, The reasonable depreciation arising from such damage or loss, but not exceeding the estimated cost of repairs. But where the ship is an actual total loss or when the cost of repairs

	Rules of 1860, 1864 and 1877	York-Antwerp Rules (1890)	York-Antwerp Rules (1924)
			average act shall be the estimated sound value of the ship after deducting therefrom the estimated cost of repairing damage which is not general average and the proceeds of sale, if any.
60.65			**Rule XIX. Undeclared or Wrongfully Declared Cargo** Damage or loss caused to goods loaded without the knowledge of the shipowner or his agent or to goods wilfully misdescribed at time of shipment shall not be allowed as general average, but such goods shall remain liable to contribute if saved. Damage or loss caused to goods which have been wrongfully declared on shipment at a value which is lower than their real value shall be contributed for at the declared value, but such goods shall contribute upon their actual value.
60.66			**Rule XX. Expenses Bearing up for Port, etc.** Fuel and stores consumed and wages and maintenance of master, officers and crew incurred, during the prolongation of the voyage occasioned by a ship entering a port or place of refuge or returning to her port or place of loading shall be admitted as general average when the expenses of entering such port or place are allowable in general average in accordance with Rule X (a). Fuel and stores consumed during extra detention in a port or place of loading, call or refuge shall also be allowed in general average

York-Antwerp Rules (1950)	York-Antwerp Rules (1974)	York-Antwerp Rules (1994)
mated sound value of the ship after deducting therefrom the estimated cost of repairing damage which is not general average and the proceeds of sale, if any.	of the damage would exceed the value of the ship when repaired, the amount to be allowed as general average shall be the difference between the estimated sound value of the ship after deducting therefrom the estimated cost of repairing damage which is not general average and the value of the ship in her damaged state which may be measured by the net proceeds of sale, if any.	of the damage would exceed the value of the ship when repaired, the amount to be allowed as general average shall be the difference between the estimated sound value of the ship after deducting therefrom the estimated cost of repairing damage which is not general average and the value of the ship in her damaged state which may be measured by the net proceeds of sale, if any.
Rule XIX. Undeclared or Wrongfully Declared Cargo	**Rule XIX. Undeclared or Wrongfully Declared Cargo**	**Rule XIX. Undeclared or Wrongfully Declared Cargo**
Damage or loss caused to goods loaded without the knowledge of the shipowner or his agent or to goods wilfully misdescribed at time of shipment shall not be allowed as general average, but such goods shall remain liable to contribute if saved.	Damage or loss caused to goods loaded without the knowledge of the shipowner or his agent or to goods wilfully misdescribed at time of shipment shall not be allowed as general average, but such goods shall remain liable to contribute if saved.	Damage or loss caused to goods loaded without the knowledge of the shipowner or his agent or to goods wilfully misdescribed at time of shipment shall not be allowed as general average, but such goods shall remain liable to contribute if saved.
Damage or loss caused to goods which have been wrongfully declared on shipment at a value which is lower than their real value shall be contributed for at the declared value, but such goods shall contribute upon their actual value.	Damage or loss caused to goods which have been wrongfully declared on shipment at a value which is lower than their real value shall be contributed for at the declared value, but such goods shall contribute upon their actual value.	Damage or loss caused to goods which have been wrongfully declared on shipment at a value which is lower than their real value shall be contributed for at the declared value, but such goods shall contribute upon their actual value.
(Corresponding provisions are to be found in Rule XI, *supra.*)	(Corresponding provisions are to be found in Rule XI, *supra.*)	(Corresponding provisions are to be found in Rule XI, *supra.*)

	Rules of 1860, 1864 and 1877	York-Antwerp Rules (1890)	York-Antwerp Rules (1924)
			for the period during which wages and maintenance of master, officers and crew are allowed in terms of Rule XI, except such fuel and stores as are consumed in effecting repairs not allowable in general average.
60.67			**Rule XXI. Provision of Funds** A commission of 2 per cent on general average disbursements shall be allowed in general average, but when the funds are not provided by any of the contributing interests, the necessary cost of obtaining the funds required by means of a bottomry bond or otherwise, or the loss sustained by owners of goods sold for the purpose, shall be allowed in general average. The cost of insuring money advanced to pay for general average disbursements shall also be allowed in general average.
60.68			**Rule XXII. Interest on Losses made good in General Average** Interest shall be allowed on expenditure, sacrifices and allowances charged to general average at the legal rate per annum prevailing at the final port of destination at which the adventure ends, or where there is no recognised legal rate, at the rate of 5 per cent per annum, until the date of the general average statement, due allowance being made for any interim reimbursement from the contributory interests or from the general average deposit fund.

York-Antwerp Rules (1950)	York-Antwerp Rules (1974)	York-Antwerp Rules (1994)
Rule XX. Provision of Funds A commission of 2 per cent on general average disbursements, other than the wages and maintenance of master, officers and crew and fuel and stores not replaced during the voyage, shall be allowed in general average, but when the funds are not provided by any of the contributing interests, the necessary cost of obtaining the funds required by means of a bottomry bond or otherwise, or the loss sustained by owners of goods sold for the purpose, shall be allowed in general average. The cost of insuring money advanced to pay for general average disbursements shall also be allowed in general average.	**Rule XX. Provision of Funds** A commission of 2 per cent on general average disbursements, other than the wages and maintenance of master, officers and crew and fuel and stores not replaced during the voyage, shall be allowed in general average, but when the funds are not provided by any of the contributing interests, the necessary cost of obtaining the funds required by means of a bottomry bond or otherwise, or the loss sustained by owners of goods sold for the purpose, shall be allowed in general average. The cost of insuring money advanced to pay for general average disbursements shall also be allowed in general average.	**Rule XX. Provision of Funds** A commission of 2 per cent on general average disbursements, other than the wages and maintenance of master, officers and crew and fuel and stores not replaced during the voyage, shall be allowed in general average. *The capital loss sustained by the owners of goods sold for the purpose of raising funds to defray general average disbursements shall be allowed in general average.* The cost of insuring money advanced to pay for general average disbursements shall also be allowed in general average.
Rule XXI. Interest on Losses made good in General Average Interest shall be allowed on expenditure, sacrifices and allowances charged to general average at the rate of 5 per cent per annum, until the date of the general average statement, due allowance being made for any interim reimbursement from the contributory interests or from the general average deposit fund.	**Rule XXI. Interest on Losses made good in General Average** Interest shall be allowed on expenditure, sacrifices and allowances charged to general average at the rate of 7 per cent per annum, until the date of the general average statement, due allowance being made for any interim reimbursement from the contributory interests or from the general average deposit fund.	**Rule XXI. Interest on Losses made good in General Average** Interest shall be allowed on expenditure, sacrifices and allowances *in* general average at the rate of 7 per cent per annum, until *three months after* the date of *issue of* the general average *adjustment*, due allowance being made for any *payment on account by* the contributory interests or from the general average deposit fund.

	Rules of 1860, 1864 and 1877	York-Antwerp Rules (1890)	York-Antwerp Rules (1924)
60.69			**Rule XXIII. Treatment of Cash Deposits** Where cash deposits have been collected in respect of cargo's liability for general average, salvage or special charges, such deposits shall be paid into a special account, earning interest where possible in the joint names of two trustees (one to be nominated on behalf of the shipowner and the other on behalf of the depositors) in a bank to be approved by such trustees. The sum so deposited, together with accrued interest, if any, shall be held as security for and upon trust for payment to the parties entitled thereto of the general average, salvage or special charges payable by the cargo in respect of which the deposits have been collected. The trustees shall have power to make payments on account or refunds of deposits which may be certified to in writing by the average adjuster. Such deposits and payments or refunds shall be without prejudice to the ultimate liability of the parties.

York-Antwerp Rules (1950)	York-Antwerp Rules (1974)	York-Antwerp Rules (1994)
Rule XXII. Treatment of Cash Deposits Where cash deposits have been collected in respect of cargo's liability for general average, salvage or special charges, such deposits shall be paid without any delay into a special account in the joint names of a representative nominated on behalf of the shipowner and a representative nominated on behalf of the depositors in a bank to be approved by both. The sum so deposited, together with accrued interest, if any, shall be held as security for payment to the parties entitled thereto of the general average, salvage or special charges payable by cargo in respect to which the deposits have been collected. Payments on account or refunds of deposits may be made, if certified to in writing by the average adjuster. Such deposits and payments or refunds shall be without prejudice to the ultimate liability of the parties.	**Rule XXII. Treatment of Cash Deposits** Where cash deposits have been collected in respect of cargo's liability for general average, salvage or special charges, such deposits shall be paid without any delay into a special account in the joint names of a representative nominated on behalf of the shipowner and a representative nominated on behalf of the depositors in a bank to be approved by both. The sum so deposited, together with accrued interest, if any, shall be held as security for payment to the parties entitled thereto of the general average, salvage or special charges payable by cargo in respect to which the deposits have been collected. Payments on account or refunds of deposits may be made, if certified to in writing by the average adjuster. Such deposits and payments or refunds shall be without prejudice to the ultimate liability of the parties.	**Rule XXII. Treatment of Cash Deposits** Where cash deposits have been collected in respect of cargo's liability for general average, salvage or special charges, such deposits shall be paid without any delay into a special account in the joint names of a representative nominated on behalf of the shipowner and a representative nominated on behalf of the depositors in a bank to be approved by both. The sum so deposited, together with accrued interest, if any, shall be held as security for payment to the parties entitled thereto of the general average, salvage or special charges payable by cargo in respect to which the deposits have been collected. Payments on account or refunds of deposits may be made, if certified to in writing by the average adjuster. Such deposits and payments or refunds shall be without prejudice to the ultimate liability of the parties.

APPENDIX 2C

FRENCH TEXT* OF THE YORK-ANTWERP RULES 1994

60.70 **RÈGLE D'INTERPRETATION**

Dans le règlement d'avaries communes, les Règles suivantes doivent s'appliquer à l'exclusion de toute loi et pratique incompatibles avec elles.

A l'exception de ce qui est prévu par la Règle "Paramount" et les Règles numérotées, l'avarie commune doit être réglée conformément aux Règles precédées de lettres.

60.71 **RÈGLE "PARAMOUNT"**

Une admission en avarie commune ne pourra être en aucun cas prononcée pour un sacrifice ou une dépense qui n'aurait pas été raisonnablement consenti.

Règle A

60.72 Il y a acte d'avarie commune quand, et seulement quand, intentionnellement et raisonnablement, un sacrifice extraordinaire est fait ou une dépense extraordinaire encourue pour le salut commun, dans le but de préserver d'un péril les propriétés engagées dans une aventure maritime commune.

Les sacrifices et dépenses d'avarie commune seront supportés par les divers intérêts appelés à contribuer sur les bases déterminées ci-après.

Règle B

60.73 Il y a aventure maritime commune lorsqu'un ou plusieurs navires remorquent ou poussent un ou plusieurs autres navires, pourvu que tous soient engagés dans des activités commerciales et non dans une opération d'assistance.

Lorsque des mesures seront prises pour préserver les navires et leurs éventuelles cargaisons d'un péril commun, les Règles seront applicables.

Un navire n'est pas en situation de péril commun avec un ou plusieurs autres navires s'il lui suffit de s'en détacher pour se trouver en sécurité; mais si le fait de s'en détacher est lui-même constitutif d'un acte d'avarie commune, l'aventure maritime commune n'est pas pour autant interrompue.

Règle C

60.74 Seuls les pertes, dommages ou dépenses qui sont la conséquence directe de l'acte d'avarie commune seront admis en avarie commune.

Une admission en avarie commune ne pourra être en aucun cas prononcée pour des dommages, pertes ou dépenses encourus au titre de dommages à l'environnement ou consécutivement à des fuites ou rejets de substances polluantes émanant des propriétés engagées dans l'aventure maritime commune.

Chômage, différence de cours, et toute perte ou dommage subi ou dépense encourue par suite du retard, soit au cours du voyage, soit postérieurement, de

* Version française établie par l'Association Française du Droit Maritime.

même que toute perte indirecte quelconque, ne seront pas admis en avarie commune.

Règle D

Lorsque l'événement qui a donné lieu au sacrifice ou à la dépense aura été la conséquence d'une faute commise par l'une des parties engagées dans l'aventure, il n'y aura pas moins lieu à contribution, mais sans préjudice des recours ou des défenses pouvant concerner cette partie à raison d'une telle faute. **60.75**

Règle E

La preuve qu'une perte ou une dépense doit effectivement être admise en avarie commune incombe à celui qui réclame cette admission. **60.76**

Les parties qui entendent présenter réclamation au titre de l'avarie commune doivent notifier par écrit au dispacheur, dans les 12 mois de la date à laquelle a pris fin l'aventure maritime commune, la perte ou la dépense pour laquelle elles réclament contribution.

A défaut d'une telle notification, ou encore à défaut, pour l'une quelconque des parties, de fournir dans les 12 mois de la date à laquelle la demande lui en est faite, les justificatifs de sa réclamation ou les précisions relatives à la valeur d'un intérêt appelé à conribuer, le dispacheur sera autorisé à estimer le montant de l'admission ou de la valeur contributive sur la base des informations dont il dispose, son estimation ne pouvant être dès lors contestée qu'en cas d'erreur manifeste.

Règle F

Toute dépense supplémentaire encourue en substitution d'une autre dépense qui aurait été admissible en avarie commune sera réputée elle même avarie commune et admise à ce titre, sans égard à l'économie éventuellement réalisée par d'autres intérêts, mais seulement jusqu'à concurrence du montant de la dépense d'avarie commune ainsi évitée. **60.77**

Règle G

Le règlement des avaries communes doit être établi, tant pour l'estimation des pertes que pour la contribution, sur la base des valeurs au moment et au lieu où se termine l'aventure. **60.78**

Cette règle est sans influence sur la détermination du lieu où le règlement doit être établi.

Quand un navire se trouve en quelque port ou lieu que ce soit, dans des circonstances qui seraient susceptibles de donner lieu à une admission en avarie commune sur la base des dispositions des Règles X et XI, et quand la cargaison ou une partie de celle-ci est acheminée à destination par d'autres moyens, les droits et obligations relatifs à l'avarie commune demeureront—sous réserve que les intérêts cargaison en soient autant que faire se peut avisés—aussi proches que possible de ce qu'ils auraient été si, en l'absence d'un tel acheminement, l'aventure s'était poursuivie sur le navire d'origine, et ce aussi longtemps que cela apparaîtra justifié en l'état du contrat et de la loi applicables au transport.

La part des admissions en avarie commune incombant à la cargaison, en application du 3ème paragraphe de la présente règle, ne pourra excéder la dépense qu'auraient supportée les propriétaires de la cargaison si celle-ci avait été acheminée à leurs frais.

Règle I. Jet de cargaison.

60.79 Aucun jet de cargaison ne sera admis en avarie commune à moins que cette cargaison n'ait été transportée conformément aux usages reconnus du commerce.

Règle II. Perte ou dommage causé par sacrifices pour le salut commun.

60.80 Sera admis en avarie commune la perte ou le dommage causé aux propriétés engagées dans l'aventure maritime commune ou en conséquence d'un sacrifice fait pour le salut commun, et par l'eau qui pénètre dans la cale par les écoutilles ouvertes ou par toute autre ouverture pratiquée en vue d'opérer un jet pour le salut commun.

Règle III. Extinction d'incendie à bord.

60.81 Sera admis en avarie commune le dommage causé au navire et à la cargaison, ou à l'un d'eux, par l'eau ou autrement, y compris le dommage causé en submergeant ou en sabordant un navire en feu, en vue d'éteindre un incendie à bord; toutefois, aucune bonification ne sera faite pour dommage causé par la fumée quelle qu'en soit la cause ou par la chaleur de l'incendie.

Règle IV. Coupement de débris.

60.82 La perte ou le dommage éprouvé en coupant des débris ou des parties du navire qui ont été enlevés ou sont effectivement perdus par accident, ne sera pas bonifié en avarie commune.

Règle V. Echouement volontaire.

60.83 Quand un navire est intentionnellement mis à la côte pour le salut commun, qu'il dût ou non y être drossé, les pertes ou dommages en résultant et subis par les propriétés engagées dans l'aventure maritime commune, seront admis en avarie commune.

Règle VI. Rémunération d'assistance.

60.84 (a) Les dépenses encourues par les parties engagées dans l'aventure et ayant le caractère d'assistance, soit en vertu d'un contrat soit autrement, seront admises en avarie commune, pourvu que les opérations d'assistance aient été effectuées dans le but de préserver du péril les propriétés engagées dans l'aventure maritime commune.
Les dépenses admises en avarie commune comprendront toute rémunératon d'assistance dans la fixation de laquelle l'habileté et les efforts des assistants pour prévenir ou limiter les dommages à l'environnement, tels qu'ils sont énoncés à l'article 13.1 (b) de la Convention Internationale de 1989 sur l'assistance, ont été pris en compte.
(b) L'indemnité spéciale payable à l'assistant par l'armateur sous l'empire de l'article 14 de la dite Convention, dans les conditions indiquées par le paragraphe 4 de cet article, ou de toute autre disposition de portée semblable ne sera pas admise en avarie commune.

Règle VII. Dommage aux machines et aux chaudières.

60.85 Le dommage causé à toute machine et chaudière d'un navire échoué dans une position périlleuse par les efforts faits pour le renflouer, sera admis en avarie commune, lorsqu'il sera établi qu'il procède de l'intention réelle de renflouer le navire pour le salut commun au risque d'un tel dommage; mais lorsqu'un navire est à flot, aucune perte ou avarie causée par le fonctionnement de l'appareil de propulsion et des chaudières ne sera, en aucune circonstance, admise en avarie commune.

Règle VIII. Dépenses pour alléger un navire échoué et dommage résultant de cette mesure.

Lorsqu'un navire est échoué et que la cargaison, ainsi que le combustible et les approvisionnements du navire, ou l'un d'eux, sont déchargés dans des circonstances telles que cette mesure constitue un acte d'avarie commune, les dépenses supplémentaires d'allègement, de location des allèges, et, le cas échéant, celles de réembarquement ainsi que toute perte ou dommage aux propriétés engagées dans l'aventure maritime commune en résultant, seront admises en avarie commune. **60.86**

Règle IX. Cargaison, objets du navire et approvisionnements utilisés comme combustibles.

La cargaison, les objets et approvisionnements du navire, ou l'un d'eux, qu'il a été nécessaire d'utiliser comme combustibles pour le salut commun en cas de péril, seront admis en avarie commune, mais lorsque le coût des objets et approvisionnements du navire est ainsi admis, l'avarie commune sera créditée du coût estimatif du combustible qui autrement aurait été consommé pour la poursuite du voyage. **60.87**

Règle X. Dépenses au port de refuge, etc.

(a) Quand un navire sera entré dans un port ou lieu de refuge ou qu'il sera retourné à son port ou lieu de chargement par suite d'accident, de sacrifice ou d'autres circonstances extraordinaires qui auront rendu cette mesure nécessaire pour le salut commun, les dépenses encourues pour entrer dans ce port ou lieu seront admises en avarie commune; et, quand il en sera reparti avec tout ou partie de sa cargaison primitive, les dépenses correspondantes pour quitter ce port ou lieu qui auront été la conséquence de cette entrée ou de ce retour seront de même admises en avarie commune. **60.88**
Quand un navire est dans un port ou lieu de refuge quelconque et qu'il est nécessairement déplacé vers un autre port ou lieu parce que les réparations ne peuvent être effectuées au premier port ou lieu, les dispositions de cette Règle s'appliqueront au deuxième port ou lieu, comme s'il était un port ou lieu de refuge, et le coût du déplacement, y compris les réparations provisoires et le remorquage, sera admis en avarie commune.
Les dispositions de la Règle XI s'appliqueront à la prolongation du voyage occasionnée par ce déplacement.

(b) Les frais pour manutentionner à bord ou pour décharger la cargaison, le combustible ou les approvisionnements, soit à un port, soit à un lieu de chargement, d'escale ou de refuge, seront admis en avarie commune si la manutention ou le déchargement était nécessaire pour le salut commun ou pour permettre de réparer les avaries au navire causées par sacrifice ou par accident si ces réparations étaient nécessaires pour permettre de continuer le voyage en sécurité, excepté si les avaries au navire sont découvertes dans un port ou lieu de chargement ou d'escale sans qu'aucun accident ou autre circonstance extraordinaire en rapport avec ces avaries ne se soit produit au cours du voyage.
Les frais pour manutentionner à bord ou pour décharger la cargaison, le combustible ou les approvisionnements ne seront pas admis en avarie

commune s'ils ont été encourus à seule fin de remédier à un désarrimage survenu au cours du voyage, à moins qu'une telle mesure soit nécessaire pour le salut commun.

(c) Toutes les fois que les frais de manutention ou de déchargement de la cargaison, du combustible ou des approvisionnements seront admissibles en avarie commune, les frais de leur magasinage, y compris l'assurance si elle a été raisonnablement conclue, de leur rechargement et de leur arrimage seront également admis en avarie commune. Les dispositions de la Règle XI s'appliqueront à la période supplémentaire d'immobilisation occasionnée par ce rechargement ou ce réarrimage.

Mais si le navire est condamné ou ne continue pas son voyage primitif, les frais de magasinage ne seront admis en avarie commune que jusqu'à la date de condamnation du navire ou de l'abandon du voyage ou bien jusqu'à la date de l'achèvement du déchargement de la cargaison en cas de condamnation du navire ou d'abandon du voyage avant cette date.

Règle XI. Salaires et entretien de l'équipage et autres dépenses pour se rendre au port de refuge, et dans ce port, etc.

60.89 (a) Les salaires et frais d'entretien du capitaine, des officiers et de l'équipage raisonnablement encourus ainsi que le combustible et les approvisionnements consommés durant la prolongation du voyage occasionnée par l'entrée du navire dans un port de refuge, ou par son retour au port ou lieu de chargement, doivent être admis en avarie commune quand les dépenses pour entrer en ce port ou lieu sont admissibles en avarie commune par application de la Règle X (a).

(b) Quand un navire sera entré ou aura été retenu dans un port ou lieu par suite d'un accident, sacrifice ou autres circonstances extraordinaires qui ont rendu cela nécessaire pour le salut commun, ou pour permettre la réparation des avaries causées au navire par sacrifice ou accident quand la réparation est nécessaire à la poursuite du voyage en sécurité, les salaires et frais d'entretien des capitaine, officiers et équipage raisonnablement encourus pendant la période supplémentaire d'immobilisation en ce port ou lieu jusqu'à ce que le navire soit ou aurait dû être mis en état de poursuivre son voyage, seront admis en avarie commune.

Le combustible et les approvisionnements consommés pendant la période supplémentaire d'immobilisation seront admis en avarie commune à l'exception du combustible et des approvisionnements consommés en effectuant des réparations non admissibles en avarie commune.

Les frais de port encourus durant cette période supplémentaire d'immobilisation seront de même admis en avarie commune, à l'exception des frais qui ne sont encourus qu'à raison de réparations non admissibles en avarie commune.

Cependant, si des avaries au navire sont découvertes dans un port ou lieu de chargement ou d'escale sans qu'aucun accident ou autre circonstance extraordinaire en rapport avec ces avaries se soit produit au cours du voyage, les salaires et frais d'entretien des capitaine, officiers et équipage, le combustible et les approvisionnements consommés ainsi que les frais de port encourus pendant l'immobilisation supplémentaire pour les besoins de la réparation des avaries ainsi découvertes, ne seront pas admis en avarie commune même si la réparation est nécessaire à la poursuite du voyage en sécurité.

Quand le navire est condamné ou ne poursuit pas son voyage primitif, les salaires et frais d'entretien des capitaine, officiers et équipage et le combustible et les approvisionnements consommés et les frais de port ne seront admis en avarie commune que jusqu'à la date de la condamnation du navire ou de l'abandon du voyage ou jusqu'à la date d'achèvement du déchargement de la cargaison en cas de condamnation du navire ou d'abandon du voyage avant cette date.

(c) Pour l'application de la présente règle ainsi que des autres règles, les salaires comprennent les paiements faits au capitaine, officiers et équipage ou à leur profit, que ces paiements soient imposés aux armateurs par la loi ou qu'ils résultent des conditions et clauses des contrats de travail.

(d) Le coût des mesures prises pour prévenir ou minimiser un dommage à l'environnement sera admis en avarie commune lorsqu'il aura été encouru dans l'une ou toutes les situations suivantes:

(i) lorsqu'il est engagé dans le cadre d'une opération conduite pour le salut commun qui, si elle avait été engagée par une partie extérieure à l'aventure maritime commune, lui aurait donné droit à une indemnité d'assistance;

(ii) lorsqu'il est une condition de l'entrée ou de la sortie d'un port ou d'un lieu quelconque dans les situations prévues à la Règle X (a);

(iii) lorsqu'il est une condition de séjour dans un port ou un lieu quelconque dans les situations prévues à la Règle XI (b), pour vu qu'en cas de fuite ou de rejet effectif de substances polluantes, le coût de toutes mesures supplémentaires prises pour prévenir ou minimiser la pollution ou le dommage à l'environnement ne soit pas admis en avarie commune;

(iv) lorsqu'il a un lien nécessaire avec le déchargement, le stockage ou le rechargement de la cargaison, chaque fois que le coût de ces opérations est admissible en avarie commune.

Règle XII. Dommage causé à la cargaison en la déchargeant, etc.

Le dommage ou la perte subis par la cargaison, le combustible ou les approvisionnements dans les opérations de manutention, déchargement, emmagasinage, rechargement et arrimage, seront admis en avarie commune lorsque le coût respectif de ces opérations sera admis en avarie commune et dans ce cas seulement. **60.90**

Règle XIII. Déduction du coût des réparations.

Les réparations à admettre en avarie commune ne seront pas sujettes à des déductions pour différence du "neuf au vieux" quand du vieux matériel sera, en totalité ou en partie, remplacé par du neuf, à moins que le navire ait plus de quinze ans; en pareil cas la déduction sera de un tiers. **60.91**

Les déductions seront fixées d'après l'âge du navire depuis le 31 décembre de l'année d'achèvement de la construction jusqu'à la date de l'acte d'avarie commune, excepté pour les isolants, canots de sauvetage et similaires, appareils et équipements de communications et de navigation, machines et chaudières, pour lesquels les déductions seront fixées d'après l'âge des différentes parties auxquelles elles s'appliquent.

Les déductions seront effectuées seulement sur le coût du matériel nouveau ou de ses parties au moment où il sera usiné et prêt à être mis en place dans le navire.

Aucune déduction ne sera faite sur les approvisionnements, matières consommables, ancres et chaînes.

Les frais de cale sèche, de slip et de déplacement du navire seront admis en entier.

Les frais de nettoyage, de peinture ou d'enduit de la coque ne seront pas admis en avarie commune à moins que la coque ait été peinte ou enduite dans les douze mois qui ont précédé la date de l'acte d'avarie commune; en pareil cas ces frais seront admis pour moitié.

Règle XIV. Réparations provisoires.

60.92 Lorsque des réparations provisoires sont effectuées à un navire, dans un port de chargement, d'escale ou de refuge, pour le salut commun ou pour des avaries causées par un sacrifice d'avarie commune, le coût de ces réparations sera bonifié en avarie commune.

Lorsque des réparations provisoires d'un dommage fortuit sont effectuées afin de permettre l'achèvement du voyage, le coût de ces réparations sera admis en avarie commune, sans égard à l'économie éventuellement réalisée par d'autres intérêts, mais seulement jusqu'à concurrence de l'économie sur les dépenses qui auraient étéx effectuées en ce lieu.

Aucune déduction pour différence du "neuf au vieux" ne sera faite du coût des réparations provisoires admissibles en avarie commune.

Règle XV. Perte de fret.

60.93 La perte de fret résultant d'une perte ou d'un dommage subi par la cargaison sera admise en avarie commune, tant si elle est causée par un acte d'avarie commune que si cette perte ou ce dommage est ainsi admis.

Devront être déduites du montant du fret brut perdu les dépenses que le propriétaire de ce fait aurait encourues pour le gagner, mais qu'il n'a pas exposées par suite du sacrifice.

Règle XVI. Valeur à admettre pour la cargaison perdue ou avariée par sacrifice.

60.94 Le montant à admettre en avarie commune pour dommage ou perte de cargaison sacrifiée sera le montant de la perte éprouvée de ce fait en prenant pour base le prix au moment du déchargement vérifié d'après la facture commerciale remise au réceptionnaire ou, à défaut d'une telle facture, d'après la valeur embarquée. Le prix au moment du déchargement inclura le coût de l'assurance et le fret, sauf si ce fret n'est pas au risque de la cargaison.

Quand une marchandise ainsi avariée est vendue et que le montant du dommage n'a pas été autrement convenu, la perte à admettre en avarie commune sera la différence entre le produit net de la vente et la valeur nette à l'état sain, telle qu'elle est calculée dans le premier paragraphe de cette Règle.

Règle XVII. Valeurs contributives.

60.95 La contribution à l'avarie commune sera établie sur les valeurs nettes réelles des propriétés à la fin du voyage sauf que la valeur de la cargaison sera le prix au moment du déchargement vérifié d'après la facture commerciale remise au réceptionnaire ou, à défaut d'une telle facture, d'après la valeur embarquée. La valeur de la cargaison comprendra le coût de l'assurance et le fret sauf si ce fret n'est pas au risque de la cargaison, et sous déduction des pertes ou avaries subies par la cargaison avant ou pendant le déchargement. La valeur du navire sera estimée sans tenir compte de la plus ou moins value résultant de l'affrètement coque nue ou à temps sous lequel il peut se trouver.

A ces valeurs sera ajouté le montant admis en avarie commune des propriétés sacrifiées, s'il n'y est pas déjà compris. Du fret et du prix de passage en risque seront déduits les frais et les gages de l'équipage qui n'auraient pas été encourus pour gagner le fret si le navire et la cargaison s'étaient totalement perdus au moment de l'acte d'avarie commune et qui n'ont pas été admis en avarie commune.

De la valeur des propriétés seront également déduits tous les frais supplémentaires y relatifs, postérieurs à l'événement qui donne ouverture à l'avarie commune, à l'exception des frais qui auront été admis en avarie commune ou qui incombent au navire en vertu d'une décision allouant l'indemnité spéciale prévue à l'article 14 de la Convention Internationale de 1989 sur l'assistance ou de toute autre disposition de portée semblable.

Dans les situations prévues au troisième paragraphe de la Règle G, la cargaison et les autres propriétés contribueront sur la base de leur valeur à leur destination d'origine à moins qu'elles n'aient été vendues ou qu'il n'en ait été autrement disposé avant l'arrivée à destination, et le navire contribuera sur sa valeur nette réelle à la fin du déchargement de la cargaison.

Quand une cargaison est vendue en cours de voyage, elle contribue sur le produit net de vente augmenté du montant admis en avarie commune.

Le courrier, les bagages des passagers, les effets personnels et les véhicules à moteur privés et accompagnés ne contribueront pas à l'avarie commune.

Règle XVIII. Avaries au navire.

Le montant à admettre en avarie commune pour dommage ou perte subis par **60.96**
le navire, ses machines et/ou ses apparaux du fait d'un acte d'avarie commune, sera le suivant:

(a) en cas de réparation ou de remplacement, le coût réel et raisonnable de la réparation ou du remplacement du dommage ou de la perte sous réserve des déductions à opérer en vertu de la Règle XIII;

(b) dans le cas contraire, la dépréciation raisonnable résultant d'un tel dommage ou d'une telle perte jusqu'à concurrence du coût estimatif des réparations.

Mais lorsqu'il y a perte totale ou que le coût des réparations du dommage dépasserait la valeur du navire une fois réparé, le montant à admettre en avarie commune sera la différence entre la valeur estimative du navire à l'état sain sous déduction du coût estimatif des réparations du dommage n'ayant pas le caractère d'avarie commune, et la valeur du navire en son état d'avarie, cette valeur pouvant être déterminée par le produit net de vente, le cas échéant.

Règle XIX. Marchandises non déclarées ou faussement déclarées.

La perte ou le dommage causé aux marchandises chargées à l'insu de l'armateur **60.97**
ou de son agent, ou à celles qui ont fait l'objet d'une désignation volontairement fausse au moment de l'embarquement, ne sera pas admis en avarie commune, mais ces marchandises resteront tenues de contribuer si elle sont sauvées.

La perte ou le dommage causé aux marchandises qui ont été faussement déclarées à l'embarquement pour une valeur moindre que leur valeur réelle sera admis sur la base de la valeur déclarée, mais ces marchandises devront contribuer sur leur valeur réelle.

Règle XX. Avance de fonds.

Une commission de deux pour cent sur les débours d'avarie commune autres **60.98**
que les salaires et frais d'entretien du capitaine, des officiers et de l'équipage et le combustible et les approvisionnements qui n'ont pas été remplacés durant le voyage, sera admise en avarie commune.

La perte financière subie par les propriétaires des marchandises vendues pour obtenir les fonds nécessaires en vue de faire face aux dépenses d'avarie commune sera admise en avarie commune.

Les frais d'assurance de l'argent avancé pour payer les dépenses d'avarie commune seront également admis en avarie commune.

Règle XXI. Intérêts sur les pertes admises en avarie commune.

60.99 Un intérêt sera alloué sur les dépenses, sacrifices et bonifications classées en avarie commune, au taux de sept pour cent par an, jusqu'à l'expiration d'un délai de trois mois à compter de la date du dépot du règlement d'avarie commune, en tenant dûment compte des paiements provisionnels effectués par ceux qui sont appelés à contribuer, ou prélevés sur le fonds des dépôts d'avarie commune.

Règle XXII. Traitement des dépôts en espèces.

60.100 Lorsque des dépôts en espèces auront été encaissés en garantie de la contribution de la cargaison à l'avarie commune, aux frais de sauvetage ou frais spéciaux, ces dépôts devront être versés, sans aucun délai, à un compte joint spécial aux noms d'un représentant désigné pour l'armateur et d'un représentant désigné pour les déposants dans une banque agréée par eux deux. La somme ainsi déposée augmentée, s'il y a lieu, des intérêts, sera conservée à titre de garantie pour le paiement aux ayants droits en raison de l'avarie commune, des frais de sauvetage ou des frais spéciaux payables par la cargaison et en vue desquels les dépôts ont été effectués. Des paiements en acompte ou des remboursements de dépôts peuvent être faits avec l'autorisation écrite du dispacheur. Ces dépôts, paiements ou remboursements, seront effectués sans préjudice des obligations définitives des parties.

Appendix 3

RULES OF PRACTICE

Adopted by the Association of Average Adjusters up to 1996

(Only the Rules relating to or having some bearing on General Average are shown here. The references in parentheses are to the printed Annual Reports of the Association)

NOTE. Some of the undermentioned Rules are, as indicated, "Customs of Lloyd's", now by resolution of the Association incorporated amongst the Rules of Practice. **70.01**

The preamble to the Customs was:

> "Nothing can be called a 'Custom of Lloyd's' which is determined by a decision of the superior courts; for whatever is thus sanctioned rests on a ground surer than Custom. A 'Custom of Lloyd's' then must relate to a point on which the law is doubtful, or not yet defined, but as to which, for practical convenience, it is necessary that there should be some uniform rule. By the term is here understood the Customs of English Adjusting, whether as affecting General or Particular Average."

SECTION "A" GENERAL RULES

A2. Interest and Commission for Advancing Funds **70.02**
(Proposed and Accepted 1906, p. 21. Confirmed 1907, p. 60.)

That, in practice, interest and commission for advancing funds are only allowable in average when, proper and necessary steps having been taken to make a collection on account, an out-of-pocket expense for interest and/or commission for advancing funds is reasonably incurred.

A3. Agency Commission and Agency **70.03**
(Proposed and Accepted 1906, p. 21. Confirmed 1907, p. 60.)

That, in practice, neither commission (except bank commission) nor any charge by way of agency or remuneration for trouble is allowed to the shipowner in average, except in respect of services rendered on behalf of cargo when such services are not involved in the contract of affreightment.

A4. Duty of Adjusters in respect of Cost of Repairs **70.04**
(Proposed and Accepted 1879, p. 24. Confirmed 1880, p. 21.)

That in adjusting particular average on ship or general average which includes repairs, it is the duty of the adjuster to satisfy himself that such reasonable and usual precautions have been taken to keep down the cost of repairs as a prudent shipowner would have taken if uninsured.

70.05 A5. Claims on Ship's Machinery

(Proposed and Accepted 1890, p. 32. Confirmed 1891, p. 32.)

That in all claims on ship's machinery for repairs, no claim for a new propeller or new shaft shall be admitted into an adjustment, unless the adjuster shall obtain and insert into his statement evidence showing what has become of the old propeller or shaft.

70.06 A6. Water Casks (Custom of Lloyd's, 1876)

Water casks or tanks carried on a ship's deck are not paid for by underwriters as general or particular average; nor are warps or other articles when improperly carried on deck.

70.07 A7. Adjustment; Policies of Insurance and Names of Underwriters

(Proposed and Accepted 1968, p. 25. Confirmed 1969, p. 22.)

That no adjustment shall be drawn up showing the amount of payments by or to the underwriters, unless the policies or copies of the policies of insurance or certificates of insurance, for which the statement is required, be produced to the average adjusters. Such statement shall set out sufficient details of the underwriters interested and the amounts due on the respective policies produced.

SECTION "B" GENERAL AVERAGE

70.08 B1. Basis of Adjustment

(Proposed and Accepted 1889, p. 60. Confirmed 1890, p. 33.)
(Addition Proposed and Accepted 1899, p. 29. Confirmed 1900, p. 20.)

That in any adjustment of general average not made in accordance with British law it shall be prefaced on what principle or according to what law the adjustment has been made, and the reason for so adjusting the claim shall be set forth.

In all cases the adjuster shall give particulars in a prominent position in the average statement of the clause or clauses contained in the charter-party and/or bills of lading with reference to the adjustment of general average.

70.09 B9. Claims arising out of Deficiency of Fuel

(Proposed and Accepted 1899, p. 50. Confirmed 1900, p. 25.)

That in adjusting general average arising out of deficiency of fuel, the facts on which the general average is based shall be set forth in the adjustment, including the material dates and distances, and particulars of fuel supplies and consumption.

70.10 B24. Contributory Value of Ship

(Proposed and Accepted 1899, p. 41. Confirmed 1900, p. 20.)

That in any adjustment of general average there shall be set forth the certificate on which the contributory value of the ship is based or, if there be no such certificate, the information adopted in lieu thereof, and any amount made good shall be specified.

B25. CONTRIBUTORY VALUE OF FREIGHT 70.11
(Original Rule of Practice 1873.—Part)
(Referred to a Special Committee 1908—Report 1909.)
(Amended 1968, p. 22. Confirmed 1969, p. 22.)

That in any adjustment of general average there shall be set forth the amount of the gross freight and the freight advanced, if any; also the charges and wages deducted and any amount made good.

B26. VESSEL IN BALLAST AND UNDER CHARTER: CONTRIBUTING INTERESTS 70.12
(Proposed and Accepted 1945, p. 53. Confirmed 1946, p. 45.)

For the purpose of ascertaining the liability of Underwriters on British policies of insurance, the following provisions shall apply:—

When a vessel is proceeding in ballast to load under a voyage charter entered into by the shipowner before the general average act, the interests contributing to the general average shall be the vessel, such items of stores and equipment as belong to parties other than the owners of the vessel (*e.g.* bunkers, wireless installation and navigational instruments) and the freight earned under the voyage charter computed in the usual way after deduction of contingent expenses subsequent to the general average act. Failing a prior termination of the adventure, the place where the adventure shall be deemed to end and at which the values for contribution to general average shall be calculated is the final port of discharge of the cargo carried under the charter but in the event of the prior loss of the vessel and freight, or either of them, the general average shall attach to any surviving interest or interests including freight advanced at the loading port deducting therefrom contingent expenses subsequent to the general average act.

When a vessel is proceeding in ballast under a time charter alone or a time charter and a voyage charter entered into by the time charterer, the general average shall attach to the vessel and such items of stores and equipment as are indicated above. Failing a prior termination of the adventure, the adventure shall be deemed to end and the values for contribution to general average calculated at the first loading port upon the commencement of loading cargo.

When the charter to which the shipowner is a party provides for York/Antwerp Rules, the general average shall be adjusted in accordance with those Rules and British law and practice and without regard to the law and practice of any foreign port at which the adventure may terminate; and in the interpretation of Rule XI it shall be immaterial whether the extra period of detention takes place at a port of loading, call or refuge, provided that the detention is in consequence of accident, sacrifice or other extraordinary circumstance occurring whilst the vessel is in ballast.

In practice neither time charter hire, as such, nor time charterer's voyage freight shall contribute to general average.

B27. CHARTERED FREIGHT (ULTERIOR): CONTRIBUTION TO GENERAL AVERAGE 70.13
(Proposed and Accepted 1891, p. 35. Confirmed 1892, p. 27.)

That when at the time of a general average act the vessel has on board cargo shipped under charter-party or bills of lading, and is also under a separate charter to load another cargo after the cargo then in course of carriage has been discharged, the ulterior chartered freight shall not contribute to the general average.

70.14 B28. Deductions from Freight at Charterer's Risk
(Original Rule of Practice, 1873.)
(Referred to a Special Committee 1908—Report 1909.)
(Amended 1968, p. 23. Confirmed 1969, p. 22.)

That freight at the risk of the charterer shall be subject to no deduction for wages and charges, except in the case of charters in which the wages or charges are payable by the charterer, in which case such freight shall be governed by the same rule as freight at the risk of the shipowner.

70.15 B29. Forwarding Charges on Advanced Freight
(Original Rule of Practice, 1873.)

That in case of wreck, the cargo being forwarded to its destination, the charterer, who has paid a lump sum on account of freight, which is not to be returned in the event of the vessel being lost, shall not be liable for any portion of the forwarding freight and charges, when the same are less than the balance of freight payable to the shipowner at the port of destination under the original charter-party.

70.16 B30. Sacrifice for the Common Safety: Direct Liability of Underwriters
(Proposed and Accepted 1890, p. 42. Confirmed 1891, p. 34.)

That in case of general average sacrifice there is, under ordinary policies of insurance, a direct liability of an underwriter on ship for loss of or damage to ship's materials, and of an underwriter on goods or freight, for loss of or damage to goods or loss of freight so sacrificed as a general average loss; that such loss not being particular average is not taken into account in computing the memorandum percentages, and that the direct liability of an underwriter for such loss is consequently unaffected by the memorandum or any other warranty respecting particular average.

70.17 B31. Sacrifice of Ship's Stores: Direct Liability of Underwriters
(Proposed and Accepted 1921, p. 50. Confirmed 1922, p. 43.)

That underwriters insuring ship's stores, bunker coal or fuel, destroyed or used as part of a general average operation, shall only be liable for those articles as a direct claim on the policy when they formed part of the property at risk at the time of the peril giving rise to the general average act.

70.18 B32. Enforcement of General Average Lien by Shipowners
(Proposed and Accepted 1890, p. 56. Confirmed 1891, p. 34.)

That in all cases where general average damage to ship is claimed direct from the underwriters on that interest, the average adjusters shall ascertain whether the shipowners have taken the necessary steps to enforce their lien for general average on the cargo, and shall insert in the average statement a note giving the result of their enquiries.

70.19 B33. Underwriter's Liability (Custom of Lloyd's 1876)

If the ship or cargo be insured for more than its contributory value, the underwriter pays what is assessed on the contributory value. But where insured for less than the contributory value, the underwriter pays on the insured value; and when there has been a particular average for damage which forms a deduction from the contributory value of the ship that must be deducted from the insured value to find upon what the underwriter contributes.

This rule does not apply to foreign adjustments, when the basis of contribution is something other than the net value of the thing insured.

(Proposed and Accepted 1922, p. 56. Confirmed 1923, p. 19.)

That in practice, in applying the above rule for the purpose of ascertaining the liability of underwriters for contribution to general average and salvage charges, deduction shall be made from the insured value of all losses and charges for which underwriters are liable and which have been deducted in arriving at the contributory value.

(Proposed and Accepted June 1926, p. 38. Confirmed November 1926, p. 7.)

In adjusting the liability of underwriters on freight for general average contribution and salvage charges, effect shall be given to section 73 of the Marine Insurance Act 1906, by comparing the gross and not the net amount of freight at risk with the insured value in the case of a valued policy or the insurable value in the case of an unvalued policy.

B34. The Duty of Adjusters in Cases involving Refunds of General Average Deposits or Apportionment of Salvage, Collision Recoveries, or other Funds **70.20**

(Proposed and Accepted 1896, p. 50. Confirmed 1897, p. 34.)

That in cases of general average where deposits have been collected and it is likely that repayments will have to be made, measures be taken by the adjuster to ascertain the names of underwriters who have reimbursed their assured in respect of such deposits; that the names of any such underwriters be set forth in the adjustment as claimants of refund, if any, to which they are apparently entitled; and that on completion of the adjustment, notice be sent to all underwriters whose names are so set forth as to any refund of which they appear as claimants and as to the steps to be taken in order to obtain payment of the same.

That in cases where the names of any underwriters are not to be ascertained on completion of the adjustment, notice be sent to the Secretary of Lloyd's, to the Institute of London Underwriters, to the Liverpool Underwriter's Association, and to the Association of Underwriters of Glasgow, notifying such interests as have not been appropriated to underwriters. And that in cases of apportionment of salvage or other funds for distribution similar measures be taken by the adjuster to safeguard the interests of any underwriters who may be entitled to benefit under the apportionment.

B35. "Memorandum" to Statements showing Refunds in respect of General Average Deposits **70.21**

(Proposed and Accepted 1904, p. 50. Confirmed 1905, p. 36.)

That the following memorandum shall appear at the end of statements which show refunds to be due in respect of General Average Deposits, *viz.*—

> Memorandum—Refunds of general average deposits shown in this statement should only be paid on production of the "original" deposit receipts.

70.22 B36. Interest on Deposits

(Proposed and Accepted 1923, p. 32. Confirmed 1924, p. 36.)

That, unless otherwise expressly provided, the interest accrued on deposits on account of salvage and/or general average and/or particular and/or other charges, or on the balance of such deposits after payments on account, if any, have been made, shall be credited to the depositor or those to whom his rights in respect of the deposits have been transferred.

70.23 B37. Apportionment of Interest on Amounts Made Good

(Proposed and Accepted 1925, p. 68. Confirmed 1926, p. 38.)

That in practice (in the absence of express agreement between the parties concerned) interest allowed on amounts made good shall be apportioned between assured and underwriters, taking into account the sums paid by underwriters and the dates when such payments were made, notwithstanding that by the addition of interest the underwriter may receive a larger sum than he has paid.

SECTION "C" YORK/ANTWERP RULES

70.24 C1. Salvage Services rendered under an Agreement

(Proposed and Accepted 1942, p. 50. Confirmed 1943, p. 39.)
(Amended 1950, p. 28. Confirmed 1951, p. 38.)

Expenses for salvage services rendered by or accepted under agreement shall in practice be treated as general average provided that such expenses were incurred for the common safety within the meaning of Rule "A" of the York-Antwerp Rules 1924 or York-Antwerp Rules 1950.

70.25 C2. Commission allowed under York/Antwerp Rules

(Proposed and Accepted 1933, p. 45. Confirmed 1934, p. 40.)
(Amended 1950, 1974 and 1996.)

That the commission of 2 per cent allowed on general average disbursements under the York-Antwerp Rules, shall be credited in full to the party who has authorised the expenditure and is liable for payment, except that where the funds for payment are provided in the first instance in whole or in part from the deposit funds, or by other parties to the adventure, or by underwriters, the commission on such advances shall be credited to the deposit funds or to the parties or underwriters providing the funds for payment.

70.26 C3. York-Antwerp Rules 1924: Rules X(a) and XX

(Proposed and Accepted 1949, p. 36. Confirmed 1950, p. 27.)

That, in practice, where a vessel is at any port or place in circumstances in which the wages and maintenance of crew during detention there for the purpose of repairs necessary for the safe prosecution of the voyage would be admissible in general average under Rule XI of the York-Antwerp Rules 1924, and the vessel is necessarily removed thence to another port or place because such repairs cannot be effected at the first port or place, the provisions of Rule X(a) shall be applied to the second port or place as if it were a port or place of refuge within that Rule and the provisions of Rule XX shall be applied to the prolongation of the voyage occasioned by such removal.

C4. YORK-ANTWERP RULES 1950, 1974 AND 1994: RULE X(A) 70.27
(Proposed and Accepted 1957, p. 24. Confirmed 1958, p. 18.)
(Amended 1974 and 1996)

That in practice, in applying the second paragraph of Rule X(a), a vessel shall be deemed to be at a port or place of refuge when she is at any port or place in circumstances in which the wages and maintenance of the Master, Officers and crew incurred during any extra period of detention there would be admissible in General Average under the provisions of Rule XI.

SECTION "F" GENERAL AVERAGE ADJUSTMENT UNDER ENGLISH LAW AND PRACTICE

F1. DECKLOAD JETTISON (CUSTOM OF LLOYD'S, AMENDED 1890–91) 70.28

The jettison of a deckload carried according to the usage of trade and not in violation of the contracts of affreightment is general average.

There is an exception to this rule in the case of cargoes of cotton, tallow, acids and some other goods.

F2. DAMAGE BY WATER USED TO EXTINGUISH FIRE 70.29
(Proposed and Accepted 1873, p. 20. Confirmed 1874, p. 18.)

That damage done by water poured down a ship's hold to extinguish a fire be treated as general average.

F3. EXTINGUISHING FIRE ON SHIPBOARD 70.30
(Proposed and Accepted 1968, p. 18. Confirmed 1969, p. 22.)
(Amended 1974.)

Damage done to a ship and cargo, or either of them, by water or otherwise, including damage by beaching or scuttling a burning ship, in extinguishing a fire on board the ship, shall be made good as general average; except that no compensation shall be made for damage by smoke or heat however caused.

F4. VOLUNTARY STRANDING 70.31
(Proposed and Accepted 1968, p. 20. Confirmed 1969, p. 22.)
(Amended 1996.)

Where a ship is intentionally run on shore for the common safety, whether or not she might have been driven on shore, the consequent loss or damage shall be allowed as general average.

F5. EXPENSES LIGHTENING A SHIP WHEN ASHORE 70.32
(*Custom of Lloyd's, Amended* 1890–91 *and* 1968–69)

When a ship is ashore in a position of peril and, in order to float her, cargo is put into lighters, and is then at once re-shipped, the whole cost of lightering, including lighter hire and re-shipping, is general average.

F6. SAILS SET TO FORCE A SHIP OFF THE GROUND 70.33
(*Custom of Lloyd's*, 1876)

Sails damaged by being set, or kept set, to force a ship off the ground or to drive her higher up the ground for the common safety, are general average.

70.34 F7. STRANDED VESSELS: DAMAGE TO ENGINES IN GETTING OFF
(Proposed and Accepted 1890, p. 64. Confirmed 1891, p. 35.)
(Amended 1906, p. 15. Confirmed 1907, p. 46.)

That damage caused to machinery and boilers of a stranded vessel, in endeavouring to refloat for the common safety, when the interests are in peril, be allowed in general average.

70.35 F8. RESORT TO PORT OF REFUGE FOR GENERAL AVERAGE REPAIRS: TREATMENT OF THE CHARGES INCURRED
(Proposed and Accepted 1888, p. 45. Confirmed 1889, p. 48.)

That when a ship puts into a port of refuge in consequence of damage which is itself the subject of general average, and sails thence with her original cargo, or a part of it, the outward as well as the inward port charges shall be treated as general average; and when cargo is discharged for the purpose of repairing such damage, the warehouse rent and reloading of the same shall, as well as the discharge, be treated as general average. (See *Attwood v. Sellar.*)

70.36 F9. RESORT TO PORT OF REFUGE ON ACCOUNT OF PARTICULAR AVERAGE REPAIRS: TREATMENT OF THE CHARGES INCURRED
(Proposed and Accepted 1888, p. 47. Confirmed 1889, p. 49.)

That when a ship puts into a port of refuge in consequence of damage which is itself the subject of particular average (or not of general average) and when the cargo has been discharged in consequence of such damage, the inward port charges and the cost of discharging the cargo shall be general average, the warehouse rent of cargo shall be a particular charge on cargo, and the cost of reloading and outward port charges shall be a particular charge on freight. (See *Svendsen v. Wallace.*)

70.37 F10. TREATMENT OF COSTS OF STORAGE AND RELOADING AT PORT OF REFUGE
(Proposed and Accepted 1886, p. 37. Confirmed 1887, p. 36.)

That when the cargo is discharged for the purpose of repairing, re-conditioning, or diminishing damage to ship or cargo which is itself the subject of general average, the cost of storage on it and of reloading it shall be treated as general average, equally with the cost of discharging it.

70.38 F11. INSURANCE ON CARGO DISCHARGED UNDER AVERAGE
(Proposed and Accepted 1924, p. 43. Confirmed 1925, p. 43.)
(Amended 1968, p. 21. Confirmed 1969, p. 22.)

That in practice, where the cost of insurance has been reasonably incurred by the shipowner, or his agents, on cargo discharged under average, such cost shall be treated as part of the cost of storage.

70.39 F12. EXPENSES AT A PORT OF REFUGE
(*Custom of Lloyd's, Amended* 1890–91)

When a ship puts into a port of refuge on account of accident and not in consequence of damage which is itself the subject of general average, then on the assumption that the ship was seaworthy at the commencement of the voyage, the Custom of Lloyd's is as follows:

(*a*)—All cost of towage, pilotage, harbour dues, and other extraordinary
1876 expenses incurred in order to bring the ship and cargo into a place of safety, are general average. Under the terms "extraordinary expenses" are not included wages or victuals of crew, coals, or engine stores, or demurrage.

(*b*)—The cost of discharging the cargo, whether for the common safety, or to
1876 repair the ship, together with the cost of conveying it to the warehouse, is general average.

The cost of discharging the cargo on account of damage to it resulting from its own *vice propre*, is chargeable to the owners of the cargo.

(*c*)—The warehouse rent, or other expenses which take the place of warehouse
1876 rent, of the cargo when so discharged, is, except as under, a special charge on the cargo.

(*d*)—The cost of reloading the cargo, and the outward port charges incurred
1876 through leaving the port of refuge, are, when the discharge of cargo falls in general average, a special charge on freight.

(*e*)—The expenses referred to in clause (*d*) are charged to the party who runs
1876 the risk of freight—that is, wholly to the charterer—if the whole freight has been prepaid; and, if part only, then in the proportion which the part prepaid bears to the whole freight.

(*f*)—When the cargo, instead of being sent ashore, is placed on board hulk or lighters during the ship's stay in port, the hulk-hire is divided between general average, cargo, and freight, in such proportions as may place the several contributing interests in nearly the same relative positions as if the cargo had been landed and stored.

F13. Treatment of Costs of Extraordinary Discharge **70.40**

(Proposed and Accepted 1886, p. 37. Confirmed 1887, p. 36.)

That no distinction be drawn in practice between discharging cargo for the common safety of ship and cargo, and discharging it for the purpose of effecting at an intermediate port or ports of refuge repairs necessary for the prosecution of the voyage.

F14. Towage from a Port of Refuge **70.41**

(Proposed and Accepted 1876, p. 26. Confirmed 1877, p. 54.)

That if a ship be in a port of refuge at which it is practicable to repair her, and if, in order to save expense, she be towed thence to some other port, then the extra cost of such towage shall be divided in proportion to the saving of expense thereby occasioned to the several parties to the adventure.

F15. Cargo Forwarded from a Port of Refuge **70.42**

(Proposed and Accepted 1876, p. 26. Confirmed 1877, p. 54.)

That if a ship be in a port of refuge at which it is practicable to repair her so as to enable her to carry on the whole cargo, but, in order to save expense, the cargo, or a portion of it, be transhipped by another vessel, or otherwise forwarded, then the cost of such transhipment (up to the amount of expense saved) shall be divided in proportion to the saving of expense thereby occasioned to the several parties to the adventure.

70.43 F16. CARGO SOLD AT A PORT OF REFUGE
(Proposed and Accepted 1902, p. 34. Confirmed 1903, p. 18.)

That if a ship be in a port of refuge at which it is practicable to repair her so as to enable her to carry on the whole cargo, or such portion of it as is fit to be carried on, but, in order to save expense, the cargo, or a portion of it, be, with the consent of the owners of such cargo, sold at the port of refuge, then the loss by sale including loss of freight on cargo so sold (up to the amount of expense saved) shall be divided in proportion to the saving of expense thereby occasioned to the several parties to the adventure; provided always that the amount so divided shall in no case exceed the cost of transhipment and/or forwarding referred to in the preceding rule of the Association.

70.44 F17. INTERPRETATION OF THE RULE RESPECTING SUBSTITUTED EXPENSES
(Proposed and Accepted 1877, p. 63. Confirmed 1878, p. 18.)

That for the purpose of avoiding any misinterpretation of the resolution relating to the apportionment of substituted expenses, it is declared that the saving of expense therein mentioned is limited to a saving or reduction of the actual outlay, including the crew's wages and provisions, if any, which would have been incurred at the port of refuge, if the vessel had been repaired there, and does not include supposed losses or expenses, such as interest, loss of market, demurrage, or assumed damage by discharging.

70.45 F18. DAMAGE TO CARGO, FUEL AND STORES IN DISCHARGING, ETC.
(Proposed and Accepted 1886, p. 37. Confirmed 1887, p. 36.)
(Amended 1996.)

Damage to or loss of cargo, fuel or stores sustained in consequence of their handling, discharging, storing, reloading and stowing shall be made good as general average, when and only when the cost of those measures respectively is admitted as general average.

70.46 F19. DEDUCTIONS FROM COST OF REPAIRS IN ADJUSTING GENERAL AVERAGE
(Proposed and Accepted 1887, p. 36. Confirmed 1888, p. 28.)
(*Referred to Special Committee* 1884, *p.* 45—*Reports, Prov.* 1885, *p.* 19, *Final* 1886, *p.* 16.)
(Amended 1934, p. 41. Confirmed 1935, p. 22.)
(Amended 1950, p. 30. Confirmed 1951, p. 38.)
(Amended 1974.)

Repairs to be allowed in general average shall not be subject to deductions in respect of "new for old" where old material or parts are replaced by new unless the ship is over fifteen years old in which case there shall be a deduction of one third. The deductions shall be regulated by the age of the ship from December 31 of the year of completion of construction to the date of the general average act, except for insulation, life and similar boats, communications and navigational apparatus and equipment, machinery and boilers for which the deductions shall be regulated by the age of the particular parts to which they apply.

The deductions shall be made only from the cost of the new material or parts when finished and ready to be installed in the ship.

No deductions shall be made in respect of provisions, stores, anchors and chain cables.

Drydock and slipway dues and costs of shifting the ship shall be allowed in full.

The costs of cleaning, painting or coating of bottom shall not be allowed in general average unless the bottom has been painted or coated within the twelve months preceding the date of the general average act in which case one half of such costs shall be allowed.

F20. FREIGHT SACRIFICED: AMOUNT TO BE MADE GOOD IN GENERAL AVERAGE **70.47**
(Proposed and Accepted 1894, p. 56. Confirmed 1895, p. 29.)

That the loss of freight to be made good in general average shall be ascertained by deducting from the amount of gross freight lost the charges which the owner thereof would have incurred to earn such freight, but has, in consequence of the sacrifice, not incurred.

F21. BASIS OF CONTRIBUTION TO GENERAL AVERAGE **70.48**
(Original Rule of Practice, 1873.)

When property saved by a general average act is injured or destroyed by subsequent accident, the contributing value of that property to a general average which is less than the total contributing value, shall, when it does not reach the port of destination, be its actual net proceeds; when it does it shall be its actual net value at the port of destination on its delivery there; and in all cases any values allowed in general average shall be added to and form part of the contributing value as above.

The above rule shall not apply to adjustments made before the adventure has terminated.

F22. CONTRIBUTORY VALUE OF FREIGHT **70.49**
(Original Rule of Practice 1873—Part.)
(Referred to a Special Committee 1908—Report 1909.)
(Amended 1968, p. 22. Confirmed 1969, p. 22.)

That freight at the risk of the shipowner shall contribute to general average upon its gross amount, deducting such charges and crew's wages as would not have been incurred in earning the freight had the ship and cargo been totally lost at the date of the general average act and have not been allowed as general average.

Uniformity Resolutions

1. YORK-ANTWERP RULES 1924: APPLICATION OF RULE XIV **70.50**
(Passed November 1928, p. 11.)

That in practice, in applying Rule XIV of the York-Antwerp Rules 1924, the cost of the temporary repair of the accidental damage there referred to shall be allowed in general average up to the saving to the general average by effecting such temporary repair, without regard to the saving (if any) to other interests.

APPENDIX 4

LLOYD'S STANDARD FORMS FOR GENERAL AVERAGE SECURITY 80.01

SALVAGE

80.02

LLOYD'S AVERAGE BOND

To ....
Owner(s) of the ....
Voyage and date ....
Port of shipment ....
Port of destination/discharge ....
Bill of lading or waybill number(s) ....

Quantity and description of goods

In consideration of the delivery to us or to our order, on payment of the freight due, of the goods noted above we agree to pay the proper proportion of any salvage and/or general average and/or special charges which may hereafter be ascertained to be due from the goods or the shippers or owners thereof under an adjustment prepared in accordance with the provisions of the contract of affreightment governing the carriage of the goods or, failing any such provision, in accordance with the law and practice of the place where the common maritime adventure ended and which is payable in respect of the goods by the shippers or owners thereof.

We also agree to:

(i) furnish particulars of the value of the goods, supported by a copy of the commercial invoice rendered to us, or, if there is no such invoice, details of the shipped value and

(ii) make a payment on account of such sum as is duly certified by the average adjusters to be due from the goods and which is payable in respect of the goods by the shippers or owners thereof.

Date .... Signature of receiver of goods ....
Full name and address ....
....
....

VALUATION FORM

80.03

To ....
Owner(s) of the ....
Voyage and date ....
Port of shipment ....
Port of destination/discharge ....
Bill of lading or waybill number(s) ....

Quantity and description of goods	Particulars of value A Invoice value (specify currency)	 B Shipped value
Currency		

1. If the goods are insured please state the following details (if known):—
   Name and address of insurers or brokers ....
   Policy or certificate number and date .... Insured value ....
2. If the goods arrived subject to loss or damage, please state nature and extent thereof
   ....
   ....
   and ensure that copies of supporting documents are forwarded either direct or through the insurers to the average adjusters named below.
3. If a general average deposit has been paid, please state:—
   (a) Amount of the deposit .... (b) Deposit receipt number ....
   (c) Whether you have made any claim on your insurers for reimbursement ....

Date .... Signature ....
Full name and address ....
....
....

NOTES

1. If the goods form the subject of a commercial transaction, fill in column A with the amount of the commercial invoice rendered to you, **and attach a copy of this invoice hereto**.
2. If there is no commercial invoice covering the goods, state the shipped value, if known to you, in column B.
3. In either case, state the currency involved.
4. The shipowners have appointed as average adjusters .... to whom this form should be sent duly completed together with a copy of the commercial invoice.

80.04 **Guarantee by Corporation of Lloyd's to the Shipowners**

In consideration of the immediate delivery to the consignees thereof of the merchandise specified below, the Corporation of Lloyd's hereby guarantees the due payment to the Shipowners of any contribution for General Average and/or Salvage and/or other Charges which may be properly chargeable against the said merchandise.

Vessel
Voyage and Date
Description of Goods

For the Corporation of Lloyd's

Dated, LLOYD'S,

Form Y

LLOYD'S GENERAL AVERAGE BOND AND GUARANTEE

Settlement of Claims Abroad

AN AGREEMENT made this day of 19 BETWEEN the Corporation of Lloyd's (hereinafter called "Lloyd's") of the first part Messrs. (hereinafter called "the Shipowner") of the second part and the other several Persons whose names or firms are subscribed hereto (hereinafter called "the Consignees") of the third part WHEREAS the ship or vessel lately arrived at the port of on a voyage from and it is alleged that during such voyage the vessel met with a casualty and sustained damage and loss and that sacrifices were made and expenditure incurred which may form a charge on the cargo or some part thereof or be the subject of a Salvage and/or a General Average Contribution but the same cannot be immediately ascertained and in the meantime it is desirable that the cargo shall be delivered NOW THEREFORE THESE PRESENTS WITNESS and the Parties hereto severally agree as follows: **80.05**

1. The Shipowner agrees with the Consignees that he will deliver to them respectively or to their order respectively their respective consignments particulars whereof are contained in the Schedule hereto on payment of the freight payable on delivery if any and the Consignees in consideration of such delivery agree for themselves severally and respectively that they will pay as herein provided the proper and respective proportion of any Salvage and/or General Average and/or Particular and/or other Charges which may be chargeable upon their respective consignments particulars whereof are contained in the Schedule hereto or to which the Shippers or Owners of such consignments may be liable to contribute in respect of such damage loss sacrifice or expenditure. And the consignees further promise and agree forthwith to furnish to the Shipowner a correct account and particulars of the amount and value of the cargo delivered to them respectively in order that any such Salvage and/or General Average and/or Particular and/or other Charges may be ascertained and adjusted in the usual manner.

2. In consideration of the delivery as aforesaid by the Shipowner of the said merchandise to the Consignees respectively without the requirement of any cash deposit Lloyd's hereby guarantees to the Shipowner the due payment by the Consignees and/or their Underwriters of the whole of the said Salvage and/or General Average and/or Particular and/or other Charges which may be properly chargeable against the said merchandise.

3. Lloyd's further agrees with the Shipowner that Lloyd's will pending the preparation of the usual Average Statement make interim payment or payments to the Shipowner in respect of the amounts which may ultimately be found due to him from the Consignees respectively in respect of the matters aforesaid. Provided always that Lloyd's shall only be liable to make any such payment upon the receipt of and to the amount shown by a Certificate in writing stating the proper amount of any such payment; such Certificate to be signed by the Adjuster or firm of Adjusters who may be employed in the preparation of the said Average Statement.

4. In consideration of these presents the Shipowner hereby assigns to Lloyd's all the sums which may be due and payable by the Consignees respectively to the Shipowner in respect of the aforesaid Salvage and/or General Average and/or Particular and/or other Charges and all his right and title to recover the same from the Consignees respectively whether under the Contract of Affreightment or under this Agreement or otherwise howsoever. And the Consignees hereby

take cognisance of and admit the receipt of notice of the assignment herein contained.

5. The Consignees in consideration of these presents hereby severally certify and warrant to Lloyd's (i) that the merchandise specified in the first column of the Schedule hereto is respectively insured by the Policy or Policies specified in the second column; (ii) that such Policy or Policies have been fully subscribed for the amount appearing in the third column. The Consignees hereby severally assign to Lloyd's all their respective rights under such Policy or Policies in respect of the recovery thereunder of the sums which may be due and payable by them respectively to the Shipowner in respect of the aforesaid Salvage and/or General Average and/or Particular and/or other Charges and severally to undertake to do all things necessary to make such assignment valid and effectual. Provided always and it is hereby declared that nothing herein contained shall in any way relieve the Consignees from their personal liability in respect of the whole or any part of the aforesaid sums which Lloyd's may not be able for any reason whatever to recover under the aforesaid Policy or Policies.

FOR THE CORPORATION OF LLOYD'S
By Special Authority

....

Lloyd's Agents at ....

....

SCHEDULE

Description and Quantity of Cargo	Number of Policy and Insurance Certificate, if any	Amount insured	Signature of Consignees

No. . . .

General Average Deposit Receipt.

LLOYD'S FORM.

Dated at . . . .

. . . . **19** . . . .

Vessel . . . .

Depositors, Messrs. . . . .

. . . .

Contributory Value (provisional) . . . .

B/L or Waybill No. . . . .

Amount of Deposit . . . .

Description of Goods:

<u>NOTE FOR DEPOSITORS:</u> <u>IF INSURED</u> you may wish to send this receipt together with the original policy or certificate of insurance to your insurers who, subject to the policy conditions, may be prepared to refund this deposit. <u>IF NOT INSURED</u> you should notify the Average Adjusters direct of your interest and retain this receipt until the adjustment is issued when any credit balance can be claimed.

<u>NOTE FOR INSURERS:</u> When a repayment of this deposit has been made, advise the Average Adjusters and thus assist in final settlement.

NO DUPLICATE OF THIS RECEIPT CAN BE ISSUED.

No. . . . .

GENERAL AVERAGE DEPOSIT RECEIPT.

LLOYD'S FORM.

Dated at . . . . 19 . . . .

Vessel . . . . from . . . . to . . . .

Nature and date of Accident . . . .

. . . .

RECEIVED from Messrs. . . . .

the sum of . . . .

deposit on account of General Average and or Salvage and or Charges,

being . . . . per cent on . . . .

provisionally accepted as the contributory value of the following goods, viz.:

. . . .

. . . .

B/L or Waybill No. . . . .

Marks and Nos. and Description of Interest to be inserted here.

£

. . . .

for and on behalf of the Trustee(s) or nominated representative(s).

N.B.—The refund, if any, will be made only to the bearer of, and in exchange for, this Receipt, and will be the whole balance of the deposit after satisfying the General Average and or Salvage and or Charges, without deduction or set off of any other claims of the Shipowner against the Shipper or Consignee.

The General Average will be adjusted in . . . . and the Shipowners have given the necessary instructions to Messrs. . . . . Average Adjusters

80.06

80.07

LLOYD'S

NOTES

1. Insert name of person signing on behalf of Owners of property to be salved. The Master should sign wherever possible.

2. The Contractor's name should always be inserted in line 4 and whenever the agreement is signed by the Master of the Salving vessel or other person on behalf of the Contractor the name of the Master or other person must also be inserted in line 4 before the words "for and on behalf of". The words "for and on behalf of" should be deleted where a Contractor signs personally.

3. Insert place if agreed in clause 1(a)(i) and currency if agreed in clause 1(3).

STANDARD FORM OF

SALVAGE AGREEMENT

(APPROVED AND PUBLISHED BY THE COUNCIL OF LLOYD'S)

NO CURE – NO PAY

On board the ....

Dated ....

**See Note 1 above* IT IS HEREBY AGREED between Captain + ... for and on behalf of the Owners of the " ...." her cargo freight bunkers stores and any other property thereon (hereinafter collectively called "the Owners")

†See Note 2 above and ....for and on behalf of .... (hereinafter called "the Contractor"*) that:-

1. (a) The Contractor shall use his best endeavours:-

#See Note 3 above (i) to salve the " ...." and/or her cargo freight bunkers stores and any other property thereon and take them to #.. or

to such other place as may hereafter be agreed either place to be deemed a place of safety or if no such place is named or agreed to a place of safety and

(ii) while performing the salvage services to prevent or minimise damage to the environment.

(b) Subject to the statutory provisions relating to special compensation the services shall be rendered and accepted as salvage services upon the principle of "no cure – no pay".

(c) The Contractor's remuneration shall be fixed by Arbitration in London in the manner hereinafter prescribed and any other difference arising out of this Agreement or the operations thereunder shall be referred to Arbitration in the same way.

(d) In the event of the services referred to in this Agreement or any part of such services having been already rendered at the date of this Agreement by the Contractor to the said vessel and/or her cargo freight bunkers stores and any other property thereon the provisions of this Agreement shall apply to such services.

#See Note 3 above (e) The security to be provided to the Council of Lloyd's (hereinafter called "the Council") the Salved Value(s) the Award and/or any Interim Award(s) and/or any Award on Appeal shall be in .... currency.

(f) If clause 1(e) is not completed then the security to be provided and the Salved Value(s) the Award and/or Interim Award(s) and/or Award on Appeal shall be in Pounds Sterling.

(g) This Agreement and Arbitration thereunder shall except as otherwise expressly provided be governed by the law of England, including the English law of salvage.

PROVISIONS AS TO THE SERVICES

2. *Definitions:* In this Agreement any reference to "Convention" is a reference to the International Convention on Salvage 1989 as incorporated in the Merchant Shipping (Salvage and Pollution) Act 1994 (and any amendment thereto). The terms "Contractor" and "services"/"salvage services" in this Agreement shall have the same meanings as the terms "salvor(s)" and "salvage operation(s)" in the Convention.

3. *Owners Co-operation*: The Owners their Servants and Agents shall co-operate fully with the Contractor in and about the salvage including obtaining entry to the place named or the place of safety as defined in clause 1. The Contractor may make reasonable use of the vessel's machinery gear equipment anchors chains stores and other appurtenances during and for the purpose of the salvage services free of expense but shall not unnecessarily damage abandon or sacrifice the same or any property the subject of this Agreement.

4. *Vessel Owners Right to Terminate*: When there is no longer any reasonable prospect of a useful result leading to a salvage reward in accordance with Convention Article 13 the owners of the vessel shall be entitled to terminate the services of the Contractor by giving reasonable notice to the Contractor in writing.

PROVISIONS AS TO SECURITY

5. (a) The Contractor shall immediately after the termination of the services or sooner notify the Council and where practicable the Owners of the amount for which he demands salvage security (inclusive of costs expenses and interest) from each of the respective Owners.

(b) Where a claim is made or may be made for special compensation the owners of the vessel shall on the demand of the Contractor whenever made provide security for the Contractor's claim for special compensation provided always that such demand is made within two years of the date of termination of the services.

(c) The amount of any such security shall be reasonable in the light of the knowledge available to the Contractor at the time when the demand is made. Unless otherwise agreed such security shall be provided (i) to the Council (ii) in a form approved by the Council and (iii) by persons firms or corporations either acceptable to the Contractor or resident in the United Kingdom and acceptable to the Council. The Council shall not be responsible for the sufficiency (whether in amount or otherwise) of any security which shall be provided nor the default or insolvency of any person firm or corporation providing the same.

(d) The owners of the vessel their Servants and Agents shall use their best endeavours to ensure that the cargo owners provide their proportion of salvage security before the cargo is released.

6. (a) Until security has been provided as aforesaid the Contractor shall have a maritime lien on the property salved for his remuneration.

(b) The property salved shall not without the consent in writing of the Contractor (which shall not be unreasonably withheld) be removed from the place to which it has been taken by the Contractor under clause 1(a). Where such consent is given by the Contractor on condition that the Contractor is provided with temporary security pending completion of the voyage the Contractor's maritime lien on the property salved shall remain in force to the extent necessary to enable the Contractor to compel the provision of security in accordance with clause 5(c).

(c) The Contractor shall not arrest or detain the property salved unless:

(i) security is not provided within 14 days (exclusive of Saturdays and Sundays or other days observed as general holidays at Lloyd's) after the date of the termination of the services or

(ii) he has reason to believe that the removal of the property salved is contemplated contrary to clause 6(b) or

(iii) any attempt is made to remove the property salved contrary to clause 6(b).

(d) The Arbitrator appointed under clause 7 or the Appeal Arbitrator(s) appointed under clause 13(d) shall have power in their absolute discretion to include in the amount awarded to the Contractor the whole or part of any expenses reasonably incurred by the Contractor in:

(i) ascertaining demanding and obtaining the amount of security reasonably required in accordance with clause 5.

(ii) enforcing and/or protecting by insurance or otherwise or taking reasonable steps to enforce and/or protect his lien.

PROVISIONS AS TO ARBITRATION

7. (a) Whether security has been provided or not the Council shall appoint an Arbitrator upon receipt of a written request made by letter telex facsimile or in any other permanent form provided that any party requesting such appointment shall if required by the Council undertake to pay the reasonable fees and expenses of the Council and/or any Arbitrator or Appeal Arbitrator(s).

(b) Where an Arbitrator has been appointed and the parties do not proceed to arbitration the Council may recover any fees costs and/or expenses which are outstanding.

8. The Contractor's remuneration and/or special compensation shall be fixed by the Arbitrator appointed under clause 7. Such remuneration shall not be diminished by reason of the exception to the principle of "no cure – no pay" in the form of special compensation.

REPRESENTATION

9. Any party to this Agreement who wishes to be heard or to adduce evidence shall nominate a person in the United Kingdom to represent him failing which the Arbitrator or Appeal Arbitrator(s) may proceed as if such party had renounced his right to be heard or adduce evidence.

CONDUCT OF THE ARBITRATION

10. (a) The Arbitrator shall have power to:

(i) admit such oral or documentary evidence or information as he may think fit

(i) conduct the Arbitration in such manner in all respects as he may think fit subject to such procedural rules as the Council may approve

(iii) order the Contractor in his absolute discretion to pay the whole or part of the expense of providing excessive security or security which has been unreasonably demanded under Clause 5(b) and to deduct such sum from the remuneration and/or special compensation

(iv) make interim Award(s) including payment(s) on account on such terms as may be fair and just

(v) make such orders as to costs fees and expenses including those of the Council charged under clauses 10(h) and 14(b) as may be fair and just.

(b) The Arbitrator and the Council may charge reasonable fees and expenses for their services whether the Arbitration proceeds to a hearing or not and all such fees and expenses shall be treated as part of the costs of the Arbitration.

(c) Any Award shall (subject to Appeal as provided in this Agreement) be final and binding on all the parties concerned whether they were represented at the Arbitration or not.

INTEREST & RATES OF EXCHANGE

11. *Interest*: Interest at rates per annum to be fixed by the Arbitrator shall (subject to Appeal as provided in this Agreement) be payable on any sum awarded taking into account any sums already paid:—

(i) from the date of termination of the services unless the Arbitrator shall in his absolute discretion otherwise decide until the date of publication by the Council of the Award and/or Interim Award(s) and

(ii) from the expiration of 21 days (exclusive of Saturdays and Sundays or other days observed as general holidays at Lloyd's) after the date of publication by the Council of the Award and/or Interim Award(s) until the date payment is received by the Contractor or the Council both dates inclusive.

For the purpose of sub-clause (ii) the expression "sum awarded" shall include the fees and expenses referred to in clause 10(b).

12. *Currency Correction*: In considering what sums of money have been expended by the Contractor in rendering the services and/or in fixing the amount of the Award and/or Interim Award(s) and/or Award on Appeal the Arbitrator or Appeal Arbitrator(s) shall to such an extent and in so far as it may be fair and just in all the circumstances give effect to the consequences of any change or changes in the relevant rates of exchange which may have occurred between the date of termination of the services and the date on which the Award and/or Interim Award(s) and/or Award on Appeal is made.

PROVISIONS AS TO APPEAL

13. (a) Notice of Appeal if any shall be given to the Council within 14 days (exclusive of Saturdays and Sundays or other days observed as general holidays at Lloyd's) after the date of the publication by the Council of the Award and/or Interim Award(s).

(b) Notice of Cross-Appeal if any shall be given to the Council within 14 days (exclusive of Saturdays and Sundays or other days observed as general holidays at Lloyd's) after notification by the Council to the parties of any Notice of Appeal. Such notification if sent by post shall be deemed received on the working day following the day of posting.

(c) Notice of Appeal or Cross-Appeal shall be given to the Council by letter telex facsimile or in any other permanent form.

(d) Upon receipt of Notice of Appeal the Council shall refer the Appeal to the hearing and determination of the Appeal Arbitrator(s) selected by it.

(e) If any Notice of Appeal or Cross-Appeal is withdrawn the Appeal hearing shall nevertheless proceed in respect of such Notice of Appeal or Cross-Appeal as may remain.

(f) Any Award on Appeal shall be final and binding on all the parties to that Appeal Arbitration whether they were represented either at the Arbitration or at the Appeal Arbitration or not.

CONDUCT OF THE APPEAL

14. (a) The Appeal Arbitrator(s) in addition to the powers of the Arbitrator under clauses 10(a) and 11 shall have power to:—

(i) admit the evidence which was before the Arbitrator together with the Arbitrator's notes and reasons for his Award and/or Interim Award(s) and any transcript of evidence and such additional evidence as he or they may think fit.

(ii) confirm increase or reduce the sum awarded by the Arbitrator and to make such order as to the payment of interest on such sum as he or they may think fit.

(iii) confirm revoke or vary any order and/or Declaratory Award made by the Arbitrator.

(iv) award interest on any fees and expenses charged under paragraph (b) of this clause from the expiration of 21 days (exclusive of Saturdays and Sundays or other days observed as general holidays at Lloyd's) after the date of publication by the Council of the Award on Appeal and/or Interim Award(s) on Appeal until the date payment is received by the Council both dates inclusive.

(b) The Appeal Arbitrator(s) and the Council may charge reasonable fees and expenses for their services in connection with the Appeal Arbitration whether it proceeds to a hearing or not and all such fees and expenses shall be treated as part of the costs of the Appeal Arbitration.

PROVISIONS AS TO PAYMENT

15. (a) In case of Arbitration of no Notice of Appeal be received by the Council in accordance with clause 13(a) the Council shall call upon the party or parties concerned to pay the amount awarded and in the event of non-payment shall subject to the Contractor first providing to the Council a satisfactory Undertaking to pay all the costs thereof realise or enforce the security and pay therefrom to the Contractor (whose receipt shall be a good discharge to it) the amount awarded to him together with interest if any. The Contractor shall reimburse the parties concerned to such extent as the Award is less than any sums paid on account or in respect of Interim Award(s).

(b) If Notice of Appeal be received by the Council in accordance with clause 13 it shall as soon as the Award on Appeal has been published by it call upon the party or parties concerned to pay the amount awarded and in the event of non-payment shall subject to the Contractor first providing to the Council a satisfactory Undertaking to pay all the costs thereof realise or enforce the security and pay therefrom to the Contractor (whose receipt shall be a good discharge to it) the amount awarded to him together with interest if any. The Contractor shall reimburse the parties concerned to such extent as the Award on Appeal is less than any sums paid on account or in respect of the Award or Interim Award(s).

(c) If any sum shall become payable to the Contractor as remuneration for his services and/or interest and/or costs as the result of an agreement made between the Contractor and the Owners or any of them the Council in the event of non-payment shall subject to the Contractor first providing to the Council a satisfactory Undertaking to pay all the costs thereof realise or enforce the security and pay therefrom to the Contractor (whose receipt shall be a good discharge to it) the said sum.

(d) If the Award and/or Interim Award(s) and/or Award on Appeal provides or provide that the costs of the Arbitration and/or of the Appeal Arbitration or any part of such costs shall be borne by the Contractor such costs may be deducted from the amount awarded or agreed before payment is made to the Contractors unless satisfactory security is provided by the Contractor for the payment of such costs.

(e) Without prejudice to the provisions of clause 5(c) the liability of the Council shall be limited in any event to the amount of security provided to it.

GENERAL PROVISIONS

16. *Scope of Authority:* The Master or other person signing this Agreement on behalf of the property to be salved enters into this Agreement as agent for the vessel her cargo freight bunkers stores and any other property thereon and the respective Owners thereof and binds each (but not the one for the other or himself personally) to the due performance thereof.

17. *Notices:* Any Award notice authority order or other document signed by the Chairman of Lloyd's or any person authorised by the Council for the purpose shall be deemed to have been duly made or given by the Council and shall have the same force and effect in all respects as if it had been signed by every member of the Council.

18. *Sub-Contractor(s):* The Contractor may claim salvage and enforce any Award or agreement made between the Contractor and the Owners against security provided under clause 5 or otherwise if any on behalf of any Sub-Contractors his or their Servants or Agents including Masters and members of the crews of vessels employed by him or by any Sub-Contractors in the services provided that he first provides a reasonably satisfactory indemnity to the Owners against all claims by or liabilities to the said persons.

19. *Inducements prohibited:* No person signing this Agreement or any party on whose behalf it is signed shall at any time or in any manner whatsoever offer provide make give or promise to provide demand or take any form of inducement for entering into this Agreement.

For and on behalf of the Contractor	**For and on behalf of the Owners of property to be salved.**
.... (To be signed by the Contractor personally or by the Master of the salving vessel or other person whose name is inserted in line 4 of this Agreement)	.... (To be signed by the Master or other person whose name is inserted in line 1 of this Agreement)

APPENDIX 5

THE FUTURE OF GENERAL AVERAGE

As the final section of this twelfth edition of *Lowndes & Rudolf*, which records 2,500 years of continuing history and development of the general average distribution system and of the York-Antwerp Rules, plus a commentary on the current law and practice on this complex subject, it is appropriate to consider the FUTURE OF GENERAL AVERAGE. Translated into rhetorical form, this title might be expressed: **90.01**

WHITHER GENERAL AVERAGE?

or, with a small printer's error, to even greater effect:

WHETHER GENERAL AVERAGE.

Is there still a continuing need and future for general average, or, as is sometimes claimed, has it possibly outgrown its original purpose and, particularly in the liner trade, become too cumbersome, time-consuming and costly for the advantages it confers? Could the mercantile community manage without it? Or is it possible to find a simpler and more efficient alternative?

The opening sentence of a magazine article in March 1989 stated that: **90.02**

> "If general average didn't exist, someone would have to invent it."

but it is most unlikely that the sentiment expressed would be received with any great acclaim or universal agreement today. Indeed, as recorded earlier in paragraph 00.11, "during the last hundred years or more there have been intermittent calls for abolition [of general average] on various grounds", and those "intermittent calls" might more accurately have been described as "strongly worded and well reasoned attacks" on the general average distribution system.[1]

The general average system is thought to have originated in the Mediterranean in about 500 B.C. at a time when it was the custom for merchants to travel with **90.03**

[1] For the benefit of interested readers, the more important attacks and other writings in the English language include the following:

1864—By the *Committee of Lloyd's* on the proposed 1864 York Rules.

1869—By *J. T. Danson*, in the February 1869 issue of the *Law Magazine* and *Law Review*. He had started life as a journalist and assistant editor to Charles Dickens on the *Daily News*, and at this time was the underwriter of the Thames and Mersey Insce. Co. in Liverpool, writing the largest marine insurance account of the day.

1877—By the *Committee of Lloyd's* on the proposed 1877 York-Antwerp Rules.

1890—By *W. H. Jarrett*, Manager of the Commercial Union Assce. Co. in a paper read before the Insurance Institute of Victoria.

1894—By (later Sir) *Douglas Owen*, Secretary of the Alliance Marine Insce. Co. and author of *Marine Insurance Notes and Clauses* and other works, in a paper read at Lloyd's on May 9, 1894. The views are sound and expressed in a style which makes entertaining reading.

1914—By *W. R. Ray*, of the Union Insce. of Canton in a paper read before the Insurance Institute of Victoria on September 16, 1914.

their cargoes in the tiny ships of those times, buying, selling and bartering their wares as the voyage progressed.

The *reason* for its introduction can easily be deduced. Any voyage in those days was a truly hazardous adventure, and occasionally a storm would spring up, or the vessel strike a rock, and it would be necessary to throw overboard part of the cargo or make some other sacrifice in order to save the adventure from shipwreck and complete disaster.

Now whilst a merchant might suffer the loss of his cargo by storm or shipwreck with some degree of equanimity, one can imagine his utter misery at seeing those goods *deliberately* thrown overboard, while his fellow merchants carried on safely with their goods to the market. Their advantage was accomplished at the expense of his ruin, and there must have been many a fierce argument between the merchants as to whose goods should be jettisoned until common sense prevailed and the custom grew up that those merchants whose goods had been jettisoned, or the shipowner whose mast was cut away, for the benefit of all, should have their loss made good by contributions from the shipowner and those merchants whose property was saved.

The equalisation of the loss served a most necessary and useful function, for the merchants had probably invested the bulk of their fortunes in the one adventure, and there were no other insurance facilities whereby they could protect themselves against loss.

90.04 The general average system, born of necessity, was eminently equitable and reasonable for those far-off days, and it would be difficult to fault it on any theoretical grounds. Indeed, none of the attacks on the general average system attempt to challenge the equitable principles of the system.

The central point of the argument for the abolitionists[2] rests upon the fact that what was once a vital commercial necessity is no longer such, but, rather, a costly and unnecessary anachronism, sometimes taking several years to sort out and settle, when only as many months would be required to resolve matters if all sacrifices and expenditures were allowed to lie where they fell, and their sufferers transfer the risks to the broad shoulders of a more than adequate marine insurance market. Further, they draw attention to the fact that the scope and extent of general average is continually being widened[3] with ever increasing types of losses and expenses, a process which could be seen to be continuing even at a meeting of A.I.D.E. held at York in September 1989.

1914—By *H. K. Fowler*, Manager of the U.S. branch of the Thames and Mersey Marine Insce. Co. in his address as Chairman of the U.S. Association of Average Adjusters in October 1914.

1925—By *C. H. Johnson*, later underwriter of the Royal Group of Insce. Cos. in a paper read before the Insurance Institute of Liverpool on February 11, 1925.

1948—A Report by I.U.M.I. (International Union of Marine Insurers).

1958—By *Knut Selmer*, Research Fellow in the Institute of Maritime Law, University of Oslo, in his book *The Survival of General Average*. This is a remarkable survey of every aspect of the subject, and required reading for anyone seriously proposing to abate the general average distribution system.

1966—An extended correspondence in *Lloyd's List* initiated by *Thomas F. Poole* on May 31, 1966, and continuing until at least December 2, 1966, with occasional parallel articles in other shipping journals.

1991/94—The Reports of U.N.C.T.A.D. and I.U.M.I. and the paper by Prof. William Tetley Q.C., referred to in para. 00.106, *ante*.

[2] *E.g.* see the list of criticisms in the 1948 I.U.M.I. Report copied in para. 90.30, *post*.

[3] Douglas Owen, writing in 1894, quoted from the 1877 Report of the *Committee of Lloyd's*: "So vast and complicated a system of general average that it has become almost intolerable" and continued:

Defence of the General Average System

The ancient principles of general average were so eminently fair and reasonable that they do not come under attack and need no defence, and if allowances in general average had remained as few and limited as under the Roman Civil Law[4] (jettison of cargo and cutting away masts, etc.), it is unlikely that any antipathy to the distribution system would have developed. With modern ships, cases of general average would have been of infrequent occurrence (probably less than 10 per cent of the present number), and even were it wished to dismantle the system, this would have caused no insuperable problem, if only by reason of its limited application. **90.05**

What has given rise to the objections during the past 130 years is the ever continuing increase in the number of situations which are held to be the proper subject of general average and the allowances which can be made. The process can be likened to the building of a wall, where each row of bricks forms the foundation for the next row. Each new allowance in general average can logically and legally be used as a sound precedent for yet further allowances.

The greatly enlarged general average system, and the consequent need for it to be brought into action far more frequently, creates the present climate of antipathy, the recurring attacks on the system, and the occasional need to defend it. Defences of the increased allowances are not offered, presumably for the reason that they have often been hallowed by the courts or are enshrined within the York-Antwerp Rules which are nominally accepted by voluntary agreement between the parties to the adventure.

A well-written apologia or defence of the basic system was offered, however, by G. R. Rudolf in *The York-Antwerp Rules* published in 1926, and subsequently incorporated verbatim as an Appendix in the 7th/9th editions of this present work. He considered there were two formidable difficulties in the way of the elimination of general average: **90.06**

> "The first is the practical difficulty of getting universal agreement to this course, and the second, the undesirability on grounds of public policy of interfering in any way with the discretion of the master in time of peril."

Rudolf considered the second difficulty to be the more important, "a matter of much greater moment", and instanced the case of a vessel aground in a position of great danger, with a falling tide and bad weather threatening.

> "The master has perhaps three alternatives before him: (1) to hire a passing steamer to tow his ship off, (2) to use his own engines to try and force the

"If this was true some 20 years ago, what is to be said of it (in 1894)? What was merely vast and complicated then has become stupendous and compound-comminuted today. The forebodings of the Committee have been more than fulfilled. The preposterous and overgrown snowball of abuses has rolled itself bigger and bigger, and still those irresponsible persons who have the rolling of it, but over whom it does not roll, exclaim enthusiastically that it must be rolled bigger yet ... Average adjusters and legal faddists vie with one another at the snowball rolling, and happy and distinguished is he who can succeed in sticking a fresh lump upon it."

[4] See App. 1, *ante*.

ship afloat, or (3) to jettison enough cargo to lighten the ship sufficiently to float off. The cost of these three alternatives is respectively: (1) £500, (2) £200, (3) £2,500. Under the principles of general average, the master's choice is left absolutely unfettered by any consideration whatever other than 'what is the best course to adopt to save ship and cargo,' knowing that the party whose property or purse is called upon to suffer for the general benefit will be recouped by all who benefit thereby. Would the master's choice be quite so free if in addition to the heavy responsibility of deciding on the best course to adopt from a nautical point of view, he had also to consider whose pocket was going to suffer?"

90.07 There is thus a strong inference that, were general average to be abolished and all losses and expenses to lie where they fell, the master might adopt the third course and jettison cargo, rather than employ methods 1 or 2 at the sole cost of his owner; in other words, the general average system acts as a watchdog or guardian angel for the protection of the cargo interests.

What may be considered as an implied slur on some shipmasters and their owners is best left to those parties to answer, but the inference is, at the least, questionable.

90.08 If a vessel runs aground while steaming ahead, and the bottom is soft, almost as a reflex action will the engine be put full astern and worked variously in efforts to refloat. Even if the bottom is of rock, after sounding the double bottom tanks and holds to check that there is no leakage, the engine will still be used in early efforts to refloat as a matter of routine seamanship, and it would appear, therefore, that the first cost of refloating is at the expense of the shipowner.

If the vessel is making more water than can be coped with by the ship's pumps, she would be better left where she is until salvage assistance and a diver to attend to the leak can be obtained. A hasty jettison, in any circumstances, will seldom achieve anything, for unless heavy anchors or ground tackle can be laid out aft, it is likely that the ship will merely drive further ashore as she is lightened. Alternatively, she could even be overcome by the leakage and sink in deep water.

90.09 The suggestion that the master might sacrifice cargo rather than incur some expense or loss which would fall upon his owner can also be tested (as a theoretical exercise, at least, for the statistics have probably long since been destroyed) by considering the case of the jettison of a deck cargo of timber in heavy weather. This can be achieved far more quickly and easily than a jettison of underdeck cargo after a stranding. Prior to 1924, such a jettison of deck cargo would not have been admissible as general average, and the loss would have fallen entirely upon the cargo interests themselves. Is it likely that there was a sudden decline in the number of deck cargo jettisons following the admission in the 1924 York-Antwerp Rules of deck cargo jettisons, thereby throwing upon the shipowner the liability to contribute to such losses?

Overall, it is seriously to be doubted whether there is much force in the public policy and guardian angel theory, but if unnecessary sacrifices of cargo were to occur, a few well-publicised law suits against any offenders would doubtless do much to discourage such action.

It is also to be noted that in many types of maritime accident, no purpose would be served or benefit arise from a sacrifice of cargo.

90.10 It is also suggested on occasion that general average should be retained for the benefit of those parties, whether cargo or ship, who do not insure or have very large deductibles in their policies of insurance. It is to be doubted whether general average losses and contributions amount to as much as 10 per cent of marine losses in general, and it hardly seems likely that a merchant who abjures insurance cover for major losses by sea perils should need the protection of the general average distribution system merely to recover the much smaller losses of a general average nature, whether as a direct sacrifice of his goods or by way of contribution. In any case, what he loses on a single sacrifice will be recompensed on the law of swings and roundabouts by the savings he will make in a further 50 cases where he is required to pay a contribution. The same argument applies to those with large deductibles in their policies of insurance.

Suggested Reforms and the Practical Difficulties of Achieving them

A number of reforms and alternative schemes have been suggested over the years, but before commenting upon them it is important to bear certain basic facts in mind: **90.11**

(1) Abolition or abatement of general average cannot be forced upon the mercantile community; it can come about only if the ship and cargo interests actively desire it, or can be persuaded of the potential benefits which will accrue to them, personally, by such abolition or abatement.
(2) Ship and cargo interests will only desire an abolition of the general average distribution system if they are placed in as good a financial position under any new scheme as they enjoy at present. In other words, the parties would expect to recover direct from their insurers any claims or allowances which they presently receive in general average (for example the shipowner would still expect to recover the wages and maintenance of his crew, etc.).
(3) Insurance premiums and freight rates should not be increased (or any increase in freight rates must be compensated by an equivalent decrease in the cargo insurance premiums).

To fulfil these essential requirements is likely to prove a herculean task, but it is reasonably evident that any new scheme must fulfil them before it can hope to be considered.

Suggested schemes have included the following.

Scheme 1

It is said that there is "nothing new under the sun", and one scheme which was actually operated over two hundred years ago is recorded in Magens' *Essays on Insurance* published in 1755: **90.12**

> "In London, where the East India Company hire all the ships they employ in their trade from private people there is a general condition in the charter-parties that every ship shall make good all damages that may happen to the goods on board her; and farther, that the Company [*i.e.* the cargo] shall contribute nothing to any damage the ship may receive by cutting away masts etc. ... so that what general custom has made a gross [or general] average to be borne by Ship and Cargo, falls solely on the owners of those vessels the Company employ."

This was abolition with a vengeance! Not only had the shipowner to bear all his own losses, but also those of the cargo. Such a scheme would be stillborn today as it would obviously necessitate increases in the rates of freight.

Scheme 2

That we should return to the "common safety" theory, that is reduce general average allowances to those permissible under, say, English law, which is **90.13** extremely strict and limited in its application of general average as compared with the very generous provisions of the York-Antwerp Rules.

This scheme is also an unlikely starter and would not command general acceptance. It would eliminate a very few general average situations, but in the vast majority of cases an adjustment would still be necessary, though with considerably reduced general average allowances. These reductions would be likely to fall largely on the shipowner, thus upsetting the present financial equilibrium between the parties, and on these grounds unacceptable. Also for consideration is the fact that although the nationals of any country may be prepared to forego their own national law in favour of some "anonymous" and international code such as the York-Antwerp Rules, they would be most unlikely to accept the law of any other single country, more particularly an "ungenerous" law such as that of England.

Scheme 3

90.14 That sacrifices (of physical property) should lie where they fall, but expenditures (of cash) should continue to be apportioned.

Such a scheme might simplify some adjustments but would hardly reduce the number prepared. It is extremely rare for any general average to consist of *sacrifice* alone and, indeed, 90 per cent or more of all general average adjustments consist only of general average *expenditure*, plus bunkers and stores consumed. Further, the total value of cargo sacrifices almost certainly exceeds the value of ship sacrifices, so that there would be an increased burden on cargo interests with resultant increases in cargo rates of premium.

Scheme 4

90.15 That all sacrifices and all expenses should be allowed to lie where they fall, that is a complete abolition of the general average distribution system.

Its simplicity recommends it, but there is certainly one grave disadvantage, even apart from the misguided fear that shipmasters would jettison cargo rather than incur an expense which would fall upon the shipowner. Assume that a ship with a residual (damaged) value of 1,000,000 was carrying a cargo worth 5,000,000. In the event of a very severe casualty, it would obviously be worth spending 2,000,000 or more to save the adventure as a whole, but under existing legal principles the shipowner would be entitled to abandon the voyage and throw in his hand if he were obliged to bear this expenditure. From his own financial standpoint, no expenditure of more than 1,000,000 could be justified.

90.16 That valuable property worth 6,000,000 should be left to rot or be lost is unthinkable, and the services of professional salvors under a Lloyd's Open Form of Salvage Agreement would no doubt be arranged. But if those salvors are obliged to seek security for and prosecute their claims for salvage against each separate property interest saved, problems similar to [or worse than] those in the existing general average distribution system will again be re-introduced.

Admittedly, it will be only in those cases in which salvage services are required that the situation is likely to arise, and other property sacrifices and expenses would still not be treated as general average, but it does raise the further serious and important problem of whether salvage assistance might be accepted more readily by a shipmaster than at present if it means that cargo interests will thereby "contribute" to the cost of an operation, rather than that the shipowner should bear the whole cost.[5]

If the general average distribution system is to be abolished, it would appear

[5] Mocatta J. touches upon this problem in *Australian Coastal Shipping v. Green* [1971] 1 Q.B. 465.

essential to ensure that such abolition could not be circumvented by an alternative distribution system such as salvage, that is, the shipowner should also be responsible for salvage applicable to the cargo. This could not be wholly achieved with current hull insurance conditions, nor within the normal insured value of any vessel, and a special and additional policy of insurance would be required by the shipowner to cover what under existing practice would be considered as general average attaching to cargo.

The question of the cost of such an insurance, and whether shipowners in general could afford the same without increasing freight rates will be considered later in paragraph 90.25.

Scheme 5

That the bill of lading should serve also as a cargo insurance policy which would pay all damage to the goods, whether caused by accident or sacrifice, and any general average contribution. Such a scheme would also avoid the general average distribution altogether. **90.17**

The scheme is undoubtedly worth exploring further, but the concept of the "Insured Bill of Lading" tends to be strenuously fought by large trading companies with a good claims experience and who prefer dealing direct with insurers of their own choosing, and with tailor-made policies to suit their own particular needs.

(It is to be noted that this form of policy is far more extensive than that referred to in Scheme 4, in paragraph 90.15, above.)

These are but a few of the reforms that have been put forward over the years. **90.18** They have all been made with the best of intentions, but it will be appreciated that intense practical difficulties face anyone who endeavours to abolish or reduce the general average distribution system.

However, and to avoid some of the potential areas of complaint and keep the wheels of commerce running smoothly, average adjusters are able to take some positive steps and are ever on the alert to spot at an early stage those situations where the cost of collecting general average security and the extra cost of preparing a full-scale adjustment is likely to exceed the contribution payable by the cargo interests. Hull insurers can then be approached with figures demonstrating that it would be more economical for them to pay the whole of the general average—usually without commission and interest—and insurers are usually most co-operative, thereby sparing cargo interests the trouble and expense on many a small general average situation.

On other occasions it is not possible to produce figures showing that hull insurers can pay the whole of a general average. However, an examination of the cargo manifest in a multi-bill of lading general average case may show that there are a number of high-valued cargo interests amongst a great many small valued interests, and the economies of the situation will quickly show that it is commercially sensible and viable for the general average to be charged only to the ship and those high-valued cargo interests. The ship's agents can then be instructed to release without general average security all separate bills of lading whose value is less than, for example, $10,000—or even $500,000!

Savings in time, trouble and expense could also be achieved on occasion if **90.19** only the Protecting and Indemnity Associations would grasp the nettle a little earlier on cases where it is fairly obvious that the shipowner is in breach of his obligations under the contract of carriage, and that the cargo interests will refuse to pay any general average contribution. It would be so very much better and cheaper in the long run in a multi-bill of lading case if the P. & I. Clubs would recognise the situation at an early stage, thus obviating the need to obtain general average security from the cargo interests and prepare a full-scale adjustment.

90.20 Shipowners are also well aware of the potential friction with shippers and consignees over small general average cases, and a number of them have clauses in their insurance policies providing for the hull insurers to pay the whole of any general average where it does not exceed a specified sum, for example £50,000. It is along these lines that one can see the smoothest path for a gradual reduction in the general average distribution system, and it is probable that the number of shipowners using such clauses, and the amounts their insurers will be willing to bear, will increase with the years.

90.21 It is particularly in the liner and ferry trades that the shipowner and/or his insurers are frequently prepared to bear the whole of any "small" general average, and if serious thought and consideration were to be given to developing and extending this idea, it would surely be possible to devise a scheme which would preserve undisturbed the current state of financial burdens on the ship and cargo interests, yet enable the shipowner to bear a much increased general average expenditure without the need to apply the distribution system.

In the multi-bill of lading liner trades, where the need to dispense with the distribution system is greatest, and the savings and benefits to all concerned would be most marked, any viable scheme would probably be received with a warm welcome. The bulk cargo and tramp trades might be left to continue undisturbed with the present system until sufficient experience and statistics had been gained from any new system.

90.22 The suggestion most consistently put forward in earlier papers has been that general average sacrifices (of physical property), at least, should be allowed to lie where they fall, and this appears to be a sensible and logical first part of any plan to dismantle the general average distribution system.

The cargo interests and their insurers would bear any losses caused by jettison, or by the means used to extinguish a fire, or by a forced discharge—as they do at present—but would relinquish their rights of recourse in general average against the shipowner and the other cargo interests. For their part, the shipowners and their insurers would bear the cost of repairing damage to the ship caused by the means used to refloat, or to extinguish a fire, etc., again without rights of recourse against the cargo.

Such a move would assist considerably in the simplification of the large fire, stranding and jettison type of adjustments, for there would no longer be any need to distinguish between accidental and intentional damage, either to the ship or cargo. (The possibility that the shipmaster might sacrifice cargo rather than incur a sacrifice or expenditure which would fall upon the shipowner is, as explained earlier in paragraphs 90.08, 90.09, most unlikely, and more particularly with reputable owners in the liner trades presently under discussion.)

90.23 However, by itself, this move suffers from two defects:

(1) It might simplify the adjustments, but it would in no way reduce the number prepared.
(2) In the liner trade, it is probable that the total value of cargo sacrifices in the occasional fire or jettison case considerably exceeds the total value of ship sacrifices, and that the cargo interests, accordingly, would be unlikely to accept it as it would throw an additional financial burden upon them.

90.24 Any suggestions to reduce the general average system must be designed with a view to preserving as nearly as possible the present financial burden on the ship and cargo interests. So that if the cargo interests were prepared to bear their own sacrifices without recourse against the ship and other interests, the shipowners and their insurers ought to make some concession of equal value. A logical proposal would be for the shipowner to bear a certain basic sum of any general average expenditure (including salvage). Only if the total general average and salvage expenditure exceeded this sum would an apportionment take place, and then only of the amount by which this sum was exceeded.

Without the necessary statistics, it is impossible to suggest what this sum might be, but in the case of the typical ocean-going cargo liner, it is possible to visualise that it could be in the $250/500,000 range. If this were so, such a scheme would obviate the need to distribute the general average in a considerable number of the cases presently undertaken.

Further, such a sum could generally be borne by the shipowner and his insurers within the normal insured value of the vessel without creating the problem mentioned in paragraphs 90.15, 90.16, above, where the shipowner would be inclined to abandon the voyage (and his vessel to insurers) because the total expenditure required to salve both ship and cargo would be greater than the residual damaged value of the ship alone.

To continue this train of thought, it is possible to visualise a supplementary move which would free the cargo interests and their insurers of the responsibility to contribute towards *any* general average or salvage expenditure: the shipowner might effect an insurance to cover only the proportion of any general average expenditure in excess of the sum already to be borne by him as suggested above. **90.25**

The premium ought to be provided by the cargo interests themselves as a surcharge on their freight, and in theory this is perfectly possible, for the cargo insurers would be able to reduce their present rates of premium by the precise amount payable by the shipowner. In practice, however, it is anticipated that the shipowner might be obliged to find the premium himself, and to this extent, the idea is likely to be stillborn. Nevertheless, and assuming that a generous rate of premium for the longest voyage undertaken by a cargo liner would be ·025 per cent, the liability attaching to cargo worth $10,000,000 could be covered for $2,500. Would this not be a cheap price to pay to avoid all the extra trouble, expense and delay to both ship and cargo interests associated with a large multi-bill of lading general average situation?

No longer would the carriage of goods by sea be subject to the anachronistic trappings of a bygone age; the costly distribution of losses and "salvage" expenses could be dispensed with, and the system brought up to date and in line with the similar carriage by road, rail or air, where losses lie where they fall and the carrier endeavours to complete the transit without the need to "pass round the hat".

POSSIBLE DRAFT CLAUSES

Bill of Lading and/or Charterparty Clause

General average to be adjusted in accordance with York-Antwerp Rules 1974 except that: **90.26**

(A) Loss of and/or damage to ship, cargo, or other property caused by general average sacrifice shall be borne by the party suffering the loss without recourse against the other contributing interests.

(B) The Shipowner to bear the first $/£. ... ... of any general average expenditure and/or salvage and only the excess of this sum to be apportioned between the contributing interests.

Hull Policy Clause (plus other existing wording)

90.27 General average to be adjusted in accordance with York-Antwerp Rules, but where the contract of affreightment so provides:

(A) Sacrifices of ship to be paid in full without recourse against cargo or other contributing interests.
(B) The first $/£. ... ... of any general average expenditure and/or salvage to be paid by hull underwriters, also the ship's proportion of any general average expenditure and/or salvage in excess of this sum (subject to the provisions of section 73 of the Marine Insurance Act 1906).

Cargo Policy Clause

90.28 Probably unnecessary with new Institute Cargo Clauses, which cover general average "according to the contract of affreightment", but if it be thought necessary for clarity or emphasis:

General Average

Where the contract of affreightment so provides, sacrifices of cargo to be paid without recourse against the other contributing interests.

Insurance by Shipowner of Cargo's Proportion of "Large" General Averages

90.29 In the event of any general average expenditure and/or salvage being incurred in excess of $/£. ... ..., this Policy to pay Cargo's proportion of the excess of this sum.

90.30 The General Average Committee of the I.U.M.I. included in a 1948 report to the Council a list of the known criticisms of the general average system, as detailed below. It should be noted, however, that the Committee did not subscribe to all the criticisms and, indeed, reported that while the criticisms were sufficiently well founded to give reason for considering ways and means of simplification and of some reform, the principle of general average could not be abolished, and that there were no adequate grounds for abolition.

Criticisms of the General Average System Recorded in the 1948 I.U.M.I. Report (see paragraph 90.04, above)

(a) The great increase in the size of ships and other developments in shipping and trade have caused highly involved and too laborious complications of adjustment.
(b) The trend has been to extend, rather than to limit the scope of general average, thus increasing the complexities of the subject instead of aiming at the rationalisation and simplification generally aspired to in modern development.
(c) Under the conditions referred to under (a), and with the trend mentioned under (b) unnecessary and sometimes excessive expenses occur too frequently. They fall under the categories of services, *e.g.* agency fees, port of refuge charges, surveys, financing advances, and printing and adjustment fees.
(d) General average deposits cause excessive clerical work for all concerned.
(e) Complicated problems of currency arise when deposits are collected in different currencies or the general average adjustment is drawn up in a currency different to that of the country from or to which the goods are shipped or to that of the ship's home port.
(f) The delays occurring in the winding up of general averages and the issue of adjustments, etc., carry with them risks of exchange fluctuations against which it is

difficult for those who have financed the deposits to protect themselves.

(g) Depositors and others are liable to become involved in insolvency of ship's agents or shipowners, this notwithstanding Rule XXIII. (Note: 1924 Y.A.R. = Rule XXII in 1994.)

(h) General average deposits are sometimes grossly over-estimated when fixing the amount to be deposited.

(i) Frequently experienced delays in the winding up of general averages, in the issue of adjustments, and in the collection of general average contributions or distribution of refunds. These delays make it necessary to keep underwriting accounts open for indefinite periods, thus often obscuring the true position of such accounts or of individual hull or cargo statistics.

(j) High costs of commission and interests. The delays mentioned above are attributed to the present rules giving inducement to defer the closing of general averages.

(k) The difficulties experienced in arriving at both the proper contributory values of ship and cargo and the amounts, to be made good in General Average. These difficulties are enhanced when shipvaluers, shipowners, and other specialists hold different views as to values for general average purposes, or where cargoes are government owned, or, through government measures, are held at artificial price levels at port of destination.

(l) Failure to bring about international unification of general average rules leads to increasing difficulties, as cargoes under the same general average are nowadays often consigned to ports of discharge in different countries where different laws are applicable.

(m) That although the York-Antwerp Rules are widely adopted, they are not always construed in the same way by jurists and average adjusters in different countries. The varying national interpretations have with the years tended to increase existing divergences in practice as well as in legal construction.

INDEX